AMERICAN CONSTITUTIONAL LAW

Volume 2
The Bill of Rights and
Subsequent Amendments

Tenth Edition

RALPH A ROSSUM
Claremont McKenna College

G. ALAN TARR
Rutgers University, Camden

WESTVIEW
PRESS

Westview Press was founded in 1975 in Boulder, Colorado, by notable publisher and intellectual Fred Praeger. Westview Press continues to publish scholarly titles and high-quality undergraduate- and graduate-level textbooks in core social science disciplines. With books developed, written, and edited with the needs of serious nonfiction readers, professors, and students in mind, Westview Press honors its long history of publishing books that matter.

Copyright © 2017 by Westview Press
Published by Westview Press,
An imprint of Perseus Books
A division of Hachette Book Group
2465 Central Avenue
Boulder, CO 80301
www.westviewpress.com

Every effort has been made to secure required permissions for all text, images, maps, and other art reprinted in this volume.

Westview Press books are available at special discounts for bulk purchases in the United States by corporations, institutions, and other organizations. For more information, please contact the Special Markets Department at the Perseus Books Group, 2300 Chestnut Street, Suite 200, Philadelphia, PA 19103, or call (800) 810-4145, ext. 5000, or e-mail special.markets@perseusbooks.com.

A CIP catalog record for the print version of this book is available from the Library of Congress
PB ISBN: 978-0-8133-4997-8
EBOOK ISBN: 978-0-8133-5031-8

10 9 8 7 6 5 4 3 2 1

AMERICAN CONSTITUTIONAL LAW
Volume 2

About the Authors

Ralph A. Rossum is Henry Salvatori Professor of American Constitutionalism at Claremont McKenna College. He earned his PhD from the University of Chicago and is the author of several books, including *The Supreme Court and Tribal Gaming:* California v. Cabazon Band of Mission Indians (2011); *Antonin Scalia's Jurisprudence: Text and Tradition* (2006); *Federalism, the Supreme Court, and the Seventeenth Amendment: The Irony of Constitutional Democracy* (2001); *Congressional Control of the Judiciary: The Article III Option* (1988); *The American Founding: Politics, Statesmanship, and the Constitution* (1981); *Reverse Discrimination: The Constitutional Debate* (1979); and *The Politics of the Criminal Justice System: An Organizational Analysis* (1978). He has served in the US Department of Justice as deputy director of its Bureau of Justice Statistics and as a board member of its National Institute of Corrections. He currently serves as a member of the California Advisory Committee, US Commission on Civil Rights.

G. Alan Tarr is Director of the Center for State Constitutional Studies and Board of Governors Professor of Political Science at Rutgers University, Camden. He received his doctorate from the University of Chicago. Professor Tarr is the author of several books, including *Judicial Process and Judicial Policymaking* (6th edition, 2013), *Without Fear or Favor: Judicial Independence and Judicial Accountability in the States* (2012), *Understanding State Constitutions* (1998), and *State Supreme Courts in State and Nation* (1988). He is coeditor of the three-volume *State Constitutions for the Twenty-First Century* (2005), *Constitutional Dynamics in Federal Systems: Subnational Perspectives* (2012), *Constitutional Origins, Structure, and Change in Federal Countries* (2005), and several other volumes. Three times the recipient of fellowships from the National Endowment for the Humanities and more recently a Fulbright Fellow, Professor Tarr has served as a consultant to the US Department of State, the American Bar Association, the National Center for State Courts, and several state governments. He has lectured on American constitutionalism and federalism throughout the United States, as well as in Africa, Asia, Europe, North America, and South America.

To the Memory of Herbert J. Storing

Contents

6   FREEDOM OF RELIGION 280

7   CRIMINAL PROCEDURE 356

CASES

Preface

American Constitutional Law, Tenth Edition, is designed as a basic text for courses in national powers and civil liberties. This substantially revised and updated edition features the major constitutional controversies and cases either not included in, or decided since the publication of, the Ninth Edition. This is perhaps our most extensive revision of the casebook from one edition to another; we have added sixteen new cases and deleted and moved twenty-six cases to our new website (www.westviewconlaw.com).

Volume I now includes: *National Labor Relations Board v. Noel Canning* (2014), which restricted the president's power to make recess appointments; *Zivotofsky v. Kerry* (2015), which affirmed the president's exclusive power to recognize foreign states; *Comptroller of the Treasurer of Maryland v. Wynne* (2015), which reflected the Court's continued embrace of the dormant commerce clause; *Adoptive Couple v. Baby Girl* (2013), which revealed the Court's increasing willingness to depart from the standard canons of construction of federal Indian law; *Taylor v. City of Gadsden* (2013), in which a federal district judge rejected a contract clause objection to a city's changes in the public pensions of police and fire personnel; and *Horne v. Department of Agriculture* (2015) and *Koons v. St. Johns River Management District* (2013)—two recent Takings Clause cases.

Volume II now includes: *McDonald v. Chicago* (2010), which incorporated the Second Amendment to apply to the states; *Walker v. Texas Division, Sons of Confederate Veterans, Inc.* (2015) and *McCullen v. Coakley* (2014), both of which addressed free speech issues; *Burwell v. Hobby Lobby Stores, Inc.* (2014), which concerned the protection of religious liberty; *Los Angeles v. Patel* (2015), *Maryland v. King* (2014), and *Riley v. California* (2014), all of which dealt with Fourth Amendment questions; *Shelby County v. Holder* (2013), which found Section 4 of the Voting Rights Act unconstitutional, and *Obergefell v. Hodges* (2015), the Court's landmark decision regarding same-sex marriage.

As in previous editions, our approach to these subjects is based on three major premises. First, the study of the Constitution and constitutional law is of fundamental importance to a full and coherent understanding of the principles, prospects, and problems of America's democratic republic. Cases should be examined not merely to foster an appreciation of what court majorities have thought of particular issues at certain points in time (although that is obviously important), but also to gain a deeper and fuller understanding of the principles at the very heart of the American constitutional system. To that end, this text emphasizes precedent-setting cases and presents comprehensive expositions of alternative constitutional positions. Substantial excerpts from cases and other constitutionally significant pronouncements have been included so that students can grapple with the arguments and justifications for these alternative positions. To ensure that the best arguments on all sides of a constitutional question are presented, we have included extensive extracts of both concurring and dissenting opinions.

Second, no interpretation of the Constitution can be evaluated properly without an appreciation of what those who initially drafted and ratified the Constitution sought to accomplish. The text incorporates documentary evidence in seeking to identify and explain the original purposes of the Constitution and the means provided for the achievement of those purposes. This inquiry into the Framers' understanding of the Constitution, in turn, furnishes one of the criteria for evaluating judicial decisions and constitutionally significant pronouncements from the executive and legislative branches.

Third, the study of the Constitution involves much more than an examination of its judicial interpretation. The Constitution is not merely what the Supreme Court says it is; its words are not so many empty vessels into which justices can pour meaning. Accordingly, this volume examines the interpretations of a variety of sources. The original intent of the framers, the original understanding of the ratifiers, and the original public meaning of the words and phrases of the Constitution are important sources. Another, equally indispensable source is, of course, the Supreme Court, whose decisions have influenced so profoundly our understanding of the Constitution and its principles. And because other governmental bodies have contributed significantly to the overall interpretation of the Constitution, this text includes decisions of the lower federal courts and state judiciaries and also extrajudicial materials of constitutional significance such as certain congressional acts and resolutions and executive orders.

As we approach constitutional questions throughout this text, we begin by turning to the Framers. We do so, however, not so much for specific answers as for general guidance concerning what the Constitution was designed to accomplish. Obviously, no interpretation can be expected to conform strictly to the expectations of the Framers. Other legitimate approaches may also contribute to an understanding of the Constitution, relying variously on analysis of the text itself, judicial precedent, constitutional doctrine, logical reasoning, adaptation of constitutional provisions to changing circumstances, and a concern for the consequences of any particular decision. All these approaches are described in Chapter 1.

The structure of the volumes might be seen as a reflection of James Madison's observation in *The Federalist*, No. 51, that "in framing a government which is to be administered by men over men, the great difficulty lies in this: you must first enable the government to control the governed; and in the next place; oblige it to control itself." Chapter 1 explores in general how the Constitution was designed to resolve this difficulty, and Chapter 2 introduces the reader to the actual process of constitutional adjudication. The remainder of this two-volume work systematically examines how the Constitution and its amendments not only grant the national and state governments sufficient power to control the governed but also oblige these governments to control themselves. Chapters 3 through 6 of Volume I consider the distribution of power in the national government, specifically exploring how the constitutional scheme of separation of powers and checks and balances both grants and controls power. Because of the importance of the distribution of power among the branches of the national government, we devote separate chapters to the judiciary, Congress, the presidency, and war and foreign affairs. Chapters 7 through 11 of Volume I consider the distribution of power between the national government and the states and between the national government and Native American tribal governments, focusing on how the division of power among various governments in the United States helps to advance the ends of the Constitution. Chapter 12 (also included as Chapter 4 in Volume II) and Chapters 3 through 11 of Volume II shift to an examination of the distribution of power between the government and the individual. The emphasis in these chapters is not so much on institutional contrivances that oblige the government to control itself as on the Bill of Rights and those subsequent amendments that guarantee specific rights and liberties, an emphasis that illuminates the way in which our most precious rights and liberties have increasingly become dependent for their vindication not upon constitutional structure but upon what *The Federalist* called mere "parchment barriers."

With the exception of the first two chapters, each chapter opens with an introductory essay that is then followed by cases and, where appropriate, extrajudicial materials. Each essay ends with extensive notes that provide valuable explanatory details and references to additional materials and a list of suggested readings, including essays in *The Federalist,* additional cases, and scholarly books and articles. Each case also has its own introductory headnote, which provides historical perspective, indicates where the case stands in relation to current law, and gives the final court vote. Some cases have endnotes that elaborate on the short- and long-term consequences of the decision. The text includes three appendixes: the Constitution of the United States, a list of Supreme Court justices, and a table of cases.

We encourage our readers to visit our newly revamped and updated website at westviewconlaw.com for additional cases and other resources in understanding the Supreme Court and constitutional law, including links to primary sources and relevant blogs and websites. The additional cases, numbering more than 150 and formatted identically to those included in the casebooks, are organized by volume and chapter. With the exceptions of Chapters 1 and 2, each of the chapters will have the deleted cases found in past editions, cases that we edited for the website in the past but were never included in subsequent editions, and new cases decided after the publication of the Tenth Edition. Check back every September for new cases and updated resources.

We would like to thank the excellent editorial staff at Westview Press for so smoothly and efficiently bringing the Tenth Edition into print. We express particular gratitude to Senior Editor Ada Fung; Associate Managing Editor, Krista Anderson; our project editor, Cisca Schreefel; and our copyeditor, George DeStefano. We would also like to thank the peer reviewers who provided us with helpful and insightful feedback, including: Joseph Knippenberg (Oglethorpe University); Vincent Muñoz (University of Notre Dame); Michael Zarkin (Westminster College); and the many others who wished to remain anonymous.

Any errors of fact or interpretation are, of course, solely our responsibility. Finally, we wish to express our gratitude to our wives, Constance and Susan, for their patience, understanding, and loving support throughout this decades-long project.

Ralph A. Rossum
G. Alan Tarr

Note to the Reader

The authors of *American Constitutional Law* have adopted a convention to inform the reader of how each justice then serving on the Supreme Court voted in each of the cases presented in these two volumes. The convention is perhaps best explained by an example. At the end of the headnote to *Kelo v. City of New London* (2005), a case found in "Economic Due Process and the Takings Clause" (Chapter 12 in Volume I and Chapter 4 in Volume II), the following language is found: "Opinion of the Court: Stevens, Kennedy, Souter, Ginsburg, Breyer. Concurring opinion: Kennedy. Dissenting opinions: O'Connor, Rehnquist, Scalia, Thomas; Thomas." This language indicates that (1) the Court in *Kelo* was divided 5–4 on the question before it; (2) Justice Stevens wrote the opinion of the Court in which Justices Kennedy, Souter, Ginsburg, and Breyer joined (for any opinion, be it the opinion of the Court, the judgment of the Court, a concurrence, or a dissent, the author's name is listed first and underscored, followed by the names of the other justices who join in that opinion—listed in order of seniority); (3) Justice Kennedy wrote a separate concurring opinion (concurring opinions are listed separately from opinions in which justices concur only in the judgment of the Court); (4) Justices O'Connor, Scalia, and Thomas and Chief Justice Rehnquist dissented; (5) Justice O'Connor wrote a dissenting opinion in which Chief Justice Rehnquist and Justices Scalia and Thomas joined; and (6) Justice Thomas wrote a separate dissenting opinion (each concurring or dissenting opinion is separated from the others by a semicolon). Throughout the casebook, the name of any justice who wrote an opinion in a case is underscored whether or not excerpts from that opinion are actually included in the text.

For additional cases and resources, please visit www.westviewconlaw.com.

1

Interpretation of the Constitution

CHAPTER OUTLINE

"We are under a Constitution, but the Constitution is what the Court says it is."[1] In the century since Charles Evans Hughes, then governor of New York and later chief justice of the United States Supreme Court, uttered these now famous words, they have been repeated so often and in so many contexts that they have assumed a prescriptive as well as a descriptive character. But exactly how valid is this prescription for understanding the US Constitution?

Hughes's observation certainly contains some truth. Many provisions of the Constitution are not self-defining and so have been the objects of judicial interpretation and construction. Various criminal procedural protections found in Amendments Four through Eight immediately spring to mind. What, after all, makes a particular search or seizure "unreasonable"? What is sufficient to establish "probable cause"? What constitutes "due process of law"? What is a "speedy" trial? What is an "excessive" fine or bail? What is "cruel and unusual punishment"? Hughes's claim also portrays accurately the perspective of lower-court judges and practicing attorneys. However erroneous they might believe the Supreme Court's understanding of a particular constitutional provision, lower-court judges feel obliged to adhere to the Court's interpretation. And lawyers usually seek to accomplish their objectives within the framework of the prevailing Court view rather than attempting to convince the justices to abandon that view.

Yet, Hughes's assertion is also misleading in several respects. Above all, it fails to recognize that governmental bodies other than the Supreme Court also contribute to an overall interpretation of the Constitution. By passing the War Powers Resolution of 1973, for example, the US Congress undertook to define the constitutional limits of the president's powers to initiate and conduct undeclared war, an issue the Supreme Court has refused to consider. Likewise, in the Speedy Trial Act of 1984, Congress took upon itself constitutional interpretation in the sphere of criminal procedure, declaring that a defendant not brought to trial within one hundred days of arrest can move for a dismissal of the charges. In so doing, it gave meaning to a constitutional provision that the Supreme Court itself has acknowledged to be vaguer than any other procedural right. And in the Voting Rights Act of 1982, Congress held that the Fifteenth Amendment (barring states from denying citizens the right to vote "on account of race, color, or previous condition of servitude") bans not only intentional discrimination against the voting rights of minorities (what the Supreme Court had held) but any electoral scheme that has the effect of preventing minority voters from electing "representatives of their choice." Constitutionally significant pronouncements have also emanated from the executive branch and from the lower federal and state courts. (Statements made by President Abraham Lincoln have had more to do with defining the outer bounds of presidential prerogative than have any statements of the Court, just as actions taken by President Franklin D. Roosevelt altered the balance of power between the national government and the states far more than any judicial opinion.)

Another problem with Hughes's assertion is that it obscures the extent to which the meaning of the Constitution is clear and uncontroversial. Most constitutional provisions are settled; what questions are raised about them pertain not to fundamental meaning but rather to specific application. Relatively few constitutional provisions have sparked protracted debate and controversy: the Commerce Clause of Article I, Section 8, authorizing Congress to regulate commerce among the several states; the First Amendment's establishment of religion and free exercise clauses as well as its guarantees of freedom of speech and of the press; the language of the Fifth and Fourteenth Amendments that no person shall be deprived of life, liberty, or property without due process of law; and the Fourteenth Amendment's pronouncement that no person shall be denied the equal protection of the laws. Although these provisions are extremely important, the intense debate over them tends to obscure how ably the Constitution has governed our political actions for the past two and a quarter centuries. By focusing exclusively on these provisions and arguing, implicitly or explicitly, that they are fundamentally without meaning until construed by the Court, some jurists and legal scholars have reinforced the view that the Constitution is deficient in decisive respects and therefore unworthy of vital public support. As a result, the Constitution is deprived of what James Madison, in *The Federalist,* No. 49, called "that veneration which time bestows on everything, and without which perhaps the wisest and freest governments would not possess the requisite stability." This is of no minor concern, for, as Madison continues, "the most rational government will not find it a superfluous advantage, to have the prejudices of the community on its side."

Still another problem with the view that the Constitution means only what the Court says it means is that it denies that the Constitution is capable of being understood not only by those who made and ratified it but also by those who continue to live under it. As Justice Joseph Story put it in his *Commentaries on the Constitution of the United States:*

> Every word employed in the Constitution is to be expounded in its plain, obvious, and common sense, unless the context provides some ground to control, qualify, or enlarge it. Constitutions are not designed for metaphysical or logical subtleties, for niceties of expression, for critical propriety, for elaborate shades of meaning, or for the exercise of philosophical acuteness or judicial research. They are instruments of a practical nature, founded on the common business of human life, adapted to common wants, designed for common use, and fitted for common understandings. The people make them; the people adopt them; the people must be supposed to read them, with the help of common sense, and cannot be presumed to admit in them any recondite meaning or extraordinary gloss.[2]

In a popular government, the people should take an active interest in the Constitution that gives form to their politics and protection to their liberties; they should not be discouraged from doing so by talk that the Constitution is some obscure document capable of being understood only by Supreme Court justices or by those trained in the law.

A related problem: the view that the Constitution is whatever the Court says it is implies that the Constitution has no meaning in and of itself. If all meaning must be poured into it by the Court, we are unlikely to turn to it for basic instruction on the principles, problems, and prospects of the American regime. The proudest claim of those responsible for framing and ratifying the Constitution was, as stated in *The Federalist,* No. 10, that it provided "a Republican remedy for the diseases most incident to Republican Government." If we strip the Constitution of all independent meaning, we are unlikely to remember the Founders' answers to the basic questions and dilemmas of democratic government—and what is even more regrettable, we are likely to forget the questions themselves.

Yet another effect of presenting the Constitution as devoid of any independent meaning is that it encourages uncritical acceptance of Supreme Court decisions. If the Constitution has only that meaning ascribed to it by the Supreme Court, on what basis, other than subjective preference, can anyone object to the Court's interpretations? On what constitutional basis, for example, can one object to the Supreme Court's decisions in *Dred Scott v. Sandford* (1857), declaring that African Americans could not be citizens, and in *Plessy v. Ferguson* (1896), upholding racial segregation? Students of the Court implicitly acknowledge this problem by routinely paying lip service to Hughes's assertion and then criticizing at length judicial interpretations that they find wanting in fidelity to the language of the Constitution, in scholarship, in craftsmanship, or in deference to the popularly elected branches.

Finally, Hughes's claim ignores the influence that political institutions can have on political behavior. The Court is seen as influencing the Constitution; rarely is the influence that the Constitution might have on the Court, or on politics more generally, even considered.

APPROACHES TO CONSTITUTIONAL INTERPRETATION

To avoid these problems, we will argue, along with Justice Felix Frankfurter, that the "ultimate touchstone of constitutionality is the Constitution itself and not what the [judges] have said about it."[3] But what, in fact, does the Constitution mean? How are we to understand its provisions and give them effect? In searching for satisfactory answers to these questions, students of the Constitution have proposed several approaches to constitutional interpretation, each of which has its own strengths and weaknesses.[4]

Textual Analysis

One approach to constitutional interpretation involves explicating the constitutional text simply on the basis of the words found there. The basic claim of this approach seems unarguable: if the Constitution is to control the outcome of a case, and if its text is plain, then constitutional interpretation should stop right there. As Justice Noah Swayne observed in *United States v. Hartwell* (1868): "If the language be clear, it is conclusive. There cannot be construction where there is nothing to construe."

On today's Supreme Court, the late Justice Antonin Scalia is most closely associated with the textualist approach. He argued that the Court is to interpret the text alone and nothing else. Thus in *Coy v. Iowa* (1988), he upheld the right of a defendant, under the Sixth Amendment, literally to "be confronted with the witnesses against him" and overturned his conviction because Iowa law allowed the two thirteen-year-old girls he was charged with sexually assaulting to testify behind a large screen that shielded them from the defendant. For Scalia, the text was unequivocal and governing: "Simply as a matter of English, it confers at least 'a right to meet face to face all those who appear and give evidence at trial.' Simply as a matter of Latin as well, since the word 'confront' ultimately derives from the prefix 'con-' (from 'contra' meaning 'against' or 'opposed') and the noun 'frons' (forehead). Shakespeare was thus describing the root meaning of confrontation when he had Richard the Second say: 'Then call them to our presence—face to face, and frowning brow to brow, ourselves will hear the accuser and the accused freely speak.'"

Textualism, however, has its limitations. Although many provisions of the Constitution are perfectly clear, others require extensive construction. Consider Article II, section 4, authorizing the impeachment of "the President, Vice President, and all civil officers of the United States" for "high Crimes and Misdemeanors"—a phrase some believe includes not only criminal offenses but also noncriminal behavior amounting to a serious dereliction of duty. Moreover, even if the meanings of all relevant words are perfectly plain, problems of emphasis remain. As Justice Stephen Breyer has noted, "All controversies of importance involve if not a conflict at least an interplay of principles."[5] In many cases, two or more constitutional provisions come into play, and the justices must decide which is to be given priority. To provide just one example of this problem, consider adverse pretrial publicity in a criminal case. Does the First Amendment guarantee of the freedom of speech and the press supersede the Sixth Amendment guarantee of a trial "by an impartial jury"? As this example indicates, the constitutional text in and of itself cannot resolve all the questions that the Constitution raises.

Precedent

When textual analysis alone is inadequate, many students of the Constitution turn to previously decided cases, searching for answers on the basis of precedent, or stare decisis ("to stand by decided matters"). That is, they seek guidance from how judges have interpreted a provision in prior cases.

Reliance on precedent, the primary mode of legal reasoning in Anglo-American law, adds stability, continuity, and predictability to the entire legal enterprise. But judges have relied on precedent only sporadically in constitutional law. Very good arguments can be adduced either to adhere to or to depart from precedent. No Supreme Court case presents these opposing arguments better than *Payne v. Tennessee* (1991), a 5–4 decision that overturned two recent precedents also decided by 5–4 votes—*Booth v. Maryland* (1987) and *South Carolina v. Gathers* (1989)—and held that "victim-impact" statements in the penalty stage of capital punishment cases do not violate the Eighth Amendment's prohibition of "cruel and unusual punishment." Justice Thurgood Marshall in dissent attacked the *Payne* majority for departing from precedent, claiming that nothing "has changed since this Court decided both *Booth* and *Gathers*" other than "this Court's own personnel" and concluding that "this truncation of the Court's duty to stand by its own precedents is astonishing." Justice Scalia in a concurring opinion replied that what would be truly astonishing is "the notion that an important constitutional decision with plainly inadequate rational support must be left in place for the sole reason that it once attracted five votes."

Many jurists and scholars believe that interpreters should look to the Constitution itself, rather than to prior interpretations of that document, in deciding cases. Then, too, constitutional cases deal with momentous social and political issues that only temporarily take the form of litigation, and there is wide recognition that these issues cannot be resolved satisfactorily on the same basis as other legal problems. To some critics, relying on precedent for constitutional interpretation is rather like driving a car down a busy street while looking only through the rearview mirror: we get a good notion of where we have been but not where we should be going. As Thomas Hobbes observed in *A Dialogue Between a Philosopher and a Student of the Common Laws of England*, "Precedents prove only what was done, but not what was well done."[6] This difficulty seems especially troublesome in constitutional law. Most areas of law lack clearly defined ends or purposes and so must evolve by way of precedent. The common law, for example, is based mainly on longstanding usage or judicial precedent. Constitutional law, on the other hand, has before it certain "directions, goals, and ideals" that are easily discernible in the Constitution. Once discerned, these guideposts make it possible for the Court to decide matters of political and social import not in terms of what previous Courts have held, but in light of what is most conducive to achieving the goals or purposes of the Constitution.[7]

Constitutional Doctrine

When neither the constitutional text nor precedent provides an adequate account of the meaning of the Constitution, arguments from "constitutional doctrine" might be raised. Constitutional doctrines are formulas—sometimes nothing more than slogans—extracted from a combination of the constitutional text and a series of related cases. The Equal Protection Clause of the Fourteenth Amendment provides several examples of the development and use of constitutional doctrines. When considered as it applies to questions of race, this clause typically is understood to prohibit discrimination (although the word *discrimination* is nowhere to be found in the amendment); when considered as it applies to questions of legislative apportionment, it typically is understood to require "one person, one vote" (another phrase not found in the text). Similarly, the First Amendment's Establishment Clause, which charges Congress to "make no law respecting an establishment of religion," has been interpreted by many as erecting a high "wall of separation" between church and state. In these illustrations, the enunciated constitutional doctrines serve as mediating principles that stand between specific controversies and the Constitution, giving meaning and content to ideals that may—or may not—be embodied in the text.

Although these examples suggest that constitutional doctrines broaden the scope of the constitutional text they reference, this is not invariably the case. Take the protection against self-incrimination. The Fifth Amendment does not use the term *self-incrimination;* rather, it reads: "No person . . . shall be compelled in any criminal case to be a witness against himself." Unlike certain other reformulations of constitutional provisions, such as "separation of church and state" for the Establishment Clause, "freedom of expression" for "the freedom of speech, or of the press," and "interstate commerce" for "commerce among the several states," this reformulation is narrower than the constitutional guarantee itself. Individuals can be witnesses against themselves in ways that do not incriminate them; they can, in criminal cases, injure their civil interests or disgrace themselves. Thus, unlike the constitutional doctrine limiting the Fifth Amendment to "self-incrimination," the words of the amendment would seem to apply as well to any disclosures that would expose either criminal defendants or witnesses to civil liability or public condemnation.

Over time, many of these doctrines have come to give the constitutional provision in question its only meaning as a guide for decision. This substitution for the original texts may have profound implications. As such doctrines become increasingly important, public debate tends to center on the meaning of the doctrines and not on the meaning of the Constitution itself. In reference to the Equal Protection Clause, for example, the contemporary debate over affirmative action and diversity has focused almost exclusively on such questions as whether this policy is discriminatory against; the question of what "equal protection of the law" truly means has been all but forgotten. Equally disturbing is the fact that reducing constitutional provisions to doctrines often interferes with thoughtful consideration of the constitutional issues.

The "one person, one vote" rule provides a case in point. On only the most elemental level does this rule have meaning; after all, the question of permitting certain voters the opportunity to vote two, five, or ten times has never been raised by any of the legislative reapportionment cases. In *Baker v. Carr* (1962), for example, the central issue was how much the voter's one vote was to be worth—a question that moved Justice Frankfurter to ask:

> What is this question of legislative apportionment? Appellants invoke the right to vote and have their votes counted. But they are permitted to vote and their votes are counted. They go to the polls, they cast their ballots, they send their representatives to the state councils. Their complaint is simply that the representatives are not sufficiently numerous or powerful—in short, that Tennessee has adopted a basis of representation with which they are not satisfied. Talk of "debasement" or "dilution" is circular talk. One cannot speak of "debasement" or "dilution" of the value of a vote until there is first defined a standard of reference as to what a vote should be worth.

Emphasis on "one person, one vote" merely obscured these questions and added to doctrinal confusion. Because of this problem, Justice Abe Fortas broke from the Court majority in the legislative reapportionment cases, declaring that such "admittedly complex and subtle" matters must be governed by "substance, not shibboleth." He complained that formulas such as "one person, one vote," "are not surgical instruments"; rather, "they have a tendency to hack deeply—to amputate."[8] The ease of applying such formulas may make them attractive, but this may come at the price of clarity in constitutional understanding.

Logical Reasoning

Another approach to constitutional interpretation emphasizes the use of logical reasoning as exemplified in the syllogism, a formal argument consisting of a major premise, a minor premise, and a conclusion.[9] The major premise sets forth a proposition, such as "A law repugnant to the Constitution is void." The minor premise contains an assertion related to the major premise: "This particular law is repugnant to the Constitution." From these premises the conclusion logically follows: "This particular law is void." The foregoing example represents the essence of Chief Justice John Marshall's reasoning in *Marbury v. Madison* (1803), which formally established the Court's power of judicial review (that is, the power to void legislative or executive acts that the Court finds unconstitutional).

Marshall himself was well aware, however, that logical analysis is an insufficient method of interpreting the Constitution. If the validity of the major premise is assumed, the soundness of the conclusion depends on whether what is asserted in the minor premise is true.[10] But logic cannot determine whether a particular law is repugnant to the Constitution. Justice Owen Roberts made things too simple in *United States v. Butler* (1936) by arguing that "when an act of Congress is appropriately challenged in the courts as not conforming to the constitutional mandate the judicial branch of the Government has only one duty—to lay the article of the Constitution which is invoked beside the statute which is challenged and to decide whether the latter squares with the former." Whether an act in fact squares with the Constitution is a question that must be left to informed opinion and judgment—informed opinion about the purposes for which the Constitution was established and judgment of as to whether the law in question is consistent with those purposes.

Logical analysis, therefore, must be supplemented with a clear understanding of what *The Federalist,* No. 10, calls the "great objects" of the Constitution. Even Marshall, the justice most commonly identified with the use of logical analysis, ultimately based his constitutional interpretations on his understanding of the ends the Constitution was designed to serve. Marshall believed that the Constitution points beyond itself to the purposes and policies that it serves; in the difficult (and most interesting) cases, constitutional interpretation must turn upon an understanding of the Constitution's proper ends. He confidently observed in *McCulloch v. Maryland* (1819) that the nature of the Constitution demands "that only its great outlines should be marked, its important objects designated." As for the "minor ingredients" that compose these objects, he was convinced that they could be "deduced from the nature of the objects themselves."

The Living Constitution

Based on changing conditions and the lessons of experience, the adaptive, or "living Constitution," approach holds that constitutional interpretation can and must be influenced by present-day values and take account of changing conditions in society. One of its critics writes that its proponents regard the Constitution as a "morphing document"[11] that means, from age to age, whatever the society, and more particularly the Court, thinks it ought to mean. The "living Constitution" approach has been enshrined in the Court's interpretation of the Eighth Amendment's prohibition against cruel and unusual punishments. The Court has held, beginning with *Trop v. Dulles* (1957), that this prohibition is not "static" but changes from generation to generation to comport with what Chief Justice Earl Warren called "the evolving standards of decency that mark the progress of a maturing society."

Proponents of this approach concede that these adaptations must be reconcilable with the language of the Constitution. But, they insist, the meaning of the Commerce Clause, or what is protected by the Fourth Amendment or by the Due Process or Equal Protection Clauses, or the reach of the Eighth Amendment can legitimately change over time. For example, no one voting to adopt or ratify the Fourteenth Amendment in 1868 would have believed that they were, therefore, requiring the states to grant licenses for same-sex marriage. However, Justice Kennedy, relying equally on a "living Constitution" interpretation of both the Due Process and Equal Protection Clauses of the Fourteenth Amendment, would conclude for a five-member majority in *Obergefell v. Hodges* (2015) that a proper contemporary understanding of the principles enshrined by these clauses in the Constitution required exactly that. As Kennedy argued, "the nature of injustice is that we may not always see it in our own times. The generations that wrote and ratified the Bill of Rights and the Fourteenth Amendment did not presume to know the extent of freedom in all of its dimensions, and so they entrusted to future generations a charter protecting the right of all persons to enjoy liberty as we learn its meaning. When new insight reveals discord between the Constitution's central protections and a received legal stricture, a claim to liberty must be addressed." And, he continued, "Indeed, in interpreting the Equal Protection Clause, the Court has recognized that new insights and societal understandings can reveal unjustified inequality within our most fundamental institutions that once passed unnoticed and unchallenged."

The rationale for the living Constitution approach is well stated by Justice Oliver Wendell Holmes in *Missouri v. Holland* (1920):

> When we are dealing with words that also are a constituent act, like the Constitution of the United States, we must realize that they have called into life a being the development of which could not have been foreseen completely by the most gifted of its begetters. It was enough for them to realize or to hope that they had created an organism; it has taken a century and has cost their successors much sweat and blood to prove that they created a nation. The case before us must be considered in the light of our whole experience and not merely in that of what was said a hundred years ago.

Defenders of this approach also like to cite Chief Justice Marshall's observation in *McCulloch* that "we must never forget that it is a constitution we are expounding," one that is "intended to endure for ages to come, and consequently, to be adapted to the various crises of human affairs." However, Marshall was not asserting in *McCulloch* that the Court should adapt the Constitution but was arguing instead that the powers of the Constitution should be understood as broad enough to provide Congress with sufficient latitude to confront various crises in the future.[12]

Like the other approaches to constitutional interpretation considered thus far, the adaptive or "living Constitution" approach has its problems. Most important, too much adaptation can render the Constitution and its various provisions so pliant that the original document is no longer able to provide guidance concerning what is to be done. Some who embrace the adaptive approach seek not merely an adaptation *within* the Constitution but rather an adaptation *of* the Constitution; they want not only to devise new means to the ends of the Constitution but to adopt entirely new ends as well.[13] Justice Byron White's frustration in *New York v. United States* (1992) with the Court's insistence that Congress act in conformity with federalism and the Tenth Amendment is a case in point:

> The Court rejects this . . . argument by resorting to generalities and platitudes about the purpose of federalism being to protect individual rights. Ultimately, I suppose, the entire structure of our federal constitutional government can be traced

to an interest in establishing checks and balances to prevent the exercise of tyranny against individuals. But these fears seem extremely far distant to me in a situation such as this. We face a crisis of national proportions in the disposal of low-level radioactive waste. . . . For me, the Court's civics lecture has a decidedly hollow ring at a time when action, rather than rhetoric, is needed to solve a national problem.

Justice William Brennan's objections to capital punishment also illustrate the problems of the adaptive approach. He consistently argued that the objective of the Cruel and Unusual Punishments Clause of the Eighth Amendment is the promotion of "human dignity" and, by insisting that capital punishment is a denial of human dignity, concluded that capital punishment is unconstitutional,[14] despite the fact that the Constitution permits capital trials when preceded by a "presentment or indictment of a Grand Jury," permits a person to be "put in jeopardy of life" provided it is not done twice "for the same offense," and permits both the national government and the states to deprive persons of their lives provided it is done with "due process of law."

The consequence of such an approach may be an increased politicization of the federal judiciary. As Justice Scalia pointed out in *A Matter of Interpretation:* "If the people come to believe that the Constitution . . . means, not what it says or what it was understood to mean, but what it *should* mean, in light of the 'evolving standards of decency that mark the progress of a maturing society'—well, then, they will look for qualifications other than impartiality, judgment, and lawyerly acumen in those whom they select to interpret it." In fact, "they will look for judges who agree with *them* as to what the evolving standards have evolved to; who agree with *them* as to what the Constitution *ought* to be."[15]

The ultimate objection to the "living Constitution" is its essentially arbitrary quality—if it evolves in a way one likes, it is the "unfolding of the American dream;" if it evolves in a way one does not, it is not only a breach of the nation's pledge to adhere to its original principles but also the unfolding of an American nightmare.

Consequentialism

A consequentialist approach to interpretation will read a constitutional or statutory text with an eye to what will be the "practical consequences" of a Court's decision on the "contemporary conditions, social, industrial, and political of the community to be affected." In his book, *Active Liberty*, Justice Breyer proudly proclaims himself a consequentialist. Thus, for example, in campaign finance reform cases, he declares that "restrictions on speech, even when political speech is at issue," are reasonable and lawful; the campaign reform law's negative consequences on "those primarily wealthier citizens who wish to engage in more electoral communication" are more than offset by its positive consequences on the "public's confidence in, and ability to communicate through, the electoral process." And, concerning federalism issues, he asks, "Why should courts try to answer difficult federalism questions on the basis of logical deduction from text or precedent alone? Why not ask about the consequences of decision-making on the active liberty that federalism seeks to further."[16] Another example: In *District of Columbia v. Heller* (2008), Breyer dissented from the Court's majority opinion that held that the Second Amendment secures an individual right to keep and bear arms for self-defense because of its "unfortunate consequences," including threatening "to leave cities without effective protection against gun violence and accidents."

Most justices who employ consequentialist arguments in constitutional cases lack Breyer's candor in admitting that they are doing so; they simply do it. Some representative examples: in *Linkletter v. Walker* (1965), Justice Tom Clark wrote for a seven-member majority refusing to apply *Mapp v. Ohio* (1961) retroactively because it would "tax the administration of justice to the utmost," that is, it would allow every person in prison serving a sentence where at trial illegally seized evidence was admitted to seek a new hearing, a new trial, or outright release. In *Planned Parenthood v. Casey* (1992), Justices O'Connor, Kennedy, and Souter in their joint plurality opinion refused to overrule *Roe v. Wade* (1972), despite their "reservations" that it was correctly decided because of the negative consequences that would have on the Court's legitimacy. "A decision to overrule *Roe's* essential holding under the existing circumstances would address error, if error there was, at the cost of both profound and unnecessary damage to the Court's legitimacy, and to the Nation's commitment to the rule of law." In *Blakely v. Washington* (2004), Justice O'Connor wrote for the four justices in dissent, rejecting the majority's decision that the right to trial by jury required that every element of a crime that increases its penalty must be submitted to a jury and proved beyond a reasonable doubt because it would "trim or eliminate altogether" federal and state sentencing guidelines schemes. In *United States v. Windsor* (2013), Justice Kennedy insisted that the Supreme Court had jurisdiction in that case to declare unconstitutional the Defense of Marriage Act (DOMA) for two consequentialist reasons. To begin with, "the costs, uncertainties, and alleged harm and injuries [inflicted by DOMA] likely would continue for a time measured in years before the issue is resolved." In addition, the Obama Administration's refusal to defend DOMA would otherwise "preclude judicial review" and would thereby make "the Court's role in determining the constitutionality of a law . . . secondary to the President's." And, in *Harris v. Quinn* (2014), Justice Kagan, in her dissent, justified the suppression of free speech for a class of public employees on the grounds that "thousands of contracts involving millions of employees" would have to be renegotiated.

Breyer admits that his approach makes it easy for a judge to be "willful, in the sense of enforcing [his] individual views."[17] It is a temptation to which many on the Court have succumbed—and for a very long time. Indeed, Justice Scalia has claimed that consequentialism "is nothing but an invitation to judicial lawmaking."[18]

Originalism

Originalism is an umbrella term, referring to original intent, original understanding, and original public meaning. While these three terms are often used interchangeably and the approaches overlap somewhat, each can be seen as a distinct approach to constitutional interpretation. The first approach, *original intent*, seeks to identify what the delegates to the Constitutional Convention in Philadelphia collectively intended to accomplish when they drafted the Constitution in the summer of 1787. Those who pursue an original intent approach do so because they believe that "interpreting a document means to attempt to discern the intent of the author."[19] Therefore, they focus on the text of the Constitution, on the records of the Constitutional Convention, on what the delegates said about the Constitution as it was being drafted. Madison's notes figure most prominently for them, but other delegates also took notes and many of the delegates wrote letters and essays during and after the Convention that provide for them insight into the Framers' intentions.

The second approach to originalism is *original understanding*. It focuses on identifying what the various provisions of the Constitution meant to those who brought the Constitution into existence, the delegates of the state ratifying conventions of 1787 and 1788. Those who pursue an original understanding approach point out that the Constitutional Convention met in secret under a rule that declared that "nothing spoken in the House be printed, or otherwise published, or communicated without leave," and, as a consequence, the public did not become aware of its records and what was said there until decades after ratification of the Constitution. Therefore, the best way to discern the original understanding of the Constitution is to look at what the delegates said at the ratifying conventions and at what arguments were made by the various Federalist and Anti-Federalist writers attempting to influence the election of those delegates. Those who advocate an original understanding approach cite James Madison, who declared on the floor of the House on April 16, 1796:

> Whatever veneration might be entertained for the body of men who formed our Constitution, the sense of that body could never be regarded as the oracular guide in expounding the Constitution. As the instrument came from them it was nothing more than the draft of a plan, nothing but a dead letter, until life and validity were breathed into it by the voice of the people, speaking through the several State Conventions. If we were to look, therefore, for the meaning of the instrument beyond the face of the instrument, we must look for it, not in the General Convention, which proposed, but in the State Conventions, which accepted and ratified the Constitution.

The third approach to originalism is *original public meaning*, which is closely tied to textualism and is most closely associated with the late Justice Scalia. This approach seeks to ascertain the meaning of the particular constitutional text in question at the time of its adoption by consulting dictionaries of the era and other founding-era documents "to discern the then-customary meaning of the word and phrases in the Constitution." As Scalia put it in *A Matter of Interpretation*:

> I will consult the writings of some men who happened to be delegates to the Constitutional Convention–Hamilton's and Madison's writings in *The Federalist*, for example. I do so, however, not because they were Framers and therefore their intent is authoritative and must be the law; but rather because their writings, like those of other intelligent and informed people of the time, display how the text of the Constitution was originally understood. Thus, I give equal weight to Jay's pieces in *The Federalist*, and to Jefferson's writings, even though neither of them was a Framer. What I look for in the Constitution is precisely what I look for in a statute: the original meaning of the text, not what the original draftsmen intended.[20]

Scalia's majority opinion in *District of Columbia v. Heller* (2008), in which he held that the Second Amendment protects an individual's right to keep and bear arms for purposes of self-defense, demonstrates his original public meaning approach to constitutional interpretation. In it, he turned to dictionaries and legal encyclopedias from the late eighteenth century to determine what such words as "keep," "bear," "arms," and "well-regulated militia" meant to those who adopted and ratified the Second Amendment.

Although original intent, original understanding, and original public meaning typically lead to the same result, they do not always do so. Consider, for example, the question of state sovereign immunity where the text of Article III, § 2 suggests the states could be sued in federal court without their consent; where Alexander Hamilton in *The Federalist*, No. 81 and John Marshall in the Virginia State Ratifying Convention said they could not; where the Supreme Court in 1793 in *Chisholm v. Georgia* said they could; and finally where Congress and the state legislatures through their adoption and ratification of the Eleventh Amendment two years later said they could not. Consider also the tension between original intent and original understanding regarding the legal effect of treaties. James Wilson was one of the most prominent delegates to the Constitutional Convention—he more than any other delegate shaped the executive branch. He chaired the important Committee on Detail that turned the various resolutions approved by the delegates into a draft of the eventual Constitution; he considered treaties to be self-executing, having "the operation of law" without requiring implementing legislation.

Wilson's original intent position differed completely from Hamilton's original understanding view in *The Federalist*, No. 75 that treaties "are not rules prescribed by the sovereign to the subject [i.e., they do not apply directly to the people and therefore do not have the operation of law], but agreements between sovereign and sovereign."

On the current Supreme Court, Justice Clarence Thomas looks simultaneously to original public meaning, original intent, and original understanding to identify what is, in fact, the Constitution's original general meaning.[21] In so doing, he incorporates Scalia's narrower original public meaning approach and also asks what the text meant to the society that adopted it, but he then widens his originalist focus to consider evidence of the original intent of the Framers and the original understanding of the ratifiers and to ask why the text was adopted. Thomas thus views the proper inquiry as being what ends did the Framers seek to achieve, what evils did they seek to avert, and what means did they employ to achieve those ends and avert those evils when they proposed and ratified those texts.

Originalism as an approach to constitutional interpretation is enjoying a revival. In 1987, Scalia's first year on the Court, originalist arguments were made in only 7 percent of constitutional cases, but twenty years later, with Scalia and Thomas together on the Court, they were made in nearly 35 percent of all cases.[22] Originalist arguments are prevailing in a variety of cases—especially in cases involving the rights of criminal defendants. There has been such a dramatic increase in the number of books, law review articles, and legal briefs advancing originalist analyses that Justice Elena Kagan, during her Senate confirmation hearings stated: "We are all originalists."

That, however, has not shielded originalism from criticism. Some object to the very idea of originalism; as Walton H. Hamilton has famously noted, "It is a little presumptuous for one generation, through a Constitution, to impose its will on posterity. Posterity has its own problems, and to deal with them adequately, it needs freedom of action, unhampered by the dead hand of the past."[23] Originalists, however, deny that they are attempting to impose the founding generation's will on posterity. Rather, they seek to understand the intentions of the Framers, the understanding of the ratifiers, and the original meaning of the words and phrases they employed not because their judgments must be embraced unreservedly, but because they wrote and ratified the very Constitution we are called on to interpret; therefore, they are the best possible guides to discovering the ends and means of the constitutional order under which we live. As long as that order remains in force, we need to know as much about the Constitution as possible, including the purposes it was designed to achieve and the evils it was designed to avert. When constitutional questions are raised, therefore, this approach turns to the founding generation not for specific answers but rather for general guidance as to what the Constitution was to accomplish and how constitutional questions can be resolved in a manner consistent with these overall intentions.

Others such as Justice William Brennan criticize originalism as "little more than arrogance cloaked as humility. It is arrogant to pretend that from our vantage we can gauge accurately the intent of the Framers on application of principle to specific, contemporary questions."[24] Or, as Justice Robert Jackson put it in *Youngstown Sheet & Tube Company v. Sawyer* (1952), "Just what our forefathers did envision, or would have envisioned had they foreseen modern conditions, must be divined from materials almost as enigmatic as the dreams Joseph was called to interpret for Pharaoh." If the problem Brennan and Jackson identify is a lack of evidence as to original intent, understanding, and meaning, it must be noted that with the tremendous outpouring of historical scholarship surrounding and following the bicentennial celebrations of the Declaration of Independence, the Constitution, and the Bill of Rights, we are awash in originalist sources. Since 1976, the Wisconsin Historical Society has published twenty-six volumes (with four more to come) of *The Documentary History of the Ratification of the Constitution*. In 1987, Philip B. Kurland and Ralph

Lerner published *The Founders' Constitution*, a five-volume work that includes original sources critical to the drafting and ratification of each article, clause, and paragraph of the US Constitution. In 1981, Herbert J. Storing published *The Complete Anti-Federalist*, a seven-volume collection of all the significant pamphlets, newspaper articles and letters, essays, and speeches that were written in opposition to the Constitution during the ratification debate. And, since 1972, the First Federal Congress Project published twenty volumes of *The Documentary History of the First Federal Congress of the United States of America*.

Still others dismiss originalism as simply a means of cloaking the justices' policy predilections. Christopher L. Eisgruber argues that originalism is flexible enough that those who employ it reach conclusions at odds with their political preferences "between very rarely and never."[25] Frank Cross agrees: "The justices are able to manipulate (or ignore) originalist materials to produce results they desire to reach on ideological or other grounds. . . . Originalism does not generally explain decisions, but is used to make them more appealing."[26] To these critics, originalists offer two responses. First, they note that this charge can be leveled against other approaches to constitutional interpretation as well. Second, they argue that a justice's consistent commitment to the originalist approach acts as a check, particularly when compared to the multiple approaches sometimes employed by other justices.

THE APPROACHES IN PERSPECTIVE

Textual analysis, precedent, constitutional doctrine, logical analysis, adaptation, consequentialism, and the identification of original intent, original understanding, and original public meaning have all been used by justices of the Supreme Court as they have engaged in constitutional interpretation, and therefore these approaches all have contributed to our contemporary understanding of the Constitution. In this book, we are especially guided by the originalist approaches to constitutional interpretation, following the prudent counsel given by Justice Joseph Story in his *Commentaries on the Constitution of the United States:*

> In construing the Constitution of the United States, we are, in the first instance, to consider, what are its nature and objects, its scope and design, as apparent from the structure of the instrument, viewed as a whole and also viewed in its component parts. Where its words are plain, clear and determinate, they require no interpretation. . . . Where the words admit of two senses, each of which is conformable to general usage, that sense is to be adopted, which without departing from the literal import of the words, best harmonizes with the nature and objects, the scope and design of the instrument. . . . In examining the Constitution, the antecedent situation of the country and its institutions, the existence and operations of the state governments, the powers and operations of the Confederation, in short all the circumstances, which had a tendency to produce, or to obstruct its formation and ratification, deserve careful attention.[27]

Originalist approaches explore what Story calls the Constitution's "nature and objects, its scope and design." They begin by identifying the ends (i.e., "objects") the Framers intended the Constitution to achieve and the means (i.e., the "scope and design") they used to achieve these ends; based on that understanding, they proceed to evaluate the decisions of the Supreme Court and the lower federal and state judiciaries and the constitutionally significant pronouncements of the executive and legislative branches. But, what are these ends and means? The remainder of this chapter is a brief introduction to this important question.

THE ENDS OF THE CONSTITUTION

In spelling out the ends of the Constitution, we can begin with the Preamble and by quoting Justice Joseph Story: "It is an admitted maxim in the ordinary course of the administration of justice, that the preamble of a statute is a key to open the mind of the makers, as to the mischiefs, which are to be remedied, and the objects, which are to be accomplished by the provisions of the statute. . . . There does not seem any reason why, in a fundamental law or constitution of government, an equal attention should not be given to the intention of the framers, as stated in the preamble."[28] The Preamble states that the Constitution was ordained and established by "We the People of the United States" in order "to form a more perfect Union, establish Justice, insure domestic Tranquility, provide for the common defense, promote the general Welfare, and secure the Blessings of Liberty to ourselves and our Posterity." The Preamble, when read in conjunction with the rest of the Constitution and the documentary history concerning its drafting and ratification, makes clear that the Founders set out to establish an efficient and powerful guarantor of rights and liberties based on the principle of qualitative majority rule, that is, the principle that the majority not only should rule but should rule well. In *The Federalist*, No. 10, James Madison explicitly stated this goal: "To secure the public good and private rights against the danger of [an overbearing majority], and at the same time to preserve the spirit and form of popular government is then the great object to which our inquiries are directed. Let me add that it is the desideratum by which alone this form of government can be rescued from the opprobrium under which it has so long labored and be recommended to the esteem and adoption of mankind."

As Madison and his colleagues were well aware, the "great object" of their inquiries presented daunting difficulties. They were irrevocably committed to popular or republican government, but, historically, popular governments led inevitably to majority tyranny. In such governments, measures were decided "not according to the rules of justice, and the rights of the minor party; but by the superior force of an interested and over-bearing majority." Minority rights were disregarded—as were the "permanent and aggregate interests of the community." Because popular governments too easily allowed for "unjust combinations of the majority as a whole," they typically had proved to be "incompatible with personal security, or the rights of property" and "as short in their lives, as they have been violent in their deaths." Such, according to Madison, was the great "opprobrium" under which "this form of government" had "so long labored."

The most commonly prescribed palliative for the problems of majority tyranny was to render the government powerless. However eager a majority might be to "concert and carry into effect its schemes of oppression," if the government were sufficiently impotent, it would pose no real threat. As William Symmes commented in the Massachusetts State Constitutional Ratifying Convention, "Power was never given . . . but it was exercised, nor ever exercised but it was finally abused."[29] The implication was clear: to prevent abuses, power must be consciously and jealously withheld.

This prescription was not without its shortcomings, however. Carried to an extreme, it rendered government not only powerless but also altogether unworkable. To this view, the leading Framers justifiably and appropriately responded that, although the spirit of jealousy was extremely valuable, when carried too far it impinged on another equally important principle of government—that of "strength and stability in the organization of our government, and vigor in its operations."[30] They understood that a strong and stable government was necessary, not only to cope with the problems that society faces, but also to render liberty fully secure. In order that popular government "be recommended to the esteem and adoption of mankind," they realized they would have to solve the twofold problem raised by majority rule: to establish a constitution capable of avoiding democratic tyranny, on the one hand, and democratic ineptitude, on the other. This problem had overwhelmed the government under the Articles of Confederation and led to the calling of the Federal Convention. Under the Articles, the member states were so powerful and their legislative assemblies so dominant and unchecked that the tyrannical impulses of the majority continually placed in jeopardy the life, liberty, and property of the citizenry; the central federal government was so infirm and its responsibilities so few and limited that its situation often "bordered on anarchy." The Framers fully appreciated the challenge they faced. As Madison noted in *The Federalist,* No. 51, "In framing a government which is to be administered by men over men, the great difficulty lies in this: You must first enable the government to control the governed; and in the next place, oblige it to control itself." As we shall see, the Framers rose to this challenge by arranging the various articles and provisions of the Constitution so that they not only granted the federal and state governments sufficient power to control the governed but also obliged them to control themselves through a number of institutional arrangements and contrivances.

CONSTITUTIONAL MEANS TO CONSTITUTIONAL ENDS

The Framers' solution to the problems of republican government was altogether consistent with republican principles. *The Federalist* is replete with references to this matter. Recognizing that "a dependence on the people is no doubt the primary control on the government," the Framers also understood that experience had "taught mankind the necessity of auxiliary precautions." This understanding was fundamentally shaped by their assessment of human nature. They believed humankind to be driven by self-interest and consumed by the desire for distinction. Humans were seen as "ambitious, rapacious, and vindictive" creatures whose passions for "power and advantage" are so powerful and basic that it is folly to expect that they can be controlled adequately by traditional republican reliance on pure patriotism; respect for character, conscience, or religion; or even the not-very-lofty maxim that "honesty is the best policy." Inevitably, human avarice and lust for power divide individuals into parties, inflame them with mutual animosity, and render them much more disposed to oppress one another than to cooperate for the common good. Humans are predictable in such matters. They will form factions, whether there are readily apparent reasons to do so or not. As their passions lead them in directions contrary to the "dictates of reason and justice," their reason is subverted into providing arguments for self-indulgence rather than incentives to virtue.

Given these sentiments, it is hardly surprising that the Framers placed little faith in improving human nature through moral reformation or in the activities of "enlightened statesmen." The only hope for republican government, they concluded, was the establishment of institutions that would depend on "the ordinary depravity of human nature." Appreciating that human passion and pride are elemental forces that can never be stifled or contained by "parchment barriers," they sought to harness and direct these forces through the process of mutual checking. Consequently, they included in the Constitution checks and controls that might "make it the interest, even of bad men, to act for the public good."[31] Self-interest, the Framers contended, was one check that nothing could overcome and the principal hope for security and stability in a republican government. The rather ignoble but always reliable inclination of people to follow their own "sober second thoughts of self-interest" would serve to minimize the likelihood of majority tyranny.[32] As the observant Alexis de Tocqueville would later describe it, the Framers relied on institutional mechanisms to check one personal interest with another and to direct the passions with the very same instruments that excite them.

What kinds of institutional mechanisms—what constitutional means—could incorporate and redirect human self-interest in such a way as to enable the federal and state governments to control the governed and, at the same time, oblige those governments to control themselves? The answer to that question can be found in the three principal concepts underpinning the Constitution: the extended republic; separation of powers and checks and balances; and federalism.

The Extended Republic

The multiplicity of interests in the extended commercial republic established by the Constitution represents one of the principal mechanisms by which the Framers sought to establish an energetic government based on the principle of qualitative majority rule. The advantages of an extended republic can be best seen by examining the defects of a small republic.

As Madison noted in *The Federalist,* No. 10, the smaller the republic, "the fewer probably will be the distinct parties and interests composing it; the fewer the distinct parties and interests, the more frequently will a majority be found of the same party; and the smaller the compass within which they are placed, the more easily will they concert and execute their plans of oppression." Thus arises democratic tyranny, which can be prevented only by rendering the government impotent and thereby fostering democratic ineptitude. In contrast, the larger the republic, the greater the variety of interests, parties, and sects present within it and the more moderate and diffused the conflict. In the words of *The Federalist,* No. 10, "Extend the sphere, and you take in a greater variety of parties and interests; you make it less probable that a majority of the whole will have a common motive to invade the rights of other citizens; or if such a common motive exists, it will be more difficult for all who feel it to discover their own strength, and to act in unison with each other."

Because of the "greater variety" of economic, geographic, religious, political, cultural, and ethnic interests that an extended republic takes in, rule by a majority is effectively replaced by rule by ever-changing coalitions of minorities that come together on one particular issue to act as a majority but break up on the next. The coalition of minorities that acts as a majority on the issue of import duties is not likely to remain intact on such issues as national defense or governmental aid to private schools. The very real possibility that allies in one coalition might be opponents in the next encourages a certain moderation in politics, in terms of both the political objectives sought and the political tactics employed. Political interests become reluctant to raise the political stakes too high: by scoring too decisive a political victory on one issue, an interest might find that it has only weakened itself by devastating a potential ally and thus rendering itself vulnerable to similar treatment in the future. Accordingly, politics is moderated not through idle appeals to conscience and beneficence, but rather through the reliance on the inclination of individuals to look after their own self-interest. As Madison observed in *The Federalist,* No. 51, this diversity of interests ensures that "a coalition of a majority of the whole society" will seldom take place "on any other principles than those of justice and the common good." The extended republic thus helped to make it possible for the Framers to give the national government sufficient power to prevent democratic ineptitude without raising the specter of democratic tyranny.

The Framers' recognition of and reliance on the moderating effects brought about by an extended republic are apparent in such constitutional provisions as the Contract Clause in Article I, Section 10, which prohibits any state from passing laws "impairing the obligation of contracts." Note that only the states are restrained, but the federal government is not— and for good reasons. It was thought that no state, however large, was or would be extensive enough to contain a variety of interests wide enough to prevent majorities from acting oppressively and using their legislative power to nullify contracts for their own advantage. Consequently, the states had to have their power to do so limited by the Constitution. The federal government, by contrast, was large enough and contained the multiplicity of interests necessary to prevent oppression of this sort and so had no need of constitutional constraint. Thus majority tyranny could be avoided simply by relying on the popular principle to operate naturally in an extended republic. The elegant simplicity of this mechanism was pointed out by Madison in *The Federalist,* No. 10: "In the extent and proper structure of the Union, therefore, we behold a Republican remedy for the disease most incident to Republican Government."

Separation of Powers and Checks and Balances

For the Framers, the "great desideratum of politics" was the formation of a "government that will, at the same time, deserve the seemingly opposite epithets—efficient and free."[33] The extended republic was one means by which they sought to realize this objective; a government of separated institutions sharing powers was another. They were aware, as Madison stated in *The Federalist,* No. 47, that "the accumulation of all powers legislative, executive, and judiciary in the same hands, whether of one, a few, or many, and whether hereditary, self-appointed, or elective may justly be pronounced the very definition of tyranny," and therefore that the preservation of liberty requires that the three great departments of power should be separate and distinct. Thus, they sought to construct a government consisting of three coordinate and equal branches, with each performing a blend of functions, thereby balancing governmental powers. Their goal was to structure the government so that, in the words of *The Federalist,* No. 51, the three branches would, "by their mutual relations, be the means of keeping each other in their proper places."

This the Framers succeeded in doing. They began by giving most legislative power to the Congress, most executive power to the president, and most judicial power to the Supreme Court and to such inferior federal courts as Congress might establish. They then set out to divide and arrange the remaining powers in such a manner that each branch could be a check on the others. Thus, they introduced the principle of bicameralism, under which Congress was divided into the House of Representatives and the Senate, and they arranged for the president to exercise certain important legislative powers by requiring yearly addresses on the State of the Union and by providing him with a conditional veto power. (Some Framers assumed that the Congress would also be restrained by the Supreme Court's unstated power of judicial review.) The Framers sought to keep the president in check by requiring senatorial confirmation of executive appointees and judicial nominees, mandating that the Senate advise on and consent to treaties, and allowing for impeachment by the Congress. Finally, they supplied the means for keeping the Supreme Court in its "proper place" by giving the Congress budgetary control over the judiciary, the power of impeachment, and the power to regulate the Court's appellate jurisdiction. On top of these specific arrangements, they provided for staggered terms of office (two years for the House, six years for the Senate, four years for the president, and tenure "for good behavior" for the judiciary) to give each branch a further "constitutional control over the others."

Because they knew that the various branches of the government, even though popularly elected, might from time to time be activated by "an official sentiment opposed to that of the General Government and perhaps to that of the people themselves,"[34] they regarded separation of powers as essential to ensure the fidelity of these popular agents. Separation of powers would provide for a "balance of the parts" that would consist "in the independent exercise of their separate powers and, when their powers are separately exercised, then in their mutual influence and operation on one another. Each part acts and is acted upon, supports and is supported, regulates and is regulated by the rest." This balance would ensure that, even if these separate parts were to become activated by separate interests, they would nonetheless move "in a line of direction somewhat different from that, which each acting by itself, would have taken; but, at the same time, in a line partaking of the natural direction of each, and formed out of the natural direction of the whole—the true line of publick liberty and happiness."[35] Not only would such a separation and balancing of powers prevent any branch of government from tyrannizing the people, but it would also thwart the majority from tyrannizing the minority. In creating an independent executive and judiciary, the Framers provided a means of temporarily blocking the will of tyrannical majorities as expressed through a compliant or demagogic legislature. Although separation of powers cannot permanently frustrate the wishes of the people, on those occasions when "the interests of the people are at variance with their inclinations," it so structures these institutions that they are able to "withstand the temporary delusions" of the people, in order to give them what *The Federalist*, No. 71, described as the "time and opportunity for more cool and sedate reflection." The prospects for democratic tyranny are dimmed accordingly.

And, in addition to keeping society free, separation of powers was seen by the Framers as helping to render the government efficient—as minimizing the prospects for democratic ineptitude. Realizing that the democratic process of mutual deliberation and consent can paralyze the government when swift and decisive action is necessary, the Framers reasoned that government would be more efficient if its various functions were performed by separate and distinct agencies. According to James Wilson, a leading Framer:

> In planning, forming, and arranging laws, deliberation is always becoming, and always useful. But in the active scenes of government, there are emergencies, in which the man . . . who deliberates is lost. Secrecy may be equally necessary as dispatch. But can either secrecy or dispatch be expected, when, to every enterprise, mutual communication, mutual consultation, and mutual agreement among men, perhaps of discordant views, of discordant tempers, and discordant interests, are indispensably necessary? How much time will be consumed! and when it is consumed, how little business will be done! . . . If, on the other hand, the executive power of government is placed in the hands of one person, who is to direct all the subordinate officers of that department; is there not reason to expect, in his plans and conduct, promptitude, activity, firmness, consistency, and energy?[36]

For the Framers, then, separation of powers not only forestalled democratic tyranny but also provided for an independent and energetic executive able to ensure what *The Federalist*, No. 37, called "that prompt and salutary execution of the laws, which enter into the very definition of good Government."

Federalism

The American constitutional system rests on a federal arrangement in which power is shared by the national government and the states. The primary purpose of this arrangement was to provide for a strong central government; however, it has also had the effect of promoting qualitative majority rule. The federalism created by the Framers can best be understood when contrasted with the confederalism that existed under the Articles of Confederation. Confederalism was characterized by three principles:

1. The central government exercised authority only over the individual governments (i.e., states) of which it was composed, never over the individual citizens of whom those governments were composed. Even this authority was limited; the resolutions of the federal authority amounted to little more than recommendations that the states could (and did) disregard.
2. The central government had no authority over the internal affairs of the individual states; its rule was limited mainly to certain external tasks of mutual interest to the member states.
3. Each individual state had an "exact equality of suffrage" derived from the equality of sovereignty shared by all states.[37]

The consequences of these principles on the operation of the federal government were disastrous. They rendered the Articles of Confederation so weak that they were reduced, in Alexander Hamilton's words from *The Federalist,* No. 9, "to the last stage of national humiliation." There was obviously a need for a "more perfect union" and for new arrangements capable of rendering the political structure "adequate to the exigencies of Government and the preservation of the Union."[38]

The new federal structure erected by the Framers corrected each of the difficulties inherent in confederalism. To begin with, the power of the new federal government was enhanced considerably. Not only could it now operate directly on the individual citizen, just as the state governments could, but it could also deal with internal matters: for example, it now could regulate commerce among the several states, establish uniform rules of bankruptcy, coin money, establish a postal system, tax, and borrow money. Moreover, the federal government was made supreme over the states. As Article VI spelled out: "This Constitution, and the laws of the United States which shall be made in pursuance thereof . . . shall be the supreme law of the land."

If the federalism the Framers created strengthened the central government, it also contributed to qualitative majority rule by preserving the presence of powerful states capable of checking and controlling not only the central government but each other as well. Federalism granted the new central government only those powers expressly or implicitly delegated to it in the Constitution and allowed the states to retain all powers not prohibited to them. The states were permitted to regulate intrastate commerce and the health, safety, and welfare of the citizenry (i.e., the police power) and even were authorized to exercise certain powers concurrently with the central government—for example, the power of taxation and the power to regulate interstate commerce—so long as these powers were not exercised in a manner inconsistent with constitutional limitations or federal regulations. Finally, the Framers' federalism also contributed to qualitative majority rule by blending federal elements into the structure and procedures of the central government itself. To take only the most obvious example, it mixed into the Senate the federal principle of equal representation of all states. When joined with bicameralism and separation of powers, this principle directly contributed to qualitative majority rule. For a measure to become law, it would have to pass the Senate—where, because of the federal principle of equal representation of all states, the presence of a nationally distributed majority (with the moderating tendencies that provides) would be virtually guaranteed.

This division of power between the federal and state governments also provided another remedy for the ills of democratic ineptitude. As James Wilson emphasized, with two levels of government at their disposal, the people are in a position to assign their sovereign power to whichever level they believe to be more productive in promoting the common good. Moreover, efficiency is gained in still another way. The federal system permits the states to serve as experimental social laboratories in which new policies and procedures can be implemented. If these experiments prove to be successful, they can be adopted elsewhere; if they fail, the damage is limited to the particular state in question. Because the risks are lessened, experimentation is encouraged, and the chances of positive reform and better governance are increased accordingly. In a wholly national or unitary system, on the other hand, experimentation can take place only on a national scale, and social inertia and a commitment to the status quo are encouraged.

The enhanced efficiency of the federal system, in turn, dims the prospect of democratic tyranny. As Madison observed in *The Federalist*, No. 20, "Tyranny has perhaps oftener grown out of the assumptions of power, called for, on pressing exigencies, by a defective constitution, than by the full exercise of the largest constitutional authorities."

The Framers saw the multiplicity of interests present in an extended republic, separation of powers and checks and balances, and federalism as contributing to a government that is at once "efficient and free." These institutional mechanisms, operating in conjunction with each other, were designed to prevent the twin evils of democratic ineptitude and democratic tyranny. The Framers' intention was to institute an energetic and efficient government based on the principle of qualitative majority rule, and they systematically and consistently employed these means to achieve that end. This understanding is at the core of the approach to constitutional interpretation, used where appropriate, in the discussion of the constitutional provisions that follows.

NOTES

1. Chief Justice Hughes subsequently qualified these remarks. "The remark has been used, regardless of its context, as if permitting the inference that I was picturing constitutional interpretation by the courts as a matter of judicial caprice. This was farthest from my thought. . . . I was speaking of the essential function of the courts under our system of interpreting and applying constitutional safeguards." *The Autobiographical Notes of Charles Evans Hughes,* edited by David J. Danielski and J. S. Tulshin (Cambridge, MA: Harvard University Press, 1973), 143.

2. Joseph Story, *Commentaries on the Constitution of the United States* (Boston: Hilliard and Gray, 1833), 1: 436–437.

3. *Graves v. O'Keefe* (1939), Justice Frankfurter concurring.

4. See book 3, chapter 5, "Rules of Interpretation," in Story, *Commentaries on the Constitution of the United States,* 1:382–442. See also Francis Lieber, *Legal and Political Hermeneutics,* 2nd ed. (Boston: Charles C. Little & James Brown, 1839), reprinted in *Cardozo Law Review* 16, no. 6 (1995): 1879–2105.

5. Stephen Breyer, *Active Liberty: Interpreting Our Democratic Constitution* (New York: Alfred A. Knopf, 2005), 19.

6. Thomas Hobbes, *A Dialogue Between a Philosopher and a Student of the Common Laws of England,* edited by Joseph Cropsey (Chicago: University of Chicago Press, 1971), 129.

7. See J. Skelly Wright, "Professor Bickel, the Scholarly Tradition, and the Supreme Court," *Harvard Law Review* 84, no. 4 (1971): 785.

8. *Avery v. Midland County* (1968), Justice Fortas dissenting.

9. Scalia and Garner state that "the most rigorous form of logic, and hence the most persuasive, is the syllogism." Antonin Scalia and Bryan A. Garner, *Making Your Case: The Art of Persuading Judges* (St. Paul, MN: Thomson, West, 2008), 41.

10. Ibid., 42.

11. The phrase is Justice Scalia's. See Antonin Scalia, *A Matter of Interpretation: Federal Courts and the Law* (Princeton, N.J.: Princeton University Press, 1997), 47.

12. See Christopher Wolfe, "A Theory of U.S. Constitutional History," *Journal of Politics* 43, no. 2 (1981): 301.

13. See Walter F. Berns, *Taking the Constitution Seriously* (New York: Simon and Schuster, 1987), 236: "The Framers . . . provided for a Supreme Court and charged it with the task, not of keeping the Constitution in tune with the times but, to the extent possible, of keeping the times in tune with the Constitution."

14. William J. Brennan, "The Constitution of the United States: Contemporary Ratification," presentation at the Text and Teaching Symposium, Georgetown University, Washington, DC, October 12, 1985.

15. Scalia, *Matter of Interpretation*, 46–47 (emphases in the original).

16. The quotations above come from Breyer, *Active Liberty*, see pp. 6, 18, 48–49, 63, and 97.

17. Ibid., pp. 97, 18.

18. Scalia, *Matter of Interpretation*, 21.

19. Lino Graglia, "Interpreting the Constitution: Posner on Bork," 44 *Stanford Law Review* (1991–1992): 1019, 1024.

20. Scalia, *Matter of Interpretation*, 34.

21. Ralph A. Rossum, *Understanding Clarence Thomas: The Jurisprudence of Constitutional Restoration* (Lawrence: University Press of Kansas, 2014).

22. Jeffrey S. Sutton, "The Role of History in Judging Disputes about the Meaning of the Constitution," *Texas Tech Law Review* 41 (2009): 1173, 1176.

23. Walton H. Hamilton, "The Constitution—Apropos of Crosskey," *University of Chicago Law Review* 21, no. 1 (1953): 82.

24. See Brennan, "Constitution of the United States."

25. Christopher L. Eisgruber, *Constitutional Self-Government* (Cambridge, MA: Harvard University Press, 2007), p. 40.

26. Frank Cross, *The Failed Promise of Originalism* (Palo Alto, CA: Stanford University Press, 2013), p. 190.

27. Story, *Commentaries on the Constitution of the United States,* 1:387–388. See also 322, 404, 412, and 417.

28. Ibid., 443–444.

29. Jonathan Elliot, ed., *The Debates in the Several State Conventions on the Adoption of the Federal Constitution as Recommended by the General Convention in Philadelphia in 1787,* 5 vols., 2nd ed. (Philadelphia: Lippincott, 1866), 2:74.

30. Alexander Hamilton in the New York State Ratifying Convention, in Elliot, *Debates in the Several State Conventions,* 2:301.

31. David Hume, *Political Essays,* edited by Charles W. Handel (Indianapolis: Bobbs-Merrill, 1953), 13.

32. The phrase is Frederick Douglass's. See his "The Destiny of Colored Americans," *North Star,* November 16, 1849.

33. Robert Green McCloskey, ed., *The Works of James Wilson* (Cambridge, MA: Belknap Press of Harvard University Press, 1967), 791.

34. James Wilson, in Farrand, *Records of the Federal Convention of 1787,* 1:359.

35. McCloskey, *Works of James Wilson,* 300.

36. Ibid., 294, 296. See also *The Federalist,* No. 70.

37. See Martin Diamond, "What the Framers Meant by Federalism," in *A Nation of States: Essays on the American Federal System,* edited by Robert A. Goldwin, 2nd ed. (Chicago: Rand McNally College Publications, 1974), 25–42.

38. Resolution of the Congress calling for the Federal Convention of 1787, in Farrand, *Records of the Federal Convention of 1787,* 3:14.

SELECTED READINGS

The Federalist, Nos. 1, 6, 9, 10, 15, 37, 39, 47–51, 63, 70–72, 78.

Amar, Akhil Reed. *America's Constitution: A Biography.* New York: Random House, 2006.

Anastaplo, George. *The Constitution of 1787: A Commentary.* Baltimore, MD: Johns Hopkins University Press, 1989.

Balkin, Jack M. *Living Originalism.* Cambridge, MA: Harvard University Press, 2011.

Barber, Sotirios A., and James E. Fleming. *Constitutional Interpretation: The Basic Questions.* New York: Oxford University Press, 2007.

Baude, William. "Is Originalism Our Law?" *Columbia Law Review* 115 (2015): 1–86.

Breyer, Stephen. *Active Liberty: Interpreting Our Democratic Constitution.* New York: Alfred A. Knopf, 2005.

Calabresi, Steven G., ed. *Originalism: A Quarter-Century of Debate.* Washington, DC: Regnery, 2007.

Cornell, Saul. *The Other Founders: Anti-Federalism and Dissenting Tradition in America, 1788–1828.*

Chapel Hill: University of North Carolina Press, 1999.

Cross, Frank. *The Failed Promise of Originalism.* Palo Alto, CA: Stanford University Press, 2013.

Diamond, Martin. "Democracy and *The Federalist*: A Reconsideration of the Framers' Intent." *American Political Science Review* 53, no. 1 (1959): 52–68.

Douglas, William O. "Stare Decisis." *Columbia Law Review* 49 (1949): 725–758.

Elliot, Jonathan, ed. *The Debates in the Several State Conventions on the Adoption of the Federal Constitution as Recommended by the General Convention in Philadelphia in 1787.* 2nd ed. 5 vols. Philadelphia: Lippincott, 1866.

Farrand, Max, ed. *The Records of the Federal Convention of 1787.* 4 vols. New Haven, CT: Yale University Press, 1937.

Faulkner, Robert K. *The Jurisprudence of John Marshall.* Princeton, NJ: Princeton University Press, 1968.

Hickok, Eugene W., ed. *The Bill of Rights: Original Meaning and Current Understanding.* Charlottesville: University Press of Virginia, 1991.

Kesler, Charles R., ed. *Saving the Revolution: The Federalist Papers and the American Founding.* New York: Free Press, 1987.

Kurland, Philip B., and Ralph Lerner, eds. *The Founders' Constitution.* 5 vols. Chicago: University of Chicago Press, 1987.

Levinson, Sanford. *Framed: America's 51 Constitutions and the Crisis of Governance.* New York: Oxford University Press, 2012

————. "On Interpretation: The Adultery Clause of the Ten Commandments." *Southern California Law Review* 58, no. 2 (1985): 719–725.

Levy, Leonard W., and Dennis J. Mahoney, eds. *The Framing and Ratification of the Constitution.* New York: Macmillan, 1987.

Maier, Pauline. *Ratification: The People Debate the Constitution, 1787–1788.* New York: Simon & Schuster, 2010.

McClellan, James. *Liberty, Order, and Justice: An Introduction to the Constitutional Principles of American Government.* 2nd ed. Indianapolis: Liberty Fund, 1999.

McDowell, Gary L. *The Language of Law and the Foundations of American Constitutionalism.* New York: Cambridge University Press, 2010.

McGinnis, John O., and Michael B. Rappaport. *Originalism and the Good Constitution.* Cambridge, MA: Harvard University Press, 2013.

Meese, Edwin. "Toward a Jurisprudence of Original Intention." *Benchmark* 2, no. 1 (1986): 1–10.

O'Connor, Mike. *A Commercial Republic: America's Enduring Debate over Democratic Capitalism.* Lawrence: University Press of Kansas, 2014.

Rehnquist, William H. "The Notion of a Living Constitution." *Texas Law Review* 54 (May 1976): 693–707.

Rossum, Ralph A. *Antonin Scalia's Jurisprudence: Text and Tradition.* Lawrence: University Press of Kansas, 2006.

————. *Understanding Clarence Thomas: The Jurisprudence of Constitutional Restoration.* Lawrence: University Press of Kansas, 2014.

Rossum, Ralph A. and Gary L. McDowell, eds. *The American Founding: Politics, Statesmanship, and the Constitution.* Port Washington, NY: Kennikat Press, 1981.

Ryan, James E., "Does It Take A Theory? Originalism, Active Liberty, and Minimalism, *Stanford Law Review* 58 (2006): 1623–1660.

Scalia, Antonin. *A Matter of Interpretation: Federal Courts and the Law.* Princeton, NJ: Princeton University Press, 1997.

Scalia, Antonin, and Bryan A. Garner. *Reading Law: Interpretation of Legal Texts.* St. Paul, MN: West, 2012.

Storing, Herbert J., ed. *The Complete Anti-Federalist.* 7 vols. Chicago: University of Chicago Press, 1981.

Strauss, David A. *The Living Constitution.* New York: Oxford University Press, 2010.

Tillman, Seth Barrett, "*The Federalist Papers* as Reliable Historical Source Materials for Constitutional Interpretation." *West Virginia Law Review* 105 (2003): 601–619.

Watson, Bradley C. S. *Living Constitution, Dying Faith: Progressivism and the New Science of Jurisprudence.* Wilmington, DE: ISI Press, 2009.

Whittington, Keith E. *Constitutional Interpretation: Textual Meaning, Original Intent, and Judicial Review.* Lawrence: University Press of Kansas, 1999.

Wolfe, Christopher. *How to Read the Constitution: Originalism, Constitutional Interpretation, and Judicial Power.* Lanham, MD: Rowman & Littlefield, 1996.

Wood, Gordon S. *The Creation of the American Republic, 1776–1787.* Chapel Hill: University of North Carolina Press, 1969.

2

Constitutional Adjudication

CHAPTER OUTLINE

M ore than 180 years ago, Alexis de Tocqueville observed that "there is hardly a political question in the United States which does not sooner or later turn into a judicial one."[1] Today, as then, Americans transform policy disputes into constitutional issues and seek resolution of those disputes in courts in general and in the United States Supreme Court in particular. The Supreme Court's political and legal roles are thus intertwined. By deciding cases that raise important issues concerning the extent, distribution, and uses of governmental power, the Court inevitably participates in governing.

The Supreme Court's dual responsibilities as an interpreter of the Constitution and as an agency of government provide the focus for this chapter. Five basic questions are considered: Who is selected to serve on the Supreme Court? What is the Supreme Court's position in the federal judicial system? How are political questions transformed into legal issues and brought before the justices? How do the justices go about deciding cases? And what happens after the Supreme Court decides? The chapter's final sections offer a framework for analyzing judicial decisions and survey source materials in constitutional law.

THE JUSTICES OF THE SUPREME COURT

Appointment and Tenure

Supreme Court justices are appointed by the president with the advice and consent of the Senate and, like other federal judges, hold office during "good behavior." Only one justice has ever been impeached by the House of Representatives (Samuel Chase in 1804), and the Senate failed to convict him. For most justices, appointment to the Court represents the culmination of their careers, and the vast majority remain on the bench until death or retirement. Justice William O. Douglas, for example, served thirty-six years on the Court, and Justice Oliver Wendell Holmes did not retire until he was ninety-one.

Historically, vacancies on the Court have occurred about every two or three years, so presidents serving two full terms often have a considerable impact on the composition of the Court. Thus President Ronald Reagan named four justices to the Court during his two terms, and Presidents Bill Clinton and Barack Obama each named two justices during their first terms. Yet openings do not occur according to a fixed schedule. Thus, Clinton did not appoint any justices during his second term, and President George W. Bush none during his first term. Recent advances in life expectancy have meant that justices tend to serve longer today than in earlier eras: three current justices—Anthony Kennedy, Ruth Bader Ginsburg, and Stephen Breyer—are more than seventy-five years old. This longevity makes the choice of who is appointed to the Court all the more crucial. When Justice Sandra Day O'Connor announced her retirement in 2005, the average tenure for currently sitting justices was more than nineteen years, and no new justice had been appointed for eleven years. Table 2.1 lists the justices serving on the Supreme Court as of 2016.

Choosing Justices

In appointing justices, presidents typically select persons with distinguished careers in public life. Among justices appointed up to 2016, twenty-five had served in Congress, and more than twenty had held cabinet posts. Although prior judicial experience is not a requirement, all but one justice appointed since 1975 had served as an appellate judge. Most important, presidents seek appointees who share their political affiliation (roughly 90 percent of appointees have been members of the president's party) and their constitutional views. Thus, President Reagan sought proponents of "judicial restraint," whereas President Clinton pledged to appoint justices sympathetic to abortion rights. Presidents also consider demographic factors in their appointments. President Lyndon Johnson chose Thurgood Marshall as the first Afri-

TABLE 2.1 Justices of the US Supreme Court, 2016

	Born	Home State	Position Before Appointment	Prior Judicial Experience	Party Affiliation	Year Appointed	Appointing President
John Roberts	1955	Indiana	US Court of Appeals	Yes	Republican	2005 (Chief)	G. W. Bush
Anthony Kennedy	1936	California	US Court of Appeals	Yes	Republican	1988	Reagan
Clarence Thomas	1948	Georgia	US Court of Appeals	Yes	Republican	1991	G. H. W. Bush
Ruth Bader Ginsburg	1933	New York	US Court of Appeals	Yes	Democrat	1993	Clinton
Stephen Breyer	1938	California	US Court of Appeals	Yes	Democrat	1994	Clinton
Samuel Alito	1950	New Jersey	US Court of Appeals	Yes	Republican	2006	G. W. Bush
Sonia Sotomayor	1954	New York	US Court of Appeals	Yes	Democrat	2009	Obama
Elena Kagan	1960	New York	Solicitor General	No	Democrat	2010	Obama

Note: When Justice Antonin Scalia died in February, 2016, President Barack Obama nominated Merrick Garland, Chief Judge of the United States Court of Appeals for the District of Columbia, to replace him. But as of July 2016, the seat remains vacant.

can American on the Supreme Court; when Marshall retired, President George H. W. Bush replaced him with another African American, Clarence Thomas. President Reagan appointed Sandra Day O'Connor as the first woman on the Court, and in 2009 President Obama selected Sonia Sotomayor as the first Latina appointee. In recent years there has been some criticism that those chosen for the Court are too similar in their backgrounds and experience. Of the current justices, all attended either Harvard or Yale Law School, and all but one had served on federal courts of appeals before their appointment to the Court.

The Impact of Appointments

Through their appointment of Supreme Court justices, presidents can influence the orientation of the Supreme Court. For example, appointments by President George W. Bush from 2001–2009 produced a more conservative Court, while those appointed by President Barack Obama aligned with the liberal wing of the Court. However, presidents do not always see their choices seated on the Court. For example, Harriet Miers asked President Bush to withdraw her nomination in 2005 following widespread criticism from the President's conservative political base. The Senate also can refuse to confirm nominees— between 1968 and 1992, six nominees were rejected by the Senate or withdrew when it became apparent they could not be confirmed. Even when the Senate does confirm nominees, the process has sometimes been contentious—for example, Justice Clarence Thomas was approved by only a 52–48 vote after accusations of sexual harassment were leveled against him during confirmation hearings. Moreover, once on the Court, justices might not behave as the president expected. The president might have misjudged the prospective justice's views, those views might change after the justice is appointed, or new issues might arise that the president did not anticipate when choosing a justice. When a justice fails to meet a president's expectations, there is nothing a president can do about it, and so presidents recognize they must be careful in whom they choose. Thus, in explaining his choice of John Roberts for Chief Justice, President Bush commented: "I believed Roberts would be a natural leader. I didn't worry about him drifting away from his principles over time."[2]

The politics of the appointment process have changed over time, particularly in the Senate. Until the 1920s, Senate deliberations on prospective justices were secret. Nominees did not testify, and they were confirmed or rejected without a roll-call vote, so it was impossible to know how individual senators had voted. Now, however, nominees testify before the Senate Judiciary Committee in public hearings, as do groups and individuals supporting or opposing the nominees. Since 1982, when President Reagan nominated Sandra Day O'Connor to the Court, these hearings have been televised. This opened up the process and made it easier for groups to mobilize opinion for and against nominees and to influence votes on confirmation by threatening to hold senators electorally accountable. Yet whether groups mobilize depends on the character and views of the nominee. When President Reagan nominated conservative jurist Robert Bork for the Supreme Court, liberal groups successfully organized to oppose him. In contrast, President Clinton's appointees to the Supreme Court, Ruth Bader Ginsburg and Stephen Breyer, were uncontroversial and overwhelmingly confirmed by the Senate. Many liberal groups mobilized in unsuccessful attempts to block George W. Bush's appointments of John Roberts and Samuel Alito to the Supreme Court; and when President Obama nominated Sonja Sotomayor and Elena Kagan for the Supreme Court, Democratic senators overwhelmingly supported the nominees, while Republican senators almost unanimously opposed them.

THE SUPREME COURT IN THE FEDERAL JUDICIAL SYSTEM

Article III of the Constitution establishes the United States Supreme Court and authorizes "such inferior Courts as the Congress may from time to time ordain and establish." Acting under this authority, Congress has created a three-tiered system of federal courts, with the Supreme Court at the apex of the system and the federal courts of appeals and federal district courts below it. During the twentieth century, Congress added to this system various specialized courts, such as the Court of Military Appeals, the Foreign Intelligence Surveillance Court, and the Court of International Trade.

The district courts are the primary trial courts of the federal judicial system, with a single judge presiding over trials in civil or criminal cases. Ninety-four federal district courts serve the fifty states, the District of Columbia, and various US territories. Every state has at least one district court, with more populous states divided into multiple districts. California, New York, and Texas each have four district courts.

The thirteen courts of appeals serve as the first-level appellate courts of the federal judicial system, hearing appeals from the district courts, from federal administrative agencies, and from various specialized courts. The courts of appeals typically hear cases as three-judge panels, which are randomly chosen for each case, and decide cases by majority vote. Occasionally, however, a court of appeals might hear a case *en banc*, that is, with the court's entire membership participating in the decision of the case. Most courts of appeals are organized into regional "circuits" made up of three or more states. The Seventh Circuit, for example, includes Wisconsin, Illinois, and Indiana. The Court of Appeals for the District of Columbia hears large numbers of appeals from federal administrative agencies and serves as a sort of state supreme court for the District of Columbia. The Court of Appeals for the Federal Circuit has a subject-matter jurisdiction, hearing cases involving international trade, veterans' benefits, and government contracts, among other matters.

The Supreme Court initially consisted of six justices. Congress changed the size of the Court several times—sometimes for political purposes—before finally establishing the number of justices at nine in 1869. When President Franklin Roosevelt proposed to increase the number of justices after the Court had struck down several New Deal laws, hoping to appoint justices more sympathetic to his views, Congress refused to expand the Court. Since then, there has been no serious effort to expand the Court or to limit the justices' tenure.

HOW CASES GET TO THE SUPREME COURT

Since 2000, the Supreme Court has annually received more than seven thousand petitions for review but decided less than 2 percent of the cases appealed to it with full opinions. In its 2013 term, for example, it received 7,541 petitions for review but decided only seventy-three cases. The cases the Court decides must fall within its jurisdiction; that is, it can decide only those cases it is empowered to hear by the Constitution or by statute. Once this requirement is met, the Court has broad discretion in determining what cases it will decide. The range of discretion available to the Court has increased over time, and this expanded discretion has led to significant shifts in its caseload.

The Jurisdiction of the Supreme Court

The Supreme Court has both an original jurisdiction (over those cases in which the Court functions as a trial court) and an appellate jurisdiction (over those cases in which the Court reviews the decisions of other courts). Article III, Section 2, of the Constitution defines the Court's original jurisdiction but confers its appellate jurisdiction subject to "such Exceptions, and under such Regulations, as Congress shall make."

Original Jurisdiction. The Supreme Court's original jurisdiction extends to cases involving foreign diplomatic personnel and to cases in which a state is a party. The Court seldom decides more than a couple of cases under its original jurisdiction each term. Two developments have minimized the number of cases initiated in the Supreme Court. First, the Eleventh Amendment, adopted in 1798, withdrew part of the Court's original jurisdiction by prohibiting those who were not citizens of a state from suing it in federal court.[3] And second, during the twentieth century, Congress deflected many potential original-jurisdiction cases to the federal district courts by giving those courts concurrent jurisdiction. Currently, the Supreme Court retains exclusive original jurisdiction over only legal disputes between two states, which commonly deal with boundaries or with water or mineral rights. Because hearing testimony in even these few cases would be a major drain on the time and energies of the Court, it typically appoints a "Special Master"—usually a retired judge—to conduct hearings and report back to it. In deciding these cases, the justices often endorse the findings of the Special Master.

Appellate Jurisdiction. The Supreme Court hears most of its cases on appeal from the federal courts of appeals—in its 2014 term, these made up 89 percent of its docket. It may also hear appeals from federal district courts or from one of the fifty state court systems. In all cases, the Court operates as the court of last resort: its decisions are final in that there is no court to which one can appeal to reverse them. The Court's interpretation of statutes can only be reversed by congressional legislation, and given political polarization, this rarely occurs.[4] Its constitutional rulings can only be overturned by constitutional amendment or by subsequent Supreme Court decisions. In the absence of such changes in the law, all courts are obliged to follow the Supreme Court's direction in matters of federal law. The Court's decisions are also final in the sense that the Court generally decides cases only after litigants have exhausted their available appeals to other courts (Figure 2.1). As Justice Robert Jackson put it in *Brown v. Allen* (1953): "We are not final because we are infallible, but we are infallible only because we are final."

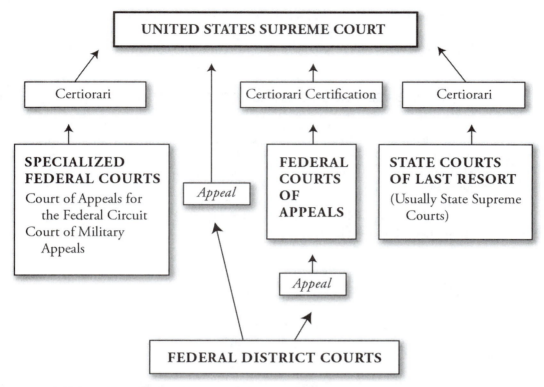

FIGURE 2.1 **How Cases Reach the Supreme Court**

Cases initiated in state courts usually reach the US Supreme Court on appeal from state supreme courts, although the Court may hear a case on appeal from another state court when no further appeal is available in the state system. In *Thompson v. City of Louisville* (1960), for example, the justices accepted a case directly from the police court of Louisville, Kentucky, because under state law the defendant's fine was too low for appeal to any higher state court.[5] Cases initiated in federal district courts normally come to the Court following review by the appropriate court of appeals, but the Court can expedite consideration of cases. In *United States v. Nixon* (1974), which involved President Richard Nixon's refusal during the Watergate Scandal to surrender tapes of his conversations subpoenaed for use in a criminal prosecution, the importance of the dispute prompted the Court to hear the case immediately after the federal district court ruled.

Over the course of time, the Supreme Court has gained virtually total discretion in determining what cases it hears. Early in the twentieth century, cases on appeal (that is, cases in which the party appealing had a right to Supreme Court review) accounted for more than 80 percent of the Court's docket. Because many of these cases raised no significant legal issue, the justices lobbied for a reduction in the burden of obligatory review. Congress responded with the Judiciary Act of 1925, which drastically reduced the categories of cases in which parties had a right of appeal to the Court. In 1988, again at the urging of the justices, Congress eliminated almost all the Court's remaining mandatory jurisdiction, thereby according the Court nearly complete control of its appellate docket.

Even before 1988, the justices had considerable control over what cases they decided. For one thing, more than 90 percent of the petitions for review came to the Court on writs of certiorari.[6] These petitions ranged from professionally drafted legal presentations in so-called paid cases to lay-drafted petitions submitted *in forma pauperis*.[7] In determining which certiorari petitions to accept, the Court has full discretion. As the Supreme Court's Rule 10 states, "A review on writ of certiorari is not a matter of right but of judicial discretion, and will be granted only when there are special and important reasons therefore."[8] In recent years, the Court has used its discretion to reduce dramatically the number of cases it hears each term. During the early 1980s, the justices granted review in more than 180 cases per term. In its 2014 term, however, the Court decided only sixty-seven cases with full opinion. Former Justice David Souter suggested that this change did not reflect a conscious choice; rather, "it just happened." Whatever the explanation, the Court's increasing selectivity underscores the importance of the process by which the justices choose what cases they will hear.

The Decision to Decide

Because the justices receive more than 7,000 petitions for certiorari each year, they have established procedures and criteria for determining which cases warrant review. It might be, as Chief Justice Earl Warren once suggested, that the standards that guide the justices' determinations "cannot be captured in any rule or guidelines that would be meaningful."[9] But if so, how does the Court decide what to decide?

The Case-Selection Process. The mechanics of case selection are clear. Each justice has several law clerks (distinguished law school graduates selected annually by the justice after they have already served a year's clerkship for another federal judge) whose duties include screening the petitions for review and preparing memos summarizing the materials. The influx of cases in recent decades has prompted eight justices to pool their clerks for memo writing, so that the case memos each clerk prepares will be distributed to the justices in the "cert pool." Justice Alito has his clerks independently evaluate all petitions for certiorari. Having evaluated the filings with the aid of the clerks' memos, the chief justice prepares a "discuss list" of the petitions he believes deserve collective consideration. Other justices can then add cases to the list. Unless a justice requests that a petition be discussed in conference, it is automatically denied. More than 70 percent of all petitions are disposed of in this manner.

Collective consideration of the petitions on the discuss list occurs during the three- or four-day conference before the beginning of the Court's term in October and at weekly conferences during the term. In the preterm conference, which is devoted exclusively to case selection, the justices dispose of the hundreds of petitions that have accumulated over the summer months. No case is accepted for review, at either the preterm or the regular weekly conference, unless at least four justices vote to hear it (the so-called rule of four).

Criteria for Case Selection. The justices do not publish or explain their votes to grant or deny review in particular cases, although occasionally a justice may file a dissent from a denial of certiorari. Although the considerations affecting case selection likely vary from justice to justice and case to case, one can identify some factors that affect the Court's decisions on petitions for certiorari.

One factor is the Court's responsibility to promote uniformity and consistency in federal law. This may involve the interpretation of federal statutes as well as of the Constitution—indeed, in its 2013 term, only twenty of the seventy-four cases the Court decided raised constitutional issues. Supreme Court Rule 10, "Considerations Governing Review on Certiorari," recognizes this supervisory responsibility in its list of the factors that might prompt the Court to grant certiorari: (1) important questions of federal law on which the Court has not previously ruled, (2) conflicting interpretations of federal law by lower courts, (3) lower-court decisions that conflict with previous Supreme Court decisions, and

(4) lower-court departures "from the accepted and usual course of judicial proceedings." This list is neither exhaustive nor binding: review may be granted on the basis of other factors or denied when a listed factor is present. At times the Court might deny review even when lower courts have reached conflicting decisions on an issue. For example, for several years the justices refused to review challenges to states' use of roadblocks to detect drunk drivers, even though state courts had disagreed about whether the roadblocks violated the constitutional prohibition on unreasonable searches and seizures. Only in 1990, after rejecting several earlier petitions for certiorari, did the Court address the issue.[10]

In denying certiorari despite disagreement among lower courts, the justices may rely on another case-selection criterion—the intrinsic importance of the issues raised in a case. Although occasionally the Court reaches out to correct a gross miscarriage of justice, the justices tend to be less concerned with correcting the errors of lower courts than with confronting "questions whose resolution will have immediate importance far beyond the particular facts and parties involved."[11] This criterion, of course, cannot be applied automatically. Some cases, because of the momentous political or legal issues they raise, seem to demand Supreme Court review. *National Federation of Independent Business v. Sebelius* (2012), which involved a challenge to President Obama's health-care reforms, fell into that category. Many other cases, including most *in forma pauperis* petitions, raise relatively minor issues that do not warrant the Court's attention. In some cases, the choice as to whether to hear a case might be controversial. For example, commentators disagreed sharply about whether the Court should have heard the case of *Bush v. Gore* (2000), which arose from the dispute over the counting of ballots in Florida in the 2000 presidential election. Whenever the choice is not so clear, additional factors come into play.

A concern in some decisions on whether to grant review is the effect the case might have on the long-term influence of the Court. The Court may seek to safeguard its influence by avoiding unproductive involvement in political disputes, as when it refused to hear cases challenging the constitutionality of the Vietnam War. But this has not always been the case, as shown by the Court's willingness in *Bush v. Gore* (2000) to involve itself in the contested presidential election of 2000. The justices also attempt to select cases in which the issues are clear and sufficiently well-defined so as to facilitate wise and persuasive constitutional decisions.

Finally, the Court sometimes seeks to avoid unnecessarily inflaming public opinion by limiting the number of controversial issues it addresses at one time and by considering public reaction in choosing cases in which to announce important rulings. Thus, for thirteen years after *Brown v. Board of Education* (1954), which outlawed state-mandated school segregation, it refused to consider constitutional challenges to state laws prohibiting interracial marriage.[12] The Court chose *Gideon v. Wainwright* (1963) to announce that indigent defendants had a right to counsel at trial in part because it involved a relatively minor offense rather than a violent crime. Yet the Court does not always avoid controversial issues, as illustrated by its decision in *Obergefell v. Hodges* (2015) to uphold a challenge to state laws prohibiting same-sex marriage.

Even more important than maintaining the Court's influence are the justices' constitutional views—their notions of which constitutional issues are most important and how those issues should be resolved. Specifically, justices might vote to hear a case when they believe that review would further their conception of desirable constitutional policy. In some cases, certain justices might favor review if they believe that a majority of the Court will support their constitutional position, particularly if they disagree with the lower court's decision. Alternatively, if they expect to be in a minority on the Court, they might oppose review rather than risk creation of an unfavorable precedent—a practice referred to as a defensive denial of certiorari.

The Changing Agenda. Our discussion of case selection has focused thus far on the factors underlying the selection of particular cases for review. However, the quotation from De Tocqueville that opens the chapter suggests a broader perspective. If political questions tend to become judicial questions, then the cases from which the justices select presumably reflect the broad political issues confronting the nation. Put differently, if the Court seeks to decide cases of national importance, then the nation's political concerns necessarily furnish the Court's basic agenda.

The historical record confirms this. Prior to the Civil War, the paramount political issue was the distribution of political power between the federal and state governments (with slavery and property rights underlying elements in many of these disputes). So the constitutional cases considered by the Court characteristically required it to define the respective spheres of the federal and state governments. After the Civil War, the nation underwent rapid industrialization and saw the growth of large corporations. Governmental efforts to deal with these developments played a major role in the Court's constitutional decisions from the 1870s until the late 1930s. In the wake of the New Deal, an expansion in the scope of governmental activity, facilitated by Court rulings permitting extensive regulation of economic activity, created new conflicts between government and the individual. Accordingly, the Court's constitutional decisions primarily involved the delineation of individual rights. Although this emphasis on rights has continued, in recent years there has been renewed concern about the reach of government, and this has been reflected in the Supreme Court's renewed attention to issues of federalism and the scope of federal power. In *Shelby County v. Holder* (2013), the Court struck down a provision of the Voting Rights Act of 1965 that required certain jurisdictions, primarily in the South, to obtain permission from the Department of Justice before putting election laws into effect. And in *National Federation of Independent Business v. Sebelius* (2012), while narrowly refusing to hold the Affordable Care Act (otherwise known as Obamacare) unconstitutional, the Court did strike down a provision involving the expansion of Medicaid on the grounds that it unduly coerced states to agree to the expansion or lose all their Medicaid funding.

HOW THE SUPREME COURT DECIDES CASES

In deciding cases, the justices first inform themselves about the facts and legal issues in the case and about the more general consequences that can be expected from a ruling. After oral argument, they discuss the case in closed conference and reach a tentative decision. Finally, through the process of opinion writing and continuing discussion, the justices confirm (or, in rare instances, reconsider) the decision reached in conference, clarify and develop the bases for the ruling, and attempt to reconcile intracourt differences.

The Court's decisions thus have a dual aspect. The litigants in a case may be most concerned with winning or losing: for a convicted felon challenging the constitutionality of a police search that uncovered incriminating evidence, avoiding prison is the primary goal. In announcing decisions, however, the Court justifies its rulings on the basis of legal principles whose ramifications extend far beyond the confines of the individual case. Indeed, the justices use their discretion to review cases that have broad societal importance. This combination of the specific and the general, of immediate results and broader implications, is a crucial aspect of the Court's decision making.

Informing and Persuading the Court

In weighing the merits of a particular case, the Court relies on three sources of information: the briefs of the contending parties, *amicus curiae* (literally, "friend of the court") briefs, and oral argument. In all cases heard by the Court, the lawyers for both parties file legal briefs and argue the case orally before the justices. Other interested parties may submit amicus briefs, which increase the range of information available to the justices.

Legal Briefs. A legal brief is first and foremost a partisan document—an attempt to persuade a court to rule in favor of one's client or position. Persuasion takes the form of marshaling and then interpreting favorably the facts and the legal materials (precedents, statutes, constitutional provisions) involved in the case. For amicus briefs and for those submitted by the litigants, the ultimate goal is to gain a favorable ruling.

Amicus briefs differ from the briefs filed by the litigants. They usually are filed by groups that are interested primarily in the general constitutional issue the case raises, rather than in the fate of the particular litigants. Some organizations file amicus briefs out of concern for the effects the Court's decision might have on them or on their members. For other organizations, the principal concern is ideological: they wish to see the Constitution interpreted in a particular way. *Grutter v. Bollinger* (2003), which involved an affirmative-action program for admission to the University of Michigan Law School, illustrates the range of groups that might be involved on one side or the other of a contentious issue. Among those filing amicus briefs urging the justices to uphold the university's program were several universities that also had affirmative-action programs, the American Psychological Association, the National Urban League, the General Motors Corporation, and several members of Congress. Among those filing briefs opposing the Michigan program were the Asian American Legal Foundation, the Center for Individual Freedom, the National Association of Scholars, and the George W. Bush administration.

Although legal briefs commonly focus on the interpretation of constitutional provisions, statutes, and precedents relevant to the case, they may also include nonlegal materials. For example, attorneys may use social science research to document conditions within society, indicate the effects of governmental policies, or forecast the likely consequences of a Court ruling. The prototype for such briefs was the famous "Brandeis brief" filed in *Muller v. Oregon* (1908). At issue in *Muller* was the constitutionality of an Oregon statute limiting female workers to a ten-hour workday, which the plaintiff challenged as an arbitrary interference with economic liberty. In response, Louis Brandeis, then counsel for the state of Oregon and later a Supreme Court justice, claimed that the law served important public purposes—a claim supported by more than one hundred pages of social and economic data demonstrating that long working hours were dangerous to the health and safety of working women. Brandeis's success in *Muller* prompted counsel in later cases to adopt a similar approach. In *Brown v. Board of Education,* for example, legal arguments for outlawing racial segregation in public education were supplemented by the results of psychological tests showing the adverse effects of segregation on African American children. More recently, contending parties in cases involving the constitutionality of the death penalty have included in their briefs extensive data on the deterrent effect of capital punishment and on the tendency to impose death sentences on those convicted of murdering white victims.

Oral Argument. In oral argument, the attorneys for each party have their last opportunity to influence the Court's decision. In the early nineteenth century, when the Court's docket was less crowded, the greatest lawyers in the country would spend several days arguing a case before the justices. Nowadays, oral presentations are usually limited to a half hour for each party, although in particularly important cases more time can be allotted. In *Bush v. Gore,* the Court allotted forty-five minutes for each side, and in *National Federation of Independent Business v. Sebelius,* it allowed each side three hours of argument over three days to address the variety of issues in the case.

Despite the time constraints, oral argument provides an opportunity for influencing the justices, many of whom view it as vital for clarifying the written arguments presented in the briefs. Through their questions, the justices test the soundness of the opposing legal positions, and weaknesses in an argument or lack of preparation by attorneys soon becomes apparent. The justices' questions can also indicate issues on which they are undecided, and effective response to their inquiries can improve a client's chances. As Justice John Marshall Harlan observed, oral argument "may in many cases make the difference between winning and losing, no matter how good the briefs are."[13]

The Decision-Making Process

On Wednesdays and Fridays during its annual term (early October to late June), the Court meets in conference to consider the cases on which it has most recently heard oral argument. The confidentiality of these deliberations is jealously guarded—only the justices themselves, without law clerks or other Court staff, are present at conference.

Deliberations begin only after the justices shake hands—a ritual meant to symbolize that the inevitable disagreements are legal, not personal. The chief justice initiates discussion by indicating his views of the case at hand and his vote. The associate justices, in descending order of seniority, similarly present their views and votes, and the tallying of votes produces a tentative decision. Although the discussion at conference can on occasion be quite heated, Chief Justice William Rehnquist noted that, for the most part, justices merely announce their conclusions rather than seek to persuade their fellow justices.[14] If the chief justice has voted with the majority, he determines who will write the opinion of the Court (majority opinion), assigning the opinion to another member of the majority or retaining it for himself. If the chief justice is in the minority, the senior justice aligned with the majority assigns the opinion of the Court. The other justices are free to express their views in concurring or dissenting opinions, and in recent decades the number of separate opinions has risen dramatically.

How do the justices decide how they will vote? Some scholars maintain that the justices' votes simply reflect their ideological orientations. According to this view, Justice Clarence Thomas votes as he does because he is a conservative, whereas Justice Ruth Bader Ginsburg votes as she does because she is a liberal. Other scholars insist that justices are not free to decide simply on the basis of their preferences—the law constrains the choices they make and directs their decisions. Still other scholars argue that the justices behave strategically: that in seeking to advance their constitutional or ideological views, they take into account the institutional context in which they operate and the likely reaction of the President, Congress, and other political actors.

Accounts of the justices' deliberations indicate that in conference, they rely on legal arguments to buttress their positions and persuade their colleagues. This emphasis on legal argument suggests that the justices acknowledge their duty to put aside their personal preferences and base their decisions on the Constitution, although whether they succeed in doing so may well be another matter. The requirement that decisions be legally justifiable rarely promotes consensus. Conscientious justices can and often do disagree about the difficult legal issues facing them. In recent terms, dissenting opinions were filed in about half of the cases the Court decided. In the Court's 2014 term, for example, 41 percent of the Court's rulings were unanimous, but in 26 percent of the cases the justices were divided 5–4. Although interaction among the justices might have some effect on their votes and opinions, the decision-making process is more individual than collective in nature. As Justice Lewis Powell put it, "For the most part, perhaps as much as 90 percent of our total time, we function as nine small, independent law firms."[15] This high degree of individuality reflects both the well-developed constitutional views the members of the Court bring to their cases and the limited resources available for changing the views of their colleagues.

The vote in conference is only the initial step. Discussion of cases continues after conference, as the opinion of the Court and any concurring or dissenting opinions are prepared and circulated among the justices for their comments. Reviewing these opinions gives the justices an opportunity to reconsider their initial positions, and a particularly persuasive opinion might lead to a change of vote. On a closely divided Court, defection by a single justice can produce a new majority and, therefore, a different decision.

The likelihood of such a vote shift should not be exaggerated. A study of one ten-year period found that the justices' final votes differed from their votes in conference only about 9 percent of the time.[16] Even if no votes are changed, the period between the conference and the announcement of the Court's decision represents a crucial stage in the decisional process. The justices who compose the majority carefully review the draft opinion of the Court, and they might require changes in its language or argument before they will endorse it. One study found that in the majority of cases the opinion of the Court went through three or more drafts.[17] Even after prolonged discussions, deep-seated differences can prevent a Court majority from coalescing behind a single opinion. In *Furman v. Georgia* (1971), all five members of the Court majority wrote separate opinions presenting quite disparate grounds for invalidating Georgia's death penalty statute. More recently, justices have taken to joining opinions of the Court only "in part," agreeing to some sections but not to others.

The justices' close scrutiny of the opinion of the Court reflects in part a concern for the soundness of the legal arguments it presents because public and congressional acceptance of a decision might be affected by the persuasiveness of the arguments supporting it. The justices also realize that the justifications for their decision play a large role in future decisions. The importance of this consideration was highlighted in the decision handed down in *United States v. Nixon,* in which the Court unanimously rejected the president's claim of executive privilege and voted to compel him to release the Watergate tapes. Before that decision was announced, several justices refused to join Chief Justice Warren Burger's opinion for the Court because they felt that it provided too much support for future claims of executive power. Only after the chief justice agreed to extensive revisions of the original opinion did all the justices join it.

THE IMPACT OF SUPREME COURT DECISIONS

Most Supreme Court decisions not only resolve disputes between particular litigants but also have consequences for the nation as a whole. In ruling on the constitutionality of a particular program or practice, the Court also indicates the likely validity of similar programs or practices. In interpreting a constitutional provision, the Court announces standards that can guide future decisions involving that provision. In elaborating constitutional principles, the Court can educate the public about what our basic principles of government require.

Yet judicial decisions do not always achieve their intended results. Decisions can be misunderstood, misrepresented, or ignored. Those responsible for carrying out the Court's mandates might seek to evade their responsibilities, or they might find ways to negate the effectiveness of the mandates; opposition to Court rulings might lead to attempts to overturn them or to limit their effects. Rather than resolving conflicts, then, Court decisions sometimes merely aggravate them.

Legal Obligation

A Supreme Court decision invalidating a governmental program imposes legal obligations on three distinct sets of actors. Most immediately, the losing party in the case must either abandon the program or remedy its constitutional defects. In a case such as *Regents of the University of California v. Bakke* (1978), in which the Court ruled that the goal of the affirmative-action plan in question (increased minority-group representation in the medical profession) was legitimate but the means employed to achieve this goal were unconstitutional, the university merely had to revise its program so that the goal could be achieved constitutionally. When the aim of an invalidated program is itself unconstitutional, however, any alternative program designed to accomplish that aim would likewise be unconstitutional.

Because of the Court's hierarchical position in the American judicial system, its decisions on matters of federal law are also binding precedent for all other courts, both federal and state. This means that should a litigant challenge a program similar to one invalidated by the Court, lower-court judges are obliged to invalidate it. Moreover, in deciding other cases in which a federal statute or constitutional provision comes into play, judges must treat the Court's interpretation as authoritative. As Judge Learned Hand of the Second Circuit Court of Appeals put it, "I have always felt that it was the duty of an inferior court to suppress its own opinions and to try to prophesy what the appellate court would do. God knows, I have often been wrong in that too; but I have at least been obedient, which is as I conceive it a judge's prime duty."[18]

Finally, by striking down a program as unconstitutional, the Court can also oblige other governmental units to discontinue programs similar to the invalidated one. This underscores the crucial importance of the opinion of the Court: the broader the basis for the ruling, the broader the range of affected programs. The progress of school-desegregation decisions illustrates this point. In a series of decisions handed down between 1938 and 1954, the Court ruled that certain racially segregated school systems had violated the Equal Protection Clause of the Fourteenth Amendment by failing to provide equal educational facilities for African American students. However, because these rulings were tied to the conditions in specific districts, their effects were not felt outside those districts. Then, in 1954 the Court ruled in *Brown v. Board of Education* that separate public school systems for African Americans and whites were *inherently* unequal, thereby obliging all states operating such systems to dismantle them. By choosing the broader basis for its decision in *Brown,* the Court ensured that its ruling would have nationwide effect.

Yet there is considerable controversy over what obligations a Court ruling imposes on government officials. Although they cannot legitimately defy the Court's decision in a specific case, officials are not obliged in every instance to endorse the Court's interpretation of the Constitution. Such a requirement would imply that the Constitution is what the Court says it is or that the Court can never err in its reading of the Constitution. For example, in the wake of the Court's infamous decision in *Dred Scott v. Sandford* (1857)—declaring that African Americans could not be citizens—Abraham Lincoln, although professing respect for the Court and acknowledging the authority of its ruling in the case, denied that the Court had correctly interpreted the Constitution and indicated his intention to seek a reversal of the Court's position. Similarly, critics of the Supreme Court's ruling in *Roe v. Wade* (1973), which recognized a constitutional right to abortion, adopted various restrictions on abortion that were susceptible to legal challenge, expecting that the resulting litigation would provide an opportunity for the Court to reconsider its position. This strategy succeeded only in part: the Court in *Planned Parenthood of Southeastern Pennsylvania v. Casey* (1992) refused to overrule *Roe,* but it did uphold some regulations of abortion. Those seeking to persuade the Court to reverse direction may also count on changes in the Court's membership to accomplish their goal. Thus, in *Stenberg v. Carhart* (2000), a 5–4 majority struck down restrictions on late-term abortions, but after the appointment of Chief Justice Roberts and Justice Alito, the Court in *Gonzales v. Carhart* (2007) upheld very similar restrictions, also by a 5–4 vote.

Response to Court Mandates

In invalidating a program or practice, the Supreme Court imposes an obligation to cease the unconstitutional activity or to take steps to remedy the constitutional violation. In most cases, those affected by the Court's rulings comply with the legal requirements. The mere existence of legal obligations does not guarantee compliance, however, and the Court's mandates have not always been carried out.

Communication of Court Mandates. If its decisions are to achieve their intended effects, the Court must identify clearly what actions are to be undertaken or what practices eliminated, and it must communicate that mandate to the appropriate officials. Rulings that are unclear or that fail to reach their intended audience are unlikely to have much effect.

Confusion over the exact scope or meaning of Court mandates can stem from disagreement on the Court. Not once during the 1960s, for example, did a majority of the justices agree on standards defining what kinds of sexually explicit materials were protected by the First Amendment. As a result, the Court handed down decisions marked by a multiplicity of opinions, each offering a different standard for determining whether movies or publications were obscene. State and local officials who tried to respect constitutional limitations while enforcing obscenity legislation consequently received little guidance from the Court.

Even when the justices agree among themselves, ambiguities in the opinion of the Court can create uncertainty about the scope of the ruling, as happened in *Escobedo v. Illinois* (1964). In *Escobedo,* the Court for the first time recognized that suspects had a right to counsel during police interrogations. However, because the opinion of the Court did not clearly define that right, lower courts developed widely divergent interpretations of the ruling. Over an eighteen-month period, 150 cases raising *Escobedo*-type issues were appealed to the Supreme Court. Only after the Court clarified its position in *Miranda v. Arizona* (1966) did lower courts consistently enforce the right to counsel prior to trial.[19]

Finally, the meaning of a Court ruling might be obscured as it is transmitted to its intended audience. The transmission to police officers of the Supreme Court's landmark criminal-justice decisions of the 1960s illustrates how such confusion can occur. In determining what the Court required, police officers typically relied on numerous sources for information, such as police training sessions, local officials, and the mass media. Often, the Court's message was simplified and distorted in the course of transmission. A study of the initial response to *Miranda* in four Wisconsin police departments, for example, found that despite the clarity of the Court's guidelines, more than half the officers in three departments incorrectly identified what the decision required.[20] However, this tends to pose a problem only in the short run.

Noncompliance. A more serious concern is noncompliance, the refusal to undertake or refrain from actions as required by Supreme Court rulings. State and federal courts at times have failed to follow or enforce Court decisions, with state supreme courts, in particular, displaying a penchant for ignoring Court precedent. More frequently, however, noncompliance crops up among state or local officials who resist Court directions to implement unpopular decisions or to observe new and potentially burdensome limitations on their powers. Southern school boards, for instance, sought to evade the Court's school desegregation requirements; in the 1970s, some northern school boards did the same. Many school districts initially ignored Court decisions requiring the elimination of prayer and Bible reading from their schools. When police officers believed that Court decisions hampered their efforts to control crime, they sought to evade limitations on their power to conduct searches and interrogate suspects.

That individuals evade, or seek to evade, their legal responsibilities is nothing new: the very existence of courts testifies to the need to enforce legal norms. Yet noncompliance, particularly if it is widespread, poses a threat to the Court's effectiveness because its capacity to enforce its decisions is limited. As Alexander Hamilton noted in *The Federalist*, No. 78, the judiciary lacks control over "either the sword or the purse" and must "ultimately depend upon the aid of the executive arm even for the efficacy of its judgments." Should the executive prove reluctant to enforce the Court's decisions vigorously, as happened initially after *Brown v. Board of Education*, the Court must depend on the willingness of litigants to initiate cases challenging instances of noncompliance. Even then, it cannot always rely on the lower courts to enforce its rulings. In sum, the Court's effectiveness ultimately depends less on its ability to punish noncompliance than on its ability to persuade the targets of its decisions to comply voluntarily.

Political Impact

In addition to imposing legal obligations, Supreme Court decisions influence public opinion, political activity, and the development of public policy. By upholding a challenged governmental enactment, the justices authoritatively dispose of constitutional objections to its validity and can thereby promote public acceptance of the law. The Court's decision in *Heart of Atlanta Motel v. United States* (1964), which upheld a controversial section of the Civil Rights Act of 1964, resolved constitutional questions about the national government's power to ban racial discrimination in public accommodations. Its decisions in *National Labor Relations Board v. Jones & Laughlin Steel Corporation* (1937) and in subsequent cases validated New Deal efforts to regulate the national economy. As these examples indicate, Supreme Court decisions have played a crucial role in legitimating the federal government's expanding exercise of power. In addition, the Court's legitimation of one state's law might dispose other states to adopt similar measures. The full development of so-called Jim Crow laws, for example, did not occur until after the Court, in *Plessy v. Ferguson* (1896), upheld a Louisiana statute establishing racial segregation in public transportation.

Even when the justices do not invalidate governmental policies, their rulings may still have political repercussions. The justices' interpretation of federal statutes has at times prompted campaigns for congressional action to overturn those interpretations. Thus, after a series of rulings during the late 1980s that narrowly construed federal civil rights statutes, civil rights groups prevailed on Congress to pass the Civil Rights Act of 1991, reversing several of those decisions. Even rulings upholding governmental action against constitutional challenge can, by focusing attention on an issue, elicit a political response. For example, after the Court, in *Goldman v. Weinberger* (1986), rejected the claim of an Orthodox Jewish psychologist that he had a constitutional right to wear a yarmulke while on active duty in a military hospital, Congress enacted legislation establishing a statutory right to do so.

Decisions invalidating state or federal policies also have produced varied effects. An adverse Court ruling may activate the political forces supporting a program to seek alternative means of accomplishing their objectives. Five constitutional amendments have been adopted, in whole or in part, to overturn Supreme Court decisions.[21] During the 1970s and 1980s, opponents of Court decisions sought, unsuccessfully, to strip the Court of its power to hear cases involving school prayer, busing, and abortion. And after the Court in *Kelo v. City of New London* (2005) ruled that states could use their power of eminent domain to condemn private residences and then transfer the property to other private landowners to promote economic development, voters in several states adopted amendments to their state constitutions prohibiting state and local officials from using eminent domain to transfer property from one private owner to another.

The response to the Supreme Court's abortion decisions illustrates the political dynamics that may be created by judicial rulings. The Supreme Court's decision in *Roe v. Wade,* striking down state restrictions on abortion, galvanized the pro-life movement, which supported legislation making it more difficult to obtain abortions as well as a constitutional amendment outlawing abortion. During the late 1980s and early 1990s, the Court's validation of state laws limiting abortion activated pro-choice forces, who attempted to blunt the effects of these decisions by supporting candidates sympathetic to their cause and by pushing for the adoption of state and federal laws protecting abortion rights. More recently, the Court's ruling in *Stenberg v. Carhart* (2000), striking down a Nebraska law outlawing certain types of late-term ("partial-birth") abortions, led pro-life advocates to push for a federal law prohibiting the practice. Congress enacted the law, and pro-choice groups immediately challenged it in federal court. Because the Supreme Court would likely rule on the law's constitutionality, both pro-life and pro-choice groups sought to influence who would fill the vacancies on the Court produced by the retirement of Justice O'Connor and the death of Chief Justice Rehnquist. As it turned out, the justices appointed to those vacancies provided crucial votes upholding the congressional statute in *Gonzales v. Carhart* (2007).

Controversial decisions may generate both support and opposition. For example, *Brown v. Board of Education* produced not only intransigent resistance by segregationists but also efforts by civil rights groups to solidify and extend the gains they had made. Such decisions have the added effect of subtly changing the political context in which conflicts between such forces occur, by giving proponents of the Court's view the political advantage of being able to claim that the Constitution supports their position. Finally, the broad public support for the Court has promoted public acceptance of politically charged decisions such as *Bush v. Gore* (2000).

In sum, Supreme Court decisions establish government policy, just as decisions made by the executive or legislative branches do, and thereby shape American society. Indeed, if the Court is to fulfill its constitutional functions, it cannot avoid making policy. The important question to ask is whether its policies can be constitutionally justified.

ANALYZING SUPREME COURT DECISIONS

Because judicial opinions provide justifications for constitutional positions, when reading cases one should bear in mind the modes of constitutional interpretation outlined in Chapter 1. Often it is helpful to "brief," or outline, a case to analyze its major elements (see Box 2.1). In general, one should look for the following elements that are common to all court cases.

Components of Supreme Court Decisions

Title and Citation. Case titles derive from the names of the parties to the controversy. The party listed first is seeking reversal of an unfavorable lower-court decision, whereas the party listed second typically wants that decision affirmed. If the case comes to the Court on appeal, the parties are referred to as the appellant and the appellee. If the case comes on a writ of certiorari, they are referred to as the petitioner and the respondent.

Facts of the Case. Because Supreme Court cases arise as disputes between particular litigants, Court decisions represent attempts to apply constitutional principles to unique situations. Full understanding of a judicial decision therefore requires an appreciation of the facts underlying the case, which have been established by testimony at trial. Supreme

BOX 2.1 A Sample Case Brief

Texas v. Johnson
491 U.S. 397 (1989)

Facts of the Case

Gregory Johnson burned an American flag as a form of political protest. He was arrested and convicted of violating a Texas statute that forbade desecration of the American flag. He appealed his conviction, claiming that his action was protected by the First Amendment. The Texas Court of Criminal Appeals overturned his conviction, and the Supreme Court granted certiorari.

The Law

The Free Speech Clause of the First Amendment, made applicable to states by the Due Process Clause of the Fourteenth Amendment.

Legal Questions

1. Does Johnson's conduct constitute expressive conduct, thus implicating the First Amendment? *Yes.*
2. Did Johnson's burning of the flag disturb the peace? *No.*
3. Is the state's interest in preserving the flag as a national symbol related to the suppression of free expression? *Yes.*
4. Does the Supreme Court's test for expressive conduct enunciated by *United States v. O'Brien* apply here? *No.*
5. Does the state have a valid interest in promoting respect for the flag as a symbol of the nation? *Yes.*
6. Can government prohibit flag desecration as a means of promoting that interest? *No.*
7. Is the Texas law constitutional? *No.*

Opinion of the Court (Brennan)

Johnson's burning of the American flag was an attempt to convey a political message. When Texas banned flag desecration to promote respect for the flag, it prevented the use of the flag to communicate messages, such as Johnson's, that are critical of the government and of the nation. However, the First Amendment forbids government from prohibiting the expression of ideas and communication of messages merely because they are offensive or disagreeable, and therefore the Texas statute is unconstitutional.

Concurring Opinion (Kennedy)

Commitment to the Constitution requires overturning Johnson's conviction, however distasteful it may be to do so.

Dissenting Opinion (Rehnquist)

The American flag's unique position as a symbol of the nation justifies special protections against its desecration. Texas's flag desecration statute does not prevent Johnson from communicating his criticism of the government, because his speech and other actions expressing that criticism were not prohibited or interfered with. The statute only prohibits one means of conveying his message, and it does so in response to the profound regard that Americans have for their flag.

Dissenting Opinion (Stevens)

The rules developed for other forms of symbolic expression do not apply here, because of the flag's status as a special symbol of the nation.

Evaluation

The Court's ruling extended the range of expressive actions entitled to First Amendment protection. Forty-eight states and the national government had statutes banning flag desecration, so the effects of the Court's ruling were felt nationwide. Efforts to amend the Constitution to overturn the Court's ruling failed, and a congressional flag-desecration statute that was passed in the wake of this decision was subsequently invalidated by the Court.

Court justices might differ in interpreting the facts, however; disagreement about the facts, as well as about the proper interpretation of the Constitution, can produce divisions on the Court. The opinion of the Court typically summarizes the relevant facts before elaborating the Court's justification for its decision. Summaries of the facts in those cases precede most of the cases presented in this volume.

The Law. Constitutional rulings by the Supreme Court involve the interpretation of three elements of law: constitutional provisions, statutes or administrative regulations (or both), and Supreme Court precedents. Large bodies of law have sprung from most constitutional provisions, so it is important to note precisely which provision the Court is interpreting. For example, if a constitutional challenge is raised under the Fourteenth Amendment, the first thing to determine is whether the challenge is based on the Due Process Clause or the Equal Protection Clause.

Legal Questions. A Court decision can be viewed as a response to a particular legal question or a series of questions. Identifying these questions is vital to proper analysis of the opinions in a case. One way to do so is to frame the questions in a yes-or-no format (see Box 2.1 for an example). Usually, the Court's answers to the legal questions in a case can be determined from a close reading of the opinion of the Court. However, in cases in which five justices are unable to agree on a single opinion, one must search all opinions in the case for points of majority agreement.

Opinion of the Court. This opinion announces the Court's decision and offers the justification for that ruling. Because the decision can serve as a precedent in future cases, close attention should be paid to the chain of reasoning supporting the decision and to its possible implications. Often the best approach is to trace how the Court arrived at its answers to each of the legal questions previously identified.

Concurring Opinions. Members of the Court majority might write concurring opinions because they agree with the Court's decision but disagree with its justification, in which case the concurring opinion will offer an alternative justification. They might also write concurring opinions even if they agree with both the decision and its justification in order either to clarify their own view of the case or to respond to arguments made in a dissenting opinion. Determining the basis for the concurrence should be the initial step in analyzing a concurring opinion.

Dissenting Opinions. Dissenting opinions attempt to demonstrate why the Court's decision is wrong. They might point to alleged errors in reasoning, misinterpretation of precedents or constitutional provisions, or misunderstanding of the facts in a case. Analysis of dissenting opinions should focus on the bases for disagreement with the opinion of the Court.

Evaluation. No analysis of a case is complete without an evaluation of the decision. Is the opinion of the Court convincing? Is the decision consistent with previous Court decisions? If not, does the Court provide persuasive reasons for departing from precedent? What are the likely effects of the Court's decision?

NOTES

1. Alexis de Tocqueville, *Democracy in America*, edited by J. P. Mayer (Garden City, NY: Doubleday, 1969), 270.

2. George W. Bush, *Decision Point* (New York: Crown, 2010), 98.

3. The Eleventh Amendment was adopted to overturn the Supreme Court's ruling in *Chisholm v. Georgia* (1793), which held that a state could be sued in federal court, by a citizen of another state, without its consent.

4. Richard L. Hasen, "End of the Dialogue? Political Polarization, the Supreme Court, and Congress," *Southern California Law Review* 86 (January 2013): 205–262.

5. "Shufflin' Sam" Thompson had been arrested for loitering while waiting in a bar for his bus and

shuffling his feet in time to music from a jukebox. When he protested his arrest, he was also charged with disorderly conduct. He was convicted on both charges and fined $10 for each. Because Kentucky law provided no opportunity to appeal fines of less than $20, Thompson petitioned for Supreme Court review. The Court accepted the case and ruled unanimously that the convictions were not supported by evidence and therefore amounted to a denial of due process of law.

6. Cases may also come to the Supreme Court by certification. Under this rarely used procedure, a lower federal court requests instruction from the Supreme Court on a point of law.

7. "Paid" cases are those in which the petitioners have paid the $300 filing fee and have supplied the prescribed copies of briefs and other legal materials. An *in forma pauperis* case is one in which an impoverished petitioner requests review of a lower-court decision. These cases generally involve criminal appeals filed by prisoners who cannot afford expert legal assistance. In such cases, the Court waives the filing fee and the other requirements.

8. The Supreme Court establishes the procedural rules governing appeals to the Court and the operations of the Court.

9. "Retired Chief Justice Warren Attacks Freund Study Group's Composition and Proposal," *American Bar Association Journal* 59 (July 1973): 728.

10. *Michigan Department of State Police v. Sitz,* 496 U.S. 444 (1990).

11. Chief Justice Fred Vinson in "Work of the U.S. Supreme Court," *Texas Bar Journal* 12 (1949): 551.

12. It eventually struck down such laws in the aptly named *Loving v. Virginia,* 388 U.S. 1 (1967).

13. Harlan's statement is reported in Lewis, *Gideon's Trumpet,* 162n23.

14. William H. Rehnquist, *The Supreme Court: How It Was, How It Is,* rev. ed. (New York: Knopf, 2001), 254–255.

15. Lewis F. Powell Jr., "What the Justices Are Saying . . . ," *American Bar Association Journal* 62 (1976): 1454.

16. Saul Brenner, "Fluidity on the United States Supreme Court: A Reexamination," *American Journal of Political Science* 24 (1980): 526–535.

17. Forrest Maltzman, James F. Spriggs II, and Paul J. Wahlbeck, *Crafting Law on the Supreme Court: The Collegial Game* (New York: Cambridge University Press, 2000), 116, table 4.2.

18. Hand's comment is contained in an intracourt memorandum quoted in Marvin Schick, *Learned Hand's Court* (Baltimore, MD: Johns Hopkins University Press, 1970), 167.

19. On the initial state-court responses to *Escobedo v. Illinois* and *Miranda v. Arizona,* see Neil T. Romans, "The Role of State Supreme Courts in Judicial Policy Making: *Escobedo, Miranda,* and the Use of Impact Analysis," *Western Political Quarterly* 27 (1974): 526–535.

20. Neil A. Milner, *The Court and Local Enforcement: The Impact of* Miranda (Beverly Hills, CA: Sage, 1971), 225, table 11–2.

21. The Eleventh Amendment overruled *Chisholm v. Georgia* (1793); the Fourteenth Amendment, *Dred Scott v. Sandford* (1857); the Sixteenth Amendment, *Pollock v. Farmers' Loan & Trust Co.* (1895); the Twenty-Fourth Amendment, *Breedlove v. Suttles* (1937); and the Twenty-Sixth Amendment, *Oregon v. Mitchell* (1970).

SELECTED READINGS

Abraham, Henry J. *Justices, Presidents, and Senators: A Political History of U.S. Supreme Court Appointments from Washington to Bush II.* Lanham, MD: Rowman & Littlefield, 2007.

Baum, Lawrence. *The Supreme Court.* 11th ed. Washington, DC: CQ Press, 2012.

Dickson, Dale, ed. *The Supreme Court in Conference (1940–1985): The Private Discussions Behind Nearly 300 Supreme Court Decisions.* New York: Oxford University Press, 2001.

Epstein, Lee, and Jack Knight. *The Choices Justices Make.* Washington, DC: CQ Press, 1998.

Farber, Daniel A., and Suzanna Sherry, *Judgment Calls: Principles and Politics in Constitutional Law.* New York: Oxford University Press, 2009.

Hall, Kermit L., James W. Ely, and Joel B. Grossman, eds. *The Oxford Companion to the Supreme Court of the United States.* 2nd ed. New York: Oxford University Press, 2005.

Hall, Matthew E. K. *The Nature of Supreme Court Power.* New York: Cambridge University Press, 2011.

Keck, Thomas M. *Judicial Politics in Polarized Times.* Chicago: University of Chicago Press, 2014.

Lewis, Anthony. *Gideon's Trumpet.* New York: Random House, 1964.

Maltz, Earl, ed. *Rehnquist Justice: Understanding the Court Dynamic.* Lawrence: University Press of Kansas, 2003.

Murphy, Walter F. *Elements of Judicial Strategy.* Chicago: University of Chicago Press, 1964.

O'Brien, David M. *Storm Center: The Supreme Court in American Politics.* 10th ed. New York: W. W. Norton, 2014.

Perry, H. W., Jr. *Deciding to Decide: Agenda Setting in the United States Supreme Court.* Cambridge, MA: Harvard University Press, 1991.

Powe, Lucas A., Jr. *The Warren Court and American Politics.* Cambridge, MA: Belknap Press of Harvard University Press, 2000.

Rehnquist, William H. *The Supreme Court: How It Was, How It Is.* Rev. ed. New York: Knopf, 2001.

Rosenberg, Gerald N. *The Hollow Hope: Can Courts Bring About Social Change?* 2nd ed. Chicago: University of Chicago Press, 2008.

Rossum, Ralph A. *Antonin Scalia's Jurisprudence: Text and Tradition.* Lawrence: University Press of Kansas, 2006.

Rossum, Ralph A. *Understanding Clarence Thomas: The Jurisprudence of Constitutional Restoration.* Lawrence: University Press of Kansas, 2014.

Segal, Jeffrey A., and Harold J. Spaeth. *The Supreme Court and the Attitudinal Model Revisited.* New York: Cambridge University Press, 2002.

Silverstein, Mark. *Judicious Choices: The New Politics of Supreme Court Confirmations.* 2nd ed. New York: W. W. Norton, 2007.

Sweet, Martin J. *Merely Judgment: Ignoring, Evading, and Trumping the Supreme Court.* Charlottesville: University Press of Virginia, 2010.

Tarr, G. Alan. *Judicial Process and Judicial Policymaking.* 6th ed. Belmont, CA: Cengage, 2014.

Tribe, Laurence, and Joshua Matz. *Uncertain Justice: The Roberts Court and the Constitution.* New York: Henry Holt & Co., 2014.

Whittington, Keith E. *Political Foundations of Judicial Supremacy: The Presidency, the Supreme Court, and Constitutional Leadership in U.S. History.* Princeton, NJ: Princeton University Press, 2007.

Wolfe, Christopher, ed. *That Eminent Tribunal: Judicial Supremacy and the Constitution.* Princeton, NJ: Princeton University Press, 2004.

3

Rights under the Constitution

The constitutional guarantees for Americans' most fundamental rights—freedom of speech, the free exercise of religion, freedom from unreasonable searches and seizures, and the like—did not appear in the original Constitution. Only with the ratification of the Bill of Rights, amendments added in 1791, were these rights given express constitutional protection. Moreover, the Bill of Rights originally protected only against violations of rights by the federal government, leaving state governments largely free to deal with rights as they thought appropriate.[1] Not until the ratification of the Thirteenth, Fourteenth, and Fifteenth Amendments after the Civil War did the Constitution impose substantial restrictions on state invasions of rights. And not until the second half of the twentieth century did the Supreme Court interpret the Fourteenth Amendment as imposing on the states most of the same requirements as were imposed only on the federal government.

This chapter analyzes these dramatic changes in the protection of rights under the Constitution. Initially, it considers why the original Constitution did not contain a bill of rights and how those guarantees became part of the Constitution. Next, it examines the adoption of the Fourteenth Amendment and its effects on the division of responsibility between federal and state governments for the protection of rights. It then traces the US Supreme Court's changing perspectives on extending constitutional protection against state violations of rights. It turns next to how war and other emergencies affect the scope of rights. Finally, it analyzes the Second Amendment to the Constitution, which protects the right to bear arms.

RIGHTS AND THE FOUNDING

The Creation and Ratification of the Constitution

The Constitution initially did not include a bill of rights because few delegates at the Constitutional Convention believed one was needed. In fact, neither the Virginia Plan nor the New Jersey Plan, the two major plans of government introduced at the convention, contained a bill of rights. During the latter stages of the convention, the delegates added various rights guarantees to the Constitution on a piecemeal basis. Among these were restrictions on suspending the privilege of the writ of habeas corpus (protecting against illegal imprisonment), a ban on *ex post facto* laws (criminalizing conduct after it has already taken place), and a ban on religious tests for federal office. But when George Mason of Virginia proposed, a week before adjournment, that a bill of rights be added to the Constitution, arguing that "it would give great quiet to the people," not a single state supported his proposal.

The absence of a bill of rights did not reflect hostility to rights. But having witnessed the failure of state declarations of rights to prevent violations of rights, most delegates were skeptical about the efficacy of "parchment barriers." Real security for rights, they believed, came not from constitutional prohibitions but from a well-constructed government that lacked the propensity or opportunity to violate rights. The creation of such a government was the delegates' main concern throughout the convention. They believed that the Constitution adequately safeguarded rights against invasion by the national government by (1) enumerating and limiting national powers; (2) making governmental officials accountable to the people; (3) promoting the establishment of an "extended republic" (see Chapter 1), in which majority factions were unlikely to form; and (4) establishing a system of separation of powers and checks and balances. These features led Alexander Hamilton to conclude in *The Federalist*, No. 84, that "the Constitution is itself, in every rational sense, and to every useful purpose, a bill of rights."

Hamilton insisted that a bill of rights was unnecessary. Because the Constitution granted only a limited legislative power to the federal government, Congress does not have the power to invade rights. In fact, he suggested, inclusion of a bill of rights could be dangerous. To prohibit Congress from invading the freedom of the press or violating other rights would seem to imply that, in the absence of these prohibitions, Congress could do just that. So instead of limiting federal power, a bill of rights might expand it. In addition, Hamilton noted that no bill of rights could hope to be comprehensive, so the failure to include a particular right in the bill of rights might seem to imply that Congress was not prohibited from invading that right. Thus, the inclusion of some rights could make other rights less secure.

Hamilton's arguments did not persuade the Anti-Federalists, who opposed the ratification of the Constitution. They responded that the Constitution itself undermined Hamilton's argument: if a noncomprehensive list of rights was dangerous, why did the Constitution already include some rights guarantees? More generally, they emphasized the need to rein in what they viewed as a dangerously powerful federal government. "Universal experience," they insisted, demonstrated "that the most express declarations and reservations are necessary to protect the just rights and liberty of mankind from the silent, powerful and ever active conspiracy of those who govern."[2] This argument proved effective. At the Massachusetts ratifying convention, the Federalists were forced to agree to introduce amendments as the price of ratification. Several subsequent ratifying conventions also suggested amendments. At least some Anti-Federalists hoped through this process of amendment to undermine the powers of the federal government.

The Creation of the Bill of Rights

As a member of the House of Representatives in the first Congress, James Madison played the leading role in the creation of the Bill of Rights. He prepared an initial list of amendments, largely culled from the proposals submitted by the various states, and pushed for their consideration in the face of widespread lack of interest in Congress. Madison himself did not believe that the lack of a bill of rights was a major defect in the Constitution. Rather, he sought both to quell the fears of citizens sincerely concerned about abuses of governmental power and to forestall the introduction of amendments by opponents of the Constitution that would subvert the new government. As he put it, "It is possible the abuse of the powers of the General Government may be guarded against in a more secure manner than is now done, while no one advantage arising from the exercise of that power shall be damaged or endangered by it."[3]

Madison's strategy succeeded, as Congress largely accepted his proposals and rejected others that would have crippled the federal government. The states quickly ratified ten of the twelve amendments sent to them, rejecting an amendment affecting representation in the House and not ratifying one regulating congressional pay raises until 1992. Ratification of the ten amendments, the Bill of Rights, reassured the populace that their rights were secure and effectively ended Anti-Federalist efforts to tamper with the Constitution.

Two aspects of the Bill of Rights are particularly noteworthy. First, Madison consciously designed the amendments to avoid the problems identified by Hamilton in *The Federalist*, No. 84. The Ninth Amendment responded to Hamilton's concern that no listing of rights could be comprehensive by noting that "the enumeration in the Constitution, of certain rights, shall not be construed to deny or disparage others retained by the people." The Tenth Amendment responded to the concern that the national government might derive additional powers from the listing of rights by emphasizing that "the powers not delegated to the United States by the Constitution, nor prohibited by it to the States, are reserved to the States respectively, or to the people."

Second, the Bill of Rights placed restrictions solely on the federal government. Concerned about abuses by factional majorities in the states, Madison had proposed that freedom of conscience, freedom of the press, and trial by jury in criminal cases be secured against state violation. The Senate, however, rejected his proposal. In part, the limited reach of the amendments reflected the perceived source of threats to rights—after all, the impetus for the amendments was the creation of a substantially stronger national government. It is also possible that some provisions of the Bill of Rights were primarily designed to protect state powers from federal invasion. To the extent that they were, the concern was federalism, not individual rights. Finally, Congress may have refused to extend the Bill of Rights to the states because state declarations of rights already protected against state violations of rights.

When the question of applying the Bill of Rights to the states first arose, in *Barron v. Baltimore* (1833), the US Supreme Court unanimously held that the Bill of Rights restricted only the federal government. In reaching this conclusion, Chief Justice John Marshall looked to the constitutional text, observing that the First Amendment begins with the phrase *Congress shall make no law* and that no subsequent provision of the Bill of Rights indicates any limitation upon state action. In addition, he reasoned that "had Congress engaged in the extraordinary occupation of improving the constitutions of the several states by affording the people additional protections from the exercise of power by their own governments in matters which concerned themselves alone, they would have declared this purpose in plain and intelligible language." The adoption of the Fourteenth Amendment in 1868 required reconsideration of the issue raised in *Barron*. Did that amendment impose on the states the same restrictions that the Bill of Rights had imposed on the federal government? If not, how did it affect the division of responsibility between nation and state for defining and protecting rights?

THE FOURTEENTH AMENDMENT

Constitutional historians disagree about the meaning of the Fourteenth Amendment. Many scholars argue that the amendment applies the Bill of Rights to the states, guarantees other rights against state infringement as well, and gives the federal government broad authority to protect those rights.[4] Reviewing the same evidence, other scholars emphasize the attachment to federalism of the amendment's authors, depict the amendment's aims as narrow, and deny that these aims encompassed the application of the Bill of Rights to the states.[5] Still other scholars occupy a middle position between these two alternatives.[6]

The Creation of the Fourteenth Amendment

The Fourteenth Amendment was the second of three amendments adopted after the Civil War during Reconstruction. Although the Thirteenth Amendment (ratified in 1865) had outlawed slavery, the Southern states sought to perpetuate the economic and social subordination of African Americans through the infamous Black Codes. These laws deprived African Americans of basic rights, such as the right to contract and to testify in court; subjected them to heavier penalties for violations of the law; and bound them to employers through harsh vagrancy and apprenticeship provisions. Congress responded to this Southern intransigence with the Civil Rights Act of 1866 and the Fourteenth Amendment. The Civil Rights Act guaranteed to "black citizens" the same rights "to make and enforce contracts, to inherit, purchase, lease, sell, hold, and convey real and personal property" and to enjoy the "full and equal benefit of all laws and proceedings for the security of person and property, as is enjoyed by white citizens." But whether Congress had constitutional authority to enact this law was unclear. Few members of Congress believed that Congress had the power to protect rights against state violation prior to the Civil War. Some concluded that the Thirteenth Amendment, which authorized Congress to enact "appropriate legislation" to enforce its provisions, provided a constitutional basis for the law. They reasoned that the amendment was designed not only to eliminate slavery but also to secure to the emancipated slaves the rights associated with their status as free persons. Others in Congress, however, doubted that the amendment conferred such broad authority, and, even after Congress had enacted the law by overriding President Andrew Johnson's veto, doubts lingered about its constitutionality.

The Fourteenth Amendment removed those doubts by expanding congressional authority to secure rights against state violation. An initial version of the amendment assigned Congress primary responsibility for protecting rights against state infringement. But ultimately Section 1 of the amendment was redrafted to ensure that initial responsibility for the protection of rights remained with the states. However, Section 1 made clear what that responsibility entailed. States were (1) prohibited from abridging the privileges and immunities of citizens of the United States; (2) required to observe due process of law in depriving any person of life, liberty, or property; and (3) prohibited from denying equal protection of the laws to any person. If the states failed to meet their obligations under the amendment, those persons whose rights had been violated could sue to vindicate their rights. More important, Congress, under Section 5 of the amendment, could enforce the provisions of the amendment "by appropriate legislation."

Although the Fourteenth Amendment served to constitutionalize the Civil Rights Act of 1866, many scholars argue that it had broader purposes. They note that the amendment speaks in general terms rather than repeating the list of rights found in the Civil Rights Act and that it guarantees rights to "all persons" rather than exclusively to those who had been enslaved. But if so, this raises important questions. What are the privileges and immunities protected against state abridgement? What constitutes due process of law? And what constitutes a denial of equal protection of the laws?

Privileges and Immunities

The framers of the Fourteenth Amendment expected that its Privileges and Immunities Clause would furnish the primary vehicle for protecting rights against state infringements. The Privileges and Immunities Clause found in the original Constitution (Article IV, Section 2) forbids states from discriminating against nonresidents. More specifically, it prohibits states from distinguishing between their citizens and those of other states in safeguarding "all Privileges and Immunities of Citizens in the several States." The Fourteenth Amendment's Privileges and Immunities Clause extends this protection by prohibiting states from distinguishing among their own citizens with regard to the privileges and immunities of citizens of the United States.

Neither the original Constitution nor the Fourteenth Amendment defines what the privileges and immunities of citizens of the United States are. Many scholars argue that they involve the rights guaranteed to all citizens, including those found in the first ten amendments. In support of this conclusion, they observe that both Representative John Bingham of Ohio, who proposed the amendment, and Senator Jacob Howard of Michigan, who presented the proposal to the Senate, expressly stated that the Fourteenth Amendment made the Bill of Rights applicable to the states. In addition, they note that in *Corfield v. Coryell* (1823), a decision quoted approvingly by many congressional proponents of the Fourteenth Amendment, Justice Bushrod Washington offered a broad interpretation of privileges and immunities as including those protections that "belong, of right, to the citizens of all free governments." Finally, they point out that members of

Congress frequently complained that the slave states had denied to opponents of slavery the freedom of speech and other basic rights, and the framers of the amendment referred directly to such concerns during the debates over the amendment.

Other scholars deny that the Privileges and Immunities Clause made the Bill of Rights applicable to the states. Dismissing Bingham as inconsistent and confused and Howard as unrepresentative of congressional views, they instead point to statements by several members of Congress that the Clause constitutionalized the Civil Rights Act of 1866. More generally, they stress that the amendment's proponents were strongly committed to federalism and would not have adopted a provision that would have compromised state sovereignty.

In *The Slaughter-House Cases* (1873), the Supreme Court's first opportunity to interpret the Fourteenth Amendment, it gave a very narrow reading to "privileges and immunities," limiting them to such rights as access to the nation's seaports and the privilege of the writ of habeas corpus. This ruling, never overturned, in effect read the Fourteenth Amendment's Privileges and Immunities Clause out of the Constitution. In subsequent cases, therefore, debate shifted from the Privileges and Immunities Clause to the Due Process Clause and its effect on the protection of rights against state violation.

DUE PROCESS AND THE BILL OF RIGHTS

Supreme Court justices have proposed three views of the appropriate relationship between the Due Process Clause and the Bill of Rights: the "fundamental rights" interpretation, total incorporation, and selective incorporation.

The "Fundamental Rights" Interpretation

Advocates of the "fundamental rights" interpretation find no necessary connection between the Fourteenth Amendment and the guarantees of the Bill of Rights. Rather, they view the Fourteenth Amendment as protecting "traditional notions" of due process, described by Justice Henry Brown in *Holden v. Hardy* (1898) as those "certain immutable principles of justice which inhere in the very idea of free government which no member of the Union may disregard" and by Justice Benjamin Cardozo in *Palko v. Connecticut* (1937) as those principles "implicit in the concept of ordered liberty."

As applied to criminal procedure, a key concern in the Bill of Rights, this interpretation obliges a state to grant the defendant "that fundamental fairness essential to the very concept of justice." The Bill of Rights may be pertinent in determining what "fundamental fairness" requires, but it is not determinative. For example, although the Fifth Amendment requires indictment by a grand jury in federal prosecutions, states could dispense with grand-jury indictment and still operate a criminal justice system that treated defendants fairly. Thus, the fundamental rights interpretation does not impose the requirement of a grand jury upon the states. Conversely, the fundamental rights interpretation recognizes that a state procedure may violate due process, even though its operation does not contravene any specific guarantee in the first eight amendments. For example, the Bill of Rights does not mandate that defendants be guilty "beyond a reasonable doubt," but the Supreme Court held in *In re Winship* (1970) that such a standard was necessary for fundamental fairness. In sum, fundamental fairness, not mere compliance with the Bill of Rights, is the touchstone.

Critics of the fundamental rights interpretation insist that the original understanding of the Fourteenth Amendment was that it would apply the Bill of Rights to the states. They also contend that the fundamental rights interpretation promotes subjective decision making by encouraging justices to rely on their personal notions of justice. Supporters of that interpretation counter that its application rests on a societal consensus about fundamental values that can be determined independently of a justice's personal views and that various "objective" factors are available to guide the Court as to whether a particular procedural right was traditionally recognized as an essential ingredient of fairness. As Justice Felix Frankfurter observed in *Joint Anti-Fascist Refugee Committee v. McGrath* (1951):

> "Due Process," unlike some legal rules, is not a technical conception with a fixed content unrelated to time, place, and circumstances. Expressing as it does in its ultimate analysis respect enforced by law for the feeling of just treatment which has been evolved through centuries of Anglo-American constitutional history and civilization, "due process" cannot be imprisoned within the treacherous limits of any formula. Representing a profound attitude of fairness between man and man, and more particularly between the individual and the government, due process is compounded of history, reason, the past course of decisions, and stout confidence in the strength of the democratic faith which we profess.

To proponents of the fundamental rights interpretation, then, judgments as to what due process requires must be made on a case-by-case basis.

Total Incorporation

According to the total incorporation interpretation, the Fourteenth Amendment was intended to extend to all persons the complete protection of the Bill of Rights. Advocates of total incorporation insist that the legislative history and language of the amendment support total incorporation and that judges are bound by that clear intent of the Founders. In addition, they make the pragmatic argument that, by restricting judges to the specific language of the Bill of Rights, total incorporation avoids the subjectivity inherent in the fundamental rights approach.

Critics of total incorporation challenge these contentions. They argue that neither the legislative history nor the language of the amendment supports incorporation. They also disparage reliance on the Due Process Clause of the Fourteenth Amendment to incorporate the Bill of Rights, noting that it merely restates a single provision of the Fifth Amendment. Thus in *Hurtado v. California* (1884), in which the Court concluded that the Fourteenth Amendment's Due Process Clause did not require indictment by grand jury in state prosecutions, Justice Stanley Matthews observed:

> According to a recognized canon of interpretation, especially applicable to formal and solemn instruments of constitutional law, we are forbidden to assume, without clear reason to the contrary, that any part of [the Fifth] Amendment is superfluous. The natural and obvious inference is, that in the sense of the Constitution, "due process of law" was not meant or intended to include the institution and procedure of a grand jury in any case. The conclusion is equally irresistible, that when the same phrase was employed in the Fourteenth Amendment to restrain the action of the States, it was used in the same sense and with no greater extent; and that if in the adoption of that amendment it had been part of its purpose to perpetuate the institution of the grand jury in all the States, it would have embodied, as to the Fifth Amendment, express declaration to that effect.

Of course, Justice Matthews's argument largely derives its force from the fact that proponents of total incorporation have had to base their arguments on the Fourteenth Amendment's Due Process Clause, given the Supreme Court's gutting of the amendment's Privileges and Immunities Clause in *The Slaughter-House Cases*.

Opponents of total incorporation also deny that it avoids subjectivity. They criticize Justice Hugo Black, total incorporation's leading judicial exponent, for merely shifting the focus of judicial inquiry from the flexible concept of fundamental fairness to equally flexible terms in the specific amendments. Such terms as *probable cause, speedy and public trial,* and *cruel and unusual punishments,* they observe, are hardly self-defining and must be interpreted in light of the same contemporary notions of fairness considered in applying the fundamental rights standard. Finally, critics contend that total incorporation imposes an undue burden on the states and deprives them of any opportunity to act as social and legal laboratories—to experiment with alternative approaches to preserving rights.

Selective Incorporation

Selective incorporation combines elements of both the fundamental rights and the total incorporation interpretations. Like the fundamental rights approach, it holds that the Fourteenth Amendment encompasses all rights, substantive and procedural, that are "of the very essence of a scheme of ordered liberty" (*Palko v. Connecticut*). It recognizes that not all rights enumerated in the Bill of Rights are fundamental and that some fundamental rights may not be specifically mentioned in the Bill of Rights. But in determining whether an enumerated right is fundamental, this interpretation, like the total incorporation view, focuses on the *total* right guaranteed by the individual amendment, not merely on the aspect of that right before the Court or the application of that right in a particular case. In other words, by deciding that a particular guarantee of the first eight amendments is fundamental, the Supreme Court incorporates that guarantee into the Fourteenth Amendment "whole and intact" and enforces it against the states according to the same standards applied to the federal government. *Duncan v. Louisiana* (1968), which incorporated the right to a jury trial, expressed this understanding: "Because trial by jury in criminal cases is fundamental to the American scheme of justice, we hold that the Fourteenth Amendment guarantees a right of jury trial in all criminal cases which—were they to be tried in a Federal court—would come within the Sixth Amendment's guarantee."

Proponents of selective incorporation maintain that it represents an improvement over competing interpretations. They argue that a fundamental right should not be denied merely because the "totality of circumstances" in a particular case does not disclose "a denial of fundamental fairness," pointing out that judicial evaluation of the factual circumstances surrounding any particular case can be extremely subjective. On the other hand, selective incorporation avoids the rigidity of total incorporation, under which, for example, the Seventh Amendment right of trial by jury in all suits at common law in excess of $20 logically would be incorporated.

According to its detractors, however, selective incorporation represents a compromise inconsistent with the logic and history supporting the two doctrines it attempts to combine. Those who embrace total incorporation charge that it is merely another example of judges picking and choosing what rights they wish to enforce. But proponents of the fundamental rights interpretation counter that selective incorporation fails to appreciate the special burdens it imposes on the administration of criminal justice. They fear that the imposition of a single standard regulating both state and federal practice would either place an unrealistic "constitutional straitjacket" on the states or result in a relaxing of standards as applied to both state and federal officials, in order to meet the special problems of the states.

When selective incorporation replaced the fundamental rights interpretation during the 1960s as the dominant view on the Court, this led to the incorporation of several constitutional guarantees, including eleven dealing with criminal procedure (see Table 3.1). By 1972, all but two criminal procedure guarantees—the Eighth Amendment prohibition of

TABLE 3.1 **Incorporation of Provisions of the Bill of Rights**

RIGHT	CASE AND YEAR
First Amendment	
Freedom of speech	*Gitlow v. New York* (1925)
Freedom of the press	*Near v. Minnesota* (1931)
Freedom of assembly	*De Jonge v. Oregon* (1937)
Free exercise of religion	*Cantwell v. Connecticut* (1940)
Establishment clause	*Everson v. Board of Education* (1947)
Second Amendment	
Right to bear arms	*McDonald v. Chicago* (2010)
Third Amendment	
Freedom from quartering of troops in peacetime	Not incorporated
Fourth Amendment	
Unreasonable search and seizure	*Wolf v. Colorado* (1947)
Exclusionary rule	*Mapp v. Ohio* (1961)
Fifth Amendment	
Grand jury clause	Not incorporated
Self-incrimination clause	*Malloy v. Hogan* (1964)
Double jeopardy clause	*Benton v. Maryland* (1969)
Takings clause	*Chicago, Burlington, & Quincy Railroad Co. v. Chicago* (1897)
Sixth Amendment	
Right to a public trial	*In re Oliver* (1948)
Notice clause	*Cole v. Arkansas* (1948)
Right to counsel	*Gideon v. Wainwright* (1963); *Argersinger v. Hamlin* (1972)
Confrontation clause	*Pointer v. Texas* (1965)
Right to an impartial jury	*Parker v. Gladden* (1966)
Right to a speedy trial	*Klopfer v. North Carolina* (1967)
Compulsory process clause	*Washington v. Texas* (1967)
Right to jury trial (criminal cases)	*Duncan v. Louisiana* (1968)
Seventh Amendment	
Right to jury trial (civil cases)	Not incorporated
Eighth Amendment	
Ban on cruel and unusual punishments	*Robinson v. California* (1962)
Ban on excessive bail	*Schlib v. Kuebel* (1971)
Ban on excessive fines	Not incorporated
Other	
Right to privacy	*Griswold v. Connecticut* (1965)

excessive fines and the Fifth Amendment requirement of prosecutions by grand-jury indictment—had been held to apply to the states. More recently, in *McDonald v. Chicago* (2010) the Court ruled that the Second Amendment's guarantee of the right to keep and bear arms applied to the states as well as to the federal government. The Court's approach is discussed in the section on the Second Amendment later in this chapter.

State Constitutional Guarantees

Although the extension of federal protection against states' violations of rights is a relatively recent phenomenon, this does not mean that previously Americans had no protection against state infringements on rights. Rather, for most of our nation's history, a rough division of labor prevailed as to the protection of rights. State laws and state constitutions served as the primary guarantees against oppressive state governments, with the federal Constitution securing fundamental rights against state violation only when state guarantees afforded no redress. But by the mid-twentieth century, this balance had begun to shift. Defendants in state courts looked primarily to the federal Constitution and federal judicial precedent for vindication of their rights, assuming that state constitutional guarantees either duplicated federal protections or were altogether irrelevant.

Beginning in the 1970s, however, lawyers and scholars rediscovered state constitutions. Motivated both by rulings of the Burger Court that narrowed rights protections and by its encouragement of reliance on state constitutional guarantees, they began to fashion legal arguments based on the distinctive text and history of those state charters. These have been the basis for innovative—and sometimes controversial—rulings as to the rights of defendants, public education funding, and same-sex marriage. Although it is unlikely that state constitutions will ever become the primary guarantors of rights, this new emphasis on state constitutions represents one approach toward reconciling federalism and the protection of rights.

RIGHTS DURING WARTIME AND OTHER EMERGENCIES

The Framers of the Constitution sought to design a system of government that could respond effectively to the demands of war and other crises. In *The Federalist*, No. 23, Alexander Hamilton acknowledged that achievement of this aim required that broad powers be granted to the federal government:

> The circumstances that endanger the safety of nations are infinite, and for this reason no constitutional shackles can wisely be imposed on the power to which the care of it is committed. This power ought to be coextensive with all the possible combinations of such circumstances; and ought to be under the direction of the same councils which are appointed to preside over the common defense.

Or as Chief Justice Charles Evans Hughes put it, "the war power of the Federal Government is a power to wage war successfully." It follows that some governmental actions that would be impermissible in peacetime might be legitimate in time of war. Quoting Chief Justice Hughes once again: "While emergency does not create power, emergency may furnish the occasion for the exercise of power."[7]

But how far does this enhanced power during war and other emergencies extend? Does it permit a temporary suspension or dilution of constitutionally protected rights? The US Constitution, unlike the constitutions in many other countries, does not answer that question directly. The primary expression of how hostilities might affect rights is found in Article I, Section 9, which authorizes suspension of the writ of habeas corpus "when in Cases of Rebellion or Invasion the public Safety may require it." The Third Amendment also prohibits the quartering of troops in private homes except in time of war and only then "in a manner to be prescribed by Law"—that is, as authorized by the people's representatives in Congress.

Nevertheless, questions about the status of rights during wartime and other emergencies have arisen throughout American history. During the Civil War, President Lincoln suspended the writ of habeas corpus to all persons "guilty of any disloyal practice" and authorized trial and punishment of such persons by courts-martial and military tribunals. Early in World War II, President Roosevelt issued an executive order, later supported by statute, that led to the forced evacuation from the West Coast of 112,000 residents of Japanese ancestry, many of whom were American citizens. During both World War I and World War II, the government imposed restrictions on speech that was viewed as detrimental to the war effort, and during the early years of the Cold War with the Soviet Union, it imposed a wide range of restrictions on freedom of speech and association (discussed in Chapter 5). Many of these actions support Justice Robert Jackson's tart observation that "it is easy, by giving way to the passion, intolerance, and suspicions of wartime, to reduce our liberties to a shadow, often in answer to exaggerated claims of security."[8]

More recently, in the wake of the 9/11 attacks on the United States, the federal government took decisive—and in some instances controversial—action to deal with the threat of terrorism. President George W. Bush issued an executive order authorizing the indefinite detention without charges, access to counsel, or hearings of alien enemy combatants at a facility in Guantánamo Bay, Cuba, and of enemy combatants with American citizenship within the United States. He also ordered trial by military tribunal for noncitizens allegedly implicated in terrorist activities. At the behest of the president, Congress enacted the Military Commissions Act of 2006, which "authorized trial by military commission for violations of the law of war, and for other purposes." It also passed the USA PATRIOT Act in 2001, which substantially augmented federal powers to investigate and gather information in order to head off future terrorist attacks. This act (1) promoted cooperation and sharing of information between law enforcement and intelligence agencies, (2) permitted government tracing and tracking of e-mails and other electronic communications when there were "reasonable grounds" for such inquiries, (3) permitted "roving" wiretaps of cell phones and other devices, (4) expanded governmental authority to conduct "sneak-and-peek" searches in which the suspect was not notified of the search, and (5) expanded governmental powers to deny admission to foreign nationals and to detain or deport them, if (among other things) they espoused terrorism or were suspected of intending to engage in activities "that could endanger the welfare, safety, or security of the United States."

Throughout American history, those who believed that their constitutional rights had been invaded have challenged such governmental actions. Two important early rulings are *Ex parte Milligan* (1866) and *Korematsu v. United States* (1944), in which the Supreme Court ruled directly on Lincoln's actions during the Civil War and on Roosevelt's during World War II. These cases elaborate four alternative views of governmental power and rights during wartime. According to the broadest interpretation of governmental power, espoused by the four concurring justices in *Milligan* and by the Court majority in *Korematsu,* the fundamental consideration is that the government's power to wage war is the power to wage war successfully. From this, it follows that the national government possesses all powers necessary and proper to the successful prosecution of the war. When an area of the country is an actual or potential theater of military operations, accordingly, the government might engage in actions that would violate the Constitution during peacetime. As long as the actions taken are "reasonably expedient military precautions" relating to national security, they are constitutionally permissible under the Necessary and Proper Clause.

The Court majority in *Milligan* took a far more restrictive view of governmental power, asserting that all constitutional limitations on governmental action apply with equal force during wartime. According to the *Milligan* majority, what is decisive is the Framers' decision not to insert exceptions for wartime in the Bill of Rights. Their judgment that the government did not need the power to suspend constitutionally protected rights, based as it was on a personal familiarity with war during the American Revolution, remains authoritative for future generations. Therefore, any action that infringes on rights during peacetime is likewise unconstitutional during wartime because "the Constitution of the United States is a law for rulers and ruled, equally in war and in peace."

Justice Frank Murphy, dissenting in *Korematsu,* offered a third approach. According to Murphy, military necessity can justify the deprivation of individual rights, but judges should not uncritically accept government assertions of necessity. When the government undertakes the radical step of suspending rights, judges must scrutinize closely the bases for this action. Only when such deprivations can be "reasonably related to a public danger that is so immediate, imminent, and impending as not to admit of delay and not to permit the intervention of ordinary constitutional processes," Murphy concluded, should they be upheld. During wartime, then, the judiciary must play a major role in enforcing constitutional limitations.

In his dissent in *Korematsu,* Justice Robert Jackson offered a distinctive interpretation of governmental power in wartime. Jackson maintained that what is expedient on military grounds might not be constitutionally permissible—a situation that obviously creates a dilemma for the Supreme Court. On the one hand, the judiciary cannot expect the federal government to refrain from actions it deems essential to the public safety merely because of judicial disapproval. On the other hand, should the Court endorse unconstitutional actions on the basis of alleged military necessity, it would provide a precedent for abuses of power whenever "any authority can bring forward a plausible claim of an urgent need." Because the Constitution does not provide sufficient power to deal with all the exigencies of war, necessity—that is, self-preservation—and not constitutionality will inevitably (and properly) be the standard for governmental action during wartime. The Supreme Court, Jackson argued, should play no role in such situations.

The government's response to the 2001 terrorist attacks on the United States has raised anew the issue of the status of rights in time of war or national emergency. Civil-liberties groups criticized various aspects of the PATRIOT Act, particularly its authorization of "sneak-and-peek" searches, its expansion of wiretapping authority, and its expansion of executive power to detain and deport aliens. In contrast, proponents of the law insisted that it gave the federal government the tools it needed to combat a serious threat to the nation's security and to safeguard its citizens. As of 2016, the Supreme Court had not ruled on the constitutionality of any provisions of the PATRIOT Act. Congress in 2001 had inserted sunset provisions in the PATRIOT Act, under which certain provisions expired at the end of 2005 unless reenacted, thus creating an opportunity for the people's representatives to assess the act's effectiveness and its effect on civil liberties. But in 2005 and again in 2011 Congress extended several controversial provisions of the PATRIOT Act.

The Bush administration's decision to hold as enemy combatants both non-Americans and American citizens apprehended during military operations in Afghanistan or on missions within the United States also prompted legal challenges. In *Rumsfeld v. Padilla* (2004), a five-member Court majority ruled that José Padilla's habeas corpus petition had been filed in the wrong court and thus did not address whether American citizens apprehended in the United States could be designated as enemy combatants and held indefinitely without charges being filed against them. But in *Hamdi v. Rumsfeld* (2004), the Court concluded that the Due Process Clause required that American citizens be informed of the basis for their designation as enemy combatants and given the opportunity to rebut the government's assertions before a neutral decision maker. The Court divided, however, on what procedures were constitutionally required. A plurality of justices, in an opinion by Justice Sandra Day O'Connor, sought to balance the individual's strong liberty interest against the government's concern that those who fought with the enemy not be released to resume hostilities. They suggested the possibility that the demands of due process "could be met by an appropriately authorized and property constituted military tribunal." Justices David Souter and Ruth Bader Ginsburg concluded that the President lacked the power to detain American citizens as enemy combatants because Congress had not authorized him to do so. Justice Antonin Scalia, joined by Justice John Paul Stevens in dissent, noted the narrow scope of what was decided: the Court's ruling applied "only to citizens accused of being enemy combatants, who are detained within the territorial jurisdiction of a federal court." Yet for these individuals, he argued, the Constitution offered the government only two options: suspend the writ of habeas corpus or commence criminal proceedings. Only Justice Clarence Thomas concluded that the Constitution authorized the president in time of war to hold Americans as enemy combatants without a hearing.

In *Rasul v. Bush* (2004), the Court considered the rights of aliens held as enemy combatants. By a 6–3 vote, the justices concluded that the federal courts had jurisdiction under the federal habeas corpus statute to hear petitions from aliens captured during hostilities in Afghanistan who were held at the US naval base at Guantánamo Bay, Cuba. Speaking for the Court, Justice Stevens distinguished *Johnson v. Eisentrager* (1950), an earlier ruling that enemy aliens detained outside the United States were not entitled to habeas corpus relief. Although Guantánamo Bay was outside the country, he argued that it was effectively under the jurisdiction of the United States. Moreover, as Justice Anthony Kennedy noted in his concurring opinion, whereas the petitioners in *Eisentrager* had received a full trial by military commission, the detainees in Guantánamo were being held indefinitely without access to counsel and without any legal proceeding to determine their status. The Court's ruling prompted an angry rejoinder from Justice Scalia, who distinguished sharply between the rights available to citizens and those available to aliens, between those available within the United States and those available beyond its borders. In the wake of the Court's ruling, the Defense Department established a Combatant Status Review Tribunal at Guantánamo Bay, before which detainees could contest their designation as enemy combatants.

Rasul depended on the interpretation of a federal statute rather than the Constitution, so it could be overturned by congressional legislation. It nonetheless represented a significant extension of judicial authority. For the first time, the Supreme Court undertook to review actions against foreign enemies taken by the executive beyond the borders of the United States. To its proponents, *Rasul* showed the judiciary meeting its responsibility to ensure due process for all those accused of wrongdoing. But to its critics, *Rasul* represented an inappropriate attempt by the judiciary to supervise the exercise of the commander-in-chief power, a power expressly conferred on the president. This judicial willingness to challenge presidential or congressional action, or both, was evident in later cases as well.

In *Hamdan v. Rumsfeld* (2006), the Supreme Court by a 5–3 vote invalidated President Bush's executive order authorizing trial of detainees by military tribunal. Speaking for the Court, Justice Stevens insisted that even if the president possessed the power to convene military commissions, those tribunals would have to be either sanctioned by the "laws of war," as codified by Congress in Article 21 of the Uniform Code of Military Justice, or authorized by statute. Congress responded to this implicit invitation by enacting the Military Commissions Act of 2006, which gave the president congressional authorization for trying enemy combatants by military commission.[9] But this law, too, was challenged, in *Boumediene v. Bush* (2008).

In *Boumediene* a five-member majority in an opinion by Justice Kennedy held that the detainees at Guantánamo Bay had the constitutional privilege of habeas corpus. It also ruled that the procedures established by the Detainee Treatment Act (DTA), under which the determinations of Combat Status Review Tribunals (military tribunals) were subject to limited review by a federal court of appeals, were inadequate. The Court in *Johnson v. Eisentrager* had held that aliens held outside American territory had no right to habeas corpus. But Justice Kennedy argued that the US government had manipulated the *Eisentrager* rule, and he insisted that its "effective control" over the base at Guantánamo Bay, rather than political sovereignty, was determinative. "The Constitution," he wrote, "grants Congress and the President the power to acquire, dispose of, and govern territory, not the power to decide when and where its terms apply." Even when the United States acts outside its borders, its powers are not "absolute and unlimited" but are subject "to such restrictions as are expressed in the Constitution." These restrictions include the right to habeas corpus, unless Congress has suspended the writ, as it had not in this instance.

Having determined that noncitizens at Guantanamo had constitutional rights that federal courts could enforce, the Court next examined whether the DTA adequately protected those rights. The Court majority concluded that it did not. Particularly troubling was the limited review allowed to the court of appeals in reviewing the rulings of Combatant Status Review Tribunals and the statute's failure to provide opportunities for detainees to present new evidence before the court of appeals. In dissent, Chief Justice John Roberts maintained that the DTA fully protected the constitutional rights of aliens held as enemy combatants, providing the combatants held at Guantánamo "greater procedural protections than have ever been afforded alleged enemy detainees—whether citizens or aliens— in our national history." In cases involving complicated national security concerns, he insisted, courts should defer to the joint judgment of Congress and the president. Otherwise, as Justice Scalia noted in his dissent, questions of "how to handle enemy prisoners in war will ultimately lie with the branch that knows the least about national security concerns." What the dissenters saw as an unseemly grasping for power on the part of the judiciary could also have serious consequences. Indeed, Justice Scalia warned that the Court's ruling would likely lead to increased casualties and greater difficulties in the war with Islamic extremists.

THE SECOND AMENDMENT

The Second Amendment states: "A well-regulated Militia, being necessary to the security of a free State, the right of the People to keep and bear Arms, shall not be infringed." The interpretation of this provision stirs strong emotions. Arrayed on the one side are those who, with Justice Joseph Story (1811–1845), regard the right to keep and bear arms as "the palladium of the liberties of a republic" and view restrictions on gun ownership as a serious infringement on individual liberty.[10] They believe that the Second Amendment recognizes a personal right to possess firearms and to use them for traditionally lawful purposes, such as hunting and self-defense. On the other side are those who favor gun control, insisting that widespread private gun ownership promotes crime and threatens public safety. They view the amendment as protecting either a right of the states to form militias or an individual right to bear arms that is exclusively tied to participation in the militia. Thus, the federal and state governments remain free to regulate or prohibit private possession of firearms. Until recently the Supreme Court had never directly addressed whether the right to keep or bear arms is an individual personal right or one that pertains only to state militias. However, in its landmark ruling in *District of Columbia v. Heller* (2008), the justices concluded that the Second Amendment safeguards an individual's right to possess firearms for private use and struck down the District of Columbia's ban on handguns and its requirement that all firearms be kept "unloaded and disassembled or bound by a trigger lock."

Both the majority and the dissenters in *Heller* recognized that in interpreting the Second Amendment, the constitutional text and the historical context out of which it arose are vitally important. Speaking for the Court, Justice Scalia pointed out that, alone among the guarantees of the Bill of Rights, the Second Amendment contains a prefatory clause ("a well-regulated Militia being necessary to the security of a free State") that helps illuminate the purpose of its operative clause ("the right of the People to keep and bear arms shall not be infringed"). For Scalia, the constitutional text codified a preexisting "right of the people to keep and bear arms." He noted that the same words, *the right of the people,* appear in the First Amendment's Assembly-and-Petition Clause and in the Fourth Amendment's Search-and-Seizure Clause and that very similar terminology is found in the Ninth Amendment. In all these instances, the words "unambiguously refer to individual rights, not 'collective' rights, or rights that may be exercised only through participation in some corporate body." Thus, "reading the Second Amendment as protecting only the right to 'keep and bear Arms' in an organized militia fits poorly with the operative clause's description of the holder of that right as 'the people.'" Rather, these words create "a strong presumption that the Second Amendment right is exercised individually and belongs to all Americans."

The Second Amendment is also closely tied to the perception, widespread at the time of the Founding, that a standing (that is, permanent, professional) army could pose a serious threat to republican government. What made a standing army dangerous was that it would form a class distinct from the general populace and that government might employ such a force to tyrannize the citizenry. During the Constitutional Convention, some delegates—mindful of the use of the British Army to quell the colonists prior to independence and aware of the warnings about professional armies voiced by various writers on republican government—favored a ban on standing armies during peacetime.[11] Although this proposal was rejected, the convention did designate a civilian, the president, as commander in chief of the armed forces, and it limited military appropriations to two years' duration to ensure that the people's representatives retained control over the military. For many Anti-Federalists, this was insufficient. During the ratification debates, they resurrected the idea of a ban on standing armies in peacetime. More successful were calls for constitutional amendments to limit the dangers of a national military. The Third Amendment forbids the quartering of troops in private homes during peacetime, lest the national government station troops within communities to intimidate the populace (as the British did in Boston in 1774). The Second Amendment ensures that the federal government does not possess a monopoly on the use of force by preventing federal elimination of or encroachment on the state militia.

To appreciate the original understanding of the Second Amendment, one must recognize how different the militia of the late eighteenth century was from a standing army. First of all, the militia was emphatically a state force, a fundamental consideration to those who believed that federalism helped secure liberty and that the states would be a natural locus for resistance should the federal government ever become tyrannical. Thus, James Madison, in *The Federalist*, No. 46, dismissed concerns that the federal government could use its standing army to oppress by noting that schemes of oppression would be opposed by state "militia of near half a million citizens with arms in their hands." The size of the force described by Madison reveals a second difference: the militia in the late eighteenth century was not a select force, like the contemporary National Guard, but, rather, included all able-bodied free men. Such a large "well regulated" (that is, well-trained) militia would be a formidable deterrent to foreign enemies, thus obviating the need for a large standing army. It could also frustrate tyrannical ambitions of the federal government, thus safeguarding (as the Second Amendment put it) "the security of a free State."

The phrase *keep and bear arms* is suggestive of a final difference between a standing army and the militia. Soldiers in a standing army "bear arms" in the course of military service, utilizing weapons furnished by the national government under its constitutional authority to "support Armies" (Article I, Section 8, Paragraph 12). One might also "bear arms" as a member of the militia, thus suggesting a right confined to militia service. However, as Justice Scalia notes, the Second Amendment also extends a right to "keep arms," a necessity in the late eighteenth century, when citizens typically used their own weapons during service in the militia. The amendment's concern for the arming of the militia thus leads to a right to the private possession of weapons.

The Court's ruling in *Heller* left two major questions unresolved. First, does the Constitution also restrict the states' power to prohibit or regulate the possession of firearms? This issue arose in *McDonald v. Chicago* (2010), which involved a challenge to a Chicago ordinance that prohibited the possession of handguns by private individuals. In an opinion that attracted four of the five majority justices, Justice Samuel Alito endorsed the Court's ruling in *Heller* that the Second Amendment protects "a personal right to keep and bear arms for lawful purposes, most notably for self-defense within the home," and held that right was incorporated by the Due Process Clause of the Fourteenth Amendment and placed limitations on the states. Applying the selective incorporation approach discussed earlier in this chapter, Alito first considered whether the right to keep and bear arms was a right "fundamental to our scheme of ordered liberty and system of justice," concluding that it was "deeply rooted in this Nation's history and tradition." In support of this, Alito noted that the right to keep and bear arms was recognized by influential English writers such as William Blackstone, championed by Federalists and Antifederalists alike, and protected in state declarations of rights dating from the Founding and from the ratification of the Fourteenth Amendment. He pointed out that armed self-defense was viewed as particularly important for protecting freed slaves against terrorism and mob violence in the post–Civil War era, noting that it was included in the Freedmen's Bureau Act and the Civil Rights Act of 1866 and was discussed in regard to the Fourteenth Amendment itself. Having determined that the right was fundamental, Alito insisted that the Court had long ago abandoned "the notion that the Fourteenth Amendment applies to the States only a watered-down, subjective version of the individual guarantees of the Bill of Rights." Instead, he emphasized that the right recognized in *Heller* was as broad when applied to the states as to the federal government.

In dissent, Justice Stephen Breyer urged the Court to reconsider its ruling in *Heller*, warning of "the reefs and shoals that lie in wait for those nonexpert judges who place virtually determinative weight upon historical considerations." Yet even if one accepted *Heller*, he argued, the right recognized there should not be incorporated. For Breyer, the issue of incorporation depended less upon history than upon practical factors, such as the extent to which modern society continued to recognize the right as fundamental and whether representative institutions were better situated to make judgments about the proper balance to be struck between private gun possession and public safety.

Breyer's concern about the balance between gun possession and public safety points to the second question unresolved by *Heller* and *McDonald*. Both those cases involved extraordinarily stringent restrictions on gun ownership. But to what extent can government regulate the right to keep and bear arms consistent with the Second Amendment? Justice Stephen Breyer argued in dissent in *Heller* that even if the Second Amendment recognizes a personal right to bear arms, the District of Columbia's handgun ban and trigger-lock requirements did not violate that right. He pointed out that during the nineteenth century, many towns and municipalities had regulated the discharge of firearms in town, the storage of gunpowder necessary for firing weapons, and the carrying of loaded weapons within their borders. From this he concluded that the amendment did not forbid reasonable regulation of the private possession and use of firearms. He proposed an "interest-balancing" approach in Second Amendment cases that "would take account both of the statute's effects upon the competing interests and the existence of any clearly superior less restrictive alternative." Employing this method, Justice Breyer concluded that "the District's objectives are compelling; its predictive judgments as to its law's tendency to achieve those objectives are adequately supported; the law does not impose a burden upon any self-defense interest that the Amendment seeks to secure; and there is no clear less restrictive alternative."

The *Heller* majority agreed that "the right secured by the Second Amendment is not unlimited," confirming the validity of, for example, "longstanding prohibitions on the possession of firearms by felons and the mentally ill, or laws forbidding the carrying of firearms in sensitive places such as schools and government buildings, or laws imposing conditions and qualifications on the commercial sale of arms." However, it insisted that government could not invade the core protection of the amendment. The very idea of an enumeration of rights was to take certain matters out of the hands of government, whatever the justification offered for regulating them. The core of the Second Amendment, Justice Scalia argued for the Court, was "the inherent right of self-defense," and so the District's handgun ban was unconstitutional because it "amount[ed] to a prohibition of an entire class of arms that is overwhelmingly chosen by American society for that lawful purpose." However, the Court in the future will have to decide what sorts of regulations are compatible with the Second Amendment.

NOTES

1. Most state constitutions contained declarations of rights, which secured rights against state governments. In addition, the original Constitution imposed some restrictions on state violations of rights. For example, Article IV, Section 2, mandates, "The Citizens of each State shall be entitled to all Privileges and Immunities of Citizens in the several States," and Article IV, Section 4, authorizes Congress to "guarantee to every State in this Union a Republican Form of Government."

2. Letter from Richard Henry Lee to Governor Edmund Randolph, October 1, 1787, in Robert A. Rutland, ed., *The Papers of George Mason, 1725–1792*, 3 vols. (Chapel Hill: University of North Carolina Press, 1970), 3: 997–999. Even some proponents of the Constitution favored the addition of a bill of rights. As Thomas Jefferson put it, "A bill of rights is what the people are entitled to against every government on earth, general or particular, and what no government should refuse, or rest on inference." Letter from Thomas Jefferson to James Madison, December 20, 1787, in Thomas Jefferson, *The Papers of Thomas Jefferson*, edited by Julian P. Boyd (Princeton, NJ: Princeton University Press, 1950–), 12: 440.

3. *The Debates and Proceedings of the Congress of the United States* (Washington, DC, 1834), 1: 432.

4. Scholars endorsing this expansive interpretation of the Fourteenth Amendment include Akhil Reed Amar, *The Bill of Rights: Creation and Reconstruction* (New Haven, CT: Yale University Press, 1998); Judith A. Baer, *Equality Under the Constitution: Reclaiming the Fourteenth Amendment* (Ithaca, NY: Cornell University Press, 1983); and Michael Kent Curtis, *No State Shall Abridge: The Fourteenth Amendment and the Bill of Rights* (Durham, NC: Duke University Press, 1986).

5. This narrow view of the scope of the Fourteenth Amendment is presented in Charles Fairman, "Does the Fourteenth Amendment Incorporate the Bill of Rights? The Original Understanding," *Stanford Law Review* 2 (1949): 5–138; and Raoul Berger, *The Fourteenth Amendment and the Bill of Rights* (Norman: University of Oklahoma Press, 1989).

6. See, for example, Earl M. Maltz, *Civil Rights, the Constitution, and Congress, 1863–1869* (Lawrence: University Press of Kansas, 1990); William E. Nelson, *The Fourteenth Amendment: From Political Principle to Judicial Doctrine* (Cambridge, MA: Harvard University Press, 1988); and Michael P. Zuckert, "Completing the Constitution: The Fourteenth Amendment and Constitutional Rights," *Publius: The Journal of Federalism* 22 (1992): 69–91.

7. Both quotes are from Chief Justice Hughes's opinion for the Court in *Home Building and Loan Association v. Blaisdell*, 290 U.S. 398 (1934).

8. Quoted in Geoffrey R. Stone, *Perilous Times: Free Speech in Wartime from the Sedition Act of 1798 to the War on Terrorism* (New York: W. W. Norton, 2004), 528.

9. In August 2008, Salim Hamdan—Osama bin Laden's driver, and the petitioner in *Hamdan v. Rumsfeld*—was convicted of "providing material support" to al-Qaeda under the first military commission trial at Guantánamo Bay. He was sentenced to sixty-six months in prison but, as of his sentencing date, had already served sixty-one months. In November 2008, Hamdan was sent to Yemen to serve out the remainder of his sentence, and he remained in that country following his release from custody.

10. Joseph Story, *Commentaries on the Constitution of the United States* (Boston: Hilliard and Gray, 1833), 1: 708. Thirty-eight state declarations of rights protect the right to bear arms, with some expressly extending that right to include private possession of weapons for self-defense. See Robert Dowlut and Janet A. Knoop, "State Constitutions and the Right to Keep and Bear Arms," *Oklahoma City University Law Review* 7 (1982): 177–241.

11. Thus Adam Smith wrote in *The Wealth of Nations*: "In a militia, the character of the labourer, artificer, or tradesman, predominates over that of the soldier; in a standing army, that of the soldier predominates over every other character." Quoted in *United States v. Miller*, 307 U.S. 174, 179 (1939).

SELECTED READINGS

The Federalist, Nos. 46, 84.

Amar, Akhil Reed. *The Bill of Rights: Creation and Reconstruction*. New Haven, CT: Yale University Press, 1998.

Baer, Judith A. *Equality Under the Constitution: Reclaiming the Fourteenth Amendment*. Ithaca, NY: Cornell University Press, 1983.

Barnett, Randy E., ed. *History and Meaning of the Ninth Amendment*. Fairfax, VA: George Mason University Press, 1989.

Berger, Raoul. *The Fourteenth Amendment and the Bill of Rights*. Norman: University of Oklahoma Press, 1989.

Bodenhamer, David J., and James W. Ely Jr. *The Bill of Rights in Modern America*. Bloomington: Indiana University Press, 2008.

Curtis, Michael Kent. *No State Shall Abridge: The Fourteenth Amendment and the Bill of Rights*. Durham, NC: Duke University Press, 1986.

Dinan, John J. *Keeping the People's Liberties: Legislators, Citizens, and Judges as Guardians of Rights*. Lawrence: University Press of Kansas, 1998.

Dudziak, Mary L. *War-Time: An Idea, Its History, Its Consequences*. New York: Oxford University Press, 2012.

Fisher, Louis. *The Constitution and 9/11: Recurring Threats to America's Freedoms*. Lawrence: University Press of Kansas, 2008.

Goldsmith, Jack. *The Terror Presidency: Law and Judgment Inside the Bush Administration*. New York: W. W. Norton, 2009.

Goldwin, Robert A. *From Parchment to Power: How James Madison Used the Bill of Rights to Save the Constitution*. Washington, DC: American Enterprise Institute, 1997.

Green, Christopher R. *Equal Citizenship, Civil Rights, and the Constitution: The Original Sense of the Privileges and Immunities Clause*. New York: Routledge, 2015.

Halbrook, Stephen P. *The Founders' Second Amendment: Origins of the Right to Bear Arms*. Chicago: Ivan R. Dee, in association with the Independent Institute, 2008.

Katz, Ellis, and G. Alan Tarr, eds. *Federalism and Rights*. Lanham, MD: Rowman & Littlefield, 1996.

Lutz, Donald S. "The State Constitutional Pedigree of the U.S. Bill of Rights." *Publius: The Journal of Federalism* 22 (1992): 19–45.

Malcolm, Joyce L. *To Keep and Bear Arms: The Origins of an Anglo-American Right*. Cambridge, MA: Harvard University Press, 1994.

Maltz, Earl M. *Civil Rights, the Constitution, and Congress, 1863–1869*. Lawrence: University Press of Kansas, 1990.

Nelson, William E. *The Fourteenth Amendment: From Political Principle to Judicial Doctrine*. Cambridge, MA: Harvard University Press, 1988.

Rehnquist, William. *All the Laws but One: Civil Liberties in Wartime*. New York: Knopf, 1998.

Richards, Peter Judson. *Extraordinary Justice: Military Tribunals in Historical and International Context*. New York: New York University Press, 2007.

Rossum, Ralph A. "Antonin Scalia and the Rule of Law: The Textualist Foundation of the 'Law of Rules.'" In *Freedom and the Rule of Law*, edited by Anthony A. Peacock. Lanham, MD: Lexington Books, 2009.

————. "*The Federalist*'s Understanding of the Constitution as a Bill of Rights." In *Saving the Revolution: The "Federalist Papers" and the American Founding*, edited by Charles R. Kesler. New York: Free Press, 1987.

Schwartz, Bernard. *The Great Rights of Mankind: A History of the American Bill of Rights.* Expanded ed. Madison, WI: Madison House, 1992.

Stone, Geoffrey R. *Perilous Times: Free Speech in Wartime from the Sedition Act of 1798 to the War on Terrorism.* New York: W. W. Norton, 2004.

Storing, Herbert J. "The Constitution and the Bill of Rights." In *How Does the Constitution Secure Rights?* edited by Robert A. Goldwin and William A. Schambra. Washington, DC: American Enterprise Institute, 1985.

Tarr, G. Alan. *Understanding State Constitutions.* Princeton, NJ: Princeton University Press, 1998.

Tushnet, Mark V. *The Constitution in Wartime: Beyond Alarmism and Complacency.* Durham, NC: Duke University Press, 2005.

Veit, Helen E., Kenneth R. Bowling, and Charles Bangs Bickford. *Creating the Bill of Rights: The Documentary Record from the First Federal Congress.* Baltimore: Johns Hopkins University Press, 1991.

Barron v. Baltimore
32 U.S. (7 Peters) 243 (1833)

In grading and paving its streets, the city of Baltimore redirected the course of several streams flowing into its harbor. As a result, deposits of sand and gravel built up near John Barron's wharf, which was rendered inaccessible to ships. This seriously diminished the wharf's commercial value, and Barron brought suit in county court against the city, alleging a violation of the Fifth Amendment clause that forbids taking private property for public use without just compensation. The county court awarded Barron $4,500 in damages, but the Maryland Court of Appeals for the Western Shore reversed that decision. Barron appealed, and the case was brought before the US Supreme Court on a writ of error. Opinion of the Court: <u>Marshall</u>*, Johnson, Duvall, Story, Thompson, McLean, Baldwin.

THE CHIEF JUSTICE delivered the opinion of the Court.

The question thus presented is, we think, of great importance, but not of much difficulty. The constitution was ordained and established by the people of the United States for themselves, for their own government, and not for the government of the individual states. Each state established a constitution for itself, and, in that constitution, provided such limitations and restrictions on the powers of its particular government as its judgment dictated. The people of the United States framed such a government for the United States as they supposed best adapted to their situation, and best calculated to promote their interests. The powers they conferred on this government were to be exercised by itself; and the limitations on power, if expressed in general terms, are naturally, and, we think, necessarily applicable to the government created by the instrument. They are limitations of power granted in the instrument itself; not of distinct governments, framed by different persons and for different purposes.

If these propositions be correct, the fifth amendment must be understood as restraining the power of the general government, not as applicable to the states. In their several constitutions they have imposed such restrictions on their respective governments as their own wisdom suggested; such as they deemed most proper for themselves. It is a subject on which they judge exclusively, and with which others interfere no farther than they are supposed to have a common interest.

Had the people of the several states, or any of them, required changes in their constitutions; had they required additional safeguards to liberty from the apprehended encroachments of their particular governments: the remedy was in their own hands, and would have been applied by themselves. A convention would have been assembled by the discontented state, and the required improvements would have been made by itself. The unwieldy and cumbrous machinery of procuring a recommendation from two-thirds of congress, and the assent of three-fourths of their sister states, could never have occurred to any human being as a mode of doing that which might be effected by the state itself. Had the framers of these amendments intended them to be limitations on the powers of the state governments, they would have imitated the framers of the original constitution, and have expressed that intention. Had congress engaged in the extraordinary occupation of improving the constitutions of the several states by affording the people additional protection from the exercise of power by their own governments in matters which concerned themselves alone, they would have declared this purpose in plain and intelligible language.

But it is universally understood, it is a part of the history of the day, that the great revolution which established the constitution of the United States, was not effected without immense opposition. Serious fears were extensively entertained that those powers which the patriot statesmen, who then watched over the interests of our country, deemed essential to union, and to the attainment of those invaluable objects for which union was sought, might be exercised in a manner dangerous to liberty. In almost every convention by which the

---

*See page xix for an explanation of the underscoring.

constitution was adopted, amendments to guard against the abuse of power were recommended. These amendments demanded security against the apprehended encroachments of the general government—not against those of the local governments.

In compliance with a sentiment thus generally expressed to quiet fears thus extensively entertained, amendments were proposed by the required majority in congress, and adopted by the states. These amendments contain no expression indicating an intention to apply them to the state governments. This court cannot so apply them.

We are of the opinion that the provision in the fifth amendment to the constitution, declaring that private property shall not be taken for public use without just compensation, is intended solely as a limitation on the exercise of power by the government of the United States, and is not applicable to the legislation of the states.

Palko v. Connecticut
302 U.S. 319 (1937)

Frank Palko was indicted for the crime of first-degree murder. A jury found him guilty of second-degree murder, and he was sentenced to life imprisonment. Thereafter, the state of Connecticut, with the permission of the trial judge, appealed to the Connecticut Supreme Court of Errors under a statute that permitted appeals from the rulings and decisions of the trial court "upon all questions of law arising on the trial of criminal cases in the same manner and to the same effect as if made by the accused." The Supreme Court of Errors set aside the trial court's judgment and ordered a new trial, at which Palko was found guilty of first-degree murder and sentenced to death. The conviction was affirmed by the Supreme Court of Errors, and the case was appealed to the US Supreme Court. Palko contended that the Connecticut statute was unconstitutional in that the Due Process Clause of the Fourteenth Amendment protected individuals from being tried twice for the same offense. Opinion of the Court: <u>Cardozo</u>, Hughes, McReynolds, Brandeis, Sutherland, Stone, Roberts, Black. Dissenting (without opinion): Butler.

JUSTICE CARDOZO delivered the opinion of the Court.

The argument for appellant is that whatever is forbidden by the Fifth Amendment is forbidden by the Fourteenth also. The Fifth Amendment, which is not directed to the states, but solely to the federal government, creates immunity from double jeopardy. No person shall be "subject for the same offense to be twice put in jeopardy of life or limb." The Fourteenth Amendment ordains, "nor shall any State deprive any person of life, liberty, or property, without due process of law." To retry a defendant, though under one indictment and only one, subjects him, it is said, to double jeopardy in violation of the Fifth Amendment, if the prosecution is one on behalf of the United States. From this the consequence is said to follow that there is a denial of life or liberty without due process of law, if the prosecution is one on behalf of the People of a State.

In appellant's view the Fourteenth Amendment is to be taken as embodying the prohibitions of the Fifth. His thesis is even broader. Whatever would be a violation of the original bill of rights (Amendments I to VIII) if done by the federal government is now equally unlawful by force of the Fourteenth Amendment if done by a state. There is no such general rule.

The Fifth Amendment provides, among other things, that no person shall be held to answer for a capital or otherwise infamous crime unless on presentment or indictment of a grand jury. This court has held that, in prosecutions by a state, presentment or indictment by a grand jury may give way to informations at the instance of a public officer. The Fifth Amendment provides also that no person shall be compelled in any criminal case to be a witness against himself. This court has said that, in prosecutions by a state the exemption will fail if the state elects to end it. The Sixth Amendment calls for a jury trial in criminal cases and the Seventh for a jury trial in civil cases at common law where the value in controversy shall exceed twenty dollars. This court has ruled that consistently with those amendments trial by jury may be modified by a state or abolished altogether.

On the other hand, the Due Process Clause of the Fourteenth Amendment may make it unlawful for a state to abridge by its statutes the freedom of speech which the First Amendment safeguards against encroachment by the Congress, or the like freedom of the press, or the free exercise of religion, or the right of peaceable assembly without which speech would be unduly trammeled, or the right of one accused of crime to the benefit of counsel. In these and other situations immunities that are valid as against the federal government by force of the specific pledges of particular amendments have been found to be implicit in the concept of ordered liberty, and thus, through the Fourteenth Amendment, become valid as against the states.

The line of division may seem to be wavering and broken if there is a hasty catalogue of the cases on the one side and the other. Reflection and analysis will induce a different view. There emerges the perception of a rationalizing principle which gives to discrete instances a proper order and coherence. The right to trial by jury and the immunity from prosecution except as the result of an indictment may have value and importance. Even so, they are not of the very essence of a scheme of ordered liberty. To abolish them is not to violate "a principle of justice so rooted in the traditions and conscience of our people as to be ranked as fundamental." Few would be so narrow or provincial as to maintain that a fair and enlightened system of justice would be impossible without them. What is true of jury trials and indictments is true also, as the cases show, of the immunity from compulsory self-incrimination. This too might be lost, and justice still be done. Indeed, today as in the past there are students of our penal system who look upon the immunity as a mischief rather than a benefit, and who would limit its scope, or destroy it altogether. No doubt there would remain the need to give protection against torture, physical or mental. Justice, however, would not perish if the accused were subject to a duty to respond to orderly inquiry. The exclusion of these immunities and privileges from the privileges and immunities protected against the action of the states has not been arbitrary or casual. It has been dictated by a study and appreciation of the meaning, the essential implications, of liberty itself.

We reach a different plane of social and moral values when we pass to the privileges and immunities that have been taken over from the earlier articles of the federal bill of rights and brought within the Fourteenth Amendment by a process of absorption. These in their origin were effective against the federal government alone. If the Fourteenth Amendment has absorbed them, the process of absorption has had its source in the belief that neither liberty nor justice would exist if they were sacrificed. This is true, for illustration, of freedom of thought, and speech. Of that freedom one may say that it is the matrix, the indispensable condition, of nearly every other form of freedom. With rare aberrations a pervasive recognition of that truth can be traced in our history, political and legal. So it has come about that the domain of liberty, withdrawn by the Fourteenth Amendment from encroachment by the states, has been enlarged by latter-day judgments to include liberty of the mind as well as liberty of action. The extension became, indeed, a logical imperative when once it was recognized, as long ago it was, that liberty is something more than exemption from physical restraint, and that even in the field of substantive rights and duties the legislative judgment, if oppressive and arbitrary, may be overridden by the courts. Fundamental too in the concept of due process, and so in that of liberty, is the thought that condemnation shall be rendered only after trial. The hearing, moreover, must be a real one, not a sham or a pretense. For that reason, ignorant defendants in a capital case were held to have been condemned unlawfully when in truth, though not in form, they were refused the aid of counsel. The decision did not turn upon the fact that the benefit of counsel would have been guaranteed to the defendants by the provisions of the Sixth Amendment if they had been prosecuted in a federal court. The decision turned upon the fact that in the particular situation laid before us in the evidence the benefit of counsel was essential to the substance of a hearing.

On which side of the line the case made out by the appellant has appropriate location must be the next inquiry and the final one. Is that kind of double jeopardy to which the statute has subjected him a hardship so acute and shocking that our polity will not endure it? Does it violate those "fundamental principles of liberty and justice which lie at the base of all our civil and political institutions"? The answer surely must be "no." What the answer would have to be if the state were permitted after a trial free from error to try the accused over again or to bring another case against him, we have no occasion to consider. We deal with the statute before us and no other. The state is not attempting to wear the accused out by a multitude of cases with accumulated trials. It asks no more than this, that the case against him shall go on until there shall be a trial free from the corrosion of substantial legal error. This is not cruelty at all, nor even vexation in any immoderate degree. If the trial had been infected with error adverse to the accused, there might have been review at his instance, and as often as necessary to purge the vicious taint. A reciprocal privilege, subject at all times to the discretion of the presiding judge, has now been granted to the state. There is here no seismic innovation. The edifice of justice stands, its symmetry, to many, greater than before.

Adamson v. California
332 U.S. 46 (1947)

The California Constitution and penal code permitted the trial judge and prosecuting attorneys to comment adversely upon, and juries to consider as evidence of guilt, a defendant's failure to testify on his own behalf. Admiral Dewey Adamson had declined to testify at his trial for first-degree murder. In the presentation of the case to the jury, the prosecuting attorneys argued that Adamson's refusal to testify was an indication of his guilt. He was convicted and sentenced to death. His conviction was affirmed by the state supreme court and appealed to the US Supreme Court. Opinion of the Court: <u>Reed</u>, Vinson, Frankfurter, Jackson, Burton. Concurring opinion: <u>Frankfurter</u>. Dissenting opinions: <u>Black</u>, Douglas; <u>Murphy</u>, Rutledge.

JUSTICE REED delivered the opinion of the Court.

Appellant urges that the provision of the Fifth Amendment that no person "shall be compelled in any criminal case to be a witness against himself" is a fundamental national privilege or immunity protected against state abridgment by the Fourteenth Amendment or a privilege or immunity secured, through the Fourteenth Amendment, against deprivation by state action because it is a personal right, enumerated in the federal Bill of Rights.

It is settled law that the clause of the Fifth Amendment, protecting a person against being compelled to be a witness against himself, is not made effective by the Fourteenth Amendment as a protection against state action on the ground that freedom from testimonial compulsion is a right of national citizenship, or because it is a personal privilege or immunity secured by the Federal Constitution as one of the rights of man that are listed in the Bill of Rights.

The reasoning that leads to those conclusions starts with the unquestioned premise that the Bill of Rights, when adopted, was for the protection of the individual against the federal government and its provisions were inapplicable to similar actions done by the states. With the adoption of the Fourteenth Amendment, it was suggested that the dual citizenship recognized by its first sentence secured for citizens federal protection for their elemental privileges and immunities of state citizenship. *The Slaughter-House Cases* decided, contrary to the suggestion, that these rights, as privileges and immunities of state citizenship, remained under the sole protection of the state governments. This Court, without the expression of a contrary view upon that phase of the issues before the Court, has approved this determination. This leaves a state free to abridge, within the limits of the due process clause, the privileges and immunities flowing from state citizenship. This reading of the Federal Constitution has heretofore found favor with the majority of this Court as a natural and logical interpretation. It accords with the constitutional doctrine of federalism by leaving to the states the responsibility of dealing with the privileges and immunities of their citizens except those inherent in national citizenship. It is the construction placed upon the amendment by justices whose own experience had given them contemporaneous knowledge of the purposes that led to the adoption of the Fourteenth Amendment. This construction has become embedded in our federal system as a functioning element in preserving the balance between national and state power. We reaffirm the conclusion that protection against self-incrimination is not a privilege or immunity of national citizenship.

JUSTICE FRANKFURTER, concurring.

The short answer to the suggestion that the provision of the Fourteenth Amendment, which ordains "nor shall any State deprive any person of life, liberty, or property, without due process of law," was a way of saying that every State must thereafter initiate prosecutions through indictment by a grand jury, must have trial by such a jury of twelve in criminal cases, and must have trial by such a jury in common law suits where the amount in controversy exceeds twenty dollars, is that it is a strange way of saying it. It would be extraordinarily strange for a Constitution to convey such specific commands in such a roundabout and inexplicit way. Those reading the English language with the meaning which it ordinarily conveys, those conversant with the political and legal history of the concept of due process, those sensitive to the relations of the States to the central government as well as the relation of some of the provisions of the Bill of Rights to the process of justice, would hardly recognize the Fourteenth Amendment as a cover for the various explicit provisions of the first eight Amendments. Some of these are enduring reflections of experience with human nature, while some express the restricted views of Eighteenth-Century England regarding the best methods for the ascertainment of facts.

It may not be amiss to restate the pervasive function of the Fourteenth Amendment in exacting from the States observance of basic liberties. The Amendment neither comprehends the specific provisions by which the founders deemed it appropriate to restrict the Federal Government nor is it confined to them. The Due Process Clause of the Fourteenth Amendment has an independent potency, precisely as does the Due Process Clause of the Fifth Amendment in relation to the Federal Government. It ought not to require argument to reject the notion that due process of law meant one thing in the Fifth Amendment and another in the Fourteenth. The Fifth Amendment specifically prohibits prosecution of an "infamous crime" except upon indictment; it forbids double jeopardy; it bars compelling a person to be a witness against himself in any criminal case; it precludes deprivation of "life, liberty, or property, without due process of law." Are Madison and his contemporaries in the framing of the Bill of Rights to be charged with writing into it a meaningless clause? To consider "due process of law" as merely a shorthand statement of other specific clauses in the same amendment is to attribute to the authors and proponents of this Amendment ignorance of, or indifference to, a historic conception which was one of the great instruments in the arsenal of constitutional freedom which the Bill of Rights was to protect and strengthen.

The relevant question is whether the criminal proceedings which resulted in conviction deprived the accused of the due process of law to which the United States Constitution entitled him. Judicial review of that guaranty of the Fourteenth Amendment inescapably imposes upon this Court an exercise of judgment upon the whole course of the proceedings in order to ascertain whether they offend those canons of decency and fairness which express the notions of justice of English-speaking peoples even toward those charged with the most heinous offenses. These standards of justice are not authoritatively formulated anywhere as though they were prescriptions in a pharmacopoeia. But neither does the application of the Due Process Clause imply that judges are wholly at large. The judicial judgment in applying the Due Process Clause must move within the limits of accepted notions of justice and is not to be based upon the idiosyncrasies of a merely personal judgment. The fact that judges among themselves may differ whether in a particular case a trial offends accepted notions of justice is not disproof that general rather than idiosyncratic standards are applied. An important safeguard against such merely individual judgment is an alert deference to the judgment of the State court under review.

JUSTICE BLACK, dissenting.

This decision reasserts a constitutional theory spelled out in *Twining v. New Jersey* [1908], that this Court is endowed by the Constitution with boundless power under "natural law" periodically to expand and contract constitutional standards to conform to the Court's conception of what at a particular time constitutes "civilized decency" and "fundamental liberty and justice." Invoking this *Twining* rule, the Court concludes that although comment upon testimony in a federal court would violate the Fifth Amendment, identical comment in a state court does not violate today's fashion in civilized decency and fundamentals and is therefore not prohibited by the Federal Constitution as amended.

I would not reaffirm the *Twining* decision. I think that decision and the "natural law" theory of the Constitution upon which it relies degrade the constitutional safeguards of the Bill of Rights and simultaneously appropriate for this Court a broad power which we are not authorized by the Constitution to exercise. My reasons for believing that the Twining decision should not be revitalized can best be understood by reference to the constitutional, judicial, and general history that preceded and followed the case. That reference must be abbreviated far more than is justified but for the necessary limitations of opinion-writing.

My study of the historical events that culminated in the Fourteenth Amendment, and the expressions of those who sponsored and favored, as well as those who opposed its submission and passage, persuades me that one of the chief objects that the provisions of the Amendment's first section, separately, and as a whole, were intended to accomplish was to make the Bill of Rights, applicable to the states.

I am attaching to this dissent an appendix which contains a résumé, by no means complete, of the Amendment's history. In my judgment that history conclusively demonstrates

that the language of the first section of the Fourteenth Amendment, taken as a whole, was thought by those responsible for its submission to the people, and by those who opposed its submission, sufficiently explicit to guarantee that thereafter no state could deprive its citizens of the privileges and protections of the Bill of Rights.

I further contend that the "natural law" formula which the Court uses to reach its conclusion in this case should be abandoned as an incongruous excrescence on our Constitution. I believe that formula to be itself a violation of our Constitution, in that it subtly conveys to courts, at the expense of legislatures, ultimate power over public policies in fields where no specific provision of the Constitution limits legislative power.

It is an illusory apprehension that literal application of some or of all the provisions of the Bill of Rights to the States would unwisely increase the sum total of the powers of this Court to invalidate state legislation. The Federal Government has not been harmfully burdened by the requirement that enforcement of federal laws affecting civil liberty conform literally to the Bill of Rights. Who would advocate its repeal? It must be conceded, of course, that the natural law-due process formula, which the Court today reaffirms, has been interpreted to limit substantially this Court's power to prevent state violations of the individual civil liberties guaranteed by the Bill of Rights. But this formula also has been used in the past, and can be used in the future, to license this Court, in considering regulatory legislation, to roam at large in the broad expanses of policy and morals and to trespass, all too freely, on the legislative domain of the states as well as the Federal Government.

JUSTICE MURPHY, with whom JUSTICE RUTLEDGE concurs, dissenting.

While in substantial agreement with the views of MR. JUSTICE BLACK, I have one reservation. I agree that the specific guarantees of the Bill of Rights should be carried over intact into the first section of the Fourteenth Amendment. But I am not prepared to say that the latter is entirely and necessarily limited by the Bill of Rights. Occasions may arise where a proceeding falls so far short of conforming to fundamental standards of procedure as to warrant constitutional condemnation in terms of a lack of due process despite the absence of a specific provision in the Bill of Rights.

Duncan v. Louisiana
391 U.S. 145 (1968)

Gary Duncan, an African American, was convicted in a Louisiana court of simple battery for slapping a white person on the elbow. Under state law, the maximum sentence for this misdemeanor was two years' imprisonment and a $300 fine. During his court proceedings, Duncan requested a jury trial, but the judge denied his request, noting that the state constitution permitted jury trials only in instances in which hard labor or capital punishment might be imposed. Sentenced to sixty days in prison and a fine of $150, Duncan unsuccessfully petitioned the Louisiana Supreme Court for review, and then he appealed to the US Supreme Court. He contended that the Sixth and Fourteenth Amendments guaranteed the right to a jury trial in state prosecutions for crimes punishable by two years' imprisonment or more. Opinion of the Court: <u>White</u>, Warren, Black, Douglas, Brennan, Fortas, Marshall. Concurring opinions: <u>Black</u>, Douglas; <u>Fortas</u>. Dissenting opinion: <u>Harlan</u>, Stewart.

JUSTICE WHITE delivered the opinion of the Court.

The test for determining whether a right extended by the Fifth and Sixth Amendments with respect to federal criminal proceedings is also protected against state action by the Fourteenth Amendment has been phrased in a variety of ways in the opinions of this Court. The question has been asked whether a right is among those "fundamental principles of liberty and justice which lie at the base of all our civil and political institutions," whether it is "basic in our system of jurisprudence," and whether it is "a fundamental right, essential to a fair trial." The claim before us is that the right to trial by jury guaranteed by the Sixth Amendment meets these tests. The position of Louisiana, on the other hand, is that the Constitution imposes upon the States no duty to give a jury trial in any criminal case, regardless of the seriousness of the crime or the size of the punishment which may be imposed. Because we believe that trial by jury in criminal cases is fundamental to the American scheme of justice, we hold that the Fourteenth Amendment guarantees a right of jury trial in all criminal cases which—were they to be tried in a federal court—would come within the Sixth Amendment's guarantee. Since we consider the appeal before us to be such a case, we hold that the Constitution was violated when appellant's demand for jury trial was refused.

The guarantees of jury trial in the Federal and State Constitutions reflect a profound judgment about the way in which law should be enforced and justice administered. A right to jury trial is granted to criminal defendants in order to prevent oppression by the Government. Those who wrote our constitutions knew from history and experience that it was necessary to protect against unfounded criminal charges brought to eliminate enemies and against judges too responsive to the voice of higher authority. The framers of the constitutions strove to create an independent judiciary but insisted upon further protection against arbitrary action. Providing an accused with the right to be tried by a jury of his peers gave him an inestimable safeguard against the corrupt or overzealous prosecutor and against the compliant, biased, or eccentric judge. If the defendant preferred the common-sense judgment of a jury to the more tutored but perhaps less sympathetic reaction of the single judge, he was to have it. Beyond this, the jury trial provisions in the Federal and State Constitutions reflect a fundamental decision about the exercise of official power—a reluctance to entrust plenary powers over the life and liberty of the citizen to one judge or to a group of judges. Fear of unchecked power, so typical of our State and Federal Governments in other respects, found expression in the criminal law in this insistence upon community participation in the determination of guilt or innocence. The deep commitment of the Nation to the right of jury trial in serious criminal cases as a defense against arbitrary law enforcement qualifies for protection under the Due Process Clause of the Fourteenth Amendment, and must therefore be respected by the States.

Louisiana's contention is that even if it must grant jury trials in serious criminal cases, the conviction before us is valid and constitutional because here the petitioner was tried for simple battery and was sentenced to only 60 days in the parish prison. We are not persuaded. It is doubtless true that there is a category of petty crimes or offenses which is not subject to the Sixth Amendment jury trial provision and should not be subject to the Fourteenth Amendment jury trial requirement here applied to the States. Crimes carrying possible penalties up to six months do not require a jury trial if they otherwise qualify as petty offenses. But the penalty authorized for a particular crime is of major relevance in determining whether it is serious or not and may in itself, if severe enough, subject the trial to the mandates of the Sixth Amendment. The penalty authorized by the law of the locality may be taken "as a gauge of its social and ethical judgments" of the crime in question. In the case before us the Legislature of Louisiana has made simple battery a criminal offense punishable by imprisonment for up to two years and a fine. The question, then, is whether a crime carrying such a penalty is an offense which Louisiana may insist on trying without a jury.

We think not. Of course the boundaries of the petty offense category have always been ill-defined, if not ambulatory. In the absence of an explicit constitutional provision, the definitional task necessarily falls on the courts, which must either pass upon the validity of legislative attempts to identify those petty offenses which are exempt from jury trial or, where the legislature has not addressed itself to the problem, themselves face the question in the first instance. In either case it is necessary to draw a line in the spectrum of crime, separating petty from serious infractions. This process, although essential, cannot be wholly satisfactory, for it requires attaching different consequences to events which, when they lie near the line, actually differ very little.

In the federal system, petty offenses are defined as those punishable by no more than six months in prison and a $500 fine. In 49 of the 50 States crimes subject to trial without a jury, which occasionally include simple battery, are punishable by not more than one year in jail. Moreover, in the late 18th century in America crimes triable without a jury were for the most part punishable by no more than a six-month prison term, although there appear to have been exceptions to this rule. We need not, however, settle in this case the exact location of the line between petty offenses and serious crimes. It is sufficient for our purposes to hold that a crime punishable by two years in prison is, based on past and contemporary standards in this country, a serious crime and not a petty offense. Consequently, appellant was entitled to a jury trial and it was error to deny it.

JUSTICE BLACK, with whom JUSTICE DOUGLAS joins, concurring.

I believe as strongly as ever that the Fourteenth Amendment was intended to make the Bill of Rights applicable to the States. I have been willing to support the selective incorporation doctrine, however, as an alternative, although perhaps less historically supportable than complete incorporation. The selective incorporation process, if used properly, does limit the Supreme Court in the Fourteenth Amendment field to specific Bill of Rights' protections only and keeps judges from roaming at will in their own notions of what policies outside the Bill of Rights are desirable and what are not. And, most importantly for me, the selective incorporation process has the virtue of having already worked to make most of the Bill of Rights' protections applicable to the States.

JUSTICE HARLAN, with whom JUSTICE STEWART joins, dissenting.

Every American jurisdiction provides for trial by jury in criminal cases. The question before us is not whether jury trial is an ancient institution, which it is; nor whether it plays a significant role in the administration of criminal justice, which it does; nor whether it will endure, which it shall. The question in this case is whether the State of Louisiana, which provides trial by jury for all felonies, is prohibited by the Constitution from trying charges of simple battery to the court alone. In my view, the answer to that question, mandated alike by our constitutional history and by the longer history of trial by jury, is clearly "no."

The Court's approach to this case is an uneasy and illogical compromise among the views of various Justices on how the Due Process Clause should be interpreted. The Court does not say that those who framed the Fourteenth Amendment intended to make the Sixth Amendment applicable to the States. And the Court concedes that it finds nothing unfair about the procedure by which the present appellant was tried. Nevertheless, the Court reverses his conviction: it holds, for some reason not apparent to me, that the Due Process Clause incorporates the particular clause of the Sixth Amendment that requires trial by jury in federal criminal cases—including, as I read its opinion, the sometimes trivial accompanying baggage of judicial interpretation in federal contexts.

A few members of the Court have taken the position that the intention of those who drafted the first section of the Fourteenth Amendment was simply, and exclusively, to make the provisions of the first eight Amendments applicable to state action. Neither history, nor sense, supports using the Fourteenth Amendment to put the States in a constitutional straitjacket with respect to their own development in the administration of criminal or civil law.

Although I therefore fundamentally disagree with the total incorporation view of the Fourteenth Amendment, it seems to me that such a position does at least have the virtue, lacking in the Court's selective incorporation approach, of internal consistency: we look to the Bill of Rights, word for word, clause for clause, precedent for precedent because, it is said, the men who wrote the Amendment wanted it that way.

Apart from the approach taken by the absolute incorporationists, I can see only one method of analysis that has any internal logic. That is to start with the words "liberty" and "due process of law" and attempt to define them in a way that accords with American traditions and our system of government. This approach, involving a much more discriminating process of adjudication than does "incorporation," is, albeit difficult, the one that was followed throughout the 19th and most of the present century. It entails a "gradual process of judicial inclusion and exclusion," seeking, with due recognition of constitutional tolerance for state experimentation and disparity, to ascertain those "immutable principles of free government which no member of the Union may disregard."

The relationship of the Bill of Rights to this "gradual process" seems to me to be twofold. In the first place it has long been clear that the Due Process Clause imposes some restrictions on state action that parallel Bill of Rights restrictions on federal action. Second, and more important than this accidental overlap, is the fact that the Bill of Rights is evidence, at various points, of the content Americans find in the term "liberty" and of American standards of fundamental fairness.

Today's Court still remains unwilling to accept the total incorporationists' view of the history of the Fourteenth Amendment. This, if accepted, would afford a cogent reason for applying the Sixth Amendment to the States. The Court is also, apparently, unwilling to face the task of determining whether denial of trial by jury in the situation before us, or in other situations, is fundamentally unfair. Consequently, the Court has compromised on the case of the incorporationist position, without its internal logic. It has simply assumed that the question before us is whether the Jury Trial Clause of the Sixth Amendment should be incorporated into the Fourteenth, jot-for-jot and case-for-case, or ignored. Then the Court merely declares that the clause in question is "in" rather than "out."

Since, as I see it, the Court has not even come to grips with the issues in this case, it is necessary to start from the beginning. When a criminal defendant contends that his state conviction lacked "due process of law," the question before this Court, in my view, is whether he was denied any element of fundamental procedural fairness.

The argument that jury trial is not a requisite of due process is quite simple. The central proposition is that "due process of law" requires only that criminal trials be fundamentally fair. As stated above, apart from the theory that it was historically intended as a mere shorthand for the Bill of Rights, I do not see what else "due process of law" can intelligibly be thought to mean. If due process of law requires only fundamental fairness, then the inquiry in each case must be whether a state trial process was a fair one. The Court has held, properly I think, that in an adversary process it is a requisite of fairness, for which there is no adequate substitute, that a criminal defendant be afforded a right to counsel and to cross-examine opposing witnesses. But it simply has not been demonstrated, nor, I think, can it be demonstrated, that trial by jury is the only fair means of resolving issues of fact.

There is a wide range of views on the desirability of trial by jury, and on the ways to make it most effective when it is used; there is also considerable variation from State to State in local conditions such as the size of the criminal caseload, the ease or difficulty of summoning jurors, and other trial conditions bearing on fairness. We have before us, therefore, an almost perfect example of a situation in which the celebrated dictum of Mr. Justice Brandeis should be invoked. It is, he said, "one of the happy incidents of the federal system that a single courageous State may, if its citizens choose, serve as a laboratory" [*New State Ice Co. v. Liebmann* (1932)]. This Court, other courts, and the political process are available to correct any experiments in criminal procedure that prove fundamentally unfair to defendants. That is not what is being done today: instead, and quite without reason, the Court has chosen to impose upon every State one means of trying criminal cases; it is a good means, but it is not the only fair means, and it is not demonstrably better than the alternatives States might devise.

Ex parte Milligan
71 U.S. (4 Wall.) 2 (1866)

In 1862, President Abraham Lincoln ordered that all persons "guilty of any disloyal practice affording aid and comfort to rebels" should be subject to trial and punishment by "courts-martial or military commissions." Two years later, a military commission acting under this authority tried and convicted Lambdin P. Milligan, a notorious Confederate sympathizer in Indiana, on charges of disloyalty. Because the civil courts were functioning and Indiana was not a battle zone, Milligan charged that the commission lacked jurisdiction over him and sought a writ of habeas corpus in circuit court. He also contended that trial before the military commission violated his constitutional right to trial by jury. After failing to reach agreement on the issues Milligan raised, the circuit court certified the questions to the Supreme Court. Note that the Court announced its ruling in 1866, after the end of the Civil War and the assassination of President Lincoln. Opinion of the Court: Davis, Nelson, Grier, Clifford, Field. Concurring on the judgment: Chase, Wayne, Swayne, Miller.

JUSTICE DAVIS delivered the opinion of the Court.

Milligan, not a resident of one of the rebellious states, or a prisoner of war, but a citizen of Indiana for twenty years past, and never in the military or naval service, is, while at his home, arrested by the military power of the United States, imprisoned and, on certain criminal charges preferred against him, tried, convicted, and sentenced to be hanged by a military commission, organized under the direction of the military commander of the military district of Indiana. Had this tribunal the legal power and authority to try and punish this man?

No graver question was ever considered by this court, nor one which more nearly concerns the rights of the whole people; for it is the birthright of every American citizen when charged with crime, to be tried and punished according to law. The provisions of [the Constitution] on the administration of criminal justice are too plain and direct to leave room for misconstruction or doubt of their true meaning. Those applicable to this case are found in that clause of the original Constitution which says "that the trial of all crimes, except in case of impeachment, shall be by jury;"

and in the fourth, fifth, and sixth articles of the amendments.

Even these provisions, expressed in such plain English words, that it would seem the ingenuity of man could not evade them, are now, after the lapse of more than seventy years, sought to be avoided. The Constitution of the United States is a law for rulers and people, equally in war and in peace, and covers with the shield of its protection all classes of men, at all times and under all circumstances. No doctrine, involving more pernicious consequences, was ever invented by the wit of man than that any of its provisions can be suspended during any of the great exigencies of government. Such a doctrine leads directly to anarchy or despotism, but the theory of necessity on which it is based is false; for the government, within the Constitution, has all the powers granted to it which are necessary to preserve its existence, as has been happily proved by the result of the great effort to throw off its just authority.

Have any of the rights guaranteed by the Constitution been violated in the case of Milligan? and if so, what are they?

Every trial involves the exercise of judicial power; and from what source did the Military Commission that tried him derive their authority? Certainly no part of the judicial power of the country was conferred on them: because the Constitution expressly vests it "in one Supreme Court and such inferior courts as the Congress may from time to time ordain and establish," and it is not pretended that the commission was a court ordained and established by Congress. They cannot justify on the mandate of the President: because he is controlled by law, and has his appropriate sphere of duty, which is to execute, not to make, the laws.

But it is said that the jurisdiction is complete under the "laws and usages of war." It can serve no useful purpose to inquire what those laws and usages are, whence they originated, where found, and on whom they operate; they can never be applied to citizens in states which have upheld the authority of the government, and where the courts are open and their process unobstructed. This court has judicial knowledge that in Indiana the Federal author-

ity was always unopposed, and its courts always open to hear criminal accusations and redress grievances; and no usage of war could sanction a military trial there for any offense whatever of a citizen in civil life, in nowise connected with the military service. Congress could grant no such power; and to the honor of our national legislature be it said, it has never been provoked by the state of the country even to attempt its exercise. One of the plainest constitutional provisions was, therefore, infringed when Milligan was tried by a court not ordained and established by Congress, and not composed of judges appointed during good behavior.

Another guarantee of freedom was broken when Milligan was denied a trial by jury. This privilege is a vital principle, underlying the whole administration of criminal justice; it is not held by sufferance, and cannot be frittered away on any plea of state or political necessity. When peace prevails, and the authority of the government is undisputed, there is no difficulty in preserving the safeguards of liberty; for the ordinary modes of trial are never neglected, and no one wishes it otherwise; but if society is disturbed by civil commotion—if the passions of men are aroused and the restraints of law weakened, if not disregarded—these safeguards need, and should receive, the watchful care of those intrusted with the guardianship of the Constitution and laws.

It is claimed that martial law covers with its broad mantle the proceedings of this Military Commission. The proposition is this: That in a time of war the commander of an armed force (if in his opinion the exigencies of the country demand it, and of which he is to judge), has the power, within the lines of his military district, to suspend all civil rights and their remedies, and subject citizens as well as soldiers to the rule of his will; and in the exercise of his lawful authority cannot be restrained, except by his superior officer or the President of the United States.

This nation, as experience has proved, cannot always remain at peace, and has no right to expect that it will always have wise and humane rulers, sincerely attached to the principles of the Constitution. Wicked men, ambitious of power, with hatred of liberty and contempt of law, may fill the place once occupied by Washington and Lincoln; and if this right is conceded, and the calamities of war again befall us, the dangers to human liberty are frightful to contemplate.

It is insisted that the safety of the country in time of war demands that this broad claim for martial law shall be sustained. If this were true, it could be well said that a country, preserved at the sacrifice of all the cardinal principles of liberty, is not worth the cost of preservation. Happily, it is not so. Martial rule can never exist where the courts are open, and in the proper and unobstructed exercise of their jurisdiction. It is also confined to the locality of actual war. Because, during the late Rebellion it could have been enforced in Virginia, where the national authority was overturned and the courts driven out, it does not follow that it should obtain in Indiana, where that authority was never disputed, and justice was always administered.

THE CHIEF JUSTICE delivered the following opinion.

The opinion which has just been read asserts not only that the Military Commission held in Indiana was not authorized by Congress, but that it was not in the power of Congress to authorize it. We cannot agree to this. We think that Congress had power, though not exercised, to authorize the Military Commission which was held in Indiana.

Congress has power to raise and support armies; to provide and maintain a navy; to make rules for the government and regulation of the land and naval forces; and to provide for governing such part of the militia as may be in the service of the United States. It is not denied that the power to make rules for the government of the army and navy is a power to provide for trial and punishment by military courts without a jury. It has been so understood and exercised from the adoption of the Constitution to the present time.

Nor, in our judgment, does the fifth or any other amendment, abridge that power. It is not necessary to attempt any precise definition of the boundaries of this power. But may it not be said that government includes protection and defense as well as the regulation of internal administration? And is it impossible to imagine cases in which citizens conspiring or attempting the destruction or great injury of the national forces may be subjected by Congress to military trial and punishment in the just exercise of this undoubted constitutional power?

But we do not put our opinion, that Congress might authorize such a military commission as was held in Indiana, upon the power to provide for the government of the national forces. Congress has the power not only to raise and support and govern armies, but to declare war. It has, therefore, the power to provide by law for carrying on war. This power necessarily extends to all legislation essential to the prosecution of war with vigor and success, except such as interferes with the command of the force and conduct of campaigns. That power and duty belong to the President as Commander-in-Chief. Both these powers are derived from the Constitution, but neither is defined by that instrument. Their extent must be determined: by their nature, and by the principles of our institutions.

Where peace exists the laws of peace must prevail. What we do maintain is that when the nation is involved in war, and some portions of the country are invaded, and all are exposed to invasion, it is within the power of Congress to determine to what states or districts such great and imminent public danger exists as justifies the authorization of military tribunals for the trial of crimes and offenses against the discipline or security of the army or against the public safety.

In Indiana, for example, at the time of the arrest of Milligan and his co-conspirators, it is established by the papers in the record, that the state was a military district, was the theater of military operations, had been actually invaded, and was constantly threatened with invasion. It appears, also, that a powerful secret association, composed of citizens and others, existed within the state, under military organization, conspiring against the draft, and plotting insurrection, the liberation of the prisoners of war at various depots, the seizure of the state and national arsenals, armed co-operation with the enemy, and war against the national government.

We cannot doubt that, in such a time or public danger, Congress had power, under the

Constitution, to provide for the organization of a military commission, and for trial by that commission of persons engaged in this conspiracy. The fact that the Federal courts were open was regarded by Congress as a sufficient reason for not exercising the power; but that fact could not deprive Congress of the right to exercise it. Those courts might be open and undisturbed in the execution of their functions, and yet wholly incompetent to avert threatened danger, or to punish, with adequate promptitude and certainty, the guilty conspirators.

In Indiana, the judges and officers of the courts were loyal to the government. But it might have been otherwise. In times of rebellion and civil war it may often happen, indeed, that judges and marshals will be in active sympathy with the rebels, and courts their most efficient allies. We think that the power of Congress, in such times and in such localities, to authorize trials for crimes against the security and safety of the national forces, may be derived from its constitutional authority to raise and support armies and to declare war, if not from its constitutional authority to provide for governing the national forces.

We have no apprehension that this power, under our American system of government, in which all official authority is derived from the people and exercised under direct responsibility to the people, is more likely to be abused than the power to regulate commerce or the power to borrow money. And we are unwilling to give our assent by silence to expressions of opinion which seem to us calculated, though not intended, to cripple the constitutional powers of the government, and to augment the public dangers in times of invasion and rebellion.

Korematsu v. United States
323 U.S. 214 (1944)

In February 1942, President Franklin Roosevelt issued Executive Order 9066, which authorized the creation of military areas from which individuals might be excluded to prevent espionage or sabotage. The order also permitted military commanders to regulate who might enter or remain in such areas. A month later, Congress passed legislation establishing criminal penalties for violations of these regulations. Acting pursuant to the authority delegated to him under the executive order, the commander of the Western Defense Command initially imposed a curfew on residents of Japanese ancestry and ultimately ordered that they be evacuated to inland detention centers. In Hirabayashi v. United States (1943), the Court upheld the curfew program in a narrow ruling that involved no consideration of the evacuation program. When Toyosaburo Korematsu, an American citizen of Japanese ancestry, refused to leave his home in California, he was convicted in federal district court of violating the exclusion order. After the conviction was upheld by the circuit court of appeals, the Supreme Court granted certiorari. Opinion of the Court: <u>Black</u>, Stone, Reed, Frankfurter, Douglas, Rutledge. Concurring opinion: <u>Frankfurter</u>. Dissenting opinions: <u>Roberts</u>; <u>Murphy</u>; <u>Jackson</u>.

JUSTICE BLACK delivered the opinion of the Court.

All legal restrictions which curtail the civil rights of a single racial group are immediately suspect. That is not to say that all such restrictions are unconstitutional. It is to say that courts must subject them to the most rigid scrutiny. Pressing public necessity may sometimes justify the existence of such restrictions; racial antagonism never can.

In the light of the principles we announced in the *Hirabayashi* case [*Hirabayashi v. United States* (1943)], we are unable to conclude that it was beyond the war power of Congress and the Executive to exclude those of Japanese ancestry from the West Coast war area at the time they did. Nothing short of apprehension by the proper military authorities of the gravest imminent danger to the public safety can constitutionally justify either. But exclusion from a threatened area has a definite and close relationship to the prevention of espionage and sabotage.

It was because we could not reject the finding of the military authorities that it was impossible to bring about an immediate segregation of the disloyal from the loyal that we sustained the validity of the curfew order as applying to the whole group. In the instant case, temporary exclusion of the entire group was rested by the military on the same ground. The judgment that exclusion of the whole group was for the same reason a military imperative answers the contention that the exclusion was in the nature of group punishment based on antagonism to those of Japanese origin.

We uphold the exclusion order as of the time it was made and when the petitioner violated it. In doing so, we are not unmindful of the hardships imposed by it upon a large group of American citizens. But hardships are part of war, and war is an aggregation of hardships. All citizens alike, both in and out of uniform, feel the impact of war in greater or lesser measure. Citizenship has its responsibilities as well as its privileges, and in time of war the burden is always heavier. Compulsory exclusion of large groups of citizens from their homes, except under circumstances of direst emergency and peril, is inconsistent with our basic governmental institutions. But when under conditions of modern warfare our shores are threatened by hostile forces, the power to protect must be commensurate with the threatened danger.

It is said that we are dealing here with the case of imprisonment of a citizen in a concentration camp solely because of his ancestry, without evidence or inquiry concerning his loyalty and good disposition towards the United States. To cast this case into outlines of racial prejudice, without reference to the real military dangers which were presented, merely confuses the issue. Korematsu was not excluded from the Military Area because of hostility to him or his race. He was excluded because we are at war with the Japanese Empire, because the properly constituted military authorities feared an invasion of our West Coast and felt constrained to take proper security measures, because they decided that the military urgency of the situation demanded that all citizens of Japanese ancestry be segregated from the West Coast temporarily, and finally, because Congress, reposing its confidence in this time of war in our military leaders—as inevitably it must—determined that they should have the power to do just this.

There was evidence of disloyalty on the part of some, the military authorities considered that the need for action was great, and time was short. We cannot—by availing ourselves of the calm perspective of hindsight—now say that at that time these actions were unjustified.

Affirmed.

JUSTICE FRANKFURTER, concurring.

The provisions of the Constitution which confer on the Congress and the President powers to enable this country to wage war are as much part of the Constitution as provisions looking to a nation at peace. And we have had recent occasion to quote approvingly the statement of former Chief Justice Hughes that the war power of the Government is "the power to wage war successfully." Therefore, the validity of action under the war power must be judged wholly in the context of war. That action is not to be stigmatized as lawless because like action in times of peace would be lawless. To talk about a military order that expresses an allowable judgment of war needs by those entrusted with the duty of conducting war as "an unconstitutional order" is to suffuse a part of the Constitution with an atmosphere of unconstitutionality. To recognize that military orders are "reasonably expedient military precautions" in time of war and yet to deny them constitutional legitimacy makes of the Constitution an instrument for dialectic subtleties not reasonably to be attributed to the hard-headed Framers, of whom a majority had had actual participation in war. If a military order such as that under review does not transcend the means appropriate for conducting war, such action by the military is as constitutional as would be any authorized action by the Interstate Commerce Commission within the limits of the constitutional power to regulate commerce. To find that the Constitution does not forbid the military measures now complained of does not carry with it approval of that which Congress and the Executive did. That is their business, not ours.

JUSTICE MURPHY, dissenting.

This exclusion of "all persons of Japanese ancestry, both alien and non-alien," from the Pacific Coast area on a plea of military necessity in the absence of martial law ought not to be approved. Such exclusion goes over "the very brink of constitutional power" and falls into the ugly abyss of racism.

In dealing with matters relating to the prosecution and progress of a war, we must accord great respect and consideration to the judgments of the military authorities who are on the scene and who have full knowledge of the military facts. The scope of their direction must, as a matter of necessity and common sense, be wide. And their judgments ought not to be overruled lightly by those whose training and duties ill-equip them to deal intelligently with matters so vital to the physical security of the nation. At the same time, however, it is essential that there be definite limits to military discretion, especially where martial law has not been declared. Individuals must not be left impoverished of their constitutional rights on a plea of military necessity that has neither substance nor support.

The judicial test of whether the Government, on a plea of military necessity, can validly deprive an individual of any of his constitutional rights is whether the deprivation is reasonably related to a public danger that is so "immediate, imminent, and impending" as not to admit of delay and not to permit the intervention of ordinary constitutional processes to alleviate the danger.

In adjudging the military action taken in light of the then apparent dangers, we must not erect too high or too meticulous standards; it is necessary only that the action have some reasonable relation to the removal of the dangers of invasion, sabotage and espionage. But the exclusion, either temporarily or permanently, of all persons with Japanese blood in their veins has no such reasonable relation. And that relation is lacking because the exclusion order necessarily must rely for its reasonableness upon the assumption that all persons of Japanese ancestry may have a dangerous tendency to commit sabotage and espionage and to aid our Japanese enemy in other ways. That this forced exclusion was the result in good measure of this erroneous assumption of racial guilt rather than bona fide military necessity is evidenced by the Commanding General's Final Report on the evacuation from the Pacific

Coast area. In it he refers to all individuals of Japanese descent as "subversive," as belonging to "an enemy race" whose "racial strains are undiluted," and as constituting over 112,000 potential enemies at large today along the Pacific Coast.* In support of this blanket condemnation of all persons of Japanese descent, however, no reliable evidence is cited to show that such individuals were generally disloyal, or had generally so conducted themselves in this area as to constitute a special menace to defense installations or war industries, or had otherwise by their behavior furnished reasonable ground for their exclusion as a group.

Justification for the exclusion is sought, instead, mainly upon questionable racial and sociological grounds not ordinarily within the realm of expert military judgment, supplemented by certain semimilitary conclusions drawn from an unwarranted use of circumstantial evidence. No adequate reason is given for the failure to treat these Japanese Americans on an individual basis by holding investigations and hearings to separate the loyal from the disloyal, as was done in the case of persons of German and Italian ancestry. It is asserted merely that the loyalties of this group "were unknown and time was of the essence." Yet nearly four months elapsed after Pearl Harbor before the first exclusion order was issued; nearly eight months went by until the last order was issued; and the last of these "subversive" persons was not actually removed until almost eleven months had elapsed. Leisure and deliberation seem to have been more of the essence than speed. And the fact that conditions were not such as to warrant a declaration of martial law adds strength to the belief that the factors of

---

*Further evidence of the Commanding General's attitude toward individuals of Japanese ancestry is revealed in his voluntary testimony: "I don't want any of them [persons of Japanese ancestry] here. They are a dangerous element. There is no way to determine their loyalty. The west coast contains too many vital installations essential to the defense of the country to allow any Japanese on this coast. The danger of the Japanese was, and is now—if they are permitted to come back—espionage and sabotage. It makes no difference whether he is an American citizen, he is still a Japanese. American citizenship does not necessarily determine loyalty. But we must worry about the Japanese all the time until he is wiped off the map. Sabotage and espionage will make problems as long as he is allowed in this area."

time and military necessity were not as urgent as they have been represented to be.

I dissent, therefore, from this legalization of racism. All residents of this nation are kin in some way by blood or culture to a foreign land. Yet they are primarily and necessarily a part of the new and distinct civilization of the United States. They must accordingly be treated at all times as the heirs of the American experiment and as entitled to all the rights and freedoms guaranteed by the Constitution.

JUSTICE JACKSON, dissenting.

It is said that if the military commander had reasonable military grounds for promulgating the orders, they are constitutional and become law, and the Court is required to enforce them. There are several reasons why I cannot subscribe to this doctrine.

It would be impracticable and dangerous idealism to expect or insist that each specific military command in an area of probable operations will conform to conventional tests of constitutionality. When an area is so beset that it must be put under military control at all, the paramount consideration is that its measures be successful, rather than legal. The armed services must protect a society, not merely its Constitution. The very essence of the military job is to marshal physical force, to remove every obstacle to its effectiveness, to give it every strategic advantage. Defense measures will not, and often should not, be held within the limits that bind civil authority in peace. No court can require such a commander in such circumstances to act as a reasonable man; he may be unreasonably cautious and exacting. Perhaps he should be. But a commander in temporarily focusing the life of a community on defense is carrying out a military program; he is not making law in the sense the courts know the term. He issues orders, and they may have a certain authority as military commands, although they may be very bad as constitutional law.

But if we cannot confine military expedients by the Constitution, neither would I distort the Constitution to approve all that the military may deem expedient. That is what the Court appears to be doing, whether consciously or not. I cannot say, from any evidence before me, that the orders of General DeWitt were not reasonably expedient military precautions, nor could I say that they were. But even if they were permissible military procedures, I deny that it follows that they are constitutional. If, as the Court holds, it does follow, then we may as well say that any military order will be constitutional and have done with it.

In the very nature of things, military decisions are not susceptible of intelligent judicial appraisal. They do not pretend to rest on evidence, but are made on information that often would not be admissible and on assumptions that could not be proved. Information in support of an order could not be disclosed to courts without danger that it would reach the enemy. Neither can courts act on communications made in confidence. Hence courts can never have any real alternative to accepting the mere declaration of the authority that issued the order that it was reasonably necessary from a military viewpoint.

Much is said of the danger to liberty from the Army program for deporting and detaining these citizens of Japanese extraction. But a judicial construction of the due process clause that will sustain this order is a far more subtle blow to liberty than the promulgation of the order itself. A military order, however unconstitutional, is not apt to last longer than the military emergency. Even during that period a succeeding commander may revoke it all. But once a judicial opinion rationalizes such an order to show that it conforms to the Constitution, or rather rationalizes the Constitution to show that the Constitution sanctions such an order, the Court for all time has validated the principle of racial discrimination in criminal procedure and of transplanting American citizens. The principle then lies about like a loaded weapon ready for the hand of any authority that can bring forward a plausible claim of an urgent need. Every repetition imbeds that principle more deeply in our law and thinking and expands it to new purposes.

I should hold that a civil court cannot be made to enforce an order which violates constitutional limitations even if it is a reasonable exercise of military authority. The courts can exercise only the judicial power, can apply only law, and must abide by the Constitution, or they cease to be civil courts and become instruments of military policy.

Of course the existence of a military power resting on force, so vagrant, so centralized, so necessarily heedless of the individual, is an inherent threat to liberty. But I would not lead people to rely on this Court for a review that seems to me wholly delusive. The military reasonableness of these orders can only be determined by military superiors. If the people ever let command of the war power fall into irresponsible and unscrupulous hands, the courts wield no power equal to its restraint. The chief restraint upon those who command the physical forces of the country, in the future as in the past, must be their responsibility to the political judgments of their contemporaries and to the moral judgments of history.

My duties as a justice as I see them do not require me to make a military judgment as to whether General DeWitt's evacuation and detention program was a reasonable military necessity. I do not suggest that the courts should

have attempted to interfere with the Army in carrying out its task. But I do not think they may be asked to execute a military expedient that has no place in law under the Constitution. I would reverse the judgment and discharge the prisoner.

[*In 1948, following condemnation by a presidential commission of the forced evacuation of Japanese Americans, Congress passed the Evacuation Claims Act, under which claimants received more than $37 million. In 1984, another governmental commission concluded that the internment resulted from "race prejudice, wartime hysteria, and a failure of political leadership" and recommended a national apology and further monetary compensation. That same year a federal district court vacated Korematsu's conviction based on newly discovered evidence that the government had deliberately withheld and falsified relevant evidence in the materials it presented in court. In 1988, Congress formally apologized for the internment and established a fund to pay reparations.*]

Hamdi v. Rumsfeld
542 U.S. 507 (2004)

After the 2001 terrorist attacks by al-Qaeda, Congress passed a resolution authorizing the president to "use all necessary and appropriate force against those nations, organizations, or persons he determines planned, authorized, committed, or aided the terrorist attacks" or "harbored such organizations or persons, in order to prevent any future acts of international terrorism against the United States by such nations, organizations or persons." Soon thereafter, the president ordered US armed forces to Afghanistan to subdue al-Qaeda and the Taliban regime that supported it. In the course of this conflict, Yaser Esam Hamdi was captured. Hamdi was imprisoned at the US naval base at Guantánamo Bay, Cuba, but upon learning that Hamdi was an American citizen, authorities transferred him to a naval brig in Norfolk, Virginia, and then to one in Charleston, South Carolina. The government contended that Hamdi was an enemy combatant and that this status justified holding him in the United States indefinitely without formal charges or proceedings. Hamdi's father filed a petition for a writ of habeas corpus

in the Eastern District of Virginia, alleging that his son's detention was not legally authorized and that detention of a US citizen without charges, access to an impartial tribunal, or assistance of counsel violated his constitutional rights.

The district court initially ordered that counsel be given access to Hamdi, but the United States Court of Appeals reversed. On remand, the government submitted a declaration from Michael Mobbs, a special adviser to the undersecretary of defense for policy, that asserted that Hamdi was a member of a Taliban military unit and had surrendered with his unit to the Northern Alliance. It claimed that because al-Qaeda and the Taliban "were and are hostile forces engaged in armed conflict with the armed forces of the United States," "individuals associated with" those groups "were and continue to be enemy combatants." Finally, it stated that Hamdi was labeled an enemy combatant "[b]ased upon his interviews and in light of his association with the Taliban."

The district court concluded that the Mobbs declaration fell "far short" of supporting Hamdi's detention and ordered the government to turn over numerous materials for in camera review, including copies of all of Hamdi's statements and the notes taken from interviews with him that related to his reasons for going to Afghanistan and his activities therein, a list of all interrogators who had questioned Hamdi and their names and addresses, statements by members of the Northern Alliance regarding Hamdi's surrender and capture, a list of the dates and locations of his capture and subsequent detentions, and the names and titles of the US government officials who made the determinations that Hamdi was an enemy combatant and that he should be moved to a naval brig. The government appealed the production order, and the court of appeals reversed. Hamdi then appealed that ruling, and the Supreme Court granted certiorari. Judgment of the Court: O'Connor, Rehnquist, Kennedy, Breyer. *Concurring in part and dissenting in part:* Souter, Ginsburg. *Dissenting opinions:* Scalia, Stevens; Thomas.

JUSTICE O'CONNOR announced the judgment of the Court and delivered an opinion, in which THE CHIEF JUSTICE, JUSTICE KENNEDY, and JUSTICE BREYER join.

II

The threshold question before us is whether the Executive has the authority to detain citizens who qualify as "enemy combatants." The Government maintains that no explicit congressional authorization is required, because the Executive possesses plenary authority to detain pursuant to Article II of the Constitution. We do not reach the question whether Article II provides such authority, however, because we agree with the Government's alternative position, that Congress has in fact authorized Hamdi's detention, through the AUMF [Authorization for the Use of Military Force].

The AUMF authorizes the President to use "all necessary and appropriate force" against "nations, organizations, or persons" associated with the September 11, 2001, terrorist attacks. We conclude that detention of individuals falling into the limited category we are considering, for the duration of the particular conflict in which they were captured, is so fundamental and accepted an incident to war as to be an exercise of the "necessary and

appropriate force" Congress has authorized the President to use.

There is no bar to this Nation's holding one of its own citizens as an enemy combatant. In *Quirin,* one of the detainees, Haupt, alleged that he was a naturalized United States citizen. We held that "citizens who associate themselves with the military arm of the enemy government, and with its aid, guidance and direction enter this country bent on hostile acts, are enemy belligerents within the meaning of the law of war." A citizen, no less than an alien, can be "part of or supporting forces hostile to the United States or coalition partners" and "engaged in an armed conflict against the United States"; such a citizen, if released, would pose the same threat of returning to the front during the ongoing conflict.

In light of these principles, it is of no moment that the AUMF does not use specific language of detention. Because detention to prevent a combatant's return to the battlefield is a fundamental incident of waging war, in permitting the use of "necessary and appropriate force," Congress has clearly and unmistakably authorized detention in the narrow circumstances considered here.

Hamdi objects, nevertheless, that Congress has not authorized the indefinite detention to which he is now subject. We understand Congress' grant of authority for the use of "necessary and appropriate force" to include the authority to detain for the duration of the relevant conflict, and our understanding is based on longstanding law-of-war principles. If the practical circumstances of a given conflict are entirely unlike those of the conflicts that informed the development of the law of war, that understanding may unravel. But that is not the situation we face as of this date. Active combat operations against Taliban fighters apparently are ongoing in Afghanistan. The United States may detain, for the duration of these hostilities, individuals legitimately determined to be Taliban combatants who "engaged in an armed conflict against the United States." If the record establishes that United States troops are still involved in active combat in Afghanistan, those detentions are part of the exercise of "necessary and appropriate force," and therefore are authorized by the AUMF.

Ex parte Milligan (1866) does not undermine our holding about the Government's authority to seize enemy combatants. In that case, the Court made repeated reference to the fact that its inquiry into whether the military tribunal had jurisdiction to try and punish Milligan turned in large part on the fact that Milligan was not a prisoner of war, but a resident of Indiana arrested while at home there. Had Milligan been captured while he was assisting Confederate soldiers by carrying a rifle against Union troops on a Confederate battlefield, the holding of the Court might well have been different. Moreover, as Justice Scalia acknowledges, the Court in *Ex parte Quirin* (1942) dismissed the language of *Milligan* that the petitioners had suggested prevented them from being subject to military process. Haupt was accused of being a spy. The Court in *Quirin* found him "subject to trial and punishment by [a] military tribunal" for those acts, and held that his citizenship did not change this result.

III

Even in cases in which the detention of enemy combatants is legally authorized, there remains the question of what process is constitutionally due to a citizen who disputes his enemy-combatant status. Hamdi argues that he is owed a meaningful and timely hearing and that "extra-judicial detention [that] begins and ends with the submission of an affidavit based on third-hand hearsay" does not comport with the Fifth and Fourteenth Amendments. The Government counters that any more process than was provided below would be both unworkable and "constitutionally intolerable."

First, the Government urges the adoption of the Fourth Circuit's holding below—that because it is "undisputed" that Hamdi's seizure took place in a combat zone, the habeas determination can be made purely as a matter of law, with no further hearing or factfinding necessary. This argument is easily rejected. As the dissenters from the denial of rehearing *en banc* noted, the circumstances surrounding Hamdi's seizure cannot in any way be characterized as "undisputed," as "those circumstances are neither conceded in fact, nor susceptible to concession in law, because Hamdi has not been permitted to speak for himself or even through counsel as to those circumstances."

The Government's second argument is that further factual exploration is unwarranted and inappropriate in light of the extraordinary constitutional interests at stake. Under the Government's most extreme rendition of this argument, "respect for separation of powers and the limited institutional capabilities of courts in matters of military decision-making in connection with an ongoing conflict" ought to eliminate entirely any individual process, restricting the courts to investigating only whether legal authorization exists for the broader detention scheme. At most, the Government argues, courts should review its determination that a citizen is an enemy combatant under a very deferential "some evidence" standard. Under this review, a court would assume the accuracy of the Government's articulated basis for Hamdi's detention, as set forth in the Mobbs Declaration, and assess only whether that articulated basis was a legitimate one. In response, Hamdi emphasizes that this Court consistently has recognized that an individual challenging his detention may not be held at the will of the Executive without recourse to some proceeding before a neutral tribunal to determine whether the Executive's asserted justifications for that detention have basis in fact and warrant in law.

Both of these positions highlight legitimate concerns. And both emphasize the tension that often exists between the autonomy that the Government asserts is necessary in order to pursue effectively a particular goal and the process that a citizen contends he is due before he is deprived of a constitutional right. The ordinary mechanism that we use for balancing such serious competing interests, and for determining the procedures that are necessary to ensure that a citizen is not "deprived of life, liberty, or property, without due process of law," is the test that we articulated in *Mathews v. Eldridge* (1976). *Mathews* dictates that the process due in any given instance is determined by weighing "the private interest that will be affected by the official action" against the Government's asserted interest, "including the function involved" and the burdens the Government would face in providing greater process. The

Mathews calculus then contemplates a judicious balancing of these concerns, through an analysis of "the risk of an erroneous deprivation" of the private interest if the process were reduced and the "probable value, if any, of additional or substitute safeguards." We take each of these steps in turn.

It is beyond question that substantial interests lie on both sides of the scale in this case. Hamdi's "private interest affected by the official action," is the most elemental of liberty interests—the interest in being free from physical detention by one's own government. Nor is the weight on this side of the *Mathews* scale offset by the circumstances of war or the accusation of treasonous behavior. The risk of erroneous deprivation of a citizen's liberty in the absence of sufficient process here is very real. Moreover, as critical as the Government's interest may be in detaining those who actually pose an immediate threat to the national security of the United States during ongoing international conflict, history and common sense teach us that an unchecked system of detention carries the potential to become a means for oppression and abuse of others who do not present that sort of threat.

On the other side of the scale are the weighty and sensitive governmental interests in ensuring that those who have in fact fought with the enemy during a war do not return to battle against the United States. Without doubt, our Constitution recognizes that core strategic matters of warmaking belong in the hands of those who are best positioned and most politically accountable for making them.

The Government also argues at some length that its interests in reducing the process available to alleged enemy combatants are heightened by the practical difficulties that would accompany a system of trial-like process. In its view, military officers who are engaged in the serious work of waging battle would be unnecessarily and dangerously distracted by litigation half a world away, and discovery into military operations would both intrude on the sensitive secrets of national defense and result in a futile search for evidence buried under the rubble of war. To the extent that these burdens are triggered by heightened procedures, they are properly taken into account in our due process analysis.

Striking the proper constitutional balance here is of great importance to the Nation during this period of ongoing combat. But it is equally vital that our calculus not give short shrift to the values that this country holds dear or to the privilege that is American citizenship. It is during our most challenging and uncertain moments that our Nation's commitment to due process is most severely tested; and it is in those times that we must preserve our commitment at home to the principles for which we fight abroad.

With due recognition of these competing concerns, we believe that neither the process proposed by the Government nor the process apparently envisioned by the District Court below strikes the proper constitutional balance when a United States citizen is detained in the United States as an enemy combatant. We therefore hold that a citizen-detainee seeking to challenge his classification as an enemy combatant must receive notice of the factual basis for his classification, and a fair opportunity to rebut the Government's factual assertions before a neutral decisionmaker. At the same time, the exigencies of the circumstances may demand that, aside from these core elements, enemy combatant proceedings may be tailored to alleviate their uncommon potential to burden the Executive at a time of ongoing military conflict. Hearsay, for example, may need to be accepted as the most reliable available evidence from the Government in such a proceeding. Likewise, the Constitution would not be offended by a presumption in favor of the Government's evidence, so long as that presumption remained a rebuttable one and fair opportunity for rebuttal were provided. Thus, once the Government puts forth credible evidence that the habeas petitioner meets the enemy-combatant criteria, the onus could shift to the petitioner to rebut that evidence with more persuasive evidence that he falls outside the criteria.

We think it unlikely that this basic process will have the dire impact on the central functions of warmaking that the Government forecasts. The parties agree that initial captures on the battlefield need not receive the process we have discussed here; that process is due only when the determination is made to continue to hold those who have been seized. The Government has made clear in its briefing that documentation regarding battlefield detainees already is kept in the ordinary course of military affairs. Any factfinding imposition created by requiring a knowledgeable affiant to summarize these records to an independent tribunal is a minimal one. Likewise, arguments that military officers ought not have to wage war under the threat of litigation lose much of their steam when factual disputes at enemy-combatant hearings are limited to the alleged combatant's acts. This focus meddles little, if at all, in the strategy or conduct of war, inquiring only into the appropriateness of continuing to detain an individual claimed to have taken up arms against the United States.

While we accord the greatest respect and consideration to the judgments of military authorities in matters relating to the actual prosecution of a war, and recognize that the scope of that discretion necessarily is wide, it does not infringe on the core role of the military for the courts to exercise their own time-honored and constitutionally mandated roles of reviewing and resolving claims like those presented here. In sum, while the full protections that accompany challenges to detentions in other settings may prove unworkable and inappropriate in the enemy-combatant setting, the threats to military operations posed by a basic system of independent review are not so weighty as to trump a citizen's core rights to challenge meaningfully the Government's case and to be heard by an impartial adjudicator.

There remains the possibility that the standards we have articulated could be met by an appropriately authorized and properly constituted military tribunal. Indeed, it is notable that military regulations already provide for such process in related instances, dictating that tribunals be made available to determine the status of enemy detainees who assert prisoner-of-war status under the Geneva Convention. In the absence of such process, however, a court that receives a petition for a writ of habeas corpus from an alleged enemy combatant must itself ensure that the minimum requirements of due process are achieved. Both courts below recognized as much, focusing their energies on the question of whether Hamdi was

due an opportunity to rebut the Government's case against him. The Government, too, proceeded on this assumption, presenting its affidavit and then seeking that it be evaluated under a deferential standard of review based on burdens that it alleged would accompany any greater process. As we have discussed, a habeas court in a case such as this may accept affidavit evidence like that contained in the Mobbs Declaration, so long as it also permits the alleged combatant to present his own factual case to rebut the Government's return. We anticipate that a District Court would proceed with the caution that we have indicated is necessary in this setting, engaging in a factfinding process that is both prudent and incremental. We have no reason to doubt that courts faced with these sensitive matters will pay proper heed both to the matters of national security that might arise in an individual case and to the constitutional limitations safeguarding essential liberties that remain vibrant even in times of security concerns.

The judgment of the United States Court of Appeals for the Fourth Circuit is vacated, and the case is remanded for further proceedings.

JUSTICE SOUTER, with whom JUSTICE GINSBURG joins, concurring in part, dissenting in part, and concurring in the judgment.

Hamdi seeks to challenge the facts claimed by the Government as the basis for holding him as an enemy combatant. And in this Court he presses the distinct argument that the Government's claim, even if true, would not implicate any authority for holding him that would satisfy 18 U.S.C. §4001(a) (Non-Detention Act), which bars imprisonment or detention of a citizen "except pursuant to an Act of Congress." The plurality accepts the Government's position that if Hamdi's designation as an enemy combatant is correct, his detention (at least as to some period) is authorized by an Act of Congress as required by §4001(a), that is, by the Authorization for Use of Military Force (hereinafter Force Resolution). Here, I disagree and respectfully dissent.

Because I find Hamdi's detention forbidden by §4001(a) and unauthorized by the Force Resolution, I would not reach any questions of what process he may be due in litigating disputed issues in a proceeding under the habeas statute or prior to the habeas enquiry itself. For me, it suffices that the Government has failed to justify holding him in the absence of a further Act of Congress, criminal charges, a showing that the detention conforms to the laws of war, or a demonstration that §4001(a) is unconstitutional. I would therefore vacate the judgment of the Court of Appeals and remand for proceedings consistent with this view.

JUSTICE SCALIA, with whom JUSTICE STEVENS joins, dissenting.

Petitioner, a presumed American citizen, has been imprisoned without charge or hearing in the Norfolk and Charleston Naval Brigs for more than two years, on the allegation that he is an enemy combatant who bore arms against his country for the Taliban. His father claims to the contrary, that he is an inexperienced aid worker caught in the wrong place at the wrong time. This case brings into conflict the competing demands of national security and our citizens' constitutional right to personal liberty. Although I share the Court's evident unease as it seeks to reconcile the two, I do not agree with its resolution.

Where the Government accuses a citizen of waging war against it, our constitutional tradition has been to prosecute him in federal court for treason or some other crime. Where the exigencies of war prevent that, the Constitution's Suspension Clause, Art. I, §9, cl. 2, allows Congress to relax the usual protections temporarily. Absent suspension, however, the Executive's assertion of military exigency has not been thought sufficient to permit detention without charge. No one contends that the congressional Authorization for Use of Military Force, on which the Government relies to justify its actions here, is an implementation of the Suspension Clause. Accordingly, I would reverse the decision below.

I

The very core of liberty secured by our Anglo-Saxon system of separated powers has been freedom from indefinite imprisonment at the will of the Executive. The gist of the Due Process Clause, as understood at the founding and since, was to force the Government to follow those common-law procedures traditionally deemed necessary before depriving a person of life, liberty, or property. When a citizen was deprived of liberty because of alleged criminal conduct, those procedures typically required committal by a magistrate followed by indictment and trial.

These due process rights have historically been vindicated by the writ of habeas corpus. The writ of habeas corpus was preserved in the Constitution—the only common-law writ to be explicitly mentioned. Hamilton lauded "the establishment of the writ of *habeas corpus*" in his Federalist defense as a means to protect against "the practice of arbitrary imprisonments in all ages, [one of] the favourite and most formidable instruments of tyranny." *The Federalist* No. 84. Indeed, availability of the writ under the new Constitution (along with the requirement of trial by jury in criminal cases) was his basis for arguing that additional, explicit procedural protections were unnecessary. See *The Federalist* No. 83.

II

The allegations here, of course, are no ordinary accusations of criminal activity. Yaser Esam Hamdi has been imprisoned because the Government believes he participated in the waging of war against the United States. The relevant question, then, is whether there is a different, special procedure for imprisonment of a citizen accused of wrongdoing by aiding the enemy in wartime.

JUSTICE O'CONNOR, writing for a plurality of this Court, asserts that captured enemy combatants (other than those suspected of war crimes) have traditionally been detained until the cessation of hostilities and then released. That is probably an accurate description of wartime practice with respect to enemy aliens. The tradition with respect to American citizens, however, has been quite different. Citizens aiding the enemy have been treated as traitors subject to the criminal process.

There are times when military exigency renders resort to the traditional criminal process impracticable. English law accommodated such exigencies by allowing legislative suspension of the writ of *habeas corpus* for brief periods. Our Federal Constitution contains a provision explicitly permitting suspension, but limiting the situations in which it may be invoked: "The privilege of the Writ of *Habeas Corpus* shall not be suspended, unless when in Cases of Rebellion or Invasion the public Safety may require it." Art. I, §9, cl. 2. Although this provision does not state that suspension must be effected by, or authorized by, a legislative act, it has been so understood, consistent with English practice and the Clause's placement in Article I.

The Suspension Clause was by design a safety valve, the Constitution's only "express provision for exercise of extraordinary authority because of a crisis," *Youngstown Sheet &Tube v. Sawyer* (1952) (Jackson, J., concurring). Very early in the Nation's history, President Jefferson unsuccessfully sought a suspension of *habeas corpus* to deal with Aaron Burr's conspiracy to overthrow the Government. During the Civil War, Congress passed its first Act authorizing Executive suspension of the writ of *habeas corpus*, to the relief of those many who thought President Lincoln's unauthorized proclamations of suspension unconstitutional. Later Presidential proclamations of suspension relied upon the congressional authorization, e.g., Proclamation No. 7 (1863). During Reconstruction, Congress passed the Ku Klux Klan Act, which included a provision authorizing suspension of the writ, invoked by President Grant in quelling a rebellion in nine South Carolina counties.

III

Of course the extensive historical evidence of criminal convictions and habeas suspensions does not necessarily refute the Government's position in this case. When the writ is suspended, the Government is entirely free from judicial oversight. It does not claim such total liberation here, but argues that it need only produce what it calls "some evidence" to satisfy a habeas court that a detained individual is an enemy combatant. Even if suspension of the writ on the one hand, and committal for criminal charges on the other hand, have been the only traditional means of dealing with citizens who levied war against their own country, it is theoretically possible that the Constitution does not require a choice between these alternatives.

I believe, however, that substantial evidence does refute that possibility. Writings from the founding generation suggest that, without exception, the only constitutional alternatives are to charge the crime or suspend the writ. Further evidence comes from this Court's decision in *Ex parte Milligan*. There, the Court issued the writ to an American citizen who had been tried by military commission for offenses that included conspiring to overthrow the Government, seize munitions, and liberate prisoners of war. The Court rejected in no uncertain terms the Government's assertion that military jurisdiction was proper "under the laws and usages of war": "It can serve no useful purpose to inquire what those laws and usages are, whence they originated, where found, and on whom they operate; they can never be applied to citizens in states which have upheld the authority of the government, and where the courts are open and their process unobstructed."

Milligan is not exactly this case, of course, since the petitioner was threatened with death, not merely imprisonment. But the reasoning and conclusion of *Milligan* logically cover the present case. The Government justifies imprisonment of Hamdi on principles of the law of war and admits that, absent the war, it would have no such authority. But if the law of war cannot be applied to citizens where courts are open, then Hamdi's imprisonment without criminal trial is no less unlawful than Milligan's trial by military tribunal.

Milligan responded to the argument, repeated by the Government in this case, that it is dangerous to leave suspected traitors at large in time of war:

> If it was dangerous, in the distracted condition of affairs, to leave Milligan unrestrained of his liberty, because he 'conspired against the government, afforded aid and comfort to rebels, and incited the people to insurrection,' the law said arrest him, confine him closely, render him powerless to do further mischief; and then present his case to the grand jury of the district, with proofs of his guilt, and, if indicted, try him according

to the course of the common law. If this had been done, the Constitution would have been vindicated, the law of 1863 enforced, and the securities for personal liberty preserved and defended.

The proposition that the Executive lacks indefinite wartime detention authority over citizens is consistent with the Founders' general mistrust of military power permanently at the Executive's disposal. In the Founders' view, the "blessings of liberty" were threatened by "those military establishments which must gradually poison its very fountain." *The Federalist* No. 45. No fewer than 10 issues of the *Federalist* were devoted in whole or part to allaying fears of oppression from the proposed Constitution's authorization of standing armies in peacetime. Many safeguards in the Constitution reflect these concerns. Congress's authority "[t]o raise and support Armies" was hedged with the proviso that "no Appropriation of Money to that Use shall be for a longer Term than two Years." U.S. Const., Art. 1, §8, cl. 12. Except for the actual command of military forces, all authorization for their maintenance and all explicit authorization for their use is placed in the control of Congress under Article I, rather than the President under Article II. As Hamilton explained, the President's military authority would be "much inferior" to that of the British King: "It would amount to nothing more than the supreme command and direction of the military and naval forces, as first general and admiral of the confederacy: while that of the British king extends to the declaring of war, and to the raising and regulating of fleets and armies; all which, by the constitution under consideration, would appertain to the legislature." *The Federalist,* No. 69. A view of the Constitution that gives the Executive authority to use military force rather than the force of law against citizens on American soil flies in the face of the mistrust that engendered these provisions.

IV

The Government argues that our more recent jurisprudence ratifies its indefinite imprisonment of a citizen within the territorial jurisdiction of federal courts. It places primary reliance upon *Ex parte Quirin* (1942), a World War II case upholding the trial by military commission of eight German saboteurs, one of whom, Hans Haupt, was a US citizen. The case was not this Court's finest hour.

Quirin would still not justify denial of the writ here. In *Quirin* it was uncontested that the petitioners were members of enemy forces. They were "admitted enemy invaders," and it was "undisputed" that they had landed in the United States in service of German forces. The specific holding of the Court was only that, "upon the conceded facts," the petitioners were "plainly within [the] boundaries" of military jurisdiction. But where those jurisdictional facts are not conceded—where the petitioner insists that he is not a belligerent—*Quirin* left the pre-existing law in place: Absent suspension of the writ, a citizen held where the courts are open is entitled either to criminal trial or to a judicial decree requiring his release.

V

It follows from what I have said that Hamdi is entitled to a habeas decree requiring his release unless (1) criminal proceedings are promptly brought, or (2) Congress has suspended the writ of *habeas corpus*. A suspension of the writ could, of course, lay down conditions for continued detention, similar to those that today's opinion prescribes under the Due Process Clause. But there is a world of difference between the people's representatives' determining the need for that suspension (and prescribing the conditions for it), and this Court's doing so.

VI

Several limitations give my views in this matter a relatively narrow compass. They apply only to citizens, accused of being enemy combatants, who are detained within the territorial jurisdiction of a federal court. This is not likely to be a numerous group; currently we know of only two, Hamdi and Jose Padilla. Where the citizen is captured outside and held outside the United States, the constitutional requirements may be different. Moreover, even within the United States, the accused citizen-enemy combatant may lawfully be detained once prosecution is in progress or in contemplation. The

Government has been notably successful in securing conviction, and hence long-term custody or execution, of those who have waged war against the state.

I frankly do not know whether these tools are sufficient to meet the Government's security needs, including the need to obtain intelligence through interrogation. It is far beyond my competence, or the Court's competence, to determine that. But it is not beyond Congress's. If the situation demands it, the Executive can ask Congress to authorize suspension of the writ—which can be made subject to whatever conditions Congress deems appropriate, including even the procedural novelties invented by the plurality today. To be sure, suspension is limited by the Constitution to cases of rebellion or invasion. But whether the attacks of September 11, 2001, constitute an "invasion," and whether those attacks still justify suspension several years later, are questions for Congress rather than this Court. If civil rights are to be curtailed during wartime, it must be done openly and democratically, as the Constitution requires, rather than by silent erosion through an opinion of this Court.

The Founders well understood the difficult tradeoff between safety and freedom. "Safety from external danger," Hamilton declared, "is the most powerful director of national conduct. Even the ardent love of liberty will, after a time, give way to its dictates. The violent destruction of life and property incident to war; the continual effort and alarm attendant on a state of continual danger, will compel nations the most attached to liberty, to resort for repose and security to institutions which have a tendency to destroy their civil and political rights. To be more safe, they, at length, become willing to run the risk of being less free." *The Federalist* No. 8. The Founders warned us about the risk, and equipped us with a Constitution designed to deal with it.

Many think it not only inevitable but entirely proper that liberty give way to security in times of national crisis—that, at the extremes of military exigency, *inter arma silent leges*. Whatever the general merits of the view that war silences law or modulates its voice, that view has no place in the interpretation and application of a Constitution designed precisely to confront war

and, in a manner that accords with democratic principles, to accommodate it. Because the Court has proceeded to meet the current emergency in a manner the Constitution does not envision, I respectfully dissent.

JUSTICE THOMAS, dissenting.

The Executive Branch, acting pursuant to the powers vested in the President by the Constitution and with explicit congressional approval, has determined that Yaser Hamdi is an enemy combatant and should be detained. This detention falls squarely within the Federal Government's war powers, and we lack the expertise and capacity to second-guess that decision. As such, petitioners' habeas challenge should fail, and there is no reason to remand the case. The plurality reaches a contrary conclusion by failing adequately to consider basic principles of the constitutional structure as it relates to national security and foreign affairs and by using the balancing scheme of *Mathews v. Eldridge* (1976). I do not think that the Federal Government's war powers can be balanced away by this Court. Arguably, Congress could provide for additional procedural protections, but until it does, we have no right to insist upon them.

But even if I were to agree with the general approach the plurality takes, I could not accept the particulars. The plurality utterly fails to account for the Government's compelling interests and for our own institutional inability to weigh competing concerns correctly. I respectfully dissent.

I

"It is 'obvious and unarguable' that no governmental interest is more compelling than the security of the Nation." *Haig v. Agee* (1981). The national security, after all, is the primary responsibility and purpose of the Federal Government. The Founders intended that the President have primary responsibility—along with the necessary power—to protect the national security and to conduct the Nation's foreign relations. They did so principally because the structural advantages of a unitary Executive are essential in these domains. "Energy in the executive is a leading character in the definition of good government. It is essential to the protec-

tion of the community against foreign attacks."
The Federalist No. 70. The principle "ingredi-ent" for "energy in the executive" is "unity." This is because "decision, activity, secrecy, and dispatch will generally characterise the pro-ceedings of one man, in a much more eminent degree, than the proceedings of any greater number."

Judicial interference in these domains de-stroys the purpose of vesting primary responsi-bility in a unitary Executive. I cannot improve on Justice Jackson's words, speaking for the Court:

The President, both as Commander-in-Chief and as the Nation's organ for foreign affairs, has available intelligence services whose reports are not and ought not to be published to the world. It would be intolerable that courts, without the relevant information, should re-view and perhaps nullify actions of the Execu-tive taken on information properly held secret. Nor can courts sit *in camera* in order to be taken into executive confidences. But even if courts could require full disclosure, the very nature of executive decisions as to foreign pol-icy is political, not judicial. Such decisions are wholly confided by our Constitution to the political departments of the government, Exec-utive and Legislative. They are delicate, com-plex, and involve large elements of prophecy. They are and should be undertaken only by those directly responsible to the people whose welfare they advance or imperil. They are deci-sions of a kind for which the Judiciary has nei-ther aptitude, facilities nor responsibility and which has long been held to belong in the do-main of political power not subject to judicial intrusion or inquiry.

Several points, made forcefully by Justice Jackson, are worth emphasizing. First, with re-spect to certain decisions relating to national security and foreign affairs, the courts simply lack the relevant information and expertise to second-guess determinations made by the Pres-ident based on information properly withheld. Second, even if the courts could compel the Executive to produce the necessary informa-tion, such decisions are simply not amenable to judicial determination because "they are deli-cate, complex, and involve large elements of prophecy." Third, the Court in *Chicago &*

Southern Air Lines and elsewhere has correctly recognized the primacy of the political branches in the foreign-affairs and national-security contexts.

Finally, and again for the same reasons, where "the President acts pursuant to an ex-press or implied authorization from Congress, he exercises not only his powers but also those delegated by Congress, and in such a case the executive action 'would be supported by the strongest of presumptions and the widest lati-tude of judicial interpretation, and the burden of persuasion would rest heavily upon any who might attack it.'" *Dames & Moore* (quoting *Youngstown* [Jackson, J., concurring]). That is why the Court has explained, in a case analo-gous to this one, that "the detention, ordered by the President in the declared exercise of his powers as Commander in Chief of the Army in time of war and of grave public danger, is not to be set aside by the courts without the clear conviction that [it is] in conflict with the Con-stitution or laws of Congress constitutionally enacted." *Ex parte Quirin* (1942).

I acknowledge that the question whether Hamdi's executive detention is lawful is a ques-tion properly resolved by the Judicial Branch, though the question comes to the Court with the strongest presumptions in favor of the Government. The plurality agrees that Hamdi's detention is lawful if he is an enemy combat-ant. But the question whether Hamdi is actu-ally an enemy combatant is "of a kind for which the Judiciary has neither aptitude, facil-ities nor responsibility and which has long been held to belong in the domain of political power not subject to judicial intrusion or in-quiry." That is, although it is appropriate for the Court to determine the judicial question whether the President has the asserted author-ity, we lack the information and expertise to question whether Hamdi is actually an enemy combatant, a question the resolution of which is committed to other branches.

IV

Although I do not agree with the plurality that the balancing approach of *Mathews v. Eldridge* (1976), is the appropriate analytical tool with which to analyze this case, I cannot help but explain that the plurality misapplies its chosen framework, one that if applied correctly would probably lead to the result I have reached. The plurality devotes two paragraphs to its discussion of the Government's interest, though much of those two paragraphs explain why the Government's concerns are misplaced. But: "It is 'obvious and unarguable' that no governmental interest is more compelling than the security of the Nation." The Government seeks to further that interest by detaining an enemy soldier not only to prevent him from rejoining the ongoing fight. Rather, as the Government explains, detention can serve to gather critical intelligence regarding the intentions and capabilities of our adversaries, a function that the Government avers has become all the more important in the war on terrorism.

Additional process, the Government explains, will destroy the intelligence gathering function. It also does seem quite likely that, under the process envisioned by the plurality, various military officials will have to take time to litigate this matter. And though the plurality does not say so, a meaningful ability to challenge the Government's factual allegations will probably require the Government to divulge highly classified information to the purported enemy combatant, who might then upon release return to the fight armed with our most closely held secrets.

The plurality manages to avoid these problems by discounting or entirely ignoring them. Ultimately, the plurality's dismissive treatment of the Government's asserted interests arises from its apparent belief that enemy-combatant determinations are not part of "the actual prosecution of a war," or one of the "central functions of warmaking." This seems wrong: Taking and holding enemy combatants is a quintessential aspect of the prosecution of war.

Undeniably, Hamdi has been deprived of a serious interest, one actually protected by the Due Process Clause. Against this, however, is the Government's overriding interest in protecting the Nation. I acknowledge that under the plurality's approach, it might, at times, be appropriate to give detainees access to counsel and notice of the factual basis for the Government's determination. But properly accounting for the Government's interests also requires concluding that access to counsel and to the factual basis would not always be warranted. Though common sense suffices, the Government thoroughly explains that counsel would often destroy the intelligence gathering function. Equally obvious is the Government's interest in not fighting the war in its own courts and protecting classified information.

For these reasons, I would affirm the judgment of the Court of Appeals.

Boumediene v. Bush
553 U.S. 723 (2008)

After the terrorist attacks on September 11, 2001, and the commencement of hostilities with Afghanistan, the United States began incarcerating aliens whom it designated as "enemy combatants" at the naval base at Guantánamo Bay, Cuba. These detainees included persons captured on the battlefield in Afghanistan and others apprehended in places far removed from the battlefield, such as Bosnia and Gambia. In Hamdi v. Rumsfeld *(2004), the Supreme Court held that the detainees were entitled to procedures that allowed them to contest their designation as enemy combatants. In response, the deputy secretary of defense established military commissions, known as Combatant Status Review Tribunals (CSRTs), to review the status of detainees. The petitioners in this case*

all denied that they were members of the al-Qaeda terrorist network that carried out the September 11, 2001, attacks or of the Taliban regime that provided sanctuary for al-Qaeda. Each appeared before a separate CSRT, was determined to be an enemy combatant, and sought a writ of habeas corpus in the United States District Court for the District of Columbia. These petitions were consolidated in two separate cases before the district court. In one a judge ruled for the government, and in the other a judge ruled for the petitioners. While these cases were on appeal, Congress passed the Detainee Treatment Act (DTA), stripping federal district courts of jurisdiction over writs of habeas corpus filed by Guantánamo detainees and giving the D.C.

Court of Appeals exclusive authority to conduct a limited review of the determinations of the CSRTs. After the Supreme Court in Hamdan v. Rumsfeld *(2006) ruled that these provisions did not apply to cases filed before the DTA was enacted, Congress passed the Military Commissions Act (MCA), which confirmed that the habeas-stripping provision of the DTA applied to pending petitions as well. The court of appeals concluded that this law removed its jurisdiction to consider petitioners' habeas corpus applications, the petitioners appealed that ruling, and the Supreme Court granted certiorari.* Opinion of the Court: <u>Kennedy</u>, Stevens, Souter, Ginsburg, Breyer. Concurring opinion: <u>Souter</u>, Ginsburg, Breyer. Dissenting opinions: <u>Roberts</u>, Scalia, Thomas, Alito; <u>Scalia</u>, Roberts, Thomas.

JUSTICE KENNEDY delivered the opinion of the Court.

Petitioners present a question not resolved by our earlier cases relating to the detention of aliens at Guantanamo: whether they have the constitutional privilege of *habeas corpus*, a privilege not to be withdrawn except in conformance with the Suspension Clause, Art. I, §9, cl. 2. We hold these petitioners do have the *habeas corpus* privilege. Congress has enacted a statute, the Detainee Treatment Act of 2005 (DTA), that provides certain procedures for review of the detainees' status. We hold that those procedures are not an adequate and effective substitute for *habeas corpus*. Therefore §7 of the Military Commissions Act of 2006 (MCA) operates as an unconstitutional suspension of the writ.

II

As a threshold matter, we must decide whether MCA §7 denies the federal courts jurisdiction to hear *habeas corpus* actions pending at the time of its enactment. We hold the statute does deny that jurisdiction, so that, if the statute is valid, petitioners' cases must be dismissed. The MCA was a direct response to *Hamdan*'s holding that the DTA's jurisdiction-stripping provision had no application to pending cases.

III

In deciding the constitutional questions now presented we must determine whether peti-

tioners are barred from seeking the writ or invoking the protections of the Suspension Clause either because of their status, *i.e.*, petitioners' designation by the Executive Branch as enemy combatants, or their physical location, *i.e.*, their presence at Guantanamo Bay. The Government contends that noncitizens designated as enemy combatants and detained in territory located outside our Nation's borders have no constitutional rights and no privilege of *habeas corpus*. Petitioners contend they do have cognizable constitutional rights and that Congress, in seeking to eliminate recourse to *habeas corpus* as a means to assert those rights, acted in violation of the Suspension Clause.

[Justice Kennedy then surveyed the history of habeas corpus, focusing particularly on whether it operated in territory over which the British government lacked sovereignty. He concluded:] Recent scholarship points to the inherent shortcomings in the historical record. And given the unique status of Guantanamo Bay and the particular dangers of terrorism in the modern age, the common-law courts simply may not have confronted cases with close parallels to this one. We decline, therefore, to infer too much, one way or the other, from the lack of historical evidence on point.

IV

Drawing from its position that at common law the writ ran only to territories over which the Crown was sovereign, the Government says the Suspension Clause affords petitioners no rights because the United States does not claim sovereignty over the place of detention. We do not question the Government's position that Cuba, not the United States, maintains sovereignty, in the legal and technical sense of the term, over Guantanamo Bay. But we take notice of the obvious and uncontested fact that the United States, by virtue of its complete jurisdiction and control over the base, maintains *de facto* sovereignty over this territory.

A

The Court has discussed the issue of the Constitution's extraterritorial application on many occasions. These decisions undermine the Government's argument that, at least as applied to noncitizens, the Constitution necessarily stops where *de jure* sovereignty ends. [After reviewing the Court's rulings in *The Insular Cases, Reid v. Covert* (1956), and *Johnson v. Eisentrager* (1950), Justice Kennedy concluded that there was:] a common thread uniting the Insular Cases, *Eisentrager,* and *Reid:* the idea that questions of extraterritoriality turn on objective factors and practical concerns, not formalism.

B

The Government's formal sovereignty-based test raises troubling separation-of-powers concerns as well. The political history of Guantanamo illustrates the deficiencies of this approach. The United States has maintained complete and uninterrupted control of the bay for over 100 years. Yet the Government's view is that the Constitution had no effect there, at least as to noncitizens, because the United States disclaimed sovereignty in the formal sense of the term. The necessary implication of the argument is that by surrendering formal sovereignty over any unincorporated territory to a third party, while at the same time entering into a lease that grants total control over the territory back to the United States, it would be possible for the political branches to govern without legal constraint.

Our basic charter cannot be contracted away like this. The Constitution grants Congress and the President the power to acquire, dispose of, and govern territory, not the power to decide when and where its terms apply. Abstaining from questions involving formal sovereignty and territorial governance is one thing. To hold the political branches have the power to switch the Constitution on or off at will is quite another. The former position reflects this Court's recognition that certain matters requiring political judgments are best left to the political branches. The latter would permit a striking anomaly in our tripartite system of government, leading to a regime in which Congress and the President, not this Court, say "what the law is." *Marbury v. Madison* (1803).

These concerns have particular bearing upon the Suspension Clause question in the cases now before us, for the writ of *habeas corpus* is itself an indispensable mechanism for monitoring the separation of powers. The test for determining the scope of this provision must not be subject to manipulation by those whose power it is designed to restrain.

C

As we recognized in *Rasul,* the outlines of a framework for determining the reach of the Suspension Clause are suggested by the factors the Court relied upon in *Eisentrager.* In addition to the practical concerns discussed above, the *Eisentrager* Court found relevant that each petitioner: "(a) is an enemy alien; (b) has never been or resided in the United States; (c) was captured outside of our territory and there held in military custody as a prisoner of war; (d) was tried and convicted by a Military Commission sitting outside the United States; (e) for offenses against laws of war committed outside the United States; (f) and is at all times imprisoned outside the United States." Based on this language from *Eisentrager,* and the reasoning in our other extraterritoriality opinions, we conclude that at least three factors are relevant in determining the reach of the Suspension Clause: (1) the citizenship and status of the detainee and the adequacy of the process through which that status determination was made; (2) the nature of the sites where apprehension and then detention took place; and (3) the practical obstacles inherent in resolving the prisoner's entitlement to the writ.

Applying this framework, we note at the onset that the status of these detainees is a matter of dispute. The petitioners, like those in *Eisentrager,* are not American citizens. But the petitioners in *Eisentrager* did not contest, it seems, the Court's assertion that they were "enemy aliens." In the instant cases, by contrast, the detainees deny they are enemy combatants. They have been afforded some process in CSRT proceedings to determine their status; but, unlike in *Eisentrager,* there has been no trial by military commission for violations of the laws of war. The difference is not trivial. The records from the *Eisentrager* trials suggest that, well before the petitioners brought their case to this Court, there had been a rigorous adversarial process to test the legality of their detention. The *Eisentrager* petitioners were charged by a bill of particulars that made detailed factual allegations against them. To rebut the accusations, they were entitled to representation by counsel, allowed to introduce evidence on their own behalf, and permitted to cross-examine the prosecution's witnesses. In comparison the procedural protections afforded to the detainees in the CSRT hearings are far more limited, and, we conclude, fall well short of the procedures and adversarial mechanisms that would eliminate the need for *habeas corpus* review. Although the detainee is assigned a "Personal Representative" to assist him during CSRT proceedings, the Secretary of the Navy's memorandum makes clear that person is not the detainee's lawyer or even his "advocate." The Government's evidence is accorded a presumption of validity. The detainee is allowed to present "reasonably available" evidence, but his ability to rebut the Government's evidence against him is limited by the circumstances of his confinement and his lack of counsel at this stage. And although the detainee can seek review of his status determination in the Court of Appeals, that review process cannot cure all defects in the earlier proceedings.

As to the second factor relevant to this analysis, the detainees here are similarly situated to the *Eisentrager* petitioners in that the sites of their apprehension and detention are technically outside the sovereign territory of the United States. But there are critical differences between Landsberg Prison, circa 1950, and the United States Naval Station at Guantanamo Bay in 2008. Unlike its present control over the naval station, the United States' control over the prison in Germany was neither absolute nor indefinite. Guantanamo Bay, on the other hand, is no transient possession. In every practical sense Guantanamo is not abroad; it is within the constant jurisdiction of the United States.

As to the third factor, we recognize, as the Court did in *Eisentrager,* that there are costs to holding the Suspension Clause applicable in a case of military detention abroad. *Habeas corpus* proceedings may require expenditure of funds by the Government and may divert the attention of military personnel from other pressing tasks. While we are sensitive to these concerns, we do not find them dispositive. Compliance with any judicial process requires some incremental expenditure of resources. Yet

civilian courts and the Armed Forces have functioned alongside each other at various points in our history. The Government presents no credible arguments that the military mission at Guantanamo would be compromised if *habeas corpus* courts had jurisdiction to hear the detainees' claims.

It is true that before today the Court has never held that noncitizens detained by our Government in territory over which another country maintains *de jure* sovereignty have any rights under our Constitution. But the cases before us lack any precise historical parallel. We hold that Art. I, §9, cl. 2, of the Constitution has full effect at Guantanamo Bay. If the privilege of *habeas corpus* is to be denied to the detainees now before us, Congress must act in accordance with the requirements of the Suspension Clause. The MCA does not purport to be a formal suspension of the writ; and the Government, in its submissions to us, has not argued that it is. Petitioners, therefore, are entitled to the privilege of *habeas corpus* to challenge the legality of their detention.

V

In light of this holding the question becomes whether the statute stripping jurisdiction to issue the writ avoids the Suspension Clause mandate because Congress has provided adequate substitute procedures for *habeas corpus.* The Government submits there has been compliance with the Suspension Clause because the DTA review process in the Court of Appeals provides an adequate substitute.

A

The DTA's jurisdictional grant is quite limited. The Court of Appeals has jurisdiction not to inquire into the legality of the detention generally but only to assess whether the CSRT complied with the "standards and procedures specified by the Secretary of Defense" and whether those standards and procedures are lawful. The differences between the DTA and the habeas statute that would govern in MCA §7's absence are likewise telling. In §2241 Congress confirmed the authority of "any justice" or "circuit judge" to issue the writ. That statute accommodates the necessity for fact-finding that will arise in some cases by allowing the appellate judge or Justice to transfer the case to a district court of competent jurisdiction, whose institutional capacity for factfinding is superior to his or her own. By granting the Court of Appeals "exclusive" jurisdiction over petitioners' cases, Congress has foreclosed that option. This choice indicates Congress intended the Court of Appeals to have a more limited role in enemy combatant status determinations than a district court has in *habeas corpus* proceedings. In passing the DTA Congress did not intend to create a process that differs from traditional *habeas corpus* process in name only. It intended to create a more limited procedure. It is against this background that we must interpret the DTA and assess its adequacy as a substitute for *habeas corpus*.

B

We do not endeavor to offer a comprehensive summary of the requisites for an adequate substitute for *habeas corpus*. We do consider it uncontroversial, however, that the privilege of *habeas corpus* entitles the prisoner to a meaningful opportunity to demonstrate that he is being held pursuant to "the erroneous application or interpretation" of relevant law. And the habeas court must have the power to order the conditional release of an individual unlawfully detained—though release need not be the exclusive remedy and is not the appropriate one in every case in which the writ is granted. These are the easily identified attributes of any constitutionally adequate *habeas corpus* proceeding. But, depending on the circumstances, more may be required. *Habeas corpus* proceedings need not resemble a criminal trial, even when the detention is by executive order. But the writ must be effective. The habeas court must have sufficient authority to conduct a meaningful review of both the cause for detention and the Executive's power to detain.

Petitioners identify what they see as myriad deficiencies in the CSRTs. The most relevant for our purposes are the constraints upon the detainee's ability to rebut the factual basis for the Government's assertion that he is an enemy combatant. As already noted, at the CSRT stage the detainee has limited means to find or present evidence to challenge the Government's case against him. He does not have the

assistance of counsel and may not be aware of the most critical allegations that the Government relied upon to order his detention. The detainee can confront witnesses that testify during the CSRT proceedings. But given that there are in effect no limits on the admission of hearsay evidence—the only requirement is that the tribunal deem the evidence "relevant and helpful"—the detainee's opportunity to question witnesses is likely to be more theoretical than real.

The Government defends the CSRT process, arguing that it was designed to conform to the procedures suggested by the plurality in *Hamdi*. Setting aside the fact that the relevant language in *Hamdi* did not garner a majority of the Court, it does not control the matter at hand. For the writ of *habeas corpus*, or its substitute, to function as an effective and proper remedy in this context, the court that conducts the habeas proceeding must have the means to correct errors that occurred during the CSRT proceedings. This includes some authority to assess the sufficiency of the Government's evidence against the detainee. It also must have the authority to admit and consider relevant exculpatory evidence that was not introduced during the earlier proceeding.

C

We now consider whether the DTA allows the Court of Appeals to conduct a proceeding meeting these standards. The DTA does not explicitly empower the Court of Appeals to order the applicant in a DTA review proceeding released should the court find that the standards and procedures used at his CSRT hearing were insufficient to justify detention. This is troubling. Yet, for present purposes, we can assume congressional silence permits a constitutionally required remedy. The more difficult question is whether the DTA permits the Court of Appeals to make requisite findings of fact. The DTA enables petitioners to request "review" of their CSRT determination in the Court of Appeals; but the "Scope of Review" provision confines the Court of Appeals' role to reviewing whether the CSRT followed the "standards and procedures" issued by the Department of Defense and assessing whether those "standards and procedures" are lawful.

Among these standards is "the requirement that the conclusion of the Tribunal be supported by a preponderance of the evidence allowing a rebuttable presumption in favor of the Government's evidence." Assuming the DTA can be construed to allow the Court of Appeals to review or correct the CSRT's factual determinations, as opposed to merely certifying that the tribunal applied the correct standard of proof, we see no way to construe the statute to allow what is also constitutionally required in this context: an opportunity for the detainee to present relevant exculpatory evidence that was not made part of the record in the earlier proceedings.

VI

Although we hold that the DTA is not an adequate and effective substitute for *habeas corpus*, it does not follow that a *habeas corpus* court may disregard the dangers the detention in these cases was intended to prevent. Certain accommodations can be made to reduce the burden *habeas corpus* proceedings will place on the military without impermissibly diluting the protections of the writ.

In the DTA Congress sought to consolidate review of petitioners' claims in the Court of Appeals. Channeling future cases to one district court would no doubt reduce administrative burdens on the Government. This is a legitimate objective that might be advanced even without an amendment to §2241. If, in a future case, a detainee files a habeas petition in another judicial district in which a proper respondent can be served, the Government can move for change of venue to the court that will hear these petitioners' cases, the United States District Court for the District of Columbia. Another of Congress' reasons for vesting exclusive jurisdiction in the Court of Appeals, perhaps, was to avoid the widespread dissemination of classified information. The Government has raised similar concerns here and elsewhere. We make no attempt to anticipate all of the evidentiary and access-to-counsel issues that will arise during the course of the detainees' *habeas corpus* proceedings. We recognize, however, that the Government has a legitimate interest in protecting sources and methods of intelligence gathering; and we expect that the District Court will use its discretion to accommodate this interest to the greatest extent possible. These and the other remaining questions are within the expertise and competence of the District Court to address in the first instance.

* * *

Our opinion does not undermine the Executive's powers as Commander in Chief. On the contrary, the exercise of those powers is vindicated, not eroded, when confirmed by the Judicial Branch. Within the Constitution's separation-of-powers structure, few exercises of judicial power are as legitimate or as necessary as the responsibility to hear challenges to the authority of the Executive to imprison a person. Some of these petitioners have been in custody for six years with no definitive judicial determination as to the legality of their detention. Their access to the writ is a necessity to determine the lawfulness of their status, even if, in the end, they do not obtain the relief they seek.

The determination by the Court of Appeals that the Suspension Clause and its protections are inapplicable to petitioners was in error. The judgment of the Court of Appeals is reversed. The cases are remanded to the Court of Appeals with instructions that it remand the cases to the District Court for proceedings consistent with this opinion.

JUSTICE SOUTER, with whom JUSTICE GINSBURG and JUSTICE BREYER join, concurring.

A fact insufficiently appreciated by the dissents is the length of the disputed imprisonments. It is in fact the very lapse of four years from the time *Rasul* put everyone on notice that habeas process was available to Guantanamo prisoners, and the lapse of six years since some of these prisoners were captured and incarcerated, that stand at odds with the repeated suggestions of the dissenters that these cases should be seen as a judicial victory in a contest for power between the Court and the political branches. The several answers to the charge of triumphalism might start with a basic fact of Anglo-American constitutional history: that the power, first of the Crown and now of the

Executive Branch of the United States, is necessarily limited by *habeas corpus* jurisdiction to enquire into the legality of executive detention. And one could explain that in this Court's exercise of responsibility to preserve *habeas corpus* something much more significant is involved than pulling and hauling between the judicial and political branches. Instead, though, it is enough to repeat that some of these petitioners have spent six years behind bars. After six years of sustained executive detentions in Guantanamo, subject to habeas jurisdiction but without any actual habeas scrutiny, today's decision is no judicial victory, but an act of perseverance in trying to make habeas review, and the obligation of the courts to provide it, mean something of value both to prisoners and to the Nation.

THE CHIEF JUSTICE, with whom JUSTICE SCALIA, JUSTICE THOMAS, and JUSTICE ALITO join, dissenting.

Today the Court strikes down as inadequate the most generous set of procedural protections ever afforded aliens detained by this country as enemy combatants. The political branches crafted these procedures amidst an ongoing military conflict, after much careful investigation and thorough debate. The Court rejects them today out of hand, without bothering to say what due process rights the detainees possess, without explaining how the statute fails to vindicate those rights, and before a single petitioner has even attempted to avail himself of the law's operation. And to what effect? The majority merely replaces a review system designed by the people's representatives with a set of shapeless procedures to be defined by federal courts at some future date. One cannot help but think, after surveying the modest practical results of the majority's ambitious opinion, that this decision is not really about the detainees at all, but about control of federal policy regarding enemy combatants.

The Court should have resolved these cases on other grounds. Habeas is most fundamentally a procedural right, a mechanism for contesting the legality of executive detention. The critical threshold question in these cases, prior to any inquiry about the writ's scope, is whether the system the political branches de-

signed protects whatever rights the detainees may possess. If so, there is no need for any additional process, whether called "habeas" or something else.

Congress entrusted that threshold question in the first instance to the Court of Appeals for the District of Columbia Circuit, as the Constitution surely allows Congress to do. But before the D. C. Circuit has addressed the issue, the Court cashiers the statute, and without answering this critical threshold question itself. The Court does eventually get around to asking whether review under the DTA is, as the Court frames it, an "adequate substitute" for habeas, but even then its opinion fails to determine what rights the detainees possess and whether the DTA system satisfies them. The majority instead compares the undefined DTA process to an equally undefined habeas right— one that is to be given shape only in the future by district courts on a case-by-case basis. This whole approach is misguided.

It is also fruitless. How the detainees' claims will be decided now that the DTA is gone is anybody's guess. But the habeas process the Court mandates will most likely end up looking a lot like the DTA system it replaces, as the district court judges shaping it will have to reconcile review of the prisoners' detention with the undoubted need to protect the American people from the terrorist threat—precisely the challenge Congress undertook in drafting the DTA. All that today's opinion has done is shift responsibility for those sensitive foreign policy and national security decisions from the elected branches to the Federal Judiciary.

I believe the system the political branches constructed adequately protects any constitutional rights aliens captured abroad and detained as enemy combatants may enjoy. I therefore would dismiss these cases on that ground. With all respect for the contrary views of the majority, I must dissent.

II

The majority's overreaching is particularly egregious given the weakness of its objections to the DTA. Simply put, the Court's opinion fails on its own terms. The majority strikes down the statute because it is not an "adequate substitute" for habeas review, but fails to show what rights the detainees have that cannot be vindicated by the DTA system.

Because the central purpose of *habeas corpus* is to test the legality of executive detention, the writ requires most fundamentally an Article III court able to hear the prisoner's claims and, when necessary, order release. Beyond that, the process a given prisoner is entitled to receive depends on the circumstances and the rights of the prisoner. After much hemming and hawing, the majority appears to concede that the DTA provides an Article III court competent to order release. The only issue in dispute is the process the Guantanamo prisoners are entitled to use to test the legality of their detention. *Hamdi* concluded that American citizens detained as enemy combatants are entitled to only limited process, and that much of that process could be supplied by a military tribunal, with review to follow in an Article III court. That is precisely the system we have here. It is adequate to vindicate whatever due process rights petitioners may have. The *Hamdi* plurality concluded that this type of review would be enough to satisfy due process, even for citizens. Congress followed the Court's lead, only to find itself the victim of a constitutional bait and switch.

Hamdi merits scant attention from the Court—a remarkable omission, as *Hamdi* bears directly on the issues before us. *Hamdi* was all about the scope of habeas review in the context of enemy combatant detentions. The petitioner, an American citizen held within the United States as an enemy combatant, invoked the writ to challenge his detention. After "a careful examination both of the writ and of the Due Process Clause," this Court enunciated the "basic process" the Constitution entitled Hamdi to expect from a habeas court under §2241. That process consisted of the right to "receive notice of the factual basis for his classification, and a fair opportunity to rebut the Government's factual assertions before a neutral decisionmaker." In light of the Government's national security responsibilities, the plurality found the process could be "tailored to alleviate [the] uncommon potential to burden the Executive at a time of ongoing military conflict." For example, the Government could rely on hearsay and could claim a presumption in favor of its own evidence.

Hamdi further suggested that this "basic process" on collateral review could be provided by a military tribunal. It pointed to prisoner-of-war tribunals as a model that would satisfy the Constitution's requirements. Only "in the absence of such process" before a military tribunal, the Court held, would Article III courts need to conduct full-dress habeas proceedings to "ensure that the minimum requirements of due process are achieved." And even then, the petitioner would be entitled to no more process than he would have received from a properly constituted military review panel, given his limited due process rights and the Government's weighty interests.

Contrary to the majority, *Hamdi* is of pressing relevance because it establishes the procedures American citizens detained as enemy combatants can expect from a habeas court proceeding under §2241. The DTA system of military tribunal hearings followed by Article III review looks a lot like the procedure *Hamdi* blessed. If nothing else, it is plain from the design of the DTA that Congress, the President, and this Nation's military leaders have made a good-faith effort to follow our precedent.

D

Despite these guarantees, the Court finds the DTA system an inadequate habeas substitute, for one central reason: Detainees are unable to introduce at the appeal stage exculpatory evidence discovered after the conclusion of their CSRT proceedings. The Court hints darkly that the DTA may suffer from other infirmities, but it does not bother to name them, making a response a bit difficult. As it stands, I can only assume the Court regards the supposed defect it did identify as the gravest of the lot.

If this is the most the Court can muster, the ice beneath its feet is thin indeed. As noted, the CSRT procedures provide ample opportunity for detainees to introduce exculpatory evidence—whether documentary in nature or from live witnesses—before the military tribunals. And if their ability to introduce such evidence is denied contrary to the Constitution or laws of the United States, the D.C. Circuit has the authority to say so on review. If that sort of procedure sounds familiar, it should. Federal appellate courts reviewing factual determinations follow just such a procedure in a variety of circumstances.

III

The majority rests its decision on abstract and hypothetical concerns. Step back and consider what, in the real world, Congress and the Executive have actually granted aliens captured by our Armed Forces overseas and found to be enemy combatants:

§ The right to hear the bases of the charges against them, including a summary of any classified evidence.

§ The ability to challenge the bases of their detention before military tribunals modeled after Geneva Convention procedures. Some 38 detainees have been released as a result of this process.

§ The right, before the CSRT, to testify, introduce evidence, call witnesses, question those the Government calls, and secure release, if and when appropriate.

§ The right to the aid of a personal representative in arranging and presenting their cases before a CSRT.

§ Before the D.C. Circuit, the right to employ counsel, challenge the factual record, contest the lower tribunal's legal determinations, ensure compliance with the Constitution and laws, and secure release, if any errors below establish their entitlement to such relief.

In sum, the DTA satisfies the majority's own criteria for assessing adequacy. This statutory scheme provides the combatants held at Guantanamo greater procedural protections than have ever been afforded alleged enemy detainees—whether citizens or aliens—in our national history. I respectfully dissent.

JUSTICE SCALIA, with whom THE CHIEF JUSTICE, JUSTICE THOMAS, and JUSTICE ALITO join, dissenting.

Today, for the first time in our Nation's history, the Court confers a constitutional right to *habeas corpus* on alien enemies detained abroad by our military forces in the course of an ongoing war. The CHIEF JUSTICE's dis-

sent, which I join, shows that the procedures prescribed by Congress in the Detainee Treatment Act provide the essential protections that *habeas corpus* guarantees; there has thus been no suspension of the writ, and no basis exists for judicial intervention beyond what the Act allows. My problem with today's opinion is more fundamental still: The writ of *habeas corpus* does not, and never has, run in favor of aliens abroad; the Suspension Clause thus has no application, and the Court's intervention in this military matter is entirely *ultra vires*.

I think it appropriate to begin with a description of the disastrous consequences of what the Court has done today. America is at war with radical Islamists. The enemy began by killing Americans and American allies abroad: 241 at the Marine barracks in Lebanon, 19 at the Khobar Towers in Dhahran, 224 at our embassies in Dar es Salaam and Nairobi, and 17 on the USS *Cole* in Yemen. On September 11, 2001, the enemy brought the battle to American soil, killing 2,749 at the Twin Towers in New York City, 184 at the Pentagon in Washington, D.C., and 40 in Pennsylvania. It has threatened further attacks against our homeland; one need only walk about buttressed and barricaded Washington, or board a plane anywhere in the country, to know that the threat is a serious one. Our Armed Forces are now in the field against the enemy, in Afghanistan and Iraq. Last week, 13 of our countrymen in arms were killed.

The game of bait-and-switch that today's opinion plays upon the Nation's Commander in Chief will make the war harder on us. It will almost certainly cause more Americans to be killed. That consequence would be tolerable if necessary to preserve a time-honored legal principle vital to our constitutional Republic. But it is this Court's blatant *abandonment* of such a principle that produces the decision today. The President relied on our settled precedent in *Johnson v. Eisentrager* (1950), when he established the prison at Guantanamo Bay for enemy aliens. Had the law been otherwise, the military surely would not have transported prisoners there, but would have kept them in Afghanistan, transferred them to another of our foreign military bases, or turned them over to allies for detention. Those other facilities might well have been worse for the detainees themselves.

In the long term, then, the Court's decision today accomplishes little, except perhaps to reduce the well-being of enemy combatants that the Court ostensibly seeks to protect. In the short term, however, the decision is devastating. At least 30 of those prisoners hitherto released from Guantanamo Bay have returned to the battlefield. Some have been captured or killed. But others have succeeded in carrying on their atrocities against innocent civilians. In one case, a detainee released from Guantanamo Bay masterminded the kidnapping of two Chinese dam workers, one of whom was later shot to death when used as a human shield against Pakistani commandoes. Another former detainee promptly resumed his post as a senior Taliban commander and murdered a United Nations engineer and three Afghan soldiers. Still another murdered an Afghan judge. It was reported only last month that a released detainee carried out a suicide bombing against Iraqi soldiers in Mosul, Iraq.

These, mind you, were detainees whom the military had concluded were not enemy combatants. Their return to the kill illustrates the incredible difficulty of assessing who is and who is not an enemy combatant in a foreign theater of operations where the environment does not lend itself to rigorous evidence collection. Astoundingly, the Court today raises the bar, requiring military officials to appear before civilian courts and defend their decisions under procedural and evidentiary rules that go beyond what Congress has specified. As the CHIEF JUSTICE's dissent makes clear, we have no idea what those procedural and evidentiary rules are, but they will be determined by civil courts and (in the Court's contemplation at least) will be more detainee-friendly than those now applied, since otherwise there would no reason to hold the congressionally prescribed procedures unconstitutional. If they impose a higher standard of proof (from foreign battlefields) than the current procedures require, the number of the enemy returned to combat will obviously increase.

But even when the military has evidence that it can bring forward, it is often foolhardy to release that evidence to the attorneys representing our enemies. And one escalation of procedures that the Court is clear about is affording the detainees increased access to witnesses (perhaps troops serving in Afghanistan?) and to classified information. During the 1995 prosecution of Omar Abdel Rahman, federal prosecutors gave the names of 200 unindicted co-conspirators to the "Blind Sheik's" defense lawyers; that information was in the hands of Osama Bin Laden within two weeks. In another case, trial testimony revealed to the enemy that the United States had been monitoring their cellular network, whereupon they promptly stopped using it, enabling more of them to evade capture and continue their atrocities.

And today it is not just the military that the Court elbows aside. A mere two Terms ago in *Hamdan v. Rumsfeld* (2006), when the Court held (quite amazingly) that the Detainee Treatment Act of 2005 had not stripped habeas jurisdiction over Guantanamo petitioners' claims, four Members of today's five-Justice majority joined an opinion saying the following: "Nothing prevents the President from returning to Congress to seek the authority [for trial by military commission] he believes necessary. Where, as here, no emergency prevents consultation with Congress, judicial insistence upon that consultation does not weaken our Nation's ability to deal with danger. To the contrary, that insistence strengthens the Nation's ability to determine—through democratic means—how best to do so. The Constitution places its faith in those democratic means."

Turns out they were just kidding. For in response, Congress, at the President's request, quickly enacted the Military Commissions Act, emphatically reasserting that it did not want these prisoners filing habeas petitions. It is therefore clear that Congress and the Executive—*both* political branches—have determined that limiting the role of civilian courts in adjudicating whether prisoners captured abroad are properly detained is important to success in the war that some 190,000 of our men and women are now fighting. But it does not matter. The Court today decrees that no good reason to accept the judgment of the other two branches is "apparent." "The Government," it declares, "presents no credible arguments that the military mission at Guantanamo would be compromised if *habeas corpus* courts had jurisdiction to hear the detainees' claims." What competence does the Court have to second-guess the judgment of Congress and the President on such a point? None whatever. But the Court blunders in nonetheless. Henceforth, as today's opinion makes unnervingly clear, how to handle enemy prisoners in this war will ultimately lie with the branch that knows least about the national security concerns that the subject entails.

The Nation will live to regret what the Court has done today. I dissent.

District of Columbia v. Heller
554 U.S. 570 (2008)

The District of Columbia makes it a crime to carry unregistered firearms, and the registration of handguns is prohibited. Wholly apart from that prohibition, no person may carry a handgun without a license, but the chief of police may issue licenses for one-year periods. District of Columbia law also requires residents to keep their lawfully owned firearms, such as registered long guns, "unloaded and dissembled or bound by a trigger lock or similar device" unless they are located in a place of business or are being used for lawful recreational activities. Dick Heller, a D.C. special police officer authorized to carry a handgun while on duty, applied for a registration certificate for a handgun that he wished to keep at home, but the District refused. He thereafter filed a lawsuit in the federal district court, seeking an injunction barring the city from enforcing the bar on the registration of handguns, the licensing requirement insofar as it prohibits the carrying of a firearm in the home without a license, and the trigger-lock requirement insofar as it prohibits the use of "functional firearms within the home." The district court dismissed the respondent's Second Amendment complaint, but the Court of Appeals for the District of Columbia Circuit reversed, and the Supreme Court granted certiorari. Opinion of the Court: Scalia, Roberts, Kennedy, Thomas, Alito. Dissenting opinions: Stevens, Souter, Ginsburg, Breyer; Breyer, Stevens, Souter, Ginsburg.

JUSTICE SCALIA delivered the opinion of the Court.

The Second Amendment provides: "A well regulated Militia, being necessary to the security of a free State, the right of the people to keep and bear Arms, shall not be infringed." In interpreting this text, we are guided by the principle that "the Constitution was written to be understood by the voters; its words and phrases were used in their normal and ordinary as distinguished from technical meaning." *United States v. Sprague* (1931). The two sides in this case have set out very different interpretations of the Amendment. Petitioners and today's dissenting Justices believe that it protects only the right to possess and carry a firearm in connection with militia service. Respondent argues that it protects an individual right to possess a firearm unconnected with service in a militia, and to use that arm for traditionally lawful purposes, such as self-defense within the home.

The Second Amendment is naturally divided into two parts: its prefatory clause and its operative clause. The former does not limit the latter grammatically, but rather announces a purpose. The Amendment could be rephrased, "Because a well regulated Militia is necessary to the security of a free State, the right of the people to keep and bear Arms shall not be infringed." Logic demands that there be a link between the stated purpose and the command. But apart from that clarifying function, a prefatory clause does not limit or expand the scope of the operative clause.

1. OPERATIVE CLAUSE.

a. "A Right of the People." The first salient feature of the operative clause is that it codifies a "right of the people." The unamended Constitution and the Bill of Rights use the phrase "right of the people" two other times, in the First Amendment's Assembly-and-Petition Clause and in the Fourth Amendment's Search-and-Seizure Clause. The Ninth Amendment uses very similar terminology. All three of these instances unambiguously refer to individual rights, not "collective" rights, or rights that may be exercised only through participation in some corporate body.

Three provisions of the Constitution refer to "the people" in a context other than "rights"— the famous preamble ("We the people"), §2 of Article I (providing that "the people" will choose members of the House), and the Tenth Amendment (providing that those powers not given the Federal Government remain with "the States" or "the people"). Those provisions arguably refer to "the people" acting collectively—but they deal with the exercise or reservation of powers, not rights. Nowhere else in the Constitution does a "right" attributed to "the people" refer to anything other than an individual right. What is more, in all six other provisions of the Constitution that mention "the people," the term unambiguously refers to all members of the political community. As we said in *United States v. Verdugo-Urquidez* (1990):

"'The people' seems to have been a term of art employed in select parts of the Constitution. Its uses suggest that 'the people' protected by the Fourth Amendment and by the First and Second Amendments, and to whom rights and powers are reserved in the Ninth and Tenth Amendments, refers to a class of persons who are part of a national community or who have otherwise developed sufficient connection with this country to be considered part of that community." This contrasts markedly with the phrase "the militia" in the prefatory clause. The "militia" in colonial America consisted of a subset of "the people"—those who were male, able bodied, and within a certain age range. Reading the Second Amendment as protecting only the right to "keep and bear Arms" in an organized militia therefore fits poorly with the operative clause's description of the holder of that right as "the people." We start therefore with a strong presumption that the Second Amendment right is exercised individually and belongs to all Americans.

b. "Keep and bear Arms." Before addressing the verbs "keep" and "bear," we interpret their object: "Arms." The 18th-century meaning is no different from the meaning today. The 1773 edition of Samuel Johnson's dictionary defined "arms" as "weapons of offence, or armour of defence." Timothy Cunningham's important 1771

legal dictionary defined "arms" as "any thing that a man wears for his defence, or takes into his hands, or useth in wrath to cast at or strike another." The term was applied, then as now, to weapons that were not specifically designed for military use and were not employed in a military capacity. For instance, Cunningham's legal dictionary gave as an example of usage: "Servants and labourers shall use bows and arrows on Sundays, &c. and not bear other arms."

Some have made the argument, bordering on the frivolous, that only those arms in existence in the 18th century are protected by the Second Amendment. We do not interpret constitutional rights that way. Just as the First Amendment protects modern forms of communications and the Fourth Amendment applies to modern forms of search, the Second Amendment extends, prima facie, to all instruments that constitute bearable arms, even those that were not in existence at the time of the founding.

We turn to the phrases "keep arms" and "bear arms." Johnson defined "keep" as, most relevantly, "to retain; not to lose," and "to have in custody." Webster defined it as "to hold; to retain in one's power or possession." No party has apprised us of an idiomatic meaning of "keep Arms." Thus, the most natural reading of "keep Arms" in the Second Amendment is to "have weapons."

The phrase "keep arms" was not prevalent in the written documents of the founding period that we have found, but there are a few examples, all of which favor viewing the right to "keep Arms" as an individual right unconnected with militia service. William Blackstone, for example, wrote that Catholics convicted of not attending service in the Church of England suffered certain penalties, one of which was that they were not permitted to "keep arms in their houses." Petitioners point to militia laws of the founding period that required militia members to "keep" arms in connection with militia service, and they conclude from this that the phrase "keep Arms" has a militia-related connotation. This is rather like saying that, since there are many statutes that authorize aggrieved employees to "file complaints" with federal agencies, the phrase "file complaints" has an employment-related connotation. "Keep arms" was simply a common way of referring to possessing arms, for militiamen and everyone else.

At the time of the founding, as now, to "bear" meant to "carry." When used with "arms," however, the term has a meaning that refers to carrying for a particular purpose—confrontation. In *Muscarello v. United States* (1998), in the course of analyzing the meaning of "carries a firearm" in a federal criminal statute, Justice Ginsburg wrote that "surely a most familiar meaning is, as the Constitution's Second Amendment indicates: 'wear, bear, or carry upon the person or in the clothing or in a pocket, for the purpose of being armed and ready for offensive or defensive action in a case of conflict with another person.'" We think that Justice Ginsburg accurately captured the natural meaning of "bear arms." Although the phrase implies that the carrying of the weapon is for the purpose of "offensive or defensive action," it in no way connotes participation in a structured military organization.

The phrase "bear Arms" also had at the time of the founding an idiomatic meaning that was significantly different from its natural meaning: "to serve as a soldier, do military service, fight" or "to wage war." But it *unequivocally* bore that idiomatic meaning only when followed by the preposition "against," which was in turn followed by the target of the hostilities. (That is how, for example, our Declaration of Independence ¶28, used the phrase: "He has constrained our fellow Citizens taken Captive on the high Seas to bear Arms against their Country.") Every example given by petitioners' *amici* for the idiomatic meaning of "bear arms" from the founding period either includes the preposition "against" or is not clearly idiomatic.

Petitioners justify their limitation of "bear arms" to the military context by pointing out the unremarkable fact that it was often used in that context—the same mistake they made with respect to "keep arms." It is especially unremarkable that the phrase was often used in a military context in the federal legal sources (such as records of congressional debate) that have been the focus of petitioners' inquiry. Those sources would have had little occasion to use it *except* in discussions about the standing army and the militia. And the phrases used primarily in those military discussions include not only "bear arms" but also "carry arms," "possess arms," and "have arms"—though no one thinks that those other phrases also had special military meanings. The common references to those "fit to bear arms" in congressional discussions about the militia are matched by use of the same phrase in the few nonmilitary federal contexts where the concept would be relevant. Other legal sources frequently used "bear arms" in nonmilitary contexts.

Justice Stevens places great weight on James Madison's inclusion of a conscientious-objector clause in his original draft of the Second Amendment: "but no person religiously scrupulous of bearing arms, shall be compelled to render military service in person." He argues that this clause establishes that the drafters of the Second Amendment intended "bear Arms" to refer only to military service. [But] what Justice Stevens would conclude from the deleted provision does not follow. It was not meant to exempt from military service those who objected to going to war but had no scruples about personal gunfights. Quakers opposed the use of arms not just for militia service, but for any violent purpose whatsoever. Thus, the most natural interpretation of Madison's deleted text is that those opposed to carrying weapons for potential violent confrontation would not be "compelled to render military service," in which such carrying would be required.

Finally, Justice Stevens suggests that "keep and bear Arms" was some sort of term of art, presumably akin to "hue and cry" or "cease and desist." (This suggestion usefully evades the problem that there is no evidence whatsoever to support a military reading of "keep arms.") Justice Stevens believes that the unitary meaning of "keep and bear Arms" is established by the Second Amendment's calling it a "right" (singular) rather than "rights" (plural). There is nothing to this. State constitutions of the founding period routinely grouped multiple (related) guarantees under a singular "right," and the First Amendment protects the "right [singular] of the people peaceably to assemble, and to petition the Government for a redress of grievances."

c. Meaning of the Operative Clause. Putting all of these textual elements together, we find that they guarantee the individual right to possess and carry weapons in case of confrontation. This meaning is strongly confirmed by the historical background of the Second Amendment. We look to this because it has always been widely understood that the Second Amendment, like the First and Fourth Amendments, codified a *pre-existing* right. The very text of the Second Amendment implicitly recognizes the pre-existence of the right and declares only that it "shall not be infringed."

Between the Restoration and the Glorious Revolution, the Stuart Kings Charles II and James II succeeded in using select militias loyal to them to suppress political dissidents, in part by disarming their opponents. These experiences caused Englishmen to be extremely wary of concentrated military forces run by the state and to be jealous of their arms. They accordingly obtained an assurance from William and Mary, in the Declaration of Right (which was codified as the English Bill of Rights), that Protestants would never be disarmed. It was clearly an individual right, having nothing whatever to do with service in a militia. Thus, the right secured in 1689 as a result of the Stuarts' abuses was by the time of the founding understood to be an individual right protecting against both public and private violence. And, of course, what the Stuarts had tried to do to their political enemies, George III had tried to do to the colonists.

There seems to us no doubt, on the basis of both text and history, that the Second Amendment conferred an individual right to keep and bear arms. Of course the right was not unlimited. Thus, we do not read the Second Amendment to protect the right of citizens to carry arms for any sort of confrontation, just as we do not read the First Amendment to protect the right of citizens to speak for *any purpose.* Before turning to limitations upon the individual right, however, we must determine whether the prefatory clause of the Second Amendment comports with our interpretation of the operative clause.

2. PREFATORY CLAUSE.

The prefatory clause reads: "A well regulated Militia, being necessary to the security of a free State."

a. "Well-Regulated Militia." In *United States v. Miller* (1939), we explained that "the Militia comprised all males physically capable of acting in concert for the common defense." That definition comports with founding-era sources. The adjective "well-regulated" implies nothing more than the imposition of proper discipline and training. See Johnson 1619 ("Regulate": "To adjust by rule or method"); cf. Va. Declaration of Rights §13 (1776), (referring to "a well-regulated militia, composed of the body of the people, trained to arms").

b. "Security of a Free State." The phrase "security of a free state" meant "security of a free polity," not security of each of the several States. It is true that the term "State" elsewhere in the Constitution refers to individual States, but the phrase "security of a free state" and close variations seem to have been terms of art in 18th-century political discourse, meaning a "'free country'" or free polity. There are many reasons why the militia was thought to be "necessary to the security of a free state." First, of course, it is useful in repelling invasions and suppressing insurrections. Second, it renders large standing armies unnecessary—an argument that Alexander Hamilton made in favor of federal control over the militia. *The Federalist* No. 29. Third, when the able-bodied men of a nation are trained in arms and organized, they are better able to resist tyranny.

3. RELATIONSHIP BETWEEN PREFATORY CLAUSE AND OPERATIVE CLAUSE.

We reach the question, then: Does the preface fit with an operative clause that creates an individual right to keep and bear arms? It fits perfectly, once one knows the history that the founding generation knew and that we have described above. That history showed that the way tyrants had eliminated a militia consisting of all the able-bodied men was not by banning the militia but simply by taking away the people's arms, enabling a select militia or standing army to suppress political opponents. This is what had occurred in England that prompted codification of the right to have arms in the English Bill of Rights.

It is therefore entirely sensible that the Second Amendment's prefatory clause announces the purpose for which the right was codified: to prevent elimination of the militia. The prefatory clause does not suggest that preserving the militia was the only reason Americans valued the ancient right; most undoubtedly thought it even more important for self-defense and hunting. But the threat that the new Federal Government would destroy the citizens' militia by taking away their arms was the reason that right—unlike some other English rights—was codified in a written Constitution. Justice Breyer's assertion that individual self-defense is merely a "subsidiary interest" of the right to keep and bear arms is profoundly mistaken. He bases that assertion solely upon the prologue—but that can only show that self-defense had little to do with the right's *codification;* it was the *central component* of the right itself.

B

Our interpretation is confirmed by analogous arms-bearing rights in state constitutions that preceded and immediately followed adoption of the Second Amendment. Four States adopted analogues to the Federal Second Amendment in the period between independence and the ratification of the Bill of Rights. The most likely reading of all four of these pre–Second Amendment state constitutional provisions is that they secured an individual right to bear arms for defensive purposes. Between 1789 and 1820, nine States adopted Second Amendment analogues. Four of them—Kentucky, Ohio, Indiana, and Missouri—referred to the right of the people to "bear arms in defence of themselves and the State." Another three States—Mississippi, Connecticut, and Alabama—used the even more individualistic phrasing that each citizen has the "right to bear arms in defence of himself and the State." Finally, two States—Tennessee and Maine—used the "common defence" language of Massachusetts. That of the nine state constitutional protections for the right to bear arms enacted immediately after 1789 at least seven unequivocally protected an individual citizen's right to self-defense is strong evidence that that is how the founding generation conceived of the right. The historical narrative that petitioners must endorse would thus treat the Federal Second

Amendment as an odd outlier, protecting a right unknown in state constitutions or at English common law.

C

Justice Stevens relies on the drafting history of the Second Amendment—the various proposals in the state conventions and the debates in Congress. It is dubious to rely on such history to interpret a text that was widely understood to codify a pre-existing right, rather than to fashion a new one. But even assuming that this legislative history is relevant, Justice Stevens flatly misreads the historical record. [His position] relies on the proposition, unsupported by any evidence, that different people of the founding period had vastly different conceptions of the right to keep and bear arms. That simply does not comport with our longstanding view that the Bill of Rights codified venerable, widely understood liberties.

D

We now address how the Second Amendment was interpreted from immediately after its ratification through the end of the 19th century. [Justice Scalia then reviews postratification commentary on the right to bear arms, pre–Civil War case law, post–Civil War legislation, and post–Civil War commentators, concluding that] virtually all interpreters of the Second Amendment in the century after its enactment interpreted the amendment as we do.

E

We now ask whether any of our precedents forecloses the conclusions we have reached about the meaning of the Second Amendment. Justice Stevens places overwhelming reliance upon this Court's decision in *United States v. Miller* (1939). Nothing so clearly demonstrates the weakness of Justice Stevens' case. *Miller* did not hold that and cannot possibly be read to have held that. The judgment in the case upheld against a Second Amendment challenge two men's federal convictions for transporting an unregistered short-barreled shotgun in interstate commerce, in violation of the National Firearms Act. It is entirely clear that the Court's basis for saying that the Second Amendment did not apply was not that the defendants were "bear[ing] arms" not "for military purposes." Rather, it was that the *type of weapon at issue* was not eligible for Second Amendment protection: "In the absence of any evidence tending to show that the possession or use of a [short-barreled shotgun] at this time has some reasonable relationship to the preservation or efficiency of a well regulated militia, we cannot say that the Second Amendment guarantees the right to keep and bear *such an instrument*."

This holding is not only consistent with, but positively suggests, that the Second Amendment confers an individual right to keep and bear arms (though only arms that "have some reasonable relationship to the preservation or efficiency of a well regulated militia"). Had the Court believed that the Second Amendment protects only those serving in the militia, it would have been odd to examine the character of the weapon rather than simply note that the two crooks were not militiamen.

Read in isolation, *Miller*'s phrase "part of ordinary military equipment" could mean that only those weapons useful in warfare are protected. That would be a startling reading of the opinion, since it would mean that the National Firearms Act's restrictions on machineguns (not challenged in *Miller*) might be unconstitutional, machineguns being useful in warfare in 1939. We think that *Miller*'s "ordinary military equipment" language must be read in tandem with what comes after: "Ordinarily when called for [militia] service [able-bodied] men were expected to appear bearing arms supplied by themselves and of the kind in common use at the time." The traditional militia was formed from a pool of men bringing arms "in common use at the time" for lawful purposes like self-defense. Indeed, that is precisely the way in which the Second Amendment's operative clause furthers the purpose announced in its preface. We therefore read *Miller* to say only that the Second Amendment does not protect those weapons not typically possessed by law-abiding citizens for lawful purposes, such as short-barreled shotguns.

III

Like most rights, the right secured by the Second Amendment is not unlimited. From Blackstone through the 19th-century cases, commentators and courts routinely explained that the right was not a right to keep and carry any weapon whatsoever in any manner whatsoever and for whatever purpose. Although we do not undertake an exhaustive historical analysis today of the full scope of the Second Amendment, nothing in our opinion should be taken to cast doubt on longstanding prohibitions on the possession of firearms by felons and the mentally ill, or laws forbidding the carrying of firearms in sensitive places such as schools and government buildings, or laws imposing conditions and qualifications on the commercial sale of arms.

We also recognize another important limitation on the right to keep and carry arms. *Miller* said, as we have explained, that the sorts of weapons protected were those "in common use at the time." We think that limitation is fairly supported by the historical tradition of prohibiting the carrying of "dangerous and unusual weapons." It may be objected that if weapons that are most useful in military service—M-16 rifles and the like—may be banned, then the Second Amendment right is completely detached from the prefatory clause. But as we have said, the conception of the militia at the time of the Second Amendment's ratification was the body of all citizens capable of military service, who would bring the sorts of lawful weapons that they possessed at home to militia duty. It may well be true today that a militia, to be as effective as militias in the 18th century, would require sophisticated arms that are highly unusual in society at large. Indeed, it may be true that no amount of small arms could be useful against modern-day bombers and tanks. But the fact that modern developments have limited the degree of fit between the prefatory clause and the protected right cannot change our interpretation of the right.

IV

We turn finally to the law at issue here. As we have said, the law totally bans handgun possession in the home. It also requires that any lawful firearm in the home be disassembled or bound by a trigger lock at all times, rendering it inoperable. The inherent right of self-defense has been central to the Second Amendment right. The handgun ban amounts to a prohibition of an entire class of "arms" that is overwhelmingly chosen by American society for that lawful purpose. The prohibition extends, moreover, to the home, where the need for defense of self, family, and property is most acute. Under any of the standards of scrutiny that we have applied to enumerated constitutional rights, banning from the home "the most preferred firearm in the nation to 'keep' and use for protection of one's home and family" would fail constitutional muster.

It is no answer to say, as petitioners do, that it is permissible to ban the possession of handguns so long as the possession of other firearms (*i.e.,* long guns) is allowed. It is enough to note that the American people have considered the handgun to be the quintessential self-defense weapon. There are many reasons that a citizen may prefer a handgun for home defense: It is easier to store in a location that is readily accessible in an emergency; it cannot easily be redirected or wrestled away by an attacker; it is easier to use for those without the upper-body strength to lift and aim a long gun; it can be pointed at a burglar with one hand while the other hand dials the police. Whatever the reason, handguns are the most popular weapon chosen by Americans for self-defense in the home, and a complete prohibition of their use is invalid.

We must also address the District's requirement (as applied to respondent's handgun) that firearms in the home be rendered and kept inoperable at all times. This makes it impossible for citizens to use them for the core lawful purpose of self-defense and is hence unconstitutional.

Justice Breyer criticizes us for declining to establish a level of scrutiny for evaluating Second Amendment restrictions. He proposes, explicitly at least, none of the traditionally expressed levels (strict scrutiny, intermediate scrutiny, rational basis), but rather a judge-empowering "interest-balancing inquiry" that "asks whether the statute burdens a protected interest in a way or to an extent that is out of proportion to the statute's salutary effects upon other important governmental interests." After an exhaustive discussion of the arguments for and against gun control, Justice Breyer arrives at his interest-balanced answer: because hand-

gun violence is a problem, because the law is limited to an urban area, and because there were somewhat similar restrictions in the founding period (a false proposition that we have already discussed), the interest-balancing inquiry results in the constitutionality of the handgun ban. QED. We know of no other enumerated constitutional right whose core protection has been subjected to a freestanding "interest-balancing" approach. The very enumeration of the right takes out of the hands of government—even the Third Branch of Government—the power to decide on a case-by-case basis whether the right is *really worth* insisting upon.

In sum, we hold that the District's ban on handgun possession in the home violates the Second Amendment, as does its prohibition against rendering any lawful firearm in the home operable for the purpose of immediate self-defense. Assuming that Heller is not disqualified from the exercise of Second Amendment rights, the District must permit him to register his handgun and must issue him a license to carry it in the home.

We are aware of the problem of handgun violence in this country, and we take seriously the concerns raised by the many *amici* who believe that prohibition of handgun ownership is a solution. The Constitution leaves the District of Columbia a variety of tools for combating that problem, including some measures regulating handguns. But the enshrinement of constitutional rights necessarily takes certain policy choices off the table. These include the absolute prohibition of handguns held and used for self-defense in the home. Undoubtedly some think that the Second Amendment is outmoded in a society where our standing army is the pride of our Nation, where well-trained police forces provide personal security, and where gun violence is a serious problem. That is perhaps debatable, but what is not debatable is that it is not the role of this Court to pronounce the Second Amendment extinct.

JUSTICE STEVENS, with whom JUSTICE SOUTER, JUSTICE GINSBURG, and JUSTICE BREYER join, dissenting.

The Second Amendment was adopted to protect the right of the people of each of the several States to maintain a well-regulated militia. It was a response to concerns raised during the ratification of the Constitution that the power of Congress to disarm the state militias and create a national standing army posed an intolerable threat to the sovereignty of the several States. Neither the text of the Amendment nor the arguments advanced by its proponents evidenced the slightest interest in limiting any legislature's authority to regulate private civilian uses of firearms. Specifically, there is no indication that the Framers of the Amendment intended to enshrine the common-law right of self-defense in the Constitution.

In 1934, Congress enacted the National Firearms Act, the first major federal firearms law. Upholding a conviction under that Act, this Court held that, "in the absence of any evidence tending to show that possession or use of a 'shotgun having a barrel of less than eighteen inches in length' at this time has some reasonable relationship to the preservation or efficiency of a well regulated militia, we cannot say that the Second Amendment guarantees the right to keep and bear such an instrument." *Miller.* The view of the Amendment we took in *Miller*—that it protects the right to keep and bear arms for certain military purposes, but that it does not curtail the Legislature's power to regulate the nonmilitary use and ownership of weapons—is both the most natural reading of the Amendment's text and the interpretation most faithful to the history of its adoption.

The opinion the Court announces today fails to identify any new evidence supporting the view that the Amendment was intended to limit the power of Congress to regulate civilian uses of weapons. Even if the textual and historical arguments on both sides of the issue were evenly balanced, respect for the well-settled views of all of our predecessors on this Court, and for the rule of law itself would prevent most jurists from endorsing such a dramatic upheaval in the law.

I

The text of the Second Amendment is brief. It provides: "A well regulated Militia, being necessary to the security of a free State, the right of the people to keep and bear Arms, shall not be infringed." Three portions of that text merit special focus: the introductory language defining the Amendment's purpose, the class of persons encompassed within its reach, and the unitary nature of the right that it protects.

"A well regulated Militia, being necessary to the security of a free State"

The preamble to the Second Amendment makes three important points. It identifies the preservation of the militia as the Amendment's purpose; it explains that the militia is necessary to the security of a free State; and it recognizes that the militia must be "well regulated." The Court today tries to denigrate the importance of this clause of the Amendment by beginning its analysis with the Amendment's operative provision and returning to the preamble merely "to ensure that our reading of the operative clause is consistent with the announced purpose." That is not how this Court ordinarily reads such texts, and it is not how the preamble would have been viewed at the time the Amendment was adopted. While the Court makes the novel suggestion that it need only find some "logical connection" between the preamble and the operative provision, it does acknowledge that a prefatory clause may resolve an ambiguity in the text. Without identifying any language in the text that even mentions civilian uses of firearms, the Court proceeds to "find" its preferred reading in what is at best an ambiguous text, and then concludes that its reading is not foreclosed by the preamble.

"The right of the people"

The centerpiece of the Court's textual argument is its insistence that the words "the people" as used in the Second Amendment must have the same meaning, and protect the same class of individuals, as when they are used in the First and Second Amendments. According to the Court, in all three provisions—as well as the Constitution's preamble, section 2 of Article I, and the Tenth Amendment—"the term unambiguously refers to all members of the political community, not an unspecified subset." But the Court *itself* reads the Second Amendment to protect a "subset" significantly narrower than the class of persons protected by the First and Fourth Amendments; when it finally drills down on the substantive meaning of the Second Amendment, the Court limits the protected class to "law-abiding, responsible citizens." But the class of persons protected by the First and Fourth Amendments is not so limited; for even felons (and presumably irresponsible citizens as well) may invoke the protections of those constitutional provisions. The Court offers no way to harmonize its conflicting pronouncements.

The words "the people" in the Second Amendment refer back to the object announced in the Amendment's preamble. They remind us that it is the collective action of individuals having a duty to serve in the militia that the text directly protects and, perhaps more importantly, that the ultimate purpose of the Amendment was to protect the States' share of the divided sovereignty created by the Constitution.

"To keep and bear Arms"

Although the Court's discussion of these words treats them as two "phrases"—as if they read "to keep" and "to bear"—they describe a unitary right: to possess arms if needed for military purposes and to use them in conjunction with military activities. The term "bear arms" is a familiar idiom; when used unadorned by any additional words, its meaning is "to serve as a soldier, do military service, fight." 1 *Oxford English Dictionary* 634 (2d ed. 1989). One 18th-century dictionary defined "arms" as "weapons of offence, or armour of defence," 1 S. Johnson, *A Dictionary of the English Language* (1755), and another contemporaneous source explained that "by *arms,* we understand those instruments of offence generally made use of in war; such as firearms, swords, &c. By *weapons,* we more particularly mean instruments of other kinds (exclusive of fire-arms), made use of as offensive, on special occasions." Had the Framers wished to expand the meaning of the phrase "bear arms" to encompass civilian possession and use, they could have done so by the addition of phrases such as "for the defense of themselves," as was done in the Pennsylvania and Vermont Declarations of Rights.

The Amendment's use of the term "keep" in no way contradicts the military meaning conveyed by the phrase "bear arms" and the Amendment's preamble. To the contrary, a number of state militia laws in effect at the time of the Second Amendment's drafting used the term "keep" to describe the requirement that militia members store their arms at their homes, ready to be used for service when necessary. This reading is confirmed by the fact that the clause protects only one right, rather than two. It does not describe a right "to keep arms" and a separate right "to bear arms." Rather, the single right that it does describe is both a duty and a right to have arms available and ready for military service, and to use them for military purposes when necessary. When each word in the text is given full effect, the Amendment is most naturally read to secure to the people a right to use and possess arms in conjunction with service in a well-regulated militia.

II

The proper allocation of military power in the new Nation was an issue of central concern for the Framers. Two themes relevant to our current interpretive task ran through the debates on the original Constitution. "On the one hand, there was a widespread fear that a national standing Army posed an intolerable threat to individual liberty and to the sovereignty of the separate States." *Perpich v. Department of Defense* (1990). On the other hand, the Framers recognized the dangers inherent in relying on inadequately trained militia members "as the primary means of providing for the common defense," *Perpich.*

The original Constitution's retention of the militia and its creation of divided authority over that body did not prove sufficient to allay fears about the dangers posed by a standing army. This sentiment was echoed at a number of state ratification conventions; indeed, it was one of the primary objections to the original Constitution voiced by its opponents. The Anti-Federalists were ultimately unsuccessful in persuading state ratification conventions to condition their approval of the Constitution upon the eventual inclusion of any particular amendment. But a number of States did propose to the first Federal Congress amendments reflecting a desire to ensure that the institution of the militia would remain protected under the new Government.

[James] Madison, charged with the task of assembling the proposals for amendments sent by the ratifying States, was the principal draftsman of the Second Amendment. Madison's first draft omitted any mention of non-military use or possession of weapons. Rather, his original draft repeated the essence of the two proposed amendments sent by Virginia, combining the substance of the two provisions succinctly into one, which read: "The right of the people to keep and bear arms shall not be infringed; a well armed, and well regulated militia being the best security of a free country; but no person religiously scrupulous of bearing arms, shall be compelled to render military service in person." Madison's decision to model the Second Amendment on the distinctly military Virginia proposal is revealing, since it is clear that he considered and rejected formulations that would have unambiguously protected civilian uses of firearms. Madison's initial inclusion of an exemption for conscientious objectors sheds revelatory light on the purpose of the Amendment. It confirms an intent to describe a duty as well as a right, and it unequivocally identifies the military character of both. The history of the adoption of the Amendment thus describes an overriding concern about the potential threat to state sovereignty that a federal standing army would pose, and a desire to protect the States' militias as the means by which to guard against that danger.

IV

For most of our history, the invalidity of Second-Amendment-based objections to firearms regulations has been well settled and uncontroversial. Indeed, the Second Amendment was not even mentioned in either full House of Congress during the legislative proceedings that led to the passage of the 1934 Act [challenged in *United States v. Miller*]. The key to that decision did not turn on the difference between muskets and sawed-off shotguns; it turned, rather, on the basic difference between the military and nonmilitary use and possession of guns. Indeed, if the Second Amendment were not limited in its coverage to military uses of weapons, why should the Court in *Miller*

have suggested that some weapons but not others were eligible for Second Amendment protection? If use for self-defense were the relevant standard, why did the Court not inquire into the suitability?

The Court is simply wrong when it intones that *Miller* contained "not a word" about the Amendment's history. The Court plainly looked to history to construe the term "Militia," and, on the best reading of *Miller,* the entire guarantee of the Second Amendment. After noting the original Constitution's grant of power to Congress and to the States over the militia, the Court explained: "With obvious purpose to assure the continuation and render possible the effectiveness of such forces the declaration and guarantee of the Second Amendment were made. It must be interpreted and applied with that end in view. The Militia which the States were expected to maintain and train is set in contrast with Troops which they were forbidden to keep without the consent of Congress. The sentiment of the time strongly disfavored standing armies; the common view was that adequate defense of country and laws could be secured through the Militia—civilians primarily, soldiers on occasion. The signification attributed to the term Militia appears from the debates in the Convention, the history and legislation of Colonies and States, and the writings of approved commentators."

JUSTICE BREYER, with whom JUSTICE STEVENS, JUSTICE SOUTER, and JUSTICE GINSBURG join, dissenting.

II

Although I adopt for present purposes the majority's position that the Second Amendment embodies a general concern about self-defense, I shall not assume that the Amendment contains a specific untouchable right to keep guns in the house to shoot burglars. The majority does not, because it cannot, convincingly show that the Second Amendment seeks to maintain the latter in pristine, unregulated form. To the contrary, colonial history itself offers important examples of the kinds of gun regulation that citizens would then have thought compatible with the "right to keep and bear arms."

And those examples include substantial regulation of firearms in urban areas, including regulations that imposed obstacles to the use of firearms for the protection of the home.

Boston, Philadelphia, and New York City, the three largest cities in America during that period, all restricted the firing of guns within city limits to at least some degree. Furthermore, several towns and cities (including Philadelphia, New York, and Boston) regulated, for fire-safety reasons, the storage of gunpowder, a necessary component of an operational firearm. Moreover, the law would, as a practical matter, have prohibited the carrying of loaded firearms anywhere in the city, unless the carrier had no plans to enter any building or was willing to unload or discard his weapons before going inside. And Massachusetts residents must have believed this kind of law compatible with the provision in the Massachusetts Constitution that granted "the people . . . a right to keep and to bear arms for the common defence"—a provision that the majority says was interpreted as "securing an individual right to bear arms for defensive purposes."

This historical evidence demonstrates that a self-defense assumption is the *beginning,* rather than the *end,* of any constitutional inquiry. That the District law impacts self-defense merely raises *questions* about the law's constitutionality. But to answer the questions that are raised (that is, to see whether the statute is unconstitutional) requires us to focus on practicalities, the statute's rationale, the problems that called it into being, its relation to those objectives—in a word, the details. There are no purely logical or conceptual answers to such questions. All of which to say that to raise a self-defense question is not to answer it.

III

I therefore begin by asking a process-based question: How is a court to determine whether a particular firearm regulation (here, the District's restriction on handguns) is consistent with the Second Amendment? What kind of constitutional standard should the court use? How high a protective hurdle does the Amendment erect?

Respondent proposes that the Court adopt a "strict scrutiny" test, which would require

reviewing with care each gun law to determine whether it is "narrowly tailored to achieve a compelling governmental interest." *Abrams v. Johnson* (1997). But the majority implicitly, and appropriately, rejects that suggestion by broadly approving a set of laws—prohibitions on concealed weapons, forfeiture by criminals of the Second Amendment right, prohibitions on firearms in certain locales, and governmental regulation of commercial firearm sales—whose constitutionality under a strict scrutiny standard would be far from clear. Indeed, adoption of a true strict-scrutiny standard for evaluating gun regulations would be impossible because almost every gun-control regulation will seek to advance (as the one here does) a "primary concern of every government—a concern for the safety and indeed the lives of its citizens." Thus, any attempt *in theory* to apply strict scrutiny to gun regulations will *in practice* turn into an interest-balancing inquiry, with the interests protected by the Second Amendment on one side and the governmental public-safety concerns on the other, the only question being whether the regulation at issue impermissibly burdens the former in the course of advancing the latter. I would simply adopt such an interest-balancing inquiry explicitly.

IV

The third District restriction prohibits (in most cases) the registration of a handgun within the District. Because registration is a prerequisite to firearm possession, the effect of this provision is generally to prevent people in the District from possessing handguns. In determining whether this regulation violates the Second Amendment, I shall ask how the statute seeks to further the governmental interests that it serves, how the statute burdens the interests that the Second Amendment seeks to protect, and whether there are practical less burdensome ways of furthering those interests. The ultimate question is whether the statute imposes burdens that, when viewed in light of the statute's legitimate objectives, are disproportionate.

A

No one doubts the constitutional importance of the statute's basic objective, saving lives. But there is considerable debate about whether the

District's statute helps to achieve that objective. First, consider the facts as the legislature saw them when it adopted the District statute. As stated by the local council committee that recommended its adoption, the major substantive goal of the District's handgun restriction is "to reduce the potentiality for gun-related crimes and gun-related deaths from occurring within the District of Columbia." The committee informed the Council that guns were "responsible for 69 deaths in this country each day," for a total of "approximately 25,000 gun-deaths each year," along with an additional 200,000 gun-related injuries. In respect to local crime, the committee observed that there were 285 murders in the District during 1974—a record number. The District's special focus on handguns thus reflects the fact that the committee report found them to have a particularly strong link to undesirable activities in the District's exclusively urban environment.

Next, consider the facts as a court must consider them looking at the matter as of today. Petitioners, and their *amici,* have presented us with more recent statistics that tell much the same story that the committee report told 30 years ago. At the least, they present nothing that would permit us to second-guess the Council in respect to the numbers of gun crimes, injuries, and deaths, or the role of handguns.

Respondent and his many *amici* for the most part do not disagree about the figures set forth in the preceding subsection, but they do disagree strongly with the District's *predictive judgment* that a ban on handguns will help solve the crime and accident problems that those figures disclose. [Their] empirically based arguments may have proved strong enough to convince many legislatures, as a matter of legislative policy, not to adopt total handgun bans. But the question here is whether they are strong enough to destroy judicial confidence in the reasonableness of a legislature that rejects them. And that they are not. In a word, the studies to which respondent's *amici* point raise policy-related questions. They succeed in proving that the District's predictive judgments are controversial. But they do not by themselves show that those judgments are incorrect; nor do they demonstrate a consensus, academic or otherwise, supporting that conclusion. Thus, it

is not surprising that the District and its *amici* support the District's handgun restriction with studies of their own. The upshot is a set of studies and counterstudies that, at most, could leave a judge uncertain about the proper policy conclusion. But legislators, not judges, have primary responsibility for drawing policy conclusions from empirical fact. For these reasons, I conclude that the District's statute properly seeks to further the sort of life-preserving and public-safety interests that the Court has called "compelling."

B

I next assess the extent to which the District's law burdens the interests that the Second Amendment seeks to protect. Respondent and his *amici,* as well as the majority, suggest that those interests include: (1) the preservation of a "well regulated Militia"; (2) safeguarding the use of firearms for sporting purposes, *e.g.,* hunting and marksmanship; and (3) assuring the use of firearms for self-defense.

The District's statute burdens the Amendment's first and primary objective hardly at all. The majority briefly suggests that the "right to keep and bear Arms" might encompass an interest in hunting. But any inability of District residents to hunt near where they live has much to do with the jurisdiction's exclusively urban character and little to do with the District's firearm laws. [Because] the District's law does not prohibit possession of rifles or shotguns, and the presence of opportunities for sporting activities in nearby States, [it] burdens any sports-related or hunting-related objectives that the Amendment may protect little, or not at all.

The District's law does prevent a resident from keeping a loaded handgun in his home. And it consequently makes it more difficult for the householder to use the handgun for self-defense in the home against intruders, such as burglars. To that extent the law burdens to some degree an interest in self-defense that for present purposes I have assumed the Amendment seeks to further.

In weighing needs and burdens, we must take account of the possibility that there are reasonable, but less restrictive alternatives. Are there *other* potential measures that might similarly promote the same goals while imposing lesser restrictions? Here I see none. The reason there is no clearly superior, less restrictive alternative to the District's handgun ban is that the ban's very objective is to reduce significantly the number of handguns in the District, say, for example, by allowing a law enforcement officer immediately to assume that *any* handgun he sees is an *illegal* handgun. And there is no plausible way to achieve that objective other than to ban the guns.

The upshot is that the District's objectives are compelling; its predictive judgments as to its law's tendency to achieve those objectives are adequately supported; the law does impose a burden upon any self-defense interest that the Amendment seeks to secure; and there is no clear less restrictive alternative. I turn now to the final portion of the "permissible regulation" question: Does the District's law *disproportionately* burden Amendment-protected interests? Several considerations, taken together, convince me that it does not.

First, the District law is tailored to the life-threatening problems it attempts to address. Second, the self-defense interest in maintaining loaded handguns in the home to shoot intruders is not the *primary* interest, but at most a subsidiary interest, that the Second Amendment seeks to serve. Further, any self-defense interest at the time of the Framing could not have focused exclusively upon urban-crime related dangers. Two hundred years ago, most Americans, many living on the frontier, would likely have thought of self-defense primarily in terms of outbreaks of fighting with Indian tribes, rebellions such as Shays' Rebellion, marauders, and crime-related dangers to travelers on the roads, on footpaths, or along waterways. And the subsequent development of modern urban police departments, by diminishing the need to keep loaded guns nearby in case of intruders, would have moved any such right even further away from the heart of the amendment's more basic protective ends.

A contrary view, as embodied in today's decision, will have unfortunate consequences. The decision will encourage legal challenges to gun regulation throughout the Nation. Because it says little about the standards used to evaluate regulatory decisions, it will leave the Nation without clear standards for resolving those challenges. And litigation over the course of many years, or the mere specter of such litigation, threatens to leave cities without effective protection against gun violence and accidents during that time. As important, the majority's decision threatens severely to limit the ability of more knowledgeable, democratically elected officials to deal with gun-related problems. With respect, I dissent.

McDonald v. Chicago
561 U.S. 742 (2010).

In District of Columbia v. Heller *(2008), the Supreme Court held that the Second Amendment protects the right to keep and bear arms for the purpose of self-defense and struck down a District of Columbia law that banned the possession of handguns in the home. Chicago and the village of Oak Park, a Chicago suburb, have laws effectively banning handgun possession by almost all private citizens. After Heller, petitioners filed suit in federal court against Chicago, alleging that the City's handgun ban had left them vulnerable to criminals. They sought a declaration that the ban and several related City ordinances violate the Second and Fourteenth Amendments. The District Court rejected petitioners' argument that the* ordinances are unconstitutional, noting that the Seventh Circuit previously had upheld the constitutionality of a handgun ban, that* Heller *had explicitly refrained from opining on whether the Second Amendment applied to the States, and that the court had a duty to follow established Circuit precedent. The Seventh Circuit affirmed, and the Supreme Court granted certiorari. Judgment and Opinion of the Court:* Alito, Roberts, Scalia, Kennedy, Thomas (in part). *Concurring opinions:* Scalia; Thomas. *Dissenting opinions:* Stevens; Breyer, Ginsburg, Sotomayor.

JUSTICE ALITO announced the judgment of the Court and delivered the opinion of the

Court with respect to Parts I, II–A, II–B, II–D, III–A, and III–B, in which THE CHIEF JUSTICE, JUSTICE SCALIA, JUSTICE KENNEDY, and JUSTICE THOMAS join, and an opinion with respect to Parts II–C, IV, and V, in which THE CHIEF JUSTICE, JUSTICE SCALIA, and JUSTICE KENNEDY join.

Two years ago, in *District of Columbia* v. *Heller* (2008), we held that the Second Amendment protects the right to keep and bear arms for the purpose of self-defense, and we struck down a District of Columbia law that banned the possession of handguns in the home. The city of Chicago (City) and the village of Oak Park, a Chicago suburb, have laws that are similar to the District of Columbia's, but Chicago and Oak Park argue that their laws are constitutional because the Second Amendment has no application to the States. We have previously held that most of the provisions of the Bill of Rights apply with full force to both the Federal Government and the States. Applying the standard that is well established in our case law, we hold that the Second Amendment right is fully applicable to the States.

II

A

Petitioners argue that the Chicago and Oak Park laws violate the right to keep and bear arms for two reasons. Petitioners' primary submission is that this right is among the "privileges or immunities of citizens of the United States" and that the narrow interpretation of the Privileges or Immunities Clause adopted in the *Slaughter-House Cases* (1873) should now be rejected. As a secondary argument, petitioners contend that the Fourteenth Amendment's Due Process Clause "incorporates" the Second Amendment right. Chicago and Oak Park maintain that a right set out in the Bill of Rights applies to the States only if that right is an indispensable attribute of *any* "civilized" legal system. If it is possible to imagine a civilized country that does not recognize the right, the municipal respondents tell us, then that right is not protected by due process. And since there are civilized countries that ban or strictly regulate the private possession of handguns, the municipal respondents maintain that due

process does not preclude such measures. In light of the parties' far-reaching arguments, we begin by recounting this Court's analysis over the years of the relationship between the provisions of the Bill of Rights and the States.

B

The Bill of Rights, including the Second Amendment, originally applied only to the Federal Government. The constitutional Amendments adopted in the aftermath of the Civil War fundamentally altered our country's federal system. The provision at issue in this case, §1 of the Fourteenth Amendment, provides, among other things, that a State may not abridge "the privileges or immunities of citizens of the United States" or deprive "any person of life, liberty, or property, without due process of law." Four years after the adoption of the Fourteenth Amendment, this Court was asked to interpret the Amendment's reference to "the privileges or immunities of citizens of the United States." The *Slaughter-House Cases* involved challenges to a Louisiana law permitting the creation of a state-sanctioned monopoly on the butchering of animals within the city of New Orleans. Justice Samuel Miller's opinion for the Court concluded that the Privileges or Immunities Clause protects only those rights "which owe their existence to the Federal government, its National character, its Constitution, or its laws." The Court held that other fundamental rights—rights that predated the creation of the Federal Government and that "the State governments were created to establish and secure"—were not protected by the Clause.

Today, many legal scholars dispute the correctness of the narrow *Slaughter-House* interpretation.

Three years after the decision in the *Slaughter-House Cases*, the Court decided [*United States v.*] *Cruikshank* (1876). In that case, the Court reviewed convictions stemming from the infamous Colfax Massacre in Louisiana on Easter Sunday 1873. Dozens of blacks, many unarmed, were slaughtered by a rival band of armed white men. Cruikshank himself allegedly marched unarmed African-American prisoners through the streets and then had them summarily executed. Ninety-seven men were indicted for participating in the massacre, but only nine went to trial. Six of the nine were acquitted of all charges; the remaining three were acquitted of murder but convicted under the Enforcement Act of 1870, for banding and conspiring together to deprive their victims of various constitutional rights, including the right to bear arms. The Court reversed all of the convictions, including those relating to the deprivation of the victims' right to bear arms. The Court wrote that the right of bearing arms for a lawful purpose "is not a right granted by the Constitution." "The second amendment," the Court continued, "declares that it shall not be infringed; but this means no more than that it shall not be infringed by Congress." Our later decisions in *Presser v. Illinois* (1886), and *Miller v. Texas* (1894), reaffirmed that the Second Amendment applies only to the Federal Government.

C

The Seventh Circuit concluded that *Cruikshank*, *Presser*, and *Miller* doomed petitioners' claims. Petitioners argue, however, that we should overrule those decisions and hold that the right to keep and bear arms is one of the "privileges or immunities of citizens of the United States." In petitioners' view, the Privileges or Immunities Clause protects all of the rights set out in the Bill of Rights, as well as some others, but petitioners are unable to identify the Clause's full scope. We see no need to reconsider that interpretation here. However, this Court's decisions in *Cruikshank*, *Presser*, and *Miller* do not preclude us from considering whether the Due Process Clause of the Fourteenth Amendment makes the Second Amendment right binding on the States.

D

1

In the late nineteenth century, the Court began to consider whether the Due Process Clause prohibits the States from infringing rights set out in the Bill of Rights. Five features of the approach taken during the ensuing era should be noted. First, the Court viewed the due process question as entirely separate from the question whether a right was a privilege or immunity of national citizenship. Second, the Court explained that the only rights protected against state infringement by the Due Process Clause were those rights "of such a nature that they are included in the conception of due process of law." Although it was "possible that some of the personal rights safeguarded by the first eight Amendments against National action [might] also be safeguarded against state action," the Court stated, this was "not because those rights are enumerated in the first eight Amendments." Third, in some cases decided during this era the Court "can be seen as having asked, when inquiring into whether some particular procedural safeguard was required of a State, if a civilized system could be imagined that would not accord the particular protection." *Duncan v. Louisiana* (1968). Fourth, the Court during this era was not hesitant to hold that a right set out in the Bill of Rights failed to meet the test for inclusion within the protection of the Due Process Clause. Finally, even when a right set out in the Bill of Rights was held to fall within the conception of due process, the protection or remedies afforded against state infringement sometimes differed from the protection or remedies provided against abridgment by the Federal Government.

3

Although Justice Black's theory [of "total incorporation" of the Bill of Rights as limits on the states] was never adopted, the Court eventually moved in that direction by initiating what has been called a process of "selective incorporation," that is, the Court began to hold that the Due Process Clause fully incorporates particular rights contained in the first eight Amendments. The Court made it clear that the governing standard is not whether any "civilized system [can] be imagined that would not accord the particular protection." Instead, the Court inquired whether a particular Bill of Rights guarantee is fundamental to our scheme of ordered liberty and system of justice. The Court also shed any reluctance to hold that rights guaranteed by the Bill of Rights met the requirements for protection under the Due Process Clause. The Court eventually incorporated almost all of the provisions of the Bill of Rights. Finally, the Court abandoned "the notion that the Fourteenth Amendment applies to the States only a watered down, subjective version of the individual guarantees of the Bill of Rights," stating that it would be "incongruous" to apply different standards "depending on whether the claim was asserted in a state or federal court." Instead, the Court held that incorporated Bill of Rights protections "are all to be enforced against the States under the Fourteenth Amendment according to the same standards that protect those personal rights against federal encroachment." Employing this approach, the Court overruled earlier decisions in which it had held that particular Bill of Rights guarantees or remedies did not apply to the States.

III

With this framework in mind, we now turn directly to the question whether the Second Amendment right to keep and bear arms is incorporated in the concept of due process. In answering that question, we must decide whether the right to keep and bear arms is fundamental to our scheme of ordered liberty, or whether this right is "deeply rooted in this Nation's history and tradition." *Washington v. Glucksberg* (1997).

A

Our decision in *Heller* points unmistakably to the answer. Self-defense is a basic right, recognized by many legal systems from ancient times to the present day, and in *Heller*, we held that individual self-defense is "the central component" of the Second Amendment right. Explaining that "the need for defense of self, family, and property is most acute" in the home, we found that this right applies to handguns because they are "the most preferred firearm in the nation to 'keep' and use for protection of one's home and family." *Heller* makes it clear that this right is "deeply rooted in this Nation's history and tradition." The 1689 English Bill of Rights explicitly protected a right to keep arms for self-defense, and that by 1765, Blackstone was able to assert that the right to keep and bear arms was "one of the fundamental rights of Englishmen." The right to keep and bear arms was considered no less fundamental by those who drafted and ratified the Bill of Rights. "During the 1788 ratifica-

tion debates, the fear that the federal government would disarm the people in order to impose rule through a standing army or select militia was pervasive in Antifederalist rhetoric." Federalists responded, not by arguing that the right was insufficiently important to warrant protection but by contending that the right was adequately protected by the Constitution's assignment of only limited powers to the Federal Government. Thus, Antifederalists and Federalists alike agreed that the right to bear arms was fundamental to the newly formed system of government. But those who were fearful that the new Federal Government would infringe traditional rights such as the right to keep and bear arms insisted on the adoption of the Bill of Rights as a condition for ratification of the Constitution. This is surely powerful evidence that the right was regarded as fundamental.

This understanding persisted in the years immediately following the ratification of the Bill of Rights. In addition to the four States that had adopted Second Amendment analogues before ratification, nine more States adopted state constitutional provisions protecting an individual right to keep and bear arms between 1789 and 1820. Founding-era legal commentators confirmed the importance of the right to early Americans.

B

1

By the 1850's, the perceived threat that had prompted the inclusion of the Second Amendment in the Bill of Rights—the fear that the National Government would disarm the universal militia—had largely faded as a popular concern, but the right to keep and bear arms was highly valued for purposes of self-defense. Abolitionist authors wrote in support of the right. And when attempts were made to disarm "Free-Soilers" in "Bloody Kansas," Senator Charles Sumner, who later played a leading role in the adoption of the Fourteenth Amendment, proclaimed that "never was [the rifle] more needed in just self-defense than now in Kansas." Indeed, the 1856 Republican Party Platform protested that in Kansas the constitutional rights of the people had been "fraudulently and violently taken from them" and the "right of the people to keep and bear arms" had been "infringed."

After the Civil War, many of the over 180,000 African Americans who served in the Union Army returned to the States of the old Confederacy, where systematic efforts were made to disarm them and other blacks. Throughout the South, armed parties, often consisting of ex-Confederate soldiers serving in the state militias, forcibly took firearms from newly freed slaves. The Report of the Joint Committee on Reconstruction—which was widely reprinted in the press and distributed by Members of the 39th Congress to their constituents shortly after Congress approved the Fourteenth Amendment—contained numerous examples of such abuses. Congress concluded that legislative action was necessary. Its efforts to safeguard the right to keep and bear arms demonstrate that the right was still recognized to be fundamental.

The most explicit evidence of Congress' aim appears in §14 of the Freedmen's Bureau Act of 1866, which provided that "the right to have full and equal benefit of all laws and proceedings concerning personal liberty, personal security, and the acquisition, enjoyment, and disposition of estate, real and personal, including the constitutional right to bear arms, shall be secured to and enjoyed by all the citizens without respect to race or color, or previous condition of slavery." The Civil Rights Act of 1866 similarly sought to protect the right of all citizens to keep and bear arms.

Congress, however, ultimately deemed these legislative remedies insufficient. Southern resistance, Presidential vetoes, and this Court's pre-Civil-War precedent persuaded Congress that a constitutional amendment was necessary to provide full protection for the rights of blacks. Today, it is generally accepted that the Fourteenth Amendment was understood to provide a constitutional basis for protecting the rights set out in the Civil Rights Act of 1866. In debating the Fourteenth Amendment, the 39th Congress referred to the right to keep and bear arms as a fundamental right deserving of protection. Evidence from the period immediately following the ratification of the Fourteenth Amendment confirms that the right to keep and bear arms was considered fundamental. In

an 1868 speech addressing the disarmament of freedmen, Representative Stevens emphasized the necessity of the right: "Disarm a community and you rob them of the means of defending life. Take away their weapons of defense and you take away the inalienable right of defending liberty." "The fourteenth amendment, now so happily adopted, settles the whole question." And in debating the Civil Rights Act of 1871, Congress routinely referred to the right to keep and bear arms and decried the continued disarmament of blacks in the South.

The right to keep and bear arms was also widely protected by state constitutions at the time when the Fourteenth Amendment was ratified. In 1868, 22 of the 37 States in the Union had state constitutional provisions explicitly protecting the right to keep and bear arms. Quite a few, moreover, explicitly protected the right to keep and bear arms as an individual right to self-defense. What is more, state constitutions adopted during the Reconstruction era by former Confederate States included a right to keep and bear arms. A clear majority of the States in 1868, therefore, recognized the right to keep and bear arms as being among the foundational rights necessary to our system of Government. In sum, it is clear that the Framers and ratifiers of the Fourteenth Amendment counted the right to keep and bear arms among those fundamental rights necessary to our system of ordered liberty.

2

Municipal respondents contend that Congress, in the years immediately following the Civil War, merely sought to outlaw "discriminatory measures taken against freedmen, which it addressed by adopting a non-discrimination principle" and that even an outright ban on the possession of firearms was regarded as acceptable, "so long as it was not done in a discriminatory manner." This argument is implausible. First, while §1 of the Fourteenth Amendment contains" an antidiscrimination rule," namely, the Equal Protection Clause, municipal respondents can hardly mean that §1 does no more than prohibit discrimination. If that were so, then the First Amendment, as applied to the States, would not prohibit nondiscriminatory abridgments of the rights to freedom of speech or freedom of religion; the Fourth Amendment, as applied to the States, would not prohibit all unreasonable searches and seizures but only discriminatory searches and seizures—and so on. We assume that this is not municipal respondents' view, so what they must mean is that the Second Amendment should be singled out for special—and specially unfavorable—treatment. We reject that suggestion.

Second, municipal respondents' argument ignores the clear terms of the Freedmen's Bureau Act of 1866, which acknowledged the existence of the right to bear arms. That law speaks of and protects "the constitutional right to bear arms," an unmistakable reference to the right protected by the Second Amendment. And it protects the "full and equal benefit" of this right in the States. It would have been nonsensical for Congress to guarantee the full and equal benefit of a constitutional right that does not exist.

Third, if the 39th Congress had outlawed only those laws that discriminate on the basis of race or previous condition of servitude, African Americans in the South would likely have remained vulnerable to attack by many of their worst abusers: the state militia and state peace officers. In the years immediately following the Civil War, a law banning the possession of guns by all private citizens would have been nondiscriminatory only in the formal sense. Any such law—like the Chicago and Oak Park ordinances challenged here—presumably would have permitted the possession of guns by those acting under the authority of the State and would thus have left firearms in the hands of the militia and local peace officers. And as the Report of the Joint Committee on Reconstruction revealed, those groups were widely involved in harassing blacks in the South.

Fourth, municipal respondents' purely antidiscrimination theory of the Fourteenth Amendment disregards the plight of whites in the South who opposed the Black Codes. If the 39th Congress and the ratifying public had simply prohibited racial discrimination with respect to the bearing of arms, opponents of the Black Codes would have been left without the means of self-defense—as had abolitionists in Kansas in the 1850's.

IV

Municipal respondents' remaining arguments are at war with our central holding in *Heller*: that the Second Amendment protects a personal right to keep and bear arms for lawful purposes, most notably for self-defense within the home. Municipal respondents, in effect, ask us to treat the right recognized in *Heller* as a second-class right, subject to an entirely different body of rules than the other Bill of Rights guarantees that we have held to be incorporated into the Due Process Clause. [Responding to municipalities' argument that private possession of handguns may jeopardize public safety,] the right to keep and bear arms is not the only constitutional right that has controversial public safety implications. All of the constitutional provisions that impose restrictions on law enforcement and on the prosecution of crimes fall into the same category.

We likewise reject municipal respondents' argument that we should depart from our established incorporation methodology on the ground that making the Second Amendment binding on the States and their subdivisions is inconsistent with principles of federalism and will stifle experimentation. This argument was made repeatedly and eloquently by Members of this Court who rejected the concept of incorporation and urged retention of the two track approach to incorporation. Time and again, however, those pleas failed. Unless we turn back the clock or adopt a special incorporation test applicable only to the Second Amendment, municipal respondents' argument must be rejected.

Municipal respondents assert that, although most state constitutions protect firearms rights, state courts have held that these rights are subject to "interest-balancing" and have sustained a variety of restrictions. In *Heller*, however, we expressly rejected the argument that the scope of the Second Amendment right should be determined by judicial interest balancing and this Court decades ago abandoned "the notion that the Fourteenth Amendment applies to the States only a watered-down, subjective version of the individual guarantees of the Bill of Rights."

V
A

Justice Breyer's conclusion that the Fourteenth Amendment does not incorporate the right to keep and bear arms appears to rest primarily on four factors: First, "there is no popular consensus" that the right is fundamental; second, the right does not protect minorities or persons neglected by those holding political power; third, incorporation of the Second Amendment right would "amount to a significant incursion on a traditional and important area of state concern, altering the constitutional relationship between the States and the Federal Government" and preventing local variations; and fourth, determining the scope of the Second Amendment right in cases involving state and local laws will force judges to answer difficult empirical questions regarding matters that are outside their area of expertise. Even if we believed that these factors were relevant to the incorporation inquiry, none of these factors undermines the case for incorporation of the right to keep and bear arms for self-defense.

First, we have never held that a provision of the Bill of Rights applies to the States only if there is a "popular consensus" that the right is fundamental, and we see no basis for such a rule. But in this case, there is evidence of such a consensus. An amicus brief submitted by 58 Members of the Senate and 251 Members of the House of Representatives urges us to hold that the right to keep and bear arms is fundamental. Another brief submitted by 38 States takes the same position.

Second, petitioners and many others who live in high crime areas dispute the proposition that the Second Amendment right does not protect minorities and those lacking political clout. Amici supporting incorporation of the right to keep and bear arms contend that the right is especially important for women and members of other groups that may be especially vulnerable to violent crime.

Third, Justice Breyer is correct that incorporation of the Second Amendment right will to some extent limit the legislative freedom of the States, but this is always true when a Bill of Rights provision is incorporated. Incorporation always restricts experimentation and local variations, but that has not stopped the Court from incorporating virtually every other provision of the Bill of Rights.

Finally, Justice Breyer is incorrect that incorporation will require judges to assess the costs and benefits of firearms restrictions and thus to make difficult empirical judgments in an area in which they lack expertise. "The very enumeration of the right takes out of the hands of government—even the Third Branch of Government—the power to decide on a case-by-case basis whether the right is really worth insisting upon." *Heller*.

* * *

We therefore hold that the Due Process Clause of the Fourteenth Amendment incorporates the Second Amendment right recognized in *Heller*. The judgment of the Court of Appeals is reversed, and the case is remanded for further proceedings.

JUSTICE THOMAS, concurring in part and concurring in the judgment.

I agree with the Court that the Fourteenth Amendment makes the right to keep and bear arms set forth in the Second Amendment "fully applicable to the States." I believe there is a more straightforward path to this conclusion, one that is more faithful to the Fourteenth Amendment's text and history. The right to keep and bear arms is a privilege of American citizenship that applies to the States through the Fourteenth Amendment's Privileges or Immunities Clause.

JUSTICE BREYER, with whom JUSTICE GINSBURG and JUSTICE SOTOMAYOR join, dissenting.

I can find nothing in the Second Amendment's text, history, or underlying rationale that could warrant characterizing it as "fundamental" insofar as it seeks to protect the keeping and bearing of arms for private self-defense purposes. Nor can I find any justification for interpreting the Constitution as transferring ultimate regulatory authority over the private uses of firearms from democratically elected legislatures to courts or from the States to the Federal Government. I therefore conclude that the Fourteenth Amendment does not "incorporate" the Second Amendment's right "to keep and bear Arms."

I

Two years ago, in *District of Columbia v. Heller* (2008), the Court rejected the preexisting judicial consensus that the Second Amendment was primarily concerned with the need to maintain a "well regulated Militia." Although the Court acknowledged that "the threat that the new Federal Government would destroy the citizens' militia by taking away their arms was the reason that right was codified in a written Constitution," the Court asserted that "individual self defense was the central component of the right itself." The Court based its conclusions almost exclusively upon its reading of history. But the relevant history in *Heller* was far from clear: Four dissenting Justices disagreed with the majority's historical analysis. And subsequent scholarly writing reveals why disputed history provides treacherous ground on which to build decisions written by judges who are not expert at history. Since *Heller*, historians, scholars, and judges have continued to express the view that the Court's historical account was flawed.

Consider as an example of these critiques an amici brief filed in this case by historians who specialize in the study of the English Civil Wars. *Heller's* conclusion that "individual self-defense" was "the central component" of the Second Amendment's right "to keep and bear Arms" rested upon its view that the Amendment "codified a pre-existing right" that had "nothing whatever to do with service in a militia." That view in turn rested in significant part upon Blackstone having described the right as "'the right of having and using arms for self preservation and defence,'" which reflected the provision in the English Declaration of Right of 1689 that gave the King's Protestant "'subjects'" the right to "'have Arms for their defence suitable to their Conditions, and as allowed by law.'" The Framers, said the majority, understood that right "as permitting a citizen to 'repel force by force' when 'the intervention of society in his behalf, may be too late to prevent an injury.'"

The historians now tell us, however, that the right to which Blackstone referred had, not nothing, but everything, to do with the militia.

As properly understood at the time of the English Civil Wars, the historians claim, the right to bear arms "ensured that Parliament had the power" to arm the citizenry: "to defend the realm" in the case of a foreign enemy, and to "secure the right of 'self preservation,'" or "self-defense," should "the sovereign usurp the English Constitution." Thus, the Declaration of Right says that private persons can possess guns only "as allowed by law." Moreover, when Blackstone referred to "'the right of having and using arms for self-preservation and defence,'" he was referring to the right of the people "to take part in the militia to defend their political liberties," and to the right of Parliament (which represented the people) to raise a militia even when the King sought to deny it that power. Nor can the historians find any convincing reason to believe that the Framers had something different in mind than what Blackstone himself meant. If history, and history alone, is what matters, why would the Court not now reconsider *Heller* in light of these more recently published historical views? At the least, where *Heller's* historical foundations are so uncertain, why extend its applicability?

My aim in referring to this history is to illustrate the reefs and shoals that lie in wait for those nonexpert judges who place virtually determinative weight upon historical considerations. In my own view, the Court should not look to history alone but to other factors as well—above all, in cases where the history is so unclear that the experts themselves strongly disagree. It should, for example, consider the basic values that underlie a constitutional provision and their contemporary significance. And it should examine as well the relevant consequences and practical justifications that might, or might not, warrant removing an important question from the democratic decision making process.

II
A

Taking *Heller* as a given, the Fourteenth Amendment does not incorporate the Second Amendment right to keep and bear arms for purposes of private self-defense. Under this Court's precedents, to incorporate the private self-defense right the majority must show that the right is, e.g., "fundamental to the American scheme of justice," *Duncan v. Louisiana* (1968). And this it fails to do. The majority here relies almost exclusively upon history to make the necessary showing. But this Court, in considering an incorporation question, has never stated that the historical status of a right is the only relevant consideration. Rather, the Court has either explicitly or implicitly made clear that the right in question has remained fundamental over time. I thus think it proper, above all where history provides no clear answer, to look to other factors in considering whether a right is sufficiently "fundamental" to remove it from the political process in every State. I would include among those factors the nature of the right; any contemporary disagreement about whether the right is fundamental; the extent to which incorporation will further other, perhaps more basic, constitutional aims; and the extent to which incorporation will advance or hinder the Constitution's structural aims, including its division of powers among different governmental institutions (and the people as well). Is incorporation needed, for example, to further the Constitution's effort to ensure that the government treats each individual with equal respect? Will it help maintain the democratic form of government that the Constitution foresees? In a word, will incorporation prove consistent, or inconsistent, with the Constitution's efforts to create governmental institutions well suited to the carrying out of its constitutional promises?

Finally, I would take account of the Framers' basic reason for believing the Court ought to have the power of judicial review. Alexander Hamilton feared granting that power to Congress alone, for he feared that Congress, acting as judges, would not overturn as unconstitutional a popular statute that it had recently enacted, as legislators. Judges, he thought, may find it easier to resist popular pressure to suppress the basic rights of an unpopular minority. That being so, it makes sense to ask whether that particular comparative judicial advantage is relevant to the case at hand.

B

How do these considerations apply here? For one thing, I would apply them only to the private self-defense right directly at issue. After all, the Amendment's militia-related purpose is primarily to protect States from federal regulation, not to protect individuals from militia-related regulation. Moreover, the Civil War Amendments, the electoral process, the courts, and numerous other institutions today help to safeguard the States and the people from any serious threat of federal tyranny. How are state militias additionally necessary? It is difficult to see how a right that, as the majority concedes, has "largely faded as a popular concern" could possibly be so fundamental that it would warrant incorporation through the Fourteenth Amendment. Hence, the incorporation of the Second Amendment cannot be based on the militia-related aspect of what *Heller* found to be more extensive Second Amendment rights. [Yet] the Framers' basic reasons for including language in the Constitution would nonetheless seem more pertinent (in deciding about the contemporary importance of a right) than the particular scope 17th-or 18th-century listeners would have then assigned to the words they used. And examination of the Framers' motivation tells us they did not think the private armed self-defense right was of paramount importance. Further, there is no popular consensus that the private self-defense right described in *Heller* is fundamental. The plurality suggests that two amici briefs filed in the case show such a consensus, but, of course, numerous amici briefs have been filed opposing incorporation as well. Moreover, every State regulates firearms extensively, and public opinion is sharply divided on the appropriate level of regulation. There is no reason here to believe that incorporation of the private self-defense right will further any other or broader constitutional objective. We are aware of no argument that gun control regulations target or are passed with the purpose of targeting "discrete and insular minorities." *Carolene Products Co.* Nor will incorporation help to assure equal respect for individuals. Unlike the First Amendment's rights of free speech, free press, assembly, and petition, the private self-defense right does not comprise a necessary part of the democratic process that the Constitution seeks to establish. Unlike the First Amendment's religious protections, the Fourth

Amendment's protection against unreasonable searches and seizures, the Fifth and Sixth Amendments' insistence upon fair criminal procedure, and the Eighth Amendment's protection against cruel and unusual punishments, the private self-defense right does not significantly seek to protect individuals who might otherwise suffer unfair or inhumane treatment at the hands of a majority. Unlike the protections offered by many of these same Amendments, it does not involve matters as to which judges possess a comparative expertise, by virtue of their close familiarity with the justice system and its operation. Finally, incorporation of the right will work a significant disruption in the constitutional allocation of decision making authority, thereby interfering with the Constitution's ability to further its objectives.

First, on any reasonable accounting, the incorporation of the right recognized in *Heller* would amount to a significant incursion on a traditional and important area of state concern, altering the constitutional relationship between the States and the Federal Government. Private gun regulation is the quintessential exercise of a State's "police power"—i.e., the power to "protect the lives, limbs, health, comfort, and quiet of all persons, and the protection of all property within the State," by enacting "all kinds of restraints and burdens" on both "persons and property." *Slaughter-House Cases* (1873). The Court has long recognized that the Constitution grants the States special authority to enact laws pursuant to this power. A decade ago, we wrote that there is "no better example of the police power" than "the suppression of violent crime." *United States v. Morrison* (2000). And examples in which the Court has deferred to state legislative judgments in respect to the exercise of the police power are legion.

Second, determining the constitutionality of a particular state gun law requires finding answers to complex empirically based questions of a kind that legislatures are better able than courts to make. And it may require this kind of analysis in virtually every case. Government regulation of the right to bear arms normally embodies a judgment that the regulation will help save lives. The determination whether a gun regulation is

constitutional would thus almost always require the weighing of the constitutional right to bear arms against the "primary concern of every government—a concern for the safety and indeed the lives of its citizens."

Suppose, for example, that after a gun regulation's adoption the murder rate went up. Without the gun regulation would the murder rate have risen even faster? How is this conclusion affected by the local recession which has left numerous people unemployed? What about budget cuts that led to a downsizing of the police force? How effective was that police force to begin with? And did the regulation simply take guns from those who use them for lawful purposes without affecting their possession by criminals?

Consider too that countless gun regulations of many shapes and sizes are in place in every State and in many local communities. Does the right to possess weapons for self-defense extend outside the home? To the car? To work? What sort of guns are necessary for self-defense? Handguns? Rifles? Semiautomatic weapons? When is a gun semi-automatic? Where are different kinds of weapons likely needed? Does time-of-day matter? Does the presence of a child in the house matter? Does the presence of a convicted felon in the house matter? Do police need special rules permitting patdowns designed to find guns? When do registration requirements become severe to the point that they amount to an unconstitutional ban? Who can possess guns and of what kind? Aliens? Prior drug offenders? Prior alcohol abusers? How would the right interact with a state or local government's ability to take special measures during, say, national security emergencies?

The difficulty of finding answers to these questions is exceeded only by the importance of doing so. In answering such questions judges cannot simply refer to judicial homilies, such as Blackstone's 18th-century perception that a man's home is his castle. Nor can the plurality so simply reject, by mere assertion, the fact that "incorporation will require judges to assess the costs and benefits of firearms restrictions." The fact is that judges do not know the answers to the kinds of empirically based questions that will often determine the need for particular forms of gun regulation. Nor do they have readily available "tools" for finding and evaluating the technical material submitted by others. At the same time, there is no institutional need to send judges off on this "mission-almost-impossible." Legislators are able to "amass the stuff of actual experience and cull conclusions from it." *United States v. Gainey*, 380 U. S. 63, 67 (1965). They are far better suited than judges to uncover facts and to understand their relevance. And legislators, unlike Article III judges, can be held democratically responsible for their empirically based and value laden conclusions. We have thus repeatedly affirmed our preference for "legislative not judicial solutions" to this kind of problem.

Third, the ability of States to reflect local preferences and conditions—both key virtues of federalism—here has particular importance. The incidence of gun ownership varies substantially as between crowded cities and uncongested rural communities, as well as among the different geographic regions of the country. The nature of gun violence also varies as between rural communities and cities.

Fourth, although incorporation of any right removes decisions from the democratic process, the incorporation of this particular right does so without strong offsetting justification—as the example of Oak Park's handgun ban helps to show. Oak Park decided to ban handguns in 1983, after a local attorney was shot to death with a handgun that his assailant had smuggled into a courtroom. A citizens committee spent months gathering information about handguns. It secured 6,000 signatures from community residents in support of a ban. And the village board enacted a ban into law. Subsequently, at the urging of ban opponents the Board held a community referendum on the matter. The public decided to keep the ban by a vote of 8,031 to 6,368. And since that time, Oak Park now tells us, crime has decreased and the community has seen no accidental handgun deaths. Given the empirical and local value-laden nature of the questions that lie at the heart of the issue, why is it so fundamental a matter as to require taking that power from the people? What is it here that the people did not know? What is it that a judge knows better?

III

The plurality, in seeking to justify incorporation, asks whether the interests the Second Amendment protects are "'deeply rooted in this Nation's history and tradition.'" It looks to selected portions of the Nation's history for the answer. And it finds an affirmative reply. As I have made clear, I do not believe history is the only pertinent consideration. Nor would I read history as broadly as the majority does. In particular, since we here are evaluating a more particular right—namely, the right to bear arms for purposes of private self-defense—general historical references to the "right to keep and bear arms" are not always helpful. That said, I can find much in the historical record that shows that some Americans in some places at certain times thought it important to keep and bear arms for private self-defense. For instance, the reader will see that many States have constitutional provisions protecting gun possession. But, as far as I can tell, those provisions typically do no more than guarantee that a gun regulation will be a reasonable police power regulation. Thus, the specific question before us is whether there is a consensus that so substantial a private self-defense right as the one described in *Heller* applies to the States.

States and localities have consistently enacted firearms regulations, including regulations similar to those at issue here, throughout our Nation's history. Courts have repeatedly upheld such regulations. And it is, at the very least, possible, and perhaps likely, that incorporation will impose on every, or nearly every, State a different right to bear arms than they currently recognize—a right that threatens to destabilize settled state legal principles. I thus cannot find a historical consensus with respect to whether the right described by *Heller* is "fundamental" as our incorporation cases use that term. Nor can I find sufficient historical support for the majority's conclusion that that right is "deeply rooted in this Nation's history and tradition." Instead, I find no more than ambiguity and uncertainty that perhaps even expert historians would find difficult to penetrate. And a historical record that is so ambiguous cannot itself provide an adequate basis for incorporating a private right of self-defense and applying it against the States.

Although the majority does not discuss 20th- or 21st century evidence concerning the Second Amendment at any length, I think that it is essential to consider the recent history of the right to bear arms for private self-defense when considering whether the right is "fundamental." To that end, many States now provide state constitutional protection for an individual's right to keep and bear arms. In determining the importance of this fact, we should keep the following considerations in mind: First, by the end of the 20th century, in every State and many local communities, highly detailed and complicated regulatory schemes governed (and continue to govern) nearly every aspect of firearm ownership: Who may sell guns and how they must be sold; who may purchase guns and what type of guns may be purchased; how firearms must be stored and where they may be used; and so on. Of particular relevance here, some municipalities ban handguns, even in States that constitutionally protect the right to bear arms. Moreover, at least seven States and Puerto Rico ban assault weapons or semiautomatic weapons. Thirteen municipalities do the same.

Second, state courts in States with constitutions that provide gun rights have almost uniformly interpreted those rights as providing protection only against unreasonable regulation of guns. When determining reasonableness those courts have normally adopted a highly deferential attitude towards legislative determinations. Third, the plurality correctly points out that only a few state courts, a "paucity" of state courts, have specifically upheld handgun bans. But which state courts have struck them down? The absence of supporting information does not help the majority find support. Silence does not show or tend to show a consensus that a private self-defense right strong enough to strike down a handgun ban is "deeply rooted in this Nation's history and tradition."

In sum, the Framers did not write the Second Amendment in order to protect a private right of armed self-defense. There has been, and is, no consensus that the right is, or was, "fundamental." No broader constitutional interest or principle supports legal treatment of that right as fundamental. To the contrary, broader constitutional concerns of an institutional nature argue strongly against that treatment. Moreover, nothing in 18th-, 19th-, 20th-, or 21st-century history shows a consensus that the right to private armed self-defense, as described in *Heller*, is "deeply rooted in this Nation's history or tradition" or is otherwise "fundamental." Indeed, incorporating the right recognized in *Heller* may change the law in many of the 50 States. Read in the majority's favor, the historical evidence is at most ambiguous. And, in the absence of any other support for its conclusion, ambiguous history cannot show that the Fourteenth Amendment incorporates a private right of self-defense against the States. With respect, I dissent.

4

Economic Due Process and the Takings Clause

CHAPTER OUTLINE

Before the Civil War, the only constitutional restrictions on the power of the states to regulate economic activity were those found in Article I, Section 10, which prohibits the states from emitting bills of credit, making anything but gold or silver a tender in payment of debts, and passing *ex post facto* laws or laws impairing obligations of contracts. With the adoption of the Fourteenth Amendment in 1868, this situation changed. As briefly pointed out in Chapter 11 of Volume I, this amendment, especially through its Due Process Clause, supplied the Supreme Court with a potent weapon for invalidating state efforts at economic regulation and for protecting vested property rights. In the early part of the twentieth century, the Court wielded the Due Process Clause to strike down state laws that, in its estimation, arbitrarily, unreasonably, and capriciously interfered with the rights of life, liberty, and property.[1] During this period, various justices used the clause to justify substantive reviews of governmental actions, scrutinizing not only how, procedurally, the government acted but also what, substantively, the government did.

As with the Contract Clause before it, substantive due process in the economic realm gradually lost its potency, and by the late 1930s it no longer represented a major obstacle to economic regulation by the states. Such obstacles as remain are now found in the limitations on punitive-damages awards established by the Court in *BMW v. Gore* (1996), the Takings Clause of the Fifth Amendment as incorporated to apply to the states, the Court's expanding interpretations of congressional power to regulate commerce among the several states, and the state constitutions themselves. Today, it is almost wholly within the realm of civil liberties that substantive due process retains its potency and continues to serve as a constitutional limitation, not only on legislative and executive procedure, but also on legislative and executive power to act at all. This chapter traces the rise and decline of substantive due process in the economic realm, as well as its subsequent revival as a strong check on the substance of legislation infringing upon civil liberties. The chapter also explores the remaining significance of the Takings Clause as a check on state regulation of property rights.

THE FOURTEENTH AMENDMENT

The Fourteenth Amendment commands that "no state shall make or enforce any law which shall abridge the privileges or immunities of citizens of the United States; nor shall any State deprive any person of life, liberty, or property, without due process of law; nor deny to any person within its jurisdiction the equal protection of the laws." Out of an acrimonious debate over the specific intentions of the members of the Thirty-Ninth Congress who framed this amendment[2] has emerged general agreement as to what overall ends the amendment was intended to advance and as to how its three major provisions were to advance these ends. As a group, the Privileges or Immunities, Due Process, and Equal Protection Clauses were intended to place economic and civil liberties on the safe and secure foundation of federal protection, as follows:

- The Privileges or Immunities Clause was to protect substantive rights (e.g., freedom of speech, religious freedom, the right to engage in lawful occupations, freedom from improper police violence).
- The Due Process and Equal Protection Clauses were to protect procedural rights, with the former guaranteeing procedural safeguards and judicial regularity in the enforcement of those rights and the latter barring legislative and executive discrimination with respect to those substantive rights.

The Fourteenth Amendment can be visualized as a platform erected above the surface of state action for the protection of economic and civil liberties. In this metaphor, the

Privileges or Immunities, Due Process, and Equal Protection Clauses represent the platform's three legs: each performs different functions, yet collectively they render the platform stable and secure. The amendment's framers believed that all three legs were essential but that the Privileges or Immunities Clause would be the most important of the three because it was designed to be the major load-bearing leg. This design is reflected clearly in Section 5 of the amendment, which provides that "Congress shall have power to enforce, by appropriate legislation, the provisions of this article." Looking at these provisions from the point of view of Congress, the Privileges or Immunities Clause provides the simplest framework for such enforcement legislation. Under that clause, Congress can set out, through a single act or a series of acts, a comprehensive list of the vast number of substantive rights that flow from US citizenship and make it unlawful for any state, or its agents, to abridge such substantive rights.[3] In contrast, the Due Process and Equal Protection Clauses, with their procedural emphases, represent far more elusive reference points for enforcement legislation because of the formidable technical difficulties one faces to avoid unconstitutional vagueness and still frame statutes that protect persons from state deprivation of their lives, liberty, or property "without due process of law" or that guarantee "equal protection of the laws" without interference with essential classificatory schemes.

Just five years after the Fourteenth Amendment was ratified, however, the Supreme Court in *The Slaughter-House Cases* (1873) effectively kicked out the critical privileges-or-immunities leg and left the protective platform precariously supported by its two spindly procedural legs—due process and equal protection. To keep the platform of protections from collapsing altogether, subsequent Courts have found it imperative to increase substantially the size and strength of these procedural legs. Through judicial interpretation, the justices have added layer upon layer of meaning and coverage to these legs, in an effort to render secure those substantive economic and civil rights that were originally to have been protected by the Privileges or Immunities Clause.

THE EVISCERATION (AND POSSIBLE RECENT RESTORATION?) OF THE PRIVILEGES OR IMMUNITIES CLAUSE

In *Butcher's Benevolent Association v. Crescent City Live-Stock Landing and Slaughter-House Company*, more commonly known as *The Slaughter-House Cases* (1873), the Court upheld an act of the Louisiana Legislature that had conferred upon one firm what was in effect a monopoly of the slaughterhouse business in New Orleans. The plaintiffs had asserted, among other things, that the law in question was in violation of the Fourteenth Amendment. In a 5–4 decision, the Court rejected this claim, principally as a result of its especially narrow construction of the Privileges or Immunities Clause. Speaking for the majority, Justice Samuel F. Miller drew a distinction between state citizenship and national citizenship and, hence, between those privileges or immunities that accrued to an individual by virtue of state citizenship and those that stemmed from national citizenship. Only the latter, he insisted, were protected by the Fourteenth Amendment.

In distinguishing the privileges or immunities of state citizenship from those of national citizenship, Justice Miller quoted earlier decisions in an effort to demonstrate that the whole body of commonly accepted civil and economic rights—including the right to pursue lawful employment in a lawful manner, which lay at the heart of *The Slaughter-House Cases*—fell within the privileges or immunities of state citizenship. Such rights included "protection by the government, with the right to acquire and possess property of every kind, and to pursue and obtain happiness and safety, subject, nevertheless, to such restraints as the [state] government may prescribe for the general good of the whole." Miller contended that the framers of the Fourteenth Amendment had not intended to transfer this whole body of rights to the protection of the federal government. To interpret the amendment otherwise, he argued, would be to accept consequences "so serious, so far-reaching and pervading" that they would alter radically "the whole theory of the relations of the state and Federal governments to each other." This the Court refused to do, "in the absence of language which expresses such a purpose too clearly to admit of doubt."

Miller and the majority did not argue that national citizenship conferred no privileges or immunities. Although declining to define them precisely, they did suggest that such privileges or immunities included the right of a citizen "to come to the seat of the government to assert any claim he may have upon that government," the "right of free access to its seaports," and the right "to demand the care and protection of the Federal government over his life, liberty, and property when on the high seas, or within the jurisdiction of a foreign government." This list, however, left the whole body of traditional economic and civil rights solely under the protection of the states. As far as the federal Constitution was concerned, therefore, the privileges or immunities of the citizens of the separate states remained exactly as they had been before the Fourteenth Amendment was adopted. Justice Miller's argument prompted a frustrated Justice Stephen B. Field to complain in his dissent that if that was all the Privileges or Immunities Clause meant, "it was a vain and idle enactment, which accomplished nothing, and most unnecessarily excited Congress and the people on its passage." For Justice Field, the clause was intended to have a "profound significance and consequence." He argued that what the Privileges and Immunities Clause of Article IV, Section 2, "did for the protection of the citizens of one State against hostile and discriminating legislation of other States, the Fourteenth Amendment does for the protection of every citizen of the United States against hostile and discriminating legislation against him in favor of others, whether they reside in the same or in different states."

The *Slaughter-House* decision knocked out the only substantive (and, therefore, the most important) leg supporting the platform of economic and civil liberties erected by the Fourteenth Amendment. It was, in the words of Michael Kent Curtis, "one of the signal disasters of American judicial history."[4] In 1935, the Court made an initial effort to prop up this substantive leg and to restore the Privileges or Immunities Clause, holding in *Colgate v. Harvey* that the right of a US citizen to do business and place a loan in a state other than that in which he resided was a privilege of national citizenship. Just five years later in *Madden v. Kentucky* (1940), however, it expressly overturned that decision and returned to the old interpretation that "the right to carry out an incident of a trade, business, or calling such as the deposit of money in banks is not a privilege of national citizenship." And four years later in *Snowden v. Hughes* (1944), it again reaffirmed its narrow *Slaughter-House* interpretation when it held that the right to become a candidate for and be elected to a state office was an attribute of state citizenship, not a privilege of national citizenship. Those who had been denied this right, the Court declared, must look to their own state constitutions and laws for redress.[5]

Until 1999 it was altogether accurate to say that, with respect to the Privileges or Immunities Clause, the Court's decision in *The Slaughter-House Cases* remained good law. However, that year in *Saenz v. Roe,* the Court once again launched a campaign to restore the Privileges or Immunities Clause, invoking its language to strike down a durational residency requirement in California's welfare statute as an impermissible infringement on the right to travel and holding further that congressional approval of such a requirement did not resuscitate its constitutionality. Justice John Stevens held for a seven-member majority that a privilege and immunity of national citizenship is the right of travelers who elect to become permanent residents of a state "to be treated like other citizens of that State." Thomas dissented, arguing that Stevens attributed a meaning to the clause that was unintended when the Fourteenth Amendment was ratified. He faulted Stevens for failing to address the clause's "historical underpinnings." Yet, he declared, "because I believe that the demise of the Privileges and Immunities Clause has contributed in no small part to the current disarray of our Fourteenth Amendment jurisprudence, I would be open to reevaluating its meaning in an appropriate case." But, he continued, "before invoking the Clause, we should endeavor to understand what the framers of the Fourteenth Amendment thought it meant." And he went further: "We should also consider whether the Clause should displace, rather than augment, portions of our equal protection and substantive due process jurisprudence." He concluded by expressing his worry about the Court's sudden invocation of the Privileges or Immunities Clause: because Stevens used it to protect a right not expressly mentioned in the Constitution, will it become "yet another convenient tool for inventing new rights, limited solely by the 'predilections of those who happen at the time to be Members of this Court'"?

Interestingly, Thomas's dissent in *Saenz* gave great encouragement to Alan Gura, the brash young attorney who successfully argued in *District of Columbia v. Heller* that the Second Amendment secures to individuals the personal right to possess a firearm unconnected with service in a militia and to use that weapon for purposes of self-defense. Gura was retained to represent Otis McDonald, the petitioner in *McDonald v. Chicago,* where the question was whether the Second Amendment was incorporated by the Fourteenth Amendment to apply to the states. Gura gambled and devoted fifty-six of his sixty-three pages of argument in his initial brief to the Privileges or Immunities Clause argument. He so alarmed the National Rifle Association (NRA) that it filed a brief making selective incorporation under the Due Process Clause much more forcefully and at much greater length than did Gura's brief, asked for (and was granted) some of Gura's time during oral argument, and hired former solicitor general Paul Clement (who argued the government's case in *Heller*) to participate in the oral argument. The NRA's action proved to be wise, as Gura's efforts to rely on the Privileges or Immunities Clause were immediately challenged during oral argument; Chief Justice Roberts quickly questioned his reliance on the clause, noting that *The Slaughter-House Cases* had been good law for 140 years and adding that "it's a heavy burden for you to carry to suggest that we ought to overrule that decision." And, soon thereafter, Scalia challenged his argument in the following colloquy:

> **JUSTICE SCALIA:** Mr. Gura, do you think it is at all easier to bring the Second Amendment under the Privileges and Immunities Clause than it is to bring it under our established law of substantive due?
>
> **MR. GURA:** It's—
>
> **JUSTICE SCALIA:** Is it easier to do it under privileges and immunities than it is under substantive due process?
>
> **MR. GURA:** It is easier in terms, perhaps, of the text and history of the original public understanding of—
>
> **JUSTICE SCALIA:** No, no. I'm not talking about whether—whether the *Slaughter-House Cases* were right or wrong. I'm saying, assuming we give, you know, the Privileges and Immunities Clause your definition, does that make it any easier to get the Second Amendment adopted with respect to the States?
>
> **MR. GURA:** Justice Scalia, I suppose the answer to that would be no, because—
>
> **JUSTICE SCALIA:** Then if the answer is no, why are you asking us to overrule 150, 140 years of prior law, when you can reach your result under substantive due [process]—I mean, you know, unless you are bucking for a—a place on some law school faculty—
>
> (Laughter.)
>
> **MR. GURA:** No. No. I have left law school some time ago and this is not an attempt to return.

JUSTICE SCALIA: What you argue is the darling of the professoriate, for sure, but it's also contrary to 140 years of our jurisprudence. Why do you want to undertake that burden instead of just arguing substantive due process, which as much as I think it's wrong, . . . even I have acquiesced in it?

(Laughter.)

Despite Roberts's and Scalia's questions, and the laughter they elicited, Thomas was unfazed. In a twenty-thousand-word solo opinion, he insisted that the right to keep and bear arms was an "inalienable right that pre-existed the Constitution's adoption" and a privilege and immunity that could be enforced against the states under the Fourteenth Amendment.

ECONOMIC REGULATION AND THE RISE OF SUBSTANTIVE DUE PROCESS

The emasculation of the Privileges or Immunities Clause left the substantive economic and civil liberties guaranteed by that clause wholly dependent for support upon the Due Process and Equal Protection Clauses. The *Slaughter-House* majority, however, also construed these clauses narrowly.[6] In response to the plaintiffs' assertion that the Louisiana statute in question deprived them of their property without due process of law, the Court observed that "under no construction of that provision that we have ever seen, or that we deem admissible, can the restraint imposed by the State of Louisiana . . . be held to be a deprivation of property within the meaning of that provision."[7] And to a plea that the act deprived the plaintiffs of equal protection of the laws, the Court responded that the Equal Protection Clause had been aimed only at laws in the states "where the newly emancipated negroes resided, which discriminated with gross injustice and hardship against them as a class."

Over time, the Court has expanded and enlarged these narrow interpretations—these spindly legs—until today the Due Process and Equal Protection Clauses solidly support the protection of a vast array of substantive rights. (This chapter and Chapters 5 through 7 of Volume II explore the Court's expansion of the Due Process Clause, first in order to protect economic rights and subsequently in order to protect civil liberties. Chapters 8 through 10 in Volume II then explore the Court's somewhat later expansion of the Equal Protection Clause and how it has enlarged this procedural leg as well into a means of protecting substantive civil liberties. Finally, Chapter 11 of Volume II explores how the Court has employed these two clauses together to create and expand a generalized right to privacy, personal autonomy, and human dignity.)

The narrow procedural interpretation given the Due Process Clause in *The Slaughter-House Cases* gave way only gradually to a broader, more substantive understanding. In the significant case of *Munn v. Illinois* (1877), the Court reaffirmed the restrictive *Slaughter-House* interpretation and refused to hold that an Illinois statute that set maximum rates for grain elevators denied the elevator operators use of their property without due process of law. Chief Justice Morrison Waite argued that, since the days of the common law, grain elevators and warehouses had been recognized as businesses "clothed with a public interest" and as such were subject to public regulation by the legislature. Although he conceded that this regulatory power might be abused, the chief justice insisted that abuse "is no argument against the [law's] existence. For protection against abuses by legislatures the people must resort to the polls, not to the courts." In dissent, Justice Field argued that there was nothing in the character of the grain-elevator business that justified state regulation, and hence Illinois's legislation was "nothing less than a bold assertion of absolute power by the State to control at its discretion the property and business of the citizen, and fix the compensation he shall receive." To Field, this "unrestrained license" to regulate was incompatible with due process of law.

Field's broader conception of due process was articulated further by Justice Joseph Bradley in his concurring opinion in *Davidson v. New Orleans* (1878). Justice Miller, writing for the majority in *Davidson,* rejected a New Orleans landowner's claim that he had been deprived of his property without due process of law by being forced to pay a special assessment whose purpose (the draining of swamplands) allegedly would not benefit him. After confessing that "the Constitutional meaning or value of the phrase 'due process of law' remains today without that satisfactory precision of definition which judicial decisions have given to nearly all the other guarantees of personal rights found in the constitutions of the several States and of the United States," Justice Miller went on to declare that the phrase's meaning, however unclear, must be understood in a procedural sense only:

> It is not possible to hold that a party has, without due process of law, been deprived of his property, when, as regards the issues affecting it, he has, by the laws of the State, a fair trial in a court of justice, according to the modes of proceedings applicable to such a case. . . . This proposition covers the present case. Before the assessment could be collected, or become effective, the statute required that the tableau of assessments should be filed in the proper District Court of the State; that personal service of notice, with reasonable time to object, should be served on all owners who were known and within reach of process, and due advertisement made as to those who were unknown, or could not be found. This was complied with; and the party complaining here appeared, and had a full and fair hearing in the court of first instance, and afterwards in the Supreme Court. If this be not due process of law, then the words can have no definite meaning as used in the Constitution.

Justice Bradley, although agreeing with the decision, insisted that the Due Process Clause had a substantive dimension as well. Making explicit what was implicit in Justice Field's dissent in *Munn,* he argued,

> I think . . . we are entitled under the fourteenth amendment, not only to see that there is some process of law, but "due process of law," provided by the State law when a citizen is deprived of his property; and that, in judging what is "due process of law," respect must be had to the cause and object of the taking, whether under the taxing power, the power of eminent domain, or the power of assessment for local improvements, or none of these: and if found to be suitable or admissible in the special case, it will be adjudged to be "due process of law;" but if found to be arbitrary, oppressive, and unjust, it may be declared to be not "due process of law."

According to this view, the Due Process Clause requires courts to review not only how, procedurally, the government acts (procedural due process), but also what, substantively, the government does (substantive due process). If the Court discerns that a law is unreasonable—that is, "arbitrary, oppressive, and unjust"—then it is justified in declaring the law to be a denial of due process and, hence, constitutionally infirm.

These substantive due-process arguments did not originate with Justices Field and Bradley. As far back as 1856, in *Wynehamer v. New York,* the New York Court of Appeals (the state's highest court) had invalidated a Prohibition law on the grounds that such an exercise of the police power infringed on the economic liberty of tavern proprietors to practice their livelihood and therefore denied them due process of law.[8] Justices Field and Bradley, however, were the first to give expression to these sentiments at the level of the United

States Supreme Court, and the arguments they introduced in *Munn* and *Davidson* gained ascendancy in *Mugler v. Kansas* (1887) and *Allgeyer v. Louisiana* (1897) and received their clearest constitutional expression in *Lochner v. New York* (1905).

In *Mugler,* the Court upheld Kansas's Prohibition law but warned that it would begin examining the reasonableness of legislation. Justice John Marshall Harlan stressed that if "a statute purporting to have been enacted to protect the public health, the public morals, or the public safety has no real or substantial relation to those objects, or is a palpable invasion of rights secured by the fundamental law, it is the duty of the Courts to so adjudge." Then, in *Allgeyer,* the Court for the first time relied on substantive due process to invalidate state legislation. Louisiana had enacted legislation designed to regulate out-of-state insurance companies doing business in the state. Justice Rufus Peckham, writing for the majority, argued that the statute in question "is not due process of law, because it prohibits an act which under the federal constitution the defendant has a right to perform." The state's legitimate exercise of its police power, he contended, did not extend to "prohibiting a citizen from making contracts of the nature involved in this case outside of the limits of the jurisdiction of the state, and which are also to be performed outside of such jurisdiction." In the course of his opinion, Justice Peckham forthrightly announced the principle that the right to make contracts was a part of the liberty guaranteed by the Due Process Clause:

> The liberty mentioned in the [Fourteenth] Amendment means not only the right of the citizen to be free from the mere physical restraint of his person, as by incarceration, but the term is deemed to embrace the right of the citizen to be free in the enjoyment of all his faculties; to be free to use them in all lawful ways; to live and work where he will; to earn his livelihood by any lawful calling; to pursue any livelihood or avocation, and for that purpose to enter into all contracts which may be proper, necessary and essential to his carrying out to a successful conclusion the purposes above mentioned.

These substantive due-process arguments received their clearest expression in *Lochner v. New York,* in which the same Justice Peckham, the most libertarian member of the Court, was assigned the writing of the majority opinion and declared that New York had unreasonably and arbitrarily interfered with the "freedom of master and employee to contract with each other in relation to their employment" by passing a law limiting the number of hours a baker could work in a bakery.[9] Finding no valid health or safety reasons that could justify such a law, Peckham ruled that it amounted to an unreasonable deprivation of liberty (i.e., the liberty to contract) and violated the Due Process Clause. Justices John Marshall Harlan and Oliver Wendell Holmes each wrote separate dissents. Justice Harlan agreed with Peckham that there is "a liberty to contract which cannot be violated even under the sanction of direct legislative enactment," but charged the majority with "enlarging the scope of the Amendment far beyond its original purpose" and with "bringing under the supervision of this court matters which have been supposed to belong exclusively to the legislative departments of the several States." Justice Holmes penned one of his most memorable passages: "The Fourteenth Amendment does not enact Mr. Spencer's *Social Statics.* [In this work, Spencer presented an account of the development of human freedom and a defense of individual liberties based on the principles of social Darwinism.] . . . A constitution . . . is made for people of fundamentally differing views."

By embracing the notion of substantive due process, Justice Peckham assumed for the Court the very role that Justice Miller had warned against in *The Slaughter-House Cases:* it made the Court a "perpetual censor," reviewing the reasonableness of state efforts at economic regulation. It continued to play this role at least through *Adkins v. Children's Hospital* (1923), when it branded the District of Columbia's minimum-wage law for women and children "the product of a naked arbitrary exercise of power" and thus a violation of the Fifth Amendment's Due Process Clause. Prior to *Adkins,* the Court rarely played this role to strike down state laws; as Charles Warren made clear in two famous at the time but now largely forgotten articles in the *Columbia Law Review,* the Court had during this entire period upheld more than 90 percent of all due-process challenges to economic legislation by the states.[10] Thus, for example, in *Muller v. Oregon* (1908) and *Bunting v. Oregon* (1917), the justices upheld the constitutionality of state legislation that, respectively, limited the workday for women to ten hours and extended the same maximum-hours limitation to all mill and factory workers. Of decisive importance in both of these decisions, however, was the Court's belief that the regulations in question were a reasonable exercise of the state's police powers—not its post-*Adkins* conviction that any judicial inquiry into the substance or reasonableness of economic legislation was inappropriate.

THE DEMISE OF SUBSTANTIVE DUE PROCESS IN THE ECONOMIC REALM

As the Court's subsequent decision in *Adkins* makes apparent, *Muller* and *Bunting* did not represent a repudiation of substantive due process—in these cases, the Court merely judged that the economic regulations in question were reasonable; it did not conclude that it was inappropriate for the Court to make such judgments in the first place. The disavowal of substantive due process began somewhat later in *Nebbia v. New York* (1934), in which the Court, by a 5–4 vote, upheld the validity of a Depression-era law regulating the price of milk. The New York legislature had sought to prevent ruinous price cutting by establishing a milk control board with power to fix minimum and maximum retail prices, and the appellant claimed that enforcement of the milk price regulations denied him due process of law by preventing him from selling his product at whatever price he desired. In rejecting this claim, Justice Owen Roberts, speaking for the majority, declared, "So far as the requirement of due process is concerned, and in the absence of other constitutional restrictions, a state is free to adopt whatever economic policy may reasonably be deemed to promote public welfare, and to enforce that policy by legislation adapted to its purpose. The courts are without authority either to declare such policy, or, when it is declared by the legislature, to override it."

What was begun in *Nebbia* was completed in *West Coast Hotel Company v. Parrish* (1937). This case arose under a Washington State minimum-wage law that had been passed in 1913 and enforced continuously thereafter, quite irrespective of *Adkins.* In the midst of the intense political controversy generated by President Franklin Roosevelt's Court-packing plan, the Court upheld the law. Chief Justice Charles Evans Hughes insisted that the state legislature had the right to use its minimum-wage requirements to help implement its policy of protecting women from exploitative employers. He noted that "the adoption of similar requirements by many States evidences a deepseated conviction both as to the presence of the evil and as to the means adopted to check it. Legislative response to that conviction cannot be regarded as arbitrary or capricious, and that is all we have to decide." The chief justice then went even further: "Even if the wisdom of the policy is regarded as debatable and its effects uncertain, still the legislature is entitled to its judgment."

The Court's refusal in *Parrish* to contradict the judgment of the legislature on economic matters and its outright repudiation of substantive due process in the economic realm through its explicit overruling of *Adkins* remain controlling precedents. Subsequent decisions, in fact, suggest a reluctance to subject economic legislation to any constitutional test at all.[11] *Day-Brite Lighting v. Missouri* (1952) provides a clear example of this trend. In reviewing a state law that provided that employees could absent themselves from their jobs for four hours on election days and forbade employers from deducting wages for their absence, the Court admitted that the social policy embodied in the law was debatable but pointed out that "our recent decisions make plain that we do not sit as a superlegislature to weigh the wisdom of legislation nor to decide whether the policy it expresses offends the public welfare." This argument was repeated in *Williamson v. Lee Optical Company* (1955), which involved a statute that forbade any person but an ophthalmologist or an optometrist from fitting lenses to the face or duplicating or replacing lenses into frames, except on the prescription of an ophthalmologist or optometrist. After acknowledging that the law was "a needless, wasteful requirement in many cases," the Court went on to insist that "the day is gone" when it would strike down "state laws regulatory of business and industrial conditions, because they may be unwise, improvident, or out of harmony with a particular school of thought." Eight years later, in *Ferguson v. Skrupa* (1963), the Court applied the same reasoning in upholding a Kansas statute prohibiting anyone except lawyers from engaging in the business of debt adjustment, with Justice Hugo Black noting in his majority opinion that "it is up to legislatures, not courts, to decide on the wisdom and utility of legislation." The *Ferguson* opinion elicited some judicial protests, however. Despite his abiding commitment to judicial self-restraint, Justice John Harlan felt compelled to protest against what he perceived to be judicial abdication. In his concurrence, he insisted that even economic legislation must bear "a rational relation to a constitutionally permissible objective"—a relationship that he found to exist in the instant case.

PUNITIVE DAMAGES: AN EXCEPTION TO THE DEMISE OF SUBSTANTIVE DUE PROCESS IN THE ECONOMIC REALM?

Justice Black's words in *Ferguson,* echoing as they do Chief Justice Waite's opinion in *Munn v. Illinois,* highlight the full circle traveled by the Court in its consideration of the Due Process Clause and economic rights. The spindly due-process leg in *Munn,* which by *Lochner* had grown enormously in size and strength, had lost its muscularity by *Parrish* and atrophied to the spindly leg it once again became by *Williamson.* So it remained, at least until *BMW v. Gore* (1996), which raises the interesting question of whether the Court is not once again embracing substantive due process—if not to limit what legislatures can do, then at least to limit the size of punitive-damages awards that civil juries can impose.

In this case, the plaintiff brought suit in an Alabama court for $500,000 in compensatory and punitive damages against the American distributor of BMWs. He alleged that the failure to disclose that the top, hood, trunk, and quarter panels of the car he had purchased had been repainted at the automobile manufacturer's US vehicle preparation center—the result of damage caused by exposure to acid rain during transit between Germany and United States—constituted fraud under Alabama law. At trial, BMW acknowledged that it followed a nationwide policy of not advising its dealers, and hence its customers, of pre-delivery damage to new cars when the cost of repair did not exceed 3 percent of the car's suggested retail price. The cost of repainting the plaintiff's vehicle was $601.37 (or about 1.5 percent of its $40,750.88 suggested retail price) and therefore fell into that category. The jury returned a verdict finding BMW liable for compensatory damages of $4,000 (its judgment of how much less the plaintiff's car was worth because it had been repainted) and assessing $4 million in punitive damages (its judgment of the appropriate punishment for BMW for selling approximately one thousand repainted cars nationally for approximately $4,000 more than each was worth). The trial judge denied BMW's post-trial motion to set aside the punitive-damages award, holding, among other things, that the award did not violate the Due Process Clause of the Fourteenth Amendment as interpreted in two earlier damages cases: *Pacific Mutual Insurance Co. v. Haslip* (1991) and *TXO Production Corp. v.*

Alliance Resources Corp. (1993). The Alabama Supreme Court agreed, but it reduced the award to $2 million on the grounds that, in computing the amount, the jury had improperly multiplied Gore's compensatory damages by the number of similar sales in all states.

The Supreme Court, however, reversed the Alabama Supreme Court and held that the Due Process Clause of the Fourteenth Amendment prohibits a state from imposing punitive-damages awards that are "grossly excessive"—in this instance, a punitive-damages award that was five hundred times compensatory damages. Justice Stevens for a five-member majority identified three "guideposts" that led the Court to the conclusion that the Alabama courts had entered "the zone of arbitrariness" and deprived the defendant of "elementary notions of fairness": the degree of reprehensibility of the defendant's conduct, the ratio between the punitive award and the plaintiff's actual harm, and the difference between the courts' sanction and legislative sanctions authorized for comparable misconduct. In his dissent, Justice Antonin Scalia complained that these guideposts "mark a road to nowhere; they provide no real guidance at all." He observed that "the elevation of 'fairness' in punishment to a principle of 'substantive due process' means that every punitive award unreasonably imposed is unconstitutional; such an award is by definition excessive, since it attaches a penalty to conduct undeserving of punishment." He drew out the consequences: "If the Court is correct, it must be that every claim that a state jury's award of compensatory damages is 'unreasonable' (because not supported by the evidence) amounts to an assertion of constitutional injury. . . . By today's logic, every dispute as to evidentiary sufficiency in a state civil suit poses a question of constitutional moment, subject to review in this Court. That is a stupefying proposition." Justice Ruth Bader Ginsburg was in fundamental agreement; in her dissent, she likewise objected to the way in which the majority "leads us into territory traditionally within the States' domain" with "only a vague concept of substantive due process, a 'raised eyebrow' test, as its ultimate guide."

Several years passed before *BMW v. Gore* figured prominently in a subsequent Supreme Court opinion, allowing for speculation to develop over whether it was the beginning of a renewed judicial infatuation with substantive due process in the economic realm or whether it was merely an isolated, if provocative, exception. However, with its decision in *State Farm Mutual Automobile Insurance Company v. Campbell* (2003), the Court made it clear that *Gore* was no exception. In *Campbell,* the Court applied the three "guideposts" from *Gore* and held that an award of $145 million in punitive damages, where full compensatory damages were $1 million, was excessive and violated due process. Justice Kennedy for the six-member majority went so far as to argue that "few awards exceeding a single-digit ratio between punitive and compensatory damages . . . will satisfy due process." Justice Ginsburg in her dissent accused him of acting like a legislator rather than a judge when he suggested that if "compensatory damages are substantial, then a lesser ratio, perhaps only equal to compensatory damages, can reach the outermost limit of the due process guarantee."

Punitive-damages cases typically raise substantive due-process questions, but *Caperton v. Massey Coal Company* (2009) raised a procedural due-process question. A West Virginia jury returned a verdict that found the Massey Coal Company fraudulently liable in a coal contract dispute and awarded Caperton $50 million in compensatory and punitive damages. After the verdict but before the appeal, West Virginia held its 2004 judicial elections, in which Don Blankenship (Massey's chairman, chief executive officer, and president) supported Brent Benjamin, who successfully challenged Justice Warren McGraw, a member of the West Virginia Supreme Court, who was running for reelection. In addition to contributing the $1,000 statutory maximum to Benjamin's campaign committee, Blankenship donated almost $2.5 million to an independent political organization that opposed McGraw and supported Benjamin and spent more than $500,000 on independent expenditures—for direct mailings and letters soliciting donations as well as television and newspaper advertisements—in support of Benjamin's candidacy. When Massey's appeal was heard by the West Virginia Supreme Court, Justice Brent Benjamin refused to recuse himself—when challenged, he insisted that there was no "objective evidence" of bias on his part but merely a "subjective belief"—and joined the Court majority in a 3–2 decision overturning the jury's verdict and award. In a 5–4 decision, the US Supreme Court held in an opinion by Justice Kennedy that in this "extraordinary" case, the Due Process Clause required recusal whether or not actual bias existed or could be proved. Chief Justice Roberts wrote a spirited dissent, raising forty unanswered questions that Kennedy's opinion "quickly [brought] to mind. Judges and litigants will surely encounter others when they are forced to apply the majority's decision in different circumstances. Today's opinion requires state and federal judges simultaneously to act as political scientists (why did candidate X win the election?), economists (was the financial support disproportionate?), and psychologists (is there likely to be a debt of gratitude?)."

THE EMERGENCE OF SUBSTANTIVE DUE PROCESS IN THE CIVIL LIBERTIES REALM

With the possible exception of the Court's punitive-damages jurisprudence, what can be said with certainty is that the Court, for whatever reason, has not embraced substantive due process simultaneously in both the economic and the civil liberties realms. When substantive due process was at its height in the economic realm in the early part of the twentieth century, it was nonexistent in the realm of civil liberties, as *Buck v. Bell* (1927) makes abundantly clear.

In *Buck* the Court denied a substantive due-process objection to a 1924 Virginia statute that, on the grounds of the "health of the patient and the welfare of society," provided for the sexual sterilization of inmates of institutions supported by the state who were found to be afflicted with hereditary forms of insanity or imbecility. The preamble of the Virginia statute declared that the commonwealth was supporting in various institutions many "defective persons" who, if discharged, would become a menace, but who, if rendered incapable of procreating, might be discharged with safety and become self-supporting, with benefits both to themselves and to society; it also declared that experience had shown that "heredity plays an important part in the transmission of insanity, imbecility, etc." Justice Holmes upheld the sterilization of Carrie Buck, whom he described as a "feeble minded white woman," "the daughter of a feeble minded mother," and herself "the mother of an illegitimate feeble minded child." He argued first that the statute met all the requirements of procedural due process: "There can be no doubt that, so far as procedure is concerned, the rights of the patient are most carefully considered, and, as every step in this case was taken in scrupulous compliance with the statute and after months of observation, there is no doubt that, in that respect, the plaintiff in error has had due process of law." But, he noted, Carrie Buck also objected on substantive due-process grounds: "The attack is [also] upon the substantive law. It seems to be contended that in no circumstances could such an order be justified." The Court, however, was unpersuaded, and so, just four years after it had found in *Adkins* that a minimum-wage law for women and children was "the product of a naked arbitrary exercise of power," it held that Virginia's eugenics-inspired statute passed constitutional muster. Justice Holmes wrote for an eight-member majority (Justice Butler dissented but did not write an opinion) when he declared:

> We have seen more than once that the public welfare may call upon the best citizens for their lives. It would be strange if it could not call upon those who already

sap the strength of the State for these lesser sacrifices, often not felt to be such by those concerned, in order to prevent our being swamped with incompetence. It is better for all the world if, instead of waiting to execute degenerate offspring for crime or to let them starve for their imbecility, society can prevent those who are manifestly unfit from continuing their kind. The principle that sustains compulsory vaccination is broad enough to cover cutting the Fallopian tubes. Three generations of imbeciles are enough.[12]

At about the time that the Court was abandoning the protection of economic rights by substantive due process, it was beginning to embrace the concept to protect civil rights. The contemptuous disregard for the civil rights of Carrie Buck was soon replaced by a particular judicial solicitude for the rights of "discrete and insular minorities." In footnote 4 of the Court's opinion in *United States v. Carolene Products Company* (1938), decided just one year after its repudiation of substantive due process in the economic realm in *West Coast Hotel v. Parrish,* Justice Harlan Fiske Stone outlined a justification for "more exacting judicial scrutiny" where infringements of civil liberties were involved. The Court's subsequent embrace of substantive due process in the realm of civil liberties is a major theme in Volume II.

THE TAKINGS CLAUSE

Just as the Due Process Clause supplanted the Contract Clause as a means of protecting property rights, so, too, the Takings Clause of the Fifth Amendment as made applicable to the states by the Fourteenth Amendment appears to have supplanted due process. It states that private property shall not "be taken for public use, without just compensation." This language tacitly recognizes the inherent power of eminent domain of the federal and state governments; as the Court said in *Boom Co. v. Patterson* (1879), this power "appertains to every independent government. It requires no constitutional recognition; it is an attribute of sovereignty."

Prior to the adoption of the Fourteenth Amendment, the power of eminent domain of state governments was unrestrained by any federal authority. In *Barron v. Baltimore* (1833), the Court held that the just compensation provision of the Fifth Amendment did not apply to the states. In *Chicago, Burlington & Quincy Railroad Co. v. Chicago* (1897), however, the Court embraced the argument that the Due Process Clause of the Fourteenth Amendment afforded property owners the same measure of protection against the states as the Fifth Amendment did against the federal government. It ruled that, although a state "legislature may prescribe a form of procedure to be observed in the taking of private property for public use, . . . it is not due process of law if provision be not made for compensation. . . . The mere form of the proceeding instituted against the owner . . . cannot convert the process used into due process of law, if the necessary result be to deprive him of his property without compensation." Although the federal and state guarantees of just compensation flow from different sources, the standards used by the Court in dealing with the issues appear to be identical, whether they arise in federal or state cases.

The decision to condemn or expropriate private property for public use upon just compensation of the owner is a legislative one, and, over time, the Court has become increasingly reluctant to question whether the confiscated property has been taken for a "public use." Initially, the courts considered the term *public use* to be synonymous with *use by the public,* and they held the exercise of the power of eminent domain to be invalid if the property taken was conveyed to private individuals instead of being used, for example, for the construction of roads, schools, or parks. Beginning with *Clark v. Nash* (1905), however, the Supreme Court began to equate public use with any use conducive of the public interest or public welfare. The result has been that the public-use limitation on governments' power of eminent domain no longer limits the uses for which governments can take private property.

In *Clark* the Supreme Court held that Utah could authorize by statute an individual to condemn a right-of-way across his neighbor's land for the enlargement of an irrigation ditch, thereby enabling him to obtain water from a stream to irrigate his land, which otherwise would remain absolutely valueless. The Court held that "the validity of such statutes may sometimes depend upon many different facts, the existence of which would make a public use, even by an individual, where, in the absence of such facts, the use would clearly be private." The facts present in this case that convinced the Court that Utah's condemnation statute served the public interest—and therefore a public use—were the "climate and soil" of the "arid and mountainous States of the West" and the recognition by these states that "the cultivation of an otherwise valueless soil, by means of irrigation," was "absolutely necessary" for their "growth and prosperity."

Applying its equation of public use with the exercise of the police power in furtherance of the public interest, the Court has approved the widespread use of the power of eminent domain by federal and state governments in conjunction with private companies to facilitate urban renewal, destruction of slums, erection of low-cost housing in place of deteriorated housing, and the promotion of aesthetic values as well as economic ones. The leading modern case in this field is *Berman v. Parker* (1954). In it, the Court sustained a federal statute for the District of Columbia granting its redevelopment agency the power to acquire privately owned land in blighted areas by the use of eminent domain to eliminate slum and substandard housing conditions and to resell that land to other private individuals subject to conditions designed to accomplish these purposes. A unanimous Court held that the judiciary's role in determining whether eminent domain is being used for a public purpose "is an extremely narrow one." Courts must defer to the legislature on questions of eminent domain no less than on all other exercises of the police power: "When the legislature has spoken, the public interest has been declared in terms well-nigh conclusive. In such cases, the legislature, not the judiciary, is the main guardian of the public needs to be served by social legislation."

Against the argument that the taking of an individual's property merely to develop a better-balanced, more attractive community was not a proper public use, Justice William O. Douglas in *Berman v. Parker* declared that the values that governments can pursue in their exercise of eminent domain "are spiritual as well as physical, aesthetic as well as monetary. It is within the power of the legislature to determine that the community should be beautiful as well as healthy, spacious as well as clean, well-balanced as well as carefully patrolled. . . . If those who govern the District of Columbia decide that the Nation's Capital should be beautiful as well as sanitary, there is nothing in the Fifth Amendment that stands in the way." And against the argument that there is no public use involved when government takes the private property of one individual only to sell it in turn to another, the Court again showed its deference to the legislative branches: not only is the power of eminent domain "merely the means to the end," "but the means of executing the project are for Congress and Congress alone to determine, once the public purpose has been established."

Under the extraordinarily deferential standard laid down in *Berman v. Parker,* eminent domain can be exercised to achieve anything that is otherwise within the power of the legislature. *Hawaii Housing Authority v. Midkiff* (1984) and *Kelo v. City of New London* (2005) are the most important recent examples. In *Midkiff,* the Supreme Court unanimously upheld Hawaii's use of its power of eminent domain to acquire property from large landowners and transfer it to lessees living on single-family residential lots on the land. The purpose of this land-condemnation scheme was to reduce the concentration of landownership, and Justice O'Connor declared for a unanimous Court that "our cases make clear that empirical debates over the wisdom of takings—no less than debates over the wisdom of other kinds of socioeconomic legislation—are not to be carried out in the federal courts." And in *Kelo,* a sharply divided Court upheld the use of eminent domain for economic-development purposes in language so sweeping that Justice O'Connor, this time in dissent, declared that it had "effectively delete[d] the words 'for public use' from the Takings Clause."

The Takings Clause requires not only a "public use" for the property that is taken but also "just compensation" to the owner. *Just compensation* was defined by the Court in *Monongahela Navigation Co. v. United States* (1893) as "a full and perfect equivalent for the property taken." This has come to mean the market value of the property—that is, what a willing buyer would pay a willing seller. Because property is ordinarily taken under a condemnation suit upon the payment of the money award by the condemner, no interest accrues. However, if the property is taken in fact before payment is made, the courts have held that just compensation requires the payment of interest.

At its simplest, just compensation requires that, if real property is condemned, the market value of that property must be paid to the owner. Things, however, are seldom that simple: the many kinds of property and many uses of property cause problems in computing just compensation. For example, if only a portion of a tract of land is taken, the owner's compensation is to include any element of value arising out of the relation of the part taken to the entire tract, unless the taking has in fact benefited the owner, in which case the benefit may be subtracted from the value of the land condemned (even then, however, any benefit that the owner receives in common with everyone else from the public use to which the property is appropriated may not be subtracted). Moreover, the Court held in *Horne v. Department of Agriculture* (2015) that the Takings Clause and its requirement that the government pay just compensation "when it 'physically takes possession of an interest in property'" applies equally to both real property and personal property. As Chief Justice Roberts pithily explained it: "The Government has a categorical duty to pay just compensation when it takes your car, just as when it takes your home." At issue in *Horne* was the US Department of Agriculture's California Raisin Marketing Order, which required raisin growers to give a percentage of their crop to the government, free of charge (in 2002–2003, it ordered raisin growers to turn over 47 percent of their crop) to help maintain a stable raisin market. An eight-member majority held that the Takings Clause barred the government from imposing such a demand on growers without just compensation.

The courts have long held that legislatures are free to decide on the nature and character of the tribunals that determine compensation; as a consequence, they may be regular courts, special legislative courts, commissions, or administrative bodies. Proceedings to condemn land for the benefit of the United States are brought in the federal district court for the district in which the land is located.

When a government itself initiates a condemnation proceeding against someone's property, the question of whether that property has been "taken," with the consequent requirement of just compensation, does not arise. However, questions of whether there has been a taking do arise when physical damage results to property because of government action or when regulatory action limits activity on the property or otherwise deprives it of value.

In *Pumpelly v. Green Bay Co.* (1872), the Court determined that land can be "taken" in the constitutional sense by physical invasion or occupation by the government, as occurs when government floods land. More recently, it held in *Griggs v. Allegheny County* (1962) that operators of airports are required to compensate the owners of adjacent land when the noise, glare, and fear of injury occasioned by the low-altitude overflights during takeoffs and landings made the land unfit for the use to which the owners had applied it. Cases such as these, where the government has not instituted formal condemnation proceedings but instead property owners have sued for just compensation claiming that governmental action or regulation has "taken" their property, are described as "inverse condemnation."

Regulation may also deprive owners of most or all beneficial use of their property or may destroy the value of the property for the purposes to which it is suited. Does such regulation also constitute a taking? Initially, the Court flatly denied the possibility of compensation for this diminution of property values; however, in *Pennsylvania Coal Co. v. Mahon* (1922), it established as a general principle that "if regulation goes too far it will be recognized as a taking." But how far is "too far"?

Although the Court confessed in *Penn Central Transportation Co. v. City of New York* (1978) that it had failed to develop a "set formula to determine where regulation ends and taking begins," it has responded to increasing governmental regulation of property over the years—in terms of zoning and land-use controls, environmental regulations, and so on— by formulating general principles for determining whether a regulatory taking has occurred. One guideline had already been announced in *Armstrong v. United States* (1960): the regulation cannot force "some people alone to bear public burdens which, in all fairness and justice, should be borne by the public as a whole." Applying that guideline in *Nollan v. California Coastal Commission* (1987), Justice Scalia declared that, even if the California Coastal Commission was right in its belief that the public interest would be served by a continuous strip of publicly accessible beach along the coast, "that does not establish that the Nollans alone can be compelled to contribute to its realization" by requiring them to provide a public-access easement across their property as a condition for obtaining a building permit. The commission was free to serve this public interest, if it wished, "by using its power of eminent domain for this 'public purpose,'" but, Scalia insisted, if it wanted "an easement across the Nollans' property, it must pay for it."

Among the members of the Rehnquist Court, Justice Scalia was the most willing to enforce this guideline. Thus, in *Pennell v. City of San Jose* (1988), a case involving a rent-control ordinance that allowed administrative reductions on rent in case of "tenant hardship," Justice Scalia dissented from Chief Justice Rehnquist's majority decision that the case was not ripe for judicial resolution, reached the merits on the hardship provision, and expanded on the themes he had advanced in *Nollan*. He denied the landlords were the cause of the problem at which the hardship provision was aimed. Rather, he insisted that the provision was drafted "to meet a quite different social problem: the existence of some renters who are too poor to afford even reasonably priced housing. But that problem is no more caused or exploited by landlords than it is by the grocers who sell needy renters their food, or the department stores that sell them their clothes, or the employers who pay them their wages, or the citizens of San Jose holding the higher-paying jobs from which they are excluded." Moreover, Scalia continued, "Even if the neediness of renters could be regarded as a problem distinctively attributable to landlords in general, it is not remotely attributable to the particular landlords that the ordinance singles out—namely, those who happen to have a 'hardship' tenant at the present time, or who may happen to rent to a 'hardship' tenant in the future, or whose current or future affluent tenants may happen to decline into the 'hardship' category." He then delivered his primary point: "The fact that government acts through the landlord-tenant relationship does not magically transform general public welfare, which must be supported by all the public, into mere 'economic regulation,' which can disproportionately burden particular individuals."

Other guidelines have followed in the wake of *Thompson*. A second was spelled out in *Penn Central* itself: courts must consider the "economic impact of the regulation on the claimant and, particularly, the extent to which the regulation has interfered with reasonable investment-backed expectations."

A third guideline, announced in *Loretto v. Teleprompter Manhattan CATV Corp.* (1982), addresses physical invasions: when government permanently occupies or authorizes someone else to occupy property, the action constitutes a taking, and compensation must be paid regardless of the public interests served by the occupation or the extent of damage to the parcel as a whole. In that case, the Supreme Court held that a New York statute requiring landlords to allow television cable companies to install cable facilities in their apartment buildings constituted a taking, even though the facilities occupied no more than one and a half cubic feet of the landlords' property.

A fourth guideline was spelled out by the Court in *Agins v. City of Tiburon* (1980): a land-use regulation must "substantially advance legitimate governmental interests." Also applying that guideline in *Nollan,* Justice Scalia held for a five-member majority that the California Coastal Commission's extraction from the Nollans of a public-access easement across a strip of their beachfront property as a condition for obtaining a permit to enlarge their beachfront home did not "substantially advance" the state's legitimate interest in preserving the public's view of the beach from the street in front of the lot.

A fifth guideline was also announced in *Agins*: the regulation cannot deny a property owner "economically viable use of his land." The Court elaborated on this guideline in *Lucas v. South Carolina Coastal Council* (1992), a case in which a landowner was deprived of all "economically viable use" of his $1 million property when the state passed a coastal zone act, designed to prevent beach erosion, that prevented him from building a beachfront home on his property: "When the owner of real property has been called upon to sacrifice all economically beneficial uses in the name of the common good, that is, to leave his property economically idle, he has suffered a taking."

A sixth guideline was provided by the Court in *Tahoe-Sierra Preservation Council v. Tahoe Regional Planning Agency* (2002). In it, the Court held that no compensation is due to property owners who are temporarily deprived of all economically viable use of their land through, as in this case, the imposition of moratoriums on development imposed by governmental agencies during the process of drafting a comprehensive land-use plan.

And, a seventh guideline was articulated in *Dolan v. City of Tigard* (1994): local governmental agencies may not condition the approval of land-use permits on owners' relinquishment of a portion of their property unless there is a "nexus" and "rough proportionality" between the government's demand and the effects of the proposed land use. In *Dolan,* Chief Justice Rehnquist declared that "we see no reason why the Takings Clause of the Fifth Amendment, as much a part of the Bill of Rights as the First Amendment or Fourth Amendment, should be relegated to the status of a poor relation" and, upon applying this guideline, concluded that the City of Tigard, Oregon, violated the constitutional rights of Florence Dolan when it held that it would approve her application to expand her plumbing and electric supply store only if she dedicated 10 percent of her land to the city. In *Koontz v. St. John River Water Management District* (2013), the Court held that the government's demand for property from a land-use permit applicant must satisfy this guideline even when the government denies the permit and even when its demand is for money.

NOTES

1. For an especially useful essay on this matter, see Edward S. Corwin, "The Supreme Court and the Fourteenth Amendment," *Michigan Law Review* 7 (June 1909): 643.

2. See Raoul Berger, *Government by Judiciary: The Transformation of the Fourteenth Amendment* (Cambridge, MA: Harvard University Press, 1977); Jacobus Tenbroek, *Equal Under Law* (New York:

Macmillan, 1965); Alexander M. Bickel, "The Original Understanding and the Segregation Decision," *Harvard Law Review* 69, no. 1 (1955); Charles Fairman, "Does the Fourteenth Amendment Incorporate the Bill of Rights?" *Stanford Law Review* 2, no. 1 (1949); William W. Van Alstyne, "The Fourteenth Amendment, the 'Right to Vote,' and the Understanding of the Thirty-Ninth

Congress," in *1966 Supreme Court Review,* edited by Philip Kurland (Chicago: University of Chicago Press, 1966); and Alford H. Kelly, "Clio and the Court: An Illicit Love Affair," in *1965 Supreme Court Review,* edited by Philip Kurland (Chicago: University of Chicago Press, 1965).

3. See Corwin, "Supreme Court and the Fourteenth Amendment"; Tenbroek, *Equal Under Law,* 236–238; M. Glenn Abernathy, *Civil Liberties Under the Constitution,* 3rd ed. (New York: Harper and Row, 1977), 32–33; and Berger, *Government by Judiciary,* 18–19.

4. Michael Kent Curtis, "Resurrecting the Privileges and Immunities Clause and Revising the *Slaughter-House Cases* Without Exhuming *Lochner:* Individual Rights and the Fourteenth Amendment," *Boston College Law Review* 38 (December 1966): 105.

5. Unsuccessful attempts to broaden the scope of privileges and immunities include *Hague v. Committee for Industrial Organization* (1939), *Edwards v. California* (1941), and *Oyama v. California* (1948).

6. It could be said that, with respect to the Due Process and Equal Protection Clauses, the Court correctly identified the intentions of the Thirty-Ninth Congress in drafting these clauses and acted accordingly. Given its concurrent construction of the Privileges or Immunities Clause, however, the Court's fidelity to the intentions of the Thirty-Ninth Congress simply served to exacerbate matters and led directly to the development of substantive due process (discussed later). For an excellent treatment of the development of substantive due process, see Eugene W. Hickok and Gary L. McDowell, *Law vs. Justice: Courts and Politics in American Society* (New York: Free Press, 1993), 80–121.

7. The Court accepted without debate the procedural interpretation of due process. For differing views of what due process could have meant, however, see *Dred Scott v. Sandford* (1857), *Hepburn v. Griswold* (1870), and Edward S. Corwin, "Due Process of Law Before the Civil War," pts. 1 and 2, *Harvard Law Review* 24 (March 1911): 366ff.; (April 1911): 460ff.

8. As Justice Comstock put the question: "Do the prohibitions and penalties of the act for the prevention of intemperance, pauperism, and crime pass the utmost boundaries of mere regulation and police, and by their own force, assuming them to be valid and faithfully obeyed and executed, work the essential loss or destruction of the property at which they are aimed? . . . In my judgment, they do plainly work this result."

9. See David E. Bernstein's important recent revisionist book on *Lochner: Rehabilitating* Lochner: *Defending Individual Rights Against Progressive Reform* (Chicago: University of Chicago Press, 2011).

10. Charles Warren, "The Progressiveness of the United States Supreme Court," *Columbia Law Review* 13 (April 1913): 294–313, and "A Bulwark to the State Police Power: The United States Supreme Court," *Columbia Law Review* 13 (December 1913): 667–695.

11. Guy Miller Struve, "The Less-Restrictive-Alternative Principle and Economic Due Process," *Harvard Law Review* 80 (1967): 1463–1488.

12. Carrie Buck also objected on equal-protection grounds. Justice Holmes was equally unpersuaded here:

"But, it is said . . . this reasoning . . . fails when it is confined to the small number who are in the institutions named and is not applied to the multitudes outside. It is the usual last resort of constitutional arguments to point out shortcomings of this sort. But the answer is that the law does all that is needed when it does all that it can, indicates a policy, applies it to all within the lines, and seeks to bring within the lines all similarly situated so far and so fast as its means allow. Of course, so far as the operations enable those who otherwise must be kept confined to be returned to the world, and thus open the asylum to others, the equality aimed at will be more nearly reached."

SELECTED READINGS

Baude, William. "Rethinking the Federal Eminent Domain Power," *Yale Law Journal* 122 (2013): 1738–1825.

Berger, Raoul. *Government by Judiciary: The Transformation of the Fourteenth Amendment.* 2nd ed. Indianapolis: Liberty Fund, 1997.

Burnett, Guy F. *The Safeguard of Liberty and Property: The Supreme Court, Kelo v. New London, and the Takings Clause.* Lanham, MD: Lexington Books, 2014.

Chapman, Nathan S., and Michael W. McConnell, "Due Process as Separation of Powers," *Yale Law Journal* 121 (2012): 1672–1807.

Curtis, Michael Kent. "Resurrecting the Privileges and Immunities Clause and Revising the *Slaughter-House Cases* Without Exhuming *Lochner:* Individual Rights and the Fourteenth Amendment." *Boston College Law Review* 38 (December 1996): 1–106.

Eagle, Steven J. "Property Tests, Due Process Tests, and Regulatory Takings Jurisprudence." *Brigham Young University Law Review* (2007): 899–958.

Easterbrook, Frank H. "Substance and Due Process." In *1982 Supreme Court Review*, edited by Philip B. Kurland, Gerhard Casper, and Dennis Hutchinson. Chicago: University of Chicago Press, 1983.

Epstein, Richard A. *Takings: Property and the Power of Eminent Domain*. Cambridge, MA: Harvard University Press, 1985.

Kitch, Edmund W., and Clara Ann Bowler. "The Facts of *Munn v. Illinois*." In *1978 Supreme Court Review*, edited by Philip B. Kurland and Gerhard Casper. Chicago: University of Chicago Press, 1979.

Krauss, Michael J. "Punitive Damages and the Supreme Court: A Tragedy in Five Acts." In *2006–2007 Supreme Court Economic Review*. Washington, DC: Cato Institute, 2007.

Labbe, Ronald M., and Jonathan Lurie, The Slaughterhouse Cases: *Regulation, Reconstruction, and the Fourteenth Amendment*. Lawrence: University Press of Kansas, 2005.

McCloskey, Robert. "Economic Due Process and the Supreme Court: An Exhumation and Reburial." In *1962 Supreme Court Review*, edited by Philip B. Kurland. Chicago: University of Chicago Press, 1962.

Nelson, William E. *The Fourteenth Amendment: From Political Principle to Judicial Doctrine*. Cambridge, MA: Harvard University Press, 1988.

Porter, Mary Cornelia. "That Commerce Shall Be Free: A New Look at the Old Laissez-Faire Court." In *1976 Supreme Court Review*, edited by Philip B. Kurland. Chicago: University of Chicago Press, 1977.

Siegan, Bernard H. *Economic Liberties and the Constitution*. Chicago: University of Chicago Press, 1981.

Smith, Douglas G. "The Privileges and Immunities Clause of Article IV, Section 2: Precursor of Section 1 of the Fourteenth Amendment." *San Diego Law Review* 34 (May–June 1997): 809–857.

Somin, Ilya. *The Grasping Hand:* Kelo v. City of New London *and the Limits of Eminent Domain*. Chicago: University of Chicago Press, 2015.

Zuckert, Michael P. "Congressional Power Under the Fourteenth Amendment: The Original Understanding of Section Five." *Constitutional Commentary* 3 (1986): 123–147.

The Slaughter-House Cases
83 U.S. (16 Wallace) 36 (1873)

In 1869, the Louisiana Legislature passed an act designed to "protect the health of the City of New Orleans" by granting to the Crescent City Live-Stock Landing and Slaughter-House Company a twenty-five-year monopoly on the sheltering and slaughtering of animals in the city and surrounding parishes. The law required that all other butchers in the New Orleans area come to that company and pay for the use of its abattoir. Although the law was in response to a cholera epidemic and represented an attempt to end contamination of the city's water supply caused by the dumping of refuse into the Mississippi River by small independent slaughterhouses, the state legislature at the time was dominated by carpetbagger elements, and charges of corruption were rampant. The Butchers' Benevolent Association, a group of small, independent slaughterers who had been deprived of their livelihood by the legislation, challenged the act on the grounds that it violated the Thirteenth Amendment and the Privileges or Immunities, Due Process, and Equal Protection Clauses of the Fourteenth Amendment. A state district court and the Louisiana Supreme Court upheld the legislation, at which point this case, along with two others involving the same controversy, was brought to the United States Supreme Court on a writ of error. These three cases have come to be known simply as The Slaughter-House Cases. *Opinion of the Court:* Miller, *Clifford, Davis, Strong, Hunt. Dissenting opinions:* Field, *Chase, Swayne, Bradley;* Bradley; *Swayne.*

JUSTICE MILLER delivered the opinion of the Court.

The plaintiffs in error . . . allege that the statute is a violation of the Constitution of the United States in these several particulars:

That it creates an involuntary servitude forbidden by the thirteenth article of amendment;

That it abridges the privileges and immunities of citizens of the United States;

That it denies to the plaintiffs the equal protection of the laws; and,

That it deprives them of their property without due process of law; contrary to the provisions of the first section of the fourteenth article of amendment. This court is thus called upon for the first time to give construction to these articles.

. . . In the light of . . . recent . . . history, . . . and on the most casual examination of the language of these amendments, no one can fail to be impressed with the one pervading purpose found in them all, lying at the foundation of each, and without which none of them would have been even suggested; we mean the freedom of the slave race, the security and firm establishment of that freedom, and the protection of the newly made freeman and citizen from the oppressions of those who had formerly exercised unlimited dominion over him. . . .

We do not say that no one else but the negro can share in this protection. . . . But what we do say, and what we wish to be understood is, that in any fair and just construction of any section or phrase of these amendments, it is necessary to look to the purpose which we have said was the pervading spirit of them all, the evil which they were designed to remedy, and the process of continued addition to the Constitution, until that purpose was supposed to be accomplished, as far as constitutional law can accomplish it.

The first section of the fourteenth article, to which our attention is more specially invited, opens with a definition of citizenship—not only citizenship of the United States, but citizenship of the States. . . . "All persons born or naturalized in the United States, and subject to the jurisdiction thereof, are citizens of the United States and of the State wherein they reside." . . .

It declares that persons may be citizens of the United States without regard to their citizenship of a particular State, and it overturns the *Dred Scott* decision by making all persons born within the United States and subject to its jurisdiction citizens of the United States. . . . Not only may a man be a citizen of the United States without being a citizen of a State, but an important element is necessary to convert the former into the latter. He must reside within the State to make him a citizen of it, but it is only necessary that he should be born or naturalized in the United States to be a citizen of the Union.

It is quite clear, then, that there is a citizenship of the United States, and a citizenship of a State, which are distinct from each other, and which depend upon different characteristics or circumstances in the individual.

We think this distinction and its explicit recognition in this amendment of great weight in this argument, because the next paragraph of this same section, which is the one mainly relied on by the plaintiffs in error, speaks only of privileges and immunities of citizens of the United States, and does not speak of those of citizens of the several States. The argument, however, in favor of the plaintiffs rests wholly on the assumption that the citizenship is the same, and the privileges and immunities guaranteed by the Clause are the same.

The language is, "No State shall make or enforce any law which shall abridge the privileges or immunities of citizens of the United States." It is a little remarkable, if this clause was intended as a protection to the citizen of a State against the legislative power of his own State, that the word citizen of the State should be left out when it is so carefully used, and used in contradistinction to citizens of the United States, in the very sentence which precedes it. It is too clear for argument that the change in phraseology was adopted understandingly and with a purpose.

Of the privileges and immunities of the citizen of the United States, and of the privileges and immunities of the citizen of the State, and what they respectively are, we will presently consider; but we wish to state here that it is only the former which are placed by this clause under the protection of the Federal Constitution, and that the latter, whatever they may be, are not intended to have any additional protection by this paragraph of the amendment.

If, then, there is a difference between the privileges and immunities belonging to a citizen of the United States as such, and those belonging to the citizen of the State as such, the latter must rest for their security and protection where they have heretofore rested; for they are not embraced by this paragraph of the amendment.

The first occurrence of the words "privileges and immunities" in our constitutional history, is to be found in the fourth of the articles of the old Confederation. It declares "that . . . the free inhabitants of each of these States . . . shall be entitled to all the privileges and immunities of free citizens in the several States." . . .

In the Constitution of the United States, which superseded the Articles of Confederation, the corresponding provision is found in section two of the fourth article, in the following words: "The citizens of each State shall be entitled to all the privileges and immunities of citizens of the several States." . . .

That constitutional provision . . . did not create those rights, which it called privileges and immunities of citizens of the States. It threw around them in that clause no security for the citizen of the State in which they were claimed or exercised. Nor did it profess to control the power of the State governments over the rights of its own citizens.

Its sole purpose was to declare to the several States, that whatever those rights, as you grant or establish them to your own citizens, or as you limit or qualify, or impose restrictions on their exercise, the same, neither more nor less, shall be the measure of the rights of citizens of other States within your jurisdiction.

It would be the vainest show of learning to attempt to prove by citations of authority, that up to the adoption of the recent amendments, no claim or pretence was set up that those rights depended on the Federal government for their existence or protection, beyond the very few express limitations which the Federal Constitution imposed upon the States—such, for instance, as the prohibition against *ex post facto* laws, bills of attainder, and laws impairing the obligation of contracts. But with the exception of these and a few other restrictions, the entire domain of the privileges and immunities of citizens of the States, as above defined, lay within the constitutional and legislative power of the States, and without that of the Federal government. Was it the purpose of the fourteenth amendment, by the simple declaration that no State should make or enforce any law which shall abridge the privileges and immunities of citizens of the United States, to transfer the security and protection of all the civil rights which we have mentioned, from the States to the Federal government? And where it is declared that Congress shall have the power to enforce that article, was it intended to bring within the power of Congress the entire domain of civil rights heretofore belonging exclusively to the States?

All this and more must follow, if the proposition of the plaintiffs in error be sound. For not only are these rights subject to the control of Congress whenever in its discretion, any of them are supposed to be abridged by State legislation, but that body may also pass laws in advance, limiting and restricting the exercise of legislative power by the States, in their most ordinary and usual functions, as in its judgment it may think proper on all such subjects. And still further, such a construction followed by the reversal of the judgments of the Supreme Court of Louisiana in these cases, would constitute this court a perpetual censor upon all legislation of the States, on the civil rights of their own citizens, with authority to nullify such as it did not approve as consistent with those rights, as they existed at the time of the adoption of this amendment. The argument we admit is not always the most conclusive which is drawn from the consequences urged against the adoption of a particular construction of an instrument. But when, as in the case before us, these consequences are so serious, so far-reaching and pervading, so great a departure from the structure and spirit of our institutions; when the effect is to fetter and degrade the State governments by subjecting them to the control of Congress, in the exercise of powers heretofore universally conceded to them of the most ordinary and fundamental character; when in fact it radically changes the whole theory of the relations of the State and Federal governments to each other and of both these governments to the people; the argument has a force that is irresistible, in the absence of language which expresses such a purpose too clearly to admit of doubt.

We are convinced that no such results were intended by the Congress which proposed these amendments, nor by the legislatures of the States which ratified them.

Having shown that the privileges and immunities relied on in the argument are those which belong to citizens of the States as such, and that they are left to the State governments for security and protection, and not by this article placed under the special care of the Federal government, we may hold ourselves excused from defining the privileges and immunities of citizens of the United States which no State can abridge, until some case involving those privileges may make it necessary to do so.

But lest it should be said that no such privileges and immunities are to be found if those we have been considering are excluded, we venture to suggest some which owe their existence to the Federal government, its National character, its Constitution, or its laws. One of these is well described in the case of *Crandall v. Nevada*. It is said to be the right of the citizen of this great country, protected by implied guarantees of its Constitution, "to come to the seat of government to assert any claim he may have upon that government, to transact any business he may have with it, to seek its protection, to share its offices, to engage in administering its functions. He has the right of free access to its seaports, through which all operations of foreign commerce are conducted, to the subtreasuries, land offices, and courts of justice in the several States." . . .

Another privilege of a citizen of the United States is to demand the care and protection of the Federal government over his life, liberty, and property when on the high seas or within the jurisdiction of a foreign government. Of this there can be no doubt, nor that the right depends upon his character as a citizen of the United States. The right to peaceably assemble and petition for redress of grievances, the privilege of the writ of *habeas corpus*, are rights of the citizen guaranteed by the Federal Constitution. The right to use the navigable waters of the United States, however they may penetrate the territory of the several States, all rights secured to our citizens by treaties with foreign nations, are dependent upon citizenship of the United States, and not citizenship of a State. One of these privileges is conferred by the very article under consideration. It is that a citizen of the United States can, of his own volition, become a citizen of any State of the Union by a *bona-fide* residence therein, with the same rights as other citizens of that State. To these may be added the rights secured by the thirteenth and fifteenth articles of amendment, and by the other clause of the fourteenth, next to be considered.

But it is useless to pursue this branch of the inquiry, since we are of opinion that the rights claimed by these plaintiffs in error, if they have any existence, are not privileges and immunities of citizens of the United States within the meaning of the clause of the fourteenth amendment under consideration. . . .

The argument has not been much pressed in these cases that the defendant's charter deprives the plaintiffs of their property without due process of law. . . . We are not without judicial interpretation, . . . both State and National, of the meaning of this clause. And it is sufficient to say that under no construction of that provision that we have ever seen, or any that we deem admissible, can the restraint imposed by the State of Louisiana upon the exercise of their trade by the butchers of New Orleans be held to be a deprivation of property within the meaning of that provision.

"Nor shall any State deny to any person within its jurisdiction the equal protection of the laws." In the light of the history of these amendments, and the pervading purpose of them, which we have already discussed, it is not difficult to give a meaning to this clause. The existence of laws in the States where the newly emancipated negroes resided, which discriminated with gross injustice and hardship against them as a class, was the evil to be remedied by this clause, and by it such laws are forbidden. . . .

The judgments of the Supreme Court of Louisiana in these cases are

Affirmed.

JUSTICE FIELD, dissenting. . . .

The question presented is . . . one of the gravest importance, not merely to the parties here, but to the whole country. It is nothing less than the question whether the recent amendments to the Federal Constitution protect the citizens of the United States against the deprivation of their common rights by State legislation. In my judgment the fourteenth amendment does afford such protection, and was so intended by the Congress which framed and the States which adopted it.

The counsel for the plaintiffs in error have contended, with great force, that the act in question is also inhibited by the thirteenth amendment. . . .

. . . I have been so accustomed to regard it as intended to meet that form of slavery which had previously prevailed in this country, and to which the recent civil war owed its existence, that I was not prepared, nor am I yet, to give to it the extent and force ascribed by counsel. Still it is evident that the language of the amendment is not used in a restrictive sense. It is not confined to African slavery alone. It is general and universal in its application. . . .

It is not necessary, however, . . . to rest my objections to the act in question upon the terms and meaning of the thirteenth amendment. The provisions of the fourteenth amendment, which is properly a supplement to the thirteenth, cover, in my judgment, the case before us, and inhibit any legislation which confers special and exclusive privileges like these under consideration. . . . It first declares that "all persons born or naturalized in the United States, and subject to the jurisdiction thereof, are citizens of the United States and of the State wherein they reside." . . .

. . . It recognizes in express terms, if it does not create, citizens of the United States, and it makes their citizenship dependent upon the place of their birth, or the fact of their adoption, and not upon the constitution or laws of any State or the condition of their ancestry. A citizen of a State is now only a citizen of the United States residing in that State. The fundamental rights, privileges, and immunities which belong to him as a free man and a free citizen, now belong to him as a citizen of the United States, and are not dependent upon his citizenship of any State. . . .

The amendment does not attempt to confer any new privileges or immunities upon citizens, or to enumerate or define those already existing. It assumes that there are such privileges and immunities which belong of right to citizens as such, and ordains that they shall not be abridged by State legislation. If this inhibition has no reference to privileges and immunities of this character, but only refers, as held by the majority of the court in their opinion, to such privileges and immunities as were before its adoption specially designated in the Constitution or necessarily implied as belonging to citizens of the United States, it was a vain and idle enactment, which accomplished nothing, and most unnecessarily excited Congress and the people on its passage. With privileges and immunities thus designated or implied no State could ever have interfered by its laws, and no new constitutional provision was required to inhibit such interference. The supremacy of the Constitution and the laws of the United States always controlled any State legislation of that character. But if the amendment refers to the natural and inalienable rights which belong to all citizens, the inhibition has a profound significance and consequence.

What, then, are the privileges and immunities which are secured against abridgment by State legislation? . . . The terms, privileges and immunities, are not new in the amendment; they were in the Constitution before the amendment was adopted. They are found in the second section of the fourth article, which declares that "the citizens of each State shall be entitled to all privileges and immunities of citizens in the several States," and they have been the subject of frequent consideration in judicial decisions. In *Corfield v. Coryell* (1825), Mr. Justice Washington said he had "no hesitation in confining these expressions to those privileges and immunities which were, in their nature, fundamental; which belong of right to citizens of all free governments, and which have at all times been enjoyed by the citizens of the several States which compose the Union, from the time of their becoming free, independent, and sovereign;" and, in considering what those fundamental privileges were, he said that perhaps it would be more tedious than difficult to enumerate them, but that they might be "all comprehended under the following general heads: protection by the government; the enjoyment of life and liberty, with the right to acquire and possess property of every kind, and to pursue and obtain happiness and safety, subject, nevertheless, to such restraints as the government may justly prescribe for the general good of the whole." This appears to me to be a sound construction of the clause in question. The privileges and immunities designated are those *which of right belong to the citizens of all free governments.* Clearly among these must be placed the right to pursue a lawful employment in a lawful manner, without other restraint than such as equally affects all persons. . . .

What the clause in question did for the protection of the citizens of one State against hostile and discriminating legislation of other States, the fourteenth amendment does for the protection of every citizen of the United States against hostile and discriminating legislation against him in favor of others, whether they reside in the same or in different States. If under the fourth article of the Constitution equality of privileges and immunities is secured between citizens of different States, under the fourteenth amendment the same equality is secured between citizens of the United States. . . .

This equality of right, with exemption from all disparaging and partial enactments, in the lawful pursuits of life, throughout the whole country, is the distinguishing privilege of citizens of the United States. To them, everywhere, all pursuits, all professions, all avocations are open without other restrictions than such as are imposed equally upon all others of the same age, sex, and condition. The State may prescribe such regulations for every pursuit and calling of life as will promote the public health, secure the good order and advance the general prosperity of society, but when once prescribed, the pursuit or calling must be free to be followed by every citizen who is within the conditions designated, and will conform to the regulations. This is the fundamental idea upon which our institutions rest, and unless adhered to in the legislation of the country our government will be a republic only in name. The fourteenth amendment, in my judgment, makes it essential to the validity of the legislation of every State that this equality of right should be respected. . . .

JUSTICE BRADLEY, dissenting. . . .

In my view, a law which prohibits a large class of citizens from adopting a lawful employment, or from following a lawful employment previously adopted, does deprive them of liberty as well as property, without due process of law. Their right of choice is a portion of their liberty; their occupation is their property. Such a law also deprives those citizens of the equal protection of the laws, contrary to the last clause of the section.

It is futile to argue that none but persons of the African race are intended to be benefited by this amendment. They may have been the primary cause of the amendment, but its language is general, embracing all citizens, and I think it was purposely so expressed.

Munn v. Illinois
94 U.S. 113 (1877)

Pursuant to Article XIII of the Illinois Constitution of 1870, which empowered the state legislature to regulate the storage of grain, the Illinois General Assembly enacted a statute in 1871 that required grain warehouses and elevators to obtain operating licenses and established the maximum rates they could charge for the handling and storage of grain. Ira Y. Munn was convicted in county court of operating a grain warehouse without a license and of charging higher rates than those allowed by the law, and he was fined $100. The Illinois Supreme Court affirmed his conviction, and Munn brought the case to the US Supreme Court on a writ of error. Opinion of the Court: Waite, Clifford, Swayne, Miller, Davis, Bradley, Hunt. Dissenting opinions: Field, Strong.

THE CHIEF JUSTICE delivered the opinion of the Court.

The question to be determined in this case is whether the general assembly of Illinois can, under the limitations upon the legislative power of the States imposed by the Constitution of the United States, fix by law the maximum of charges for the storage of grain in warehouses at Chicago and other places in the State. . . .

It is claimed that such a law is repugnant— To that part of Amendment 14 which ordains that no State shall "deprive any person of life, liberty, or property, without due process of law." . . .

The Constitution contains no definition of the word "deprive," as used in the Fourteenth Amendment. To determine its signification, therefore, it is necessary to ascertain the effect which usage has given it, when employed in the same or a like connection.

While this provision of the amendment is new in the Constitution of the United States, as a limitation upon the powers of the States, it is old as a principle of civilized government. It is found in Magna Charta, and, in substance if not in form, in nearly or quite all the constitutions that have been from time to time adopted by the several States of the Union. By the Fifth Amendment, it was introduced into the Constitution of the United States as a limitation upon the powers of the national government, and by the Fourteenth, as a guaranty against any encroachment upon an acknowledged right of citizenship by the legislatures of the States. . . .

When one becomes a member of society, he necessarily parts with some rights or privileges which, as an individual not affected by his relations to others, he might retain. . . . This does not confer power upon the whole people to control rights which are purely and exclusively private, . . . but it does authorize the establishment of laws requiring each citizen to so conduct himself, and so use his own property, as not unnecessarily to injure another. . . . From this source come the police powers. . . . Under these powers the government regulates the conduct of its citizens one towards another, and the manner in which each shall use his own property, when such regulation becomes necessary for the public good. In their exercise it has been customary in England from time immemorial, and in this country from its first colonization, to regulate ferries, common carriers, hackmen, bakers, millers, wharfingers, innkeepers, &c., and in so doing to fix a maximum of charge to be made for services rendered, accommodations furnished, and articles sold. To this day, statutes are to be found in many of the States upon some or all these subjects; and we think it has never yet been successfully contended that such legislation came within any of the constitutional prohibitions against interference with private property. . . .

This brings us to inquire as to the principles upon which this power of regulation rests, in order that we may determine what is within and what without its operative effect. Looking, then, to the common law, from whence came the right which the Constitution protects, we find that when private property is "affected with a public interest, it ceases to be *juris privati* only." This was said by Lord Chief Justice Hale more than two hundred years ago, in his treatise *De Portibus Maris,* . . . and has been accepted without objection as an essential element in the law of property ever since. Property does become clothed with a public interest when used in a manner to make it of public consequence, and affect the community at large. When, therefore, one devotes his property to a use in which the public has an interest, he, in effect, grants to the public an interest in that use, and must submit to be controlled by the public for the common good, to the extent of the interest he has thus created. He may withdraw his grant by discontinuing the use; but, so long as he maintains the use, he must submit to the control. . . .

. . . When private property is devoted to a public use, it is subject to public regulation. It remains only to ascertain whether the warehouses of these plaintiffs in error, and the business which is carried on there, come within the operation of this principle.

. . . It is difficult to see why, if the common carrier, or the miller, or the ferryman, or the innkeeper, or the wharfinger, or the baker, or the cartman, or the hackney-coachman, pursues a public employment and exercises "a sort of public office," these plaintiffs in error do not. They stand . . . in the very "gateway of commerce," and take toll from all who pass. Their business most certainly "tends to a common charge, and is become a thing of public interest and use." Every bushel of grain for its passage "pays a toll, which is a common charge," and, therefore, according to Lord Hale, every such warehouseman "ought to be under public regulation, viz., that he . . . take but reasonable toll." Certainly, if any business can be clothed "with a public interest, and cease to be *juris private* only," this has been. . . .

. . . For our purposes we must assume that, if a state of facts could exist that would justify such legislation, it actually did exist when the statute now under consideration was passed. For us the question is one of power, not of expediency. If no state of circumstances could exist to justify such a statute, then we may declare this one void, because in excess of the legislative power of the State. But if it could, we must presume it did. Of the propriety of legislative interference within the scope of legislative power, the legislature is the exclusive judge. . . .

We know that this is a power which may be abused; but that is no argument against its existence. For protection against abuses by legislatures the people must resort to the polls, not to the courts. . . .

We conclude, therefore, that the statute in question is not repugnant to the Constitution of the United States, and that there is no error in the judgment. . . .

Judgment affirmed.

JUSTICE FIELD, dissenting.

. . . I am compelled to dissent from the decision of the court in this case, and from the reasons upon which that decision is founded. The principle upon which the opinion of the majority proceeds is, in my judgment, subversive of the rights of private property, heretofore believed to be protected by constitutional guaranties against legislative interference. . . .

The question presented . . . is one of the greatest importance,—whether it is within the competency of a State to fix the compensation which an individual may receive for the use of his own property in his private business, and for his services in connection with it. . . .

. . . The court holds that property loses something of its private character when employed in such a way as to be generally useful. The doctrine declared is that property "becomes clothed with a public interest when used in a manner to make it of public consequence, and affect the community at large;" and from such clothing the right of the legislature is deduced to control the use of the property, and to determine the compensation which the owner may receive for it. When Sir Matthew Hale, and the sages of the law in his day, spoke of property as affected by a public interest, and ceasing from that cause to be *juris privati* solely, that is, ceasing to be held merely in private right, they referred to property dedicated by the owner to public uses, or to property the use of which was granted by the government, or in connection with which special privileges were conferred. Unless the property was thus dedicated, or some right bestowed by the government was held with the property, either by specific grant or by prescription of so long a time as to imply a grant originally, the property was not affected by any public interest so as to be taken out of the category of property held in private right. But it is not in any such sense that the terms "clothing property with a public interest" are used in this case. From the nature of the business under consideration—the storage of grain—which, in any sense in which the words can be used, is a private business, in which the public are interested only as they are interested in the storage of other products of the soil, or in articles of manufacture, it is clear that the court intended to declare that, whenever one devotes his property to a business which is useful to the public,—"affects the community at large,"—the legislature can regulate the compensation which the owner may receive for its use, and for his own services in connection with it.

If this be sound law, if there be no protection, either in the principles upon which our republican government is founded, or in the prohibitions of the Constitution against such invasion of private rights, all property and all business in the State are held at the mercy of a majority of its legislature. . . .

. . . It is only where some right or privilege is conferred by the government or municipality upon the owner, which he can use in connection with his property, or by means of which the use of his property is rendered more valuable to him, or he thereby enjoys an advantage over others, that the compensation to be received by him becomes a legitimate matter of regulation. Submission to the regulation of compensation in such cases is an implied condition of the grant, and the State, in exercising its power of prescribing the compensation, only determines the conditions upon which its concession shall be enjoyed. When the privilege ends, the power of regulation ceases.

There is nothing in the character of the business of the defendants as warehousemen which called for the interference complained of in this case. Their buildings are not nuisances; their occupation of receiving and storing grain infringes upon no rights of others, disturbs no neighborhood, infects not the air, and in no respect prevents others from using and enjoying their property as to them may seem best. The legislation in question is nothing less than a bold assertion of absolute power by the State to control at its discretion the property and business of the citizen, and fix the compensation he shall receive. The will of the legislature is made the condition upon which the owner shall receive the fruits of his property and the just reward of his labor, industry, and enterprise. . . . The decision of the court in this case gives unrestrained license to legislative will. . . . I am of opinion that the judgment of the Supreme Court of Illinois should be reversed.

Lochner v. New York
198 U.S. 45 (1905)

Joseph Lochner, a Utica, New York, bakery proprietor, was found guilty and fined $50 for violating an 1897 New York law that limited the hours of employment in bakeries and confectionery establishments to ten hours a day and sixty hours a week. When his conviction was sustained by the New York appellate courts, Lochner brought the case to the Supreme Court on a writ of error. Opinion of the Court: Peckham,

Fuller, Brewer, Brown, McKenna. Dissenting opinions: Harlan, Day, White; Holmes.

JUSTICE PECKHAM delivered the opinion of the Court.

The statute necessarily interferes with the right of contract between the employer and employees, concerning the number of hours in which the latter may labor in the bakery of the employer. The general right to make a contract in relation to his business is part of the liberty of the individual protected by the Fourteenth Amendment of the Federal Constitution. . . . Under that provision no State can deprive any person of life, liberty or property without due process of law. The right to purchase or to sell labor is part of the liberty protected by this amendment, unless there are circumstances which exclude the right. There are, however, certain powers, existing in the sovereignty of each State in the Union, somewhat vaguely termed police powers, the exact description and limitation of which have not been attempted by the courts. Those powers, broadly stated, . . . relate to the safety, health, morals and general welfare of the public. Both property and liberty are held on such reasonable conditions as may be imposed by the governing power of the State in the exercise of those powers, and with such conditions the Fourteenth Amendment was not designed to interfere. . . .

It must, of course, be conceded that there is a limit to the valid exercise of the police power by the State. There is no dispute concerning this general proposition. Otherwise the Fourteenth Amendment would have no efficacy and the legislatures of the States would have unbounded power, and it would be enough to say that any piece of legislation was enacted to conserve the morals, the health or the safety of the people; such legislation would be valid, no matter how absolutely without foundation the claim might be. The claim of the police power would be a mere pretext—become another and delusive name for the supreme sovereignty of the State to be exercised free from constitutional restraint. This is not contended for. In every case that comes before this court, therefore, where legislation of this character is concerned and where the protection of the Federal Constitution is sought, the question necessarily arises: Is this a fair, reasonable and appropriate exercise of the police power of the State, or is it an unreasonable, unnecessary and arbitrary interference with the right of the individual to his personal liberty or to enter into those contracts in relation to labor which may seem to him appropriate or necessary for the support of himself and his family? Of course the liberty of

contract relating to labor includes both parties to it. The one has as much right to purchase as the other to sell labor.

This is not a question of substituting the judgment of the court for that of the legislature. If the act be within the power of the State it is valid, although the judgment of the court might be totally opposed to the enactment of such a law. But the question would still remain: Is it within the police power of the State? and that question must be answered by the court.

The question whether this act is valid as a labor law, pure and simple, may be dismissed in a few words. There is no reasonable ground for interfering with the liberty of person or the right of free contract, by determining the hours of labor, in the occupation of a baker. There is no contention that bakers as a class are not equal in intelligence and capacity to men in other trades or manual occupations, or that they are not able to assert their rights and care for themselves without the protecting arm of the State, interfering with their independence of judgment and of action. They are in no sense wards of the State. Viewed in the light of a purely labor law, with no reference whatever to the question of health, we think that a law like the one before us involves neither the safety, the morals nor the welfare of the public, and that the interest of the public is not in the slightest degree affected by such an act. The law must be upheld, if at all, as a law pertaining to the health of the individual engaged in the occupation of a baker. It does not affect any other portion of the public than those who are engaged in that occupation. Clean and wholesome bread does not depend upon whether the baker works but ten hours per day or only sixty hours a week. . . .

We think the limit of the police power has been reached and passed in this case. There is, in our judgment, no reasonable foundation for holding this to be necessary or appropriate as a health law to safeguard the public health or the health of the individuals who are following the trade of a baker. . . .

We think that there can be no fair doubt that the trade of a baker, in and of itself, is not an unhealthy one to that degree which would authorize the legislature to interfere with the right to labor, and with the right of free contract on the part of the individual, either as employer or employee. In looking through statistics regarding all trades and occupations, it may be true that the trade of a baker does not appear to be as healthy as some other trades, and is also vastly more healthy than still others. . . .

. . . The act is not, within any fair meaning of the term, a health law, but is an illegal interference with the rights of individuals, both employers and employees, to make contracts regarding labor upon such terms as they may think best, or which they may agree upon with the other parties to such contracts. Statutes of the nature of that under review, limiting the hours in which grown and intelligent men may labor to earn their living, are mere meddlesome interferences with the rights of the individual, and they are not saved from condemnation by the claim that they are passed in the exercise of the police power and upon the subject of the health of the individual whose rights are interfered with, unless there be some fair ground, reasonable in and of itself, to say that there is material danger to the public health or to the health of the employees, if the hours of labor are not curtailed. . . .

It was further urged on the argument that restricting the hours of labor in the case of bakers was valid because it tended to cleanliness on the part of the workers, as a man was more apt to be cleanly when not overworked, and if cleanly then his "output" was also more likely to be so. . . . The connection, if any exists, is too shadowy and thin to build any argument for the interference of the legislature. If the man works ten hours a day it is all right, but if ten and a half or eleven his health is in danger and his bread may be unhealthful, and, therefore, he shall not be permitted to do it. This, we think, is unreasonable and entirely arbitrary. . . .

It is manifest to us that the limitation of the hours of labor as provided for in this section of the statute . . . has no such direct relation to and no such substantial effect upon the health of the employee, as to justify us in regarding the section as really a health law. It seems to us that the real object and purpose were simply to regulate the hours of labor between the master and his employees . . . in a private business, not dangerous in any degree to morals or in any

real and substantial degree, to the health of the employees. Under such circumstances the freedom of master and employee to contract with each other in relation to their employment, and in defining the same, cannot be prohibited or interfered with, without violating the Federal Constitution. . . .

Reversed.

JUSTICE HARLAN, with whom JUSTICE WHITE and JUSTICE DAY concur, dissenting.

I take it to be firmly established that what is called the liberty of contract may, within certain limits, be subjected to regulations designed and calculated to promote the general welfare or to guard the public health, the public morals or the public safety. . . .

Granting . . . that there is a liberty of contract which cannot be violated even under the sanction of direct legislative enactment, but assuming, as according to settled law we may assume, that such liberty of contract is subject to such regulations as the State may reasonably prescribe for the common good and the well-being of society, what are the conditions under which the judiciary may declare such regulations to be in excess of legislative authority and void? Upon this point there is no room for dispute; for, the rule is universal that a legislative enactment, Federal or state, is never to be disregarded or held invalid unless it be, beyond question, plainly and palpably in excess of legislative power. . . . If there be doubt as to the validity of the statute, that doubt must therefore be resolved in favor of its validity, and the courts must keep their hands off, leaving the legislature to meet the responsibility for unwise legislation. If the end which the legislature seeks to accomplish be one to which its power extends, and if the means employed to that end, although not the wisest or best, are yet not plainly and palpably unauthorized by law, then the court cannot interfere. In other words, when the validity of a statute is questioned, the burden of proof, so to speak, is upon those who assert it to be unconstitutional. . . . Let these principles be applied to the present case. . . .

It is plain that this statute was enacted in order to protect the physical well-being of those who work in bakery and confectionery establishments. . . . I find it impossible, in view of common experience, to say that there is here no real or substantial relation between the means employed by the State and the end sought to be accomplished by its legislation. . . . Nor can I say that the statute has no appropriate or direct connection with that protection to health which each State owes to her citizens, . . . or that it is not promotive of the health of the employees in question, . . . or that the regulation prescribed by the State is utterly unreasonable and extravagant or wholly arbitrary. . . . Still less can I say that the statute is, beyond question, a plain, palpable invasion of rights secured by the fundamental law. . . . Therefore I submit that this court will transcend its functions if it assumes to annul the statute of New York. It must be remembered that this statute does not apply to all kinds of business. It applies only to work in bakery and confectionery establishments, in which, as all know, the air constantly breathed by workmen is not as pure and healthful as that to be found in some other establishments or out of doors. . . .

. . . There are many reasons of a weighty, substantial character, based upon the experience of mankind, in support of the theory that, all things considered, more than ten hours' steady work each day, from week to week, in a bakery or confectionery establishment, may endanger the health, and shorten the lives of the workmen, thereby diminishing their physical and mental capacity to serve the State, and to provide for those dependent upon them.

If such reasons exist that ought to be the end of this case, for the State is not amenable to the judiciary, in respect of its legislative enactments, unless such enactments are plainly, palpably, beyond all question, inconsistent with the Constitution of the United States. We are not to presume that the state of New York has acted in bad faith. Nor can we assume that its legislature acted without due deliberation, or that it did not determine this question upon the fullest attainable information, and for the common good. We cannot say that the State has acted without reason nor ought we to proceed upon the theory that its action is a mere sham. Our duty, I submit, is to sustain the statute as not being in conflict with the Federal Constitution, for the reason—and such is an all-sufficient reason—it is not shown to be plainly and palpably inconsistent with that instrument. . . .

I take leave to say that the New York statute, in the particulars here involved, cannot be held to be in conflict with the Fourteenth Amendment, without enlarging the scope of the Amendment far beyond its original purpose and without bringing under the supervision of this court matters which have been supposed to belong exclusively to the legislative departments of the several States when exerting their conceded power to guard the health and safety of their citizens by such regulations as they in their wisdom deem best. . . .

JUSTICE HOLMES, dissenting. . . .

This case is decided upon an economic theory which a large part of the country does not entertain. If it were a question whether I agreed with that theory, I should desire to study it further and long before making up my mind. But I do not conceive that to be my duty, because I strongly believe that my agreement or disagreement has nothing to do with the right of a majority to embody their opinions in law. It is settled by various decisions of this court that state constitutions and state laws may regulate life in many ways which we as legislators might think as injudicious or if you like as tyrannical as this, and which equally with this interfere with the liberty to contract. Sunday laws and usury laws are ancient examples. A more modern one is the prohibition of lotteries. . . . The Fourteenth Amendment does not enact Mr. Herbert Spencer's *Social Statics*. . . . A constitution is not intended to embody a particular economic theory, whether of paternalism and the organic relation of the citizen to the State or of *laissez faire*. It is made for people of fundamentally differing views, and the accident of our finding certain opinions natural and familiar or novel and even shocking ought not to conclude our judgment upon the question whether statutes embodying them conflict with the Constitution of the United States.

. . . I think that the word liberty in the Fourteenth Amendment is perverted when it is held to prevent the natural outcome of a dominant opinion, unless it can be said that a rational and fair man necessarily would admit that the statute proposed would infringe fundamental principles as they have been understood by the traditions of our people and our law. It does not need research to show that no such sweeping condemnation can be passed upon the statute before us. A reasonable man might think it a proper measure on the score of health. Men whom I certainly could not pronounce unreasonable would uphold it as a first installment of a general regulation of the hours of work. . . .

West Coast Hotel Company v. Parrish
300 U.S. 379 (1937)

In 1913, the state legislature of Washington enacted a minimum-wage law covering women and minors. The law provided for the establishment of an Individual Welfare Commission, which was authorized "to establish such standards of wages and conditions of labor for women and minors employed within the State of Washington as shall be held hereunder to be reasonable and not detrimental to health and morals, and which shall be sufficient for the decent maintenance of women." Elsie Parrish, employed as a chambermaid by the West Coast Hotel Company, together with her husband brought suit to recover the difference between the wages paid her and the minimum wage fixed pursuant to the state law. The minimum wage for her job was $14.50 for a forty-eight-hour week. The trial court decided against Parrish and declared the law to be repugnant to the Due Process Clause of the Fourteenth Amendment. The Washington Supreme Court reversed the trial court and sustained the statute. The hotel company brought the case to the US Supreme Court on appeal. Opinion of the Court: <u>Hughes</u>, Brandeis, Stone, Roberts, Cardozo. Dissenting opinion: <u>Sutherland</u>, Van Devanter, McReynolds, Butler.

THE CHIEF JUSTICE delivered the opinion of the Court.

This case presents the question of the constitutional validity of the minimum wage law of the State of Washington. . . .

The appellant relies upon the decision of this Court in *Adkins v. Children's Hospital* (1923), which held invalid the District of Columbia Minimum Wage Act, which was attacked under the due process clause of the Fifth Amendment. . . . The state court has refused to regard the decision in the *Adkins* case as determinative and has pointed to our decisions both before and since that case as justifying its position. We are of the opinion that this ruling of the state court demands on our part a reexamination of the *Adkins* case. The importance of the question, in which many States having similar laws are concerned, the close division by which the decision in the *Adkins* case was reached, and the economic conditions which have supervened, and in the light of which the reasonableness of the exercise of the protective power of the State must be considered, make it not only appropriate, but we think imperative, that in deciding the present case the subject should receive fresh consideration. . . .

. . . The violation alleged by those attacking minimum wage regulation for women is deprivation of freedom of contract. What is this freedom? The Constitution does not speak of freedom of contract. It speaks of liberty and prohibits the deprivation of liberty without due process of law. In prohibiting that deprivation the Constitution does not recognize an absolute and uncontrollable liberty. Liberty in each of its phases has its history and connotation. But the liberty safeguarded is liberty in a social organization which requires the protection of law against the evils which menace the health, safety, morals and welfare of the people. Liberty under the Constitution is thus necessarily subject to the restraints of due process, and regulation which is reasonable in relation to its subject and is adopted in the interests of the community is due process.

. . . What can be closer to the public interest than the health of women and their protection from unscrupulous and overreaching employers? And if the protection of women is a legitimate end of the exercise of state power, how can it be said that the requirement of the payment of a minimum wage fairly fixed in order to meet the very necessities of existence is not an admissible means to that end? The legislature of the State was clearly entitled to consider the situation of women in employment, the fact that they are in the class receiving the least pay, that their bargaining power is relatively weak, and that they are the ready victims of those who would take advantage of their necessitous circumstances. The legislature was entitled to adopt measures to reduce the evils of the "sweating system," the exploiting of workers at wages so low as to be insufficient to meet the bare cost of living, thus making their very helplessness the occasion of a most injurious competition. The legislature had the right to consider that its minimum wage requirements would be an important aid in carrying out its policy of protection. The adoption of similar requirements by many States evidences a deepseated conviction both as to the presence of the evil and as to the means adapted to check it. Legislative response to that conviction cannot be regarded as arbitrary or capricious, and that is all we have to decide. Even if the wisdom of the policy be regarded as debatable and its effects uncertain, still the legislature is entitled to its judgment.

There is an additional and compelling consideration which recent economic experience has brought into a strong light. The exploitation of a class of workers who are in an unequal position with respect to bargaining power and are thus relatively defenceless against the denial of a living wage is not only detrimental to their health and well being but casts a direct burden for their support upon the community. What these workers lose in wages the taxpayers are called upon to pay. The bare cost of living must be met. . . . The community is not bound to provide what is in effect a subsidy for unconscionable employers. The community may direct its law-making power to correct the abuse which springs from their selfish disregard of the public interest. . . .

Our conclusion is that the case of *Adkins v. Children's Hospital* . . . should be, and it is, overruled. The judgment of the Supreme Court of the State of Washington is

Affirmed.

JUSTICE SUTHERLAND, dissenting.

It is urged that the question involved should now receive fresh consideration, among other reasons, because of "the economic conditions which have supervened"; but the meaning of the Constitution does not change with the ebb and flow of economic events. We frequently are told in more general words that the Constitution must be construed in the light of the present. If by that it is meant that the Constitution is made up of living words that apply to every new condition which they include, the statement is quite true. But to say, if that be intended, that the words of the Constitution mean today what they did not mean when written—that is, that they do not apply to a situation now to which they would have applied then—is to rob that instrument of the essential element which continues it in force as the people have made it until they, and not their official agents, have made it otherwise. . . .

The judicial function is that of interpretation; it does not include the power of amendment under the guise of interpretation. To miss the point of difference between the two is to miss all that the phrase "supreme law of the land" stands for and to convert what was intended as inescapable and enduring mandates into mere moral reflections. . . .

Coming, then, to a consideration of the Washington statute, it first is to be observed that it is in every substantial respect identical with the statute involved in the *Adkins* case. Such vices as existed in the latter are present in the former. And if the *Adkins* case was properly decided, as we who join in this opinion think it was, it necessarily follows that the Washington statute is invalid. . . .

Neither the statute involved in the *Adkins* case nor the Washington statute, so far as it is involved here, has the slightest relation to the capacity or earning power of the employee, to the number of hours which constitute the day's work, the character of the place where the work is to be done, or the circumstances or surroundings of the employment. The sole basis upon which the question of validity rests is the assumption that the employee is entitled to receive a sum of money sufficient to provide a living for her, keep her in health and preserve her morals. . . .

What we said further, in that case . . . is equally applicable here . . . : "A statute which prescribes payment without regard to any of these things and solely with relation to circumstances apart from the contract of employment, the business affected by it and the work done under it, is so clearly the product of a naked, arbitrary exercise of power that it cannot be allowed to stand under the Constitution of the United States." . . .

Williamson v. Lee Optical Company
348 U.S. 483 (1955)

In 1953, the Oklahoma Legislature passed a law that made it unlawful for any person other than a licensed ophthalmologist or optometrist to fit lenses to the face or to duplicate or replace lenses, except upon written prescriptive authority of a licensed ophthalmologist or optometrist. Lee Optical challenged the constitutionality of this law before a federal district court of three judges, alleging in part that it violated the Due Process Clause of the Fourteenth Amendment. The district court agreed, holding portions of the act unconstitutional, and the State of Oklahoma appealed to the Supreme Court. Opinion of the Court: <u>Douglas</u>, Warren, Black, Reed, Burton, Clark, Frankfurter, Minton. Not participating: Harlan.

JUSTICE DOUGLAS delivered the opinion of the Court.

An ophthalmologist is a duly licensed physician who specializes in the care of the eyes. An optometrist examines eyes for refractive error, recognizes (but does not treat) diseases of the eye, and fills prescriptions for eyeglasses. The optician is an artisan qualified to grind lenses, fill prescriptions, and fit frames.

The effect of §2 is to forbid the optician from fitting or duplicating lenses without a prescription from an ophthalmologist or optometrist. In practical effect, it means that no optician can fit old glasses into new frames or supply a lens, whether it be a new lens or one to duplicate a lost or broken lens, without a prescription. The District Court . . . rebelled at the notion that a State could require a prescription from an optometrist or ophthalmologist "to take old lenses and place them in new frames and then fit the completed spectacles to the *face* of the eyeglass wearer." . . . It held that such a requirement was not "reasonably and rationally related to the health and welfare of the people." . . . It was, accordingly, the opinion of the court that this provision of the law violated the Due Process Clause by arbitrarily interfering with the optician's right to do business.

The Oklahoma law may exact a needless, wasteful requirement in many cases. But it is for the legislature, not the courts, to balance the advantages and disadvantages of the new requirement. It appears that in many cases the optician can easily supply the new frames or new lenses without reference to the old written prescription. It also appears that many written prescriptions contain no directive data in regard to fitting spectacles to the face. But in some cases the directions contained in the prescription are essential, if the glasses are to be fitted so as to correct the particular defects of vision or alleviate the eye condition. The legislature might have concluded that the frequency of occasions when a prescription is necessary was sufficient to justify this regulation of the fitting of eyeglasses. Likewise, when it is necessary to duplicate a lens, a written prescription may or may not be necessary. But the legislature might have concluded that one was needed often enough to require one in every case. Or the legislature may have concluded that eye examinations were so critical, not only for correction of vision but also for detection of latent ailments or diseases, that every change in frames and every duplication of a lens should be accompanied by a prescription from a medical expert. To be sure, the present law does not require a new examination of the eyes every time the frames are changed or the lenses duplicated. For if the old prescription is on file with the optician, he can go ahead and make the new fitting or duplicate the lenses. But the law need not be in every respect logically consistent with its aims to be constitutional. It is enough that there is an evil at hand for correction, and that it might be thought that the particular legislative measure was a rational way to correct it.

The day is gone when this Court uses the Due Process Clause of the Fourteenth Amendment to strike down state laws, regulatory of business and industrial conditions, because they may be unwise, improvident, or out of harmony with a particular school of thought. . . . We emphasize again what Chief Justice Waite said in *Munn v. Illinois*, . . . "For protection against abuses by legislatures the people must resort to the polls, not to the courts." . . .

State Farm Mutual Automobile Insurance Company v. Campbell
538 U.S. 408 (2003)

In 1981, Curtis Campbell attempted to pass six vans traveling ahead of him on a two-lane Utah highway. To avoid a head-on collision with Campbell, a driver of a small car approaching from the opposite direction swerved onto the shoulder, lost control of his automobile, and collided with another vehicle, killing him and permanently disabling the driver of the vehicle into which he crashed. Campbell escaped without damage to his automobile or injury to himself. Although investigators and witnesses concluded that Campbell caused the accident, Campbell's insurer, State Farm Mutual Automobile Insurance Company, contested liability, declined to settle the ensuing claims for the $50,000 policy limit ($25,000 per claimant), ignored its own investigators' advice, and took the case to trial, assuring Campbell and his wife that they had no liability for the accident, that State Farm would represent their interests, and that they did not need separate counsel. In the ensuing wrongful-death and tort action, a Utah jury returned a judgment for $185,849—more than three times the policy limit—and State Farm refused to appeal. When the Utah Supreme Court denied Campbell's own appeal, State Farm agreed to pay the entire judgment; however, Campbell sued State Farm for bad faith, fraud, and intentional infliction of emotional distress. The trial court's initial ruling granting State Farm summary judgment was reversed on appeal. On remand, the court denied State Farm's motion to exclude evidence of similar out-of-state conduct, whereupon the jury found State Farm's decision not to settle to be unreasonable and awarded Campbell's estate (he had subsequently died) $2.6 million in compensatory damages and $145 million in punitive damages, which the trial court reduced to $1 million and $25 million, respectively. When the Utah Supreme Court reinstated the $145 million punitive-damages award, the Supreme Court granted certiorari. Opinion of the Court: Kennedy, Rehnquist, Stevens, O'Connor, Souter, Breyer. Dissenting opinions: Scalia; Thomas; Ginsburg.

JUSTICE KENNEDY delivered the opinion of the Court.

We address once again the measure of punishment, by means of punitive damages, a State may impose upon a defendant in a civil case. The question is whether . . . an award of $145 million in punitive damages, where full compensatory damages are $1 million, is excessive and in violation of the Due Process Clause of the Fourteenth Amendment to the Constitution of the United States. . . .

[I]n our judicial system compensatory and punitive damages, although usually awarded at the same time by the same decisionmaker, serve different purposes. Compensatory damages "are intended to redress the concrete loss that the plaintiff has suffered by reason of the defendant's wrongful conduct." By contrast, punitive damages serve a broader function; they are aimed at deterrence and retribution.

While States possess discretion over the imposition of punitive damages, it is well established that there are procedural and substantive constitutional limitations on these awards. The Due Process Clause of the Fourteenth Amendment prohibits the imposition of grossly excessive or arbitrary punishments on a tortfeasor. The reason is that "elementary notions of fairness enshrined in our constitutional jurisprudence dictate that a person receive fair notice not only of the conduct that will subject him to punishment, but also of the severity of the penalty that a State may impose." To the extent an award is grossly excessive, it furthers no legitimate purpose and constitutes an arbitrary deprivation of property.

Although these awards serve the same purposes as criminal penalties, defendants subjected to punitive damages in civil cases have not been accorded the protections applicable in a criminal proceeding. This increases our concerns over the imprecise manner in which punitive damages systems are administered. . . . Our concerns are heightened when the decisionmaker is presented . . . with evidence that has little bearing as to the amount of punitive damages that should be awarded. Vague instructions, or those that merely inform the jury to avoid "passion or prejudice," do little to aid the decisionmaker in its task of assigning appropriate weight to evidence that is relevant and evidence that is tangential or only inflammatory.

In light of these concerns, in [BMW v.] Gore [(1996)], we instructed courts reviewing punitive damages to consider three guideposts: (1) the degree of reprehensibility of the defendant's misconduct; (2) the disparity between the actual or potential harm suffered by the plaintiff and the punitive damages award; and (3) the difference between the punitive damages awarded by the jury and the civil penalties authorized or imposed in comparable cases. . . .

Under the principles outlined in BMW v. Gore, this case is neither close nor difficult. It was error to reinstate the jury's $145 million punitive damages award. We address each guidepost of Gore in some detail.

"The most important indicium of the reasonableness of a punitive damages award is the degree of reprehensibility of the defendant's conduct." We have instructed courts to determine the reprehensibility of a defendant by considering whether: the harm caused was physical as opposed to economic; the tortious conduct evinced an indifference to or a reckless disregard of the health or safety of others; the target of the conduct had financial vulnerability; the conduct involved repeated actions or was an isolated incident; and the harm was the result of intentional malice, trickery, or deceit, or mere accident. The existence of any one of these factors weighing in favor of a plaintiff may not be sufficient to sustain a punitive damages award; and the absence of all of them renders any award suspect. It should be presumed a plaintiff has been made whole for his injuries by compensatory damages, so punitive damages should only

be awarded if the defendant's culpability, after having paid compensatory damages, is so reprehensible as to warrant the imposition of further sanctions to achieve punishment or deterrence.

Applying these factors in the instant case, we must acknowledge that State Farm's handling of the claims against the Campbells merits no praise. The trial court found that State Farm's employees altered the company's records to make Campbell appear less culpable. State Farm disregarded the overwhelming likelihood of liability and the near-certain probability that, by taking the case to trial, a judgment in excess of the policy limits would be awarded. . . . While we do not suggest there was error in awarding punitive damages based upon State Farm's conduct toward the Campbells, a more modest punishment for this reprehensible conduct could have satisfied the State's legitimate objectives, and the Utah courts should have gone no further.

This case, instead, was used as a platform to expose, and punish, the perceived deficiencies of State Farm's operations throughout the country. The Utah Supreme Court's opinion makes explicit that State Farm was being condemned for its nationwide policies rather than for the conduct direct toward the Campbells. . . .

A State cannot punish a defendant for conduct that may have been lawful where it occurred. . . . A basic principle of federalism is that each State may make its own reasoned judgment about what conduct is permitted or proscribed within its borders, and each State alone can determine what measure of punishment, if any, to impose on a defendant who acts within its jurisdiction.

For a more fundamental reason, however, the Utah courts erred in relying upon this and other evidence: The courts awarded punitive damages to punish and deter conduct that bore no relation to the Campbells' harm. A defendant's dissimilar acts, independent from the acts upon which liability was premised, may not serve as the basis for punitive damages. A defendant should be punished for the conduct that harmed the plaintiff, not for being an unsavory individual or business. Due process does not permit courts, in the calculation of punitive damages, to adjudicate the merits of other parties' hypothetical claims against a defendant under the guise of the reprehensibility analysis, but we have no doubt the Utah Supreme Court did that here. . . .

Turning to the second *Gore* guidepost, we have been reluctant to identify concrete constitutional limits on the ratio between harm, or potential harm, to the plaintiff and the punitive damages award. We decline again to impose a bright-line ratio which a punitive damages award cannot exceed. Our jurisprudence and the principles it has now established demonstrate, however, that, in practice, few awards exceeding a single-digit ratio between punitive and compensatory damages, to a significant degree, will satisfy due process. In [*Pacific Mutual Life Insurance Co. v.*] *Haslip* [(1991)], in upholding a punitive damages award, we concluded that an award of more than four times the amount of compensatory damages might be close to the line of constitutional impropriety. We cited that 4-to-1 ratio again in *Gore*. The Court further referenced a long legislative history, dating back over 700 years and going forward to today, providing for sanctions of double, treble, or quadruple damages to deter and punish. While these ratios are not binding, they are instructive. They demonstrate what should be obvious: Single-digit multipliers are more likely to comport with due process, while still achieving the State's goals of deterrence and retribution, than awards with ratios in range of 500 to 1, or, in this case, of 145 to 1.

Nonetheless, because there are no rigid benchmarks that a punitive damages award may not surpass, ratios greater than those we have previously upheld may comport with due process where "a particularly egregious act has resulted in only a small amount of economic damages." The converse is also true, however. When compensatory damages are substantial, then a lesser ratio, perhaps only equal to compensatory damages, can reach the outermost limit of the due process guarantee. The precise award in any case, of course, must be based upon the facts and circumstances of the defendant's conduct and the harm to the plaintiff.

In sum, courts must ensure that the measure of punishment is both reasonable and proportionate to the amount of harm to the plaintiff

and to the general damages recovered. In the context of this case, we have no doubt that there is a presumption against an award that has a 145-to-1 ratio. The compensatory award in this case was substantial; the Campbells were awarded $1 million for a year and a half of emotional distress. This was complete compensation. The harm arose from a transaction in the economic realm, not from some physical assault or trauma; there were no physical injuries; and State Farm paid the excess verdict before the complaint was filed, so the Campbells suffered only minor economic injuries for the 18-month period in which State Farm refused to resolve the claim against them. The compensatory damages for the injury suffered here, moreover, likely were based on a component which was duplicated in the punitive award. Much of the distress was caused by the outrage and humiliation the Campbells suffered at the actions of their insurer; and it is a major role of punitive damages to condemn such conduct. Compensatory damages, however, already contain this punitive element. . . .

The third guidepost in *Gore* is the disparity between the punitive damages award and the "civil penalties authorized or imposed in comparable cases." . . . Here, we need not dwell long on this guidepost. The most relevant civil sanction under Utah state law for the wrong done to the Campbells appears to be a $10,000 fine for an act of fraud, an amount dwarfed by the $145 million punitive damages award. . . .

An application of the *Gore* guideposts to the facts of this case, especially in light of the substantial compensatory damages awarded (a portion of which contained a punitive element), likely would justify a punitive damages award at or near the amount of compensatory damages. The punitive award of $145 million, therefore, was neither reasonable nor proportionate to the wrong committed, and it was an irrational and arbitrary deprivation of the property of the defendant. The proper calculation of punitive damages under the principles we have discussed should be resolved, in the first instance, by the Utah courts.

The judgment of the Utah Supreme Court is reversed, and the case is remanded for proceedings not inconsistent with this opinion.

JUSTICE SCALIA, dissenting.

I adhere to the view expressed in my dissenting opinion in *BMW of North America, Inc. v. Gore* that the Due Process Clause provides no substantive protections against "excessive" or "'unreasonable'" awards of punitive damages. I am also of the view that the punitive damages jurisprudence which has sprung forth from *BMW v. Gore* is insusceptible of principled application; accordingly, I do not feel justified in giving the case *stare decisis* effect. I would affirm the judgment of the Utah Supreme Court.

JUSTICE GINSBURG, dissenting.

. . . In *Gore,* I stated why I resisted the Court's foray into punitive damages "territory traditionally within the States' domain." I adhere to those views. . . .

The large size of the award upheld by the Utah Supreme Court in this case indicates why damage-capping legislation may be altogether fitting and proper. Neither the amount of the award nor the trial record, however, justifies this Court's substitution of its judgment for that of Utah's competent decisionmakers. In this regard, I count it significant that, on the key criterion "reprehensibility," there is a good deal more to the story than the Court's abbreviated account tells. . . .

When the Court first ventured to override state-court punitive damages awards, it did so moderately. The Court recalled that "in our federal system, States necessarily have considerable flexibility in determining the level of punitive damages that they will allow in different classes of cases and in any particular case." Today's decision exhibits no such respect and restraint. No longer content to accord state-court judgments "a strong presumption of validity," the Court announces that "few awards exceeding a single-digit ratio between punitive and compensatory damages, to a significant degree, will satisfy due process." Moreover, the Court adds, when compensatory damages are substantial, doubling those damages "can reach the outermost limit of the due process guarantee." In a legislative scheme or a state high court's design to cap punitive damages, the handiwork in setting single-digit and 1-to-1 benchmarks could hardly be questioned; in a judicial decree imposed on the States by this Court under the banner of substantive due process, the numerical controls today's decision installs seem to me boldly out of order. . . .

United States v. Carolene Products Company
304 U.S. 144 (1938)

In what has become a famous footnote in an otherwise unimportant case, Justice Stone developed the justification for "more exacting judicial scrutiny" where infringements of civil liberties (as opposed to economic rights) are involved. Opinion of the Court: <u>Stone</u>, Hughes, Brandeis, Roberts. Concurring opinions: <u>Butler</u>; <u>Black</u>. Dissenting opinion: <u>McReynolds</u>. Not participating: Cardozo and Reed.

JUSTICE STONE delivered the opinion of the Court.

Regulatory legislation affecting ordinary commercial transactions is not to be pronounced unconstitutional unless in the light of the facts made known or generally assumed it is of such a character as to preclude the assumption that it rests upon some rational basis within the knowledge and experience of the legislators.[4]

---

4. There may be narrower scope for operation of the presumption of constitutionality when legislation appears on its face to be within a specific prohibition of the Constitution, such as those of the first ten Amendments, which are deemed equally specific when held to be embraced within the Fourteenth. It is unnecessary to consider now whether legislation which restricts those political processes which can ordinarily be expected to bring about repeal of undesirable legislation, is to be subjected to more exacting judicial scrutiny under the general prohibitions of the Fourteenth Amendment than are most other types of legislation. Nor need we enquire whether similar considerations enter into the review of statutes directed at particular religious, or national, or racial minorities; whether prejudice against discrete and insular minorities may be a special condition, which tends seriously to curtail the operation of those political processes ordinarily to be relied upon to protect minorities, and which may call for a correspondingly more searching judicial inquiry.

Kelo v. City of New London
545 U.S. 469 (2005)

In 2000, New London, Connecticut, approved an integrated economic development plan designed to revitalize its Fort Trumbull area. The pharmaceutical company Pfizer, Inc., had announced that it would build a $300 million global research facility on a site immediately adjacent to Fort Trumbull, and the city, expecting the Pfizer facility to be a catalyst to the area's rejuvenation, included in its development plan the acquisition of land for new businesses that it hoped would be drawn to the area. With the plan approved, New London, through its development agent, purchased most of the property earmarked for the project from willing sellers and initiated condemnation proceedings against the owners of the rest of the property who refused to sell. Susette Kelo and eight other petitioners brought suit in New London Superior Court claiming that the taking of their properties violated the "public use" restriction in the Fifth Amendment's Takings Clause. The trial court granted a permanent restraining order prohibiting the taking of some of the properties. When the Connecticut Supreme Court, relying on Hawaii Housing Authority v. Midkiff *(1984) and* Berman v. Parker *(1954), reversed and upheld all of the proposed takings, the US Supreme Court granted certiorari.* Opinion of the Court: <u>Stevens</u>, Kennedy, Souter, Ginsburg, Breyer. Concurring opinion: <u>Kennedy</u>. Dissenting opinions: <u>O'Connor</u>, Rehnquist, Scalia, Thomas; <u>Thomas</u>.

JUSTICE STEVENS delivered the opinion of the Court.

In 2000, the city of New London approved a development plan that, in the words of the Supreme Court of Connecticut, was "projected to create in excess of 1,000 jobs, to increase tax and other revenues, and to revitalize an economically distressed city, including its downtown and waterfront areas." In assembling the land needed for this project, the city's development agent has purchased property from willing sellers and proposes to use the power of eminent domain to acquire the remainder of the property from unwilling owners in exchange for just compensation. The question presented is whether the city's proposed disposition of this property qualifies as a "public use" within the meaning of the Takings Clause of the Fifth Amendment to the Constitution. . . .

Petitioner Susette Kelo has lived in the Fort Trumbull area since 1997. She has made extensive improvements to her house, which she prizes for its water view. Petitioner Wilhelmina Dery was born in her Fort Trumbull house in 1918 and has lived there her entire life. Her husband Charles (also a petitioner) has lived in the house since they married some 60 years ago. In all, the nine petitioners own 15 properties in Fort Trumbull. Ten of the parcels are occupied by the owner or a family member; the other five are held as investment properties. There is no allegation that any of these properties is blighted or otherwise in poor condition; rather, they were condemned only because they happen to be located in the development area.

. . . Two polar propositions are perfectly clear. On the one hand, it has long been accepted that the sovereign may not take the property of *A* for the sole purpose of transferring it to another private party *B,* even though *A* is paid just compensation. On the other hand, it is equally clear that a State may transfer property from one private party to another if future "use by the public" is the purpose of the taking; the condemnation of land for a railroad with common-carrier duties is a familiar example. Neither of these propositions, however, determines the disposition of this case.

As for the first proposition, the City would no doubt be forbidden from taking petitioners' land for the purpose of conferring a private benefit on a particular private party. . . . On the other hand, this is not a case in which the City is planning to open the condemned land—at least not in its entirety—to use by the general public. Nor will the private lessees of the land in any sense be required to operate like common carriers, making their services available to all comers. But although such a projected use would be sufficient to satisfy the public use requirement, this "Court long ago rejected any literal requirement that condemned property be put into use for the general public." . . . The disposition of this case therefore turns on the question whether the City's development plan serves a "public purpose." Without exception, our cases have defined that concept broadly, reflecting our longstanding policy of deference to legislative judgments in this field.

In *Berman v. Parker* (1954), this Court upheld a redevelopment plan targeting a blighted area of Washington, D. C., in which most of the housing for the area's 5,000 inhabitants was beyond repair. Under the plan, the area would be condemned and part of it utilized for the construction of streets, schools, and other public facilities. The remainder of the land would be leased or sold to private parties for the purpose of redevelopment, including the construction of low-cost housing.

The owner of a department store located in the area challenged the condemnation, pointing out that his store was not itself blighted and arguing that the creation of a "better balanced, more attractive community" was not a valid public use. Writing for a unanimous Court, Justice Douglas refused to evaluate this claim in isolation, deferring instead to the legislative and agency judgment that the area "must be planned as a whole" for the plan to be successful. The Court explained that "community redevelopment programs need not, by force of the Constitution, be on a piecemeal basis—lot by lot, building by building."

In *Hawaii Housing Authority v. Midkiff* (1984), the Court considered a Hawaii statute whereby fee title was taken from lessors and transferred to lessees (for just compensation) in order to reduce the concentration of land ownership. We unanimously upheld the statute and rejected the Ninth Circuit's view that it was "a naked attempt on the part of the state of Hawaii to take the property of A and transfer it to B solely for B's private use and benefit." Reaffirming *Berman*'s deferential approach to legislative judgments in this field, we concluded that the State's purpose of eliminating the "social and economic evils of a land oligopoly" qualified as a valid public use. Our opinion also rejected the contention that the mere fact that the State immediately transferred the properties to private individuals upon condemnation somehow diminished the public character of the taking. "It is only the taking's

purpose, and not its mechanics," we explained, that matters in determining public use. . . .

Those who govern the City were not confronted with the need to remove blight in the Fort Trumbull area, but their determination that the area was sufficiently distressed to justify a program of economic rejuvenation is entitled to our deference. The City has carefully formulated an economic development plan that it believes will provide appreciable benefits to the community, including—but by no means limited to—new jobs and increased tax revenue. As with other exercises in urban planning and development, the City is endeavoring to coordinate a variety of commercial, residential, and recreational uses of land, with the hope that they will form a whole greater than the sum of its parts. To effectuate this plan, the City has invoked a state statute that specifically authorizes the use of eminent domain to promote economic development. Given the comprehensive character of the plan, the thorough deliberation that preceded its adoption, and the limited scope of our review, it is appropriate for us, as it was in *Berman,* to resolve the challenges of the individual owners, not on a piecemeal basis, but rather in light of the entire plan. Because that plan unquestionably serves a public purpose, the takings challenged here satisfy the public use requirement of the Fifth Amendment.

To avoid this result, petitioners urge us to adopt a new bright-line rule that economic development does not qualify as a public use. Putting aside the unpersuasive suggestion that the City's plan will provide only purely economic benefits, neither precedent nor logic supports petitioners' proposal. Promoting economic development is a traditional and long accepted function of government. There is, moreover, no principled way of distinguishing economic development from the other public purposes that we have recognized. In our cases upholding takings that facilitated agriculture and mining, for example, we emphasized the importance of those industries to the welfare of the States in question; in *Berman,* we endorsed the purpose of transforming a blighted area into a "well-balanced" community through redevelopment; [and] in *Midkiff,* we upheld the interest in breaking up a land oligopoly that "created artificial deterrents to the normal functioning of the State's residential land market." . . . It would be incongruous to hold that the City's interest in the economic benefits to be derived from the development of the Fort Trumbull area has less of a public character than any of those other interests. Clearly, there is no basis for exempting economic development from our traditionally broad understanding of public purpose.

Petitioners contend that using eminent domain for economic development impermissibly blurs the boundary between public and private takings. Again, our cases foreclose this objection. Quite simply, the government's pursuit of a public purpose will often benefit individual private parties. For example, in *Midkiff,* the forced transfer of property conferred a direct and significant benefit on those lessees who were previously unable to purchase their homes. . . .

It is further argued that without a bright-line rule nothing would stop a city from transferring citizen *A*'s property to citizen *B* for the sole reason that citizen *B* will put the property to a more productive use and thus pay more taxes. Such a one-to-one transfer of property, executed outside the confines of an integrated development plan, is not presented in this case. While such an unusual exercise of government power would certainly raise a suspicion that a private purpose was afoot, the hypothetical cases posited by petitioners can be confronted if and when they arise. They do not warrant the crafting of an artificial restriction on the concept of public use.

Alternatively, petitioners maintain that for takings of this kind we should require a "reasonable certainty" that the expected public benefits will actually accrue. Such a rule, however, would represent an even greater departure from our precedents. "When the legislature's purpose is legitimate and its means are not irrational, our cases make clear that empirical debates over the wisdom of takings—no less than debates over the wisdom of other kinds of socioeconomic legislation—are not to be carried out in the federal courts." The disadvantages of a heightened form of review are especially pronounced in this type of case. Orderly implementation of a comprehensive redevelopment plan obviously requires that the legal rights of all interested parties be established before new construction can be commenced. A constitutional rule that required postponement of the judicial approval of every condemnation until the likelihood of success of the plan had been assured would unquestionably impose a significant impediment to the successful consummation of many such plans.

Just as we decline to second-guess the City's considered judgments about the efficacy of its development plan, we also decline to second-guess the City's determinations as to what lands it needs to acquire in order to effectuate the project. "It is not for the courts to oversee the choice of the boundary line nor to sit in review on the size of a particular project area. Once the question of the public purpose has been decided, the amount and character of land to be taken for the project and the need for a particular tract to complete the integrated plan rests in the discretion of the legislative branch."

In affirming the City's authority to take petitioners' properties, we do not minimize the hardship that condemnations may entail, notwithstanding the payment of just compensation. We emphasize that nothing in our opinion precludes any State from placing further restrictions on its exercise of the takings power. Indeed, many States already impose "public use" requirements that are stricter than the federal baseline. . . .

The judgment of the Supreme Court of Connecticut is affirmed.

JUSTICE O'CONNOR, with whom THE CHIEF JUSTICE, JUSTICE SCALIA, and JUSTICE THOMAS join, dissenting.

Over two centuries ago, just after the Bill of Rights was ratified, Justice Chase wrote:

> An ACT of the Legislature (for I cannot call it a law) contrary to the great first principles of the social compact, cannot be considered a rightful exercise of legislative authority. . . . A few instances will suffice to explain what I mean. . . . [A] law that takes property from A. and gives it to B: It is against all reason and justice, for a people to entrust a Legislature with SUCH powers; and, therefore, it cannot

be presumed that they have done it. *Calder v. Bull* (1798).

Today the Court abandons this long-held, basic limitation on government power. Under the banner of economic development, all private property is now vulnerable to being taken and transferred to another private owner, so long as it might be upgraded—*i.e.,* given to an owner who will use it in a way that the legislature deems more beneficial to the public—in the process. To reason, as the Court does, that the incidental public benefits resulting from the subsequent ordinary use of private property render economic development takings "for public use" is to wash out any distinction between private and public use of property—and thereby effectively to delete the words "for public use" from the Takings Clause of the Fifth Amendment. Accordingly I respectfully dissent.

. . . The Fifth Amendment to the Constitution, made applicable to the States by the Fourteenth Amendment, provides that "private property [shall not] be taken for public use, without just compensation." When interpreting the Constitution, we begin with the unremarkable presumption that every word in the document has independent meaning, "that no word was unnecessarily used, or needlessly added." In keeping with that presumption, we have read the Fifth Amendment's language to impose two distinct conditions on the exercise of eminent domain: "the taking must be for a 'public use' and 'just compensation' must be paid to the owner."

These two limitations serve to protect "the security of Property," which Alexander Hamilton described to the Philadelphia Convention as one of the "great objects of Government." Together they ensure stable property ownership by providing safeguards against excessive, unpredictable, or unfair use of the government's eminent domain power—particularly against those owners who, for whatever reasons, may be unable to protect themselves in the political process against the majority's will. While the Takings Clause presupposes that government can take private property without the owner's consent, the just compensation requirement spreads the cost of condemnations

and thus "prevents the public from loading upon one individual more than his just share of the burdens of government." The public use requirement, in turn, imposes a more basic limitation, circumscribing the very scope of the eminent domain power: Government may compel an individual to forfeit her property for the *public's* use, but not for the benefit of another private person. . . .

Where is the line between "public" and "private" property use? We give considerable deference to legislatures' determinations about what governmental activities will advantage the public. But were the political branches the sole arbiters of the public-private distinction, the Public Use Clause would amount to little more than hortatory fluff. An external, judicial check on how the public use requirement is interpreted, however limited, is necessary if this constraint on government power is to retain any meaning.

Our cases have generally identified three categories of takings that comply with the public use requirement, though it is in the nature of things that the boundaries between these categories are not always firm. Two are relatively straightforward and uncontroversial. First, the sovereign may transfer private property to public ownership—such as for a road, a hospital, or a military base. Second, the sovereign may transfer private property to private parties, often common carriers, who make the property available for the public's use—such as with a railroad, a public utility, or a stadium. But "public ownership" and "use-by-the-public" are sometimes too constricting and impractical ways to define the scope of the Public Use Clause. Thus we have allowed that, in certain circumstances and to meet certain exigencies, takings that serve a public purpose also satisfy the Constitution even if the property is destined for subsequent private use.

This case . . . presents an issue of first impression: Are economic development takings constitutional? I would hold that they are not. We are guided by two precedents about the taking of real property by eminent domain. In *Berman,* we upheld takings within a blighted neighborhood of Washington, D.C. The neighborhood had so deteriorated that, for example, 64.3% of its dwellings were beyond repair. It had become burdened with "over-crowding of dwellings," "lack of adequate streets and alleys," and "lack of light and air." Congress had determined that the neighbor-hood had become "injurious to the public health, safety, morals, and welfare" and that it was necessary to "eliminate all such injurious conditions by employing all means necessary and appropriate for the purpose," including eminent domain. Mr. Berman's department store was not itself blighted. Having approved of Congress' decision to eliminate the harm to the public emanating from the blighted neigh-borhood, however, we did not second-guess its decision to treat the neighborhood as a whole rather than lot-by-lot.

In *Midkiff,* we upheld a land condemnation scheme in Hawaii whereby title in real prop-erty was taken from lessors and transferred to lessees. At that time, the State and Federal Governments owned nearly 49% of the State's land, and another 47% was in the hands of only 72 private landowners. Concentration of land ownership was so dramatic that on the State's most urbanized island, Oahu, 22 land-owners owned 72.5% of the fee simple titles. The Hawaii Legislature had concluded that the oligopoly in land ownership was "skewing the State's residential fee simple market, inflating land prices, and injuring the public tranquility and welfare," and therefore enacted a condem-nation scheme for redistributing title.

In those decisions, we emphasized the im-portance of deferring to legislative judgments about public purpose. . . . Yet for all the em-phasis on deference, *Berman* and *Midkiff* hewed to a bedrock principle without which our public use jurisprudence would collapse: "A purely private taking could not withstand the scrutiny of the public use requirement; it would serve no legitimate purpose of govern-ment and would thus be void."

The Court's holdings in *Berman* and *Midkiff* were true to the principle underlying the Public Use Clause. In both those cases, the extraordi-nary, precondemnation use of the targeted property inflicted affirmative harm on society—in *Berman* through blight resulting from ex-treme poverty and in *Midkiff* through oligopoly resulting from extreme wealth. And in both cases, the relevant legislative body had found

that eliminating the existing property use was necessary to remedy the harm. Thus a public purpose was realized when the harmful use was eliminated. Because each taking *directly* achieved a public benefit, it did not matter that the property was turned over to private use. Here, in contrast, New London does not claim that Susette Kelo's and Wilhelmina Dery's well-maintained homes are the source of any social harm. Indeed, it could not so claim with-out adopting the absurd argument that any single-family home that might be razed to make way for an apartment building, or any church that might be replaced with a retail store, or any small business that might be more lucrative if it were instead part of a national franchise, is in-herently harmful to society and thus within the government's power to condemn.

In moving away from our decisions sanc-tioning the condemnation of harmful property use, the Court today significantly expands the meaning of public use. It holds that the sover-eign may take private property currently put to ordinary private use, and give it over for new, ordinary private use, so long as the new use is predicted to generate some secondary benefit for the public—such as increased tax revenue, more jobs, maybe even aesthetic pleasure. But nearly any lawful use of real private property can be said to generate some incidental benefit to the public. Thus, if predicted (or even guar-anteed) positive side-effects are enough to ren-der transfer from one private party to another constitutional, then the words "for public use" do not realistically exclude *any* takings, and thus do not exert any constraint on the emi-nent domain power. . . .

Finally, in a coda, the Court suggests that property owners should turn to the States, who may or may not choose to impose appropriate limits on economic development takings. This is an abdication of our responsibility. States play many important functions in our system of dual sovereignty, but compensating for our refusal to enforce properly the Federal Consti-tution (and a provision meant to curtail state action, no less) is not among them.

JUSTICE THOMAS, dissenting.

. . . I do not believe that this Court can eliminate liberties expressly enumerated in the

Constitution and therefore join [Justice O'Connor's] dissenting opinion. Regrettably, however, the Court's error runs deeper than this. Today's decision is simply the latest in a string of our cases construing the Public Use Clause to be a virtual nullity, without the slightest nod to its original meaning. In my view, the Public Use Clause, originally understood, is a meaningful limit on the government's eminent domain power. Our cases have strayed from the Clause's original meaning, and I would reconsider them. . . .

The most natural reading of the Clause is that it allows the government to take property only if the government owns, or the public has a legal right to use, the property, as opposed to taking it for any public purpose or necessity whatsoever. At the time of the founding, dictionaries primarily defined the noun "use" as "the act of employing any thing to any purpose." The term "use," moreover, "is from the Latin *utor*, which means 'to use, make use of, avail one's self of, employ, apply, enjoy, etc.'" When the government takes property and gives it to a private individual, and the public has no right to use the property, it strains language to say that the public is "employing" the property, regardless of the incidental benefits that might accrue to the public from the private use. The term "public use," then, means that either the government or its citizens as a whole must actually "employ" the taken property.

Granted, another sense of the word "use" was broader in meaning, extending to "convenience" or "help," or "qualities that make a thing proper for any purpose." Nevertheless, read in context, the term "public use" possesses the narrower meaning. Elsewhere, the Constitution twice employs the word "use," both times in its narrower sense. Article 1, §10 provides that "the net Produce of all Duties and Imposts, laid by any State on Imports or Exports, shall be for the Use of the Treasury of the United States," meaning the Treasury itself will control the taxes, not use it to any beneficial end. And Article I, §8 grants Congress power "to raise and support Armies, but no Appropriation of Money to that Use shall be for a longer Term than two Years." Here again, "use" means "employed to raise and support Armies," not anything directed to achieving any military

end. The same word in the Public Use Clause should be interpreted to have the same meaning.

Tellingly, the phrase "public use" contrasts with the very different phrase "general Welfare" used elsewhere in the Constitution. See Article I, §8 ("Congress shall have Power To . . . provide for the common Defence and general Welfare of the United States"); preamble (Constitution established "to promote the general Welfare"). The Framers would have used some such broader term if they had meant the Public Use Clause to have a similarly sweeping scope. . . . The Constitution's text, in short, suggests that the Takings Clause authorizes the taking of property only if the public has a right to employ it, not if the public realizes any conceivable benefit from the taking.

The Constitution's common-law background reinforces this understanding. The common law provided an express method of eliminating uses of land that adversely impacted the public welfare: nuisance law. Blackstone and Kent, for instance, both carefully distinguished the law of nuisance from the power of eminent domain. Blackstone rejected the idea that private property could be taken solely for purposes of any public benefit. "So great . . . is the regard of the law for private property," he explained, "that it will not authorize the least violation of it; no, not even for the general good of the whole community." . . . When the public took property, in other words, it took it as an individual buying property from another typically would: for one's own use. The Public Use Clause, in short, embodied the Framers' understanding that property is a natural, fundamental right, prohibiting the government from "taking *property* from A. and giving it to B."

. . . There is no justification . . . for affording almost insurmountable deference to legislative conclusions that a use serves a "public use." To begin with, a court owes no deference to a legislature's judgment concerning the quintessentially legal question of whether the government owns, or the public has a legal right to use, the taken property. Even under the "public purpose" interpretation, moreover, it is most implausible that the Framers intended to defer to legislatures as to what satisfies the Public Use Clause, uniquely among all the express provisions of the Bill of Rights. We would not defer to a legislature's determination of the various circumstances that establish, for example, when a search of a home would be reasonable. . . . The Court has elsewhere recognized "the overriding respect for the sanctity of the home that has been embedded in our traditions since the origins of the Republic" when the issue is only whether the government may search a home. Yet today the Court tells us that we are not to "second-guess the City's considered judgments" when the issue is, instead, whether the government may take the infinitely more intrusive step of tearing down petitioners' homes. Something has gone seriously awry with this Court's interpretation of the Constitution. Though citizens are safe from the government in their homes, the homes themselves are not. Once one accepts, as the Court at least nominally does, that the Public Use Clause is a limit on the eminent domain power of the Federal Government and the States, there is no justification for the almost complete deference it grants to legislatures as to what satisfies it.

. . . *Berman* and *Midkiff* erred by equating the eminent domain power with the police power of States. Traditional uses of that regulatory power, such as the power to abate a nuisance, required no compensation whatsoever, in sharp contrast to the takings power, which has always required compensation. The question whether the State can take property using the power of eminent domain is therefore distinct from the question whether it can regulate property pursuant to the police power. In *Berman,* for example, if the slums at issue were truly "blighted," then state nuisance law, not the power of eminent domain, would provide the appropriate remedy. To construe the Public Use Clause to overlap with the States' police power conflates these two categories.

The "public purpose" test applied by *Berman* and *Midkiff* also cannot be applied in principled manner. "When we depart from the natural import of the term 'public use,' and substitute for the simple idea of a public possession and occupation, that of public utility, public interest, common benefit, general advantage or convenience . . . we are afloat without any certain principle to guide us." Once one permits takings for public purposes in

addition to public uses, no coherent principle limits what could constitute a valid public use. . . . I share the Court's skepticism about a public use standard that requires courts to second-guess the policy wisdom of public works projects. The "public purpose" standard this Court has adopted, however, demands the use of such judgment, for the Court concedes that the Public Use Clause would forbid a purely private taking. It is difficult to imagine how a court could find that a taking was purely private except by determining that the taking did not, in fact, rationally advance the public interest. The Court is therefore wrong to criticize the "actual use" test as "difficult to administer." It is far easier to analyze whether the government owns or the public has a legal right to use the taken property than to ask whether the taking has a "purely private purpose"—unless the Court means to eliminate public use scrutiny of takings entirely. Obliterating a provision of the Constitution, of course, guarantees that it will not be misapplied.

For all these reasons, I would revisit our Public Use Clause cases and consider returning to the original meaning of the Public Use Clause: that the government may take property only if it actually uses or gives the public a legal right to use the property.

The consequences of today's decision are not difficult to predict, and promise to be harmful. So-called "urban renewal" programs provide some compensation for the properties they take, but no compensation is possible for the subjective value of these lands to the individuals displaced and the indignity inflicted by uprooting them from their homes. Allowing the government to take property solely for public purposes is bad enough, but extending the concept of public purpose to encompass any economically beneficial goal guarantees that these losses will fall disproportionally on poor communities. Those communities are not only systematically less likely to put their lands to the highest and best social use, but are also the least politically powerful. If ever there were justification for intrusive judicial review of constitutional provisions that protect "discrete and insular minorities," *United States v. Carolene Products Co.* (1938), surely that principle would apply with great force to the powerless groups and individuals the Public Use Clause protects. The deferential standard this Court has adopted for the Public Use Clause is therefore deeply perverse. It encourages "those citizens with disproportionate influence and power in the political process, including large corporations and development firms" to victimize the weak.

Those incentives have made the legacy of this Court's "public purpose" test an unhappy one. In the 1950s, no doubt emboldened in part by the expansive understanding of "public use" this Court adopted in *Berman,* cities "rushed to draw plans" for downtown development. "Of all the families displaced by urban renewal from 1949 through 1963, 63 percent of those whose race was known were nonwhite, and of these families, 56 percent of nonwhites and 38 percent of whites had incomes low enough to qualify for public housing, which, however, was seldom available to them." Public works projects in the 1950s and 1960s destroyed predominantly minority communities in St. Paul, Minnesota, and Baltimore, Maryland. In 1981, urban planners in Detroit, Michigan, uprooted the largely "lower-income and elderly" Pole-

town neighborhood for the benefit of the General Motors Corporation. Urban renewal projects have long been associated with the displacement of blacks; "in cities across the country, urban renewal came to be known as 'Negro removal.'" Over 97 percent of the individuals forcibly removed from their homes by the "slum-clearance" project upheld by this Court in *Berman* were black. Regrettably, the predictable consequence of the Court's decision will be to exacerbate these effects.

The Court relies almost exclusively on this Court's prior cases to derive today's far-reaching, and dangerous, result. When faced with a clash of constitutional principle and a line of unreasoned cases wholly divorced from the text, history, and structure of our founding document, we should not hesitate to resolve the tension in favor of the Constitution's original meaning. For the reasons I have given, and for the reasons given in Justice O'Connor's dissent, the conflict of principle raised by this boundless use of the eminent domain power should be resolved in petitioners' favor. I would reverse the judgment of the Connecticut Supreme Court.

Horne v. Department of Agriculture
576 U.S. ___ (2015)

The Agricultural Marketing Agreement Act of 1937 authorizes the Secretary of Agriculture to promulgate "marketing orders" to help maintain stable markets for particular agricultural products. The marketing order for raisins established a Raisin Administrative Committee that imposes a reserve requirement—a requirement that growers set aside a certain percentage of their crop for the Government, free of charge. The Government then sells those raisins in noncompetitive markets, donates them, or otherwise disposes of them in a manner consistent with the purposes of the program. If any profits remain after subtracting the Government's expenses from administering the program, the net proceeds are distributed back to the raisin growers. In 2002–2003, raisin growers were required to set aside 47 percent of their raisin crop under the reserve requirement. In 2003–2004, 30 percent. The Horne family, raisin

growers in California, refused to set aside any raisins for the Government on the ground that the reserve requirement was an unconstitutional taking of their property for public use without just compensation. The Government fined the Hornes the fair market value of the raisins as well as additional civil penalties for their failure to obey the raisin marketing order.

The Hornes sought relief in federal court, arguing that the reserve requirement was an unconstitutional taking of their property under the Fifth Amendment. The Ninth Circuit rejected their argument that the reserve requirement was a Fifth Amendment taking; it determined that the requirement was not a per se taking because personal property is afforded less protection under the Takings Clause than real property and because the Hornes, who retained an interest in any net proceeds, were not completely divested of their property. The Ninth Circuit held that, as in cases allowing the government to set conditions on land use and development, the Government imposed a condition (the reserve requirement) in exchange for a Government benefit (an orderly raisin market). It also held that the Hornes could avoid relinquishing large percentages of their crop by "planting different crops." The Supreme Court granted certiorari. Opinion of the Court: <u>Roberts</u>, Scalia, Kennedy, Thomas, Ginsburg (as to Parts I and II), Breyer (as to Parts I and II), Alito, Kagan (as to Parts I and II). Concurring opinion: <u>Thomas.</u> Concurring in part and dissenting in part: <u>Breyer</u>, Ginsburg, Kagan. Dissenting opinion: <u>Sotomayor.</u>

CHIEF JUSTICE ROBERTS delivered the opinion of the Court.

Under the United States Department of Agriculture's California Raisin Marketing Order, a percentage of a grower's crop must be physically set aside in certain years for the account of the Government, free of charge. The Government then sells, allocates, or otherwise disposes of the raisins in ways it determines are best suited to maintaining an orderly market. The question is whether the Takings Clause of the Fifth Amendment bars the Government from imposing such a demand on the growers without just compensation.

I

The Agricultural Marketing Agreement Act of 1937 authorizes the Secretary of Agriculture to promulgate "marketing orders" to help maintain stable markets for particular agricultural products. The marketing order for raisins requires growers in certain years to give a percentage of their crop to the Government, free of charge. The required allocation is determined by the Raisin Administrative Committee, a Government entity composed largely of growers and others in the raisin business appointed by the Secretary of Agriculture. In 2002–2003, this Committee ordered raisin growers to turn over 47 percent of their crop. In 2003–2004, 30 percent.

Growers generally ship their raisins to a raisin "handler," who physically separates the raisins due the Government (called "reserve

raisins"), pays the growers only for the remainder ("free-tonnage raisins"), and packs and sells the free-tonnage raisins. The Raisin Committee acquires title to the reserve raisins that have been set aside, and decides how to dispose of them in its discretion. It sells them in noncompetitive markets, for example to exporters, federal agencies, or foreign governments; donates them to charitable causes; releases them to growers who agree to reduce their raisin production; or disposes of them by "any other means" consistent with the purposes of the raisin program. Proceeds from Committee sales are principally used to subsidize handlers who sell raisins for export (not including the Hornes, who are not raisin exporters). Raisin growers retain an interest in any net proceeds from sales the Raisin Committee makes, after deductions for the export subsidies and the Committee's administrative expenses. In the years at issue in this case, those proceeds were less than the cost of producing the crop one year, and nothing at all the next.

. . . In 2002, the Hornes refused to set aside any raisins for the Government, believing they were not legally bound to do so. The Government sent trucks to the Hornes' facility at eight o'clock one morning to pick up the raisins, but the Hornes refused entry. The Government then assessed against the Hornes a fine equal to the market value of the missing raisins—some $480,000—as well as an additional civil penalty of just over $200,000 for disobeying the order to turn them over.

When the Government sought to collect the fine, the Hornes turned to the courts, arguing that the reserve requirement was an unconstitutional taking of their property under the Fifth Amendment. Their case eventually made it to this Court when . . . the Ninth Circuit . . . rejected the Hornes' argument that the reserve requirement was a per se taking, reasoning that "the Takings Clause affords less protection to personal than to real property," and concluding that the Hornes "are not completely divested of their property rights," because growers retain an interest in the proceeds from any sale of reserve raisins by the Raisin Committee. [It] . . . instead viewed the reserve requirement as a use restriction, similar to a government condition on the grant of a land use permit. See *Dolan v. City of Tigard*, (1994); *Nollan v. California Coastal Commission* (1987). As in such permit cases, the Court of Appeals explained, the Government here imposed a condition (the reserve requirement) in exchange for a Government benefit (an orderly raisin market). And just as a landowner was free to avoid the government condition by forgoing a permit, so too the Hornes could avoid the reserve requirement by "planting different crops." Under that analysis, the court found that the reserve requirement was a proportional response to the Government's interest in ensuring an orderly raisin market, and not a taking under the Fifth Amendment. We granted certiorari.

II

The petition for certiorari poses three questions, which we answer in turn.

A

The first question presented asks "Whether the government's 'categorical duty' under the Fifth Amendment to pay just compensation when it 'physically takes possession of an interest in property' applies only to real property and not to personal property." The answer is no.

1

There is no dispute that the "classic taking [is one] in which the government directly appropriates private property for its own use." Nor is there any dispute that, in the case of real property, such an appropriation is a per se taking that requires just compensation. Nothing in the text or history of the Takings Clause, or our precedents, suggests that the rule is any different when it comes to appropriation of personal property. The Government has a categorical duty to pay just compensation when it takes your car, just as when it takes your home.

The Takings Clause . . . protects "private property" without any distinction between different types. The principle reflected in the Clause goes back at least 800 years to Magna Carta, which specifically protected agricultural crops from uncompensated takings. Clause 28 of that charter forbade any "constable or other bailiff" from taking "corn or other provisions from any one without immediately tendering money therefor, unless he can have postponement thereof by permission of the seller."

The colonists brought the principles of Magna Carta with them to the New World, including that charter's protection against uncompensated takings of personal property. In 1641, for example, Massachusetts adopted its Body of Liberties, prohibiting "mans Cattel or goods of what kinde soever" from being "pressed or taken for any publique use or service, unless it be by warrant grounded upon some act of the generall Court, nor without such reasonable prices and hire as the ordinarie rates of the Countrie do afford." Virginia allowed the seizure of surplus "live stock, or beef, pork, or bacon" for the military, but only upon "paying or tendering to the owner the price so estimated by the appraisers." And South Carolina authorized the seizure of "necessaries" for public use, but provided that "said articles so seized shall be paid for agreeable to the prices such and the like articles sold for on the ninth day of October last."

. . . Nothing in this history suggests that personal property was any less protected against physical appropriation than real property. . . .

2

The reserve requirement imposed by the Raisin Committee is a clear physical taking. Actual raisins are transferred from the growers to the Government. . . . The Committee disposes of what become its raisins as it wishes, to promote the purposes of the raisin marketing order.

Raisin growers subject to the reserve requirement thus lose the entire "bundle" of property rights in the appropriated raisins . . . with the exception of the speculative hope that some residual proceeds may be left when the Government is done with the raisins and has deducted the expenses of implementing all aspects of the marketing order. The Government's "actual taking of possession and control" of the reserve raisins gives rise to a taking as clearly "as if the Government held full title and ownership," as it essentially does. . . .

B

The second question presented asks "Whether the government may avoid the categorical duty to pay just compensation for a physical taking of property by reserving to the property owner a contingent interest in a portion of the value of the property, set at the government's discretion." The answer is no.

The Government and dissent argue that raisins are fungible goods whose only value is in the revenue from their sale. According to the Government, the raisin marketing order leaves that interest with the raisin growers: After selling reserve raisins and deducting expenses and subsidies for exporters, the Raisin Committee returns any net proceeds to the growers. The Government contends that because growers are entitled to these net proceeds, they retain the most important property interest in the reserve raisins, so there is no taking in the first place. The dissent agrees, arguing that this possible future revenue means there has been no taking . . . That is not an issue here: The Hornes did not receive any net proceeds from Raisin Committee sales for the years at issue, because they had not set aside any reserve raisins in those years (and, in any event, there were no net proceeds in one of them).

C

The third question presented asks "Whether a governmental mandate to relinquish specific, identifiable property as a 'condition' on permission to engage in commerce effects a per se taking." The answer, at least in this case, is yes.

The Government contends that the reserve requirement is not a taking because raisin growers voluntarily choose to participate in the raisin market. According to the Government, if raisin growers don't like it, they can "plant different crops," or "sell their raisin-variety grapes as table grapes or for use in juice or wine."

"Let them sell wine" is probably not much more comforting to the raisin growers than similar retorts have been to others throughout history. . . . [P]roperty rights "cannot be so easily manipulated." . . . The Government and dissent rely heavily on *Ruckelshaus v. Monsanto Co.* (1984). There we held that the Environmental Protection Agency could require companies manufacturing pesticides, fungicides, and rodenticides to disclose health, safety, and environmental information about their prod-

ucts as a condition to receiving a permit to sell those products. While such information included trade secrets in which pesticide manufacturers had a property interest, those manufacturers were not subjected to a taking because they received a "valuable Government benefit" in exchange—a license to sell dangerous chemicals.

The taking here cannot reasonably be characterized as part of a similar voluntary exchange. In one of the years at issue here, the Government insisted that the Hornes turn over 47 percent of their raisin crop, in exchange for the "benefit" of being allowed to sell the remaining 53 percent. The next year, the toll was 30 percent. We have already rejected the idea that *Monsanto* may be extended by regarding basic and familiar uses of property as a "Government benefit" on the same order as a permit to sell hazardous chemicals. Selling produce in interstate commerce, although certainly subject to reasonable government regulation, is similarly not a special governmental benefit that the Government may hold hostage, to be ransomed by the waiver of constitutional protection. Raisins are not dangerous pesticides; they are a healthy snack. A case about conditioning the sale of hazardous substances on disclosure of health, safety, and environmental information related to those hazards is hardly on point.

III

[T]he Government briefly argues that if we conclude that the reserve requirement effects a taking, we should remand for the Court of Appeals to calculate "what compensation would have been due if petitioners had complied with the reserve requirement." The Government contends that the calculation must consider what the value of the reserve raisins would have been without the price support program, as well as "other benefits . . . from the regulatory program, such as higher consumer demand for raisins spurred by enforcement of quality standards and promotional activities." Indeed, according to the Government, the Hornes would "likely" have a net gain under this theory.

The best defense may be a good offense, but the Government cites no support for its hypothetical-based approach, or its notion that general regulatory activity such as enforcement of quality standards can constitute just compensation for a specific physical taking. Instead, our cases have set forth a clear and administrable rule for just compensation: "The Court has repeatedly held that just compensation normally is to be measured by 'the market value of the property at the time of the taking.'" The Government has already calculated the amount of just compensation in this case, when it fined the Hornes the fair market value of the raisins: $483,843.53. The Government cannot now disavow that valuation and does not suggest that the marketing order affords the Hornes compensation in that amount. There is accordingly no need for a remand; the Hornes should simply be relieved of the obligation to pay the fine and associated civil penalty they were assessed when they resisted the Government's effort to take their raisins. This case, in litigation for more than a decade, has gone on long enough.

The judgment of the United States Court of Appeals for the Ninth Circuit is reversed.

It is so ordered.

JUSTICE BREYER, with whom JUSTICE GINSBURG and JUSTICE KAGAN join, concurring in part and dissenting in part.

I agree with Parts I and II of the Court's opinion. However, I cannot agree with the Court's rejection, in Part III, of the Government's final argument. The Government contends that we should remand the case for a determination of whether any compensation would have been due if the Hornes had complied with the California Raisin Marketing Order's reserve requirement. In my view, a remand for such a determination is necessary.

The question of just compensation was not presented in the Hornes' petition for certiorari. It was barely touched on in the briefs. And the courts below did not decide it. . . . In my view, . . . the Takings Clause requires compensation in an amount equal to the value of the reserve raisins adjusted to account for the benefits received. And the Government does, indeed, suggest that the marketing order affords just compensation. Further, the Hornes have not demonstrated the contrary. Before granting judgment in favor of the Hornes, a court

should address the issue in light of all of the relevant facts and law.

* * *

Given the precedents, the parties should provide full briefing on this question. I would remand the case, permitting the lower courts to consider argument on the question of just compensation.

JUSTICE SOTOMAYOR, dissenting.

. . . Because the Order does not deprive the Hornes of all of their property rights, it does not effect a per se taking. I respectfully dissent from the Court's contrary holding.

. . . In my view, [w]here some property right is retained by the owner, no per se taking . . . has occurred. . . .

The Hornes . . . retain at least one meaningful property interest in the reserve raisins: the right to receive some money for their disposition. The Order explicitly provides that raisin producers retain the right to "[t]he net proceeds from the disposition of reserve tonnage raisins" and ensures that reserve raisins will be sold "at prices and in a manner intended to maxim[ize] producer returns," According to the Government, of the 49 crop years for which a reserve pool was operative, producers received equitable distributions of net proceeds from the disposition of reserve raisins in 42.

Granted, this equitable distribution may represent less income than what some or all of the reserve raisins could fetch if sold in an unregulated market. In some years, it may even turn out (and has turned out) to represent no net income. But whether and when that occurs turns on market forces for which the Government cannot be blamed and to which all commodities—indeed, all property—are subject. In any event, we have emphasized that "a reduction in the value of property is not necessarily equated with a taking," that even "a significant restriction . . . imposed on one means of disposing" of property is not necessarily a taking, and that not every "'injury to property by governmental action'" amounts to a taking. . . . I take us at our word: [An] action can[not] be called a per se taking . . . if there remains a property interest that is at most merely damaged. That is the case here; accordingly, no per se taking has occurred.

Nollan v. California Coastal Commission
483 U.S. 825 (1987)

The California Coastal Commission granted a permit to James and Marilyn Nollan to replace a small bungalow on their beachfront lot with a larger house upon the condition that they allow the public an easement to pass across their beach, which was located between two public beaches. The Nollans filed a petition for writ of administrative mandamus, asking the Ventura County Superior Court to invalidate the access condition. They argued that the condition could not be imposed absent evidence that their proposed development would have a direct adverse impact on public access to the beach. The court agreed and remanded the case to the commission for a full evidentiary hearing on that issue. On remand, the commission held a public hearing and made further factual findings; it reaffirmed its imposition of the condition, finding that the new house would increase blockage of the view of the ocean, thus contributing to the development of "a 'wall' of residential structures" that would prevent the public "psychologically . . . from realizing a stretch of coastline exists nearby that they have every right to visit." The Nollans filed a supplemental petition for a writ of administrative mandamus with the California Superior Court, arguing that imposition of the access condition violated the Takings Clause of the Fifth Amendment, as incorporated against the states by the Fourteenth Amendment. The superior court avoided the constitutional question but ruled in their favor on statutory grounds. In its view, the administrative record did not provide an adequate factual basis for concluding that replacement of the bungalow with the house would create a direct or cumulative burden on public access to the ocean. The commission appealed to the California Court of Appeals, which reversed, holding that the access condition violated neither California statutes nor the Takings Clause of the US Constitution. The Nollans appealed to the US Supreme Court. Opinion of the Court: Scalia, Rehnquist, White, Powell, O'Connor. Dissenting opinions: Brennan, Marshall; Blackmun; Stevens, Blackmun.

JUSTICE SCALIA delivered the opinion of the Court.

Had California simply required the Nollans to make an easement across their beachfront available to the public on a permanent basis in order to increase public access to the beach, rather than conditioning their permit to rebuild their house on their agreeing to do so, we have no doubt there would have been a taking. To say that the appropriation of a public easement across a landowner's premises does not constitute the taking of a property interest but rather (as Justice Brennan contends) "a mere restriction on its use," is to use words in a manner that deprives them of all their ordinary meaning. Indeed, one of the principal uses of the eminent domain power is to assure that the government be able to require conveyance of just such interests, so long as it pays for them. . . . Perhaps because the point is so obvious, we have never been confronted with a controversy that required us to rule upon it, but our cases' analysis of the effect of other governmental action leads to the same conclusion. We have repeatedly held that, as to property reserved by its owner for private use, "the right to exclude [others is] 'one of the most essential sticks in the bundle of rights that are commonly characterized as property.'" . . .

Given, then, that requiring uncompensated conveyance of the easement outright would violate the Fourteenth Amendment, the question becomes whether requiring it to be conveyed as a condition for issuing a land-use permit alters the outcome. We have long recognized that land-use regulation does not effect a taking if it "substantially advance[s] legitimate state interests" and does not "den[y]" an owner economically viable use of his land," *Agins v. Tiburon* (1980). Our cases have not elaborated on the standards for determining what constitutes a "legitimate state interest" or what type of connection between the regulation and the state interest satisfies the requirement that the former "substantially advance" the latter. They have made clear, however, that a broad range of governmental purposes and regulations satisfies these requirements. . . . The Commission argues that among these permissible purposes are protecting the public's ability to see the beach, assisting the public in overcoming the "psychological barrier" to using the beach created by a developed shorefront, and preventing congestion on the public beaches. We assume, without deciding, that this is so—in which case the Commission unquestionably would be able to deny the Nollans their permit outright if their new house (alone, or by reason of the cumulative impact produced in conjunction with other construction) would substantially impede these purposes, unless the denial would interfere so drastically with the Nollans' use of their property as to constitute a taking. . . .

The Commission argues that a permit condition that serves the same legitimate police power purpose as a refusal to issue the permit should not be found to be a taking if the refusal to issue the permit would not constitute a taking. We agree. Thus, if the Commission attached to the permit some condition that would have protected the public's ability to see the beach notwithstanding construction of the new house—for example, a height limitation, a width restriction, or a ban on fences—so long as the Commission could have exercised its police power (as we have assumed it could) to forbid construction of the house altogether, imposition of the condition would also be constitutional. Moreover (and here we come closer to the facts of the present case), the condition would be constitutional even if it consisted of the requirement that the Nollans provide a viewing spot on their property for passersby with whose sighting of the ocean their new house would interfere. Although such a requirement, constituting a permanent grant of continuous access to the property, would have to be considered a taking if it were not attached to a development permit, the Commission's assumed power to forbid construction of the house in order to protect the public's view of the beach must surely include the power to condition construction upon some concession by the owner, even a concession of property rights, that serves the same end. If a prohibition designed to accomplish that purpose would be a legitimate exercise of the police power rather

than a taking, it would be strange to conclude that providing the owner an alternative to that prohibition which accomplishes the same purpose is not.

The evident constitutional propriety disappears, however, if the condition substituted for the prohibition utterly fails to further the end advanced as the justification for the prohibition. When that essential nexus is eliminated, the situation becomes the same as if California law forbade shouting fire in a crowded theater, but granted dispensations to those willing to contribute $100 to the state treasury. While a ban on shouting fire can be a core exercise of the State's police power to protect the public safety, and can thus meet even our stringent standards for regulation of speech, adding the unrelated condition alters the purpose to one which, while it may be legitimate, is inadequate to sustain the ban. Therefore, even though, in a sense, requiring a $100 tax contribution in order to shout fire is a lesser restriction on speech than an outright ban, it would not pass constitutional muster. Similarly here, the lack of nexus between the condition and the original purpose of the building restriction converts that purpose to something other than what it was. The purpose then becomes, quite simply, the obtaining of an easement to serve some valid governmental purpose, but without payment of compensation. Whatever may be the outer limits of "legitimate state interests" in the takings and land-use context, this is not one of them. In short, unless the permit condition serves the same governmental purpose as the development ban, the building restriction is not a valid regulation of land use but "an out-and-out plan of extortion." . . .

The Commission claims that it concedes as much, and that we may sustain the condition at issue here by finding that it is reasonably related to the public need or burden that the Nollans' new house creates or to which it contributes. We can accept, for purposes of discussion, the Commission's proposed test as to how close a "fit" between the condition and the burden is required, because we find that this case does not meet even the most untailored standards. The Commission's principal contention to the contrary essentially turns on a play on the word "access." The Nollans' new house, the Commission found, will interfere with "visual access" to the beach. That in turn (along with other shorefront development) will interfere with the desire of people who drive past the Nollans' house to use the beach, thus creating a "psychological barrier" to "access." The Nollans' new house will also, by a process not altogether clear from the Commission's opinion but presumably potent enough to more than offset the effects of the psychological barrier, increase the use of the public beaches, thus creating the need for more "access." These burdens on "access" would be alleviated by a requirement that the Nollans provide "lateral access" to the beach.

Rewriting the argument to eliminate the play on words makes clear that there is nothing to it. It is quite impossible to understand how a requirement that people already on the public beaches be able to walk across the Nollans' property reduces any obstacles to viewing the beach created by the new house. It is also impossible to understand how it lowers any "psychological barrier" to using the public beaches, or how it helps to remedy any additional congestion on them caused by construction of the Nollans' new house. We therefore find that the Commission's imposition of the permit condition cannot be treated as an exercise of its land-use power for any of these purposes. Our conclusion on this point is consistent with the approach taken by every other court that has considered the question, with the exception of the California state courts.

Justice Brennan argues that imposition of the access requirement is not irrational. In his version of the Commission's argument, the reason for the requirement is that in its absence, a person looking toward the beach from the road will see a street of residential structures including the Nollans' new home and conclude that there is no public beach nearby. If, however, that person sees people passing and repassing along the dry sand behind the Nollans' home, he will realize that there is a public beach somewhere in the vicinity. . . . The Commission's action, however, was based on the opposite factual finding that the wall of houses completely blocked the view of the beach and that a person looking from the road would not be able to see it at all.

Even if the Commission had made the finding that Justice Brennan proposes, however, it is not certain that it would suffice. We do not share Justice Brennan's confidence that the Commission "should have little difficulty in the future in utilizing its expertise to demonstrate a specific connection between provisions for access and burdens on access," . . . that will avoid the effect of today's decision. We view the Fifth Amendment's Property Clause to be more than a pleading requirement, and compliance with it to be more than an exercise in cleverness and imagination. As indicated earlier, our cases describe the condition for abridgment of property rights through the police power as a "*substantial* advanc[ing]" of a legitimate state interest. We are inclined to be particularly careful about the adjective where the actual conveyance of property is made a condition to the lifting of a land-use restriction, since in that context there is heightened risk that the purpose is avoidance of the compensation requirement, rather than the stated police power objective.

We are left, then, with the Commission's justification for the access requirement unrelated to land-use regulation: The Commission notes that there are several existing provisions of pass and repass lateral access benefits already given by past Faria Beach Tract applicants as a result of prior coastal permit decisions. The access required as a condition of this permit is part of a comprehensive program to provide continuous public access along Faria Beach as the lots undergo development or redevelopment. . . .

That is simply an expression of the Commission's belief that the public interest will be served by a continuous strip of publicly accessible beach along the coast. The Commission may well be right that it is a good idea, but that does not establish that the Nollans (and other coastal residents) alone can be compelled to contribute to its realization. Rather, California is free to advance its "comprehensive program," if it wishes, by using its power of eminent domain for this "public purpose," but if it wants an easement across the Nollans' property, it must pay for it.

Reversed.

JUSTICE BRENNAN, with whom JUSTICE MARSHALL joins, dissenting.

Appellants in this case sought to construct a new dwelling on their beach lot that would both diminish visual access to the beach and move private development closer to the public tidelands.

The Commission reasonably concluded that such "buildout," both individually and cumulatively, threatens public access to the shore. It sought to offset this encroachment by obtaining assurance that the public may walk along the shoreline in order to gain access to the ocean. The Court finds this an illegitimate exercise of the police power, because it maintains that there is no reasonable relationship between the effect of the development and the condition imposed.

The first problem with this conclusion is that the Court imposes a standard of precision for the exercise of a State's police power that has been discredited for the better part of this century. Furthermore, even under the Court's cramped standard, the permit condition imposed in this case directly responds to the specific type of burden on access created by appellants' development. Finally, a review of those factors deemed most significant in takings analysis makes clear that the Commission's action implicates none of the concerns underlying the Takings Clause.

Even if we accept the Court's unusual demand for a precise match between the condition imposed and the specific type of burden on access created by the appellants, the State's action easily satisfies this requirement. First, the lateral access condition serves to dissipate the impression that the beach that lies behind the wall of homes along the shore is for private use only. It requires no exceptional imaginative powers to find plausible the Commission's point that the average person passing along the road in front of a phalanx of imposing permanent residences, including the appellants' new home, is likely to conclude that this particular portion of the shore is not open to the public. If, however, that person can see that numerous people are passing and repassing along the dry sand, this conveys the message that the beach is in fact open for use by the public. Furthermore, those persons who go down to the public beach a quarter-mile away will be able to look down the coastline and see that persons have continuous access to the tidelands, and will observe signs that proclaim the public's right of access over the dry sand. The burden produced by the diminution in visual access—the impression that the beach is not open to the public—is thus directly alleviated by the provision for public access over the dry sand. The Court therefore has an unrealistically limited conception of what measures could reasonably be chosen to mitigate the burden produced by a diminution of visual access. . . .

The fact that the Commission's action is a legitimate exercise of the police power does not, of course, insulate it from a takings challenge, for when "regulation goes too far it will be recognized as a taking." Conventional takings analysis underscores the implausibility of the Court's holding, for it demonstrates that this exercise of California's police power implicates none of the concerns that underlie our takings jurisprudence. . . .

. . . The character of the regulation in this case is not unilateral government action, but a condition on approval of a development request submitted by appellants. The state has not sought to interfere with any pre-existing property interest, but has responded to appellants' proposal to intensify development on the coast. Appellants themselves chose to submit a new development application, and could claim no property interest in its approval. They were aware that approval of such development would be conditioned on preservation of adequate public access to the ocean. The State has initiated no action against appellants' property; had the Nollans' not proposed more intensive development in the coastal zone, they would never have been subject to the provision that they challenge.

Examination of the economic impact of the Commission's action reinforces the conclusion that no taking has occurred. Allowing appellants to intensify development along the coast in exchange for ensuring public access to the ocean is a classic instance of government action that produces a "reciprocity of advantage." . . . Appellants have been allowed to replace a one-story 521-square-foot beach home with a two-story 1,674-square-foot residence and an attached two-car garage, resulting in development covering 2,464 square feet of the lot.

Such development obviously significantly increases the value of appellants' property; appellants make no contention that this increase is offset by any diminution in value resulting from the deed restriction, much less that the restriction made the property less valuable than it would have been without the new construction. Furthermore, appellants gain an additional benefit from the Commission's permit condition program. They are able to walk along the beach beyond the confines of their own property only because the Commission has required deed restrictions as a condition of approving other new beach developments. Thus appellants benefit both as private landowners and as members of the public from the fact that new development permit requests are conditioned on preservation of public access. . . .

. . . State agencies therefore require considerable flexibility in responding to private desires for development in a way that guarantees the preservation of public access to the coast. They should be encouraged to regulate development in the context of the overall balance of competing uses of the shoreline. The Court today does precisely the opposite, overruling an eminently reasonable exercise of an expert state agency's judgment, substituting its own narrow view of how this balance should be struck. Its reasoning is hardly suited to the complex reality of natural resource protection in the 20th century. I can only hope that today's decision is an aberration, and that a broader vision ultimately prevails. I dissent.

Lucas v. South Carolina Coastal Council
505 U.S. 1003 (1992)

In 1986, David Lucas paid $975,000 for two residential lots on the Isle of Palms, a barrier island situated to the east of Charleston, South Carolina. He intended to build single-family houses on them, such as were found on the immediately adjacent lots. At the time, Lucas's lots were not subject to South Carolina's coastal-zone building-permit requirements. In 1988, however, the South Carolina Legislature enacted the Beachfront Management Act, which had the direct effect of prohibiting Lucas from erecting any permanent habitable structures on his land. He filed suit against the newly created Coastal Council in the South Carolina Court of Common Pleas, contending that the Beachfront Management Act's ban on construction effected a taking of his property under the Fifth and Fourteenth Amendments and therefore required the payment of just compensation. He did not deny the validity of the act as a lawful exercise of South Carolina's police power; he simply contended that the act deprived him of all "economically viable use" of his property and that he was entitled to compensation, regardless of whether the legislature had acted in furtherance of a legitimate police-power objective. The state trial court agreed, finding that the ban had rendered Lucas's parcels "valueless," and ordered the Coastal

Council to pay Lucas "just compensation" in the amount of $1,232,387.50. The Supreme Court of South Carolina reversed. Because Lucas had not attacked the validity of the statute as such, it found itself bound to accept the uncontested findings of the South Carolina Legislature that new construction in the coastal zone of the sort that Lucas intended threatened South Carolina's beaches. It concluded, on the basis of Mugler v. Kansas *(1887) and a long line of cases that followed it, that when regulation is necessary to prevent "harmful or noxious uses" of property akin to public nuisances, no compensation is owed under the Takings Clause, regardless of the regulation's effect on the property's value. The US Supreme Court granted certiorari. Opinion of the Court:* <u>Scalia</u>, *Rehnquist, White, O'Connor, Thomas. Concurring in the judgment:* <u>Kennedy</u>. *Dissenting opinions:* <u>Blackmun</u>; <u>Stevens</u>. *Separate statement voting to dismiss the writ of certiorari:* <u>Souter</u>.

JUSTICE SCALIA delivered the opinion of the Court.

. . . Prior to Justice Holmes' exposition in *Pennsylvania Coal Co. v. Mahon* (1922), it was generally thought that the Takings Clause reached only a "direct appropriation" of property, *Legal Tender Cases* (1871), or the functional equivalent of a "practical ouster of [the owner's] possession." *Transportation Co. v. Chicago* (1879). Justice Holmes recognized in *Mahon*, however, that if the protection against physical appropriations of private property was to be meaningfully enforced, the government's power to redefine the range of interests included in the ownership of property was necessarily constrained by constitutional limits. If, instead, the uses of private property were subject to unbridled, uncompensated qualification under the police power, "the natural tendency of human nature [would be] to extend the qualification more and more until at last private property disappear[ed]." These considerations gave birth in that case to the oft-cited maxim that, "while property may be regulated to a certain extent, if regulation goes too far it will be recognized as a taking." Nevertheless, our decision in *Mahon* offered little insight into when, and under what circumstances, a given regulation would be seen as going "too far" for purposes of the Fifth Amendment. In 70-odd years of succeeding "regulatory takings" jurisprudence, we have generally eschewed any "set formula" for determining how far is too far, preferring to "engag[e] in . . . essentially *ad hoc,* factual inquiries," *Penn Central Transportation Co. v. New York City* (1978). We have, however, described at least two discrete categories of regulatory action as compensable without case-specific inquiry into the public interest advanced in support of the restraint. The first encompasses regulations that compel the property owner to suffer a physical "invasion" of his property. In general (at least with regard to permanent invasions), no matter how minute the intrusion, and no matter how weighty the public purpose behind it, we have required compensation. For example, in *Loretto v. Teleprompter Manhattan CATV Corp.* (1982), we determined that New York's law requiring landlords to allow television cable companies to emplace cable facilities in their apartment buildings constituted a taking, even though the facilities occupied at most only 1 1/2 cubic feet of the landlords' property.

The second situation in which we have found categorical treatment appropriate is where regulation denies all economically beneficial or productive use of land. As we have said on numerous occasions, the Fifth Amendment is violated when land-use regulation "does not substantially advance legitimate state interests or denies an owner economically viable use of his land." We have never set forth the justification for this rule. Perhaps it is simply, as Justice Brennan suggested, that total deprivation of beneficial use is, from the landowner's point of view, the equivalent of a physical appropriation.

. . . On the other side of the balance, affirmatively supporting a compensation requirement, is the fact that regulations that leave the owner of land without economically beneficial or productive options for its use—typically, as here, by requiring land to be left substantially in its natural state—carry with them a heightened risk that private property is being pressed into some form of public service under the guise of mitigating serious public harm. We think, in short, that there are good reasons for our frequently expressed belief that when the owner of real property has been called upon to sacrifice all economically beneficial uses in the name of the common good, that is, to leave his property economically idle, he has suffered a taking.

The trial court found Lucas's two beachfront lots to have been rendered valueless by respondent's enforcement of the coastal-zone construction ban. Under Lucas's theory of the case, which rested upon our "no economically viable use" statements, that finding entitled him to compensation. Lucas believed it unnecessary to take issue with either the purposes behind the Beachfront Management Act, or the means chosen by the South Carolina Legislature to effectuate those purposes. The South Carolina Supreme Court, however, thought otherwise. In its view, the Beachfront Management Act was no ordinary enactment, but involved an exercise of South Carolina's "police powers" to mitigate the harm to the public interest that petitioner's use of his land might occasion. By neglecting to dispute the findings enumerated in the Act or otherwise to challenge the legislature's purposes, petitioner "concede[d] that the beach/dune area of South Carolina's shores is an extremely valuable public resource; that the erection of new construction, *inter alia,* contributes to the erosion and destruction of this public resource; and that discouraging new construction in close proximity to the beach/dune area is necessary to prevent a great public harm." In the court's view, these concessions brought petitioner's challenge within a long line of this Court's cases sustaining against Due Process and Takings Clause challenges the State's use of its "police powers" to enjoin a property owner from activities akin to public nuisances. . . .

It is correct that many of our prior opinions have suggested that "harmful or noxious uses" of property may be proscribed by government regulation without the requirement of compensation. However, we think the South Carolina Supreme Court was too quick to conclude that that principle decides the present case. . . .

A fortiori the legislature's recitation of a noxious-use justification cannot be the basis for departing from our categorical rule that total regulatory takings must be compensated. If it were, departure would virtually always be allowed. The South Carolina Supreme Court's approach would essentially nullify *Mahon's* affirmation of limits to the noncompensable exercise of the police power. . . .

Where the State seeks to sustain regulation that deprives land of all economically beneficial use, we think it may resist compensation only if the logically antecedent inquiry into the nature of the owner's estate shows that the proscribed use interests were not part of his title to begin with. This accords, we think, with our "takings" jurisprudence, which has traditionally been guided by the understandings of our citizens regarding the content of, and the State's power over, the "bundle of rights" that they acquire when they obtain title to property. Confiscatory regulations, i.e., regulations that prohibit all economically beneficial use of land, cannot be newly legislated or decreed (without compensation), but must inhere in the title itself, in the restrictions that background principles of the State's law of property and nuisance already place upon land ownership. . . .

On this analysis, the owner of a lake bed, for example, would not be entitled to compensation when he is denied the requisite permit to engage in a landfilling operation that would have the effect of flooding others' land. Nor the corporate owner of a nuclear generating plant, when it is directed to remove all improvements from its land upon discovery that the plant sits astride an earthquake fault. Such regulatory action may well have the effect of eliminating the land's only economically productive use, but it does not proscribe a productive use that was previously permissible under relevant property and nuisance principles. The use of these properties for what are now expressly prohibited purposes was always unlawful, and (subject to other constitutional limitations) it was open to the State at any point to make the implication of those background principles of nuisance and property law explicit. When, however, a regulation that declares "off-limits" all economically productive or beneficial uses of land goes beyond what the relevant background principles would dictate, compensation must be paid to sustain it. The "total taking" inquiry we require today will ordinarily entail (as the application of state nuisance law ordinarily entails) analysis of, among other things, the degree of harm to public lands and resources, or adjacent private property, posed by the claimant's proposed activities, the social value of the claimant's activities and their suitability to the locality in question, and the relative ease with which the alleged harm can be avoided through measures taken by the claimant and the government (or adjacent private landowners) alike. The fact that a particular use has long been engaged in by similarly situated owners ordinarily imports a lack of any common-law prohibition. So also does the fact that other landowners, similarly situated, are permitted to continue the use denied to the claimant.

We emphasize that to win its case South Carolina must do more than proffer the legislature's declaration that the uses Lucas desires are inconsistent with the public interest. As we have said, a "State, by *ipse dixit,* may not transform private property into public property without compensation. . . ." Instead, as it would be required to do if it sought to restrain Lucas in a common-law action for public nuisance, South Carolina must identify background principles of nuisance and property law that prohibit the uses he now intends in the circumstances in which the property is presently found. Only on this showing can the State fairly claim that, in proscribing all such beneficial uses, the Beachfront Management Act is taking nothing. . . .

The judgment is reversed and the cause remanded for proceedings not inconsistent with this opinion.

JUSTICE BLACKMUN, dissenting.

. . . This Court repeatedly has recognized the ability of government, in certain circumstances, to regulate property without compensation no matter how adverse the financial effect on the owner may be. More than a century ago, the Court explicitly upheld the right of States to prohibit uses of property injurious to public health, safety, or welfare without paying compensation: "A prohibition simply upon the use

of property for purposes that are declared, by valid legislation, to be injurious to the health, morals, or safety of the community, cannot, in any just sense, be deemed a taking or an appropriation of property." *Mugler v. Kansas* (1887). On this basis, the Court upheld an ordinance effectively prohibiting operation of a previously lawful brewery, although the "establishments will become of no value as property."

Mugler was only the beginning in a long line of cases. In none of the cases did the Court suggest that the right of a State to prohibit certain activities without paying compensation turned on the availability of some residual valuable use. Instead, the cases depended on whether the government interest was sufficient to prohibit the activity, given the significant private cost.

Koontz v. St. Johns River Water Management District
570 U.S. ___ (2013)

The estate of Coy Koontz Sr. sought permits to develop a section of his property from the St. Johns River Water Management District, which, under Florida law, requires permit applicants wishing to build on wetlands to offset the resulting environmental damage. Koontz offered to mitigate the environmental effects of his development proposal by deeding to the District a conservation easement on nearly three-quarters of his property. The District rejected Koontz's proposal and informed him that it would approve construction only if he (1) reduced the size of his development and deeded to the District a conservation easement on the resulting larger remainder of his property or (2) hired contractors to make improvements to District-owned wetlands several miles away. Believing the District's demands to be excessive in light of the environmental effects his proposal would have caused, Koontz filed suit under a state law that provides money damages for agency action that is an "unreasonable exercise of the state's police power constituting a taking without just compensation." The trial court found the District's actions unlawful because they failed the requirements of Nollan v. California Coastal Commission *(1987) and* Dolan v. City of Tigard *(1994). Those cases held that the govern-*

ment may not condition the approval of a land-use permit on the owner's relinquishment of a portion of his property unless there is a nexus and rough proportionality between the government's demand and the effects of the proposed land use. The District Court of Appeal affirmed, but the State Supreme Court reversed on two grounds. First, it held that petitioner's claim failed because, unlike in Nollan *or* Dolan, *the District denied the application; and second, it held that a demand for money cannot give rise to a claim under* Nollan *and* Dolan. *Koontz petitioned the Supreme Court, which granted certiorari. Opinion of the Court:* Alito, *Roberts, Scalia, Kennedy, Thomas. Dissenting opinion:* Kagan, *Ginsburg, Breyer, Sotomayor.*

JUSTICE ALITO delivered the opinion of the Court.

Our decisions in *Nollan v. California Coastal Commission* (1987) and *Dolan v. City of Tigard* (1994) provide important protection against the misuse of the power of land-use regulation. In those cases, we held that a unit of government may not condition the approval of a land-use permit on the owner's relinquishment of a portion of his property unless there is a "nexus" and "rough proportionality" between the government's demand and the effects of the proposed land use. In this case, the St. Johns River Water Management District (District) believes that it circumvented *Nollan* and *Dolan* because of the way in which it structured its handling of a permit application submitted by Coy Koontz, Sr., whose estate is represented in this Court by Coy Koontz, Jr. The District did not approve his application on the condition that he surrender an interest in his land. Instead, the District, after suggesting that he could obtain approval by signing over such an interest, denied his application because he refused to yield. The Florida Supreme Court blessed this maneuver and thus effectively interred those important decisions. Because we conclude that *Nollan* and *Dolan* cannot be evaded in this way, the Florida Supreme Court's decision must be reversed.

I

A

In 1972, petitioner purchased an undeveloped 14.9-acre tract of land on the south side of Florida State Road 50, a divided four-lane highway east of Orlando. The property is located less than 1,000 feet from that road's intersection with Florida State Road 408, a tolled expressway that is one of Orlando's major thoroughfares. . . . Although largely classified as wetlands by the State, the northern section drains well. . . .

In 1984, in an effort to protect the State's rapidly diminishing wetlands, the Florida Legislature passed the Warren S. Henderson Wetlands Protection Act, which made it illegal for anyone to "dredge or fill in, on, or over surface waters" without a Wetlands Resource Management (WRM) permit. Under the Henderson Act, permit applicants are required to provide "reasonable assurance" that proposed construction on wetlands is "not contrary to the public interest," as defined by an enumerated list of criteria. Consistent with the Henderson Act, the St. Johns River Water Management District, the district with jurisdiction over petitioner's land, requires that permit applicants wishing to build on wetlands offset the result-

ing environmental damage by creating, enhancing, or preserving wetlands elsewhere.

Petitioner decided to develop the 3.7-acre northern section of his property, and in 1994 he applied to the District for MSSW and WRM permits. Under his proposal, petitioner would have raised the elevation of the northernmost section of his land to make it suitable for a building, graded the land from the southern edge of the building site . . . , and installed a dry-bed pond for retaining and gradually releasing stormwater runoff from the building and its parking lot. To mitigate the environmental effects of his proposal, petitioner offered to foreclose any possible future development of the approximately 11-acre southern section of his land by deeding to the District a conservation easement on that portion of his property.

The District considered the 11-acre conservation easement to be inadequate, and it informed petitioner that it would approve construction only if he agreed to one of two concessions. First, the District proposed that petitioner reduce the size of his development to 1 acre and deed to the District a conservation easement on the remaining 13.9 acres. To reduce the development area, the District suggested that petitioner could eliminate the dry-bed pond from his proposal and instead install a more costly subsurface stormwater management system beneath the building site. The District also suggested that petitioner install retaining walls rather than gradually sloping the land from the building site down to the elevation of the rest of his property to the south.

In the alternative, the District told petitioner that he could proceed with the development as proposed, building on 3.7 acres and deeding a conservation easement to the government on the remainder of the property, if he also agreed to hire contractors to make improvements to District-owned land several miles away. Specifically, petitioner could pay to replace culverts on one parcel or fill in ditches on another. Either of those projects would have enhanced approximately 50 acres of District-owned wetlands. When the District asks permit applicants to fund offsite mitigation work, its policy is never to require any particular offsite project, and it did not do so here. Instead, the District said that it "would also favorably consider" alternatives to its suggested offsite mitigation projects if petitioner proposed something "equivalent."

Believing the District's demands for mitigation to be excessive in light of the environmental effects that his building proposal would have caused, petitioner filed suit in state court. Among other claims, he argued that he was entitled to relief under Fla. Stat. §373.617(2), which allows owners to recover "monetary damages" if a state agency's action is "an unreasonable exercise of the state's police power constituting a taking without just compensation."

II

A

We have said in a variety of contexts that "the government may not deny a benefit to a person because he exercises a constitutional right." *Regan v. Taxation With Representation of Washington* (1983). . . . *Nollan* and *Dolan* "involve a special application" of this doctrine that protects the Fifth Amendment right to just compensation for property the government takes when owners apply for land-use permits. Our decisions in those cases reflect two realities of the permitting process. The first is that land-use permit applicants are especially vulnerable to the type of coercion that the unconstitutional conditions doctrine prohibits because the government often has broad discretion to deny a permit that is worth far more than property it would like to take. By conditioning a building permit on the owner's deeding over a public right-of-way, for example, the government can pressure an owner into voluntarily giving up property for which the Fifth Amendment would otherwise require just compensation. So long as the building permit is more valuable than any just compensation the owner could hope to receive for the right-of-way, the owner is likely to accede to the government's demand, no matter how unreasonable. Extortionate demands of this sort frustrate the Fifth Amendment right to just compensation, and the unconstitutional conditions doctrine prohibits them.

A second reality of the permitting process is that many proposed land uses threaten to impose costs on the public that dedications of property can offset. Where a building proposal would substantially increase traffic congestion, for example, officials might condition permit approval on the owner's agreement to deed over the land needed to widen a public road. Respondent argues that a similar rationale justifies the exaction at issue here: petitioner's proposed construction project, it submits, would destroy wetlands on his property, and in order to compensate for this loss, respondent demands that he enhance wetlands elsewhere. Insisting that landowners internalize the negative externalities of their conduct is a hallmark of responsible land-use policy, and we have long sustained such regulations against constitutional attack.

Nollan and *Dolan* accommodate both realities by allowing the government to condition approval of a permit on the dedication of property to the public so long as there is a "nexus" and "rough proportionality" between the property that the government demands and the social costs of the applicant's proposal. Our precedents thus enable permitting authorities to insist that applicants bear the full costs of their proposals while still forbidding the government from engaging in "out-and-out . . . extortion" that would thwart the Fifth Amendment right to just compensation. Under *Nollan* and *Dolan* the government may choose whether and how a permit applicant is required to mitigate the impacts of a proposed development, but it may not leverage its legitimate interest in mitigation to pursue governmental ends that lack an essential nexus and rough proportionality to those impacts.

B

The principles that undergird our decisions in *Nollan* and *Dolan* do not change depending on whether the government approves a permit on the condition that the applicant turn over property or denies a permit because the applicant refuses to do so. We have often concluded that denials of governmental benefits were impermissible under the unconstitutional conditions doctrine. In so holding, we have recognized that regardless of whether the government ultimately succeeds in pressuring someone into forfeiting a constitutional right, the unconstitutional conditions doctrine forbids burdening the Constitution's enumerated rights by coercively withholding benefits from those who exercise them.

A contrary rule would be especially untenable in this case because it would enable the government to evade the limitations of *Nollan* and *Dolan* simply by phrasing its demands for property as conditions precedent to permit approval. Under the Florida Supreme Court's approach, a government order stating that a permit is "approved if" the owner turns over property would be subject to *Nollan* and *Dolan*, but an identical order that uses the words "denied until" would not. Our unconstitutional conditions cases have long refused to attach significance to the distinction between conditions precedent and conditions subsequent. To do so here would effectively render *Nollan* and *Dolan* a dead letter.

The Florida Supreme Court puzzled over how the government's demand for property can violate the Takings Clause even though "'no property of any kind was ever taken,'" but the unconstitutional conditions doctrine provides a ready answer. Extortionate demands for property in the land-use permitting context run afoul of the Takings Clause not because they take property but because they impermissibly burden the right not to have property taken without just compensation. As in other unconstitutional conditions cases in which someone refuses to cede a constitutional right in the face of coercive pressure, the impermissible denial of a governmental benefit is a constitutionally cognizable injury.

Nor does it make a difference, as respondent suggests, that the government might have been able to deny petitioner's application outright without giving him the option of securing a permit by agreeing to spend money to improve public lands. Virtually all of our unconstitutional conditions cases involve a gratuitous governmental benefit of some kind. Yet we have repeatedly rejected the argument that if the government need not confer a benefit at all, it can withhold the benefit because someone refuses to give up constitutional rights. Even if respondent would have been entirely

within its rights in denying the permit for some other reason, that greater authority does not imply a lesser power to condition permit approval on petitioner's forfeiture of his constitutional rights. . . .

III

We turn to the Florida Supreme Court's alternative holding that petitioner's claim fails because respondent asked him to spend money rather than give up an easement on his land. A predicate for any unconstitutional conditions claim is that the government could not have constitutionally ordered the person asserting the claim to do what it attempted to pressure that person into doing. For that reason, we began our analysis in both *Nollan* and *Dolan* by observing that if the government had directly seized the easements it sought to obtain through the permitting process, it would have committed a per se taking. The Florida Supreme Court held that petitioner's claim fails at this first step because the subject of the exaction at issue here was money rather than a more tangible interest in real property. Respondent and the dissent take the same position. . . .

. . . [I]f we accepted this argument it would be very easy for land-use permitting officials to evade the limitations of *Nollan* and *Dolan*. Because the government need only provide a permit applicant with one alternative that satisfies the nexus and rough proportionality standards, a permitting authority wishing to exact an easement could simply give the owner a choice of either surrendering an easement or making a payment equal to the easement's value. Such so-called "in lieu of" fees are utterly commonplace, and they are functionally equivalent to other types of land use exactions. For that reason . . . , we reject respondent's argument and hold that so-called "monetary exactions" must satisfy the nexus and rough proportionality requirements of *Nollan* and *Dolan*.

* * *

We hold that the government's demand for property from a land-use permit applicant must satisfy the requirements of *Nollan* and *Dolan* even when the government denies the permit and even when its demand is for money. The Court expresses no view on the merits of petitioner's claim that respondent's actions here failed to comply with the principles set forth in this opinion and those two cases. The Florida Supreme Court's judgment is reversed, and this case is remanded for further proceedings not inconsistent with this opinion.

JUSTICE KAGAN, with whom JUSTICE GINSBURG, JUSTICE BREYER, and JUSTICE SOTOMAYOR join, dissenting.

In the paradigmatic case triggering review under *Nollan* and *Dolan*, the government approves a building permit on the condition that the landowner relinquish an interest in real property, like an easement. The significant legal questions that the Court resolves today are whether *Nollan* and *Dolan* also apply when that case is varied in two ways. First, what if the government does not approve the permit, but instead demands that the condition be fulfilled before it will do so? Second, what if the condition entails not transferring real property, but simply paying money? . . .

I think the Court gets the first question it addresses right. The *Nollan-Dolan* standard applies not only when the government approves a development permit conditioned on the owner's conveyance of a property interest (i.e., imposes a condition subsequent), but also when the government denies a permit until the owner meets the condition (i.e., imposes a condition precedent). That means an owner may challenge the denial of a permit on the ground that the government's condition lacks the "nexus" and "rough proportionality" to the development's social costs that *Nollan* and *Dolan* require. Still, the condition-subsequent and condition-precedent situations differ in an important way. When the government grants a permit subject to the relinquishment of real property, and that condition does not satisfy *Nollan* and *Dolan*, then the government has taken the property and must pay just compensation under the Fifth Amendment. But when the government denies a permit because an owner has refused to accede to that same demand, nothing has actually been taken. The owner is entitled to have the improper condition removed; and he may be entitled to a monetary remedy created by state law for imposing such a condition; but he cannot be entitled to constitutional compensation for a taking of property. So far, we all agree.

Our core disagreement concerns the second question the Court addresses. The majority extends *Nollan* and *Dolan* to cases in which the government conditions a permit not on the transfer of real property, but instead on the payment or expenditure of money. . . . The boundaries of the majority's new rule are uncertain. But it threatens to subject a vast array of land-use regulations, applied daily in States and localities throughout the country, to heightened constitutional scrutiny. I would not embark on so unwise an adventure, and would affirm the Florida Supreme Court's decision.

I also would affirm for two independent reasons establishing that Koontz cannot get the money damages he seeks. First, respondent St. Johns River Water Management District (District) never demanded anything (including money) in exchange for a permit; the *Nollan-Dolan* standard therefore does not come into play (even assuming that test applies to demands for money). Second, no taking occurred in this case because Koontz never acceded to a demand (even had there been one), and so no property changed hands; as just noted, Koontz therefore cannot claim just compensation under the Fifth Amendment. The majority does not take issue with my first conclusion, and affirmatively agrees with my second. But the majority thinks Koontz might still be entitled to money damages, and remands to the Florida Supreme Court on that question. I do not see how, and expect that court will so rule.

I

. . . Koontz claims that the District demanded that he spend money to improve public wetlands, not that he hand over a real property interest. I assume for now that the District made that demand (although I think it did not). The key question then is: Independent of the permitting process, does requiring a person to pay money to the government, or spend money on its behalf, constitute a taking requiring just compensation? Only if the answer is yes does the *Nollan-Dolan* test apply. . . . [But] a requirement that a person pay money to repair public wetlands is not a taking. Such an order does not affect a "specific and identified propert[y] or property right"; it simply "imposes an obligation to perform an act" (the improvement of wetlands) that costs money. To be sure, when a person spends money on the government's behalf, or pays money directly to the government, it "will reduce [his] net worth"—but that "can be said of any law which has an adverse economic effect" on someone. Because the government is merely imposing a "general liability" to pay money—and therefore is "indifferent as to how the regulated entity elects to comply or the property it uses to do so"—the order to repair wetlands, viewed independent of the permitting process, does not constitute a taking. And that means the order does not trigger the *Nollan-Dolan* test, because it does not force Koontz to relinquish a constitutional right. . . .

The majority's approach . . . threatens significant practical harm. By applying *Nollan* and *Dolan* to permit conditions requiring monetary payments—with no express limitation except as to taxes—the majority extends the Takings Clause, with its notoriously "difficult" and "perplexing" standards, into the very heart of local land-use regulation and service delivery. Cities and towns across the nation impose many kinds of permitting fees every day. Some enable a government to mitigate a new development's impact on the community, like increased traffic or pollution—or destruction of wetlands. Others cover the direct costs of providing services like sewage or water to the development. Still others are meant to limit the number of landowners who engage in a certain activity, as fees for liquor licenses do. All now must meet *Nollan* and *Dolan*'s nexus and proportionality tests. The Federal Constitution thus will decide whether one town is overcharging for sewage, or another is setting the price to sell liquor too high. And the flexibility of state and local governments to take the most routine actions to enhance their communities will diminish accordingly. That problem becomes still worse because the majority's distinction between monetary "exactions" and taxes is so hard to apply. The majority acknowledges, as it must, that taxes are not takings. But once the majority decides that a simple demand to pay money—the sort of thing often viewed as a

tax—can count as an impermissible "exaction," how is anyone to tell the two apart? . . .

At bottom, the majority's analysis seems to grow out of a yen for a prophylactic rule: Unless *Nollan* and *Dolan* apply to monetary demands, the majority worries, "land-use permitting officials" could easily "evade the limitations" on exaction of real property interests that those decisions impose. But that is a prophylaxis in search of a problem. No one has presented evidence that in the many States declining to apply heightened scrutiny to permitting fees, local officials routinely short-circuit *Nollan* and *Dolan* to extort the surrender of real property interests having no relation to a development's costs. And if officials were to impose a fee as a contrivance to take an easement (or other real property right), then a court could indeed apply *Nollan* and *Dolan*. That situation does not call for a rule extending, as the majority's does, to all monetary exactions. Finally, a court can use the *Penn Central* framework, the Due Process Clause, and (in many places) state law to protect against monetary demands, whether or not imposed to evade *Nollan* and *Dolan*, that simply "go too far."

In sum, *Nollan* and *Dolan* restrain governments from using the permitting process to do what the Takings Clause would otherwise prevent—i.e., take a specific property interest without just compensation. Those cases have no application when governments impose a general financial obligation as part of the permitting process. . . . By extending *Nollan* and *Dolan*'s heightened scrutiny to a simple payment demand, the majority threatens the heartland of local land-use regulation and service delivery, at a bare minimum depriving state and local governments of "necessary predictability." That decision is unwarranted—and deeply unwise. I would keep *Nollan* and *Dolan* in their intended sphere and affirm the Florida Supreme Court. . . .

III

Nollan and *Dolan* are important decisions, designed to curb governments from using their power over land-use permitting to extract for free what the Takings Clause would otherwise require them to pay for. But for no fewer than three independent reasons, this case does not present that problem. First and foremost, the government commits a taking only when it appropriates a specific property interest, not when it requires a person to pay or spend money. Here, the District never took or threatened such an interest; it tried to extract from Koontz solely a commitment to spend money to repair public wetlands. Second, *Nollan* and *Dolan* can operate only when the government makes a demand of the permit applicant; the decisions' prerequisite, in other words, is a condition. Here, the District never made such a demand: It informed Koontz that his applications did not meet legal requirements; it offered suggestions for bringing those applications into compliance; and it solicited further proposals from Koontz to achieve the same end. That is not the stuff of which an unconstitutional condition is made. And third, the Florida statute at issue here does not, in any event, offer a damages remedy for imposing such a condition. It provides relief only for a consummated taking, which did not occur here. The majority's errors here are consequential. The majority turns a broad array of local land-use regulations into federal constitutional questions. It deprives state and local governments of the flexibility they need to enhance their communities—to ensure environmentally sound and economically productive development. It places courts smack in the middle of the most everyday local government activity. As those consequences play out across the country, I believe the Court will rue today's decision. I respectfully dissent.

5

Freedom of Speech, Press, and Association

CHAPTER OUTLINE

The First Amendment speaks in strikingly absolute terms: "Congress shall make no law abridging the freedom of speech, or of the press." The Supreme Court's interpretation of these guarantees has been both broader and narrower than a literal reading of the amendment might suggest. The Court has ruled that the amendment protects channels of communication other than speech and press, including those such as television and the Internet invented since the amendment's adoption. It has also extended some protection to actions undertaken with communicative intent such as political demonstrations and symbolic acts, even if they do not involve speech. Acknowledging that "effective advocacy of both public and private points of view, particularly controversial ones, is undeniably enhanced by group association," the Court recognized in *NAACP v. Alabama* (1958) a First Amendment right to freedom of association for expressive purposes. Most important, in *Gitlow v. New York* (1925) and *Near v. Minnesota* (1931), the justices ruled that under the Due Process Clause of the Fourteenth Amendment, the First Amendment's restrictions likewise apply to state regulations of speech and of the press. In fact, most free speech cases have involved challenges to state or local enactments.

But the Court has never held that the First Amendment prohibits all regulation of speech and the press. It has upheld restrictions on the time, place, and manner of expression—for instance, regulations governing the use of loudspeakers and limiting the distribution of leaflets in airports. It has denied constitutional protection altogether to some categories of expression ("the lewd and the obscene, the profane, the libelous, and the insulting or 'fighting' words") and extended protection only in a limited way to others, such as commercial advertising.[1] Finally, it has concluded that the protection accorded expression depends on the effects it is likely to produce. As Justice Oliver Wendell Holmes noted in *Schenck v. United States* (1919), "The most stringent protection of free speech would not protect a man in falsely shouting fire in a theater and causing a panic."

General acceptance of these propositions has not precluded disagreements about the standards to be applied in evaluating First Amendment claims, about the application of these standards in individual cases, and about the level of deference to be accorded statutes that impinge on speech and the press. This chapter examines how the differing interpretations of the ends of the First Amendment have found expression in the standards that the Court has employed in press and speech cases.

THE MEANING OF THE FIRST AMENDMENT

The First Amendment prohibits all laws abridging the freedom of speech and of the press, so the meaning of the amendment depends on the definition and scope of those freedoms. Because the Framers in the Bill of Rights were concerned more with protecting existing freedoms than with forging new liberties, the treatment of those freedoms in English law may be relevant to understanding the meaning of the First Amendment. William Blackstone in *Commentaries on the Law of England* summarized the English law on freedom of the press immediately before the American Revolution:

> The liberty of the press consists in laying no previous restraints upon publications, and not in freedom from censure for criminal matter when published. To punish (as the law does at present) any dangerous or offensive writings, which when published, shall on a fair and impartial trial be adjudged of a pernicious tendency, is necessary for the preservation of peace and good order, a government and religion, the only solid foundations of civil liberty.

Under English law, then, freedom of the press did not mean the right to publish whatever one chose without fear of punishment, for that could jeopardize peace and good order. Freedom of the press merely meant the right to be free from prior censorship. Trial by jury, involving judgment by one's peers, was expected to ensure that the power to punish abuses would not be used to suppress legitimate publications.

The Framers undoubtedly sought to provide protection as extensive as existed in England, but their aims may have been broader. Proponents of a broader view argue that because the First Amendment protects not only freedom of the press but also freedom of speech, which cannot be subjected to prior censorship, it must prohibit more than prior restraints on expression. In addition, they note that under English law, writers could be punished for seditious libel (criticism of the government)—a position inconsistent with the system of republican government created by the Constitution. And indeed, when Congress outlawed seditious libel in the Sedition Act of 1798, opponents of the act contended that it violated the First Amendment. Within three years the act was repealed, and President Thomas Jefferson pardoned all those convicted under the act.[2]

This focus on the character of the government established by the Constitution leads to a more expansive interpretation of the First Amendment. As Justice Harlan Stone noted in his famous *Carolene Products* footnote (see Chapter 4), restrictions on political expression are constitutionally suspect because they cripple the political process, hampering the defeat of incumbents and the repeal of undesirable legislation. Only through the unfettered discussion of political alternatives can the citizenry reach informed judgments about what policies government should pursue. Justice Louis Brandeis eloquently invoked the political importance of freedom of expression in *Whitney v. California* (1927):

> [The Framers] believed that freedom to think as you will and to speak as you think are means indispensable to the discovery of political truth; that without free speech and assembly, discussion would be futile; that with them, discussion affords ordinarily adequate protection against the dissemination of noxious doctrine; that the greatest menace to freedom is an inert people; that public discussion is a political duty; and that this should be a fundamental principle of the American government.

Justice Brandeis's statement leaves crucial questions unanswered. If the First Amendment protects political speech because it is a prerequisite for self-government, does that protection extend only to speech advocating political alternatives consistent with a system of self-government? More specifically, does the First Amendment protect advocacy of unlawful actions or of the violent overthrow of the government? Brandeis also referred to free discussion as affording "ordinarily adequate protection against the dissemination of noxious doctrines," implying that free discussion sometimes will not be adequate. Under what conditions, then, may other measures, including the suppression of speech, be employed to combat the spread of "noxious doctrines"? Finally, in *Whitney*, Brandeis dealt solely with political speech and its importance for self-government. He thus left open the question whether nonpolitical speech is entitled to the same First Amendment protection. On the one hand, some of the same arguments used to support political expression can be applied to nonpolitical expression: the suppression of unpopular moral or scientific ideas, like the suppression of political views, can enshrine error and thwart the search for truth. On the other hand, much nonpolitical speech—for example, commercial advertising and movies—does not involve a search for truth. Does the First Amendment extend protection to speech on all subjects? And if so, does it provide equally broad protection regardless of the subject of the speech? As these questions suggest, there may be quite different understandings of what ends the First Amendment was designed to serve, and these divergent views have been reflected in the various standards that the Supreme Court has used in deciding First Amendment cases.

FIRST AMENDMENT STANDARDS

The Bad-Tendency Test

The bad-tendency test was the prevailing standard in state courts during the nineteenth century and was adopted by the Supreme Court when it began to address First Amendment issues early in the twentieth century. During the decade following World War I, in such cases as *Abrams v. United States* (1919), *Gitlow v. New York* (1925), and *Whitney v. California* (1927), the Court employed this test in upholding the convictions of political radicals who advocated violent action. Underlying the bad-tendency test is the assumption that the First Amendment, like other constitutional provisions, is designed to promote the public good. It follows that types of speech that have good effects are entitled to constitutional protection, whereas speech that threatens the security, order, or morals of the society may be regulated. The decisive consideration, then, is whether the regulated speech is likely to produce bad effects—and this, the Court held, is primarily a matter for the legislature to decide. Thus, the Court in *Gitlow* embraced judicial restraint, declaring that "every presumption is to be indulged in favor of the validity of the statute."

In adopting the bad-tendency test, the Court maintained that the First Amendment was never intended to protect all speech and publications; rather, like other provisions of the Bill of Rights, it merely embodied guarantees that had existed under English law. Because English law permitted prosecutions for abuses of freedom of the press, so did the First Amendment. And because legislators are popularly elected and are more familiar than judges with societal conditions, legislative judgments about the types of speech that are harmful generally should prevail. The bad-tendency test thus gives laws affecting speech and press no closer judicial scrutiny than is accorded to any other laws.

The Clear-and-Present-Danger Test

Dissatisfaction with the suppression of speech and press possible under the bad-tendency test, as shown in the prosecution of opponents of World War I and of political radicals during the Red Scare after the war, led to the development of an alternative test. This was the clear-and-present-danger test, first enunciated by Justice Holmes in *Schenck v. United States* (1919). In Holmes's words, "The question in every case is whether the words are used in such circumstances and are of such a nature as to create a clear and present danger that they will bring about the substantive evils that Congress has a right to prevent." This test resembles the bad-tendency test in permitting the punishment of speech that produces harmful effects, but it imposes more exacting criteria for determining harm. The clear-and-present-danger test requires the government to demonstrate that the *specific speech,* in the context in which it occurred, created a danger to the achievement of permissible governmental objectives and that the likelihood of harm was both substantial ("clear") and proximate ("present").

In the decade following *Schenck,* Justices Holmes and Brandeis refined the test and clarified its constitutional foundations. Dissenting in *Abrams v. United States* (1919), Holmes asserted that the "theory of our Constitution" was that the public interest was best served by a "free trade in ideas." The First Amendment, he argued, reflected the conviction that "the best test of truth is the power of thought to get itself accepted in the competition of the market." When government intervenes in this marketplace, suppressing harmful speech, it interferes with society's best mechanism for discovering truth. Such intervention can be justified only when speech leads to substantial harm so immediately that there is no opportunity for further discussion to exert a corrective effect.

For more than a decade, the clear-and-present-danger test proved singularly ineffective in protecting speech and press. In no case was the test used to overturn a conviction, and only in *Schenck,* in which the Court upheld a conviction under the Espionage Act, did a majority of the justices endorse it. In *Herndon v. Lowry* (1937), however, the Court relied on the test in reversing a conviction for distributing Communist Party literature. From that point until the early 1950s, the justices regularly employed the clear-and-present-danger test in deciding First Amendment questions, often invalidating restrictions on speech and the press.

Dennis v. United States (1951) marked a fundamental shift away from the clear-and-present-danger test. In *Dennis* the Supreme Court upheld the conviction of several Communist Party leaders for conspiring to advocate the overthrow of the government. The case arose in the aftermath of World War II, when the Cold War between the United States and the Soviet Union generated national security concerns and fears of domestic subversion, leading to a greater willingness to curtail speech. Chief Justice Fred Vinson asserted that the situation in *Dennis* required a reformulation of Holmes's test: "In each case [judges] must ask whether the gravity of the evil, discounted by its improbability, justifies such invasion of free speech as is necessary to avoid the danger." In dissent Justices Hugo Black and William Douglas observed that faithful application of Holmes's test required that the convictions be overturned. This in fact explains Vinson's modification of the test. Having determined that the clear-and-present-danger test offered too much protection—"the words cannot mean that before the Government may act, it must wait until the *putsch* is about to be executed, the plans have been laid and the signal is awaited"—Vinson sought to reconcile it with the community's need to deal with perceived threats to its safety. This perception that the clear-and-present-danger test protected too much, together with the dissenters' belief that it protected too little, led the Court to abandon the test. Nevertheless, the Court's opinions in *Brandenburg v. Ohio* (1969) and more recent cases have continued to reflect the concerns, if not the language, of Holmes and Brandeis.

The Balancing Test

In *Kovacs v. Cooper* (1949), Justice Felix Frankfurter proposed the balancing test as an alternative to the clear-and-present-danger test, and during the 1950s and early 1960s it became the prevailing approach to free speech claims, particularly in cases involving persons or groups viewed as subversive. The balancing test is more of an approach than a standard. First Amendment cases typically pit individual rights against the attainment of other governmental ends. Critics of the clear-and-present-danger test asserted that it automatically elevated individual rights above other governmental ends, thereby oversimplifying issues and predetermining outcomes. They contended that concentration on the single goal of protecting speech had no constitutional basis because the Constitution was designed to promote a variety of ends. What was necessary, rather, was an impartial balancing of competing claims on a case-by-case basis. Proponents of balancing urged that in undertaking this task, judges assign great weight to the balancing already undertaken by the legislative branch. *Barenblatt v. United States* (1959), in which the Court upheld the contempt conviction of a teacher who refused to disclose to a congressional committee whether he belonged to the Communist Party, exemplifies this approach. It also demonstrates the difficulty inherent in attempting to compare the interest in free speech with other governmental interests.

The Court's Current Approach

In assessing regulations restricting speech or publication, the Court now focuses on whether the enactments regulating speech are content-neutral. Government may seek to achieve legitimate ends through enactments that are neutral with regard to the content of the speech that is regulated—for example, the laws might regulate the time, place, and manner of expression without regard to the message being conveyed. In such cases, the Court typically balances the competing claims of government and of those affected by the regulation. But when government seeks to achieve its ends by restricting the subject matter, viewpoint, or extent of expression, the Court adopts a more stringent standard ("strict scrutiny"): government must demonstrate that its enactment is necessary to protect a compelling government interest and that it is the least-restrictive means of doing so. Thus, in *Elrod v. Burns* (1976), the Court noted that "the interest advanced must be paramount, one of vital importance," in invalidating the patronage dismissal of government workers. And in *Reno v. American Civil Liberties Union* (1997), it noted that a statute "is unacceptable if less restrictive alternatives would be at least as effective in achieving the legitimate purpose that the statute was enacted to serve." Although the requirement of a compelling government interest can be met, the Court's approach affords broad protection for the freedom of speech and of the press.

Auxiliary Doctrines

The Court sometimes decides First Amendment issues on the basis of narrower auxiliary doctrines that focus on the means government has used to achieve its ends. Among the most important of these are the overbreadth and void-for-vagueness doctrines.

A statute is overbroad if it outlaws both unprotected and constitutionally protected speech. The basic defect of such statutes is their excessive deterrent effect. Speakers must guess whether their speech is constitutionally protected despite being proscribed by the statute and may refrain from speaking rather than risk punishment for violating the law. As a result, the statute achieves its valid purpose only by infringing on First Amendment rights. *Coates v. City of Cincinnati* (1971) illustrates how the Court employs the overbreadth doctrine. In invalidating a city ordinance that made it a criminal offense for "three or more persons to assemble on any of the sidewalks and then conduct themselves in a manner annoying to persons passing by," the Court did not concern itself with the details of Coates's conduct. Even if Coates's actions were not constitutionally protected, it ruled, the ordinance could not be upheld because it established a standard for restricting the right of assembly that invaded First Amendment rights.

Closely related to the overbreadth standard is the void-for-vagueness doctrine. A statute is void for vagueness when, as noted in *Connally v. General Construction Co.* (1926), it "either forbids or requires the doing of an act in terms so vague that men of common intelligence must necessarily guess at its meaning and differ as to its application." By not providing adequate notice of what constitutes illegal behavior, vague statutes "chill" the exercise of First Amendment rights and give too much discretion to the officials charged with their enforcement. However, the government can replace a law invalidated as overbroad or void for vagueness with a more narrowly or precisely drawn statute that meets constitutional requirements.

POLITICAL EXPRESSION

Speaking for the Court in *New York Times v. Sullivan* (1964), Justice William Brennan proclaimed that the nation was committed to the "principle that debate on public issues should be uninhibited, robust, and wide open." Yet advocacy of political change through violence or other undemocratic means may threaten the very foundations of government. Restrictions on political expression may also be deemed necessary to prevent corruption of the political process or to serve other important societal purposes. This section details how the Court has dealt with governmental restrictions on political expression.

National Security

Governmental attempts to limit political expression have been most pronounced during periods of national crisis. The first major conflict over political expression took place in the late 1790s, when the Sedition Act provoked a bitter controversy (see "Libel and the Invasion of Privacy," page 203).

The next significant clash between political expression and the perceived requirements of national security occurred during and immediately after World War I. After the assassination of President William McKinley by an anarchist in 1902, several states enacted laws making it a crime to advocate the violent overthrow of government; by 1921 two-thirds of the states had such laws. In 1917, Congress passed the Espionage Act, which prohibited expression that interfered with the war effort. During the war, almost two thousand persons were prosecuted under the Espionage Act, and many others under similar state laws.[3] As *Schenck v. United States* and *Gitlow v. New York* illustrate, in the decade following the end of the war, the Court consistently upheld convictions in national security cases against First Amendment challenges.

Following World War II, the Cold War between the United States and the Soviet Union intensified concern about the activities of the Communist Party and so-called Communist front groups. The federal government responded by prosecuting Communist Party officials under the Smith Act, which forbade advocating or organizing to advocate the overthrow of the government by force or violence. When the Supreme Court sustained the convictions of twelve Communist Party leaders in *Dennis v. United States* (1951), it encouraged the government to initiate prosecutions against other Communist Party officials. However, later judicial interpretation of the Smith Act limited its usefulness. In *Yates v. United States* (1957), the Court ruled that the act proscribed only advocacy of participation in overthrowing the government: "Those to whom the advocacy is addressed must be urged to *do* something, now or in the future, rather than merely to *believe in* something." And in *Scales v. United States* (1961), the Court concluded that mere membership in an organization advocating governmental overthrow was insufficient to sustain a conviction. Noting that members might disagree with positions taken by an organization, the Court ruled that the act applied only to "knowing" and "active" members who specifically intended to advance the organization's illegal aims. Thus, without directly addressing the constitutionality of the Smith Act, the Court essentially ended prosecutions under it. Ultimately, the Court's decision in *Brandenburg v. Ohio* (1969) cast serious doubt on the continuing authority of *Dennis*.

During the Cold War, the federal and state governments either instituted or expanded loyalty programs designed to deny positions to those who might use them for subversive purposes. The Court initially endorsed most loyalty requirements. In *Adler v. Board of Education* (1952), it upheld a New York law that authorized the dismissal of teachers belonging to proscribed organizations, and in *Konigsberg v. State Bar of California* (1961), it ruled that persons who refused to answer questions about Communist Party membership could be denied admission to the bar. But over time the Court restricted governmental loyalty programs by extending procedural protections to public employees threatened with dismissal and by using the overbreadth and void-for-vagueness doctrines to limit the scope of loyalty inquiries. In *United States v. Robel* (1967), it struck down as overbroad a federal statute prohibiting members of Communist organizations from working in defense facilities, and in *Keyishian v. Board of Regents* (1967), it overruled *Adler,* observing that the New York oath was unconstitutionally vague and penalized mere membership in the Communist Party.

Legislative investigations into subversive activities also raised First Amendment issues. During the 1950s, scores of witnesses were summoned before congressional and state legislative committees to testify about their past and present political associations, and witnesses who refused to testify were cited for contempt. In reviewing contempt convictions, the Supreme Court imposed procedural limitations on the conduct of investigations, announcing that it would not tolerate "exposure for the sake of exposure." Not until *Barenblatt v. United States* (1959), however, did the Court consider the question of whether witnesses compelled to testify about political associations and beliefs were denied their First Amendment rights. The five-member majority in *Barenblatt* ruled that because the Communist Party was not "an ordinary political party" but an organization committed to the overthrow of the government, Congress's need for information about its activities overrode First Amendment objections. But when the Communist Party was not involved, the Court scrutinized the actions of legislative committees more closely. Thus, in *Gibson v. Florida Legislative Investigating Committee* (1963), the Court concluded that the head of the Miami chapter of the National Association for the Advancement of Colored People (NAACP) could not be compelled to furnish membership lists to a state committee investigating possible Communist infiltration of the organization.

In 1996, Congress responded to the increasing threat of terrorism by enacting the Antiterrorism and Effective Death Penalty Act, which made it a crime to "knowingly provide material support or resources" to foreign terrorist organizations. Material support was defined as including not only weapons but also, among other things, funds, training, and personnel. This law was challenged by groups that wished to support the humanitarian and political activities of organizations designated by the secretary of state as foreign terrorist organizations. In *Holder v. Humanitarian Law Project* (2010), the Supreme Court rejected their claim that the law violated their First Amendment rights of freedom of speech and freedom of association. Writing for the Court, Chief Justice John Roberts noted that the law regulated speech based on its content, and thus strict scrutiny was warranted. But because it was clear that combating terrorism was a compelling interest, the case turned on whether the means Congress had chosen was necessary to achieve that end. The Court majority concluded that it was, noting that support for even a terrorist organization's legitimate activities ran the risk of furthering terrorism. It also noted that in dealing with issues of terrorism, it was appropriate to defer to the combined judgment of the executive and legislative branches because "conclusions must often be based on informed judgment rather than concrete evidence." The Court concluded that the law did not unduly burden political speech because individuals remained free to advocate independently the political causes supported by the terrorist groups.

In his dissenting opinion, Justice Stephen Breyer claimed the primary aim of the First Amendment was to protect political speech. Yet the statute prohibited "communication and advocacy of political ideas and lawful means of achieving political ends" because it was undertaken in coordination with groups that also used violence to achieve their goals. The law, he argued, was incompatible with Court precedents that safeguarded the right to speak and to organize in support of the lawful ends of groups which also pursued unlawful objectives or did so in an unlawful fashion. He pointed in particular to cases involving the Communist Party, in which the Court held that persons had the right to join groups that espoused the violent overthrow of government as long as they did not share or advance that unlawful purpose.

Government Service

Even when national security is not implicated, government's special interest in safeguarding the effectiveness and fairness of its operations may justify some restrictions on political expression by public employees. Thus, in *U.S. Civil Service Commission v. National Association of Letter Carriers* (1973), the Supreme Court upheld restrictions on partisan political activity by federal civil servants. Yet in cases dealing with government employees not protected by a civil service system, the Court has made clear that public servants do not forfeit their right to express opinions on political matters. In *Elrod v. Burns* (1976), the justices struck a major blow at the spoils system by invalidating patronage dismissals of non-policy-making public employees. In the face of claims that patronage was necessary for strong political parties, the Court held that removals based on political affiliation violated government workers' rights of freedom of association and freedom of political belief. And in *Republican Party of Minnesota v. White* (2002), the Court ruled that if states elect their judges, they cannot prohibit the candidates for judicial office from expressing their views on political or legal questions during the campaign, even when such prohibitions are designed to preserve judicial impartiality. However, in *Williams-Yulee v. Florida Bar* (2015) a five-member majority backtracked, upholding the Florida Bar Association's ban on judicial candidates personally soliciting funds for their election campaigns.

The Electoral Process

The Court has recognized that government may act to protect the political process from corruption. Therefore, laws regulating lobbying and punishing election fraud do not violate the First Amendment. More problematic, however, are regulations of the electoral process, such as the Federal Election Campaign Act Amendments of 1974. This law, enacted in response to the Watergate scandal and to the spiraling costs of election campaigns, (1) restricted the size of individual and group contributions to political campaigns, (2) limited the amounts that candidates could spend in those campaigns, (3) required disclosure of campaign contributions and expenditures, (4) provided for public financing of presidential campaigns, and (5) established the Federal Election Commission to administer the act. In *Buckley v. Valeo* (1976), the Court upheld the act's disclosure requirements and its limits on campaign contributions, maintaining that they served an important purpose (elimination of corruption). But it invalidated limits on campaign expenditures, concluding that they restricted the communication of political views without contributing significantly to the control of corruption. The Court acknowledged, however, that government could require candidates to limit their campaign expenditures as a condition for receiving public financing.

Perhaps the most controversial aspect of *Buckley* was its invalidation of limits on spending by candidates or groups to promote their views. Proponents of such limits argue that there is a need to intervene in the marketplace of ideas to correct "distortions" resulting from the unequal distribution of wealth in society. Limiting the participation of wealthy groups and individuals in the marketplace of ideas, they argue, will encourage the dissemination of diverse viewpoints by equalizing opportunities to influence the electorate. Although acknowledging that increasing access to the marketplace of ideas is a legitimate goal, the Court in *Buckley* held that the government cannot limit the freedom of speech of groups or individuals in order to achieve it. The Court emphasized the potential for abuse inherent in permitting government to control the flow of political communication. Thus, in rulings such as *Federal Election Commission v. National Conservative Political Action Committee* (1985) and *Colorado Republican Federal Campaign Committee v. Federal Election*

Commission (1996), the Court adhered to the position it announced in *Buckley.* But in *Austin v. Michigan State Chamber of Commerce* (1990), a narrow Court majority held that government could prevent "the corrosive and distorting effects of immense aggregations of wealth that are accumulated with the help of the corporate form and that have little or no correlation to the public's support for the corporation's political ideas."

In 2002, Congress enacted the Bipartisan Campaign Finance Reform Act (BCRA)— also known as the McCain-Feingold Act—the most far-reaching regulation of election practices in three decades. This statute limited the contributions that corporations, labor unions, and individuals could make to political parties, often referred to as "soft-money contributions," insisting that such contributions were a source of corruption or apparent corruption. It also prohibited corporations and unions from financing "electioneering" ads pertaining to candidates for federal office during the last sixty days before a general election and the last thirty days before a primary election. These ads, Congress contended, were designed to influence election outcomes and therefore were subject to regulation just as were ads endorsing specific candidates. In *McConnell v. Federal Election Commission* (2003), a badly divided Court upheld these provisions of the act, claiming in doing so to be following the precedent of *Buckley v. Valeo.*

After the appointments of Chief Justice John Roberts and Justice Samuel Alito, the Court in *Citizens United v. Federal Election Commission* (2010) reconsidered its position, overruling *Austin* and parts of *McConnell.* Speaking for a five-member majority, Justice Anthony Kennedy struck down the provision of the BCRA that prohibited corporations and labor unions from spending funds to run ads during the final stages of an election campaign. Kennedy argued that persons do not lose their First Amendment rights when they associate themselves with others in order to make their speech more effective. (As Justice Scalia put it in his concurring opinion, "The First Amendment is written in terms of 'speech,' not speakers, and offers no foothold for excluding any category of speaker.") Beyond that Kennedy maintained that restrictions on corporate and union speech "interfere with the open marketplace of ideas protected by the First Amendment," depriving the public of viewpoints and information it might use in making its political choices. The government has no role, he insisted, in protecting citizens in this marketplace, as it is up to the public "to determine for itself what speech and speakers are worthy of consideration." Although government may outlaw *quid pro quo* corruption, it cannot act to prevent alleged "distortions" in the marketplace of ideas. Indeed, "the concept that government can restrict the speech of some elements of our society in order to enhance the relative voice of others is wholly foreign to the First Amendment." Thus, *Citizens United* protected the right of corporations and unions to speak and spend independently of candidates throughout elections.

Speaking for the four dissenters, Justice John Paul Stevens rejected the notion that the BCRA's prohibition banned speech, noting that corporations and unions remained free to form political action committees to engage in electioneering. Beyond that, he argued that the restriction on the use of corporate funds for independent expenditures in support of or in opposition to political candidates was "viewpoint-neutral" because it did not depend on the identity or ideology of the candidates supported by those funds. He maintained that corporate participation in the electoral process raised "special concerns" because of corporations' "immense aggregations of wealth." The funds they have available can lead to "corporate domination of the airwaves prior to an election," even though this disproportionate presence is "not an indication of popular support for the corporation's political ideas." Beyond that, their expenditures may give them what he termed "undue influence," a form of corruption beyond quid pro quo arrangements that government can likewise seek to prevent. He concluded that "while American democracy is imperfect, few outside the majority of this Court would have thought its flaws included a dearth of corporate money in politics."

The Court's ruling in *Citizens United* proved highly controversial. President Barack Obama took the unusual step of criticizing the ruling in his 2010 State of the Union message, and sixteen state legislatures adopted resolutions urging a constitutional amendment to overturn the decision. But the reaction was not all negative: the decision was praised by the American Civil Liberties Union (ACLU), and Mitch McConnell, majority leader of the Senate, claimed that "it struck a blow for the First Amendment." In later cases the Court has reaffirmed its commitment to *Citizens United*. In *Arizona Free Enterprise Club's Freedom Club PAC v. Bennett* (2011), the Court struck down an Arizona law under which publicly financed candidates received extra funding if they were outspent by their privately funded opponents. And in *McCutcheon v. FEC* (2014), it held that Congress may not limit the total amount that donors can contribute to candidates and political committees during an election cycle.

THE REGULATION OF SPEECH AND ASSOCIATION

In *Kunz v. New York* (1951), Justice Robert Jackson noted that "the vulnerability of various forms of communication to community control must be proportioned to their impact upon other community interests." This explains why government may impose more stringent limitations on speech and expressive conduct than on publication. Because a speaker can address larger numbers of people simultaneously, speech is likely to have a more immediate impact than the press would have. And because expressive conduct ("symbolic speech") has an action component, it is more likely to interfere with legitimate governmental ends unrelated to the suppression of speech. This section examines to what extent, and for what purposes, government can regulate speech and expressive conduct.

Coerced Speech

Freedom of speech includes not only the right to express one's views but also the right not to be compelled to affirm beliefs that one does not share. Thus, in *West Virginia Board of Education v. Barnette* (1943), the Supreme Court held that Jehovah's Witness schoolchildren could not be required to salute the American flag (see Chapter 6), and in *Wooley v. Maynard* (1977), it ruled that New Hampshire could not penalize residents who covered the slogan "Live Free or Die" on their license plates. Religious convictions motivated Barnette and Maynard, but they were not decisive for the Court. As Justice Jackson declared in *Barnette,* "If there is any fixed star in our constitutional constellation, it is that no official, high or petty, can prescribe what shall be orthodox in politics, nationalism, religion, or other matters of opinion or force citizens to confess by word or act their faith therein." However, in *Board of Regents of the University of Wisconsin v. Southworth* (2000), the Court ruled that students were not compelled to affirm views they disagreed with when they were required to pay a student fee used to support student organizations that took positions on controversial issues. Even if Southworth's fees helped subsidize speech he found objectionable, the Court held that the university's program of promoting extracurricular speech did not violate the First Amendment as long as its funding of student organizations was viewpoint-neutral, that is, not based on the content of the opinions they were expressing.

The Supreme Court has recognized that the First Amendment protects the right to join together with others to communicate one's views—what might be called a right of expressive association. One way that members of an organization can ensure that it continues to reflect their ideas is by controlling its membership, restricting it to like-minded persons. However, government may have valid reasons unrelated to the suppression of speech, such as preventing discrimination, for regulating the membership policies of organizations. The

Supreme Court has confronted these competing concerns in three cases: *Roberts v. United States Jaycees* (1984), *Hurley v. Irish-American Gay, Lesbian and Bisexual Group of Boston (GLIB)* (1995), and *Boy Scouts of America v. Dale* (2000). In *Roberts*, the Court ruled that Minnesota could compel the Jaycees, an all-male organization, to admit women as members. Although the Jaycees claimed that this invaded their rights of freedom of speech and association, the Court noted that the Jaycees had failed to show that the admission of women would interfere with the organization's ability to convey its views and values. But in *Hurley*, the Court unanimously upheld the right of the organization sponsoring Boston's St. Patrick's Day Parade to refuse to include a group of gay, lesbian, and bisexual marchers in the parade. "The parade's overall message is distilled from the individual presentations along the way," Justice David Souter wrote for the Court, "and each unit's expression is perceived by spectators as part of the whole." Thus, for the state to require the inclusion of the excluded group would alter the expression of the parade organizers and compel them to convey a message of which they disapproved. Finally, in *Dale* a closely divided Court upheld the right of the Boy Scouts to exclude gays from leadership positions. The justices agreed on the applicable standard: "The forced inclusion of an unwanted person in a group infringes the group's freedom of expressive association if the presence of that person affects in a significant way the group's ability to advocate public or private viewpoints." But they disagreed on its application, disputing whether homosexual conduct was inconsistent with the values that the Boy Scouts proclaimed and sought to instill. In 2015, the Boy Scouts abandoned its blanket ban on gay leaders, although it continued to allow church-sponsored units to select leaders who subscribed to their moral positions.

Symbolic Speech

Conduct, as well as speech, can promote the ends of the First Amendment. Demonstrations and picketing, by combining conduct with speech, can often be more effective than speech alone. Even conduct without speech—a refusal to salute a flag, for instance—can be an eloquent form of expression. Accordingly, the Court has long recognized that symbolic speech is entitled to some First Amendment protection. On the other hand, the Court has never ruled that the mere presence of a communicative element immunizes harmful conduct from regulation. In each case the Court must balance the claims of free expression against the pursuit of other governmental objectives.

In *United States v. O'Brien* (1968), the Court upheld David O'Brien's conviction for burning his draft card to protest the Vietnam War. Chief Justice Earl Warren proposed a four-part test for determining when government may regulate expressive conduct:

> [A] government regulation is sufficiently justified if it is within the constitutional power of the Government; if it furthers an important or substantial governmental interest; if the governmental interest is unrelated to the suppression of free expression; and if the incidental restriction of alleged First Amendment freedoms is no greater than is essential to the furtherance of that interest.

So when expression and conduct are intertwined, government can regulate the non-speech element to achieve valid governmental ends. Thus, in *O'Brien* the government's interest in the smooth operation of the Selective Service System justified the incidental burden imposed on free expression. In *Clark v. Community for Creative Non-Violence* (1984), the Court relied on *O'Brien* to uphold the National Park Service's ban on sleeping in national parks. Rejecting the challenge of a group that sought to conduct a "sleep-in" in parks near the Capitol to dramatize the plight of the homeless, the Court observed that the prohibition was not designed to restrict expression and served the valid purpose of maintaining parks "in an attractive and intact condition."

For a governmental regulation to be valid, however, it must be viewpoint-neutral and not regulate conduct as a means of restricting the expression of particular ideas. This requirement was decisive in *Texas v. Johnson* (1989), in which a sharply divided Court struck down the conviction of a political protester who had violated Texas's flag-desecration statute by burning the American flag. According to the Court's five-member majority, the flaw in the Texas law was that it permitted the use of the flag to show support for the nation and its institutions but prohibited its use to register dissent. Because the ban on flag desecration was not viewpoint-neutral, it violated the First Amendment.

Unprotected Speech

In *Chaplinsky v. New Hampshire* (1942), the Supreme Court held that certain categories of speech were not protected by the First Amendment. Among these were what it termed "fighting words," that is, verbal provocations that amount to an invitation to fight and thus by their very character pose an immediate threat to public order. In subsequent cases the Court has construed "fighting words" narrowly. It is not enough that speech be offensive, or invite dispute, or provoke hostility; only face-to-face personal insults enjoy no First Amendment protection.

In recent decades the issue of what speech is unprotected by the First Amendment has arisen due to campus restrictions on racist and sexist expression. Some universities concluded that the First Amendment does not protect such speech, even if it does not involve "fighting words," and established speech codes on their campuses banning such speech. The University of Michigan, for example, prohibited speech that "stigmatized or victimized an individual on the basis of race, ethnicity, religion, sex, sexual orientation" or several other factors and "created an intimidating, hostile, or demeaning environment for educational pursuits." Other universities prohibited "fighting words" that vilify individuals on the basis of their membership in various groups. Stanford University, for example, banned "fighting words" that insulted or stigmatized persons "on the basis of their sex, race, color, handicap, religion, sexual orientation, or national and ethnic origin." Advocates of speech codes claim that the speech banned by those codes harms the members of targeted groups. In making this claim, they depart from traditional First Amendment analysis, which views harm as coming not from speech itself but from its close connection to action. They further argue that speech codes, by creating a more congenial environment on campus, encourage minority students to express their ideas, thereby fostering the interchange of ideas.

In *Doe v. University of Michigan* (1989), a federal district court struck down the University of Michigan's speech code on First Amendment grounds. This decision, however, did not affect university speech codes that restricted only "fighting words." Although the Supreme Court has never addressed the constitutionality of such speech codes, in *R. A. V. v. City of St. Paul* (1992), it invalidated a municipal ordinance that outlawed the display of symbols known to "arouse anger, alarm or resentment in others on the basis of race, color, creed, religion, or gender." Speaking for the Court, Justice Antonin Scalia held that St. Paul's ordinance was invalid, even if it merely outlawed "fighting words." For although government can ban "fighting words" altogether, it cannot distinguish among "fighting words" based on hostility toward their ideological content. St. Paul's ordinance was invalid, therefore, because it involved a viewpoint-based distinction: it outlawed "fighting words" on the basis of race or gender but not, for example, on the basis of political affiliation or sexual preference. Because most speech codes make similar viewpoint-based distinctions, they too are constitutionally suspect under the standard announced in *R. A. V.*

The Supreme Court followed *R. A. V.* in *Virginia v. Black* (2003), striking down a Virginia law that outlawed cross burning with an intent to intimidate. Although the Court majority conceded that Virginia could outlaw acts designed to intimidate, it held that the First Amendment protected cross burning, if it was used as a means to convey a racist political viewpoint, however distasteful the message might be. The question then became how one determined whether the aim of the cross burning was intimidation, and the Court concluded that Virginia could not assume that all cross burnings were meant to intimidate. The constitutional defect of the Virginia statute was that it was overbroad, in that it outlawed both protected and unprotected symbolic expression. In dissent Justice Thomas argued that the history of cross burning showed that it was a form of racial intimidation and that Virginia could rely on that history in outlawing the practice.

Public Order

Government has a basic responsibility to maintain public order, and all states have statutes punishing disorderly conduct, breach of the peace, incitement to riot, and similar offenses. When "fighting words" are not involved, the threat to public order usually arises when proponents of unpopular or controversial views use some form of public assembly—meetings, parades, demonstrations—to reach a broad audience. But that very fact complicates the issue: to penalize speakers merely because their views excite opposition would give unsympathetic listeners a "heckler's veto" over speech. The Supreme Court has repeatedly confronted this issue. In *Feiner v. New York* (1951), it upheld the conviction of a speaker who disobeyed police orders to end a speech that had produced some crowd hostility. But in *Edwards v. South Carolina* (1963) and *Cox v. Louisiana* (1965), it overturned the breach-of-the-peace convictions of civil-rights activists whose demonstrations had also stirred crowd unrest. More recently, in *Snyder v. Phelps* (2011), the Supreme Court upheld the right of protesters to picket the funeral of a soldier, despite the emotional distress it caused, to express their view that the death of American soldiers was a divine judgment on the nation for its tolerance of homosexuality.

Time, Place, and Manner Regulations

Government can regulate the time, place, and manner of speech on public property to promote effective communication or accommodate other legitimate uses of that property. But in imposing such restrictions, it cannot discriminate on the basis of the content or viewpoint of expression. As the Supreme Court noted in *Police Department of Chicago v. Mosley* (1972), "Once a forum is opened up to assembly or speaking by some groups, government may not prohibit others from assembling or speaking on the basis of what they intend to say." Thus, the Court has struck down permit systems that distinguish on the basis of the content of speech (*Carey v. Brown* [1980]) or that give excessive discretion, and thus the opportunity to discriminate, to local officials (*Lakewood v. Plain Dealer Publishing Co.* [1988]).

Even nondiscriminatory regulations may be constitutionally suspect. Although government can regulate speech on public property to accommodate other interests, it may not deny all access to public property for expression. As Justice Owen Roberts emphasized in *Hague v. C.I.O.* (1939), "Wherever the title of streets and parks may rest, they have immemorially been held in trust for the use of the public. The privilege of a citizen of the United States to use the street and parks for communication of views on national questions may be regulated in the interest of all, but it must not, in the guise of regulation, be abridged or denied." On the question of what property must be made available for communicative purposes, the justices have divided. In *Adderley v. Florida* (1966), Justice Black, speaking for the Court, indicated that government could limit expression to property that had traditionally been used as a public forum. However, in *Tinker v. Des Moines* (1969), a case involving the First Amendment rights of students, Justice Abraham Fortas, speaking for the Court, insisted that the decisive consideration was whether the use of governmental property as a public forum significantly interfered with the purposes to which the property was dedicated.

Antiabortion protesters have on several occasions challenged the constitutionality of restrictions on their activities outside abortion clinics. Clearly, government can prohibit protesters from obstructing access to such facilities or harassing those attempting to enter them. But when protests occur on sidewalks or other public property outside the clinics, can it shield women entering the clinics from unwanted communications or regulate how protesters convey their views? In *Hill v. Colorado* (2001), the Court upheld a Colorado statute that prohibited any person from approaching within eight feet of another person, without his or her consent, to engage in protest, counseling, or education, in an area within one hundred feet of the entrance of any health care facility. Speaking for the Court, Justice Stevens argued that the law was a content-neutral regulation of time, place, and manner that served the important governmental interests of ensuring access to health facilities and protecting unwilling listeners from unwanted messages. In sharply worded dissents, Justices Scalia and Anthony Kennedy challenged the Court's position. They contended that far from being content neutral, the law targeted abortion protesters and that the right to present one's views in a public forum outweighed the desire to avoid unwelcome communications. Justice Kennedy concluded that "for the first time, the Court has approved a law which bars a private citizen from passing a message, in a peaceful manner and on a profound moral issue, to a fellow citizen on a public sidewalk."

The justices revisited the issue in *McCullen v. Coakley* (2014), a constitutional challenge to a Massachusetts law that provided that "no person shall knowingly enter or remain on a public way or sidewalk adjacent to a reproductive health care facility within a radius of 35 feet." Chief Justice Roberts, writing for the Court, viewed the law as a content-neutral restriction on speech. But he invalidated the law because the fixed buffer zones outside abortion clinics restricted "substantially more speech than necessary to achieve the Commonwealth's asserted interests." In a concurring opinion, Justice Scalia insisted that the law was more than a poorly conceived regulation of time, place, and manner. The fact that the law applied only at abortion clinics—and thus, as a practical matter, only to abortion-related speech—was enough to indicate that it was content based, having as its purpose restricting speech in opposition to abortion.

Government Sponsorship

Government can promote freedom of speech not only by making its property available for communicative purposes but also by providing financial support for speech. For example, the National Endowment for the Arts underwrites the creation and display of artistic work, and the National Science Foundation awards grants for scientific research. Yet the power to encourage speech by underwriting it also entails the power to discourage speech by refusing to sponsor it. More specifically, through its funding decisions government promotes some ideas and discourages others. This may raise First Amendment concerns. Government obviously has a valid interest in ensuring that its programs achieve their goals, and thus it can limit its support to only that speech that promotes a program's goals. In addition, a governmental refusal to fund speech has less dire consequences than a statute outlawing speech because those denied funding remain free to communicate their views. Nonetheless, government's power to grant or withhold funding may significantly influence the speech of recipients or potential recipients of governmental largesse. Moreover, if government cannot favor particular viewpoints in making its property available for communicative purposes, can it make viewpoint-based decisions in allocating public funds?

In *Rust v. Sullivan* (1991) and *Legal Services Corporation v. Velazquez* (2001), the Court considered limitations on speech imposed by government on those receiving government funding. In *Rust*, the Court by a 5–4 vote upheld federal regulations banning abortion counseling at federally funded clinics. Speaking for the Court, Chief Justice William Rehnquist emphasized that government can define the limits of programs it establishes with public funds. However, in *Velazquez* the Court struck down a congressional enactment that prohibited attorneys funded by the Legal Services Corporation from challenging the validity of state or federal welfare programs in court. Four members of the *Rust* majority dissented in *Velazquez*, insisting it was indistinguishable from the Court's earlier decision. Speaking for the Court, Justice Kennedy sought to distinguish *Rust* by contending that attorneys who represent clients seeking welfare benefits are not engaged in government speech, even though they receive funding from the government. He also argued that precluding attorneys from challenging the validity of welfare programs impaired the judicial function because judges would not be exposed to all pertinent legal arguments.

In the unusual case of *Walker v. Texas Division, Sons of Confederate War Veterans, Inc.* (2015), the Court was obliged to determine whether speech was by the government or by a private group. Texas issues license plates for all vehicles but allows nonprofit groups for a fee to display their own insignia and messages on their plates, while reserving the authority to veto proposed specialty plates. When Texas refused to issue a plate containing the Confederate battle flag, the Sons of Confederate War Veterans sued, charging that this constituted censorship of their views. They argued that once the state had opened up its property—in this case, license plates—for speech, it could not censor the messages posted on them because it disagreed with those messages. But by a 5–4 vote the Court rejected this claim of viewpoint discrimination, arguing that "when government speaks, it is not barred by the Free Speech Clause from determining the content of what it says." Because Texas issued the plates, it could control the messages that appeared on them.

RESTRAINTS ON THE PRESS

Prior Restraints

Prior restraints, which may involve either governmental licensing of publications or bans on publication of particular information, impose a particularly severe burden on communication. To require governmental approval prior to publication brings more materials under official scrutiny and, at a minimum, delays even constitutionally protected expression. In addition, the decision to censor is typically reached without the adversarial proceedings and procedural safeguards that accompany criminal prosecutions. For these reasons, by the late seventeenth century English law had recognized that freedom from prior restraints was essential to freedom of the press.

Recognizing that the First Amendment was meant to secure at least as much press freedom as prevailed in England, the Supreme Court has ruled that prior restraints are constitutionally suspect. In *Near v. Minnesota* (1931), the Court struck down a Minnesota law that permitted judges to enjoin publication of "malicious, scandalous and defamatory" newspapers. Speaking for the Court, Chief Justice Charles Evans Hughes recognized that the state had a legitimate interest in curbing such publications and could prosecute those who published them, but argued that this interest did not justify prior restraints against publication, as such restraints could be tolerated only in "exceptional cases." To Hughes, prior restraints were impermissible unless the publication involved jeopardized the country's safety in wartime, threatened public decency (obscenity), incited violence or governmental overthrow, or invaded private rights (libel).

The Court has refused to add to the exceptions Hughes identified in *Near*. Thus, in *Nebraska Press Association v. Stuart* (1976), it overturned a judicial "gag order" designed to prevent prejudicial publicity in a murder case, and in *United States v. Stevens* (2010) it struck down a congressional statute outlawing the creation or possession of videos depicting the torture and killing of animals. The Court has also construed Hughes's exceptions narrowly. In *New York Times v. United States* (1971), the justices lifted an injunction restraining publication of the Pentagon Papers, a top-secret account of the nation's involvement in the Vietnam War, despite objections that publication would threaten national security. In *Snepp v. United States* (1980), on the other hand, they upheld a contract requiring a former CIA agent to submit his writings for prepublication clearance by the agency.

Governmental Regulation of Newsgathering

Some governmental regulations, even if adopted for legitimate purposes and applicable to all citizens, may restrict reporters' access to information or deter sources from confiding in them. By making newsgathering more difficult, these regulations may deprive the citizenry of information about matters of public concern.

In *Richmond Newspapers Inc. v. Virginia* (1980), the Supreme Court recognized that, "absent a need to further a state interest of the highest order," the press cannot be prosecuted for publishing truthful information of public interest that is lawfully obtained. This does not mean that reporters have a right to obtain all newsworthy information. Government can classify information to prevent its disclosure. In addition, as the Court noted in *Nixon v. Warner Communications* (1978), the First Amendment gives the media no right to information beyond that possessed by the general public. On that basis the justices in *Houchins v. KQED* (1978) upheld correctional authorities' refusal to grant reporters special access to prison facilities and to prisoners. But government cannot arbitrarily shield its proceedings from public scrutiny, particularly when those proceedings have historically been open to the public. Thus, the Court recognized a right of public access to criminal trials in *Richmond Newspapers* and to preliminary hearings in criminal cases in *Press-Enterprise Co. v. Superior Court* (1986). Although reporters were accorded no special access, their status as members of the public served to guarantee their admission.

The Court has also maintained that government may impose the same obligations on the press as on other citizens, even when those requirements may affect newsgathering. In *Branzburg v. Hayes* (1972), for example, the Court ruled that reporters must supply relevant information to grand juries, despite the alleged effects of such action on reporters' relationships with confidential sources. Similarly, in *Zurcher v. Stanford Daily* (1978), it upheld a warrant under which police searched a newsroom for evidence, despite claims that the search disrupted the newsroom and could lead to the disclosure of confidential sources and information.

Underlying the Court's reluctance to grant special privileges to the press is the difficulty of differentiating members of the press from other members of the public who wish to communicate their views. The problem has become particularly complicated with the development of the Internet and blogging, as large numbers of nonjournalists regularly publish information and opinions on the Internet. This blurs the distinction between the press and the public and so makes special privileges for the press more problematic.

In the face of the Court's failure to provide special protection for the press, other institutions have acted to facilitate newsgathering. Passage of the Freedom of Information Act by Congress in 1966 and of "sunshine" legislation by state legislatures has expanded the availability of information about governmental activities to the press as well as to the general public. Many states have also enacted legislation shielding reporters from grand-jury questioning. Finally, in the wake of *Zurcher,* Congress enacted the Privacy Protection Act of 1980, which narrowly defined the circumstances under which federal, state, and local law-enforcement officers could conduct unannounced searches of newsrooms.

Governmental Regulation of Broadcast Media

In *Miami Herald Publishing Co. v. Tornillo* (1974), the Supreme Court unanimously invalidated a statute requiring newspapers to print replies by political candidates they had attacked. But in *Red Lion Broadcasting Co. v. Federal Communications Commission* (1969), it unanimously upheld the commission's "fairness doctrine," which required broadcasters to provide balanced coverage of controversial issues and to permit victims of personal attacks a right to reply. The contrast between the two cases illustrates the Court's view that the First Amendment permits greater control by government over the broadcast media than it does over print media.

Federal control over broadcasting began with the Radio Act of 1927, which established a licensing scheme under which the federal government determined who could broadcast over the airwaves and, to some extent, what could be broadcast. Later statutes extended this regulatory authority to cover television and then cable. The Federal Radio Commission and its successor, the Federal Communications Commission (FCC), were authorized to ensure that broadcasting served the "public interest, convenience or necessity." Acting under this authority, the FCC developed content guidelines, ranging from expectations that stations carry public affairs and children's programs to requirements like the "fairness doctrine." Broadcasters had to adhere to FCC guidelines because failure to do so could jeopardize renewal of their broadcasting licenses. In 1984, Congress enacted the Cable Communications Policy Act, which gave state and local governments control over who would be permitted to erect and operate cable systems. Acting under this authority, local governments devised licensing (franchise) systems for cable companies, often imposing content requirements as a condition for receiving a franchise.

The initial rationale for this disparate treatment of the broadcast media was spectrum scarcity. As the Supreme Court put it in *Red Lion,* "Broadcast frequencies constituted a scarce resource whose use could be regulated and rationalized only by the Government. Without government control, the medium would be of little use because of the cacophony of competing voices, none of which could be clearly and predictably heard." Thus, much like time, place, and manner regulations, government regulation of the airwaves was justified as necessary to promote effective communication. In addition, because government allocation of licenses excluded some potential licensees, it was argued that government could regulate use of the airwaves to safeguard the public interest and the interests of those without direct access to them.

Technological advances have eliminated spectrum scarcity, so recent arguments for regulation have stressed the need to ensure a diversity of views over the airwaves and to prevent the owners of radio and television stations from exercising excessive influence through their programming decisions. (This argument for governmental regulation to increase access to the marketplace of ideas and curtail the influence of the wealthy thus resembles the arguments offered for restrictions on campaign spending.) Opponents of regulation counter that the multiplicity of broadcasters ensures diverse perspectives and prevents any broadcaster from exerting excessive influence and that the Internet offers unlimited opportunities to communicate one's views. More generally, opponents of regulation insist that the First Amendment places the same restrictions on government in dealing with all communications media, whether broadcast or print or Internet. Although the Supreme Court has never reconsidered *Red Lion* in the light of changing technologies, in 1987 the Federal

Communications Commission repudiated the spectrum-scarcity rationale for regulation and abolished the "fairness doctrine."

LIBEL AND THE INVASION OF PRIVACY

The Sedition Act of 1798, passed by the Federalist-dominated Congress in an effort to limit criticism of the Adams administration, provoked a serious First Amendment dispute by outlawing "seditious libel," that is, defamation of government and its officials. The Jeffersonian Republicans challenged the act's constitutionality on two grounds: that with the ratification of the First Amendment, only the states had the authority to punish abuses of freedom of the press, and that the crime of seditious libel was inconsistent with republican self-government. Although the Supreme Court never had occasion to rule on the act's constitutionality, President Thomas Jefferson expressed his constitutional judgment by pardoning all those who had been convicted under the act.

The political impetus for the Sedition Act distinguishes it from most libel laws, which protect persons from unfair damage to their reputations by authorizing criminal penalties or civil suits for damages. In *Chaplinsky v. New Hampshire* (1942), the Court recognized libel as a category of expression not protected by the First Amendment. But because libel laws restrict the flow of information, the justices have had to reconcile the full discussion of public issues with adequate protection for personal reputations.

New York Times v. Sullivan (1964) marked the Court's first attempt to distinguish libel from protected expression. Sullivan, a police commissioner in Montgomery, Alabama, had been awarded $500,000 in damages stemming from a newspaper advertisement that contained partially erroneous statements criticizing police mistreatment of African Americans. In unanimously overturning the libel judgment, the Court provided broad protection for criticism of public officials. The First Amendment, it asserted, abolished the crime of seditious libel and permits even "vehement, caustic, and unpleasantly sharp attacks on government and public officials." Because erroneous statements are unavoidable in the heat of public debate, "a rule compelling the critic of official conduct to guarantee the truth of all his factual assertions" would unjustifiably inhibit discussion of public affairs. Even false statements about official conduct, therefore, enjoy constitutional protection, unless they are made with "actual malice," that is, "with knowledge that [they were] false or with a reckless disregard of whether or not [they were] false."

In *New York Times,* proof of malice was required for articles dealing with the official conduct of an elected official. To promote uninhibited discussion of public issues, however, the Court in subsequent cases extended the *New York Times* standard to statements made about candidates for public office, nonelected government employees with authority over the conduct of governmental affairs, and "public figures" in general—that is, individuals who "have thrust themselves to the forefront of particular public controversies in order to influence the resolution of the issues involved."[4] However, the Court continues to distinguish between public figures and private individuals, rejecting the applicability of the *New York Times* standard to publications about those involuntarily involved in events of public interest.

A related concern is whether the First Amendment protects publications that violate the privacy of the individual or inflict emotional distress but do not contain malicious falsehoods. *Hustler Magazine v. Falwell* (1988) involved a parody of an advertisement depicting Jerry Falwell, a prominent religious leader, as having had sexual relations with his mother. The Supreme Court unanimously ruled that Falwell, as a public figure, could not collect damages for infliction of emotional distress because the parody did not pretend to be factual and hence did not involve "actual malice." A second case, *Florida Star v. B. J. F.* (1989), involved a suit for invasion of privacy by a rape victim whose name was published in a newspaper, contrary to Florida law. In contrast to *Falwell,* the victim was not a public figure, but the publication contained information that was both accurate and legally obtained. A divided Court held that Florida could prohibit publication of such information only by a law narrowly tailored to achieve "a state interest of the highest order" and that the Florida law failed that demanding test.

OBSCENITY AND VIDEO GAMES

Obscenity (pornography) has long been regarded as not protected by the First Amendment. But because not all publications dealing with sex are obscene, the Supreme Court has had to determine what sexually oriented materials enjoy First Amendment protection. This has proved difficult. For sixteen years after it decided *Roth v. United States* (1957), its first major obscenity case, the Court was unable to agree on standards for distinguishing obscene from nonobscene materials. Finally, in *Miller v. California* (1973), a five-member majority adopted a test for identifying obscenity:

> (a) Whether "the average person, applying contemporary community standards" would find that the work, taken as a whole, appeals to the prurient interest [that is, arouses lustful thoughts and desires]; (b) whether the work depicts or describes, in a patently offensive way, sexual conduct specifically defined by the applicable state law; and (c) whether the work, taken as a whole, lacks serious literary, artistic, political, or scientific value.

This test remains the Court's standard in obscenity cases. But given changes in social norms, prosecutions are rare for the distribution to adults of even hard-core pornography, and thus the cases since *Miller* have focused on other issues. First, to what extent can localities regulate nonobscene adult entertainment? In *Erznoznik v. City of Jacksonville* (1975), the Court invalidated an ordinance forbidding drive-in theaters from showing films containing nudity when the screen was visible to the general public, and in *Schad v. Mount Ephraim* (1981), it struck down on overbreadth grounds a conviction for commercial displays of nude dancing in violation of a community ban on live entertainment. But in *Renton v. Playtime Theaters* (1986), the justices upheld a zoning ordinance that prohibited adult motion picture theaters from locating within one thousand feet of any residential zone, church, park, or school. Taken together, these decisions suggest that localities can regulate sexually oriented expression, based on its content, as long as the regulation does not altogether suppress the expression and is closely related to a legitimate governmental objective.

Second, what steps can government take to protect children from obscenity and from sexual exploitation? In *New York v. Ferber* (1982), the Court unanimously held that government could ban the dissemination of materials that showed children engaged in sexual activity. But the development of new forms of communication, such as cable television and the Internet, poses a more difficult problem: how can one maintain free speech for adults and protect children in a medium that is available to both? The Court and Congress have engaged in an extended colloquy over this issue. In *Reno v. American Civil Liberties Union* (1997), the Court struck down a statute designed to regulate "indecent" material on the Internet, and in *United States v. Playboy Entertainment Group* (2000), it invalidated regulations designed to control access by minors to sexually explicit programming on cable television. These rulings emphasized that restrictions designed to protect children should not restrict the availability to adults of materials protected by the First Amendment. The Court's position encouraged noncensorial approaches to protecting children from inappropriate material, such as rating systems on television programs and technological restrictions on access to sexually explicit websites. But in

United States v. American Library Association (2003), the Court upheld provisions of the Children's Internet Protection Act, under which a public library could not receive federal assistance to provide Internet access unless it installed software to block images of obscenity and prevented minors from obtaining access to harmful material. Finally, in *Ashcroft v. Free Speech Coalition* (2002), the Court struck down as overbroad a prohibition on computer-generated images that appear to be minors engaged in sexual activity. Although acknowledging the encouragement given to pedophiles by this material, the justices held that government could proscribe only material that failed *Miller's* three-part test for obscenity.

Third, what penalties can government impose on those who violate obscenity laws? In *Fort Wayne Books v. Indiana* (1989), the Court upheld application of a state "racketeering" law to those guilty of multiple obscenity offenses. Under such laws, those convicted not only face stiff fines and jail sentences but may also forfeit real and personal property used or acquired in the course of committing the offenses. *Alexander v. United States* (1989), in which the Court upheld the application of the Racketeer Influenced and Corrupt Organizations Act (RICO) to the owner of several bookstores and theaters specializing in sexually explicit material, illustrates the effect of these laws. When his conviction on seventeen obscenity counts led to his conviction on three RICO counts, Alexander was ordered to forfeit all his businesses and real estate used to conduct his racketeering enterprise, plus almost $9 million acquired through racketeering activity.

Feminist opponents of pornography have proposed a different approach to its regulation. Pornography is objectionable, they claim, because it degrades and harms women by justifying their treatment as sexual objects. Because it differentially harms women, trafficking in pornography constitutes a form of sexual discrimination, and women should be able to sue those who engage in such discrimination. Thus, whereas the traditional regulation of obscenity focused on the explicit portrayal of sexual activity, feminist critics are concerned with its implicit endorsement of sexual subordination, and whereas traditional regulation relied on criminal penalties, feminists have sought to control it through the threat of civil suits. This critique of pornography represents a fundamental challenge to First Amendment jurisprudence because it asserts that some views are so clearly erroneous and harmful that they should be banished from the marketplace of ideas. In contrast, the Supreme Court has held that the First Amendment does not permit the outlawing of ideas, however loathsome. When the city council of Indianapolis enacted an ordinance incorporating the feminist approach to pornography regulation, lower federal courts quickly invalidated the law, and the Supreme Court affirmed.

More recently, in *Brown v. Entertainment Merchants Association* (2011), the Court for the first time addressed First Amendment protection for video games. Concerned about the proliferation of violent video games and their possible effects on behavior, California enacted a law that restricted the sale of violent games to those under age eighteen without their parents' consent. By a 7–2 margin, the Court struck down this law as unconstitutional. Speaking for the Court, Justice Scalia argued that video games were entitled to First Amendment protection because "like the protected books, plays, and movies that preceded them, video games communicate ideas—and even social messages—through many familiar literary devices (such as characters, dialogue, plot, and music) and through features distinctive to the medium (such as the player's interaction with the virtual world)." Because "minors are entitled to a significant measure of First Amendment protection," states must demonstrate a compelling interest in restricting their access to materials protected by the amendment, and in *Brown* California had failed to do so. Although it claimed that violent video games had detrimental effects on children, Scalia insisted that social science research did not bear this out. Moreover, the fact that California allowed minors access to such materials with their parents' consent undermined its claim that exposure to such materials had dire effects. In sum, the Court refused to liken violent videos to obscenity and thereby justify an exception to First Amendment protection.

CONCLUSIONS

Over time, the Supreme Court has substantially expanded the range of expression that enjoys First Amendment protection. In large measure, this broadening of the amendment's coverage resulted from the incorporation of the speech and press guarantees. In addition, the Court has ruled that some previously excluded categories of expression are entitled to First Amendment protection. Rulings involving symbolic speech, commercial speech, and freedom of association have been particularly important in extending the scope of the First Amendment.

The Court has also progressively narrowed its definitions of the categories of speech—"the lewd and the obscene, the profane, the libelous, and the insulting or 'fighting' words"—that are not entitled to First Amendment protection. Despite the Court's ruling in *Miller v. California* (1973), a broad range of sexually explicit materials enjoy constitutional protection, and the Court has rejected claims that violent video games should likewise be outside First Amendment protection. The Court's rulings in *New York Times v. Sullivan* (1964) and succeeding cases have rewritten the law of libel to provide broad protection for criticisms of governmental officials. In addition, its substantive rulings and its use of the void-for-vagueness and overbreadth doctrines have largely eliminated prosecutions for "fighting words."

Yet as controversies over campaign financing, speech codes, and obscenity illustrate, the Court's extension of broad protections for expression has recently come under attack. Rejecting the notion of a self-correcting marketplace of ideas, some commentators have called for intervention by government to ensure what they deem more equitable outcomes. Some critics, fearful that the wealthy can dominate the marketplace of ideas not by the quality of their arguments but by monopolizing communications, want government to act to reduce their influence. Other critics insist that racist and sexist expression harms members of minority groups and therefore should be regulated or banned. Although these arguments have not been accepted by the Court, they do challenge proponents of a broad reading of the First Amendment to clarify the grounds for their position.

Finally, advances in technology have raised new questions about the scope of freedom of speech and of the press. These changes have required the Court to apply established principles to new contexts. At times, they have led the justices to reconsider those principles—for example, the Court has permitted a level of government licensing and regulation for radio and television that would be impermissible for print media. The Internet has already produced several cases involving the regulation of obscenity, and it seems likely to raise a host of questions relating to copyright, privacy, and other matters.

NOTES

1. *Chaplinsky v. New Hampshire*, 315 U.S. 568, 572 (1942). For a discussion of the protection accorded commercial speech, see *Central Hudson Gas Company v. Public Service Commission*, 447 U.S. 557 (1980).

2. Those who opposed the Sedition Act on First Amendment grounds did not necessarily believe that prosecution for seditious libel was inconsistent with democratic government. Because the First Amendment imposed limitations only on Congress, state legislatures remained free to punish the crime.

3. As Zechariah Chaffee observed:

It became criminal to advocate heavier taxation instead of bond issues, to state that conscription was unconstitutional though the Supreme Court had not yet held it valid, to say that the sinking of merchant ships was legal, to urge that a referendum should have preceded our declaration of war, to say that the war was contrary to the teachings of Christ. Men have been punished for criticizing the Red Cross and the Y.M.C.A., while under the Minnesota Espionage Act it has been held a crime to discourage women from knitting by the remark, "No soldier ever sees those socks."

Chaffee, *Free Speech in the United States* (Cambridge, MA: Harvard University Press, 1941), 51–52n12.

4. This definition of a "public figure" is from *Gertz v. Robert Welch, Inc.*, 418 U.S. 323, 345 (1974).

SELECTED READINGS

Anastaplo, George. *Reflections on Freedom of Speech and the First Amendment.* Lexington: University Press of Kentucky, 2007.

Bork, Robert H. "Neutral Principles and Some First Amendment Problems." *Indiana Law Journal* 47 (1971): 1–35.

Downs, Donald A. *Restoring Free Speech and Liberty on Campus.* Cambridge: Cambridge University Press, 2005.

Fish, Stanley. *There's No Such Thing as Free Speech.* New York: Oxford University Press, 1994.

Graber, Mark A. *Transforming Free Speech: The Ambiguous Legacy of Civil Libertarianism.* Berkeley: University of California Press, 1991.

Hyman, Steven J. *Free Speech and Human Dignity.* New Haven, CT: Yale University Press, 2008.

Lakier, Genevieve. "The Invention of Low-Value Speech," *Harvard Law Review* 128 (June 2015): 2166–2232.

Levy, Leonard W. *Emergence of a Free Press.* New York: Oxford University Press, 1985.

MacKinnon, Catherine. *Only Words.* Cambridge, MA: Harvard University Press, 1993.

Meiklejohn, Alexander. *Political Freedom: The Constitutional Powers of the People.* New York: Harper & Row, 1960.

Nelson, Samuel P. *Beyond the First Amendment: The Politics of Free Speech and Pluralism.* Baltimore: Johns Hopkins University Press, 2005.

Post, Robert C. *Citizens Divided: Campaign Finance Reform and the Constitution.* Cambridge, MA: Harvard University Press, 2014.

Shiell, Timothy C. *Campus Hate Speech on Trial.* 2nd ed. Lawrence: University Press of Kansas, 2009.

Stein, Laura L. *Speech Rights in America: The First Amendment, Democracy, and the Media.* Urbana: University of Illinois Press, 2006.

Stone, Geoffrey R. *Perilous Times: Free Speech in Wartime from the Sedition Act of 1798 to the War on Terror.* New York: W. W. Norton, 2004.

Sullivan, Kathleen M. "Two Concepts of Freedom of Speech." *Harvard Law Review* 124 (November 2011): 143–177.

Sunstein, Cass R. *Democracy and the Problem of Free Speech.* New York: Free Press, 1993.

Vile, John R., David L. Hudson, and David Schultz, eds. *Encyclopedia of the First Amendment.* Washington, DC: CQ Press, 2009.

Gitlow v. New York
268 U.S. 652 (1925)

Benjamin Gitlow, a member of the Left Wing Section of the Socialist Party, was convicted of violating the New York criminal anarchy law by advocating the forceful overthrow of the government and circulating a paper advocating governmental overthrow. The specific basis for the indictment was Gitlow's publication of The Left Wing Manifesto, *which proclaimed that the goal of so-called revolutionary socialism was to destroy the "bourgeois state" through "revolutionary mass action" and depicted capitalism as "in the process of disintegration and collapse." No evidence of any effects following from circulation of Gitlow's publication was introduced at trial. When the New York Court of Appeals affirmed his conviction, Gitlow appealed his case to the Supreme Court.* Opinion of the Court: <u>Sanford</u>, Taft, Van Devanter, McReynolds, Sutherland, Butler, Stone. Dissenting opinion: <u>Holmes</u>, Brandeis.

JUSTICE SANFORD delivered the opinion of the Court.

The sole contention here is, essentially, that as there was no evidence of any concrete result flowing from the publication of the *Manifesto* or of circumstances showing the likelihood of such result, the statute as construed and applied by the trial court penalizes the mere utterance, as such, of "doctrine" having no quality of incitement, without regard either to the circumstances of its utterance or to the likelihood of unlawful sequences; and that, as the exercise of the right of free expression with relation to government is only punishable "in circumstances involving likelihood of substantive evil," the statute contravenes the due process clause of the Fourteenth Amendment. The argument in support of this contention rests primarily upon the following propositions: 1st, That the "liberty" protected by the Fourteenth Amendment includes the liberty of speech and of the press; and 2nd, That while liberty of expression "is not absolute," it may be restrained "only in circumstances where its exercise bears a causal relation with some substantive evil, consummated, attempted or likely," and as the statute "takes no account of circumstances," it unduly restrains this liberty and is therefore unconstitutional.

The statute does not penalize the utterance or publication of abstract "doctrine" or academic discussion having no quality of incitement to any concrete action. It is not aimed against mere historical or philosophical essays. It does not restrain the advocacy of changes in the form of government by constitutional and lawful means. What it prohibits is language advocating, advising or teaching the overthrow of organized government by unlawful means. These words imply urging to action.

The *Manifesto*, plainly, is neither the statement of abstract doctrine nor, as suggested by counsel, mere prediction that industrial disturbances and revolutionary mass strikes will result spontaneously in an inevitable process of evolution in the economic system. It advocates and urges in fervent language mass action which shall progressively foment industrial disturbances and through political mass strikes and revolutionary mass action overthrow and destroy organized parliamentary government.

The means advocated for bringing about the destruction of organized parliamentary government, namely, mass industrial revolts usurping the functions of municipal government, political mass strikes directed against the parliamentary state, and revolutionary mass action for its final destruction, necessarily imply the use of force and violence, and in their essential nature are inherently unlawful in a constitutional government of law and order. That the jury were warranted in finding that the *Manifesto* advocated not merely the abstract doctrine of overthrowing organized government by force, violence and unlawful means, but action to that end, is clear.

For present purposes we may and do assume that freedom of speech and of the press—which are protected by the First Amendment from abridgment by Congress—are among the fundamental personal rights and "liberties" protected by the due process clause of the Fourteenth Amendment from impairment by the States.

It is a fundamental principle, long established, that the freedom of speech and of the press which is secured by the Constitution, does not confer an absolute right to speak or publish, without responsibility, whatever one may choose, or an unrestricted and unbridled license that gives immunity for every possible use of language and prevents the punishment of those who abuse this freedom. That a State in the exercise of its police power may punish those who abuse this freedom by utterances inimical to the public welfare, tending to corrupt public morals, incite to crime, or disturb the public peace, is not open to question.

By enacting the present statute the State has determined, through its legislative body, that utterances advocating the overthrow of organized government by force, violence and unlawful means, are so inimical to the general welfare and involve such danger of substantive evil that they may be penalized in the exercise of its police power. That determination must be given great weight. Every presumption is to be indulged in favor of the validity of the statute. The State cannot reasonably be required to measure the danger from every such utterance in the nice balance of a jeweler's scale. A single revolutionary spark may kindle a fire that, smouldering for a time, may burst into a sweeping and destructive conflagration. It cannot be said that the State is acting arbitrarily or unreasonably when in the exercise of its judgment as to the measures necessary to protect the public peace and safety, it seeks to extinguish the spark without waiting until it has enkindled the flame or blazed into the conflagration. It cannot reasonably be required to defer the adoption of measures for its own peace and safety until the revolutionary utterances lead to actual disturbances of the public peace or imminent and immediate danger of its own destruction; but it may, in the exercise of its judgment, suppress the threatened danger in its incipiency.

We cannot hold that the present statute is an arbitrary or unreasonable exercise of the police power of the State unwarrantably infringing the freedom of speech or press; and we must

and do sustain its constitutionality. This being so it may be applied to every utterance—not too trivial to be beneath the notice of the law—which is of such a character and used with such intent and purpose as to bring it within the prohibition of the statute. In other words, when the legislative body has determined generally, in the constitutional exercise of its discretion, that utterances of a certain kind involve such danger of substantive evil that they may be punished, the question whether any specific utterance coming within the prohibited class is likely, in and of itself, to bring about the substantive evil, is not open to consideration. It is sufficient that the statute itself be constitutional and that the use of the language comes within its prohibition.

JUSTICE HOLMES, dissenting.

Justice Brandeis and I are of opinion that this judgment should be reversed. If what I think the correct test is applied, it is manifest that there was no present danger of an attempt to overthrow the government by force on the part of the admittedly small minority who shared the defendant's views. It is said that this manifesto was more than a theory, that it was an incitement. Every idea is an incitement. It offers itself for belief and if believed it is acted on unless some other belief outweighs it or some failure of energy stifles the movement at its birth. The only difference between the expression of an opinion and an incitement in the narrower sense is the speaker's enthusiasm for the result. Eloquence may set fire to reason. But whatever may be thought of the redundant discourse before us it had no chance of starting a present conflagration. If in the long run the beliefs expressed in proletarian dictatorship are destined to be accepted by the dominant forces of the community, the only meaning of free speech is that they should be given their chance and have their way.

Schenck v. United States
249 U.S. 47 (1919)

Charles Schenck, general secretary of the Socialist Party, was convicted of violating the various provisions of the Espionage Act of 1917 by conspiring to obstruct military recruitment and cause

insubordination in the armed forces. The charges stemmed from the fact that Schenck had mailed to fifteen thousand men who were eligible for military service leaflets that claimed that the draft was unconstitutional and urged the potential draftees to "assert your rights." Opinion of the Court: <u>Holmes</u>, White, McKenna, Day, Van Devanter, Pitney, McReynolds, Brandeis, Clarke.

JUSTICE HOLMES delivered the opinion of the Court.

The document in question upon its first printed side recited the first section of the Thirteenth Amendment, said that the idea embodied in it was violated by the conscription act and that a conscript is little better than a convict. In impassioned language it intimated that conscription was despotism in its worst form and a monstrous wrong against humanity in the interest of Wall Street's chosen few. It said "Do not submit to intimidation," but in form at least confined itself to peaceful measures such as a petition for the repeal of the act. The other and later printed side of the sheet was headed "Assert Your Rights." It stated reasons for alleging that any one violated the Constitution when he refused to recognize "your right to assert your opposition to the draft," and went on "If you do not assert and support your rights, you are helping to deny or disparage rights which it is the solemn duty of all citizens and residents of the United States to retain." It described the arguments on the other side as coming from cunning politicians and a mercenary capitalist press, and even silent consent to the conscription law as helping to support an infamous conspiracy. It denied the power to send our citizens away to foreign shores to shoot up the people of other lands, and added that words could not express the condemnation such cold-blooded ruthlessness deserves, &c., &c., winding up, "You must do your share to maintain, support and uphold the rights of the people of this country." Of course the document would not have been sent unless it had been intended to have some effect, and we do not see what effect it could be expected to have upon persons subject to the draft except to influence them to obstruct the carrying of it out. The defendants do not deny that the jury might find against them on this point.

But it is said, suppose that that was the tendency of this circular, it is protected by the First Amendment to the Constitution. Two of the strongest expressions are said to be quoted respectively from well-known public men. It well may be that the prohibition of laws abridging the freedom of speech is not confined to previous restraints, although to prevent them may have been the main purpose. We admit that in many places and in ordinary times the defendants in saying all that was said in the circular would have been within their constitutional rights. But the character of every act depends upon the circumstances in which it is done. The most stringent protection of free speech would not protect a man in falsely shouting fire in a theatre and causing a panic. It does not even protect a man from an injunction against uttering words that may have all the effect of force. The question in every case is whether the words used are used in such circumstances and are of such a nature as to create a clear and present danger that they will bring about the substantive evils that Congress has a right to prevent. It is a question of proximity and degree. When a nation is at war many things that might be said in time of peace are such a hindrance to its effort that their utterance will not be endured so long as men fight and that no Court could regard them as protected by any constitutional right. It seems to be admitted that if an actual obstruction of the recruiting service were proved, liability for words that produced that effect might be enforced. The statute of 1917 in §4 punishes conspiracies to obstruct as well as actual obstruction. If the act, (speaking, or circulating a paper,) its tendency and the intent with which it is done are the same, we perceive no ground for saying that success alone warrants making the act a crime.

Judgments affirmed.

Dennis v. United States
341 U.S. 494 (1951)

In 1940, Congress enacted the Smith Act, under which persons could be punished for advocating the overthrow of the government by force or violence or for organizing a group that advocated such action. In 1948, Eugene Dennis and ten other leaders of the Communist Party were indicted under the Smith Act for willfully and knowingly conspiring "(1) to organize as the Communist Party of the United States a society, group and assembly of persons who teach and advocate the overthrow and destruction of the Government of the United States by force and violence, and (2) knowingly and willfully to advocate and teach the duty and necessity of overthrowing and destroying the Government of the United States by force and violence." After a long and contentious trial marked by intense conflict between the judge and the defense attorneys, all the defendants were convicted. When the convictions were upheld on appeal, the Supreme Court granted certiorari but limited its review to whether the relevant provisions of the Smith Act violated the First Amendment or were void for vagueness. Judgment of the Court: <u>Vinson</u>, Reed, Burton, Minton. Concurring opinions: <u>Frankfurter</u>; <u>Jackson</u>. Dissenting opinions: <u>Black</u>; <u>Douglas</u>. Not participating: Clark.

THE CHIEF JUSTICE announced the judgment of the Court and an opinion in which JUSTICE REED, JUSTICE BURTON and JUSTICE MINTON join.

The obvious purpose of the statute is to protect existing Government, not from change by peaceable, lawful and constitutional means, but from change by violence, revolution and terrorism. That it is within the *power* of the Congress to protect the Government of the United States from armed rebellion is a proposition which requires little discussion. The question with which we are concerned here is whether the *means* which it has employed conflict with the First and Fifth Amendments to the Constitution.

One of the bases for the contention that the means which Congress has employed are invalid takes the form of an attack on the face of the statute on the grounds that by its terms it prohibits academic discussion of the merits of Marxism-Leninism, that it stifles ideas and is contrary to all concepts of a free speech and a free press. The very language of the Smith Act negates the interpretation which petitioners would have us impose on that Act. It is directed at advocacy, not discussion. Thus, the

trial judge properly charged the jury that they could not convict if they found that petitioners did "no more than pursue peaceful studies and discussions or teaching and advocacy in the realm of ideas." Congress did not intend to eradicate the free discussion of political theories, to destroy the traditional rights of Americans to discuss and evaluate ideas without fear of governmental sanction.

Speech is not an absolute, above and beyond control by the legislature when its judgment, subject to review here, is that certain kinds of speech are so undesirable as to warrant criminal sanction. Nothing is more certain in modern society than the principle that there are no absolutes, that a name, a phrase, a standard has meaning only when associated with the considerations which gave birth to the nomenclature. To those who would paralyze our Government in the face of impending threat by encasing it in a semantic straitjacket we must reply that all concepts are relative.

In this case we are squarely presented with the application of the "clear and present danger" test, and must decide what that phrase imports. Overthrow of the Government by force and violence is certainly a substantial enough interest for the Government to limit speech. Indeed, this is the ultimate value of any society, for if a society cannot protect its very structure from armed internal attack, it must follow that no subordinate value can be protected. If, then, this interest may be protected, the literal problem which is presented is what has been meant by the use of the phrase "clear and present danger" of the utterances bringing about the evil within the power of Congress to punish.

Obviously, the words cannot mean that before the Government may act, it must wait until the *putsch* is about to be executed, the plans have been laid and the signal is awaited. If Government is aware that a group aiming at its overthrow is attempting to indoctrinate its members and to commit them to a course whereby they will strike when the leaders feel the circumstances permit, action by the Government is required. The argument that there is no need for Government to concern itself, for Government is strong, it possesses ample powers to put down a rebellion, it may defeat the revolution with ease needs no answer. For that is not the question. Certainly an attempt to overthrow the Government by force, even though doomed from the outset because of inadequate numbers or power of the revolutionists, is a sufficient evil for Congress to prevent. The damage which such attempts create both physically and politically to a nation makes it impossible to measure the validity in terms of the probability of success, or the immediacy of a successful attempt. In the instant case the trial judge charged the jury that they could not convict unless they found that petitioners intended to overthrow the Government "as speedily as circumstances would permit." This does not mean, and could not properly mean, that they would not strike until there was certainty of success. What was meant was that the revolutionists would strike when they thought the time was ripe. We must therefore reject the contention that success or probability of success is the criterion.

Chief Judge Learned Hand, writing for the majority below, interpreted the phrase as follows: "In each case [courts] must ask whether the gravity of the 'evil,' discounted by its improbability, justifies such invasion of free speech as is necessary to avoid the danger." We adopt this statement of the rule. As articulated by Chief Judge Hand, it is as succinct and inclusive as any other we might devise at this time. It takes into consideration those factors which we deem relevant, and relates their significances. More we cannot expect from words.

Likewise, we are in accord with the court below, which affirmed the trial court's finding that the requisite danger existed. The mere fact that from the period 1945 to 1948 petitioners' activities did not result in an attempt to overthrow the Government by force and violence is of course no answer to the fact that there was a group that was ready to make the attempt. The formation by petitioners of such a highly organized conspiracy, with rigidly disciplined members subject to call when the leaders, these petitioners, felt that the time had come for action, coupled with the inflammable nature of world conditions, similar uprisings in other countries, and the touch-and-go nature of our relations with countries with whom petitioners were in the very least ideologically attuned, convince us that their convictions were justi-

fied on this score. And this analysis disposes of the contention that a conspiracy to advocate, as distinguished from the advocacy itself, cannot be constitutionally restrained, because it comprises only the preparation. It is the existence of the conspiracy which creates the danger. If the ingredients of the reaction are present, we cannot bind the Government to wait until the catalyst is added.

We hold that §§2 (a) (1), 2 (a) (3) and 3 of the Smith Act do not violate the First Amendment and other provisions of the Bill of Rights, or the First and Fifth Amendments because of indefiniteness. Petitioners intended to overthrow the Government of the United States as speedily as the circumstances would permit. Their conspiracy to organize the Communist Party and to teach and advocate the overthrow of the Government of the United States by force and violence created a "clear and present danger" of an attempt to overthrow the Government by force and violence. They were properly and constitutionally convicted for violation of the Smith Act. The judgments of conviction are

Affirmed.

JUSTICE FRANKFURTER, concurring.

Few questions of comparable import have come before this Court in recent years. The appellants maintain that they have a right to advocate a political theory, so long, at least, as their advocacy does not create an immediate danger of obvious magnitude to the very existence of our present scheme of society. On the other hand, the Government asserts the right to safeguard the security of the Nation by such a measure as the Smith Act. Our judgment is thus solicited on a conflict of interests of the utmost concern to the well-being of the country. This conflict of interests cannot be resolved by a dogmatic preference for one or the other, nor by a sonorous formula which is in fact only a euphemistic disguise for an unresolved conflict. If adjudication is to be a rational process, we cannot escape a candid examination of the conflicting claims with full recognition that both are supported by weighty title-deeds.

But how are competing interests to be assessed? Since they are not subject to quantitative ascertainment, the issue necessarily resolves itself into asking, who is to make the adjustment?—who is to balance the relevant factors and ascertain which interest is in the circumstances to prevail? Full responsibility for the choice cannot be given to the courts. Courts are not representative bodies. They are not designed to be a good reflex of a democratic society. Their judgment is best informed, and therefore most dependable, within narrow limits. Primary responsibility for adjusting the interests which compete in the situation before us of necessity belongs to the Congress. We are to set aside the judgment of those whose duty it is to legislate only if there is no reasonable basis for it. It is not for us to decide how we would adjust the clash of interests which this case presents were the primary responsibility for reconciling it ours. Congress has determined that the danger created by advocacy of overthrow justifies the ensuing restriction on freedom of speech. The determination was made after due deliberation, and the seriousness of the congressional purpose is attested by the volume of legislation passed to effectuate the same ends.

Can we then say that the judgment Congress exercised was denied it by the Constitution? Can we establish a constitutional doctrine which forbids the elected representatives of the people to make this choice? Can we hold that the First Amendment deprives Congress of what it deemed necessary for the Government's protection? To make validity of legislation depend on judicial reading of events still in the womb of time—a forecast, that is, of the outcome of forces at best appreciated only with knowledge of the topmost secrets of nations—is to charge the judiciary with duties beyond its equipment.

The wisdom of the assumptions underlying the legislation and prosecution is another matter. Civil liberties draw at best only limited strength from legal guaranties. Preoccupation by our people with the constitutionality, instead of with the wisdom, of legislation or of executive action is preoccupation with a false value. Focusing attention on constitutionality tends to make constitutionality synonymous with wisdom. When legislation touches freedom of thought and freedom of speech, such a tendency is a formidable enemy of the free spirit. Much that should be rejected as illiberal, because repressive and envenoming, may well be not unconstitutional. The ultimate reliance for the deepest needs of civilization must be found outside their vindication in courts of law.

JUSTICE JACKSON, concurring.

The "clear and present danger" test was an innovation by Mr. Justice Holmes in the *Schenck* [*v. United States* (1919)] case, reiterated and refined by him and Mr. Justice Brandeis in later cases, all arising before the era of World War II that revealed the subtlety and efficacy of modernized revolutionary techniques used by totalitarian parties. In those cases, they were faced with convictions under so-called criminal syndicalism statutes aimed at anarchists but which, loosely construed, had been applied to punish socialism, pacifism, and left-wing ideologies, the charges often resting on farfetched inferences which, if true, would establish only technical or trivial violations. They proposed "clear and present danger" as a test for the sufficiency of evidence in particular cases. I would save it, unmodified, for application as a "rule of reason" in the kind of case for which it was devised.

But its recent expansion has extended, in particular to Communists, unprecedented immunities. Unless we are to hold our Government captive in a judge-made verbal trap, we must approach the problem of a well-organized, nation-wide conspiracy, such as I have described, as realistically as our predecessors faced the trivialities that were being prosecuted until they were checked with a rule of reason. I think reason is lacking for applying that test to this case.

JUSTICE BLACK, dissenting.

At the outset I want to emphasize what the crime involved in this case is, and what it is not. These petitioners were not charged with an attempt to overthrow the Government. They were not charged with overt acts of any kind designed to overthrow the Government. They were not even charged with saying anything or writing anything designed to overthrow the Government. The charge was that they agreed to assemble and to talk and publish certain ideas at a later date. The indictment is that they conspired to organize the Communist Party and to use newspapers and other publications in the future to teach and advocate the forcible overthrow of the Government. No matter how it is worded, this is a virulent form of prior censorship of speech and press, which I believe the First Amendment forbids.

The opinions for affirmance indicate that the chief reason for jettisoning the [clear-and-present-danger] rule is the expressed fear that advocacy of Communist doctrine endangers the safety of the Republic. Undoubtedly, a governmental policy of unfettered communication of ideas does entail dangers. To the Founders of this Nation, however, the benefits derived from free expression were worth the risk. They embodied this philosophy in the First Amendment's command that "Congress shall make no law abridging the freedom of speech, or of the press." I have always believed that the First Amendment is the keystone of our Government, that the freedoms it guarantees provide the best insurance against destruction of all freedom. At least as to speech in the realm of public matters, I believe that the "clear and present danger" test does not "mark the furthermost constitutional boundaries of protected expression" but does "no more than recognize a minimum compulsion of the Bill of Rights." *Bridges v. California* (1941).

So long as this Court exercises the power of judicial review of legislation, I cannot agree that the First Amendment permits us to sustain laws suppressing freedom of speech and press on the basis of Congress' or our own notions of mere "reasonableness." Such a doctrine waters down the First Amendment so that it amounts to little more than an admonition to Congress. The Amendment as so construed is not likely to protect any but those "safe" or orthodox views which rarely need its protection.

Public opinion being what it now is, few will protest the conviction of these Communist petitioners. There is hope, however, that in calmer times, when present pressures, passions and fears subside, this or some later Court will restore the First Amendment liberties to the high preferred place where they belong in a free society.

JUSTICE DOUGLAS, dissenting.

If this were a case where those who claimed protection under the First Amendment were teaching the techniques of sabotage, the assassination of the President, the filching of documents from public files, the planting of bombs, the art of street warfare, and the like, I would have no doubts. The freedom to speak is not absolute; the teaching of methods of terror and other seditious conduct should be beyond the pale along with obscenity and immorality. This case was argued as if those were the facts. The argument imported much seditious conduct into the record. That is easy and it has popular appeal, for the activities of Communists in plotting and scheming against the free world are common knowledge. But the fact is that no such evidence was introduced at the trial.

There is a statute which makes a seditious conspiracy unlawful. Petitioners, however, were not charged with a "conspiracy to overthrow" the Government. They were charged with a conspiracy to form a party and groups and assemblies of people who teach and advocate the overthrow of our Government by force or violence and with a conspiracy to advocate and teach its overthrow by force and violence. It may well be that indoctrination in the techniques of terror to destroy the Government would be indictable under either statute. But the teaching which is condemned here is of a different character.

There comes a time when even speech loses its constitutional immunity. Yet free speech is the rule, not the exception. The restraint to be constitutional must be based on more than fear, on more than passionate opposition against the speech, on more than a revolted dislike for its contents. There must be some immediate injury to society that is likely if speech is allowed.

The nature of Communism as a force on the world scene would, of course, be relevant to the issue of clear and present danger of petitioners' advocacy within the United States. But the primary consideration is the strength and tactical position of petitioners and their converts in this country. On that there is no evidence in the record. If we are to take judicial notice of the threat of Communists within the nation, it should not be difficult to conclude that *as a political party* they are of little consequence. In America they are miserable merchants of unwanted ideas; their wares remain unsold. The fact that their ideas are abhorrent does not make them powerful.

The political impotence of the Communists in this country does not, of course, dispose of the problem. Their numbers; their positions in industry and government; the extent to which they have in fact infiltrated the police, the armed services, transportation, stevedoring, power plants, munitions works, and other critical places—these facts all bear on the likelihood that their advocacy of the Soviet theory of revolution will endanger the Republic. But the record is silent on these facts. If we are to proceed on the basis of judicial notice, it is impossible for me to say that the Communists in this country are so potent or so strategically deployed that they must be suppressed for their speech.

Free speech—the glory of our system of government—should not be sacrificed on anything less than plain and objective proof of danger that the evil advocated is imminent. On this record no one can say that petitioners and their converts are in such a strategic position as to have even the slightest chance of achieving their aims.

Barenblatt v. United States
360 U.S. 109 (1959)

Lloyd Barenblatt, who had previously served as a psychology instructor at the University of Michigan and at Vassar College, was subpoenaed to testify by a subcommittee of the House Un-American Activities Committee, which was conducting hearings dealing with alleged Communist infiltration into the field of education. He refused to answer subcommittee questions pertaining to his past or present membership in the Communist Party and other groups, asserting that the First Amendment barred a legislative inquiry into his political beliefs and associations. After being convicted of contempt of Congress, he appealed the conviction primarily on First Amendment grounds. Opinion of the Court: <u>Harlan</u>, Frankfurter, Clark, Whittaker, Stewart. Dissenting opinions: <u>Black</u>, Warren, Douglas; <u>Brennan</u>.

JUSTICE HARLAN delivered the opinion of the Court.

The power of inquiry has been employed by Congress throughout our history, over the whole range of the national interests concerning which Congress might legislate or decide upon due investigation not to legislate; it has similarly been utilized in determining what to appropriate from the national purse, or whether to appropriate. The scope of the power of inquiry, in short, is as penetrating and far-reaching as the potential power to enact and appropriate under the Constitution.

Broad as it is, the power is not, however, without limitations. Since Congress may only investigate into those areas in which it may potentially legislate or appropriate, it cannot inquire into matters which are within the exclusive province of one of the other branches of the Government. And the Congress, in common with all branches of the Government, must exercise its powers subject to the limitations placed by the Constitution on governmental action, more particularly in the context of this case the relevant limitations of the Bill of Rights.

Petitioner's various contentions resolve themselves into three propositions: First, the compelling of testimony by the Subcommittee was neither legislatively authorized nor constitutionally permissible because of the vagueness of Rule XI of the House of Representatives, Eighty-third Congress, the charter of authority of the parent Committee. Second, petitioner was not adequately apprised of the pertinency of the Subcommittee's questions to the subject matter of the inquiry. Third, the questions petitioner refused to answer infringed rights protected by the First Amendment.

Rule XI authorized this Subcommittee to compel testimony within the framework of the investigative authority conferred on the Un-American Activities Committee. Petitioner contends that *Watkins v. United States* [1957] nevertheless held the grant of this power in all circumstances ineffective because of the vagueness of Rule XI in delineating the Committee jurisdiction to which its exercise was to be appurtenant. Petitioner also contends, independently of *Watkins,* that the vagueness of Rule XI deprived the Subcommittee of the right to compel testimony in this investigation into Communist activity.

Granting the vagueness of the Rule, we may not read it in isolation from its long history in the House of Representatives. Just as legislation is often given meaning by the gloss of legislative reports, administrative interpretation, and long usage, so the proper meaning of an authorization to a congressional committee is not to be derived alone from its abstract terms unrelated to the definite content furnished them by the course of congressional actions. The Rule comes to us with a "persuasive gloss of legislative history," which shows beyond doubt that in pursuance of its legislative concerns in the domain of "national security" the House has clothed the Un-American Activities Committee with pervasive authority to investigate Communist activities in this country. From the beginning, without interruption to the present time, and with the undoubted knowledge and approval of the House, the Committee has devoted a major part of its energies to the investigation of Communist activities. In the context of these unremitting pursuits, the House has steadily continued the life of the Committee at the commencement of each new Congress; it has never narrowed the powers of the Committee, whose authority has remained throughout identical with that contained in Rule XI; and it has continuingly supported the Committee's activities with substantial appropriations. Beyond this, the Committee was raised to the level of a standing committee of the House in 1945, it having been but a special committee prior to that time. In light of this long and illuminating history it can hardly be seriously argued that the investigation of Communist activities generally, and the attendant use of compulsory process, was beyond the purview of the Committee's intended authority under Rule XI.

Undeniably a conviction for contempt cannot stand unless the questions asked are pertinent to the subject matter of the investigation. What we deal with here is whether petitioner was sufficiently apprised of "the topic under inquiry" thus authorized "and the connective reasoning whereby the precise questions asked related to it." *Watkins.* In light of his prepared memorandum of constitutional objections there can be no doubt that this petitioner was well aware of the Subcommittee's authority and purpose to question him as it did. The subject matter of the inquiry had been identified at the commencement of the investigation as Communist infiltration into the field of education. Further, petitioner had stood mute in the face of the Chairman's statement as to why he had been called as a witness by the Subcommittee. And, lastly, petitioner refused to answer questions as to his own Communist Party affiliations, whose pertinency of course was clear beyond doubt.

The precise constitutional issue confronting us is whether the Subcommittee's inquiry into petitioner's past or present membership in the Communist Party transgressed the provisions of the First Amendment, which of course reach and limit congressional investigations. Undeniably, the First Amendment in some circumstances protects an individual from being compelled to disclose his associational relationships. However, the protections of the First Amendment, unlike a proper claim of the privilege against self-incrimination under the Fifth Amendment, do not afford a witness the right to resist inquiry in all circumstances. Where First Amendment rights are asserted to bar governmental interrogation, resolution of the issue always involves a balancing by the courts of the competing private and public interests at stake in the particular circumstances shown.

The first question is whether this investigation was related to a valid legislative purpose, for Congress may not constitutionally require an individual to disclose his political relationships or other private affairs except in relation to such a purpose. That Congress has wide power to legislate in the field of Communist activity in this Country, and to conduct appropriate investigations in aid thereof, is hardly debatable. The existence of such power has never been questioned by this Court, and it is sufficient to say, without particularization, that Congress has enacted or considered in this field a wide range of legislative measures, not a few of which have stemmed from recommendations of the very Committee whose actions have been drawn in question here. In the last analysis this power rests on the right of self-preservation, "the ultimate value of any society." *Dennis v. United States* [1951]. Justification for its exercise in turn rests on the long and widely accepted view that the tenets of the Communist Party include the ultimate overthrow of the Government of the United States by force and violence, a view which has been given formal expression by the Congress.

To suggest that because the Communist Party may also sponsor peaceable political reforms the constitutional issues before us should now be judged as if that Party were just an ordinary political party from the standpoint of national security, is to ask this Court to blind itself to world affairs which have determined the whole course of our national policy since the close of World War II. Nor can we accept the further contention that this investigation should not be deemed to have been in furtherance of a legislative purpose because the true objective of the Committee and of the Congress was purely "exposure." So long as Congress acts in pursuance of its constitutional power, the Judiciary lacks authority to intervene on the basis of the motives which spurred the exercise of that power. Having scrutinized this record we cannot say that the unanimous panel of the Court of Appeals which first considered this case was wrong in concluding that "the primary purposes of the inquiry were in aid of legislative processes."

We conclude that the balance between the individual and the governmental interests here at stake must be struck in favor of the latter, and that therefore the provisions of the First Amendment have not been offended. We hold that petitioner's conviction for contempt of Congress discloses no infirmity, and that the judgment of the Court of Appeals must be

Affirmed.

JUSTICE BLACK, with whom THE CHIEF JUSTICE and JUSTICE DOUGLAS concur, dissenting.

It goes without saying that a law to be valid must be clear enough to make its commands understandable. For obvious reasons, the standard of certainty required in criminal statutes is more exacting than in noncriminal statutes. This is simply because it would be unthinkable to convict a man for violating a law he could not understand. This Court has recognized that the stricter standard is as much required in criminal contempt cases as in all other criminal cases, and has emphasized that the "vice of vagueness" is especially pernicious where legislative power over an area involving speech, press, petition and assembly is involved.

Measured by the foregoing standards, Rule XI cannot support any conviction for refusal to testify. On the Court's own test, the issue is whether Barenblatt can know with sufficient certainty, at the time of his interrogation, that there is so compelling a need for his replies that infringement of his rights of free association is justified. The record does not disclose where Barenblatt can find what that need is. There is certainly no clear congressional statement of it in Rule XI. Perhaps if Barenblatt had had time to read all the reports of the Committee to the House, and in addition had examined the appropriations made to the Committee he, like the Court, could have discerned an intent by Congress to allow an investigation of communism in education. Even so he would be hard put to decide what the need for this investigation is since Congress expressed it neither when it enacted Rule XI nor when it acquiesced in the Committee's assertions of power. Yet it is knowledge of this need—what is wanted from him and why it is wanted—that a witness must have if he is to be in a position to comply with the Court's rule that he balance individual rights against the requirements of the State. I cannot see how that knowledge can exist under Rule XI. I would hold that Rule XI is too broad to be meaningful and cannot support petitioner's conviction.

The First Amendment says in no equivocal language that Congress shall pass no law abridging freedom of speech, press, assembly or petition. The activities of this Committee, authorized by Congress, do precisely that, through exposure, obloquy and public scorn.

To apply the Court's balancing test under [present] circumstances is to read the First Amendment to say "Congress shall pass no law abridging freedom of speech, press, assembly and petition, unless Congress and the Supreme Court reach the joint conclusion that on balance the interest of the Government in stifling these freedoms is greater than the interest of the people in having them exercised." This is closely akin to the notion that neither the First Amendment nor any other provision of the Bill of Rights should be enforced unless the Court believes it is reasonable to do so. This violates the genius of our written Constitution.

But even assuming what I cannot assume, that some balancing is proper in this case, I feel that the Court after stating the test ignores it completely. At most it balances the right of the Government to preserve itself, against Barenblatt's right to refrain from revealing Communist affiliations. Such a balance, however, mistakes the factors to be weighed. In the first place, it completely leaves out the real interest in Barenblatt's silence, the interest of the people as a whole in being able to join organizations, advocate causes and make political "mistakes" without later being subjected to governmental penalties for having dared to think for themselves. It is this right, the right to err politically, which keeps us strong as a Nation. For no number of laws against communism can have as much effect as the personal conviction which comes from having heard its arguments and rejected them, or from having once accepted its tenets and later recognized their worthlessness. Instead, the obloquy which results from investigations such as this not only stifles "mistakes" but prevents all but the most courageous from hazarding any views which might at some later time become disfavored. This result, whose importance cannot be overestimated, is doubly crucial when it affects the universities, on which we must largely rely for the experimentation and development of new ideas essential to our country's welfare. It is these interests of society, rather than Barenblatt's own right to silence, which I think the Court should put on the balance against the demands of the Government, if any balancing process is to be tolerated. Instead they are not mentioned, while on the other side the demands of the Government are vastly overstated and called ""self-preservation." It is admitted that this Committee can only seek information for the purpose of suggesting laws, and that Congress' power to make laws in the realm of speech and association is quite limited, even on the Court's test. Its interest in making such laws in the field of education, primarily a state function, is clearly narrower still. Yet the Court styles this attenuated interest self-preservation, and allows it to overcome the need our country has to let us all think, speak, and associate politically as we like and without fear of reprisal. Such a result reduces "balancing" to a mere play on words.

Finally, I think Barenblatt's conviction violates the Constitution because the chief aim, purpose and practice of the House Un-American Activities Committee, as disclosed by its many reports, is to try witnesses and punish them because they are or have been Communists or because they refuse to admit or deny Communist affiliations. The punishment imposed is generally punishment by humiliation and public shame.

The same intent to expose and punish is manifest in the Committee's investigation which led to Barenblatt's conviction. The declared purpose of the investigation was to identify to the people of Michigan the individuals responsible for the, alleged, Communist success there. As a result of its Michigan investigation, the Committee called upon American labor unions to amend their constitutions, if necessary, in order to deny membership to any Communist Party member. This would, of course, prevent many workers from getting or holding the only kind of jobs their particular skills qualified them for. The Court, today, barely mentions these statements, which, especially when read in the context of past reports by the Committee, show unmistakably what the Committee was doing. I do not question the Committee's patriotism and sincerity in doing all this. I merely feel that it cannot be done by Congress under our Constitution.

Brandenburg v. Ohio
395 U.S. 444 (1969)

Charles Brandenburg, a local Ku Klux Klan leader, was convicted under Ohio's Criminal Syndicalism Act, which prohibited "advocating the duty, necessity, or propriety of crime, sabotage, violence, or unlawful methods of terrorism as a means of accomplishing industrial or political reform." The evidence in the case included two television films that showed Brandenburg addressing two Klan meetings. The most provocative element in his speeches was the statement that "if our President, our Congress, our Supreme Court, continues to suppress the white, Caucasian race, it's possible that there might have to be some revengence taken." Per Curiam: Warren, Black, Douglas, Harlan, Brennan, Stewart, White, Fortas, Marshall. Concurring opinions: Black; Douglas, Black.

PER CURIAM.

The Ohio Criminal Syndicalism Statute was enacted in 1919. From 1917 to 1920, identical or quite similar laws were adopted by 20 States and two territories. In 1927, this Court sustained the constitutionality of California's Criminal Syndicalism Act, the text of which is quite similar to that of the laws of Ohio. *Whitney v. California* [1927]. The Court upheld the statute on the ground that, without more, "advocating" violent means to effect political and economic change involves such danger to the security of the State that the State may outlaw it. But *Whitney* has been thoroughly discredited by later decisions. These later decisions have fashioned the principle that the constitutional guarantees of free speech and free press do not permit a State to forbid or proscribe advocacy of the use of force or of law violation except where such advocacy is directed to inciting or producing imminent lawless action and is likely to incite or produce such action.

Measured by this test, Ohio's Criminal Syndicalism Act cannot be sustained. The Act punishes persons who "advocate or teach the duty, necessity, or propriety" of violence "as a means of accomplishing industrial or political reform"; or who publish or circulate or display any book or paper containing such advocacy; or who "justify" the commission of violent acts "with intent to exemplify, spread or advocate the propriety of the doctrines of criminal syndicalism"; or who "voluntarily assemble" with a group formed "to teach or advocate the doctrines of criminal syndicalism." Neither the indictment nor the trial judge's instructions to the jury in any way refined the statute's bald definition of the crime in terms of mere advocacy not distinguished from incitement to imminent lawless action.

Accordingly, we are here confronted with a statute which, by its own words and as applied, purports to punish mere advocacy and to forbid, on pain of criminal punishment, assembly with others merely to advocate the described type of action. Such a statute falls within the condemnation of the First and Fourteenth Amendments. The contrary teaching of *Whitney v. California* cannot be supported, and that decision is therefore overruled.

JUSTICE DOUGLAS, concurring.

While I join the opinion of the Court, I see no place in the regime of the First Amendment for any "clear and present danger" test, whether strict and tight as some would make it, or free-wheeling as the Court in *Dennis* [*v. United States* (1951)] rephrased it.

When one reads the opinions closely and sees when and how the "clear and present danger" test has been applied, great misgivings are aroused. First, the threats were often loud but always puny and made serious only by judges so wedded to the status quo that critical analysis made them nervous. Second, the test was so twisted and perverted in Dennis as to make the trial of those teachers of Marxism an all-out political trial which was part and parcel of the cold war that has eroded substantial parts of the First Amendment.

One's beliefs have long been thought to be sanctuaries which government could not invade. *Barenblatt* [*v. United States* (1959)] is one example of the ease with which that sanctuary can be violated. The lines drawn by the Court between the criminal act of being an "active"

Communist and the innocent act of being a nominal or inactive Communist mark the difference only between deep and abiding belief and casual or uncertain belief. But I think that all matters of belief are beyond the reach of subpoenas or the probings of investigators. That is why the invasions of privacy made by investigating committees were notoriously unconstitutional. That is the deep-seated fault in the infamous loyalty-security hearings which, since 1947 when President Truman launched them, have processed 20,000,000 men and women. Those hearings were primarily concerned with one's thoughts, ideas, beliefs, and convictions. They were the most blatant violations of the First Amendment we have ever known.

The line between what is permissible and not subject to control and what may be made impermissible and subject to regulation is the line between ideas and overt acts. The example usually given by those who would punish speech is the case of one who falsely shouts fire in a crowded theatre. This is, however, a classic case where speech is brigaded with action. They are indeed inseparable and a prosecution can be launched for the overt acts actually caused. Apart from rare instances of that kind, speech is, I think, immune from prosecution. Certainly there is no constitutional line between advocacy of abstract ideas as in *Yates* [*v. United States* (1957)] and advocacy of political action as in *Scales* [*v. United States* (1961)]. The quality of advocacy turns on the depth of the conviction; and government has no power to invade that sanctuary of belief and conscience.

Holder v. Humanitarian Law Project
561 U.S. 1 (2010)

Federal law makes it a crime to knowingly provide "material support or resources" to organizations that the secretary of state has designated as foreign terrorist organizations (18 U.S.C. §2339B[a][1]). The statute defines "material support or resources" as including "any property, tangible or intangible, or service, including currency or monetary instruments or financial securities, financial services, lodging, training, expert advice or assistance, safe houses, false documentation or identification, communications equipment, facilities, weapons, lethal substances, explosives, personnel." The Humanitarian Law Project (HLR), as well as other groups and individuals involved in the case, sought to provide support to two organizations—the Kurdistan Workers' Party (PKK) and the Liberation Tigers of Tamil Eelam (LTTE), both of which had been identified by the secretary of state as terrorist organizations. However, the HLR claimed that it wished to assist only the lawful, nonviolent purposes of these groups, through monetary contributions, provision of legal training, and political advocacy. It argued that the statute, in preventing it from engaging in these activities, violated its rights to freedom of speech and freedom of association under the First Amendment. After several *years of litigation, during which Congress amended the law to clarify its meaning, the federal district court partially enjoined the enforcement of the law, the court of appeals affirmed, and the Supreme Court granted certiorari. Opinion of the Court:* Roberts, *Stevens, Scalia, Kennedy, Thomas, Alito. Dissenting opinion:* Breyer, *Ginsburg, Sotomayor.*

THE CHIEF JUSTICE delivered the opinion of the Court.

The plaintiffs in this litigation seek to provide support to two organizations [designated as terrorist groups]. Plaintiffs claim that they seek to facilitate only the lawful, nonviolent purposes of those groups, and that applying the material-support law to prevent them from doing so violates the Constitution. In particular, they claim that the statute infringes their rights to freedom of speech and association, in violation of the First Amendment. We conclude that the material-support statute is constitutional as applied to the particular activities plaintiffs have told us they wish to pursue. We do not, however, address the resolution of more difficult cases that may arise under the statute in the future.

II

Given the complicated 12-year history of this litigation, we pause to clarify the questions before us. Plaintiffs challenge §2339B's prohibition on four types of material support—"training," "expert advice or assistance," "service," and "personnel." They raise three constitutional claims. First, plaintiffs claim that §2339B violates the Due Process Clause of the Fifth Amendment because these four statutory terms are impermissibly vague. Second, plaintiffs claim that §2339B violates their freedom of speech under the First Amendment. Third, plaintiffs claim that §2339B violates their First Amendment freedom of association. Plaintiffs claim that §2339B is invalid to the extent it prohibits them from engaging in certain specified activities. Those activities are: (1) "training members of the PKK on how to use humanitarian and international law to peacefully resolve disputes"; (2) "engaging in political advocacy on behalf of Kurds who live in Turkey"; and (3) "teaching PKK members how to petition various representative bodies such as the United Nations for relief." With respect to the other plaintiffs, those activities are: (1) "training members of the LTTE to present claims for tsunami-related aid to mediators and international bodies"; (2) "offering their legal expertise in negotiating peace agreements between the LTTE and the Sri Lankan government"; and (3) "engaging in political advocacy on behalf of Tamils who live in Sri Lanka."

III

Plaintiffs claim, as a threshold matter, that we should affirm the Court of Appeals without reaching any issues of constitutional law. They contend that we should interpret the material-support statute, when applied to speech, to require proof that a defendant intended to further a foreign terrorist organization's illegal activities. We reject plaintiffs' interpretation of §2339B because it is inconsistent with the text of the statute. Section 2339B(a)(1) prohibits "knowingly" providing material support. It then specifically describes the type of knowledge that is required: "To violate this paragraph, a person must have knowledge that the

organization is a designated terrorist organization, that the organization has engaged or engages in terrorist activity, or that the organization has engaged or engages in terrorism." Congress plainly spoke to the necessary mental state for a violation of §2339B, and it chose knowledge about the organization's connection to terrorism, not specific intent to further the organization's terrorist activities.

V

We next consider whether the material-support statute, as applied to plaintiffs, violates the freedom of speech guaranteed by the First Amendment. Both plaintiffs and the Government take extreme positions on this question. Plaintiffs claim that Congress has banned their "pure political speech." Under the material-support statute, plaintiffs may say anything they wish on any topic. They may speak and write freely about the PKK and LTTE, the governments of Turkey and Sri Lanka, human rights, and international law. They may advocate before the United Nations. As the Government states: "The statute does not prohibit independent advocacy or expression of any kind." Section 2339B also "does not prevent [plaintiffs] from becoming members of the PKK and LTTE or impose any sanction on them for doing so." Congress has not, therefore, sought to suppress ideas or opinions in the form of "pure political speech." Rather, Congress has prohibited "material support," which most often does not take the form of speech at all. And when it does, the statute is carefully drawn to cover only a narrow category of speech to, under the direction of, or in coordination with foreign groups that the speaker knows to be terrorist organizations.

For its part, the Government takes the foregoing too far, claiming that the only thing truly at issue in this litigation is conduct, not speech. Section 2339B is directed at the fact of plaintiffs' interaction with the PKK and LTTE, the Government contends, and only incidentally burdens their expression. The Government argues that the proper standard of review is therefore the one set out in *United States v. O'Brien* (1968). In that case, the Court rejected a First Amendment challenge to a conviction under a generally applicable prohibition on destroying draft cards, even though O'Brien had burned his card in protest against the draft. In so doing, we applied what we have since called "intermediate scrutiny," under which a "content-neutral regulation will be sustained under the First Amendment if it advances important governmental interests unrelated to the suppression of free speech and does not burden substantially more speech than necessary to further those interests." *Turner Broadcasting System, Inc. v. FCC* (1997). [But] *O'Brien* does not provide the applicable standard for reviewing a content-based regulation of speech, and §2339B regulates speech on the basis of its content. Plaintiffs want to speak to the PKK and the LTTE, and whether they may do so under §2339B depends on what they say. If plaintiffs' speech to those groups imparts a "specific skill" or communicates advice derived from "specialized knowledge"—for example, training on the use of international law or advice on petitioning the United Nations—then it is barred.

The Government argues that §2339B should nonetheless receive intermediate scrutiny because it generally functions as a regulation of conduct. That argument runs headlong into a number of our precedents, most prominently *Cohen v. California* (1971). *Cohen* also involved a generally applicable regulation of conduct, barring breaches of the peace. But when *Cohen* was convicted for wearing a jacket bearing an epithet, we did not apply *O'Brien.* Instead, we recognized that the generally applicable law was directed at Cohen because of what his speech communicated—he violated the breach of the peace statute because of the offensive content of his particular message. We accordingly applied more rigorous scrutiny and reversed his conviction.

This suit falls into the same category. The law here may be described as directed at conduct, as the law in *Cohen* was directed at breaches of the peace, but as applied to plaintiffs the conduct triggering coverage under the statute consists of communicating a message. As we explained in *Texas v. Johnson:* "If the [Government's] regulation is not related to expression, then the less stringent standard we announced in *United States v. O'Brien* for regulations of

noncommunicative conduct controls. If it is, then we are outside of *O'Brien's* test, and we must [apply] a more demanding standard."

The First Amendment issue before us is not whether the Government may prohibit pure political speech, or may prohibit material support in the form of conduct. It is instead whether the Government may prohibit what plaintiffs want to do—provide material support to the PKK and LTTE in the form of speech. Everyone agrees that the Government's interest in combating terrorism is an urgent objective of the highest order. Plaintiffs' complaint is that the ban on material support, applied to what they wish to do, is not "necessary to further that interest." The objective of combating terrorism does not justify prohibiting their speech, plaintiffs argue, because their support will advance only the legitimate activities of the designated terrorist organizations, not their terrorism.

Whether foreign terrorist organizations meaningfully segregate support of their legitimate activities from support of terrorism is an empirical question. When it enacted §2339B, Congress made specific findings regarding the serious threat posed by international terrorism. One of those findings explicitly rejects plaintiffs' contention that their support would not further the terrorist activities of the PKK and LTTE: "Foreign organizations that engage in terrorist activity are so tainted by their criminal conduct that any contribution to such an organization facilitates that conduct." Plaintiffs argue that the reference to "any contribution" in this finding meant only monetary support. There is no reason to read the finding to be so limited. Congress's use of the term "contribution" is best read to reflect a determination that any form of material support furnished "to" a foreign terrorist organization should be barred, which is precisely what the material-support statute does. Congress considered and rejected the view that ostensibly peaceful aid would have no harmful effects.

We are convinced that Congress was justified in rejecting that view. The PKK and the LTTE are deadly groups. The PKK's insurgency has claimed more than 22,000 lives. The LTTE has engaged in extensive suicide bombings and political assassinations, including killings of the

Sri Lankan President, Security Minister, and Deputy Defense Minister. It is not difficult to conclude as Congress did that the "taint" of such violent activities is so great that working in coordination with or at the command of the PKK and LTTE serves to legitimize and further their terrorist means.

Material support meant to "promote peaceable, lawful conduct" can further terrorism by foreign groups in multiple ways. "Material support" is a valuable resource by definition. Such support frees up other resources within the organization that may be put to violent ends. It also importantly helps lend legitimacy to foreign terrorist groups—legitimacy that makes it easier for those groups to persist, to recruit members, and to raise funds—all of which facilitate more terrorist attacks.

Money is fungible, and "when foreign terrorist organizations that have a dual structure raise funds, they highlight the civilian and humanitarian ends to which such moneys could be put." But "there is reason to believe that foreign terrorist organizations do not maintain legitimate financial firewalls between those funds raised for civil, nonviolent activities, and those ultimately used to support violent, terrorist operations." Thus, "funds raised ostensibly for charitable purposes have in the past been redirected by some terrorist groups to fund the purchase of arms and explosives." There is evidence that the PKK and the LTTE, in particular, have not "respected the line between humanitarian and violent activities."

The dissent argues that there is "no natural stopping place" for the proposition that aiding a foreign terrorist organization's lawful activity promotes the terrorist organization as a whole. But Congress has settled on just such a natural stopping place: The statute reaches only material support coordinated with or under the direction of a designated foreign terrorist organization. Independent advocacy that might be viewed as promoting the group's legitimacy is not covered.

Providing foreign terrorist groups with material support in any form also furthers terrorism by straining the United States' relationships with its allies and undermining cooperative efforts between nations to prevent terrorist attacks. We see no reason to question Congress's

finding that "international cooperation is required for an effective response to terrorism, as demonstrated by the numerous multilateral conventions in force providing universal prosecutive jurisdiction over persons involved in a variety of terrorist acts. The material-support statute furthers this international effort by prohibiting aid for foreign terrorist groups that harm the United States' partners abroad: "A number of designated foreign terrorist organizations have attacked moderate governments with which the United States has vigorously endeavored to maintain close and friendly relations," and those attacks "threaten [the] social, economic and political stability" of such governments.

In analyzing whether it is possible in practice to distinguish material support for a foreign terrorist group's violent activities and its nonviolent activities, we do not rely exclusively on our own inferences drawn from the record evidence. We have before us an affidavit stating the Executive Branch's conclusion on that question. The State Department informs us that "the experience and analysis of the U. S. government agencies charged with combating terrorism strongly support" Congress's finding that all contributions to foreign terrorist organizations further their terrorism. That evaluation of the facts by the Executive, like Congress's assessment, is entitled to deference. When it comes to collecting evidence and drawing factual inferences in this area, "the lack of competence on the part of the courts is marked," *Rostker,* and respect for the Government's conclusions is appropriate.

One reason for that respect is that national security and foreign policy concerns arise in connection with efforts to confront evolving threats in an area where information can be difficult to obtain and the impact of certain conduct difficult to assess. The dissent slights these real constraints in demanding hard proof—with "detail," "specific facts," and "specific evidence"—that plaintiffs' proposed activities will support terrorist attacks. That would be a dangerous requirement. In this context, conclusions must often be based on informed judgment rather than concrete evidence, and that reality affects what we may reasonably insist on from the Government. The material-support statute is, on its face, a preventive measure—it criminalizes not terrorist attacks themselves, but aid that makes the attacks more likely to occur. The Government, when seeking to prevent imminent harms in the context of international affairs and national security, is not required to conclusively link all the pieces in the puzzle before we grant weight to its empirical conclusions. Congress and the Executive are uniquely positioned to make principled distinctions between activities that will further terrorist conduct and undermine United States foreign policy, and those that will not.

We also find it significant that Congress has been conscious of its own responsibility to consider how its actions may implicate constitutional concerns. First, §2339B only applies to designated foreign terrorist organizations. There is, and always has been, a limited number of those organizations designated by the Executive Branch, and any groups so designated may seek judicial review of the designation. Second, in response to the lower courts' holdings in this litigation, Congress added clarity to the statute by providing narrowing definitions of the terms "training," "personnel," and "expert advice or assistance," as well as an explanation of the knowledge required to violate §2339B. Third, in effectuating its stated intent not to abridge First Amendment rights, Congress has also displayed a careful balancing of interests in creating limited exceptions to the ban on material support. The definition of material support, for example, excludes medicine and religious materials. In this area perhaps more than any other, the Legislature's superior capacity for weighing competing interests means that "we must be particularly careful not to substitute our judgment of what is desirable for that of Congress." Finally, and most importantly, Congress has avoided any restriction on independent advocacy, or indeed any activities not directed to, coordinated with, or controlled by foreign terrorist groups. At bottom, plaintiffs simply disagree with the considered judgment of Congress and the Executive that providing material support to a designated foreign terrorist organization— even seemingly benign support—bolsters the terrorist activities of that organization.

We turn to the particular speech plaintiffs propose to undertake. First, plaintiffs propose to "train members of the PKK on how to use humanitarian and international law to peacefully resolve disputes." Congress can, consistent with the First Amendment, prohibit this direct training. It is wholly foreseeable that the PKK could use the "specific skills" that plaintiffs propose to impart, as part of a broader strategy to promote terrorism. The PKK could, for example, pursue peaceful negotiation as a means of buying time to recover from short-term setbacks, lulling opponents into complacency, and ultimately preparing for renewed attacks. A foreign terrorist organization introduced to the structures of the international legal system might use the information to threaten, manipulate, and disrupt. This possibility is real, not remote.

Second, plaintiffs propose to "teach PKK members how to petition various representative bodies such as the United Nations for relief." The Government acts within First Amendment strictures in banning this proposed speech because it teaches the organization how to acquire "relief," which plaintiffs never define with any specificity, and which could readily include monetary aid.

Finally, plaintiffs propose to "engage in political advocacy on behalf of Kurds who live in Turkey," and "engage in political advocacy on behalf of Tamils who live in Sri Lanka." Plaintiffs do not specify their expected level of coordination with the PKK or LTTE or suggest what exactly their "advocacy" would consist of. Plaintiffs' proposals are phrased at such a high level of generality that they cannot prevail in this pre-enforcement challenge.

The dissent fails to address the real dangers at stake. It instead considers only the possible benefits of plaintiffs' proposed activities in the abstract. The dissent seems unwilling to entertain the prospect that training and advising a designated foreign terrorist organization on how to take advantage of international entities might benefit that organization in a way that facilitates its terrorist activities. In the dissent's world, such training is all to the good. Congress and the Executive, however, have concluded that we live in a different world: one in which the designated foreign terrorist organizations "are so tainted by their criminal conduct that any contribution to such an organization facilitates that conduct." One in which, for example, "the United Nations High Commissioner for Refugees was forced to close a Kurdish refugee camp in northern Iraq because the camp had come under the control of the PKK, and the PKK had failed to respect its 'neutral and humanitarian nature.'" Training and advice on how to work with the United Nations could readily have helped the PKK in its efforts to use the United Nations camp as a base for terrorist activities.

VI

Plaintiffs' final claim is that the material-support statute violates their freedom of association under the First Amendment. Plaintiffs argue that the statute criminalizes the mere fact of their associating with the PKK and the LTTE, thereby running afoul of decisions like *De Jonge v. Oregon* (1937), and cases in which we have overturned sanctions for joining the Communist Party. [But] the statute does not penalize mere association with a foreign terrorist organization. As the Ninth Circuit put it: "The statute does not prohibit being a member of one of the designated groups or vigorously promoting and supporting the political goals of the group. What [it] prohibits is the act of giving material support."

The judgment of the United States Court of Appeals for the Ninth Circuit is affirmed in part and reversed in part, and the cases are remanded for further proceedings consistent with this opinion.

JUSTICE BREYER, with whom JUSTICES GINSBURG and SOTOMAYOR join, dissenting.

I cannot agree with the Court's conclusion that the Constitution permits the Government to prosecute the plaintiffs criminally for engaging in coordinated teaching and advocacy furthering the designated organizations' lawful political objectives. In my view, the Government has not met its burden of showing that an interpretation of the statute that would prohibit this speech- and association-related activity serves the Government's compelling interest in combating terrorism. And I would interpret

the statute as normally placing activity of this kind outside its scope.

The statute before us forbids "knowingly providing" "a foreign terrorist organization" with "material support or resources," defined to include, among other things, "training," "expert advice or assistance," "personnel," and "service." All these activities are of a kind that the First Amendment ordinarily protects. All involve the communication and advocacy of political ideas and lawful means of achieving political ends. Even the subjects the plaintiffs wish to teach—using international law to resolve disputes peacefully or petitioning the United Nations, for instance—concern political speech.

That this speech and association for political purposes is the kind of activity to which the First Amendment ordinarily offers its strongest protection is elementary. Although in the Court's view the statute applies only where the PKK helps to coordinate a defendant's activities, the simple fact of "coordination" alone cannot readily remove protection that the First Amendment would otherwise grant. That amendment, after all, also protects the freedom of association.

"Coordination" with a group that engages in unlawful activity also does not deprive the plaintiffs of the First Amendment's protection under any traditional "categorical" exception to its protection. The plaintiffs do not propose to solicit a crime. They will not engage in fraud or defamation or circulate obscenity. And the First Amendment protects advocacy even of unlawful action so long as that advocacy is not "directed to inciting or producing imminent lawless action and likely to incite or produce such action." *Brandenburg v. Ohio* (1969). Here the plaintiffs seek to advocate peaceful, lawful action to secure political ends; and they seek to teach others how to do the same. Moreover, the Court has previously held that a person who associates with a group that uses unlawful means to achieve its ends does not thereby necessarily forfeit the First Amendment's protection for freedom of association. *Scales v. United States* (1961).

Not even the "serious and deadly problem" of international terrorism can require automatic forfeiture of First Amendment rights.

After all, this Court has recognized that not "even the war power removes constitutional limitations safeguarding essential liberties." *United States v. Robel* (1967). There is no general First Amendment exception that applies here.

It is not surprising that the majority, in determining the constitutionality of criminally prohibiting the plaintiffs proposed activities, would apply, not the kind of intermediate First Amendment standard that applies to conduct, but "a more demanding standard." Indeed, where, as here, a statute applies criminal penalties and at least arguably does so on the basis of content-based distinctions, I should think we would scrutinize the statute and justifications "strictly"—to determine whether the prohibition is justified by a "compelling" need that cannot be "less restrictively" accommodated. But, even if we assume for argument's sake that "strict scrutiny" does not apply, no one can deny that we must at the very least "measure the validity of the means adopted by Congress against both the goal it has sought to achieve and the specific prohibitions of the First Amendment." And here I need go no further, for I doubt that the statute, as the Government would interpret it, can survive any reasonably applicable First Amendment standard.

The Government does identify a compelling countervailing interest, namely, the interest in protecting the security of the United States and its nationals from the threats that foreign terrorist organizations pose by denying those organizations financial and other fungible resources. I do not dispute the importance of this interest. But I do dispute whether the interest can justify the statute's criminal prohibition. To put the matter more specifically, precisely how does application of the statute to the protected activities before us help achieve that important security-related end?

The Government makes two efforts to answer this question. First, the Government says that the plaintiffs' support for these organizations is "fungible" in the same sense as other forms of banned support. Being fungible, the plaintiffs' support could, for example, free up other resources, which the organization might put to terrorist ends. The proposition that the two very different kinds of "support" are "fungible," however, is not obviously true. There is

no obvious way in which undertaking advocacy for political change through peaceful means or teaching the PKK and LTTE, say, how to petition the United Nations for political change is fungible with other resources that might be put to more sinister ends in the way that donations of money, food, or computer training are fungible. It is far from obvious that these advocacy activities can themselves be redirected, or will free other resources that can be directed, towards terrorist ends. The Government has provided us with no empirical information that might convincingly support this claim. Instead, the Government cites only to evidence that Congress was concerned about the "fungible" nature in general of resources, predominately money and material goods.

Second, the Government says that the plaintiffs' proposed activities will "bolster a terrorist organization's efficacy and strength in a community" and "undermine this nation's efforts to delegitimize and weaken those groups." In the Court's view, too, the Constitution permits application of the statute to activities of the kind at issue in part because those activities could provide a group that engages in terrorism with "legitimacy." Yet the Government does not claim that the statute forbids any speech "legitimating" a terrorist group. Rather, it reads the statute as permitting (1) membership in terrorist organizations, (2) "peaceably assembling with members of the PKK and LTTE for lawful discussion," or (3) "independent advocacy" on behalf of these organizations.

This "legitimacy" justification cannot by itself warrant suppression of political speech, advocacy, and association. Speech, association, and related activities on behalf of a group will often, perhaps always, help to legitimate that group. Thus, were the law to accept a "legitimating" effect, in and of itself and without qualification, as providing sufficient grounds for imposing such a ban, the First Amendment battle would be lost in untold instances where it should be won. Once one accepts this argument, there is no natural stopping place. The argument applies as strongly to "independent" as to "coordinated" advocacy.

The "legitimacy" justification itself is inconsistent with critically important First Amendment case law. Consider the cases involving the protection the First Amendment offered those who joined the Communist Party intending only to further its peaceful activities. In those cases, this Court took account of congressional findings that the Communist Party not only advocated theoretically but also sought to put into practice the overthrow of our Government through force and violence. Nonetheless, the Court held that the First Amendment protected an American's right to belong to that party—despite whatever "legitimating" effect membership might have had—as long as the person did not share the party's unlawful purposes.

I am not aware of any case in this Court—not *Gitlow v. New York* (1925), not *Schenck v. United States* (1919), not *Abrams,* not the later Communist Party cases decided during the heat of the Cold War—in which the Court accepted anything like a claim that speech or teaching might be criminalized lest it, e.g., buy negotiating time for an opponent who would put that time to bad use.

In sum, these cases require us to consider how to apply the First Amendment where national security interests are at stake. When deciding such cases, courts are aware and must respect the fact that the Constitution entrusts to the Executive and Legislative Branches the power to provide for the national defense, and that it grants particular authority to the President in matters of foreign affairs. Nonetheless, this Court has also made clear that authority and expertise in these matters do not automatically trump the Court's own obligation to secure the protection that the Constitution grants to individuals. In these cases, I believe the Court has failed to examine the Government's justifications with sufficient care. It has failed to insist upon specific evidence, rather than general assertion. It has failed to require tailoring of means to fit compelling ends. And ultimately it deprives the individuals before us of the protection that the First Amendment demands. That is why, with respect, I dissent.

Citizens United v. Federal Election Commission
558 U.S. 50 (2010)

Federal law prohibits corporations and unions from using general treasury funds to make direct contributions to candidates or independent expenditures that expressly advocate the election or defeat of a candidate in a federal election. The Bipartisan Campaign Reform Act of 2002 (BCRA) extended this prohibition to any "electioneering communication," which it defined as "any broadcast, cable, or satellite communication" that "refers to a clearly identified candidate for Federal office" and is made within thirty days of a primary or sixty days of a general election. Although corporations and unions are barred from using their general treasury funds for express advocacy or electioneering, they may establish a "separate segregated fund" (known as a political action committee, or PAC) for these purposes, funded by donations from stockholders and employees in the case of a corporation or members in the case of a union. In January 2008, Citizens United, a nonprofit corporation, released Hillary: The Movie, *which was highly critical of then senator Hillary Clinton.* Hillary *played in theaters and was available on DVD, but Citizens United*

wanted to increase distribution by making it available for free through video-on-demand. In order to promote the film, it produced two ten-second ads and one thirty-second ad for Hillary, *which it sought to run on broadcast and cable television. Citizens United wanted to make* Hillary *available through video-on-demand within thirty days of the 2008 primary elections, but it feared that both the film and the ads would be covered by §441b of BCRA, which banned corporate-funded independent expenditures. It therefore sued in federal district court, claiming that the §441b ban, at least as applied to* Hillary, *violated the First Amendment. The district court denied Citizens United's motion for a preliminary injunction and granted the Federal Election Commission's motion for summary judgment. The Supreme Court then noted probable jurisdiction. The case was reargued before the Supreme Court after the Court requested supplemental briefs addressing whether it should overrule* Austin v. Michigan Chamber of Commerce *(1990) and/ or the part of* McConnell v. Federal Election Commission *(2003) that addressed the validity of*

§441b of BCRA. Opinion of the Court: <u>Kennedy</u>, Scalia, Roberts, Alito, Thomas (in part). Concurring opinions: <u>Roberts</u>, Alito; <u>Scalia</u>, Alito, Thomas (in part). Concurring in part and dissenting in part: <u>Stevens</u>, Ginsburg, Breyer, Sotomayor; <u>Thomas</u>.

JUSTICE KENNEDY delivered the opinion of the Court.

Federal law prohibits corporations and unions from using their general treasury funds to make independent expenditures for speech defined as an "electioneering communication" or for speech expressly advocating the election or defeat of a candidate. Limits on electioneering communications were upheld in *McConnell v. Federal Election Comm'n.* (2003). The holding of *McConnell* rested to a large extent on an earlier case, *Austin v. Michigan Chamber of Commerce* (1990). *Austin* had held that political speech may be banned based on the speaker's corporate identity. In this case we are asked to reconsider *Austin* and, in effect, *McConnell.* It has been noted that "*Austin* was a significant departure from ancient First Amendment principles," *Federal Election Comm'n v. Wisconsin Right to Life, Inc.* (WRTL). We agree with that conclusion. The Government may regulate corporate political speech through disclaimer and disclosure requirements, but it may not suppress that speech altogether.

II

In the exercise of its judicial responsibility, it is necessary for the Court to consider the facial validity of §441b. Any other course of decision would prolong the substantial, nation-wide chilling effect caused by §441b's prohibitions on corporate expenditures. Consideration of the facial validity of §441b is further supported by the following reasons.

First is the uncertainty caused by the litigating position of the Government. When the Government holds out the possibility of ruling for Citizens United on a narrow ground yet refrains from adopting that position, the added uncertainty demonstrates the necessity to address the question of statutory validity.

Second, substantial time would be required to bring clarity to the application of the statutory provision in order to avoid any chilling

effect caused by some improper interpretation. It is well known that the public begins to concentrate on elections only in the weeks immediately before they are held. There are short timeframes in which speech can have influence. The need or relevance of the speech will often first be apparent at this stage in the campaign. The decision to speak is made in the heat of political campaigns, when speakers react to messages conveyed by others. A speaker's ability to engage in political speech that could have a chance of persuading voters is stifled if the speaker must first commence a protracted lawsuit. By the time the lawsuit concludes, the election will be over and the litigants in most cases will have neither the incentive nor, perhaps, the resources to carry on, even if they could establish that the case is not moot because the issue is "capable of repetition, yet evading review." Here, Citizens United decided to litigate its case to the end. Today, Citizens United finally learns, two years after the fact, whether it could have spoken during the 2008 Presidential primary—long after the opportunity to persuade primary voters has passed.

Third is the primary importance of speech itself to the integrity of the election process. As additional rules are created for regulating political speech, any speech arguably within their reach is chilled. Campaign finance regulations now impose "unique and complex rules" on "71 distinct entities." These entities are subject to separate rules for 33 different types of political speech. The F[ederal] E[lection] C[omission] has adopted 568 pages of regulations, 1,278 pages of explanations and justifications for those regulations, and 1,771 advisory opinions since 1975. In fact, after this Court in *WRTL* adopted an objective "appeal to vote" test for determining whether a communication was the functional equivalent of express advocacy, the FEC adopted a two-part, 11-factor balancing test to implement *WRTL*'s ruling.

This regulatory scheme may not be a prior restraint on speech in the strict sense of that term, for prospective speakers are not compelled by law to seek an advisory opinion from the FEC before the speech takes place. As a practical matter, however, given the complexity of the regulations and the deference courts show to administrative determinations, a speaker who wants to avoid threats of criminal liability and the heavy costs of defending against FEC enforcement must ask a governmental agency for prior permission to speak. These onerous restrictions thus function as the equivalent of prior restraint by giving the FEC power analogous to licensing laws implemented in 16th- and 17th-century England, laws and governmental practices of the sort that the First Amendment was drawn to prohibit.

The ongoing chill upon speech that is beyond all doubt protected makes it necessary in this case to invoke the earlier precedents that a statute which chills speech can and must be invalidated where its facial invalidity has been demonstrated. For these reasons we find it necessary to reconsider *Austin*.

III

The law before us is an outright ban, backed by criminal sanctions. Section 441b makes it a felony for all corporations—including nonprofit advocacy corporations—either to expressly advocate the election or defeat of candidates or to broadcast electioneering communications within 30 days of a primary election and 60 days of a general election. Thus, the following acts would all be felonies under §441b: The Sierra Club runs an ad, within the crucial phase of 60 days before the general election, that exhorts the public to disapprove of a Congressman who favors logging in national forests; the National Rifle Association publishes a book urging the public to vote for the challenger because the incumbent U. S. Senator supports a handgun ban; and the American Civil Liberties Union creates a Web site telling the public to vote for a Presidential candidate in light of that candidate's defense of free speech. These prohibitions are classic examples of censorship.

Section 441b is a ban on corporate speech notwithstanding the fact that a PAC created by a corporation can still speak. A PAC is a separate association from the corporation. So the PAC exemption from §441b's expenditure ban does not allow corporations to speak. Even if a PAC could somehow allow a corporation to speak—and it does not—the option to form PACs does not alleviate the First Amendment problems with §441b. PACs are burdensome alternatives; they are expensive to administer and subject to extensive regulations. This might explain why fewer than 2,000 of the millions of corporations in this country have PACs. PACs, furthermore, must exist before they can speak. Given the onerous restrictions, a corporation may not be able to establish a PAC in time to make its views known regarding candidates and issues in a current campaign.

Section 441b's prohibition on corporate independent expenditures is thus a ban on speech. As a "restriction on the amount of money a person or group can spend on political communication during a campaign," that statute "necessarily reduces the quantity of expression by restricting the number of issues discussed, the depth of their exploration, and the size of the audience reached." *Buckley v. Valeo* (1976). Were the Court to uphold these restrictions, the Government could repress speech by silencing certain voices at any of the various points in the speech process. If §441b applied to individuals, no one would believe that it is merely a time, place, or manner restriction on speech. Its purpose and effect are to silence entities whose voices the Government deems to be suspect.

Speech is an essential mechanism of democracy, for it is the means to hold officials accountable to the people. The right of citizens to inquire, to hear, to speak, and to use information to reach consensus is a precondition to enlightened self-government and a necessary means to protect it. For these reasons, political speech must prevail against laws that would suppress it, whether by design or inadvertence. Laws that burden political speech are "subject to strict scrutiny," which requires the Government to prove that the restriction "furthers a compelling interest and is narrowly tailored to achieve that interest."

Premised on mistrust of governmental power, the First Amendment stands against attempts to disfavor certain subjects or viewpoints. Prohibited, too, are restrictions distinguishing among different speakers, allowing speech by some but not others. See *First Nat. Bank of Boston v. Bellotti* (1978). As instruments to censor, these categories are interrelated: Speech restrictions based on the identity of the speaker are all too often simply a means to control content.

Quite apart from the purpose or effect of regulating content, moreover, the Government may commit a constitutional wrong when by law it identifies certain preferred speakers. By taking the right to speak from some and giving it to others, the Government deprives the disadvantaged person or class of the right to use speech to strive to establish worth, standing, and respect for the speaker's voice. The Government may not by these means deprive the public of the right and privilege to determine for itself what speech and speakers are worthy of consideration.

The Court has upheld a narrow class of speech restrictions that operate to the disadvantage of certain persons, but these rulings were based on an interest in allowing governmental entities to perform their functions. See, e.g., *Bethel School Dist. No. 403 v. Fraser* (1986) (protecting the "function of public school education"); *Jones v. North Carolina Prisoners' Labor Union, Inc.* (1977) (furthering "the legitimate penological objectives of the corrections system"); *Parker v. Levy* (1974) (ensuring "the capacity of the Government to discharge its [military] responsibilities"); *Civil Service Comm'n v. Letter Carriers* (1973) ("[F]ederal service should depend upon meritorious performance rather than political service"). The corporate independent expenditures at issue in this case, however, would not interfere with governmental functions, so these cases are inapposite.

A-1

The Court has recognized that First Amendment protection extends to corporations. This protection has been extended by explicit holdings to the context of political speech. Under the rationale of these precedents, political speech does not lose First Amendment protection "simply because its source is a corporation." *Bellotti.*

A-2

In *Buckley,* the Court addressed various challenges to the Federal Election Campaign Act of 1971 (FECA) as amended in 1974. These amendments created 18 U. S. C. §608(e), an independent expenditure ban that applied to individuals as well as corporations and labor unions. Before addressing the constitutionality

of §608(e)'s independent expenditure ban, *Buckley* first upheld §608(b), FECA's limits on direct contributions to candidates. The *Buckley* Court recognized a "sufficiently important" governmental interest in "the prevention of corruption and the appearance of corruption." This followed from the Court's concern that large contributions could be given "to secure a political quid pro quo." The *Buckley* Court explained that the potential for quid pro quo corruption distinguished direct contributions to candidates from independent expenditures. The Court emphasized that "the independent expenditure ceiling fails to serve any substantial governmental interest in stemming the reality or appearance of corruption in the electoral process," because "the absence of prearrangement and coordination alleviates the danger that expenditures will be given as a quid pro quo for improper commitments from the candidate."

Less than two years after *Buckley,* *Bellotti* reaffirmed the First Amendment principle that the Government cannot restrict political speech based on the speaker's corporate identity. The reasoning and holding of *Bellotti* did not rest on the existence of a viewpoint-discriminatory statute. It rested on the principle that the Government lacks the power to ban corporations from speaking. *Bellotti* did not address the constitutionality of the State's ban on corporate independent expenditures to support candidates. In our view, however, that restriction would have been unconstitutional under *Bellotti*'s central principle: that the First Amendment does not allow political speech restrictions based on a speaker's corporate identity.

A-3

Thus the law stood until *Austin. Austin* "upheld a direct restriction on the independent expenditure of funds for political speech for the first time in [this Court's] history." There, the Michigan Chamber of Commerce sought to use general treasury funds to run a newspaper ad supporting a specific candidate. Michigan law, however, prohibited corporate independent expenditures that supported or opposed any candidate for state office. A violation of the law was punishable as a felony. The Court sustained the speech prohibition. The Court is thus confronted with conflicting lines of precedent: a pre-*Austin* line that forbids restrictions on political speech based on the speaker's corporate identity and a post-*Austin* line that permits them.

B-1

As for *Austin*'s antidistortion rationale, the Government does little to defend it. And with good reason, for if the First Amendment has any force, it prohibits Congress from fining or jailing citizens, or associations of citizens, for simply engaging in political speech. Political speech is "indispensable to decisionmaking in a democracy, and this is no less true because the speech comes from a corporation rather than an individual." This protection for speech is inconsistent with *Austin*'s antidistortion rationale. *Austin* sought to defend the antidistortion rationale as a means to prevent corporations from obtaining "an unfair advantage in the political marketplace" by using "resources amassed in the economic marketplace." But *Buckley* rejected the premise that the Government has an interest "in equalizing the relative ability of individuals and groups to influence the outcome of elections." *Buckley* was specific in stating that "the skyrocketing cost of political campaigns" could not sustain the governmental prohibition.

Austin's antidistortion rationale would produce the dangerous, and unacceptable, consequence that Congress could ban political speech of media corporations. Media corporations are now exempt from §441b's ban on corporate expenditures. Yet media corporations accumulate wealth with the help of the corporate form, the largest media corporations have "immense aggregations of wealth," and the views expressed by media corporations often "have little or no correlation to the public's support" for those views. Thus, under the Government's reasoning, wealthy media corporations could have their voices diminished to put them on par with other media entities. There is no precedent for permitting this under the First Amendment.

When Government seeks to use its full power, including the criminal law, to command where a person may get his or her information or what distrusted source he or she may not hear, it uses censorship to control thought. This is unlawful. The First Amendment confirms the freedom to think for ourselves.

B-2

The Government falls back on the argument that corporate political speech can be banned in order to prevent corruption or its appearance. In *Buckley,* the Court found this interest "sufficiently important" to allow limits on contributions but did not extend that reasoning to expenditure limits. When *Buckley* examined an expenditure ban, it found "that the governmental interest in preventing corruption and the appearance of corruption [was] inadequate to justify [the ban] on independent expenditures."

"The absence of prearrangement and coordination of an expenditure with the candidate or his agent not only undermines the value of the expenditure to the candidate, but also alleviates the danger that expenditures will be given as a quid pro quo for improper commitments from the candidate." *Buckley.* Limits on independent expenditures, such as §441b, have a chilling effect extending well beyond the Government's interest in preventing quid pro quo corruption.

When *Buckley* identified a sufficiently important governmental interest in preventing corruption or the appearance of corruption, that interest was limited to quid pro quo corruption. The fact that speakers may have influence over or access to elected officials does not mean that these officials are corrupt. Reliance on a "generic favoritism or influence theory is at odds with standard First Amendment analyses because it is unbounded and susceptible to no limiting principle."

The *McConnell* record was "over 100,000 pages" long, yet it "does not have any direct examples of votes being exchanged for expenditures." This confirms *Buckley*'s reasoning that independent expenditures do not lead to, or create the appearance of, quid pro quo corruption. In fact, there is only scant evidence that independent expenditures even ingratiate. Ingratiation and access, in any event, are not corruption.

B-3

The Government contends further that corporate independent expenditures can be limited because of its interest in protecting dissenting shareholders from being compelled to fund corporate political speech. This asserted interest, like *Austin's* antidistortion rationale, would allow the Government to ban the political speech even of media corporations. The First Amendment does not allow that power. There is, furthermore, little evidence of abuse that cannot be corrected by shareholders "through the procedures of corporate democracy."

B-4

We need not reach the question whether the Government has a compelling interest in preventing foreign individuals or associations from influencing our Nation's political process. Section 441b is not limited to corporations or associations that were created in foreign countries or funded predominately by foreign shareholders. Section 441b therefore would be overbroad even if we assumed, *arguendo,* that the Government has a compelling interest in limiting foreign influence over our political process.

C

Austin is undermined by experience since its announcement. Political speech is so ingrained in our culture that speakers find ways to circumvent campaign finance laws. Our Nation's speech dynamic is changing, and informative voices should not have to circumvent onerous restrictions to exercise their First Amendment rights. Rapid changes in technology—and the creative dynamic inherent in the concept of free expression—counsel against upholding a law that restricts political speech in certain media or by certain speakers. Today, 30-second television ads may be the most effective way to convey a political message. Soon, however, it may be that Internet sources, such as blogs and social networking Web sites, will provide citizens with significant information about political candidates and issues. Yet, §441b would seem to ban a blog post expressly advocating the election or defeat of a candidate if that blog were created with corporate funds.

Due consideration leads to this conclusion: *Austin* should be and now is overruled. We return to the principle established in *Buckley* and

Bellotti that the Government may not suppress political speech on the basis of the speaker's corporate identity. No sufficient governmental interest justifies limits on the political speech of nonprofit or for-profit corporations.

IV
A

Citizens United next challenges BCRA's disclaimer and disclosure provisions as applied to *Hillary* and the three advertisements for the movie. Under BCRA §311, televised electioneering communications funded by anyone other than a candidate must include a disclaimer that "_____ is responsible for the content of this advertising." The required statement must be made in a "clearly spoken manner," and displayed on the screen in a "clearly readable manner" for at least four seconds. It must state that the communication "is not authorized by any candidate or candidate's committee"; it must also display the name and address (or Web site address) of the person or group that funded the advertisement. Under BCRA §201, any person who spends more than $10,000 on electioneering communications within a calendar year must file a disclosure statement with the FEC. That statement must identify the person making the expenditure, the amount of the expenditure, the election to which the communication was directed, and the names of certain contributors.

Disclaimer and disclosure requirements may burden the ability to speak, but they "impose no ceiling on campaign-related activities," and "do not prevent anyone from speaking." The Court has subjected these requirements to "exacting scrutiny," which requires a "substantial relation" between the disclosure requirement and a "sufficiently important" governmental interest. In *Buckley,* the Court explained that disclosure could be justified based on a governmental interest in "providing the electorate with information" about the sources of election-related spending. The *McConnell* Court applied this interest in rejecting facial challenges to BCRA §§201 and 311. There was evidence in the record that independent groups were running election-related advertisements "while hiding behind dubious and misleading names." The Court therefore upheld BCRA §§201 and

311 on the ground that they would help citizens "make informed choices in the political marketplace."

Although both provisions were facially upheld, the Court acknowledged that as-applied challenges would be available if a group could show a "reasonable probability" that disclosure of its contributors' names "will subject them to threats, harassment, or reprisals from either Government officials or private parties."

V

When word concerning the plot of the movie *Mr. Smith Goes to Washington* reached the circles of Government, some officials sought, by persuasion, to discourage its distribution. Under *Austin,* though, officials could have done more than discourage its distribution—they could have banned the film. After all, it, like *Hillary,* was speech funded by a corporation that was critical of Members of Congress. *Mr. Smith Goes to Washington* may be fiction and caricature; but fiction and caricature can be a powerful force.

Modern day movies, television comedies, or skits on Youtube.com might portray public officials or public policies in unflattering ways. Yet if a covered transmission during the blackout period creates the background for candidate endorsement or opposition, a felony occurs solely because a corporation, other than an exempt media corporation, has made the "purchase, payment, distribution, loan, advance, deposit, or gift of money or anything of value" in order to engage in political speech. Speech would be suppressed in the realm where its necessity is most evident: in the public dialogue preceding a real election. Governments are often hostile to speech, but under our law and our tradition it seems stranger than fiction for our Government to make this political speech a crime. Yet this is the statute's purpose and design.

The judgment of the District Court is reversed with respect to the constitutionality of 2 U. S. C. §441b's restrictions on corporate independent expenditures. The judgment is affirmed with respect to BCRA's disclaimer and disclosure requirements. The case is remanded for further proceedings consistent with this opinion.

JUSTICE SCALIA, with whom JUSTICE ALITO joins, and with whom JUSTICE THOMAS joins in part, concurring.

I write separately to address Justice Stevens' discussion of "Original Understandings." This section of the dissent purports to show that today's decision is not supported by the original understanding of the First Amendment. The dissent attempts this demonstration, however, in splendid isolation from the text of the First Amendment. It never shows why "the freedom of speech" that was the right of Englishmen did not include the freedom to speak in association with other individuals, including association in the corporate form.

Instead of taking this straightforward approach to determining the Amendment's meaning, the dissent embarks on a detailed exploration of the Framers' views about the "role of corporations in society." The Framers didn't like corporations, the dissent concludes, and therefore it follows (as night the day) that corporations had no rights of free speech. Of course the Framers' personal affection or disaffection for corporations is relevant only insofar as it can be thought to be reflected in the understood meaning of the text they enacted—not, as the dissent suggests, as a freestanding substitute for that text. But the dissent's distortion of proper analysis is even worse than that. Though faced with a constitutional text that makes no distinction between types of speakers, the dissent feels no necessity to provide even an isolated statement from the founding era to the effect that corporations are not covered, but places the burden on petitioners to bring forward statements showing that they are.

The Amendment is written in terms of "speech," not speakers. Its text offers no foothold for excluding any category of speaker, from single individuals to partnerships of individuals, to unincorporated associations of individuals, to incorporated associations of individuals—and the dissent offers no evidence about the original meaning of the text to support any such exclusion. We are therefore simply left with the question whether the speech at issue in this case is "speech" covered by the First Amendment. No one says otherwise. A documentary film critical of a potential

Presidential candidate is core political speech, and its nature as such does not change simply because it was funded by a corporation.

JUSTICE STEVENS, with whom JUSTICE GINSBURG, JUSTICE BREYER, and JUSTICE SOTOMAYOR join, concurring in part and dissenting in part.

The real issue in this case concerns how, not if, the appellant may finance its electioneering. Citizens United is a wealthy nonprofit corporation that runs a political action committee (PAC) with millions of dollars in assets. Under the Bipartisan Campaign Reform Act of 2002 (BCRA), it could have used those assets to televise and promote *Hillary: The Movie* wherever and whenever it wanted to. It also could have spent unrestricted sums to broadcast *Hillary* at any time other than the 30 days before the last primary election. Neither Citizens United's nor any other corporation's speech has been "banned." All that the parties dispute is whether Citizens United had a right to use the funds in its general treasury to pay for broadcasts during the 30-day period. The notion that the First Amendment dictates an affirmative answer to that question is, in my judgment, profoundly misguided.

The basic premise underlying the Court's ruling is that the First Amendment bars regulatory distinctions based on a speaker's identity, including its "identity" as a corporation. While that glittering generality has rhetorical appeal, it is not a correct statement of the law. In the context of election to public office, the distinction between corporate and human speakers is significant. They cannot vote or run for office. Because they may be managed and controlled by nonresidents, their interests may conflict in fundamental respects with the interests of eligible voters. The financial resources, legal structure, and instrumental orientation of corporations raise legitimate concerns about their role in the electoral process. Our lawmakers have a compelling constitutional basis, if not also a democratic duty, to take measures designed to guard against the potentially deleterious effects of corporate spending in local and national races.

The majority's approach to corporate electioneering marks a dramatic break from our past. Congress has placed special limitations on campaign spending by corporations ever since the passage of the Tillman Act in 1907. The Court today rejects a century of history when it treats the distinction between corporate and individual campaign spending as an invidious novelty born of *Austin v. Michigan Chamber of Commerce*.

III
The So-Called "Ban"

Pervading the Court's analysis is the ominous image of a "categorical ban" on corporate speech. This characterization is highly misleading, and needs to be corrected. Our cases have repeatedly pointed out that, "contrary to the [majority's] critical assumptions," the statutes upheld in *Austin* and *McConnell* do "not impose an absolute ban on all forms of corporate political spending." For starters, both statutes provide exemptions for PACs, separate segregated funds established by a corporation for political purposes. At the time Citizens United brought this lawsuit, the only types of speech that could be regulated under §203 were: (1) broadcast, cable, or satellite communications; (2) capable of reaching at least 50,000 persons in the relevant electorate; (3) made within 30 days of a primary or 60 days of a general federal election; (4) by a labor union or a non-MCFL, nonmedia corporation; (5) paid for with general treasury funds; and (6) "susceptible of no reasonable interpretation other than as an appeal to vote for or against a specific candidate." The category of communications meeting all of these criteria is not trivial, but the notion that corporate political speech has been "suppressed altogether," that corporations have been "excluded from the general public dialogue," or that a work of fiction such as *Mr. Smith Goes to Washington* might be covered is nonsense.

In many ways, then, §203 functions as a source restriction or a time, place, and manner restriction. It applies in a viewpoint-neutral fashion to a narrow subset of advocacy messages about clearly identified candidates for federal office, made during discrete time periods through discrete channels. In the case at hand, all Citizens United needed to do to broadcast *Hillary* right before the primary was to abjure business contributions or use the funds in its PAC, which by its own account is "one of the most active conservative PACs in America."

Identity-Based Distinctions

The second pillar of the Court's opinion is its assertion that "the Government cannot restrict political speech based on the speaker's identity." Yet in a variety of contexts, we have held that speech can be regulated differentially on account of the speaker's identity, when identity is understood in categorical or institutional terms. The Government routinely places special restrictions on the speech rights of students, prisoners, members of the Armed Forces, foreigners, and its own employees. When such restrictions are justified by a legitimate governmental interest, they do not necessarily raise constitutional problems. In contrast to the blanket rule that the majority espouses, our cases recognize that the Government's interests may be more or less compelling with respect to different classes of speakers. "[D]ifferential treatment" is constitutionally suspect "unless justified by some special characteristic" of the regulated class of speakers, and that the constitutional rights of certain categories of speakers, in certain contexts, "are not automatically coextensive with the rights" that are normally accorded to members of our society, *Morse v. Frederick* (2007).

The election context is distinctive in many ways, and the Court, of course, is right that the First Amendment closely guards political speech. But in this context, too, the authority of legislatures to enact viewpoint-neutral regulations based on content and identity is well settled. We have, for example, allowed state-run broadcasters to exclude independent candidates from televised debates. *Arkansas Ed. Television Comm'n v. Forbes* (1998). We have upheld statutes that prohibit the distribution or display of campaign materials near a polling place. *Burson v. Freeman* (1992). Although we have not reviewed them directly, we have never cast doubt on laws that place special restrictions on campaign spending by foreign nationals. And we have consistently approved laws that bar Government employees, but not others, from contributing to or participating in

political activities. These statutes burden the political expression of one class of speakers, namely, civil servants. Yet we have sustained them on the basis of longstanding practice and Congress' reasoned judgment that certain regulations which leave "untouched full participation in political decisions at the ballot box," *Civil Service Comm'n v. Letter Carriers* (1973), help ensure that public officials are "sufficiently free from improper influences," and that "confidence in the system of representative Government is not eroded to a disastrous extent."

The same logic applies to this case with additional force because it is the identity of corporations, rather than individuals, that the Legislature has taken into account. Campaign finance distinctions based on corporate identity tend to be less worrisome, in other words, because the "speakers" are not natural persons, much less members of our political community, and the governmental interests are of the highest order. Furthermore, when corporations, as a class, are distinguished from noncorporations, as a class, there is a lesser risk that regulatory distinctions will reflect invidious discrimination or political favoritism. In short, the Court dramatically overstates its critique of identity-based distinctions, without ever explaining why corporate identity demands the same treatment as individual identity. Only the most wooden approach to the First Amendment could justify the unprecedented line it seeks to draw.

Our First Amendment Tradition

A third fulcrum of the Court's opinion is the idea that *Austin* and *McConnell* are radical outliers, "aberrations," in our First Amendment tradition. The Court has it exactly backwards.

1. Original Understandings

The Court invokes "ancient First Amendment principles" and original understandings, to defend today's ruling, yet it makes only a perfunctory attempt to ground its analysis in the principles or understandings of those who drafted and ratified the Amendment. Perhaps this is because there is not a scintilla of evidence to support the notion that anyone believed it would preclude regulatory distinctions based on the corporate form. To the extent that the

Framers' views are discernible and relevant to the disposition of this case, they would appear to cut strongly against the majority's position.

This is not only because the Framers and their contemporaries conceived of speech more narrowly than we now think of it, but also because they held very different views about the nature of the First Amendment right and the role of corporations in society. Those few corporations that existed at the founding were authorized by grant of a special legislative charter. Corporate sponsors would petition the legislature, and the legislature, if amenable, would issue a charter that specified the corporation's powers and purposes and "authoritatively fixed the scope and content of corporate organization," including "the internal structure of the corporation." Corporations were created, supervised, and conceptualized as quasi-public entities, "designed to serve a social function for the state." It was "assumed that [they] were legally privileged organizations that had to be closely scrutinized by the legislature because their purposes had to be made consistent with public welfare."

The Framers thus took it as a given that corporations could be comprehensively regulated in the service of the public welfare. Even "the notion that business corporations could invoke the First Amendment would probably have been quite a novelty," given that "at the time, the legitimacy of every corporate activity was thought to rest entirely in a concession of the sovereign." Shelledy, "Autonomy, Debate, and Corporate Speech," 18 *Hastings Const. L. Q.* 541, 578 (1991); cf. *Trustees of Dartmouth College v. Woodward* (1819) (Marshall, C. J.) ("A corporation is an artificial being, invisible, intangible, and existing only in contemplation of law. Being the mere creature of law, it possesses only those properties which the charter of its creation confers upon it"). In light of these background practices and understandings, it seems to me implausible that the Framers believed "the freedom of speech" would extend equally to all corporate speakers, much less that it would preclude legislatures from taking limited measures to guard against corporate capture of elections.

Justice Scalia criticizes the foregoing discussion for failing to adduce statements from the founding era showing that corporations were understood to be excluded from the First Amendment's free speech guarantee. Of course, Justice Scalia adduces no statements to suggest the contrary proposition, or even to suggest that the contrary proposition better reflects the kind of right that the drafters and ratifiers of the Free Speech Clause thought they were enshrining. Although Justice Scalia makes a perfectly sensible argument that an individual's right to speak entails a right to speak with others for a common cause, he does not explain why those two rights must be precisely identical, or why that principle applies to electioneering by corporations that serve no "common cause." Nothing in his account dislodges my basic point that members of the founding generation held a cautious view of corporate power and a narrow view of corporate rights (not that they "despised" corporations), and that they conceptualized speech in individualistic terms. If no prominent Framer bothered to articulate that corporate speech would have lesser status than individual speech, that may well be because the contrary proposition—if not also the very notion of "corporate speech"—was inconceivable.

Justice Scalia also emphasizes the unqualified nature of the First Amendment text. Yet the text only leads us back to the questions who or what is guaranteed "the freedom of speech," and, just as critically, what that freedom consists of and under what circumstances it may be limited. The truth is we cannot be certain how a law such as BCRA §203 meshes with the original meaning of the First Amendment. Nothing in our constitutional history dictates today's outcome. To the contrary, this history helps illuminate just how extraordinarily dissonant the decision is.

2. Legislative and Judicial Interpretation

A century of more recent history puts to rest any notion that today's ruling is faithful to our First Amendment tradition. At the federal level, the express distinction between corporate and individual political spending on elections stretches back to 1907, when Congress passed the Tillman Act, banning all corporate contributions to candidates. By the time Congress passed FECA in 1971, the bar on corporate contributions and expenditures had become such an accepted part of federal campaign finance regulation that when a large number of plaintiffs, including several nonprofit corporations, challenged virtually every aspect of the Act in *Buckley,* no one even bothered to argue that the bar as such was unconstitutional. *Buckley* famously (or infamously) distinguished direct contributions from independent expenditures, but its silence on corporations only reinforced the understanding that corporate expenditures could be treated differently from individual expenditures.

3. Buckley *and* Bellotti

Against this extensive background of congressional regulation of corporate campaign spending and our repeated affirmation of this regulation as constitutionally sound, the majority dismisses *Austin* as "a significant departure from ancient First Amendment principles." How does the majority attempt to justify this claim? Selected passages from two cases, *Buckley* and *Bellotti,* do all of the work. In the Court's view, *Buckley* and *Bellotti* decisively rejected the possibility of distinguishing corporations from natural persons in the 1970's; it just so happens that in every single case in which the Court has reviewed campaign finance legislation in the decades since, the majority failed to grasp this truth.

The majority emphasizes *Buckley*'s statement that "the concept that government may restrict the speech of some elements of our society in order to enhance the relative voice of others is wholly foreign to the First Amendment." But this elegant phrase cannot bear the weight that our colleagues have placed on it. The *Buckley* Court used this line in evaluating "the ancillary governmental interest in equalizing the relative ability of individuals and groups to influence the outcome of elections." But we made it clear in *Austin* (as in several cases before and since) that a restriction on the way corporations spend their money is no mere exercise in disfavoring the voice of some elements of our society in preference to others. Indeed, we expressly ruled that the compelling interest supporting Michigan's statute was not one of "equalizing the relative influence of speakers on elections,"

but rather the need to confront the distinctive corrupting potential of corporate electoral advocacy financed by general treasury dollars.

The case on which the majority places even greater weight is *Bellotti,* claiming it "could not have been clearer" that *Bellotti*'s holding forbade distinctions between corporate and individual expenditures like the one at issue here. The Court's reliance is odd. *Bellotti* ruled, in an explicit limitation on the scope of its holding, that "our consideration of a corporation's right to speak on issues of general public interest implies no comparable right in the quite different context of participation in a political campaign for election to public office." *Bellotti,* in other words, did not touch the question presented in *Austin* and *McConnell,* and the opinion squarely disavowed the proposition for which the majority cites it.

The majority attempts to explain away the distinction *Bellotti* drew—between general corporate speech and campaign speech intended to promote or prevent the election of specific candidates for office—as inconsistent with the rest of the opinion and with *Buckley.* Yet the basis for this distinction is perfectly coherent: The anticorruption interests that animate regulations of corporate participation in candidate elections, the "importance" of which "has never been doubted," do not apply equally to regulations of corporate participation in referenda. A referendum cannot owe a political debt to a corporation, seek to curry favor with a corporation, or fear the corporation's retaliation.

The majority grasps a quotational straw from *Bellotti,* that speech does not fall entirely outside the protection of the First Amendment merely because it comes from a corporation. Of course not, but no one suggests the contrary and neither *Austin* nor *McConnell* held otherwise. They held that even though the expenditures at issue were subject to First Amendment scrutiny, the restrictions on those expenditures were justified by a compelling state interest. *Austin* and *McConnell,* then, sit perfectly well with *Bellotti.*

IV

The majority recognizes that *Austin* and *McConnell* may be defended on anticorruption, antidistortion, and shareholder protection rationales. It badly errs both in explaining the nature of these rationales, which overlap and complement each other, and in applying them to the case at hand.

The Anticorruption Interest

Undergirding the majority's approach to the merits is the claim that the only "sufficiently important governmental interest in preventing corruption or the appearance of corruption" is one that is "limited to quid pro quo corruption." This is the same "crabbed view of corruption" that was espoused by Justice Kennedy in *McConnell* and squarely rejected by the Court in that case. On numerous occasions we have recognized Congress' legitimate interest in preventing the money that is spent on elections from exerting an "undue influence on an officeholder's judgment" and from creating "the appearance of such influence." Corruption operates along a spectrum, and the majority's apparent belief that quid pro quo arrangements can be neatly demarcated from other improper influences does not accord with the theory or reality of politics.

Quid Pro Quo Corruption

Even under the majority's "crabbed view of corruption," the Government should not lose this case. We have never suggested that such quid pro quo debts must take the form of outright vote buying or bribes, which have long been distinct crimes. Rather, they encompass the myriad ways in which outside parties may induce an officeholder to confer a legislative benefit in direct response to, or anticipation of, some outlay of money the parties have made or will make on behalf of the officeholder. Of almost equal concern as the danger of actual quid pro quo arrangements is the impact of the appearance of corruption. Congress may "legitimately conclude that the avoidance of the appearance of improper influence is also critical if confidence in the system of representative Government is not to be eroded to a disastrous extent."

The majority appears to think it decisive that the BCRA record does not contain "direct examples of votes being exchanged for expenditures." It would have been quite remarkable if Congress had created a record detailing such behavior by its own Members. Proving that a specific vote was exchanged for a specific expenditure has always been next to impossible. Yet, even if "ingratiation and access are not corruption" themselves, they are necessary prerequisites to it; they can create both the opportunity for, and the appearance of, quid pro quo arrangements. The influx of unlimited corporate money into the electoral realm also creates new opportunities for the mirror image of quid pro quo deals: threats, both explicit and implicit. Starting today, corporations with large war chests to deploy on electioneering may find democratically elected bodies becoming much more attuned to their interests.

Deference and Incumbent Self-Protection

Rather than show any deference to a coordinate branch of Government, the majority thus rejects the anticorruption rationale without serious analysis. Today's opinion provides no clear rationale for being so dismissive of Congress, but the prior individual opinions on which it relies have offered one: the incentives of the legislators who passed BCRA. In my view, we should instead start by acknowledging that Congress surely has both wisdom and experience in these matters that is far superior to ours. In America, incumbent legislators pass the laws that govern campaign finance, just like all other laws. To apply a level of scrutiny that effectively bars them from regulating electioneering whenever there is the faintest whiff of self-interest, is to deprive them of the ability to regulate electioneering.

Austin and Corporate Expenditures

Just as the majority gives short shrift to the general societal interests at stake in campaign finance regulation, it also overlooks the distinctive considerations raised by the regulation of corporate expenditures. The majority fails to appreciate that *Austin*'s antidistortion rationale is itself an anticorruption rationale, tied to the special concerns raised by corporations. Understood properly, "antidistortion" is a variant on the classic governmental interest in protecting against improper influences on officeholders that debilitate the democratic process. It is manifestly not just an "equalizing" ideal in disguise.

1. Antidistortion

The fact that corporations are different from human beings might seem to need no elaboration, except that the majority opinion almost completely elides it. Corporations have no consciences, no beliefs, no feelings, no thoughts, no desires. Corporations help structure and facilitate the activities of human beings, to be sure, and their "personhood" often serves as a useful legal fiction. But they are not themselves members of "We the People" by whom and for whom our Constitution was established.

These basic points help explain why corporate electioneering is not only more likely to impair compelling governmental interests, but also why restrictions on that electioneering are less likely to encroach upon First Amendment freedoms. One fundamental concern of the First Amendment is to "protect the individual's interest in self-expression." Freedom of speech helps "make men free to develop their faculties," *Whitney v. California* (1927) (Brandeis, J., concurring), it respects their "dignity and choice," *Cohen v. California* (1971), and it facilitates the value of "individual self-realization." Corporate speech, however, is derivative speech, speech by proxy. A regulation such as BCRA §203 may affect the way in which individuals disseminate certain messages through the corporate form, but it does not prevent anyone from speaking in his or her own voice.

In short, regulations such as §203 and the statute upheld in *Austin* impose only a limited burden on First Amendment freedoms not only because they target a narrow subset of expenditures and leave untouched the broader "public dialogue," but also because they leave untouched the speech of natural persons.

2. Shareholder Protection

There is yet another way in which laws such as §203 can serve First Amendment values. Interwoven with *Austin*'s concern to protect the integrity of the electoral process is a concern to protect the rights of shareholders from a kind of coerced speech: electioneering expenditures that do not "reflec[t] [their] support." The Court

dismisses this interest on the ground that abuses of shareholder money can be corrected "through the procedures of corporate democracy," and, it seems, through Internet-based disclosures. I fail to understand how this addresses the concerns of dissenting union members, who will also be affected by today's ruling, and I fail to understand why the Court is so confident in these mechanisms. By "corporate democracy," presumably the Court means the rights of shareholders to vote and to bring derivative suits for breach of fiduciary duty. In practice, however, these rights are so limited as to be almost nonexistent, given the internal authority wielded by boards and managers and the expansive protections afforded by the business judgment rule.

V

At bottom, the Court's opinion is thus a rejection of the common sense of the American people, who have recognized a need to prevent corporations from undermining self-government since the founding, and who have fought against the distinctive corrupting potential of corporate electioneering since the days of Theodore Roosevelt. It is a strange time to repudiate that common sense. While American democracy is imperfect, few outside the majority of this Court would have thought its flaws included a dearth of corporate money in politics. I would affirm the judgment of the District Court.

JUSTICE THOMAS, concurring in part and dissenting in part.

I dissent from Part IV of the Court's opinion, because the disclosure, disclaimer, and reporting requirements in BCRA §§201 and 311 are unconstitutional. In continuing to hold otherwise, the Court misapprehends the import of "recent events" that some *amici* describe "in which donors to certain causes were blacklisted, threatened, or otherwise targeted for retaliation." *Amici*'s examples relate principally to Proposition 8, a state ballot proposition that amended California's constitution to provide that "only marriage between a man and a woman is valid or recognized in California. Any donor who gave more than $100 to any committee supporting or opposing Proposition

8 was required to disclose his full name, street address, occupation, employer's name (or business name, if self-employed), and the total amount of his contributions. The California Secretary of State was then required to post this information on the Internet. Some opponents of Proposition 8 compiled this information and created Web sites with maps showing the locations of homes or businesses of Proposition 8 supporters. Many supporters (or their customers) suffered property damage, or threats of physical violence or death, as a result. I cannot endorse a view of the First Amendment that subjects citizens of this Nation to death threats, ruined careers, damaged or defaced property, or pre-emptive and threatening warning letters as the price for engaging in "core political speech, the primary object of First Amendment protection." *McConnell* (Thomas, J.).

Texas v. Johnson
491 U.S. 397 (1989)

During the Republican National Convention in Dallas in 1984, Gregory Johnson participated in a demonstration, dubbed the "Republican War Chest Tour," to protest the policies of the Reagan administration and of certain Dallas-based corporations. The demonstrators marched through the Dallas streets chanting slogans and staged "die-ins" outside various corporate locations to dramatize the consequences of nuclear war. The demonstration ended in front of Dallas City Hall, where Johnson unfurled an American flag given to him by a fellow demonstrator (who had taken it from outside a building along the route), doused it with kerosene, and set it on fire. While the flag burned, the protesters chanted: "America, the red, white, and blue, we spit on you." Johnson was subsequently arrested and convicted of violating a Texas law prohibiting the "desecration of venerated objects," including the national flag. The law defined "desecrate" as "deface, damage, or otherwise physically mistreat in a way that the actor knows will seriously offend one or more persons likely to observe or discover his action." The opinion of the Court applies the "O'Brien test," derived from United States v. O'Brien *(1968), for determining the constitutionality of governmental regulations of expressive conduct. Under that test, "a governmental regulation is sufficiently justified if it is within the constitutional power of the government; if it furthers an important or substantial governmental interest; if the governmental interest is unrelated to the suppression of free expression; and if the incidental restriction of alleged First Amendment freedoms is no greater than is essential to the furtherance of that interest." Opinion of the Court:* Brennan, *Marshall,*

Blackmun, Scalia, Kennedy. *Concurring opinion:* Kennedy. *Dissenting opinions:* Rehnquist, *White, O'Connor;* Stevens.

JUSTICE BRENNAN delivered the opinion of the Court.

After publicly burning an American flag as a means of political protest, Gregory Lee Johnson was convicted of desecrating a flag in violation of Texas law. This case presents the question whether his conviction is consistent with the First Amendment. We hold that it is not.

Johnson was convicted of flag desecration for burning the flag rather than for uttering insulting words. This fact somewhat complicates our consideration of his conviction under the First Amendment. We must first determine whether Johnson's burning of the flag constituted expressive conduct, permitting him to invoke the First Amendment in challenging his conviction. If his conduct was expressive, we next decide whether the State's regulation is related to the suppression of free expression. If the State's regulation is not related to expression, then the less stringent standard we announced in *United States v. O'Brien* for regulations of noncommunicative conduct controls. If it is, then we are outside of *O'Brien*'s test, and we must ask whether this interest justifies Johnson's conviction under a more demanding standard.

In deciding whether particular conduct possesses sufficient communicative elements to bring the First Amendment into play, we have asked whether "an intent to convey a particularized message was present, and [whether] the likelihood was great that the message would be understood by those who viewed it." The State of Texas conceded for purposes of its oral argument in this case that Johnson's conduct was expressive conduct, Johnson burned an American flag as part—indeed, as the culmination—of a political demonstration that coincided with the convening of the Republican Party and its renomination of Ronald Reagan for President. The expressive, overtly political nature of this conduct was both intentional and overwhelmingly apparent. In these circumstances, Johnson's burning of the flag was conduct "sufficiently imbued with elements of communication," to implicate the First Amendment.

In order to decide whether *O'Brien's* test applies here, therefore, we must decide whether Texas has asserted an interest in support of Johnson's conviction that is unrelated to the suppression of expression. The State offers two separate interests to justify this conviction: preventing breaches of the peace, and preserving the flag as a symbol of nationhood and national unity. We hold that the first interest is not implicated on this record and that the second is related to the suppression of expression.

Texas claims that its interest in preventing breaches of the peace justifies Johnson's conviction for flag desecration. However, no disturbance of the peace actually occurred or threatened to occur because of Johnson's burning of the flag. The only evidence offered by the State at trial to show the reaction to Johnson's actions was the testimony of several persons who had been seriously offended by the flag-burning. The State's position, therefore, amounts to a claim that an audience that takes serious offense at particular expression is necessarily likely to disturb the peace and that the expression may be prohibited on this basis. Our precedents do not countenance such a presumption. Thus, we have not permitted the Government to assume that every expression of a provocative idea will incite a riot, but have instead required careful consideration of the actual circumstances surrounding such expression, asking whether the expression "is directed to inciting or producing imminent lawless action and is likely to incite or produce such action." *Brandenburg v. Ohio* (1969). We conclude that the State's interest in maintaining order is not implicated on these facts.

The State also asserts an interest in preserving the flag as a symbol of nationhood and national unity. The State, apparently, is concerned that such conduct will lead people to believe either that the flag does not stand for nationhood and national unity, but instead reflects other, less positive concepts, or that the concepts reflected in the flag do not in fact, exist, that is, we do not enjoy unity as a Nation. These concerns blossom only when a person's treatment of the flag communicates some message, and thus are related "to the suppression of free expression" within the meaning of *O'Brien*. We are thus outside of *O'Brien's* test altogether.

It remains to consider whether the State's interest in preserving the flag as a symbol of nationhood and national unity justifies Johnson's conviction. According to Texas, if one physically treats the flag in a way that would tend to cast doubt on either the idea that nationhood and national unity are the flag's referents or that national unity actually exists, the message conveyed thereby is a harmful one and therefore may be prohibited. If there is a bedrock principle underlying the First Amendment, it is that the Government may not prohibit the expression of an idea simply because society finds the idea itself offensive or disagreeable. We have not recognized an exception to this principle even where our flag has been involved. In *Street v. New York* (1969), we held that a State may not criminally punish a person for uttering words critical of the flag. Nor may the Government, we have held in *West Virginia State Board of Education v. Barnette* (1943), in which the Court invalidated a compulsory flag salute law, compel conduct that would evince respect for the flag.

In short, nothing in our precedents suggests that a State may foster its own view of the flag by prohibiting expressive conduct relating to it. To conclude that the Government may permit designated symbols to be used to communicate only a limited set of messages would be to enter territory having no discernible or defensible boundaries. Could the Government, on this theory, prohibit the burning of state flags? Of copies of the Presidential seal? Of the Constitution? In evaluating these choices under the First Amendment, how would we decide which symbols were sufficiently special to warrant this unique status? To do so, we would be forced to consult our own political preferences, and impose them on the citizenry, in the very way that the First Amendment forbids us to do.

It is not the State's ends, but its means, to which we object. It cannot be gainsaid that there is a special place reserved for the flag in this Nation, and thus we do not doubt that the Government has a legitimate interest in making efforts to "preserve the national flag as an unalloyed symbol of our country." We reject the suggestion, urged at oral argument by counsel for Johnson, that the Government lacks "any state interest whatsoever" in regulating the manner in which the flag may be displayed. Congress has, for example, enacted precatory regulations describing the proper treatment of the flag, and we cast no doubt on the legitimacy of its interest in making such recommendations. To say that the Government has an interest in encouraging proper treatment of the flag, however, is not to say that it may criminally punish a person for burning a flag as a means of political protest.

"National unity as an end which officials may foster by persuasion and example is not in question. The problem is whether under our Constitution compulsion as here employed is a permissible means for its achievement." *Barnette.*

THE CHIEF JUSTICE, with whom JUSTICE WHITE and JUSTICE O'CONNOR join, dissenting.

In holding this Texas statute unconstitutional, the Court ignores Justice Holmes' familiar aphorism that "a page of history is worth a volume of logic." *New York Trust Co. v. Eisner* (1921). For more than 200 years, the American flag has occupied a unique position as the symbol of our Nation, a uniqueness that justifies a governmental prohibition against flag burning in the way respondent Johnson did here.

The American flag does not represent the views of any particular political party, and it does not represent any particular political philosophy. The flag is not simply another "idea" or "point of view" competing for recognition in the marketplace of ideas. Millions and millions of Americans regard it with an almost mystical reverence regardless of what sort of social, political, or philosophical beliefs they may have. I cannot agree that the First Amendment invalidates the Act of Congress, and the laws of 48 of the 50 States, which make criminal the public burning of the flag.

The Court insists that the Texas statute prohibiting the public burning of the American flag infringes on respondent Johnson's freedom of expression. Johnson was free to make any verbal denunciation of the flag that he wished; indeed, he was free to burn the flag in private. He could publicly burn other symbols of the Government or effigies of political leaders. He did lead a march through the streets of Dallas, and conducted a rally in front of the Dallas City Hall. He engaged in a "die-in" to protest nuclear weapons. He shouted out various slogans during the march, including: "Reagan, Mondale which will it be? Either one means World War III"; "Ronald Reagan, killer of the hour, Perfect example of US power"; and "red, white and blue, we spit on you, you stand for plunder, you will go under." For none of these acts was he arrested or prosecuted; it was only when he proceeded to burn publicly an American flag stolen from its rightful owner that he violated the Texas statute. The Texas statute deprived Johnson of only one rather inarticulate symbolic form of protest—a form of protest that was profoundly offensive to many—and left him with a full panoply of other symbols and every conceivable form of verbal expression to express his deep disapproval of national policy. Thus, in no way can it be said that Texas is punishing him because his hearers—or any other group of people—were profoundly opposed to the message that he sought to convey. Such opposition is no proper basis for restricting speech or expression under the First Amendment. It was Johnson's use of this particular symbol, and not the idea that he sought to convey by it or by his many other expressions, for which he was punished.

But the Court today will have none of this. The uniquely deep awe and respect for our flag felt by virtually all of us are bundled off under the rubric of "designated symbols," that the First Amendment prohibits the government from "establishing." But the government has not "established" this feeling; 200 years of history have done that. The government is simply recognizing as a fact the profound regard for the American flag created by that history when it enacts statutes prohibiting the disrespectful public burning of the flag.

R. A. V. v. City of St. Paul
505 U.S. 377 (1992)

R. A. V., together with several other teenagers, constructed a crude cross out of broken chair legs and burned the cross in the yard of a black family. He was arrested and charged with, among other things, violating St. Paul's Bias-Motivated Crime Ordinance, which forbade the display of a symbol "including, but not limited to, a burning cross or Nazi swastika, which one knows or has reasonable grounds to know arouses anger, alarm or resentment in others on the basis of race, color, creed, religion, or gender." The trial court dismissed this charge, ruling that the St. Paul ordinance violated the First Amendment because it was substantially overbroad and impermissibly restricted expression based on its content. The Minnesota Supreme Court reversed this ruling, contending that the ordinance restricted only "fighting words," which the US Supreme Court in Chaplinsky v. New Hampshire *(1942) had ruled were not entitled to First Amendment protection. The US Supreme Court then granted certiorari.* Opinion of the Court: <u>Scalia</u>, Rehnquist, Kennedy, Souter, Thomas. Concurring opinions: <u>White</u>, Blackmun, O'Connor, Stevens (in part); Blackmun; <u>Stevens</u>, White (in part), Blackmun (in part).

JUSTICE SCALIA delivered the opinion of the Court.

Assuming, *arguendo,* that all of the expression reached by the ordinance is proscribable under the "fighting words" doctrine, we nonetheless conclude that the ordinance is facially unconstitutional in that it prohibits otherwise permitted speech solely on the basis of the subjects the speech addresses.

The First Amendment generally prevents government from proscribing speech, see, e.g., *Cantwell v. Connecticut* (1940), or even expressive conduct, see, e.g., *Texas v. Johnson* (1989), because of disapproval of the ideas expressed. Content-based regulations are presumptively invalid. From 1791 to the present, however,

our society, like other free but civilized societies, has permitted restrictions upon the content of speech in a few limited areas, which are "of such slight social value as a step to truth that any benefit that may be derived from them is clearly outweighed by the social interest in order and morality." *Chaplinsky* [*v. New Hampshire* (1942)].

These areas of speech can, consistently with the First Amendment, be regulated because of their constitutionally proscribable contents (obscenity, defamation, etc.), not that they are categories of speech entirely invisible to the Constitution, so that they may be made the vehicles for content discrimination unrelated to their distinctively proscribable content. Thus, the government may proscribe libel; but it may not make the further content discrimination of proscribing only libel critical of the government.

The proposition that a particular instance of speech can be proscribable on the basis of one feature (e.g., obscenity) but not on the basis of another (e.g., opposition to the city government) is commonplace, and has found application in many contexts. We have long held, for example, that nonverbal expressive activity can be banned because of the action it entails, but not because of the ideas it expresses—so that burning a flag in violation of an ordinance against outdoor fires could be punishable, whereas burning a flag in violation of an ordinance against dishonoring the flag is not. Similarly, we have upheld reasonable "time, place, or manner" restrictions, but only if they are "justified without reference to the content of the regulated speech." *Ward v. Rock Against Racism* (1989).

Even the prohibition against content discrimination that we assert the First Amendment requires is not absolute. It applies differently in the context of proscribable speech than in the area of fully protected speech.

When the basis for the content discrimination consists entirely of the very reason the entire class of speech at issue is proscribable, no significant danger of idea or viewpoint discrimination exists. Such a reason, having been adjudged neutral enough to support exclusion of the entire class of speech from First Amendment protection, is also neutral enough to form the basis of distinction within the class. To illustrate: A State might choose to prohibit only that obscenity which is the most patently offensive in its prurience—i.e., that which involves the most lascivious displays of sexual activity. But it may not prohibit, for example, only that obscenity which includes offensive political messages.

II

Applying these principles to the St. Paul ordinance, we conclude that, even as narrowly construed by the Minnesota Supreme Court, the ordinance is facially unconstitutional. Although the phrase in the ordinance, "arouses anger, alarm or resentment in others," has been limited by the Minnesota Supreme Court's construction to reach only those symbols or displays that amount to "fighting words," the remaining, unmodified terms make clear that the ordinance applies only to "fighting words" that insult, or provoke violence, "on the basis of race, color, creed, religion or gender." Displays containing abusive invective, no matter how vicious or severe, are permissible unless they are addressed to one of the specified disfavored topics. Those who wish to use "fighting words" in connection with other ideas—to express hostility, for example, on the basis of political affiliation, union membership, or homosexuality—are not covered. The First Amendment does not permit St. Paul to impose special prohibitions on those speakers who express views on disfavored subjects.

In its practical operation, moreover, the ordinance goes even beyond mere content discrimination, to actual viewpoint discrimination. Displays containing some words—odious racial epithets, for example—would be prohibited to proponents of all views. But "fighting words" that do not themselves invoke race, color, creed, religion, or gender—aspersions upon a person's mother, for example—would seemingly be usable *ad libitum* in the placards of those arguing in favor of racial, color, etc. tolerance and equality, but could not be used by that speaker's opponents. One could hold up a sign saying, for example, that all "anti-Catholic bigots" are misbegotten; but not that all "papists" are, for that would insult and provoke violence "on the basis of religion." St. Paul has no such authority to license one side of a debate to fight freestyle, while requiring the other to follow Marquis of Queensbury Rules.

Finally, St. Paul and its *amici* defend the conclusion of the Minnesota Supreme Court that, even if the ordinance regulates expression based on hostility towards its protected ideological content, this discrimination is nonetheless justified because it is narrowly tailored to serve compelling state interests. Specifically, they assert that the ordinance helps to ensure the basic human rights of members of groups that have historically been subjected to discrimination, including the right of such group members to live in peace where they wish. We do not doubt that these interests are compelling, and that the ordinance can be said to promote them. But the "danger of censorship" presented by a facially content-based statute requires that that weapon be employed only where it is "necessary to serve the asserted [compelling] interest." *Burson v. Freeman* (1992). The existence of adequate content-neutral alternatives thus "undercuts significantly" any defense of such a statute, casting considerable doubt on the government's protestations that "the asserted justification is in fact an accurate description of the purpose and effect of the law." The dispositive question in this case, therefore, is whether content discrimination is reasonably necessary to achieve St. Paul's compelling interests; it plainly is not. An ordinance not limited to the favored topics, for example, would have precisely the same beneficial effect. In fact the only interest distinctively served by the content limitation is that of displaying the city council's special hostility toward the particular biases thus singled out. That is precisely what the First Amendment forbids. The politicians of St. Paul are entitled to express that hostility—but not through the means of imposing unique limitations upon speakers who (however benightedly) disagree.

Let there be no mistake about our belief that burning a cross in someone's front yard is reprehensible. But St. Paul has sufficient means at its disposal to prevent such behavior without adding the First Amendment to the fire.

The judgment of the Minnesota Supreme Court is reversed, and the case is remanded for proceedings not inconsistent with this opinion.

JUSTICE WHITE, with whom JUSTICE BLACKMUN and JUSTICE O'CONNOR join, and with whom JUSTICE STEVENS joins [in part], concurring in the judgment.

I agree with the majority that the judgment of the Minnesota Supreme Court should be reversed. However, our agreement ends there. This Court's decisions have plainly stated that expression falling within certain limited categories so lacks the values the First Amendment was designed to protect that the Constitution affords no protection to that expression. *Chaplinsky v. New Hampshire* (1942), made the point in the clearest possible terms:

There are certain well-defined and narrowly limited classes of speech, the prevention and punishment of which have never been thought to raise any Constitutional problem. It has been well observed that such utterances are no essential part of any exposition of ideas, and are of such slight social value as a step to truth that any benefit that may be derived from them is clearly outweighed by the social interest in order and morality.

This categorical approach has provided a principled and narrowly focused means for distinguishing between expression that the government may regulate freely and that which it may regulate on the basis of content only upon a showing of compelling need.

In its decision today, the majority holds that the First Amendment protects those narrow categories of expression long held to be undeserving of First Amendment protection—at least to the extent that lawmakers may not regulate some fighting words more strictly than others because of their content. The Court announces that such content-based distinctions violate the First Amendment because "the government may not regulate use based on hostility—or favoritism—towards the underlying message expressed." Should the government

want to criminalize certain fighting words, the Court now requires it to criminalize all fighting words.

Fighting words are not a means of exchanging views, rallying supporters, or registering a protest; they are directed against individuals to provoke violence or to inflict injury. Therefore, a ban on all fighting words or on a subset of the fighting words category would restrict only the social evil of hate speech, without creating the danger of driving viewpoints from the marketplace.

As I see it, the Court's theory does not work and will do nothing more than confuse the law. Its selection of this case to rewrite First Amendment law is particularly inexplicable, because the whole problem could have been avoided by deciding this case under settled First Amendment principles. I would decide the case on overbreadth grounds. We have emphasized time and again that overbreadth doctrine is an exception to the established principle that "a person to whom a statute may constitutionally be applied will not be heard to challenge that statute on the ground that it may conceivably be applied unconstitutionally to others, in other situations not before the Court." *Broadrick v. Oklahoma* [1973]. A defendant being prosecuted for speech or expressive conduct may challenge the law on its face if it reaches protected expression, even when that person's activities are not protected by the First Amendment. This is because "the possible harm to society in permitting some unprotected speech to go unpunished is outweighed by the possibility that protected speech of others may be muted."

I agree with petitioner that the ordinance is invalid on its face. Although the ordinance as construed reaches categories of speech that are constitutionally unprotected, it also criminalizes a substantial amount of expression that—however repugnant—is shielded by the First Amendment. In attempting to narrow the scope of the St. Paul anti-bias ordinance, the Minnesota Supreme Court relied upon two of the categories of speech and expressive conduct that fall outside the First Amendment's protective sphere: words that incite "imminent lawless action," *Brandenburg v. Ohio* (1969), and "fighting" words, *Chaplinsky v. New Hampshire.* [T]he Minnesota Supreme Court drew upon the definition of fighting words that appears in *Chaplinsky*—words "which by their very utterance inflict injury or tend to incite an immediate breach of the peace." However, the Minnesota court emphasized (tracking the language of the ordinance) that "the ordinance censors only those displays that one knows or should know will create anger, alarm or resentment based on racial, ethnic, gender or religious bias."

Our fighting words cases have made clear, however, that such generalized reactions are not sufficient to strip expression of its constitutional protection. The mere fact that expressive activity causes hurt feelings, offense, or resentment does not render the expression unprotected. The ordinance is therefore fatally overbroad and invalid on its face.

Walker v. Texas Division, Sons of Confederate War Veterans, Inc.
576 U.S. ___ (2015)

Texas law requires all motor vehicles to display valid license plates. Drivers may choose the standard Texas plate or may for a fee choose a specialty plate, either one authorized by the state legislature or one proposed by a nonprofit organization seeking to sponsor a specialty plate. Texas law vests in the Department of Motor Vehicles Board the authority to approve or disapprove proposed plates. In 2009, the Sons of Confederate Veterans, Texas Division (SCV) applied to sponsor a specialty license plate. At the bottom of the proposed plate were the words "SONS OF CONFEDERATE VETERANS." At the side was the organization's logo, a square Confederate battle flag framed by the words "Sons of Confederate Veterans 1896." A faint Confederate battle flag appeared in the background on the lower portion of the plate. The Board voted unanimously against issuing the plate "because public comments had shown that many members of the general public find the design offensive, and because such comments are reasonable." SCV sued the chairman and members of the Board, arguing that the Board's decision violated the Free Speech Clause of the First Amendment. The District Court ruled for the Board, but the Court of Appeals for the Fifth Circuit reversed, and the Supreme Court granted certiorari. Opinion of the Court: Breyer, *Thomas, Ginsburg, Sotomayor, Kagan. Dissenting opinion:* Alito, *Roberts, Scalia, Kennedy.*

JUSTICE BREYER delivered the opinion of the Court.

II

When government speaks, it is not barred by the Free Speech Clause from determining the content of what it says. *Pleasant Grove City* v. *Summum* (2009). Were the Free Speech Clause interpreted otherwise, government would not work. How could a city government create a successful recycling program if officials, when writing householders asking them to recycle cans and bottles, had to include in the letter a long plea from the local trash disposal enterprise demanding the contrary? How could a state government effectively develop programs designed to encourage and provide vaccinations, if officials also had to voice the perspective of those who oppose this type of immunization? We have therefore refused "to hold that the Government unconstitutionally discriminates on the basis of viewpoint when it chooses to fund a program dedicated to advance certain permissible goals, because the program in advancing those goals necessarily discourages alternative goals." *Rust* v. *Sullivan* (1991). That is not to say that a government's ability to express itself is without restriction. Constitutional and statutory provisions outside of the Free Speech Clause may limit government speech. And the Free Speech Clause itself may constrain the government's speech if, for example, the government seeks to compel private persons to convey the government's speech. But, as a general matter, when the government speaks it is entitled to promote a program, to espouse a policy, or to take a position. In doing so, it represents its citizens and it carries out its duties on their behalf.

III

In our view, specialty license plates issued pursuant to Texas's statutory scheme convey government speech. Our reasoning rests primarily on our analysis in *Summum*, a recent case that presented a similar problem. In *Summum*, we considered a religious organization's request to erect in a 2.5-acre city park a monument setting forth the organization's religious tenets. In the park were 15 other permanent displays. At least 11 of these—including a wishing well, a September 11 monument, a historic granary, the city's first fire station, and a Ten Commandments monument—had been donated to the city by private entities. The religious organization argued that the Free Speech Clause required the city to display the organization's proposed monument because, by accepting a broad range of permanent exhibitions at the park, the city had created a forum for private speech in the form of monuments. This Court rejected the organization's argument. We held that the city, even when "accepting a privately donated monument and placing it on city property," had "engaged in expressive conduct." The speech at issue was "best viewed as a form of government speech" and "therefore not subject to scrutiny under the Free Speech Clause." And, in reaching that conclusion, the Court rejected the premise that the involvement of private parties in designing the monuments was sufficient to prevent the government from controlling which monuments it placed in its own public park.

B

Our analysis in *Summum* leads us to the conclusion that here, too, government speech is at issue. First, the history of license plates shows that, insofar as license plates have conveyed more than state names and vehicle identification numbers, they long have communicated messages from the States. Second, Texas license plate designs "are often closely identified in the public mind with the [State]." Texas license plates are, essentially, government IDs. And issuers of ID "typically do not permit" the placement on their IDs of "message[s] with which they do not wish to be associated." Third, Texas maintains direct control over the messages conveyed on its specialty plates. Texas law provides that the State "has sole control over the design, typeface, color, and alphanumeric pattern for all license plates." The Board must approve

every specialty plate design proposal before the design can appear on a Texas plate. And the Board and its predecessor have actively exercised this authority. Texas asserts, and SCV concedes, that the State has rejected at least a dozen proposed designs. Accordingly, like the city government in *Summum*, Texas "has effectively controlled the messages conveyed by exercising final approval authority over their selection." This final approval authority allows Texas to choose how to present itself and its constituency. Thus, Texas offers plates celebrating the many educational institutions attended by its citizens. But it need not issue plates deriding schooling. Texas offers plates that pay tribute to the Texas citrus industry. But it need not issue plates praising Florida's oranges as far better. And Texas offers plates that say "Fight Terrorism." But it need not issue plates promoting al Qaeda.

C

SCV believes that Texas's specialty license plate designs are not government speech, at least with respect to the designs (comprising slogans and graphics) that were initially proposed by private parties. According to SCV, the State does not engage in expressive activity through such slogans and graphics, but rather provides a forum for private speech by making license plates available to display the private parties' designs. We cannot agree.

We have previously used what we have called "forum analysis" to evaluate government restrictions on purely private speech that occurs on government property. *Cornelius v. NAACP Legal Defense & Ed. Fund, Inc.* (1985). But forum analysis is misplaced here. Because the State is speaking on its own behalf, the First Amendment strictures that attend the various types of government-established forums do not apply.

The parties agree that Texas's specialty license plates are not a "traditional public forum," such as a street or a park, "which has immemorially been held in trust for the use of the public and, time out of mind, has been used for purposes of assembly, communicating thoughts between citizens, and discussing public questions." *Perry Ed. Assn. v. Perry Local Educators' Assn.*, (1983). "The Court has rejected the view that traditional public forum status extends beyond its historic confines." *Arkansas Ed. Television Comm'n* v. *Forbes* (1998). And state-issued specialty license plates lie far beyond those confines.

It is equally clear that Texas's specialty plates are neither a "'designated public forum,'" which exists where "government property that has not traditionally been regarded as a public forum is intentionally opened up for that purpose," *Summum*, nor a "limited public forum," which exists where a government has "reserv[ed a forum] for certain groups or for the discussion of certain topics," *Rosenberger* v. *Rector and Visitors of Univ. of Va.*(1995). A government "does not create a public forum by inaction or by permitting limited discourse, but only by intentionally opening a nontraditional forum for public discourse." *Cornelius*. And in order "to ascertain whether [a government] intended to designate a place not traditionally open to assembly and debate as a public forum," this Court "has looked to the policy and practice of the government" and to "the nature of the property and its compatibility with expressive activity."

Texas's policies and the nature of its license plates indicate that the State did not intend its specialty license plates to serve as either a designated public forum or a limited public forum. First, the State exercises final authority over each specialty license plate design. This authority militates against a determination that Texas has created a public forum. Second, Texas takes ownership of each specialty plate design, making it particularly untenable that the State intended specialty plates to serve as a forum for public discourse. Finally, Texas license plates have traditionally been used for government speech, are primarily used as a form of government ID, and bear the State's name. These features of Texas license plates indicate that Texas explicitly associates itself with the speech on its plates.

For similar reasons, we conclude that Texas's specialty license plates are not a "nonpublic forum," which exists "where the government is acting as a proprietor, managing its internal operations." *International Soc. for Krishna Consciousness, Inc.* v. *Lee* (1992). With respect to specialty license plate designs, Texas is not simply managing government property, but instead is engaging in expressive conduct. As we have described, we reach this conclusion based on the historical context, observers' reasonable interpretation of the messages conveyed by Texas specialty plates, and the effective control that the State exerts over the design selection process. Texas's specialty license plate designs "are meant to convey and have the effect of conveying a government message." They "constitute government speech." *Summum*.

The fact that private parties take part in the design and propagation of a message does not extinguish the governmental nature of the message or transform the government's role into that of a mere forum-provider. In *Summum*, private entities "financed and donated monuments that the government accepted and displayed to the public." Here, similarly, private parties propose designs that Texas may accept and display on its license plates. In this case, as in *Summum*, the "government entity may exercise its freedom to express its views" even "when it receives assistance from private sources for the purpose of delivering a government-controlled message."

Of course, Texas allows many more license plate designs than the city in *Summum* allowed monuments. But our holding in *Summum* was not dependent on the precise number of monuments found within the park. Indeed, we indicated that the permanent displays in New York City's Central Park also constitute government speech. And an *amicus* brief had informed us that there were, at the time, 52 such displays. Further, there may well be many more messages that Texas wishes to convey through its license plates than there were messages that the city in *Summum* wished to convey through its monuments. Texas's desire to communicate numerous messages does not mean that the messages conveyed are not Texas's own.

Additionally, the fact that Texas vehicle owners pay annual fees in order to display specialty license plates does not imply that the plate designs are merely a forum for private speech. While some nonpublic forums provide governments the opportunity to profit from speech, see, *e.g., Lehman* v. *Shaker Heights* (1974), the existence of government profit alone is insufficient to trigger forum analysis. Thus, if the city in *Summum* had established a rule that organizations wishing to donate monuments must also pay fees to assist in park maintenance, we do not believe that the result in that case would have been any different. Here, too, we think it sufficiently clear that Texas is speaking through its specialty license plate designs, such that the existence of annual fees does not convince us that the specialty plates are a nonpublic forum.

IV

Our determination that Texas's specialty license plate designs are government speech does not mean that the designs do not also implicate the free speech rights of private persons. We have acknowledged that drivers who display a State's selected license plate designs convey the messages communicated through those designs. See *Wooley* v. *Maynard* (1977). And we have recognized that the First Amendment stringently limits a State's authority to compel a private party to express a view with which the private party disagrees. See *Hurley* v. *Irish-American Gay, Lesbian and Bisexual Group of Boston, Inc.* (1995); *West Virginia Bd. of Ed.* v. *Barnette*, (1943). But here, compelled private speech is not at issue. And just as Texas cannot require SCV to convey "the State's ideological message," SCV cannot force Texas to include a Confederate battle flag on its specialty license plates.

For the reasons stated, we hold that Texas's specialty license plate designs constitute government speech and that Texas was consequently entitled to refuse to issue plates featuring SCV's proposed design. Accordingly, the judgment of the United States Court of Appeals for the Fifth Circuit is

Reversed.

JUSTICE ALITO, with whom THE CHIEF JUSTICE, JUSTICE SCALIA, and JUSTICE KENNEDY join, dissenting.

Here is a test. Suppose you sat by the side of a Texas highway and studied the license plates on the vehicles passing by. You would see, in addition to the standard Texas plates, an impressive array of specialty plates. (There are now more than 350 varieties.) You would likely observe plates that honor numerous colleges and universities. You might see plates bearing the name of a high school, a fraternity or sorority, the Masons, the Knights of Columbus, the

Daughters of the American Revolution, a realty company, a favorite soft drink, a favorite burger restaurant, and a favorite NASCAR driver.

As you sat there watching these plates speed by, would you really think that the sentiments reflected in these specialty plates are the views of the State of Texas and not those of the owners of the cars? If a car with a plate that says "Rather Be Golfing" passed by at 8:30 am on a Monday morning, would you think: "This is the official policy of the State—better to golf than to work?" If you did your viewing at the start of the college football season and you saw Texas plates with the names of the University of Texas's out-of-state competitors in upcoming games—Notre Dame, Oklahoma State, the University of Oklahoma, Kansas State, Iowa State—would you assume that the State of Texas was officially (and perhaps treasonously) rooting for the Longhorns' opponents? And when a car zipped by with a plate that reads "NASCAR-24 Jeff Gordon," would you think that Gordon (born in California, raised in Indiana, resides in North Carolina), is the official favorite of the State government?

The Court says that all of these messages are government speech. This capacious understanding of government speech takes a large and painful bite out of the First Amendment. Specialty plates may seem innocuous. They make motorists happy, and they put money in a State's coffers. But the precedent this case sets is dangerous. While all license plates unquestionably contain *some* government speech (*e.g.*, the name of the State and the numbers and/or letters identifying the vehicle), the State of Texas has converted the remaining space on its specialty plates into little mobile billboards on which motorists can display their own messages. And what Texas did here was to reject one of the messages that members of a private group wanted to post on some of these little billboards because the State thought that many of its citizens would find the message offensive. That is blatant viewpoint discrimination.

If the State can do this with its little mobile billboards, could it do the same with big, stationary billboards? Suppose that a State erected electronic billboards along its highways. Suppose that the State posted some government messages on these billboards and then, to raise money, allowed private entities and individuals to purchase the right to post their own messages. And suppose that the State allowed only those messages that it liked or found not too controversial. Would that be constitutional?

What if a state college or university did the same thing with a similar billboard or a campus bulletin board or dorm list serve? What if it allowed private messages that are consistent with prevailing views on campus but banned those that disturbed some students or faculty? Can there be any doubt that these examples of viewpoint discrimination would violate the First Amendment? I hope not, but the future uses of today's precedent remain to be seen.

Relying almost entirely on one precedent— *Pleasant Grove City* v. *Summum*—the Court holds that messages that private groups succeed in placing on Texas license plates are government messages. The Court badly misunderstands *Summum*. In *Summum*, a private group claimed the right to erect a large stone monument in a small city park. The 2.5-acre park contained 15 permanent displays, 11 of which had been donated by private parties. The central question concerned the nature of the municipal government's conduct when it accepted privately donated monuments for placement in its park: Had the city created a forum for private speech, or had it accepted donated monuments that expressed a government message? We held that the monuments represented government speech, and we identified several important factors that led to this conclusion.

First, governments have long used monuments as a means of expressing a government message. Here in the United States, important public monuments like the Statue of Liberty, the Washington Monument, and the Lincoln Memorial, express principles that inspire and bind the Nation together. Thus, long experi-

ence has led the public to associate public monuments with government speech. Second, there is no history of landowners allowing their property to be used by third parties as the site of large permanent monuments that do not express messages that the landowners wish to convey. Third, spatial limitations played a prominent part in our analysis. Because only a limited number of monuments can be built in any given space, governments do not allow their parks to be cluttered with monuments that do not serve a government purpose, a point well understood by those who visit parks and view the monuments they contain. These characteristics, which rendered public monuments government speech in *Summum*, are not present in Texas's specialty plate program.

III

What Texas has done by selling space on its license plates is to create what we have called a limited public forum. It has allowed state property (*i.e.,* motor vehicle license plates) to be used by private speakers according to rules that the State prescribes. Under the First Amendment, however, those rules cannot discriminate on the basis of viewpoint. But that is exactly what Texas did here. The Confederate battle flag is a controversial symbol. To the Texas Sons of Confederate Veterans, it is said to evoke the memory of their ancestors and other soldiers who fought for the South in the Civil War. To others, it symbolizes slavery, segregation, and hatred. Whatever it means to motorists who display that symbol and to those who see it, the flag expresses a viewpoint. The Board rejected the plate design because it concluded that many Texans would find the flag symbol offensive. That was pure viewpoint discrimination. Because the Court approves this violation of the First Amendment, I respectfully dissent.

McCullen v. Coakley
573 U.S. (2014)

In 2000, the Massachusetts Legislature enacted the Massachusetts Reproductive Health Care Facilities Act in order to address clashes between abortion opponents and advocates of abortion rights outside clinics where abortions were per- *formed. The Act established a defined area with an eighteen-foot radius around the entrances and driveways of such facilities. Anyone could enter that area, but once within it, no one could approach within six feet of another person—unless* that person consented—"for the purpose of passing a leaflet or handbill to, displaying a sign to, or engaging in oral protest, education, or counseling with such other person." A separate provision subjected to criminal punishment anyone who "knowingly obstructs, detains, hinders, impedes or blocks another person's entry to or exit from a reproductive health care facility." The Massachusetts Legislature amended the statute in 2007, replacing the six-foot no-approach zones (within the eighteen-foot area) with a thirty-five-foot fixed buffer zone from which individuals are categorically excluded. The statute exempted four classes of individuals: (1) "persons entering or leaving such facility"; (2) "employees or agents of such facility acting within the scope of their employment"; (3) "law enforcement, ambulance, firefighting, construction, utilities, public works and other municipal agents acting within the scope of their employment"; and (4) "persons using the public sidewalk or street right-of-way adjacent to such facility solely for the purpose of reaching a destination other than such facility." The Act thus made it more difficult for those who attempt to engage women approaching the clinics in "sidewalk counseling," which involves offering information about alternatives to abortion and help pursuing those options. In 2008, pro-life advocates sued Attorney General Martha Coakley and other Massachusetts officials to enjoin enforcement of the Act, alleging that it violates the First and Fourteenth Amendments. The District Court denied petitioners' challenge, the Court of Appeals for the First Circuit affirmed, and the Supreme Court granted certiorari. Opinion of the Court: <u>Roberts</u>, Ginsburg, Breyer, Sotomayor, Kagan. Concurring in the judgment: <u>Scalia</u>, Kennedy, Thomas; <u>Alito</u>.

CHIEF JUSTICE ROBERTS delivered the opinion of the Court.

A Massachusetts statute makes it a crime to knowingly stand on a "public way or sidewalk" within 35 feet of an entrance or driveway to any place, other than a hospital, where abortions are performed. Petitioners are individuals who approach and talk to women outside such facilities, attempting to dissuade them from having abortions. The statute prevents petitioners from doing so near the facilities' entrances. The question presented is whether the statute violates the First Amendment.

II

By its very terms, the Massachusetts Act regulates access to "public ways" and "sidewalks." Such areas occupy a "special position in terms of First Amendment protection" because of their historic role as sites for discussion and debate. These places—which we have labeled "traditional public fora"—"have immemorially been held in trust for the use of the public and, time out of mind, have been used for purposes of assembly, communicating thoughts between citizens, and discussing public questions." Even though the Act says nothing about speech on its face, there is no doubt—and respondents do not dispute—that it restricts access to traditional public fora and is therefore subject to First Amendment scrutiny.

Consistent with the traditionally open character of public streets and sidewalks, we have held that the government's ability to restrict speech in such locations is "very limited." In particular, the guiding First Amendment principle that the "government has no power to restrict expression because of its message, its ideas, its subject matter, or its content" applies with full force in a traditional public forum. We have, however, afforded the government somewhat wider leeway to regulate features of speech unrelated to its content. "Even in a public forum the government may impose reasonable restrictions on the time, place, or manner of protected speech, provided the restrictions are justified without reference to the content of the regulated speech, that they are narrowly tailored to serve a significant governmental interest, and that they leave open ample alternative channels for communication of the information."

While the parties agree that this test supplies the proper framework for assessing the constitutionality of the Massachusetts Act, they disagree about whether the Act satisfies the test's three requirements.

III

Petitioners contend that the Act is not content neutral. First, they argue that it discriminates against abortion-related speech because it establishes buffer zones only at clinics that perform abortions. Second, petitioners contend that the Act, by exempting clinic employees and agents, favors one viewpoint about abortion over the other. If either of these arguments is correct, then the Act must satisfy strict scrutiny—that is, it must be the least restrictive means of achieving a compelling state interest. Respondents do not argue that the Act can survive this exacting standard.

Justice Scalia objects to our decision to consider whether the statute is content based and thus subject to strict scrutiny, given that we ultimately conclude that it is not narrowly tailored. But we think it unexceptional to perform the first part of a multipart constitutional analysis first. The content-neutrality prong of the test is logically antecedent to the narrow-tailoring prong, because it determines the appropriate level of scrutiny.

A

The Act applies only at a "reproductive health care facility," defined as "a place, other than within or upon the grounds of a hospital, where abortions are offered or performed." Given this definition, petitioners argue, "virtually all speech affected by the Act is speech concerning abortion," thus rendering the Act content based. We disagree. To begin, the Act does not draw content-based distinctions on its face. Whether petitioners violate the Act "depends" not "on what they say," but simply on where they say it. Indeed, petitioners can violate the Act merely by standing in a buffer zone, without displaying a sign or uttering a word.

It is true, of course, that by limiting the buffer zones to abortion clinics, the Act has the "inevitable effect" of restricting abortion-related speech more than speech on other subjects. But a facially neutral law does not become content based simply because it may disproportionately affect speech on certain topics. On the contrary, "a regulation that serves purposes unrelated to the content of expression is deemed neutral, even if it has an incidental effect on some speakers or messages but not others." The question in such a case is whether the law is "justified without reference to the content of the regulated speech." *Renton* v. *Playtime Theatres, Inc.* (1986).

The Massachusetts Act's stated purpose is to "increase forthwith public safety at reproductive health care facilities." Respondents have articulated similar purposes before this Court—namely, "public safety, patient access to healthcare, and the unobstructed use of public sidewalks and roadways." We have previously deemed the foregoing concerns to be content neutral. Obstructed access and congested sidewalks are problems no matter what caused them. A group of individuals can obstruct clinic access and clog sidewalks just as much when they loiter as when they protest abortion or counsel patients.

To be clear, the Act would not be content neutral if it were concerned with undesirable effects that arise from "the direct impact of speech on its audience" or "listeners' reactions to speech." If, for example, the speech outside Massachusetts abortion clinics caused offense or made listeners uncomfortable, such offense or discomfort would not give the Commonwealth a content-neutral justification to restrict the speech. All of the problems identified by the Commonwealth here, however, arise irrespective of any listener's reactions. Whether or not a single person reacts to abortion protestors' chants or petitioners' counseling, large crowds outside abortion clinics can still compromise public safety, impede access, and obstruct sidewalks.

Petitioners do not really dispute that the Commonwealth's interests in ensuring safety and preventing obstruction are, as a general matter, content neutral. But petitioners note that these interests "apply outside every building in the State that hosts any activity that might occasion protest or comment," not just abortion clinics. By choosing to pursue these interests only at abortion clinics, petitioners argue, the Massachusetts Legislature evinced a purpose to "single out for regulation speech about one particular topic: abortion." We cannot infer such a purpose from the Act's limited scope. The Massachusetts Legislature amended the Act in 2007 in response to a problem that was, in its experience, limited to abortion clinics.

B

Petitioners also argue that the Act is content based because it exempts four classes of individuals, one of which comprises "employees or agents of [a reproductive healthcare] facility acting within the scope of their employment." This exemption, petitioners say, favors one side in the abortion debate and thus constitutes viewpoint discrimination—an "egregious form of content discrimination," *Rosenberger* v. *Rector and Visitors of Univ. of Va.* (1995). In particular, petitioners argue that the exemption allows clinic employees and agents—including the volunteers who "escort" patients arriving at the Boston clinic—to speak inside the buffer zones.

It is of course true that "an exemption from an otherwise permissible regulation of speech may represent a governmental attempt to give one side of a debatable public question an advantage in expressing its views to the people." *City of Ladue* v. *Gilleo* (1994). At least on the record before us, however, the statutory exemption for clinic employees and agents acting within the scope of their employment does not appear to be such an attempt. There is nothing inherently suspect about providing some kind of exemption to allow individuals who work at the clinics to enter or remain within the buffer zones. In particular, the exemption cannot be regarded as simply a carve-out for the clinic escorts; it also covers employees such as the maintenance worker shoveling a snowy sidewalk or the security guard patrolling a clinic entrance. Given the need for an exemption for clinic employees, the "scope of their employment" qualification simply ensures that the exemption is limited to its purpose of allowing the employees to do their jobs. It performs the same function as the identical "scope of their employment" restriction on the exemption for "law enforcement, ambulance, fire-fighting, construction, utilities, public works and other municipal agents." There is no suggestion in the record that any of the clinics authorize their employees to speak about abortion in the buffer zones. The "scope of their employment" limitation thus seems designed to protect against exactly the sort of conduct that petitioners and Justice Scalia fear. We thus conclude that the Act is neither content nor viewpoint based and therefore need not be analyzed under strict scrutiny.

IV

Even though the Act is content neutral, it still must be "narrowly tailored to serve a significant governmental interest." For a content-neutral time, place, or manner regulation to be narrowly tailored, it must not "burden substantially more speech than is necessary to further the government's legitimate interests." Such a regulation, unlike a content-based restriction of speech, "need not be the least restrictive or least intrusive means of" serving the government's interests. But the government still "may not regulate expression in such a manner that a substantial portion of the burden on speech does not serve to advance its goals."

A

Respondents claim that the Act promotes "public safety, patient access to healthcare, and the unobstructed use of public sidewalks and roadways." Petitioners do not dispute the significance of these interests. At the same time, the buffer zones impose serious burdens on petitioners' speech. At each of the three Planned Parenthood clinics where petitioners attempt to counsel patients, the zones carve out a significant portion of the adjacent public sidewalks, pushing petitioners well back from the clinics' entrances and driveways. The zones thereby compromise petitioners' ability to initiate the close, personal conversations that they view as essential to "sidewalk counseling." The buffer zones have also made it substantially more difficult for petitioners to distribute literature to arriving patients. The Court of Appeals and respondents are wrong to downplay these burdens on petitioners' speech.

Respondents also emphasize that the Act does not prevent petitioners from engaging in various forms of "protest"—such as chanting slogans and displaying signs—outside the buffer zones. That misses the point. Petitioners are not protestors. They seek not merely to express their opposition to abortion, but to inform women of various alternatives and to provide help in pursuing them. Petitioners believe that they can accomplish this objective only through personal, caring, consensual conversations. And for good reason: It is easier to ignore a strained voice or a waving hand than a direct greeting or an outstretched arm.

B

1

The buffer zones burden substantially more speech than necessary to achieve the Commonwealth's asserted interests. At the outset, we note that the Act is truly exceptional: No other State [has] a law that creates fixed buffer zones around abortion clinics. That of course does not mean that the law is invalid. It does, however, raise concern that the Commonwealth has too readily forgone options that could serve its interests just as well, without substantially burdening the kind of speech in which petitioners wish to engage. That is the case here. The Commonwealth's interests include ensuring public safety outside abortion clinics, preventing harassment and intimidation of patients and clinic staff, and combating deliberate obstruction of clinic entrances. The Act itself contains a separate provision, subsection (e)—unchallenged by petitioners—that prohibits much of this conduct. That provision subjects to criminal punishment "any person who knowingly obstructs, detains, hinders, impedes or blocks another person's entry to or exit from a reproductive health care facility." The Commonwealth points to a substantial public safety risk created when protestors obstruct driveways leading to the clinics. That is, however, an example of its failure to look to less intrusive means of addressing its concerns. Any such obstruction can readily be addressed through existing local ordinances. All of the foregoing measures are, of course, in addition to available generic criminal statutes forbidding assault, breach of the peace, trespass, vandalism, and the like. The Commonwealth has available to it a variety of approaches that appear capable of serving its interests, without excluding individuals from areas historically open for speech and debate.

2

Respondents have but one reply: "We have tried other approaches, but they do not work." We cannot accept that contention. Although respondents claim that Massachusetts "tried other laws already on the books," they identify not a single prosecution brought under those laws within at least the last 17 years. And while they also claim that the Commonwealth "tried injunctions," the last injunctions they cite date to the 1990s. In short, the Commonwealth has not shown that it seriously undertook to address the problem with less intrusive tools readily available to it. Nor has it shown that it considered different methods that other jurisdictions have found effective.

Respondents contend that the alternatives we have discussed suffer from two defects: First, given the "widespread" nature of the problem, it is simply not "practicable" to rely on individual prosecutions and injunctions. But far from being "widespread," the problem appears from the record to be limited principally to the Boston clinic on Saturday mornings. Moreover, by their own account, the police appear perfectly capable of singling out lawbreakers. The second supposed defect in the alternatives we have identified is that laws like subsection (e) of the Act requires a showing of intentional or deliberate obstruction, intimidation, or harassment, which is often difficult to prove. As Captain Evans predicted in his legislative testimony, fixed buffer zones would "make our job so much easier." Of course they would. But that is not enough to satisfy the First Amendment. To meet the requirement of narrow tailoring, the government must demonstrate that alternative measures that burden substantially less speech would fail to achieve the government's interests, not simply that the chosen route is easier.

* * *

Petitioners wish to converse with their fellow citizens about an important subject on the public streets and sidewalks—sites that have hosted discussions about the issues of the day throughout history. Respondents assert undeniably significant interests in maintaining public safety on those same streets and sidewalks, as well as in preserving access to adjacent healthcare facilities. But here the Commonwealth has pursued those interests by the extreme step of closing a substantial portion of a traditional public forum to all speakers. It has done so without seriously addressing the problem through alternatives that leave the forum open for its time-honored purposes. The Commonwealth may not do that consistent with the First Amendment. The judgment of the Court of Appeals for the First Circuit is reversed, and the case is remanded for further proceedings consistent with this opinion.

JUSTICE SCALIA, with whom JUSTICE KENNEDY and JUSTICE THOMAS join, concurring in the judgment.

Today's opinion carries forward this Court's practice of giving abortion-rights advocates a pass when it comes to suppressing the free-speech rights of their opponents. There is an entirely separate, abridged edition of the First Amendment applicable to speech against abortion. See, *e.g.*, *Hill v. Colorado* (2000); *Madsen v. Women's Health Center, Inc.* (1994). The second half of the Court's analysis today, invalidating the law at issue because of inadequate "tailoring," is certainly attractive to those of us who oppose an abortion-speech edition of the First Amendment. But think again. This is an opinion that has Something for Everyone, and the more significant portion continues the onward march of abortion-speech-only jurisprudence. That is the first half of the Court's analysis, which concludes that a statute of this sort is not content based and hence not subject to so-called strict scrutiny. The Court reaches out to decide that question unnecessarily—or at least unnecessarily insofar as legal analysis is concerned.

I. THE COURT'S CONTENT-NEUTRALITY DISCUSSION IS UNNECESSARY

The gratuitous portion of today's opinion is Part III, which concludes that subsection (b) of the Massachusetts Reproductive Health Care Facilities Act is not specifically directed at speech opposing (or even concerning) abortion and hence need not meet the strict-scrutiny standard applicable to content-based speech regulations. Inasmuch as Part IV holds that the Act is unconstitutional because it does not survive the lesser level of scrutiny associated with content-neutral "time, place, and manner" regulations, there is no principled reason for the majority to decide whether the statute is subject to strict scrutiny.

II. THE STATUTE IS CONTENT BASED AND FAILS STRICT SCRUTINY

Having eagerly volunteered to take on the level-of-scrutiny question, the Court provides the wrong answer. Petitioners argue for two reasons that subsection (b) articulates a content-based speech restriction—and that we must therefore evaluate it through the lens of strict scrutiny.

A. Application to Abortion Clinics Only

First, petitioners maintain that the Act targets abortion-related—for practical purposes, abortion-opposing—speech because it applies outside abortion clinics only (rather than outside other buildings as well). It blinks reality to say, as the majority does, that a blanket prohibition on the use of streets and sidewalks where speech on only one politically controversial topic is likely to occur—and where that speech can most effectively be communicated—is not content based. Would the Court exempt from strict scrutiny a law banning access to the streets and sidewalks surrounding the site of the Republican National Convention? Or those used annually to commemorate the 1965 Selma-to-Montgomery civil rights marches? Or those outside the Internal Revenue Service? Surely not.

Every objective indication shows that the provision's primary purpose is to restrict speech that opposes abortion. I begin with the fact that the Act burdens only the public spaces outside abortion clinics. One might have expected the majority to defend the statute's peculiar targeting by arguing that those locations regularly face the safety and access problems that it says the Act was designed to solve. But the majority does not make that argument because it would be untrue. The structure of the Act also indicates that it rests on content-based concerns. The goals of "public safety, patient access to healthcare, and the unobstructed use of public sidewalks and roadways," are already achieved by an earlier-enacted subsection of the statute, which provides criminal penalties for "any person who knowingly obstructs, detains, hinders, impedes or blocks another person's entry to or exit from a reproductive health care facility." Thus, the speech-free zones carved out by subsection (b) add nothing to safety and access; what they achieve, and what they were obviously designed to achieve, is the suppression of speech opposing abortion.

Further contradicting the Court's fanciful defense of the Act is the fact that subsection (b) was enacted as a more easily enforceable substitute for a prior provision. That provision did not exclude people entirely from the restricted areas around abortion clinics; rather, it forbade people in those areas to approach within six feet of another person *without that person's consent* "for the purpose of passing a leaflet or handbill to, displaying a sign to, or engaging in oral protest, education or counseling with such other person." As the majority acknowledges, that provision was "modeled on a Colorado law that this Court had upheld in *Hill*." And in that case, the Court recognized that the statute in question was directed at the suppression of unwelcome speech, vindicating what *Hill* called "the unwilling listener's interest in avoiding unwanted communication." The provision at issue here was indisputably meant to serve the same interest in protecting citizens' supposed right to avoid speech that they would rather not hear. In concluding that the statute is content based and therefore subject to strict scrutiny, I necessarily conclude that *Hill* should be overruled. Protecting people from speech they do not want to hear is not a function that the First Amendment allows the government to undertake in the public streets and sidewalks.

B. Exemption for Abortion-Clinic Employees or Agents

Petitioners contend that the Act targets speech opposing abortion (and thus constitutes a presumptively invalid viewpoint-discriminatory restriction) for another reason as well: It exempts "employees or agents" of an abortion clinic "acting within the scope of their employment." Is there any serious doubt that *abortion-clinic employees or agents* "acting within the scope of their employment" near clinic entrances may—indeed, often will—speak in favor of abortion ("You are doing the right thing")? Or speak in opposition to the message of abortion opponents—saying, for example, that "this is a safe facility" to rebut the statement that it is not?

C. Conclusion

In sum, the Act should be reviewed under the strict-scrutiny standard applicable to content-based legislation. That standard requires that a regulation represent "the least restrictive means" of furthering "a compelling Government interest." Respondents do not even attempt to argue that subsection (b) survives this test. "Suffice it to say that if protecting people from unwelcome communications"—the actual purpose of the provision—"is a compelling state interest, the First Amendment is a dead letter." *Hill*. The provision is thus unconstitutional root and branch. I concur only in the judgment that the statute is unconstitutional under the First Amendment.

Near v. Minnesota
283 U.S. 697 (1931)

The Saturday Press published a series of articles charging that various Minneapolis public officials were dishonest and incompetent and that they were responsible for the racketeering and bootlegging in the city. The publication also called for a special grand jury to investigate the situation. Under a state law that authorized abatement of a "malicious, scandalous and defamatory newspaper," the state secured a court order that required the Saturday Press to cease publication. When the state *supreme court affirmed the court order, the case was appealed to the US Supreme Court.* Opinion of the Court: <u>Hughes</u>, Holmes, Brandeis, Stone, Roberts. Dissenting opinion: <u>Butler</u>, Van Devanter, McReynolds, Sutherland.

THE CHIEF JUSTICE delivered the opinion of the Court.

Without attempting to summarize the contents of the voluminous exhibits attached to the complaint, we deem it sufficient to say that the articles charged in substance that a Jewish gangster was in control of gambling, bootlegging and racketeering in Minneapolis, and that law enforcing officers and agencies were not energetically performing their duties. Most of the charges were directed against the Chief of Police; he was charged with gross neglect of duty, illicit relations with gangsters, and with participation in graft. The County Attorney was charged with knowing the existing conditions and with failure to take adequate measures to remedy them. The Mayor was accused of inefficiency and dereliction. One member of the grand jury was stated to be in sympathy with the gangsters. A special grand jury and a special prosecutor were demanded to deal with the situation in general, and, in particular, to investigate an attempt to assassinate one Guilford, one of the original defendants, who, it appears from the articles, was shot by gangsters after the first issue of the periodical had been published. There is no question but that the articles made serious accusations against the public officers named and others in connection with the prevalence of crimes and the failure to expose and punish them.

This statute, for the suppression as a public nuisance of a newspaper or periodical, is unusual, if not unique, and raises questions of grave importance transcending the local interests involved in the particular action. It is no longer open to doubt that the liberty of the press, and of speech, is within the liberty safeguarded by the due process clause of the Fourteenth Amendment from invasion by state action. In maintaining this guaranty, the authority of the State to enact laws to promote the health, safety, morals and general welfare of its people is necessarily admitted. The limits of this sovereign power must always be determined with appropriate regard to the particular subject of its exercise. It is important to note precisely the purpose and effect of the statute as the state court has construed it.

First. The statute is not aimed at the redress of individual or private wrongs. Remedies for libel remain available and unaffected. The statute, said the state court, "is not directed at threatened libel but at an existing business which, generally speaking, involves more than

libel." It is aimed at the distribution of scandalous matter as "detrimental to public morals and to the general welfare," tending "to disturb the peace of the community" and "to provoke assaults and the commission of crime."

Second. The statute is directed not simply at the circulation of scandalous and defamatory statements with regard to private citizens, but at the continued publication by newspapers and periodicals of charges against public officers of corruption, malfeasance in office, or serious neglect of duty. Such charges by their very nature create a public scandal. They are scandalous and defamatory within the meaning of the statute, which has its normal operation in relation to publications dealing prominently and chiefly with the alleged derelictions of public officers.

Third. The object of the statute is not punishment, in the ordinary sense, but suppression of the offending newspaper or periodical. Under this statute, a publisher of a newspaper or periodical, undertaking to conduct a campaign to expose and to censure official derelictions, and devoting his publication principally to that purpose, must face not simply the possibility of a verdict against him in a suit or prosecution for libel, but a determination that his newspaper or periodical is a public nuisance to be abated, and that this abatement and suppression will follow unless he is prepared with legal evidence to prove the truth of the charges and also to satisfy the court that, in addition to being true, the matter was published with good motives and for justifiable ends. This suppression is accomplished by enjoining publication and that restraint is the object and effect of the statute.

Fourth. The statute not only operates to suppress the offending newspaper or periodical but to put the publisher under an effective censorship. When a newspaper or periodical is found to be "malicious, scandalous and defamatory," and is suppressed as such, resumption of publication is punishable as a contempt of court by fine or imprisonment.

The question is whether a statute authorizing such proceedings in restraint of publication is consistent with the conception of the liberty of the press as historically conceived and guaranteed. In determining the extent of the constitutional protection, it has been generally, if not universally, considered that it is the chief purpose of the guaranty to prevent previous restraints upon publication. The struggle in England, directed against the legislative power of the licenser, resulted in renunciation of the censorship of the press. The liberty deemed to be established was thus described by Blackstone: "The liberty of the press is indeed essential to the nature of a free state; but this consists in laying no previous restraints upon publications, and not in freedom from censure for criminal matter when published. Every freeman has an undoubted right to lay what sentiments he pleases before the public; to forbid this, is to destroy the freedom of the press; but if he publishes what is improper, mischievous or illegal, he must take the consequence of his own temerity."

The criticism upon Blackstone's statement has not been because immunity from previous restraint upon publication has not been regarded as deserving of special emphasis, but chiefly because that immunity cannot be deemed to exhaust the conception of the liberty guaranteed by state and federal constitutions. The objection has also been made that the principle as to immunity from previous restraint is stated too broadly, if every such restraint is deemed to be prohibited. That is undoubtedly true; the protection even as to previous restraint is not absolutely unlimited. But the limitation has been recognized only in exceptional cases.

No one would question but that a government might prevent actual obstruction to its recruiting service or the publication of the sailing dates of transports or the number and location of troops. On similar grounds, the primary requirements of decency may be enforced against obscene publications. The security of the community life may be protected against incitements to acts of violence and the overthrow by force of orderly government. The constitutional guaranty of free speech does not "protect a man from an injunction against uttering words that may have all the effect of force." These limitations are not applicable here. Nor are we now concerned with questions as to the extent of authority to prevent publications in order to protect private rights according to the principles governing the exercise of the jurisdiction of courts of equity.

The exceptional nature of its limitations places in a strong light the general conception that liberty of the press, historically considered and taken up by the Federal Constitution, has meant, principally although not exclusively, immunity from previous restraints or censorship. The conception of the liberty of the press in this country had broadened with the exigencies of the colonial period and with the efforts to secure freedom from oppressive administration. That liberty was especially cherished for the immunity it afforded from previous restraint of the publication of censure of public officers and charges of official misconduct.

For these reasons we hold the statute, so far as it authorized the proceedings in this action under clause (b) of section one, to be an infringement of the liberty of the press guaranteed by the Fourteenth Amendment.

New York Times Company v. United States
403 U.S. 713 (1971)

In late March 1971, the New York Times *obtained from Daniel Ellsberg, who was associated with the Pentagon, a copy of the Pentagon Papers (a classified Defense Department study of US involvement in Indochina). On June 12, 1971, after prolonged editorial consideration of the material, the* Times *began publication of excerpts from the multivolume study. When the* Times *ignored a Justice Department request to halt further publication, the attorney general obtained an injunction in federal district court—the first federal injunction ever sought against a newspaper publication. From this point the case proceeded with extraordinary speed through the federal courts. By June 19, both the* Times *and the* Washington Post, *which had also begun publication of the materials, were under restraining orders imposed by federal courts of appeal. The Supreme Court agreed to hear the cases on June 25, heard oral argument a day later, and on June*

29 announced its decision. Per Curiam: Black, Douglas, Brennan, Stewart, White, Marshall. Concurring opinions: Black, Douglas; Douglas, Black; Brennan; Stewart, White; White, Stewart; Marshall. Dissenting opinions: Burger; Harlan, Burger, Blackmun; Blackmun.

PER CURIAM.

"Any system of prior restraints of expression comes to this Court bearing a heavy presumption against its constitutional validity." *Bantam Books, Inc. v. Sullivan* [1963]. The Government "thus carries a heavy burden of showing justification for the imposition of such a restraint." *Organization for a Better Austin v. Keefe* [1971]. The District Court for the Southern District of New York in the *New York Times* case and the District Court for the District of Columbia and the Court of Appeals for the District of Columbia Circuit in the *Washington Post* case held that the Government had not met that burden. We agree.

JUSTICE BLACK, with whom JUSTICE DOUGLAS joins, concurring.

I adhere to the view that the Government's case against the *Washington Post* should have been dismissed and that the injunction against the *New York Times* should have been vacated without oral argument when the cases were first presented to this Court. I believe that every moment's continuance of the injunctions against these newspapers amounts to a flagrant, indefensible, and continuing violation of the First Amendment.

In the First Amendment the Founding Fathers gave the free press the protection it must have to fulfill its essential role in our democracy. The press was to serve the governed, not the governors. The Government's power to censor the press was abolished so that the press would remain forever free to censure the Government. The press was protected so that it could bare the secrets of government and inform the people. Only a free and unrestrained press can effectively expose deception in government. And paramount among the responsibilities of a free press is the duty to prevent any part of the government from deceiving the people and sending them off to distant lands to die of foreign fevers and foreign shot and shell.

In my view, far from deserving condemnation for their courageous reporting, the *New York Times,* the *Washington Post,* and other newspapers should be commended for serving the purpose that the Founding Fathers saw so clearly. In revealing the workings of government that led to the Vietnam war, the newspapers nobly did precisely that which the Founders hoped and trusted they would do.

We are asked to hold that despite the First Amendment's emphatic command, the Executive Branch, the Congress, and the Judiciary can make laws enjoining publication of current news and abridging freedom of the press in the name of "national security." The word "security" is a broad, vague generality whose contours should not be invoked to abrogate the fundamental law embodied in the First Amendment. The guarding of military and diplomatic secrets at the expense of informed representative government provides no real security for our Republic. The Framers of the First Amendment, fully aware of both the need to defend a new nation and the abuses of the English and Colonial governments, sought to give this new society strength and security by providing that freedom of speech, press, religion, and assembly should not be abridged.

JUSTICE BRENNAN, concurring.

The error that has pervaded these cases from the outset was the granting of any injunctive relief whatsoever, interim or otherwise. The entire thrust of the Government's claim throughout these cases has been that publication of the material sought to be enjoined "could," or "might," or "may" prejudice the national interest in various ways. But the First Amendment tolerates absolutely no prior judicial restraints of the press predicated upon surmise or conjecture that untoward consequences may result. Our cases have thus far indicated that such cases may arise only when the Nation "is at war," during which times "no one would question but that a government might prevent actual obstruction to its recruiting service or the publication of the sailing dates of transports or the number and location of troops." *Near v. Minnesota* [1931]. Even if the present world situation were assumed to be tantamount to a time of war, or if the power of presently available armaments would justify even in peacetime the suppression of information that would set in motion a nuclear holocaust, in neither of these actions has the Government presented or even alleged that publication of items from or based upon the material at issue would cause the happening of an event of that nature.

JUSTICE STEWART, with whom JUSTICE WHITE joins, concurring.

In the absence of the governmental checks and balances present in other areas of our national life, the only effective restraint upon executive policy and power in the areas of national defense and international affairs may lie in an enlightened citizenry—in an informed and critical public opinion which alone can here protect the values of democratic government. For this reason, it is perhaps here that a press that is alert, aware, and free most vitally serves the basic purpose of the First Amendment. For without an informed and free press there cannot be an enlightened people.

Yet it is elementary that the successful conduct of international diplomacy and the maintenance of an effective national defense require both confidentiality and secrecy. Other nations can hardly deal with this Nation in an atmosphere of mutual trust unless they can be assured that their confidences will be kept. And within our own executive departments, the development of considered and intelligent international policies would be impossible if those charged with their formulation could not communicate with each other freely, frankly, and in confidence. In the area of basic national defense the frequent need for absolute secrecy is, of course, self-evident.

I think there can be but one answer to this dilemma, if dilemma it be. The responsibility must be where the power is. If the Constitution gives the Executive a large degree of unshared power in the conduct of foreign affairs and the maintenance of our national defense, then under the Constitution the Executive must have the largely unshared duty to determine and preserve the degree of internal security necessary to exercise that power successfully. It is an awesome responsibility, requiring judgment and wisdom of a high order. I should

suppose that moral, political, and practical considerations would dictate that a very first principle of that wisdom would be an insistence upon avoiding secrecy for its own sake. But be that as it may, it is clear to me that it is the constitutional duty of the Executive—as a matter of sovereign prerogative and not as a matter of law as the courts know law—through the promulgation and enforcement of executive regulations, to protect the confidentiality necessary to carry out its responsibilities in the fields of international relations and national defense.

This is not to say that Congress and the courts have no role to play. Undoubtedly Congress has the power to enact specific and appropriate criminal laws to protect government property and preserve government secrets. And if a criminal prosecution is instituted, it will be the responsibility of the courts to decide the applicability of the criminal law under which the charge is brought. But in the cases before us we are asked neither to construe specific regulations nor to apply specific laws. We are asked, instead, to perform a function that the Constitution gave to the Executive, not the Judiciary. We are asked, quite simply, to prevent the publication by two newspapers of material that the Executive Branch insists should not, in the national interest, be published. I am convinced that the Executive is correct with respect to some of the documents involved. But I cannot say that disclosure of any of them will surely result in direct, immediate, and irreparable damage to our Nation or its people. That being so, there can under the First Amendment be but one judicial resolution of the issues before us. I join the judgments of the Court.

JUSTICE WHITE, with whom JUSTICE STEWART joins, concurring.

The Government's position is simply stated: The responsibility of the Executive for the conduct of the foreign affairs and for the security of the Nation is so basic that the President is entitled to an injunction against publication of a newspaper story whenever he can convince a court that the information to be revealed threatens "grave and irreparable" injury to the public interest; and the injunction should issue whether or not the material to be published is classified, whether or not publication would be lawful under relevant criminal statutes enacted by Congress, and regardless of the circumstances by which the newspaper came into possession of the information.

At least in the absence of legislation by Congress, based on its own investigations and findings, I am quite unable to agree that the inherent powers of the Executive and the courts reach so far as to authorize remedies having such sweeping potential for inhibiting publications by the press. Terminating the ban on publication of the relatively few sensitive documents the Government now seeks to suppress does not mean that the law either requires or invites newspapers or others to publish them or that they will be immune from criminal action if they do.

Congress has addressed itself to the problems of protecting the security of the country and the national defense from unauthorized disclosure of potentially damaging information. It has not, however, authorized the injunctive remedy against threatened publication. It has apparently been satisfied to rely on criminal sanctions and their deterrent effect on the responsible as well as the irresponsible press.

THE CHIEF JUSTICE, dissenting.

In these cases, the imperative of a free and unfettered press comes into collision with another imperative, the effective functioning of a complex modern government and specifically the effective exercise of certain constitutional powers of the Executive. Only those who view the First Amendment as an absolute in all circumstances—a view I respect, but reject—can find such cases as these to be simple or easy.

It is not disputed that the *Times* has had unauthorized possession of the documents for three to four months, during which it has had its expert analysts studying them, presumably digesting them and preparing the material for publication. No doubt this was for a good reason; the analysis of 7,000 pages of complex material drawn from a vastly greater volume of material would inevitably take time and the writing of good news stories takes time. But why should the United States Government, from whom this information was illegally acquired by someone, along with all the counsel,

trial judges, and appellate judges be placed under needless pressure? After these months of deferral, the alleged "right to know" has somehow and suddenly become a right that must be vindicated instanter.

As I see it, we have been forced to deal with litigation concerning rights of great magnitude without an adequate record, and surely without time for adequate treatment either in the prior proceedings or in this Court. I am not prepared to reach the merits [of the case]. I would affirm the Court of Appeals for the Second Circuit and allow the District Court to complete the trial aborted by our grant of *certiorari,* meanwhile preserving the status quo in the *Post* case.

JUSTICE HARLAN, with whom THE CHIEF JUSTICE and JUSTICE BLACKMUN join, dissenting.

The scope of the judicial function in passing upon the activities of the Executive Branch of the Government in the field of foreign affairs is very narrowly restricted. This view is, I think, dictated by the concept of separation of powers upon which our constitutional system rests.

In a speech on the floor of the House of Representatives, Chief Justice John Marshall, then a member of that body, stated: "The President is the sole organ of the nation in its external relations, and its sole representative with foreign nations." From that time, shortly after the founding of the Nation, to this, there has been no substantial challenge to this description of the scope of executive power.

From this constitutional primacy in the field of foreign affairs, it seems to me that certain conclusions necessarily follow. Some of these were stated concisely by President Washington, declining the request of the House of Representatives for the papers leading up to the negotiation of the Jay Treaty: "The nature of foreign negotiations requires caution, and their success must often depend on secrecy; and even when brought to a conclusion a full disclosure of all the measures, demands, or eventual concessions which may have been proposed or contemplated would be extremely impolitic; for this might have a pernicious influence on future negotiations, or produce immediate inconveniences, perhaps danger and mischief, in relation to other powers." The power to evaluate the "pernicious influence" of premature disclosure is not, however, lodged in the Executive alone. I agree that, in performance of its duty to protect the values of the First Amendment against political pressures, the judiciary must review the initial Executive determination to the point of satisfying itself that the subject matter of the dispute does lie within the proper compass of the President's foreign relations power. Constitutional considerations forbid "a complete abandonment of judicial control." Cf. *United States v. Reynolds* [1953]. Moreover, the judiciary may properly insist that the determination that disclosure of the subject matter would irreparably impair the national security be made by the head of the Executive Department concerned—here the Secretary of State or the Secretary of Defense—after actual personal consideration by that officer. This safeguard is required in the analogous area of executive claims of privilege for secrets of state. But in my judgment the judiciary may not properly go beyond these two inquiries and redetermine for itself the probable impact of disclosure on the national security.

Even if there is some room for the judiciary to override the executive determination, it is plain that the scope of review must be exceedingly narrow. I can see no indication in the opinions of either the District Court or the Court of Appeals in the *Post* litigation that the conclusions of the Executive were given even the deference owing to an administrative agency, much less that owing to a co-equal branch of the Government operating within the field of its constitutional prerogative. Accordingly, I would vacate the judgment of the Court of Appeals for the District of Columbia Circuit on this ground and remand the case for further proceedings in the District Court. Before the commencement of such further proceedings, due opportunity should be afforded the Government for procuring from the Secretary of State or the Secretary of Defense or both an expression of their views on the issue of national security. The ensuing review by the District Court should be in accordance with the views expressed in this opinion. And for the reasons stated above I would affirm the judgment of the Court of Appeals for the Second Circuit.

Branzburg v. Hayes
408 U.S. 665 (1972)

In Branzburg, the Court considered together three cases involving reporters' refusal to testify before grand juries. In one case, Paul Branzburg, a reporter for the Louisville Courier-Journal, *refused to answer grand jury questions about the identity of persons he had observed processing hashish from marijuana. In the other two cases, Paul Pappas and Earl Caldwell refused to testify before grand juries investigating the activities of the Black Panthers, a radical group.* Opinion of the Court: White, Burger, Blackmun, Powell, Rehnquist. Concurring opinion: Powell. Dissenting opinions: Douglas; Stewart, Brennan, Marshall.

JUSTICE WHITE delivered the opinion of the Court.

The issue in these cases is whether requiring newsmen to appear and testify before state or federal grand juries abridges the freedom of speech and press guaranteed by the First Amendment. We hold that it does not.

Petitioners Branzburg and Pappas and respondent Caldwell press First Amendment claims that may be simply put: that to gather news it is often necessary to agree either not to identify the source of information published or to publish only part of the facts revealed, or both; that if the reporter is nevertheless forced to reveal these confidences to a grand jury, the source so identified and other confidential sources of other reporters will be measurably deterred from furnishing publishable information, all to the detriment of the free flow of information protected by the First Amendment. The heart of the claim is that the burden on news gathering resulting from compelling reporters to disclose confidential information outweighs any public interest in obtaining the information.

It is clear that the First Amendment does not invalidate every incidental burdening of the press that may result from the enforcement of civil or criminal statutes of general applicability. It has generally been held that the First Amendment does not guarantee the press a constitutional right of special access to information not available to the public generally. Despite the fact that news gathering may be hampered, the press is regularly excluded from grand jury proceedings, our own conferences, the meetings of other official bodies gathered in executive session, and the meetings of private organizations. Newsmen have no constitutional right of access to the scenes of crime or disaster when the general public is excluded, and they may be prohibited from attending or publishing information about trials if such restrictions are necessary to assure a defendant a fair trial before an impartial tribunal.

It is thus not surprising that the great weight of authority is that newsmen are not exempt from the normal duty of appearing before a grand jury and answering questions relevant to a criminal investigation. A number of States have provided newsmen a statutory privilege of varying breadth, but the majority have not done so, and none has been provided by federal statute. Until now the only testimonial privilege for unofficial witnesses that is rooted in the Federal Constitution is the Fifth Amendment privilege against compelled self-incrimination. We are asked to create another by interpreting the First Amendment to grant newsmen a testimonial privilege that other citizens do not enjoy. This we decline to do. Fair and effective law enforcement aimed at providing security for the person and property of the individual is a fundamental function of government, and the grand jury plays an important, constitutionally mandated role in this process. We perceive no basis for holding that the public interest in law enforcement and in ensuring effective grand jury proceedings is insufficient to override the consequential, but uncertain, burden on news gathering that is said to result from insisting that reporters, like other citizens, respond to relevant questions put to them in the course of a valid grand jury investigation or criminal trial.

The administration of a constitutional newsman's privilege would present practical and conceptual difficulties of a high order. Sooner or later, it would be necessary to define those categories of newsmen who qualified for the privilege, a questionable procedure in light of the traditional doctrine that liberty of the press is the right of the lonely pamphleteer who uses carbon paper or a mimeograph just as much as of the large metropolitan publisher who utilizes the latest photocomposition methods. Freedom of the press is a "fundamental personal right" which "is not confined to newspapers and periodicals. It necessarily embraces pamphlets and leaflets. The press in its historic connotation comprehends every sort of publication which affords a vehicle of information and opinion." *Lovell v. Griffin* [1938]. The informative function asserted by representatives of the organized press in the present cases is also performed by lecturers, political pollsters, novelists, academic researchers, and dramatists. Almost any author may quite accurately assert that he is contributing to the flow of information to the public, that he relies on confidential sources of information, and that these sources will be silenced if he is forced to make disclosures before a grand jury.

Finally, news gathering is not without its First Amendment protections, and grand jury investigations if instituted or conducted other than in good faith, would pose wholly different issues for resolution under the First Amendment. Official harassment of the press undertaken not for purposes of law enforcement but to disrupt a reporter's relationship with his news sources would have no justification. Grand juries are subject to judicial control and subpoenas to motions to quash. We do not expect courts will forget that grand juries must operate within the limits of the First Amendment as well as the Fifth.

JUSTICE STEWART, with whom JUSTICE BRENNAN and JUSTICE MARSHALL join, dissenting.

The Court's crabbed view of the First Amendment reflects a disturbing insensitivity to the critical role of an independent press in our society. The Court in these cases holds that a newsman has no First Amendment right to protect his sources when called before a grand jury. The Court thus invites state and federal authorities to undermine the historic independence of the press by attempting to annex the journalistic profession as an investigative arm of government. Not only will this decision impair performance of the press' constitutionally protected functions, but it will, I am convinced, in the long run harm rather than help the administration of justice.

The reporter's constitutional right to a confidential relationship with his source stems from the broad societal interest in a full and free flow of information to the public. It is this basic concern that underlies the Constitution's protection of a free press.

Enlightened choice by an informed citizenry is the basic ideal upon which an open society is premised, and a free press is thus indispensable to a free society. Not only does the press enhance personal self-fulfillment by providing the people with the widest possible range of fact and opinion, but it also is an incontestable precondition of self-government. As private and public aggregations of power burgeon in size and the pressures for conformity necessarily mount, there is obviously a continuing need for an independent press to disseminate a robust variety of information and opinion through reportage, investigation, and criticism, if we are to preserve our constitutional tradition of maximizing freedom of choice by encouraging diversity of expression.

In keeping with this tradition, we have held that the right to publish is central to the First Amendment and basic to the existence of constitutional democracy. No less important to the news dissemination process is the gathering of information. News must not be unnecessarily cut off at its source, for without freedom to acquire information the right to publish would be impermissibly compromised. Accordingly, a right to gather news, of some dimensions, must exist.

The right to gather news implies, in turn, a right to a confidential relationship between a reporter and his source. This proposition follows as a matter of simple logic once three factual predicates are recognized: (1) newsmen require informants to gather news; (2) confidentiality—the promise or understanding that names or certain aspects of communications will be kept off the record—is essential to the creation and maintenance of a news-gathering relationship with informants; and (3) an unbridled subpoena power—the absence of a constitutional right protecting, in any way, a confidential relationship from compulsory process—will either deter sources from divulging information or deter reporters from gathering and publishing information.

Posed against the First Amendment's protection of the newsman's confidential relationships in these cases is society's interest in the use of the grand jury to administer justice fairly and effectively. Yet the longstanding rule making every person's evidence available to the grand jury is not absolute. The rule has been limited by the Fifth Amendment, the Fourth Amendment, and the evidentiary privileges of the common law.

In striking the proper balance between the public interest in the efficient administration of justice and the First Amendment guarantee of the fullest flow of information, we must begin with the basic proposition that because of their "delicate and vulnerable" nature and their transcendent importance for the just functioning of our society, First Amendment rights require special safeguards. Accordingly, when a reporter is asked to appear before a grand jury and reveal confidences, I would hold that the government must (1) show that there is probable cause to believe that the newsman has information which is clearly relevant to a specific probable violation of law; (2) demonstrate that the information sought cannot be obtained by alternative means less destructive of First Amendment rights; and (3) demonstrate a compelling and overriding interest in the information.

New York Times v. Sullivan
376 U.S. 254 (1964)

L. B. Sullivan, commissioner of public affairs in Montgomery, Alabama, brought suit charging *that he had been libeled by an advertisement that a civil rights group published in the* New York

Times. *The ad, which criticized the treatment of blacks by the Montgomery police, contained several minor factual errors. A jury in Alabama awarded Sullivan $500,000 in damages, and the state supreme court affirmed the trial judgment. Meanwhile, similar suits were filed by other plaintiffs in Alabama against the* Times *and the Columbia Broadcasting Company for combined damages of $7 million.* Opinion of the Court: Brennan, Warren, Clark, Harlan, Stewart, White. Concurring opinions: Black, Douglas; Goldberg, Douglas.

JUSTICE BRENNAN delivered the opinion of the Court.

We are required in this case to determine for the first time the extent to which the constitutional protections for speech and press limit a State's power to award damages in a libel action brought by a public official against critics of his official conduct.

Under Alabama law as applied in this case, a publication is "libelous per se" if the words "tend to injure a person in his reputation" or to "bring him into public contempt"; the trial court stated that the standard was met if the words are such as to "injure him in his public office, or impute misconduct to him in his office, or want of official integrity, or want of fidelity to a public trust." The jury must find that the words were published "of and concerning" the plaintiff, but where the plaintiff is a public official his place in the governmental hierarchy is sufficient evidence to support a finding that his reputation has been affected by statements that reflect upon the agency of which he is in charge. Once "libel per se" has been established, the defendant has no defense as to stated facts unless he can persuade the jury that they were true in all their particulars. Unless he can discharge the burden of proving truth, general damages are presumed, and may be awarded without proof of pecuniary injury. The question before us is whether this rule of liability, as applied to an action brought by a public official against critics of his official conduct, abridges the freedom of speech and of the press that is guaranteed by the First and Fourteenth Amendments.

We consider this case against the background of a profound national commitment to the principle that debate on public issues should be uninhibited, robust, and wide-open, and that it may well include vehement, caustic, and sometimes unpleasantly sharp attacks on government and public officials. Authoritative interpretations of the First Amendment guarantees have consistently refused to recognize an exception for any test of truth—whether administered by judges, juries, or administrative officials—and especially one that puts the burden of proving truth on the speaker. Erroneous statement is inevitable in free debate, and it must be protected if the freedoms of expression are to have the "breathing space" that they "need to survive," *N.A.A.C.P. v. Button* (1963).

Injury to official reputation affords no more warrant for repressing speech that would otherwise be free than does factual error. Criticism of official conduct does not lose its constitutional protection merely because it is effective criticism and hence diminishes official reputations.

If neither factual error nor defamatory content suffices to remove the constitutional shield from criticism of official conduct, the combination of the two elements is no less inadequate. This is the lesson to be drawn from the great controversy over the Sedition Act of 1798, which first crystallized a national awareness of the central meaning of the First Amendment. Although the Sedition Act was never tested in this Court, the attack upon its validity has carried the day in the court of history. Fines levied in its prosecution were repaid by Act of Congress on the ground that it was unconstitutional. A broad consensus has developed that the Act, because of the restraint it imposed upon criticism of government and public officials, was inconsistent with the First Amendment.

What a State may not constitutionally bring about by means of a criminal statute is likewise beyond the reach of its civil law of libel. The fear of damage awards under a rule such as that invoked by the Alabama courts here may be markedly more inhibiting than the fear of prosecution under a criminal statute. The judgment awarded in this case—without the need for any proof of actual pecuniary loss—was one thousand times greater than the maximum fine provided by the Alabama criminal statute, and one hundred times greater than that provided by the Sedition Act.

The state rule of law is not saved by its allowance of the defense of truth. A rule compelling the critic of official conduct to guarantee the truth of all his factual assertions—and to do so on pain of libel judgments virtually unlimited in amount—leads to "self-censorship." Allowance of the defense of truth, with the burden of proving it on the defendant, does not mean that only false speech will be deterred. Under such a rule, would-be critics of official conduct may be deterred from voicing their criticism, even though it is believed to be true and even though it is in fact true, because of doubt whether it can be proved in court or fear of the expense of having to do so. They tend to make only statements which "steer far wider of the unlawful zone." *Speiser v. Randall* [1958]. The rule thus dampens the vigor and limits the variety of public debate. It is inconsistent with the First and Fourteenth Amendments.

The constitutional guarantees require, we think, a federal rule that prohibits a public official from recovering damages for a defamatory falsehood relating to his official conduct unless he proves that the statement was made with "actual malice"—that is, with knowledge that it was false or with reckless disregard of whether it was false or not.

Since respondent may seek a new trial, we deem that considerations of effective judicial administration require us to review the evidence in the present record to determine whether it could constitutionally support a judgment for respondent. Applying these standards, we consider that the proof presented to show actual malice lacks the convincing clarity which the constitutional standard demands, and hence that it would not constitutionally sustain the judgment for respondent under the proper rule of law.

Reversed and remanded.

JUSTICE BLACK, with whom JUSTICE DOUGLAS joins, concurring.

I concur in reversing this half-million-dollar judgment against the New York Times Company and the four individual defendants. I vote to reverse exclusively on the ground that the *Times* and the individual defendants had an absolute, unconditional constitutional right to publish in the *Times* advertisement their criticisms of the Montgomery agencies and officials. The half-million-dollar verdict gives dramatic proof that state libel laws threaten the very existence of an American press virile enough to publish unpopular views on public affairs and bold enough to criticize the conduct of public officials.

In my opinion the Federal Constitution has dealt with this deadly danger to the press in the only way possible without leaving the free press open to destruction—by granting the press an absolute immunity for criticism of the way public officials do their public duty. To punish the exercise of this right to discuss public affairs or to penalize it through libel judgments is to abridge or shut off discussion of the very kind most needed. This Nation, I suspect, can live in peace without libel suits based on public discussions of public affairs and public officials. But I doubt that a country can live in freedom where its people can be made to suffer physically or financially for criticizing their government, its actions, or its officials.

Reno v. American Civil Liberties Union
521 U.S. 844 (1997)

Congress enacted the Telecommunications Act of 1996 to encourage the rapid deployment of new telecommunications technologies. After committee hearings on the act, amendments were added in executive committee and on the floor of Congress with the purpose of protecting minors from harmful materials on the Internet. These amendments came to be known as the Communications Decency Act of 1996 (CDA). Section 223(a)(1) of the CDA criminalized the "knowing" transmission of "obscene or indecent" messages to any recipient under eighteen years of age. Section 223(d) prohibited the "knowing" sending or displaying to minors of any message that, "in context, depicts or describes, in terms patently offensive as measured by contemporary community standards, sexual or excretory activities or organs." The CDA also established defenses against prosecution under the act for those who took "good faith, effective actions" to restrict access to minors and for those who restricted access by requiring designated forms of age proof, such as a verified credit card or an adult identification number. Immediately after enactment of the CDA, several plaintiffs filed suit, challenging Sections 223(a)(1) and 223(d) as violations of the First Amendment. A three-judge district court convened pursuant to the act entered a preliminary injunction against enforcement of both challenged provisions, and the government appealed this ruling to the Supreme Court under the act's special review provisions. Opinion of the Court: <u>Stevens</u>, *Scalia, Kennedy, Souter, Thomas, Ginsburg, Breyer. Opinion concurring in the judgment in part and dissenting in part:* <u>O'Connor</u>, *Rehnquist.*

JUSTICE STEVENS delivered the opinion of the Court.

At issue is the constitutionality of two statutory provisions enacted to protect minors from "indecent" and "patently offensive" communications on the Internet. Notwithstanding the legitimacy and importance of the congressional goal of protecting children from harmful materials, we agree with the three-judge District Court that the statute abridges "the freedom of speech" protected by the First Amendment.

We begin with a summary of the undisputed facts. Sexually explicit material on the Internet includes text, pictures, and chat and "extends from the modestly titillating to the hardest core." Though such material is widely available, users seldom encounter such content accidentally. "A document's title or a description of the document will usually appear before the document itself, and in many cases the user will receive detailed information about a site's content before he or she need take the step to access the document. Almost all sexually explicit images are preceded by warnings as to the content." For that reason, the "odds are slim" that a user would enter a sexually explicit site by accident. Unlike communications received by radio or television, "the receipt of information on the Internet requires a series of affirmative steps more deliberate and directed than merely turning a dial. A child requires some sophistication and some ability to read to retrieve material and thereby to use the Internet unattended."

Systems have been developed to help parents control the material that may be available on a home computer with Internet access. "Although parental control software currently can screen for certain suggestive words or for known sexually explicit sites, it cannot now screen for sexually explicit images." Nevertheless, the evidence indicates that "a reasonably effective method by which parents can prevent their children from accessing sexually explicit and other material which parents may believe is inappropriate for their children will soon be available."

The problem of age verification differs for different uses of the Internet. The District Court categorically determined that there "is no effective way to determine the identity or the age of a user who is accessing material through e-mail, mail exploders, newsgroups or chat rooms." The Government offered no evidence that there was a reliable way to screen recipients and participants in such fora for age. Moreover, even if it were technologically feasible to block minors' access to newsgroups and chat rooms containing discussions of art, politics or other subjects that potentially elicit "indecent" or "patently offensive" contributions, it would not be possible to block their access to that material and "still allow them access to the remaining content, even if the overwhelming majority of that content was not indecent."

Technology exists by which an operator of a Web site may condition access on the verification of requested information such as a credit card number or an adult password. Credit card verification is only feasible, however, either in connection with a commercial transaction in which the card is used, or by payment to a verification agency. Using credit card possession as a surrogate for proof of age would impose costs on noncommercial Web sites that would require many of them to shut down. For that reason, at the time of the trial, credit card verification was "effectively unavailable to a substantial number of Internet content providers." Moreover, the imposition of such a requirement "would completely bar adults who do not have a credit card and lack the resources to obtain one from accessing any blocked material."

Commercial pornographic sites that charge their users for access have assigned them passwords as a method of age verification. The record does not contain any evidence concerning the reliability of these technologies. Even if passwords are effective for commercial purveyors of indecent material, the District Court found that an adult password requirement would impose significant burdens on noncommercial sites, both because they would discourage users from accessing their sites and because the cost of creating and maintaining such screening systems would be "beyond their reach."

In sum, the District Court found: "Even if credit card verification or adult password verification were implemented, the Government presented no testimony as to how such systems could ensure that the user of the password or credit card is in fact over 18. The burdens imposed by credit card verification and adult password verification systems make them effectively unavailable to a substantial number of Internet content providers."

In arguing for reversal, the Government contends that the CDA is plainly constitutional under three of our prior decisions: (1) *Ginsberg v. New York* (1968); (2) *FCC v. Pacifica Foundation* (1978); and (3) *Renton v. Playtime Theatres, Inc.* (1986). A close look at these cases, however, raises—rather than relieves—doubts concerning the constitutionality of the CDA.

In *Ginsberg,* we upheld the constitutionality of a New York statute that prohibited selling to minors under 17 years of age material that was considered obscene as to them even if not obscene as to adults. In four important respects, the statute upheld in *Ginsberg* was narrower than the CDA. First, we noted in *Ginsberg* that "the prohibition against sales to minors does not bar parents who so desire from purchasing the magazines for their children." Under the CDA, by contrast, neither the parents' consent—nor even their participation—in the communication would avoid the application of the statute. Second, the New York statute applied only to commercial transactions, whereas the CDA contains no such limitation. Third, the New York statute cabined its definition of material that is harmful to minors with the requirement that it be "utterly without redeeming social importance for minors." The CDA fails to provide us with any definition of the term "indecent" as used in 223(a)(1) and, importantly, omits any requirement that the "patently offensive" material covered by 223(d) lack serious literary, artistic, political, or scientific value. Fourth, the New York statute defined a minor as a person under the age of 17, whereas the CDA, in applying to all those under 18 years, includes an additional year of those nearest majority.

In *Pacifica,* we upheld a declaratory order of the Federal Communications Commission, holding that the broadcast of a recording of a 12-minute monologue entitled "Filthy Words" that had previously been delivered to a live audience "could have been the subject of administrative sanctions." There are significant differences between the order upheld in *Pacifica* and the CDA. First, the order in *Pacifica,* issued by an agency that had been regulating radio stations for decades, targeted a specific broadcast that represented a rather dramatic departure from traditional program content in order to designate when—rather than whether—it would be permissible to air such a program in that particular medium. The CDA's broad categorical prohibitions are not limited to particular times and are not dependent on any evaluation by an agency familiar with the unique characteristics of the Internet.

Second, unlike the CDA, the Commission's declaratory order was not punitive; we expressly refused to decide whether the indecent broadcast "would justify a criminal prosecution." Finally, the Commission's order applied to a medium which as a matter of history had "received the most limited First Amendment protection," in large part because warnings could not adequately protect the listener from unexpected program content. The Internet, however, has no comparable history. Moreover, the District Court found that the risk of encountering indecent material by accident is remote because a series of affirmative steps is required to access specific material.

In *Renton,* we upheld a zoning ordinance that kept adult movie theaters out of residential neighborhoods. The ordinance was aimed, not at the content of the films shown in the theaters, but rather at the "secondary effects"—such as crime and deteriorating property values—that these theaters fostered. According to the Government, the CDA is constitutional because it constitutes a sort of "cyberzoning" on the Internet. But the CDA applies broadly to the entire universe of cyberspace. And the purpose of the CDA is to protect children from the primary effects of "indecent" and "patently offensive" speech, rather than any "secondary" effect of such speech. These precedents, then, surely do not require us to uphold the CDA and are fully consistent with the application of the most stringent review of its provisions.

Regardless of whether the CDA is so vague that it violates the Fifth Amendment, the many ambiguities concerning the scope of its coverage render it problematic for purposes of the First Amendment. For instance, each of the two parts of the CDA uses a different linguistic form. The first uses the word "indecent," while the second speaks of material that "in context, depicts or describes, in terms patently offensive as measured by contemporary community standards, sexual or excretory activities or organs." Given the absence of a definition of either term, this difference in language will provoke uncertainty among speakers about how the two standards relate to each other and just what they mean.

The vagueness of the CDA is a matter of special concern for two reasons. First, the CDA is a content-based regulation of speech. The vagueness of such a regulation raises special First Amendment concerns because of its obvious chilling effect on free speech. Second, the CDA is a criminal statute. In addition to the opprobrium and stigma of a criminal conviction, the CDA threatens violators with penalties including up to two years in prison for each act of violation. The severity of criminal sanctions may well cause speakers to remain silent rather than communicate even arguably unlawful words, ideas, and images.

The Government argues that the statute is no more vague than the obscenity standard this Court established in *Miller v. California* (1973). But that is not so. Just because a definition including three limitations is not vague, it does not follow that one of those limitations, standing by itself, is not vague. Each of *Miller*'s additional two prongs—(1) that, taken as a whole, the material appeal to the "prurient" interest,

and (2) that it "lack serious literary, artistic, political, or scientific value"—critically limits the uncertain sweep of the obscenity definition. The second requirement is particularly important because, unlike the "patently offensive" and "prurient interest" criteria, it is not judged by contemporary community standards. This "societal value" requirement, absent in the CDA, allows appellate courts to impose some limitations and regularity on the definition by setting, as a matter of law, a national floor for socially redeeming value.

We are persuaded that the CDA lacks the precision that the First Amendment requires when a statute regulates the content of speech. In order to deny minors access to potentially harmful speech, the CDA effectively suppresses a large amount of speech that adults have a constitutional right to receive and to address to one another. That burden on adult speech is unacceptable if less restrictive alternatives would be at least as effective in achieving the legitimate purpose that the statute was enacted to serve. It is true that we have repeatedly recognized the governmental interest in protecting children from harmful materials. But that interest does not justify an unnecessarily broad suppression of speech addressed to adults. "Regardless of the strength of the government's interest" in protecting children, "the level of discourse reaching a mailbox simply cannot be limited to that which would be suitable for a sandbox."

In arguing that the CDA does not so diminish adult communication, the Government relies on the incorrect factual premise that prohibiting a transmission whenever it is known that one of its recipients is a minor would not interfere with adult-to-adult communication. The findings of the District Court make clear that this premise is untenable. Given the size of the potential audience for most messages, in the absence of a viable age verification process, the sender must be charged with knowing that one or more minors will likely view it. Knowledge that, for instance, one or more members of a 100-person chat group will be minor—and therefore that it would be a crime to send the group an indecent message—would surely burden communication among adults.

The District Court found that at the time of trial existing technology did not include any effective method for a sender to prevent minors from obtaining access to its communications on the Internet without also denying access to adults. The Court found no effective way to determine the age of a user who is accessing material through e-mail, mail exploders, newsgroups, or chat rooms. As a practical matter, the Court also found that it would be prohibitively expensive for noncommercial—as well as some commercial—speakers who have Web sites to verify that their users are adults. These limitations must inevitably curtail a significant amount of adult communication on the Internet. By contrast, the District Court found that "despite its limitations, currently available *user-based* software suggests that a reasonably effective method by which *parents* can prevent their children from accessing sexually explicit and other material which *parents* may believe is inappropriate for their children will soon be widely available."

The breadth of this content-based restriction of speech imposes an especially heavy burden on the Government to explain why a less restrictive provision would not be as effective as the CDA. It has not done so. Particularly in the light of the absence of any detailed findings by the Congress, or even hearings, addressing the special problems of the CDA, we are persuaded that the CDA is not narrowly tailored if that requirement has any meaning at all. We agree with the District Court's conclusion that the CDA places an unacceptably heavy burden on protected speech, and that the defenses do not constitute the sort of "narrow tailoring" that will save an otherwise patently invalid unconstitutional provision. For the foregoing reasons, the judgment of the district court is affirmed.

JUSTICE O'CONNOR, with whom THE CHIEF JUSTICE joins, concurring in the judgment in part and dissenting in part.

I write separately to explain why I view the Communications Decency Act of 1996 (CDA) as little more than an attempt by Congress to create "adult zones" on the Internet. The creation of "adult zones" is by no means a novel concept. States have long denied minors access to certain establishments frequented by adults. The Court has previously sustained such zoning laws, but only if they respect the First Amendment rights of adults and minors. That is to say, a zoning law is valid if (i) it does not unduly restrict adult access to the material; and (ii) minors have no First Amendment right to read or view the banned material. As applied to the Internet as it exists in 1997, the "display" provision and some applications of the "indecency transmission" and "specific person" provisions fail to adhere to the first of these limiting principles by restricting adults' access to protected materials in certain circumstances. Unlike the Court, however, I would invalidate the provisions only in those circumstances.

Our cases make clear that a "zoning" law is valid only if adults are still able to obtain the regulated speech. If the law does not unduly restrict adults' access to constitutionally protected speech, however, it may be valid. In *Ginsberg v. New York* (1968), for example, the Court sustained a New York law that barred store owners from selling pornographic magazines to minors in part because adults could still buy those magazines. The Court in *Ginsberg* concluded that the New York law created a constitutionally adequate adult zone simply because, on its face, it denied access only to minors. The Court did not question—and therefore necessarily assumed—that an adult zone, once created, would succeed in preserving adults' access while denying minors' access to the regulated speech. Before today, there was no reason to question this assumption, for the Court has previously only considered laws that operated in the physical world, a world that with the twin characteristics of geography and identity enable the establishment's proprietor to prevent children from entering the establishment, but to let adults inside.

The electronic world is fundamentally different. Since users can transmit and receive messages on the Internet without revealing anything about their identities or ages, it is not currently possible to exclude persons from accessing certain messages on the basis of their identity. Cyberspace differs from the physical world in another basic way: Cyberspace is malleable. Thus, it is possible to construct barriers in cyberspace and use them to screen for identity, making cyberspace more like the physical world and, consequently, more amenable to zoning laws. This transformation of cyberspace is already underway. Internet speakers (users who post material on the Internet) have begun to zone cyberspace itself through the use of "gateway" technology. Such technology requires Internet users to enter information about themselves—perhaps an adult identification number or a credit card number—before they can access certain areas of cyberspace, much like a bouncer checks a person's driver's license before admitting him to a nightclub.

Despite this progress, the transformation of cyberspace is not complete. Although gateway technology has been available on the World Wide Web for some time now, it is not ubiquitous in cyberspace, and because without it "there is no means of age verification," cyberspace still remains largely unzoned—and unzoneable. User based zoning is also in its infancy. Although the prospects for the eventual zoning of the Internet appear promising, I agree with the Court that we must evaluate the constitutionality of the CDA as it applies to the Internet as it exists today.

Given the present state of cyberspace, I agree with the Court that the "display" provision cannot pass muster. Until gateway technology is available throughout cyberspace, and it is not in 1997, a speaker cannot be reasonably assured that the speech he displays will reach only adults because it is impossible to confine speech to an "adult zone." Thus, the only way for a speaker to avoid liability under the CDA is to refrain completely from using indecent speech. But this forced silence impinges on the First Amendment right of adults to make and obtain this speech and, for all intents and purposes, "reduce[s] the adult population [on the Internet] to reading only what is fit for children." As a result, the "display" provision cannot withstand scrutiny.

The "indecency transmission" and "specific person" provisions present a closer issue, for they are not unconstitutional in all of their applications. Both provisions are constitutional as applied to a conversation involving only an adult and one or more minors, e.g., when an adult speaker sends an e-mail knowing the addressee is a minor, or when an adult and minor

converse by themselves or with other minors in a chat room. In this context, these provisions are no different from the law we sustained in *Ginsberg*. The analogy to *Ginsberg* breaks down, however, when more than one adult is a party to the conversation. If a minor enters a chat room otherwise occupied by adults, the CDA effectively requires the adults in the room to stop using indecent speech. If they did not, they could be prosecuted under the "indecency transmission" and "specific person" provisions for any indecent statements they make to the group, since they would be transmitting an indecent message to specific persons, one of whom is a minor. The CDA is therefore akin to a law that makes it a crime for a bookstore owner to sell pornographic magazines to anyone once a minor enters his store. Even assuming such a law might be constitutional in the physical world as a reasonable alternative to excluding minors completely from the store, the absence of any means of excluding minors from chat rooms in cyberspace restricts the rights of adults to engage in indecent speech in those rooms.

There is no question that Congress intended to prohibit certain communications between one adult and one or more minors. There is also no question that Congress would have enacted a narrower version of these provisions had it known a broader version would be declared unconstitutional. I would therefore sustain the "indecency transmission" and "specific person" provisions to the extent they apply to the transmission of Internet communications where the party initiating the communication knows that all of the recipients are minors.

Whether the CDA substantially interferes with the First Amendment rights of minors, and thereby runs afoul of the second characteristic of valid zoning laws, presents a closer question. Because the CDA denies minors the right to obtain material that is "patently offensive"—even if it has some redeeming value for minors and even if it does not appeal to their prurient interests—Congress' rejection of the *Ginsberg* "harmful to minors" standard means that the CDA could ban some speech that is "indecent" (i.e., "patently offensive") but that is not obscene as to minors. I do not deny this possibility, but to prevail in a facial challenge, it is not enough for a plaintiff to show "some" overbreadth. Our cases require a proof of "real" and "substantial" overbreadth, *Broadrick v. Oklahoma* (1973), and appellees have not carried their burden in this case. In my view, the universe of speech constitutionally protected as to minors but banned by the CDA—i.e., the universe of materials that is "patently offensive," but which nonetheless has some redeeming value for minors or does not appeal to their prurient interest—is a very small one. Appellees cite no examples of speech falling within this universe and do not attempt to explain why that universe is substantial "in relation to the statute's plainly legitimate sweep." Accordingly, in my view, the CDA does not burden a substantial amount of minors' constitutionally protected speech.

Thus, the constitutionality of the CDA as a zoning law hinges on the extent to which it substantially interferes with the First Amendment rights of adults. Because the rights of adults are infringed only by the "display" provision and by the "indecency transmission" and "specific person" provisions as applied to communications involving more than one adult, I would invalidate the CDA only to that extent. Insofar as the "indecency transmission" and "specific person" provisions prohibit the use of indecent speech in communications between an adult and one or more minors, however, they can and should be sustained. The Court reaches a contrary conclusion, and from that holding I respectfully dissent.

Indianapolis Anti-Pornography Ordinance (1984)

In 1984, the City-County Council of Indianapolis and Marion County, Indiana, pioneered a new approach to regulating pornography. The council concluded that pornography's implicit endorsement of the sexual subordination of women constitutes a form of sex discrimination that degrades and harms all women. It therefore authorized any woman to sue those trafficking in pornography for violating her civil rights. The ordinance was struck down by a federal district court in American Booksellers Association, Inc. v. Hudnut, *and the Supreme Court summarily affirmed that ruling.*

Be it ordered by the City-County Council of the City of Indianapolis and of Marion County, Indiana:

(a) Findings. The City-County Council hereby makes the following findings:

(2) Pornography is a discriminatory practice based on sex because its effect is to deny women equal opportunities in society. Pornography is central in creating and maintaining sex as a basis of discrimination. Pornography is a systematic practice of exploitation and subordination based on sex which differentially harms women. The bigotry and contempt it promotes, with the acts of aggression it fosters, harm women's opportunities for equality of rights in employment, education, access to and use of public accommodations, and acquisition

of real property, and contribute significantly to restricting women in particular from full exercise of citizenship and participation in public life, including in neighborhoods.

(b) It is the purpose of this ordinance

(8) To prevent and prohibit all discriminatory practices of sexual subordination or inequality through pornography.

(g) Discriminatory practice shall mean and include the following:

(4) Trafficking in pornography: The production, sale, exhibition, or distribution of pornography.

(A) City, state and federally funded public libraries or private and public university and college libraries in which pornography is available for study, including on open shelves, shall not be construed to be trafficking in pornography, but special display presentations of pornography in said places is sex discrimination.

(B) The formation of private clubs or associations for purposes of trafficking in pornography is illegal and shall be considered a conspiracy to violate the civil rights of women.

(C) Any woman has a cause of action hereunder as a woman acting against the subordination of women. Any man, child or transsexual who alleges injury by pornography in the way women are injured by it shall also have a cause of action under this chapter.

(5) Coercion into pornographic performance.

(6) Forcing pornography on a person: The forcing of pornography on any woman, man, child or transsexual in any place of employment, in education, in a home, or in any public place, except that a man, child or transsexual must allege and prove injury in the same way that a woman is injured in order to have a cause of action.

(7) Assault or physical attack due to pornography: The assault, physical attack, or injury of any woman, man, child, or transsexual in a way that is directly caused by specific pornography. The injured party shall have a claim for damages against the perpetrator(s), maker(s), distributor(s), seller(s), and exhibitor(s), and for an injunction against the specific pornography's further exhibition, distribution, or sale.

(8) Defenses. Where the materials which are the subject matter of a cause of action under (4), (5), (6), or (7) of this section are pornography, it shall not be a defense that the defendant did not know or intend that the materials were pornography or sex discrimination.

(v) Pornography shall mean the sexually explicit subordination of women, graphically depicted, whether in pictures or words, that includes one or more of the following:

(1) Women are presented as sexual objects who enjoy pain or humiliation; or

(2) Women are presented as sexual objects who experience sexual pleasure in being raped; or

(3) Women are presented as sexual objects tied up or cut up or mutilated or bruised or physically hurt, or as dismembered or truncated or fragmented or severed into body parts; or

(4) Women are presented being penetrated by objects or animals; or

(5) Women are presented in scenarios of degradation, injury, abasement, torture, shown as filthy or inferior, bleeding, bruised, or hurt in a context that makes these conditions sexual.

(bb) Sexually explicit shall mean actual or simulated:

(1) Sexual intercourse, including genital-genital, oral-genital, anal-genital or oral-anal, whether between persons of the same or opposite sex or between women and animals; or

(2) Uncovered exhibition of the genitals, pubic region, buttocks or anus of any person.

Brown v. Entertainment Merchants Association
564 U.S. ___ (2011)

Entertainment Merchants Association, representing the video-games and software industries, filed a pre-enforcement challenge to a California law that restricted the sale or rental of violent video games to minors. The Act covered games "in which the range of options available to a player includes killing, maiming, dismembering, or sexually assaulting an image of a human being, if those acts are depicted" in a manner that "[a] reasonable person, considering the game as a whole, would find appeals to a deviant or morbid interest of minors," that is "patently offensive to prevailing standards in the community as to what is suitable for minors," and that "causes the game, as a whole, to lack serious literary, artistic, political, or scientific value for minors." The District Court concluded that the Act violated the First Amendment and permanently enjoined its enforcement, the Ninth Circuit Court of Appeals affirmed, and the Supreme Court granted certiorari. Opinion of the

Court: Scalia, Kennedy, Ginsburg, Sotomayor, Kagan. Concurring in the judgment: Alito, Roberts. Dissenting opinions: Thomas, Breyer.

JUSTICE SCALIA delivered the opinion of the Court.

California correctly acknowledges that video games qualify for First Amendment protection. The Free Speech Clause exists principally to protect discourse on public matters, but we have long recognized that it is difficult to distinguish politics from entertainment, and dangerous to try. "Everyone is familiar with instances of propaganda through fiction. What is one man's amusement, teaches another's doctrine." *Winters v. New York* (1948). Like the protected books, plays, and movies that preceded them, video games communicate ideas—and even social messages—through many familiar literary devices (such as characters, dialogue, plot, and music) and through features distinctive to the medium (such as the player's interaction with the virtual world). That suffices to confer First Amendment protection. Under our Constitution, "esthetic and moral judgments about art and literature are for the individual to make, not for the Government to decree, even with the mandate or approval of a majority." *United States v. Playboy Entertainment Group, Inc.* (2000). And whatever the challenges of applying the Constitution to ever-advancing technology, "the basic principles of freedom of speech and the press, like the First Amendment's command, do not vary" when a new and different medium for communication appears. *Joseph Burstyn, Inc. v. Wilson* (1952).

The most basic of those principles is this: "As a general matter, government has no power to restrict expression because of its message, its ideas, its subject matter, or its content." *Ashcroft v. American Civil Liberties Union* (2002). There are of course exceptions. These limited areas—such as obscenity, incitement, and fighting words—represent "well-defined and narrowly limited classes of speech, the prevention and punishment of which have never been thought to raise any Constitutional problem."

Last Term, in [*United States v. Stevens* (2010)], we held that new categories of unprotected speech may not be added to the list by a legislature that concludes certain speech is too harmful to be tolerated. *Stevens* concerned a federal statute purporting to criminalize the creation, sale, or possession of certain depictions of animal cruelty. The statute covered depictions "in which a living animal is intentionally maimed, mutilated, tortured, wounded, or killed" if that harm to the animal was illegal where the "the creation, sale, or possession took place." A saving clause largely borrowed from our obscenity jurisprudence, exempted depictions with "serious religious, political, scientific, educational, journalistic, historical, or artistic value." We held that statute to be an impermissible content-based restriction on speech. There was no American tradition of forbidding the depiction of animal cruelty—though States have long had laws against committing it.

The Government argued in *Stevens* that lack of a historical warrant did not matter; that it could create new categories of unprotected speech by applying a "simple balancing test" that weighs the value of a particular category of speech against its social costs and then punishes that category of speech if it fails the test. We emphatically rejected that "startling and dangerous" proposition. Without persuasive evidence that a novel restriction on content is part of a long (if heretofore unrecognized) tradition of proscription, a legislature may not revise the "judgment of the American people," embodied in the First Amendment, "that the benefits of its restrictions on the Government outweigh the costs." That holding controls this case. As in *Stevens*, California has tried to make violent-speech regulation look like obscenity regulation by appending a saving clause required for the latter. That does not suffice. Our cases have been clear that the obscenity exception to the First Amendment does not cover whatever a legislature finds shocking, but only depictions of "sexual conduct."

Because speech about violence is not obscene, it is of no consequence that California's statute mimics the New York statute regulating obscenity-for-minors that we upheld in *Ginsberg v. New York* (1968). That case approved a prohibition on the sale to minors of sexual material that would be obscene from the perspective of a child. We held that the legislature could "adjust the definition of obscenity 'to social realities by permitting the appeal of this type of material to be assessed in terms of the sexual interests' of minors." And because "obscenity is not protected expression," the New York statute could be sustained so long as the legislature's judgment that the proscribed materials were harmful to children "was not irrational."

The California Act is something else entirely. It does not adjust the boundaries of an existing category of unprotected speech to ensure that a definition designed for adults is not uncritically applied to children. California does not argue that it is empowered to prohibit selling offensively violent works to adults—and it is wise not to, since that is but a hair's breadth from the argument rejected in *Stevens*. Instead, it wishes to create a wholly new category of content-based regulation that is permissible only for speech directed at children. That is unprecedented and mistaken. "Minors are entitled to a significant measure of First Amendment protection, and only in relatively narrow and well-defined circumstances may government bar public dissemination of protected materials to them." *Erznoznik v. Jacksonville* (1975). No doubt a State possesses legitimate power to protect children from harm, but that does not include a free-floating power to restrict the ideas to which children may be exposed.

California's argument would fare better if there were a longstanding tradition in this country of specially restricting children's access to depictions of violence, but there is none. Certainly the books we give children to read— or read to them when they are younger—contain no shortage of gore. Grimm's Fairy Tales, for example, are grim indeed. As her just deserts for trying to poison Snow White, the wicked queen is made to dance in red hot slippers "till she fell dead on the floor, a sad example of envy and jealousy." Cinderella's evil stepsisters have their eyes pecked out by doves. And Hansel and Gretel (children!) kill their captor by baking her in an oven. High-school reading lists are full of similar fare.

California claims that video games present special problems because they are "interactive," in that the player participates in the violent action on screen and determines its outcome. The latter feature is nothing new: Since at least the publication of "The Adventures of You: Sugarcane Island" in 1969, young readers of choose-your-own-adventure stories have been able to make decisions that determine the plot by following instructions about which page to turn to. As for the argument that video games enable participation in the violent action, that seems to us more a matter of degree than of kind. As Judge Posner has observed, all literature is interactive. "The better it is, the more interactive. Literature when it is successful draws the reader into the story, makes him identify with the characters, invites him to judge them and quarrel with them, to experience their joys and sufferings as the reader's own." *American Amusement Machine Assn. v. Kendrick* (CA7 2001).

Justice Alito has done considerable independent research to identify video games in which "the violence is astounding." "Victims are

dismembered, decapitated, disemboweled, set on fire, and chopped into little pieces. Blood gushes, splatters, and pools." He recounts all these disgusting video games in order to disgust us—but disgust is not a valid basis for restricting expression. And the same is true of Justice Alito's description of those video games he has discovered that have a racial or ethnic motive for their violence—"ethnic cleansing of African Americans, Latinos, or Jews." To what end does he relate this? Does it increase the "aggressiveness" that California wishes to suppress? Who knows? But it does arouse the reader's ire, and the reader's desire to put an end to this horrible message. Thus, ironically, Justice Alito's argument highlights the precise danger posed by the California Act: that the ideas expressed by speech—whether it be violence, or gore, or racism—and not its objective effects, may be the real reason for governmental proscription.

Because the Act imposes a restriction on the content of protected speech, it is invalid unless California can demonstrate that it passes strict scrutiny—that is, unless it is justified by a compelling government interest and is narrowly drawn to serve that interest. The State must specifically identify an "actual problem" in need of solving, and the curtailment of free speech must be actually necessary to the solution. California cannot meet that standard. At the outset, it acknowledges that it cannot show a direct causal link between violent video games and harm to minors. Rather, relying upon our decision in *Turner Broadcasting System, Inc. v. FCC* (1994), the State claims that it need not produce such proof because the legislature can make a predictive judgment that such a link exists, based on competing psychological studies. But reliance on *Turner Broadcasting* is misplaced. That decision applied intermediate scrutiny to a content-neutral regulation. California's burden is much higher, and because it bears the risk of uncertainty, ambiguous proof will not suffice. The State's evidence is not compelling. California relies primarily on the research of Dr. Craig Anderson and a few other research psychologists whose studies purport to show a connection between exposure to violent video games and harmful effects on children. These studies have been rejected by every court to consider them, and with good reason: They do not prove that violent video games cause minors to act aggressively (which would at least be a beginning). Instead, nearly all of the research is based on correlation, not evidence of causation, and most of the studies suffer from significant, admitted flaws in methodology. They show at best some correlation between exposure to violent entertainment and minuscule real-world effects, such as children's feeling more aggressive or making louder noises in the few minutes after playing a violent game than after playing a nonviolent game.

Even taking for granted Dr. Anderson's conclusions that violent video games produce some effect on children's feelings of aggression, those effects are both small and indistinguishable from effects produced by other media. In his testimony in a similar lawsuit, Dr. Anderson admitted that the "effect sizes" of children's exposure to violent video games are "about the same" as that produced by their exposure to violence on television. And he admits that the same effects have been found when children watch cartoons starring Bugs Bunny or the Road Runner, or when they play video games like Sonic the Hedgehog that are rated "E" (appropriate for all ages), or even when they "view a picture of a gun."

Of course, California has (wisely) declined to restrict Saturday morning cartoons, the sale of games rated for young children, or the distribution of pictures of guns. The consequence is that its regulation is wildly underinclusive when judged against its asserted justification, which in our view is alone enough to defeat it. Underinclusiveness raises serious doubts about whether the government is in fact pursuing the interest it invokes, rather than disfavoring a particular speaker or viewpoint. Here, California has singled out the purveyors of video games for disfavored treatment—at least when compared to booksellers, cartoonists, and movie producers—and has given no persuasive reason why.

The Act is also seriously underinclusive in another respect—and a respect that renders irrelevant the contentions of the concurrence and the dissents that video games are qualitatively different from other portrayals of vio-

lence. The California Legislature is perfectly willing to leave this dangerous, mind-altering material in the hands of children so long as one parent (or even an aunt or uncle) says it's OK. And there are not even any requirements as to how this parental or avuncular relationship is to be verified; apparently the child's or putative parent's, aunt's, or uncle's say-so suffices. That is not how one addresses a serious social problem.

California claims that the Act is justified in aid of parental authority: By requiring that the purchase of violent video games can be made only by adults, the Act ensures that parents can decide what games are appropriate. At the outset, we note our doubts that punishing third parties for conveying protected speech to children just in case their parents disapprove of that speech is a proper governmental means of aiding parental authority. Accepting that position would largely vitiate the rule that "only in relatively narrow and well-defined circumstances may government bar public dissemination of protected materials to minors." But leaving that aside, California cannot show that the Act's restrictions meet a substantial need of parents who wish to restrict their children's access to violent video games but cannot do so. The video-game industry has in place a voluntary rating system designed to inform consumers about the content of games. The system, implemented by the Entertainment Software Rating Board (ESRB), assigns age-specific ratings to each video game submitted. The Video Software Dealers Association encourages retailers to prominently display information about the ESRB system in their stores; to refrain from renting or selling adults-only games to minors; and to rent or sell "M" rated games to minors only with parental consent. In 2009, the Federal Trade Commission (FTC) found that, as a result of this system, "the video game industry outpaces the movie and music industries" in "(1) restricting target-marketing of mature-rated products to children; (2) clearly and prominently disclosing rating information; and (3) restricting children's access to mature-rated products at retail." This system does much to ensure that minors cannot purchase seriously violent games on their own, and that parents who care about the matter can readily evaluate the games their children bring home. Filling the remaining modest gap in concerned-parents' control can hardly be a compelling state interest.

And finally, the Act's purported aid to parental authority is vastly overinclusive. Not all of the children who are forbidden to purchase violent video games on their own have parents who care whether they purchase violent video games. While some of the legislation's effect may indeed be in support of what some parents of the restricted children actually want, its entire effect is only in support of what the State thinks parents ought to want. This is not the narrow tailoring to "assisting parents" that restriction of First Amendment rights requires.

California's effort to regulate violent video games is the latest episode in a long series of failed attempts to censor violent entertainment for minors. While we have pointed out above that some of the evidence brought forward to support the harmfulness of video games is unpersuasive, we do not mean to demean or disparage the concerns that underlie the attempt to regulate them—concerns that may and doubtless do prompt a good deal of parental oversight. We have no business passing judgment on the view of the California Legislature that violent video games (or, for that matter, any other forms of speech) corrupt the young or harm their moral development. Our task is only to say whether or not such works constitute a "well-defined and narrowly limited class of speech, the prevention and punishment of which have never been thought to raise any Constitutional problem," *Chaplinsky*[*v. New Hampshire*], (the answer plainly is no); and if not, whether the regulation of such works is justified by that high degree of necessity we have described as a compelling state interest (it is not). Even where the protection of children is the object, the constitutional limits on governmental action apply. We affirm the judgment below.

JUSTICE ALITO, with whom THE CHIEF JUSTICE joins, concurring in the judgment.

The California statute in this case represents a pioneering effort to address what the state legislature and others regard as a potentially serious social problem: the effect of exceptionally violent video games on impressionable minors, who often spend countless hours immersed in the alternative worlds that these games create. Although the California statute is well intentioned, its terms are not framed with the precision that the Constitution demands, and I therefore agree with the Court that this particular law cannot be sustained.

I disagree, however, with the approach taken in the Court's opinion. In the view of the Court, all those concerned about the effects of violent video games—federal and state legislators, educators, social scientists, and parents—are unduly fearful, for violent video games really present no serious problem. Spending hour upon hour controlling the actions of a character who guns down scores of innocent victims is not different in "kind" from reading a description of violence in a work of literature.

The Court is sure of this; I am not. When all of the characteristics of video games are taken into account, there is certainly a reasonable basis for thinking that the experience of playing a video game may be quite different from the experience of reading a book, listening to a radio broadcast, or viewing a movie. And if this is so, then for at least some minors, the effects of playing violent video games may also be quite different. The Court acts prematurely in dismissing this possibility out of hand. I would hold only that the particular law at issue here fails to provide the clear notice that the Constitution requires. I would not squelch legislative efforts to deal with what is perceived by some to be a significant and developing social problem. If differently framed statutes are enacted by the States or by the Federal Government, we can consider the constitutionality of those laws when cases challenging them are presented to us.

JUSTICE THOMAS, dissenting.

The Court's decision today does not comport with the original public understanding of the First Amendment. When interpreting a constitutional provision, "the goal is to discern the most likely public understanding of that provision at the time it was adopted." *McDonald v. Chicago* (2010). As originally understood, the First Amendment's protection against laws "abridging the freedom of speech" did not extend to all speech. "There are certain well-defined and narrowly limited classes of speech, the prevention and punishment of which have never been thought to raise any Constitutional problem." *Chaplinsky v. New Hampshire* (1942). Laws regulating such speech do not "abridge the freedom of speech" because such speech is understood to fall outside "the freedom of speech." In my view, the "practices and beliefs held by the Founders" reveal another category of excluded speech: speech to minor children bypassing their parents. The historical evidence shows that the founding generation believed parents had absolute authority over their minor children and expected parents to use that authority to direct the proper development of their children. It would be absurd to suggest that such a society understood "the freedom of speech" to include a right to speak to minors (or a corresponding right of minors to access speech) without going through the minors' parents. The founding generation would not have considered it an abridgment of "the freedom of speech" to support parental authority by restricting speech that bypasses minors' parents.

Admittedly, the original public understanding of a constitutional provision does not always comport with modern sensibilities. This, however, is not such a case. Although much has changed in this country since the Revolution, the notion that parents have authority over their children and that the law can support that authority persists today. For example, at least some States make it a crime to lure or entice a minor away from the minor's parent. Every State in the Union still establishes a minimum age for marriage without parental or judicial consent. Minors remain subject to curfew laws across the country and cannot unilaterally consent to most medical procedures.

JUSTICE BREYER, dissenting.

In determining whether the statute is unconstitutional, I would apply both this Court's "vagueness" precedents and a strict form of First Amendment scrutiny. In doing so, the special First Amendment category I find relevant is not (as the Court claims) the category of "depictions of violence," but rather the category of "protection of children." This Court

has held that the "power of the state to control the conduct of children reaches beyond the scope of its authority over adults." *Prince v. Massachusetts* (1944). And the "regulation of communication addressed to [children] need not conform to the requirements of the First Amendment in the same way as those applicable to adults." *Ginsberg v. New York.*

II

In my view, California's statute provides "fair notice of what is prohibited," and consequently it is not impermissibly vague. *United States v. Williams* (2008). *Ginsberg* explains why that is so. The Court there considered a New York law that forbade the sale to minors of a "picture, photograph, drawing, sculpture, motion picture film, or similar visual representation or image of a person or portion of the human body which depicts nudity" that "predominately appeals to the prurient, shameful or morbid interest of minors," and "is patently offensive to prevailing standards in the adult community as a whole with respect to what is suitable material for minors," and "is utterly without redeeming social importance for minors." This Court wrote that the statute was sufficiently clear.

Comparing the language of California's statute with the language of New York's statute, it is difficult to find any vagueness-related difference. Why are the words "kill," "maim," and "dismember" any more difficult to understand than the word "nudity?" All that is required for vagueness purposes is that the terms "kill," "maim," and "dismember" give fair notice as to what they cover, which they do. The remainder of California's definition copies, almost word for word, the language this Court used in *Miller v. California* (1973), in permitting a total ban on material that satisfied its definition (one enforced with criminal penalties). Consequently, for purposes of this facial challenge, I would not find the statute unconstitutionally vague.

III

Like the majority, I believe that the California law must be "narrowly tailored" to further a "compelling interest," without there being a "less restrictive" alternative that would be "at least as effective." *Reno v. American Civil Liberties Union* (1997). I would not apply this strict standard "mechanically." Rather, I would evaluate the degree to which the statute injures speech-related interests, the nature of the potentially-justifying "compelling interests," the degree to which the statute furthers that interest, the nature and effectiveness of possible alternatives, and, in light of this evaluation, whether, overall, "the statute works speech-related harm out of proportion to the benefits that the statute seeks to provide."

California's law imposes no more than a modest restriction on expression. The statute prevents no one from playing a video game, it prevents no adult from buying a video game, and it prevents no child or adolescent from obtaining a game provided a parent is willing to help. All it prevents is a child or adolescent from buying, without a parent's assistance, a gruesomely violent video game of a kind that the industry itself tells us it wants to keep out of the hands of those under the age of 17.

The interest that California advances in support of the statute is compelling. It consists of both (1) the "basic" parental claim "to authority in their own household to direct the rearing of their children," which makes it proper to enact "laws designed to aid discharge of [parental] responsibility," and (2) the State's "independent interest in the well-being of its youth." And where these interests work in tandem, it is not fatally "underinclusive" for a State to advance its interests in protecting children against the special harms present in an interactive video game medium through a default rule that still allows parents to provide their children with what their parents wish.

There is considerable evidence that California's statute significantly furthers this compelling interest. [Justice Breyer then reviews several studies.] Experts debate the conclusions of all these studies. Like many, perhaps most, studies of human behavior, each study has its critics, and some of those critics have produced studies of their own in which they reach different conclusions. I, like most judges, lack the social science expertise to say definitively who is right. But associations of public health professionals who do possess that expertise have reviewed many of these studies and found a significant risk that violent video games, when compared with more passive media, are particularly likely to cause children harm. I would find sufficient grounds in these studies and expert opinions for this Court to defer to an elected legislature's conclusion that the video games in question are particularly likely to harm children. For these reasons, I respectfully dissent.

6

Freedom of Religion

CHAPTER OUTLINE

"Congress shall make no law respecting an establishment of religion, or prohibiting the free exercise thereof." The religion clauses of the First Amendment thus impose two restrictions: the Establishment Clause requires a degree of separation between church and state, and the Free Exercise Clause recognizes a sphere of religious liberty that Congress cannot invade. For almost 150 years, the Supreme Court had little occasion to construe these constitutional provisions, but since then it has decided more than eighty religion cases. The expansion of governmental activity impinging on religious practices and religiously motivated action has contributed to the rise in litigation; so has increasing religious diversity in the United States. Most important was the incorporation of the religion clauses in *Cantwell v. Connecticut* (1940) and *Everson v. Board of Education* (1947), which brought state and local enactments under federal constitutional scrutiny for the first time. The Court's greater involvement in disputes over religion has led to intense controversy. This chapter analyzes the continuing debate over the meaning of the Establishment and Free Exercise Clauses.

ESTABLISHMENT OF RELIGION

Everson and the Purposes of the Establishment Clause

In *Everson v. Board of Education* (1947), the Supreme Court outlined the interpretation of the Establishment Clause that guided its decisions for several decades. Although the justices split 5–4 in upholding New Jersey's program of covering the cost of bus transportation for students attending private (including sectarian) schools, all the justices agreed that the Establishment Clause was meant to erect a "wall of separation" between church and state. Justice Hugo Black summarized the Court's position:

> The "establishment of religion" clause of the First Amendment means at least this: Neither a state nor the Federal Government can set up a church. Neither can pass laws which aid one religion, aid all religions, or prefer one religion over another. Neither can force nor influence a person to go to or to remain away from church against his will or force him to profess a belief or disbelief in any religion. No person can be punished for entertaining or professing religious beliefs or disbeliefs, for church attendance or non-attendance. No tax in any amount, large or small, can be levied to support any religious activities or institutions, whatever they may be called, or whatever form they may adopt to teach or practice religion. Neither a state nor the Federal Government can, openly or secretly, participate in the affairs of any religious organizations or groups and vice versa.

Three aspects of Black's statement deserve particular emphasis. First, the Court held that the Establishment Clause imposes restrictions on state activity as stringent as those imposed on the federal government. Second, it ruled that the Establishment Clause prohibits any aid to religion and requires strict neutrality not only among religions but also between religion and irreligion. Finally, as the divisions on the Court in *Everson* show, Black's standard did not lend itself to automatic application, and thus its endorsement by the Court did not foreclose disagreement in future Establishment Clause cases.

To support its interpretation of the Establishment Clause, the Court looked to the Founders' aims in adopting this provision. Yet in seeking those aims, the justices focused not on the constitutional text or the debates in the First Congress but on the struggle for religious liberty in Virginia during the 1780s. Why did this struggle, which culminated in the disestablishment of the Episcopal Church, offer the key to understanding the

Establishment Clause? According to the Court, the long dispute in Virginia had engaged the attention of the other states, several of which were influenced by its outcome to eliminate their own religious establishments. Thus, the Court reasoned, the victory for religious liberty in Virginia created a national climate of opinion favorable to the separation of church and state. Even more important, the leaders of the antiestablishment forces in Virginia, particularly James Madison, played a key role in the creation and adoption of the Bill of Rights. The Court therefore concluded that the views in favor of a strict separation of church and state expressed by Madison and others during the Virginia campaign were incorporated into the First Amendment.

Although the Court proposed various standards for detecting violations of the Establishment Clause, the decisions handed down until the 1980s largely reflected the view of the clause's purposes outlined in *Everson*. Therefore, the Court consistently ruled against government attempts to promote particular religious views. Examples include *School District of Abington Township v. Schempp* (1963), in which the Court invalidated requirements for Bible reading and the recitation of the Lord's Prayer in the public schools, and *Epperson v. Arkansas* (1968), in which it overturned an Arkansas law that prohibited teaching about evolution. The Court also struck down enactments penalizing individuals for their religious beliefs or disbelief: in *Torasco v. Watkins* (1961), it unanimously invalidated a Maryland constitutional provision that established a religious test for public office, and in *McDaniel v. Paty* (1978), it struck down a Tennessee law that disqualified clergy from serving as state legislators. Finally, the justices invalidated more evenhanded efforts to aid religion on the ground that they violated governmental neutrality between religion and irreligion. New York's establishment of a nondenominational prayer for public school children, struck down in *Engel v. Vitale* (1962), fell into this category, as did a Champaign, Illinois, program of releasing students from classes for religious instruction on school premises, invalidated in *McCollum v. Board of Education* (1948).

Alternatives to *Everson*

Ever since *Everson,* some scholars have insisted that the justices' focus on the Virginia struggle for religious liberty led them to misinterpret the religion clauses of the First Amendment.[1] Drawing upon this research in his dissent in *Wallace v. Jaffree* (1985), Justice William Rehnquist presented a substantially different account of the Establishment Clause. According to Rehnquist, the debate in the First Congress showed that the Founders did not envision a "wall of separation" between church and state. Because most members of the Founding generation believed that political liberty was more secure where religion flourished, they did not oppose using religious means, including nondiscriminatory aid to religion, to achieve valid governmental ends. Nor did they object to governmental accommodation of the religious character of the American people. According to Rehnquist, governmental practice for more than a century after the ratification of the First Amendment reflected this view. As long as the federal government neither established a national church nor gave preference to a particular religion, its actions supporting or accommodating religion did not violate the Establishment Clause.

Acceptance of this alternative interpretation of the Establishment Clause does not require repudiation of all the Court's decisions. If laws mandating prayer and Bible reading in public schools entail governmental support for particular religious views, then their invalidation by the Court was correct. Equally unexceptionable were the Court's decisions in *McGowan v. Maryland* (1961), upholding Sunday closing laws, and in *Walz v. Tax Commission* (1970), upholding tax exemptions for churches, in that the challenged programs served legitimate governmental purposes. And rulings that are difficult to square with *Everson*—such as *Lynch v. Donnelly* (1984), permitting inclusion of a crèche in a Christmas display on public property, and *Town of Grace v. Galloway* (2014), upholding prayers held at the beginning of meetings of a town board—might be upheld as accommodations of the populace's religious beliefs.

On the other hand, some Court rulings cannot be reconciled with Chief Justice Rehnquist's interpretation of the Establishment Clause. The Court's invalidation of Alabama's moment-of-silence statute in *Jaffree* is a prime example because government merely accommodated students' religious beliefs without favoring any particular creed. The same could be said of *Lee v. Weisman* (1992), in which the Court struck down the practice of having clergy offer prayers at public school graduations, and *McCreary County v. American Civil Liberties Union* (2005), in which the Court invalidated a display of the Ten Commandments in a courthouse. Even more important deviations are the Court's rulings on aid to nonpublic schools, to which we shall turn shortly.

Other justices have also sought an alternative to the strict separation of church and state endorsed in *Everson*. Several have suggested that the basic concern underlying the Establishment Clause is not separation but governmental neutrality both among religions and between religion and nonreligion. According to this view, governmental endorsement of particular religions or religion in general violates the Establishment Clause. Yet not every governmental action that benefits religion or religious groups violates neutrality. Indeed, a concern for governmental neutrality explains some Court rulings invalidating state policies that discriminated against religion, even though the states argued that failure to do so would violate the separation of church and state. In *Zobrest v. Catalina Foothills School District* (1993), for example, the Court rejected the state's claim that its provision of a sign-language interpreter to a deaf child attending a parochial school would violate the Establishment Clause because it would aid in the transmission of religious teaching to the student. According to the Court, governmental neutrality required that the state provide this service evenhandedly to all deaf students, regardless of whether they chose a secular or a religious education. Similarly, in *Rosenberger v. University of Virginia* (1995), the Court upheld a challenge to the university's refusal to subsidize publication of a religious magazine published by a student group. If the university funded secular publications by student groups, the Court held, its failure to fund the religious publications based on their content discriminated against religious expression and thus violated neutrality.

Aid to Education

Perhaps the most difficult Establishment Clause question faced by the justices has been the validity of governmental aid to programs that benefit both sectarian and nonsectarian institutions. *Everson v. Board of Education* illustrates the difficulties. On the one hand, the state's reimbursement for the cost of transporting children to sectarian schools in *Everson* facilitates attendance at those schools and thus seems inconsistent with the no-aid standard announced in *Everson*. On the other hand, for the state to deny transportation to students merely because they attend religious schools would appear to reflect governmental hostility to, rather than neutrality toward, religion. As the expansion of governmental aid programs has made the consequences of exclusion from them more severe, conflicts over such programs have increased in both frequency and intensity.

Initially, the Court concluded that some aid programs were constitutionally permissible. In *Everson* itself, the Court upheld New Jersey's transportation program, and in *Board of Education v. Allen* (1968) it rejected a challenge to a New York law requiring local school boards to lend textbooks to students in private and parochial schools.[2] Although these programs arguably facilitated attendance at sectarian schools, the Court noted that the aid served legitimate secular purposes, went to the students rather than to religious institutions, and did not directly assist those institutions in accomplishing their religious objectives. However, dissenters in these cases insisted that the programs violated the Establishment Clause's no-aid requirement and that the textbooks at issue in *Allen,* whatever their content, could be used to promote religious belief. Apparently, these arguments had some effect, for the Court in subsequent cases struck down various programs providing instructional materials and auxiliary services to parochial schools.

The Court first reviewed major aid programs to private (including sectarian) schools in *Lemon v. Kurtzman* (1971). At issue were Pennsylvania's program directly reimbursing nonpublic elementary and secondary schools for the costs of teachers' salaries, textbooks, and instructional materials in specific secular subjects, and Rhode Island's providing a 15 percent salary supplement to teachers of secular subjects in nonpublic elementary and secondary schools. With only a single dissent, the Court invalidated both programs. Speaking for the Court, Chief Justice Warren Burger announced a three-pronged test, culled from prior Court decisions, for programs challenged under the Establishment Clause: "First, the statute must have a secular legislative purpose; second, its principal or primary effect must be one that neither advances nor inhibits religion; finally, the statute must not foster an excessive entanglement with religion." Applying this test to the programs in *Lemon,* Burger concluded that although both had secular legislative purposes, both involved excessive governmental entanglement with the sectarian schools. Sectarian elementary and secondary education, he noted, seeks to inculcate religious belief, not only through religious instruction but also by creating a pervasively religious atmosphere in the schools. And because all aspects of sectarian elementary and secondary education promote the schools' religious goals, aid to such schools unconstitutionally involves government in fostering religious belief. Even if a school sought to compartmentalize its religious and secular instruction, intrusive governmental policing of the school's operations would be required to ensure that the aid served only secular purposes. Finally, such aid programs had the effect of promoting political divisions along religious lines, "one of the principal evils against which the First Amendment was intended to protect."

Nevertheless, in *Tilton v. Richardson* (1971), the Court sustained the constitutionality of the Higher Education Facilities Act of 1963, under which private colleges received federal grants and loans to construct buildings to be used solely for secular purposes.[3] Over the protests of three members of the *Lemon* majority, Chief Justice Burger distinguished the program in *Tilton* from those invalidated in *Lemon* on two bases: the colleges receiving funds did not inject religious teaching into their secular courses or view religious indoctrination as one of their primary functions, and the character of the aid—one time, single purpose, and nonideological—precluded both political divisions along sectarian lines and excessive administrative entanglements.

In cases involving aid to nonpublic elementary and secondary education decided by the Court from 1971 to 1997, *Lemon's* emphasis on the educational mission of the schools receiving aid played a crucial role. When states attempt to ensure that aid is not used to advance religion by policing its use, their programs run the risk of invalidation on entanglement grounds. However, state aid without policing may have a primary effect of advancing religion because the Court has held that religious education and secular education are inextricably mixed in sectarian elementary and secondary schools. Although this appears to preclude any aid to sectarian schools violates the Constitution, the Court did not take that position. Instead, it attempted to distinguish between aid that advanced the schools' religious mission and aid that did not.

However, the Court splintered badly in considering specific aid programs. Its rulings were difficult to reconcile and, insofar as they were reconcilable, seemed to rest on rather tenuous distinctions. For example, in *Board of Education v. Allen* (1968), the Court upheld lending textbooks to students in nonpublic schools, but in *Wolman v. Walter* (1977), it invalidated lending other instructional materials, such as maps, films, and laboratory equipment. In *Levitt v. Committee for Public Education* (1973), it struck down reimbursement for state-mandated testing when the tests were prepared by parochial school personnel, but in *Committee for Public Education v. Regan* (1980), it upheld reimbursement when the tests were prepared by the state. Finally, in *Zobrest v. Catalina Foothills School District* (1993), it upheld state provision of a sign-language interpreter to a deaf student attending a sectarian school, but in *Aguilar v. Felton* (1985), it struck down state provision of remedial and enrichment programs by public school personnel in sectarian schools. As Justice Byron White wryly noted in *Committee for Public Education v. Regan*, the Court's rulings "sacrifice[d] clarity and predictability for flexibility." This, of course, created problems for states attempting to provide aid to students in sectarian schools without running afoul of constitutional limitations. Indeed, the number of school-aid cases coming before the Court testified to the difficulties that states had in discerning the line between permissible and impermissible programs.

The problem was not merely that the three-pronged test developed in *Lemon* was difficult to apply or that its requirement of monitoring aid without entanglement created, in Chief Justice Rehnquist's words, an "insoluble paradox." Critics both on and off the Court complained that the problem went much deeper. The Court's approach prevented government from pursuing legitimate secular ends, such as provision of education, through programs that benefit religious institutions (among other institutions) but are neutral between religion and nonreligion.

A fundamental shift in the Court's approach occurred in *Zelman v. Simmons-Harris* (2002), in which a five-member majority upheld a system of tuition vouchers that enabled students in Cleveland to attend a school of their parents' choosing, whether public or private. In his opinion for the Court, Chief Justice Rehnquist repudiated three key components of the Court's position in *Lemon v. Kurtzman*. First, Rehnquist maintained that in evaluating programs of governmental aid, the Court should uphold them if they meet the first two criteria enunciated in *Lemon* (secular purpose and a primary effect that neither advances nor inhibits religion). In doing so, he downgraded the third *Lemon* criterion (excessive entanglement between government and religion), arguing that it was merely one element relevant in determining a program's primary effect. Second, Rehnquist insisted that governmental aid to religious schools, if provided as part of a general program of aid to education and distributed without regard to the religious or nonreligious character of the recipient schools, satisfied the constitutional requirement of neutrality. Government programs that do not employ religion as a criterion in determining what schools or students receive aid should not, he argued, be seen as having a primary effect of advancing religion. Finally, Rehnquist shifted the focus from whether the schools receiving aid were pervasively religious, a crucial factor in *Lemon*, to whether funds went to such schools as a result of "true private choice." When private choice operates, any religious indoctrination that students receive is the result of their own (or their parents') free choice and thus cannot be ascribed to the government.

FREE EXERCISE OF RELIGION

The Free Exercise Clause ensures that individuals can pursue their religious convictions without impediment, and the multiplicity of thriving denominations in the United States today indicates that religious liberty is flourishing. This is not primarily the result of Supreme Court rulings. On occasion, the Court has confronted discrimination against a particular religious group—in *Church of Lukumi Babalu Aye v. Hialeah* (1993), for example, it struck down an ordinance directed against the Santeria religion, which employs animal sacrifice as one of its rites. But perhaps because no single denomination is predominant, overt governmental hostility toward particular religions has seldom posed a serious problem. The free-exercise cases coming to the Court typically involve a more delicate issue: how to resolve conflicts between governmental regulations serving secular ends and the demands of individuals' religious beliefs.

Governmental regulations can burden or conflict with the claims of conscience in various ways. Some regulations may place an indirect burden on particular groups of believers. An example is the Pennsylvania Sunday closing law, upheld in *Braunfeld v. Brown* (1961). The law put Orthodox Jews and other Sabbatarians at an economic disadvantage because it obliged them to close their businesses on a second day, in addition to the one required by their religious beliefs, whereas Christians could meet the demands of both law and religion by closing on Sunday. Other regulations establish eligibility requirements for governmental benefits that force believers to choose between their religious convictions and those benefits. Thus, South Carolina denied unemployment compensation to a Seventh-Day Adventist who refused jobs that required her to work on Saturday (her Sabbath), based on a state law requiring potential recipients to accept "available suitable work." (The Court in *Sherbert v. Verner* [1963] ruled that this denial of benefits violated the free exercise of religion.) Still other laws oblige individuals to perform or refrain from actions in violation of their religious convictions. Among the cases raising such issues are *Jacobson v. Massachusetts* (1905), in which the Court upheld compulsory vaccination for smallpox despite resistance on religious grounds, and *Goldman v. Weinberger* (1986), in which the Court rejected the claim of an Orthodox Jewish psychologist that he should be permitted to wear a yarmulke while on duty in uniform at a military hospital. Finally, governmental actions may make it difficult for adherents of site-specific religions to practice their faith. In *Lyng v. Northwest Indian Cemetery Protective Association* (1988), for example, the Court refused to block development of portions of a national forest, even though Native American groups viewed the land as sacred.

Braunfeld and *Sherbert* signaled a major shift in the Court's interpretation of the Free Exercise Clause. Before 1960, the Court relied on the secular regulation rule in evaluating free-exercise claims. Under this rule, a law was invalid if it did not serve legitimate, nonreligious governmental ends or if it was directed against particular sects. If those requirements were met, however, the fact that the law conflicted with some persons' perceived religious obligations did not invalidate it or qualify them for exemptions. According to this interpretation, the Constitution does not require government to accord special recognition to religious beliefs or religiously motivated behavior. To hold that religious claims should prevail over the accomplishment of government's legitimate aims, the Court maintained, would be to admit their superior validity—a position that conflicts with the neutrality toward religion enjoined by the First Amendment. By granting religious exemptions from general legislation, moreover, government in effect could be providing an inducement for individuals to profess particular religious beliefs. Thus, even when striking down enactments challenged on religious grounds, as in *West Virginia Board of Education v. Barnette* (1943), the Court emphasized that believers and nonbelievers alike were exempt from their requirements.

In *Braunfeld*, Chief Justice Earl Warren enunciated a more exacting standard for evaluating legislation challenged on free-exercise grounds. In upholding Pennsylvania's Sunday closing law, he emphasized that the state could not achieve its important secular goal of a uniform day of rest through any alternative means that was less burdensome on religious practice. Thus, laws that imposed a substantial burden on religious practices would be upheld only if they served an important state aim and that aim could not be advanced by a less restrictive means. The latter criterion provided the basis of the *Sherbert* ruling, in which Justice William Brennan, speaking for the Court, observed that even if South Carolina's aim of deterring fraudulent claims was a compelling one, it had not demonstrated that less restrictive means of preventing fraud were ineffective. In *Wisconsin v. Yoder* (1972), the Court emphasized the first aspect of Warren's test, ruling that requiring Amish children to attend school beyond the eighth grade did not serve an important state purpose.

This more stringent free-exercise standard sought to reduce conflicts between legal and religious obligations by extending greater protection to religiously motivated conduct. Proponents hailed the standard's emphasis on accommodation as consistent with the solicitude for religious commitments and respect for the autonomy of religious organizations mandated by the First Amendment. They emphasized that such accommodations were needed because the expanding scope of governmental regulation increased the frequency of collisions between secular and religious requirements. And adoption of this standard did have an immediate beneficial effect on legislation, stimulating governmental efforts to accommodate religious convictions in designing programs.

The consequences of the Court's new approach were not all positive, however. The Court's approach required the justices to balance the claims of government against those of religious adherents and thus suffered from the difficulty common to balancing tests: the outcome of the balancing often depends on who is doing it. In addition, if religious beliefs qualify an individual for otherwise unavailable benefits or exemptions, this may provide an inducement to profess such beliefs and government must judge the validity of individual claims. This in turn raises two problems. First, officials must judge the sincerity of an individual's beliefs because religious beliefs may be professed solely in order to escape obligations or prohibitions. As the problems encountered in administering the conscientious-objector exemption to the military draft reveal, such determinations can be difficult. Second, even if an individual's beliefs are sincere, officials must determine whether the beliefs are religious in character: nonreligious beliefs, however strongly held, do not justify an exemption from legal obligations. This judgment has been complicated by the broad definition of religion given by the Court in *United States v. Seeger* (1965) in interpreting the conscientious-objector exemption, under which nontheistic and purely personal beliefs may qualify as religious. Paradoxically, then, the Court's aim of freeing religious belief from the burden of government regulation can be accomplished only by a much deeper governmental intrusion in the religious realm: defining what constitutes a religion and judging the sincerity of individuals' beliefs.

These considerations led the Court to resurrect the secular regulation rule in *Employment Division, Department of Human Resources of Oregon v. Smith* (1990). At issue in *Smith* was Oregon's refusal to grant unemployment benefits to two employees who had been fired for using peyote, an illegal hallucinogenic drug, as part of the ritual of the Native American Church. Speaking for the Court, Justice Antonin Scalia denied that the Free Exercise Clause required government to grant exemptions from neutral, generally applicable laws. Such a requirement, he insisted, would make "each conscience a law unto itself." However, Justice Scalia's position drew intense criticism. In her concurring opinion in *Smith*, Justice O'Connor charged that the opinion of the Court diverged from "well-settled First Amendment jurisprudence." Other critics charged that the Court had embraced an unduly narrow conception of religious liberty. They also maintained that although on its face the Court's position seemed neutral among religions, in fact it worked to the disadvantage of minority religions. Mainstream religions would be able to protect themselves in the political process, by blocking legislation that impinged on their religious practices or by obtaining statutory exemptions. But government would enact laws that inadvertently burdened the practice of minority religions because their adherents lack the numbers and influence necessary to prevail in the political process.[4]

At the urging of a wide spectrum of religious groups, Congress in 1993 responded to *Smith* by enacting the Religious Freedom Restoration Act (RFRA), which was designed to restore the free-exercise standard enunciated in *Sherbert.* More specifically, the act forbade actions by both the federal government and state governments that burdened a person's exercise of religion, unless it could be demonstrated that imposing the burden "(1) is in furtherance of a compelling governmental interest; and (2) is the least restrictive means of furthering that compelling governmental interest." As the constitutional basis for imposing such requirements on the states, Congress cited Section 5 of the Fourteenth Amendment, which gave it the "power to enforce, by appropriate legislation" the rights protected by the Fourteenth Amendment (including the free exercise of religion). However, in *City of Boerne v. Flores, Archbishop of San Antonio* (1997), the Supreme Court struck down those portions of RFRA that imposed requirements on state governments. The power to enforce the obligations of the Fourteenth Amendment, the Court reasoned, does not include the power to alter the meaning of those obligations. Otherwise, Congress could change the meaning of the Constitution by statute, thus undermining the Constitution's status as "superior paramount law, unchangeable by ordinary means." If Congress wished to overturn *Smith,* it had to do so by constitutional amendment, not by statute.

The Court's ruling in *Boerne,* however, left open two possibilities. First, a state might choose to impose on itself a requirement to grant to religious adherents exemptions from state policies that burden their free exercise of religion. Thus, more than twenty states have adopted their own versions of RFRA, granting believers exemptions from general legal requirements that impinge on their religious practices, unless it can be shown that the challenged requirements are the least-restrictive means available for serving a compelling state interest. Second, Congress might require that federal statutes meet the requirements of RFRA. In *Gonzales v. O Centro Espírita Beneficente União do Vegetal* (2006), which involved the use of an otherwise illegal substance in a religious ceremony, the Court unanimously upheld RFRA as applied to the federal government. The justices concluded that RFRA applied to federal drug laws and required individualized exemptions for religious purposes. As Chief Justice Roberts concluded for the Court, "RFRA plainly contemplates that courts would recognize exceptions—that is how the law works."

The Free Exercise Clause also protects religious institutions from undue interference in their internal affairs. One way government can avoid such interference is by crafting exceptions for religious groups into statutes. For example, during Prohibition government banned the consumption of alcoholic beverages but granted churches an exception for wine used for sacramental purposes. But as the scope of government regulation increases, so does the potential for collisions, raising questions about whether such exemptions may sometimes be required by the First Amendment. In *Hosanna-Tabor Evangelical Lutheran Church and School v. EEOC* (2012), the issue was whether a church school's firing of an employee violated the Americans with Disabilities Act. The Supreme Court unanimously recognized that the First Amendment requires that religious organizations enjoy wide latitude in conducting their own affairs and specifically mandates a "ministerial exception" in laws dealing with employment so that government does not interfere with a church's choice of religious leaders.

Controversy has also erupted over a provision of the 2010 Patient Protection and Affordable Care Act (PPACA) that mandated that birth-control services for women be included as part of any employer-provided health insurance plan. Regulations proposed by the Department of Health and Human Services (HHS) in pursuance of that law required all employers, including church-sponsored and-affiliated enterprises, to provide those services, which included contraception, sterilization, and abortion-inducing drugs. The rule thus required some faith-based employers—including Catholic charities, schools, universities, and hospitals—to provide services they deemed immoral. The regulations provided an exemption for "religious institutions" if their primary purpose was to "inculcate religious values," but religious groups protested that the exception was too narrow and that the government would determine which institutions qualified for the exemption. A compromise was proposed under which, if charities or hospitals indicated that they had a religious objection to providing birth-control services as part of their health plan, they would not be obliged to do so; but the insurance company would be required to offer those services free of charge. However, this compromise did not satisfy all critics of the HHS regulations. Wheaton College, a religious college, sought an injunction against being required to file a form certifying that it was a religious institution that objected to the distribution of contraceptives. It claimed that the requirement violated the Religious Freedom Restoration Act (RFRA) because it made the college complicit in the provision of contraceptives by triggering the obligation for someone else to provide the services to which it objected. In *Wheaton College v. Burwell* (2014), the Supreme Court upheld a temporary injunction against enforcing the requirement until the justices could rule on the question, and in 2016, the Court heard arguments in *Zubik v. Burwell* addressing the issue.

Another question is what institutions might qualify for exemptions from generally applicable laws under RFRA. In *Burwell v. Hobby Lobby Stores, Inc.* (2014), two privately held corporations, whose owners had religious objections to the provision of contraceptives that they deemed abortifacients, sought exemption under RFRA from the requirements imposed by the PPACA. Speaking for a five-member majority, Justice Samuel Alito noted that RFRA's requirement extends to associations of persons who avail themselves of the corporate form, just as it does to individuals. Thus, under RFRA, the federal government had an obligation to accommodate Hobby Lobby's religiously motivated action, absent the need to serve a compelling governmental interest that could not be served by alternative means. Although the case involved a clash between the government's compelling interest in securing women's reproductive health and Hobby Lobby's sincere belief that facilitating access to abortifacients violated their religious convictions, Alito noted that there was a means to reconcile the conflict. The government could extend to corporations whose owners had religious objections the same accommodation that it provided for nonprofit organizations with religious objections. Thus, there was an alternative means of meeting the government's compelling interest that did not intrude on religious commitments.

RECONCILING THE RELIGION CLAUSES

In interpreting the Establishment Clause, the Supreme Court has held that government may neither favor nor disfavor religion. Yet in free-exercise cases before *Smith,* it insisted that government must exempt believers from some general legal requirements, in effect using religion as a criterion for granting exemptions. Thus, the aims of the religion clauses, at least under these interpretations, seem inconsistent. How can one reconcile the Establishment Clause's mandate of neutrality between religion and irreligion with the Free Exercise Clause's demand for accommodation of religiously motivated actions?

One possibility is to admit that the Court's interpretations are inconsistent but to insist that this inconsistency reflects a tension between the Establishment and Free Exercise Clauses. Thus, in striking down aid to religion while requiring the accommodation of religious beliefs in the application of general legislation, the Court is merely fulfilling the somewhat opposed purposes of the two provisions. Although this view prevailed on the Court before *Smith,* it is subject to two objections. First, it depreciates the Constitution by assuming that it incorporates an incoherent understanding of the proper relation between government and religion. Second, it offers no guidance for determining whether one should opt for neutrality or accommodation in resolving particular disputes.

Many justices and constitutional scholars therefore find the problem not in the Constitution but in the Court's interpretation of it. According to one view, the Court had interpreted the Establishment Clause in an overly rigid fashion that unduly restricted governmental efforts to promote the free exercise of religion. Justice Potter Stewart, dissenting in the school-prayer cases, voiced this criticism when he insisted that in providing opportunities for voluntary religious observances in the public schools, government merely accommodated the religious convictions of the populace. Justice Byron White dissented from the Court's aid-to-education cases on similar grounds, asserting that governmental programs that made it possible for individuals to pursue a religious education constituted an accommodation consistent with—and indeed, appropriate to—the First Amendment's primary concern, which is religious liberty.

Other observers concluded that the Court had improperly interpreted the Free Exercise Clause before *Smith.* According to this view, best expressed in Justice John Marshall Harlan's dissent in *Sherbert,* the requirement that statutes must accommodate religious convictions violates the neutrality between religion and irreligion sought by the First Amendment. Only by reinstitution of the secular-regulation rule, this argument went, could the Court properly reconcile its establishment and free-exercise positions.

Finally, Chief Justice Rehnquist and Justices Scalia and Thomas proposed a reconsideration of the Court's approach to both the Establishment and the Free Exercise Clauses. Agreeing with Justice Harlan that the secular-regulation rule is the appropriate standard in free-exercise cases, they have maintained that government is not constitutionally required to accommodate believers in designing legislation. Yet because their interpretation of the Establishment Clause does not require governmental neutrality between religion and irreligion, there is no constitutional bar to governmental efforts to accommodate religion. Their position thus permits government wide discretion in determining whether and when to grant exemptions from general statutory requirements. The adoption of the Religious Freedom Restoration Act as a restriction on the federal government, as well as the adoption of similar laws in several states, has shifted much of the focus of litigation from constitutional interpretation to interpretation of those statutes and their implications. Congress and state legislatures will have to consider to what extent religious scruples can be accommodated without compromising important statutory objectives.

NOTES

1. Works criticizing the Court's historical scholarship include Philip Hamburger, *Separation of Church and State* (Cambridge, MA: Harvard University Press, 2002); V. Phillip Munoz, *God and the Founders: Madison, Washington, Jefferson* (New York: Cambridge University Press, 2009); and Steven D. Smith, *The Rise and Decline of American Religious Freedom* (Cambridge, MA: Harvard University Press, 2014).

2. Interestingly, Justice Hugo Black, who wrote the opinion of the Court in *Everson,* dissented in *Allen*—as did Justice William Douglas, the only other member of the *Everson* majority still on the Court when *Allen* was decided.

3. The Court did invalidate a provision of the law that permitted colleges to use the buildings for religious purposes twenty years after receiving the funds.

4. Critical assessments of the Court's approach in *Smith* include Michael W. McConnell, "Free Exercise Revisionism and the *Smith* Decision," *University of Chicago Law Review* 57 (1990): 1609–1654; and Douglas Laycock, "Formal, Substantive, and Disaggregated Neutrality Toward Religion," *DePaul Law Review* 39 (1990): 993–1018.

SELECTED READINGS

Carter, Stephen L. *The Culture of Disbelief: How American Law and Politics Trivialize Religious Devotion.* New York: Basic Books, 1993.

Curry, Thomas J. *The First Freedoms: Church and State in America to the Passage of the First Amendment.* New York: Oxford University Press, 1986.

Drakeman, Donald L. *Church, State, and Original Intent*. Cambridge: Cambridge University Press, 2010.

Dreisbach, Daniel L., Mark D. Hall, and Jeffry H. Morrison, eds. *The Founders on God and Government*. Lanham, MD: Rowman & Littlefield, 2004.

Hamburger, Philip. *Separation of Church and State*. Cambridge, MA: Harvard University Press, 2002.

Horwitz, Paul. "The *Hobby Lobby* Moment," *Harvard Law Review* 128 (November 2014): 154–189.

Laycock, Douglas. *Same-Sex Marriage and Religious Liberty*. Lanham, MD: Rowman & Littlefield, 2008.

Levy, Leonard W. *The Establishment Clause: Religion and the First Amendment*. New York: Macmillan, 1986.

McConnell, Michael W. "The Origins and Historical Understanding of Free Exercise of Religion." *Harvard Law Review* 103 (1990): 1409–1517.

Miller, William Lee. *The First Liberty: America's Foundation in Religious Freedom*. Washington, DC: Georgetown University Press, 2003.

Munoz, V. Phillip. *God and the Founders: Madison, Washington, Jefferson*. New York: Cambridge University Press, 2009.

Putnam, Robert D., and David E. Campbell. *American Grace: How Religion Divides and Unites Us*. New York: Simon & Schuster, 2010.

Smith, Steven D. *The Rise and Decline of American Religious Freedom*. Cambridge, MA: Harvard University Press, 2014.

Tarr, G. Alan. "Church and State in the States." *Washington Law Review* 64 (1989): 73–110.

Viteritti, Joseph P. *The Last Freedom: Religion from Public School to the Public Square*. Princeton, NJ: Princeton University Press, 2007.

Witte, John, Jr. *Religion and the American Constitutional Experiment: Essential Rights and Liberties*. 3rd ed. Boulder, CO: Westview Press, 2010.

Everson v. Board of Education
330 U.S. 1 (1947)

A New Jersey statute authorized local school boards to make rules and contracts for the transportation of students to and from schools. Acting under this statute, the Ewing Township Board of Education authorized reimbursement to parents of money spent for transportation to Catholic parochial schools as well as to public schools. Arch Everson, a taxpayer in the school district, challenged the transportation program as a violation of the state constitution (a claim rejected by the state supreme court) and the federal Constitution. Opinion of the Court: Black, Vinson, Reed, Douglas, Murphy. Dissenting opinions: Jackson, Frankfurter; Rutledge, Frankfurter, Jackson, Burton.

JUSTICE BLACK delivered the opinion of the Court.

This Court has previously recognized that the provisions of the First Amendment, in the drafting and adoption of which Madison and Jefferson played such leading roles, had the same objective and were intended to provide the same protection against governmental intrusion on religious liberty as the Virginia [Bill for Religious Liberty].

The "establishment of religion" clause of the First Amendment means at least this: Neither a state nor the Federal Government can set up a church. Neither can pass laws which aid one religion, aid all religions, or prefer one religion over another. Neither can force nor influence a person to go to or to remain away from church against his will or force him to profess a belief or disbelief in any religion. No person can be punished for entertaining or professing religious beliefs or disbeliefs, for church attendance or non-attendance. No tax in any amount, large or small, can be levied to support any religious activities or institutions, whatever they may be called, or whatever form they may adopt to teach or practice religion. Neither a state nor the Federal Government can, openly or secretly, participate in the affairs of any religious organizations or groups and vice versa. In the words of Jefferson, the clause against establishment of religion by law was intended to erect "a wall of separation between church and State."

New Jersey cannot consistently with the "establishment of religion" clause of the First Amendment contribute tax-raised funds to the support of an institution which teaches the tenets and faith of any church. On the other hand, other language of the amendment commands that New Jersey cannot hamper its citizens in the free exercise of their own religion. Consequently, it cannot exclude individual Catholics, Lutherans, Mohammedans, Baptists, Jews, Methodists, Non-believers, Presbyterians, or the members of any other faith, *because of their faith, or lack of it,* from receiving the benefits of public welfare legislation. While we do not mean to intimate that a state could not provide transportation only to children attending public schools, we must be careful, in protecting the citizens of New Jersey against state-established churches, to be sure that we do not inadvertently prohibit New Jersey from extending its general state law benefits to all its citizens without regard to their religious belief.

Measured by these standards, we cannot say that the First Amendment prohibits New Jersey from spending tax-raised funds to pay the bus fares of parochial school pupils as a part of a general program under which it pays the fares of pupils attending public and other schools. It is undoubtedly true that children are helped to get to church schools. There is even a possibility that some of the children might not be sent to the church schools if the parents were compelled to pay their children's bus fares out of their own pockets when transportation to a public school would have been paid for by the State. The same possibility exists where the state requires a local transit company to provide reduced fares to school children including those attending parochial schools, or where a municipally owned transportation system undertakes to carry all school children free of charge. Moreover, state-paid policemen, detailed to protect children going to and from church schools from the very real hazards of traffic, would serve much the same purpose and accomplish much the same result as state provisions intended to guarantee free transportation of a kind which the state deems to be best for the school children's welfare. And parents might refuse to risk their children to the serious danger of traffic accidents going to and from parochial schools, the approaches to which were not protected by policemen. Similarly, parents might be reluctant to permit their children to attend schools which the state had cut off from such general government services as ordinary police and fire protection, connections for sewage disposal, public highways and sidewalks. Of course, cutting off church schools from these services, so separate and so indisputably marked off from the religious function, would make it far more difficult for the schools to operate. But such is obviously not the purpose of the First Amendment. That Amendment requires the state to be neutral in its relations with groups of religious believers and non-believers; it does not require the state to be their adversary. State power is no more to be used so as to handicap religions than it is to favor them.

The First Amendment has erected a wall between church and state. That wall must be kept high and impregnable. We could not approve the slightest breach. New Jersey has not breached it here.

JUSTICE JACKSON, dissenting.

The Court's opinion marshals every argument in favor of state aid and puts the case in its most favorable light, but much of its reasoning confirms my conclusions that there are no good grounds upon which to support the present legislation. In fact, the undertones of the opinion, advocating complete and uncompromising separation of Church from State, seem utterly discordant with its conclusion yielding support to their commingling in educational matters. The case which irresistibly comes to mind as the most fitting precedent is that of Julia who, according to Byron's reports, "whispering 'I will ne'er consent,'—consented."

The Court sustains this legislation by assuming two deviations from the facts of this particular case. The Court concludes that this "legislation, as applied, does no more than provide a general program to help parents get their children, regardless of their religion, safely and expeditiously to and from accredited schools,"

and it draws a comparison between "state provisions intended to guarantee free transportation" for school children with services such as police and fire protection, and implies that we are here dealing with "laws authorizing new types of public services." This hypothesis permeates the opinion. The facts will not bear that construction.

The Township of Ewing is not furnishing transportation to the children in any form; it is not operating school buses itself or contracting for their operation; and it is not performing any public service of any kind with this taxpayer's money. All school children are left to ride as ordinary paying passengers on the regular buses operated by the public transportation system. What the Township does, and what the taxpayer complains of, is at stated intervals to reimburse parents for the fares paid, provided the children attend either public schools or Catholic Church schools. This expenditure of tax funds has no possible effect on the child's safety or expedition in transit. As passengers on the public buses they travel as fast and no faster, and are as safe and no safer, since their parents are reimbursed as before.

In addition to thus assuming a type of service that does not exist, the Court also insists that we must close our eyes to a discrimination which does exist. The resolution which authorizes disbursement of this taxpayer's money limits reimbursement to those who attend public schools and Catholic schools. That is the way the Act is applied to this taxpayer.

The New Jersey Act in question makes the character of the school, not the needs of the children, determine the eligibility of parents to reimbursement. The Act permits payment for transportation to parochial schools or public schools but prohibits it to private schools operated in whole or in part for profit.

JUSTICE RUTLEDGE, with whom JUSTICE FRANKFURTER, JUSTICE JACKSON and JUSTICE BURTON agree, dissenting.

The Amendment's purpose was not to strike merely at the official establishment of a single sect, creed or religion, outlawing only a formal relation such as had prevailed in England and some of the colonies. Necessarily it was to uproot all such relationships. But the object was broader than separating church and state in this narrow sense. It was to create a complete and permanent separation of the spheres of religious activity and civil authority by comprehensively forbidding every form of public aid or support for religion.

No provision of the Constitution is more closely tied to or given content by its generating history than the religious clause of the First Amendment. It is at once the refined product and the terse summation of that history. The history includes not only Madison's authorship and the proceedings before the First Congress, but also the long and intensive struggle for religious freedom in America, more especially in Virginia, of which the Amendment was the direct culmination.

All the great instruments of the Virginia struggle for religious liberty thus became warp and woof of our constitutional tradition, not simply by the course of history, but by the common unifying force of Madison's life, thought and sponsorship. He epitomized the whole of that tradition in the Amendment's compact, but nonetheless comprehensive, phrasing. Madison opposed every form and degree of official relation between religion and civil authority. For him religion was a wholly private matter beyond the scope of civil power either to restrain or to support. In no phase was he more unrelentingly absolute than in opposing state support or aid by taxation. Not even "three pence" contribution was thus to be exacted from any citizen for such a purpose. In view of this history no further proof is needed that the Amendment forbids any appropriation, large or small, from public funds to aid or support any and all religious exercises.

New Jersey's action exactly fits the type of exaction and the kind of evil at which Madison and Jefferson struck. Under the test they framed it cannot be said that the cost of transportation is no part of the cost of education or of the religious instruction given. That it is a substantial and a necessary element is shown most plainly by the continuing and increasing demand for the state to assume it. Nor is there pretense that it relates only to the secular instruction given in religious schools or that any attempt is or could be made toward allocating proportional shares as between the secular and the religious instruction. It is precisely because the instruction is religious and relates to a particular faith, whether one or another, that parents send their children to religious schools. And the very purpose of the state's contribution to defray the cost of conveying the pupil to the place where he will receive not simply secular, but also and primarily religious, teaching and guidance.

The matter is not one of quantity, to be measured by the amount of money expended. Now as in Madison's day it is one of principle, to keep separate the separate spheres as the First Amendment drew them; to prevent the first experiment upon our liberties; and to keep the question from becoming entangled in corrosive precedents.

School District of Abington Township v. Schempp
374 U.S. 203 (1963)

One year after the Court in Engel v. Vitale *invalidated the use of a government-composed prayer for voluntary recitation in New York public schools, it considered the more widespread practice of Bible reading in the public schools. A Pennsylvania law required daily Bible reading, and a Baltimore school board regulation required both Bible reading and daily recitation of the Lord's Prayer. Both programs permitted students to absent themselves from the religious exercises on parental request. Perhaps to allay the intense criticism that greeted the Engel decision, the opinion of the Court was assigned to*

Justice Clark, an elder in the Presbyterian Church, and concurring opinions were filed by Justice Brennan, a Catholic, and Justice Goldberg, a Jew. Opinion of the Court: Clark, Warren, Black, Douglas, Harlan, Brennan, White, Goldberg. Concurring opinions: Douglas; Brennan; Goldberg; Harlan. Dissenting opinion: Stewart.

JUSTICE CLARK delivered the opinion of the Court.

The wholesome "neutrality" of which this Court's cases speak stems from a recognition of the teachings of history that powerful sects or groups might bring about a fusion of governmental and religious functions or a concert or dependency of one upon the other to the end that official support of the State or Federal Government would be placed behind the tenets of one or of all orthodoxies. This the Establishment Clause prohibits. And a further reason for neutrality is found in the Free Exercise Clause, which recognizes the value of religious training, teaching and observance and, more particularly, the right of every person to freely choose his own course with reference thereto, free of any compulsion from the state. This the Free Exercise Clause guarantees. Thus, as we have seen, the two clauses may overlap. The Establishment Clause has been directly considered by this Court eight times in the past score of years and, with only one Justice dissenting on the point, it has consistently held that the clause withdrew all legislative power respecting religious belief or the expression thereof. The test may be stated as follows: what are the purpose and the primary effect of the enactment? If either is the advancement or inhibition of religion then the enactment exceeds the scope of legislative power as circumscribed by the Constitution. That is to say that to withstand the strictures of the Establishment Clause there must be a secular legislative purpose and a primary effect that neither advances nor inhibits religion. The distinction between the two clauses is apparent—a violation of the Free Exercise Clause is predicated on coercion while the Establishment Clause violation need not be so attended.

Applying the Establishment Clause principles to the cases at bar we find that the States are requiring the selection and reading at the opening of the school day of verses from the Holy Bible and the recitation of the Lord's Prayer by the students in unison. These exercises are prescribed as part of the curricular activities of students who are required by law to attend school.

Surely the place of the Bible as an instrument of religion cannot be gainsaid, and the State's recognition of the pervading religious character of the ceremony is evident from the rule's specific permission of the alternative use of the Catholic Douay version as well as the recent amendment permitting nonattendance at the exercises. None of these factors is consistent with the contention that the Bible is here used either as an instrument for nonreligious moral inspiration or as a reference for the teaching of secular subjects. The conclusion follows that in both cases the laws require religious exercises and such exercises are being conducted in direct violation of the rights of the appellees and petitioners.

It is insisted that unless these religious exercises are permitted a "religion of secularism" is established in the schools. We agree of course that the State may not establish a "religion of secularism" in the sense of affirmatively opposing or showing hostility to religion, thus "preferring those who believe in no religion over those who do believe." *Zorach v. Clauson* [1952]. We do not agree, however, that this decision in any sense has that effect. In addition, it might well be said that one's education is not complete without a study of comparative religion or the history of religion and its relationship to the advancement of civilization. It certainly may be said that the Bible is worthy of study for its literary and historic qualities. Nothing we have said here indicates that such study of the Bible or of religion, when presented objectively as part of a secular program of education, may not be effected consistently with the First Amendment. But the exercises here are religious exercises, required by the States in violation of the command of the First Amendment that the Government maintain strict neutrality, neither aiding nor opposing religion.

Finally, we cannot accept that the concept of neutrality, which does not permit a State to require a religious exercise even with the consent of the majority of those affected, collides with the majority's right to free exercise of religion. While the Free Exercise Clause clearly prohibits the use of state action to deny the rights of free exercise to anyone, it has never meant that a majority could use the machinery of the State to practice its beliefs.

JUSTICE BRENNAN, concurring.

The specific question before us has aroused vigorous dispute whether the architects of the First Amendment—James Madison and Thomas

Jefferson particularly—understood the prohibition against any "law respecting an establishment of religion" to reach devotional exercises in the public schools. But I doubt that their view, even if perfectly clear one way or the other, would supply a dispositive answer to the question presented by these cases. A more fruitful inquiry, it seems to me, is whether the practices here challenged threaten those consequences which the Framers deeply feared; whether, in short, they tend to promote that type of interdependence between religion and state which the First Amendment was designed to prevent.

A too literal quest for the advice of the Founding Fathers upon the issues of these cases seems to me futile and misdirected for several reasons: First, on our precise problem the historical record is at best ambiguous, and statements can readily be found to support either side of the proposition. The ambiguity of history is understandable if we recall the nature of the problems uppermost in the thinking of the statesmen who fashioned the religious guarantees; they were concerned with far more flagrant intrusions of government into the realm of religion than any that our century has witnessed.

Second, the structure of American education has greatly changed since the First Amendment was adopted. In the context of our modern emphasis upon public education available to all citizens, any views of the eighteenth century as to whether the exercises at bar are an "establishment" offer little aid to decision.

Third, our religious composition makes us a vastly more diverse people than were our forefathers. They knew differences chiefly among Protestant sects. Today the Nation is far more heterogeneous religiously, including as it does substantial minorities not only of Catholics and Jews but as well of those who worship according to no version of the Bible and those who worship no God at all. In the face of such profound changes, practices which may have been objectionable to no one in the time of Jefferson and Madison may today be highly offensive to many persons, the deeply devout and the nonbelievers alike.

Fourth, the American experiment in free public education available to all children has been guided in large measure by the dramatic evolution of the religious diversity among the population which our public schools serve. It is implicit in the history and character of American public education that the public schools serve a uniquely public function: the training of American citizens in an atmosphere free of parochial, divisive, or separatist influences of any sort—an atmosphere in which children may assimilate a heritage common to all American groups and religions. This is a heritage neither theistic nor atheistic, but simply civic and patriotic.

JUSTICE STEWART, dissenting.

While in many contexts the Establishment Clause and the Free Exercise Clause fully complement each other, there are areas in which a doctrinaire reading of the Establishment Clause leads to irreconcilable conflict with the Free Exercise Clause. A single obvious example should suffice to make the point. Spending federal funds to employ chaplains for the armed forces might be said to violate the Establishment Clause. Yet a lonely soldier stationed at some faraway outpost could surely complain that a government which did not provide him the opportunity for pastoral guidance was affirmatively prohibiting the free exercise of his religion. And such examples could readily be multiplied. The short of the matter is simply that the two relevant clauses of the First Amendment cannot accurately be reflected in a sterile metaphor which by its very nature may distort rather than illumine the problems involved in a particular case.

That the central value embodied in the First Amendment—and, more particularly, in the guarantee of "liberty" contained in the Fourteenth—is the safeguarding of an individual's right to free exercise of his religion has been consistently recognized. It is this concept of constitutional protection which makes the cases before us such difficult ones for me. For there is involved in these cases a substantial free exercise claim on the part of those who affirmatively desire to have their children's school day open with the reading of passages from the Bible.

It might be argued that parents who want their children exposed to religious influences can adequately fulfill that wish off school property and outside school time. With all its surface persuasiveness, however, this argument seriously misconceives the basic constitutional justification for permitting the exercises at issue in these cases. For a compulsory state educational system so structures a child's life that if religious exercises are held to be an impermissible activity in schools, religion is placed at an artificial and state-created disadvantage. Viewed in this light, permission of such exercises for those who want them is necessary if the schools are truly to be neutral in the matter of religion. And a refusal to permit religious exercises thus is seen, not as the realization of state neutrality, but rather as the establishment of a religion of secularism, or at the least, as government support of the beliefs of those who think that religious exercises should be conducted only in private.

What our Constitution indispensibly protects is the freedom of each of us, be he Jew or Agnostic, Atheist, Buddhist or Freethinker, to believe or disbelieve, to worship or not worship, to pray or keep silent, according to his own conscience, uncoerced and unrestrained by government. It is conceivable that these school boards, or even all school boards, might eventually find it impossible to administer a system of religious exercises during school hours in such a way as to meet this constitutional standard—in such a way as completely to free from any kind of official coercion those who do not affirmatively want to participate. But I think we must not assume that school boards so lack the qualities of inventiveness and good will as to make impossible the achievement of that goal.

Lemon v. Kurtzman
403 U.S. 602 (1971)

Lemon *marked the Supreme Court's first consideration of the constitutionality of state programs providing financial aid to church-affiliated elementary and secondary schools. Under the Pennsylvania Nonpublic Elementary and Secondary Education Act, Pennsylvania purchased specified secular educational services from nonpublic schools by reimbursing them for the cost of teachers' salaries, textbooks, and instructional materials in various secular subjects. A three-judge federal district court dismissed the complaint regarding the program in* Lemon v. Kurtzman. *Under the Rhode Island Salary Supplement Act, Rhode Island paid teachers of secular subjects in nonpublic elementary schools a supplement of 15 percent of their annual salary. In* Earley v. DiCenso *(1970), a three-judge federal district court struck down the act as a violation of the Establishment Clause. The Court consolidated these cases for argument with* Tilton v. Richardson, *which involved the constitutionality of a congressional grant program to public and private colleges for building construction. Opinion of the Court:* Burger, Black, Douglas, Harlan, Stewart, Blackmun. *Concurring opinions:* Douglas, Black; Brennan. *Dissenting opinion:* White. *Not participating:* Marshall.

THE CHIEF JUSTICE delivered the opinion of the Court.

Every analysis in this area must begin with consideration of the cumulative criteria developed by the Court over many years. Three such tests may be gleaned from our cases. First, the statute must have a secular legislative purpose; second, its principal or primary effect must be one that neither advances nor inhibits religion; finally, the statute must not foster "an excessive government entanglement with religion."

Inquiry into the legislative purposes of the Pennsylvania and Rhode Island statutes affords no basis for a conclusion that the legislative intent was to advance religion. On the contrary, the statutes themselves clearly state that they are intended to enhance the quality of the secular education in all schools covered by the compulsory attendance laws. There is no reason to believe that the legislatures meant anything else. A State always has a legitimate concern for maintaining minimum standards in all schools it allows to operate.

The two legislatures, however, have recognized that church-related elementary and secondary schools have a significant religious mission and that a substantial portion of their activities is religiously oriented. They have therefore sought to create statutory restrictions designed to guarantee the separation between secular and religious educational functions and to ensure that State financial aid supports only the former. We need not decide whether these legislative precautions restrict the principal or primary effect of the programs to the point where they do not offend the Religion Clauses, for we conclude that the cumulative impact of the entire relationship arising under the statutes in each State involves excessive entanglement between government and religion.

In order to determine whether the government entanglement with religion is excessive, we must examine the character and purposes of the institutions that are benefited, the nature of the aid that the State provides, and the resulting relationship between the government and the religious authority.

RHODE ISLAND PROGRAM

The District Court made extensive findings on the grave potential for excessive entanglement that inheres in the religious character and purpose of the Roman Catholic elementary schools of Rhode Island, to date the sole beneficiaries of the Rhode Island Salary Supplement Act. The church schools involved in the program are located close to parish churches. This understandably permits convenient access for religious exercises since instruction in faith and morals is part of the total educational process. The school buildings contain identifying religious symbols such as crosses on the exterior and crucifixes, and religious paintings and statues either in the classrooms or hallways. Although only approximately 30 minutes a day are devoted to direct religious instruction, there are religiously oriented extracurricular activities. Approximately two-thirds of the teachers in these schools are nuns of various religious orders. Their dedicated efforts provide an atmosphere in which religious instruction and religious vocations are natural and proper parts of life in such schools.

On the basis of these findings the District Court concluded that the parochial schools constituted "an integral part of the religious mission of the Catholic Church." The dangers and corresponding entanglements are enhanced by the particular form of aid that the Rhode Island Act provides.

In [*Board of Education v.*] *Allen* [1968], the Court refused to make assumptions, on a meager record, about the religious content of the textbooks that the State would be asked to provide. We cannot, however, refuse here to recognize that teachers have a substantially different ideological character from books. In terms of potential for involving some aspect of faith or morals in secular subjects, a textbook's content is ascertainable, but a teacher's handling of a subject is not. We need not and do not assume that teachers in parochial schools will be guilty of bad faith or any conscious design to evade the limitations imposed by the statute and the First Amendment. We simply recognize that a dedicated religious person, teaching in a school affiliated with his or her faith and operated to inculcate its tenets, will inevitably experience great difficulty in remaining religiously neutral.

To ensure that no trespass occurs, the State has therefore carefully conditioned its aid with pervasive restrictions. An eligible recipient must teach only those courses that are offered in the public schools and use only those texts and materials that are found in the public schools. In addition the teacher must not engage in teaching any course in religion.

A comprehensive, discriminating, and continuing state surveillance will inevitably be required to ensure that these restrictions are obeyed and the First Amendment otherwise respected. Unlike a book, a teacher cannot be inspected once so as to determine the extent and intent of his or her personal beliefs and subjective acceptance of the limitations imposed by the First Amendment. These prophylactic contacts will involve excessive and enduring entanglement between state and church.

There is another area of entanglement in the Rhode Island program that gives concern. The statute excludes teachers employed by nonpublic schools whose average per-pupil expenditures on secular education equal or exceed the comparable figures for public schools. In the event that the total expenditures of an otherwise eligible school exceed this norm, the program requires the government to examine the school's records in order to determine how much of the total expenditures is attributable to secular education and how much to religious activity. This kind of state inspection and evaluation of the religious content of a religious organization is fraught with the sort of entanglement that the Constitution forbids. It is a relationship pregnant with dangers of excessive government direction of church schools and hence of churches.

PENNSYLVANIA PROGRAM

The very restrictions and surveillance necessary to ensure that teachers play a strictly non-ideological role give rise to entanglements between church and state. The Pennsylvania statute, like that of Rhode Island, fosters this kind of relationship. The Pennsylvania statute, moreover, has the further defect of providing state financial aid directly to the church-related school. The history of government grants of a continuing cash subsidy indicates that such programs have almost always been accompanied by varying measures of control and surveillance. The government cash grants before us now provide no basis for predicting that comprehensive measures of surveillance and controls will not follow. In particular the government's post-audit power to inspect and evaluate a church-related school's financial records and to determine which expenditures are religious and which are secular creates an intimate and continuing relationship between church and state.

A broader base of entanglement of yet a different character is presented by the divisive political potential of these state programs. In a community where such a large number of pupils are served by church-related schools, it can be assumed that state assistance will entail considerable political activity. Partisans of parochial schools, understandably concerned with rising costs and sincerely dedicated to both the religious and secular educational mission of their schools, will inevitably champion this cause and promote political action to achieve their goals. Those who oppose state aid, whether for constitutional, religious, or fiscal reasons, will inevitably respond and employ all of the usual political campaign techniques to prevail. Candidates will be forced to declare

and voters to choose. It would be unrealistic to ignore the fact that many people confronted with issues of this kind will find their votes aligned with their faith.

Ordinarily political debate and division, however vigorous or even partisan, are normal and healthy manifestations of our democratic system of government, but political division along religious lines was one of the principal evils against which the First Amendment was intended to protect. The potential divisiveness of such conflict is a threat to the normal political process. The potential for political divisiveness related to religious belief and practice is aggravated in these two statutory programs by the need for continuing annual appropriations and the likelihood of larger and larger demands as costs and populations grow.

JUSTICE WHITE, dissenting.

Our prior cases have recognized the dual role of parochial schools in American society: they perform both religious and secular functions. It is enough for me that the States and the Federal Government are financing a separable secular function of overriding importance in order to sustain the legislation here challenged. That religion and private interests other than education may substantially benefit does not convert these laws into impermissible establishments of religion.

Where a state program seeks to ensure the proper education of its young, in private as well as public schools, free exercise considerations at least counsel against refusing support for students attending parochial schools simply because in that setting they are also being instructed in the tenets of the faith they are constitutionally free to practice.

The Court strikes down the Rhode Island statute on its face. No fault is found with the secular purpose of the program; there is no suggestion that the purpose of the program was aid to religion disguised in secular attire. Nor does the Court find that the primary effect of the program is to aid religion rather than to implement secular goals. The Court nevertheless finds that impermissible "entanglement" will result from administration of the program. The Court thus creates an insoluble paradox for the State and the parochial schools. The

State cannot finance secular instruction if it permits religion to be taught in the same classroom; but if it exacts a promise that religion not be so taught—a promise the school and its teachers are quite willing and on this record able to give—and enforces it, it is then entangled in the "no entanglement" aspect of the Court's Establishment Clause jurisprudence.

With respect to Pennsylvania, the Court, accepting as true the factual allegations of the complaint, as it must for purpose of a motion to dismiss, would reverse the dismissal of the complaint and invalidate the legislation. The critical allegations, as paraphrased by the Court, are that "the church-related elementary and secondary schools are controlled by religious organizations, have the purpose of propagating and promoting a particular religious faith, and conduct their operations to fulfill that purpose." From these allegations the Court concludes that forbidden entanglements would follow from enforcing compliance with the secular purpose for which the state money is being paid.

I disagree. There is no specific allegation in the complaint that sectarian teaching does or would invade secular classes supported by state funds. That the schools are operated to promote a particular religion is quite consistent with the view that secular teaching devoid of religious instruction can successfully be maintained. I would no more here than in the Rhode Island case substitute presumption for proof that religion is or would be taught in state-financed secular courses or assume that enforcement measures would be so extensive as to border on a free exercise violation. I would reverse the judgment of the District Court and remand the case for trial, thereby holding the Pennsylvania legislation valid on its face but leaving open the question of its validity as applied to the particular facts of this case.

Wallace v. Jaffree
472 U.S. 38 (1985)

Beginning in the late 1970s, roughly half the states enacted laws authorizing a "moment of silence" at the outset of classes in public schools. This case provided the Supreme Court its first opportunity to consider the constitutionality of such laws. At issue was a 1981 Alabama law under which "a period of silence not to exceed one minute in duration shall be observed for meditation or voluntary prayer." (This law superseded a 1978 Alabama enactment that authorized a moment of silence but did not mention prayer.) Ishmael Jaffree, who had three children in Alabama public schools, challenged the 1981 law, claiming that it violated the First Amendment, made applicable to the states by the Fourteenth Amendment. The district court, in an unusual opinion, ruled against Jaffree, claiming that the Establishment Clause did not bar states from establishing a religion. The court of appeals reversed, ruling that the statute did not serve a secular purpose, and the state appealed to the Supreme Court. Opinion of the Court: Stevens, Brennan, Marshall, Blackmun, Powell. Concurring opinions: Powell; O'Connor. Dissenting opinions: Burger; White; Rehnquist.

JUSTICE STEVENS delivered the opinion of the Court.

When the Court has been called upon to construe the breadth of the Establishment Clause, it has examined the criteria developed over a period of many years. Thus, in *Lemon v. Kurtzman* (1971), we wrote: "Three such tests may be gleaned from our cases. First, the statute must have a secular legislative purpose; second, its principal or primary effect must be one that neither advances nor inhibits religion; finally, the statute must not foster 'an excessive government entanglement with religion.'" It is the first of these three criteria that is most plainly implicated by this case. As the District Court correctly recognized, no consideration of the second or third criteria is necessary if a statute does not have a clearly secular purpose.

In applying the purpose test, it is appropriate to ask "whether government's actual purpose is to endorse or disapprove of religion." In this case, the answer to that question is dispositive. For the record not only provides us with an unambiguous affirmative answer, but it also reveals that the enactment of § 16-1-20.1 was not motivated by any clearly secular purpose—indeed, the statute had *no* secular purpose. The sponsor of the bill that became § 16-1-20.1, Senator Donald Holmes, inserted into the legislative record—apparently without dissent—a statement indicating that the legislation was an "effort to return voluntary prayer" to the public schools. Later Senator Holmes confirmed this purpose before the District Court. In response to the question whether he had any purpose for the legislation other than returning voluntary prayer to public schools, he stated, "No, I did not have no other purpose in mind." The State did not present evidence of *any* secular purpose.

The legislative intent to return prayer to the public schools is, of course, quite different from merely protecting every student's right to engage in voluntary prayer during an appropriate moment of silence during the school day. The 1978 statute already protected that right, containing nothing that prevented any student from engaging in voluntary prayer during a silent minute of meditation. Appellants have not identified any secular purpose that was not fully served by § 16-1-20 before the enactment of § 16-1-20.1. Thus, only two conclusions are consistent with the text of § 16-1-20.1: (1) the statute was enacted to convey a message of State endorsement and promotion of prayer; or (2) the statute was enacted for no purpose. No one suggests that the statute was nothing but a meaningless or irrational act. The Legislature enacted § 16-1-20.1 despite the existence of § 16-1-20 for the sole purpose of expressing the State's endorsement of prayer activities for one minute at the beginning of each school day. The addition of "or voluntary prayer" indicates that the State intended to characterize prayer as a favored practice. Such an endorsement is not consistent with the established principle that the government must pursue a course of complete neutrality toward religion.

JUSTICE O'CONNOR, concurring in the judgment.

A state sponsored moment of silence in the public schools is different from state sponsored vocal prayer or Bible reading. First, a moment of silence is not inherently religious. Silence, unlike prayer or Bible reading, need not be associated with a religious exercise. Second, a pupil who participates in a moment of silence need not compromise his or her beliefs. During a moment of silence, a student who objects to prayer is left to his or her own thoughts, and is not compelled to listen to the prayers or thoughts of others. For these simple reasons, a moment of silence statute does not stand or fall under the Establishment Clause according to how the Court regards vocal prayer or Bible reading.

The analysis above suggests that moment of silence laws in many States should pass Establishment Clause scrutiny because they do not favor the child who chooses to pray during a moment of silence over the child who chooses to meditate or reflect. Alabama Code § 16-1-20.1 does not stand on the same footing. However deferentially one examines its text and legislative history, however objectively one views the message attempted to be conveyed to the public, the conclusion is unavoidable that the purpose of the statute is to endorse prayer in public schools. I accordingly agree with the Court of Appeals that the Alabama statute has a purpose which is in violation of the Establishment Clause, and cannot be upheld.

JUSTICE REHNQUIST, dissenting.

Thirty-eight years ago this Court, in *Everson v. Board of Education* summarized its exegesis of Establishment Clause doctrine thus: "In the words of Jefferson, the clause against establishment of religion by law was intended to erect 'a wall of separation between church and State.'"

It is impossible to build sound constitutional doctrine upon a mistaken understanding of constitutional history, but unfortunately the Establishment Clause has been expressly freighted with Jefferson's misleading metaphor for nearly forty years. When we turn to the record of the proceedings in the First Congress leading up to the adoption of the Establishment Clause of the Constitution, including Madison's significant contributions thereto, we see a far different picture of its purpose than the highly simplified "wall of separation between church and State." On the basis of record of these proceedings in the House of Representatives, James Madison was undoubtedly the most important architect among the members of the House of the amendments which became the Bill of Rights, but it was James Madison speaking as an advocate of sensible legislative compromise, not as an advocate of incorporating the Virginia Statute of Religious Liberty into the United States Constitution. His original language "nor shall any national religion be established" obviously does not conform to the "wall of separation" between church and State idea which latter day commentators have ascribed to him. His explanation on the floor of the meaning of his language—"that Congress should not establish a religion, and enforce the legal observation of it by law" is of the same ilk. When he replied to Huntington in the debate over the proposal which came from the Select Committee of the House, he urged that the language "no religion shall be established by law" should be amended by inserting the word "national" in front of the word "religion."

It seems indisputable from these glimpses of Madison's thinking, as reflected by actions on the floor of the House in 1789, that he saw the amendment as designed to prohibit the establishment of a national religion, and perhaps to prevent discrimination among sects. He did not see it as requiring neutrality on the part of government between religion and irreligion. Thus the Court's opinion in *Everson*—while correct in bracketing Madison and Jefferson together in their exertions in their home state leading to the enactment of the Virginia Statute of Religious Liberty—is totally incorrect in suggesting that Madison carried these views onto the floor of the United States House of Representatives when he proposed the language which would ultimately become the Bill of Rights.

None of the other Members of Congress who spoke during the August 15th debate expressed the slightest indication that they thought the language before them from the Select Committee, or the evil to be aimed at, would require that the Government be absolutely neutral as between religion and irreligion. The evil to be aimed at, so far as those who spoke were concerned, appears to have been the establishment of a national church, and perhaps the preference of one religious sect over another; but it was definitely not concern about whether the Government might aid all religions evenhandedly.

The actions of the First Congress, which re-enacted the Northwest Ordinance for the governance of the Northwest Territory in 1789, confirm the view that Congress did not mean that the Government should be neutral between religion and irreligion. [This Ordinance] provided that "[r]eligion, morality, and knowledge, being necessary to good government and the happiness of mankind, schools and the means of education shall forever be encouraged." Land grants for schools in the Northwest Territory were not limited to public schools. It was not until 1845 that Congress limited land grants in the new States and Territories to nonsectarian schools.

As the United States moved from the 18th into the 19th century, Congress appropriated time and again public moneys in support of sectarian Indian education carried on by religious organizations. Typical of these was Jefferson's treaty with the Kaskaskia Indians, which provided annual cash support for the Tribe's Roman Catholic priest and church. It was not until 1897, when aid to sectarian education for Indians had reached $500,000 annually, that Congress decided thereafter to cease appropriating money for education in sectarian schools. This history shows the fallacy of the notion found in *Everson* that "no tax in any amount" may be levied for religious activities in any form.

Joseph Story, a member of this Court from 1822 to 1845, and during much of that time a professor at the Harvard Law School, published by far the most comprehensive treatise on the United States Constitution that had then appeared. Volume 2 of Story's *Commentaries on the Constitution of the United States* discussed the meaning of the Establishment Clause of the First Amendment this way: "Probably at the time of the adoption of the Constitution, and of the amendment to it now under consideration [First Amendment], the general if not the universal sentiment in America was, that Christianity ought to receive encouragement from the State so far as was not incompatible with the private rights of conscience and the freedom of religious worship.

An attempt to level all religions, and to make it a matter of state policy to hold all in utter indifference, would have created universal disapprobation, if not universal indignation."

It would seem from this evidence that the Establishment Clause of the First Amendment had acquired a well-accepted meaning: it forbade establishment of a national religion, and forbade preference among religious sects or denominations. There is simply no historical foundation for the proposition that the Framers intended to build the "wall of separation" that was constitutionalized in *Everson*.

Notwithstanding the absence of an historical basis for this theory of rigid separation, the wall idea might well have served as a useful albeit misguided analytical concept, had it led this Court to unified and principled results in Establishment Clause cases. The opposite, unfortunately, has been true; in the 38 years since *Everson* our Establishment Clause cases have been neither principled nor unified. Whether due to its lack of historical support or its practical unworkability, the *Everson* "wall" has proven all but useless as a guide to sound constitutional adjudication. It should be frankly and explicitly abandoned.

The Framers intended the Establishment Clause to prohibit the designation of any church as a "national" one. The Clause was also designed to stop the Federal Government from asserting a preference for one religious denomination or sect over others. Given the "incorporation" of the Establishment Clause as against the States via the Fourteenth Amendment in *Everson*, States are prohibited as well from establishing a religion or discriminating between sects. As its history abundantly shows, however, nothing in the Establishment Clause requires government to be strictly neutral between religion and irreligion, nor does that Clause prohibit Congress or the States from pursuing legitimate secular ends through nondiscriminatory sectarian means.

Lee v. Weisman
505 U.S. 577 (1992)

For many years, the public middle schools and high schools in Providence, Rhode Island, invited members of the clergy to offer prayers at graduation ceremonies. In line with that practice, Robert E. Lee, principal of the Bishop Middle School, invited Rabbi Leslie Gutterman to offer an invocation and benediction as part of the school's graduation ceremony. The principal sent him a pamphlet entitled "Guidelines for Civic Occasions," prepared by the National Conference of Christians and Jews, which recommended that public prayers at nonsectarian civic events be composed with "inclusiveness and sensitivity." Four days before the ceremony, Daniel Weisman, the father of Deborah Weisman, who was graduating, sought a temporary restraining order in the United States District Court for the District of Rhode Island to prohibit school officials from including an invocation and benediction in the graduation ceremony. The court denied the motion for lack of adequate time to consider it. Although attendance was not mandatory, Deborah and her family attended the graduation, where the prayers were recited. Rabbi Gutterman's invocation was: "God of the Free, Hope of the Brave: For the legacy of America where diversity is celebrated and the rights of minorities are protected, we thank You. May these young men and women grow up to enrich it. For the liberty of America, we thank You. May these new graduates grow up to guard it. For the political process of America in which all its citizens may participate, for its court system where all may seek justice, we thank You. May those we honor this morning always turn to it in trust. For the destiny of America, we thank You. May the graduates of Nathan Bishop Middle School so live that they might help to share it. May our aspirations for our country and for these young people, who are our hope for the future, be richly fulfilled. Amen." His benediction was: "O God, we are grateful to You for having endowed us with the capacity for learning which we have celebrated on this joyous commencement. Happy families give thanks for seeing their children achieve an important milestone. Send Your blessings upon the teachers and administrators who helped prepare them. The graduates now need strength and guidance for the future;

help them to understand that we are not complete with academic knowledge alone. We must each strive to fulfill what You require of us all: to do justly, to love mercy, to walk humbly. We give thanks to You, Lord, for keeping us alive, sustaining us, and allowing us to reach this special, happy occasion. Amen."

After the graduation, Daniel Weisman sought a permanent injunction barring school officials from inviting the clergy to deliver prayers at future graduations. He noted that his daughter was enrolled in high school in the district and argued that prayers would likely be offered at her high school graduation. The district court ruled that the practice of including prayers in public school graduations violated the Establishment Clause. The court of appeals affirmed, and the Supreme Court granted certiorari. Opinion of the Court: <u>Kennedy</u>, Blackmun, Stevens, O'Connor, Souter. Concurring opinions: <u>Blackmun</u>, Stevens, O'Connor; <u>Souter</u>, Stevens, O'Connor. Dissenting opinion: <u>Scalia</u>, Rehnquist, White, Thomas.

JUSTICE KENNEDY delivered the opinion of the Court.

The government involvement with religious activity in this case is pervasive, to the point of creating a state-sponsored and state-directed religious exercise in a public school. Conducting this formal religious observance conflicts with settled rules pertaining to prayer exercises for students, and that suffices to determine the question before us. The principle that government may accommodate the free exercise of religion does not supersede the fundamental limitations imposed by the Establishment Clause. It is beyond dispute that, at a minimum, the Constitution guarantees that government may not coerce anyone to support or participate in religion or its exercise, or otherwise act in a way which "establishes a [state] religion or religious faith, or tends to do so." *Everson v. Board of Education of Ewing* (1947). The State's involvement in the school prayers challenged today violates these central principles.

That involvement is as troubling as it is undenied. A school official, the principal, decided that an invocation and a benediction should be given; this is a choice attributable to the State, and from a constitutional perspective it is as if

a state statute decreed that prayers should occur. The principal chose the religious participant, here a rabbi, and that choice is also attributable to the State. The State's role did not end with the decision to include a prayer and with the choice of clergyman. Principal Lee provided Rabbi Gutterman with a copy of the "Guidelines for Civic Occasions," and advised him that his prayers should be nonsectarian. Through these means the principal directed and controlled the content of the prayer. Though the efforts of the school officials in this case to find common ground appear to have been a good-faith attempt to recognize the common aspects of religions and not the divisive ones, our precedents do not permit school officials to assist in composing prayers as an incident to a formal exercise for their students. *Engel v. Vitale* (1962). And these same precedents caution us to measure the idea of a civic religion against the central meaning of the Religion Clauses of the First Amendment, which is that all creeds must be tolerated and none favored. The suggestion that government may establish an official or civic religion as a means of avoiding the establishment of a religion with more specific creeds strikes us as a contradiction that cannot be accepted.

The degree of school involvement here made it clear that the graduation prayers bore the imprint of the State and thus put school-age children who objected in an untenable position. We turn our attention now to consider the position of the students, both those who desired the prayer and she who did not. To endure the speech of false ideas or offensive content and then to counter it is part of learning how to live in a pluralistic society, a society which insists upon open discourse towards the end of a tolerant citizenry. And tolerance presupposes some mutuality of obligation. It is argued that our constitutional vision of a free society requires confidence in our own ability to accept or reject ideas of which we do not approve, and that prayer at a high school graduation does nothing more than offer a choice. By the time they are seniors, high school students no doubt have been required to attend classes and assemblies and to complete assignments exposing them to ideas they find distasteful or immoral or absurd or all of these. Against this background, students may consider it an odd measure of justice to be subjected during the course of their education to ideas deemed offensive and irreligious, but to be denied a brief, formal prayer ceremony that the school offers in return. This argument cannot prevail, however. It overlooks a fundamental dynamic of the Constitution.

The First Amendment protects speech and religion by quite different mechanisms. Speech is protected by insuring its full expression even when the government participates, for the very object of some of our most important speech is to persuade the government to adopt an idea as its own. The method for protecting freedom of worship and freedom of conscience in religious matters is quite the reverse. In religious debate or expression the government is not a prime participant, for the Framers deemed religious establishment antithetical to the freedom of all. The Free Exercise Clause embraces a freedom of conscience and worship that has close parallels in the speech provisions of the First Amendment, but the Establishment Clause is a specific prohibition on forms of state intervention in religious affairs with no precise counterpart in the speech provisions. The explanation lies in the lesson of history that was and is the inspiration for the Establishment Clause, the lesson that in the hands of government what might begin as a tolerant expression of religious views may end in a policy to indoctrinate and coerce. A state-created orthodoxy puts at grave risk that freedom of belief and conscience which are the sole assurance that religious faith is real, not imposed.

There are heightened concerns with protecting freedom of conscience from subtle coercive pressure in the elementary and secondary public schools. Our decisions in *Engel v. Vitale* (1962) and *Abington Township School District* [*v. Schempp* (1963)] recognize, among other things, that prayer exercises in public schools carry a particular risk of indirect coercion. What to most believers may seem nothing more than a reasonable request that the nonbeliever respect their religious practices, in a school context may appear to the nonbeliever or dissenter to be an attempt to employ the machinery of the State to enforce a religious orthodoxy.

We need not look beyond the circumstances of this case to see the phenomenon at work. The undeniable fact is that the school district's supervision and control of a high school graduation ceremony places public pressure, as well as peer pressure, on attending students to stand as a group or, at least, maintain a respectful silence during the Invocation and Benediction. This pressure, though subtle and indirect, can be as real as any overt compulsion. Of course, in our culture standing or remaining silent can signify adherence to a view or simple respect for the views of others. And no doubt some persons who have no desire to join a prayer have little objection to standing as a sign of respect for those who do. But for the dissenter of high school age, who has a reasonable perception that she is being forced by the State to pray in a manner her conscience will not allow, the injury is no less real. There can be no doubt that for many, if not most, of the students at the graduation, the act of standing or remaining silent was an expression of participation in the Rabbi's prayer. That was the very point of the religious exercise. It is of little comfort to a dissenter, then, to be told that for her the act of standing or remaining in silence signifies mere respect, rather than participation. What matters is that, given our social conventions, a reasonable dissenter in this milieu could believe that the group exercise signified her own participation or approval of it.

Finding no violation under these circumstances would place objectors in the dilemma of participating, with all that implies, or protesting. We do not address whether that choice is acceptable if the affected citizens are mature adults, but we think the State may not, consistent with the Establishment Clause, place primary and secondary school children in this position. Research in psychology supports the common assumption that adolescents are often susceptible to pressure from their peers toward conformity, and that the influence is strongest in matters of social convention. To recognize that the choice imposed by the State constitutes an unacceptable constraint only acknowledges that the government may no more use social pressure to enforce orthodoxy than it may use more direct means.

The injury caused by the government's action, and the reason why Daniel and Deborah Weisman object to it, is that the State, in a school setting, in effect required participation in a religious exercise. It is, we concede, a brief exercise during which the individual can concentrate on joining its message, meditate on her own religion, or let her mind wander. But the embarrassment and the intrusion of the religious exercise cannot be refuted by arguing that these prayers, and similar ones to be said in the future, are of a *de minimis* character. To do so would be an affront to the Rabbi who offered them and to all those for whom the prayers were an essential and profound recognition of divine authority.

Attendance at graduation and promotional ceremonies is voluntary. Petitioners and the United States, as *amicus,* made this a center point of the case, arguing that the option of not attending the graduation excuses any inducement or coercion in the ceremony itself. The argument lacks all persuasion. Everyone knows that in our society and in our culture high school graduation is one of life's most significant occasions. A school rule which excuses attendance is beside the point. Attendance may not be required by official decree, yet it is apparent that a student is not free to absent herself from the graduation exercise in any real sense of the term "voluntary," for absence would require forfeiture of those intangible benefits which have motivated the student through youth and all her high school years. Graduation is a time for family and those closest to the student to celebrate success and express mutual wishes of gratitude and respect, all to the end of impressing upon the young person the role that it is his or her right and duty to assume in the community and all of its diverse parts.

The Government's argument gives insufficient recognition to the real conflict of conscience faced by the young student. The essence of the Government's position is that with regard to a civic, social occasion of this importance it is the objector, not the majority, who must take unilateral and private action to avoid compromising religious scruples, here by electing to miss the graduation exercise. This turns conventional First Amendment analysis on its head. It is a tenet of the First Amendment that the State cannot require one of its citizens to forfeit his or her rights and benefits as the price of resisting conformance to state-sponsored religious practice. To say that a student must remain apart from the ceremony at the opening invocation and closing benediction is to risk compelling conformity in an environment analogous to a classroom setting, where we have said that the risk of compulsion is especially high.

Inherent differences between the public school system and a session of a State Legislature distinguish this case from *Marsh v. Chambers* (1983). The atmosphere at the opening of a session of a state legislature where adults are free to enter and leave with little comment and for any number of reasons cannot compare with the constraining potential of the one school event most important for the student to attend. The influence and force of a formal exercise in a school graduation are far greater than the prayer exercise condoned in *Marsh.* The *Marsh* majority in fact gave specific recognition to this distinction and placed particular reliance on it in upholding the prayers at issue there. For the reasons we have stated, the judgment of the Court of Appeals is

Affirmed.

JUSTICE SOUTER, with whom JUSTICE STEVENS and JUSTICE O'CONNOR join, concurring.

Whatever else may define the scope of accommodation permissible under the Establishment Clause, one requirement is clear: accommodation must lift a discernible burden on the free exercise of religion. Concern for the position of religious individuals in the modern regulatory state cannot justify official solicitude for a religious practice unburdened by general rules; such gratuitous largesse would effectively favor religion over disbelief. By these lights one easily sees that, in sponsoring the graduation prayers at issue here, the State has crossed the line from permissible accommodation to unconstitutional establishment.

Religious students cannot complain that omitting prayers from their graduation ceremony would, in any realistic sense, "burden" their spiritual callings. To be sure, many of them invest this rite of passage with spiritual significance, but they may express their religious feelings about it before and after the ceremony. They may even organize a privately sponsored baccalaureate if they desire the company of like-minded students. Because they accordingly have no need for the machinery of the State to affirm their beliefs, the government's sponsorship of prayer at the graduation ceremony is most reasonably understood as an official endorsement of religion and, in this instance, of theistic religion.

Petitioners would deflect this conclusion by arguing that graduation prayers are no different from presidential religious proclamations and similar official "acknowledgments" of religion in public life. But religious invocations in Thanksgiving Day addresses and the like, rarely noticed, ignored without effort, conveyed over an impersonal medium, and directed at no one in particular, inhabit a pallid zone worlds apart from official prayers delivered to a captive audience of public school students and their families. Madison himself respected the difference between the trivial and the serious in constitutional practice. Realizing that his contemporaries were unlikely to take the Establishment Clause seriously enough to forgo a legislative chaplainship, he suggested that "[r]ather than let this step beyond the landmarks of power have the effect of a legitimate precedent, it will be better to apply to it the legal aphorism *de minimis non curat lex.*" But that logic permits no winking at the practice in question here. When public school officials, armed with the State's authority, convey an endorsement of religion to their students, they strike near the core of the Establishment Clause. However "ceremonial" their messages may be, they are flatly unconstitutional.

JUSTICE SCALIA, with whom THE CHIEF JUSTICE, JUSTICE WHITE, and JUSTICE THOMAS join, dissenting.

In holding that the Establishment Clause prohibits invocations and benedictions at public school graduation ceremonies, the Court—with nary a mention that it is doing so—lays waste a tradition as old as public-school graduation ceremonies themselves, and that is a component of an even more longstanding American tradition of nonsectarian prayer to God at public celebrations generally. As its instrument of destruction, the bulldozer of its social engineering, the Court invents a boundless, and boundlessly manipulable, test of psychological coercion. Today's opinion shows more forcefully than volumes of argumentation why our Nation's protection, that fortress which is our Constitution, cannot possibly rest upon the changeable philosophical predilections of the Justices of this Court, but must have deep foundations in the historic practices of our people.

The Court presumably would separate graduation invocations and benedictions from other instances of public "preservation and transmission of religious beliefs" on the ground that they involve "psychological coercion." A few citations of "research in psychology" that have no particular bearing upon the precise issue here cannot disguise the fact that the Court has gone beyond the realm where judges know what they are doing. The Court's argument that state officials have "coerced" students to take part in the invocation and benediction at graduation ceremonies is, not to put too fine a point on it, incoherent.

The Court declares that students' "attendance and participation in the [invocation and benediction] are in a fair and real sense obligatory." But what exactly is this "fair and real sense"? According to the Court, students at graduation who want "to avoid the fact or appearance of participation" in the invocation and benediction are psychologically obligated by "public pressure, as well as peer pressure, to stand as a group or, at least, maintain respectful silence" during those prayers. The Court's notion that a student who simply sits in "respectful silence" during the invocation and benediction (when all others are standing) has somehow joined—or would somehow be perceived as having joined—in the prayers is nothing short of ludicrous. We indeed live in a vulgar age. But surely "our social conventions" have not coarsened to the point that anyone who does not stand on his chair and shout obscenities can reasonably be deemed to have assented to everything said in his presence. Since the Court does not dispute that students exposed to prayers at graduation ceremonies retain (despite "subtle coercive pressures") the free will to sit, there is absolutely no basis for the Court's decision. It is fanciful enough to say that "a reasonable dissenter," standing head erect in a class of bowed heads, "could believe that the group exercise signified her own participation or approval of it." It is beyond the absurd to say that she could entertain such a belief while pointedly declining to rise.

But let us assume the very worst, that the nonparticipating graduate is "subtly coerced" to stand! The Court acknowledges that "in our culture standing can signify adherence to a view or simple respect for the views of others." But if it is a permissible inference that one who is standing is doing so simply out of respect for the prayers of others that are in progress, then how can it possibly be said that a "reasonable dissenter could believe that the group exercise signified her own participation or approval"? Quite obviously, it cannot. I may add, moreover, that maintaining respect for the religious observances of others is a fundamental civic virtue that government (including the public schools) can and should cultivate—so that even if it were the case that the displaying of such respect might be mistaken for taking part in the prayer, I would deny the dissenter's interest in avoiding even the false appearance of participation constitutionally trumps the government's interest in fostering respect for religion generally.

The opinion manifests that the Court itself has not given careful consideration to its test of psychological coercion. For if it had, how could it observe, with no hint of concern or disapproval, that students stood for the Pledge of Allegiance, which immediately preceded Rabbi Gutterman's invocation? The government can, of course, no more coerce political orthodoxy than religious orthodoxy. Moreover, since the Pledge of Allegiance has been revised since [*West Virginia Board of Education v.*] *Barnette* to include the phrase "under God," recital of the Pledge would appear to raise the same Establishment Clause issue as the invocation and benediction. If students were psychologically coerced to remain standing during invocation, they must also have been psychologically coerced, moments before, to stand for (and thereby, in the Court's view, take part in or

appear to take part in) the Pledge. Must the Pledge therefore be barred from the public schools (both from graduation ceremonies and from the classroom)? In *Barnette* we held that a public-school student could not be compelled to recite the Pledge; we did not even hint that she could not be compelled to observe respectful silence—indeed, even to stand in respectful silence—when those who wished to recite it did so. Logically, this ought to be the next project for the Court's bulldozer.

The other "dominant fact" identified by the Court is that "state officials direct the performance of a formal religious exercise at school graduation ceremonies." All the record shows is that principals of the Providence public schools, acting within their delegated authority, have invited clergy to deliver invocations and benedictions at graduations; and that Principal Lee invited Rabbi Gutterman, provided him a two-page flyer, prepared by the National Conference of Christians and Jews, giving general advice on inclusive prayer for civic occasions, and advised him that his prayers at graduation should be nonsectarian. The Court identifies nothing in the record remotely suggesting that school officials have ever drafted, edited, screened, or censored graduation prayers, or that Rabbi Gutterman was a mouthpiece of the school officials.

The deeper flaw in the Court's opinion does not lie in its wrong answer to the question whether there was state-induced "peer-pressure" coercion; it lies, rather, in the Court's making violation of the Establishment Clause hinge on such a precious question. The coercion that was a hallmark of historical establishments of religion was coercion of religious orthodoxy and of financial support *by force of law and threat of penalty.* The Establishment Clause was adopted to prohibit such an establishment of religion at the federal level (and to protect state establishments of religion from federal interference). I will further acknowledge for the sake of argument that, as some scholars have argued, by 1790 the term "establishment" had acquired an additional meaning—financial support of religion generally, by public taxation—that reflected the development of "general or multiple" establishments, not limited to a single church. But that would still be an establishment coerced by *force of law.* But there is simply no support for the proposition that the officially sponsored nondenominational invocation and benediction read by Rabbi Gutterman—with no one legally coerced to recite them—violated the Constitution of the United States. To the contrary, they are so characteristically American they could have come from the pen of George Washington or Abraham Lincoln himself.

Thus, while I have no quarrel with the Court's general proposition that the Establishment Clause "guarantees that government may not coerce anyone to support or participate in religion or its exercise," I see no warrant for expanding the concept of coercion beyond acts backed by threat of penalty—a brand of coercion that, happily, is readily discernible to those of us who have made a career of reading the disciples of Blackstone rather than of Freud. The Framers were indeed opposed to coercion of religious worship by the National Government; but, as their own sponsorship of nonsectarian prayer in public events demonstrates, they understood that "speech is not coercive; the listener may do as he likes."

This historical discussion places in revealing perspective the Court's extravagant claim that the State has "for all practical purposes" and "in every practical sense" compelled students to participate in prayers at graduation. Beyond the fact, stipulated to by the parties, that attendance at graduation is voluntary, there is nothing in the record to indicate that failure of attending students to take part in the invocation or benediction was subject to any penalty or discipline.

The reader has been told much in this case about the personal interest of Mr. Weisman and his daughter, and very little about the personal interests on the other side. They are not inconsequential. Church and state would not be such a difficult subject if religion were, as the Court apparently thinks it to be, some purely personal avocation that can be indulged entirely in secret, like pornography, in the privacy of one's room. For most believers it is not that, and has never been. Religious men and women of almost all denominations have felt it necessary to acknowledge and beseech the blessing of God as a people, and not just as individuals, because they believe in the "protection of divine Providence," as the Declaration of Independence put it, not just for individuals but for societies; because they believe God to be, as Washington's first Thanksgiving Proclamation put it, the "Great Lord and Ruler of Nations." One can believe in the effectiveness of such public worship, or one can deprecate and deride it. But the longstanding American tradition of prayer at official ceremonies displays with unmistakable clarity that the Establishment Clause does not forbid the government to accommodate it.

McCreary County v. American Civil Liberties Union
545 U.S. 844 (2005)

In 1999, McCreary County and Pulaski County, Kentucky, posted a version of the Ten Commandments on the walls of their courthouses. After suits were filed charging that the exhibit violated the Establishment Clause, the exhibits were twice changed. The final version of the display was entitled The Foundations of American Law and Government Display and included various documents, including the Magna Carta, the Declaration of Independence, the Bill of Rights, the lyrics of the "Star Spangled Banner," the Mayflower Compact, the National Motto, the Preamble to the Kentucky Constitution, and a picture of Lady Justice. Each document had a statement about its historical and legal significance. The comment on the (King James version of the) Ten Commandments reads: "The Ten Commandments have profoundly influenced the formation of Western legal thought and the formation of our country. That influence is clearly seen in the Declaration of Independence, which declared that `We hold these truths to be self-evident, that all men are created equal, that they are endowed by their Creator with certain unalienable Rights, that among these are Life, Liberty, and the pursuit of Happiness.' The Ten Commandments provide the moral background of the Declaration of Independence and the foundation of our legal tradition." The

American Civil Liberties Union obtained a preliminary injunction to enjoin the counties' display in federal district court as in violation of the Establishment Clause, a divided court of appeals affirmed, and the Supreme Court granted certiorari. Opinion of the Court: Souter, Stevens, O'Connor, Ginsburg, Breyer. Concurring opinion: O'Connor. Dissenting opinion: Scalia, Rehnquist, Thomas, Kennedy (in part).

JUSTICE SOUTER delivered the opinion of the Court.

Twenty-five years ago in a case prompted by posting the Ten Commandments in Kentucky's public schools, this Court recognized that the Commandments "are undeniably a sacred text in the Jewish and Christian faiths" and held that their display in public classrooms violated the First Amendment's bar against establishment of religion. *Stone [v. Graham]* (1980). *Stone* found a predominantly religious purpose in the government's posting of the Commandments, "given their prominence as an instrument of religion." The Counties ask for a different approach here by arguing that official purpose is unknowable and the search for it inherently vain. In the alternative, the Counties would avoid the District Court's conclusion by having us limit the scope of the purpose enquiry so severely that any trivial rationalization would suffice, under a standard oblivious to the history of religious government action like the progression of exhibits in this case.

Ever since *Lemon v. Kurtzman* summarized the three familiar considerations for evaluating Establishment Clause claims, looking to whether government action has "a secular legislative purpose" has been a common, albeit seldom dispositive, element of our cases. The touchstone for our analysis is the principle that the "First Amendment mandates governmental neutrality between religion and religion, and between religion and nonreligion." *Epperson v. Arkansas,* (1968). When the government acts with the ostensible and predominant purpose of advancing religion, it violates that central Establishment Clause value of official religious neutrality, there being no neutrality when the government's ostensible object is to take sides.

Despite the intuitive importance of official purpose to the realization of Establishment Clause values, the Counties ask us to abandon *Lemon's* purpose test, or at least to truncate any enquiry into purpose here. Their first argument is that the very consideration of purpose is deceptive: according to them, true "purpose" is unknowable, and its search merely an excuse for courts to act selectively and unpredictably in picking out evidence of subjective intent. The assertions are as seismic as they are unconvincing. Examination of purpose is a staple of statutory interpretation that makes up the daily fare of every appellate court in the country. With enquiries into purpose this common, if they were nothing but hunts for mares' nests deflecting attention from bare judicial will, the whole notion of purpose in law would have dropped into disrepute long ago.

But scrutinizing purpose does make practical sense, where an understanding of official objective emerges from readily discoverable fact, without any judicial psychoanalysis of a drafter's heart of hearts. The cases with findings of a predominantly religious purpose point to the straightforward nature of the test. In *Wallace [v. Jaffree]*, for example, we inferred purpose from a change of wording from an earlier statute to a later one, each dealing with prayer in schools. And in *Edwards [v. Aguillard]*, we relied on a statute's text and the detailed public comments of its sponsor, when we sought the purpose of a state law requiring creationism to be taught alongside evolution. In other cases, the government action itself bespoke the purpose, as in *[School District of] Abington [Township v. Schempp]*, where the object of required Bible study in public schools was patently religious; in *Stone,* the Court held that the "posting of religious texts on the wall served no educational function," and found that if "the posted copies of the Ten Commandments [were] to have any effect at all, it [would] be to induce the schoolchildren to read, meditate upon, perhaps to venerate and obey, the Commandments." In each case, the government's action was held unconstitutional only because openly available data supported a common-sense conclusion that a religious objective permeated the government's action.

After declining the invitation to abandon concern with purpose wholesale, we also have to avoid the Counties' alternative tack of trivializing the enquiry into it. The Counties would read the cases as if the purpose enquiry were so naive that any transparent claim to secularity would satisfy it, and they would cut context out of the enquiry, to the point of ignoring history, no matter what bearing it actually had on the significance of current circumstances. There is no precedent for the Counties' arguments, or reason supporting them.

The Counties' second proffered limitation can be dispatched quickly. They argue that purpose in a case like this one should be inferred, if at all, only from the latest news about the last in a series of governmental actions, however close they may all be in time and subject. But the world is not made brand new every morning, and the Counties are simply asking us to ignore perfectly probative evidence. Hence, we look to the record of evidence showing the progression leading up to the third display of the Commandments.

The display rejected in *Stone* had two obvious similarities to the first one in the sequence here: both set out a text of the Commandments as distinct from any traditionally symbolic representation, and each stood alone, not part of an arguably secular display. The display in *Stone* had no context that might have indicated an object beyond the religious character of the text, and the Counties' solo exhibit here did nothing more to counter the sectarian implication than the postings at issue in *Stone*. The reasonable observer could only think that the Counties meant to emphasize and celebrate the Commandments' religious message.

Once the Counties were sued, they modified the exhibits and invited additional insight into their purpose in a display that hung for about six months. This new one was the product of forthright and nearly identical Pulaski and Mc-Creary County resolutions listing a series of American historical documents with theistic and Christian references, which were to be posted in order to furnish a setting for displaying the Ten Commandments and any "other Kentucky and American historical document" without raising concern about "any Christian or religious references" in them. The display's unstinting focus was on religious passages, showing that the Counties were posting the Commandments precisely because of their

sectarian content. That demonstration of the government's objective was enhanced by serial religious references and the accompanying resolution's claim about the embodiment of ethics in Christ. Together, the display and resolution presented an indisputable, and undisputed, showing of an impermissible purpose. The Counties make no attempt to defend their undeniable objective, but instead hopefully describe version two as "dead and buried."

After the Counties changed lawyers, they mounted a third display, without a new resolution or repeal of the old one. The result was the "Foundations of American Law and Government" exhibit, which placed the Commandments in the company of other documents the Counties thought especially significant in the historical foundation of American government. In trying to persuade the District Court to lift the preliminary injunction, the Counties cited several new purposes for the third version, including a desire "to educate the citizens of the county regarding some of the documents that played a significant role in the foundation of our system of law and government." These new statements of purpose were presented only as a litigating position, there being no further authorizing action by the Counties' governing boards. And although repeal of the earlier county authorizations would not have erased them from the record of evidence bearing on current purpose, the extraordinary resolutions for the second display passed just months earlier were not repealed or otherwise repudiated. No reasonable observer could swallow the claim that the Counties had cast off the objective so unmistakable in the earlier displays.

In holding the preliminary injunction adequately supported by evidence that the Counties' purpose had not changed at the third stage, we do not decide that the Counties' past actions forever taint any effort on their part to deal with the subject matter. We hold only that purpose needs to be taken seriously under the Establishment Clause and needs to be understood in light of context. Nor do we have occasion here to hold that a sacred text can never be integrated constitutionally into a governmental display on the subject of law, or American history. We do not forget, and in this litigation have frequently been reminded, that our own courtroom frieze was deliberately designed in the exercise of governmental authority so as to include the figure of Moses holding tablets exhibiting a portion of the Hebrew text of the later, secularly phrased Commandments; in the company of 17 other lawgivers, most of them secular figures, there is no risk that Moses would strike an observer as evidence that the National Government was violating neutrality in religion.

The importance of neutrality as an interpretive guide is no less true now than it was when the Court broached the principle in *Everson v. Board of Ed. of Ewing* (1947), and a word needs to be said about the different view taken in today's dissent. The dissent puts forward a limitation on the application of the neutrality principle, with citations to historical evidence said to show that the Framers understood the ban on establishment of religion as sufficiently narrow to allow the government to espouse submission to the divine will. The dissent identifies God as the God of monotheism, all of whose three principal strains (Jewish, Christian, and Muslim) acknowledge the religious importance of the Ten Commandments. On the dissent's view, it apparently follows that even rigorous espousal of a common element of this common monotheism, is consistent with the establishment ban.

But the dissent's argument for the original understanding is flawed from the outset by its failure to consider the full range of evidence showing what the Framers believed. The dissent is certainly correct in putting forward evidence that some of the Framers thought some endorsement of religion was compatible with the establishment ban. But there is also evidence supporting the proposition that the Framers intended the Establishment Clause to require governmental neutrality in matters of religion, including neutrality in statements acknowledging religion. The fair inference is that there was no common understanding about the limits of the establishment prohibition, and the dissent's conclusion that its narrower view was the original understanding, stretches the evidence beyond tensile capacity. What the evidence does show is a group of statesmen, like others before and after them, who proposed a guarantee with contours not wholly

worked out, leaving the Establishment Clause with edges still to be determined. And none the worse for that. Indeterminate edges are the kind to have in a constitution meant to endure, and to meet "exigencies which, if foreseen at all, must have been seen dimly, and which can be best provided for as they occur." *McCulloch v. Maryland* (1819).

While the dissent fails to show a consistent original understanding from which to argue that the neutrality principle should be rejected, it does manage to deliver a surprise. [It] says that the deity the Framers had in mind was the God of monotheism, with the consequence that government may espouse a tenet of traditional monotheism. This is truly a remarkable view. Other members of the Court have dissented on the ground that the Establishment Clause bars nothing more than governmental preference for one religion over another, but at least religion has previously been treated inclusively. Today's dissent, however, apparently means that government should be free to approve the core beliefs of a favored religion over the tenets of others, a view that should trouble anyone who prizes religious liberty.

Given the ample support for the District Court's finding of a predominantly religious purpose behind the Counties' third display, we affirm the Sixth Circuit in upholding the preliminary injunction.

JUSTICE SCALIA, with whom THE CHIEF JUSTICE and JUSTICE THOMAS join, and with whom JUSTICE KENNEDY joins as to Parts II and III, dissenting.

On September 11, 2001 I was attending in Rome, Italy an international conference of judges and lawyers, principally from Europe and the United States. That night and the next morning virtually all of the participants watched, in their hotel rooms, the address to the Nation by the President of the United States concerning the murderous attacks upon the Twin Towers and the Pentagon, in which thousands of Americans had been killed. The address ended, as Presidential addresses often do, with the prayer "God bless America." The next afternoon I was approached by one of the judges from a European country, who, after extending his profound condolences for my country's loss, sadly observed "How I wish that the Head of State of my country, at a similar time of national tragedy and distress, could conclude his address 'God bless _____.' It is of course absolutely forbidden."

That is one model of the relationship between church and state—a model spread across Europe by the armies of Napoleon, and reflected in the Constitution of France, which begins "France is a secular Republic." Religion is to be strictly excluded from the public forum. This is not, and never was, the model adopted by America. George Washington added to the form of Presidential oath prescribed by Art. II, §1, c1.8, of the Constitution, the concluding words "so help me God." The Supreme Court under John Marshall opened its sessions with the prayer, "God save the United States and this Honorable Court." The First Congress instituted the practice of beginning its legislative sessions with a prayer. The same week that Congress submitted the Establishment Clause as part of the Bill of Rights for ratification by the States, it enacted legislation providing for paid chaplains in the House and Senate. The day after the First Amendment was proposed, the same Congress that had proposed it requested the President to proclaim "a day of public thanksgiving and prayer, to be observed, by acknowledging, with grateful hearts, the many and signal favours of Almighty God." President Washington offered the first Thanksgiving Proclamation shortly thereafter, devoting November 26, 1789 on behalf of the American people "to the service of that great and glorious Being who is the beneficent author of all the good that is, that was, or that will be." The same Congress also reenacted the Northwest Territory Ordinance of 1787, Article III of which provided: "Religion, morality, and knowledge, being necessary to good government and the happiness of mankind, schools and the means of education shall forever be encouraged." And of course the First Amendment itself accords religion (and no other manner of belief) special constitutional protection.

These actions of our First President and Congress and the Marshall Court were not idiosyncratic; they reflected the beliefs of the period. Those who wrote the Constitution believed that morality was essential to the well-being of society and that encouragement of religion was the best way to foster morality. Nor have the views of our people on this matter significantly changed. Presidents continue to conclude the Presidential oath with the words "so help me God." Our legislatures, state and national, continue to open their sessions with prayer led by official chaplains. The sessions of this Court continue to open with the prayer "God save the United States and this Honorable Court." Invocation of the Almighty by our public figures, at all levels of government, remains commonplace. Our coinage bears the motto "IN GOD WE TRUST." And our Pledge of Allegiance contains the acknowledgment that we are a Nation "under God." As one of our Supreme Court opinions rightly observed, "We are a religious people whose institutions presuppose a Supreme Being." *Zorach v. Clauson* (1952).

With all of this reality (and much more) staring it in the face, how can the Court *possibly* assert that "the First Amendment mandates governmental neutrality between religion and nonreligion," and that "manifesting a purpose to favor adherence to religion generally," is unconstitutional? Who says so? Surely not the words of the Constitution. Surely not the history and traditions that reflect our society's constant understanding of those words. Surely not even the current sense of our society, recently reflected in an Act of Congress adopted *unanimously* by the Senate and with only 5 nays in the House of Representatives, criticizing a Court of Appeals opinion that had held "under God" in the Pledge of Allegiance unconstitutional. Nothing stands behind the Court's assertion that governmental affirmation of the society's belief in God is unconstitutional except the Court's own say-so, citing as support only the unsubstantiated say-so of earlier Courts going back no farther than the mid-20th century.

Besides appealing to the demonstrably false principle that the government cannot favor religion over irreligion, today's opinion suggests that the posting of the Ten Commandments violates the principle that the government cannot favor one religion over another. That is indeed a valid principle where public aid or assistance to religion is concerned, or where the free exercise of religion is at issue, but it necessarily applies in a more limited sense to public acknowledgment of the Creator. If religion in the public forum had to be entirely nondenominational, there could be no religion in the public forum at all. One cannot say the word "God," or "the Almighty," one cannot offer public supplication or thanksgiving, without contradicting the beliefs of some people that there are many gods, or that God or the gods pay no attention to human affairs. With respect to public acknowledgment of religious belief, it is entirely clear from our Nation's historical practices that the Establishment Clause permits this disregard of polytheists and believers in unconcerned deities, just as it permits the disregard of devout atheists. The Thanksgiving Proclamation issued by George Washington at the instance of the First Congress was scrupulously nondenominational—but it was monotheistic. In *Marsh v. Chambers,* we said that the fact the particular prayers offered in the Nebraska Legislature were "in the Judeo-Christian tradition," posed no additional problem, because "there is no indication that the prayer opportunity has been exploited to proselytize or advance any one, or to disparage any other, faith or belief."

Historical practices thus demonstrate that there is a distance between the acknowledgment of a single Creator and the establishment of a religion. The former is, as *Marsh v. Chambers* put it, "a tolerable acknowledgment of beliefs widely held among the people of this country." The three most popular religions in the United States, Christianity, Judaism, and Islam—which combined account for 97.7% of all believers—are monotheistic. All of them, moreover (Islam included), believe that the Ten Commandments were given by God to Moses, and are divine prescriptions for a virtuous life. Publicly honoring the Ten Commandments is thus indistinguishable, insofar as discriminating against other religions is concerned, from publicly honoring God. Both practices are recognized across such a broad and diverse range of the population—from Christians to Muslims—that they cannot be reasonably understood as a government endorsement of a particular religious viewpoint.

Van Orden v. Perry
545 U.S. 677 (2005)

---

*Among the twenty-one historical markers and seventeen monuments surrounding the Texas State Capitol is a six-foot-high monolith inscribed with the Ten Commandments. The engraved quotation on the monument is framed by religious symbols: two tablets with what appears to be ancient script on them, two Stars of David, and the superimposed Greek letters chi and rho as the familiar monogram of Christ. The monument was donated to the state by the Fraternal Order of Eagles, which is a national social, civic, and patriotic organization. After the monument was accepted, the state selected a site for the monument based on the recommendation of the state organization responsible for maintaining the capitol grounds. The Eagles paid the cost of erecting the monument, the dedication of which was presided over by two state legislators. Forty years after the monument's erection, a resident of Austin who frequently was on the capitol grounds, Thomas Van Orden, sued state officials, seeking both a declara-*tion that the monument's placement violates the Establishment Clause and an injunction requiring its removal. The district court held that the monument did not contravene the Establishment Clause, the court of appeals affirmed, and the Supreme Court granted certiorari. Judgment of the Court: <u>Rehnquist</u>, Scalia, Kennedy, Thomas. Concurring opinions: <u>Scalia</u>; <u>Thomas</u>. Concurring in the judgment: <u>Breyer</u>. Dissenting opinions: <u>Stevens</u>, Ginsburg; <u>Souter</u>, Stevens, Ginsburg; <u>O'Connor</u>.*

THE CHIEF JUSTICE announced the judgment of the Court and delivered an opinion, in which JUSTICE SCALIA, JUSTICE KENNEDY, and JUSTICE THOMAS join.

The question here is whether the Establishment Clause of the First Amendment allows the display of a monument inscribed with the Ten Commandments on the Texas State Capitol grounds. We hold that it does.

Our cases, Januslike, point in two directions in applying the Establishment Clause. One face looks toward the strong role played by religion and religious traditions throughout our Nation's history. The other face looks toward the principle that governmental intervention in religious matters can itself endanger religious freedom.

This case, like all Establishment Clause challenges, presents us with the difficulty of respecting both faces. Our institutions presuppose a Supreme Being, yet these institutions must not press religious observances upon their citizens. One face looks to the past in acknowledgment of our Nation's heritage, while the other looks to the present in demanding a separation between church and state. Reconciling these two faces requires that we neither abdicate our responsibility to maintain a division between church and state nor evince a hostility to religion by disabling the government from in some ways recognizing our religious heritage:

Over the last 25 years, we have sometimes pointed to *Lemon v. Kurtzman* (1971), as providing the governing test in Establishment Clause challenges. Whatever may be the fate of the *Lemon* test in the larger scheme of Establishment Clause jurisprudence, we think it not useful in dealing with the sort of passive monument that Texas has erected on its Capitol grounds. Instead, our analysis is driven both by the nature of the monument and by our Nation's history. As we explained in *Lynch v. Donnelly* (1984): "There is an unbroken history of official acknowledgment by all three branches of government of the role of religion in American life from at least 1789." For example, both Houses passed resolutions in 1789 asking President George Washington to issue a Thanksgiving Day Proclamation to "recommend to the people of the United States a day of public thanksgiving and prayer, to be observed by acknowledging, with grateful hearts, the many and signal favors of Almighty God." President Washington's proclamation directly attributed to the Supreme Being the foundations and successes of our young Nation. Recognition of the role of God in our Nation's heritage has also been reflected in our decisions.

In this case we are faced with a display of the Ten Commandments on government property outside the Texas State Capitol. Such acknowledgments of the role played by the Ten Commandments in our Nation's heritage are common throughout America. We need only look within our own Courtroom. Since 1935, Moses has stood, holding two tablets that reveal portions of the Ten Commandments written in Hebrew, among other lawgivers in the south frieze. Representations of the Ten Commandments adorn the metal gates lining the north and south sides of the Courtroom as well as the doors leading into the Courtroom. Moses also sits on the exterior east facade of the building holding the Ten Commandments tablets.

Similar acknowledgments can be seen throughout a visitor's tour of our Nation's Capital. For example, a large statue of Moses holding the Ten Commandments, alongside a statue of the Apostle Paul, has overlooked the rotunda of the Library of Congress' Jefferson Building since 1897. And the Jefferson Building's Great Reading Room contains a sculpture of a woman beside the Ten Commandments with a quote above her from the Old Testament (Micah 6:8). A medallion with two tablets depicting the Ten Commandments decorates the floor of the National Archives. Inside the Department of Justice, a statue entitled "The Spirit of Law" has two tablets representing the Ten Commandments lying at its feet. In front of the Ronald Reagan Building is another sculpture that includes a depiction of the Ten Commandments. So too a 24-foot-tall sculpture, depicting, among other things, the Ten Commandments and a cross, stands outside the federal courthouse that houses both the Court of Appeals and the District Court for the District of Columbia. Moses is also prominently featured in the Chamber of the United States House of Representatives. These displays and recognitions of the Ten Commandments bespeak the rich American tradition of religious acknowledgments.

Of course, the Ten Commandments are religious—they were so viewed at their inception and so remain. The monument, therefore, has religious significance. According to Judeo-Christian belief, the Ten Commandments were given to Moses by God on Mt. Sinai. But Moses was a lawgiver as well as a religious leader. And the Ten Commandments have an undeniable historical meaning, as the foregoing examples demonstrate. Simply having religious content or promoting a message consistent with a religious doctrine does not run afoul of the Establishment Clause.

There are, of course, limits to the display of religious messages or symbols. For example, we held unconstitutional a Kentucky statute requiring the posting of the Ten Commandments in every public schoolroom. *Stone v. Graham* (1980). In the classroom context, we found that the Kentucky statute had an improper and plainly religious purpose. The placement of the Ten Commandments monument on the Texas State Capitol grounds is a far more passive use of those texts than was the case in *Stone,* where the text confronted elementary school students every day. Indeed, Van Orden, the petitioner here, apparently walked by the monument for a number of years before bringing this lawsuit. The monument is therefore also quite different from the prayers involved in *Schempp* and *Lee v. Weisman.* Texas has treated her Capitol grounds monuments as representing the several strands in the State's political and legal history. The inclusion of the Ten Commandments monument in this group has a dual significance, partaking of both religion and government. We cannot say that Texas' display of this monument violates the Establishment Clause of the First Amendment. The judgment of the Court of Appeals is affirmed.

JUSTICE THOMAS, concurring.

Our task would be far simpler if we returned to the original meaning of the word "establishment" than it is under the various approaches this Court now uses. Establishment at the founding involved, for example, mandatory observance or mandatory payment of taxes supporting ministers. And "government practices that have nothing to do with creating or maintaining coercive state establishments" simply do not "implicate the possible liberty interest of being free from coercive state establishments."

There is no question that, based on the original meaning of the Establishment Clause, the Ten Commandments display at issue here is

constitutional. In no sense does Texas compel petitioner Van Orden to do anything. The only injury to him is that he takes offense at seeing the monument as he passes it on his way to the Texas Supreme Court Library. He need not stop to read it or even to look at it, let alone to express support for it or adopt the Commandments as guides for his life. The mere presence of the monument along his path involves no coercion and thus does not violate the Establishment Clause. While the Court correctly rejects the challenge to the Ten Commandments monument on the Texas Capitol grounds, a more fundamental rethinking of our Establishment Clause jurisprudence remains in order.

JUSTICE BREYER, concurring in the judgment.

In *School Dist. of Abington Township* v. *Schempp* (1963), Justice Goldberg wrote, in respect to the First Amendment's Religion Clauses, that there is "no simple and clear measure which by precise application can readily and invariably demark the permissible from the impermissible." One must refer instead to the basic purposes of those Clauses. They seek to "assure the fullest possible scope of religious liberty and tolerance for all." They seek to avoid that divisiveness based upon religion that promotes social conflict, sapping the strength of government and religion alike. They seek to maintain that "separation of church and state" that has long been critical to the "peaceful dominion that religion exercises in this country," where the "spirit of religion" and the "spirit of freedom" are productively "united," "reigning together" but in separate spheres "on the same soil." A. de Tocqueville, Democracy in America.

If the relation between government and religion is one of separation, but not of mutual hostility and suspicion, one will inevitably find difficult borderline cases. And in such cases, I see no test-related substitute for the exercise of legal judgment. The case before us is a borderline case. It concerns a large granite monument bearing the text of the Ten Commandments located on the grounds of the Texas State Capitol. On the one hand, the Commandments' text undeniably has a religious message, invoking, indeed emphasizing, the Deity. On the other hand, focusing on the text of the Commandments alone cannot conclusively resolve this case. Rather, to determine the message that the text here conveys, we must examine how the text is *used*. And that inquiry requires us to consider the context of the display.

In certain contexts, a display of the tablets of the Ten Commandments can convey not simply a religious message but also a secular moral message (about proper standards of social conduct). And in certain contexts, a display of the tablets can also convey a historical message (about a historic relation between those standards and the law)—a fact that helps to explain the display of those tablets in dozens of courthouses throughout the Nation, including the Supreme Court of the United States. Here the tablets have been used as part of a display that communicates not simply a religious message, but a secular message as well. The circumstances surrounding the display's placement on the capitol grounds and its physical setting suggest that the State itself intended the latter, nonreligious aspects of the tablets' message to predominate.

A further factor is determinative here. As far as I can tell, 40 years passed in which the presence of this monument, legally speaking, went unchallenged (until the single legal objection raised by petitioner). And I am not aware of any evidence suggesting that this was due to a climate of intimidation. Hence, those 40 years suggest more strongly than can any set of formulaic tests that few individuals, whatever their system of beliefs, are likely to have understood the monument as amounting, in any significantly detrimental way, to a government effort to favor a particular religious sect, primarily to promote religion over nonreligion, to "engage in" any "religious practice," to "compel" any "religious practice," or to "work deterrence" of any "religious belief." *Schempp* (Goldberg, J., concurring). Those 40 years suggest that the public visiting the capitol grounds has considered the religious aspect of the tablets' message as part of what is a broader moral and historical message reflective of a cultural heritage.

This case, moreover, is distinguishable from instances where the Court has found Ten Commandments displays impermissible. The display is not on the grounds of a public school, where, given the impressionability of the young, government must exercise particular care in separating church and state. This case also differs from *McCreary County*, where the short (and stormy) history of the courthouse Commandments' displays demonstrates the substantially religious objectives of those who mounted them, and the effect of this readily apparent objective upon those who view them. That history there indicates a governmental effort substantially to promote religion, not simply an effort primarily to reflect, historically, the secular impact of a religiously inspired document. And, in today's world, in a Nation of so many different religious and comparable nonreligious fundamental beliefs, a more contemporary state effort to focus attention upon a religious text is certainly likely to prove divisive in a way that this longstanding, pre-existing monument has not.

I recognize the danger of the slippery slope. Still, where the Establishment Clause is at issue, we must "distinguish between real threat and mere shadow." Here, we have only the shadow. I concur in the judgment of the Court.

JUSTICE STEVENS, with whom JUSTICE GINSBURG joins, dissenting.

The sole function of the monument on the grounds of Texas' State Capitol is to display the full text of one version of the Ten Commandments. The monument is not a work of art and does not refer to any event in the history of the State. It is significant because, and only because, it communicates the following message:

I AM the LORD thy God.
Thou shalt have no other gods before me.
Thou shalt not make to thyself any graven
  images.
Thou shalt not take the Name of the Lord
  thy God in vain.
Remember the Sabbath day, to keep it holy.
Honor thy father and thy mother, that thy
  days may be long upon the land which the
  Lord thy God giveth thee.
Thou shalt not kill.
Thou shalt not commit adultery.
Thou shalt not steal.

*Thou shalt not bear false witness against thy
neighbor.*
Thou shalt not covet thy neighbor's house.
*Thou shalt not covet thy neighbor's wife,
nor his manservant, nor his maidservant,
nor his cattle, nor anything that is thy
neighbor's.*

Viewed on its face, Texas' display has no purported connection to God's role in the formation of Texas or the founding of our Nation;
nor does it provide the reasonable observer
with any basis to guess that it was erected to
honor any individual or organization. The
message transmitted by Texas' chosen display is
quite plain: This State endorses the divine code
of the "Judeo-Christian" God.

For those of us who learned to recite the King
James version of the text long before we understood the meaning of some of its words, God's
Commandments may seem like wise counsel.
The question before this Court, however, is
whether it is counsel that the State of Texas may
proclaim without violating the Establishment
Clause of the Constitution. If any fragment of
Jefferson's metaphorical "wall of separation between church and State" is to be preserved—if
there remains any meaning to the "wholesome

'neutrality' of which this Court's [Establish-
ment Clause] cases speak," *School Dist. of
Abington Township v. Schempp* (1963)—a negative answer to that question is mandatory.

The Eagles may donate as many monuments
as they choose to be displayed in front of Protestant churches, benevolent organizations'
meeting places, or on the front lawns of private
citizens. The expurgated text of the King James
version of the Ten Commandments that they
have crafted is unlikely to be accepted by Catholic parishes, Jewish synagogues, or even some
Protestant denominations, but the message
they seek to convey is surely more compatible
with church property than with property that
is located on the government side of the metaphorical wall.

The judgment of the Court in this case
stands for the proposition that the Constitution permits governmental displays of sacred
religious texts. This makes a mockery of the
constitutional ideal that government must remain neutral between religion and irreligion. If
a State may endorse a particular deity's command to "have no other gods before me," it is
difficult to conceive of any textual display that
would run afoul of the Establishment Clause. I
respectfully dissent.

Rosenberger v. University of Virginia
515 U.S. 819 (1995)

*The Student Activity Fund (SAF) at the Univer-
sity of Virginia receives its money from mandatory
student fees and supports extracurricular student
activities related to the university's educational
purposes. In order to qualify for SAF support, a
student organization must be recognized as a
"contracted independent organization" (CIO) by
the university. CIOs are required by university
regulation to include in their dealings with third
parties and in all written materials a disclaimer,
stating that the CIO is independent of the university and that the university is not responsible for
the CIO. The University of Virginia authorizes
payment from the SAF to outside contractors for
the printing costs of student publications. The
university's guidelines recognize various categories
of CIOs that can receive such payment, including
"student news, information, opinion, entertain-*

*ment, or academic communications media
groups." The guidelines, however, specify that the
costs of certain activities of CIOs that are otherwise eligible for funding, including religious activities, cannot be reimbursed by the SAF.*

*Wide Awake Productions (WAP), which was
formed by Ronald Rosenberger and other under-
graduates in 1990, qualified as a CIO. The organization published a newspaper,* Wide Awake: A
Christian Perspective at the University of Virginia, *whose mission was "to challenge Christians
to live, in word and deed, according to the faith
they proclaim and to encourage students to consider
what a personal relationship with Jesus Christ
means." When WAP requested the SAF to pay the
costs of printing the newspaper, the SAF denied the
request on the grounds that* Wide Awake *was a
"religious activity." After appeals of the decision*

within the university proved unavailing, WAP, Wide Awake, and three of its editors filed suit in federal court, charging that the refusal to authorize payment of the printing costs solely on the basis of Wide Awake's religious orientation violated their rights to freedom of speech and press, to the free exercise of religion, and to equal protection of the laws. In response, the University of Virginia contended that underwriting the printing costs of a religious publication would violate the Establishment Clause. After the district court and the court of appeals ruled for the university, the US Supreme Court granted certiorari. Opinion of the Court: <u>Kennedy</u>, Rehnquist, O'Connor, Scalia, Thomas. Concurring opinions: <u>O'Connor</u>; <u>Thomas</u>. Dissenting opinion: <u>Souter</u>, Stevens, Ginsburg, Breyer.

JUSTICE KENNEDY delivered the opinion of the Court.

It is axiomatic that the government may not regulate speech based on its substantive content or the message it conveys. *Police Department of Chicago v. Mosley* (1972). Other principles follow from this precept. In the realm of private speech or expression, government regulation may not favor one speaker over another. Discrimination against speech because of its message is presumed to be unconstitutional. These rules informed our determination that the government offends the First Amendment when it imposes financial burdens on certain speakers based on the content of their expression.

These principles provide the framework forbidding the State from exercising viewpoint discrimination, even when the limited public forum is one of its own creation. In a case involving a school district's provision of school facilities for private uses, we declared that "there is no question that the District, like the private owner of property, may legally preserve the property under its control for the use to which it is dedicated." *Lamb's Chapel v. Center Moriches Union Free School District* (1993). The necessities of confining a forum to the limited and legitimate purposes for which it was created may justify the State in reserving it for certain groups or for the discussion of certain topics. Once it has opened a limited forum, however, the State must respect the lawful boundaries it has itself set. The State may not

exclude speech where its distinction is not "reasonable in light of the purpose served by the forum," nor may it discriminate against speech on the basis of its viewpoint. Thus, in determining whether the State is acting to preserve the limits of the forum it has created so that the exclusion of a class of speech is legitimate, we have observed a distinction between, on the one hand, content discrimination, which may be permissible if it preserves the purposes of that limited forum, and, on the other hand, viewpoint discrimination, which is presumed impermissible when directed against speech otherwise within the forum's limitations.

The most recent and most apposite case is our decision in *Lamb's Chapel*. There, a school district had opened school facilities for use after school hours by community groups for a wide variety of social, civic, and recreational purposes. The district, however, had enacted a formal policy against opening facilities to groups for religious purposes. Invoking its policy, the district rejected a request from a group desiring to show a film series addressing various child-rearing questions from a "Christian perspective." Our conclusion was unanimous: "It discriminates on the basis of viewpoint to permit school property to be used for the presentation of all views about family issues and child-rearing except those dealing with the subject matter from a religious standpoint."

The University tries to escape the consequences of our holding in *Lamb's Chapel* by urging that this case involves the provision of funds rather than access to facilities. To this end the University relies on our assurance in *Widmar v. Vincent*. There, in the course of striking down a public university's exclusion of religious groups from use of school facilities made available to all other student groups, we stated: "Nor do we question the right of the University to make academic judgments as to how best to allocate scarce resources." The quoted language in Widmar was but a proper recognition of the principle that when the State is the speaker, it may make content-based choices.

The distinction between the University's own favored message and the private speech of students is evident in the case before us. The University itself has taken steps to ensure the distinction in the agreement each CIO must sign. The University declares that the student groups eligible for SAF support are not the University's agents, are not subject to its control, and are not its responsibility. Having offered to pay the third-party contractors on behalf of private speakers who convey their own messages, the University may not silence the expression of selected viewpoints.

Vital First Amendment speech principles are at stake here. The first danger to liberty lies in granting the State the power to examine publications to determine whether or not they are based on some ultimate idea and if so for the State to classify them. The second, and corollary, danger is to speech from the chilling of individual thought and expression. That danger is especially real in the University setting, where the State acts against a background and tradition of thought and experiment that is at the center of our intellectual and philosophic tradition. For the University, by regulation, to cast disapproval on particular viewpoints of its students risks the suppression of free speech and creative inquiry in one of the vital centers for the nation's intellectual life, its college and university campuses.

Based on the principles we have discussed, we hold that the regulation invoked to deny SAF support, both in its terms and in its application to these petitioners, is a denial of their right of free speech guaranteed by the First Amendment. It remains to be considered whether the violation following from the University's action is excused by the necessity of complying with the Constitution's prohibition against state establishment of religion. We turn to that question.

A central lesson of our decisions is that a significant factor in upholding governmental programs in the face of Establishment Clause attack is their neutrality towards religion. The governmental program here is neutral toward religion. There is no suggestion that the University created it to advance religion or adopted some ingenious device with the purpose of aiding a religious cause. The object of the SAF is to open a forum for speech and to support various student enterprises, including the publication of newspapers, in recognition of the diversity and creativity of student life. The

neutrality of the program distinguishes the student fees from a tax levied for the direct support of a church or group of churches. A tax of that sort, of course, would run contrary to Establishment Clause concerns dating from the earliest days of the Republic. It does not violate the Establishment Clause for a public university to grant access to its facilities on a religion-neutral basis to a wide spectrum of student groups, including groups which use meeting rooms for sectarian activities, accompanied by some devotional exercises. There is no difference in logic or principle, and no difference of constitutional significance, between a school using its funds to operate a facility to which students have access, and a school paying a third-party contractor to operate the facility on its behalf. The latter occurs here. The University provides printing services to a broad spectrum of student newspapers qualified as CIOs by reason of their officers and membership. Any benefit to religion is incidental to the government's provision of secular services for secular purposes on a religion-neutral basis.

To obey the Establishment Clause, it was not necessary for the University to deny eligibility to student publications because of their viewpoint. The neutrality commanded of the State by the separate Clauses of the First Amendment was compromised by the University's course of action. The viewpoint discrimination inherent in the University's regulation required public officials to scan and interpret student publications to discern their underlying philosophic assumptions respecting religious theory and belief. That course of action was a denial of the right of free speech and would risk fostering a pervasive bias or hostility to religion, which could undermine the very neutrality the Establishment Clause requires. There is no Establishment Clause violation in the University's honoring its duties under the Free Speech Clause.

The judgment of the Court of Appeals must be, and is, reversed.

JUSTICE O'CONNOR, concurring.

"We have time and again held that the government generally may not treat people differently based on the God or gods they worship, or don't worship." *Board of Education of Kiryas Joel Village School District v. Grumet* (1994). As

JUSTICE SOUTER demonstrates, however, there exists another axiom in the history and precedent of the Establishment Clause. "Public funds may not be used to endorse the religious message." *Bowen v. Kendrick* (1988). This case lies at the intersection of the principle of government neutrality and the prohibition on state funding of religious activities. It is clear that the University has established a generally applicable program to encourage the free exchange of ideas by its students, an expressive marketplace that includes some 15 student publications with predictably divergent viewpoints. It is equally clear that petitioners' viewpoint is religious and that publication of *Wide Awake* is a religious activity, under both the University's regulation and a fair reading of our precedents. Not to finance *Wide Awake,* according to petitioners, violates the principle of neutrality by sending a message of hostility toward religion. To finance *Wide Awake,* argues the University, violates the prohibition on direct state funding of religious activities.

When bedrock principles collide, they test the limits of categorical obstinacy and expose the flaws and dangers of a Grand Unified Theory that may turn out to be neither grand nor unified. The Court today does only what courts must do in many Establishment Clause cases— focus on specific features of a particular government action to ensure that it does not violate the Constitution. By withholding from *Wide Awake* assistance that the University provides generally to all other student publications, the University has discriminated on the basis of the magazine's religious viewpoint in violation of the Free Speech Clause. And particular features of the University's program— such as the explicit disclaimer, the disbursement of funds directly to third-party vendors, the vigorous nature of the forum at issue, and the possibility for objecting students to opt out— convince me that providing such assistance in this case would not carry the danger of impermissible use of public funds to endorse *Wide Awake*'s religious message.

JUSTICE SOUTER, with whom JUSTICE STEVENS, JUSTICE GINSBURG and JUSTICE BREYER join, dissenting.

The Court today, for the first time, approves direct funding of core religious activities by an arm of the State. It does so, however, only after erroneous treatment of some familiar principles of law implementing the First Amendment's Establishment and Speech Clauses, and by viewing the very funds in question as beyond the reach of the Establishment Clause's funding restrictions as such. Because there is no warrant for distinguishing among public funding sources for purposes of applying the First Amendment's prohibition of religious establishment, I would hold that the University's refusal to support petitioners' religious activities is compelled by the Establishment Clause. I would therefore affirm.

This writing is no merely descriptive examination of religious doctrine or even of ideal Christian practice in confronting life's social and personal problems. Nor is it merely the expression of editorial opinion that incidentally coincides with Christian ethics and reflects a Christian view of human obligation. It is straightforward exhortation to enter into a relationship with God as revealed in Jesus Christ, and to satisfy a series of moral obligations derived from the teachings of Jesus Christ. These are not the words of "student news, information, opinion, entertainment, or academic communication" (in the language of the University's funding criterion), but the words of "challenge to Christians to live, in word and deed, according to the faith they proclaim and to consider what a personal relationship with Jesus Christ means" (in the language of *Wide Awake*'s founder). The subject is not the discourse of the scholar's study or the seminar room, but of the evangelist's mission station and the pulpit. It is nothing other than the preaching of the word, which (along with the sacraments) is what most branches of Christianity offer those called to the religious life.

Using public funds for the direct subsidization of preaching the word is categorically forbidden under the Establishment Clause, and if the Clause was meant to accomplish nothing else, it was meant to bar this use of public money. Evidence on the subject antedates even the Bill of Rights itself, as may be seen in the writings of Madison, whose authority on questions about the meaning of the Establishment

Clause is well settled. Four years before the First Congress proposed the First Amendment, Madison gave his opinion on the legitimacy of using public funds for religious purposes, in the Memorial and Remonstrance Against Religious Assessments, which played the central role in ensuring the defeat of the Virginia tax assessment bill in 1786 and framed the debate upon which the Religion Clauses stand "Who does not see that the same authority which can force a citizen to contribute three pence only of his property for the support of any one establishment, may force him to conform to any other establishment in all cases whatsoever?"

Madison wrote against a background in which nearly every Colony had exacted a tax for church support, the practice having become "so commonplace as to shock the freedom-loving colonials into a feeling of abhorrence." Madison's Remonstrance captured the colonists' "conviction that individual religious liberty could be achieved best under a government which was stripped of all power to tax, to support, or otherwise to assist any or all religions, or to interfere with the beliefs of any religious individual or group." Their sentiment as expressed by Madison in Virginia, led not only to the defeat of Virginia's tax assessment bill but also directly to passage of the Virginia Bill for Establishing Religious Freedom, written by Thomas Jefferson. That bill's preamble declared that "to compel a man to furnish contributions of money for the propagation of opinions which he disbelieves, is sinful and tyrannical," and its text provided "that no man shall be compelled to frequent or support any religious worship, place, or ministry whatsoever." We have "previously recognized that the provisions of the First Amendment, in the drafting and adoption of which Madison and Jefferson played such leading roles, had the same objective and were intended to provide the same protection against governmental intrusion on religious liberty as the Virginia statute."

The principle against direct funding with public money is patently violated by the contested use of today's student activity fee. Like today's taxes generally, the fee is Madison's three pence. The University exercises the power of the State to compel a student to pay it, and the use of any part of it for the direct support

of religious activity thus strikes at what we have repeatedly held to be the heart of the prohibition on establishment. The Court, accordingly, has never before upheld direct state funding of the sort of proselytizing published in *Wide Awake* and, in fact, has categorically condemned state programs directly aiding religious activity. Even when the Court has upheld aid to an institution performing both secular and sectarian functions, it has always made a searching enquiry to ensure that the institution kept the secular activities separate from its sectarian ones, with any direct aid flowing only to the former and never the latter.

Why does the Court not apply this clear law to these clear facts and conclude, as I do, that the funding scheme here is a clear constitutional violation? The answer is that the Court focuses on a subsidiary body of law, which it correctly states but ultimately misapplies. The relationship between the prohibition on direct aid and the requirement of evenhandedness when affirmative government aid does result in some benefit to religion reflects the relationship between basic rule and marginal criterion. At the heart of the Establishment Clause stands the prohibition against direct public funding, but that prohibition does not answer the questions that occur at the margins of the Clause's application. Is any government activity that provides any incidental benefit to religion likewise unconstitutional? Would it be wrong to put out fires in burning churches, wrong to pay the bus fares of students on the way to parochial schools, wrong to allow a grantee of special education funds to spend them at a religious college? These are the questions that call for drawing lines, and it is in drawing them that evenhandedness becomes important.

Evenhandedness as one element of a permissibly attenuated benefit is, of course, a far cry from evenhandedness as a sufficient condition of constitutionality for direct financial support of religious proselytization, and our cases have unsurprisingly repudiated any such attempt to cut the Establishment Clause down to a mere prohibition against unequal direct aid.

Since I cannot see the future I cannot tell whether today's decision portends much more than making a shambles out of student activity fees in public colleges. Still, my apprehension is whetted by Chief Justice Burger's warning in *Lemon v. Kurtzman* (1971): "in constitutional adjudication some steps, which when taken were thought to approach 'the verge,' have become the platform for yet further steps. A certain momentum develops in constitutional theory and it can be a 'downhill thrust' easily set in motion but difficult to retard or stop."

Zelman v. Simmons-Harris
536 U.S. 639 (2002)

Cleveland's public schools have been among the worst-performing public schools in the nation. In 1995, a federal district court declared a "crisis of magnitude" and placed the entire Cleveland school district under state control. To deal with this educational crisis, Ohio enacted its Pilot Project Scholarship Program. The program provides tuition aid for students in kindergarten through third grade, expanding each year through eighth grade, to attend a participating public or private school of their parents' choosing. It also provides tutorial aid for students who choose to remain enrolled in public school. The program is part of a broader attempt to enhance educational options for Cleveland's schoolchildren, including provision for community schools (which are funded under state law but are run by their own school boards and can hire their own teachers and determine their own curriculum) and magnet schools (which are operated by a local school board and emphasize a particular subject area, teaching method, or service to students). Any private school, whether religious or nonreligious, may participate in the Pilot Project Scholarship Program, so long as it agrees not to discriminate on the basis of race, religion, or ethnic background, or to "advocate or foster unlawful behavior or teach hatred of any person or group on the basis of race, ethnicity, national origin, or religion." Any public school in a district adjacent to the Cleveland district may also participate in the program. Tuition aid is distributed to parents according to financial need, and the aid goes to the school in which parents enroll their child. If parents choose a private school, checks are made payable to the parents, who then endorse the checks over to the chosen school. In the 1999–2000 school year, fifty-six private schools participated in the program, forty-six (or 82 percent) of which had a religious affiliation. None of the public schools in districts adjacent to Cleveland have elected to participate. More than thirty-seven
hundred students participated in the scholarship program, most of whom (96 percent) enrolled in religiously affiliated schools. In July 1999, respondents filed suit in federal district court, claiming that the tuition-aid program violated the Establishment Clause. The district court agreed, a divided panel of the court of appeals affirmed that judgment, and the Supreme Court granted certiorari. Opinion of the Court: <u>Rehnquist</u>, O'Connor, Scalia, Kennedy, Thomas. Concurring opinions: <u>O'Connor</u>; <u>Thomas</u>. Dissenting opinions: <u>Stevens</u>; <u>Souter</u>, Stevens, Ginsburg, Breyer; <u>Breyer</u>, Stevens, Souter.

THE CHIEF JUSTICE delivered the opinion of the Court.

The State of Ohio has established a pilot program designed to provide educational choices to families with children who reside in the Cleveland City School District. The question presented is whether this program offends the Establishment Clause of the United States Constitution. We hold that it does not.

The Establishment Clause of the First Amendment, applied to the States through the Fourteenth Amendment, prevents a State from enacting laws that have the "purpose" or "effect" of advancing or inhibiting religion. *Agostini v. Felton* (1997). There is no dispute that the program challenged here was enacted for the valid secular purpose of providing educational assistance to poor children in a demonstrably failing public school system. Thus, the question presented is whether the Ohio program nonetheless has the forbidden "effect" of advancing or inhibiting religion. To answer that question, our decisions have drawn a consistent distinction between government programs that provide aid directly to religious schools, *Mitchell v. Helms* (2000); *Rosenberger v. Rector and Visitors of Univ. of Va.* (1995), and programs of true private choice, in which government aid reaches religious schools only as a result of the genuine and independent choices of private individuals, *Witters v. Washington Dept. of Servs. for Blind* (1986); *Zobrest v. Catalina Foothills School Dist.* (1993). While our jurisprudence with respect to the constitutionality of direct aid programs has "changed significantly" over the past two decades, our jurisprudence with respect to true private choice programs has remained consistent and unbroken. Three times we have confronted Establishment Clause challenges to neutral government programs that provide aid directly to a broad class of individuals, who, in turn, direct the aid to religious schools or institutions of their own choosing. Three times we have rejected such challenges.

In *Mueller v. Allen* (1983), we rejected an Establishment Clause challenge to a Minnesota program authorizing tax deductions for various educational expenses, including private school tuition costs, even though the great majority of the program's beneficiaries (96%) were parents of children in religious schools. In *Witters,* we used identical reasoning to reject an Establishment Clause challenge to a vocational scholarship program that provided tuition aid to a student studying at a religious institution to become a pastor. Finally, in *Zobrest,* we applied *Mueller* and *Witters* to reject an Establishment Clause challenge to a federal program that permitted sign-language interpreters to assist deaf children enrolled in religious schools. Reviewing our earlier decisions, we stated that "government programs that neutrally provide benefits to a broad class of citizens defined without reference to religion are not readily subject to an Establishment Clause challenge." Looking once again to the challenged program as a whole, we observed that the program "distributes benefits neutrally to any child qualifying as 'disabled.'" Its "primary beneficiaries," we said, were "disabled children, not sectarian schools."

Mueller, Witters, and *Zobrest* thus make clear that where a government aid program is neutral with respect to religion, and provides assistance directly to a broad class of citizens who, in turn, direct government aid to religious schools wholly as a result of their own genuine and independent private choice, the program is not readily subject to challenge under the Establishment Clause. A program that shares these features permits government aid to reach religious institutions only by way of the deliberate choices of numerous individual recipients. The incidental advancement of a religious mission, or the perceived endorsement of a religious message, is reasonably attributable to the individual recipient, not to the government, whose role ends with the disbursement of benefits.

We believe that the program challenged here is a program of true private choice, consistent with *Mueller, Witters,* and *Zobrest,* and thus constitutional. As was true in those cases, the Ohio program is neutral in all respects toward religion. It is part of a general and multifaceted undertaking by the State of Ohio to provide educational opportunities to the children of a failed school district. It confers educational assistance directly to a broad class of individuals defined without reference to religion, i.e., any parent of a school-age child who resides in the Cleveland City School District. The program permits the participation of all schools within the district, religious or nonreligious. Adjacent public schools also may participate and have a financial incentive to do so. Program benefits are available to participating families on neutral terms, with no reference to religion. The only preference stated anywhere in the program is a preference for low-income families, who receive greater assistance and are given priority for admission at participating schools.

There are no "financial incentives" that "skew" the program toward religious schools. Such incentives "are not present where the aid is allocated on the basis of neutral, secular criteria that neither favor nor disfavor religion, and is made available to both religious and secular beneficiaries on a nondiscriminatory basis." *Agostini.* The program here in fact creates financial disincentives for religious schools, with private schools receiving only half the government assistance given to community schools and one-third the assistance given to magnet schools. Adjacent public schools, should any choose to accept program students, are also eligible to receive two to three times the state funding of a private religious school. Families too have a financial disincentive to choose a private religious school over other schools. Parents that choose to participate in the scholarship program and then to enroll their children in a private school (religious or nonreligious) must copay a portion of the school's tuition. Families that choose a community school, magnet school, or traditional public school pay nothing. Although such features of the program are not necessary to its constitutionality, they clearly dispel the claim that the program "creates financial incentives for parents to choose a sectarian school." *Zobrest.*

Respondents suggest that even without a financial incentive for parents to choose a religious school, the program creates a "public perception that the State is endorsing religious practices and beliefs." But no reasonable observer would think a neutral program of private choice, where state aid reaches religious schools solely as a result of the numerous independent decisions of private individuals, carries with it the *imprimatur* of government endorsement.

There also is no evidence that the program fails to provide genuine opportunities for Cleveland parents to select secular educational options for their school-age children. Cleveland schoolchildren enjoy a range of educational choices: They may remain in public school as before, remain in public school with publicly funded tutoring aid, obtain a scholarship and choose a religious school, obtain a scholarship and choose a nonreligious private school, enroll in a community school, or enroll in a magnet school. That 46 of the 56 private schools now participating in the program are religious schools does not condemn it as a violation of the Establishment Clause. The Establishment Clause question is whether Ohio is coercing parents into sending their children to religious schools, and that question must be answered by evaluating *all* options Ohio provides Cleveland schoolchildren, only one of which is to obtain a program scholarship and then choose a religious school.

JUSTICE SOUTER speculates that because more private religious schools currently participate in the program, the program itself must somehow discourage the participation of private nonreligious schools. But Cleveland's

preponderance of religiously affiliated private schools certainly did not arise as a result of the program; it is a phenomenon common to many American cities. Indeed, by all accounts the program has captured a remarkable cross-section of private schools, religious and nonreligious. It is true that 82% of Cleveland's participating private schools are religious schools, but it is also true that 81% of private schools in Ohio are religious schools. To attribute constitutional significance to this figure, moreover, would lead to the absurd result that a neutral school-choice program might be permissible in some parts of Ohio, such as Columbus, where a lower percentage of private schools are religious schools, but not in inner-city Cleveland, where Ohio has deemed such programs most sorely needed, but where the preponderance of religious schools happens to be greater. Likewise, an identical private choice program might be constitutional in some States, such as Maine or Utah, where less than 45% of private schools are religious schools, but not in other States, such as Nebraska or Kansas, where over 90% of private schools are religious schools. The constitutionality of a neutral educational aid program simply does not turn on whether and why, in a particular area, at a particular time, most private schools are run by religious organizations, or most recipients choose to use the aid at a religious school.

In sum, the Ohio program is entirely neutral with respect to religion. It provides benefits directly to a wide spectrum of individuals, defined only by financial need and residence in a particular school district. It permits such individuals to exercise genuine choice among options public and private, secular and religious. The program is therefore a program of true private choice. In keeping with an unbroken line of decisions rejecting challenges to similar programs, we hold that the program does not offend the Establishment Clause. The judgment of the Court of Appeals is reversed.

JUSTICE THOMAS, concurring.

Frederick Douglass once said that "education means emancipation. It means light and liberty. It means the uplifting of the soul of man into the glorious light of truth, the light by which men can only be made free." Today many of our inner city public schools deny emancipation to urban minority students. Despite this Court's observation nearly 50 years ago in *Brown v. Board of Education,* that "it is doubtful that any child may reasonably be expected to succeed in life if he is denied the opportunity of an education," urban children have been forced into a system that continually fails them. These cases present an example of such failures. Besieged by escalating financial problems and declining academic achievement, the Cleveland City School District was in the midst of an academic emergency when Ohio enacted its scholarship program. The dissents and respondents wish to invoke the Establishment Clause of the First Amendment, as incorporated through the Fourteenth, to constrain a State's neutral efforts to provide greater educational opportunity for underprivileged minority students. Today's decision properly upholds the program as constitutional, and I join it in full.

I

The Fourteenth Amendment fundamentally restructured the relationship between individuals and the States and ensured that States would not deprive citizens of liberty without due process of law. It guarantees citizenship to all individuals born or naturalized in the United States and provides that "[n]o State shall make or enforce any law which shall abridge the privileges or immunities of citizens of the United States; nor shall any State deprive any person of life, liberty, or property, without due process of law; nor deny to any person within its jurisdiction the equal protection of the laws." As Justice Harlan noted, the Fourteenth Amendment "added greatly to the dignity and glory of American citizenship, and to the security of personal liberty." *Plessy v. Ferguson* (1896) (dissenting opinion). When rights are incorporated against the States through the Fourteenth Amendment they should advance, not constrain, individual liberty.

Consequently, in the context of the Establishment Clause, it may well be that state action should be evaluated on different terms than similar action by the Federal Government. "States, while bound to observe strict neutrality, should be freer to experiment with involvement [in religion]—on a neutral basis—than the Federal Government." *Walz v. Tax Comm'n of City of New York* (1970) (Harlan, J., concurring). Thus, while the Federal Government may "make no law respecting an establishment of religion," the States may pass laws that include or touch on religious matters so long as these laws do not impede free exercise rights or any other individual religious liberty interest. By considering the particular religious liberty right alleged to be invaded by a State, federal courts can strike a proper balance between the demands of the Fourteenth Amendment on the one hand and the federalism prerogatives of States on the other.

Whatever the textual and historical merits of incorporating the Establishment Clause, I can accept that the Fourteenth Amendment protects religious liberty rights. But I cannot accept its use to oppose neutral programs of school choice through the incorporation of the Establishment Clause. There would be a tragic irony in converting the Fourteenth Amendment's guarantee of individual liberty into a prohibition on the exercise of educational choice.

II

The wisdom of allowing States greater latitude in dealing with matters of religion and education can be easily appreciated in this context. Respondents advocate using the Fourteenth Amendment to handcuff the State's ability to experiment with education. But without education one can hardly exercise the civic, political, and personal freedoms conferred by the Fourteenth Amendment. Faced with a severe educational crisis, the State of Ohio enacted wide-ranging educational reform that allows voluntary participation of private and religious schools in educating poor urban children otherwise condemned to failing public schools. The program does not force any individual to submit to religious indoctrination or education. It simply gives parents a greater choice as to where and in what manner to educate their children. This is a choice that those with greater means have routinely exercised.

In addition to expanding the reach of the scholarship program, the inclusion of religious schools makes sense given Ohio's purpose of increasing educational performance and opportunities. Religious schools, like other private schools, achieve far better educational results than their public counterparts. But the success of religious and private schools is in the end beside the point, because the State has a constitutional right to experiment with a variety of different programs to promote educational opportunity. That Ohio's program includes successful schools simply indicates that such reform can in fact provide improved education to underprivileged urban children.

Although one of the purposes of public schools was to promote democracy and a more egalitarian culture, failing urban public schools disproportionately affect minority children most in need of educational opportunity. At the time of Reconstruction, blacks considered public education "a matter of personal liberation and a necessary function of a free society." J. Anderson, *Education of Blacks in the South, 1860–1935* (1988). Today, however, the promise of public school education has failed poor inner-city blacks. While in theory providing education to everyone, the quality of public schools varies significantly across districts. Just as blacks supported public education during Reconstruction, many blacks and other minorities now support school choice programs because they provide the greatest educational opportunities for their children in struggling communities. Opponents of the program raise formalistic concerns about the Establishment Clause but ignore the core purposes of the Fourteenth Amendment.

While the romanticized ideal of universal public education resonates with the cognoscenti who oppose vouchers, poor urban families just want the best education for their children, who will certainly need it to function in our high-tech and advanced society. The failure to provide education to poor urban children perpetuates a vicious cycle of poverty, dependence, criminality, and alienation that continues for the remainder of their lives. If society cannot end racial discrimination, at least it can arm minorities with the education to defend themselves from some of discrimination's effects.

Ten States have enacted some form of publicly funded private school choice as one means of raising the quality of education provided to underprivileged urban children. These programs address the root of the problem with failing urban public schools that disproportionately affect minority students. Society's other solution to these educational failures is often to provide racial preferences in higher education. Such preferences, however, run afoul of the Fourteenth Amendment's prohibition against distinctions based on race. By contrast, school choice programs that involve religious schools appear unconstitutional only to those who would twist the Fourteenth Amendment against itself by expansively incorporating the Establishment Clause. Converting the Fourteenth Amendment from a guarantee of opportunity to an obstacle against education reform distorts our constitutional values and disserves those in the greatest need. As Frederick Douglass poignantly noted "no greater benefit can be bestowed upon a long benighted people, than giving to them, as we are here earnestly this day endeavoring to do, the means of an education."

JUSTICE STEVENS, dissenting.

I am convinced that the Court's decision is profoundly misguided. Admittedly, in reaching that conclusion I have been influenced by my understanding of the impact of religious strife on the decisions of our forbears to migrate to this continent, and on the decisions of neighbors in the Balkans, Northern Ireland, and the Middle East to mistrust one another. Whenever we remove a brick from the wall that was designed to separate religion and government, we increase the risk of religious strife and weaken the foundation of our democracy. I respectfully dissent.

JUSTICE SOUTER, with whom JUSTICE STEVENS, JUSTICE GINSBURG, and JUSTICE BREYER join, dissenting.

The Court's majority holds that the Establishment Clause is no bar to Ohio's payment of tuition at private religious elementary and middle schools under a scheme that systematically provides tax money to support the schools' religious missions. The occasion for the legislation thus upheld is the condition of public education in the city of Cleveland. The record indicates that the schools are failing to serve their objective, and the vouchers in issue here are said to be needed to provide adequate alternatives to them. If there were an excuse for giving short shrift to the Establishment Clause, it would probably apply here. But there is no excuse. Constitutional limitations are placed on government to preserve constitutional values in hard cases, like these. I therefore respectfully dissent.

The applicability of the Establishment Clause to public funding of benefits to religious schools was settled in *Everson v. Board of Ed. of Ewing* (1947), which inaugurated the modern era of establishment doctrine. The Court stated the principle in words from which there was no dissent: "No tax in any amount, large or small, can be levied to support any religious activities or institutions, whatever they may be called, or whatever form they may adopt to teach or practice religion."

Today, however, the majority holds that the Establishment Clause is not offended by Ohio's Pilot Project Scholarship Program, under which students may be eligible to receive as much as $2,250 in the form of tuition vouchers transferable to religious schools. In the city of Cleveland the overwhelming proportion of large appropriations for voucher money must be spent on religious schools if it is to be spent at all, and will be spent in amounts that cover almost all of tuition. The money will thus pay for eligible students' instruction not only in secular subjects but in religion as well, in schools that can fairly be characterized as founded to teach religious doctrine and to imbue teaching in all subjects with a religious dimension. Public tax money will pay at a systemic level for teaching the covenant with Israel and Mosaic law in Jewish schools, the primacy of the Apostle Peter and the Papacy in Catholic schools, the truth of reformed Christianity in Protestant schools, and the revelation to the Prophet in Muslim schools, to speak only of major religious groupings in the Republic.

How can a Court consistently leave *Everson* on the books and approve the Ohio vouchers? The answer is that it cannot. It is only by ignoring *Everson* that the majority can claim to rest on traditional law in its invocation of neutral aid provisions and private choice to

sanction the Ohio law. It is, moreover, only by ignoring the meaning of neutrality and private choice themselves that the majority can even pretend to rest today's decision on those criteria.

I

The majority's statements of Establishment Clause doctrine cannot be appreciated without some historical perspective on the Court's announced limitations on government aid to religious education, and its repeated repudiation of limits previously set. Viewed with the necessary generality, the cases can be categorized in three groups. In the period from 1947 to 1968, the basic principle of no aid to religion through school benefits was unquestioned. Thereafter for some 15 years, the Court termed its efforts as attempts to draw a line against aid that would be divertible to support the religious, as distinct from the secular, activity of an institutional beneficiary. Then, starting in 1983, concern with divertibility was gradually lost in favor of approving aid in amounts unlikely to afford substantial benefits to religious schools, when offered evenhandedly without regard to a recipient's religious character, and when channeled to a religious institution only by the genuinely free choice of some private individual. Now, the three stages are succeeded by a fourth, in which the substantial character of government aid is held to have no constitutional significance, and the espoused criteria of neutrality in offering aid, and private choice in directing it, are shown to be nothing but examples of verbal formalism.

II

Although it has taken half a century since *Everson* to reach the majority's twin standards of neutrality and free choice, the facts show that, in the majority's hands, even these criteria cannot convincingly legitimize the Ohio scheme.

A

Consider first the criterion of neutrality. Neutrality in this sense refers, of course, to evenhandedness in setting eligibility as between potential religious and secular recipients of public money. Thus, for example, the aid scheme in *Witters* provided an eligible recipient with a scholarship to be used at any institution within a practically unlimited universe of schools; it did not tend to provide more or less aid depending on which one the scholarship recipient chose, and there was no indication that the maximum scholarship amount would be insufficient at secular schools. Neither did any condition of Zobrest's interpreter's subsidy favor religious education.

In order to apply the neutrality test, then, it makes sense to focus on a category of aid that may be directed to religious as well as secular schools, and ask whether the scheme favors a religious direction. Here, one would ask whether the voucher provisions, allowing for as much as $2,250 toward private school tuition (or a grant to a public school in an adjacent district), were written in a way that skewed the scheme toward benefiting religious schools.

This, however, is not what the majority asks. The majority looks not to the provisions for tuition vouchers, but to every provision for educational opportunity. The illogic is patent. If regular, public schools (which can get no voucher payments) "participate" in a voucher scheme with schools that can, and public expenditure is still predominantly on public schools, then the majority's reasoning would find neutrality in a scheme of vouchers available for private tuition in districts with no secular private schools at all. Why the majority does not simply accept the fact that the challenge here is to the more generous voucher scheme and judge its neutrality in relation to religious use of voucher money seems very odd. It seems odd, that is, until one recognizes that comparable schools for applying the criterion of neutrality are also the comparable schools for applying the other majority criterion, whether the immediate recipients of voucher aid have a genuinely free choice of religious and secular schools to receive the voucher money. And in applying this second criterion, the consideration of "*all* schools" is ostensibly helpful to the majority position.

B

The majority addresses the issue of choice the same way it addresses neutrality, by asking whether recipients or potential recipients of voucher aid have a choice of public schools among secular alternatives to religious schools. Again, however, the majority asks the wrong question and misapplies the criterion. The majority has confused choice in spending scholarships with choice from the entire menu of possible educational placements, most of them open to anyone willing to attend a public school. I say "confused" because the majority's new use of the choice criterion, which it frames negatively as "whether Ohio is coercing parents into sending their children to religious schools," ignores the reason for having a private choice enquiry in the first place. Cases since *Mueller* have found private choice relevant under a rule that aid to religious schools can be permissible so long as it first passes through the hands of students or parents. The majority's view that all educational choices are comparable for purposes of choice thus ignores the whole point of the choice test: it is a criterion for deciding whether indirect aid to a religious school is legitimate because it passes through private hands that can spend or use the aid in a secular school. The question is whether the private hand is genuinely free to send the money in either a secular direction or a religious one.

Defining choice as choice in spending the money or channeling the aid is, moreover, necessary if the choice criterion is to function as a limiting principle at all. If "choice" is present whenever there is any educational alternative to the religious school to which vouchers can be endorsed, then there will always be a choice and the voucher can always be constitutional, even in a system in which there is not a single private secular school as an alternative to the religious school. And because it is unlikely that any participating private religious school will enroll more pupils than the generally available public system, it will be easy to generate numbers suggesting that aid to religion is not the significant intent or effect of the voucher scheme.

That is, in fact, just the kind of rhetorical argument that the majority accepts in these cases. In addition to secular private schools (129 students), the majority considers public schools with tuition assistance (roughly 1,400 students), magnet schools (13,000 students), and community schools (1,900 students), and concludes that fewer than 20% of pupils receive state vouchers to attend religious schools. If the choice of relevant alternatives is an open one, proponents of voucher aid will always win, because they will always be able to find a "choice" somewhere that will show the bulk of public spending to be secular. The choice enquiry will be diluted to the point that it can screen out nothing, and the result will always be determined by selecting the alternatives to be treated as choices.

If, contrary to the majority, we ask the right question about genuine choice to use the vouchers, the answer shows that something is influencing choices in a way that aims the money in a religious direction: of 56 private schools in the district participating in the voucher program (only 53 of which accepted voucher students in 1999–2000), 46 of them are religious; 96.6% of all voucher recipients go to religious schools, only 3.4% to nonreligious ones. Unfortunately for the majority position, there is no explanation for this that suggests the religious direction results simply from free choices by parents. One answer to these statistics, for example, which would be consistent with the genuine choice claimed to be operating, might be that 96.6% of families choosing to avail themselves of vouchers choose to educate their children in schools of their own religion. This would not, in my view, render the scheme constitutional, but it would speak to the majority's choice criterion. Evidence shows, however, that almost two out of three families using vouchers to send their children to religious schools did not embrace the religion of those schools. The families made it clear they had not chosen the schools because they wished their children to be proselytized in a religion not their own, or in any religion, but because of educational opportunity.

Even so, the fact that some 2,270 students chose to apply their vouchers to schools of other religions might be consistent with true choice if the students "chose" their religious schools over a wide array of private nonreligious options, or if it could be shown generally that Ohio's program had no effect on educational choices and thus no impermissible effect of advancing religious education. But both possibilities are contrary to fact. First, even if all existing nonreligious private schools in Cleveland were willing to accept large numbers of voucher students, only a few more than the 129 currently enrolled in such schools would be able to attend, as the total enrollment at all nonreligious private schools in Cleveland for kindergarten through eighth grade is only 510 children, and there is no indication that these schools have many open seats. Second, the $2,500 cap that the program places on tuition for participating low-income pupils has the effect of curtailing the participation of nonreligious schools: "nonreligious schools with higher tuition (about $4,000) stated that they could afford to accommodate just a few voucher students." By comparison, the average tuition at participating Catholic schools in Cleveland in 1999–2000 was $1,592, almost $1,000 below the cap.

There is, in any case, no way to interpret the 96.6% of current voucher money going to religious schools as reflecting a free and genuine choice by the families that apply for vouchers. The 96.6% reflects, instead, the fact that too few nonreligious school desks are available and few but religious schools can afford to accept more than a handful of voucher students. And contrary to the majority's assertion, public schools in adjacent districts hardly have a financial incentive to participate in the Ohio voucher program, and none has. For the overwhelming number of children in the voucher scheme, the only alternative to the public schools is religious.

III

The scale of the aid to religious schools approved today is unprecedented, both in the number of dollars and in the proportion of systemic school expenditure supported. It is virtually superfluous to point out that every objective underlying the prohibition of religious establishment is betrayed by this scheme, but something has to be said about the enormity of the violation. I anticipated these objectives earlier, in discussing *Everson*, which cataloged them, the first being respect for freedom of conscience. Jefferson described it as the idea that no one "shall be compelled to support any religious worship, place, or ministry whatsoever," A Bill for Establishing Religious

Freedom, and Madison thought it violated by any "'authority which can force a citizen to contribute three pence of his property for the support of any establishment.'" Madison's objection to three pence has simply been lost in the majority's formalism.

As for the second objective, to save religion from its own corruption, Madison wrote of the "'experience that ecclesiastical establishments, instead of maintaining the purity and efficacy of Religion, have had a contrary operation.'" In Madison's time, the manifestations were "pride and indolence in the Clergy; ignorance and servility in the laity, in both, superstition, bigotry and persecution;" in the 21st century, the risk is one of "corrosive secularism" to religious schools, and the specific threat is to the primacy of the schools' mission to educate the children of the faithful according to the unaltered precepts of their faith.

Increased voucher spending is not, however, the sole portent of growing regulation of religious practice in the school, for state mandates to moderate religious teaching may well be the most obvious response to the third concern behind the ban on establishment, its inextricable link with social conflict. As appropriations for religious subsidy rise, competition for the money will tap sectarian religion's capacity for discord. The intensity of the expectable friction can be gauged by realizing that the scramble for money will energize not only contending sectarians, but taxpayers who take their liberty of conscience seriously. Religious teaching at taxpayer expense simply cannot be cordoned from taxpayer politics, and every major religion currently espouses social positions that provoke intense opposition. Not all taxpaying Protestant citizens, for example, will be content to underwrite the teaching of the Roman Catholic Church condemning the death penalty. Nor will all of America's Muslims acquiesce in paying for the endorsement of the religious Zionism taught in many religious Jewish schools, which combines "a nationalistic sentiment" in support of Israel with a "deeply religious" element. Nor will every secular taxpayer be content to support Muslim views on differential treatment of the sexes, or, for that matter, to fund the espousal of a wife's obligation of obedience to her husband, presumably taught in any schools adopting the articles of faith of the Southern Baptist Convention. Views like these, and innumerable others, have been safe in the sectarian pulpits and classrooms of this Nation not only because the Free Exercise Clause protects them directly, but because the ban on supporting religious establishment has protected free exercise, by keeping it relatively private. With the arrival of vouchers in religious schools, that privacy will go, and along with it will go confidence that religious disagreement will stay moderate.

If the divisiveness permitted by today's majority is to be avoided in the short term, it will be avoided only by action of the political branches at the state and national levels. Legislatures not driven to desperation by the problems of public education may be able to see the threat in vouchers negotiable in sectarian schools. Perhaps even cities with problems like Cleveland's will perceive the danger, now that they know a federal court will not save them from it.

West Virginia Board of Education v. Barnette
319 U.S. 624 (1943)

In 1942, the West Virginia Board of Education adopted a regulation requiring the flag salute and Pledge of Allegiance as a part of regular public school activities. Students who refused to participate were deemed insubordinate and expelled, with readmission denied until compliance. During their expulsion, such students were considered "unlawfully absent," and both they and their parents were subject to prosecution. Walter Barnette, a Jehovah's

Witness, brought suit to enjoin the compulsory flag salute, contending that it required his children to violate the religious commandment not to worship graven images. The Supreme Court had considered the flag-salute issue only three years previously, in Minersville School District v. Gobitis. In Gobitis, Justice Felix Frankfurter, speaking for an 8–1 majority, held that the compulsory flag salute did not violate the Free Exercise Clause of the First

Amendment. Since Gobitis, *however, Justices Robert Jackson and Wiley Rutledge had replaced two members of the Court majority. In addition, two other members of the* Gobitis *majority, Justices Hugo Black and William Douglas, had repudiated their* Gobitis *votes in* Jones v. Opelika *(1942). When a three-judge district court enjoined enforcement of the regulation, the Court agreed to hear the case on appeal.* Opinion of the Court: Jackson, Stone, Black, Douglas, Murphy, Rutledge. Concurring opinion: Black, Douglas. Dissenting opinions: Roberts, Reed; Frankfurter.

JUSTICE JACKSON delivered the opinion of the Court.

The freedom asserted by these appellees does not bring them into collision with rights asserted by any other individual. The sole conflict is between authority and rights of the individual. The State asserts power to condition access to public education on making a prescribed sign and profession and at the same time to coerce attendance by punishing both parent and child. The latter stand on a right of self-determination in matters that touch individual opinion and personal attitude.

As the present Chief Justice said in dissent in the *Gobitis* case, the State may "require teaching by instruction and study of all in our history and in the structure and organization of our government, including the guaranties of civil liberty, which tend to inspire patriotism and love of country." Here, however, we are dealing with a compulsion of students to declare a belief. They are not merely made acquainted with the flag salute so that they may be informed as to what it is or even what it means. The issue here is whether this slow and easily neglected route to aroused loyalties constitutionally may be short-cut by substituting a compulsory salute and slogan.

There is no doubt that, in connection with the pledges, the flag salute is a form of utterance. Symbolism is a primitive but effective way of communicating ideas. The use of an emblem or flag to symbolize some system, idea, institution, or personality, is a short cut from mind to mind. It is also to be noted that the compulsory flag salute and pledge requires affirmation of a belief and an attitude of mind.

It is not clear whether the regulation contemplates that pupils forego any contrary convictions of their own and become unwilling converts to the prescribed ceremony or whether it will be acceptable if they simulate assent by words without belief and by a gesture barren of meaning. It is now a commonplace that censorship or suppression of expression of opinion is tolerated by our Constitution only when the expression presents a clear and present danger of action of a kind the State is empowered to prevent and punish. It would seem that involuntary affirmation could be commanded only on even more immediate and urgent grounds than silence. But here the power of compulsion is invoked without any allegation that remaining passive during a flag salute ritual creates a clear and present danger that would justify an effort even to muffle expression. To sustain the compulsory flag salute we are required to say that a Bill of Rights which guards the individual's right to speak his own mind, left it open to public authorities to compel him to utter what is not in his mind.

Nor does the issue as we see it turn on one's possession of particular religious views or the sincerity with which they are held. While religion supplies appellees' motive for enduring the discomforts of making the issue in this case, many citizens who do not share these religious views hold such a compulsory rite to infringe constitutional liberty of the individual. It is not necessary to inquire whether nonconformist beliefs will exempt from the duty to salute unless we first find power to make the salute a legal duty.

It was said that the flag-salute controversy confronted the Court with "the problem which Lincoln cast in memorable dilemma: 'Must a government of necessity be too *strong* for the liberties of its people, or too *weak* to maintain its own existence?'" and that the answer must be in favor of strength. If validly applied to this problem, the utterance cited would resolve every issue of power in favor of those in authority and would require us to override every liberty thought to weaken or delay execution of their policies. To enforce those rights today is not to choose weak government over strong government. It is only to adhere as a means of strength to individual freedom of mind in preference to officially disciplined uniformity for which history indicates a disappointing and disastrous end.

It was also considered in the *Gobitis* case that functions of educational officers in States, counties and school districts were such that to interfere with their authority "would in effect make us the school board for the country." The Fourteenth Amendment, as now applied to the States, protects the citizen against the State itself and all of its creatures—Boards of Education not excepted. These have, of course, important, delicate, and highly discretionary functions, but none that they may not perform within the limits of the Bill of Rights. Such Boards are numerous and their territorial jurisdiction often small. But small and local authority may feel less sense of responsibility to the Constitution, and agencies of publicity may be less vigilant in calling it to account. The action of Congress in making flag observance voluntary and respecting the conscience of the objector in a matter so vital as raising the Army contrasts sharply with these local regulations in matters relatively trivial to the welfare of the nation.

The *Gobitis* opinion reasoned that this is a field "where courts possess no marked and certainly no controlling competence," that it is committed to the legislatures as well as the courts to guard cherished liberties and that it is constitutionally appropriate to "fight out the wise use of legislative authority in the forum of public opinion and before legislative assemblies rather than to transfer such a contest to the judicial arena," since all the "effective means of inducing political changes are left free." The very purpose of a Bill of Rights was to withdraw certain subjects from the vicissitudes of political controversy, to place them beyond the reach of majorities and officials and to establish them as legal principles to be applied by the courts. One's right to life, liberty, and property, to free speech, a free press, freedom of worship and assembly, and other fundamental rights may not be submitted to vote; they depend on the outcome of no elections. They are susceptible of restriction only to prevent grave and immediate danger to interests which the State may lawfully protect.

Lastly, and this is the very heart of the *Gobitis* opinion, it reasons that "National unity is the basis of national security," that the authorities have "the right to select appropriate means for its attainment," and hence reaches the conclusion that such compulsory measures toward "national unity" are constitutional. If there is any fixed star in our constitutional constellation, it is that no official, high or petty, can prescribe what shall be orthodox in politics, nationalism, religion, or other matters of opinion or force citizens to confess by word or act their faith therein. If there are any circumstances which permit an exception, they do not now occur to us.

The decision of this Court in *Minersville School District v. Gobitis* is overruled, and the judgment enjoining enforcement of the West Virginia regulation is

Affirmed.

JUSTICE FRANKFURTER, dissenting.

One who belongs to the most vilified and persecuted minority in history is not likely to be insensible to the freedoms guaranteed by our Constitution. Were my purely personal attitude relevant I should wholeheartedly associate myself with the general libertarian views in the Court's opinion, representing as they do the thought and action of a lifetime. But as judges we are neither Jew nor Gentile, neither Catholic nor agnostic. We owe equal attachment to the Constitution and are equally bound by our judicial obligations whether we derive our citizenship from the earliest or the latest immigrants to these shores. As a member of this Court I am not justified in writing my private notions of policy into the Constitution, no matter how deeply I may cherish them or how mischievous I may deem their disregard. The duty of a judge who must decide which of two claims before the Court shall prevail, that of a State to enact and enforce laws within its general competence or that of an individual to refuse obedience because of the demands of his conscience, is not that of the ordinary person. It can never be emphasized too much that one's own opinion about the wisdom or evil of a law should be excluded altogether when one is doing one's duty on the bench. The only opinion of our own even looking in that direction that is material is our opinion whether legislators could in reason have enacted such a law. In the light of all the circumstances, including the history of this question in this Court, it would require more daring than I possess to deny that reasonable legislators could have taken the action which is before us for review. Most unwillingly, therefore, I must differ from my brethren with regard to legislation like this. I cannot bring my mind to believe that the "liberty" secured by the Due Process Clause gives this Court authority to deny to the State of West Virginia the attainment of that which we all recognize as a legitimate legislative end, namely, the promotion of good citizenship, by employment of the means here chosen.

Under our constitutional system the legislature is charged solely with civil concerns of society. If the avowed or intrinsic legislative purpose is either to promote or to discourage some religious community or creed, it is clearly within the constitutional restrictions imposed on legislatures and cannot stand. But it by no means follows that legislative power is wanting whenever a general nondiscriminatory civil regulation in fact touches conscientious scruples or religious beliefs of an individual or a group. Were this so, instead of the separation of church and state, there would be the subordination of the state on any matter deemed within the sovereignty of the religious conscience.

We are told that a flag salute is a doubtful substitute for adequate understanding of our institutions. The states that require such a school exercise do not have to justify it as the only means for promoting good citizenship in children, but merely as one of diverse means for accomplishing a worthy end. We may deem it a foolish measure, but the point is that this Court is not the organ of government to resolve doubts as to whether it will fulfill its purpose. Only if there be no doubt that any reasonable mind could entertain can we deny to the states the right to resolve doubts their way and not ours.

Of course patriotism cannot be enforced by the flag salute. But neither can the liberal spirit be enforced by judicial invalidation of illiberal legislation. Our constant preoccupation with the constitutionality of legislation rather than with its wisdom tends to preoccupation of the American mind with a false value. The tendency of focusing attention on constitutionality is to make constitutionality synonymous with wisdom, to regard a law as all right if it is constitutional. Such an attitude is a great enemy of liberalism. Particularly in legislation affecting freedom of thought and freedom of speech much which should offend a free-spirited society is constitutional. Reliance for the most precious interests of civilization, therefore, must be found outside of their vindication in courts of law. Only a persistent positive translation of the faith of a free society into the convictions and habits and actions of a community is the ultimate reliance against unabated temptations to fetter the human spirit.

Sherbert v. Verner
374 U.S. 398 (1963)

---

*Under South Carolina's unemployment compensation act, a worker was considered ineligible for benefits if although able to work and available for work, he "failed, without good cause to accept available suitable work when offered him by the employment office or the employer." Adell Sherbert, a Seventh-Day Adventist, was fired from her job and then refused other jobs because those jobs required her to work on Saturday, her Sabbath. Her application for unemployment compensation was denied because she had refused "available suitable work." She then sued the South Carolina Unem-*ployment *Security Commission, contending that the denial of benefits infringed upon the free exercise of her religion. Opinion of the Court: Brennan, Warren, Black, Clark, Goldberg. Concurring opinions: Douglas; Stewart. Dissenting opinion: Harlan, White.*

JUSTICE BRENNAN delivered the opinion of the Court.

We turn first to the question whether the disqualification for benefits imposes any burden on the free exercise of appellant's religion.

We think it is clear that it does. Here not only is it apparent that appellant's declared ineligibility for benefits derives solely from the practice of her religion, but the pressure upon her to forego that practice is unmistakable. The ruling forces her to choose between following the precepts of her religion and forfeiting benefits, on the one hand, and abandoning one of the precepts of her religion in order to accept work, on the other hand. Governmental imposition of such a choice puts the same kind of burden upon the free exercise of religion as would a fine imposed against appellant for her Saturday worship.

Nor may the South Carolina court's construction of the statute be saved from constitutional infirmity on the ground that unemployment compensation benefits are not appellant's "right" but merely a "privilege." It is too late in the day to doubt that the liberties of religion and expression may be infringed by the denial of or placing of conditions upon a benefit or privilege. Conditions upon public benefits cannot be sustained if they so operate, whatever their purpose, as to inhibit or deter the exercise of First Amendment freedoms.

We must next consider whether some compelling state interest enforced in the eligibility provisions of the South Carolina statute justifies the substantial infringement of appellant's First Amendment right. It is basic that no showing merely of a rational relationship to some colorable state interest would suffice; in this highly sensitive constitutional area, "only the gravest abuses, endangering paramount interests, give occasion for permissible limitation." *Thomas v. Collins* (1945). No such abuse or danger has been advanced in the present case. The appellees suggest no more than a possibility that the filing of fraudulent claims by unscrupulous claimants feigning religious objections to Saturday work might not only dilute the unemployment compensation fund but also hinder the scheduling by employers of necessary Saturday work. There is no proof whatever to warrant such fears of malingering or deceit as those which the respondents now advance. It is highly doubtful whether such evidence would be sufficient to warrant a substantial infringement of religious liberties. For even if the possibility of spurious claims did threaten to dilute the fund and disrupt the scheduling of work, it would plainly be incumbent upon the appellees to demonstrate that no alternative forms of regulation would combat such abuses without infringing First Amendment rights.

In holding as we do, plainly we are not fostering the "establishment" of the Seventh-day Adventist religion in South Carolina, for the extension of unemployment benefits to Sabbatarians in common with Sunday worshippers reflects nothing more than the governmental obligation of neutrality in the face of religious differences. Our holding today is only that South Carolina may not constitutionally apply the eligibility provisions so as to constrain a worker to abandon his religious convictions respecting the day of rest. This holding but reaffirms a principle that we announced a decade and a half ago, namely that no State may "exclude individual Catholics, Lutherans, Mohammedans, Baptists, Jews, Methodists, Non-believers, Presbyterians, or the members of any other faith, *because of their faith, or lack of it,* from receiving the benefits of public welfare legislation." *Everson v. Board of Education* [1947]. The judgment of the South Carolina Supreme Court is reversed and the case is remanded for further proceeding not inconsistent with this opinion.

JUSTICE STEWART, concurring in the result.

Although fully agreeing with the result which the Court reaches in this case, I cannot join the Court's opinion. This case presents a double-barreled dilemma, which in all candor I think the Court's opinion has not succeeded in papering over. The dilemma ought to be resolved.

I am convinced that no liberty is more essential to the continued vitality of the free society which our Constitution guarantees than is the religious liberty protected by the Free Exercise Clause explicit in the First Amendment and imbedded in the Fourteenth. There are many situations where legitimate claims under the Free Exercise Clause will run into head-on collision with the Court's insensitive and sterile construction of the Establishment Clause. The controversy now before us is clearly such a case. If the appellant's refusal to work on Saturdays were based on indolence, or on a compulsive desire to watch the Saturday television programs, no one would say that South Carolina could not hold that she was not "available for work" within the meaning of its statute. That being so, the Establishment Clause as construed by this Court not only *permits* but affirmatively *requires* South Carolina equally to deny the appellant's claim for unemployment compensation when her refusal to work on Saturdays is based upon her religious creed.

This poses no problem for me, because I think the Court's mechanistic concept of the Establishment Clause is historically unsound and constitutionally wrong. I think that the guarantee of religious liberty embodied in the Free Exercise Clause affirmatively requires government to create an atmosphere of hospitality and accommodation to individual belief or disbelief. In short, I think our Constitution commands the positive protection by government of religious freedom—not only for a minority, however small—not only for the majority, however large—but for each of us.

JUSTICE HARLAN, whom JUSTICE WHITE joins, dissenting.

What the Court is holding is that if the State chooses to condition unemployment compensation on the applicant's availability for work, it is constitutionally compelled to *carve out an exception*—and to provide benefits—for those whose unavailability is due to their religious convictions. Such a holding has particular significance in two respects. First, despite the Court's protestations to the contrary, the decision necessarily overrules *Braunfeld v. Brown*. The secular purpose of the statute before us today is even clearer than that involved in *Braunfeld*. And just as in *Braunfeld*—where exceptions to the Sunday closing laws for Sabbatarians would have been inconsistent with the purpose to achieve a uniform day of rest and would have required case-by-case inquiry into religious beliefs—so here, an exception to the rules of eligibility based on religious convictions would necessitate judicial examination of those convictions and would be at odds with the limited purpose of the statute to smooth out the economy during periods of industrial instability.

Second, the State must single out for financial assistance those whose behavior is religiously motivated, even though it denies such assistance to others whose identical behavior (in this case, inability to work on Saturdays) is not religiously motivated. I cannot subscribe to the conclusion that the State is constitutionally compelled to carve out an exception to its general rule of eligibility in the present case. Those situations in which the Constitution may require special treatment on account of religion are, in my view, few and far between. Such compulsion in the present case is particularly inappropriate in light of the indirect, remote, and insubstantial effect of the decision below on the exercise of appellant's religion and in light of the direct financial assistance to religion that today's decision requires.

Employment Division, Department of Human Resources of Oregon v. Smith
494 U.S. 872 (1990)

Alfred Smith and Galen Black, members of the Native American Church, were fired from their jobs with a private drug-rehabilitation organization when it became known that they ingested peyote, an illegal hallucinogenic drug, for sacramental purposes at the church's religious ceremonies. Their application for unemployment compensation was denied under a state law disqualifying employees discharged for work-related misconduct. After the Oregon Court of Appeals and the Oregon Supreme Court ruled that the denials violated Smith's and Black's free-exercise rights, the US Supreme Court *vacated the judgment, remanding the case for a determination of whether the sacramental use of peyote violated Oregon's controlled-substance law. The Oregon Supreme Court concluded that it did but ruled that such an application of the law violated the Free Exercise Clause. The US Supreme Court then granted certiorari. Opinion of the Court:* <u>Scalia</u>, *Rehnquist, White, Stevens, Kennedy. Concurring in the judgment:* <u>O'Connor</u>, *joined in part by Brennan, Marshall, Blackmun. Dissenting opinion:* <u>Blackmun</u>, *Brennan, Marshall.*

JUSTICE SCALIA delivered the opinion of the Court.

This case requires us to decide whether the Free Exercise Clause of the First Amendment permits the State of Oregon to include religiously inspired peyote use within the reach of its general criminal prohibition on use of that drug, and thus permits the State to deny unemployment benefits to persons dismissed from their jobs because of such religiously inspired use.

The free exercise of religion means, first and foremost, the right to believe and profess whatever religious doctrine one desires. Thus, the First Amendment obviously excludes all "governmental regulation of religious *beliefs* as such." But the "exercise of religion" often involves not only belief and profession but the performance of (or abstention from) physical acts: assembling with others for a worship service, participating in sacramental use of bread and wine, proselytizing, abstaining from certain foods or certain modes of transportation. It would be true, we think (though no case of ours has involved the point), that a state would be "prohibiting the free exercise [of religion]" if it sought to ban such acts or abstentions only when they are engaged in for religious reasons, or only because of the religious belief that they display. It would doubtless be unconstitutional, for example, to ban the casting of "statues that are to be used for worship purposes" or to prohibit bowing down before a golden calf.

Respondents in the present case, however, seek to carry the meaning of "prohibiting the free exercise [of religion]" one large step further. They contend that their religious motivation for using peyote places them beyond the reach of a criminal law that is not specifically directed at their religious practice, and that is concededly constitutional as applied to those who use the drug for other reasons. They assert, in other words, that "prohibiting the free exercise [of religion]" includes requiring any individual to observe a generally applicable law that requires (or forbids) the performance of an act that his religious belief forbids (or requires). As a textual matter, we do not think the words must be given that meaning. It is no more necessary to regard the collection of a general tax, for example, as "prohibiting the free exercise [of religion]" by those citizens who believe support of organized government to be sinful, than it is to regard the same tax as "abridging the freedom of the press" of those publishing companies that must pay the tax as a condition of staying in business. It is a permissible reading of the text, in one case as in the other, to say that if prohibiting the exercise of religion (or burdening the activity of printing) is not the object of the tax but merely the incidental effect of a generally applicable and otherwise valid provision, the First Amendment has not been offended.

Our decisions reveal that the latter reading is the correct one. We have never held that an individual's religious beliefs excuse him from compliance with an otherwise valid law prohibiting conduct that the State is free to regulate. On the contrary, the record of more than a century of our free exercise jurisprudence contradicts that proposition. The only decisions in which we have held that the First Amendment bars application of a neutral, generally applicable law to religiously motivated action have involved not the Free Exercise Clause alone, but the Free Exercise Clause in conjunction with other constitutional protections, such as freedom of speech and of the press, or the right of parents to direct the education of their children. The present case does not present such a hybrid situation, but a free-exercise claim unconnected with any communicative activity or parental right. Respondents urge us to hold, quite simply, that when otherwise prohibitable conduct is accompanied by religious convictions, not only the convictions but the conduct itself must be free from governmental regulation. We have never held that, and decline to do so now. There being no contention that Oregon's drug law represents an attempt to regulate religious beliefs, the communication of religious beliefs, or the raising of one's children in those beliefs, the rule to which we have adhered ever since *Reynolds* [*v. United States* (1878)] plainly controls.

Respondents argue that even though exemption from generally applicable criminal laws need not automatically be extended to religiously motivated actors, at least the claim for a religious exemption must be evaluated under the balancing test set forth in *Sherbert v. Verner*

(1963). Under the *Sherbert* test, governmental actions that substantially burden a religious practice must be justified by a compelling governmental interest. Applying that test we have, on three occasions, invalidated state unemployment compensation rules that conditioned the availability of benefits upon an applicant's willingness to work under conditions forbidden by his religion. We have never invalidated any governmental action on the basis of the *Sherbert* test except the denial of unemployment compensation. Although we have sometimes purported to apply the *Sherbert* test in contexts other than that, we have always found the test satisfied. In recent years we have abstained from applying the Sherbert test (outside the unemployment compensation field) at all.

We conclude today that the sounder approach, the approach in accord with the vast majority of our precedents, is to hold the test inapplicable to such challenges. The government's ability to enforce generally applicable prohibitions of socially harmful conduct, like its ability to carry out other aspects of public policy, "cannot depend on measuring the effects of a governmental action on a religious objector's spiritual development." To make an individual's obligation to obey such a law contingent upon the law's coincidence with his religious beliefs, except where the State's interest is "compelling"—permitting him, by virtue of his beliefs, "to become a law unto himself," *Reynolds v. United States*—contradicts both constitutional tradition and common sense.

The "compelling government interest" requirement seems benign, because it is familiar from other fields. But using it as the standard that must be met before the government may accord different treatment on the basis of race, or before the government may regulate the content of speech, is not remotely comparable to using it for the purpose asserted here. What it produces in those other fields—equality of treatment, and an unrestricted flow of contending speech—are constitutional norms; what it would produce here—a private right to ignore generally applicable laws—is a constitutional anomaly.

Values that are protected against government interference through enshrinement in the Bill of Rights are not thereby banished from the political process. Just as a society that believes in the negative protection accorded to the press by the First Amendment is likely to enact laws that affirmatively foster the dissemination of the printed word, so also a society that believes in the negative protection accorded to religious belief can be expected to be solicitous of that value in its legislation as well. It is therefore not surprising that a number of States have made an exception to their drug laws for sacramental peyote use. But to say that a nondiscriminatory religious-practice exemption is permitted, or even that it is desirable, is not to say that it is constitutionally required, and that the appropriate occasions for its creation can be discerned by the courts. It may fairly be said that leaving accommodation to the political process will place at a relative disadvantage those religious practices that are not widely engaged in; but that unavoidable consequence of democratic government must be preferred to a system in which each conscience is a law unto itself or in which judges weigh the social importance of all laws against the centrality of all religious beliefs.

Because respondents' ingestion of peyote was prohibited under Oregon law, and because that prohibition is constitutional, Oregon may, consistent with the Free Exercise Clause, deny respondents unemployment compensation when their dismissal results from use of the drug. The decision of the Oregon Supreme Court is accordingly reversed.

JUSTICE O'CONNOR, concurring in the judgment.

Although I agree with the result the Court reaches in this case, I cannot join its opinion. In my view, today's holding dramatically departs from well-settled First Amendment jurisprudence, appears unnecessary to resolve the question presented, and is incompatible with our Nation's fundamental commitment to individual religious liberty.

The Court today interprets the [Free Exercise] Clause to permit the government to prohibit, without justification, conduct mandated by an individual's religious beliefs, so long as that prohibition is generally applicable. But a law that prohibits certain conduct—conduct that happens to be an act of worship for someone—manifestly does prohibit that person's free exercise of his religion. A person who is barred from engaging in religiously motivated conduct is barred from freely exercising his religion regardless of whether the law prohibits the conduct only when engaged in for religious reasons, only by members of that religion, or by all persons. It is difficult to deny that a law that prohibits religiously motivated conduct, even if the law is generally applicable, does not at least implicate First Amendment concerns.

The Court responds that generally applicable laws are "one large step" removed from laws aimed at specific religious practices. The First Amendment, however, does not distinguish between laws that are generally applicable and laws that target particular religious practices. Indeed, few States would be so naive as to enact a law directly prohibiting or burdening a religious practice as such. Our free exercise cases have all concerned generally applicable laws that had the effect of significantly burdening a religious practice. If the First Amendment is to have any vitality, it ought not be construed to cover only the extreme and hypothetical situation in which a State directly targets a religious practice.

To say that a person's right to free exercise has been burdened, of course, does not mean that he has an absolute right to engage in the conduct. Under our established First Amendment jurisprudence, we have recognized that the freedom to act, unlike the freedom to believe, cannot be absolute. Instead, we have respected both the First Amendment's express textual mandate and the governmental interest in regulation of conduct by requiring the Government to justify any substantial burden on religiously motivated conduct by a compelling state interest and by means narrowly tailored to achieve that interest. The compelling interest test effectuates the First Amendment's command that religious liberty is an independent liberty, that it occupies a preferred position, and that the Court will not permit encroachments upon this liberty, whether direct or indirect, unless required by clear and compelling governmental interests "of the highest order." The Court attempts to support its narrow reading of the Clause by claiming that "[w]e have

never held that an individual's religious beliefs excuse him from compliance with an otherwise valid law prohibiting conduct that the State is free to regulate." But as the Court later notes, as it must, in cases such as *Cantwell* [*v. Connecticut* (1940)] and [*Wisconsin v.*] *Yoder* we have in fact interpreted the Free Exercise Clause to forbid application of a generally applicable prohibition to religiously motivated conduct. The Court endeavors to escape from our decisions in *Cantwell* and *Yoder* by labeling them "hybrid" decisions, but there is no denying that both cases expressly relied on the Free Exercise Clause, and that we have consistently regarded those cases as part of the mainstream of our free exercise jurisprudence. Moreover, in each of the other cases cited by the Court to support its categorical rule, we rejected the particular constitutional claims before us only after carefully weighing the competing interests. That we rejected the free exercise claims in those cases hardly calls into question the applicability of First Amendment doctrine in the first place. Indeed, it is surely unusual to judge the vitality of a constitutional doctrine by looking to the win-loss record of the plaintiffs who happen to come before us.

The Court today gives no convincing reason to depart from settled First Amendment jurisprudence. There is nothing talismanic about neutral laws of general applicability or general criminal prohibitions, for laws neutral toward religion can coerce a person to violate his religious conscience or intrude upon his religious duties just as effectively as laws aimed at religion. Although the Court suggests that the compelling interest test, as applied to generally applicable laws, would result in a "constitutional anomaly," the First Amendment unequivocally makes freedom of religion, like freedom from race discrimination and freedom of speech, a "constitutional nor[m]," not an "anomaly." As the language of the Clause itself makes clear, an individual's free exercise of religion is a preferred constitutional activity.

There is no dispute that Oregon's criminal prohibition of peyote places a severe burden on the ability of respondents to freely exercise their religion. Peyote is a sacrament of the Native American Church, and is regarded as vital to respondents' ability to practice their religion. There is also no dispute that Oregon has a significant interest in enforcing laws that control the possession and use of controlled substances by its citizens. As we recently noted, drug abuse is "one of the greatest problems affecting the health and welfare of our population" and thus "one of the most serious problems confronting our society today." *Treasury Employees v. Von Raab* (1989). Thus, the critical question in this case is whether exempting respondents from the State's general criminal prohibition "will unduly interfere with fulfillment of the governmental interest."

Although the question is close, I would conclude that uniform application of Oregon's criminal prohibition is "essential to accomplish" its overriding interest in preventing the physical harm caused by the use of a Schedule I controlled substance. Oregon's criminal prohibition represents that State's judgment that the possession and use of controlled substances, even by only one person, is inherently harmful and dangerous. Because the health effects caused by the use of controlled substances exist regardless of the motivation of the user, the use of such substances, even for religious purposes, violates the very purpose of the laws that prohibit them. Moreover, in view of the societal interest in preventing trafficking in controlled substances, uniform application of the criminal prohibition at issue is essential to the effectiveness of Oregon's stated interest in preventing any possession of peyote.

JUSTICE BLACKMUN, with whom JUSTICE BRENNAN and JUSTICE MARSHALL join, dissenting.

I agree with Justice O'Connor's analysis of the applicable free exercise doctrine. As she points out, "the critical question in this case is whether exempting respondents from the State's general criminal prohibition 'will unduly interfere with fulfillment of the governmental interest.'" I do disagree, however, with her specific answer to that question.

In weighing respondents' clear interest in the free exercise of their religion against Oregon's asserted interest in enforcing its drug laws, it is important to articulate in precise terms the state interest involved. It is not the State's broad interest in fighting the critical "war on drugs" that must be weighed against respondents' claim, but the State's narrow interest in refusing to make an exception for the religious, ceremonial use of peyote.

The State's interest in enforcing its prohibition, in order to be sufficiently compelling to outweigh a free exercise claim, cannot be merely abstract or symbolic. The State cannot plausibly assert that unbending application of a criminal prohibition is essential to fulfill any compelling interest, if it does not, in fact, attempt to enforce that prohibition. In this case, the State actually has not evinced any concrete interest in enforcing its drug laws against religious users of peyote. Oregon has never sought to prosecute respondents, and does not claim that it has made significant enforcement efforts against other religious users of peyote. The State's asserted interest thus amounts only to the symbolic preservation of an unenforced prohibition. But a government interest in "symbolism, even symbolism for so worthy a cause as the abolition of unlawful drugs," *Treasury Employees v. Von Raab* (1989) (Scalia, J., dissenting), cannot suffice to abrogate the constitutional rights of individuals.

Similarly, this Court's prior decisions have not allowed a government to rely on mere speculation about potential harms, but have demanded evidentiary support for a refusal to allow a religious exception. The State proclaims an interest in protecting the health and safety of its citizens from the dangers of unlawful drugs. It offers, however, no evidence that the religious use of peyote has ever harmed anyone. The actual findings of other courts cast doubt on the State's assumption that religious use of peyote is harmful. The fact that peyote is classified as a Schedule I controlled substance does not, by itself, show that any and all uses of peyote, in any circumstance, are inherently harmful and dangerous. The Federal Government, which created the classifications of unlawful drugs from which Oregon's drug laws are derived, apparently does not find peyote so dangerous as to preclude an exemption for religious use.

The carefully circumscribed ritual context in which respondents used peyote is far removed from the irresponsible and unrestricted recreational use of unlawful drugs. The Native

American Church's internal restrictions on, and supervision of, its members' use of peyote substantially obviate the State's health and safety concerns. Moreover, just as in *Yoder*, the values and interests of those seeking a religious exemption in this case are congruent to a great degree, with those the State seeks to promote through its drug laws. Not only does the Church's doctrine forbid nonreligious use of peyote; it also generally advocates self-reliance, familial responsibility, and abstinence from alcohol. There is considerable evidence that the spiritual and social support provided by the Church has been effective in combating the tragic effects of alcoholism of the Native American population. Far from promoting the lawless and irresponsible use of drugs, Native American Church members' spiritual code exemplifies values that Oregon's drug laws are presumably intended to foster.

The State also seeks to support its refusal to make an exception for religious use of peyote by invoking its interest in abolishing drug trafficking. There is, however, practically no illegal traffic in peyote. Peyote simply is not a popular drug; its distribution for use in religious rituals has nothing to do with the vast and violent traffic in illegal narcotics that plagues this country.

Finally, the State argues that granting an exception for religious peyote use would erode its interest in the uniform, fair, and certain enforcement of its drug laws. The State fears that, if it grants an exemption for religious peyote use, a flood of other claims to religious exemptions will follow. It would then be placed in a dilemma, it says, between allowing a patchwork of exemptions that would hinder its law enforcement efforts, and risking a violation of the Establishment Clause by arbitrarily limiting its religious exemptions. The State's apprehension of a flood of other religious claims is purely speculative. Almost half the States, and the Federal Government, have maintained an exemption for religious peyote use for many years, and apparently have not found themselves overwhelmed by claims to other religious exemptions. Allowing an exemption for religious peyote use would not necessarily oblige the State to grant a similar exemption to other religious groups. The unusual circumstances that make the religious use of peyote compatible with the State's interests in health and safety and in preventing drug trafficking would not apply to other religious claims. That the State might grant an exemption for religious peyote use, but deny other religious claims arising in different circumstances, would not violate the Establishment Clause. Though the State must treat all religions equally, and not favor one over another, this obligation is fulfilled by the uniform application of the "compelling interest" *test* to all free exercise claims, not by reaching uniform *results* as to all claims. . . .

For these reasons, I conclude that Oregon's interest in enforcing its drug laws against religious use of peyote is not sufficiently compelling to outweigh respondents' right to the free exercise of their religion. Since the State could not constitutionally enforce its criminal prohibition against respondents, the interests underlying the State's drug laws cannot justify its denial of unemployment benefits.

City of Boerne v. Flores, Archbishop of San Antonio
521 U.S. 507 (1997)

In Sherbert v. Verner *(1963), the Court ruled that the Free Exercise Clause required government to exempt religious believers from generally applicable laws that burdened their religious practices, unless the laws were justified by a compelling governmental interest and were narrowly tailored to achieve that interest. However, in* Department of Human Resources of Oregon v. Smith, *the Supreme Court abandoned that position. In 1993,* Congress responded to *Smith* by enacting the Religious Freedom Restoration Act (RFRA), which was "to restore the compelling interest test set forth in* Sherbert v. Verner *and to guarantee its application in all cases where free exercise of religion is substantially burdened."* St. Peter Catholic Church, *located in Boerne, Texas, was built in 1923 to seat about 230 worshippers and was too small to accommodate the parish's growing* *congregation. The archbishop of San Antonio therefore applied for a building permit to enlarge the church. A few months previous, however, the Boerne City Council had authorized the city's Historic Landmark Commission to prepare a preservation plan with proposed historic landmarks and districts. Under the plan, the commission had to approve in advance construction affecting historic landmarks or buildings in historic districts. Relying on the ordinance and the designation of a historic district that included the church, the commission denied the application to enlarge the church. The archbishop filed suit in federal district court, relying primarily on RFRA in challenging the permit denial. The district court concluded that RFRA exceeded Congress's enforcement power under Section 5 of the Fourteenth Amendment. The Fifth Circuit reversed, finding RFRA to be constitutional, and the Supreme Court granted certiorari. Opinion of the Court:* Kennedy, *Rehnquist, Stevens, Thomas, Ginsburg, Scalia (in part). Concurring opinion:* Stevens. *Concurring in part:* Scalia, *Stevens. Dissenting opinions:* O'Connor, *Breyer (in part);* Souter, *Breyer.*

JUSTICE KENNEDY delivered the opinion of the Court.

[*Employment Division v.*] *Smith* held that neutral, generally applicable laws may be applied to religious practices even when not supported by a compelling governmental interest. Members of Congress in hearings and floor debates criticized the Court's reasoning, and this disagreement resulted in the passage of RFRA. The Act's mandate applies to any "branch, department, agency, instrumentality, and official (or other person acting under color of law) of the United States," as well as to any "State, or subdivision of a State." The Act's universal coverage is confirmed in section 2000bb-3(a), under which RFRA "applies to all Federal and State law, and the implementation of that law, whether statutory or otherwise, and whether adopted before or after [RFRA's enactment]." Congress relied on its Fourteenth Amendment enforcement power in enacting the most far reaching and substantial of RFRA's provisions, those which impose its requirements on the States. The parties disagree over whether RFRA is a proper exercise

of Congress' section 5 power "to enforce" by "appropriate legislation" the constitutional guarantee that no State shall deprive any person of "life, liberty, or property, without due process of law" nor deny any person "equal protection of the laws."

In defense of the Act respondent contends that RFRA is permissible enforcement legislation. Congress, it is said, is only protecting by legislation one of the liberties guaranteed by the Fourteenth Amendment's Due Process Clause, the free exercise of religion, beyond what is necessary under *Smith.* It is said the congressional decision to dispense with proof of deliberate or overt discrimination and instead concentrate on a law's effects accords with the settled understanding that section 5 includes the power to enact legislation designed to prevent as well as remedy constitutional violations. It is further contended that Congress' section 5 power is not limited to remedial or preventive legislation.

All must acknowledge that section 5 is "a positive grant of legislative power" to Congress, *Katzenbach v. Morgan* (1966). Legislation which deters or remedies constitutional violations can fall within the sweep of Congress' enforcement power even if in the process it prohibits conduct which is not itself unconstitutional and intrudes into "legislative spheres of autonomy previously reserved to the States." *Fitzpatrick v. Bitzer* (1976). For example, the Court upheld a suspension of literacy tests and similar voting requirements under Congress' parallel power to enforce the provisions of the Fifteenth Amendment, as a measure to combat racial discrimination in voting, *South Carolina v. Katzenbach* (1966), despite the facial constitutionality of the tests under *Lassiter v. Northampton County Bd. of Elections* (1959). We have also concluded that other measures protecting voting rights are within Congress' power to enforce the Fourteenth and Fifteenth Amendments, despite the burdens those measures placed on the State. It is also true, however, that "as broad as the congressional enforcement power is, it is not unlimited." *Oregon v. Mitchell* (1970) (opinion of Black, J.).

In assessing the breadth of section 5's enforcement power, we begin with its text. Congress' power under section 5 extends only to "enforc[ing]" the provisions of the Fourteenth Amendment. The design of the Amendment and the text of section 5 are inconsistent with the suggestion that Congress has the power to decree the substance of the Fourteenth Amendment's restrictions on the States. Legislation which alters the meaning of the Free Exercise Clause cannot be said to be enforcing the Clause. Congress does not enforce a constitutional right by changing what the right is. It has been given the power "to enforce," not the power to determine what constitutes a violation. Were it not so, what Congress would be enforcing would no longer be, in any meaningful sense, the "provisions of [the Fourteenth Amendment]."

The Fourteenth Amendment's history confirms the remedial, rather than substantive, nature of the Enforcement Clause. In February [1866], Republican Representative John Bingham of Ohio reported the following draft amendment to the House of Representatives on behalf of the Joint Committee [on Reconstruction]: "The Congress shall have power to make all laws which shall be necessary and proper to secure to the citizens of each State all privileges and immunities of citizens in the several States, and to all persons in the several States equal protection in the rights of life, liberty, and property." The proposal encountered immediate opposition . . . [because] the proposed Amendment gave Congress too much legislative power at the expense of the existing constitutional structure. The House voted to table the proposal until April, which was seen as marking the defeat of the proposal. The Joint Committee began drafting a new article of Amendment, which it reported to Congress on April 30, 1866. Under the revised Amendment, Congress' power was no longer plenary but remedial. Congress was granted the power to make the substantive constitutional prohibitions against the States effective. The new measure passed both Houses and was ratified in July 1868 as the Fourteenth Amendment.

The remedial and preventive nature of Congress' enforcement power, and the limitation inherent in the power, were confirmed in our earliest cases on the Fourteenth Amendment. In the *Civil Rights Cases* (1883), the Court invalidated sections of the Civil Rights Act of 1875 which prescribed criminal penalties for denying to any person "the full enjoyment of" public accommodations and conveyances, on the grounds that it exceeded Congress' power by seeking to regulate private conduct. The Enforcement Clause, the Court said, did not authorize Congress to pass "general legislation upon the rights of the citizen, but corrective legislation; that is, such as may be necessary and proper for counteracting such laws as the State may adopt or enforce, and which, by the amendment, they are prohibited from making or enforcing." Although the specific holdings of these early cases might have been superseded or modified, their treatment of Congress' section 5 power as corrective or preventive, not definitional, has not been questioned.

If Congress could define its own powers by altering the Fourteenth Amendment's meaning, no longer would the Constitution be "superior paramount law, unchangeable by ordinary means." It would be "on a level with ordinary legislative acts, and, like other acts, alterable when the legislature shall please to alter it." *Marbury v. Madison* [1803]. Under this approach, it is difficult to conceive of a principle that would limit congressional power. Shifting legislative majorities could change the Constitution and effectively circumvent the difficult and detailed amendment process contained in Article V.

Respondent contends that RFRA is a proper exercise of Congress' remedial or preventive power. The Act, it is said, is a reasonable means of protecting the free exercise of religion as defined by *Smith*. It prevents and remedies laws which are enacted with the unconstitutional object of targeting religious beliefs and practices. RFRA is so out of proportion to a supposed remedial or preventive object that it cannot be understood as responsive to, or designed to prevent, unconstitutional behavior. It appears, instead, to attempt a substantive change in constitutional protections. Preventive measures prohibiting certain types of laws may be appropriate when there is reason to believe that many of the laws affected by the congressional enactment have a significant likelihood of being unconstitutional. RFRA is not so confined. Sweeping coverage ensures its intrusion at every level of government, displacing laws and prohibiting official actions of almost every description and regardless of subject matter. RFRA's restrictions apply to every agency and official of the Federal, State, and local Governments. RFRA applies to all federal and state law, statutory or otherwise, whether adopted before or after its enactment. RFRA has no termination date or termination mechanism. Any law is subject to challenge at any time by any individual who alleges a substantial burden on his or her free exercise of religion.

The reach and scope of RFRA distinguish it from other measures passed under Congress' enforcement power, even in the area of voting rights. The stringent test RFRA demands of state laws reflects a lack of proportionality or congruence between the means adopted and the legitimate end to be achieved. The substantial costs RFRA exacts, both in practical terms of imposing a heavy litigation burden on the States and in terms of curtailing their traditional general regulatory power, far exceed any pattern or practice of unconstitutional conduct under the Free Exercise Clause as interpreted in *Smith*. Simply put, RFRA is not designed to identify and counteract state laws likely to be unconstitutional because of their treatment of religion. When Congress acts within its sphere of power and responsibilities, it has not just the right but the duty to make its own informed judgment on the meaning and force of the Constitution. Were it otherwise, we could not afford Congress the presumption of validity its enactments now enjoy. [B]ut as the provisions of the federal statute here invoked are beyond congressional authority, it is this Court's precedent, not RFRA, which must control.

It is for Congress in the first instance to "determine whether and what legislation is needed to secure the guarantees of the Fourteenth Amendment," and its conclusions are entitled to much deference. Congress' discretion is not unlimited, however, and the courts retain the power, as they have since *Marbury v. Madison,* to determine if Congress has exceeded its authority under the Constitution. Broad as the power of Congress is under the Enforcement Clause of the Fourteenth Amendment, RFRA contradicts vital principles necessary to maintain separation of powers and the federal

balance. The judgment of the Court of Appeals sustaining the Act's constitutionality is reversed.

JUSTICE STEVENS, concurring.

In my opinion, the Religious Freedom Restoration Act of 1993 (RFRA) is a "law respecting an establishment of religion" that violates the First Amendment to the Constitution. If the historic landmark on the hill in Boerne happened to be a museum or an art gallery owned by an atheist, it would not be eligible for an exemption from the city ordinances that forbid an enlargement of the structure. Because the landmark is owned by the Catholic Church, it is claimed that RFRA gives its owner a federal statutory entitlement to an exemption from a generally applicable, neutral civil law. Whether the Church would actually prevail under the statute or not, the statute has provided the Church with a legal weapon that no atheist or agnostic can obtain. This government preference for religion, as opposed to irreligion, is forbidden by the First Amendment.

JUSTICE O'CONNOR, with whom JUSTICE BREYER [joins in part], dissenting.

I dissent from the Court's disposition of this case. I agree with the Court that the issue before us is whether the Religious Freedom Restoration Act (RFRA) is a proper exercise of Congress' power to enforce § 5 of the Fourteenth Amendment. But as a yardstick for measuring the constitutionality of RFRA, the Court uses its holding in Employment Division, Department of Human Resources of *Oregon v. Smith* (1990), the decision that prompted Congress to enact RFRA as a means of more rigorously enforcing the Free Exercise Clause. I remain of the view that *Smith* was wrongly decided, and I would use this case to reexamine the Court's holding there. If the Court were to correct the misinterpretation of the Free Exercise Clause set forth in *Smith,* it would simultaneously put our First Amendment jurisprudence back on course and allay the legitimate concerns of a majority in Congress who believe that *Smith* improperly restricted religious liberty. We would then be in a position to review RFRA in light of a proper interpretation of the Free Exercise Clause.

Burwell v. Hobby Lobby Stores, Inc.
573 U.S. ___ (2014)

Congress enacted the Religious Freedom Restoration Act (RFRA) in 1993 in response to Employment Div., Dept. of Human Resources of Ore. v. Smith *(1990), in which the Supreme Court had held that "neutral, generally applicable laws may be applied to religious practices even when not supported by a compelling governmental interest." RFRA provides that "Government shall not substantially burden a person's exercise of religion even if the burden results from a rule of general applicability." If the Government substantially burdens a person's exercise of religion, under the Act that person is entitled to an exemption from the rule unless the Government "demonstrates that application of the burden to the person—(1) is in furtherance of a compelling governmental interest; and (2) is the least restrictive means of furthering that compelling governmental interest." At issue here are HHS regulations promulgated under the Patient Protection and Affordable Care Act of 2010 (ACA). ACA requires employers with 50 or more full-time employees to offer "a group health plan or group health insurance coverage" that provides "minimum essential coverage," unless a pre-existing plan was "grandfathered" in. That coverage includes "preventive care and screenings" for women without "any cost sharing requirements," although Congress did not specify what types of preventive care must be covered but instead authorized the Health Resources and Services Administration (HRSA), a component of HHS, to make that decision. After consulting the Institute of Medicine, a nonprofit group of volunteer advisers, HRSA promulgated the Women's Preventive Services Guidelines, which required employers to provide "coverage, without cost sharing" for "all Food and Drug Administration [FDA] approved contraceptive methods, sterilization procedures, and patient education and counseling." Although many of the required, FDA-approved methods of contraception work by preventing the fertilization of an egg, four of those methods (those specifically at issue here) may have the effect of preventing an already fertilized egg from developing any further by inhibiting its attachment to the uterus. HHS also authorized the HRSA to establish exemptions from the contraceptive mandate for "religious employers" and certain religious nonprofit organizations. This case involves two challenges to the HRSA guidelines. Norman and Elizabeth Hahn and their three sons are sole owners of Conestoga Wood Specialties, a for-profit corporation with 950 employees organized under Pennsylvania law. They are also devout members of the Mennonite Church, which opposes abortion, and they have therefore excluded from the group-health insurance plan they offer to their employees certain contraceptive methods that they consider to be abortifacients. The Hahns and Conestoga sued HHS and other federal officials and agencies under RFRA and the Free Exercise Clause of the First Amendment, seeking to enjoin application of ACA's contraceptive mandate insofar as it requires them to provide health-insurance coverage for four FDA-approved contraceptives—two forms of "morning after pills" and two forms of intrauterine devices—that may operate after the fertilization of an egg. The District Court denied a preliminary injunction, and the Third Circuit affirmed. David and Barbara Green and their three children are sole owners of a nationwide chain called Hobby Lobby, a for-profit corporation organized under Oklahoma law that has 500 Hobby Lobby stores and more than 13,000 employees. One son has founded a subsidiary company, Mardel. Hobby Lobby's statement of purpose commits the Greens to "honoring the Lord in all [they] do by operating the company in a manner consistent with Biblical principles." Like the Hahns, the Greens believe that life begins at conception and that it would violate their religion to facilitate access to contraceptive drugs or devices that operate after that point. They specifically object to the same four contraceptive methods as the Hahns. The Greens, Hobby Lobby, and Mardel sued HHS and other federal agencies and officials to challenge the contraceptive mandate under RFRA and the Free Exercise Clause. The District Court denied a preliminary injunction, but the Tenth Circuit reversed. The Supreme Court then granted certiorari in both cases.* Opinion of the Court: Alito, Roberts, Scalia, Kennedy, Thomas. Concurring opinion: Kennedy. Dissenting opinions: Ginsburg, Sotomayor, Breyer, Kagan (except for Part III-C-1); Breyer, Kagan.

JUSTICE ALITO delivered the opinion of the Court.

We must decide in these cases whether the Religious Freedom Restoration Act of 1993 (RFRA), permits the United States Department of Health and Human Services (HHS) to demand that three closely held corporations provide health-insurance coverage for methods of contraception that violate the sincerely held religious beliefs of the companies' owners. We hold that the regulations that impose this obligation violate RFRA, which prohibits the Federal Government from taking any action that substantially burdens the exercise of religion unless that action constitutes the least restrictive means of serving a compelling government interest.

In holding that the HHS mandate is unlawful, we reject HHS's argument that the owners of the companies forfeited all RFRA protection when they decided to organize their businesses as corporations rather than sole proprietorships or general partnerships. The plain terms of RFRA make it perfectly clear that Congress did not discriminate in this way against men and women who wish to run their businesses as for-profit corporations in the manner required by their religious beliefs. Since RFRA applies in these cases, we must decide whether the challenged HHS regulations substantially burden the exercise of religion, and we hold that they do.

The owners of the businesses have religious objections to abortion, and according to their religious beliefs the four contraceptive methods at issue are abortifacients. If the owners comply with the HHS mandate, they believe they will be facilitating abortions, and if they do not comply, they will pay a very heavy price—as much as $1.3 million per day, or about $475 million per year, in the case of one of the companies. If these consequences do not amount to a substantial burden, it is hard to see what would.

Under RFRA, a Government action that imposes a substantial burden on religious exercise must serve a compelling government interest, and we assume that the HHS regulations satisfy this requirement. But in order for the HHS mandate to be sustained, it must also constitute the least restrictive means of serving that interest, and the mandate plainly fails that test. There are other ways in which Congress or HHS could equally ensure that every woman has cost-free access to the particular contraceptives at issue here and, indeed, to all FDA-approved contraceptives. In fact, HHS has already devised and implemented a system that seeks to respect the religious liberty of religious nonprofit corporations while ensuring that the employees of these entities have precisely the same access to all FDA-approved contraceptives as employees of companies whose owners have no religious objections to providing such coverage. The employees of these religious nonprofit corporations still have access to insurance coverage without cost sharing for all FDA-approved contraceptives; and according to HHS, this system imposes no net economic burden on the insurance companies that are required to provide or secure the coverage.

Although HHS has made this system available to religious nonprofits that have religious objections to the contraceptive mandate, HHS has provided no reason why the same system cannot be made available when the owners of for-profit corporations have similar religious objections. We therefore conclude that this system constitutes an alternative that achieves all of the Government's aims while providing greater respect for religious liberty. And under RFRA, that conclusion means that enforcement of the HHS contraceptive mandate against the objecting parties in these cases is unlawful.

As this description of our reasoning shows, our holding is very specific. We do not hold, as the principal dissent alleges, that for-profit corporations and other commercial enterprises can "opt out of any law (saving only tax laws) they judge incompatible with their sincerely held religious beliefs." Nor do we hold, as the dissent implies, that such corporations have free rein to take steps that impose "disadvantages on others" or that require "the general public [to] pick up the tab." And we certainly do not hold or suggest that "RFRA demands accommodation of a for-profit corporation's religious beliefs no matter the impact that accommodation may have on . . . thousands of women employed by Hobby Lobby." The effect of the HHS-created accommodation on the women employed by Hobby Lobby and the other companies involved in these cases would be precisely zero. Under that accommodation, these women would still be entitled to all FDA-approved contraceptives without cost sharing.

III

A

The first question that we must address is whether [RFRA] applies to regulations that govern the activities of for-profit corporations like Hobby Lobby, Conestoga, and Mardel. HHS contends that neither these companies nor their owners can even be heard under RFRA. According to HHS, the companies cannot sue because they seek to make a profit for their owners, and the owners cannot be heard because the regulations, at least as a formal matter, apply only to the companies and not to the owners as individuals.

HHS's argument would have dramatic consequences. Consider this Court's decision in *Braunfeld* v. *Brown* (1961). In that case, five Orthodox Jewish merchants who ran small retail businesses in Philadelphia challenged a Pennsylvania Sunday closing law as a violation of the Free Exercise Clause. Because of their faith, these merchants closed their shops on Saturday, and they argued that requiring them to remain shut on Sunday threatened them with financial ruin. The Court entertained their claim (although it ruled against them on the merits), and if a similar claim were raised today under RFRA, the merchants would be entitled to be heard. According to HHS, however, if these merchants chose to incorporate their businesses—without in any way changing the size or nature of their businesses—they would forfeit all RFRA (and free-exercise) rights. HHS would put these merchants to a difficult choice: either give up the right to seek judicial protection of their religious liberty or forgo the benefits, available to their competitors, of operating as corporations.

RFRA was designed to provide very broad protection for religious liberty. By enacting RFRA, Congress went far beyond what this Court has held is constitutionally required. Is there any reason to think that the Congress that enacted such sweeping protection put small-business owners to the choice that HHS

suggests? Congress provided protection for people like the Hahns and Greens by employing a familiar legal fiction: It included corporations within RFRA's definition of "persons." But it is important to keep in mind that the purpose of this fiction is to provide protection for human beings. A corporation is simply a form of organization used by human beings to achieve desired ends. An established body of law specifies the rights and obligations of the *people* (including shareholders, officers, and employees) who are associated with a corporation in one way or another. When rights, whether constitutional or statutory, are extended to corporations, the purpose is to protect the rights of these people.

B

1

RFRA applies to "a person's" exercise of religion, and RFRA itself does not define the term "person." We therefore look to the Dictionary Act, which we must consult "in determining the meaning of any Act of Congress, unless the context indicates otherwise." Under the Dictionary Act, "the word 'person' includes corporations, companies, associations, firms, partnerships, societies, and joint stock companies, as well as individuals." Thus, unless there is something about the RFRA context that "indicates otherwise," the Dictionary Act provides a quick, clear, and affirmative answer to the question whether the companies involved in these cases may be heard. We see nothing in RFRA that suggests a congressional intent to depart from the Dictionary Act definition, and HHS makes little effort to argue otherwise. We have entertained RFRA and free-exercise claims brought by nonprofit corporations, and HHS concedes that a nonprofit corporation can be a "person" within the meaning of RFRA. This concession effectively dispatches any argument that the term "person" as used in RFRA does not reach the closely held corporations involved in these cases. No known understanding of the term "person" includes *some* but not all corporations.

2

The principal argument advanced by HHS and the principal dissent regarding RFRA protection for Hobby Lobby, Conestoga, and Mardel focuses not on the statutory term "person," but on the phrase "exercise of religion." According to HHS and the dissent, these corporations are not protected by RFRA because they cannot exercise religion. Neither HHS nor the dissent, however, provides any persuasive explanation for this conclusion. Is it because of the corporate form? The corporate form alone cannot provide the explanation because HHS concedes that nonprofit corporations can be protected by RFRA. If the corporate form is not enough, what about the profit-making objective? In *Braunfeld*, we entertained the free-exercise claims of individuals who were attempting to make a profit as retail merchants, and the Court never even hinted that this objective precluded their claims. Some lower court judges have suggested that RFRA does not protect for-profit corporations because the purpose of such corporations is simply to make money. This argument flies in the face of modern corporate law. While it is certainly true that a central objective of for-profit corporations is to make money, modern corporate law does not require for-profit corporations to pursue profit at the expense of everything else, and many do not do so. For-profit corporations, with ownership approval, support a wide variety of charitable causes. If for-profit corporations may pursue such worthy objectives, there is no apparent reason why they may not further religious objectives as well.

HHS would draw a sharp line between nonprofit corporations (which, HHS concedes, are protected by RFRA) and for-profit corporations (which HHS would leave unprotected), but the actual picture is less clear-cut. Not all corporations that decline to organize as nonprofits do so in order to maximize profit. In any event, the objectives that may properly be pursued by the companies in these cases are governed by the laws of the States in which they were incorporated—Pennsylvania and Oklahoma—and the laws of those States permit for-profit corporations to pursue "any lawful purpose" or "act," including the pursuit of profit in conformity with the owners' religious principles.

4

Finally, HHS contends that Congress could not have wanted RFRA to apply to for-profit corporations because it is difficult as a practical matter to ascertain the sincere "beliefs" of a corporation. HHS goes so far as to raise the specter of "divisive, polarizing proxy battles over the religious identity of large, publicly traded corporations such as IBM or General Electric." These cases, however, do not involve publicly traded corporations, and it seems unlikely that the sort of corporate giants to which HHS refers will often assert RFRA claims. HHS has not pointed to any example of a publicly traded corporation asserting RFRA rights, and numerous practical restraints would likely prevent that from occurring. For example, the idea that unrelated shareholders—including institutional investors with their own set of stakeholders—would agree to run a corporation under the same religious beliefs seems improbable. In any event, we have no occasion in these cases to consider RFRA's applicability to such companies. The companies in the cases before us are closely held corporations, each owned and controlled by members of a single family, and no one has disputed the sincerity of their religious beliefs. HHS has also provided no evidence that the purported problem of determining the sincerity of an asserted religious belief moved Congress to exclude for-profit corporations from RFRA's protection.

For all these reasons, we hold that a federal regulation's restriction on the activities of a for-profit closely held corporation must comply with RFRA.

IV

Because RFRA applies in these cases, we must next ask whether the HHS contraceptive mandate "substantially burdens" the exercise of religion.

A

The Hahns and Greens have a sincere religious belief that life begins at conception. They therefore object on religious grounds to providing health insurance that covers methods of birth control that, as HHS acknowledges, may result in the destruction of an embryo. By requiring the Hahns and Greens and their companies to arrange for such coverage, the HHS mandate demands that they engage in conduct that seriously violates their religious beliefs.

If the Hahns and Greens and their companies do not yield to this demand, the economic consequences will be severe. If the companies continue to offer group health plans that do not cover the contraceptives at issue, they will be taxed $100 per day for each affected individual. For Hobby Lobby, the bill could amount to $1.3 million per day or about $475 million per year; for Conestoga, the assessment could be $90,000 per day or $33 million per year; and for Mardel, it could be $40,000 per day or about $15 million per year. It is true that the plaintiffs could avoid these assessments by dropping insurance coverage altogether and thus forcing their employees to obtain health insurance on one of the exchanges established under ACA. But if at least one of their full-time employees were to qualify for a subsidy on one of the government-run exchanges, this course would also entail substantial economic consequences. The companies could face penalties of $2,000 per employee each year. These penalties would amount to roughly $26 million for Hobby Lobby, $1.8 million for Conestoga, and $800,000 for Mardel.

C

In taking the position that the HHS mandate does not impose a substantial burden on the exercise of religion, HHS's main argument (echoed by the principal dissent) is that the connection between what the objecting parties must do (provide health insurance coverage for four methods of contraception that may operate after the fertilization of an egg) and the end that they find to be morally wrong (destruction of an embryo) is simply too attenuated. HHS and the dissent note that providing the coverage would not itself result in the destruction of an embryo; that would occur only if an employee chose to take advantage of the coverage and to use one of the four methods at issue.

This argument dodges the question that RFRA presents (whether the HHS mandate imposes a substantial burden on the ability of the objecting parties to conduct business in accordance with *their religious beliefs*) and instead addresses a very different question that the federal courts have no business addressing (whether the religious belief asserted in a RFRA case is reasonable). The Hahns and Greens believe that providing the coverage demanded by the HHS regulations is connected to the destruction of an embryo in a way that is sufficient to make it immoral for them to provide the coverage. This belief implicates a difficult and important question of religion and moral philosophy, namely, the circumstances under which it is wrong for a person to perform an act that is innocent in itself but that has the effect of enabling or facilitating the commission of an immoral act by another. Arrogating the authority to provide a binding national answer to this religious and philosophical question, HHS and the principal dissent in effect tell the plaintiffs that their beliefs are flawed. For good reason, we have repeatedly refused to take such a step.

Moreover, in *Thomas* v. *Review Bd. of Indiana Employment Security Div.* (1981), we considered and rejected an argument that is nearly identical to the one now urged by HHS and the dissent. In *Thomas*, a Jehovah's Witness was initially employed making sheet steel for a variety of industrial uses, but he was later transferred to a job making turrets for tanks. Because he objected on religious grounds to participating in the manufacture of weapons, he lost his job and sought unemployment compensation. Ruling against the employee, the state court had difficulty with the line that the employee drew between work that he found to be consistent with his religious beliefs (helping to manufacture steel that was used in making weapons) and work that he found morally objectionable (helping to make the weapons themselves). This Court, however, held that "it is not for us to say that the line he drew was an unreasonable one." Similarly, in these cases, the Hahns and Greens and their companies sincerely believe that providing the insurance coverage demanded by the HHS regulations lies on the forbidden side of the line, and it is not for us to say that their religious beliefs are mistaken or insubstantial. Instead, our "narrow function . . . in this context is to determine" whether the line drawn reflects "an honest conviction," and there is no dispute that it does.

V

Since the HHS contraceptive mandate imposes a substantial burden on the exercise of religion, we must move on and decide whether HHS has shown that the mandate both "(1) is in furtherance of a compelling governmental interest; and (2) is the least restrictive means of furthering that compelling governmental interest."

A

HHS asserts that the contraceptive mandate serves a variety of important interests, but many of these are couched in very broad terms, such as promoting "public health" and "gender equality." RFRA, however, contemplates a "more focused" inquiry: It "requires the Government to demonstrate that the compelling interest test is satisfied through application of the challenged law 'to the person'—the particular claimant whose sincere exercise of religion is being substantially burdened." In addition to asserting these very broadly framed interests, HHS maintains that the mandate serves a compelling interest in ensuring that all women have access to all FDA-approved contraceptives without cost sharing.

The objecting parties contend that HHS has not shown that the mandate serves a compelling government interest, and it is arguable that there are features of ACA that support that view. As we have noted, many employees—those covered by grandfathered plans and those who work for employers with fewer than 50 employees—may have no contraceptive coverage without cost sharing at all. HHS responds that many legal requirements have exceptions and the existence of exceptions does not in itself indicate that the principal interest served by a law is not compelling.

We find it unnecessary to adjudicate this issue. We will assume that the interest in guaranteeing cost-free access to the four challenged contraceptive methods is compelling within the meaning of RFRA, and we will proceed to consider the final prong of the RFRA test, *i.e.*, whether HHS has shown that the contraceptive mandate is "the least restrictive means of

furthering that compelling governmental interest."

B

The least-restrictive-means standard is not satisfied here. HHS has not shown that it lacks other means of achieving its desired goal without imposing a substantial burden on the exercise of religion by the objecting parties in these cases. HHS itself has demonstrated that it has at its disposal an approach that is less restrictive than requiring employers to fund contraceptive methods that violate their religious beliefs. HHS has already established an accommodation for nonprofit organizations with religious objections. The principal dissent identifies no reason why this accommodation would fail to protect the asserted needs of women as effectively as the contraceptive mandate, and there is none. Under the accommodation, the plaintiffs' female employees would continue to receive contraceptive coverage without cost sharing for all FDA-approved contraceptives, and they would continue to "face minimal logistical and administrative obstacles," because their employers' insurers would be responsible for providing information and coverage.

C

HHS and the principal dissent argue that a ruling in favor of the objecting parties in these cases will lead to a flood of religious objections regarding a wide variety of medical procedures and drugs, such as vaccinations and blood transfusions, but HHS has made no effort to substantiate this prediction. In any event, our decision in these cases is concerned solely with the contraceptive mandate. Our decision should not be understood to hold that an insurance-coverage mandate must necessarily fall if it conflicts with an employer's religious beliefs. Other coverage requirements, such as immunizations, may be supported by different interests (for example, the need to combat the spread of infectious diseases) and may involve different arguments about the least restrictive means of providing them.

The principal dissent raises the possibility that discrimination in hiring, for example on the basis of race, might be cloaked as religious practice to escape legal sanction. Our decision today provides no such shield. The Government has a compelling interest in providing an equal opportunity to participate in the workforce without regard to race, and prohibitions on racial discrimination are precisely tailored to achieve that critical goal.

* * *

The contraceptive mandate, as applied to closely held corporations, violates RFRA. Our decision on that statutory question makes it unnecessary to reach the First Amendment claim raised by Conestoga and the Hahns.

JUSTICE GINSBURG, with whom JUSTICE SOTOMAYOR joins, and with whom JUSTICE BREYER and JUSTICE KAGAN join as to all but Part III-C-1, dissenting.

In a decision of startling breadth, the Court holds that commercial enterprises, including corporations, along with partnerships and sole proprietorships, can opt out of any law (saving only tax laws) they judge incompatible with their sincerely held religious beliefs. Compelling governmental interests in uniform compliance with the law, and disadvantages that religion-based opt-outs impose on others, hold no sway, the Court decides, at least when there is a "less restrictive alternative." And such an alternative, the Court suggests, there always will be whenever, in lieu of tolling an enterprise claiming a religion-based exemption, the government, *i.e.,* the general public, can pick up the tab. Persuaded that Congress enacted RFRA to serve a far less radical purpose, and mindful of the havoc the Court's judgment can introduce, I dissent.

I

"The ability of women to participate equally in the economic and social life of the Nation has been facilitated by their ability to control their reproductive lives." *Planned Parenthood of Southeastern Pa. v. Casey* (1992). Congress acted on that understanding when, as part of a nationwide insurance program intended to be comprehensive, it called for coverage of preventive care responsive to women's needs. Carrying out Congress' direction, the Department of Health and Human Services (HHS), in consultation with public health experts, promulgated regulations requiring group health plans to cover all forms of contraception approved by the Food and Drug Administration (FDA). The genesis of this coverage should enlighten the Court's resolution of these cases.

As altered by the Women's Health Amendment's passage, the ACA requires new insurance plans to include coverage without cost sharing of "such additional preventive care and screenings as provided for in comprehensive guidelines supported by the Health Resources and Services Administration [(HRSA)]," a unit of HHS. The HRSA adopted guidelines recommending coverage of "all FDA-approved contraceptive methods, sterilization procedures, and patient education and counseling for all women with reproductive capacity."

While the Women's Health Amendment succeeded, a countermove proved unavailing. The Senate voted down the so-called "conscience amendment," which would have enabled any employer or insurance provider to deny coverage based on its asserted "religious beliefs or moral convictions." Congress left health care decisions—including the choice among contraceptive methods—in the hands of women, with the aid of their health care providers.

II

Any Free Exercise Clause claim Hobby Lobby or Conestoga might assert is foreclosed by this Court's decision in *Employment Div., Dept. of Human Resources of Ore. v. Smith* (1990). Even if *Smith* did not control, the Free Exercise Clause would not require the exemption Hobby Lobby and Conestoga seek. Accommodations to religious beliefs or observances, the Court has clarified, must not significantly impinge on the interests of third parties. The exemption sought by Hobby Lobby and Conestoga would override significant interests of the corporations' employees and covered dependents. It would deny legions of women who do not hold their employers' beliefs access to contraceptive coverage that the ACA would otherwise secure.

III

A

Lacking a tenable claim under the Free Exercise Clause, Hobby Lobby and Conestoga rely on RFRA, a statute instructing that "government shall not substantially burden a person's exercise of religion even if the burden results from a rule of general applicability" unless the government shows that application of the burden is "the least restrictive means" to further a "compelling governmental interest." RFRA's purpose is specific and written into the statute itself. The Act was crafted to "restore the compelling interest test as set forth in *Sherbert* v. *Verner* (1963) and *Wisconsin* v. *Yoder* (1972) and to guarantee its application in all cases where free exercise of religion is substantially burdened."

Despite these authoritative indications, the Court sees RFRA as a bold initiative departing from, rather than restoring, pre-*Smith* jurisprudence.

C

With RFRA's restorative purpose in mind, I turn to the Act's application to the instant lawsuits. That task, in view of the positions taken by the Court, requires consideration of several questions, each potentially dispositive of Hobby Lobby's and Conestoga's claims: Do for-profit corporations rank among "persons" who "exercise religion"? Assuming that they do, does the contraceptive coverage requirement "substantially burden" their religious exercise? If so, is the requirement "in furtherance of a compelling government interest"? And last, does the requirement represent the least restrictive means for furthering that interest? Misguided by its errant premise that RFRA moved beyond the pre-*Smith* case law, the Court falters at each step of its analysis.

1

RFRA's compelling interest test applies to government actions that "substantially burden *a person's exercise of religion.*" This reference, the Court submits, incorporates the definition of "person" found in the Dictionary Act. The Dictionary Act's definition, however, controls only where "context" does not "indicate otherwise." Here, context does so indicate. RFRA speaks of "a person's *exercise of religion.*" Whether a corporation qualifies as a "person" capable of exercising religion is an inquiry one cannot answer without reference to the "full

body" of pre-*Smith* "free-exercise case law." There is in that case law no support for the notion that free exercise rights pertain to for-profit corporations.

Until this litigation, no decision of this Court recognized a for-profit corporation's qualification for a religious exemption from a generally applicable law, whether under the Free Exercise Clause or RFRA. The absence of such precedent is just what one would expect, for the exercise of religion is characteristic of natural persons, not artificial legal entities. The First Amendment's free exercise protections, the Court has indeed recognized, shelter churches and other nonprofit religion-based organizations. The Court's "special solicitude to the rights of religious organizations," *Hosanna-Tabor Evangelical Lutheran Church and School* v. *EEOC* (2012), however, is just that. No such solicitude is traditional for commercial organizations.

The reason why is hardly obscure. Religious organizations exist to foster the interests of persons subscribing to the same religious faith. Not so of for-profit corporations. Workers who sustain the operations of those corporations commonly are not drawn from one religious community. Indeed, by law, no religion-based criterion can restrict the work force of for-profit corporations. The distinction between a community made up of believers in the same religion and one embracing persons of diverse beliefs, clear as it is, constantly escapes the Court's attention.

Reading RFRA, as the Court does, to require extension of religion-based exemptions to for-profit corporations surely is not grounded in the pre-*Smith* precedent Congress sought to preserve. Had Congress intended RFRA to initiate a change so huge, a clarion statement to that effect likely would have been made in the legislation. Moreover, history is not on the Court's side. Recognition of the discrete characters of "ecclesiastical and lay" corporations dates back to Blackstone, and was reiterated by this Court centuries before the enactment of the Internal Revenue Code. Citing *Braunfeld* v. *Brown* (1961), the Court questions why, if "a sole proprietorship that seeks to make a profit may assert a free-exercise claim, [Hobby Lobby and Conestoga] can't do the same?" But even accepting, *arguendo*, the premise that unincorporated business enterprises may gain religious accommodations under the Free Exercise Clause, the Court's conclusion is unsound. In a sole proprietorship, the business and its owner are one and the same. By incorporating a business, however, an individual separates herself from the entity and escapes personal responsibility for the entity's obligations. One might ask why the separation should hold only when it serves the interest of those who control the corporation. In any event, *Braunfeld* is hardly impressive authority for the entitlement Hobby Lobby and Conestoga seek. The free exercise claim asserted there was promptly rejected on the merits.

2

Even if Hobby Lobby and Conestoga were deemed RFRA "persons," to gain an exemption, they must demonstrate that the contraceptive coverage requirement "substantially burdens [their] exercise of religion." Congress no doubt meant the modifier "substantially" to carry weight. The Court barely pauses to inquire whether any burden imposed by the contraceptive coverage requirement is substantial. Instead, it rests on the Greens' and Hahns' "belief that providing the coverage demanded by the HHS regulations is connected to the destruction of an embryo in a way that is sufficient to make it immoral for them to provide the coverage." I agree with the Court that the Green and Hahn families' religious convictions regarding contraception are sincerely held. But those beliefs, however deeply held, do not suffice to sustain a RFRA claim. RFRA, properly understood, distinguishes between "factual allegations that [plaintiffs'] beliefs are sincere and of a religious nature," which a court must accept as true, and the "legal conclusion that [plaintiffs'] religious exercise is substantially burdened," an inquiry the court must undertake. *Kaemmerling* v. *Lappin* (CADC 2008).

Undertaking the inquiry that the Court forgoes, I would conclude that the connection between the families' religious objections and the contraceptive coverage requirement is too attenuated to rank as substantial. The requirement carries no command that Hobby Lobby or Conestoga purchase or provide the contraceptives they find objectionable. Instead, it calls on the companies covered by the requirement to direct money into undifferentiated funds that finance a wide variety of benefits under comprehensive health plans. Those plans, in order to comply with the ACA must offer contraceptive coverage without cost sharing, just as they must cover an array of other preventive services. Importantly, the decisions whether to claim benefits under the plans are made not by Hobby Lobby or Conestoga, but by the covered employees and dependents, in consultation with their health care providers. Should an employee of Hobby Lobby or Conestoga share the religious beliefs of the Greens and Hahns, she is of course under no compulsion to use the contraceptives in question. It is doubtful that Congress, when it specified that burdens must be "substantial," had in mind a linkage thus interrupted by independent decisionmakers (the woman and her health counselor) standing between the challenged government action and the religious exercise claimed to be infringed. Any decision to use contraceptives made by a woman covered under Hobby Lobby's or Conestoga's plan will not be propelled by the Government, it will be the woman's autonomous choice, informed by the physician she consults.

3

Even if one were to conclude that Hobby Lobby and Conestoga meet the substantial burden requirement, the Government has shown that the contraceptive coverage for which the ACA provides furthers compelling interests in public health and women's well being. Those interests are concrete, specific, and demonstrated by a wealth of empirical evidence. To recapitulate, the mandated contraception coverage enables women to avoid the health problems unintended pregnancies may visit on them and their children. That Hobby Lobby and Conestoga resist coverage for only 4 of the 20 FDA approved contraceptives does not lessen these compelling interests. Notably, the corporations exclude intrauterine devices (IUDs), devices significantly more effective, and significantly more expensive than other contraceptive methods. Moreover, the Court's reasoning appears to permit commercial enterprises like Hobby Lobby and Conestoga to exclude from their group health plans all forms of contraceptives.

Perhaps the gravity of the interests at stake has led the Court to assume, for purposes of its RFRA analysis, that the compelling interest criterion is met in these cases. It bears note in this regard that the cost of an IUD is nearly equivalent to a month's fulltime pay for workers earning the minimum wage. Stepping back from its assumption that compelling interests support the contraceptive coverage requirement, the Court notes that small employers and grandfathered plans are not subject to the requirement. If there is a compelling interest in contraceptive coverage, the Court suggests, Congress would not have created these exclusions. Federal statutes often include exemptions for small employers, and such provisions have never been held to undermine the interests served by these statutes.

4

After assuming the existence of compelling government interests, the Court holds that the contraceptive coverage requirement fails to satisfy RFRA's least restrictive means test. But the Government has shown that there is no less restrictive, equally effective means that would both (1) satisfy the challengers' religious objections to providing insurance coverage for certain contraceptives (which they believe cause abortions); and (2) carry out the objective of the ACA's contraceptive coverage requirement, to ensure that women employees receive, at no cost to them, the preventive care needed to safeguard their health and well being. A "least restrictive means" cannot require employees to relinquish benefits accorded them by federal law in order to ensure that their commercial employers can adhere unreservedly to their religious tenets.

Then let the government pay (rather than the employees who do not share their employer's faith), the Court suggests. The ACA, however, requires coverage of preventive services through the existing employer-based system of health insurance "so that employees face minimal logistical and administrative obstacles." Impeding women's receipt of benefits "by

requiring them to take steps to learn about, and to sign up for, a new [government funded and administered] health benefit" was scarcely what Congress contemplated. Moreover, Title X of the Public Health Service Act is the nation's only dedicated source of federal funding for safety net family planning services. Safety net programs like Title X are not designed to absorb the unmet needs of insured individuals. Note, too, that Congress declined to write into law the preferential treatment Hobby Lobby and Conestoga describe as a less restrictive alternative. And where is the stopping point to the "let the government pay" alternative? Suppose an employer's sincerely held religious belief is offended by health coverage of vaccines, or paying the minimum wage, or according women equal pay for substantially similar work? Does it rank as a less restrictive alternative to require the government to provide the money or benefit to which the employer has a religion-based objection? Because the Court cannot easily answer that question, it proposes something else: Extension to commercial enterprises of the accommodation already afforded to nonprofit religion-based organizations. I have already discussed the "special solicitude" generally accorded nonprofit religion-based organizations that exist to serve a community of believers, solicitude never before accorded to commercial enterprises comprising employees of diverse faiths. In sum, in view of what Congress sought to accomplish, *i.e.,* comprehensive preventive care for women furnished through employer-based health plans, none of the proffered alternatives would satisfactorily serve the compelling interests to which Congress responded.

IV

Among the pathmarking pre-*Smith* decisions RFRA preserved is *United States* v. *Lee* (1982). Lee, a sole proprietor engaged in farming and carpentry, was a member of the Old Order Amish. He sincerely believed that withholding Social Security taxes from his employees or paying the employer's share of such taxes would violate the Amish faith. This Court held that, although the obligations imposed by the Social Security system conflicted with Lee's religious beliefs, the burden was not unconstitutional.

The Government urges that *Lee* should control the challenges brought by Hobby Lobby and Conestoga. In contrast, today's Court dismisses *Lee* as a tax case. But the *Lee* Court made two key points one cannot confine to tax cases. "When followers of a particular sect enter into commercial activity as a matter of choice," the Court observed, "the limits they accept on their own conduct as a matter of conscience and faith are not to be superimposed on statutory schemes which are binding on others in that activity." The statutory scheme of employer-based comprehensive health coverage involved in these cases is surely binding on others engaged in the same trade or business as the corporate challengers here, Hobby Lobby and Conestoga. Further, the Court recognized in *Lee* that allowing a religion-based exemption to a commercial employer would "operate to impose the employer's religious faith on the employees." No doubt the Greens and Hahns and all who share their beliefs may decline to acquire for themselves the contraceptives in question. But that choice may not be imposed on employees who hold other beliefs. Working for Hobby Lobby or Conestoga, in other words, should not deprive employees of the preventive care available to workers at the shop next door, at least in the absence of directions from the Legislature or Administration to do so.

7

Criminal Procedure

CHAPTER OUTLINE

The Constitution strongly emphasizes the protection of the rights of defendants in the criminal process. The original document contains no fewer than nine provisions specifically addressed to this matter—these are in keeping with the Founders' concern to protect minorities (in this case, unpopular criminal defendants) from the tyrannical excesses of an oppressive outraged majority. Article I, Section 9, restricts suspension of the privilege of the writ of habeas corpus "unless when in cases of rebellion or invasion the public safety may require it" and prohibits Congress from passing bills of attainder, or *ex post facto* laws. Article I, Section 10, repeats language from Section 9 and similarly prohibits the states from passing bills of attainder, or *ex post facto* laws. Article II, Section 2, provides the president with the power to grant reprieves and pardons. Article III, Section 2, provides for trial by jury for "all crimes except in cases of impeachment" and further directs that the trial "shall be held in the state where the said crimes shall have been committed." Article III, Section 3, narrowly and precisely defines what constitutes treason against the United States. Finally, Article IV, Section 2, specifies the procedure for the extradition of criminal defendants.

The Bill of Rights places an even greater stress on criminal procedure. Of the twenty-three separate rights enumerated in the first eight amendments, thirteen relate to the treatment of criminal defendants. The Fourth Amendment guarantees the right of the people to be secure "in their persons, houses, papers, and effects" against unreasonable searches and seizures and prohibits the issuance of warrants without probable cause. The Fifth Amendment requires prosecution by grand-jury indictment for all "capital, or otherwise infamous" crimes (excepting certain military cases) and prohibits placing a person "twice in jeopardy of life or limb" for the same offense or compelling him to be "a witness against himself." The Sixth Amendment lists several rights that the accused shall enjoy "in all criminal prosecutions": a speedy and public trial by an impartial jury of the state and district in which the crime has been committed, notice of the "nature and cause of the accusation," confrontation of hostile witnesses, compulsory process for obtaining favorable witnesses, and assistance of counsel. The Eighth Amendment adds prohibitions against the imposition of excessive bails and fines and the infliction of cruel and unusual punishments. And in addition to these specific guarantees, the Fifth Amendment adds a general prohibition against deprivation of life, liberty, or property without due process of law.

Those provisions as spelled out in the original Constitution were obviously understood to apply only to the federal government, and initially, so were the criminal procedural protections spelled out in the Bill of Rights. When the question of applying the Bill of Rights to the states first arose, Chief Justice John Marshall declared in *Barron v. Baltimore* (1833) that the first ten amendments were enacted as limitations upon the national government alone. Marshall observed that the opening sentence of the First Amendment begins with the phrase *Congress shall make no law . . .* and that nowhere in the subsequent provisions of the Bill of Rights can be found any limitations upon state action. Further, he reasoned,

> had the framers of these amendments intended them to be limitations on the powers of the state governments, they would have imitated the framers of the original Constitution, and have expressed that intention. Had Congress engaged in the extraordinary occupation of improving the constitutions of the several states by affording the people additional protection from the exercise of power by their own governments in matters which concerned themselves alone, they would have declared this purpose in plain and intelligible language.

Since the adoption of the Fourteenth Amendment in 1868, however, all of this has changed. Through a series of decisions, the Supreme Court has held that the Fourteenth

Amendment incorporates most of the criminal procedural guarantees of the Bill of Rights and has applied them equally to the states as to the federal government. (See Chapter 3 for a full discussion of how the Court has incorporated these guarantees.) The only two Bill of Rights guarantees directly related to criminal procedure that have not been held by the Court to apply to the states are the Eighth Amendment prohibition against excessive fines and the Fifth Amendment requirement of prosecution by grand-jury indictment. Remarkably, the Supreme Court has never been presented with an opportunity to rule on the prohibition against excessive fines, but it is generally assumed that this guarantee will be incorporated if the issue is squarely presented. The Fifth Amendment requirement of grand-jury indictment, on the other hand, was specifically held not to be guaranteed by the Fourteenth Amendment in *Hurtado v. California* (1884), which continues to be followed as valid precedent. The following sections outline the development and current legal status of the major criminal procedural protections of the original Constitution and Amendments Four through Eight.

THE *EX POST FACTO* CLAUSES

Article I, Section 9, prohibits Congress, and Article I, Section 10, prohibits the states, from passing *ex post facto* laws. In *Calder v. Bull* (1798), the Supreme Court held that the Constitution's prohibition against *ex post facto* laws extended only to criminal, and not to civil, cases. Justice William Paterson explained why:

> The words, *ex post facto,* when applied to a law, have a technical meaning, and in legal phraseology, refer to crimes, pains, and penalties. Judge Blackstone's description of the terms is clear and accurate. "There is," says he, "a still more unreasonable method than this, which is called making of laws *ex post facto,* when after an action, indifferent in itself, is committed, the Legislator, then, for the first time, declares it to have been a crime, and inflicts a punishment upon the person who has committed it. Here it is impossible, that the party could foresee that an action, innocent when it was done, should be afterwards converted to guilt by a subsequent law; he had, therefore, no cause to abstain from it; and all punishment for not abstaining, must, of consequence, be cruel and unjust." *Blackstone's Commentaries* 46. Here the meaning annexed to the terms *ex post facto* laws, unquestionably refers to crimes, and nothing else. The historic page abundantly evinces, that the power of passing such laws should be withheld from legislators; as it is a dangerous instrument in the hands of bold, unprincipled, aspiring, and party men, and has been too often used to effect the most detestable purposes.

Through the years, the Court has recognized four categories of *ex post facto* laws: laws that "punish as a crime an act previously committed, which was innocent when done"; laws that "aggravate a crime, or make it greater than it was, when committed"; laws that increase the punishment for a criminal act after the act was committed; and laws that deprive one charged with a crime of any defense available according to the law at the time when the act was committed.

The two most important recent *ex post facto* cases to reach the Supreme Court both dealt with sex offenses: *Stogner v. California* (2003) and *Smith v. Doe* (2003). *Stogner* involved the emotionally charged issue of sexual child abuse. In 1993, as the issue of sexual child abuse by certain pedophile Catholic priests was gaining notoriety, the California Legislature enacted a new criminal statute of limitations that permitted a defendant to be prosecuted for sex-related child abuse where the prior limitations period had expired if the prosecution was begun within one year of a victim's report to police. In 1998, Marion Stogner was indicted for sex-related child abuse of his two daughters committed between 1955 and 1973. At the time those crimes were allegedly committed, the statute of limitations period was three years.

Was Stogner's prosecution under this law barred by the *Ex Post Facto* Clause of Article I, Section 10? A five-member majority concluded that it was. Justice Breyer quoted Judge Learned Hand that extending a limitations period after the state has assured "a man that he has become safe from its pursuit . . . seems to most of us unfair and dishonest." Breyer insisted that in this case, California had refused "to play by its own rules." Among other things, it had deprived the defendant of the "fair warning" that might have led him to preserve exculpatory evidence.

Interestingly, the three Catholic justices on the Court at the time (Justices Scalia, Kennedy, and Thomas) all dissented. Chief Justice Rehnquist joined as well in Kennedy's argument that the California statute did not violate the *Ex Post Facto* Clause because it did not "criminalize conduct which was innocent when done," allowed "the prosecutor to seek the same punishment as the law authorized at the time the offense was committed and no more," and did not "alter the government's burden to establish the elements of the crime."

Smith v. Doe involved Alaska's version of "Megan's Law," named for Megan Kanka, a seven-year-old New Jersey girl who had been sexually assaulted and murdered by a neighbor who, unknown to the victim's family, had prior convictions for sex offenses against children. Alaska's version contained two components: it required persons convicted of sex or child-kidnapping offenses to register with state or local law-enforcement authorities, and it required the Alaska Department of Public Safety, to whom this registration information was forwarded, to make available to the public their names, addresses, photographs, physical descriptions, criminal histories, and other pertinent information; the department chose to meet this notification requirement by posting this information on the Internet. Both the registration and the notification requirements were retroactive. Two individuals convicted of aggravated sex offenses prior to the statute's enactment brought suit claiming that the state's sex-offender registration and notification law constituted retroactive punishment forbidden by the *Ex Post Facto* Clause. A six-member majority of the Supreme Court, however, rejected their claim, finding the statute was civil and regulatory (as opposed to criminal and punitive) in nature, and therefore that "its retroactive application does not violate the *Ex Post Facto* Clause." (See also *Connecticut Department of Public Safety v. Doe* [2003], discussed later in this chapter, in which Connecticut's version of Megan's Law is challenged on due-process grounds.)

SEARCH AND SEIZURE

Legal Parameters

The Fourth Amendment forbids "unreasonable searches and seizures"—not all searches and seizures, only those that are "unreasonable." In general, the Supreme Court has followed the rule that searches are reasonable if they are based on a warrant obtained from a magistrate, who may issue the warrant only if law-enforcement officials have demonstrated, through introduction of evidence, that there is probable cause to believe that the search will uncover evidence of criminal activity. (In *Aguilar v. Texas* [1964], the Court ruled that probable-cause standards are the same for state and federal magistrates.)

Failure to obtain a warrant does not automatically render a search or seizure unreasonable. The Supreme Court has provided a number of exceptions to the requirement that a warrant be obtained, the most important of which is a search incident to a lawful arrest.[1]

The rationale for this exception is that an arresting officer needs to be free to search a defendant in order to remove weapons (to protect the officer's safety) and evidence (to prevent its destruction). Officers are not permitted, however, to search just anybody and then use the evidence thereby obtained to justify the original arrest. Generally speaking, officers cannot use the fruits of a search as justification for the arrest; grounds for arrest must exist for the search incident to the arrest to be valid. And as *Chimel v. California* (1968) made clear, neither do the officers have much latitude in searching premises under the control of validly arrested defendants. The officers in *Chimel* arrested the defendant in his house and, over his objections and without a search warrant, proceeded to search his entire three-bedroom house, including attic, garage, and workshop. Items obtained from this search were subsequently admitted in evidence against the defendant during his trial for burglary, and he was convicted. The Supreme Court, in a 7–2 decision, declared that such a widespread search was unreasonable and overturned his conviction. Justice Potter Stewart, speaking for the Court, noted that although there is solid justification for a search of the arrestee's person and of "the area 'within his immediate control'—construing that phrase to mean the area within which he might gain possession of a weapon or destructible evidence"—there is no comparable justification for "routinely searching any room other than that in which an arrest occurs—or, for that matter, for searching through all the desk drawers or other closed or concealed areas in that room itself. Such searches, in the absence of well-organized exceptions, may be made only under the authority of a search warrant."

A second exception to the warrant requirement is the "plain view" doctrine. As the Court held in *Harris v. United States* (1968), "It has long been settled that objects falling in the plain view of an officer who has a right to be in the position to have that view are subject to seizure and may be introduced in evidence." This doctrine covers observations made by officers standing on public property and peering into car windows or the windows of dwellings, as well as observations made by officers who are on a defendant's property in the pursuit of legitimate business.[2] It also appears to cover aerial surveillance. In *California v. Ciraolo* (1985), the Supreme Court, in a 5–4 decision, upheld the use of an airplane flying at 1,000 feet to confirm an anonymous tip that marijuana was being grown in the petitioner's backyard. Chief Justice Burger noted that the police observations took place within public navigable airspace in a physically nonintrusive manner. He argued that "in an age where private and commercial flight in the public airways is routine, it is unreasonable for respondent to expect that his marijuana plants were constitutionally protected from being observed with the naked eye from an altitude of 1,000 feet." Stressing that any member of the flying public in this airspace who cared to glance down could have seen everything that the officer observed, he concluded that "the Fourth Amendment simply does not require the police traveling in the public airways at this altitude to obtain a warrant in order to observe what is visible to the naked eye." Justice Powell dissented; he argued that the petitioner did have a reasonable expectation of privacy, as "the actual risk to privacy from commercial or pleasure aircraft is virtually nonexistent. Travelers on commercial flights, as well as private planes used for business or personal reasons, normally obtain at most a fleeting, anonymous, and nondiscriminating glimpse of the landscape and buildings over which they pass. The risk that a passenger on such a plane might observe private activities, and might connect those activities with particular people, is simply too trivial to protect against." And in *Florida v. Riley* (1989), it upheld as reasonable the use of a helicopter that at 400 feet circled twice over a greenhouse, allowing a deputy sheriff to make naked-eye observations through the openings of the greenhouse's roof and through its open sides of marijuana plants. Justice White acknowledged that the helicopter was flying below the lower limits of navigable airspace allowed for fixed-wing aircraft but insisted that "any member of the public could legally have been flying over Riley's property in a helicopter at the altitude of 400 feet and could have observed Riley's greenhouse." Justice

O'Connor supplied the critical fifth vote, but only by concurring in the judgment; she observed that "public use of altitudes lower than that—particularly public observations from helicopters circling over the curtilage of a home—may be sufficiently rare that police surveillance from such altitudes would violate reasonable expectations of privacy."[3] Modern drone technology is certain to keep the question of what is in plain view before future Courts.

Law officers are also permitted to search a vehicle on probable cause without a warrant. The Court first recognized this right during the Prohibition era, in *Carroll v. United States* (1925), citing as its justification the fact that a vehicle can be moved quickly out of the locality or jurisdiction in which the warrant must be sought. The so-called automobile exception has spawned considerable litigation, and the Court has repeatedly been obliged to clarify this area of the law and to determine whether particular warrantless searches have been justified. Unfortunately, its efforts at clarification have often been unsatisfactory, providing inadequate or even contradictory advice to police, prosecutors, and courts attempting to discharge their responsibilities in a manner consistent with the Fourth Amendment. Nowhere is this failure to provide specific guidance more apparent than in the cases of *Robbins v. California* (1981) and *New York v. Belton* (1981), both decided on the same day. In *Robbins* the justices held that a warrantless search of a package wrapped in opaque plastic and stored in the luggage area of a station wagon violated the Fourth Amendment, but in *Belton,* they ruled that a warrantless search of a zippered pocket of a jacket found in an automobile's passenger compartment did not violate the amendment. Following a public outcry over such vacillation, the Court addressed this matter again in *United States v. Ross* (1982). This time a six-member majority set forth the ground rules for the "automobile exception." To begin with, the *Ross* majority announced, the exception applies to vehicle searches that are supported by probable cause to believe that the vehicle contains contraband or other evidence of criminality. In these cases, a search is reasonable if it is based on objective facts that would justify the issuance of a warrant by a magistrate. When police officers have probable cause to search an entire vehicle, the justices continued, they may conduct a warrantless search of every part of the vehicle and its contents, including all containers and packages that may conceal the object of the search. In such cases, the scope of the search is not defined by the nature of the container in which the contraband or evidence of criminality is secreted, but rather by the object of the search and the places in which there is probable cause to believe that it may be found. As Justice Stevens noted for the majority, "Probable cause to believe that undocumented aliens are being transported in a van will not justify a warrantless search of a suitcase."

Obtaining consent to search constitutes a fourth exception to the warrant requirement. Fourth Amendment rights, like other criminal procedural rights, can be waived by the individual. In two recent cases, the Supreme Court has had the occasion to determine whether defendants have in fact voluntarily given their consent to be searched. In *Florida v. Bostick* (1991), the Supreme Court held that the Fourth Amendment permits police officers to approach bus passengers at random and ask them questions and request their consent to searches of their luggage or persons, provided that "a reasonable person would feel free to decline the officer's requests or otherwise terminate the encounter." In its determination that the passenger had voluntarily consented to be searched, it found "particularly worth noting" the fact that "the officer advised the passenger that he could refuse consent to the search." In *United States v. Drayton* (2002), the Court went further and held that the consent to be searched can be voluntarily given even if the police do not advise bus passengers of their right not to cooperate and to refuse consent to be searched. Speaking for a six-member majority, Justice Kennedy rejected the suggestion that "police officers must always inform citizens of their right to refuse when seeking permission to conduct a warrantless consent search." Nor, he continued, has the Court ever held that "even though there are no *per se* rules, a presumption of invalidity attaches if a citizen consented without explicit notification that he or she was free to refuse to cooperate. Instead, the Court has repeated that the totality of the circumstances must control, without giving extra weight to the absence of this type of warning." Although the police officer in question did not inform the respondents of their right to refuse the search, Kennedy noted that "he did request permission to search, and the totality of the circumstances indicates that their consent was voluntary, so the searches were reasonable."

The Court has also addressed the question of whether consent can be given by third parties. In *Matlock v. United States* (1974) and *Illinois v. Rodriguez* (1990), it held that police officers may search jointly occupied premises if one of the occupants consents. In *Georgia v. Randolph* (2006), it created a narrow exception to this rule, holding that a warrantless search was, in this instance, unlawful, because, although an occupant of the premises consented, the physically present co-occupant, who was the subject of the search, refused to consent. In *Fernandez v. California* (2014), however, the Court refused to extend *Randolph* to a situation where consent to a warrantless search was provided by an abused woman well after her male partner, who refused to consent, had been arrested and removed from the apartment they shared.

The Court's 1985 decision in *New Jersey v. T. L. O.* identified a fifth exception, permitting school officials to search students who are under their authority without a warrant. Justice White held for the Court majority that the legality of a search of a student should depend not on a showing of probable cause but simply on the reasonableness, under all the circumstances, of the search. Determining the reasonableness of any search involves a determination of whether the search was justified at its inception and whether, as conducted, it was reasonably related in scope to the circumstances that justified the school official's intervention in the first place. *Vernonia School District v. Acton* (1995) built on *T. L. O.* and upheld a school drug policy that authorized random urinalysis drug testing of student athletes. Justice Scalia held for the Court that "Fourth Amendment rights, no less than First and Fourteenth Amendment rights, are different in public schools than elsewhere" and that the "reasonableness" of a search "cannot disregard the schools' custodial and tutelary responsibility for children." He noted, "For their own good and that of their classmates, public school children are routinely required to submit to various physical examinations, and to be vaccinated against various diseases. . . . Particularly with regard to medical examinations and procedures, therefore, students within the school environment have a lesser expectation of privacy than members of the population generally."

The language just quoted would seem broad enough to render constitutional random urinalysis drug testing of all students, but, as Scalia continued, "it must not be lost sight of" that Vernonia's program was "directed more narrowly to drug use by school athletes, where the risk of immediate physical harm to the drug user or those with whom he is playing his sport is particularly high. Apart from psychological effects, which include impairment of judgment, slow reaction time, and a lessening of the perception of pain, the particular drugs screened by the District's Policy have been demonstrated to pose substantial physical risks to athletes." Interestingly, however, when the Supreme Court, in *Board of Education of Independent School District No. 92 of Pottawatomie County v. Earls* (2002), applied the principles of *Vernonia* to the Student Activities Drug Testing Policy of the Tecumseh, Oklahoma, School District (requiring all middle and high school students to consent to urinalysis testing for drugs in order to participate in any competitive extracurricular activity), it concluded that "Tecumseh's Policy is also constitutional." In his majority opinion, Justice Thomas rejected the respondents' argument that "the testing of nonathletes does not implicate any safety concern." As he emphasized, "The safety interest furthered by drug testing is undoubtedly substantial for all children, athletes and nonathletes alike. We know all too well that drug use carries a variety of health risks for children, including death from overdose." He then proceeded to open even wider the door for the drug testing of all students by declaring, "*Vernonia* did not require the school to test the group of students most likely to use drugs, but rather considered the constitutionality of the program in the context of the public school's custodial responsibilities."

Yet another exception, established in *Warden v. Hayden* (1967), allows the police to enter premises without an arrest or search warrant when in "hot pursuit" of a fleeing suspect and, having entered, to seize evidence uncovered in the search for the suspect.

The seventh exception to the warrant requirement is the investigative technique known as "stop and frisk," the long-established police practice of stopping suspicious persons on the street or in other public places for purposes of questioning them or conducting some other form of investigation and, incident to the stoppings, of searching ("frisking") the suspects for dangerous weapons. Because such searches were commonly employed when there were no grounds to arrest the suspect and to search him incident to arrest, their constitutionality was challenged in the courts. In *Terry v. Ohio* (1968), Chief Justice Earl Warren provided a clear answer to this question. Speaking for an eight-member majority (only Justice William Douglas dissented), he declared:

> When an officer is justified in believing that the individual whose suspicious behavior he is investigating at close range is armed and presently dangerous to the officer or to others, it would appear completely unreasonable to deny the officer the power to take necessary measures to determine whether the person is in fact carrying a weapon and to neutralize the threat of physical harm. . . . There must be a narrowly drawn authority to permit a reasonable search for weapons for the protection of the police officer, where he has reason to believe that he is dealing with an armed and dangerous individual, regardless of whether he has probable cause to arrest the individual for a crime. The officer need not be absolutely certain that the individual is armed; the issue is whether a reasonably prudent man in the circumstances would be warranted in the belief that his safety or that of others was in danger.

The Court's recognition of the reasonableness of protecting the officer's safety is also apparent in *Pennsylvania v. Mimms* (1977) and *Maryland v. Wilson* (1997). In *Mimms*, the Court held that a police officer may as a matter of course order the driver of a lawfully stopped car to exit the vehicle. It declared, "The touchstone of our analysis under the Fourth Amendment is always 'the reasonableness in all the circumstances of the particular governmental invasion of a citizen's personal security'" and held that reasonableness "depends 'on a balance between the public interest and the individual's right to personal security free from arbitrary interference by law officers.'" On the public-interest side of the balance, the Court found the officer's "practice to order all drivers [stopped in traffic stops] out of their vehicles as a matter of course" as a "precautionary measure" to protect his safety to be "both legitimate and weighty." On the other side of the balance, it noted that the driver's car was already validly stopped for a traffic infraction, and it deemed the additional intrusion of asking him to step outside his car "*de minimis*." Accordingly, it concluded that "once a motor vehicle has been lawfully detained for a traffic violation, the police officers may order the driver to get out of the vehicle without violating the Fourth Amendment's proscription of unreasonable seizures." In *Wilson*, it extended the same rule to passengers as well. After stopping a passenger car for speeding, a Maryland state trooper observed Wilson, "very nervous" and sitting in the front seat, and ordered him from the car. As Wilson exited the car, a quantity of crack cocaine fell to the ground, whereupon he was arrested and charged with possession of cocaine with intent to distribute. Wilson sought to suppress the evidence, arguing that the trooper's order to step out of the car was an unreasonable seizure under the Fourth Amendment. Rejecting Wilson's contention,

Chief Justice Rehnquist noted for a seven-member majority that "danger to an officer from a traffic stop is likely to be greater when there are passengers in addition to the driver in the stopped car." And "while there is not the same basis for ordering the passengers out of the car as there is for ordering the driver out, the additional intrusion on the passenger is minimal." Furthermore, "as a practical matter, the passengers are already stopped by virtue of the stop of the vehicle. The only change in their circumstances which will result from ordering them out of the car is that they will be outside of, rather than inside of, the stopped car. Outside the car, the passengers will be denied access to any possible weapon that might be concealed in the interior of the passenger compartment."

The 1973 decisions in *United States v. Robinson* and *Gustafson v. Florida* had previously modified the general rule that a warrantless search is valid only if it is incident to a lawful arrest. Both cases involved arrests for motor vehicle violations, and in both, subsequent searches of the offenders uncovered narcotics, and the evidence so obtained was later used to obtain convictions. In affirming both convictions, Justice William Rehnquist, writing for the majority in *Robinson* and a plurality in *Gustafson,* expanded the permissible limits of *Terry*'s stop-and-frisk doctrine. Under the circumstances of these cases, he held, a search incident to a valid arrest was not limited to a pat-down of the outer garments for weapons. These searches were not unreasonable, he continued, even though the arresting officers did not suspect either that the offenders were armed or that they might destroy evidence of the crime for which the arrests had been made. As Rehnquist declared in *Robinson,* "As custodial arrest of a suspect based on probable cause is a reasonable intrusion under the Fourth Amendment, that intrusion being lawful, a search incident to the arrest requires no additional justification."

An eighth exception to the warrant requirement involves administrative searches. "Anyone who has been stopped at a sobriety checkpoint, screened at an international border, scanned by a metal detector at an airport or government building, or drug tested for public employment has been subjected to an administrative search."[4] In *Camara v. Municipal Court* (1967), the Supreme Court held that administrative searches of homes and businesses for health and safety violations require a warrant based on probable cause of a violation of the law, but in *Marshall v. Barlow's, Inc.* (1978), it carved out an exception for "closely regulated" businesses, typically those that require a license of operate, which must "accept the burdens as well as the benefits of their trade." One of the "burdens" is to be subject to warrantless searches. In *New York v. Burger* (1987), the Court spelled out three criteria that must be met for warrantless searches of closely regulated businesses to be reasonable: (1) There must be a substantial government interest that informs the regulatory scheme pursuant to which the inspection is made; (2) the warrantless inspections must be 'necessary to further the regulatory scheme; and (3) the statute's inspection program, in terms of the certainty and regularity of its application, must provide a constitutionally adequate substitute for a warrant. In *Los Angeles v. Patel* (2015), the Court addressed the question of whether hotels are closely regulated businesses and whether a municipal ordinance allowing for the police to engage in warrantless searches of hotel registries violates the Fourth Amendment.

A ninth exception to the warrant requirement involves suspicionless searches based solely on an individual's status as a probationer or parolee. In *Samson v. California* (2006), in a 6–3 opinion, Justice Thomas reaffirmed for the Court its previous ruling in *United States v. Knights* (2001) and held that "a State's interests in reducing recidivism and thereby promoting reintegration and positive citizenship among probationers and parolees warrant privacy intrusions that would not otherwise be tolerated under the Fourth Amendment."

A tenth exception to the warrant requirement has also been introduced by the Court: drug and DNA testing. In *Skinner v. Railway Labor Executives Association* (1989), the Court sustained drug testing of railroad employees involved in train accidents and held that, in certain circumstances, reasonableness does not require a warrant, probable cause, or even any measure of individualized suspicion. The Court concluded that the demonstrated frequency of drug and alcohol use by railroad employees and the demonstrated connection between such use and grave harm rendered the drug testing a reasonable means of protecting society.

In *National Treasury Employees Union v. Von Raab,* decided the same day, the Court went even further and sustained the constitutionality of urine testing for those US Customs Service employees involved directly in drug interdiction or whose positions required them to carry firearms. Justice Kennedy concluded for a five-member majority that the government had a "compelling interest" in "safeguarding our borders" and that public safety outweighs the privacy expectations of the Customs Service employees.

Justice Scalia, who concurred in *Skinner,* filed a sharp dissent. "I joined the Court's opinion [in *Skinner*] because the demonstrated frequency of drug and alcohol use by the targeted class of employees, and the demonstrated connection between such use and grave harm, rendered the search a reasonable means of protecting society. I decline to join the Court's opinion in the present case because neither frequency of use nor connection to harm is demonstrated or even likely. In my view the Customs Service rules are a kind of immolation of privacy and human dignity in symbolic opposition to drug use." Scalia pointed out that "what is absent in the Government's justifications—notably absent, revealingly absent, and as far as I am concerned dispositively absent—is the recitation of *even a single instance* in which any of the speculated horribles actually occurred, that is, in which the cause of bribe-taking, or of poor aim, or of unsympathetic law enforcement, or of compromise of classified information, was drug use." The only plausible explanation for the program, in his view, was found in the Customs Service memorandum to its employees announcing the program: "Implementation of the drug screening program would set an important example in our country's struggle with this most serious threat to our national health and security." As Scalia sneered: "What better way to show that the Government is serious about its 'war on drugs' than to subject its employees on the front line of that war to this invasion of their privacy and affront to their dignity?" But that justification was totally unacceptable under the Fourth Amendment: "The impairment of individual liberties cannot be the means of making a point; symbolism, even symbolism for so worthy a cause as the abolition of unlawful drugs, cannot validate an otherwise unreasonable search."

As *Chandler v. Miller* (1997) makes clear, not all drug-testing schemes pass constitutional muster. In an 8–1 decision, the Court held unconstitutional a Georgia statute that required candidates for state office to certify that they have taken a urinalysis drug test within thirty days prior to qualifying for nomination or election and that the test result was negative. Georgia relied heavily on *Von Raab,* but Justice Ginsburg's majority opinion denied that *Von Raab* opened "broad vistas for suspicionless searches" and insisted that it "must be read in its unique context." She then proceeded to note "a telling difference between *Von Raab* and Georgia's candidate drug-testing program." In *Von Raab,* the Court concluded that it was "not feasible to subject employees [required to carry firearms or concerned with interdiction of controlled substances] and their work product to the kind of day-to-day scrutiny that is the norm in more traditional office environments." In contrast, candidates for public office "are subject to relentless scrutiny—by their peers, the public, and the press. Their day-to-day conduct attracts attention notably beyond the norm in ordinary work environments." She concluded that although "the candidate drug test Georgia has devised" was "well-meant," it nevertheless diminished "personal privacy for a symbol's sake. The Fourth Amendment shields society against that state action."

In *Maryland v. King* (2013), the Court upheld the constitutionality of the warrantless collection of DNA samples from felony arrestees. Writing for a five-member majority, Justice Kennedy insisted that the DNA samples were being taken only to aid in the identification of the arrestee, not to solve past crimes, and he concluded that "when officers make an arrest supported by probable cause to hold for a serious offense and they bring the suspect to the station to be detained in custody, taking and analyzing a cheek swab of the arrestee's DNA is, like fingerprinting and photographing, a legitimate police booking procedure that is reasonable under the Fourth Amendment." Justice Scalia wrote a fiery dissent, finding Kennedy's assertion that DNA was not being taken to solve crimes taxed even "the credulity of the credulous." The Fourth Amendment, he insisted, "forbids searching a person for evidence of a crime when there is no basis for believing the person is guilty of the crime or is in possession of incriminating evidence. That prohibition is categorical and without exception; it lies at the very heart of the Fourth Amendment."

An eleventh and final exception to the warrant requirement involves the use of certain kinds of highway checkpoint programs. In *Michigan Department of State Police v. Sitz* (1990), the Supreme Court held that Michigan's highway sobriety checkpoint program was "consistent with the Fourth Amendment." In his majority opinion, Chief Justice Rehnquist relied heavily on *United States v. Martinez-Fuerte* (1976), which used a balancing test in upholding checkpoints for detecting illegal aliens, and on *Von Raab* to argue that, whereas a Fourth Amendment "seizure" occurs when a vehicle is stopped at a checkpoint, on balance the seizure is reasonable. "The balance of the State's interest in preventing drunken driving, the extent to which this system can reasonably be said to advance that interest, and the degree of intrusion upon individual motorists who are briefly stopped, weighs in favor of the state program." And in *Illinois v. Lidster* (2004), the Court held, in an opinion by Justice Breyer, that police stops of motorists at a highway checkpoint set up at the location of a recent hit-and-run accident to ask for information about that accident was valid under the Fourth Amendment. As *Indianapolis v. Edmond* (2000) makes clear, however, the Court will draw the line when it comes to checkpoint programs "whose primary purpose" is "to detect evidence of ordinary criminal wrongdoing." When Indianapolis initiated a checkpoint program under which the police, acting without individualized suspicion, stopped a predetermined number of vehicles at roadblocks in various locations on city roads for the primary purpose of the discovery and interdiction of illegal narcotics, the Court refused to "credit the 'general interest in crime control' as justification for a regime of suspicionless stops" and concluded that "the program contravenes the Fourth Amendment."

Electronic Surveillance and the Protection of Digital Privacy

The Supreme Court first confronted the issue of electronic surveillance in *Olmstead v. United States* (1928), which involved the wiretapping of a gang of rumrunners. Here the justices concluded that the Fourth Amendment was not applicable, because there had been no trespass of a constitutionally protected area and no seizure of a physical object. The *Olmstead* doctrine was not repudiated until *Katz v. United States* (1967), in which the Court declared that the Fourth Amendment "protects people, not places" and held that electronic surveillance conducted outside the judicial process, whether or not it involves trespass, is per se unreasonable. In an attempt to limit *Katz* and to clarify exactly what was expected of law-enforcement personnel, Congress included in the Omnibus Crime Control and Safe Streets Act of 1968 a title on the interception and disclosure of wire or oral communication, which provided for a system of judicially approved interceptions at the request of the attorney general.

Olmstead and *Katz* dealt with old technology—landline telephones. Recently, the Court has been obliged to apply the Fourth Amendment to new wireless technologies and address questions concerning digital privacy. Its decisions have generally protected the privacy rights of those spied on by government. Thus, when the federal government engaged in the warrantless use of a thermal-imaging device to detect heat within a house that suggested the use of halide lights to grow marijuana indoors, Scalia found for a divided Court in *Kyllo v. United States* (2001) that the search was "unreasonable," because it violated "that degree of privacy against government that existed when the Fourth Amendment was adopted." The Court's duty was, he insisted, to prevent "advancing technology" capable of "discern[ing] all human activity in the home" from "shrink[ing] the realm of guaranteed privacy." By contrast, in *City of Ontario v. Quon* (2010), Kennedy held for a unanimous Court that a search by a government employer of text messages sent and received on a pager the employer owned and issued to an employee was reasonable, and therefore permissible under of the Fourth Amendment, because it was motivated by a legitimate work-related purpose and because it was not excessive in scope. And it also concluded that the search would be "regarded as reasonable and normal in the private-employer context."

Outside the employment context, the Court has continued to protect the electronic privacy of individuals. In *United States v. Jones* (2012) the Court unanimously held that the attachment of a Global Positioning System tracking device to an individual's vehicle, and subsequent use of that device to monitor the vehicle's movements on public streets, constitutes a search or seizure within the meaning of the Fourth Amendment. Scalia's majority opinion relied on the reasoning of *Kyllo* and the need to prevent backsliding from "that degree of privacy against government that existed when the Fourth Amendment was adopted." He declared, "It is important to be clear about what occurred in this case: The Government physically occupied private property for the purpose of obtaining information. We have no doubt that such a physical intrusion would have been considered a 'search' within the meaning of the Fourth Amendment when it was adopted." Justice Alito wrote an opinion for himself and three others that only concurred in the judgment; he rejected Scalia's physical-trespass argument and reliance on *Kyllo* and grounded his argument on *Katz*: "I would analyze the question presented in this case by asking whether respondent's reasonable expectations of privacy were violated by the long-term monitoring of the movements of the vehicle he drove."

In *Riley v. California* (2014), the Court addressed the question of whether the police may, without a warrant, search digital information on a cell phone seized from an individual who has been arrested. The government had argued that a search of data stored on arrestees' cell phones is "materially indistinguishable" from permissible searches of their wallets, purses, and address books. In his majority opinion, Chief Justice Roberts replied that this "is like saying a ride on horseback is materially indistinguishable from a flight to the moon. Both are ways of getting from point A to point B, but little else justifies lumping them together." He pointed out that "cell phones differ in both a quantitative and a qualitative sense" from other objects that might be kept on an arrestee's person. He noted that the term "cell phone" is itself "misleading shorthand; many of these devices are in fact minicomputers that also happen to have the capacity to be used as a telephone. They could just as easily be called cameras, video players, rolodexes, calendars, tape recorders, libraries, diaries, albums, televisions, maps, or newspapers." Because of all cell phones "contain and all they may reveal, they hold for many Americans 'the privacies of life,'" and, therefore, Roberts continued, require full Fourth Amendment protection. "The fact that technology now allows an individual to carry such information in his hand does not make the information any less worthy of the protection for which the Founders fought." All of this led Roberts to conclude as follows: "Our answer to the question of what police must do before searching a cell phone seized incident to an arrest is accordingly simple—get a warrant."

Remedies for Violations

Although the Fourth Amendment forbids unreasonable searches and seizures, it does not prescribe a remedy for those whose rights have been violated. Addressing this issue for the first time in *Weeks v. United States* (1914), the Supreme Court declared that the appropriate remedy was exclusion of the illegally obtained evidence. The justices did not hold that the Fourth Amendment of its own force barred from criminal prosecutions the use of illegally seized, or "tainted," items; that is, they did not consider the Fourth Amendment to constitute a rule of evidence. But without such an exclusionary rule, they argued, the Fourth Amendment would present no effective deterrent to improper searches and seizures. This holding meant that as a federal rule of evidence—which in its supervisory function the Court could impose on the entire federal judiciary—illegally obtained evidence could not be used in federal prosecutions.

The *Weeks* decision, however, dealt only with federal prosecutions. Because the Fourth Amendment had not yet been incorporated through the Fourteenth Amendment to apply to the states, most states continued to follow the old common-law rule that relevant evidence obtained under any circumstances was admissible. Not until *Wolf v. Colorado* (1949) did the Supreme Court have occasion to rule on these state practices. In that decision the Court concluded, in an opinion written by Justice Frankfurter, that "the security of one's privacy against arbitrary intrusion by the police—which is at the core of the Fourth Amendment—is basic to a free society. It is therefore implicit in 'the concept of ordered liberty' and as such enforceable against the States through the Due Process Clause." Although holding that the Fourth Amendment guarantee against unreasonable searches and seizures was enforceable against the states through the Fourteenth Amendment, the *Wolf* majority did not consider the exclusionary rule announced in *Weeks* to be an "essential ingredient" of that guarantee. The Court denied that the exclusionary rule had any constitutional status, asserting instead that it was merely a pragmatic remedy developed under the Court's powers to supervise the federal judicial system. Not until *Mapp v. Ohio* (1961) did the Court finally abandon the *Wolf* doctrine and impose the exclusionary rule on state proceedings as well. In *Mapp* it concluded that the exclusionary rule, by removing the incentive to disregard the Fourth Amendment, constituted "the only effectively available way . . . to compel respect for the constitutional guarantee."

Ever since *Mapp,* the exclusionary rule has been under heavy attack.[5] In his dissent in *Bivens v. Six Unknown Named Agents* (1971), Chief Justice Burger proposed its elimination and an end to what he called the "universal capital punishment we inflict on all evidence when police error is shown in its acquisition." He urged Congress to enact a statute that would waive sovereign immunity as to the illegal acts of law-enforcement officials committed in the performance of assigned tasks; create a cause of action for damages sustained by any persons aggrieved by the conduct of government agents in violation of the Fourth Amendment or statutes regulating official conduct; create a quasi-judicial tribunal, patterned after the then existing US Court of Claims, to adjudicate all claims under the statute; substitute this remedy for the exclusionary rule; and direct that no evidence, otherwise admissible, would be excluded from any criminal proceeding because of a violation of the Fourth Amendment. He believed this would provide a more "meaningful and effective remedy against unlawful conduct by governmental officials" and that it would afford "some remedy to completely innocent persons who are sometimes the victims of illegal police conduct."

Although a majority of the Court has never accepted Chief Justice Burger's argument for the complete elimination of the exclusionary rule, it has come to recognize a "good-faith" exception to it. In *United States v. Leon* (1984), *Arizona v. Evans* (1995), *Herring v. United States* (2009), and *Heien v. North Carolina* (2014), the Court has held that the exclusionary rule should not be applied so as to suppress the introduction at a criminal trial of evidence obtained in the reasonable belief that the search and seizure at issue was consistent with the Fourth Amendment. As Justice White wrote for a six-member majority in *Leon,* a case in which the defendant claimed that the police had obtained a warrant on the basis of an affidavit that was insufficient to establish probable cause, the exclusionary rule "cannot be expected, and should not be applied, to deter objectively reasonable law enforcement activity."

> This is particularly true, we believe, when an officer acting in objective good faith has obtained a search warrant from a judge or magistrate and acted within its scope. In most such cases, there is no police illegality and thus nothing to deter. It is the magistrate's responsibility to determine whether the officer's allegations establish probable cause and if so, to issue a warrant comporting in form with the requirements of the Fourth Amendment. In the ordinary case, an officer cannot be expected to question the magistrate's probable cause determination or his judgment that the form of the warrant is technically sufficient. "[O]nce the warrant issues, there is literally nothing more the policeman can do in seeking to comply with the law. . . . " Penalizing the officer for the magistrate's error, rather than his own, cannot logically contribute to the deterrence of Fourth Amendment violations.

Leon dealt with a violation of Fourth Amendment rights not by the police but by the courts. So, too, did *Evans,* which dealt with the question of whether evidence seized in violation of the Fourth Amendment by a police officer who acted in reliance on a police computer record indicating the existence of an outstanding arrest warrant—a record that was subsequently determined to be erroneous—must be suppressed by virtue of the exclusionary rule regardless of the source of error. As it turned out, the arrest warrant had previously been quashed, but court personnel had failed to notify the police of this fact so that they could correct their computer records. In a 7–2 opinion, Chief Justice Rehnquist held that the evidence need not be excluded. He made three principal points. First, the exclusionary rule exists to deter "police misconduct, not mistakes by court employees"; second, there was no evidence that "court employees are inclined to ignore or subvert the Fourth Amendment or that lawlessness among these actors requires application of the extreme sanction of exclusion"; and third, there was no reason to believe that applying the exclusionary rule "will have a significant effect on court employees responsible for informing the police that a warrant has been quashed." He continued, "Court clerks are not adjuncts to the law enforcement team engaged in the often competitive enterprise of ferreting out crime" and therefore "have no stake in the outcome of particular criminal prosecutions."

In *Herring v. United States*, the Court extended the "good-faith" exception to "a negligent bookkeeping error" by police officers not involved in the search itself. Officers in Coffee County, Alabama, arrested Bennie Dean Herring based on a warrant listed in neighboring Dale County's database. A search incident to that arrest yielded drugs and a gun. It was then revealed that the warrant had been recalled months earlier, though this information had never been entered into the database. When Herring was indicted on federal gun and drug possession charges, he moved to suppress the evidence on the ground that his initial arrest had been illegal. Assuming that there was a Fourth Amendment violation, the district court concluded that the exclusionary rule did not apply and denied the motion to suppress. The Eleventh Circuit affirmed, finding that the arresting officers were innocent of any wrongdoing and that Dale County's failure to update the records was merely negligent. The court therefore concluded that the benefit of suppression would be marginal or nonexistent and that the evidence was admissible under the good-faith rule of *Leon*. Chief Justice Roberts for a five-member majority agreed, holding that when police mistakes leading to an unlawful search are the result of isolated negligence attenuated from the search, rather than systemic error or reckless disregard of constitutional requirements, the exclusionary rule does not apply. "The fact that a Fourth Amendment violation occurred—*i.e.*, that a search or arrest was unreasonable—does not necessarily mean that the exclusionary rule applies. Indeed, exclusion 'has always been our last resort, not our first impulse,' and our precedents establish important principles that constrain application of the exclusionary rule. . . . [T]he exclusionary rule is not an individual right and applies only where it 'result[s] in appreciable deterrence.' We have repeatedly rejected the argument that exclusion is a necessary consequence of a Fourth Amendment violation."

Finally, in *Heien v. North Carolina*, the Court extended the good-faith exception to the actions of a police officer based on his mistaken understanding of the law. While issuing a warning ticket to Nicholas Heien because one of his car's two brake lights was broken, a police officer became suspicious of Heien's actions and answers to his questions. When he secured Heien's consent to search the vehicle, the officer found cocaine and arrested Heien, who was subsequently convicted of drug trafficking. The North Carolina Court of Appeals, however, overturned his conviction, holding that the relevant state code provision required only a single brake light, (which Heien's vehicle had) and therefore the justification for the stop was objectively unreasonable. The state's Supreme Court reversed; it held that the officer's mistaken understanding of the law was reasonable, and thus the stop was valid. The U.S. Supreme Court affirmed; consistent with his opinion in *Herring*, Chief Justice Roberts wrote: "A traffic stop for a suspected violation of law is a 'seizure' of the occupants of the vehicle and therefore must be conducted in accordance with the Fourth Amendment. All parties agree that to justify this type of seizure, officers need only 'reasonable suspicion'—that is, 'a particularized and objective basis for suspecting the particular person stopped' of breaking the law. The question here is whether reasonable suspicion can rest on a mistaken understanding of the scope of a legal prohibition. We hold that it can."

SELF-INCRIMINATION AND COERCED CONFESSIONS

The Fifth Amendment provides that no person "shall be compelled in any criminal case to be a witness against himself." Along with other provisions of the Bill of Rights, this privilege was originally restricted to federal prosecutions. And in both *Twining v. New Jersey* (1908) and *Adamson v. California* (1947), the Supreme Court rejected the argument that the exception to compulsory self-incrimination was a "fundamental right" and hence necessary to a system of "ordered liberty." In the 1964 case of *Malloy v. Hogan,* however, it overruled those precedents and, through the Fourteenth Amendment, extended this protection to the states. As Justice William Brennan stated for the Court, "The Fourteenth Amendment secures against state invasion the same privilege that the Fifth Amendment guarantees against federal infringement—the right of a person to remain silent unless he chooses to speak in the unfettered exercise of his own will, and to suffer no penalty—for such silence."

Long before *Malloy*, the Court had placed limitations upon police interrogation techniques and the admissibility of confessions thereby obtained. In *Brown v. Mississippi* (1936), the Court overturned the conviction of three defendants whom police had physically tortured in order to extort confessions. Chief Justice Charles Evans Hughes made abundantly clear in *Brown* the Court's belief that the use of such confessions violated the Due Process Clause of the Fourteenth Amendment: "The freedom of the state in establishing its policy is the freedom of constitutional government and is limited by the requirement of due process of law. Because a state may dispense with a jury trial,[6] it does not follow that it may substitute a trial by ordeal. The rack and torture chamber may not be substituted for the witness stand." *Brown* was extended in *Chambers v. Florida* (1940), in which the Court again overturned a state conviction—this time because the defendant had been arrested on suspicion, without a warrant; denied contact with friends or attorneys; and questioned for long periods of time by different squads of police officers.

Brown and *Chambers* were followed by a long line of cases in which the Court addressed questions concerning the admissibility of confession on an ad hoc basis, employing the "totality of circumstances" rule. Under this guideline, the Court sought to determine whether the specific circumstances surrounding the obtaining of a particular confession (the nature of the charge; the age, maturity, and educational achievements of the defendant; the degree of pressure put upon him or her; the length of interrogation; and so on) constituted coercion and thereby rendered the confession inadmissible. This guideline suffered from one major drawback: it provided the police and the prosecution with little guidance as to what practices did or did not pass constitutional muster. As a consequence, the Court found itself confronted with a barrage of "coerced confessions" cases dealing with such police practices as attempts to gain the sympathy of the defendant through a childhood friend on the police force,[7] threats to bring a defendant's wife into custody for questioning,[8] threats to place the defendant's children in the custody of welfare officials,[9] and interrogations of wounded defendants under the influence of so-called truth serums.[10] To free itself from this perpetual stream of litigation, the Warren Court in *Miranda v. Arizona* (1966) broke completely with past cases and, rejecting the ad hoc "totality of circumstances" rule, announced specific procedures that the police would have to follow during interrogations and declared that any statements elicited in violation of these procedures would be inadmissible.

Miranda was a highly controversial decision. The Democratic-controlled Congress responded swiftly and directly, declaring in Section 3501 of the Omnibus Safe Streets and Crime Control Act of 1968 that a voluntary confession was admissible, irrespective of its conformity to *Miranda*. That provision proclaimed, "[A] confession . . . shall be admissible in evidence if it is voluntarily given" and that voluntariness shall be determined on the basis "of all the circumstances surrounding the giving of the confession, including . . . whether or not [the] defendant was advised or knew that he was not required to make any statement . . .; whether or not [the] defendant had been advised prior to questioning of his right to the assistance of counsel; and . . . whether or not [the] defendant was without the assistance of counsel when questioned." To remove all doubt, it continued: "The presence or absence of any of the above-mentioned factors . . . need not be conclusive on the issue of voluntariness of the confession." Interestingly, however, as Justice Scalia pointed out in *Davis v. United States* (1994), Section 3501 had "been studiously avoided by every Administration, not only in this Court but in the lower courts, since its enactment more than 25 years ago." Scalia noted, "The United States' repeated refusal to invoke Section 3501, combined with the courts' traditional (albeit merely prudential) refusal to consider arguments not raised, has caused the federal judiciary to confront a host of *Miranda* issues that might be entirely irrelevant under federal law. Worse still, it may have produced—during an era of intense national concern about the problem of runaway crime—the acquittal and the nonprosecution of many dangerous felons, enabling them to continue their depredations upon our citizens. There is no excuse for this." He therefore announced that "I will no longer be open to the argument that this Court should continue to ignore the commands of Section 3501 simply because the Executive declines to insist that we observe them."

Scalia's wish to consider "the commands of Section 3501" was finally realized in *Dickerson v. United States* (2000), but with a result not at all to his satisfaction. Chief Justice Rehnquist held for a seven-member majority that "*Miranda*, being a constitutional decision of this Court, may not be in effect overruled by an Act of Congress, and we decline to overrule *Miranda* ourselves. We therefore hold that *Miranda* and its progeny in this Court govern the admissibility of statements made during custodial interrogation in both state and federal courts." Justice Scalia was reduced to composing a spirited dissent:

One will search today's opinion in vain, however, for a statement (surely simple enough to make) that what 18 U.S.C. §3501 prescribes—the use at trial of a voluntary confession, even when a *Miranda* warning or its equivalent has failed to be given—violates the Constitution. The reason the statement does not appear is not only (and perhaps not so much) that it would be absurd, inasmuch as §3501 excludes from trial precisely what the Constitution excludes from trial, viz., compelled confessions; but also that Justices whose votes are needed to compose today's majority are on record as believing that a violation of *Miranda* is not a violation of the Constitution. And so, to justify today's agreed-upon result, the Court must adopt a significant new, if not entirely comprehensible, principle of constitutional law. . . . As I shall discuss in some detail, the only thing that can possibly mean in the context of this case is that this Court has the power, not merely to apply the Constitution but to expand it, imposing what it regards as useful "prophylactic" restrictions upon Congress and the States. That is an immense and frightening antidemocratic power, and it does not exist.

Although the Burger and Rehnquist Courts have refused to overturn the *Miranda* decision, and although the Rehnquist Court even held in *Dickerson* that *Miranda* is "a constitutional decision of this Court [and] may not be in effect overruled by an Act of Congress," they have, nevertheless, modified *Miranda* in such decisions as *Harris v. New York* (1971), *Oregon v. Hass* (1975), *Nix v. Williams* (1984), *New York v. Quarles* (1984), and *Duckworth v. Eagan* (1989). The six-member majority in *Harris* held that, although statements made to the police by defendants who have not been advised of their *Miranda* rights cannot be introduced as evidence for the prosecution's case-in-chief, they can be employed to impeach the credibility of defendants who testify in their own behalf and, in so doing, contradict earlier statements. In so ruling, the Court refused to construe the privilege against self-incrimination to include the right to commit perjury.[11] At issue in *Hass* were the rights of a suspect in police custody who, having received and accepted the full warnings prescribed by *Miranda,* later stated that he would like to telephone a lawyer; after being told he could not do so before reaching the station, he then provided inculpatory information. Such information, the Court ruled, was admissible in evidence at the suspect's trial solely for impeachment purposes after he had taken the stand and testified to the contrary, knowing that such information had been ruled inadmissible for the prosecution's case-in-chief.

In *Williams,* the Court held in a 7–2 vote that evidence obtained in violation of the *Miranda* decision need not be suppressed if it would have been inevitably discovered by lawful means. And, in *Quarles,* the Court recognized a "public safety exception" to the requirement that *Miranda* warnings be given before a suspect's answers may be admitted into evidence. As Justice Rehnquist reasoned:

The police, in this case, in the very act of apprehending a suspect, were confronted with the immediate necessity of ascertaining the whereabouts of a gun which they had every reason to believe the suspect had just removed from his empty holster and discarded in the supermarket. So long as the gun was concealed somewhere in the supermarket, with its actual whereabouts unknown, it obviously posed more than one danger to the public safety: an accomplice might make use of it, a customer or employee might later come upon it.

To ensure that further danger to the public did not result from the concealment of the gun in a public area, the Court held that the police did not have to advise the suspect of his *Miranda* rights before questioning him about the whereabouts of the gun and that the suspect's response, in which he pointed out the gun's location, did not have to be excluded.

Finally, in *Duckworth,* the Court held that informing a suspect that an attorney would be appointed for him "if and when you go to court" does not render *Miranda* warnings inadequate. Chief Justice Rehnquist argued for a five-member majority that *Miranda* warnings need not be given in the exact form described in *Miranda* but simply must reasonably convey to suspects their rights.

It should be noted that not all self-incrimination cases are concerned with trial court procedures or pretrial police interrogation techniques. A case in point is *South Dakota v. Neville* (1983), in which Justice O'Connor held for a seven-member majority that admission into evidence of a defendant's refusal to submit to a blood-alcohol test does not offend his privilege against self-incrimination and that it is not fundamentally unfair in violation of due process to use a defendant's refusal to take the blood-alcohol test as evidence of guilt, even though the police failed to warn him that refusal could be used against him at trial. Another example is *Selective Service System v. Minnesota Public Interest Research Group* (1984), in which the Court held, 6–2, that a statute denying federal financial aid to male students who failed to register for the draft did not violate the privilege against self-incrimination of nonregistrants. And as *Chavez v. Martinez* (2003) illustrates, even abusive police interrogation does not offend the Constitution if the person being interrogated is never charged with a crime.

While Oliverio Martinez was being treated for gunshot wounds received during an altercation with police, he was interrogated by Ben Chavez, a patrol supervisor. Martinez admitted that he used heroin and had taken an officer's gun during the incident. At no point was Martinez given *Miranda* warnings. Although he was never charged with a crime, and his answers were never used against him in any criminal proceeding, Martinez filed a 42 U.S.C. §1983 suit, maintaining, among other things, that Chavez's actions violated his Fifth Amendment right not to be "compelled in any criminal case to be a witness against himself" and his Fourteenth Amendment substantive due-process right to be free from coercive questioning.

For a badly fragmented Court, Justice Thomas rejected both of Martinez's contentions. "We fail to see how, based on the text of the Fifth Amendment, Martinez can allege a violation of this right, since Martinez was never prosecuted for a crime, let alone compelled to be a witness against himself in a criminal case." Martinez argued that the meaning of "criminal case" should encompass the entire criminal investigatory process, including police interrogations, but Thomas disagreed. "In our view, a 'criminal case' at the very least requires the initiation of legal proceedings. We need not decide today the precise moment when a 'criminal case' commences; it is enough to say that police questioning does not constitute a 'case' any more than a private investigator's precomplaint activities constitute a 'civil case.' Statements compelled by police interrogations of course may not be used against a defendant at trial, but it is not until their use in a criminal case that a violation of the Self-Incrimination Clause occurs."

Thomas also rejected Martinez's due-process argument. *Rochin v. California* (1952) had established the Court's standard in this area: "Convictions based on evidence obtained by methods that are 'so brutal and so offensive to human dignity' that they 'shock the conscience' violate the Due Process Clause." And, applying the *Rochin* standard in this case, Thomas found that Chavez's persistent questioning of Martinez was not "conscience shocking." "We can find no basis in our prior jurisprudence or in our Nation's history and traditions to suppose that freedom from unwanted police questioning is a right so fundamental that it cannot be abridged absent a 'compelling state interest.' We have never required such a justification for a police interrogation, and we decline to do so here."

DUE PROCESS OF LAW

The Due Process Clauses of the Fifth and Fourteenth Amendments declare that neither the federal government nor the states shall deprive any person "of life, liberty, or property, without due process of law." As Chapters 3 and 4 have pointed out, these clauses have been employed by the Supreme Court to apply most of the provisions (including most of the criminal procedural provisions) of the Bill of Rights to the states and to invalidate various federal and state laws held by the justices to trench on economic and civil liberties. Occasionally, although typically unsuccessfully, the principle of due process is invoked directly, not to incorporate some other criminal procedural protection but to protect a criminal defendant directly, as in *Rogers v. Tennessee* (2001), *Connecticut Department of Public Safety v. Doe* (2003), and *District Attorney's Office for the Third Judicial District v. Osborne* (2009).

In *Rogers v. Tennessee,* a defendant was tried and convicted of second-degree murder for a stabbing incident that caused the death of the victim fifteen months later. Even though the statute under which he was convicted made no mention of any exceptions based on the duration between the incident causing the death and the death itself, the defendant argued on appeal that his conviction was precluded by the common-law "year-and-a-day" rule under which no defendant could be convicted of murder unless the victim died as a result of the defendant's act within a year and a day of the act. The Tennessee Supreme Court rejected his argument. Although it acknowledged that the year-and-a-day rule had long been recognized in the state, it announced that it was retroactively abolishing it, finding that the reasons for recognizing the rule at common law no longer existed. It disagreed with Rogers's contention that the application of its decision abolishing the rule in his case violated the *Ex Post Facto* Clause, observing that the provision referred only to legislative acts.

In a 6–3 decision, the Supreme Court affirmed the decision of the Tennessee Supreme Court and held that its retroactive application of its decision abolishing the year-and-a-day rule violated neither the *Ex Post Facto* Clause (in her majority opinion, Justice O'Connor agreed with the Tennessee Supreme Court that the provision applied only to legislatures) nor Rogers's due-process rights (in her opinion, O'Connor found the Tennessee Supreme Court's decision to be a routine exercise of common-law decision making in which the law was being brought "into conformity with reason and common sense").

Justice Scalia filed a strident dissent: "The Court today approves the conviction of a man for a murder that was not murder (but only manslaughter) when the offense was committed. It thus violates a principle . . . which 'dates from the ancient Greeks' and has been described as one of the most 'widely held value-judgments in the entire history of human thought.'" He declared that the Court's opinion produced "a curious constitution that only a judge could love. One in which (by virtue of the *Ex Post Facto* Clause) the elected representatives of all the people cannot retroactively make murder what was not murder when the act was committed; but in which unelected judges can do precisely that." He continued: "I do not believe this is the system that the Framers envisioned—or, for that matter, that any reasonable person would imagine." He insisted that the Tennessee Supreme Court's "retroactive revision of a concededly valid legal rule" was "unheard-of" in criminal cases in the late eighteenth century and was therefore "contrary to the judicial traditions embraced within the concept of due process of law."

In *Connecticut Department of Public Safety v. Doe,* the Court unanimously upheld Connecticut's version of "Megan's Law," which required persons convicted of sexual offenses to register with the state upon their release into the community and required the state to post a sex-offender registry containing the registrants' names, addresses, photographs, and descriptions on an Internet website and to make the registry available to the public in certain state offices. The respondent, a convicted sex offender subject to the law, filed suit in federal court, claiming that the law violated the Due Process Clause of the Fourteenth Amendment because it deprived registered sex offenders of a "liberty interest" and because it did not afford registrants a predeprivation hearing to determine whether they were likely to be "currently dangerous." Chief Justice Rehnquist, however, rejected this claim: "Due process does not entitle him to a hearing to establish a fact that is not material under the Connecticut statute. . . . [T]he fact that respondent seeks to prove—that he is not currently dangerous—is of no consequence under Connecticut's Megan's Law. As the [state's] Website explains, the law's requirements turn on an offender's conviction alone—a fact that a convicted offender has already had a procedurally safeguarded opportunity to contest. No other fact is relevant to the disclosure of registrants' information. Indeed, the disclaimer on the Website explicitly states that respondent's alleged nondangerousness simply does not matter."

In *District Attorney's Office for the Third Judicial District v. Osborne*, the defendant was convicted in Alaska state court of a brutal sexual assault that occurred in 1993. At trial, his defense attorney declined to have DNA testing done on a semen sample found at the scene of the crime, explaining later that her decision was made based on her fear that the testing would provide further evidence of Osborne's guilt. After conviction, in an unsuccessful attempt to obtain parole, he confessed in detail to the crime. Years later he filed suit in federal district court under 42 U.S.C. §1983, which gives a cause of action to those who challenge a state's "deprivation of any rights . . . secured by the Constitution"; he claimed he had a liberty interest in demonstrating his innocence with new evidence and therefore a due-process right to access the evidence used against him in order to subject it to DNA testing at his own expense. Having prevailed in the lower courts, Osborne lost at the Supreme Court by a 5–4 vote. Justice Alito's majority opinion made clear the limited reach of the Due Process Clause for convicted defendants:

> A criminal defendant proved guilty after a fair trial does not have the same liberty interests as a free man. At trial, the defendant is presumed innocent and may demand that the government prove its case beyond reasonable doubt. But "[o]nce a defendant has been afforded a fair trial and convicted of the offense for which he was charged, the presumption of innocence disappears." "Given a valid conviction, the criminal defendant has been constitutionally deprived of his liberty." The State accordingly has more flexibility in deciding what procedures are needed in the context of post-conviction relief. "[W]hen a State chooses to offer help to those seeking relief from convictions," due process does not "dictat[e] the exact form such assistance must assume." Osborne's right to due process is not parallel to a trial right, but rather must be analyzed in light of the fact that he has already been found guilty at a fair trial, and has only a limited interest in post-conviction relief.

THE RIGHT TO COUNSEL

The Sixth Amendment declares that "in all criminal prosecutions, the accused shall enjoy the right . . . to have Assistance of Counsel for his defense." Until well into the twentieth century, this language was construed to guarantee only that the accused could employ and bring to trial a lawyer of his own choosing. No provision was made for the indigent defendant who might want and even badly need assistance of counsel, but was unable to afford an attorney. The language was permissive only; it imposed no duty on the government to provide free counsel.

In 1932, the Court began to expand this interpretation, holding in *Powell v. Alabama* that in capital felony cases, right to counsel is secured by the Due Process Clause of the Fourteenth Amendment. Six years later, in *Johnson v. Zerbst,* the Court further broadened the right to counsel to include appointment of counsel for indigent defendants in all federal criminal proceedings, capital or noncapital: "The Sixth Amendment," the Court declared, "withholds from federal courts, in all criminal proceedings, the power and authority to deprive an accused of his life or liberty unless he has or waives the assistance of counsel."

Although the Court held that the Sixth Amendment required appointment of counsel for indigent criminal defendants in federal prosecutions, it was reluctant to interpret the Fourteenth Amendment's Due Process Clause in such a way as to impose the same requirements on the states. When presented with the opportunity to do so in *Betts v. Brady* (1942), Justice Owen Roberts examined the constitutional, judicial, and legislative history of the states from colonial days and concluded for a six-member majority that "this material demonstrates that, in the great majority of States, it has been the considered judgment of the people, their representatives and their courts that appointment of counsel is not a fundamental right essential to a fair trial. On the contrary, the matter has generally been deemed one of legislative policy. In the light of this evidence, we are unable to say that the concept of due process incorporated in the Fourteenth Amendment obligates the States, whatever may be their own views, to furnish counsel in every such case." In dissent, Justice Black stressed that "whether a man is innocent cannot be determined from a trial in which, as here, denial of counsel has made it impossible to conclude, with any satisfactory degree of certainty, that the defendant's case was adequately presented."

Justice Black's dissent eventually was vindicated in the celebrated case of *Gideon v. Wainwright* (1963), in which the Court overruled *Betts* and unanimously concluded that an indigent defendant's right to court-appointed counsel is fundamental and essential to a fair trial in state as well as federal felony prosecutions. Justice Black declared for the Court that precedent, reason, and reflection "require us to recognize that in our adversary system of criminal justice, any person hauled into court, who is too poor to hire a lawyer, cannot be assured a fair trial unless counsel is provided for him." Observing that the government hires lawyers to prosecute and that defendants with money hire lawyers to defend, he concluded that "lawyers in criminal courts are necessities, not luxuries." The *Gideon* ruling did not extend the right to assistance of counsel to all criminal prosecutions, however. Misdemeanor offenses were excluded from coverage until *Argersinger v. Hamlin* (1972), in which the Court unanimously held that "absent a knowing and intelligent waiver, no person may be imprisoned for any offense, whether classified as petty, misdemeanor, or felony, unless he was represented by counsel at his trial."[12]

The Court has not only held that the right to assistance of counsel must be guaranteed in all trials where defendants can be sentenced to a term of imprisonment but also held that this constitutional principle is not limited simply to the presence of counsel at trial. As it declared in *United States v. Wade* (1967): "it is central to that principle that in addition to counsel's presence at trial, the accused is guaranteed that he need not stand alone against the state at any stage of the prosecution, formal or informal, in court or out, where counsel's absence might derogate from the accused's right to a fair trial."

On the basis of this principle, the Court has ruled that the accused has the right to counsel at such "critical stages" as in-custody police interrogation following arrest (*Escobedo v. Illinois* and *Miranda v. Arizona*), the police lineup held for eyewitness identification (*United States v. Wade* and *Gilbert v. California*), the preliminary hearing (*Coleman v. Alabama*), the arraignment (*Hamilton v. Alabama*), the appeal (*Douglas v. California*), and even at a post-trial proceeding for the revocation of probation and parole (*Mempa v. Rhay*).[13]

The Court's decisions from *Powell* to *Argersinger* raised a serious question: does a defendant in a criminal trial have a constitutional right to proceed without counsel when he voluntarily and intelligently elects to do so? Stated another way, can a state constitutionally haul a person into its criminal courts and there force a lawyer upon him, even when he insists that he wants to conduct his own defense? The Court gave a negative answer to this question in *Faretta v. California* (1975). Justice Stewart, speaking for a six-member majority, stressed that the language of the provision provides for "assistance" of counsel and that "an assistant, however expert, is still an assistant." Developing this argument further, he concluded that to thrust counsel upon an unwilling defendant would violate the logic of the amendment: "In such a case, counsel is not an assistant, but a master; and the right to make a defense is stripped of the personal character upon which the Amendment insists."

Justice Harry Blackmun challenged this conclusion in his dissent: "The Court seems to suggest that so long as the accused is willing to pay the consequences of his folly, there is no reason for not allowing a defendant the right to self-representation. . . . That view ignores the established principle that the interest of the State in a criminal prosecution 'is not that it shall win a case, but that justice shall be done.'"

Chaplin & Drysdale, Chartered v. United States (1989) posed for the Court an interesting right-to-counsel question arising out of the federal government's ongoing war against drugs: can the federal government constitutionally enforce a statute authorizing forfeiture to the government of assets acquired as a result of drug-law violations if the criminal defendant intends to use these assets to pay legal fees for his defense? In a 5–4 decision, Justice White concluded for the Court that the government can; he observed, among other things, that a defendant in a drug case has no more Sixth Amendment right to use funds obtained from an illegal drug enterprise to pay for his defense than a robbery suspect has "to use funds he has stolen from a bank." Justice Blackmun's dissent called into question the adequacy of the very guarantee of right to court-appointed counsel secured by the Court in *Gideon v. Wainwright*:

> The main effect of forfeitures under the [Continuing Criminal Enterprise] Act, of course, will be to deny the defendant the right to retain counsel, and therefore the right to have his defense designed and presented by an attorney he has chosen and trusts. If the Government restrains the defendant's assets before trial, private counsel will be unwilling to continue to take on the defense. . . . The resulting relationship between the defendant and his court-appointed counsel will likely begin in distrust, and be exacerbated to the extent that the defendant perceives his new-found "indigency" as a form of punishment imposed by the Government in order to weaken his defense. If the defendant had been represented by private counsel earlier in the proceedings, the defendant's sense that the Government has stripped him of his defenses will be sharpened by the concreteness of his loss. Appointed counsel may be inexperienced and undercompensated and, for that reason, may not have adequate opportunity or resources to deal with the special problems presented by what is likely to be a complex trial. The already scarce resources of the public defender's office will be stretched to the limit. Facing a lengthy trial against a better-armed adversary, the temptation to recommend a guilty plea will be great. The result, if the defendant is convicted, will be a sense, often well grounded, that justice was not done.

THE INSANITY DEFENSE

The criminal law justifies holding individuals responsible for their actions on the assumption that they have the ability to choose between acceptable and unacceptable behavior. This assumption provides the rationale for the insanity defense: criminal law should not punish those who are unable to choose between acceptable and unacceptable behavior. But what defines the inability to choose? The oldest insanity defense, and one initially adopted by many states, is the *M'Naghten* test. It was established in England in 1843 and declares that a defendant is responsible for criminal actions unless "the party accused was laboring under such a defect of reason, from disease of the mind, as not to know the nature and quality of the act he was doing; or, if he did know it, that he did not know he was doing what was wrong." Under this defense, as under other insanity defenses, the incapacity must come from mental disease—incapacity as a result of drunkenness or drug addiction does not excuse criminal conduct. What is distinctive of the *M'Naghten* test is its emphasis on cognitive capacity (i.e., defendants' inability to understand what they did) and moral capacity (i.e., their inability to distinguish right from wrong). Their inability to understand, not their inability to control their behavior, is decisive. The test lacks any volitional element: defendants are judged insane only if they lack the ability to understand what they did and to distinguish right from wrong, not if mental illness prevents them from choosing socially acceptable behavior.

As a consequence, many states (and the federal government) subsequently adopted the "irresistible impulse" test as a supplement to the *M'Naghten* test—allowing for the acquittal of defendants who cannot control their behavior, even though they know it is wrong. A version of this combined test was also incorporated by the American Law Institute into its Model Penal Code.

However, in 1982 when John Hinckley, in a federal court, was found not guilty by reason of insanity in his attempt to assassinate President Ronald Reagan, the resulting outrage led both the federal government and many states to rethink the insanity defense. In the Comprehensive Crime Control Act of 1984, Congress shifted the burden of proof on the issue of insanity, requiring defendants to prove they were insane at the time of the crime instead of the government having to prove that they were not. The act also narrowed the legal definition of insanity, effectively resurrecting the *M'Naghten* test in federal prosecutions. Eleven states followed Michigan's lead and established the verdict of "guilty but mentally ill." Three states abolished the insanity test altogether. In 1993 Arizona, which had previously adopted the *M'Naghten* test, passed legislation restricting it simply to moral incapacity. In *Clark v. Arizona* (2006), the Supreme Court considered the question of whether an insanity test narrower than the *M'Naghten* test violates due process. Justice Souter wrote the majority opinion in which he declared: "History shows no deference to *M'Naghten* that could elevate its formula to the level of fundamental principle, so as to limit the traditional recognition of a State's capacity to define crimes and defenses."

THE ENTRAPMENT DEFENSE

Entrapment may be defined as "the conception and planning of an offense by an officer, and his procurement of its commission by one who would not have perpetrated it except for the trickery, persuasion, or fraud of the officer."[14] Two opposing versions of the entrapment defense have been formulated and defended by various members of the Court. The first may be referred to as the federal approach because it has been adopted by a majority of the Court in each of the major entrapment decisions[15] and is generally followed by the lower federal courts. The federal approach focuses on the conduct and propensities of the particular defendant in each individual case. If defendants are not predisposed to commit crimes of the nature charged, they may avail themselves of the defense. If they are ready and willing to commit such an offense at any favorable opportunity, however, then the entrapment defense will fail, regardless of the nature and extent of the government's participation. Because of the focus on the defendant's predisposition, this approach is frequently referred to as the "subjective" test.

The other version of the entrapment defense may be labeled the "hypothetical person" approach. Expressed in the concurring and dissenting opinions of the same Supreme Court cases that employ the federal approach, this approach concentrates on the quality of police or government conduct rather than on the predisposition of the accused. It subscribes to the view that governmental conduct that falls below certain minimum standards will not be tolerated, thus relieving from criminal responsibility a defendant who commits a crime as a result of such conduct. This approach will not condone conduct by law-enforcement officials that presents too great a risk that a hypothetical law-abiding person will be induced to commit a crime that he or she would not otherwise have committed. Thus, the individual who commits the criminal offense, although technically guilty, will be relieved of criminal responsibility, and further prosecution will be barred. Proponents of this approach hope to deter unlawful governmental activity in the instigation of crime and to preserve the purity of the criminal justice system. As with all questions involving the legality of law-enforcement methods, the hypothetical-person defense submits the issue of entrapment to the judge, whereas the jury decides the issue under the federal defense. Because of its exclusive concentration on the conduct of the police and its disregard of the defendant's predisposition, this approach is often referred to as the "objective" test.

In *Jacobson v. United States* (1992), the Supreme Court's latest consideration of the entrapment defense, all of the justices employed the federal approach, but split over whether the defendant was predisposed to purchase child pornography when he was induced to do so by an undercover police sting operation. Five justices concluded that the police had implanted in Jacobson the disposition to purchase illegal child pornography; four insisted that he was already predisposed to make such a purchase (because he had purchased child pornography in the past when it illegal for him to do so), and that all the government did was induce him to act on that predisposition—that is, provide him the opportunity to do so.

TRIAL BY JURY

The right to trial by jury in criminal cases is mentioned in the text of both Article III, Section 2, and the Sixth Amendment. It is the only guarantee to appear in both the body of the Constitution and the Bill of Rights and has been called "the spinal column of American democracy."[16] Reserving the function of determining criminal guilt to the people themselves, sitting as jurors, it reflects the Framers' suspicion of the power of government. As Justice Scalia observed in *Blakely v. Washington* (2004), "Just as suffrage ensures the people's ultimate control in the legislative and executive branches, jury trial is meant to ensure their control in the judiciary."

As discussed in Chapter 3, the Sixth Amendment right to trial by jury was incorporated to apply to the states in *Duncan v. Louisiana* (1968). In *Baldwin v. New York* (1970), the Supreme Court held that the right extends to all trials for crimes that can result in imprisonment of six months or more.

Traditionally, a jury consisted of twelve members, but in *Williams v. Florida* (1970), the Court held that this number was "a historical accident" and was "unnecessary to effect the purposes of the jury system" when it denied a constitutional objection to the use of a six-person jury in a state criminal trial. It concluded that reducing its size to six persons did not prevent the jury from interposing "the common sense judgment of a group of laymen" between the accused and accuser and still promoted that "community participation and shared responsibility that results from the group's determination of guilt or innocence." In *Ballew v. Georgia* (1978), by contrast, the Court held that a five-member jury violated the Constitution; Justice Blackmun asserted that five persons were unlikely to engage in "meaningful deliberation, . . . remember all the facts and arguments, and truly represent the common sense of the entire community."

Also traditionally, a jury verdict in a criminal case had to be unanimous. However, in *Johnson v. Louisiana* (1972) and *Apodaca v. Oregon* (1972), the Court upheld nonunanimous jury verdicts in state-court criminal trials—in *Johnson* it refused to strike down a

Louisiana statute authorizing 9–3 verdicts. In *Burch v. Louisiana* (1979), the Court confronted the question of how *Williams,* authorizing six-person juries, related to *Johnson* and *Apodaca,* authorizing nonunanimous verdicts. The Court held in the *Williams* case that a Louisiana statute allowing for nonunanimous verdicts in criminal cases by a six-member jury was unconstitutional. To date the Court has not determined the precise constitutional intersection of jury size and the number of jurors necessary to reach a verdict.

The right to trial by jury was dispositive in *Blakely v. Washington* (2004), in which the Supreme Court struck down Washington State's sentencing-guidelines provisions that allowed judges, not juries, to decide facts resulting in enhanced sentences. In this case, the trial judge had sentenced Blakely, who had been found guilty by a jury of kidnapping his estranged wife, to ninety months (thirty-seven months more than the fifty-three-month statutory maximum of the standard range of Washington's sentencing guidelines) because he found the defendant to have acted with "deliberate cruelty," a statutorily enumerated ground for departing from the standard range. By doing so, however, the Supreme Court held that he had violated the Sixth Amendment rights of Blakely, for he had ordered a punishment that "the jury's verdict alone does not allow" and therefore "exceed[ed] his proper authority." As Justice Scalia held for a five-member majority, the right to trial by jury in a criminal case means the right of a defendant to have the jury determine his guilt of the crime charged, and that necessarily means his commission of every element of the crime charged. (In *Southern Union Company v. United States* [2012], the Court applied the same rule to the imposition of criminal fines.)

The four dissenting justices in *Blakely* (and especially Justice O'Connor) objected that Scalia's reading of the Sixth Amendment would effectively eliminate all determinate sentencing schemes, including the Federal Sentencing Guidelines. Scalia responded first, in a footnote, "The Federal Guidelines are not before us, and we express no opinion on them." He continued, but what he said could have given O'Connor little comfort: "This case is not about whether determinate sentencing is constitutional, only about how it can be implemented in a way that respects the Sixth Amendment." Every defendant, Scalia insisted, has the right under the Sixth Amendment to compel the prosecutor to prove to a jury "all facts legally essential to the punishment." Yet, he scolded his colleagues, under the Federal Sentencing Guidelines, a defendant with "no warning in either his indictment or plea" can "see his maximum potential sentence balloon from as little as five years to as much as life imprisonment based not on facts proved to his peers beyond a reasonable doubt, but on facts extracted after trial from a report compiled by a probation officer who the judge thinks more likely got it right than got it wrong. . . . Suffice it to say that, if such a measure exists, it is not the one the Framers left us with."

What the dissenters predicted in *Blakely* came to pass in *United States v. Booker* (2005). A five-member majority of the Court (which included Scalia) concluded that the Sixth Amendment as construed in *Blakely* applied to the Federal Sentencing Guidelines. What no one could have predicted, however, was that the guidelines would escape unscathed. A different five-member majority (Justice Ruth Bader Ginsburg switched sides) concluded that what made the guidelines unconstitutional was not that they allowed judges rather than juries to decide facts that resulted in enhanced sentences, but that they were mandatory; it therefore severed those provisions of the Sentencing Reform Act that made them mandatory and saved their constitutionality by making them advisory—that is, by requiring only that a sentencing court consider the guidelines but permitting it to tailor the sentence in light of other statutory concerns. But, of course, the second majority opinion in *Booker* was a non sequitur: a judge who consults the guidelines (whether they are mandatory or not) and proceeds to enhance the sentence of a defendant on the basis of facts not found to be true beyond a reasonable doubt by a jury is still, according to *Blakely,* violating the defendant's Sixth Amendment rights. Justice Stevens pointed this out in his dissent. In his own dissent to the second majority opinion, Scalia found it "wonderfully ironic: In order to rescue from nullification a statutory scheme designed to eliminate discretionary sentencing, it discards the provisions that eliminate discretionary sentencing."

THE RIGHT TO A SPEEDY TRIAL

The Sixth Amendment assures the accused the right to a speedy trial. However, as Justice Powell remarked in *Barker v. Wingo* (1972), this right "is a more vague concept than other procedural rights. It is, for example, impossible to determine with precision when the right has been denied. We cannot definitely say how long is too long in a system where justice is supposed to be swift but deliberate." The vague quality of the right to a speedy trial led the Court in *Barker* to embrace a "balancing test" to determine whether the right had been violated. Four factors were to be weighed in the balance: length of delay, the reason for the delay, the defendant's assertion of his right, and prejudice to the defendant.

Conceding that this "difficult and sensitive balancing process" necessarily would compel the courts to approach speedy trial cases on an ad hoc basis, the Court insisted that this way of proceeding comported with the requirements of the judicial process. The Court was reluctant to go so far as to hold that the Constitution required a criminal defendant to be offered a trial within a specified time period. Against the undoubted clarity and definiteness of a time limit, the Court observed, must be weighed the fact that it would "require this Court to engage in legislative or rulemaking activity, rather than in the adjudicative process to which we should confine our efforts." It went on to note that although legislatures were free to prescribe reasonable periods of time, consistent with constitutional standards, within which criminal trials must begin, its own approach had to be less precise. Seeking such precision, Congress passed the Speedy Trial Act of 1974, which ordered that criminal defendants be brought to trial within one hundred days.

Doggett v. United States (1992) represents the Court's most recent consideration of the "speedy trial" provision. In it the Court reversed the defendant's conviction for conspiracy to import and distribute cocaine on the grounds that an eight-and-a-half-year period between indictment and trial denied him of his constitutional right to a speedy trial; it condemned the "Government's egregious persistence in failing to prosecute" the defendant, even though the defendant was not held in detention during that period and claimed to be unaware he was under indictment, and despite the fact that the government was unaware of his whereabouts. (It was believed he was in prison in Panama.) Justice Thomas was prompted to observe in dissent that "so engrossed is the Court in applying the multifactor balancing test set forth in *Barker* that it loses sight of the nature and purpose of the speedy trial guarantee set forth in the Sixth Amendment."

THE RIGHT TO CONFRONTATION

The Confrontation Clause of the Sixth Amendment guarantees an accused person the right "to be confronted with witnesses against him." It is one of two clauses in the Bill of Rights (the other being the Compulsory Process Clause) that explicitly address the right of criminal defendants to elicit evidence in their defense from witnesses at trial. As Justice Stewart said in *Faretta v. California* (1975), "When taken together, [they] guarantee that a criminal charge may be answered in a manner now considered fundamental to the fair administration of American justice—through the calling and interrogation of favorable witnesses, the cross-examination of adverse witnesses, and the orderly introduction of evidence. In short, the[y] . . . constitutionalize the right in an adversary criminal trial to make a defense as we know it." In *Pointer v. Texas* (1965), the Court incorporated the Confrontation Clause to apply to the states.

In *Coy v. Iowa* (1988), Justice Scalia for the majority held that the Confrontation Clause literally guarantees "the defendant a face-to-face meeting with witnesses appearing before the trier of fact"; consequently, it overturned the conviction of a criminal defendant (in this case, a man convicted of two counts of engaging in lascivious acts with a child) because an Iowa statute allowed the two thirteen-year-old girls he was charged with sexually assaulting to testify behind a large screen that shielded them from the defendant. Although Justice O'Connor joined the majority opinion in *Coy*, she made clear in her concurrence that she believed that certain exceptions existed to Scalia's literalist interpretation; she had in mind "use of one- or two-way closed circuit television," which for her raised no Confrontation Clause problems. Scalia finessed this issue by announcing that "we leave for another day . . . the question whether any exceptions exist." That day came two years later in *Maryland v. Craig* (1990), when Justice O'Connor declared for a six-member majority that the right to "a face-to-face meeting" is not absolute, that the central concern of the Confrontation Clause is to ensure the reliability of the evidence against a criminal defendant by subjecting it to rigorous testing in the context of an adversary proceeding, and that use of one-way closed-circuit television testimony for child victims in sexual abuse cases is consistent with the central concern of the right to confrontation. Justice Scalia dissented, complaining, "Seldom has this Court failed so conspicuously to sustain a categorical guarantee of the Constitution against the tide of prevailing current opinions."

The Supreme Court has also held that the right to confrontation severely limits the use of "hearsay" evidence (although the Court has allowed for such exceptions as the introduction of prior testimony of former witnesses who die before trial); limits the admissibility, at a trial of two or more defendants, of a confession that implicates a defendant other than the confessor; and includes the accused's right to cross-examine those witnesses who are produced by the state.

On this last point, in *Crawford v. Washington* (2004), the Supreme Court held that the Confrontation Clause flatly bars "testimonial statements of a witness who did not appear at trial unless he was unavailable to testify, and the defendant had had a prior opportunity for cross examination." The text of the clause alone did not compel this conclusion; as Scalia noted for a unanimous Court, "One could plausibly read 'witnesses against' a defendant to mean those who actually testify at trial." But, he continued, when the text was supplemented by the "historical background of the Clause," the conclusion became obvious, and the Court therefore reversed the assault and attempted-murder convictions of the defendant because the trial court had allowed the state to play for the jury a tape-recorded statement in which the defendant's wife (who did not testify at trial because of the state's marital privilege that bars one spouse from testifying against the other without the other's consent) had described, during a police interrogation, her husband's stabbing of the victim. The state insisted that her statement should not be barred because it bore "particularized guarantees of trustworthiness," but Scalia concluded, "Where testimonial statements are at issue, the only indicium of reliability sufficient to satisfy constitutional demands is the one the Constitution actually prescribes: confrontation." Two years later, in *Davis v. Washington* (2006), Scalia had the occasion to clarify exactly what was meant by the phrase *testimonial statements*. "Statements are nontestimonial when made in the course of police interrogation under circumstances objectively indicating that the primary purpose of the interrogation is to enable police assistance to meet an ongoing emergency. They are testimonial when the circumstances objectively indicate that there is no such ongoing emergency, and that the primary purpose of the interrogation is to establish or prove past events potentially relevant to later criminal prosecution." However, as *Michigan v. Bryant* (2011) makes clear, applying that definition is by no means easy.

The *Crawford* decision figured prominently in *Melendez-Diaz v. Massachusetts* (2009) and *Bullcoming v. New Mexico* (2011), where a sharply divided Court held that the affidavits of laboratory analysts who tested samples for drugs and the level of alcohol in blood samples were testimonial statements, that the analysts were witnesses for purposes of the Sixth Amendment, and that criminal defendants were entitled to be confronted with the analysts at trial. However, in *Williams v. Illinois* (2012), Justice Alito held for a five-member majority that the Confrontation Clause was not violated when a forensic specialist at the Illinois State Police lab testified that she had matched a DNA profile produced by an outside laboratory, Cellmark, to a profile the state laboratory produced using a sample of the petitioner's blood. She testified that Cellmark was an accredited laboratory and that business records showed that vaginal swabs taken from the victim were sent to Cellmark and returned. She offered no other statement for the purpose of identifying the sample used for Cellmark's profile or establishing how Cellmark handled or tested the sample, and she did not vouch for the accuracy of Cellmark's profile. Justice Kagan filed a strenuous dissent:

> Some years ago, the State of California prosecuted a man named John Kocak for rape. At a preliminary hearing, the State presented testimony from an analyst at the Cellmark Diagnostics Laboratory—the same facility used to generate DNA evidence in this case. The analyst had extracted DNA from a bloody sweatshirt found at the crime scene and then compared it to two control samples—one from Kocak and one from the victim. The analyst's report identified a single match: As she explained on direct examination, the DNA found on the sweatshirt belonged to Kocak. But after undergoing cross-examination, the analyst realized she had made a mortifying error. She took the stand again, but this time to admit that the report listed the victim's control sample as coming from Kocak, and Kocak's as coming from the victim. So the DNA on the sweatshirt matched not Kocak, but the victim herself. In trying Kocak, the State would have to look elsewhere for its evidence.
>
> Our Constitution contains a mechanism for catching such errors—the Sixth Amendment's Confrontation Clause. That Clause, and the Court's recent cases interpreting it, require that testimony against a criminal defendant be subject to cross-examination. And that command applies with full force to forensic evidence of the kind involved in both the Kocak case and this one. In two decisions issued in the last three years [*Melendez-Diaz* and *Bullcoming*], this Court held that if a prosecutor wants to introduce the results of forensic testing into evidence, he must afford the defendant an opportunity to cross-examine an analyst responsible for the test. Forensic evidence is reliable only when properly produced, and the Confrontation Clause prescribes a particular method for determining whether that has happened. The Kocak incident illustrates how the Clause is designed to work: Once confronted, the analyst discovered and disclosed the error she had made. That error would probably not have come to light if the prosecutor had merely admitted the report into evidence or asked a third party to present its findings. Hence the genius of an 18th-century device as applied to 21st-century evidence: cross-examination of the analyst is especially likely to reveal whether vials have been switched, samples contaminated, tests incompetently run, or results inaccurately recorded.

Justice Alito's disdain for *Crawford* and its rejection of all hearsay evidence, so apparent in *Williams*, resurfaced in his majority opinion in *Ohio v. Clark* (2015), in which he held that statements made by a three-year old boy (L. P.) to his preschool teacher explaining how he had sustained various injuries and introduced at Clark's trial for child abuse were not testimonial and therefore did not implicate the Confrontation Clause. Dismissing *Crawford*'s relevance and relying instead on *Michigan v. Bryant*, he concluded that because neither L. P. nor his teachers had the primary purpose of assisting in Clark's prosecution, L. P.'s statements were admissible at trial. "L. P.'s statements occurred in the context of an ongoing emergency involving suspected child abuse. When L. P.'s teachers noticed his injuries, they rightly became worried that the three-year-old was the victim of serious violence. Because the teachers needed to know whether it was safe to release L. P. to his guardian at the end of the day, they needed to determine who might be abusing the child. Thus, the immediate concern was to protect a vulnerable child who needed help." Since L. P.'s teachers were not sure who had abused him or how best to secure his safety, and because they did not know whether any other children might be at risk, "their questions and L. P.'s answers were primarily aimed at identifying and ending the threat." The teachers' questions were meant "to identify the abuser in order to protect the victim from future attacks. Whether the teachers thought that this would be done by apprehending the abuser or by some other means is irrelevant." Scalia concurred only in the judgment. "I write separately . . . to protest the Court's shoveling of fresh dirt upon the Sixth Amendment right of confrontation so recently rescued from the grave in *Crawford*." *Crawford*, he reminded Alito, "remains the law." Alito, Scalia charged, "unabashedly displays his hostility to *Crawford* and its progeny, perhaps aggravated by inability to muster the votes to overrule them." *Crawford*, Scalia continued, does not rank on Alito's "top-ten list of favorite precedents—and [he] could not restrain [himself] from saying (and saying and saying) so."

PLEA BARGAINING

Plea bargaining, in which a defendant agrees to plead guilty in return for a reduced charge or sentence, has become such a central feature of the criminal justice system that it currently occurs in approximately 90 percent of all criminal cases in the United States. In *Brady v. United States* (1970), the Supreme Court gave its approval to most forms of plea bargaining. Speaking for the Court majority, Justice Byron White announced the Court's refusal to hold that "a guilty plea is compelled and invalid under the Fifth Amendment whenever motivated by the defendant's desire to accept the certainty or probability of a lesser penalty rather than face a wider range of possibilities extending from acquittal to conviction and a higher penalty authorized by law for the crime charged. . . . We cannot hold that it is unconstitutional for the State to extend a benefit to a defendant who in turn extends a substantial benefit to the State. . . . "

After *Brady* the Court sought to formalize the procedures for plea bargaining. In *Santo Bello v. New York* (1971), for example, it held that if a defendant, relying on a prosecutor's promise, enters a guilty plea, due process of law requires that the prosecutor's promise be kept or that the defendant be given some form of relief—typically, an opportunity to withdraw the guilty plea. Later, in its most comprehensive effort to define plea-bargaining procedures, the Court issued and sent to Congress for approval a set of amendments to Rule 11 of the Federal Rules of Criminal Procedure. These amendments were approved, with several changes, by Congress and became effective in 1975.

Issues concerning plea bargaining have recently gained the Supreme Court's attention. In divided opinions in *Lafler v. Cooper* (2012) and *Missouri v. Fyre* (2012), Kennedy held that the standards of *Washington v. Strickland* (1984) guaranteeing criminal defendants "effective assistance of counsel" applies to all "critical stages of the criminal proceedings" and were not met when the attorneys in question refused to accept or allowed to lapse plea bargains that led to trials at which the defendants were convicted (at jury and bench trials) and received harsher sentences than they would have received under the plea bargains proffered. In his dissent in *Lafler*, Scalia observed, "The Court today opens a whole new field of constitutionalized criminal procedure." He noted, "The ordinary criminal process has become too long, too expensive, and unpredictable, in no small part as a consequence of an intricate federal Code of Criminal Procedure imposed on the States by this Court in pursuit of perfect justice. The Court now moves to bring perfection to the alternative in which prosecutors and defendants have sought relief." While *Lafler* and *Fyre* dealt with certain "aspects of counsel's plea-bargaining inadequacy" and left "other aspects (who knows what they might be?) to be worked out in further constitutional litigation," he declared that "it would be foolish to think that 'constitutional' rules governing counsel's behavior will not be followed by rules governing the prosecution's behavior in the plea-bargaining process." Offering examples, he wondered whether it would be constitutional for the prosecution to withdraw a plea offer that has already been accepted, or to withdraw an offer before the defense has had adequate time to consider and accept it, or to make no plea offer at all, even though its case is weak.

BAIL AND PRETRIAL DETENTION

Bail and pretrial detention have perhaps raised fewer constitutional questions than any other practices in the criminal justice system. This is in part because the "excessive fines and bails" clause of the Eighth Amendment has never been incorporated to apply to the states and in part because the Supreme Court has never established an absolute right to bail. In determining whether bail will be granted and the conditions under which it will be granted, courts have traditionally asked just one question: will the accused abscond or appear as required at his trial? Increasingly, however, a second question is also being asked: will the accused constitute a danger to the community and the safety of others by committing additional crimes while free on bail? Both the Supreme Court and Congress have given their endorsement to the asking of this second question and to the use of preventive detention when the answer to this second question mandates it.

In *Schall v. Martin* (1984), the Supreme Court upheld by a vote of 7–2 the preventive-detention provision of the New York Family Court Act that authorized pretrial detention of juveniles accused of acts of delinquency based on the finding that there was "serious risk" that the juvenile "may before the return date commit an act that, if committed by an adult, would constitute a crime." Justice Rehnquist held for the majority that preventive detention under the statute served the legitimate state objective of protecting both the juvenile and the society from the hazards of pretrial crime and that it was therefore "compatible with the 'fundamental fairness' demanded by the Due Process Clause." And, in the Comprehensive Crime Control Act of 1984, passed later that same year, Congress provided that if, after a hearing pursuant to the provisions of that act, a "judicial officer finds that no condition or combination of conditions will reasonably assure the appearance of the person as required and the safety of any other person and the community, he shall order the detention of the person prior to trial." Interestingly, given this chapter's previous discussion of the exclusionary rule, Congress specifically declared that "the rules concerning admissibility of evidence in criminal trials do not apply to the presentation and consideration of information" at the preventive-detention hearing. These preventive-detention provisions were upheld by the Supreme Court in *United States v. Salerno* (1987).

CRUEL AND UNUSUAL PUNISHMENTS

The Eighth Amendment protects against the infliction of "cruel and unusual punishments." This phraseology, derived from the English Bill of Rights of 1689, originally was understood to refer to such ancient practices as branding, drawing and quartering, burning alive, and crucifixion. But as Chief Justice Warren noted in *Trop v. Dulles* (1958), the Court must determine the meaning of the Eighth Amendment from the "evolving standards of decency that mark the progress of a maturing society." Put simply, whatever the amendment was originally intended to mean must be of less importance to the Court than what "evolving standards of decency" require. How the Court views these standards is of as much interest to the states as to the federal government because *Robinson v. California* (1962), which invalidated a California statute that made it a misdemeanor to be "addicted to the use of narcotics," made this particular provision applicable to the states through the Fourteenth Amendment.

Perhaps the most dramatic issue arising out of *Robinson* and its incorporation of the protection against cruel and unusual punishments has been that of capital punishment. In *Furman v. Georgia* (1972), a badly split Court rendered invalid every state death-penalty statute then in existence. In a brief *per curiam* order, the five members of the majority were able to agree that "the imposition and the carrying out of the death penalty in these cases constitute cruel and unusual punishment in violation of the Eighth and Fourteenth Amendments." They could agree on little more, however—as attested by the fact that each member of the majority wrote a separate opinion.

Although *Furman* foreclosed executions under state statutes then in existence, it did not declare that capital punishment inevitably was unconstitutional. Encouraged by the fact that only Justices William Brennan and Thurgood Marshall regarded all death-penalty statutes as per se unconstitutional, state legislatures were quick to adopt new capital-punishment statutes designed to meet the objections of the other members of the *Furman* majority. Ultimately, new death-penalty schemes were adopted by at least thirty-seven states. With the enactment of these new laws, the Court was forced once again to confront the question of the constitutionality of the death penalty. And in 1976, by a 7–2 vote in *Gregg v. Georgia,* it held the death penalty to be a constitutionally permissible punishment, at least for carefully defined categories of murder. The same plurality that spoke for the Court on this basic issue, however, went on to say that the Eighth Amendment requires that the sentencing authority be provided with carefully controlled discretion; a bifurcated trial was seen as the ideal procedure. Mandatory death-penalty statutes were regarded as unconstitutional.

Since *Gregg v. Georgia,* a solid majority of the Supreme Court has refused to reconsider the general constitutionality of capital punishment. In fact, in *Barefoot v. Estelle* (1983), it upheld expedited procedures to review habeas corpus petitions filed by death-row inmates, displaying an increasing impatience with the endless stays of execution that defense attorneys were securing in the lower courts. In *Pulley v. Harris* (1984), it rejected the contention that the Eighth Amendment requires that, before a state appellate court affirms a death sentence, it must engage in a comparative proportionality review, in which it compares the sentence in the case before it with the penalties imposed in similar cases to determine whether they are proportional. To inquire whether a penalty in a particular case is unacceptable because it is disproportionate to the punishment imposed on others convicted of the same crime would, Justice White wrote for a seven-member majority, depart from *Gregg* and the provisions for the exercise of controlled discretion approved there. In *McCleskey v. Kemp* (1987), the Court found no merit in the contention that Georgia's capital-punishment process violated the Eighth and Fourteenth Amendments because a statistical study purported to show a disparity in Georgia's imposition of the death sentence based on the race of the murder victim. In *Payne v. Tennessee* (1991), the Court voted 6–3 to overturn its recent decisions of *Booth v. Maryland* (1988) and *South Carolina v. Gathers* (1989) and declared that the Eighth Amendment does not prohibit a capital-sentencing jury from considering "victim impact" evidence relating to the personal characteristics of the victim and the emotional impact of the crimes on the victim's family. In *Felker v. Turpins* (1996), the Supreme Court upheld the Antiterrorism and Effective Death Penalty Act of 1996, which required dismissal of a claim presented in a state prisoner's second or successive federal habeas application if the claim was also presented in a prior application, compelled dismissal of a claim that was not presented in a prior federal application, and created a "gatekeeping" mechanism in the federal courts of appeal requiring prospective applicants to establish a *prima facie* showing that their applications satisfy the act's other requirements. And, in *Baze v. Rees* (2008) and *Glossip v. Gore* (2015), it upheld the constitutionality of two different methods of lethal injection used for capital punishment; the governing legal standard required that lethal injection must not inflict "unnecessary pain," and the petitioners in these cases argued unsuccessfully that the lethal chemicals used carried an unnecessary risk of inflicting pain during the execution.

Through the years since *Gregg*, however, the Court has also imposed a long list of substantive and procedural requirements that impede imposition of the death penalty. They include the prohibition of the death penalty for rape of an adult woman (*Coker v. Georgia* [1977]), for "ordinary" murder (*Godfrey v. Georgia* [1980]), and for felony murder absent a showing that the defendant possessed a sufficiently culpable state of mind (*Enmund v. Florida* [1982]); the prohibition of the death penalty as the mandatory punishment for any crime (*Woodson v. North Carolina* [1976] and *Sumner v. Shuman* [1987]); a requirement that the sentencer be empowered to take into account all mitigating circumstances (*Lockett v. Ohio* [1978] and *Eddings v. Oklahoma* [1982]); a requirement that the accused receive a judicial evaluation of his claim of insanity before the sentence can be executed (*Ford v. Wainwright* [1986]); a requirement that in a sentencing proceeding where the jury is asked to decide between the death penalty and a life sentence, a defendant is entitled to a jury instruction that he would be ineligible for parole under a life sentence (*Kelly v. South Carolina* [2002]); the prohibition of the death penalty for any person found to be mentally retarded (*Atkins v. Virginia* [2002]); the prohibition of a rigid rule allowing the imposition of the death penalty for anyone with an IQ test above 70 (*Hall v. Florida* [2014]); the prohibition of the use of visible shackles during a capital trial's guilt and penalty phases unless that use is "justified by an essential state interest" (*Deck v. Missouri* [2005]); and the prohibition of the death penalty for the rape of a child under the age of twelve (*Kennedy v. Louisiana* [2008]).

In recent years, the Supreme Court has focused particular attention of how the Eighth Amendment applies to juvenile offenders. In *Roper v. Simmons* (2005), it overturned *Stanford v. Kentucky* (1989) and held that the Cruel and Unusual Punishments Clause barred the death penalty for any person under the age of eighteen at the time of the crime. In *Graham v. Florida* (2010), it held that it is "grossly disproportionate" and hence unconstitutional for any judge or jury to impose a sentence of life without parole on a juvenile offender for a nonhomicide case. And in *Miller v. Alabama* (2012), it held that the Eighth Amendment is violated when a juvenile convicted of murder receives a mandatory sentence of life without parole. Speaking for a five-member majority, Justice Kagan declared, "*Graham, Roper,* and our individualized sentencing decisions make clear that a judge or jury must have the opportunity to consider mitigating circumstances before imposing the harshest possible penalty for juveniles."

The Court has also addressed other issues that have raised questions concerning cruel and unusual punishments. In *Ingraham v. Wright* (1977), it held that the Cruel and Unusual Punishments Clause did not apply to "traditional practices in public schools" such as paddling. In *Hudson v. McMillian* (1992), it held that use of "excessive physical force" by prison guards subjected a prisoner to "cruel and unusual punishment" even though no serious physical injury resulted. In dissent Justice Thomas noted that "for generations, judges and commentators regarded the Eighth Amendment as applying only to torturous punishments meted out by statutes or sentencing judges, and not generally to any hardship that might befall a prisoner during incarceration"; he dismissed the majority opinion as an unfortunate consequence of the Court having "cut the Eighth Amendment loose from its historical moorings" and argued instead that the prisoner should have sought, and the Court should have provided, relief under the Due Process Clause of the Fourteenth Amendment. In *Solem v. Helm* (1983), the Court held that the Eighth Amendment prohibits sentences that are disproportionate to the crime committed and ruled that a sentence of life imprisonment without possibility of parole imposed under a South Dakota recidivist statute upon a defendant who was convicted of uttering a "no account" check for $100 and who had three prior convictions for third-degree burglary, one prior conviction for obtaining money under false pretenses, one prior conviction for larceny, and one prior conviction for third-offense driving while intoxicated, was significantly disproportionate to his crime and prohibited by the Cruel and Unusual Punishments Clause. In *Harmelin v. Michigan* (1991), a five-member majority held that the Eighth Amendment does not prohibit the imposition of a mandatory term of life in prison without possibility of parole for possessing more than 650 grams of cocaine. The majority divided on whether *Solem v. Helm,* which had concluded that the Eighth Amendment contains a proportionality principle, should be overturned. Justice Scalia, making a textualist argument, said that it should; Justice Kennedy, wishing to adhere to precedent and therefore arguing implausibly that the Michigan law somehow passed *Solem*'s proportionality test, said it should not. Finally, in *Ewing v. California* (2003), the Court held, in a 5–4 decision, that California's three-strikes law, under which a defendant who is convicted of a felony and has previously been convicted of two or more serious or violent felonies must receive an indeterminate sentence of twenty-five years to life, does not violate the Eighth Amendment.

PRISONERS' RIGHTS

On conviction and imprisonment, a profound change occurs in a person's legal status. Duly convicted prisoners lose entirely many freedoms enjoyed by free persons; however, they do not relinquish all rights. As the Supreme Court noted in *Wolf v. McDonell* (1974), "Though his rights may be diminished by the needs and exigencies of the institutional environment, a prisoner is not wholly stripped of constitutional protections when he is imprisoned for crime. There is no iron curtain drawn between the Constitution and the prisons of this country."

There is no question that prisoners always retain the right to the minimal conditions necessary for human survival (i.e., the right to food, clothing, shelter, and medical care). The right of prisoners to a non-life-threatening environment goes beyond the provision of life's necessities; it includes their right to be protected from one another and from themselves. On this last point, lower courts have been more responsive to prisoners' claims than the Supreme Court and have found that prison crowding is unconstitutional. As a federal district court in Florida asserted in *Costello v. Wainwright* (1975), prison crowding "endangers the very lives of the inmates" and therefore violates the Eighth Amendment's guarantee against cruel and unusual punishments. The Supreme Court's reluctance to follow the lower courts is understandable, for empirical studies flatly contradict the assertion that crowding is life threatening. Not only are the overall death rates, accidental death rates, and homicide and suicide rates of inmates two to three times lower than for comparable groups of parolees (controlling for age, race, and sex), but no statistically significant correlations exist between measures of crowding (density and occupancy) and inmate death rates.[17]

Beyond agreement that inmates have the minimal right to a non-life-threatening environment, legal debate rages. Some courts and legal scholars have taken their cues from the Sixth Circuit Court of Appeals in *Coffin v. Reichard* (1944) and have declared that prisoners retain all the rights of ordinary citizens except those expressly or by necessary implication taken by law. The Supreme Court's decision in *Procunier v. Martinez* (1974) followed this line of reasoning when it held that it would employ a strict-scrutiny standard of review to evaluate claims that the rights of prisoners were being denied. It declared that it would sustain limitations of prisoners' rights only if they furthered an important or substantial governmental interest and if they were no greater than necessary to protect that interest.

Fundamentally opposed to *Coffin* and *Procunier* is the view, now dominant on the Supreme Court, that inmates are without rights except for those conferred by law or necessarily implied and that, as a consequence, courts should employ the reasonableness test to assess the legitimacy of restrictions on what prisoners assert to be their rights. In *Turner v. Safley* (1987), the Supreme Court articulated this position and rejected the use of strict scrutiny in prisoners' rights cases. Writing for a five-member majority, Justice O'Connor declared that "when a prison regulation impinges on inmates' constitutional rights, the regulation is valid if it is reasonably related to legitimate penological interests." O'Connor announced a four-prong test for measuring reasonableness: (1) Is there "a 'valid, rational connection' between the prison regulation and the legitimate government interest put forward to justify it"? (2) "[A]re alternative means of exercising the right . . . open to prison inmates"? (3) What is "the impact [that] accommodation of the asserted constitutional right will have on guards and other inmates, and on the allocation of prison resources generally"? and (4) Is "the absence of ready alternatives . . . evidence of the reasonableness of the prison regulation"? Employing this four-prong test, Justice O'Connor rejected a First Amendment challenge to a Missouri ban on inmate-to-inmate correspondence because the prohibition on correspondence was "logically connected" to legitimate security concerns. In *O'Lone v. Shabazz* (1987), the Court applied the same reasonableness test to sustain New Jersey prison policies that resulted in Muslim inmates' inability to attend weekly congregational services.[18]

Security concerns generally trump the claims of prisoners' rights; the Court is hesitant to recognize inmate claims that have the potential of putting at risk the prison itself, the guards, other inmates, or the petitioner. Justice Rehnquist in *Jones v. North Carolina Prisoners' Union* (1977) summarized well the Court's deferential approach to these issues: "It is enough to say that they [prison officials] have not been conclusively shown to be wrong in this view. The interest in preserving order and authority in prisons is self-evident."

Applying this reasoning, the Court has denied inmates' claims to a First Amendment right to organize as a prisoners' labor union and has rejected the contention that an inmate's right to privacy protects against routine strip and body-cavity searches. In *Moody v. Daggett* (1976), it refused to recognize any inmate legal rights in the ordinary classification process or interprison transfer, declaring that there are no due-process issues implicated by "the discretionary transfer of state prisoners to a substantially less agreeable prison, even where the transfer visit[s] a 'grievous loss' upon the inmate. The same is true of prisoner classification and eligibility for rehabilitative programs." In *Wilkinson v. Austin* (2005), it unanimously concluded that the procedures contained in Ohio's formal policy for determining whether to classify an inmate for placement in the state's only "Supermax" facility (a maximum-security prison with highly restrictive conditions designed to segregate the most dangerous prisoners from the general prison population) provided inmates sufficient procedural protection to comply with due process. The procedures were designed to remove from the state's other prisons the leadership of prison gangs, and Justice Kennedy balanced the security interest of other inmates, prison staff members, and the public at large against the limited procedural protections afforded these inmates as they sought to avoid confinement in a facility where almost every aspect of their lives is controlled and monitored, where incarceration is synonymous with extreme isolation, where opportunities for visitation are rare and are always conducted through glass walls, and where they are deprived of almost any environmental or sensory stimuli and of almost all human contact: "Prison security, imperiled by the brutal reality of prison gangs, provides the backdrop of the State's interest. Clandestine, organized, fueled by race-based hostility, and committed to fear and violence as a means of disciplining their own members and their rivals, gangs seek nothing less than to control prison life and to extend their power outside prison walls. Murder of an inmate, a guard, or one of their family members on the outside is a common form of gang discipline and control, as well as a condition for membership in some gangs. Testifying against, or otherwise informing on, gang activities can invite one's own death sentence."

Beyond ensuring life's necessities for inmates, the Court has consistently recognized inmates' claims in only two areas: their due-process right of access to the courts and their liberty interest in retaining "good time" and avoiding solitary confinement. Concerning the former, the Court has repeatedly insisted that inmates have the right to access to legal redress and that this right of access to the courts requires either an adequate law library or assistance from persons trained in the law (although not necessarily lawyers). Concerning the latter, the Court held in *Wolf v. McDonnell* that inmates have a liberty interest in the good-time credit they have acquired and that they may not be stripped of these credits without a hearing before an impartial tribunal. The Court has not considered either of these rights to jeopardize prison security. Access to the courts poses no problems at all, and, as the Court made explicit in *Hewitt v. Helms* (1978) and *Superintendent v. Hill* (1985), prison disciplinary proceedings can follow (and need not precede) solitary confinement and can impose sanctions based on the lax evidentiary standard of "some evidence."

RETROACTIVE APPLICATION OF
CRIMINAL PROCEDURE GUARANTEES

In interpreting the provisions of the Bill of Rights in such a manner as to expand the procedural protections of criminal defendants and incorporating those provisions through the Fourteenth Amendment to apply to the states, the Court has been forced to consider whether its interpretations and incorporations should be given retroactive effect—that is, whether they should be made available to criminal defendants whose cases had already been litigated under rules deemed constitutionally permissible at the time. Until 1965 this question was always answered in the affirmative, for reasons cited by Professor Herman Schwartz: "New constitutional doctrines are not conceptions but rather reflections of principles of 'ordered liberty' fundamental to our legal system. Such principles are equally applicable to past and present trials, for an ethical society cannot seek to retain the fruits of past defaults."[19]

Nevertheless, this commitment to unlimited retroactivity was abandoned in *Linkletter v. Walker* (1965), in which Justice Tom Clark concluded for a seven-member majority that the "Constitution neither prohibits nor requires retrospective effect." Instead, he argued, "We must . . . weigh the merits and demerits in each case by looking to the prior history of the rule in question, its purpose, effect, and whether retrospective operation will further or retard its operation." Several factors contributed to the Court's shift in this matter. The most important, perhaps, was the essentially activist character of the Warren Court. Ineluctable retroactivity was an automatic check, an inherent restraint, on judicial innovations because it required that the new rule be applied to all relevant previous cases and that judicial hearings be granted to all those convicted under the old rule to determine whether their rights had been violated and whether, as a consequence, they were eligible for a new trial, outright release, return of all fines, or even damages. It compelled the Court to confront in a most direct manner the possible undesirable consequences of adopting a new rule. A second factor in the Court's departure from unlimited retroactivity was its desire to forestall hostile public reaction to its more controversial decisions. A case in point was *Johnson v. New Jersey* (1966), which limited the retroactive effect of *Escobedo v. Illinois* and *Miranda v. Arizona* to those cases in which the trials had actually begun after the dates on which *Escobedo* and *Miranda* were decided. *Johnson* was an intensely practical decision by a Court attempting to minimize the hostility that *Escobedo* and *Miranda* had generated. A third, and closely related, factor behind the Court's shift was the volatile and provocative problem of federalism. The need to sustain and, indeed, encourage viable and healthy federal-state relationships often intruded on the Court's considerations of retroactivity. Each time the Court incorporated another Bill of Rights guarantee to apply to the states, it imposed new responsibilities on the states in the realm of criminal procedure. The inevitable consequence was hostility to federal court intervention. Aware of this exacerbating influence on already strained federal-state relations, the Court frequently sought to mitigate the tension by limiting the impact of its decisions to prospective application. Such Court awareness was apparent in *Linkletter v. Walker,* in which Justice Clark announced that retroactive application of *Mapp* would not "add harmony to the delicate state-federal relationship."

With virtually all the provisions of the Bill of Rights eventually incorporated to apply to the states, and with the advent of the more judicially restrained Burger and Rehnquist Courts, the problems posed by full retroactive application of criminal procedural guarantees largely disappeared. So, too, has the Court's adherence to *Linkletter*. In *Teague v. Lane* (1989), a majority of the Court rejected the *Linkletter* approach to retroactivity and agreed to apply the approach set forth by Justice Harlan in his opinions in *Desist v. United States* (1969) and *Mackey v. United States* (1971), pursuant to which new constitutional rules are to be applied to all cases on direct review that are not yet final but are not to be applied to previous final judgments attacked on collateral review, except in extraordinary cases in which "fundamental fairness" would be denied by not applying the new rule.

BASIC THEMES IN THE COURT'S CRIMINAL PROCEDURE DECISIONS

Four basic themes emerge from our review of what the Supreme Court has done in the realm of criminal procedure. In the first place, the Court has been required to pour meaning into the many ambiguous provisions of the Bill of Rights—a task it has accomplished through its power of judgment.

A second theme is the emphasis the Court has placed on protecting minority interests from the potentially tyrannical tendencies of the majority. Recognizing the unequal impact that criminal procedure has had on the poor and on racial minorities, the Court has undertaken to eliminate the official aspects of this inequality.

A third basic theme is the Court's growing insistence on uniform constitutional standards applicable in both state and federal systems. In so insisting, the justices have all but repudiated the traditional view that states are to serve as laboratories, experimenting with novel social and legal schemes and thereby sparing the nation as a whole of the need to suffer the consequences of failure. Although the Court's approach has ensured a certain uniformity of criminal procedure throughout the land, it has also stifled creativity, checked innovation, and jeopardized federalism—an important means to the overall ends of the Constitution.

But the movement toward broadly stated rulings is not an unmixed blessing, for it represents a substantial departure from the "judicial" function. Instead of judging the merits of a particular "case or controversy," as charged by Article III of the Constitution, the

Court has become increasingly involved in general lawmaking. The consequences of this shift are far-reaching. Lawmaking typically emphasizes the formulation and general administration of society-wide policies; it is not concerned with the fates of particular individuals or the alleviation of specific instances of injustice. Traditionally, the latter concerns have been left to the judiciary, which understood its function to be the dispensation of justice and equity on an individual, case-by-case level. As the Court abandons this traditional role, there appears to be no other institution ready to step in and take its place.

NOTES

1. *California v. Hodari D.* (1991) dealt with the question of when an arrest actually takes place. Hodari D., a juvenile, fled when a police car approached him. An officer gave chase on foot, whereupon the juvenile tossed away what appeared to be a small rock. The officer tackled and handcuffed the juvenile; recovered the discarded rock, which was found to be crack cocaine; and charged him with drug possession. The juvenile's attorneys sought to suppress the evidence of cocaine, claiming that it was the fruit of an illegal search. They claimed that the juvenile was "seized" or placed under arrest at the moment the officer made a "show of authority" by beginning to run toward him, that at that time the police officer did not have reasonable grounds to suspect that the juvenile had crack cocaine in his possession, and that therefore the discarded cocaine could not be introduced as evidence because the grounds for the arrest must exist for the search incident to the arrest to be valid. The prosecution contended that the juvenile, by fleeing, ignored the police officer's "show of authority" and was not "seized" or arrested until he was tackled, that the crack cocaine was discarded prior to the arrest, and that therefore the recovered drug could be used as a valid basis for the arrest. The Supreme Court, in a 7–2 opinion, overturned a California court of appeals decision and agreed with the prosecution. Justice Scalia declared, "An arrest requires either physical force or, where that is absent, submission to the assertion of authority."

2. *Chimel* did not qualify the "plain view" exception: incident to arrest, instrumentalities of crime can be seized if they are in plain view, even if they are not within the immediate control of the person arrested. *Arizona v. Hicks* (1987) makes clear, however, that there is a "distinction between 'looking' at a suspicious object in plain view and 'moving' it even a few inches." In a 6–3 decision, the Court overturned the conviction of the defendant for armed robbery because, although the police officer had a right to be in the room where a turntable was in plain view, his suspicion that the turntable was stolen and his movement of the turntable several

inches so that he could read the serial number on its back constituted an unreasonable search in the absence of a search warrant.

3. A related issue is whether the Fourth Amendment prohibits a warrantless search and seizure of garbage left for collection on the street curb. In *California v. Greenwood* (1988), the Court held in a 7–2 decision that the respondents, who were convicted of narcotic trafficking based on evidence found in garbage they had placed at their curb, had no "objectively reasonable" expectation of privacy in their garbage, as "it is common knowledge that plastic garbage bags left on or at the side of a public street are readily accessible to animals, children, scavengers, snoops, and other members of the public. . . . Moreover, respondents placed their refuse at the curb for the express purpose of conveying it to a third party, the trash collector, who might himself have sorted through respondents' trash or permitted others, such as the police, to do so."

4. Eve Brensike Primus, "Disentangling Administrative Searches," *Columbia Law Review* 111 (2011): 255.

5. See Dallin H. Oaks, "Studying the Exclusionary Rule in Search and Seizure," *University of Chicago Law Review* 37 (1970): 665–753; John Kaplan, "The Limits of the Exclusionary Rule," *Stanford Law Review* 26 (1974): 1027–1055; and Steven Schlesinger, *Exclusionary Injustice* (New York: Marcel Dekker, 1977).

6. This, of course, was to change in *Duncan v. Louisiana*, 391 U.S. 145 (1968). See Chapter 3.

7. *Spano v. New York* (1959).

8. *Rodgers v. Richmond* (1961).

9. *Lynumn v. Illinois* (1963).

10. *Townsend v. Sain* (1963).

11. *Harris* raises serious questions: Will not juries who hear statements, introduced as evidence, that the defendant is lying on the witness stand simply treat these statements as evidence of guilt? Will they be able to govern their thoughts by this subtle distinction?

12. Because the defendant in *Argersinger* had been convicted of carrying a concealed weapon

and sentenced to ninety days in jail, the Court left unconsidered the question of whether counsel was required even in cases in which there was no prospect of imprisonment (i.e., in which only a fine was imposed). That issue was resolved in *Scott v. Illinois* (1979), in which the Court limited the *Argersinger* holding to instances in which the defendant is in fact sentenced to a term of imprisonment. See also *Alabama v. Shelton* (2002), in which the Court held, 5–4, that a suspended sentence that may "end up in the actual deprivation of a person's liberty" may not be imposed unless the indigent defendant has been provided the assistance of court-appointed counsel.

13. See *McNeil v. Wisconsin* (1991), in which the Court held that individuals have two separate and distinct rights to counsel. They have a Sixth Amendment right, which is offense specific and does not attach until the initiation of adversary judicial proceedings, and a *Miranda,* or Fifth Amendment, right, which is not offense specific and is intended to protect a suspect's "desire to deal with the police only through counsel."

14. *Sorrells v. United States* (1932).

15. *Hampton v. United States* (1976), *United States v. Russell* (1973), *Sherman v. United States* (1958), and *Sorrells v. United States* (1932).

16. *Neder v. United States* (1999), Justice Scalia dissenting.

17. Ralph A. Rossum, "The Problem of Prison Crowding: On the Limits of Prison Capacity and Judicial Capacity," *Benchmark* 1, no. 6 (1984): 22–30.

18. However, in *Johnson v. California* (2005), the Court rejected the *Turner* reasonableness test it has consistently used in cases involving the First Amendment and decided, 6–2, that strict scrutiny was the proper standard for reviewing a Fourteenth Amendment Equal Protection Clause challenge to California's unwritten policy of racially segregating prisoners in double cells in reception centers for up to sixty days each time they enter a new correctional facility to prevent violence caused by racial gangs.

19. Herman Schwartz, "Retroactivity, Reliability, and Due Process," *University of Chicago Law Review* 33 (1966): 753.

SELECTED READINGS

Amar, Akhil Reed. "Double Jeopardy Law Made Simple," *Yale Law Journal* 106 (April 1997): 1807–1848.

———. *The Constitution and Criminal Procedure.* New Haven, CT: Yale University Press, 1997.

Berger, Raoul. *Death Penalties: The Supreme Court's Obstacle Course.* Cambridge, MA: Harvard University Press, 1982.

Berns, Walter F. *For Capital Punishment: Crime and the Morality of the Death Penalty.* New York: Basic Books, 1979.

Black, Charles L. *Capital Punishment: The Inevitability of Caprice and Mistake.* New York: Norton, 1974.

Bodenhamer, David J. *Fair Trial: Rights of the Accused in American History.* New York: Oxford University Press, 1992.

Brennan, William J. "Constitutional Adjudication and the Death Penalty: A View from the Court." *Harvard Law Review* 100 (December 1986): 313–331.

Calabresi, Steven G., and Stephanie Dotson Zimdahl. "The Supreme Court and Foreign Sources of Law: Two Hundred Years of Practice and the Juvenile Death Penalty Decision." *William and Mary Law Review* 47 (December 2005): 743–909.

Chemerinsky, Erwin. "The Court Should Have Remained Silent: Why the Court Erred in De-ciding *Dickerson v. United States.*" *University of Pennsylvania Law Review* 149 (November 2000): 287–308.

Davies, Thomas Y. "'Not 'the Framers' Design': How the Framing-Era Ban Against Hearsay Evidence Refutes the *Crawford-Davis* 'Testimonial' Formulation of the Scope of the Original Confrontation Clause." *Journal of Law and Policy* 15 (2007): 349–469.

Hickok, Eugene W., ed. *The Bill of Rights: Original Meaning and Current Understanding.* University Press of Virginia, 1991.

Israel, Jerold H., Yale Kamisar, Wayne R. LaFave, and Nancy J. King. *Criminal Procedure and the Constitution: Leading Supreme Court Cases and Introductory Text.* St. Paul, MN: West Publishing, 2016.

Kamisar, Yale. "Is the Exclusionary Rule an 'Illogical' or 'Unnatural' Interpretation of the Fourth Amendment?" *Judicature* 62 (April 1978): 66–84.

Keenan, Dylan O. "Confronting *Crawford v. Washington* in the Lower Courts." *Yale Law Journal* 122 (2012): 782–836.

Kennedy, Randall. *Race, Crime, and the Law.* New York: *Pantheon* Books, 1997.

Levy, Leonard. *Origins of the Fifth Amendment: The Right Against Self-Incrimination.* New York: Ivan R. Dee, 1999.

_____. *The Palladium of Justice: Origins of Trial by Jury.* New York: Ivan R. Dee, 2000.

Lewis, Anthony. *Gideon's Trumpet.* New York: Vintage, 1964.

Long, Carolyn N. *Mapp v. Ohio: Guarding Against Unreasonable Searches and Seizures.* Lawrence: University Press of Kansas, 2006.

Morse, Stephen J., and Morris B. Hoffman. "The Uneasy Entente Between Legal Insanity and Mens Rea: Beyond *Clark v. Arizona.*" *Journal of Criminal Law and Criminology* 97 (2007): 1071–1149.

Oaks, Dallin H. "Studying the Exclusionary Rule in Search and Seizure." *University of Chicago Law Review* 37 (1970): 665–753.

Palmer, Louis J., Jr. *The Death Penalty in the United States: A Complete Guide to Federal and State Laws.* Jefferson: NC: McFarland & Company, 2014.

Rossum, Ralph A. "The Entrapment Defense and the Teaching of Political Responsibility: The Supreme Court as Republican Schoolmaster." *American Journal of Criminal Law* 6 (1978): 287–306.

_____. *The Politics of the Criminal Justice System: An Organizational Analysis.* New York: Marcel Dekker, 1978.

Scheb, John M., and John M. Scheb II, *Criminal Law and Procedure.* Belmont, CA: Wadsworth, 2013.

Schlesinger, Steven R. *Exclusionary Injustice.* New York: Marcel Dekker, 1977.

Schulhofer, Stephen J. *More Essential Than Ever: The Fourth Amendment in the Twenty-First Century.* New York: Oxford University Press, 2012.

Tarr, G. Alan, and Mary Cornelia Porter. *State Supreme Courts in State and Nation.* New Haven, CT: Yale University Press, 1988.

Turner, Ronald. "The Juvenile Death Penalty and the Court's Consensus-Plus Eighth Amendment." *George Mason University Civil Rights Law Journal* 17 (Winter 2006): 157–197.

Vollum, Scott, Rolando del Carmen, Durant Frantzen, Claudio San Miguel, and Kelly Cheeseman, *The Death Penalty: Constitutional Issues, Commentaries, and Case Briefs.* New York: Routledge, 2014.

Wilbanks, William. *The Myth of a Racist Criminal Justice System.* Monterey, CA: Brooks/Cole, 1987.

Stogner v. California
539 U.S. 607 (2003)

In 1993, California enacted a new criminal statute of limitations permitting prosecution for sex-related child abuse where the prior limitations period has expired if the prosecution is begun within one year of a victim's report to police. In 1996, it subsequently added a provision making it clear that this law revives causes of action barred by prior limitations statutes. In 1998, Marion Stogner was indicted for sex-related child abuse of his two daughters committed between 1955 and 1973. At the time those crimes were allegedly committed, the limitations period was three years. Stogner moved to dismiss the complaint on the ground that the Ex Post Facto *Clause forbids revival of a previously time-barred prosecution. The trial court agreed, but the California Court of Appeals reversed. The trial court denied Stogner's subsequent dismissal motion, in which he argued that his prosecution violated the* Ex Post Facto *and Due Process Clauses. The court of appeals affirmed Stogner's conviction, and the US Supreme Court granted certiorari.* Opinion of the Court: <u>Breyer</u>, Stevens, O'Connor, Souter, Ginsburg. Dissenting opinion: <u>Kennedy</u>, Rehnquist, Scalia, Thomas.

JUSTICE BREYER delivered the opinion of the Court.

The Constitution's two *Ex Post Facto* Clauses prohibit the Federal Government and the States from enacting laws with certain retroactive effects. The law at issue here created a new criminal limitations period that extends the time in which prosecution is allowed. It authorized criminal prosecutions that the passage of time had previously barred. Moreover, it was enacted after prior limitations periods for Stogner's alleged offenses had expired. Do these features of the law, taken together, produce the kind of retroactivity that the Constitution forbids? We conclude that they do.

First, the new statute threatens the kinds of harm that, in this Court's view, the *Ex Post Facto* Clause seeks to avoid. Long ago the Court pointed out that the Clause protects liberty by preventing governments from enacting statutes with "manifestly *unjust and oppressive*" retroactive effects. *Calder v. Bull* (1798). Judge

Learned Hand later wrote that extending a limitations period after the State has assured "a man that he has become safe from its pursuit . . . seems to most of us unfair and dishonest." *Falter v. United States* (1928). In such a case, the government has refused "to play by its own rules." It has deprived the defendant of the "fair warning" that might have led him to preserve exculpatory evidence.

Second, the kind of statute at issue falls literally within the categorical descriptions of *ex post facto* laws set forth by Justice Chase more than 200 years ago in *Calder v. Bull*—a categorization that this Court has recognized as providing an authoritative account of the scope of the *Ex Post Facto* Clause. Drawing substantially on Richard Wooddeson's 18th-century commentary on the nature of *ex post facto* laws and past parliamentary abuses, Chase divided *ex post facto* laws into categories that he described in two alternative ways. He wrote:

> I will state what laws I consider *ex post facto* laws, within the words and the intent of the prohibition. 1st. Every law that makes an action done before the passing of the law, and which was innocent when done, criminal; and punishes such action. *2d. Every law that aggravates a crime, or makes it greater than it was, when committed.* 3d. Every law that changes the punishment, and inflicts a greater punishment, than the law annexed to the crime, when committed. *4th. Every law that alters the legal rules of evidence, and receives less, or different, testimony, than the law required at the time of the commission of the offence, in order to convict the offender.* All these, and similar laws, are manifestly unjust and oppressive. (emphasis altered from original)

In his alternative description, Chase traced these four categories back to Parliament's earlier abusive acts, as follows: Category 1: "Sometimes they respected the crime, by declaring acts to be treason, which were not treason, when committed." Category 2: "*At other times they inflicted punishments, where the party was not, by law, liable to any punishment."* Category 3: "In other cases, they inflicted greater punishment, than the law annexed to the offence." Category 4: *"At other times, they violated the rules of evidence (to supply a deficiency of legal proof) by admitting one witness, when the existing law required two; by receiving evidence without oath; or the oath of the wife against the husband; or other testimony, which the courts of justice would not admit."* (emphasis altered from original.)

The second category—including any "law that *aggravates a crime,* or makes it *greater* than it was, when committed"—describes California's statute as long as those words are understood as Justice Chase understood them—*i.e.,* as referring to a statute that "inflicts *punishments,* where the party was not, by *law,* liable to *any punishment."* After (but not before) the original statute of limitations had expired, a party such as Stogner was not "liable to any punishment." California's new statute therefore "aggravated" Stogner's alleged crime, or made it "greater than it was, when committed," in the sense that, and to the extent that, it "inflicted punishment" for past criminal conduct that (when the new law was enacted) did not trigger any such liability. . . .

In finding that California's law falls within the literal terms of Justice Chase's second category, we do not deny that it may fall within another category as well. Justice Chase's fourth category, for example, includes any "law that alters the *legal* rules of *evidence,* and receives less, or different, testimony, than the law required at the time of the commission of the offence, *in order to convict the offender."* This Court has described that category as including laws that diminish "the quantum of evidence required to convict."

Significantly, a statute of limitations reflects a legislative judgment that, after a certain time, no quantum of evidence is sufficient to convict. And that judgment typically rests, in large part, upon evidentiary concerns—for example, concern that the passage of time has eroded memories or made witnesses or other evidence unavailable. Indeed, this Court once described statutes of limitations as creating "a presumption which renders proof unnecessary."

Consequently, to resurrect a prosecution after the relevant statute of limitations has expired is to eliminate a currently existing conclusive presumption forbidding prosecution, and thereby to permit conviction on a quantum of evidence where that quantum, at the time the new law is enacted, would have been legally insufficient. And, in that sense, the new law would "violate" previous evidence-related legal rules by authorizing the courts to "receive evidence . . . which the courts of justice would not [previously have] admitted" as sufficient proof of a crime. Nonetheless, given Justice Chase's description of the second category, we need not explore the fourth category, or other categories, further.

Third, likely for the reasons just stated, numerous legislators, courts, and commentators have long believed it well settled that the *Ex Post Facto* Clause forbids resurrection of a time-barred prosecution. Such sentiments appear already to have been widespread when the Reconstruction Congress of 1867—the Congress that drafted the Fourteenth Amendment—rejected a bill that would have revived time-barred prosecutions for treason that various Congressmen wanted brought against Jefferson Davis and "his coconspirators." Radical Republicans such as Roscoe Conkling and Thaddeus Stevens, no friends of the South, opposed the bill because, in their minds, it proposed an *"ex post facto* law" and threatened an injustice tantamount to "judicial murder." In this instance, Congress ultimately passed a law extending *unexpired* limitations periods—a tailored approach to extending limitations periods that has also been taken in modern statutes.

Further, Congressmen such as Conkling were not the only ones who believed that laws reviving time-barred prosecutions are *ex post facto.* That view was echoed in roughly contemporaneous opinions by State Supreme Courts. . . .

This Court itself has not previously spoken decisively on this matter. . . . [W]e believe that the outcome of this case is determined by the nature of the harms that California's law creates, by the fact that the law falls within Justice Chase's second category as Chase understood that category, and by a long line of authority holding that a law of this type violates the *Ex Post Facto* Clause. . . .

We disagree strongly with the dissent's ultimate conclusion about the fairness of resurrecting a long-dead prosecution. Rather, like Judge Learned Hand, we believe that this retroactive application of a later-enacted law is unfair. And, like most other judges who have addressed this issue, we find the words *"ex post facto"* applicable to describe this kind of unfairness. . . . In our view, th[e dissent's] reading is too narrow; it is unsupported by precedent; and it would deny liberty where the Constitution gives protection. . . .

[T]he dissent ignores the potentially lengthy period of time (in this case, 22 years) during which the accused lacked notice that he might be prosecuted and during which he was unaware, for example, of any need to preserve evidence of innocence. Memories fade, and witnesses can die or disappear. Such problems can plague child abuse cases, where recollection after so many years may be uncertain, and "recovered" memories faulty, but may nonetheless lead to prosecutions that destroy families.

. . . [W]e agree that the State's interest in prosecuting child abuse cases is an important one. But there is also a predominating constitutional interest in forbidding the State to revive a long-forbidden prosecution. And to hold that such a law is *ex post facto* does not prevent the State from extending time limits for the prosecution of future offenses, or for prosecutions not yet time barred.

The statute before us is unfairly retroactive as applied to Stogner. A long line of judicial authority supports characterization of this law as *ex post facto.* For the reasons stated, we believe the law falls within Justice Chase's second category of *ex post facto* laws. We conclude that a law enacted after expiration of a previously applicable limitations period violates the *Ex Post Facto* Clause when it is applied to revive a previously time-barred prosecution. The California court's judgment to the contrary is reversed.

JUSTICE KENNEDY, with whom THE CHIEF JUSTICE, JUSTICE SCALIA, and JUSTICE THOMAS join, dissenting.

California has enacted a retroactive extension of statutes of limitations for serious sexual offenses committed against minors. The new period includes cases where the limitations period has expired before the effective date of the legislation. To invalidate the statute in the latter circumstance, the Court tries to force it into the second category of *Calder v. Bull* which prohibits a retroactive law "'that *aggravates a crime,* or makes it *greater* than it was, when committed.'" These words, in my view, do not permit the Court's holding, but indeed foreclose it. A law which does not alter the definition of the crime but only revives prosecution does not make the crime "greater than it was, when committed." Until today, a plea in bar has not been thought to form any part of the definition of the offense. . . .

The majority seems to suggest that retroactive extension of expired limitations periods is "'arbitrary and potentially vindictive legislation,'" but does not attempt to support this accusation. And it could not do so. The California statute can be explained as motivated by legitimate concerns about the continuing suffering endured by the victims of childhood abuse.

The California Legislature noted that "young victims often delay reporting sexual abuse because they are easily manipulated by offenders in positions of authority and trust, and because children have difficulty remembering the crime or facing the trauma it can cause." The concern is amply supported by empirical studies.

The problem the legislature sought to address is illustrated well by this case. Petitioner's older daughter testified she did not report the abuse because she was afraid of her father and did not believe anyone would help her. After she left petitioner's home, she tried to forget the abuse. Petitioner's younger daughter did not report the abuse because she was scared. He tried to convince her it was a normal way of life. Even after she moved out of petitioner's house, she was afraid to speak for fear she would not be believed. She tried to pretend she had a normal childhood. It was only her realization that the father continued to abuse other children in the family that led her to disclose the abuse, in order to protect them.

The Court tries to counter by saying the California statute is "'unfair and dishonest'" because it violated the State's initial assurance to the offender that "'he has become safe from its pursuit'" and deprived him of "the 'fair warning.'" The fallacy of this rationale is apparent when we recall that the Court is careful to leave in place the uniform decisions by state and federal courts to uphold retroactive extension of unexpired statutes of limitations against an *ex post facto* challenge. . . .

When a child molester commits his offense, he is well aware the harm will plague the victim for a lifetime. The victims whose interests [that the California law] takes into consideration have been subjected to sexual abuse within the confines of their own homes and by people they trusted and relied upon for protection. A familial figure of authority can use a confidential relation to conceal a crime. The violation of this trust inflicts deep and lasting hurt. Its only poor remedy is that the law will show its compassion and concern when the victim at last can find the strength, and know the necessity, to come forward. When the criminal has taken distinct advantage of the tender years and perilous position of a fearful victim, it is the victim's lasting hurt, not the perpetrator's fictional reliance, that the law should count the higher. The victims whose cause is now before the Court have at last overcome shame and the desire to repress these painful memories. They have reported the crimes so that the violators are brought to justice and harm to others is prevented. The Court now tells the victims their decision to come forward is in vain.

The gravity of the crime was known, and is being measured, by its wrongfulness when committed. It is a common policy for States to suspend statutes of limitations for civil harms against minors, in order to "protect minors during the period when they are unable to protect themselves." Some States toll the limitations periods for minors even where a guardian is appointed and even when the tolling conflicts with statutes of repose. The difference between suspension and reactivation is so slight

that it is fictional for the Court to say, in the given context, the new policy somehow alters the magnitude of the crime. The wrong was made clear by the law at the time of the crime's commission. The criminal actor knew it, even reveled in it. It is the commission of the then-unlawful act that the State now seeks to punish. The gravity of the crime is left unchanged by altering a statute of limitations of which the actor was likely not at all aware.

The California statute does not fit any of the remaining *Calder* categories: It does not criminalize conduct which was innocent when done; it allows the prosecutor to seek the same punishment as the law authorized at the time the offense was committed and no more; and it does not alter the government's burden to establish the elements of the crime. Any concern about stale evidence can be addressed by the judge and the jury, and by the requirement of proof beyond reasonable doubt. [The California law], moreover, contains an additional safeguard: It conditions prosecution on a presentation of independent evidence that corroborates the victim's allegations by clear and convincing evidence. These protections, as well as the general protection against oppressive prosecutions offered by the Due Process Clause, should assuage the majority's fear that the statute will have California overrun by vindictive prosecutions resting on unreliable recovered memories. . . .

The Court's stretching of *Calder's* second category contradicts the historical understanding of that category, departs from established precedent, and misapprehends the purposes of the *Ex Post Facto* Clause. The Court also disregards the interests of those victims of child abuse who have found the courage to face their accusers and bring them to justice. The Court's opinion harms not only our *ex post facto* jurisprudence but also these and future victims of child abuse, and so compels my respectful dissent.

Smith v. Doe
538 U.S. 84 (2003)

Like all other states, Alaska enacted a version of "Megan's Law," named for Megan Kanka, a seven-year-old New Jersey girl who was sexually *assaulted and murdered by a neighbor who, unknown to the victim's family, had prior convictions for sex offenses against children. Alaska's version, the Alaska Sex Offender Registration Act, was passed in 1994 and contains two components: a registration requirement and a notification requirement. It requires persons convicted of sex or child-kidnapping offenses to register with state or local law-enforcement authorities (offenders convicted of a single nonaggravated sex crime must provide annual verification of registration information for fifteen years; offenders convicted of aggravated sex crimes or of two or more sex offenses must register for life and verify information quarterly), and it requires the Alaska Department of Public Safety, to whom this registration information is forwarded, to make available to the public their names, aliases, addresses, photographs, physical descriptions, driver's license numbers, motor vehicle identification numbers, places of employment, dates of birth, crimes, dates and places of conviction, lengths and conditions of sentences, and statements as to whether the offenders are in compliance with the act's requirements or cannot be located. The act does not specify how this information is to be made available to the public, and the Department of Public Safety chose to meet this notification requirement by posting this information on the Internet. Both the act's registration and notification requirements were retroactive. Two individuals convicted of aggravated sex offenses prior to the statute's enactment, together with the wife of one of these offenders, brought suit in the United States District Court for the District of Alaska, seeking a declaration that the act was void under the* Ex Post Facto *Clause of Article I, Section 10. The district court granted summary judgment against these three individuals; however, on appeal, the United States Court of Appeals for the Ninth Circuit reversed, holding the Alaska statute violated the* Ex Post Facto *Clause, because, although the Alaska Legislature had intended that this statute would provide a nonpunitive and civil regulatory scheme, the statute's effects were punitive. The Supreme Court granted certiorari.* Opinion of the Court: <u>Kennedy</u>, Rehnquist, O'Connor, Scalia, Thomas. Concurring opinion: <u>Thomas</u>. Concurring in the judgment: <u>Souter</u>. Dissenting opinions: <u>Stevens</u>; <u>Ginsburg</u>, Breyer.

JUSTICE KENNEDY delivered the opinion of the Court.

This is the first time we have considered a claim that a sex offender registration and noti-fication law constitutes retroactive punishment forbidden by the *Ex Post Facto* Clause. The framework for our inquiry, however, is well established. We must "ascertain whether the legislature meant the statute to establish 'civil' proceedings." *Kansas v. Hendricks* (1997). If the intention of the legislature was to impose punishment, that ends the inquiry. If, however, the intention was to enact a regulatory scheme that is civil and nonpunitive, we must further examine whether the statutory scheme is "'so punitive either in purpose or effect as to negate [the State's] intention' to deem it 'civil.'" Because we "ordinarily defer to the legislature's stated intent," "'only the clearest proof' will suffice to override legislative intent and transform what has been denominated a civil remedy into a criminal penalty."

Whether a statutory scheme is civil or criminal "is first of all a question of statutory construction." We consider the statute's text and its structure to determine the legislative objective. A conclusion that the legislature intended to punish would satisfy an *ex post facto* challenge without further inquiry into its effects, so considerable deference must be accorded to the intent as the legislature has stated it.

The courts "must first ask whether the legislature, in establishing the penalizing mechanism, indicated either expressly or impliedly a preference for one label or the other." Here, the Alaska Legislature expressed the objective of the law in the statutory text itself. The legislature found that "sex offenders pose a high risk of reoffending," and identified "protecting the public from sex offenders" as the "primary governmental interest" of the law. The legislature further determined that "release of certain information about sex offenders to public agencies and the general public will assist in protecting the public safety." As we observed in *Hendricks*, where we examined an *ex post facto* challenge to a post-incarceration confinement of sex offenders, an imposition of restrictive measures on sex offenders adjudged to be dangerous is "a legitimate nonpunitive governmental objective and has been historically so regarded." In this case . . . , "nothing on the face of the statute suggests that the legislature sought to create anything other than a civil . . . scheme designed to protect the public from harm." . . .

We conclude, as did the District Court and the Court of Appeals, that the intent of the Alaska Legislature was to create a civil, nonpunitive regime.

In analyzing the effects of the Act we refer to the seven factors noted in *Kennedy v. Mendoza-Martinez* (1963), as a useful framework. . . . The factors most relevant to our analysis are whether, in its necessary operation, the regulatory scheme: has been regarded in our history and traditions as a punishment; imposes an affirmative disability or restraint; promotes the traditional aims of punishment; has a rational connection to a nonpunitive purpose; or is excessive with respect to this purpose.

A historical survey can be useful because a State that decides to punish an individual is likely to select a means deemed punitive in our tradition, so that the public will recognize it as such. The Court of Appeals observed that the sex offender registration and notification statutes "are of fairly recent origin," which suggests that the statute was not meant as a punitive measure, or, at least, that it did not involve a traditional means of punishing. Respondents argue, however, that the Act—and, in particular, its notification provisions—resemble shaming punishments of the colonial period.

Some colonial punishments indeed were meant to inflict public disgrace. Humiliated offenders were required "to stand in public with signs cataloguing their offenses." At times the labeling would be permanent: A murderer might be branded with an "M," and a thief with a "T." The aim was to make these offenders suffer "permanent stigmas, which in effect cast the person out of the community." The most serious offenders were banished, after which they could neither return to their original community nor, reputation tarnished, be admitted easily into a new one. Respondents contend that Alaska's compulsory registration and notification resemble these historical punishments, for they publicize the crime, associate it with his name, and, with the most serious offenders, do so for life.

Any initial resemblance to early punishments is, however, misleading. Punishments such as whipping, pillory, and branding inflicted physical pain and staged a direct confrontation between the offender and the public. Even punishments that lacked the corporal component, such as public shaming, humiliation, and banishment, involved more than the dissemination of information. They either held the person up before his fellow citizens for face-to-face shaming or expelled him from the community. By contrast, the stigma of Alaska's Megan's Law results not from public display for ridicule and shaming but from the dissemination of accurate information about a criminal record, most of which is already public. Our system does not treat dissemination of truthful information in furtherance of a legitimate governmental objective as punishment. On the contrary, our criminal law tradition insists on public indictment, public trial, and public imposition of sentence. Transparency is essential to maintaining public respect for the criminal justice system, ensuring its integrity, and protecting the rights of the accused. The publicity may cause adverse consequences for the convicted defendant, running from mild personal embarrassment to social ostracism. In contrast to the colonial shaming punishments, however, the State does not make the publicity and the resulting stigma an integral part of the objective of the regulatory scheme.

The fact that Alaska posts the information on the Internet does not alter our conclusion. It must be acknowledged that notice of a criminal conviction subjects the offender to public shame, the humiliation increasing in proportion to the extent of the publicity. And the geographic reach of the Internet is greater than anything which could have been designed in colonial times. These facts do not render Internet notification punitive. The purpose and the principal effect of notification are to inform the public for its own safety, not to humiliate the offender. Widespread public access is necessary for the efficacy of the scheme, and the attendant humiliation is but a collateral consequence of a valid regulation.

The State's website does not provide the public with means to shame the offender by, say, posting comments underneath his record. An individual seeking the information must take the initial step of going to the Department of Public Safety's website, proceed to the sex offender registry, and then look up the desired information. The process is more analogous to a visit to an official archive of criminal records than it is to a scheme forcing an offender to appear in public with some visible badge of past criminality. The Internet makes the document search more efficient, cost effective, and convenient for Alaska's citizenry.

We next consider whether the Act subjects respondents to an "affirmative disability or restraint." Here, we inquire how the effects of the Act are felt by those subject to it. If the disability or restraint is minor and indirect, its effects are unlikely to be punitive.

The Act imposes no physical restraint, and so does not resemble the punishment of imprisonment, which is the paradigmatic affirmative disability or restraint. The Act's obligations are less harsh than the sanctions of occupational debarment, which we have held to be nonpunitive. The Act does not restrain activities sex offenders may pursue but leaves them free to change jobs or residences. . . .

The Court of Appeals held that the registration system is parallel to probation or supervised release in terms of the restraint imposed. This argument has some force, but, after due consideration, we reject it. Probation and supervised release entail a series of mandatory conditions and allow the supervising officer to seek the revocation of probation or release in case of infraction. By contrast, offenders subject to the Alaska statute are free to move where they wish and to live and work as other citizens, with no supervision. Although registrants must inform the authorities after they change their facial features (such as growing a beard), borrow a car, or seek psychiatric treatment, they are not required to seek permission to do so. . . .

In concluding the Act was excessive in relation to its regulatory purpose, the Court of Appeals relied in large part on two propositions: first, that the statute applies to all convicted sex offenders without regard to their future dangerousness; and, second, that it places no limits on the number of persons who have access to the information. Neither argument is persuasive.

Alaska could conclude that a conviction for a sex offense provides evidence of substantial risk of recidivism. The legislature's findings are consistent with grave concerns over the high rate of recidivism among convicted sex offenders and their dangerousness as a class. . . .

The Court of Appeals' reliance on the wide dissemination of the information is also unavailing. The Ninth Circuit highlighted that the information was available "world-wide" and "broadcas[t]" in an indiscriminate manner. As we have explained, however, the notification system is a passive one: An individual must seek access to the information. . . .

Our examination of the Act's effects leads to the determination that respondents cannot show, much less by the clearest proof, that the effects of the law negate Alaska's intention to establish a civil regulatory scheme. The Act is nonpunitive, and its retroactive application does not violate the *Ex Post Facto* Clause. The judgment of the Court of Appeals for the Ninth Circuit is reversed, and the case is remanded for further proceedings consistent with this opinion.

JUSTICE SOUTER, concurring in the judgment.

. . . To me, the indications of punitive character . . . and the civil indications weighed heavily by the Court are in rough equipoise. Certainly the formal evidence of legislative intent does not justify requiring the "clearest proof" of penal substance in this case, and the substantial evidence does not affirmatively show with any clarity that the Act is valid. What tips the scale for me is the presumption of constitutionality normally accorded a State's law. That presumption gives the State the benefit of the doubt in close cases like this one, and on that basis alone I concur in the Court's judgment.

JUSTICE STEVENS, dissenting.

. . . No matter how often the Court may repeat and manipulate multifactor tests that have been applied in wholly dissimilar cases involving only one or two of these three aspects of these statutory sanctions, it will never persuade me that the registration and reporting obligations that are imposed on convicted sex offenders *and on no one else* as a result of their convictions are not part of their punishment. In my opinion, a sanction that (1) is imposed on everyone who commits a criminal offense, (2) is not imposed on anyone else, and (3) severely impairs a person's liberty is punishment. . . .

JUSTICE GINSBURG, with whom JUSTICE BREYER joins, dissenting.

Measured by the *Mendoza-Martinez* factors, I would hold Alaska's Act punitive in effect. Beyond doubt, the Act involves an "affirmative disability or restraint." Alaska's Act imposes onerous and intrusive obligations on convicted sex offenders; and it exposes registrants, through aggressive public notification of their crimes, to profound humiliation and community-wide ostracism. . . .

Telling too . . . past crime alone, not current dangerousness, is the "touchstone" triggering the Act's obligations. This touchstone adds to the impression that the Act retributively targets past guilt, *i.e.*, that it "revisits past crimes [more than it] prevents future ones."

What ultimately tips the balance for me is the Act's excessiveness in relation to its nonpunitive purpose. . . . The Act applies to all convicted sex offenders, without regard to their future dangerousness. And the duration of the reporting requirement is keyed not to any determination of a particular offender's risk of reoffending, but to whether the offense of conviction qualified as aggravated. The reporting requirements themselves are exorbitant: The Act requires aggravated offenders to engage in perpetual quarterly reporting, even if their personal information has not changed. And meriting heaviest weight in my judgment, the Act makes no provision whatever

for the possibility of rehabilitation: Offenders cannot shorten their registration or notification period, even on the clearest demonstration of rehabilitation or conclusive proof of physical incapacitation. However plain it may be that a former sex offender currently poses no threat of recidivism, he will remain subject to long-term monitoring and inescapable humiliation. John Doe I, for example, pleaded *nolo contendere* to a charge of sexual abuse of a minor nine years before the Alaska Act was enacted. He successfully completed a treatment program, and gained early release on supervised probation in part because of his compliance with the program's requirements and his apparent low risk of re-offense. He subsequently remarried, established a business, and was reunited with his family. He was also granted custody of a minor daughter, based on a court's determination that he had been successfully rehabilitated. The court's determination rested in part on psychiatric evaluations concluding that Doe had "a very low risk of re-offending" and is "not a pedophile." Notwithstanding this strong evidence of rehabilitation, the Alaska Act requires Doe to report personal information to the State four times per year, and permits the State publicly to label him a "Registered Sex Offender" for the rest of his life.

Satisfied that the Act is ambiguous in intent and punitive in effect, I would hold its retroactive application incompatible with the *Ex Post Facto* Clause, and would therefore affirm the judgment of the Court of Appeals.

Board of Education of Independent School District No. 92 of Pottawatomie County v. Earls
536 U.S. 822 (2002)

With evidence of increased drug use among its students, the Tecumseh, Oklahoma, school district adopted a Student Activities Drug Testing Policy, requiring all middle and high school students to consent to urinalysis testing for drugs in order to participate in any extracurricular activity. In practice, however, the policy was applied only to competitive extracurricular activities. Lindsay Earls was a student at Tecumseh High School and a member of the show choir, the marching band, *the Academic Team, and the National Honor Society. She and her parents brought a 42 U.S.C. §1983 action against the school district, alleging that its policy violated the Fourth Amendment. Applying Vernonia School District v. Acton (1995), in which the Supreme Court had upheld the suspicionless drug testing of school athletes, the US District Court granted the school district summary judgment. The Court of Appeals for the Tenth Circuit reversed. It announced that, before*

imposing a suspicionless drug testing program, a school "must demonstrate that there is some identifiable drug abuse problem among a sufficient number of those subject to the testing, such that testing that group of students will actually redress its drug problem." The court then held that the school district had failed to demonstrate such a problem among Tecumseh students participating in competitive extracurricular activities and declared the policy to violate the Fourth Amendment. The Supreme Court granted certiorari.
Opinion of the Court: Thomas, Rehnquist, Scalia, Kennedy, Breyer. Concurring opinion: Breyer. Dissenting opinions: O'Connor, Souter; Ginsburg, Stevens, O'Connor, Souter.

JUSTICE THOMAS delivered the opinion of the Court.

The Student Activities Drug Testing Policy implemented by the Board of Education of Independent School District No. 92 of Pottawatomie County (School District) requires all students who participate in competitive extracurricular activities to submit to drug testing. Because this Policy reasonably serves the School District's important interest in detecting and preventing drug use among its students, we hold that it is constitutional. . . .

The Fourth Amendment to the United States Constitution protects "the right of the people to be secure in their persons, houses, papers, and effects, against unreasonable searches and seizures." Searches by public school officials, such as the collection of urine samples, implicate Fourth Amendment interests. We must therefore review the School District's Policy for "reasonableness," which is the touchstone of the constitutionality of a governmental search.

In the criminal context, reasonableness usually requires a showing of probable cause. The probable-cause standard, however, "is peculiarly related to criminal investigations" and may be unsuited to determining the reasonableness of administrative searches where the "Government seeks to *prevent* the development of hazardous conditions." The Court has also held that a warrant and finding of probable cause are unnecessary in the public school context because such requirements "would unduly interfere with the maintenance of the swift and

informal disciplinary procedures [that are] needed." . . .

While schoolchildren do not shed their constitutional rights when they enter the schoolhouse, "Fourth Amendment rights . . . are different in public schools than elsewhere; the 'reasonableness' inquiry cannot disregard the schools' custodial and tutelary responsibility for children." *Vernonia.* In particular, a finding of individualized suspicion may not be necessary when a school conducts drug testing.

In *Vernonia,* this Court held that the suspicionless drug testing of athletes was constitutional. The Court, however, did not simply authorize all school drug testing, but rather conducted a fact-specific balancing of the intrusion on the children's Fourth Amendment rights against the promotion of legitimate governmental interests. Applying the principles of *Vernonia* to the somewhat different facts of this case, we conclude that Tecumseh's Policy is also constitutional.

We first consider the nature of the privacy interest allegedly compromised by the drug testing. As in *Vernonia,* the context of the public school environment serves as the backdrop for the analysis of the privacy interest at stake and the reasonableness of the drug testing policy in general. . . . A student's privacy interest is limited in a public school environment where the State is responsible for maintaining discipline, health, and safety. Schoolchildren are routinely required to submit to physical examinations and vaccinations against disease. Securing order in the school environment sometimes requires that students be subjected to greater controls than those appropriate for adults. . . .

Respondents argue that because children participating in nonathletic extracurricular activities are not subject to regular physicals and communal undress, they have a stronger expectation of privacy than the athletes tested in *Vernonia.* This distinction, however, was not essential to our decision in *Vernonia,* which depended primarily upon the school's custodial responsibility and authority.

In any event, students who participate in competitive extracurricular activities voluntarily subject themselves to many of the same intrusions on their privacy as do athletes. Some of these clubs and activities require occasional off-campus travel and communal undress. All of them have their own rules and requirements for participating students that do not apply to the student body as a whole. For example, each of the competitive extracurricular activities governed by the Policy must abide by the rules of the Oklahoma Secondary Schools Activities Association, and a faculty sponsor monitors the students for compliance with the various rules dictated by the clubs and activities. This regulation of extracurricular activities further diminishes the expectation of privacy among schoolchildren. We therefore conclude that the students affected by this Policy have a limited expectation of privacy.

Next, we consider the character of the intrusion imposed by the Policy. Urination is "an excretory function traditionally shielded by great privacy." But the "degree of intrusion" on one's privacy caused by collecting a urine sample "depends upon the manner in which production of the urine sample is monitored."

Under the Policy, a faculty monitor waits outside the closed restroom stall for the student to produce a sample and must "listen for the normal sounds of urination in order to guard against tampered specimens and to insure an accurate chain of custody." The monitor then pours the sample into two bottles that are sealed and placed into a mailing pouch along with a consent form signed by the student. This procedure is virtually identical to that reviewed in *Vernonia,* except that it additionally protects privacy by allowing male students to produce their samples behind a closed stall. Given that we considered the method of collection in *Vernonia* a "negligible" intrusion, the method here is even less problematic.

In addition, the Policy clearly requires that the test results be kept in confidential files separate from a student's other educational records and released to school personnel only on a "need to know" basis. . . .

Moreover, the test results are not turned over to any law enforcement authority. Nor do the test results here lead to the imposition of discipline or have any academic consequences. Rather, the only consequence of a failed drug test is to limit the student's privilege of participating in extracurricular activities. Indeed, a student may test positive for drugs twice and still be allowed to participate in extracurricular activities. After the first positive test, the school contacts the student's parent or guardian for a meeting. The student may continue to participate in the activity if within five days of the meeting the student shows proof of receiving drug counseling and submits to a second drug test in two weeks. For the second positive test, the student is suspended from participation in all extracurricular activities for 14 days, must complete four hours of substance abuse counseling, and must submit to monthly drug tests. Only after a third positive test will the student be suspended from participating in any extracurricular activity for the remainder of the school year, or 88 school days, whichever is longer. Given the minimally intrusive nature of the sample collection and the limited uses to which the test results are put, we conclude that the invasion of students' privacy is not significant.

Finally, this Court must consider the nature and immediacy of the government's concerns and the efficacy of the Policy in meeting them. This Court has already articulated in detail the importance of the governmental concern in preventing drug use by schoolchildren. The drug abuse problem among our Nation's youth has hardly abated since *Vernonia* was decided in 1995. In fact, evidence suggests that it has only grown worse. As in *Vernonia,* "the necessity for the State to act is magnified by the fact that this evil is being visited not just upon individuals at large, but upon children for whom it has undertaken a special responsibility of care and direction." The health and safety risks identified in *Vernonia* apply with equal force to Tecumseh's children. Indeed, the nationwide drug epidemic makes the war against drugs a pressing concern in every school.

Additionally, the School District in this case has presented specific evidence of drug use at Tecumseh schools. Teachers testified that they had seen students who appeared to be under the influence of drugs and that they had heard students speaking openly about using drugs. . . . We decline to second-guess the finding of the District Court that "viewing the evidence as a whole, it cannot be reasonably disputed that the [School District] was faced with a 'drug problem' when it adopted the Policy." . . .

Furthermore, this Court has not required a particularized or pervasive drug problem before allowing the government to conduct suspicionless drug testing. For instance, in [*Treasury Employees v.*] *Von Raab* (1989), the Court upheld the drug testing of customs officials on a purely preventive basis, without any documented history of drug use by such officials. . . .

Given the nationwide epidemic of drug use, and the evidence of increased drug use in Tecumseh schools, it was entirely reasonable for the School District to enact this particular drug testing policy. We reject the Court of Appeals' novel test that "any district seeking to impose a random suspicionless drug testing policy as a condition to participation in a school activity must demonstrate that there is some identifiable drug abuse problem among a sufficient number of those subject to the testing, such that testing that group of students will actually redress its drug problem." Among other problems, it would be difficult to administer such a test. As we cannot articulate a threshold level of drug use that would suffice to justify a drug testing program for schoolchildren, we refuse to fashion what would in effect be a constitutional quantum of drug use necessary to show a "drug problem."

Respondents also argue that the testing of nonathletes does not implicate any safety concerns, and that safety is a "crucial factor" in applying the special needs framework. . . . [B]ut the safety interest furthered by drug testing is undoubtedly substantial for all children, athletes and nonathletes alike. We know all too well that drug use carries a variety of health risks for children, including death from overdose.

We also reject respondents' argument that drug testing must presumptively be based upon an individualized reasonable suspicion of wrongdoing because such a testing regime would be less intrusive. In this context, the Fourth Amendment does not require a finding of individualized suspicion, and we decline to impose such a requirement on schools attempting to prevent and detect drug use by students. Moreover, we question whether testing based on individualized suspicion in fact would be less intrusive. Such a regime would place an additional burden on public school teachers who are already tasked with the difficult job of maintaining order and discipline. A program of individualized suspicion might unfairly target members of unpopular groups. The fear of lawsuits resulting from such targeted searches may chill enforcement of the program, rendering it ineffective in combating drug use. In any case, this Court has repeatedly stated that reasonableness under the Fourth Amendment does not require employing the least intrusive means, because "the logic of such elaborate less-restrictive-alternative arguments could raise insuperable barriers to the exercise of virtually all search-and-seizure powers."

Finally, we find that testing students who participate in extracurricular activities is a reasonably effective means of addressing the School District's legitimate concerns in preventing, deterring, and detecting drug use. While in *Vernonia* there might have been a closer fit between the testing of athletes and the trial court's finding that the drug problem was "fueled by the 'role model' effect of athletes' drug use," such a finding was not essential to the holding. *Vernonia* did not require the school to test the group of students most likely to use drugs, but rather considered the constitutionality of the program in the context of the public school's custodial responsibilities. Evaluating the Policy in this context, we conclude that the drug testing of Tecumseh students who participate in extracurricular activities effectively serves the School District's interest in protecting the safety and health of its students.

Within the limits of the Fourth Amendment, local school boards must assess the desirability of drug testing schoolchildren. In upholding the constitutionality of the Policy, we express no opinion as to its wisdom. Rather, we hold only that Tecumseh's Policy is a reasonable means of furthering the School District's important interest in preventing and deterring drug use among its schoolchildren. Accordingly, we reverse the judgment of the Court of Appeals.

JUSTICE BREYER, concurring.

I agree with the Court that *Vernonia* governs this case and requires reversal of the Tenth

Circuit's decision. The school's drug testing program addresses a serious national problem by focusing upon demand, avoiding the use of criminal or disciplinary sanctions, and relying upon professional counseling and treatment. In my view, this program does not violate the Fourth Amendment's prohibition of "unreasonable searches and seizures." I reach this conclusion primarily for the reasons given by the Court, but I would emphasize several underlying considerations, which I understand to be consistent with the Court's opinion.

In respect to the school's need for the drug testing program, I would emphasize [that] . . . the program at issue here seeks to discourage demand for drugs by changing the school's environment in order to combat the single most important factor leading school children to take drugs, namely, peer pressure. It offers the adolescent a nonthreatening reason to decline his friend's drug-use invitations, namely, that he intends to play baseball, participate in debate, join the band, or engage in any one of half a dozen useful, interesting, and important activities.

In respect to the privacy-related burden that the drug testing program imposes upon students, I would emphasize [that] . . . the testing program avoids subjecting the entire school to testing. And it preserves an option for a conscientious objector. He can refuse testing while paying a price (nonparticipation) that is serious, but less severe than expulsion from the school. . . .

I cannot know whether the school's drug testing program will work. But, in my view, the Constitution does not prohibit the effort. . . . I conclude that the school's drug testing program, constitutionally speaking, is not "unreasonable." And I join the Court's opinion.

JUSTICE GINSBURG, with whom JUSTICE STEVENS, JUSTICE O'CONNOR, and JUSTICE SOUTER join, dissenting. . . .

"The legality of a search of a student," this Court has instructed, "should depend simply on the reasonableness, under all the circumstances, of the search." Although "'special needs' inhere in the public school context," those needs are not so expansive or malleable as to render reasonable any program of student drug testing a school district elects to install.

The particular testing program upheld today is not reasonable, it is capricious, even perverse: Petitioners' policy targets for testing a student population least likely to be at risk from illicit drugs and their damaging effects. I therefore dissent. . . .

This case presents circumstances dispositively different from those of *Vernonia*. . . .

The Vernonia district . . . had good reasons for testing athletes: Sports team members faced special health risks and they "were the leaders of the drug culture." No similar reason, and no other tenable justification, explains Tecumseh's decision to target for testing all participants in every competitive extracurricular activity.

Nationwide, students who participate in extracurricular activities are significantly less likely to develop substance abuse problems than are their less-involved peers. Even if students might be deterred from drug use in order to preserve their extracurricular eligibility, it is at least as likely that other students might forgo their extracurricular involvement in order to avoid detection of their drug use. Tecumseh's policy thus falls short doubly if deterrence is its aim: It invades the privacy of students who need deterrence least, and risks steering students at greatest risk for substance abuse away from extracurricular involvement that potentially may palliate drug problems.

To summarize, this case resembles *Vernonia* only in that the School Districts in both cases conditioned engagement in activities outside the obligatory curriculum on random subjection to urinalysis. The defining characteristics of the two programs, however, are entirely dissimilar. The Vernonia district sought to test a subpopulation of students distinguished by their reduced expectation of privacy, their special susceptibility to drug-related injury, and their heavy involvement with drug use. The Tecumseh district seeks to test a much larger population associated with none of these factors. It does so, moreover, without carefully safeguarding student confidentiality and without regard to the program's untoward effects. A program so sweeping is not sheltered by *Vernonia;* its unreasonable reach renders it impermissible under the Fourth Amendment.

In *Chandler* [*v. Miller* (1997)], this Court inspected "Georgia's requirement that candidates for state office pass a drug test"; we held that the requirement "did not fit within the closely guarded category of constitutionally permissible suspicionless searches." Georgia's testing prescription, the record showed, responded to no "concrete danger," was supported by no evidence of a particular problem, and targeted a group not involved in "high-risk, safety-sensitive tasks." We concluded: "What is left, after close review of Georgia's scheme, is the image the State seeks to project. By requiring candidates for public office to submit to drug testing, Georgia displays its commitment to the struggle against drug abuse. . . . The need revealed, in short, is symbolic, not 'special,' as that term draws meaning from our case law."

Close review of Tecumseh's policy compels a similar conclusion. That policy was not shown to advance the "'special needs' [existing] in the public school context [to maintain] . . . swift and informal disciplinary procedures . . . [and] order in the schools." What is left is the School District's undoubted purpose to heighten awareness of its abhorrence of, and strong stand against, drug abuse. But the desire to augment communication of this message does not trump the right of persons—even of children within the schoolhouse gate—to be "se-

cure in their persons . . . against unreasonable searches and seizures."

In *Chandler*, the Court referred to a path-marking dissenting opinion in which "Justice Brandeis recognized the importance of teaching by example: 'Our Government is the potent, the omnipresent teacher. For good or for ill, it teaches the whole people by its example.'" (quoting *Olmstead v. United States* (1928)). That wisdom should guide decision-makers in the instant case: The government is nowhere more a teacher than when it runs a public school.

It is a sad irony that the petitioning School District seeks to justify its edict here by trumpeting "the schools' custodial and tutelary responsibility for children." In regulating an athletic program or endeavoring to combat an exploding drug epidemic, a school's custodial obligations may permit searches that would otherwise unacceptably abridge students' rights. When custodial duties are not ascendant, however, schools' tutelary obligations to their students require them to "teach by example" by avoiding symbolic measures that diminish constitutional protections. . . .

For the reasons stated, I would affirm the judgment of the Tenth Circuit declaring the testing policy at issue unconstitutional.

Los Angeles v. Patel
576 U.S. ___ (2015)

The City of Los Angeles approved a municipal ordinance requiring hotel operators to record and keep specific information about their guests on the premises for a ninety-day period. These records "shall be made available to any officer of the Los Angeles Police Department for inspection . . . at a time and in a manner that minimizes any interference with the operation of the business," and a hotel operator's failure to make the records available is a criminal misdemeanor. Respondents, a group of motel operators and a lodging association, entered US District Court and brought a facial challenge to the ordinance on Fourth Amendment grounds. The court entered judgment for Los Angeles, finding that respondents lacked a reasonable expectation of privacy in their records. The Ninth Circuit subsequently

reversed, determining that inspections under the ordinance are Fourth Amendment searches and that such searches are unreasonable under the Fourth Amendment because hotel owners are subjected to punishment for failure to turn over their records without first being afforded the opportunity for pre-compliance review. The Supreme Court granted certiorari. Opinion of the Court: Sotomayor, *Kennedy, Ginsburg, Breyer, Kagan. Dissenting opinions:* Scalia, *Roberts, Thomas;* Alito, *Thomas.*

JUSTICE SOTOMAYOR delivered the opinion of the Court.

. . . We . . . hold that the provision of the Los Angeles Municipal Code that requires hotel operators to make their registries available to the police on demand is facially unconstitutional because it penalizes them for declining to turn over their records without affording them any opportunity for pre-compliance review.

I

Los Angeles Municipal Code requires hotel operators to record information about their guests, including: the guest's name and address; the number of people in each guest's party; the make, model, and license plate number of any guest's vehicle parked on hotel property; the guest's date and time of arrival and scheduled departure date; the room number assigned to the guest; the rate charged and amount collected for the room; and the method of payment. Guests without reservations, those who pay for their rooms with cash, and any guests who rent a room for less than 12 hours must present photographic identification at the time of check-in, and hotel operators are required to record the number and expiration date of that document. For those guests who check in using an electronic kiosk, the hotel's records must also contain the guest's credit card information. This information can be maintained in either electronic or paper form, but it must be "kept on the hotel premises in the guest reception or guest check-in area or in an office adjacent" thereto for a period of 90 days. . . . A hotel operator's failure to make his or her guest records available for police inspection is a misdemeanor punishable by up to six months in jail and a $1,000 fine. . . .

III

A

The *Fourth Amendment* protects "[t]he right of the people to be secure in their persons, houses, papers, and effects, against unreasonable searches and seizures." It further provides that "no Warrants shall issue, but upon probable cause." Based on this constitutional text, the Court has repeatedly held that "searches conducted outside the judicial process, without prior approval by [a] judge or [a] magistrate [judge], are per se unreasonable . . . subject only to a few specifically established and well-delineated exceptions." This rule "applies to commercial premises as well as to homes."

Search regimes where no warrant is ever required may be reasonable where "special needs . . . make the warrant and probable-cause requirement impracticable" and where the "primary purpose" of the searches is "[d]istinguishable from the general interest in crime control." *Indianapolis v. Edmond* (2000). Here, we assume that the searches authorized by [the ordinance] serve a "special need" other than conducting criminal investigations: They ensure compliance with the recordkeeping requirement, which in turn deters criminals from operating on the hotels' premises. The Court has referred to this kind of search as an "administrative searc[h]." *Camara v. Municipal Court of City and County of San Francisco* (1967). Thus, we consider whether [the ordinance] falls within the administrative search exception to the warrant requirement.

The Court has held that absent consent, exigent circumstances, or the like, in order for an administrative search to be constitutional, the subject of the search must be afforded an opportunity to obtain pre-compliance review before a neutral decision-maker. And, we see no reason why this minimal requirement is inapplicable here. While the Court has never attempted to prescribe the exact form an opportunity for pre-compliance review must take, the City does not even attempt to argue that [the ordinance] affords hotel operators any opportunity whatsoever. [It] is, therefore, facially invalid.

A hotel owner who refuses to give an officer access to his or her registry can be arrested on the spot. The Court has held that business owners cannot reasonably be put to this kind of choice. Absent an opportunity for pre-compliance review, the ordinance creates an intolerable risk that searches authorized by it will exceed statutory limits, or be used as a pretext to harass hotel operators and their guests. Even if a hotel has been searched 10 times a day, every day, for three months, without any violation being found, the operator can only refuse to comply with an officer's demand to turn over the registry at his or her own peril.

To be clear, we hold only that a hotel owner must be afforded an opportunity to have a neutral decision-maker review an officer's demand to search the registry before he or she faces penalties for failing to comply. Actual review need only occur in those rare instances where a hotel operator objects to turning over the registry. Moreover, this opportunity can be provided without imposing onerous burdens on those charged with an administrative scheme's enforcement. For instance, respondents accept that the searches authorized by [the ordinance] would be constitutional if they were performed pursuant to an administrative subpoena. These subpoenas, which are typically a simple form, can be issued by the individual seeking the record—here, officers in the field—without probable cause that a regulation is being infringed. Issuing a subpoena will usually be the full extent of an officer's burden because "the great majority of businessmen can be expected in normal course to consent to inspection without warrant." Indeed, the City has cited no evidence suggesting that without an ordinance authorizing on-demand searches, hotel operators would regularly refuse to cooperate with the police.

In those instances, however, where a subpoenaed hotel operator believes that an attempted search is motivated by illicit purposes, respondents suggest it would be sufficient if he or she could move to quash the subpoena before any search takes place. A neutral decision-maker, including an administrative law judge, would then review the subpoenaed party's objections before deciding whether the subpoena is enforceable. Given the limited grounds on which a motion to quash can be granted, such challenges will likely be rare. And, in the even rarer event that an officer reasonably suspects that a hotel operator may tamper with the registry while the motion to quash is pending, he or she can guard the registry until the required hearing can occur, which ought not take long. . . .

Of course administrative subpoenas are only one way in which an opportunity for pre-compliance review can be made available. But whatever the precise form, the availability of pre-compliance review alters the dynamic between the officer and the hotel to be searched, and reduces the risk that officers will use these administrative searches as a pretext to harass business owners.

Finally, we underscore the narrow nature of our holding. Respondents have not challenged

and nothing in our opinion calls into question those parts of [the ordinance] that require hotel operators to maintain guest registries containing certain information. And, even absent legislative action to create a procedure along the lines discussed above, police will not be prevented from obtaining access to these documents. As they often do, hotel operators remain free to consent to searches of their registries and police can compel them to turn them over if they have a proper administrative warrant—including one that was issued ex parte—or if some other exception to the warrant requirement applies, including exigent circumstances. . . .

JUSTICE SCALIA, with whom The Chief Justice and Justice Thomas join, dissenting.

The city of Los Angeles, like many jurisdictions across the country, has a law that requires motels, hotels, and other places of overnight accommodation (hereinafter motels) to keep a register containing specified information about their guests. The purpose of this recordkeeping requirement is to deter criminal conduct, on the theory that criminals will be unwilling to carry on illicit activities in motel rooms if they must provide identifying information at check-in. Because this deterrent effect will only be accomplished if motels actually do require guests to provide the required information, the ordinance also authorizes police to conduct random spot checks of motels' guest registers to ensure that they are properly maintained. The ordinance limits these spot checks to the four corners of the register, and does not authorize police to enter any nonpublic area of the motel. To the extent possible, police must conduct these spot checks at times that will minimize any disruption to a motel's business.

The parties do not dispute the governmental interests at stake. Motels not only provide housing to vulnerable transient populations, they are also a particularly attractive site for criminal activity ranging from drug dealing and prostitution to human trafficking. Offering privacy and anonymity on the cheap, they have been employed as prisons for migrants smuggled across the border and held for ransom, and rendezvous sites where child sex workers meet their clients on threat of violence from their procurers. Nevertheless, the Court today concludes that Los Angeles's ordinance is "unreasonable" inasmuch as it permits police to flip through a guest register to ensure it is being filled out without first providing an opportunity for the motel operator to seek judicial review. Because I believe that such a limited inspection of a guest register is eminently reasonable under the circumstances presented, I dissent.

II

The *Fourth Amendment* provides, in relevant part, that "[t]he right of the people to be secure in their persons, houses, papers, and effects, against unreasonable searches and seizures, shall not be violated, and no Warrants shall issue, but upon probable cause." Grammatically, the two clauses of the Amendment seem to be independent—and directed at entirely different actors. The former tells the executive what it must do when it conducts a search, and the latter tells the judiciary what it must do when it issues a search warrant. But in an effort to guide courts in applying the Search-and-Seizure Clause's indeterminate reasonableness standard, and to maintain coherence in our case law, we have used the Warrant Clause as a guidepost for assessing the reasonableness of a search, and have erected a framework of presumptions applicable to broad categories of searches conducted by executive officials. Our case law has repeatedly recognized, however, that these are mere presumptions, and the only constitutional requirement is that a search be reasonable.

When, for example, a search is conducted to enforce an administrative regime rather than to investigate criminal wrongdoing, we have been willing to modify the probable-cause standard so that a warrant may issue absent individualized suspicion of wrongdoing. Thus, our cases say a warrant may issue to inspect a structure for fire-code violations on the basis of such factors as the passage of time, the nature of the building, and the condition of the neighborhood. *Camara v. Municipal Court* (1967). As we recognized in that case, "reasonableness is still the ultimate standard. If a valid public interest justifies the intrusion contemplated, then there is probable cause to issue a suitably

restricted search warrant." And precisely "because the ultimate touchstone of the Fourth Amendment is 'reasonableness,'" even the presumption that the search of a home without a warrant is unreasonable "is subject to certain exceptions."

One exception to normal warrant requirements applies to searches of closely regulated businesses. "[W]hen an entrepreneur embarks upon such a business, he has voluntarily chosen to subject himself to a full arsenal of governmental regulation," and so a warrantless search to enforce those regulations is not unreasonable. Recognizing that warrantless searches of closely regulated businesses may nevertheless become unreasonable if arbitrarily conducted, we have required laws authorizing such searches to satisfy three criteria: (1) There must be a "'substantial' government interest that informs the regulatory scheme pursuant to which the inspection is made"; (2) "the warrantless inspections must be 'necessary to further [the] regulatory scheme'"; and (3) "the statute's inspection program, in terms of the certainty and regularity of its application, [must] provid[e] a constitutionally adequate substitute for a warrant." *New York* v. *Burger* (1987). Los Angeles's ordinance easily meets these standards.

A

In determining whether a business is closely regulated, this Court has looked to factors including the duration of the regulatory tradition; the comprehensiveness of the regulatory regime; and the imposition of similar regulations by other jurisdictions. These factors are not talismans but shed light on the expectation of privacy the owner of a business may reasonably have, which in turn affects the reasonableness of a warrantless search.

Reflecting the unique public role of motels and their commercial forebears, governments have long subjected these businesses to unique public duties, and have established inspection regimes to ensure compliance. As Blackstone observed, "Inns, in particular, being intended for the lodging and receipt of travellers, may be indicted, suppressed, and the inn-keepers fined, if they refuse to entertain a traveller without a very sufficient cause: for thus to frustrate the end of their institution is held to be disorderly behavior." 4 W. Blackstone, *Commentaries on the Laws of England* 168 (1765). Justice Story similarly recognized "[t]he soundness of the public policy of subjecting particular classes of persons to extraordinary responsibility, in cases where an extraordinary confidence is necessarily reposed in them, and there is an extraordinary temptation to fraud, or danger of plunder." J. Story, *Commentaries on the Law of Bailments* §464, pp. 487–488 (5th ed. 1851). Accordingly, in addition to the obligation to receive any paying guest, "innkeepers are bound to take, not merely ordinary care, but uncommon care, of the goods, money, and baggage of their guests," as travellers "are obliged to rely almost implicitly on the good faith of inn-holders, whose education and morals are none of the best, and who might have frequent opportunities of associating with ruffians and pilferers."

These obligations were not merely aspirational. At the time of the founding, searches—indeed, warrantless searches—of inns and similar places of public accommodation were commonplace. For example, although Massachusetts was perhaps the State most protective against government searches, "the state code of 1788 still allowed tithingmen to search public houses of entertainment on every Sabbath without any sort of warrant."

As this evidence demonstrates, the regulatory tradition governing motels is not only longstanding, but comprehensive. And the tradition continues in Los Angeles. The City imposes an occupancy tax upon transients who stay in motels and makes the motel owner responsible for collecting it. It authorizes city officials "to enter [a motel], free of charge, during business hours" in order to "inspect and examine" them to determine whether these tax provisions have been complied with. It requires all motels to obtain a "Transient Occupancy Registration Certificate," which must be displayed on the premises. State law requires motels to "post in a conspicuous place . . . a statement of rate or range of rates by the day for lodging," and forbids any charges in excess of those posted rates. Hotels must change bed linens between guests, and they must offer guests the option not to have towels and linens laundered

daily. "Multiuse drinking utensils" may be placed in guest rooms only if they are "thoroughly washed and sanitized after each use" and "placed in protective bags." And state authorities, like their municipal counterparts, "may at reasonable times enter and inspect any hotels, motels, or other public places" to ensure compliance.

. . . The regulations we have described above reach into the "minutest detail[s]" of motel operations, and those who enter that business today (like those who have entered it over the centuries) do so with an expectation that they will be subjected to especially vigilant governmental oversight.

Finally, this ordinance is not an outlier. The City has pointed us to more than 100 similar register-inspection laws in cities and counties across the country, and that is far from exhaustive. In all, municipalities in at least 41 States have laws similar to Los Angeles's, and at least 8 States have their own laws authorizing register inspections. This copious evidence is surely enough to establish that "[w]hen a [motel operator] chooses to engage in this pervasively regulated business . . . he does so with the knowledge that his business records . . . will be subject to effective inspection." And that is the relevant constitutional test—not whether this regulatory superstructure is "the same as laws subjecting inns to warrantless searches," or whether, as an historical matter, government authorities not only required these documents to be kept but permitted them to be viewed on demand without a motel's consent.

B

The City's ordinance easily satisfies the remaining requirements: It furthers a substantial governmental interest, it is necessary to achieving that interest, and it provides an adequate substitute for a search warrant.

Neither respondents nor the Court question the substantial interest of the City in deterring criminal activity. The private pain and public costs imposed by drug dealing, prostitution, and human trafficking are beyond contention, and motels provide an obvious haven for those who trade in human misery.

Warrantless inspections are also necessary to advance this interest. Although the Court acknowledges that law enforcement can enter a motel room without a warrant when exigent circumstances exist, the whole reason criminals use motel rooms in the first place is that they offer privacy and secrecy, so that police will never come to discover these exigencies. The recordkeeping requirement, which all parties admit is permissible, therefore operates by deterring crime. Criminals, who depend on the anonymity that motels offer, will balk when confronted with a motel's demand that they produce identification. And a motel's evasion of the recordkeeping requirement fosters crime. In San Diego, for example, motel owners were indicted for collaborating with members of the Crips street gang in the prostitution of underage girls; the motel owners "set aside rooms apart from the rest of their legitimate customers where girls and women were housed, charged the gang members/pimps a higher rate for the rooms where 'dates' or 'tricks' took place, and warned the gang members of inquiries by law enforcement." The warrantless inspection requirement provides a necessary incentive for motels to maintain their registers thoroughly and accurately: They never know when law enforcement might drop by to inspect.

Respondents and the Court acknowledge that inspections are necessary to achieve the purposes of the recordkeeping regime, but insist that warrantless inspections are not. They have to acknowledge, however, that the motel operators who conspire with drug dealers and procurers may demand pre-compliance judicial review simply as a pretext to buy time for making fraudulent entries in their guest registers. The Court therefore must resort to arguing that warrantless inspections are not "necessary" because other alternatives exist.

The Court suggests that police could obtain an administrative subpoena to search a guest register and, if a motel moves to quash, the police could "guar[d] the registry pending a hearing" on the motion. This proposal is equal parts *1984* and *Alice in Wonderland*. It protects motels from government inspection of their registers by authorizing government agents to seize the registers (if "guarding" entails forbidding the register to be moved) or to upset guests by a prolonged police presence at the motel. The Court also notes that police can obtain an ex parte warrant before conducting a register inspection. Presumably such warrants could issue without probable cause of wrongdoing by a particular motel; otherwise, this would be no alternative at all. Even so, under this regime police would have to obtain an ex parte warrant before every inspection. That is because law enforcement would have no way of knowing ahead of time which motels would refuse consent to a search upon request; and if they wait to obtain a warrant until consent is refused, motels will have the opportunity to falsify their guest registers while the police jump through the procedural hoops required to obtain a warrant. It is quite plausible that the costs of this always-get-a-warrant "alternative" would be prohibitive for a police force in one of America's largest cities, juggling numerous law-enforcement priorities, and confronting more than 2,000 motels within its jurisdiction. To be sure, the fact that obtaining a warrant might be costly will not by itself render a warrantless search reasonable under the Fourth Amendment; but it can render a warrantless search necessary in the context of an administrative-search regime governing closely regulated businesses.

But all that discussion is in any case irrelevant. The administrative search need only be reasonable. It is not the burden of Los Angeles to show that there are no less restrictive means of achieving the City's purposes. . . .

Finally, the City's ordinance provides an adequate substitute for a warrant. . . . Los Angeles's ordinance provides that the guest register must be kept in the guest reception or guest check-in area, or in an adjacent office, and that it "be made available to any officer of the Los Angeles Police Department for inspection. Whenever possible, the inspection shall be conducted at a time and in a manner that minimizes any interference with the operation of the business." Nothing in the ordinance authorizes law enforcement to enter a nonpublic part of the motel. . . . The Los Angeles ordinance—which limits warrantless police searches to the pages of a guest register in a public part of a motel—circumscribes police discretion in much more exacting terms than the laws we have approved in our earlier cases. . . .

Because I believe that the limited warrantless searches authorized by Los Angeles's ordinance are reasonable under the circumstances, I respectfully dissent.

Maryland v. King
569 U.S. ___ (2013)

After his 2009 arrest on first-and second-degree assault charges, respondent King was processed through a Wicomico County, Maryland, facility, where booking personnel used a cheek swab to take a DNA sample pursuant to the Maryland DNA Collection Act. The swab was matched to an unsolved 2003 rape, and King was charged with that crime. He moved to suppress the DNA match, arguing that the act violated the Fourth Amendment, but the trial court judge found it constitutional, and King was convicted of rape. The Maryland Court of Appeals set aside the conviction, finding unconstitutional the portions of the act authorizing DNA collection from felony arrestees. The Supreme Court granted certiorari to address that finding. Opinion of the Court: <u>Kennedy</u>, Roberts, Thomas, Breyer, Alito. Dissenting opinion: <u>Scalia</u>, Ginsburg, Sotomayor, Kagan.

JUSTICE KENNEDY delivered the opinion of the Court.

II

The advent of DNA technology is one of the most significant scientific advancements of our era. The full potential for use of genetic markers in medicine and science is still being explored, but the utility of DNA identification in the criminal justice system is already undisputed. Since the first use of forensic DNA analysis to catch a rapist and murderer in England in 1986, law enforcement, the defense bar, and the courts have acknowledged DNA testing's "unparalleled ability both to exonerate the wrongly convicted and to identify the guilty. It has the potential to significantly improve both the criminal justice system and police investigative practices."

B

Respondent's identification as the rapist resulted in part through the operation of a national project to standardize collection and storage of DNA profiles. Authorized by Congress and supervised by the Federal Bureau of Investigation, the Combined DNA Index System (CODIS) connects DNA laboratories at the local, state, and national level. Since its authorization in 1994, the CODIS system has grown to include all fifty States and a number of federal agencies. CODIS collects DNA profiles provided by local laboratories taken from arrestees, convicted offenders, and forensic evidence found at crime scenes. To participate in CODIS, a local laboratory must sign a memorandum of understanding agreeing to adhere to quality standards and submit to audits to evaluate compliance with the federal standards for scientifically rigorous DNA testing.

One of the most significant aspects of CODIS is the standardization of the points of comparison in DNA analysis. . . . CODIS sets uniform national standards for DNA matching and then facilitates connections between local law enforcement agencies who can share more specific information about matched STR profiles.

All fifty States require the collection of DNA from felony convicts, and respondent does not dispute the validity of that practice. Twenty-eight States and the Federal Government have adopted laws similar to the Maryland Act authorizing the collection of DNA from some or all arrestees. Although those statutes vary in their particulars, such as what charges require a DNA sample, their similarity means that this case implicates more than the specific Maryland law. At issue is a standard, expanding technology already in widespread use throughout the Nation.

III
A

Although the DNA swab procedure used here presents a question the Court has not yet addressed, the framework for deciding the issue is well established. The Fourth Amendment, binding on the States by the Fourteenth Amendment, provides that "[t]he right of the people to be secure in their persons, houses, papers, and effects, against unreasonable searches and seizures, shall not be violated." It can be agreed that using a buccal swab on the inner tissues of a person's cheek in order to obtain DNA samples is a search. . . . A buccal swab is a far more gentle process than a venipuncture to draw blood. It involves but a light touch on the inside of the cheek; and although it can be deemed a search within the body of the arrestee, it requires no "surgical intrusions beneath the skin." The fact than an intrusion is negligible is of central relevance to determining reasonableness, although it is still a search as the law defines that term.

B

To say that the Fourth Amendment applies here is the beginning point, not the end of the analysis. . . . In some circumstances, such as "[w]hen faced with special law enforcement needs, diminished expectations of privacy, minimal intrusions, or the like, the Court has found that certain general, or individual, circumstances may render a warrantless search or seizure reasonable." . . . The instant case can be addressed with this background. The Maryland DNA Collection Act provides that, in order to obtain a DNA sample, all arrestees charged with serious crimes must furnish the sample on a buccal swab applied, as noted, to the inside of the cheeks. The arrestee is already in valid police custody for a serious offense supported by probable cause. The DNA collection is not subject to the judgment of officers. . . . [T]he search effected by the buccal swab of respondent falls within the category of cases this Court has analyzed by reference to the proposition that the "touchstone of the Fourth Amendment is reasonableness, not individualized suspicion."

Even if a warrant is not required, a search is not beyond Fourth Amendment scrutiny; for it must be reasonable in its scope and manner of execution. . . . To say that no warrant is required is merely to acknowledge that "rather than employing a per se rule of unreasonableness, we balance the privacy-related and law enforcement-related concerns to determine if the intrusion was reasonable." This application of "traditional standards of reasonableness"

requires a court to weigh "the promotion of legitimate governmental interests" against "the degree to which [the search] intrudes upon an individual's privacy." An assessment of reasonableness to determine the lawfulness of requiring this class of arrestees to provide a DNA sample is central to the instant case.

IV

A

The legitimate government interest served by the Maryland DNA Collection Act is one that is well established: the need for law enforcement officers in a safe and accurate way to process and identify the persons and possessions they must take into custody. . . .

. . . "[I]n every criminal case, it is known and must be known who has been arrested and who is being tried." . . . A suspect's criminal history is a critical part of his identity that officers should know when processing him for detention. . . . Police already seek this crucial identifying information. They use routine and accepted means as varied as comparing the suspect's booking photograph to sketch artists' depictions of persons of interest, showing his mugshot to potential witnesses, and of course making a computerized comparison of the arrestee's fingerprints against electronic databases of known criminals and unsolved crimes. In this respect the only difference between DNA analysis and the accepted use of fingerprint databases is the unparalleled accuracy DNA provides.

The task of identification necessarily entails searching public and police records based on the identifying information provided by the arrestee to see what is already known about him. The DNA collected from arrestees is an irrefutable identification of the person from whom it was taken. Like a fingerprint, . . . [a] DNA profile is useful to the police because it gives them a form of identification to search the records already in their valid possession. In this respect the use of DNA for identification is no different than matching an arrestee's face to a wanted poster of a previously unidentified suspect; or matching tattoos to known gang symbols to reveal a criminal affiliation; or matching the arrestee's fingerprints to those recovered from a crime scene. . . . Finding occurrences of the arrestee's CODIS profile in outstanding cases is consistent with this common practice. It uses a different form of identification than a name or fingerprint, but its function is the same.

Second, law enforcement officers bear a responsibility for ensuring that the custody of an arrestee does not create inordinate "risks for facility staff, for the existing detainee population, and for a new detainee." DNA identification can provide untainted information to those charged with detaining suspects and detaining the property of any felon. For these purposes officers must know the type of person whom they are detaining, and DNA allows them to make critical choices about how to proceed. . . .

Third, looking forward to future stages of criminal prosecution, "the Government has a substantial interest in ensuring that persons accused of crimes are available for trials." A person who is arrested for one offense but knows that he has yet to answer for some past crime may be more inclined to flee the instant charges, lest continued contact with the criminal justice system expose one or more other serious offenses. . . .

Fourth, an arrestee's past conduct is essential to an assessment of the danger he poses to the public, and this will inform a court's determination whether the individual should be released on bail. . . . Even if an arrestee is released on bail, development of DNA identification revealing the defendant's unknown violent past can and should lead to the revocation of his conditional release.

Finally, in the interests of justice, the identification of an arrestee as the perpetrator of some heinous crime may have the salutary effect of freeing a person wrongfully imprisoned for the same offense. "[P]rompt [DNA] testing . . . would speed up apprehension of criminals before they commit additional crimes, and prevent the grotesque detention of . . . innocent people."

B

DNA identification represents an important advance in the techniques used by law enforcement to serve legitimate police concerns for as long as there have been arrests, concerns the courts have acknowledged and approved for more than a century. . . . Perhaps the most direct historical analogue to the DNA technology used to identify respondent is the familiar practice of fingerprinting arrestees. From the advent of this technique, courts had no trouble determining that fingerprinting was a natural part of "the administrative steps incident to arrest. . . . DNA identification is an advanced technique superior to fingerprinting in many ways, so much so that to insist on fingerprints as the norm would make little sense to either the forensic expert or a layperson. The additional intrusion upon the arrestee's privacy beyond that associated with fingerprinting is not significant, and DNA is a markedly more accurate form of identifying arrestees. A suspect who has changed his facial features to evade photographic identification or even one who has undertaken the more arduous task of altering his fingerprints cannot escape the revealing power of his DNA.

The respondent's primary objection to this analogy is that DNA identification is not as fast as fingerprinting, and so it should not be considered to be the 21st-century equivalent. . . . The question of how long it takes to process identifying information obtained from a valid search goes only to the efficacy of the search for its purpose of prompt identification, not the constitutionality of the search. Given the importance of DNA in the identification of police records pertaining to arrestees and the need to refine and confirm that identity for its important bearing on the decision to continue release on bail or to impose of new conditions, DNA serves an essential purpose despite the existence of delays such as the one that occurred in this case. Even so, the delay in processing DNA from arrestees is being reduced to a substantial degree by rapid technical advances. . . .

In sum, there can be little reason to question "the legitimate interest of the government in knowing for an absolute certainty the identity of the person arrested, in knowing whether he is wanted elsewhere, and in ensuring his identification in the event he flees prosecution." . . . In the balance of reasonableness required by the Fourth Amendment, therefore, the Court must give great weight both to the significant government interest at stake in the identification of arrestees and to the unmatched potential of DNA identification to serve that interest.

V

A

By comparison to this substantial government interest and the unique effectiveness of DNA identification, the intrusion of a cheek swab to obtain a DNA sample is a minimal one. True, a significant government interest does not alone suffice to justify a search. The government interest must outweigh the degree to which the search invades an individual's legitimate expectations of privacy. . . .

The reasonableness of any search must be considered in the context of the person's legitimate expectations of privacy. . . . The expectations of privacy of an individual taken into police custody "necessarily [are] of a diminished scope." A search of the detainee's person when he is booked into custody may "'involve a relatively extensive exploration,'" including "requir[ing] at least some detainees to lift their genitals or cough in a squatting position." . . . Once an individual has been arrested on probable cause for a dangerous offense that may require detention before trial, his or her expectations of privacy and freedom from police scrutiny are reduced. DNA identification like that at issue here thus does not require consideration of any unique needs that would be required to justify searching the average citizen. The special needs cases, though in full accord with the result reached here, do not have a direct bearing on the issues presented in this case, because unlike the search of a citizen who has not been suspected of a wrong, a detainee has a reduced expectation of privacy. . . .

* * *

In light of the context of a valid arrest supported by probable cause respondent's expectations of privacy were not offended by the minor intrusion of a brief swab of his cheeks. By contrast, that same context of arrest gives rise to significant state interests in identifying respondent not only so that the proper name can be attached to his charges but also so that the criminal justice system can make informed decisions concerning pretrial custody. Upon these considerations the Court concludes that DNA identification of arrestees is a reasonable search that can be considered part of a routine booking procedure. When officers make an arrest supported by probable cause to hold for a serious offense and they bring the suspect to the station to be detained in custody, taking and analyzing a cheek swab of the arrestee's DNA is, like fingerprinting and photographing, a legitimate police booking procedure that is reasonable under the Fourth Amendment.

The judgment of the Court of Appeals of Maryland is reversed.

JUSTICE SCALIA, with whom JUSTICE GINSBURG, JUSTICE SOTOMAYOR, and JUSTICE KAGAN join, dissenting.

The Fourth Amendment forbids searching a person for evidence of a crime when there is no basis for believing the person is guilty of the crime or is in possession of incriminating evidence. That prohibition is categorical and without exception; it lies at the very heart of the Fourth Amendment. Whenever this Court has allowed a suspicionless search, it has insisted upon a justifying motive apart from the investigation of crime.

It is obvious that no such noninvestigative motive exists in this case. The Court's assertion that DNA is being taken, not to solve crimes, but to identify those in the State's custody, taxes the credulity of the credulous. And the Court's comparison of Maryland's DNA searches to other techniques, such as fingerprinting, can seem apt only to those who know no more than today's opinion has chosen to tell them about how those DNA searches actually work.

I

A

. . . [W]hile the Court is correct to note that there are instances in which we have permitted searches without individualized suspicion, "[i]n none of these cases . . . did we indicate approval of a [search] whose primary purpose was to detect evidence of ordinary criminal wrongdoing." *Indianapolis v. Edmond* (2000). That limitation is crucial. It is only when a governmental purpose aside from crime-solving is at stake that we engage in the free-form "reasonableness" inquiry that the Court indulges at length today. To put it another way, both the legitimacy of the Court's method and the correctness of its outcome hinge entirely on the truth of a single proposition: that the primary purpose of these DNA searches is something other than simply discovering evidence of criminal wrongdoing. As I detail below, that proposition is wrong.

B

The Court alludes at several points to the fact that King was an arrestee, and arrestees may be validly searched incident to their arrest. But the Court does not really rest on this principle, and for good reason: The objects of a search incident to arrest must be either (1) weapons or evidence that might easily be destroyed, or (2) evidence relevant to the crime of arrest. Neither is the object of the search at issue here.

. . . No matter the degree of invasiveness, suspicionless searches are never allowed if their principal end is ordinary crime-solving. A search incident to arrest either serves other ends (such as officer safety, in a search for weapons) or is not suspicionless (as when there is reason to believe the arrestee possesses evidence relevant to the crime of arrest).

Sensing (correctly) that it needs more, the Court elaborates at length the ways that the search here served the special purpose of "identifying" King. But that seems to me quite wrong—unless what one means by "identifying" someone is "searching for evidence that he has committed crimes unrelated to the crime of his arrest." At points the Court does appear to use "identifying" in that peculiar sense—claiming, for example, that knowing "an arrestee's past conduct is essential to an assessment of the danger he poses." If identifying someone means finding out what unsolved crimes he has committed, then identification is indistinguishable from the ordinary law-enforcement aims that have never been thought to justify a suspicionless search. Searching every lawfully stopped car, for example, might turn up information about unsolved crimes the driver had committed, but no one would say that such a search was aimed at "identifying" him, and no court would hold such a search lawful. I will therefore assume that the Court means that the DNA search at issue here was useful to "identify" King in the normal sense of that word—in the sense that would identify the author of Introduction to the Principles of Morals and Legislation as Jeremy Bentham.

1

The portion of the Court's opinion that explains the identification rationale is strangely silent on the actual workings of the DNA search at issue here. To know those facts is to be instantly disabused of the notion that what happened had anything to do with identifying King.

King was arrested on April 10, 2009, on charges unrelated to the case before us. That same day, April 10, the police searched him and seized the DNA evidence at issue here. What happened next? Reading the Court's opinion, particularly its insistence that the search was necessary to know "who [had] been arrested," one might guess that King's DNA was swiftly processed and his identity thereby confirmed—perhaps against some master database of known DNA profiles, as is done for fingerprints. After all, was not the suspicionless search here crucial to avoid "inordinate risks for facility staff" or to "existing detainee population"? Surely, then—surely—the State of Maryland got cracking on those grave risks immediately, by rushing to identify King with his DNA as soon as possible.

Nothing could be further from the truth. Maryland officials did not even begin the process of testing King's DNA that day. Or, actually, the next day. Or the day after that. And that was for a simple reason: Maryland law forbids them to do so. A "DNA sample collected from an individual charged with a crime . . . may not be tested or placed in the statewide DNA data base system prior to the first scheduled arraignment date." And King's first appearance in court was not until three days after his arrest. (I suspect, though, that they did not wait three days to ask his name or take his fingerprints.)

This places in a rather different light the Court's solemn declaration that the search here was necessary so that King could be identified at "every stage of the criminal process." I hope that the Maryland officials who read the

Court's opinion do not take it seriously. Acting on the Court's misperception of Maryland law could lead to jail time. (punishing by up to five years' imprisonment anyone who obtains or tests DNA information except as provided by statute). Does the Court really believe that Maryland did not know whom it was arraigning? The Court's response is to imagine that release on bail could take so long that the DNA results are returned in time, or perhaps that bail could be revoked if the DNA test turned up incriminating information. That is no answer at all. If the purpose of this Act is to assess "whether [King] should be released on bail," why would it possibly forbid the DNA testing process to begin until King was arraigned? Why would Maryland resign itself to simply hoping that the bail decision will drag out long enough that the "identification" can succeed before the arrestee is released? The truth, known to Maryland and increasingly to the reader: this search had nothing to do with establishing King's identity.

It gets worse. King's DNA sample was not received by the Maryland State Police's Forensic Sciences Division until April 23, 2009—two weeks after his arrest. It sat in that office, ripening in a storage area, until the custodians got around to mailing it to a lab for testing on June 25, 2009—two months after it was received, and nearly three since King's arrest. After it was mailed, the data from the lab tests were not available for several more weeks, until July 13, 2009, which is when the test results were entered into Maryland's DNA database, together with information identifying the person from whom the sample was taken. Meanwhile, bail had been set, King had engaged in discovery, and he had requested a speedy trial—presumably not a trial of John Doe. It was not until August 4, 2009—four months after King's arrest—that the forwarded sample transmitted (without identifying information) from the Maryland DNA database to the Federal Bureau of Investigation's national database was matched with a sample taken from the scene of an unrelated crime years earlier. . . .

A more specific description of exactly what happened at this point illustrates why, by definition, King could not have been identified by this match. The FBI's DNA database (known as CODIS) consists of two distinct collections. One of them, the one to which King's DNA was submitted, consists of DNA samples taken from known convicts or arrestees. I will refer to this as the "Convict and Arrestee Collection." The other collection consists of samples taken from crime scenes; I will refer to this as the "Unsolved Crimes Collection." The Convict and Arrestee Collection stores "no names or other personal identifiers of the offenders, arrestees, or detainees." Rather, it contains only the DNA profile itself, the name of the agency that submitted it, the laboratory personnel who analyzed it, and an identification number for the specimen. This is because the submitting state laboratories are expected already to know the identities of the convicts and arrestees from whom samples are taken. (And, of course, they do.)

Moreover, the CODIS system works by checking to see whether any of the samples in the Unsolved Crimes Collection match any of the samples in the Convict and Arrestee Collection. That is sensible, if what one wants to do is solve those cold cases, but note what it requires: that the identity of the people whose DNA has been entered in the Convict and Arrestee Collection already be known. If one wanted to identify someone in custody using his DNA, the logical thing to do would be to compare that DNA against the Convict and Arrestee Collection: to search, in other words, the collection that could be used (by checking back with the submitting state agency) to identify people, rather than the collection of evidence from unsolved crimes, whose perpetrators are by definition unknown. But that is not what was done. And that is because this search had nothing to do with identification.

In fact, if anything was "identified" at the moment that the DNA database returned a match, it was not King—his identity was already known. (The docket for the original criminal charges lists his full name, his race, his sex, his height, his weight, his date of birth, and his address.) Rather, what the August 4 match "identified" was the previously-taken sample from the earlier crime. That sample was genuinely mysterious to Maryland; the State knew that it had probably been left by the victim's attacker, but nothing else. King was not identified by his association with the sample; rather, the sample was identified by its association with King. The Court effectively destroys its own "identification" theory when it acknowledges that the object of this search was "to see what [was] already known about [King]." King was who he was, and volumes of his biography could not make him any more or any less King. No minimally competent speaker of English would say, upon noticing a known arrestee's similarity "to a wanted poster of a previously unidentified suspect," that the arrestee had thereby been identified. It was the previously unidentified suspect who had been identified—just as, here, it was the previously unidentified rapist.

2

That taking DNA samples from arrestees has nothing to do with identifying them is confirmed not just by actual practice (which the Court ignores) but by the enabling statute itself (which the Court also ignores). The Maryland Act at issue has a section helpfully entitled "Purpose of collecting and testing DNA samples." (One would expect such a section to play a somewhat larger role in the Court's analysis of the Act's purpose—which is to say, at least some role.) That provision lists five purposes for which DNA samples may be tested. By this point, it will not surprise the reader to learn that the Court's imagined purpose is not among them.

Instead, the law provides that DNA samples are collected and tested, as a matter of Maryland law, "as part of an official investigation into a crime." (Or, as our suspicionless-search cases would put it: for ordinary law-enforcement purposes.) That is certainly how everyone has always understood the Maryland Act until today. . . .

More devastating still for the Court's "identification" theory, the statute does enumerate two instances in which a DNA sample may be tested for the purpose of identification: "to help identify human remains," and "to help identify missing individuals." No mention of identifying arrestees. *Inclusio unius est exclusio alterius.* And note again that Maryland forbids using DNA records "for any purposes other than those specified"—it is actually a crime to do so.

The Maryland regulations implementing the Act confirm what is now monotonously obvious. . . . So, to review: DNA testing does not even begin until after arraignment and bail decisions are already made. The samples sit in storage for months, and take weeks to test. When they are tested, they are checked against the Unsolved Crimes Collection—rather than the Convict and Arrestee Collection, which could be used to identify them. The Act forbids the Court's purpose (identification), but prescribes as its purpose what our suspicionless-search cases forbid ("official investigation into a crime"). Against all of that, it is safe to say that if the Court's identification theory is not wrong, there is no such thing as error.

II

The Court also attempts to bolster its identification theory with a series of inapposite analogies. Is not taking DNA samples the same, asks the Court, as taking a person's photograph? No—because that is not a Fourth Amendment search at all. It does not involve a physical intrusion onto the person, and we have never held that merely taking a person's photograph invades any recognized "expectation of privacy."

But is not the practice of DNA searches, the Court asks, the same as taking "Bertillon" measurements—noting an arrestee's height, shoe size, and so on, on the back of a photograph? No, because that system was not, in the ordinary case, used to solve unsolved crimes. It is possible, I suppose, to imagine situations in which such measurements might be useful to generate leads. (If witnesses described a very tall burglar, all the "tall man" cards could then be pulled.) But the obvious primary purpose of such measurements, as the Court's description of them makes clear, was to verify that, for example, the person arrested today is the same person that was arrested a year ago. Which is to say, Bertillon measurements were actually used as a system of identification, and drew their primary usefulness from that task.

It is on the fingerprinting of arrestees, however, that the Court relies most heavily. The Court does not actually say whether it believes that taking a person's fingerprints is a Fourth Amendment search, and our cases provide no ready answer to that question. Even assuming so, however, law enforcement's post-arrest use of fingerprints could not be more different from its post-arrest use of DNA. Fingerprints of arrestees are taken primarily to identify them (though that process sometimes solves crimes); the DNA of arrestees is taken to solve crimes (and nothing else).

The Court asserts that the taking of fingerprints was "constitutional for generations prior to the introduction" of the FBI's rapid computer-matching system. This bold statement is bereft of citation to authority because there is none for it. The "great expansion in fingerprinting came before the modern era of Fourth Amendment jurisprudence," and so we were never asked to decide the legitimacy of the practice. As fingerprint databases expanded from convicted criminals, to arrestees, to civil servants, to immigrants, to everyone with a driver's license, Americans simply "became accustomed to having our fingerprints on file in some government database." But it is wrong to suggest that this was uncontroversial at the time, or that this Court blessed universal fingerprinting for "generations" before it was possible to use it effectively for identification. . . .

***

The Court disguises the vast (and scary) scope of its holding by promising a limitation it cannot deliver. The Court repeatedly says that DNA testing, and entry into a national DNA registry, will not befall thee and me, dear reader, but only those arrested for "serious offense[s]." I cannot imagine what principle could possibly justify this limitation, and the Court does not attempt to suggest any. If one believes that DNA will "identify" someone arrested for assault, he must believe that it will "identify" someone arrested for a traffic offense. This Court does not base its judgments on senseless distinctions. At the end of the day,

logic will out. When there comes before us the taking of DNA from an arrestee for a traffic violation, the Court will predictably (and quite rightly) say, "We can find no significant difference between this case and *King*." Make no mistake about it: As an entirely predictable consequence of today's decision, your DNA can be taken and entered into a national DNA database if you are ever arrested, rightly or wrongly, and for whatever reason.

The most regrettable aspect of the suspicionless search that occurred here is that it proved to be quite unnecessary. All parties concede that it would have been entirely permissible, as far as the Fourth Amendment is concerned, for Maryland to take a sample of King's DNA as a consequence of his conviction for second-degree assault. So the ironic result of the Court's error is this: The only arrestees to whom the outcome here will ever make a difference are those who have been acquitted of the crime of arrest (so that their DNA could not have been taken upon conviction). In other words, this Act manages to burden uniquely the sole group for whom the Fourth Amendment's protections ought to be most jealously guarded: people who are innocent of the State's accusations.

Today's judgment will, to be sure, have the beneficial effect of solving more crimes; then again, so would the taking of DNA samples from anyone who flies on an airplane (surely the Transportation Security Administration needs to know the "identity" of the flying public), applies for a driver's license, or attends a public school. Perhaps the construction of such a genetic panopticon is wise. But I doubt that the proud men who wrote the charter of our liberties would have been so eager to open their mouths for royal inspection.

I therefore dissent, and hope that today's incursion upon the Fourth Amendment . . . will some day be repudiated

Riley v. California
573 U.S. ___ (2014)

In this combined opinion, the Court resolved two separate cases raising similar Fourth Amendment questions. In Riley v. California, *the defendant was*

stopped for driving with expired registration tags eventually leading to his arrest on weapons charges. (In the course of the stop, the officer also learned

that Riley's license had been suspended and im-
pounded Riley's car; pursuant to department policy,
another officer conducted an inventory search of the
car. Riley was arrested for possession of concealed
and loaded firearms when that search turned up
two handguns under the car's hood.) An officer
searching Riley incident to the arrest seized a smart
phone from Riley's pants pocket, accessed information on the phone, and noticed the repeated use of a
term, "CK," a label that, he believed, stood for
"Crip Killers"—a slang term for members of the
Bloods gang. At the police station two hours later, a
detective specializing in gangs further examined the
phone's digital contents. Based in part on photographs and videos that the detective found, the police charged Riley in connection with a shooting
that had occurred a few weeks earlier and sought an
enhanced sentence based on Riley's gang membership. Riley moved to suppress all evidence that the
police had obtained from his cell phone. The trial
court denied the motion, Riley was convicted, and
the California Court of Appeal affirmed.

In the companion case of United States v.
Wurie, the defendant was arrested after police observed him participate in an apparent drug sale.
At the police station, the officers seized Wurie's
"flip phone"—a kind of phone that is flipped
open for use and that generally has a smaller
range of features than a smart phone—and noticed that it was receiving multiple calls from a
source identified as "my house" on its external
screen. The officers opened the phone, accessed its
call log, determined the number associated with
the "my house" label, and traced that number to
what they suspected was Wurie's apartment. They
secured a search warrant and found drugs, a firearm and ammunition, and cash in the ensuing
search. Wurie was then charged with drug and firearm offenses. He moved to suppress the evidence
obtained from the search of the apartment. The
District Court denied the motion, and Wurie was
convicted, whereupon the First Circuit reversed the
denial of the motion to suppress and vacated the
relevant convictions. The Supreme Court granted
certiorari in both cases. Opinion of the Court:
Roberts, Scalia, Kennedy, Thomas, Ginsburg,
Breyer, Sotomayor, Kagan. Concurring in part
and concurring in the judgment: Alito.

CHIEF JUSTICE ROBERTS delivered the
opinion of the Court.

These two cases raise a common question:
whether the police may, without a warrant,
search digital information on a cell phone
seized from an individual who has been
arrested.

II

. . . The two cases before us concern the reasonableness of a warrantless search incident to
a lawful arrest. In 1914, this Court first acknowledged in dictum "the right on the part of
the Government, always recognized under English and American law, to search the person of
the accused when legally arrested to discover
and seize the fruits or evidences of crime."
Weeks v. *United States* (1914). Since that time,
it has been well accepted that such a search
constitutes an exception to the warrant requirement. Indeed, the label "exception" is
something of a misnomer in this context, as
warrantless searches incident to arrest occur
with far greater frequency than searches conducted pursuant to a warrant.

Although the existence of the exception for
such searches has been recognized for a century, its scope has been debated for nearly as
long. That debate has focused on the extent to
which officers may search property found on
or near the arrestee. Three related precedents
set forth the rules governing such searches:

The first, *Chimel* v. *California* (1969), laid
the groundwork for most of the existing search
incident to arrest doctrine. Police officers in
that case arrested Chimel inside his home and
proceeded to search his entire three-bedroom
house, including the attic and garage. In particular rooms, they also looked through the
contents of drawers.

The Court crafted the following rule for assessing the reasonableness of a search incident
to arrest:

> When an arrest is made, it is reasonable
> for the arresting officer to search the per-
> son arrested in order to remove any
> weapons that the latter might seek to use
> in order to resist arrest or effect his es-
> cape. Otherwise, the officer's safety might
> well be endangered, and the arrest itself
> frustrated. In addition, it is entirely rea-
> sonable for the arresting officer to search

for and seize any evidence on the arrestee's person in order to prevent its concealment or destruction. . . . . There is ample justification, therefore, for a search of the arrestee's person and the area "within his immediate control"—construing that phrase to mean the area from within which he might gain possession of a weapon or destructible evidence.

The extensive warrantless search of Chimel's home did not fit within this exception, because it was not needed to protect officer safety or to preserve evidence.

Four years later, in *United States* v. *Robinson* (1973), the Court applied the *Chimel* analysis in the context of a search of the arrestee's person. A police officer had arrested Robinson for driving with a revoked license. The officer conducted a patdown search and felt an object that he could not identify in Robinson's coat pocket. He removed the object, which turned out to be a crumpled cigarette package, and opened it. Inside were 14 capsules of heroin.

Th[is] Court . . . concluded that the search of Robinson was reasonable even though there was no concern about the loss of evidence, and the arresting officer had no specific concern that Robinson might be armed. In doing so, the Court did not draw a line between a search of Robinson's person and a further examination of the cigarette pack found during that search. It merely noted that, "[h]aving in the course of a lawful search come upon the crumpled package of cigarettes, [the officer] was entitled to inspect it." A few years later, the Court clarified that this exception was limited to "personal property . . . immediately associated with the person of the arrestee." *United States* v. *Chadwick* (1977) (200-pound, locked footlocker could not be searched incident to arrest).

The search incident to arrest trilogy concludes with *Gant* [*v. Arizona* (2009)], which analyzed searches of an arrestee's vehicle. *Gant*, like *Robinson*, recognized that the *Chimel* concerns for officer safety and evidence preservation underlie the search incident to arrest exception. As a result, the Court concluded that *Chimel* could authorize police to search a vehicle "only when the arrestee is unsecured and within reaching distance of the passenger compartment at the time of the search." . . .

III

These cases require us to decide how the search incident to arrest doctrine applies to modern cell phones, which are now such a pervasive and insistent part of daily life that the proverbial visitor from Mars might conclude they were an important feature of human anatomy. A smart phone of the sort taken from Riley was unheard of ten years ago; a significant majority of American adults now own such phones. Even less sophisticated phones like Wurie's, which have already faded in popularity since Wurie was arrested in 2007, have been around for less than 15 years. Both phones are based on technology nearly inconceivable just a few decades ago, when *Chimel* and *Robinson* were decided.

Absent more precise guidance from the founding era, we generally determine whether to exempt a given type of search from the warrant requirement "by assessing, on the one hand, the degree to which it intrudes upon an individual's privacy and, on the other, the degree to which it is needed for the promotion of legitimate governmental interests." *Wyoming* v. *Houghton* (1999). Such a balancing of interests supported the search incident to arrest exception in *Robinson*, and a mechanical application of *Robinson* might well support the warrantless searches at issue here.

But while *Robinson*'s categorical rule strikes the appropriate balance in the context of physical objects, neither of its rationales has much force with respect to digital content on cell phones. On the government interest side, *Robinson* concluded that the two risks identified in *Chimel*—harm to officers and destruction of evidence—are present in all custodial arrests. There are no comparable risks when the search is of digital data. In addition, *Robinson* regarded any privacy interests retained by an individual after arrest as significantly diminished by the fact of the arrest itself. Cell phones, however, place vast quantities of personal information literally in the hands of individuals. A search of the information on a cell phone bears little resemblance to the type of brief physical search considered in *Robinson*.

We therefore decline to extend *Robinson* to searches of data on cell phones, and hold instead that officers must generally secure a warrant before conducting such a search.

A

We first consider each *Chimel* concern in turn. . . .

1

Digital data stored on a cell phone cannot itself be used as a weapon to harm an arresting officer or to effectuate the arrestee's escape. Law enforcement officers remain free to examine the physical aspects of a phone to ensure that it will not be used as a weapon—say, to determine whether there is a razor blade hidden between the phone and its case. Once an officer has secured a phone and eliminated any potential physical threats, however, data on the phone can endanger no one.

Perhaps the same might have been said of the cigarette pack seized from Robinson's pocket. Once an officer gained control of the pack, it was unlikely that Robinson could have accessed the pack's contents. But unknown physical objects may always pose risks, no matter how slight, during the tense atmosphere of a custodial arrest. The officer in *Robinson* testified that he could not identify the objects in the cigarette pack but knew they were not cigarettes. Given that, a further search was a reasonable protective measure. No such unknowns exist with respect to digital data. As the First Circuit explained, the officers who searched Wurie's cell phone "knew exactly what they would find therein: data. They also knew that the data could not harm them." . . .

2

The United States and California focus primarily on the second *Chimel* rationale: preventing the destruction of evidence.

Both Riley and Wurie concede that officers could have seized and secured their cell phones to prevent destruction of evidence while seeking a warrant. And once law enforcement officers have secured a cell phone, there is no longer any risk that the arrestee himself will be able to delete incriminating data from the phone.

The United States and California argue that information on a cell phone may nevertheless be vulnerable to two types of evidence destruction unique to digital data—remote wiping and data encryption. Remote wiping occurs when a phone, connected to a wireless network, receives a signal that erases stored data. This can happen when a third party sends a remote signal or when a phone is preprogrammed to delete data upon entering or leaving certain geographic areas (so-called "geofencing"). Encryption is a security feature that some modern cell phones use in addition to password protection. When such phones lock, data becomes protected by sophisticated encryption that renders a phone all but "unbreakable" unless police know the password.

As an initial matter, these broader concerns about the loss of evidence are distinct from *Chimel's* focus on a defendant who responds to arrest by trying to conceal or destroy evidence within his reach. With respect to remote wiping, the Government's primary concern turns on the actions of third parties who are not present at the scene of arrest. And data encryption is even further afield. There, the Government focuses on the ordinary operation of a phone's security features, apart from *any* active attempt by a defendant or his associates to conceal or destroy evidence upon arrest. . . .

Moreover, in situations in which an arrest might trigger a remote-wipe attempt or an officer discovers an unlocked phone, it is not clear that the ability to conduct a warrantless search would make much of a difference. The need to effect the arrest, secure the scene, and tend to other pressing matters means that law enforcement officers may well not be able to turn their attention to a cell phone right away. Cell phone data would be vulnerable to remote wiping from the time an individual anticipates arrest to the time any eventual search of the phone is completed, which might be at the station house hours later. Likewise, an officer who seizes a phone in an unlocked state might not be able to begin his search in the short time remaining before the phone locks and data becomes encrypted.

In any event, as to remote wiping, law enforcement is not without specific means to address the threat. Remote wiping can be fully prevented by disconnecting a phone from the network. There are at least two simple ways to do this: First, law enforcement officers can turn the phone off or remove its battery. Second, if they are concerned about encryption or other potential problems, they can leave a phone powered on and place it in an enclosure that isolates the phone from radio waves. Such devices are commonly called "Faraday bags," after the English scientist Michael Faraday. They are essentially sandwich bags made of aluminum foil: cheap, lightweight, and easy to use. They may not be a complete answer to the problem, but at least for now they provide a reasonable response. In fact, a number of law enforcement agencies around the country already encourage the use of Faraday bags.

To the extent that law enforcement still has specific concerns about the potential loss of evidence in a particular case, there remain more targeted ways to address those concerns. If "the police are truly confronted with a 'now or never' situation,"—for example, circumstances suggesting that a defendant's phone will be the target of an imminent remote-wipe attempt—they may be able to rely on exigent circumstances to search the phone immediately. *Missouri* v. *McNeely* (2013). Or, if officers happen to seize a phone in an unlocked state, they may be able to disable a phone's automatic-lock feature in order to prevent the phone from locking and encrypting data.

B

The search incident to arrest exception rests not only on the heightened government interests at stake in a volatile arrest situation, but also on an arrestee's reduced privacy interests upon being taken into police custody. . . . The fact that an arrestee has diminished privacy interests does not mean that the *Fourth Amendment* falls out of the picture entirely. Not every search "is acceptable solely because a person is in custody." *Maryland* v. *King* (2013). To the contrary, when "privacy-related concerns are weighty enough" a "search may require a warrant, notwithstanding the diminished expectations of privacy of the arrestee." One such example, of course, is *Chimel*. *Chimel* refused to "characteriz[e] the invasion of privacy that results from a top-to-bottom search of a man's

house as 'minor.'" Because a search of the arrestee's entire house was a substantial invasion beyond the arrest itself, the Court concluded that a warrant was required.

Robinson is the only decision from this Court applying *Chimel* to a search of the contents of an item found on an arrestee's person. . . . Lower courts applying *Robinson* and *Chimel*, however, have approved searches of a variety of personal items carried by an arrestee [including a] billfold and address book; wallet; [and] purse.

The United States asserts that a search of all data stored on a cell phone is "materially indistinguishable" from searches of these sorts of physical items. That is like saying a ride on horseback is materially indistinguishable from a flight to the moon. Both are ways of getting from point A to point B, but little else justifies lumping them together. Modern cell phones, as a category, implicate privacy concerns far beyond those implicated by the search of a cigarette pack, a wallet, or a purse. A conclusion that inspecting the contents of an arrestee's pockets works no substantial additional intrusion on privacy beyond the arrest itself may make sense as applied to physical items, but any extension of that reasoning to digital data has to rest on its own bottom.

1

Cell phones differ in both a quantitative and a qualitative sense from other objects that might be kept on an arrestee's person. The term "cell phone" is itself misleading shorthand; many of these devices are in fact minicomputers that also happen to have the capacity to be used as a telephone. They could just as easily be called cameras, video players, rolodexes, calendars, tape recorders, libraries, diaries, albums, televisions, maps, or newspapers.

One of the most notable distinguishing features of modern cell phones is their immense storage capacity. Before cell phones, a search of a person was limited by physical realities and tended as a general matter to constitute only a narrow intrusion on privacy. Most people cannot lug around every piece of mail they have received for the past several months, every picture they have taken, or every book or article they have read—nor would they have any reason to attempt to do so. And if they did, they would have to drag behind them a trunk of the sort held to require a search warrant in *Chadwick*, rather than a container the size of the cigarette package in *Robinson*.

But the possible intrusion on privacy is not physically limited in the same way when it comes to cell phones. The current top-selling smart phone has a standard capacity of 16 gigabytes (and is available with up to 64 gigabytes). Sixteen gigabytes translates to millions of pages of text, thousands of pictures, or hundreds of videos. Cell phones couple that capacity with the ability to store many different types of information: Even the most basic phones that sell for less than $20 might hold photographs, picture messages, text messages, Internet browsing history, a calendar, a thousand-entry phone book, and so on. We expect that the gulf between physical practicability and digital capacity will only continue to widen in the future.

The storage capacity of cell phones has several interrelated consequences for privacy. First, a cell phone collects in one place many distinct types of information—an address, a note, a prescription, a bank statement, a video—that reveal much more in combination than any isolated record. Second, a cell phone's capacity allows even just one type of information to convey far more than previously possible. The sum of an individual's private life can be reconstructed through a thousand photographs labeled with dates, locations, and descriptions; the same cannot be said of a photograph or two of loved ones tucked into a wallet. Third, the data on a phone can date back to the purchase of the phone, or even earlier. A person might carry in his pocket a slip of paper reminding him to call Mr. Jones; he would not carry a record of all his communications with Mr. Jones for the past several months, as would routinely be kept on a phone.

Finally, there is an element of pervasiveness that characterizes cell phones but not physical records. Prior to the digital age, people did not typically carry a cache of sensitive personal information with them as they went about their day. Now it is the person who is not carrying a cell phone, with all that it contains, who is the exception. According to one poll, nearly three-quarters of smart phone users report being within five feet of their phones most of the time, with 12% admitting that they even use their phones in the shower. A decade ago police officers searching an arrestee might have occasionally stumbled across a highly personal item such as a diary. But those discoveries were likely to be few and far between. Today, by contrast, it is no exaggeration to say that many of the more than 90% of American adults who own a cell phone keep on their person a digital record of nearly every aspect of their lives—from the mundane to the intimate. Allowing the police to scrutinize such records on a routine basis is quite different from allowing them to search a personal item or two in the occasional case.

Although the data stored on a cell phone is distinguished from physical records by quantity alone, certain types of data are also qualitatively different. An Internet search and browsing history, for example, can be found on an Internet-enabled phone and could reveal an individual's private interests or concerns—perhaps a search for certain symptoms of disease, coupled with frequent visits to WebMD. Data on a cell phone can also reveal where a person has been. Historic location information is a standard feature on many smart phones and can reconstruct someone's specific movements down to the minute, not only around town but also within a particular building.

Mobile application software on a cell phone, or "apps," offer a range of tools for managing detailed information about all aspects of a person's life. There are apps for Democratic Party news and Republican Party news; apps for alcohol, drug, and gambling addictions; apps for sharing prayer requests; apps for tracking pregnancy symptoms; apps for planning your budget; apps for every conceivable hobby or pastime; apps for improving your romantic life. There are popular apps for buying or selling just about anything, and the records of such transactions may be accessible on the phone indefinitely. There are over a million apps available in each of the two major app stores; the phrase "there's an app for that" is now part of the popular lexicon. The average smart phone user has installed 33 apps, which together can form a revealing montage of the user's life. . . .

2

To further complicate the scope of the privacy interests at stake, the data a user views on many modern cell phones may not in fact be stored on the device itself. . . . Cloud computing is the capacity of Internet-connected devices to display data stored on remote servers rather than on the device itself. Cell phone users often may not know whether particular information is stored on the device or in the cloud, and it generally makes little difference. Moreover, the same type of data may be stored locally on the device for one user and in the cloud for another.

The United States concedes that the search incident to arrest exception may not be stretched to cover a search of files accessed remotely—that is, a search of files stored in the cloud. Such a search would be like finding a key in a suspect's pocket and arguing that it allowed law enforcement to unlock and search a house. But officers searching a phone's data would not typically know whether the information they are viewing was stored locally at the time of the arrest or has been pulled from the cloud.

Although the Government recognizes the problem, its proposed solutions are unclear. It suggests that officers could disconnect a phone from the network before searching the device—the very solution whose feasibility it contested with respect to the threat of remote wiping. Alternatively, the Government proposes that law enforcement agencies "develop protocols to address" concerns raised by cloud computing. Probably a good idea, but the Founders did not fight a revolution to gain the right to government agency protocols. The possibility that a search might extend well beyond papers and effects in the physical proximity of an arrestee is yet another reason that the privacy interests here dwarf those in *Robinson*. . . .

IV

We cannot deny that our decision today will have an impact on the ability of law enforcement to combat crime. Cell phones have become important tools in facilitating coordination and communication among members of criminal enterprises, and can provide valuable incriminating information about dangerous criminals. Privacy comes at a cost.

Our holding, of course, is not that the information on a cell phone is immune from search; it is instead that a warrant is generally required before such a search, even when a cell phone is seized incident to arrest. Our cases have historically recognized that the warrant requirement is "an important working part of our machinery of government," not merely "an inconvenience to be somehow 'weighed' against the claims of police efficiency." *Coolidge* v. *New Hampshire* (1971). Recent technological advances similar to those discussed here have, in addition, made the process of obtaining a warrant itself more efficient.

Moreover, even though the search incident to arrest exception does not apply to cell phones, other case-specific exceptions may still justify a warrantless search of a particular phone. "One well-recognized exception applies when '"the exigencies of the situation" make the needs of law enforcement so compelling that [a] warrantless search is objectively reasonable under the *Fourth Amendment*.'" *Kentucky* v. *King*. Such exigencies could include the need to prevent the imminent destruction of evidence in individual cases, to pursue a fleeing suspect, and to assist persons who are seriously injured or are threatened with imminent injury. In *Chadwick*, for example, the Court held that the exception for searches incident to arrest did not justify a search of the trunk at issue, but noted that "if officers have reason to believe that luggage contains some immediately dangerous instrumentality, such as explosives, it would be foolhardy to transport it to the station house without opening the luggage."

In light of the availability of the exigent circumstances exception, there is no reason to believe that law enforcement officers will not be able to address some of the more extreme hypotheticals that have been suggested: a suspect texting an accomplice who, it is feared, is preparing to detonate a bomb, or a child abductor who may have information about the child's location on his cell phone. The defendants here recognize—indeed, they stress—that such fact-specific threats may justify a warrantless search of cell phone data. The critical point is that, unlike the search incident to arrest exception, the exigent circumstances exception requires a court to examine whether an emergency justified a warrantless search in each particular case.

***

Our cases have recognized that the *Fourth Amendment* was the founding generation's response to the reviled "general warrants" and "writs of assistance" of the colonial era, which allowed British officers to rummage through homes in an unrestrained search for evidence of criminal activity. Opposition to such searches was in fact one of the driving forces behind the Revolution itself. In 1761, the patriot James Otis delivered a speech in Boston denouncing the use of writs of assistance. A young John Adams was there, and he would later write that "[e]very man of a crowded audience appeared to me to go away, as I did, ready to take arms against writs of assistance."

Modern cell phones are not just another technological convenience. With all they contain and all they may reveal, they hold for many Americans "the privacies of life." The fact that technology now allows an individual to carry such information in his hand does not make the information any less worthy of the protection for which the Founders fought. Our answer to the question of what police must do before searching a cell phone seized incident to an arrest is accordingly simple—get a warrant.

It is so ordered.

JUSTICE ALITO, concurring in part and concurring in the judgment.

I agree with the Court that law enforcement officers, in conducting a lawful search incident to arrest, must generally obtain a warrant before searching information stored or accessible on a cell phone. . . .

I agree that we should not mechanically apply the rule used in the predigital era to the search of a cell phone. Many cell phones now in use are capable of storing and accessing a quantity of information, some highly personal, that no person would ever have had on his person in hard-copy form. This calls for a new balancing of law enforcement and privacy interests.

The Court strikes this balance in favor of privacy interests with respect to all cell phones and all information found in them, and this approach leads to anomalies. For example, the Court's broad holding favors information in digital form over information in hard-copy form. Suppose that two suspects are arrested. Suspect number one has in his pocket a monthly bill for his land-line phone, and the bill lists an incriminating call to a long-distance number. He also has in his a wallet a few snapshots, and one of these is incriminating. Suspect number two has in his pocket a cell phone, the call log of which shows a call to the same incriminating number. In addition, a number of photos are stored in the memory of the cell phone, and one of these is incriminating. Under established law, the police may seize and examine the phone bill and the snapshots in the wallet without obtaining a warrant, but under the Court's holding today, the information stored in the cell phone is out.

While the Court's approach leads to anomalies, I do not see a workable alternative. Law enforcement officers need clear rules regarding searches incident to arrest, and it would take many cases and many years for the courts to develop more nuanced rules. And during that time, the nature of the electronic devices that ordinary Americans carry on their persons would continue to change.

II

. . . While I agree with the holding of the Court, I would reconsider the question presented here if either Congress or state legislatures, after assessing the legitimate needs of law enforcement and the privacy interests of cell phone owners, enact legislation that draws reasonable distinctions based on categories of information or perhaps other variables.

The regulation of electronic surveillance provides an instructive example. After this Court held that electronic surveillance constitutes a search even when no property interest is invaded, see *Katz* v. *United States* (1967), Congress responded by enacting Title III of the Omnibus Crime Control and Safe Streets Act of 1968. Since that time, electronic surveillance has been governed primarily, not by decisions of this Court, but by the statute, which authorizes but imposes detailed restrictions on electronic surveillance.

Modern cell phones are of great value for both lawful and unlawful purposes. They can be used in committing many serious crimes, and they present new and difficult law enforcement problems. At the same time, because of the role that these devices have come to play in contemporary life, searching their contents implicates very sensitive privacy interests that this Court is poorly positioned to understand and evaluate. Many forms of modern technology are making it easier and easier for both government and private entities to amass a wealth of information about the lives of ordinary Americans, and at the same time, many ordinary Americans are choosing to make public much information that was seldom revealed to outsiders just a few decades ago.

In light of these developments, it would be very unfortunate if privacy protection in the 21st century were left primarily to the federal courts using the blunt instrument of the Fourth Amendment. Legislatures, elected by the people, are in a better position than we are to assess and respond to the changes that have already occurred and those that almost certainly will take place in the future.

Mapp v. Ohio
367 U.S. 643 (1961)

On May 23, 1957, Cleveland police officers came to Dollree Mapp's residence, acting on information that a bombing-case suspect and betting equipment might be found there. They requested entrance, but Mapp refused to admit them without a search warrant. When she refused a second time, the police forced their way into her duplex apartment and subdued and handcuffed her when she grabbed and placed in her bosom a paper that they informed her was a valid search warrant. The officers subjected her entire residence and its contents to a thorough search and in a basement trunk found materials that provided the basis for her conviction of possessing obscene materials. The Ohio Supreme Court affirmed her conviction, and the US Supreme Court granted certiorari. Opinion of the Court: Clark, Warren, Black, Douglas, Brennan. Concurring opinions: Black; Douglas. Dissenting opinion: Harlan, Frankfurter, Whittaker. Separate memorandum: Stewart.

JUSTICE CLARK delivered the opinion of the Court.

Appellant stands convicted of knowingly having had in her possession and under her control certain lewd and lascivious books, pictures, and photographs in violation [of Ohio law]. . . . The Supreme Court of Ohio found that her conviction was valid though "based primarily upon the introduction in evidence of lewd and lascivious books and pictures unlawfully seized during an unlawful search of defendant's home." . . .

The State says that even if the search were made without authority, or otherwise unreasonably, it is not prevented from using the unconstitutionally seized evidence at trial, citing *Wolf v. Colorado,* . . . (1949), in which this Court did indeed hold "that in a prosecution in a State court for a State crime the Fourteenth Amendment does not forbid the admission of evidence obtained by an unreasonable search and seizure." . . .

. . . In the year 1914, in *Weeks [v. United States,]* this Court "for the first time" held that "in a federal prosecution the Fourth Amendment barred the use of evidence secured through an illegal search and seizure." . . . This Court has ever since required of federal law officers a strict adherence to that command which this Court has held to be a clear, specific, and constitutionally required—even if judicially implied—deterrent safeguard without insistence upon which the Fourth Amendment would have been reduced to "a form of words." . . .

In 1949, 35 years after *Weeks* was announced, this Court, in *Wolf v. Colorado,* again for the first time, discussed the effect of the Fourth Amendment upon the States through the operation of the Due Process Clause of the Fourteenth Amendment. Nevertheless, after declaring that the "security of one's privacy against arbitrary intrusion by the police" is "implicit in 'the concept of ordered liberty' and as such enforceable against the States through the Due Process Clause." . . . and announcing that it "stoutly adhere[d]" to the *Weeks* decision, the Court decided that the *Weeks* exclusionary rule would not then be imposed upon the States as "an essential ingredient of the right." . . .

Today we once again examine *Wolf*'s constitutional documentation of the right to privacy free from unreasonable state intrusion, and after its dozen years on our books, are led by it to close the only courtroom door remaining open to evidence secured by official lawlessness in flagrant abuse of that basic right, reserved to all persons as a specific guarantee against that very same unlawful conduct. We hold that all evidence obtained by searches and seizures in violation of the Constitution is, by that same authority, inadmissible in a state court. . . .

Since the Fourth Amendment's right of privacy has been declared enforceable against the States through the Due Process Clause of the Fourteenth, it is enforceable against them by the same sanction of exclusion as is used against the Federal Government. Were it otherwise, then just as without the *Weeks* rule the assurance against unreasonable federal searches and seizures would be "a form of words," valueless and undeserving of mention in a perpetual charter of inestimable human liberties, so too, without that rule the freedom from state invasions of privacy would be so ephemeral and so neatly severed from its conceptual nexus with the freedom from all brutish means of coercing evidence as not to merit this Court's high regard as a freedom "implicit in the concept of ordered liberty."

. . . This Court has not hesitated to enforce as strictly against the States as it does against the Federal Government the rights of free speech and of a free press, the rights to notice and to a fair, public trial, including, as it does, the right not to be convicted by use of a coerced confession, however logically relevant it be, and without regard to its reliability. . . . Why should not the same rule apply to what is tantamount to coerced testimony by way of unconstitutional seizure of goods, papers, effects, documents, etc.? We find that as to the Federal Government, the Fourth and Fifth Amendments and, as to the States, the freedom from unconscionable invasions of privacy

and the freedom from convictions based upon coerced confessions do enjoy an "intimate relation" in their perpetuation of "principles of humanity and civil liberty [secured] . . . only after years of struggle." . . . The very least that together they assure in either sphere is that no man is to be convicted on unconstitutional evidence. . . . Moreover, our holding that the exclusionary rule is an essential part of both the Fourth and Fourteenth Amendments is not only the logical dictate of prior cases, but it also makes very good sense. There is no war between the Constitution and common sense. Presently, a federal prosecutor may make no use of evidence illegally seized, but a State's attorney across the street may, although he supposedly is operating under the enforceable prohibitions of the same Amendment. Thus the State, by admitting evidence unlawfully seized, serves to encourage disobedience to the Federal Constitution which it is bound to uphold. . . . In nonexclusionary States, federal officers, being human, were by it invited to and did, as our cases indicate, step across the street to the State's attorney with their unconstitutionally seized evidence. Prosecution on the basis of that evidence was then had in a state court in utter disregard of the enforceable Fourth Amendment. If the fruits of an unconstitutional search had been inadmissible in both state and federal courts, this inducement to evasion would have been sooner eliminated. . . .

There are those who say, as did Justice (then Judge) Cardozo, that under our constitutional exclusionary doctrine "[t]he criminal is to go free because the constable has blundered." . . . In some cases this will undoubtedly be the result. But . . . "there is another consideration—the imperative of judicial integrity." . . . The criminal goes free, if he must, but it is the law that sets him free. Nothing can destroy a government more quickly than its failure to observe its own laws, or worse, its disregard of the charter of its own existence. . . .

The ignoble shortcut to conviction left open to the State tends to destroy the entire system of constitutional restraints on which the liberties of the people rest. Having once recognized that the right to privacy embodied in the Fourth Amendment is enforceable against the States, and that the right to be secure against rude invasions of privacy by state officers is, therefore, constitutional in origin, we can no longer permit that right to remain an empty promise. Because it is enforceable in the same manner and to like effect as other basic rights secured by the Due Process Clause, we can no longer permit it to be revocable at the whim of any police officer who, in the name of law enforcement itself, chooses to suspend its enjoyment. Our decision, founded on reason and truth, gives to the individual no more than that which the Constitution guarantees him, to the police officer no less than that to which honest law enforcement is entitled, and, to the courts, that judicial integrity so necessary in the true administration of justice. . . .

JUSTICE BLACK, concurring . . .

I am still not persuaded that the Fourth Amendment, standing alone, would be enough to bar the introduction into evidence against an accused of papers and effects seized from him in violation of its commands. For the Fourth Amendment does not itself contain any provision expressly precluding the use of such evidence, and I am extremely doubtful that such a provision could properly be inferred from nothing more than the basic command against unreasonable searches and seizures. Reflection on the problem, however, in the light of cases coming before the Court since *Wolf,* has led me to conclude that when the Fourth Amendment's ban against unreasonable searches and seizures is considered together with the Fifth Amendment's ban against compelled self-incrimination, a constitutional basis emerges which not only justifies but actually requires the exclusionary rule. . . .

JUSTICE HARLAN, whom JUSTICE FRANKFURTER and JUSTICE WHITTAKER join, dissenting.

In overruling the *Wolf* case the Court, in my opinion, has forgotten the sense of judicial restraint which, with due regard for *stare decisis,* is one element that should enter into deciding whether a past decision of this Court should be overruled. Apart from that I also believe that the *Wolf* rule represents sounder Constitutional doctrine than the new rule which now replaces it. . . .

From the Court's statement of the case one would gather that the central, if not controlling, issue on this appeal is whether illegally state-seized evidence is Constitutionally admissible in a state prosecution, an issue which would of course face us with the need for re-examining *Wolf.* However, such is not the situation. For, although that question was indeed raised here and below among appellant's subordinate points, the new and pivotal issue brought to the Court by this appeal is whether § 2905.34 of the Ohio Revised Code making criminal the *mere* knowing possession or control of obscene material, and under which appellant has been convicted, is consistent with the rights of free thought and expression assured against state action by the Fourteenth Amendment. That was the principal issue which was decided by the Ohio Supreme Court, which was tendered by appellant's Jurisdictional Statement, and which was briefed and argued in this Court. . . .

In this posture of things, I think it fair to say that five members of this Court have simply "reached out" to overrule *Wolf.* With all respect for the views of the majority, and recognizing that *stare decisis* carries different weight in Constitutional adjudication than it does in nonconstitutional decision, I can perceive no justification for regarding this case as an appropriate occasion for re-examining *Wolf.* . . .

The occasion which the Court has taken here is in the context of a case where the question was briefed not at all and argued only extremely tangentially. The unwisdom of overruling *Wolf* without full-dress argument is aggravated by the circumstance that that decision is a comparatively recent one (1949) to which three members of the present majority have at one time or other expressly subscribed, one to be sure with explicit misgivings. I would think that our obligation to the States, on whom we impose this new rule, as well as the obligation of orderly adherence to our own processes would demand that we seek that aid which adequate briefing and argument lends to the determination of an important issue. It certainly has never been a postulate of judicial power that mere altered disposition, or subsequent membership on the Court, is sufficient warrant for overturning a deliberately decided rule of Constitutional law. . . .

I am bound to say that what has been done is not likely to promote respect either for the Court's adjudicatory process or for the stability of its decisions. Having been unable, however, to persuade any of the majority to a different procedural course, I now turn to the merits of the present decision. . . .

I would not impose upon the States this federal exclusionary remedy. The reasons given by the majority for now suddenly turning its back on *Wolf* seem to me notably unconvincing.

First, it is said that "the factual grounds upon which *Wolf* was based" have since changed, in that more States now follow the *Weeks* exclusionary rule than was so at the time *Wolf* was decided. While that is true, a recent survey indicates that at present one-half of the States still adhere to the common-law non-exclusionary rule . . . But in any case surely all this is beside the point, as the majority itself indeed seems to recognize. Our concern here, as it was in *Wolf,* is not with the desirability of that rule but only with the question whether the States are Constitutionally free to follow it or not as they may themselves determine, and the relevance of the disparity of views among the States on this point lies simply in the fact that the judgment involved is a debatable one. . . .

The preservation of a proper balance between state and federal responsibility in the administration of criminal justice demands patience on the part of those who might like to see things move faster among the States in this respect. Problems of criminal law enforcement vary widely from State to State. One State, in considering the totality of its legal picture, may conclude that the need for embracing the *Weeks* rule is pressing because other remedies are unavailable or inadequate to secure compliance with the substantive Constitutional principle involved. Another, though equally solicitous of Constitutional rights, may choose to pursue one purpose at a time, allowing all evidence relevant to guilt to be brought into a criminal trial, and dealing with Constitutional infractions by other means. Still another may consider the exclusionary rule too rough-and-ready a remedy, in that it reaches only unconstitutional intrusions which eventuate in criminal prosecution

of the victims. Further, a State after experimenting with the *Weeks* rule for a time may, because of unsatisfactory experience with it, decide to revert to a nonexclusionary rule. And so on. From the standpoint of Constitutional permissibility in pointing a State in one direction or another, I do not see at all why "time has set its face against" the considerations which led Mr. Justice Cardozo, then chief judge of the New York Court of Appeals, to reject for New York in *People v. Defore,* . . . the *Weeks* exclusionary rule. For us the question remains, as it has always been, one of state power, not one of passing judgment on the wisdom of one state course or another. . . .

Further, we are told that imposition of the *Weeks* rule on the States makes "very good sense," in that it will promote recognition by state and federal officials of their "mutual obligation to respect the same fundamental criteria" in their approach to law enforcement, and will avoid "'needless conflict between state and federal courts.'" . . .

An approach which regards the issue as one of achieving procedural symmetry or of serving administrative convenience surely disfigures the boundaries of this Court's functions in relation to the state and federal courts. Our role in promulgating the *Weeks* rule and its extensions . . . was quite a different one than it is here. There, in implementing the Fourth Amendment, we occupied the position of a tribunal having the ultimate responsibility for developing the standards and procedures of judicial administration within the judicial system over which it presides. Here we review state procedures whose measure is to be taken not against the specific substantive commands of the Fourth Amendment but under the flexible contours of the Due Process Clause. . . .

I regret that I find so unwise in principle and so inexpedient in policy a decision motivated by the high purpose of increasing respect for Constitutional rights. But in the last analysis I think this Court can increase respect for the Constitution only if it rigidly respects the limitations which the Constitution places upon it, and respects as well the principles inherent in its own processes. In the present case I think we exceed both, and that our voice becomes only a voice of power, not of reason.

Memorandum of JUSTICE STEWART . . .

. . . I would . . . reverse the judgment in this case because I am persuaded that the provision of . . . the Ohio [obscenity law], upon which the petitioner's conviction was based, is, in the words of Mr. Justice Harlan, not "consistent with the rights of free thought and expression assured against state action by the Fourteenth Amendment."

Olmstead v. United States
277 U.S. 438 (1928)

Roy Olmstead and several accomplices were convicted in federal district court of conspiring to violate the National Prohibition Act by unlawfully possessing, transporting, and importing intoxicating liquors. At trial the government presented incriminating evidence obtained by federal agents who wiretapped telephone lines at points between the defendants' homes and their offices. The Court of Appeals for the Ninth Circuit affirmed the convictions over objections that this wiretap evidence was inadmissible under the Fourth Amendment protection from unreasonable searches and seizures and the Fifth Amendment guarantee against self-incrimination. The Supreme Court granted certiorari. Opinion of the Court: Taft, Van Devanter, McReynolds, Sutherland, Sanford. Dissenting opinions: Holmes; Brandeis; Butler; Stone.

THE CHIEF JUSTICE delivered the opinion of the Court.

There is no room in the present case for applying the Fifth Amendment unless the Fourth Amendment was first violated. There was no evidence of compulsion to induce the defendants to talk over their many telephones. They were continually and voluntarily transacting business without knowledge of the interception. Our consideration must be confined to the Fourth Amendment. . . .

The well known historical purpose of the Fourth Amendment, directed against general warrants and writs of assistance, was to prevent the use of governmental force to search a man's house, his person, his papers and his effects; and to prevent their seizure against his will. . . .

The Amendment itself shows that the search is to be of material things—the person, the house, his papers or his effects. The description of the warrant necessary to make the proceeding lawful, is that it must specify the place to be searched and the person or *things* to be seized. . . .

. . . The Amendment does not forbid what was done here. There was no searching. There was no seizure. The evidence was secured by the use of the sense of hearing and that only. There was no entry of the houses or offices of the defendants.

By the invention of the telephone, fifty years ago, and its application for the purpose of extending communications, one can talk with another at a far distant place. The language of the Amendment cannot be extended and expanded to include telephone wires reaching to the whole world from the defendant's house or office. The intervening wires are not part of his house or office any more than are the highways along which they are stretched. . . .

Congress may of course protect the secrecy of telephone messages by making them, when intercepted, inadmissible in evidence in federal criminal trials, by direct legislation, and thus depart from the common law of evidence. But the courts may not adopt such a policy by attributing an enlarged and unusual meaning to the Fourth Amendment. The reasonable view is that one who installs in his house a telephone instrument with connecting wires intends to project his voice to those quite outside, and that the wires beyond his house and messages while passing over them are not within protection of the Fourth Amendment. Here those who intercepted the projected voices were not in the house of either party to the conversation.

Neither the cases we have cited nor any of the many federal decisions brought to our attention hold the Fourth Amendment to have been violated as against a defendant unless there has been an official search and seizure of his person, or such a seizure of his papers or his tangible material effects, or an actual physical invasion of his house "or curtilage" for the purpose of making a seizure.

We think, therefore, that the wire tapping here disclosed did not amount to a search or seizure within the meaning of the Fourth Amendment.

What has been said disposes of the only question that comes within the terms of our order granting *certiorari* in these cases. But some of our number, departing from that order, have concluded that there is merit in the two-fold objection overruled in both courts below that evidence obtained through intercepting of telephone messages by government agents was inadmissible because the mode of obtaining it was unethical and a misdemeanor under the law of Washington. To avoid any misrepresentation of our views of that objection we shall deal with it in both of its phases.

While a Territory, the English common law prevailed in Washington and thus continued after her admission in 1889. The rules of evidence in criminal cases in courts of the United States sitting there, consequently are those of the common law. . . .

The common law rule is that the admissibility of evidence is not affected by the illegality of the means by which it was obtained. . . .

Nor can we, without the sanction of congressional enactment, subscribe to the suggestion that the courts have a discretion to exclude evidence, the admission of which is not unconstitutional, because unethically secured. This would be at variance with the common law doctrine generally supported by authority. There is no case that sustains, nor any recognized textbook that gives color to such a view. Our general experience shows that much evidence has always been receivable although not obtained by conformity to the highest ethics. The history of criminal trials shows numerous cases of prosecutions of oath-bound conspiracies for murder, robbery, and other crimes, where officers of the law have disguised themselves and joined the organizations, taken the oaths and given themselves every appearance of active members engaged in the promotion of crime, for the purpose of securing evidence. Evidence secured by such means has always been received.

A standard which would forbid the reception of evidence if obtained by other than nice ethical conduct by government officials would make society suffer and give criminals greater immunity than has been known heretofore. In the absence of controlling legislation by Congress, those who realize the difficulties in bringing offenders to justice may well deem it wise that the exclusion of evidence should be confined to cases where rights under the Constitution would be violated by admitting it.

JUSTICE HOLMES, dissenting.

. . . It is desirable that criminals should be detected, and to that end that all available evidence should be used. It also is desirable that the Government should not itself foster and pay for other crimes, when they are the means by which the evidence is to be obtained. We have to choose, and for my part I think it a less evil that some criminals should escape than that the Government should play an ignoble part. . . .

JUSTICE BRANDEIS, dissenting. . . .

The Government makes no attempt to defend the methods employed by its officers. Indeed, it concedes that if wire-tapping can be deemed a search and seizure within the Fourth Amendment, such wire-tapping as was practiced in the case at bar was an unreasonable search and seizure, and that the evidence thus obtained was inadmissible. But it relies on the language of the Amendment; and it claims that the protection given thereby cannot properly be held to include a telephone conversation.

"We must never forget," said Mr. Chief Justice Marshall in *McCulloch v. Maryland,* "that it is a constitution we are expounding." Since then, this Court has repeatedly sustained the exercise of power by Congress, under various clauses of that instrument, over objects of which the Fathers could not have dreamed. . . . We have likewise held the general limitations on the powers of Government, like those embodied in the due process clauses of the Fifth and Fourteenth Amendments, do not forbid the United States or the States from meeting modern conditions by regulations which "a century ago, or even half a century ago, probably would have been rejected as arbitrary and oppressive." . . . Clauses guaranteeing to the individual protection against specific abuses of power, must have similar capacity of adaptation to a changing world.

When the Fourth and Fifth Amendments were adopted, "the form that evil had theretofore taken," had been necessarily simple. Force and violence were then the only means known to man by which a Government could directly effect self-incrimination. It could compel the individual to testify—a compulsion effected, if need be, by torture. It could secure possession of his papers and other articles incident to his private life—a seizure effected, if need be, by breaking and entry. Protection against such invasion of "the sanctities of a man's home and the privacies of life" was provided in the Fourth and Fifth Amendments by specific language. . . . But "time works changes, brings into existence new conditions and purposes." Subtler and more far-reaching means of invading privacy have become available to the Government. Discovery and invention have made it possible for the Government, by means far more effective than stretching upon the rack, to obtain disclosure in court of what is whispered in the closet.

Moreover, "in the application of a constitution, our contemplation cannot be only of what has been but of what may be." The progress of science in furnishing the Government with means of espionage is not likely to stop with wire-tapping. Ways may some day be developed by which the Government, without removing papers from secret drawers, can reproduce them in court, and by which it will be enabled to expose to a jury the most intimate occurrences of the home. Advances in the psychic and related sciences may bring means of exploring unexpressed beliefs, thoughts and emotions. . . . Can it be that the Constitution affords no protection against such invasions of individual security?

. . . The makers of our Constitution undertook to secure conditions favorable to the pursuit of happiness. They recognized the significance of man's spiritual nature, of his feelings and of his intellect. They knew that only a part of the pain, pleasure and satisfactions of life are to be found in material things. They sought to protect Americans in their beliefs, their thoughts, their emotions and their sensations. They conferred, as against the Government, the right to be let alone—the most comprehensive of rights and the right most valued by civilized men. To protect that right, every unjustifiable intrusion by the Government upon the privacy of the individual, whatever the means employed, must be deemed a violation of the Fourth Amendment. And the use, as evidence in a criminal proceeding, of facts ascertained by such intrusion must be deemed a violation of the Fifth.

Applying to the Fourth and Fifth Amendments the established rule of construction, the defendants' objections to the evidence obtained by wiretapping must, in my opinion, be sustained. It is, of course, immaterial where the physical connection with the telephone wires leading into the defendants' premises was made. And it is also immaterial that the intrusion was in aid of law enforcement. Experience should teach us to be most on our guard to protect liberty when the Government's purposes are beneficent.

Men born to freedom are naturally alert to repel invasion of their liberty by evil-minded rulers. The greatest dangers to liberty lurk in insidious encroachment by men of zeal, well-meaning but without understanding.

Independently of the constitutional question, I am of opinion that the judgment should be reversed. By the laws of Washington, wire-tapping is a crime. . . . To prove its case, the Government was obliged to lay bare the crimes committed by its officers on its behalf. A federal court should not permit such a prosecution to continue. . . .

Decency, security and liberty alike demand that government officials shall be subjected to the same rules of conduct that are commands to the citizen. In a government of laws, existence of the government will be imperiled if it fails to observe the law scrupulously. Our Government is the potent, the omnipresent teacher. For good or for ill, it teaches the whole people by its example. Crime is contagious. If the Government becomes a lawbreaker, it breeds contempt for law; it invites every man to become a law unto himself; it invites anarchy. To declare that in the administration of the criminal law the end justifies the means—to declare that the Government may commit crimes in order to secure the conviction of a private criminal—would bring terrible retribution. Against that pernicious doctrine this Court should resolutely set its face.

Katz v. United States
389 U.S. 342 (1967)

Charles Katz was convicted in federal district court of violating a federal statute by transmitting wagering information to Miami and Boston from a telephone booth in Los Angeles. At trial the government introduced a recording of his phone conversations made by FBI agents using an electronic listening device attached to the outside of the booth. The court of appeals, in affirming Katz's conviction, rejected his contention that the recording had been obtained in violation of the Fourth Amendment, on the grounds that there was no physical entrance into the area occupied by the defendant. The Supreme Court granted certiorari. Opinion of the Court: Stewart, Warren, Douglas, Harlan, Brennan, White, Fortas. Concurring opinions: Douglas, Brennan; Harlan; White. Dissenting opinion: Black. Not participating: Marshall.

JUSTICE STEWART delivered the opinion of the Court.

. . . The petitioner has strenuously argued that the booth was a "constitutionally protected area." The Government has maintained with equal vigor that it was not. But this effort to decide whether or not a given "area," viewed in the abstract, is "constitutionally protected" deflects attention from the problem presented by this case. For the Fourth Amendment protects people, not places. What a person knowingly exposes to the public, even in his own home or office, is not a subject of Fourth Amendment protection. . . . But what he seeks to preserve as private, even in an area accessible to the public, may be constitutionally protected. . . .

The Government stresses the fact that the telephone booth from which the petitioner made his calls was constructed partly of glass, so that he was as visible after he entered it as he would have been if he had remained outside. But what he sought to exclude when he entered the booth was not the intruding eye—it was the uninvited ear. He did not shed his right to do so simply because he made his calls from a place where he might be seen. No less than an individual in a business office, in a friend's apartment, or in a taxicab, a person in a telephone booth may rely upon the protection of the Fourth Amendment. One who occupies it, shuts the door behind him, and pays the toll that permits him to place a call is surely entitled to assume that the words he utters into the mouthpiece will not be broadcast to the world. To read the Constitution more narrowly is to ignore the vital role that the public telephone has come to play in private communication.

The Government contends, however, that the activities of its agents in this case should not be tested by Fourth Amendment requirements, for the surveillance technique they employed involved no physical penetration of the telephone booth from which the petitioner placed his calls. It is true that the absence of such penetration was at one time thought to foreclose further Fourth Amendment inquiry, *Olmstead v. United States*. . . .

. . . The underpinnings of *Olmstead* [*v. United States* (1928)] and *Goldman* [*v. United States* (1942)] have been so eroded by our subsequent decisions that the "trespass" doctrine there enunciated can no longer be regarded as controlling. The Government's activities in electronically listening to and recording the petitioner's words violated the privacy upon which he justifiably relied while using the telephone booth and thus constituted a "search and seizure" within the meaning of the Fourth Amendment. The fact that the electronic device employed to achieve that end did not happen to penetrate the wall of the booth can have no constitutional significance.

The question remaining for decision, then, is whether the search and seizure conducted in this case complied with constitutional standards. In that regard, the Government's position is that its agents acted in an entirely defensible manner: They did not begin their electronic surveillance until investigation of the petitioner's activities had established a strong probability that he was using the telephone in question to transmit gambling information to persons in other States, in violation of federal law. Moreover, the surveillance was limited, both in scope and in duration, to the specific purpose of establishing the contents of the petitioner's unlawful telephonic communications. The agents confined their surveillance to the brief periods during which he used the telephone booth, and they took great care to overhear only the conversations of the petitioner himself. . . .

The Government urges that, because its agents relied upon the decisions in *Olmstead* and *Goldman,* and because they did no more here than they might properly have done with prior judicial sanction, we should retroactively validate their conduct. That we cannot do. It is apparent that the agents in this case acted with restraint. Yet the inescapable fact is that this restraint was imposed by the agents themselves, not by a judicial officer. They were not required, before commencing the search, to present their estimate of probable cause for detached scrutiny by a neutral magistrate. They were not compelled, during the conduct of the search itself, to observe precise limits established in advance by a specific court order. Nor were they directed, after the search had been completed, to notify the authorizing magistrate in detail of all that had been seized. In the absence of such safeguards, this Court has never sustained a search upon the sole ground that officers reasonably expected to find evidence of a particular crime and voluntarily confined their activities to the least intrusive means consistent with that end. . . . "Over and again this Court has emphasized that the mandate of the [Fourth] Amendment requires adherence to judicial processes," . . . and that searches conducted outside the judicial process, without prior approval by judge or magistrate, are *per se* unreasonable under the Fourth Amendment—subject only to a few specifically established and well-delineated exceptions. . . .

JUSTICE BLACK, dissenting. . . .

While I realize that an argument based on the meaning of words lacks the scope, and no doubt the appeal, of broad policy discussions and philosophical discourses on such nebulous subjects as privacy, for me the language of the Amendment is the crucial place to look in construing a written document such as our Constitution. The Fourth Amendment . . . protects "persons, houses, papers, and effects, against unreasonable searches and seizures. . . ." These words connote the idea of tangible things with size, form, and weight, things capable of being searched, seized, or both. . . . The Amendment further establishes its Framers' purpose to limit its protection to tangible things by providing that no warrants shall issue but those "particularly describing the place to be searched, and the persons or things to be seized." A conversation overheard by eavesdropping, whether by plain snooping or wiretapping, is not tangible and, under the normally accepted meanings of the words, can neither be searched nor seized. In addition the language of the second clause indicates that the Amendment refers not only to something tangible so it can be seized but to something already in existence so it can be described. Yet the Court's interpretation would have the Amendment apply to overhearing future conversations which by their own nature are nonexistent until they take place. How can one "describe" a future conversation, and, if one cannot, how can a magistrate issue a warrant to eavesdrop one in the future? It is argued that information showing what is expected to be said is sufficient to limit the boundaries of what later can be admitted into evidence; but does such general information really meet the specific language of the Amendment which says "particularly describing"? Rather than using language in a completely artificial way, I must conclude that the Fourth Amendment simply does not apply to eavesdropping. . . .

Miranda v. Arizona
384 U.S. 436 (1966)

Miranda consolidates for decision four cases, all of which raised the issue of the admissibility into evidence of statements obtained from defendants during pretrial custodial police interrogation. In each of these cases, the defendants were convicted on the basis of confessions made after periods of police questioning during which they were not informed of their rights to counsel and to remain silent. The crimes for which they were convicted included murder, kidnapping, rape, and robbery.

Opinion of the Court: <u>Warren</u>, Black, Douglas, Brennan, Fortas. Dissenting opinions: <u>Clark</u>; <u>Harlan</u>, Stewart, White; <u>White</u>, Harlan, Stewart.

THE CHIEF JUSTICE delivered the opinion of the Court.

The cases before us raise questions which go to the roots of our concepts of American criminal jurisprudence: the restraints society must observe consistent with the Federal Constitution in prosecuting individuals for crime. More specifically, we deal with the admissibility of statements obtained from an individual who is subjected to custodial police interrogation and the necessity for procedures which assure that the individual is accorded his privilege under the Fifth Amendment to the Constitution not to be compelled to incriminate himself. . . .

Our holding will be spelled out with some specificity in the pages which follow but briefly stated it is this: the prosecution may not use statements, whether exculpatory or inculpatory, stemming from custodial interrogation of the defendant unless it demonstrates the use of procedural safeguards effective to secure the privilege against self-incrimination. By custodial interrogation, we mean questioning initiated by law enforcement officers after a person has been taken into custody or otherwise deprived of his freedom of action in any significant way. As for the procedural safeguards to be employed, unless other fully effective means are devised to inform accused persons of their right of silence and to assure a continuous opportunity to exercise it, the following measures are required. Prior to any questioning, the person must be warned that he has a right to remain silent, that any statement he does make may be used as evidence against him, and that he has a right to the presence of an attorney, either retained or appointed. The defendant may waive effectuation of these rights, provided the waiver is made voluntarily, knowingly and intelligently. If, however, he indicates in any manner and at any stage of the process that he wishes to consult with an attorney before speaking there can be no questioning. Likewise, if the individual is alone and indicates in any manner that he does not wish to be interrogated, the police may not question him. The mere fact that he may have answered some questions or volunteered some statements on his own does not deprive him of the right to refrain from answering any further inquiries until he has consulted with an attorney and thereafter consents to be questioned.

The constitutional issue we decide in each of these cases is the admissibility of statements obtained from a defendant questioned while in custody or otherwise deprived of his freedom of action in any significant way. In each, the defendant was questioned by police officers, detectives, or a prosecuting attorney in a room in which he was cut off from the outside world. In none of these cases was the defendant given a full and effective warning of his rights at the outset of the interrogation process. In all the cases, the questioning elicited oral admissions, and in three of them, signed statements as well which were admitted at their trials. They all thus share salient features—incommunicado interrogation of individuals in a police-dominated atmosphere, resulting in self-incriminating statements without full warnings of constitutional rights. . . .

An understanding of the nature and setting of this in-custody interrogation is essential to our decisions today. The difficulty in depicting what transpires at such interrogations stems from the fact that in this country they have largely taken place incommunicado. . . .

. . . Interrogation still takes place in privacy. Privacy results in secrecy and this in turn results in a gap in our knowledge as to what in fact goes on in the interrogation rooms. A valuable source of information about present police practices, however, may be found in various police manuals and texts, which document procedures employed with success in the past, and which recommend various other effective tactics. These texts are used by law enforcement agencies themselves as guides. It should be noted that these texts professedly present the most enlightened and effective means presently used to obtain statements through custodial interrogation. By considering these texts and other data, it is possible to describe procedures observed and noted around the country. . . .

From these representative samples of interrogation techniques, the setting prescribed by the manuals and observed in practice becomes clear. In essence, it is this: To be alone with the subject is essential to prevent distraction and to deprive him of any outside support. The aura of confidence in his guilt undermines his will to resist. He merely confirms the preconceived story the police seek to have him describe. Patience and persistence, at times relentless questioning, are employed. To obtain a confession, the interrogator must "patiently maneuver himself or his quarry into a position from which the desired objective may be attained." When normal procedures fail to produce the needed result, the police may resort to deceptive stratagems such as giving false legal advice. It is important to keep the subject off balance, for example, by trading on his insecurity about himself or his surroundings. The police then persuade, trick or cajole him out of exercising his constitutional rights. . . .

In the cases before us today, given this background, we concern ourselves primarily with this interrogation atmosphere and the evils it can bring. In No. 759, *Miranda v. Arizona,* the police arrested the defendant and took him to a special interrogation room where they secured a confession. In No. 760, *Vignera v. New York,* the defendant made oral admissions to the police after interrogation in the afternoon, and then signed an inculpatory statement upon being questioned by an assistant district attorney later the same evening. In No. 761, *Westover v. United States,* the defendant was handed over to the Federal Bureau of Investigation by local authorities after they had detained and interrogated him for a lengthy period, both at night and the following morning. After some two hours of questioning, the federal officers had obtained signed statements from the defendant. Lastly, in No. 584, *California v. Stewart,* the local police held the defendant five days in the station and interrogated him on nine separate occasions before they secured his inculpatory statement.

In these cases, we might not find the defendants' statements to have been involuntary in traditional terms. Our concern for adequate safeguards to protect precious Fifth Amendment rights is, of course, not lessened in the slightest. In each of the cases, the defendant was thrust into an unfamiliar atmosphere and run through menacing police interrogation

procedures. The potentiality for compulsion is forcefully apparent, for example, in *Miranda,* where the indigent Mexican defendant was a seriously disturbed individual with pronounced sexual fantasies, and in *Stewart,* in which the defendant was an indigent Los Angeles Negro who had dropped out of school in the sixth grade. To be sure, the records do not evince overt physical coercion or patent psychological ploys. The fact remains that in none of these cases did the officers undertake to afford appropriate safeguards at the outset of the interrogation to insure that the statements were truly the product of free choice.

It is obvious that such an interrogation environment is created for no purpose other than to subjugate the individual to the will of his examiner. This atmosphere carries its own badge of intimidation. To be sure, this is not physical intimidation, but it is equally destructive of human dignity. The current practice of incommunicado interrogation is at odds with one of our Nation's most cherished principles—that the individual may not be compelled to incriminate himself. Unless adequate protective devices are employed to dispel the compulsion inherent in custodial surroundings, no statement obtained from the defendant can truly be the product of his free choice. . . .

From the foregoing, we can readily perceive an intimate connection between the privilege against self-incrimination and police custodial questioning. . . . We have recently noted that the privilege against self-incrimination—the essential mainstay of our adversary system—is founded on a complex of values. . . . All these policies point to one overriding thought: the constitutional foundation underlying the privilege is the respect a government—state or federal—must accord to the dignity and integrity of its citizens. To maintain a "fair state-individual balance," to require the government "to shoulder the entire load," . . . to respect the inviolability of human personality, our accusatory system of criminal justice demands that the government seeking to punish an individual produce the evidence against him by its own independent labors, rather than by the cruel, simple expedient of compelling it from his own mouth. . . . In sum, the privilege is fulfilled only when the person is guaranteed the right "to remain silent unless he chooses to speak in the unfettered exercise of his own will."

The question in these cases is whether the privilege is fully applicable during a period of custodial interrogation. In this Court, the privilege has consistently been accorded a liberal construction. . . . We are satisfied that all the principles embodied in the privilege apply to informal compulsion exerted by law-enforcement officers during in-custody questioning. An individual swept from familiar surroundings into police custody, surrounded by antagonistic forces, and subjected to the techniques of persuasion described above cannot be otherwise than under compulsion to speak. As a practical matter, the compulsion to speak in the isolated setting of the police station may well be greater than in courts or other official investigations, where there are often impartial observers to guard against intimidation or trickery. . . .

Today, then, there can be no doubt that the Fifth Amendment privilege is available outside of criminal court proceedings and serves to protect persons in all settings in which their freedom of action is curtailed in any significant way from being compelled to incriminate themselves. We have concluded that without proper safeguards the process of in-custody interrogation of persons suspected or accused of crime contains inherently compelling pressures which work to undermine the individual's will to resist and to compel him to speak where he would not otherwise do so freely. In order to combat these pressures and to permit a full opportunity to exercise the privilege against self-incrimination, the accused must be adequately and effectively apprised of his rights and the exercise of those rights must be fully honored.

It is impossible for us to foresee the potential alternatives for protecting the privilege which might be devised by Congress or the States in the exercise of their creative rule-making capacities. Therefore we cannot say that the Constitution necessarily requires adherence to any particular solution for the inherent compulsions of the interrogation process as it is presently conducted. Our decision in no way creates a constitutional straitjacket which will handicap sound efforts at reform, nor is it intended to have this effect. We encourage Congress and the States to continue their laudable search for increasingly effective ways of protecting the rights of the individual while promoting efficient enforcement of our criminal laws. However, unless we are shown other procedures which are at least as effective in apprising accused persons of their right of silence and in assuring a continuous opportunity to exercise it, the following safeguards must be observed.

At the outset, if a person in custody is to be subjected to interrogation, he must first be informed in clear and unequivocal terms that he has the right to remain silent. For those unaware of the privilege, the warning is needed simply to make them aware of it—the threshold requirement for an intelligent decision as to its exercise. More important, such a warning is an absolute prerequisite in overcoming the inherent pressures of the interrogation atmosphere. It is not just the subnormal or woefully ignorant who succumb to an interrogator's imprecations, whether implied or expressly stated, that the interrogation will continue until a confession is obtained or that silence in the face of accusation is itself damning and will bode ill when presented to a jury. Further, the warning will show the individual that his interrogators are prepared to recognize his privilege should he choose to exercise it.

The Fifth Amendment privilege is so fundamental to our system of constitutional rule and the expedient of giving an adequate warning as to the availability of the privilege so simple, we will not pause to inquire in individual cases whether the defendant was aware of his rights without a warning being given. Assessments of the knowledge the defendant possessed, based on information as to his age, education, intelligence, or prior contact with authorities, can never be more than speculation; a warning is a clear-cut fact. More important, whatever the background of the person interrogated, a warning at the time of the interrogation is indispensable to overcome its pressures and to insure that the individual knows he is free to exercise the privilege at that point in time. The warning of the right to remain silent must be accompanied by the explanation that anything said can and will be used against the individual in court. This warning is needed in order to make him aware not only of the privilege, but also of the consequences of forgoing it. It is only through an awareness of these consequences that there can be any assurance of real understanding and intelligent exercise of the privilege. Moreover, this warning may serve to make the individual more acutely aware that he is faced with a phase of the adversary system—that he is not in the presence of persons acting solely in his interest.

The circumstances surrounding in-custody interrogation can operate very quickly to overbear the will of one merely made aware of his privilege by his interrogators. Therefore, the right to have counsel present at the interrogation is indispensable to the protection of the Fifth Amendment privilege under the system we delineate today. Our aim is to assure that the individual's right to choose between silence and speech remains unfettered throughout the interrogation process. A once-stated warning, delivered by those who will conduct the interrogation, cannot itself suffice to that end among those who most require knowledge of their rights. A mere warning given by the interrogators is not alone sufficient to accomplish that end. . . . Thus, the need for counsel to protect the Fifth Amendment privilege comprehends not merely a right to consult with counsel prior to questioning, but also to have counsel present during any questioning if the defendant so desires. . . .

In order fully to apprise a person interrogated of the extent of his rights under this system then, it is necessary to warn him not only that he has the right to consult with an attorney, but also that if he is indigent a lawyer will be appointed to represent him. Without this additional warning, the admonition of the right to consult with counsel would often be understood as meaning only that he can consult with a lawyer if he has one or has the funds to obtain one. The warning of a right to counsel would be hollow if not couched in terms that would convey to the indigent—the person most often subjected to interrogation—the knowledge that he too has a right to have counsel present. As with the warnings of the right to remain silent and of the general right

to counsel, only by effective and express explanation to the indigent of this right can there be assurance that he was truly in a position to exercise it. . . .

If the interrogation continues without the presence of an attorney and a statement is taken, a heavy burden rests on the government to demonstrate that the defendant knowingly and intelligently waived his privilege against self-incrimination and his right to retained or appointed counsel. This Court has always set high standards of proof for the waiver of constitutional rights, and we re-assert these standards as applied to in-custody interrogation. Since the State is responsible for establishing the isolated circumstances under which the interrogation takes place and has the only means of making available corroborated evidence of warnings given during incommunicado interrogation, the burden is rightly on its shoulders.

Whatever the testimony of the authorities as to waiver of rights by an accused, the fact of lengthy interrogation or incommunicado incarceration before a statement is made is strong evidence that the accused did not validly waive his rights. . . .

The warnings required and the waiver necessary in accordance with our opinion today are, in the absence of a fully effective equivalent, prerequisites to the admissibility of any statement made by a defendant. . . .

Our decision is not intended to hamper the traditional function of police officers in investigating crime. . . . When an individual is in custody on probable cause, the police may, of course, seek out evidence in the field to be used at trial against him. Such investigation may include inquiry of persons not under restraint. General on-the-scene questioning as to facts surrounding a crime or other general questioning of citizens in the fact-finding process is not affected by our holding. It is an act of responsible citizenship for individuals to give whatever information they may have to aid in law enforcement. In such situations the compelling atmosphere inherent in the process of in-custody interrogation is not necessarily present. . . .

Over the years the Federal Bureau of Investigation has compiled an exemplary record of effective law enforcement while advising any suspect or arrested person, at the outset of an interview, that he is not required to make a statement, that any statement may be used against him in court, that the individual may obtain the services of an attorney of his own choice and, more recently, that he has a right to free counsel if he is unable to pay. . . .

The practice of the FBI can readily be emulated by state and local enforcement agencies. The argument that the FBI deals with different crimes than are dealt with by state authorities does not mitigate the significance of the FBI experience.

The experience in some other countries also suggests that the danger to law enforcement in curbs on interrogation is overplayed. . . .

Because of the nature of the problem and because of its recurrent significance in numerous cases, we have to this point discussed the relationship of the Fifth Amendment privilege to police interrogation without specific concentration on the facts of the cases before us. We turn now to these facts to consider the application to these cases of the constitutional principles discussed above. In each instance, we have concluded that statements were obtained from the defendant under circumstances that did not meet constitutional standards for protection of privilege. . . .

JUSTICE HARLAN, with whom JUSTICE STEWART and JUSTICE WHITE join, dissenting.

I believe the decision of the Court represents poor constitutional law and entails harmful consequences for the country at large. How serious these consequences may prove to be only time can tell. But the basic flaws in the Court's justification seem to me readily apparent now once all sides of the problem are considered. . . .

While the fine points of this scheme are far less clear than the Court admits, the tenor is quite apparent. The new rules are not designed to guard against police brutality or other unmistakably banned forms of coercion. Those who use third-degree tactics and deny them in court are equally able and destined to lie as skillfully about warnings and waivers. Rather, the thrust of the new rules is to negate all pressures, to reinforce the nervous or ignorant suspect, and ultimately to

discourage any confession at all. The aim in short is toward "voluntariness" in a utopian sense, or to view it from a different angle, voluntariness with a vengeance.

Without at all subscribing to the generally black picture of police conduct painted by the Court, I think it must be frankly recognized at the outset that police questioning allowable under due process precedents may inherently entail some pressure on the suspect and may seek advantage in his ignorance or weaknesses. The atmosphere and questioning techniques, proper and fair though they be, can in themselves exert a tug on the suspect to confess, and in this light "[t]o speak of any confessions of crime made after arrest as being 'voluntary' or 'uncoerced' is somewhat inaccurate, although traditional. A confession is wholly and incontestably voluntary only if a guilty person gives himself up to the law and becomes his own accuser." . . . Until today, the role of the Constitution has been only to sift out *undue* pressure, not to assure spontaneous confessions.

The Court's new rules aim to offset these minor pressures and disadvantages intrinsic to any kind of police interrogation. The rules do not serve due process interests in preventing blatant coercion since, as I noted earlier, they do nothing to contain the policeman who is prepared to lie from the start. The rules work for reliability in confessions almost only in the Pickwickian sense that they can prevent some from being given at all. . . .

How much harm this decision will inflict on law enforcement cannot fairly be predicted with accuracy. Evidence on the role of confessions is notoriously incomplete . . . and little is added by the Court's reference to the FBI experience and the resources believed wasted in interrogation. . . . We do know that some crimes cannot be solved without confessions, that ample expert testimony attests to their importance in crime control, and that the Court is taking a real risk with society's welfare in imposing its new regime on the country. The social costs of crime are too great to call the new rules anything but a hazardous experimentation. . . .

The Court in closing its general discussion invokes the practice in federal and foreign jurisdictions as lending weight to its new curbs on confessions for all the States. A brief résumé will suffice to show that none of these jurisdictions has struck so one-sided a balance as the Court does today. Heaviest reliance is placed on the FBI practice. Differing circumstances may make this comparison quite untrustworthy, but in any event the FBI falls sensibly short of the Court's formalistic rules. For example, there is no indication that FBI agents must obtain an affirmative "waiver" before they pursue their questioning. Nor is it clear that one invoking his right to silence may not be prevailed upon to change his mind. And the warning as to appointed counsel apparently indicates only that one will be assigned by the judge when the suspect appears before him; the thrust of the Court's rules is to induce the suspect to obtain appointed counsel before continuing the interview. . . .

In conclusion: Nothing in the letter or the spirit of the Constitution or in the precedents squares with the heavy-handed and one-sided action that is so precipitously taken by the court in the name of fulfilling its constitutional responsibilities. . . .

JUSTICE WHITE, with whom JUSTICE HARLAN and JUSTICE STEWART join, dissenting. . . .

. . . The Court's duty to assess the consequences of its action is not satisfied by the utterance of the truth that a value of our system of criminal justice is "to respect the inviolability of the human personality" and to require government to produce the evidence against the accused by its own independent labors. . . . More than the human dignity of the accused is involved; the human personality of others in the society must also be preserved. Thus the values reflected by the privilege are not the sole desideratum; society's interest in the general security is of equal weight.

The obvious underpinning of the Court's decision is a deep-seated distrust of all confessions. As the Court declares that the accused may not be interrogated without counsel present, absent a waiver of the right to counsel, and as the Court all but admonishes the lawyer to advise the accused to remain silent, the result adds up to a judicial judgment that evidence from the accused should not be used against him in any way, whether compelled or not. This is the not so subtle overtone of the opinion—that it is inherently wrong for the police to gather evidence from the accused himself. And this is precisely the nub of this dissent. I see nothing wrong or immoral, and certainly nothing unconstitutional, in the police's asking a suspect whom they have reasonable cause to arrest whether or not he killed his wife or in confronting him with the evidence on which the arrest was based, at least where he has been plainly advised that he may remain completely silent. . . . Until today, "the admissions or confessions of the prisoner, when voluntarily and freely made, have always ranked high in the scale of incriminating evidence." . . . Particularly when corroborated, as where the police have confirmed the accused's disclosure of the hiding place of implements or fruits of the crime, such confessions have the highest reliability and significantly contribute to the certitude with which we may believe the accused is guilty. Moreover, it is by no means certain that the process of confessing is injurious to the accused. To the contrary it may provide psychological relief and enhance the prospects for rehabilitation. . . .

The most basic function of any government is to provide for the security of the individual and of his property. . . . These ends of society are served by the criminal laws which for the most part are aimed at the prevention of crime. Without the reasonably effective performance of the task of preventing private violence and retaliation, it is idle to talk about human dignity and civilized values. . . . There is, in my view, every reason to believe that a good many criminal defendants who otherwise would have been convicted on what this Court has previously thought to be the most satisfactory kind of evidence will now, under this new version of the Fifth Amendment, either not be tried at all or will be acquitted if the State's evidence, minus the confession, is put to the test of litigation.

I have no desire whatsoever to share the responsibility for any such impact on the present criminal process.

In some unknown number of cases the Court's rule will return a killer, a rapist or other criminal to the streets and to the environment which produced him, to repeat his crime whenever it pleases him. As a consequence, there will not be a gain, but a loss, in human dignity. The real concern is not the unfortunate consequences of this new decision on the criminal law as an abstract, disembodied series of authoritative proscriptions, but the impact on those who rely on the public authority for protection and who without it can only engage in violent self-help with guns, knives and the help of their neighbors similarly inclined. There is, of course, a saving factor: the next victims are uncertain, unnamed and unrepresented in this case. . . .

Much of the trouble with the Court's new rule is that it will operate indiscriminately in all criminal cases, regardless of the severity of the crime or the circumstances involved. It applies to every defendant, whether the professional criminal or one committing a crime of momentary passion who is not part and parcel of organized crime. It will slow down the investigation and the apprehension of confederates in those cases where time is of the essence, such as kidnapping, . . . and some of those involving organized crime. In the latter context the lawyer who arrives may also be the lawyer for the defendant's colleagues and can be relied upon to insure that no breach of the organiza-tion's security takes place even though the accused may feel that the best thing he can do is to cooperate.

At the same time, the Court's *per se* approach may not be justified on the ground that it provides a "bright line" permitting the authorities to judge in advance whether interrogation may safely be pursued without jeopardizing the admissibility of any information obtained as a consequence. Nor can it be claimed that judicial time and effort, assuming that is a relevant consideration, will be conserved because of the ease of application of the new rule. Today's decision leaves open such questions as whether the accused was in custody, whether his statements were spontaneous or the product of interrogation, whether the accused has effectively waived his rights, and whether nontestimonial evidence introduced at trial is the fruit of statements made during a prohibited interrogation, all of which are certain to prove productive of uncertainty during investigation and litigation during prosecution. For all these reasons, if further restrictions on police interrogation are desirable at this time, a more flexible approach makes much more sense than the Court's constitutional straitjacket which forecloses more discriminating treatment by legislative or rule-making pronouncements.

Nix v. Williams
467 U.S. 431 (1984)

The facts of this criminal case and its lengthy and intricate appellate history are summarized in the opinion below. Opinion of the Court: Burger, White, Blackmun, Powell, Rehnquist, O'Connor. Concurring opinion: White. Concurring in the judgment: Stevens. Dissenting opinion: Brennan, Marshall.

THE CHIEF JUSTICE delivered the opinion of the Court.

We granted *certiorari* to consider whether, at respondent Williams' second murder trial in state court, evidence pertaining to the discovery and condition of the victim's body was properly admitted on the ground that it would ultimately or inevitably have been discovered even if no violation of any constitutional or statutory provision had taken place.

On December 24, 1968, 10-year-old Pamela Powers disappeared from a YMCA building in Des Moines, Iowa, where she had accompanied her parents to watch an athletic contest. Shortly after she disappeared, Williams was seen leaving the YMCA carrying a large bundle wrapped in a blanket; a 14-year-old boy who had helped Williams open his car door reported that he had seen "two legs in it and they were skinny and white."

Williams' car was found the next day 160 miles east of Des Moines in Davenport, Iowa. Later several items of clothing belonging to the child, some of Williams' clothing, and an army blanket like the one used to wrap the bundle that Williams carried out of the YMCA were found at a rest stop on Interstate 80 near Grinnell, between Des Moines and

Davenport. A warrant was issued for Williams' arrest.

Police surmised that Williams had left Pamela Powers or her body somewhere between Des Moines and the Grinnell rest stop where some of the young girl's clothing had been found. On December 26, the Iowa Bureau of Criminal Investigation initiated a large-scale search. Two hundred volunteers divided into teams began the search 21 miles east of Grinnell, covering an area several miles to the north and south of Interstate 80. They moved westward from Poweshiek County, in which Grinnell was located, into Jasper County. Searchers were instructed to check all roads, abandoned farm buildings, ditches, culverts, and any other place in which the body of a small child could be hidden.

Meanwhile, Williams surrendered to local police in Davenport, where he was promptly arraigned. Williams contacted a Des Moines attorney who arranged for an attorney in Davenport to meet Williams at the Davenport police station. Des Moines police informed counsel they would pick Williams up in Davenport and return him to Des Moines without questioning him. Two Des Moines detectives then drove to Davenport, took Williams into custody, and proceeded to drive him back to Des Moines.

During the return trip, one of the policemen, Detective Leaming, began a conversation with Williams, saying: "I want to give you something to think about while we're traveling down the road. . . . They are predicting several inches of snow for tonight, and I feel that you yourself are the only person that knows where this little girl's body is . . . and if you get a snow on top of it you yourself may be unable to find it. And since we will be going right past the area [where the body is] on the way into Des Moines, I feel that we could stop and locate the body, that the parents of this little girl should be entitled to a Christian burial for the little girl who was snatched away from them on Christmas [E]ve and murdered. . . . [A]fter a snow storm [we may not be] able to find it at all."

Leaming told Williams he knew the body was in the area of Mitchellville—a town they would be passing on the way to Des Moines.

He concluded the conversation by saying, "I do not want you to answer me. . . . Just think about it. . . . "

Later, as the police car approached Grinnell, Williams asked Leaming whether the police had found the young girl's shoes. After Leaming replied that he was unsure, Williams directed the police to a point near a service station where he said he had left the shoes; they were not found. As they continued to drive to Des Moines, Williams asked whether the blanket had been found and then directed the officers to a rest area in Grinnell where he said he had disposed of the blanket; they did not find the blanket. At this point Leaming and his party were joined by the officers in charge of the search. As they approached Mitchellville, Williams, without any further conversation, agreed to direct the officers to the child's body.

The officers directing the search had called off the search at 3 p.m., when they left the Grinnell Police Department to join Leaming at the rest area. At that time, one search team near the Jasper County–Polk County line was only two and one-half miles from where Williams soon guided Leaming and his party to the body. The child's body was found next to a culvert in a ditch beside a gravel road in Polk County, about two miles south of Interstate 80, and essentially within the area to be searched.

FIRST TRIAL

In February 1969 Williams was indicted for first-degree murder. Before trial in the Iowa court, his counsel moved to suppress evidence of the body and all related evidence including the condition of the body as shown by the autopsy. The ground for the motion was that such evidence was the "fruit" or product of Williams' statements made during the automobile ride from Davenport to Des Moines and prompted by Leaming's statements. The motion to suppress was denied.

The jury found Williams guilty of first-degree murder; the judgment of conviction was affirmed by the Iowa Supreme Court. . . . Williams then sought release on *habeas corpus* in the United States District Court for the Southern District of Iowa. That court concluded that the evidence in question had been wrongly admitted at Williams' trial; . . . a divided panel of the Court of Appeals for the Eighth Circuit agreed. . . .

We granted *certiorari* . . . and a divided Court affirmed, holding that Detective Leaming had obtained incriminating statements from Williams by what was viewed as interrogation in violation of his right to counsel. *Brewer v. Williams* (1977). . . .

SECOND TRIAL

At Williams' second trial in 1977 in the Iowa court, the prosecution did not offer Williams' statements into evidence, nor did it seek to show that Williams had directed the police to the child's body. However, evidence of the condition of her body as it was found, articles and photographs of her clothing, and the results of post mortem medical and chemical tests on the body were admitted. The trial court concluded that the State had proved by a preponderance of the evidence that, if the search had not been suspended and Williams had not led the police to the victim, her body would have been discovered "*within a short time*" in essentially the same condition as it was actually found. The trial court also ruled that if the police had not located the body, "the search would clearly have been taken up again where it left off, given the extreme circumstances of this case and the body would [have] been found *in short order.*" . . .

In finding that the body would have been discovered in essentially the same condition as it was actually found, the court noted that freezing temperatures had prevailed and tissue deterioration would have been suspended. . . . The challenged evidence was admitted and the jury again found Williams guilty of first-degree murder; he was sentenced to life in prison.

On appeal, the Supreme Court of Iowa again affirmed. . . . That court held that there was in fact a "hypothetical independent source" exception to the Exclusionary Rule.

. . . The Iowa court then reviewed the evidence *de novo* and concluded that the State had shown by a preponderance of the evidence that, even if Williams had not guided police to the child's body, it would inevitably have been found by lawful activity of the search party before its condition had materially changed.

In 1980 Williams renewed his attack on the state-court conviction by seeking a writ of *habeas corpus* in the United States District Court for the Southern District of Iowa. The District Court conducted its own independent review of the evidence and concluded, as had the state courts, that the body would inevitably have been found by the searchers in essentially the same condition it was in when Williams led police to its discovery. The District Court denied Williams' petition. . . .

The Court of Appeals for the Eighth Circuit reversed. . . .

We granted the State's petition for *certiorari*, . . . and we reverse.

The Iowa Supreme Court correctly stated that the "vast majority" of all courts, both state and federal, recognize an inevitable discovery exception to the Exclusionary Rule. We are now urged to adopt and apply the so-called ultimate or inevitable discovery exception to the Exclusionary Rule.

. . . The Exclusionary Rule applies not only to the illegally obtained evidence itself, but also to other incriminating evidence derived from the primary evidence. . . .

The core rationale consistently advanced by this Court for extending the Exclusionary Rule to evidence that is the fruit of unlawful police conduct has been that this admittedly drastic and socially costly course is needed to deter police from violations of constitutional and statutory protections. This Court has accepted the argument that the way to ensure such protections is to exclude evidence seized as a result of such violations notwithstanding the high social cost of letting persons obviously guilty go unpunished for their crimes. On this rationale, the prosecution is not to be put in a better position than it would have been in if no illegality had transpired.

By contrast, the derivative evidence analysis ensures that the prosecution is not put in a *worse* position simply because of some earlier police error or misconduct. The independent source doctrine allows admission of evidence that has been discovered by means wholly independent of any constitutional violation. That doctrine, although closely related to the inevitable discovery doctrine, does not apply here; Williams' statements to Leaming indeed led police to the child's body, but that is not the whole story. The independent source doctrine teaches us that the interest of society in deterring unlawful police conduct and the public interest in having juries receive all probative evidence of a crime are properly balanced by putting the police in the same, not a *worse,* position than they would have been in if no police error or misconduct had occurred. . . . When the challenged evidence has an independent source, exclusion of such evidence would put the police in a worse position than they would have been in absent any error or violation. There is a functional similarity between these two doctrines in that exclusion of evidence that would inevitably have been discovered would also put the government in a worse position, because the police would have obtained that evidence if no misconduct had taken place. Thus, while the independent source exception would not justify admission of evidence in this case, its rationale is wholly consistent with and justifies our adoption of the ultimate or inevitable discovery exception to the Exclusionary Rule.

It is clear that the cases implementing the Exclusionary Rule "begin with the premise that the challenged evidence is *in some sense* the product of illegal governmental activity." . . . Of course, this does not end the inquiry. If the prosecution can establish by a preponderance of the evidence that the information ultimately or inevitably would have been discovered by lawful means—here the volunteers' search—then the deterrence rationale has so little basis that the evidence should be received. Anything less would reject logic, experience, and common sense.

Williams contends that because he did not waive his right to the assistance of counsel, the Court may not balance competing values in deciding whether the challenged evidence was properly admitted. He argues that, unlike the Exclusionary Rule in the Fourth Amendment context, the essential purpose of which is to deter police misconduct, the Sixth Amendment Exclusionary Rule is designed to protect the right to a fair trial and the integrity of the fact-finding process. Williams contends that, when those interests are at stake, the societal costs of excluding evidence obtained from responses presumed involuntary are irrelevant in determining whether such evidence should be excluded. We disagree.

Exclusion of physical evidence that would inevitably have been discovered adds nothing to either the integrity or fairness of a criminal trial. The Sixth Amendment right to counsel protects against unfairness by preserving the adversary process in which the reliability of proffered evidence may be tested in cross-examination. . . . Here, however, Detective Leaming's conduct did nothing to impugn the reliability of the evidence in question—the body of the child and its condition as it was found, articles of clothing found on the body, and the autopsy. No one would seriously contend that the presence of counsel in the police car when Leaming appealed to Williams' decent human instincts would have had any bearing on the reliability of the body as evidence. Suppression, in these circumstances, would do nothing whatever to promote the integrity of the trial process, but would inflict a wholly unacceptable burden on the administration of criminal justice.

Nor would suppression ensure fairness on the theory that it tends to safeguard the adversary system of justice. To assure the fairness of trial proceedings, this Court has held that assistance of counsel must be available at pretrial confrontations where "the subsequent trial [cannot] cure a[n otherwise] one-sided confrontation between prosecuting authorities and the uncounseled defendant." . . . Fairness can be assured by placing the State and the accused in the same positions they would have been in had the impermissible conduct not taken place. However, if the government can prove that the evidence would have been obtained inevitably and, therefore, would have been admitted regardless of any overreaching by the police, there is no rational basis to keep that evidence from the jury in order to ensure the fairness of the trial proceedings. In that situation, the State has gained no advantage at trial and the defendant has suffered no prejudice. Indeed, suppression of the evidence would operate to undermine the adversary system by putting the State in a *worse* position than it would have occupied without any police misconduct. Williams' argument that inevitable discovery constitutes impermissible balancing of values is without merit.

. . . Three courts independently reviewing the evidence have found that the body of the child inevitably would have been found by the searchers. Williams challenges these findings, asserting that the record contains only the "*post hoc* rationalization" that the search efforts would have proceeded two and one-half miles into Polk County where Williams had led police to the body.

When that challenge was made at the suppression hearing preceding Williams' second trial, the prosecution offered the testimony of Agent Ruxlow of the Iowa Bureau of Criminal Investigation. Ruxlow had organized and directed some 200 volunteers who were searching for the child's body. . . . The searchers were instructed "to check all the roads, the ditches, any culverts. . . . If they came upon any abandoned farm buildings, they were instructed to go onto the property and search those abandoned farm buildings or any other places where a small child could be secreted." . . . Ruxlow testified that he marked off highway maps of Poweshiek and Jasper Counties in grid fashion, divided the volunteers into teams of four to six persons, and assigned each team to search specific grid areas. . . . Ruxlow also testified that, if the search had not been suspended because of Williams' promised cooperation, it would have continued into Polk County, using the same grid system. . . . Although he had previously marked off into grids only the highway maps of Poweshiek and Jasper Counties, Ruxlow had obtained a map of Polk County, which he said he would have marked off in the same manner had it been necessary for the search to continue. . . .

The search had commenced at approximately 10 a.m. and moved westward through Poweshiek County into Jasper County. At approximately 3 p.m., after Williams had volunteered to cooperate with the police, Officer Leaming, who was in the police car with Williams, sent word to Ruxlow and the other Special Agent directing the search to meet him at the Grinnell truck stop and the search was suspended at that time. . . . Ruxlow also stated that he was "under the impression that there was a possibility" that Williams would lead them to the child's body at that time. . . . The search was not resumed once it was learned that Williams had led the police to the body, . . . which was found two and one-half miles from where the search had stopped in what would have been the easternmost grid to be searched in Polk County. . . . There was testimony that it would have taken an additional three to five hours to discover the body if the search had been continued; . . . the body was found near a culvert, one of the kinds of places the teams had been specifically directed to search.

On this record it is clear that the search parties were approaching the actual location of the body and we are satisfied, along with three courts earlier, that the volunteer search teams would have resumed the search had Williams not earlier led the police to the body and the body inevitably would have been found. The evidence asserted by Williams as newly discovered, i.e., certain photographs of the body and deposition testimony of Agent Ruxlow made in connection with the federal *habeas* proceeding, does not demonstrate that the material facts were inadequately developed in the suppression hearing in state court or that Williams was denied a full, fair, and adequate opportunity to present all relevant facts at the suppression hearing.

The judgment of the Court of Appeals is reversed, and the case is remanded for further proceedings consistent with this opinion.

JUSTICE BRENNAN, with whom JUSTICE MARSHALL joins, dissenting.

. . . The Court concludes that unconstitutionally obtained evidence may be admitted at trial if it inevitably would have been discovered in the same condition by an independent line of investigation that was already being pursued when the constitutional violation occurred. As has every federal Court of Appeals previously addressing this issue, . . . I agree that in these circumstances the "inevitable discovery" exception to the exclusionary rule is consistent with the requirements of the Constitution.

In its zealous efforts to emasculate the exclusionary rule, however, the Court loses sight of the crucial difference between the "inevitable discovery" doctrine and the "independent source" exception from which it is derived. When properly applied, the "independent source" exception allows the prosecution to use evidence only if it was, in fact, obtained by fully lawful means. It therefore does no violence to the constitutional protections that the exclusionary rule is meant to enforce. The "inevitable discovery" exception is likewise compatible with the Constitution, though it differs in one key respect from its next of kin: specifically, the evidence sought to be introduced at trial has not actually been obtained from an independent source, but rather would have been discovered as a matter of course if independent investigations were allowed to proceed. In my view, this distinction should require that the government satisfy a heightened burden of proof before it is allowed to use such evidence. The inevitable discovery exception necessarily implicates a hypothetical finding that differs in kind from the factual finding

that precedes application of the independent source rule. To ensure that this hypothetical finding is narrowly confined to circumstances that are functionally equivalent to an independent source, and to protect fully the fundamental rights served by the exclusionary rule, I would require clear and convincing evidence before concluding that the government had met its burden of proof on this issue. . . .

. . . Because the lower courts did not impose such a requirement, I would remand this case for application of this heightened burden of proof by the lower courts in the first instance. I am therefore unable to join either the Court's opinion or its judgment.

Connecticut Department of Public Safety v. Doe
538 U.S. 1 (2003)

Like all other states, Connecticut enacted its own version of "Megan's Law." Connecticut's version requires persons convicted of sexual offenses to register with the Department of Public Safety (DPS) upon their release into the community and requires the DPS to post a sex-offender registry containing the registrants' names, addresses, photographs, and descriptions on an Internet website and to make the registry available to the public in certain state offices. Respondent Doe, a convicted sex offender subject to the law, filed an action in US District Court for the District of Connecticut on behalf of himself and others similarly situated, claiming that the law violated the Due Process Clause of the Fourteenth Amendment. The district court granted the respondent summary judgment, certified a class of individuals subject to the law, and permanently enjoined the law's public disclosure provisions, and the Court of Appeals for the Second Circuit affirmed. The Supreme Court granted certiorari. Opinion of the Court: Rehnquist, O'Connor, Scalia, Kennedy, Souter, Thomas, Ginsburg, Breyer. Concurring opinions: Scalia; Souter, Ginsburg. Concurring in the judgment: Stevens.

THE CHIEF JUSTICE delivered the opinion of the Court.

We granted certiorari to determine whether the United States Court of Appeals for the

Second Circuit properly enjoined the public disclosure of Connecticut's sex offender registry. The Court of Appeals concluded that such disclosure both deprived registered sex offenders of a "liberty interest," and violated the Due Process Clause because officials did not afford registrants a predeprivation hearing to determine whether they are likely to be "currently dangerous." Connecticut, however, has decided that the registry requirement shall be based on the fact of previous conviction, not the fact of current dangerousness. Indeed, the public registry explicitly states that officials have not determined that any registrant is currently dangerous. We therefore reverse the judgment of the Court of Appeals because due process does not require the opportunity to prove a fact that is not material to the State's statutory scheme.

In *Paul v. Davis* (1976), we held that mere injury to reputation, even if defamatory, does not constitute the deprivation of a liberty interest. Petitioners urge us to reverse the Court of Appeals on the ground that, under *Paul v. Davis,* respondent has failed to establish that petitioners have deprived him of a liberty interest. We find it unnecessary to reach this question, however, because even assuming, *arguendo,* that respondent has been deprived of a liberty interest, due process does not entitle him to a hearing to establish a fact that is not material under the Connecticut statute. . . . [T]he fact that respondent seeks to prove—that he is not currently dangerous—is of no consequence under Connecticut's Megan's Law. As the DPS Website explains, the law's requirements turn on an offender's conviction alone—a fact that a convicted offender has already had a procedurally safeguarded opportunity to contest. No other fact is relevant to the disclosure of registrants' information. Indeed, the disclaimer on the Website explicitly states that respondent's alleged nondangerousness simply does not matter.

In short, even if respondent could prove that he is not likely to be currently dangerous, Connecticut has decided that the registry information of *all* sex offenders—currently dangerous or not—must be publicly disclosed. Unless respondent can show that that *substantive* rule of law is defective (by conflicting with a provision of the Constitution), any hearing on current dangerousness is a bootless exercise. It may be that respondent's claim is actually a substantive challenge to Connecticut's statute "recast in 'procedural due process' terms." Nonetheless, respondent expressly disavows any reliance on the substantive component of the Fourteenth Amendment's protections and maintains, as he did below, that his challenge is strictly a procedural one. But States are not barred by principles of "*procedural* due process" from drawing such classifications. Such claims "must ultimately be analyzed" in terms of substantive,

not procedural, due process. Because the question is not properly before us, we express no opinion as to whether Connecticut's Megan's Law violates principles of substantive due process.

Plaintiffs who assert a right to a hearing under the Due Process Clause must show that the facts they seek to establish in that hearing are relevant under the statutory scheme. Respondent cannot make that showing here. The judgment of the Court of Appeals is therefore

Reversed.

JUSTICE SCALIA, concurring.

I join the Court's opinion, and add that even if the requirements of Connecticut's sex offender registration law implicate a liberty interest of respondent, the categorical abrogation of that liberty interest by a validly enacted statute suffices to provide all the process that is "due"—just as a state law providing that no one under the age of 16 may operate a motor vehicle suffices to abrogate that liberty interest. Absent a claim (which respondent has not made here) that the liberty interest in question is so fundamental as to implicate so-called "substantive" due process, a properly enacted law can eliminate it. That is ultimately why, as the Court's opinion demonstrates, a convicted sex offender has no more right to additional "process" enabling him to establish that he is not dangerous than (in the analogous case just suggested) a 15-year-old has a right to "process" enabling him to establish that he is a safe driver.

Powell v. Alabama
287 U.S. 45 (1932)

In 1931, Ozie Powell and six other black defendants were convicted in Scottsboro, Alabama, for the rape of two white girls. Their trial lasted one day, and they were all sentenced to death. They had been arrested, tried, and sentenced in what Justice Sutherland was to call "an atmosphere of tense, hostile, and excited public sentiment." The defendants were too poor to retain counsel, and the trial judge vaguely appointed all members of the Alabama bar to represent them. The Alabama Supreme Court affirmed their conviction, with the chief justice writing a strong dissent on the grounds that the defendants had not been given a fair trial. The US Supreme Court granted certiorari. The Powell case is the first of a series referred to as The Scottsboro Cases, so termed because of the location of the trial. *Opinion of the Court: Sutherland, Hughes, Van Devanter, Brandeis, Stone, Roberts, Cardozo. Dissenting opinion: Butler, McReynolds.*

JUSTICE SUTHERLAND delivered the opinion of the Court.

The record shows that immediately upon the return of the indictment defendants were arraigned and pleaded not guilty. Apparently they were not asked whether they had, or were able to employ, counsel, or wished to have counsel appointed; or whether they had friends or relatives who might assist in that regard if communicated with. That it would not have been an idle ceremony to have given the defendants reasonable opportunity to communicate with their families and endeavor to obtain counsel is demonstrated by the fact that, very soon after conviction, able counsel appeared in their behalf. This was pointed out by Chief Justice Anderson in the course of his dissenting opinion. "They were nonresidents," he said, "and had little time or opportunity to get in touch with their families and friends who were scattered throughout two other states, and time has demonstrated that they could or would have been represented by able counsel had a better opportunity been given by a reasonable delay in the trial of the cases, judging from the number and activity of counsel that appeared immediately or shortly after their conviction." . . .

It is hardly necessary to say that, the right to counsel being conceded, a defendant should be afforded a fair opportunity to secure counsel of his own choice. Not only was that not done here, but such designation of counsel as was attempted was either so indefinite or so close upon the trial as to amount to a denial of effective and substantial aid in that regard.

. . . Until the very morning of the trial no lawyer had been named or definitely designated to represent the defendants. Prior to that time, the trial judge had "appointed all the members of the bar" for the limited "purpose of arraigning the defendants." Whether they would represent the defendants thereafter if no counsel appeared in their behalf, was a matter of speculation only, or, as the judge indicated, of mere anticipation on the part of the court. Such a designation, even if made for all purposes, would, in our opinion, have fallen short of meeting, in any proper sense, a requirement for the appointment of counsel. How many lawyers were members of the bar does not appear; but, in the very nature of things, whether many or few, they would not, thus collectively named, have been given that clear appreciation of responsibility or impressed with that individual sense of duty which should and naturally would accompany the appointment of a selected member of the bar, specifically named and assigned. . . .

. . . The Constitution of Alabama provides that in all criminal prosecutions the accused shall enjoy the right to have the assistance of counsel; and a state statute requires the court in a capital case, where the defendant is unable to employ counsel, to appoint counsel for him. The state supreme court held that these provisions had not been infringed, and with that holding we are powerless to interfere. The question, however, which it is our duty, and within our power, to decide, is whether the denial of the assistance of counsel contravenes the due process clause of the Fourteenth Amendment to the federal Constitution. . . .

One test which has been applied to determine whether due process of law has been accorded in given instances is to ascertain what were the settled usages and modes of proceeding under the common and statute law of England before the Declaration of Independence, subject, however, to the qualification that they be shown not to have been unsuited to the civil and political conditions of our ancestors by having been followed in this country after it became a nation. . . . Plainly, . . . this test, as thus qualified, has not been met in the present case. . . .

It never has been doubted by this court, or any other so far as we know, that notice and hearing are preliminary steps essential to the passing of an enforceable judgment, and that they, together with a legally competent tribunal having jurisdiction of the case, constitute basic elements of the constitutional requirement of due process of law. . . .

What, then, does a hearing include? Historically and in practice, in our country at least, it has always included the right to the aid of counsel when desired and provided by the party asserting the right. The right to be heard would be, in many cases, of little avail if it did not comprehend the right to be heard by counsel. Even the intelligent and educated layman has small and sometimes no skill in the science of law. If charged with crime, he is incapable, generally, of determining for himself whether the indictment is good or bad. He is unfamiliar with the rules of evidence. Left without the aid of counsel he may be put on trial without a proper charge, and convicted upon incompetent evidence, or evidence irrelevant to the issue or otherwise inadmissible. He lacks both the skill and knowledge adequately to prepare his defense, even though he have a perfect one. He requires the guiding hand of counsel at every step in the proceedings against him. Without it, though he be not guilty, he faces the danger of conviction because he does not know how to establish his innocence. If that be true of men of intelligence, how much more true is it of the ignorant and illiterate, or those of feeble intelligence. If in any case, civil or criminal, a state or federal court were arbitrarily to refuse to hear a party by counsel, employed by and appearing for him, it reasonably may not be doubted that such a refusal would be a denial of a hearing, and, therefore, of due process in the constitutional sense. . . .

In the light of the facts . . . —the ignorance and illiteracy of the defendants, their youth, the circumstances of public hostility, the imprisonment and the close surveillance of the defendants by the military forces, the fact that their friends and families were all in other states and communication with them necessarily difficult, and above all that they stood in deadly peril of their lives—we think the failure of the trial court to give them reasonable time and opportunity to secure counsel was a clear denial of due process.

But passing that, and assuming their inability, even if opportunity had been given, to employ counsel, as the trial court evidently did assume, we are of opinion that, under the circumstances just stated, the necessity of counsel was so vital and imperative that the failure of the trial court to make an effective appointment of counsel was likewise a denial of due process within the meaning of the Fourteenth Amendment. Whether this would be so in other criminal prosecutions, or under other circumstances, we need not determine. All that it is necessary now to decide, as we do decide, is that in a capital case, where the defendant is unable to employ counsel, and is incapable adequately of making his own defense because of ignorance, feeble mindedness, illiteracy, or the like, it is the duty of the court, whether requested or not, to assign counsel for him as a necessary requisite of due process of law; and that duty is not discharged by an assignment at such a time or under such circumstances as to preclude the giving of effective aid in the preparation and trial of the case. To hold otherwise would be to ignore the fundamental postulate, already adverted to, "that there are certain immutable principles of justice which inhere in the very idea of free government which no member of the Union may disregard." . . . In a case such as this, whatever may be the rule in other cases, the right to have counsel appointed, when necessary, is a logical corollary from the constitutional right to be heard by counsel. . . .

The judgments must be reversed and the causes remanded for further proceedings not inconsistent with this opinion.

Gideon v. Wainwright
372 U.S. 335 (1963)

Clarence Gideon was charged in Florida state court with breaking into a pool hall with the intent to commit a misdemeanor—a felony under Florida law. Gideon appeared at his trial without a lawyer and without the funds necessary to retain one, and he requested the trial judge to appoint a lawyer for him. The trial judge refused, citing a Florida statute that permitted the appointment of counsel only in capital cases. Gideon then proceeded to conduct his own defense, and he was found guilty by the jury and sentenced to five years in prison by the judge. Once in prison, Gideon sought release by suing out a writ of habeas corpus against Wainwright, the state director of corrections. The Florida Supreme Court denied relief, and Gideon presented an in forma pauperis petition to the US Supreme Court, asserting that the trial judge's refusal to appoint counsel for him was a denial of rights guaranteed by the Sixth and Fourteenth Amendments.

The Supreme Court granted certiorari and appointed Abe Fortas, later to serve as an associate justice of the Supreme Court, to represent him in this proceeding. Opinion of the Court: <u>Black</u>, Warren, Douglas, Brennan, Stewart, Goldberg, White. Concurring opinion: <u>Douglas</u>. Concurring in the result:<u> Clark</u>; <u>Harlan</u>.

JUSTICE BLACK delivered the opinion of the Court.

. . . Since 1942, when *Betts v. Brady* was decided by a divided Court, the problem of a defendant's federal constitutional right to counsel in a state court has been a continuing source of controversy and litigation in both state and federal courts. To give this problem another review here, we granted *certiorari*. . . . [We] requested both sides to discuss in their briefs and oral arguments the following: "Should this Court's holding in *Betts v. Brady* be reconsidered?" . . .

The Sixth Amendment provides, "In all criminal prosecutions, the accused shall enjoy the right . . . to have the Assistance of Counsel for his defence." We have construed this to mean that in federal courts counsel must be provided for defendants unable to employ counsel unless the right is competently and intelligently waived. *Betts* argued that this right is extended to indigent defendants in state courts by the Fourteenth Amendment. . . . The Court concluded that "appointment of counsel is not a fundamental right, essential to a fair trial." . . . It was for this reason the *Betts* Court refused to accept the contention that the Sixth Amendment's guarantee of counsel for indigent federal defendants was extended to or, in the words of that Court, "made obligatory upon the States by the Fourteenth Amendment." . . .

We think the Court in *Betts* was wrong . . . in concluding that the Sixth Amendment's guarantee of counsel is not one of these fundamental rights. Ten years before *Betts v. Brady,* this Court, after full consideration of all the historical data examined in *Betts,* had unequivocally declared that "the right to the aid of counsel is of this fundamental character." *Powell v. Alabama* . . . (1932). While the Court at the close of its *Powell* opinion did by its language, as this Court frequently does, limit its holding to the particular facts and circumstances of that case, its conclusions about the fundamental nature of the right to counsel are

unmistakable. Several years later, in 1936, the Court reemphasized what it had said about the fundamental nature of the right to counsel in this language:

> "We concluded that certain fundamental rights, safeguarded by the first eight amendments against federal action, were also safeguarded against state action by the due process of law clause of the Fourteenth Amendment, and among them the fundamental right of the accused to the aid of counsel in a criminal prosecution." *Grosjean v. American Press Co.* (1936).

And again in 1938 this Court said:

> "[The assistance of counsel] is one of the safeguards of the Sixth Amendment deemed necessary to insure fundamental human rights of life and liberty" . . . *Johnson v. Zerbst* . . . (1938). . . .

. . . In deciding as it did—that "appointment of counsel is not a fundamental right, essential to a fair trial"—the Court in *Betts v. Brady* made an abrupt break with its own well-considered precedents. In returning to these old precedents, sounder we believe than the new, we but restore constitutional principles established to achieve a fair system of justice. Not only these precedents but also reason and reflection require us to recognize that in our adversary system of criminal justice, any person haled into court, who is too poor to hire a lawyer, cannot be assured a fair trial unless counsel is provided for him. This seems to us to be an obvious truth. Governments, both state and federal, quite properly spend vast sums of money to establish machinery to try defendants accused of crime. Lawyers to prosecute are everywhere deemed essential to protect the public's interest in an orderly society. Similarly, there are few defendants charged with crime, few indeed, who fail to hire the best lawyers they can get to prepare and present their defenses. That government hires lawyers to prosecute and defendants who have the money hire lawyers to defend are the strongest indications of the widespread belief that lawyers in criminal courts are necessities, not luxuries. The right of one charged with crime to counsel may not be deemed fundamental and essential to fair trials in some countries, but it is in ours. From the very beginning, our state and national constitutions and laws have laid great emphasis on procedural and substantive safeguards designed to assure fair trials before impartial tribunals in which every defendant stands equal before the law. This noble ideal cannot be realized if the poor man charged with crime has to face his accusers without a lawyer to assist him. . . .

The judgment is reversed and the cause is remanded to the Supreme Court of Florida for further action not inconsistent with this opinion.

Blakely v. Washington
542 U.S. 296 (2004)

Ralph Howard Blakely Jr. pleaded guilty to kidnapping his estranged wife. Under Washington's Sentencing Reform Act, the facts admitted in his plea, standing alone, supported a maximum sentence of fifty-three months, but the judge imposed a ninety-month sentence after finding that Blakely had acted with deliberate cruelty, a statutorily enumerated ground for departing from the standard range. The Washington Court of Appeals affirmed, rejecting Blakely's argument that the sentencing procedure deprived him of his federal constitutional right to have a jury determine beyond a reasonable doubt all facts legally essential to his sentence. The Washington Supreme Court denied discretionary review, and the US Supreme Court granted certiorari. Opinion of the Court: <u>Scalia</u>, Stevens, Souter, Thomas, Ginsburg. Dissenting opinions: <u>O'Connor</u>, Rehnquist, Kennedy, Breyer; Kennedy, Breyer; <u>Breyer</u>, O'Connor.

JUSTICE SCALIA delivered the opinion of the Court.

Petitioner Ralph Howard Blakely, Jr., pleaded guilty to the kidnaping of his estranged wife. The facts admitted in his plea, standing alone, supported a maximum sentence of 53 months. Pursuant to state law, the court imposed an "exceptional" sentence of 90 months after making a judicial determination that he had acted with "deliberate cruelty." We consider whether this violated petitioner's Sixth Amendment right to trial by jury. . . .

This case requires us to apply the rule we expressed in *Apprendi v. New Jersey* (2000): "Other than the fact of a prior conviction, any fact that increases the penalty for a crime beyond the prescribed statutory maximum must be submitted to a jury, and proved beyond a reasonable doubt." . . . In this case, petitioner was sentenced to more than three years above the 53-month statutory maximum of the standard range because he had acted with "deliberate cruelty." The facts supporting that finding were neither admitted by petitioner nor found by a jury. The State nevertheless contends that there was no *Apprendi* violation because the relevant "statutory maximum" is not 53 months, but the 10-year maximum for class B felonies. It observes that no exceptional sentence may exceed that limit. . . . [H]owever, the "statutory maximum" for *Apprendi* purposes is the maximum sentence a judge may impose solely on the basis of the facts reflected in the jury verdict or admitted by the defendant. In other words, the relevant "statutory maximum" is not the maximum sentence a judge may impose after finding additional facts, but the maximum he may impose without any additional findings. When a judge inflicts punishment that the jury's verdict alone does not allow, the jury has not found all the facts "which the law makes essential to the punishment," and the judge exceeds his proper authority. . . . Because the State's sentencing procedure did not comply with the Sixth Amendment, petitioner's sentence is invalid.

Our commitment to *Apprendi* in this context reflects not just respect for longstanding precedent, but the need to give intelligible content to the right of jury trial. That right is no mere procedural formality, but a fundamental reservation of power in our constitutional structure. Just as suffrage ensures the people's ultimate control in the legislative and executive branches, jury trial is meant to ensure their control in the judiciary. *Apprendi* carries out this design by ensuring that the judge's authority to sentence derives wholly from the jury's verdict. Without that restriction, the jury would not exercise the control that the Framers intended.

Those who would reject *Apprendi* are resigned to one of two alternatives. The first is that the jury need only find whatever facts the legislature chooses to label elements of the crime, and that those it labels sentencing factors—no matter how much they may increase the punishment—may be found by the judge. This would mean, for example, that a judge could sentence a man for committing murder even if the jury convicted him only of illegally possessing the firearm used to commit it—or of making an illegal lane change while fleeing the death scene. Not even *Apprendi*'s critics would advocate this absurd result. The jury could not function as circuitbreaker in the State's machinery of justice if it were relegated to making a determination that the defendant at some point did something wrong, a mere preliminary to a judicial inquisition into the facts of the crime the State actually seeks to punish.

The second alternative is that legislatures may establish legally essential sentencing factors within limits—limits crossed when, perhaps, the sentencing factor is a "tail which wags the dog of the substantive offense." What this means in operation is that the law must not go too far—it must not exceed the judicial estimation of the proper role of the judge.

The subjectivity of this standard is obvious. Petitioner argued below that second-degree kidnaping with deliberate cruelty was essentially the same as first-degree kidnaping, the very charge he had avoided by pleading to a lesser offense. The court conceded this might be so but held it irrelevant. Petitioner's 90-month sentence exceeded the 53-month standard maximum by almost 70%; the Washington Supreme Court in other cases has upheld exceptional sentences 15 times the standard maximum. Did the court go too far in any of these cases? There is no answer that legal analysis can provide. With too far as the yardstick, it is always possible to disagree with such judgments and never to refute them.

Whether the Sixth Amendment incorporates this manipulable standard rather than *Appren-*

di's bright-line rule depends on the plausibility of the claim that the Framers would have left definition of the scope of jury power up to judges' intuitive sense of how far is too far. We think that claim not plausible at all, because the very reason the Framers put a jury-trial guarantee in the Constitution is that they were unwilling to trust government to mark out the role of the jury.

By reversing the judgment below, we are not, as the State would have it, "finding determinate sentencing schemes unconstitutional." This case is not about whether determinate sentencing is constitutional, only about how it can be implemented in a way that respects the Sixth Amendment. Several policies prompted Washington's adoption of determinate sentencing, including proportionality to the gravity of the offense and parity among defendants. Nothing we have said impugns those salutary objectives.

Justice O'Connor argues that, because determinate sentencing schemes involving judicial factfinding entail less judicial discretion than indeterminate schemes, the constitutionality of the latter implies the constitutionality of the former. This argument is flawed on a number of levels. First, the Sixth Amendment by its terms is not a limitation on judicial power, but a reservation of jury power. It limits judicial power only to the extent that the claimed judicial power infringes on the province of the jury. Indeterminate sentencing does not do so. It increases judicial discretion, to be sure, but not at the expense of the jury's traditional function of finding the facts essential to lawful imposition of the penalty. Of course indeterminate schemes involve judicial factfinding, in that a judge (like a parole board) may implicitly rule on those facts he deems important to the exercise of his sentencing discretion. But the facts do not pertain to whether the defendant has a legal right to a lesser sentence—and that makes all the difference insofar as judicial impingement upon the traditional role of the jury is concerned. In a system that says the judge may punish burglary with 10 to 40 years, every burglar knows he is risking 40 years in jail. In a system that punishes burglary with a 10-year sentence, with another 30 added for use of a gun, the burglar who enters a home unarmed is *entitled* to no more than a 10-year sentence—and by reason of the Sixth Amendment the facts bearing upon that entitlement must be found by a jury.

Justice Breyer argues that *Apprendi* works to the detriment of criminal defendants who plead guilty by depriving them of the opportunity to argue sentencing factors to a judge. But nothing prevents a defendant from waiving his *Apprendi* rights. When a defendant pleads guilty, the State is free to seek judicial sentence enhancements so long as the defendant either stipulates to the relevant facts or consents to judicial factfinding. If appropriate waivers are procured, States may continue to offer judicial factfinding as a matter of course to all defendants who plead guilty. Even a defendant who stands trial may consent to judicial factfinding as to sentence enhancements, which may well be in his interest if relevant evidence would prejudice him at trial. We do not understand how *Apprendi* can possibly work to the detriment of those who are free, if they think its costs outweigh its benefits, to render it inapplicable. . . .

Justice Breyer's more general argument—that *Apprendi* undermines alternatives to adversarial factfinding—is not so much a criticism of *Apprendi* as an assault on jury trial generally. His esteem for "non-adversarial" truth-seeking processes supports just as well an argument against either. Our Constitution and the common-law traditions it entrenches, however, do not admit the contention that facts are better discovered by judicial inquisition than by adversarial testing before a jury. Justice Breyer may be convinced of the equity of the regime he favors, but his views are not the ones we are bound to uphold.

Ultimately, our decision cannot turn on whether or to what degree trial by jury impairs the efficiency or fairness of criminal justice. One can certainly argue that both these values would be better served by leaving justice entirely in the hands of professionals; many nations of the world, particularly those following civil-law traditions, take just that course. There is not one shred of doubt, however, about the Framers' paradigm for criminal justice: not the civil-law ideal of administrative perfection, but the common-law ideal of limited state power accomplished by strict division of authority between judge and jury. As *Apprendi* held, every defendant has the *right* to insist that the prosecutor prove to a jury all facts legally essential to the punishment. Under the dissenters' alternative, he has no such right. That should be the end of the matter.

Petitioner was sentenced to prison for more than three years beyond what the law allowed for the crime to which he confessed, on the basis of a disputed finding that he had acted with "deliberate cruelty." The Framers would not have thought it too much to demand that, before depriving a man of three more years of his liberty, the State should suffer the modest inconvenience of submitting its accusation to "the unanimous suffrage of twelve of his equals and neighbours" rather than a lone employee of the State.

The judgment of the Washington Court of Appeals is reversed, and the case is remanded for further proceedings not inconsistent with this opinion.

JUSTICE O'CONNOR, with whom JUSTICE BREYER joins, and with whom THE CHIEF JUSTICE and JUSTICE KENNEDY join as to all but Part IV-B, dissenting.

The legacy of today's opinion, whether intended or not, will be the consolidation of sentencing power in the State and Federal Judiciaries. The Court says to Congress and state legislatures: If you want to constrain the sentencing discretion of judges and bring some uniformity to sentencing, it will cost you—dearly. Congress and States, faced with the burdens imposed by the extension of *Apprendi* to the present context, will either trim or eliminate altogether their sentencing guidelines schemes and, with them, 20 years of sentencing reform. It is thus of little moment that the majority does not expressly declare guidelines schemes unconstitutional; for, as residents of "*Apprendi*-land" are fond of saying, "the relevant inquiry is one not of form, but of effect." The "effect" of today's decision will be greater judicial discretion and less uniformity in sentencing. Because I find it implausible that the Framers would have considered such a result to be required by the Due Process Clause or the Sixth Amendment, and because the practical consequences of today's decision may be disastrous, I respectfully dissent.

One need look no further than the history leading up to and following the enactment of Washington's guidelines scheme to appreciate the damage that today's decision will cause. Prior to 1981, Washington, like most other States and the Federal Government, employed an indeterminate sentencing scheme. Washington's criminal code separated all felonies into three broad categories: "class A," carrying a sentence of 20 years to life; "class B," carrying a sentence of 0 to 10 years; and "class C," carrying a sentence of 0 to 5 years. Sentencing judges, in conjunction with parole boards, had virtually unfettered discretion to sentence defendants to prison terms falling anywhere within the statutory range, including probation—*i.e.,* no jail sentence at all.

This system of unguided discretion inevitably resulted in severe disparities in sentences received and served by defendants committing the same offense and having similar criminal histories. . . . To counteract these trends, the state legislature passed the Sentencing Reform Act of 1981. The Act had the laudable purposes of "making the criminal justice system accountable to the public," and "ensur[ing] that the punishment for a criminal offense is proportionate to the seriousness of the offense . . . [and] commensurate with the punishment imposed on others committing similar offenses." The Act neither increased any of the statutory sentencing ranges for the three types of felonies (though it did eliminate the statutory mandatory minimum for class A felonies), nor reclassified any substantive offenses. It merely placed meaningful constraints on discretion to sentence offenders within the statutory ranges, and eliminated parole. There is thus no evidence that the legislature was attempting to manipulate the statutory elements of criminal offenses or to circumvent the procedural protections of the Bill of Rights. Rather, lawmakers were trying to bring some much-needed uniformity, transparency, and accountability to an otherwise "'labyrinthine' sentencing and corrections system that 'lacked any principle except unguided discretion.'"

Far from disregarding principles of due process and the jury trial right, as the majority today suggests, Washington's reform has served them. Before passage of the Act, a defendant charged with second degree kidnapping, like petitioner, had no idea whether he would receive a 10-year sentence or probation. The ultimate sentencing determination could turn as much on the idiosyncracies of a particular judge as on the specifics of the defendant's crime or background. . . . After passage of the Act, a defendant charged with second degree kidnaping knows what his presumptive sentence will be; he has a good idea of the types of factors that a sentencing judge can and will consider when deciding whether to sentence him outside that range; he is guaranteed meaningful appellate review to protect against an arbitrary sentence.

Washington's move to a system of guided discretion has served equal protection principles as well. Over the past 20 years, there has been a substantial reduction in racial disparity in sentencing across the State. The reduction is directly traceable to the constraining effects of the guidelines—namely, its "presumptive ranges" and limits on the imposition of "exceptional sentences" outside of those ranges. . . .

The majority does not, because it cannot, disagree that determinate sentencing schemes, like Washington's, serve important constitutional values. Thus, the majority says: "this case is not about whether determinate sentencing is constitutional, only about how it can be implemented in a way that respects the Sixth Amendment." But extension of *Apprendi* to the present context will impose significant costs on a legislature's determination that a particular fact, not historically an element, warrants a higher sentence. While not a constitutional prohibition on guidelines schemes, the majority's decision today exacts a substantial constitutional tax.

The costs are substantial and real. Under the majority's approach, any fact that increases the upper bound on a judge's sentencing discretion is an element of the offense. Thus, facts that historically have been taken into account by sentencing judges to assess a sentence within a broad range—such as drug quantity, role in the offense, risk of bodily harm—all must now be charged in an indictment and submitted to a jury simply because it is the legislature, rather than the judge, that constrains the extent to which such facts may be used to impose a sentence within a pre-existing statutory range.

While that alone is enough to threaten the continued use of sentencing guidelines schemes, there are additional costs. For example, a legislature might rightly think that some factors bearing on sentencing, such as prior bad acts or criminal history, should not be considered in a jury's determination of a defendant's guilt—such "character evidence" has traditionally been off limits during the guilt phase of criminal proceedings because of its tendency to inflame the passions of the jury. If a legislature desires uniform consideration of such factors at sentencing, but does not want them to impact a jury's initial determination of guilt, the State may have to bear the additional expense of a separate, full-blown jury trial during the penalty phase proceeding. . . . The majority may be correct that States and the Federal Government will be willing to bear some of these costs. But simple economics dictate that they will not, and cannot, bear them all. To the extent that they do not, there will be an inevitable increase in judicial discretion with all of its attendant failings. . . . Given these observations, it is difficult for me to discern what principle besides doctrinaire formalism actually motivates today's decision. . . .

The majority claims the mantle of history and original intent. But . . . broad judicial sentencing discretion was foreign to the Framers[;] they were never faced with the constitutional choice between submitting every fact that increases a sentence to the jury or vesting the sentencing judge with broad discretionary authority to account for differences in offenses and offenders.

IV-B

The consequences of today's decision will be as far reaching as they are disturbing. Washington's sentencing system is by no means unique. Numerous other States have enacted guidelines systems, as has the Federal Government. Today's decision casts constitutional doubt over them all and, in so doing, threatens an untold number of criminal judgments. Every sentence imposed under such guidelines in cases currently pending on direct appeal is in jeopardy. . . . The numbers available from the federal system alone are staggering. On March 31, 2004, there were 8,320 federal criminal appeals pending in which the defendant's sentence was at issue. Between June 27, 2000, when *Apprendi* was decided, and March 31, 2004, there have been 272,191 defendants sentenced in federal court. Given that nearly all federal sentences are governed by the Federal Sentencing Guidelines, the vast majority of these cases are Guidelines cases.

The practical consequences for trial courts, starting today, will be equally unsettling: How are courts to mete out guidelines sentences? Do courts apply the guidelines as to mitigating factors, but not as to aggravating factors? Do they jettison the guidelines altogether? The Court ignores the havoc it is about to wreak on trial courts across the country. . . . What I have feared most has now come to pass: Over 20 years of sentencing reform are all but lost, and tens of thousands of criminal judgments are in jeopardy. I respectfully dissent.

JUSTICE BREYER, with whom JUSTICE O'CONNOR joins, dissenting.

. . . As a result of the majority's rule, sentencing must now take one of three forms, each of which risks either impracticality, unfairness, or harm to the jury trial right the majority purports to strengthen. This circumstance shows that the majority's Sixth Amendment interpretation cannot be right.

A first option for legislators is to create a simple, pure or nearly pure "charge offense" or "determinate" sentencing system. In such a system, an indictment would charge a few facts which, taken together, constitute a crime, such as robbery. Robbery would carry a single sentence, say, five years' imprisonment. And every person convicted of robbery would receive that sentence—just as, centuries ago, everyone convicted of almost any serious crime was sentenced to death.

Such a system assures uniformity, but at intolerable costs. First, simple determinate sentencing systems impose identical punishments on people who committed their crimes in very different ways. When dramatically different conduct ends up being punished the same way, an injustice has taken place. . . . Second, in a world of statutorily fixed mandatory sentences for many crimes, determinate sentencing gives tremendous power to prosecutors to manipulate sentences through their choice of charges. Prosecutors can simply charge, or threaten to charge, defendants with crimes bearing higher mandatory sentences. . . .

A second option for legislators is to return to a system of indeterminate sentencing, such as California had before the recent sentencing reform movement. When such systems were in vogue, they were criticized, and rightly so, for producing unfair disparities, including race-based disparities, in the punishment of similarly situated defendants. . . .

A third option is that which the Court seems to believe legislators will in fact take. That is the option of retaining structured schemes that attempt to punish similar conduct similarly and different conduct differently, but modifying them to conform to *Apprendi*'s dictates. Judges would be able to depart *downward* from presumptive sentences upon finding that mitigating factors were present, but would not be able to depart *upward* unless the prosecutor charged the aggravating fact to a jury and proved it beyond a reasonable doubt. . . .

This option can be implemented in one of two ways. The first way would be for legislatures to subdivide each crime into a list of complex crimes, each of which would be defined to include commonly found sentencing factors such as drug quantity, type of victim, presence of violence, degree of injury, use of gun, and so on. . . . This "complex charge offense" system . . . prejudices defendants who seek trial, for it can put them in the untenable position of contesting material aggravating facts in the guilt phases of their trials. Consider a defendant who is charged, not with mere possession of cocaine, but with the specific offense of possession of more than 500 grams of cocaine. Or consider a defendant charged, not with murder, but with the new crime of murder using a machete. Or consider a defendant whom the prosecution wants to claim was a "supervisor," rather than an ordinary gang member. How can a Constitution that guarantees due process put these defendants, as a matter of course, in the position of arguing, "I did not sell drugs, and if I did, I did not sell more

than 500 grams" or, "I did not kill him, and if I did, I did not use a machete," or "I did not engage in gang activity, and certainly not as a supervisor" to a single jury?

The second way to make sentencing guidelines *Apprendi*-compliant would be to require at least two juries for each defendant whenever aggravating facts are present: one jury to determine guilt of the crime charged, and an additional jury to try the disputed facts that, if found, would aggravate the sentence. Our experience with bifurcated trials in the capital punishment context suggests that requiring them for run-of-the-mill sentences would be costly, both in money and in judicial time and resources. . . . The majority refers to an *amicus curiae* brief filed by the Kansas Appellate Defender Office, which suggests that a two-jury system has proved workable in Kansas. And that may be so. But in all likelihood, any such workability reflects an uncomfortable fact, a fact at which the majority hints, but whose constitutional implications it does not seem to grasp. The uncomfortable fact that could make the system seem workable—even desirable in the minds of some, including defense attorneys—is called "plea bargaining." The Court can announce that the Constitution requires at least two jury trials for each criminal defendant—one for guilt, another for sentencing—but only because it knows full well that more than 90% of defendants will not go to trial even once, much less insist on two or more trials.

Is there [another] option? Perhaps. Congress and state legislatures might, for example, rewrite their criminal codes, attaching astronomically high sentences to each crime, followed by long lists of mitigating facts, which, for the most part, would consist of the absence of aggravating facts. But political impediments to legislative action make such rewrites difficult to achieve; and it is difficult to see why the Sixth Amendment would require legislatures to undertake them.

It may also prove possible to find combinations of, or variations upon, my . . . three options. But I am unaware of any variation that does not involve (a) the shift of power to the prosecutor (weakening the connection between real conduct and real punishment) inherent in any charge offense system, (b) the lack of uniformity inherent in any system of pure judicial discretion, or (c) the complexity, expense, and increased reliance on plea bargains involved in a "two-jury" system. The simple fact is that the design of any fair sentencing system must involve efforts to make practical compromises among competing goals. The majority's reading of the Sixth Amendment makes the effort to find those compromises—already difficult—virtually impossible. . . . For the reasons given, I dissent.

Michigan v. Bryant
562 U.S. ___ (2011)

Michigan police dispatched to a gas station parking lot found Anthony Covington mortally wounded. Covington told them that he had been shot by respondent Bryant outside Bryant's house and had then driven himself to the lot. At trial, which occurred before Crawford v. Washington *(2004) and* Davis v. Washington *(2006) were decided, the officers testified about what Covington said. Bryant was found guilty of second-degree murder. Ultimately, the Michigan Supreme Court reversed his conviction, holding that the Sixth Amendment's Confrontation Clause, as explained in* Crawford *and* Davis*, rendered Covington's statements inadmissible testimonial hearsay. The Supreme Court granted certiorari.* Opinion of the Court: <u>Sotomayor</u>, Roberts, Kennedy, Breyer, Alito. Concurring in the judgment: <u>Thomas</u>. Dissenting opinions: <u>Scalia</u>; <u>Ginsburg</u>. Not participating: Kagan.

JUSTICE SOTOMAYOR delivered the opinion of the Court.

At respondent Richard Bryant's trial, the court admitted statements that the victim, Anthony Covington, made to police officers who discovered him mortally wounded in a gas station parking lot. A jury convicted Bryant of second-degree murder. On appeal, the Supreme Court of Michigan held that the Sixth Amendment's Confrontation Clause, as explained in our decisions in *Crawford v. Washington* (2004), and *Davis v. Washington* (2006), rendered Covington's statements inadmissible testimonial hearsay, and the court reversed Bryant's conviction. We granted the State's petition for a writ of certiorari to consider whether the Confrontation Clause barred the admission at trial of Covington's statements to the police. We hold that the circumstances of the interaction between Covington and the police objectively indicate that the "primary purpose of the interrogation" was "to enable police assistance to meet an ongoing emergency." Therefore, Covington's identification and description of the shooter and the location of the shooting were not testimonial statements, and their admission at Bryant's trial did not violate the Confrontation Clause. We vacate the judgment of the Supreme Court of Michigan and remand.

I

Around 3:25 a.m. on April 29, 2001, Detroit, Michigan police officers responded to a radio dispatch indicating that a man had been shot. At the scene, they found the victim, Anthony Covington, lying on the ground next to his car in a gas station parking lot. Covington had a gunshot wound to his abdomen, appeared to be in great pain, and spoke with difficulty.

The police asked him "what had happened, who had shot him, and where the shooting had occurred." Covington stated that "Rick" shot him at around 3 a.m. He also indicated that he had a conversation with Bryant, whom he recognized based on his voice, through the back door of Bryant's house. Covington explained that when he turned to leave, he was shot through the door and then drove to the gas station, where police found him.

Covington's conversation with the police ended within 5 to 10 minutes when emergency medical services arrived. Covington was transported to a hospital and died within hours. The police left the gas station after speaking with Covington, called for backup, and traveled to Bryant's house. They did not find Bryant there but did find blood and a bullet on the back porch and an apparent bullet hole in the back door. Police also found Covington's wallet and identification outside the house.

At trial, which occurred prior to our decisions in *Crawford* and *Davis*, the police officers who spoke with Covington at the gas station testified about what Covington had told them. The jury returned a guilty verdict on charges of second-degree murder, being a felon in possession of a firearm, and possession of a firearm during the commission of a felony. Bryant appealed, and the Michigan Court of Appeals affirmed his conviction. Bryant then appealed to the Supreme Court of Michigan, arguing that the trial court erred in admitting Covington's statements to the police. The Supreme Court of Michigan eventually remanded the case to the Court of Appeals for reconsideration in light of our 2006 decision in *Davis*. On remand, the Court of Appeals again affirmed, holding that Covington's statements were properly admitted because they were not testimonial. Bryant again appealed to the Supreme Court of Michigan, which reversed his conviction.

Before the Supreme Court of Michigan, Bryant argued that Covington's statements to the police were testimonial under *Crawford* and *Davis* and were therefore inadmissible. The State, on the other hand, argued that the statements were admissible as "excited utterances" under the Michigan Rules of Evidence. There was no dispute that Covington was unavailable at trial and Bryant had no prior opportunity to cross-examine him. The court therefore assessed whether Covington's statements to the police identifying and describing the shooter and the time and location of the shooting were testimonial hearsay for purposes of the Confrontation Clause. The court concluded that the circumstances "clearly indicate that the 'primary purpose' of the questioning was to establish the facts of an event that had *already* occurred; the 'primary purpose' was not to enable police assistance to meet an ongoing emergency." The court explained that, in its view, Covington was describing past events and as such, his "primary purpose in making these statements to the police . . . was . . . to tell the police who had committed the crime against him, where the crime had been committed, and where the police could find the criminal." Noting that the officers' actions did not suggest that they perceived an ongoing emergency at the gas station, the court held that there was in fact no ongoing emergency. The court distinguished the facts of this case from those in *Davis*, where we held a declarant's statements in a 911 call to be nontestimonial. It instead analogized this case to *Hammon v. Indiana*, which we decided jointly with *Davis* and in which we found testimonial a declarant's statements to police just after an assault. Based on this analysis, the Supreme Court of Michigan held that the admission of Covington's statements constituted prejudicial plain error warranting reversal and ordered a new trial. The court did not address whether, absent a Confrontation Clause bar, the statements' admission would have been otherwise consistent with Michigan's hearsay rules or due process. . . . We granted certiorari to determine whether the Confrontation Clause barred admission of Covington's statements.

II

In *Crawford v. Washington*, the Court held that the Confrontation Clause allows the admission of "[t]estimonial statements of witnesses absent from trial . . . only where the declarant is unavailable, and only where the defendant has had a prior opportunity to cross-examine."] . . . In 2006, the Court in *Davis v. Washington* and *Hammon v. Indiana*, [both cases involving domestic violence] took a further step to "determine more precisely which police interrogations produce testimony" and therefore implicate a Confrontation Clause bar. We . . . expanded upon the meaning of "testimonial" that we first employed in *Crawford* and discussed the concept of an ongoing emergency. . . .

Deciding this case . . . requires further explanation of the "ongoing emergency" circumstance addressed in *Davis*. Because *Davis* and *Hammon* arose in the domestic violence context, that was the situation "we had immediately in mind (for that was the case before us)." We now face a new context: a nondomestic dispute, involving a victim found in a public location, suffering from a fatal gunshot wound, and a perpetrator whose location was unknown at the time the police located the victim. Thus, we confront for the first time circumstances in which the "ongoing emergency" discussed in *Davis* extends beyond an initial victim to a potential threat to the responding police and the public at large. This new context requires us to provide additional clarification with regard to what *Davis* meant by "the primary purpose of the interrogation is to enable police assistance to meet an ongoing emergency."

III

To determine whether the "primary purpose" of an interrogation is "to enable police assistance to meet an ongoing emergency," which would render the resulting statements nontestimonial, we objectively evaluate the circumstances in which the encounter occurs and the statements and actions of the parties.

A

An objective analysis of the circumstances of an encounter and the statements and actions of the parties to it provides the most accurate assessment of the "primary purpose of the interrogation." The circumstances in which an encounter occurs—*e.g.*, at or near the scene of the crime versus at a police station, during an ongoing emergency or afterwards—are clearly matters of objective fact. The statements and actions of the parties must also be objectively evaluated. That is, the relevant inquiry is not the subjective or actual purpose of the individuals involved in a particular encounter, but rather the purpose that reasonable participants would have had, as ascertained from the individuals' statements and actions and the circumstances in which the encounter occurred.

B

As our recent Confrontation Clause cases have explained, the existence of an "ongoing emergency" at the time of an encounter between an individual and the police is among the most important circumstances informing the "primary purpose" of an interrogation. The existence of an ongoing emergency is relevant to determining the primary purpose of the interrogation because an emergency focuses the participants on something other than "prov[ing] past events potentially relevant to later criminal prosecution." Rather, it focuses them on "end[ing] a threatening situation." Implicit in *Davis* is the idea that because the prospect of fabrication in statements given for the primary purpose of resolving that emergency is presumably significantly diminished, the Confrontation Clause does not require such statements to be subject to the crucible of cross-examination. . . .

IV

As we suggested in *Davis*, when a court must determine whether the Confrontation Clause bars the admission of a statement at trial, it should determine the "primary purpose of the interrogation" by objectively evaluating the statements and actions of the parties to the encounter, in light of the circumstances in which the interrogation occurs. The existence of an emergency or the parties' perception that an emergency is ongoing is among the most important circumstances that courts must take into account in determining whether an interrogation is testimonial because statements made to assist police in addressing an ongoing emergency presumably lack the testimonial purpose that would subject them to the requirement of confrontation. As the context of this case brings into sharp relief, the existence and duration of an emergency depend on the type and scope of danger posed to the victim, the police, and the public. . . .

This is . . . the first of our post-*Crawford* Confrontation Clause cases to involve a gun. . . . At no point during the questioning did either Covington or the police know the location of the shooter. In fact, Bryant was not at home by the time the police searched his house at approximately 5:30 a.m. At some point between 3 a.m. and 5:30 a.m., Bryant left his house. At bottom, there was an ongoing emergency here where an armed shooter, whose motive for and location after the shooting were unknown, had mortally wounded Covington within a few blocks and a few minutes of the location where the police found Covington. . . .

Because the circumstances of the encounter as well as the statements and actions of Covington and the police objectively indicate that the "primary purpose of the interrogation" was "to enable police assistance to meet an ongoing emergency," Covington's identification and description of the shooter and the location of the shooting were not testimonial hearsay. The

Confrontation Clause did not bar their admission at Bryant's trial.

* * *

For the foregoing reasons, we hold that Covington's statements were not testimonial and that their admission at Bryant's trial did not violate the Confrontation Clause. We leave for the Michigan courts to decide on remand whether the statements' admission was otherwise permitted by state hearsay rules. The judgment of the Supreme Court of Michigan is vacated, and the case is remanded for further proceedings not inconsistent with this opinion.

JUSTICE THOMAS, concurring in the judgment.

I agree with the Court that the admission of Covington's out-of-court statements did not violate the Confrontation Clause, but I reach this conclusion because Covington's questioning by police lacked sufficient formality and solemnity for his statements to be considered "testimonial." See *Crawford v. Washington* (2004).

In determining whether Covington's statements to police implicate the Confrontation Clause, the Court evaluates the "'primary purpose'" of the interrogation. The majority's analysis which relies on, *inter alia,* what the police knew when they arrived at the scene, the specific questions they asked, the particular information Covington conveyed, the weapon involved, and Covington's medical condition illustrates the uncertainty that this test creates for law enforcement and the lower courts. I have criticized the primary-purpose test as "an exercise in fiction" that is "disconnected from history" and "yields no predictable results." *Davis v. Washington* (2006) (opinion concurring in judgment in part and dissenting in part).

Rather than attempting to reconstruct the "primary purpose" of the participants, I would consider the extent to which the interrogation resembles those historical practices that the Confrontation Clause addressed. See [my opinion in *Davis*], (describing "practices that occurred under the English bail and committal statutes passed during the reign of Queen Mary").

As the majority notes, Covington interacted with the police under highly informal circum-

stances, while he bled from a fatal gunshot wound. The police questioning was not "a formalized dialogue," did not result in "formalized testimonial materials" such as a deposition or affidavit, and bore no "indicia of solemnity." Nor is there any indication that the statements were offered at trial "in order to evade confrontation." This interrogation bears little if any resemblance to the historical practices that the Confrontation Clause aimed to eliminate. Covington thus did not "bea[r] testimony" against Bryant, and the introduction of his statements at trial did not implicate the Confrontation Clause. I concur in the judgment.

JUSTICE SCALIA, dissenting.

Today's tale—a story of five officers conducting successive examinations of a dying man with the primary purpose, not of obtaining and preserving his testimony regarding his killer, but of protecting him, them, and others from a murderer somewhere on the loose—is so transparently false that professing to believe it demeans this institution. But reaching a patently incorrect conclusion on the facts is a relatively benign judicial mischief; it affects, after all, only the case at hand. In its vain attempt to make the incredible plausible, however—or perhaps as an intended second goal—today's opinion distorts our Confrontation Clause jurisprudence and leaves it in a shambles. Instead of clarifying the law, the Court makes itself the obfuscator of last resort. Because I continue to adhere to the Confrontation Clause that the People adopted, as described in *Crawford v. Washington* (2004), I dissent.

I

C

Worse still for the repute of today's opinion this is an absurdly easy case even if one (erroneously) takes the interrogating officers' purpose into account. The five officers interrogated Covington primarily to investigate past criminal events. None—absolutely none—of their actions indicated that they perceived an imminent threat. They did not draw their weapons, and indeed did not immediately search the gas station for potential shooters. To the contrary, all five testified that they questioned Covington *before conducting any investigation at the scene*. Would this have made any sense if they feared the presence of a shooter? Most tellingly, none of the officers started his interrogation by asking what would have been the obvious first question if any hint of such a fear existed: Where is the shooter?

But do not rely solely on my word about the officers' primary purpose. Listen to Sergeant Wenturine, who candidly admitted that he interrogated Covington because he "ha[d] a man here that [he] believe[d] [was] dying [so he was] gonna find out who did this, period." In short, he needed to interrogate Covington to solve a crime. Wenturine never mentioned an interest in ending an ongoing emergency.

D

A final word about the Court's active imagination. The Court invents a world where an ongoing emergency exists whenever "an armed shooter, whose motive for and location after the shooting [are] unknown, . . . mortally wound[s]" one individual "within a few blocks and [25] minutes of the location where the police" ultimately find that victim. Breathlessly, it worries that a shooter could leave the scene armed and ready to pull the trigger again. Nothing suggests the five officers in this case shared the Court's dystopian view of Detroit, where drug dealers hunt their shooting victim down and fire into a crowd of police officers to finish him off, or where spree killers shoot through a door and then roam the streets leaving a trail of bodies behind. Because almost 90 percent of murders involve a single victim, it is much more likely—indeed, I think it certain— that the officers viewed their encounter with Covington for what it was: an investigation into a past crime with no ongoing or immediate consequences.

The Court's distorted view creates an expansive exception to the Confrontation Clause for violent crimes. Because Bryant posed a continuing threat to public safety in the Court's imagination, the emergency persisted for confrontation purposes at least until the police learned his "motive for and location after the shooting." It may have persisted in this case until the police "secured the scene of the shooting" two-and-a-half hours later This is a

dangerous definition of emergency. Many individuals who testify against a defendant at trial first offer their accounts to police in the hours after a violent act. If the police can plausibly claim that a "potential threat to . . . the public" persisted through those first few hours (and if the claim is plausible here it is always plausible), a defendant will have no constitutionally protected right to exclude the uncross-examined testimony of such witnesses. His conviction could rest (as perhaps it did here) solely on the officers' recollection at trial of the witnesses' accusations. . . .

II

A

But today's decision is not only a gross distortion of the facts. It is a gross distortion of the law—a revisionist narrative in which reliability continues to guide our Confrontation Clause jurisprudence, at least where emergencies and faux emergencies are concerned.

Is it possible that the Court does not recognize the contradiction between its focus on reliable statements and *Crawford's* focus on testimonial ones? Does it not realize that the two cannot coexist? Or does it intend, by following today's illogical roadmap, to resurrect *Roberts* by a thousand unprincipled distinctions without ever explicitly overruling *Crawford?* After all, honestly overruling *Crawford* would destroy the illusion of judicial minimalism and restraint. And it would force the Court to explain how the Justices' preference comports with the meaning of the Confrontation Clause that the People adopted—or to confess that only the Justices' preference really matters.

B

The Court recedes from *Crawford* in a second significant way. It requires judges to conduct "open-ended balancing tests" and "amorphous, if not entirely subjective," inquiries into the totality of the circumstances bearing upon reliability. Where the prosecution cries "emergency," the admissibility of a statement now turns on "a highly context-dependent inquiry" into the type of weapon the defendant wielded; the type of crime the defendant committed; the medical condition of the declarant; if the declarant is injured, whether paramedics have arrived on the scene; whether the encounter takes place in an "exposed public area"; whether the encounter appears disorganized; whether the declarant is capable of forming a purpose; whether the police have secured the scene of the crime; the formality of the statement; and finally, whether the statement strikes us as reliable. This is no better than the nine-factor balancing test we rejected in *Crawford*. I do not look forward to resolving conflicts in the future over whether knives and poison are more like guns or fists for Confrontation Clause purposes, or whether rape and armed robbery are more like murder or domestic violence.

* * *

Judicial decisions, like the Constitution itself, are nothing more than "parchment barriers." Both depend on a judicial culture that understands its constitutionally assigned role, has the courage to persist in that role when it means announcing unpopular decisions, and has the modesty to persist when it produces results that go against the judges' policy preferences. Today's opinion falls far short of living up to that obligation—short on the facts, and short on the law.

For all I know, Bryant has received his just deserts. But he surely has not received them pursuant to the procedures that our Constitution requires. And what has been taken away from him has been taken away from us all.

Gregg v. Georgia
428 U.S. 153 (1976)

In Furman v. Georgia *(1972), the Supreme Court in effect struck down all capital punishment laws as they then existed in the states. The reasons for the Court's action are summarized in the following opinion. In an effort to conform to what it understood to be the requirements of Furman, the Georgia Legislature immediately revised its death-penalty statute.*

Under the provisions of this revised statute, Troy Leon Gregg was charged with two counts of armed robbery and two counts of murder. At the trial stage of the bifurcated proceeding now required by the statute, the jury found Gregg guilty of all the charges against him. At the penalty stage, the judge instructed the jury that it could recommend either a sentence of death or a sentence of life in prison on each count; that it was free to consider mitigating or aggravating circumstances, if any, as presented by the parties; and that it would not be authorized to consider imposing the death sentence unless it first found beyond a reasonable doubt (1) that the murders were committed while Gregg was engaged in the commission of other capital felonies, namely, the armed robberies of the victims; (2) that he committed the murders for the purpose of receiving the victims' money and automobile; or (3) that the murders were "outrageously and wantonly vile, horrible, and inhuman" in that they

"involved the depravity of the mind of the defendant." The jury found the first and second of these aggravating circumstances and returned a sentence of death. Under Georgia's revised statute, the Georgia Supreme Court was required to review Gregg's conviction. After reviewing the trial transcript and record and considering the evidence and sentence in similar cases, the court upheld the death sentence for the murders, concluding that they had not resulted from prejudice or any other arbitrary factor and were not excessive or disproportionate to the penalty applied in similar cases. It vacated the armed robbery sentences, however, on the ground that the death penalty had rarely been imposed in Georgia for that offense. Gregg petitioned the Supreme Court for a writ of certiorari, charging that imposition of the death sentence under the Georgia statute was "cruel and unusual" punishment under the Eighth and Fourteenth Amendments. Judgment of the Court: <u>Stewart</u>, Powell, Stevens. Concurring in the judgment: <u>White</u>, Burger, Rehnquist; <u>Blackmun</u>. Dissenting opinions: <u>Brennan</u>; <u>Marshall</u>.

JUSTICE STEWART, JUSTICE POWELL, and JUSTICE STEVENS announced the judgment of the Court and filed an opinion delivered by JUSTICE STEWART. . . .

We address initially the basic contention that the punishment of death for the crime of murder is, under all circumstances, "cruel and unusual" in violation of the Eighth and Fourteenth Amendments of the Constitution. . . . Until *Furman v. Georgia* (1972), the Court never confronted squarely the fundamental claim that the punishment of death always, regardless of the enormity of the offense or the procedure followed in imposing the sentence, is cruel and unusual punishment in violation of the Constitution.

Although this issue was presented and addressed in *Furman,* it was not resolved by the Court. Four Justices [Burger, Blackmun, Powell, Rehnquist] would have held that capital punishment is not unconstitutional *per se*; two Justices [Brennan, Marshall] would have reached the opposite conclusion; and three Justices [Douglas, Stewart, White], while agreeing that the statutes then before the Court were invalid as applied, left open the question whether such punishment may ever be imposed. We now hold that the punishment of death does not invariably violate the Constitution.

. . . The Eighth Amendment has not been regarded as a static concept. As Chief Justice Warren said, in an oft-quoted phrase, "[t]he Amendment must draw its meaning from the evolving standards of decency that mark the progress of a maturing society." . . . Thus, an assessment of contemporary values concerning the infliction of a challenged sanction is relevant to the application of the Eighth Amendment. As we develop below more fully, . . . this assessment does not call for a subjective judgment. It requires, rather, that we look to objective *indicia* that reflect the public attitude toward a given sanction.

But our cases also make clear that public perceptions of standards of decency with respect to criminal sanctions are not conclusive. A penalty also must accord with "the dignity of man," which is the "basic concept underlying the Eighth Amendment." . . . This means, at least, that the punishment not be "excessive." When a form of punishment in the abstract (in this case, whether capital punishment may ever be imposed as a sanction for murder) rather than in the particular (the propriety of death as a penalty to be applied to a specific defendant

for a specific crime) is under consideration, the inquiry into "excessiveness" has two aspects. First, the punishment must not involve the unnecessary and wanton infliction of pain. . . . Second, the punishment must not be grossly out of proportion to the severity of the crime. . . .

Of course, the requirements of the Eighth Amendment must be applied with an awareness of the limited role to be played by the courts. . . .

. . . In assessing a punishment selected by a democratically elected legislature against the constitutional measure, we presume its validity. We may not require the legislature to select the least severe penalty possible so long as the penalty selected is not cruelly inhumane or disproportionate to the crime involved. And a heavy burden rests on those who would attack the judgment of the representatives of the people.

. . . We now consider specifically whether the sentence of death for the crime of murder is a *per se* violation of the Eighth and Fourteenth Amendments to the Constitution. We note first that history and precedent strongly support a negative answer to this question. . . .

The imposition of the death penalty for the crime of murder has a long history of acceptance both in the United States and in England. The common-law rule imposed a mandatory death sentence on all convicted murderers. . . . And the penalty continued to be used into the 20th century by most American States, although the breadth of the common-law rule was diminished, initially by narrowing the class of murders to be punished by death and subsequently by widespread adoption of laws expressly granting juries the discretion to recommend mercy. . . .

It is apparent from the text of the Constitution itself that the existence of capital punishment was accepted by the Framers. At the time the Eighth Amendment was ratified, capital punishment was a common sanction in every State. Indeed, the First Congress of the United States enacted legislation providing death as the penalty for specified crimes. . . . The Fifth Amendment, adopted at the same time as the Eighth, contemplated the continued existence of the capital sanction by imposing certain limits on the prosecution of capital cases: "No person shall be held to answer for a capital, or otherwise infamous crime, unless on a presentment or indictment of a Grand Jury . . . ; nor shall any person be subject for the same offense to be twice put in jeopardy of life or limb; . . . nor be deprived of life, liberty, or property, without due process of law. . . . " And the Fourteenth Amendment, adopted over three-quarters of a century later, similarly contemplates the existence of the capital sanction in providing that no State shall deprive any person of "life, liberty, or property" without due process of law.

For nearly two centuries, this Court, repeatedly and often expressly, has recognized that capital punishment is not invalid *per se*. . . .

Four years ago, the petitioners in *Furman* and its companion cases predicated their argument primarily upon the asserted proposition that standards of decency had evolved to the point where capital punishment no longer could be tolerated. The petitioners in those cases said, in effect, that the evolutionary process had come to an end, and that standards of decency required that the Eighth Amendment be construed finally as prohibiting capital punishment for any crime regardless of its depravity and impact on society. This view was accepted by two Justices. Three other Justices were unwilling to go so far; focusing on the procedures by which convicted defendants were selected for the death penalty rather than on the actual punishment inflicted, they joined in the conclusion that the statutes before the Court were constitutionally invalid.

The petitioners in the capital cases before the Court today renew the "standards of decency" argument, but developments during the four years since *Furman* have undercut substantially the assumptions upon which their argument rested. Despite the continuing debate, dating back to the 19th century, over the morality and utility of capital punishment, it is now evident that a large proportion of American society continues to regard it as an appropriate and necessary criminal sanction.

The most marked indication of society's endorsement of the death penalty for murder is the legislative response to *Furman*. The legislatures of at least 35 States have enacted new statutes that provide for the death penalty for at least some crimes that result in the death of another person. And the Congress of the United States, in 1974, enacted a statute providing the death penalty for aircraft piracy that results in death. . . . All of the post-*Furman* statutes make clear that capital punishment itself has not been rejected by the elected representatives of the people.

The jury also is a significant and reliable objective index of contemporary values because it is so directly involved. . . . The action of juries in many States since *Furman* is fully compatible with the legislative judgments, reflected in the new statutes, as to the continued utility and necessity of capital punishment in appropriate cases. At the close of 1974 at least 254 persons had been sentenced to death since *Furman*, and by the end of March 1976, more than 460 persons were subject to death sentences.

As we have seen, however, the Eighth Amendment demands more than that a challenged punishment be acceptable to contemporary society. The Court also must ask whether it comports with the basic concept of human dignity at the core of the Amendment. . . . The sanction imposed cannot be so totally without penological justification that it results in the gratuitous infliction of suffering. . . .

The death penalty is said to serve two principal social purposes: retribution and deterrence of capital crimes by prospective offenders. In part, capital punishment is an expression of society's moral outrage at particularly offensive conduct. This function may be unappealing to many, but it is essential in an ordered society that asks its citizens to rely on legal processes rather than self-help to vindicate their wrongs.

. . . "Retribution is no longer the dominant objective of the criminal law," . . . but neither is it a forbidden objective nor one inconsistent with our respect for the dignity of men. . . . Indeed, the decision that capital punishment may be the appropriate sanction in extreme cases is an expression of the community's belief that certain crimes are themselves so grievous an affront to humanity that the only adequate response may be the penalty of death. Statistical attempts to evaluate the worth of the death penalty as a deterrent to crimes by potential offenders have occasioned a great deal of debate. The results simply have been inconclusive. . . .

Although some of the studies suggest that the death penalty may not function as a significantly greater deterrent than lesser penalties, there is no convincing empirical evidence either supporting or refuting this view. We may nevertheless assume safely that there are murderers, such as those who act in passion, for whom the threat of death has little or no deterrent effect. But for many others, the death penalty undoubtedly is a significant deterrent. There are carefully contemplated murders, such as murder for hire, where the possible penalty of death may well enter into the cold calculus that precedes the decision to act. And there are some categories of murder, such as murder by a life prisoner, where other sanctions may not be adequate.

The value of capital punishment as a deterrent of crime is a complex factual issue the resolution of which properly rests with the legislatures, which can evaluate the results of statistical studies in terms of their own local conditions and with a flexibility of approach that is not available to the courts. . . . Indeed, many of the post-*Furman* statutes reflect just such a responsible effort to define those crimes and those criminals for which capital punishment is most probably an effective deterrent. . . . Considerations of federalism, as well as respect for the ability of a legislature to evaluate, in terms of its particular state, the moral consensus concerning the death penalty and its social utility as a sanction, require us to conclude, in the absence of more convincing evidence, that the infliction of death as a punishment for murder is not without justification and thus is not unconstitutionally severe.

Finally, we must consider whether the punishment of death is disproportionate in relation to the crime for which it is imposed. There is no question that death as a punishment is unique in its severity and irrevocability. . . . When a defendant's life is at stake, the Court has been particularly sensitive to insure that every safeguard is observed. . . . But we are concerned here only with the imposition of capital punishment for the crime of murder, and when a life has been taken deliberately by the offender, we cannot say that the punishment is invariably disproportionate to the crime. It is an extreme sanction, suitable to the most extreme of crimes.

We hold that the death penalty is not a form of punishment that may never be imposed, regardless of the circumstances of the offense, regardless of the character of the offender, and regardless of the procedure followed in reaching the decision to impose it. . . .

While *Furman* did not hold that the infliction of the death penalty *per se* violates the Constitution's ban on cruel and unusual punishments, it did recognize that the penalty of death is different in kind from any other punishment imposed under our system of criminal justice. Because of the uniqueness of the death penalty, *Furman* held that it could not be imposed under sentencing procedures that created a substantial risk that it would be inflicted in an arbitrary and capricious manner.

. . . The concerns expressed in *Furman* that the penalty of death not be imposed in an arbitrary or capricious manner can be met by a carefully drafted statute that ensures that the sentencing authority is given adequate information and guidance. As a general proposition these concerns are best met by a system that provides for a bifurcated proceeding at which the sentencing authority is apprised of the information relevant to the imposition of sentence and provided with standards to guide its use of the information.

. . . Georgia's new sentencing procedures require as a prerequisite to the imposition of the death penalty, specific jury findings as to the circumstances of the crime or the character of the defendant. Moreover to guard further against a situation comparable to that presented in *Furman,* the Supreme Court of Georgia compares each death sentence with the sentences imposed on similarly situated defendants to ensure that the sentence of death in a particular case is not disproportionate. On their face these procedures seem to satisfy the concerns of *Furman.* No longer should there be "no meaningful basis for distinguishing the few cases in which [the death penalty] is imposed from the many cases in which it is not." . . .

The basic concern of *Furman* centered on those defendants who were being condemned to death capriciously and arbitrarily. Under the procedures before the Court in that case, sentencing authorities were not directed to give attention to the nature or circumstances of crime committed or to the character or record of the defendant. Left unguided, juries imposed the death sentence in a way that could only be called freakish. The new Georgia sentencing procedures, by contrast, focus the jury's attention on the particularized nature of the crime and the particularized characteristics of the individual defendant. While the jury is permitted to consider any aggravating or mitigating circumstances, it must find and identify at least one statutory aggravating factor before it may impose a penalty of death. In this way the jury's discretion is channeled. No longer can a jury wantonly and freakishly impose the death sentence; it is always circumscribed by the legislative guidelines. In addition, the review function of the Supreme Court of Georgia affords additional assurance that the concerns that prompted our decision in *Furman* are not present to any significant degree in the Georgia procedure applied here.

For the reasons expressed in this opinion, we hold that the statutory system under which Gregg was sentenced to death does not violate the Constitution. Accordingly, the judgment of the Georgia Supreme Court is affirmed.

JUSTICE BRENNAN, dissenting.

. . . Death for whatever crime and under all circumstances "is truly an awesome punishment. The calculated killing of a human being by the State involves, by its very nature, a denial of the executed person's humanity. . . . An executed person has indeed 'lost the right to have rights.'" Death is not only an unusually severe punishment, unusual in its pain, in its finality, and in its enormity, but it serves no penal purpose more effectively than a less severe punishment; therefore the principle inherent in the Clause that prohibits pointless infliction of excessive punishment when less severe punishment can adequately achieve the same purposes invalidates the punishment. . . .

The fatal constitutional infirmity in the punishment of death is that it treats "members of the human race as nonhumans, as objects to be toyed with and discarded. [It is] thus inconsistent with the fundamental premise of the Clause that even the vilest criminal remains a human being possessed of common human dignity." . . . As such it is a penalty that "subjects the individual to a fate forbidden by the principle of civilized treatment guaranteed by the [Clause]." I therefore would hold, on that ground alone, that death is today a cruel and unusual punishment prohibited by the Clause. "Justice of this kind is obviously no less shocking than the crime itself, and the new 'official' murder, far from offering redress for the offense committed against society, adds instead a second defilement to the first." . . .

JUSTICE MARSHALL, dissenting. . . .

In *Furman* I concluded that the death penalty is constitutionally invalid for two reasons. First, the death penalty is excessive. . . . And second, the American people, fully informed as to the purposes of the death penalty and its liabilities would in my view reject it as morally unacceptable. . . .

Since the decision in *Furman,* the legislatures of 35 States have enacted new statutes authorizing the imposition of the death sentence for certain crimes, and Congress has enacted a law providing the death penalty for air piracy resulting in death. . . . I would be less than candid if I did not acknowledge that these developments have a significant bearing on a realistic assessment of the moral acceptability of the death penalty to the American people. But if the constitutionality of the death penalty turns, as I have urged, on the opinion of an *informed* citizenry, then even the enactment of new death statutes cannot be viewed as conclusive. In *Furman,* I observed that the American people are largely unaware of the information critical to a judgment on the morality of the death penalty, and concluded that if they were better informed they would consider it shocking, unjust, and unacceptable. . . . A recent study, conducted after the enactment of the post-*Furman* statutes, has confirmed that the American people know little about the death penalty, and that the opinions of an informed public would differ significantly from those of a public unaware of the consequences and effects of the death penalty.

Even assuming, however, that the post-*Furman* enactment of statutes authorizing the death penalty renders the prediction of the views of an informed citizenry an uncertain basis for a constitutional decision, the enactment of those statutes has no bearing whatsoever on the conclusion that the death penalty is unconstitutional because it is excessive. An excessive penalty is invalid under the Cruel and Unusual Punishments Clause "even though popular sentiment may favor" it. . . . The inquiry here, then, is simply whether the death penalty is necessary to accomplish the legitimate legislative purposes in punishment, or whether a less severe penalty—life imprisonment—would do as well. . . .

The two purposes that sustain the death penalty as nonexcessive in the Court's view are general deterrence and retribution. . . . The evidence I reviewed in *Furman* remains convincing, in my view, that "capital punishment is not necessary as a deterrent to crime in our

society." The justification for the death penalty must be found elsewhere.

The other principal purpose said to be served by the death penalty is retribution. The notion that retribution can serve as a moral justification for the sanction of death finds credence in the opinion of my Brothers Stewart, Powell, and Stevens. . . . It is this notion that I find to be the most disturbing aspect of today's unfortunate decision. . . . To be sustained under the Eighth Amendment, the death penalty must "[comport] with the basic concept of human dignity at the core of the Amendment." . . . The objective in imposing it must be "[consistent] with our respect for the dignity of other men." . . . Under these standards, the taking of life "because the wrong-doer deserves it" surely must fall, for such a punishment has as its very basis the total denial of the wrong-doer's dignity and worth. . . .

Kennedy v. Louisiana
554 U.S. 407 (2008)

Louisiana charged Patrick Kennedy with the aggravated rape of his then eight-year-old stepdaughter. He was convicted and sentenced to death under a state statute authorizing capital punishment for the rape of a child under the age of twelve. When the Louisiana Supreme Court affirmed, rejecting the petitioner's reliance on Coker v. Georgia *(1977), which barred the use of the death penalty as punishment for the rape of an adult woman but left open the question of which, if any, other nonhomicide crimes can be punished by death consistent with the Eighth Amendment, the US Supreme Court granted certiorari. Opinion of the Court: Kennedy, Stevens, Souter, Ginsburg, Breyer. Dissenting opinion: Alito, Roberts, Scalia, Thomas.*

JUSTICE KENNEDY delivered the opinion of the Court.

. . . This case presents the question whether the Constitution bars respondent from imposing the death penalty for the rape of a child where the crime did not result, and was not intended to result, in death of the victim. We hold the Eighth Amendment prohibits the death penalty for this offense. The Louisiana statute is unconstitutional.

I

Petitioner's crime was one that cannot be recounted in these pages in a way sufficient to capture in full the hurt and horror inflicted on his victim or to convey the revulsion society, and the jury that represents it, sought to express by sentencing petitioner to death. . . . An expert in pediatric forensic medicine testified that [the victim's] injuries were the most severe he had seen from a sexual assault in his four years of practice. A laceration to the left wall of the vagina had separated her cervix from the back of her vagina, causing her rectum to protrude into the vaginal structure. Her entire perineum was torn from the posterior fourchette to the anus. The injuries required emergency surgery. . . .

II

The Eighth Amendment, applicable to the States through the Fourteenth Amendment, provides that "[e]xcessive bail shall not be required, nor excessive fines imposed, nor cruel and unusual punishments inflicted." The Amendment proscribes "all excessive punishments, as well as cruel and unusual punishments that may or may not be excessive." . . . The Eight Amendment's protection against excessive or cruel and unusual punishments flows from the basic "precept of justice that punishment for [a] crime should be graduated and proportioned to [the] offense." Whether this requirement has been fulfilled is determined not by the standards that prevailed when the Eighth Amendment was adopted in 1791 but by the norms that "currently prevail." The Amendment "draw[s] its meaning from the evolving standards of decency that mark the progress of a maturing society." This is because "[t]he standard of extreme cruelty is not merely descriptive, but necessarily embodies a moral judgment. The standard itself remains the same, but its applicability must change as the basic mores of society change."

Evolving standards of decency must embrace and express respect for the dignity of the person, and the punishment of criminals must conform to that rule. As we shall discuss, punishment is justified under one or more of three principal rationales: rehabilitation, deterrence, and retribution. It is the last of these, retribution, that most often can contradict the law's own ends. This is of particular concern when the Court interprets the meaning of the Eighth Amendment in capital cases. When the law punishes by death, it risks its own sudden descent into brutality, transgressing the constitutional commitment to decency and restraint.

For these reasons we have explained that capital punishment must "be limited to those offenders who commit 'a narrow category of the most serious crimes' and whose extreme culpability makes them 'the most deserving of execution.'" Though the death penalty is not invariably unconstitutional, the Court insists upon confining the instances in which the punishment can be imposed.

Applying this principle, we held in *Roper* [*v. Simmons*] and *Atkins* [*v. Virginia*] that the execution of juveniles and mentally retarded persons are punishments violative of the Eighth Amendment because the offender had a diminished personal responsibility for the crime. In *Coker*, for instance, the Court held it would be unconstitutional to execute an offender who had raped an adult woman. In these cases the Court has been guided by "objective indicia of society's standards, as expressed in legislative enactments and state practice with respect to executions."

Based both on consensus and our own independent judgment, our holding is that a death sentence for one who raped but did not kill a child, and who did not intend to assist another in killing the child, is unconstitutional under the Eighth and Fourteenth Amendments.

III

The existence of objective indicia of consensus against making a crime punishable by death [is] a relevant concern, and we follow the approach . . . here.

Louisiana reintroduced the death penalty for rape of a child in 1995. Five States have since followed Louisiana's lead: Georgia, Montana, Oklahoma, South Carolina, and Texas. . . . By contrast, 44 States have not made child rape a capital offense. As for federal law, Congress in the Federal Death Penalty Act of 1994 expanded the number of federal crimes for which the death penalty is a permissible sentence, including certain nonhomicide offenses; but it did not do the same for child rape or abuse. . . .

The evidence of a national consensus with respect to the death penalty for child rapists, as with respect to juveniles, mentally retarded offenders, and vicarious felony murderers, shows divided opinion but, on balance, an opinion against it. Thirty-seven jurisdictions—36 States plus the Federal Government—have the death penalty. As mentioned above, only six of those jurisdictions authorize the death penalty for rape of a child. Though our review of national consensus is not confined to tallying the number of States with applicable death penalty legislation, it is of significance that, in 45 jurisdictions, petitioner could not be executed for child rape of any kind.*

Respondent insists that the six States where child rape is a capital offense, along with the

---

*When issued and announced on June 25, 2008, the Court's decision neither noted nor discussed the military penalty for rape under the Uniform Code of Military Justice. In a petition for rehearing respondent argues that the military penalty bears on our consideration of the question in this case. For the reasons set forth in the statement respecting the denial of rehearing, we find that the military penalty does not affect our reasoning or conclusions.

States that have proposed but not yet enacted applicable death penalty legislation, reflect a consistent direction of change in support of the death penalty for child rape. Consistent change might counterbalance an otherwise weak demonstration of consensus. . . . [I]t is true that in the last 13 years there has been change towards making child rape a capital offense. This is evidenced by six new death penalty statutes, three enacted in the last two years. But this showing . . . is not an indication of a trend or change in direction. . . .

There are measures of consensus other than legislation. Statistics about the number of executions may inform the consideration whether capital punishment for the crime of child rape is regarded as unacceptable in our society. These statistics confirm our determination from our review of state statutes that there is a social consensus against the death penalty for the crime of child rape. Nine States—Florida, Georgia, Louisiana, Mississippi, Montana, Oklahoma, South Carolina, Tennessee, and Texas—have permitted capital punishment for adult or child rape for some length of time between the Court's 1972 decision in Furman and today. Yet no individual has been executed for the rape of an adult or child since 1964, and no execution for any other nonhomicide offense has been conducted since 1963. Louisiana is the only State since 1964 that has sentenced an individual to death for the crime of child rape; and petitioner and Richard Davis, who was convicted and sentenced to death for the aggravated rape of a 5-year-old child by a Louisiana jury in December 2007 are the only two individuals now on death row in the United States for a nonhomicide offense.

After reviewing the authorities informed by contemporary norms, including the history of the death penalty for this and other nonhomicide crimes, current state statutes and new enactments, and the number of executions since 1964, we conclude there is a national consensus against capital punishment for the crime of child rape.

IV

As we have said in other Eighth Amendment cases, objective evidence of contemporary values as it relates to punishment for child rape is entitled to great weight, but it does not end our inquiry. "[T]he Constitution contemplates that in the end our own judgment will be brought to bear on the question of the acceptability of the death penalty under the Eighth Amendment." We turn, then, to the resolution of the question before us, which is informed by our precedents and our own understanding of the Constitution and the rights it secures. . . .

The constitutional prohibition against excessive or cruel and unusual punishments mandates that the State's power to punish "be exercised within the limits of civilized standards." Evolving standards of decency that mark the progress of a maturing society counsel us to be most hesitant before interpreting the Eighth Amendment to allow the extension of the death penalty, a hesitation that has special force where no life was taken in the commission of the crime. It is an established principle that decency, in its essence, presumes respect for the individual and thus moderation or restraint in the application of capital punishment. . . .

Our concern here is limited to crimes against individual persons. We do not address, for example, crimes defining and punishing treason, espionage, terrorism, and drug kingpin activity, which are offenses against the State. As it relates to crimes against individuals, though, the death penalty should not be expanded to instances where the victim's life was not taken. . . .

Consistent with evolving standards of decency and the teachings of our precedents we conclude that, in determining whether the death penalty is excessive, there is a distinction between intentional first-degree murder on the one hand and nonhomicide crimes against individual persons, even including child rape, on the other. The latter crimes may be devastating in their harm, as here, but "in terms of moral depravity and of the injury to the person and to the public," they cannot be compared to murder in their "severity and irrevocability."

In reaching our conclusion we find significant the number of executions would be allowed under respondent's approach. The crime of child rape, considering its reported incidents, occurs more often than first-degree murder. Approximately 5,702 incidents of vaginal, anal, or oral rape of a child under the age of 12 were reported nationwide in 2005; this is almost twice the total incidents of intentional murder for victims of all ages (3,405) reported during the same period. Although we have no reliable statistics on convictions for child rape, we can surmise that, each year, there are hundreds, or more, of these convictions just in jurisdictions that permit capital punishment. . . . [U]nder respondent's approach, the 36 States that permit the death penalty could sentence to death all persons convicted of raping a child less than 12 years of age. This could not be reconciled with our evolving standards of decency and the necessity to constrain the use of the death penalty.

It might be said that narrowing aggravators could be used in this context, as with murder offenses, to ensure the death penalty's restrained application. We find it difficult to identify standards that would guide the decisionmaker so the penalty is reserved for the most severe cases of child rape and yet not imposed in an arbitrary way. . . . It is not a solution simply to apply to this context the aggravating factors developed for capital murder. The Court has said that a State may carry out its obligation to ensure individualized sentencing in capital murder cases by adopting sentencing processes that rely upon the jury to exercise wide discretion so long as there are narrowing factors that have some "'common-sense core of meaning . . . that criminal juries should be capable of understanding.'" . . . [T]he resulting imprecision and the tension between evaluating the individual circumstances and consistency of treatment have been tolerated where the victim dies. It should not be introduced into our justice system, though, where death has not occurred. . . .

The goal of retribution, which reflects society's and the victim's interests in seeing that the offender is repaid for the hurt he caused does not justify the harshness of the death penalty here. In measuring retribution, as well as other objectives of criminal law, it is appropriate to distinguish between a particularly depraved murder that merits death as a form of retribution and the crime of child rape.

There is an additional reason for our conclusion that imposing the death penalty for child rape would not further retributive purposes. In considering whether retribution is served, among other factors we have looked to whether capital punishment "has the potential . . . to allow the community as a whole, including the surviving family and friends of the victim, to affirm its own judgment that the culpability of the prisoner is so serious that the ultimate penalty must be sought and imposed" . . . It is not at all evident that the child rape victim's hurt is lessened when the law permits the death of the perpetrator. Capital cases require a long-term commitment by those who testify for the prosecution, especially when guilt and sentencing determinations are in multiple proceedings. In cases like this the key testimony is not just from the family but from the victim herself. During formative years of her adolescence, made all the more daunting for having to come to terms with the brutality of her experience, [the victim] was required to discuss the case at length with law enforcement personnel. In a public trial she was required to recount once more all the details of the crime to a jury as the State pursued the death of her stepfather. Society's desire to inflict the death penalty for child rape by enlisting the child victim to assist it over the course of years in asking for capital punishment forces a moral choice on the child, who is not of mature age to make that choice. The way the death penalty here involves the child victim in its enforcement can compromise a decent legal system; and this is but a subset of fundamental difficulties capital punishment can cause in the administration and enforcement of laws proscribing child rape.

There are, moreover, serious systemic concerns in prosecuting the crime of child rape that are relevant to the constitutionality of making it a capital offense. The problem of unreliable, induced, and even imagined child testimony means there is a "special risk of wrongful execution" in some child rape cases. This undermines, at least to some degree, the meaningful contribution of the death penalty to legitimate goals of punishment. Studies conclude that children are highly susceptible to suggestive questioning techniques like repetition, guided imagery, and selective reinforcement.

Similar criticisms pertain to other cases involving child witnesses; but child rape cases present heightened concerns because the central narrative and account of the crime often comes from the child herself. She and the accused are, in most instances, the only ones present when the crime was committed. And the question in a capital case is not just the fact of the crime, including, say, proof of rape as distinct from abuse short of rape, but details bearing upon brutality in its commission. These matters are subject to fabrication or exaggeration, or both. Although capital punishment does bring retribution, and the legislature here has chosen to use it for this end, its judgment must be weighed, in deciding the constitutional question, against the special risks of unreliable testimony with respect to this crime.

With respect to deterrence, if the death penalty adds to the risk of non-reporting, that, too, diminishes the penalty's objectives. Underreporting is a common problem with respect to child sexual abuse. Although we know little about what differentiates those who report from those who do not report, one of the most commonly cited reasons for nondisclosure is fear of negative consequences for the perpetrator, a concern that has special force where the abuser is a family member. As a result, punishment by death may not result in more deterrence or more effective enforcement.

In addition, by in effect making the punishment for child rape and murder equivalent, a State that punishes child rape by death may remove a strong incentive for the rapist not to kill the victim. Assuming the offender behaves in a rational way, as one must to justify the penalty on grounds of deterrence, the penalty in some respects gives less protection, not more, to the victim, who is often the sole witness to the crime. . . .

Each of these propositions, standing alone, might not establish the unconstitutionality of the death penalty for the crime of child rape. Taken in sum, however, they demonstrate the serious negative consequences of making child rape a capital offense. These considerations lead us to conclude, in our independent judgment, that the death penalty is not a proportional punishment for the rape of a child.

V

Our determination that there is a consensus against the death penalty for child rape raises the question whether the Court's own institutional position and its holding will have the effect of blocking further or later consensus in favor of the penalty from developing. The Court, it will be argued, by the act of addressing the constitutionality of the death penalty, intrudes upon the consensus-making process. By imposing a negative restraint, the argument runs, the Court makes it more difficult for consensus to change or emerge. The Court, according to the criticism, itself becomes enmeshed in the process, part judge and part the maker of that which it judges.

These concerns overlook the meaning and full substance of the established proposition that the Eighth Amendment is defined by "the evolving standards of decency that mark the progress of a maturing society." Confirmed by repeated, consistent rulings of this Court, this principle requires that use of the death penalty be restrained. The rule of evolving standards of decency with specific marks on the way to full progress and mature judgment means that resort to the penalty must be reserved for the worst of crimes and limited in its instances of application. In most cases justice is not better served by terminating the life of the perpetrator rather than confining him and preserving the possibility that he and the system will find ways to allow him to understand the enormity of his offense. Difficulties in administering the penalty to ensure against its arbitrary and capricious application require adherence to a rule reserving its use, at this stage of evolving standards and in cases of crimes against individuals, for crimes that take the life of the victim.

The judgment of the Supreme Court of Louisiana upholding the capital sentence is reversed. This case is remanded for further proceedings not inconsistent with this opinion.

JUSTICE ALITO, with whom THE CHIEF JUSTICE, JUSTICE SCALIA, and JUSTICE THOMAS join, dissenting.

The Court today holds that the Eighth Amendment categorically prohibits the imposition of the death penalty for the crime of raping a child. This is so, according to the Court, no matter how young the child, no matter how many times the child is raped, no matter how many children the perpetrator rapes, no matter how sadistic the crime, no matter how much physical or psychological trauma is inflicted, and no matter how heinous the perpetrator's prior criminal record may be. The Court provides two reasons for this sweeping conclusion: First, the Court claims to have identified "a national consensus" that the death penalty is never acceptable for the rape of a child; second, the Court concludes, based on its "independent judgment," that imposing the death penalty for child rape is inconsistent with "'the evolving standards of decency that mark the progress of a maturing society.'" Because neither of these justifications is sound, I respectfully dissent.

I

I turn first to the Court's claim that there is "a national consensus" that it is never acceptable to impose the death penalty for the rape of a child. . . . In assessing current norms, the Court relies primarily on the fact that only 6 of the 50 States now have statutes that permit the death penalty for this offense. But this statistic is a highly unreliable indicator of the views of state lawmakers and their constituents. . . . [D]icta in this Court's decision *Coker* has stunted legislative consideration of the question whether the death penalty for the targeted offense of raping a young child is consistent with prevailing standards of decency. The *Coker* dicta gave state legislators and others good reason to fear that any law permitting the imposition of the death penalty for this crime would meet precisely the fate that has now befallen the Louisiana statute that is currently before us, and this threat strongly discouraged state legislators—regardless of their own values and those of their constituents—from supporting the enactment of such legislation. . . .

The enactment and implementation of any new state death penalty statute—and particularly a new type of statute such as one that specifically targets the rape of young children—imposes many costs. There is the burden of drafting an innovative law that must take into account this Court's exceedingly complex Eighth Amendment jurisprudence. Securing passage of controversial legislation may interfere in a variety of ways with the enactment of other bills on the legislative agenda. Once the statute is enacted, there is the burden of training and coordinating the efforts of those who must implement the new law. Capital prosecutions are qualitatively more difficult than noncapital prosecutions and impose special emotional burdens on all involved. When a capital sentence is imposed under the new law, there is the burden of keeping the prisoner on death row and the lengthy and costly project of defending the constitutionality of the statute on appeal and in collateral proceedings. And if the law is eventually overturned, there is the burden of new proceedings on remand. Moreover, conscientious state lawmakers, whatever their personal views about the morality of imposing the death penalty for child rape, may defer to this Court's dicta, either because they respect our authority and expertise in interpreting the Constitution or merely because they do not relish the prospect of being held to have violated the Constitution and contravened prevailing "standards of decency." Accordingly, the *Coker* dicta gave state legislators a strong incentive not to push for the enactment of new capital child-rape laws even though these legislators and their constituents may have believed that the laws would be appropriate and desirable.

The Court expresses doubt that the *Coker* dicta had this effect, but the skepticism is unwarranted. It would be quite remarkable if state legislators were not influenced by the considerations noted above. And although state legislatures typically do not create legislative materials like those produced by Congress, there is evidence that proposals to permit the imposition of the death penalty for child rape were opposed on the ground that enactment would be futile and costly. . . .

Because of the effect of the *Coker* dicta, the Court is plainly wrong in comparing the situation here to that in *Atkins* or *Roper*. . . . When state lawmakers believe that their decision will prevail on the question whether to permit the death penalty for a particular crime or class of offender, the legislators' resolution of the issue can be interpreted as an expression of their own judgment, informed by whatever weight they attach to the values of their constituents. But when state legislators think that the enactment of a new death penalty law is likely to be futile, inaction cannot reasonably be interpreted as an expression of their understanding of prevailing societal values. In that atmosphere, legislative inaction is more likely to evidence acquiescence.

If anything can be inferred from state legislative developments, the message is very different from the one that the Court perceives. In just the past few years, despite the shadow cast by the *Coker* dicta, five States have enacted targeted capital child-rape laws. If, as the Court seems to think, our society is "[e]volving" toward ever higher "standards of decency," these enactments might represent the beginning of a new evolutionary line.

Such a development would not be out of step with changes in our society's thinking since *Coker* was decided. During that time, reported instances of child abuse have increased dramatically; and there are many indications of growing alarm about the sexual abuse of children . . . [A]t least 21 States and the District of Columbia now have statutes permitting the involuntary commitment of sexual predators, and at least 12 States have enacted residency restrictions for sex offenders.

Aside from its misleading tally of current state laws, the Court points to two additional "objective indicia" of a "national consensus," but these arguments are patent makeweights. The Court notes that Congress has not enacted a law permitting a federal district court to impose the death penalty for the rape of a child, but due to the territorial limits of the relevant federal statutes, very few rape cases, not to mention child-rape cases, are prosecuted in federal court. Congress' failure to enact a death penalty statute for this tiny set of cases is hardly evidence of Congress' assessment of our society's values.

Finally, the Court argues that statistics about the number of executions in rape cases support its perception of a "national consensus," but here too the statistics do not support the Court's position. The Court notes that the last execution for the rape of a child occurred in 1964, but the Court fails to mention that litigation regarding the constitutionality of the death penalty brought executions to a halt across the board in the late 1960's. In 1965 and 1966, there were a total of eight executions for all offenses, and from 1968 until 1977, the year when *Coker* was decided, there were no executions for any crimes. The Court also fails to mention that in Louisiana, since the state law was amended in 1995 to make child rape a capital offense, prosecutors have asked juries to return death verdicts in four cases. This 50% record is hardly evidence that juries share the Court's view that the death penalty for the rape of a young child is unacceptable under even the most aggravated circumstances.

In light of the points discussed above, I believe that the "objective indicia" of our society's "evolving standards of decency" can be fairly summarized as follows. Neither Congress nor juries have done anything that can plausibly be interpreted as evidencing the "national consensus" that the Court perceives. State legislatures, for more than 30 years, have operated under the ominous shadow of the Coker dicta and thus have not been free to express their own understanding of our society's standards of decency. And in the months following our grant of certiorari in this case, state legislatures have had an additional reason to pause. Yet despite the inhibiting legal atmosphere that has prevailed since 1977, six States have recently enacted new, targeted child-rape laws.

I do not suggest that six new state laws necessarily establish a "national consensus" or even that they are sure evidence of an ineluctable trend. In terms of the Court's metaphor of moral evolution, these enactments might have turned out to be an evolutionary dead end. But they might also have been the beginning of a strong new evolutionary line. We will never know, because the Court today snuffs out the line in its incipient stage.

II

The Court is willing to block the potential emergence of a national consensus in favor of permitting the death penalty for child rape because, in the end, what matters is the Court's "own judgment" regarding "the acceptability of the death penalty." Although the Court has much to say on this issue, most of the Court's discussion is not pertinent to the Eighth Amendment question at hand. And once all of the Court's irrelevant arguments are put aside, it is apparent that the Court has provided no coherent explanation for today's decision.

In the next section of this opinion, I will attempt to weed out the arguments that are not germane to the Eighth Amendment inquiry, and in the final section, I will address what remains.

A major theme of the Court's opinion is that permitting the death penalty in child-rape cases is not in the best interests of the victims of these crimes and society at large. . . . These policy arguments, whatever their merits, are simply not pertinent to the question whether the death penalty is "cruel and unusual" punishment. The Eighth Amendment protects the right of an accused. It does not authorize this Court to strike down federal or state criminal laws on the ground that they are not in the best interests of crime victims or the broader society. The Court's policy arguments concern matters that legislators should—and presumably do—take into account in deciding whether to enact a capital child-rape statute, but these arguments are irrelevant to the question that is before us in this case. Our cases have cautioned against using "'the aegis of the Cruel and Unusual Punishment Clause' to cut off the normal democratic processes."

The Court also contends that laws permitting the death penalty for the rape of a child create serious procedural problems. Specifically, the Court maintains that it is not feasible to channel the exercise of sentencing discretion in child-rape cases, and that the unreliability of the testimony of child victims creates a danger that innocent defendants will be convicted and executed. Neither of these contentions provides a basis for striking down all capital child-rape laws no matter how carefully and narrowly they are crafted.

The Court's argument regarding the structuring of sentencing discretion is hard to comprehend. The Court finds it "difficult to identify standards that would guide the decisionmaker so the penalty is reserved for the most severe cases of child rape and yet not imposed in an arbitrary way." Even assuming that the age of a child is not alone a sufficient factor for limiting sentencing discretion, the Court need only examine the child-rape laws recently enacted in Texas, Oklahoma, Montana, and South Carolina, all of which use a concrete factor to limit quite drastically the number of cases in which the death penalty may be imposed. In those States, a defendant convicted of the rape of a child may be sentenced to death only if the defendant has a prior conviction for a specified felony sex offense.

Moreover, it takes little imagination to envision other limiting factors that a State could use to structure sentencing discretion in child rape cases. Some of these might be: whether the victim was kidnapped, whether the defendant inflicted severe physical injury on the victim, whether the victim was raped multiple times, whether the rapes occurred over a specified extended period, and whether there were multiple victims.

The Court refers to limiting standards that are "indefinite and obscure," ante, at 30, but there is nothing indefinite or obscure about any of the above-listed aggravating factors. Indeed, they are far more definite and clear-cut than aggravating factors that we have found to be adequate in murder cases. For these reasons, concerns about limiting sentencing discretion provide no support for the Court's blanket condemnation of all capital child-rape statutes.

That sweeping holding is also not justified by the Court's concerns about the reliability of the testimony of child victims. First, the Eighth Amendment provides a poor vehicle for addressing problems regarding the admissibility or reliability of evidence, and problems presented by the testimony of child victims are not unique to capital cases. Second, concerns about the reliability of the testimony of child witnesses are not present in every child-rape case. In the case before us, for example, there was undisputed medical evidence that the victim was brutally raped, as well as strong independent evidence that petitioner was the perpetrator. Third, if the Court's evidentiary concerns have Eighth Amendment relevance, they could be addressed by allowing the death penalty in only those child-rape cases in which the independent evidence is sufficient to prove all the elements needed for conviction and imposition of a death sentence. There is precedent for requiring special corroboration in certain criminal cases. . . .

After all the arguments noted above are put aside, what is left? What remaining grounds does the Court provide to justify its independent judgment that the death penalty for child rape is categorically unacceptable? I see two.

The first is the proposition that we should be "most hesitant before interpreting the Eighth Amendment to allow the extension of the death penalty." But holding that the Eighth Amendment does not categorically prohibit the death penalty for the rape of a young child would not "extend" or "expand" the death penalty. Laws enacted by the state legislatures are presumptively constitutional. Consequently, upholding the constitutionality of such a law would not "extend" or "expand" the death penalty; rather, it would confirm the status of presumptive constitutionality that such laws have enjoyed up to this point. . . .

The Court's final—and, it appears, principal—justification for its holding is that murder, the only crime for which defendants have been executed since this Court's 1976 death penalty decisions, is unique in its moral depravity and in the severity of the injury that it inflicts on the victim and the public. But the Court makes little attempt to defend these conclusions.

With respect to the question of moral depravity, is it really true that every person who is convicted of capital murder and sentenced to death is more morally depraved than every child rapist? Consider the following two cases. In the first, a defendant robs a convenience store and watches as his accomplice shoots the store owner. The defendant acts recklessly, but was not the triggerman and did not intend the killing. In the second case, a previously convicted child rapist kidnaps, repeatedly rapes, and tortures multiple child victims. Is it clear that the first defendant is more morally depraved than the second?

The Court's decision here stands in stark contrast to *Atkins* and *Roper*, in which the Court concluded that characteristics of the affected defendants—mental retardation in *Atkins* and youth in *Roper*—diminished their culpability. . . . I have little doubt that, in the eyes of ordinary Americans, the very worst child rapists—predators who seek out and inflict serious physical and emotional injury on defenseless young children—are the epitome of moral depravity.

With respect to the question of the harm caused by the rape of child in relation to the harm caused by murder, it is certainly true that the loss of human life represents a unique harm, but that does not explain why other grievous harms are insufficient to permit a death sentence. And the Court does not take the position that no harm other than the loss of life is sufficient. The Court takes pains to limit its holding to "crimes against individual persons" and to exclude "offenses against the State," a category that the Court stretches—without explanation—to include "drug kingpin activity." But the Court makes no effort to explain why the harm caused by such crimes is necessarily greater than the harm caused by the rape of young children. . . .

The harm that is caused to the victims and to society at large by the worst child rapists is grave. It is the judgment of the Louisiana lawmakers and those in an increasing number of other States that these harms justify the death penalty. The Court provides no cogent explanation why this legislative judgment should be overridden. Conclusory references to "decency," "moderation," "restraint," "full progress," and "moral judgment" are not enough.

III

In summary, the Court holds that the Eighth Amendment categorically rules out the death penalty in even the most extreme cases of child rape even though: (1) This holding is not supported by the original meaning of the Eighth Amendment; (2) neither *Coker* nor any other prior precedent commands this result; (3) there are no reliable "objective indicia" of a "national consensus" in support of the Court's position; (4) sustaining the constitutionality of the state law before us would not "extend" or "expand" the death penalty; (5) this Court has previously rejected the proposition that the Eighth Amendment is a one-way ratchet that prohibits legislatures from adopting new capital punishment statutes to meet new problems; (6) the worst child rapists exhibit the epitome of moral depravity; and (7) child rape inflicts grievous injury on victims and on society in general.

The party attacking the constitutionality of a state statute bears the "heavy burden" of establishing that the law is unconstitutional. That burden has not been discharged here, and I would therefore affirm the decision of the Louisiana Supreme Court.

POSTSCRIPT:

Subsequent to the Court's decision in Kennedy v. Louisiana, *in which the majority asserted the lack of a national consensus concerning the imposition of the death penalty for the rape of a child, a letter signed by eighty-five members of Congress was sent to the Court pointing out that in 2006, Congress had passed language in the National Defense Authorization Act, which authorized the death penalty in military courts-martial for the rape of a child, passed the Senate by a vote of 95–0 and the House by a vote of 374–41, with the votes of a majority of each state's delegation, and was signed by President George W. Bush. This prompted a petition by Louisiana for a rehearing. On October 1, 2008, the same five-member Court majority denied that rehearing but modified its original opinion to include a new footnote, reprinted in the opinion above as the footnote on page 470. Justices Alito and Thomas voted to grant the petition for rehearing; the remaining seven did not. In two separate statements, Justice Kennedy defended his original majority opinion, and Justice Scalia criticized it.*

Statement of JUSTICE KENNEDY, with whom JUSTICE STEVENS, JUSTICE SOUTER, JUSTICE GINSBURG, and JUSTICE BREYER join.

In its petition for rehearing respondent argues that the military penalty for rape, a congressional amendment of the Uniform Code of Military Justice (UCMJ) in 2006, and a related executive order in 2007 should alter the Court's analysis of the Eighth Amendment question in this case. After considering the petition as well as supplemental briefs from the parties and the

United States, the Court has determined that rehearing is not warranted.

In 2006, Congress passed the National Defense Authorization Act, which authorized that year's appropriations for military and national-security activities. Pub L. 109–163. Also in that bill, Congress revised the military's sexual-assault statutes, in part by reclassifying the UCMJ's offense of rape as two separate crimes: adult rape and child rape. It is unclear what effect, if any, that reclassification worked on the availability of the military death penalty. . . .

In any event, authorization of the death penalty in the military sphere does not indicate that the penalty is constitutional in the civilian context. . . . That the Manual for Courts-Martial retains the death penalty for rape of a child or an adult when committed by a member of the military does not draw into question our conclusions that there is a consensus against the death penalty for the crime in the civilian context and that the penalty here is unconstitutional. . . . The more relevant federal benchmark is federal criminal law that applies to civilians, and that law does not permit the death penalty for child rape. Until the petition for rehearing, none of the briefs or submissions filed by the parties or the *amici* in this case cited or discussed the UCMJ provisions.

Statement of JUSTICE SCALIA, with whom THE CHIEF JUSTICE joins, respecting the denial of rehearing.

Respondent has moved for rehearing of this case because there has come to light a federal statute enacted in 2006 permitting the death sentence under the Uniform Code of Military Justice for rape of a minor. This provision was not cited by either party, nor by any of the numerous *amici* in the case; it was first brought to the Court's attention after the opinion had issued, in a letter signed by 85 Members of Congress. Respondent asserts that rehearing is justified because this statute calls into question the majority opinion's conclusion that there is a national consensus against capital punishment for rape of a child.

I am voting against the petition for rehearing because the views of the American people on the death penalty for child rape were, to tell the truth, irrelevant to the majority's decision in this case. The majority opinion, after an unpersuasive attempt to show that a consensus against the penalty existed, in the end came down to this: "[T]he Constitution contemplates that in the end our own judgment will be brought to bear on the question of the acceptability of the death penalty under the Eighth Amendment." Of course the Constitution contemplates no such thing; the proposed Eighth Amendment would have been laughed to scorn if it had read "no criminal penalty shall be imposed which the Supreme Court deems unacceptable." But that is what the majority opinion said, and there is no reason to believe that absence of a national consensus would provoke second thoughts.

While the new evidence of American opinion is ultimately irrelevant to the majority's decision, let there be no doubt that it utterly destroys the majority's claim to be discerning a national consensus and not just giving effect to the majority's own preference. As noted in the letter from Members of Congress, the bill providing the death penalty for child rape passed the Senate 95–0; it passed the House 374–41, with the votes of a majority of each State's delegation; and was signed by the President. Justice Kennedy's statement posits two reasons why this act by Congress proves nothing about the national consensus regarding permissible penalties for child rape. First, it claims the statute merely "reclassif[ied]" the offense of child rape. But the law did more than that; it

specifically *established* (as it would have to do) the penalty for the *new offense* of child rape—and that penalty was death: "For an offense under subsection (a) (rape) or subsection (b) (rape of a child), *death or such other punishment as a court-martial may direct.*" By separate executive order, the President later expressly reauthorized the death penalty as a punishment for child rape. Based on these acts, there is infinitely more reason to think that Congress and the President made a judgment regarding the appropriateness of the death penalty for child rape than there is to think that the many *non*-enacting state legislatures upon which the majority relies did so—especially since it was widely believed that *Coker* took the capital-punishment option off the table.

Second, Justice Kennedy speculates that the Eighth Amendment may permit subjecting a member of the military to a means of punishment that would be cruel and unusual if inflicted upon a civilian for the same crime. That is perhaps so where the fact of the malefactor's membership in the Armed Forces makes the offense more grievous. One can imagine, for example, a social judgment that treason by a military officer who has sworn to defend his country deserves the death penalty even though treason by a civilian does not. (That is not the social judgment our society has made, but one can imagine it.) It is difficult to imagine, however, how rape of a child could sometimes be deserving of death for a soldier but never for a civilian.

Roper v. Simmons
543 U.S. 551 (2005)

At age seventeen, Christopher Simmons planned and committed a capital murder described in gruesome detail in Justice Kennedy's majority opinion. After he had turned eighteen, he was sentenced to death. His direct appeal and subsequent petitions for state and federal postconviction relief were rejected. However, when the Supreme Court held in Atkins v. Virginia *(2002), that the Eighth Amendment prohibits the execution of a mentally retarded person, Simmons filed a new petition for state postconviction relief, arguing that Atkins's reasoning established that the Constitution*

prohibits the execution of a juvenile who was under eighteen when he committed his crime. The Missouri Supreme Court agreed and set aside Simmons's death sentence in favor of life imprisonment without eligibility for release; it held that although Stanford v. Kentucky *(1989) rejected the proposition that the Constitution bars capital punishment for juvenile offenders younger than eighteen, a national consensus had developed against the execution of those offenders since Stanford. The Supreme Court granted certiorari. Opinion of the Court:* <u>Kennedy</u>, Stevens, Souter,

Ginsburg, Breyer. Concurring opinion: <u>Stevens</u>, Ginsburg. Dissenting opinions: <u>O'Connor</u>; <u>Scalia</u>, Rehnquist, Thomas.

JUSTICE KENNEDY delivered the opinion of the Court.

This case requires us to address, for the second time in a decade and a half, whether it is permissible under the Eighth and Fourteenth Amendments to the Constitution of the United States to execute a juvenile offender who was older than 15 but younger than 18 when he committed a capital crime. In *Stanford v. Kentucky* (1989), a divided Court rejected the proposition that the Constitution bars capital punishment for juvenile offenders in this age group. We reconsider the question.

At the age of 17, when he was still a junior in high school, Christopher Simmons, the respondent here, committed murder. About nine months later, after he had turned 18, he was tried and sentenced to death. There is little doubt that Simmons was the instigator of the crime. Before its commission Simmons said he wanted to murder someone. In chilling, callous terms he talked about his plan, discussing it for the most part with two friends, Charles Benjamin and John Tessmer, then aged 15 and 16 respectively. Simmons proposed to commit burglary and murder by breaking and entering, tying up a victim, and throwing the victim off a bridge. Simmons assured his friends they could "get away with it" because they were minors.

The three met at about 2 a.m. on the night of the murder, but Tessmer left before the other two set out. (The State later charged Tessmer with conspiracy, but dropped the charge in exchange for his testimony against Simmons.) Simmons and Benjamin entered the home of the victim, Shirley Crook, after reaching through an open window and unlocking the back door. Simmons turned on a hallway light. Awakened, Mrs. Crook called out, "Who's there?" In response Simmons entered Mrs. Crook's bedroom, where he recognized her from a previous car accident involving them both. Simmons later admitted this confirmed his resolve to murder her.

Using duct tape to cover her eyes and mouth and bind her hands, the two perpetrators put Mrs. Crook in her minivan and drove to a state park. They reinforced the bindings, covered her head with a towel, and walked her to a railroad trestle spanning the Meramec River. There they tied her hands and feet together with electrical wire, wrapped her whole face in duct tape and threw her from the bridge, drowning her in the waters below.

By the afternoon of September 9, Steven Crook had returned home from an overnight trip, found his bedroom in disarray, and reported his wife missing. On the same afternoon fishermen recovered the victim's body from the river. Simmons, meanwhile, was bragging about the killing, telling friends he had killed a woman "because the bitch seen my face."

The next day, after receiving information of Simmons' involvement, police arrested him at his high school and took him to the police station in Fenton, Missouri. They read him his *Miranda* rights. Simmons waived his right to an attorney and agreed to answer questions. After less than two hours of interrogation, Simmons confessed to the murder and agreed to perform a videotaped reenactment at the crime scene.

The State charged Simmons with burglary, kidnaping, stealing, and murder in the first degree. As Simmons was 17 at the time of the crime, he was outside the criminal jurisdiction of Missouri's juvenile court system. He was tried as an adult. At trial the State introduced Simmons' confession and the videotaped reenactment of the crime, along with testimony that Simmons discussed the crime in advance and bragged about it later. The defense called no witnesses in the guilt phase. The jury having returned a verdict of murder, the trial proceeded to the penalty phase.

The State sought the death penalty. As aggravating factors, the State submitted that the murder was committed for the purpose of receiving money; was committed for the purpose of avoiding, interfering with, or preventing lawful arrest of the defendant; and involved depravity of mind and was outrageously and wantonly vile, horrible, and inhuman. The State called Shirley Crook's husband, daughter, and two sisters, who presented moving evidence of the devastation her death had brought to their lives.

In mitigation Simmons' attorneys first called an officer of the Missouri juvenile justice system, who testified that Simmons had no prior convictions and that no previous charges had been filed against him. Simmons' mother, father, two younger half brothers, a neighbor, and a friend took the stand to tell the jurors of the close relationships they had formed with Simmons and to plead for mercy on his behalf. Simmons' mother, in particular, testified to the responsibility Simmons demonstrated in taking care of his two younger half brothers and of his grandmother and to his capacity to show love for them.

During closing arguments, both the prosecutor and defense counsel addressed Simmons' age, which the trial judge had instructed the jurors they could consider as a mitigating factor. Defense counsel reminded the jurors that juveniles of Simmons' age cannot drink, serve on juries, or even see certain movies, because "the legislatures have wisely decided that individuals of a certain age aren't responsible enough." Defense counsel argued that Simmons' age should make "a huge difference to [the jurors] in deciding just exactly what sort of punishment to make." In rebuttal, the prosecutor gave the following response: "Age, he says. Think about age. Seventeen years old. Isn't that scary? Doesn't that scare you? Mitigating? Quite the contrary I submit. Quite the contrary."

The jury recommended the death penalty after finding the State had proved each of the three aggravating factors submitted to it. Accepting the jury's recommendation, the trial judge imposed the death penalty.

Simmons obtained new counsel, who moved in the trial court to set aside the conviction and sentence. The trial court . . . denied the motion for postconviction relief [and] the Missouri Supreme Court affirmed. After these proceedings in Simmons' case had run their course, this Court held that the Eighth and Fourteenth Amendments prohibit the execution of a mentally retarded person. *Atkins v. Virginia* (2003). Simmons filed a new petition for state postconviction relief, arguing that the reasoning of *Atkins* established that the Constitution prohibits the execution of a juvenile who was under 18 when the crime was committed. The

Missouri Supreme Court agreed. We granted certiorari and now affirm.

The Eighth Amendment provides: "Excessive bail shall not be required, nor excessive fines imposed, nor cruel and unusual punishments inflicted." The provision is applicable to the States through the Fourteenth Amendment. As the Court explained in *Atkins,* the Eighth Amendment guarantees individuals the right not to be subjected to excessive sanctions. The right flows from the basic "precept of justice that punishment for crime should be graduated and proportioned to [the] offense." By protecting even those convicted of heinous crimes, the Eighth Amendment reaffirms the duty of the government to respect the dignity of all persons.

The prohibition against "cruel and unusual punishments," like other expansive language in the Constitution, must be interpreted according to its text, by considering history, tradition, and precedent, and with due regard for its purpose and function in the constitutional design. To implement this framework we have established the propriety and affirmed the necessity of referring to "the evolving standards of decency that mark the progress of a maturing society" to determine which punishments are so disproportionate as to be cruel and unusual.

In *Thompson v. Oklahoma* (1988), a plurality of the Court determined that our standards of decency do not permit the execution of any offender under the age of 16 at the time of the crime. The plurality opinion explained that no death penalty State that had given express consideration to a minimum age for the death penalty had set the age lower than 16. . . . The next year, in *Stanford,* the Court . . . referred to contemporary standards of decency in this country and concluded the Eighth and Fourteenth Amendments did not proscribe the execution of juvenile offenders over 15 but under 18. The Court noted that 22 of the 37 death penalty States permitted the death penalty for 16-year-old offenders, and, among these 37 States, 25 permitted it for 17-year-old offenders. These numbers, in the Court's view, indicated there was no national consensus "sufficient to label a particular punishment cruel and unusual." A plurality of the Court also "emphatically reject[ed]" the suggestion that the Court should bring its own judgment to bear on the acceptability of the juvenile death penalty.

The same day the Court decided *Stanford*, it held that the Eighth Amendment did not mandate a categorical exemption from the death penalty for the mentally retarded. *Penry v. Lynaugh* (1989). In reaching this conclusion it stressed that only two States had enacted laws banning the imposition of the death penalty on a mentally retarded person convicted of a capital offense. According to the Court, "the two state statutes prohibiting execution of the mentally retarded, even when added to the 14 States that have rejected capital punishment completely, [did] not provide sufficient evidence at present of a national consensus."

Three Terms ago the subject was reconsidered in *Atkins*. We held that standards of decency have evolved since *Penry* and now demonstrate that the execution of the mentally retarded is cruel and unusual punishment. The Court noted objective indicia of society's standards, as expressed in legislative enactments and state practice with respect to executions of the mentally retarded. When *Atkins* was decided only a minority of States permitted the practice, and even in those States it was rare. On the basis of these indicia the Court determined that executing mentally retarded offenders "has become truly unusual, and it is fair to say that a national consensus has developed against it."

The inquiry into our society's evolving standards of decency did not end there. The *Atkins* Court neither repeated nor relied upon the statement in *Stanford* that the Court's independent judgment has no bearing on the acceptability of a particular punishment under the Eighth Amendment. Instead we returned to the rule, established in decisions predating *Stanford*, that "the Constitution contemplates that in the end our own judgment will be brought to bear on the question of the acceptability of the death penalty under the Eighth Amendment." . . . Just as the *Atkins* Court reconsidered the issue decided in *Penry*, we now reconsider the issue decided in *Stanford*. The beginning point is a review of objective indicia of consensus, as expressed in particular by the enactments of legislatures that have addressed the question. This data gives us essential instruction. We then must determine, in the exercise of our own independent judgment, whether the death penalty is a disproportionate punishment for juveniles.

The evidence of national consensus against the death penalty for juveniles is similar, and in some respects parallel, to the evidence *Atkins* held sufficient to demonstrate a national consensus against the death penalty for the mentally retarded. When *Atkins* was decided, 30 States prohibited the death penalty for the mentally retarded. This number comprised 12 that had abandoned the death penalty altogether, and 18 that maintained it but excluded the mentally retarded from its reach. By a similar calculation in this case, 30 States prohibit the juvenile death penalty, comprising 12 that have rejected the death penalty altogether and 18 that maintain it but, by express provision or judicial interpretation, exclude juveniles from its reach. *Atkins* emphasized that even in the 20 States without formal prohibition, the practice of executing the mentally retarded was infrequent. Since *Penry*, only five States had executed offenders known to have an IQ under 70. In the present case, too, even in the 20 States without a formal prohibition on executing juveniles, the practice is infrequent. Since *Stanford*, six States have executed prisoners for crimes committed as juveniles. In the past 10 years, only three have done so. In December 2003 the Governor of Kentucky decided to spare the life of Kevin Stanford, and commuted his sentence to one of life imprisonment without parole, with the declaration that "[w]e ought not be executing people who, legally, were children." By this act the Governor ensured Kentucky would not add itself to the list of States that have executed juveniles within the last 10 years even by the execution of the very defendant whose death sentence the Court had upheld in *Stanford* v. *Kentucky*.

There is, to be sure, at least one difference between the evidence of consensus in *Atkins* and in this case. Impressive in *Atkins* was the rate of abolition of the death penalty for the mentally retarded. Sixteen States that permitted the execution of the mentally retarded at the time of *Penry* had prohibited the practice by the time we heard *Atkins*. By contrast, the rate of change in reducing the incidence of the juvenile death penalty, or in taking specific steps to abolish it, has been slower. Five States that allowed the juvenile death penalty at the time of *Stanford* have abandoned it in the intervening 15 years—four through legislative enactments and one through judicial decision.

Though less dramatic than the change from *Penry* to *Atkins,* we still consider the change from *Stanford* to this case to be significant. . . . The number of States that have abandoned capital punishment for juvenile offenders since *Stanford* is smaller than the number of States that abandoned capital punishment for the mentally retarded after *Penry*; yet we think the same consistency of direction of change has been demonstrated. Since *Stanford,* no State that previously prohibited capital punishment for juveniles has reinstated it. . . .

A majority of States have rejected the imposition of the death penalty on juvenile offenders under 18, and we now hold this is required by the Eighth Amendment.

Because the death penalty is the most severe punishment, the Eighth Amendment applies to it with special force. Capital punishment must be limited to those offenders who commit "a narrow category of the most serious crimes" and whose extreme culpability makes them "the most deserving of execution." . . . Three general differences between juveniles under 18 and adults demonstrate that juvenile offenders cannot with reliability be classified among the worst offenders. First, as any parent knows and as the scientific and sociological studies respondent and his *amici* cite tend to confirm, "[a] lack of maturity and an underdeveloped sense of responsibility are found in youth more often than in adults and are more understandable among the young. . . . The second area of difference is that juveniles are more vulnerable or susceptible to negative influences and outside pressures, including peer pressure. . . . The third broad difference is that the character of a juvenile is not as well formed as that of an adult. The personality traits of juveniles are more transitory, less fixed. . . . These differences render suspect any conclusion that a juvenile falls among the worst offenders. The susceptibility of juveniles to immature and irresponsible behavior means their irresponsible

conduct is not as morally reprehensible as that of an adult. . . .

Once the diminished culpability of juveniles is recognized, it is evident that the penological justifications for the death penalty apply to them with lesser force than to adults. We have held there are two distinct social purposes served by the death penalty: "retribution and deterrence of capital crimes by prospective offenders." . . . Whether viewed as an attempt to express the community's moral outrage or as an attempt to right the balance for the wrong to the victim, the case for retribution is not as strong with a minor as with an adult. Retribution is not proportional if the law's most severe penalty is imposed on one whose culpability or blameworthiness is diminished, to a substantial degree, by reason of youth and immaturity. . . . As for deterrence, it is unclear whether the death penalty has a significant or even measurable deterrent effect on juveniles . . . [T]he absence of evidence of deterrent effect is of special concern because the same characteristics that render juveniles less culpable than adults suggest as well that juveniles will be less susceptible to deterrence. . . . To the extent the juvenile death penalty might have residual deterrent effect, it is worth noting that the punishment of life imprisonment without the possibility of parole is itself a severe sanction, in particular for a young person. . . . Drawing the line at 18 years of age is subject, of course, to the objections always raised against categorical rules. The qualities that distinguish juveniles from adults do not disappear when an individual turns 18. By the same token, some under 18 have already attained a level of maturity some adults will never reach. . . . [H]owever, a line must be drawn. The plurality opinion in *Thompson* drew the line at 16. . . . The logic of *Thompson* extends to those who are under 18. The age of 18 is the point where society draws the line for many purposes between childhood and adulthood. It is, we conclude, the age at which the line for death eligibility ought to rest.

. . . Our determination that the death penalty is disproportionate punishment for offenders under 18 finds confirmation in the stark reality that the United States is the only country in the world that continues to give official sanction to the juvenile death penalty. . . .

As respondent and a number of *amici* emphasize, Article 37 of the United Nations Convention on the Rights of the Child, which every country in the world has ratified save for the United States and Somalia, contains an express prohibition on capital punishment for crimes committed by juveniles under 18. . . . [I]t is fair to say that the United States now stands alone in a world that has turned its face against the juvenile death penalty.

Though the international covenants prohibiting the juvenile death penalty are of more recent date, it is instructive to note that the United Kingdom abolished the juvenile death penalty before these covenants came into being. The United Kingdom's experience bears particular relevance here in light of the historic ties between our countries and in light of the Eighth Amendment's own origins. The Amendment was modeled on a parallel provision in the English Declaration of Rights of 1689 . . .

It is proper that we acknowledge the overwhelming weight of international opinion against the juvenile death penalty, resting in large part on the understanding that the instability and emotional imbalance of young people may often be a factor in the crime. The opinion of the world community, while not controlling our outcome, does provide respected and significant confirmation for our own conclusions. . . . It does not lessen our fidelity to the Constitution or our pride in its origins to acknowledge that the express affirmation of certain fundamental rights by other nations and peoples simply underscores the centrality of those same rights within our own heritage of freedom.

The Eighth and Fourteenth Amendments forbid imposition of the death penalty on offenders who were under the age of 18 when their crimes were committed. The judgment of the Missouri Supreme Court setting aside the sentence of death imposed upon Christopher Simmons is affirmed.

JUSTICE SCALIA, with whom THE CHIEF JUSTICE and JUSTICE THOMAS join, dissenting.

In urging approval of a constitution that gave life-tenured judges the power to nullify laws enacted by the people's representatives, Alexander Hamilton assured the citizens of New York that there was little risk in this, since "[t]he judiciary . . . ha[s] neither FORCE nor WILL but merely judgment." *The Federalist* No. 78. But Hamilton had in mind a traditional judiciary, "bound down by strict rules and precedents which serve to define and point out their duty in every particular case that comes before them." Bound down, indeed. What a mockery today's opinion makes of Hamilton's expectation, announcing the Court's conclusion that the meaning of our Constitution has changed over the past 15 years—not, mind you, that this Court's decision 15 years ago was *wrong*, but that the Constitution *has changed*. The Court reaches this implausible result by purporting to advert, not to the original meaning of the Eighth Amendment, but to "the evolving standards of decency" of our national society. It then finds, on the flimsiest of grounds, that a national consensus which could not be perceived in our people's laws barely 15 years ago now solidly exists. Worse still, the Court says in so many words that what our people's laws say about the issue does not, in the last analysis, matter: "[I]n the end our own judgment will be brought to bear on the question of the acceptability of the death penalty under the Eighth Amendment." The Court thus proclaims itself sole arbiter of our Nation's moral standards—and in the course of discharging that awesome responsibility purports to take guidance from the views of foreign courts and legislatures. Because I do not believe that the meaning of our Eighth Amendment, any more than the meaning of other provisions of our Constitution, should be determined by the subjective views of five Members of this Court and like-minded foreigners, I dissent.

In determining that capital punishment of offenders who committed murder before age 18 is "cruel and unusual" under the Eighth Amendment, the Court first considers, in accordance with our modern (though in my view mistaken) jurisprudence, whether there is a "national consensus" that laws allowing such executions contravene our modern "standards of decency." We have held that this determination should be based on "objective indicia that reflect the public attitude toward a given sanction"—namely, "statutes passed by society's elected representatives." . . . [T]he Court dutifully recites this test and claims halfheartedly that a national consensus has emerged since our decision in *Stanford,* because 18 States—or 47% of States that permit capital punishment—now have legislation prohibiting the execution of offenders under 18, and because all of four States have adopted such legislation since *Stanford.*

Words have no meaning if the views of less than 50% of death penalty States can constitute a national consensus. . . . In an attempt to keep afloat its implausible assertion of national consensus, the Court . . . has counted, as States supporting a consensus in favor of that limitation, States that have eliminated the death penalty entirely. . . . Consulting States that bar the death penalty concerning the necessity of making an exception to the penalty for offenders under 18 is rather like including old-order Amishmen in a consumer-preference poll on the electric car. Of *course* they don't like it, but that sheds no light whatever on the point at issue. That 12 States favor *no* executions says something about consensus against the death penalty, but nothing—absolutely nothing—about consensus that offenders under 18 deserve special immunity from such a penalty. In repealing the death penalty, those 12 States considered *none* of the factors that the Court puts forth as determinative of the issue before us today—lower culpability of the young, inherent recklessness, lack of capacity for considered judgment, etc. What might be relevant, perhaps, is how many of those States permit 16- and 17-year-old offenders to be treated as adults with respect to noncapital offenses. (They all do; indeed, some even *require* that juveniles as young as 14 be tried as adults if they are charged with murder.) The attempt by the Court to turn its remarkable minority consensus into a faux majority by counting Amishmen is an act of nomological desperation.

Recognizing that its national-consensus argument was weak compared with our earlier cases, the *Atkins* Court found additional support in the fact that 16 States had prohibited execution of mentally retarded individuals since *Penry.* Now, the Court says a legislative change in four States is "significant" enough to trigger a constitutional prohibition. It is amazing to think that this subtle shift in numbers can take the issue entirely off the table for legislative debate. I also doubt whether many of the legislators who voted to change the laws in those four States would have done so if they had known their decision would (by the pronouncement of this Court) be rendered irreversible. After all, legislative support for capital punishment, in any form, has surged and ebbed throughout our Nation's history. . . .

Relying on such narrow margins is especially inappropriate in light of the fact that a number of legislatures and voters have expressly affirmed their support for capital punishment of 16- and 17-year-old offenders since *Stanford.* Though the Court is correct that no State has lowered its death penalty age, both the Missouri and Virginia Legislatures—which, at the time of *Stanford,* had no minimum age requirement—expressly established 16 as the minimum. The people of Arizona and Florida have done the same by ballot initiative. Thus, even States that have not executed an under-18 offender in recent years unquestionably favor the possibility of capital punishment in some circumstances.

. . . Of course, the real force driving today's decision is not the actions of four state legislatures, but the Court's "own judgment" that murderers younger than 18 can never be as morally culpable as older counterparts. The Court claims that this usurpation of the role of moral arbiter is simply a "retur[n] to the rul[e]" established in decisions predating *Stanford.* That supposed rule—which is reflected solely in dicta and never once in a *holding* that purports to supplant the consensus of the American people with the Justices' views—was repudiated in *Stanford* for the very good reason that it has no foundation in law or logic. If the Eighth Amendment set forth an ordinary rule of law, it would indeed be the role of this Court to say what the law is. But the Court having pronounced that the Eighth Amendment is an ever-changing reflection of "the evolving standards of decency" of our society, it makes no sense for the Justices then to *prescribe* those standards rather than discern them from the practices of our people. On the evolving-standards hypothesis, the only legitimate function of this Court is to identify a moral consensus of the American people. By what conceivable warrant can nine lawyers presume to be the authoritative conscience of the Nation?

. . . Today's opinion provides a perfect example of why judges are ill equipped to make the type of legislative judgments the Court insists on making here. To support its opinion that States should be prohibited from imposing the death penalty on anyone who committed murder before age 18, the Court looks to scientific and sociological studies, picking and choosing those that support its position. It never explains why those particular studies are methodologically sound; none was ever entered into evidence or tested in an adversarial proceeding. . . . In other words, all the Court has done today, to borrow from another context, is to look over the heads of the crowd and pick out its friends. . . .

The Court's contention that the goals of retribution and deterrence are not served by executing murderers under 18 is also transparently false. . . . The facts of this very case show the proposition to be false. Before committing the crime, Simmons encouraged his friends to join him by assuring them that they could "get away with it" because they were minors. This fact may have influenced the jury's decision to impose capital punishment despite Simmons' age. Because the Court refuses to entertain the possibility that its own unsubstantiated generalization about juveniles could be wrong, it ignores this evidence entirely.

Though the views of our own citizens are essentially irrelevant to the Court's decision today, the views of other countries and the so-called international community take center stage.

The Court begins by noting that "Article 37 of the United Nations Convention on the Rights of the Child, which every country in the world has ratified *save for the United States* and Somalia, contains an express prohibition on capital punishment for crimes committed by juveniles under 18." . . . Unless the Court has added to its arsenal the power to join and ratify treaties on behalf of the United States, I cannot see how this evidence favors, rather than refutes, its position. That the Senate and the President—

those actors our Constitution empowers to enter into treaties—have declined to join and ratify treaties prohibiting execution of under-18 offenders can only suggest that *our country* has either not reached a national consensus on the question, or has reached a consensus contrary to what the Court announces. . . .

More fundamentally, however, the basic premise of the Court's argument—that American law should conform to the laws of the rest of the world—ought to be rejected out of hand. In fact the Court itself does not believe it. In many significant respects the laws of most other countries differ from our law—including not only such explicit provisions of our Constitution as the right to jury trial and grand jury indictment, but even many interpretations of the Constitution prescribed by this Court itself. The Court-pronounced exclusionary rule, for example, is distinctively American. When we adopted that rule in *Mapp v. Ohio,* (1961), it was "unique to American Jurisprudence." Since then a categorical exclusionary rule has been "universally rejected" by other countries, including those with rules prohibiting illegal searches and police misconduct, despite the fact that none of these countries "appears to have any alternative form of discipline for police that is effective in preventing search violations." England, for example, rarely excludes evidence found during an illegal search or seizure and has only recently begun excluding evidence from illegally obtained confessions. Canada rarely excludes evidence and will only do so if admission will "bring the administration of justice into disrepute." The European Court of Human Rights has held that introduction of illegally seized evidence does not violate the "fair trial" requirement in Article 6, § 1, of the European Convention on Human Rights.

The Court has been oblivious to the views of other countries when deciding how to interpret our Constitution's requirement that "Congress shall make no law respecting an establishment of religion." Most other countries—including those committed to religious neutrality—do not insist on the degree of separation between church and state that this Court requires. For example, whereas "we have recognized special Establishment Clause dangers where the government makes direct money payments to sectarian institutions," countries such as the Netherlands, Germany, and Australia allow direct government funding of religious schools on the ground that "the state can only be truly neutral between secular and religious perspectives if it does not dominate the provision of so key a service as education, and makes it possible for people to exercise their right of religious expression within the context of public funding." England permits the teaching of religion in state schools. Even in France, which is considered "America's only rival in strictness of church-state separation," "[t]he practice of contracting for educational services provided by Catholic schools is very widespread."

And let us not forget the Court's abortion jurisprudence, which makes us one of only six countries that allow abortion on demand until the point of viability. . . .

The Court's special reliance on the laws of the United Kingdom is perhaps the most indefensible part of its opinion. It is of course true that we share a common history with the United Kingdom, and that we often consult English sources when asked to discern the meaning of a constitutional text written against the backdrop of 18th-century English law and legal thought. . . . The Court has, however—I think wrongly—long rejected a purely originalist approach to our Eighth Amendment, and that is certainly not the approach the Court takes today. Instead, the Court undertakes the majestic task of determining (and thereby prescribing) *our* Nation's *current* standards of decency. It is beyond comprehension why we should look, for that purpose, to a country that has developed, in the centuries since the Revolutionary War—and with increasing speed since the United Kingdom's recent submission to the jurisprudence of European courts dominated by continental jurists—a legal, political, and social culture quite different from our own. If we took the Court's directive seriously, we would also consider relaxing our double jeopardy prohibition, since the British Law Commission recently published a report that would significantly extend the rights of the prosecution to appeal cases where an acquittal was the result of a judge's ruling that was legally incorrect. We would also curtail our right to jury trial in criminal cases since, despite the jury system's deep roots in our shared common law, England now permits all but the most serious offenders to be tried by magistrates without a jury.

The Court should either profess its willingness to reconsider all these matters in light of the views of foreigners, or else it should cease putting forth foreigners' views as part of the *reasoned basis* of its decisions. To invoke alien law when it agrees with one's own thinking, and ignore it otherwise, is not reasoned decisionmaking, but sophistry.

The Court responds that "[i]t does not lessen our fidelity to the Constitution or our pride in its origins to acknowledge that the express affirmation of certain fundamental rights by other nations and peoples simply underscores the centrality of those same rights within our own heritage of freedom." . . . [T]he Court's statement flatly misdescribes what is going on here. Foreign sources are cited today, *not* to underscore our "fidelity" to the Constitution, our "pride in its origins," and "our own [American] heritage." To the contrary, they are cited *to set aside* the centuries-old American practice—a practice still engaged in by a large majority of the relevant States—of letting a jury of 12 citizens decide whether, in the particular case, youth should be the basis for withholding the death penalty. What these foreign sources "affirm," rather than repudiate, is the Justices' own notion of how the world ought to be, and their diktat that it shall be so henceforth in America. . . .

Miller v. Alabama
567 U.S. ___ (2012)

This case was heard along with the companion case of Jackson v. Hobbs. *In both of these cases, fourteen-year-olds were convicted of murder and sentenced to mandatory terms of life imprisonment without the possibility of parole. In Jackson, the petitioner accompanied two other boys to a video store to commit a robbery; on the way to the store, he learned that one of the boys was carrying a shotgun. Jackson stayed outside the store for most of the robbery, but after he entered, one of his coconspirators shot and killed the store clerk. Arkansas charged Jackson as an adult with capital felony murder and aggravated robbery, and a jury convicted him of both crimes. The trial court imposed a statutorily mandated sentence of life imprisonment without the possibility of parole. Jackson filed a state habeas petition, arguing that a mandatory life-without-parole term for a fourteen-year-old violates the Eighth Amendment. Disagreeing, the court granted the state's motion to dismiss, and the Arkansas Supreme Court affirmed.*

In Miller the petitioner along with a friend beat Miller's neighbor and set fire to his trailer after an evening of drinking and drug use. The neighbor died. Miller was initially charged as a juvenile, but his case was removed to adult court, where he was charged with murder in the course of arson. A jury found Miller guilty, and the trial court imposed a statutorily mandated punishment of life without parole. The Alabama Court of Criminal Appeals affirmed, holding that Miller's sentence was not overly harsh when compared to his crime and that its mandatory nature was permissible under the Eighth Amendment. The Supreme Court granted certiorari. Opinion of the Court: <u>Kagan</u>, Kennedy, Ginsburg, Breyer, Sotomayor. Concurring opinion: <u>Breyer</u>, Sotomayor. Dissenting opinions: <u>Roberts</u>, Scalia, Thomas, Alito; <u>Thomas</u>, Scalia; <u>Alito</u>, Scalia.

JUSTICE KAGAN delivered the opinion of the Court.

The two 14-year-old offenders in these cases were convicted of murder and sentenced to life imprisonment without the possibility of parole. In neither case did the sentencing authority have any discretion to impose a different punishment. State law mandated that each juvenile die in prison even if a judge or jury would have thought that his youth and its attendant characteristics, along with the nature of his crime, made a lesser sentence (for example, life with the possibility of parole) more appropriate. Such a scheme prevents those meting out punishment from considering a juvenile's "lessened culpability" and greater "capacity for

change," *Graham v. Florida* (2010), and runs afoul of our cases' requirement of individualized sentencing for defendants facing the most serious penalties. We therefore hold that mandatory life without parole for those under the age of 18 at the time of their crimes violates the Eighth Amendment's prohibition on "cruel and unusual punishments."

II

The Eighth Amendment's prohibition of cruel and unusual punishment "guarantees individuals the right not to be subjected to excessive sanctions." That right, we have explained, "flows from the basic 'precept of justice that punishment for crime should be graduated and proportioned'" to both the offender and the offense. As we noted the last time we considered life-without-parole sentences imposed on juveniles, "[t]he concept of proportionality is central to the Eighth Amendment." *Graham.* And we view that concept less through a historical prism than according to "'the evolving standards of decency that mark the progress of a maturing society.'"

The cases before us implicate two strands of precedent reflecting our concern with proportionate punishment. The first has adopted categorical bans on sentencing practices based on mismatches between the culpability of a class of offenders and the severity of a penalty. So, for example, we have held that imposing the death penalty for nonhomicide crimes against individuals, or imposing it on mentally retarded defendants, violates the Eighth Amendment. See *Kennedy v. Louisiana* (2008); *Atkins v. Virginia* (2002). Several of the cases in this group have specially focused on juvenile offenders, because of their lesser culpability. Thus, *Roper* [*v. Simmons* (2005)] held that the Eighth Amendment bars capital punishment for children, and *Graham* concluded that the Amendment also prohibits a sentence of life without the possibility of parole for a child who committed a nonhomicide offense. *Graham* further likened life without parole for juveniles to the death penalty itself, thereby evoking a second line of our precedents. In those cases, we have prohibited mandatory imposition of capital punishment, requiring that sentencing authorities consider the characteristics of a defendant and the details of his offense before sentencing him to death. See *Woodson v. North Carolina* (1976). Here, the confluence of these two lines of precedent leads to the conclusion that mandatory life-without-parole sentences for juveniles violate the Eighth Amendment.

To start with the first set of cases: *Roper* and *Graham* establish that children are constitutionally different from adults for purposes of sentencing. Because juveniles have diminished culpability and greater prospects for reform, we explained, "they are less deserving of the most severe punishments." Those cases relied on three significant gaps between juveniles and adults. First, children have a "'lack of maturity and an underdeveloped sense of responsibility,'" leading to recklessness, impulsivity, and heedless risk-taking. Second, children "are more vulnerable . . . to negative influences and outside pressures," including from their family and peers; they have limited "contro[l] over their own environment" and lack the ability to extricate themselves from horrific, crime-producing settings. And third, a child's character is not as "well formed" as an adult's; his traits are "less fixed" and his actions less likely to be "evidence of irretrievabl[e] deprav[ity]."

Our decisions rested not only on common sense—on what "any parent knows"—but on science and social science as well. . . .

Roper and *Graham* emphasized that the distinctive attributes of youth diminish the penological justifications for imposing the harshest sentences on juvenile offenders, even when they commit terrible crimes. . . .

Graham concluded from this analysis that life-without-parole sentences, like capital punishment, may violate the Eighth Amendment when imposed on children. To be sure, *Graham*'s flat ban on life without parole applied only to nonhomicide crimes, and the Court took care to distinguish those offenses from murder, based on both moral culpability and consequential harm. But none of what it said about children—about their distinctive (and transitory) mental traits and environmental vulnerabilities—is crime-specific. Those features are evident in the same way, and to the same degree, when (as in both cases here) a botched robbery turns into a killing. So *Gra*-

ham's reasoning implicates any life-without-parole sentence imposed on a juvenile, even as its categorical bar relates only to nonhomicide offenses.

Most fundamentally, *Graham* insists that youth matters in determining the appropriateness of a lifetime of incarceration without the possibility of parole. In the circumstances there, juvenile status precluded a life-without-parole sentence, even though an adult could receive it for a similar crime. And in other contexts as well, the characteristics of youth, and the way they weaken rationales for punishment, can render a life-without-parole sentence disproportionate. . . .

But the mandatory penalty schemes at issue here prevent the sentencer from taking account of these central considerations. By removing youth from the balance—by subjecting a juvenile to the same life-without-parole sentence applicable to an adult—these laws prohibit a sentencing authority from assessing whether the law's harshest term of imprisonment proportionately punishes a juvenile offender. That contravenes *Graham*'s (and also *Roper*'s) foundational principle: that imposition of a State's most severe penalties on juvenile offenders cannot proceed as though they were not children.

And *Graham* makes plain these mandatory schemes' defects in another way: by likening life-without-parole sentences imposed on juveniles to the death penalty itself. Life-without-parole terms, the Court wrote, "share some characteristics with death sentences that are shared by no other sentences." Imprisoning an offender until he dies alters the remainder of his life "by a forfeiture that is irrevocable." And this lengthiest possible incarceration is an "especially harsh punishment for a juvenile," because he will almost inevitably serve "more years and a greater percentage of his life in prison than an adult offender." The penalty when imposed on a teenager, as compared with an older person, is therefore "the same . . . in name only." All of that suggested a distinctive set of legal rules: In part because we viewed this ultimate penalty for juveniles as akin to the death penalty, we treated it similarly to that most severe punishment. We imposed a categorical ban on the sentence's use, in a way unprecedented for a term of imprisonment.

That correspondence—*Graham*'s "[t]reat[ment] [of] juvenile life sentences as analogous to capital punishment"—makes relevant here a second line of our precedents, demanding individualized sentencing when imposing the death penalty. In *Woodson*, we held that a statute mandating a death sentence for first-degree murder violated the Eighth Amendment. We thought the mandatory scheme flawed because it gave no significance to "the character and record of the individual offender or the circumstances" of the offense, and "exclud[ed] from consideration . . . the possibility of compassionate or mitigating factors." Subsequent decisions have elaborated on the requirement that capital defendants have an opportunity to advance, and the judge or jury a chance to assess, any mitigating factors, so that the death penalty is reserved only for the most culpable defendants committing the most serious offenses. . . .

In light of *Graham*'s reasoning, these decisions too show the flaws of imposing mandatory life-without-parole sentences on juvenile homicide offenders. Such mandatory penalties, by their nature, preclude a sentencer from taking account of an offender's age and the wealth of characteristics and circumstances attendant to it. Under these schemes, every juvenile will receive the same sentence as every other—the 17-year-old and the 14-year-old, the shooter and the accomplice, the child from a stable household and the child from a chaotic and abusive one. And still worse, each juvenile (including these two 14-year-olds) will receive the same sentence as the vast majority of adults committing similar homicide offenses—but really, as *Graham* noted, a greater sentence than those adults will serve. In meting out the death penalty, the elision of all these differences would be strictly forbidden. And once again, Graham indicates that a similar rule should apply when a juvenile confronts a sentence of life (and death) in prison. . . .

Graham, *Roper*, and our individualized sentencing decisions make clear that a judge or jury must have the opportunity to consider mitigating circumstances before imposing the harshest possible penalty for juveniles. By requiring that all children convicted of homicide receive lifetime incarceration without possibility of parole, regardless of their age and age-related characteristics and the nature of their crimes, the mandatory sentencing schemes before us violate this principle of proportionality, and so the Eighth Amendment's ban on cruel and unusual punishment. We accordingly reverse the judgments of the Arkansas Supreme Court and Alabama Court of Criminal Appeals and remand the cases for further proceedings not inconsistent with this opinion.

THE CHIEF JUSTICE, with whom JUSTICE SCALIA, JUSTICE THOMAS, and JUSTICE ALITO join, dissenting.

Determining the appropriate sentence for a teenager convicted of murder presents grave and challenging questions of morality and social policy. Our role, however, is to apply the law, not to answer such questions. The pertinent law here is the Eighth Amendment to the Constitution, which prohibits "cruel and unusual punishments." Today, the Court invokes that Amendment to ban a punishment that the Court does not itself characterize as unusual, and that could not plausibly be described as such. I therefore dissent.

The parties agree that nearly 2,500 prisoners are presently serving life sentences without the possibility of parole for murders they committed before the age of 18. The Court accepts that over 2,000 of those prisoners received that sentence because it was mandated by a legislature. And it recognizes that the Federal Government and most States impose such mandatory sentences. Put simply, if a 17-year-old is convicted of deliberately murdering an innocent victim, it is not "unusual" for the murderer to receive a mandatory sentence of life without parole. That reality should preclude finding that mandatory life imprisonment for juvenile killers violates the Eighth Amendment.

Our precedent supports this conclusion. When determining whether a punishment is cruel and unusual, this Court typically begins with "'objective indicia of society's standards, as expressed in legislative enactments and state practice.'" We look to these "objective indicia" to ensure that we are not simply following our own subjective values or beliefs. Such tangible evidence of societal standards enables us to determine whether there is a "consensus against" a given sentencing practice. If there is, the punishment may be regarded as "unusual." But when, as here, most States formally require and frequently impose the punishment in question, there is no objective basis for that conclusion.

Our Eighth Amendment cases have also said that we should take guidance from "evolving standards of decency that mark the progress of a maturing society." Mercy toward the guilty can be a form of decency, and a maturing society may abandon harsh punishments that it comes to view as unnecessary or unjust. But decency is not the same as leniency. A decent society protects the innocent from violence. A mature society may determine that this requires removing those guilty of the most heinous murders from its midst, both as protection for its other members and as a concrete expression of its standards of decency. As judges we have no basis for deciding that progress toward greater decency can move only in the direction of easing sanctions on the guilty.

In this case, there is little doubt about the direction of society's evolution: For most of the 20th century, American sentencing practices emphasized rehabilitation of the offender and the availability of parole. But by the 1980's, outcry against repeat offenders, broad disaffection with the rehabilitative model, and other factors led many legislatures to reduce or eliminate the possibility of parole, imposing longer sentences in order to punish criminals and prevent them from committing more crimes. Statutes establishing life without parole sentences in particular became more common in the past quarter century. And the parties agree that most States have changed their laws relatively recently to expose teenage murderers to mandatory life without parole. . . .

* * *

It is a great tragedy when a juvenile commits murder—most of all for the innocent victims. But also for the murderer, whose life has gone so wrong so early. And for society as well, which has lost one or more of its members to deliberate violence, and must harshly punish another. In recent years, our society has moved toward requiring that the murderer, his age

notwithstanding, be imprisoned for the remainder of his life. Members of this Court may disagree with that choice. Perhaps science and policy suggest society should show greater mercy to young killers, giving them a greater chance to reform themselves at the risk that they will kill again. But that is not our decision to make. Neither the text of the Constitution nor our precedent prohibits legislatures from requiring that juvenile murderers be sentenced to life without parole. I respectfully dissent.

JUSTICE THOMAS, with whom JUSTICE SCALIA joins, dissenting.

Today, the Court holds that "mandatory life without parole for those under the age of 18 at the time of their crimes violates the Eighth Amendment's prohibition on 'cruel and unusual punishments.'" To reach that result, the Court relies on two lines of precedent. The first involves the categorical prohibition of certain punishments for specified classes of offenders. The second requires individualized sentencing in the capital punishment context. Neither line is consistent with the original understanding of the Cruel and Unusual Punishments Clause. The Court compounds its errors by combining these lines of precedent and extending them to reach a result that is even less legitimate than the foundation on which it is built. Because the Court upsets the legislatively enacted sentencing regimes of 29 jurisdictions without constitutional warrant, I respectfully dissent. . . .

The Eighth Amendment . . . provides that: "Excessive bail shall not be required, nor excessive fines imposed, nor cruel and unusual punishments inflicted." As I have previously explained, "the Cruel and Unusual Punishments Clause was originally understood as prohibiting torturous methods of punishment—specifically methods akin to those that had been considered cruel and unusual at the time the Bill of Rights was adopted." *Graham*, (dissenting opinion). The clause does not contain a "proportionality principle." In short, it does not authorize courts to invalidate any punishment they deem disproportionate to the severity of the crime or to a particular class of offenders. Instead, the clause "leaves the unavoidably moral question of who 'deserves' a particular nonprohibited method of punishment to the judgment of the legislatures that authorize the penalty."

The legislatures of Arkansas and Alabama, like those of 27 other jurisdictions, have determined that all offenders convicted of specified homicide offenses, whether juveniles or not, deserve a sentence of life in prison without the possibility of parole. Nothing in our Constitution authorizes this Court to supplant that choice.

To invalidate mandatory life-without-parole sentences for juveniles, the Court also relies on its cases "prohibit[ing] mandatory imposition of capital punishment." The Court reasons that, because *Graham* compared juvenile life-without-parole sentences to the death penalty, the "distinctive set of legal rules" that this Court has imposed in the capital punishment context, including the requirement of individualized sentencing, is "relevant" here. But even accepting an analogy between capital and juvenile life-without-parole sentences, this Court's cases prohibiting mandatory capital sentencing schemes have no basis in the original understanding of the Eighth Amendment, and, thus, cannot justify a prohibition of sentencing schemes that mandate life-without-parole sentences for juveniles. . . .

In my view, *Woodson* and its progeny were wrongly decided. As discussed above, the Cruel and Unusual Punishments Clause, as originally understood, prohibits "torturous methods of punishment." It is not concerned with whether a particular lawful method of punishment—whether capital or noncapital—is imposed pursuant to a mandatory or discretionary sentencing regime. In fact, "[i]n the early days of the Republic," each crime generally had a defined punishment "prescribed with specificity by the legislature." Capital sentences, to which the Court analogizes, were treated no differently. . . . Accordingly, the idea that the mandatory imposition of an otherwise-constitutional sentence renders that sentence cruel and unusual finds "no support in the text and history of the Eighth Amendment."

Moreover, mandatory death penalty schemes were "a perfectly reasonable legislative response to the concerns expressed in Furman" regarding unguided sentencing discretion, in that they "eliminat[ed] explicit jury discretion and treat[ed] all defendants equally." . . . Thus, there is no basis for concluding that a mandatory capital sentencing scheme is unconstitutional. Because the Court's cases requiring individualized sentencing in the capital context are wrongly decided, they cannot serve as a valid foundation for the novel rule regarding mandatory life-without-parole sentences for juveniles that the Court announces today.

In any event, this Court has already declined to extend its individualized-sentencing rule beyond the death penalty context. In *Harmelin*, the defendant was convicted of possessing a large quantity of drugs. In accordance with Michigan law, he was sentenced to a mandatory term of life in prison without the possibility of parole. Citing the same line of death penalty precedents on which the Court relies today, the defendant argued that his sentence, due to its mandatory nature, violated the Cruel and Unusual Punishments Clause.

The Court rejected that argument, explaining that "[t]here can be no serious contention . . . that a sentence which is not otherwise cruel and unusual becomes so simply because it is 'mandatory.'" In so doing, the Court refused to analogize to its death penalty cases. The Court noted that those cases had "repeatedly suggested that there is no comparable [individualized-sentencing] requirement outside the capital context, because of the qualitative difference between death and all other penalties." The Court observed that, "even where the difference" between a sentence of life without parole and other sentences of imprisonment "is the greatest," such a sentence "cannot be compared with death." Therefore, the Court concluded that the line of cases requiring individualized sentencing had been drawn at capital cases, and that there was "no basis for extending it further."

Harmelin's reasoning logically extends to these cases. Obviously, the younger the defendant, "the great[er]" the difference between a sentence of life without parole and other terms of imprisonment. But under *Harmelin*'s rationale, the defendant's age is immaterial to the Eighth Amendment analysis. Thus, the result in today's cases should be the same as that in *Harmelin*. Petitioners, like the defendant in

Harmelin, were not sentenced to death. Accordingly, this Court's cases "creating and clarifying the individualized capital sentencing doctrine" do not apply.

Nothing about our Constitution, or about the qualitative difference between any term of imprisonment and death, has changed since *Harmelin* was decided 21 years ago. What has changed (or, better yet, "evolved") is this Court's ever-expanding line of categorical proportionality cases. The Court now uses *Roper* and *Graham* to jettison *Harmelin*'s clear distinction between capital and noncapital cases

and to apply the former to noncapital juvenile offenders. The Court's decision to do so is even less supportable than the precedents used to reach it. . . .

* * *

Today's decision invalidates a constitutionally permissible sentencing system based on nothing more than the Court's belief that "its own sense of morality . . . pre-empts that of the people and their representatives." Because nothing in the Constitution grants the Court the authority it exercises today, I respectfully dissent.

Harmelin v. Michigan
501 U.S. 957 (1991)

Ronald Allen Harmelin was convicted under Michigan law of possessing more than 650 grams of cocaine and was sentenced to a mandatory term of life in prison without possibility of parole. The Michigan Court of Appeals rejected his contention that the sentence violated the Cruel and Unusual Punishments Clause of the Eighth Amendment and affirmed his conviction. The US Supreme Court granted certiorari. Judgment of the Court: <u>Scalia</u>, Rehnquist. Concurring in part and concurring in the judgment: <u>Kennedy</u>, O'Connor, Souter. Dissenting opinions: <u>White</u>, Blackmun, Stevens; <u>Marshall</u>; <u>Stevens</u>, Blackmun.

JUSTICE SCALIA delivered the opinion of the Court.

Petitioner claims that his sentence is unconstitutionally "cruel and unusual" for two reasons. First, because it is "significantly disproportionate" to the crime he committed. Second, because the sentencing judge was statutorily required to impose it, without taking into account the particularized circumstances of the crime and of the criminal.

The Eighth Amendment, which applies against the States by virtue of the Fourteenth Amendment, see *Robinson v. California* (1962), provides: "Excessive bail shall not be required, nor excessive fines imposed, nor cruel and unusual punishments inflicted."

In *Solem v. Helm* (1983), [we] set aside under the Eighth Amendment, because it was disproportionate, a sentence of life imprisonment

without possibility of parole, imposed under a South Dakota recidivist statute for successive offenses that included three convictions of third-degree burglary, one of obtaining money by false pretenses, one of grand larceny, one of third-offense driving while intoxicated, and one of writing a "no account" check with intent to defraud.

Solem based its conclusion principally upon the proposition that a right to be free from disproportionate punishments was embodied within the "cruell and unusuall Punishments" provision of the English Declaration of Rights of 1689, and was incorporated, with that language, in the Eighth Amendment. As a textual matter, of course, it does not: a disproportionate punishment can perhaps always be considered "cruel," but it will not always be (as the text also requires) "unusual." The error of *Solem*'s assumption is confirmed by the historical context and contemporaneous understanding of the English guarantee.

We think it most unlikely that the English Cruel and Unusual Punishments Clause was meant to forbid "disproportionate" punishments. There is even less likelihood that the proportionality of punishment was one of the traditional "rights and privileges of Englishmen" apart from the Declaration of Rights, which happened to be included in the Eighth Amendment. Indeed, even those scholars who believe the principle to have been included within the Declaration of Rights do not contend that such a prohibition was reflected in English practice—nor could they. For in 1791, England punished over 200 crimes with death (until 1826, all felonies, except mayhem and petty larceny, were punishable by death). By 1830 the class of offenses punishable by death was narrowed to include "only" murder, attempts to murder by poisoning, stabbing, shooting etc.; administering poison to procure abortion; sodomy; rape; statutory rape; and certain classes of forgery.

Unless one accepts the notion of a blind incorporation, however, the ultimate question is not what "cruell and unusuall punishments" meant in the Declaration of Rights, but what its meaning was to the Americans who adopted the Eighth Amendment. Even if one assumes that the Founders knew the precise meaning of that English antecedent, a direct transplant of the English meaning to the soil of American constitutionalism would in any case have been impossible. There were no common-law punishments in the federal system, so that the provision must have been meant as a check not upon judges but upon the Legislature.

Wrenched out of its common-law context, and applied to the actions of a legislature, the word "unusual" could hardly mean "contrary to law." But it continued to mean (as it continues to mean today) "such as [does not] occu[r] in ordinary practice," Webster's 1828 edition, "[s]uch as is [not] in common use," Webster's 2d International. According to its terms, then, by forbidding "cruel *and unusual* punishments," the Clause disables the Legislature from authorizing particular forms or "modes" of punishment—specifically, cruel methods of punishment that are not regularly or customarily employed.

The language bears the construction, however—and here we come to the point crucial to resolution of the present case—that "cruelty and unusualness" are to be determined not solely with reference to the punishment at issue ("Is life imprisonment a cruel and unusual punishment?") but with reference to the crime for which it is imposed as well ("Is life imprisonment cruel and unusual punishment for possession of unlawful drugs?"). The latter interpretation would make the provision a form

of proportionality guarantee. The arguments against it, however, seem to us conclusive.

First of all, to use the phrase "cruel and unusual punishment" to describe a requirement of proportionality would have been an exceedingly vague and oblique way of saying what Americans were well accustomed to saying more directly. The notion of "proportionality" was not a novelty (though then as now there was little agreement over what it entailed). In 1778, for example, the Virginia Legislature narrowly rejected a comprehensive "Bill for Proportioning Punishments" introduced by Thomas Jefferson. Proportionality provisions had been included in several state constitutions. See, *e.g.,* Pa. Const., § 38 (1776) (punishments should be "in general more proportionate to the crimes"); S.C. Const., Art. XL (1778) (same); N.H. Bill of Rights, Pt. 1, Art. XVIII (1784) ("all penalties ought to be proportioned to the nature of the offence"). There is little doubt that those who framed, proposed, and ratified the Bill of Rights were aware of such provisions, yet chose not to replicate them. Both the New Hampshire Constitution, adopted 8 years before ratification of the Eighth Amendment, and the Ohio Constitution, adopted 12 years after, contain, in separate provisions, a prohibition of "cruel and unusual punishments" ("cruel or unusual," in New Hampshire's case) and a requirement that "all penalties ought to be proportioned to the nature of the offence." N.H. Bill of Rights, Arts. XVIII, XXXIII (1784). Ohio Const., Art. VIII, §§ 13, 14 (1802).

Secondly, it would seem quite peculiar to refer to cruelty and unusualness *for the offense in question,* in a provision having application only to a new government that had never before defined offenses, and that would be defining new and peculiarly national ones. Finally and most conclusively, as we proceed to discuss, the fact that what was "cruel and unusual" under the Eighth Amendment was to be determined without reference to the particular offense is confirmed by all available evidence of contemporary understanding.

The Eighth Amendment received little attention during the proposal and adoption of the Federal Bill of Rights. However, what evidence exists from debates at the state ratifying conventions that prompted the Bill of Rights as well as the Floor debates in the First Congress which proposed it "confirm[s] the view that the cruel and unusual punishments clause was directed at prohibiting certain *methods* of punishment."

The early commentary on the Clause contains no reference to disproportionate or excessive sentences, and again indicates that it was designed to outlaw particular *modes* of punishment. One commentator wrote:

> Under the [Eighth] amendment the infliction of cruel and unusual punishments, is also prohibited. The various barbarous and cruel punishments inflicted under the laws of some other countries, and which profess not to be behind the most enlightened nations on earth in civilization and refinement, furnish sufficient reasons for this express prohibition. Breaking on the wheel, flaying alive, rending assunder with horses, various species of horrible tortures inflicted in the inquisition, maiming, mutilating and scourging to death, are wholly alien to the spirit of our humane general constitution. B. Oliver, *The Rights of an American Citizen* 186 (1832).

We think it enough that *those who framed and approved the Federal Constitution* chose, for whatever reason, not to include within it the guarantee against disproportionate sentences that some State Constitutions contained. It is worth noting, however, that there was good reason for that choice—a reason that reinforces the necessity of overruling *Solem*. While there are relatively clear historical guidelines and accepted practices that enable judges to determine which *modes* of punishment are "cruel and unusual," *proportionality* does not lend itself to such analysis. Neither Congress nor any state legislature has ever set out with the objective of crafting a penalty that is "disproportionate," yet as some of the examples mentioned above indicate, many enacted dispositions seem to be so—because they were made for other times or other places, with different social attitudes, different criminal epidemics, different public fears, and different prevailing

theories of penology. This is not to say that there are no absolutes; one can imagine extreme examples that no rational person, in no time or place, could accept. But for the same reason these examples are easy to decide, they are certain never to occur.* The real function of a constitutional proportionality principle, if it exists, is to enable judges to evaluate a penalty that *some* assemblage of men and women *has* considered proportionate—and to say that it is not. For that real-world enterprise, the standards seem so inadequate that the proportionality principle becomes an invitation to imposition of subjective values.

Our 20th-century jurisprudence has not remained entirely in accord with the proposition that there is no proportionality requirement in the Eighth Amendment, but neither has it departed to the extent that *Solem* suggests. In *Weems v. United States* (1910), a government disbursing officer convicted of making false entries of small sums in his account book was sentenced by Philippine courts to 15 years of *cadena temporal*. That punishment, based upon the Spanish Penal Code, called for incarceration at "'hard and painful labor'" with chains fastened to the wrists and ankles at all times. Several "accessor[ies]" were superadded, including permanent disqualification from holding any position of public trust, subjection to "[government] surveillance" for life, and "civil interdiction," which consisted of deprivation of "'the rights of parental authority,

---

*Justice White argues that the Eighth Amendment must contain a proportionality principle because otherwise legislatures could "mak[e] overtime parking a felony punishable by life imprisonment." We do not in principle oppose the "parade of horribles" form of argumentation, see Scalia, "Assorted Canards of Contemporary Legal Analysis," 40 *Case W. Res. L. Rev.* 581, 590–93 (1989–1990). Justice White's argument has force only for those who believe that the Constitution prohibited everything that is intensely undesirable. As Justice Frankfurter reminded us, "[t]he process of Constitutional adjudication does not thrive on conjuring up horrible possibilities that never happen in the real world and devising doctrines sufficiently comprehensive in detail to cover the remotest contingency." *New York v. United States* (1946). It seems to us no more reasonable to hold that the Eighth Amendment forbids "disproportionate punishment" because otherwise the State could impose life imprisonment for a parking offense, than it would be to hold that the Takings Clause forbids "disproportionate taxation" because otherwise the State could tax away all income above the subsistence level.

guardianship of person or property, participation in the family council [, etc.]'."

Justice McKenna, writing for himself and three others, held that the imposition of *cadena temporal* was "Cruel and Unusual Punishment." (Justice White, joined by Justice Holmes, dissented.) That holding, and some of the reasoning upon which it was based, was not at all out of accord with the traditional understanding of the provision we have described above. The punishment was both (1) severe *and* (2) unknown to Anglo-American tradition. . . .

Other portions of the opinion, however, suggest that mere disproportionality, by itself, might make a punishment cruel and unusual. . . .

Since it contains language that will support either theory, our later opinions have used *Weems,* as the occasion required, to represent either the principle that "the Eighth Amendment bars not only those punishments that are 'barbaric' but also those that are 'excessive' in relation to the crime committed," or the principle that only a "unique . . . punishmen[t]," a form of imprisonment different from the "more traditional forms . . . imposed under the Anglo-Saxon system," can violate the Eighth Amendment.

Petitioner claims that his sentence violates the Eighth Amendment for a reason in addition to its disproportionality. He argues that it is "cruel and unusual" to impose a mandatory sentence of such severity, without any consideration of so-called mitigating factors such as, in his case, the fact that he had no prior felony convictions. He apparently contends that the Eighth Amendment requires Michigan to create a sentencing scheme whereby life in prison without possibility of parole is simply the most severe of a range of available penalties that the sentencer may impose after hearing evidence in mitigation and aggravation.

As our earlier discussion should make clear, this claim has no support in the text and history of the Eighth Amendment. Severe, mandatory penalties may be cruel, but they are not unusual in the constitutional sense, having been employed in various forms throughout our Nation's history. As noted earlier, mandatory death sentences abounded in our first Penal Code. They were also common in the several States—both at the time of the founding and throughout the 19th century. See *Woodson v. North Carolina.* There can be no serious contention, then, that a sentence which is not otherwise cruel and unusual becomes so simply because it is "mandatory."

Petitioner's "required mitigation" claim, like his proportionality claim, does find support in our death-penalty jurisprudence. We have held that a capital sentence is cruel and unusual under the Eighth Amendment if it is imposed without an individual determination that that punishment is "appropriate"—whether or not the sentence is "grossly disproportionate." Petitioner asks us to extend this so-called "individualized capital sentencing doctrine" to an "individualized mandatory life in prison without parole sentencing doctrine." We refuse to do so.

Our cases creating and clarifying the "individualized capital sentencing doctrine" have repeatedly suggested that there is no comparable requirement outside the capital context, because of the qualitative difference between death and all other penalties. We have drawn the line of required individualized sentencing at capital cases, and see no basis for extending it further.

The judgment of the Michigan Court of Appeals is

Affirmed.

JUSTICE KENNEDY, with whom JUSTICE O'CONNOR and JUSTICE SOUTER join, concurring in part and concurring in the judgment.

I write this separate opinion because my approach to the Eighth Amendment proportionality analysis differs from Justice Scalia's. Regardless of whether Justice Scalia or the dissent has the best of the historical argument, *stare decisis* counsels our adherence to the narrow proportionality principle that has existed in our Eighth Amendment jurisprudence for 80 years. Although our proportionality decisions have not been clear or consistent in all respects, they can be reconciled, and they require us to uphold petitioner's sentence.

Our decisions recognize that the Cruel and Unusual Punishments Clause encompasses a narrow proportionality principle.

The Eighth Amendment proportionality principle also applies to noncapital sentences. Close analysis of our decisions yields some common principles that give content to the uses and limits of proportionality review.

The first of these principles is that the fixing of prison terms for specific crimes involves a substantive penological judgment that, as a general matter, is "properly within the province of legislatures, not courts."

The second principle is that the Eighth Amendment does not mandate adoption of any one penological theory.

Third, marked divergences both in underlying theories of sentencing and in the length of prescribed prison terms are the inevitable, often beneficial, result of the federal structure. . . .

The fourth principle at work in our cases is that proportionality review by federal courts should be informed by "'objective factors to the maximum possible extent.'" The most prominent objective factor is the type of punishment imposed.

All of these principles—the primacy of the legislature, the variety of legitimate penological schemes, the nature of our federal system, and the requirement that proportionality review be guided by objective factors—inform the final one: the Eighth Amendment does not require strict proportionality between crime and sentence. Rather, it forbids only extreme sentences that are "grossly disproportionate" to the crime.

With these considerations stated, it is necessary to examine the challenged aspects of petitioner's sentence: its severe length and its mandatory operation.

In light of the gravity of petitioner's offense, a comparison of his crime with his sentence does not give rise to an inference of gross disproportionality. To set aside petitioner's mandatory sentence would require rejection of the collective wisdom of the Michigan Legislature and, as a consequence, the Michigan citizenry. We have never invalidated a penalty mandated by a legislature based only on the length of sentence, and, especially with a crime as severe as this one, we should do so only in the most extreme circumstance.

For the foregoing reasons, I conclude that petitioner's sentence of life imprisonment without parole for his crime of possession of more than 650 grams of cocaine does not violate the Eighth Amendment.

JUSTICE WHITE, with whom JUSTICE BLACKMUN and JUSTICE STEVENS join, dissenting.

The Eighth Amendment provides that "[e]xcessive bail shall not be required, nor excessive fines imposed, nor cruel and unusual punishments inflicted."

The language of the Amendment does not refer to proportionality in so many words, but it does forbid "excessive" fines, a restraint that suggests that a determination of excessiveness should be based at least in part on whether the fine imposed is disproportionate to the crime committed.

Justice Scalia argues that all of the available evidence of the day indicated that *those who drafted and approved the Amendment* "chose . . . not to include within it the guarantee against disproportionate sentences that some State Constitutions contained." Even if one were to accept the argument that the First Congress did not have in mind the proportionality issue, the evidence would hardly be strong enough to come close to proving an affirmative decision against the proportionality component. Had there been an intention to exclude it from the reach of the words that otherwise could reasonably be construed to include it, perhaps as plain-speaking Americans, the Members of the First Congress would have said so.

Two dangers lurk in Justice Scalia's analysis. First, he provides no mechanism for addressing a situation in which a legislature makes overtime parking a felony punishable by life imprisonment. He concedes that "one can imagine extreme examples that no rational person, in no time or place, could accept," but attempts to offer reassurance by claiming that "for the same reason these examples are easy to decide, they are certain never to occur." This is cold comfort indeed, for absent a proportionality guarantee, there would be no basis for deciding such cases should they arise.

Second, as I have indicated, Justice Scalia's position that the Eighth Amendment addresses only modes or methods of punishment is quite inconsistent with our capital punishment cases, which do not outlaw death as a mode or method of punishment, but instead put limits on its application. If the concept of proportionality is downgraded in the Eighth Amendment calculus, much of this Court's capital penalty jurisprudence will rest on quicksand.

Petitioner, a first-time offender, was convicted of possession of 672 grams of cocaine. The statute under which he was convicted provides that a person who knowingly or intentionally possesses any of various narcotics, including cocaine, "[w]hich is in an amount of 650 grams or more of any mixture containing that substance is guilty of a felony and shall be imprisoned for life." No particular degree of drug purity is required for a conviction. There is no room for judicial discretion in the imposition of the life sentence upon conviction. The asserted purpose of the legislative enactment of these statutes was to "'stem drug traffic'" and reach "'drug dealers.'"

Application of *Solem*'s proportionality analysis leaves no doubt that the Michigan statute at issue fails constitutional muster. The statutorily mandated penalty of life without possibility of parole for possession of narcotics is unconstitutionally disproportionate in that it violates the Eighth Amendment's prohibition against cruel and unusual punishment.

Consequently, I would reverse the decision of the Michigan Court of Appeals.

JUSTICE MARSHALL, dissenting.

I agree with Justice White's dissenting opinion, except insofar as it asserts that the Eighth Amendment's Cruel and Unusual Punishments Clause does not proscribe the death penalty. I adhere to my view that capital punishment is in all instances unconstitutional. See *Gregg v. Georgia* (1976) (Justice Marshall, dissenting).

JUSTICE STEVENS, with whom JUSTICE BLACKMUN joins, dissenting.

A mandatory sentence of life imprisonment without the possibility of parole must rest on a rational determination that the punished "criminal conduct is so atrocious that society's interest in deterrence and retribution wholly outweighs any considerations of reform or rehabilitation of the perpetrator." Serious as this defendant's crime was, I believe it is irrational to conclude that every similar offender is wholly incorrigible.

Ewing v. California
538 U.S. 11 (2003)

Under California's three-strikes law, a defendant who is convicted of a felony and has previously been convicted of two or more serious or violent felonies must receive an indeterminate life-imprisonment term. Such a defendant becomes eligible for parole on a date calculated by reference to a minimum term, which, in this case, was twenty-five years. Gary Ewing was convicted in California of first-degree robbery and three counts of residential burglary and was sentenced to prison. In 2000, while on parole from his prison term, he stole three golf clubs worth $399 apiece. In a California trial court, Ewing was ultimately convicted of one count of felony grand theft of personal property in connection with the theft of the golf clubs. The prosecutor formally alleged—and the trial court found—that the defendant had been convicted previously of four serious or violent felonies, namely, the three burglaries and the robbery. In sentencing him to twenty-five years to life, the court refused to exercise its discretion to reduce the conviction to a misdemeanor—under a state law that permits certain offenses, known as "wobblers," to be classified as either misdemeanors or felonies—or to dismiss the allegations of some or all of his prior relevant convictions. The state court of appeals affirmed; relying on Rummel v. Estelle *(1980), it rejected Ewing's claim that his sentence was grossly disproportionate and therefore violated the Eighth Amendment's prohibition of cruel and unusual punishments. It reasoned that enhanced sentences under the three-strikes law served the state's legitimate goal of deterring and incapacitating repeat offenders. After the California Supreme Court denied review, the US Supreme Court granted certiorari. Judgment of the Court:* O'Connor, Rehnquist, Kennedy. *Concurring in the judgment:* Scalia; Thomas. *Dissenting opinions:* Stevens, *Souter, Ginsburg, Breyer;* Breyer, *Stevens, Souter, Ginsburg.*

JUSTICE O'CONNOR announced the judgment of the Court and delivered an opinion in which THE CHIEF JUSTICE and JUSTICE KENNEDY join.

In this case, we decide whether the Eighth Amendment prohibits the State of California from sentencing a repeat felon to a prison term of 25 years to life under the State's "Three Strikes and You're Out" law.

California's three strikes law [the result of Proposition 184] reflects a shift in the State's sentencing policies toward incapacitating and deterring repeat offenders who threaten the public safety. The law was designed "to ensure longer prison sentences and greater punishment for those who commit a felony and have been previously convicted of serious and/or violent felony offenses."

On October 1, 1993, 12-year-old Polly Klaas was kidnaped from her home in Petaluma, California. Her admitted killer, Richard Allen Davis, had a long criminal history that included two prior kidnaping convictions. Davis had served only half of his most recent sentence (16 years for kidnaping, assault, and burglary). Had Davis served his entire sentence, he would still have been in prison on the day that Polly Klaas was kidnaped.

Polly Klaas' murder galvanized support for the three strikes initiative. Within days, Proposition 184 was on its way to becoming the fastest qualifying initiative in California history. On January 3, 1994, the sponsors of Assembly Bill 971 resubmitted an amended version of the bill that conformed to Proposition 184. On January 31, 1994, Assembly Bill 971 [a bill that conformed to Proposition 184] passed the Assembly by a 63 to 9 margin. The Senate passed it by a 29 to 7 margin on March 3, 1994. Governor Pete Wilson signed the bill into law on March 7, 1994. California voters approved Proposition 184 by a margin of 72 to 28 percent on November 8, 1994.

California thus became the second State to enact a three strikes law. In November 1993, the voters of Washington State approved their own three strikes law, Initiative 593, by a margin of 3 to 1. Between 1993 and 1995, 24 States and the Federal Government enacted three strikes laws. Though the three strikes laws vary from State to State, they share a common goal of protecting the public safety by providing lengthy prison terms for habitual felons.

Under California law, certain offenses may be classified as either felonies or misdemeanors. These crimes are known as "wobblers." Some crimes that would otherwise be misdemeanors become "wobblers" because of the defendant's prior record. For example, petty theft, a misdemeanor, becomes a "wobbler" when the defendant has previously served a prison term for committing specified theft-related crimes. Other crimes, such as grand theft, are "wobblers" regardless of the defendant's prior record. Both types of "wobblers" are triggering offenses under the three strikes law only when they are treated as felonies. Under California law, a "wobbler" is presumptively a felony and "remains a felony except when the discretion is actually exercised" to make the crime a misdemeanor.

In California, prosecutors may exercise their discretion to charge a "wobbler" as either a felony or a misdemeanor. Likewise, California trial courts have discretion to reduce a "wobbler" charged as a felony to a misdemeanor either before preliminary examination or at sentencing to avoid imposing a three strikes sentence. . . . California trial courts can also vacate allegations of prior "serious" or "violent" felony convictions, either on motion by the prosecution or *sua sponte*. In ruling whether to vacate allegations of prior felony convictions, courts consider whether, "in light of the nature and circumstances of [the defendant's] present felonies and prior serious and/or violent felony convictions, and the particulars of his background, character, and prospects, the defendant may be deemed outside the [three strikes'] scheme's spirit, in whole or in part." Thus, trial courts may avoid imposing a three strikes sentence in two ways: first, by reducing "wobblers" to misdemeanors (which do not qualify as triggering offenses), and second, by vacating allegations of prior "serious" or "violent" felony convictions. . . .

Ewing is no stranger to the criminal justice system. In 1984, at the age of 22, he pleaded guilty to theft. The court sentenced him to six months in jail (suspended), three years' probation, and a $300 fine. In 1988, he was convicted of felony grand theft auto and sentenced to one year in jail and three years' probation. After Ewing completed probation, however, the sentencing court reduced the crime to a misdemeanor, permitted Ewing to withdraw his guilty plea, and dismissed the case. In 1990, he was convicted of petty theft with a prior and sentenced to 60 days in the county jail and three years' probation. In 1992, Ewing was convicted of battery and sentenced to 30 days in the county jail and two years' summary probation. One month later, he was convicted of theft and sentenced to 10 days in the county jail and 12 months' probation. In January 1993, Ewing was convicted of burglary and sentenced to 60 days in the county jail and one year's summary probation. In February 1993, he was convicted of possessing drug paraphernalia and sentenced to six months in the county jail and three years' probation. In July 1993, he was convicted of appropriating lost property and sentenced to 10 days in the county jail and two years' summary probation. In September 1993, he was convicted of unlawfully possessing a firearm and trespassing and sentenced to 30 days in the county jail and one year's probation.

In October and November 1993, Ewing committed three burglaries and one robbery at a Long Beach, California, apartment complex over a 5-week period. He awakened one of his victims, asleep on her living room sofa, as he tried to disconnect her video cassette recorder from the television in that room. When she screamed, Ewing ran out the front door. On another occasion, Ewing accosted a victim in the mailroom of the apartment complex. Ewing claimed to have a gun and ordered the victim to hand over his wallet. When the victim resisted, Ewing produced a knife and forced the victim back to the apartment itself. While Ewing rifled through the bedroom, the victim fled the apartment screaming for help. Ewing absconded with the victim's money and credit cards.

On December 9, 1993, Ewing was arrested on the premises of the apartment complex for trespassing and lying to a police officer. The knife used in the robbery and a glass cocaine pipe were later found in the back seat of the patrol car used to transport Ewing to the police station. A jury convicted Ewing of first-degree robbery and three counts of residential burglary. Sentenced to nine years and eight months in prison, Ewing was paroled in 1999.

Only 10 months later, Ewing stole the golf clubs at issue in this case. He was charged with, and ultimately convicted of, one count of felony grand theft of personal property in excess of $400. As required by the three strikes law, the prosecutor formally alleged, and the trial court later found, that Ewing had been convicted previously of four serious or violent felonies for the three burglaries and the robbery in the Long Beach apartment complex.

At the sentencing hearing, Ewing asked the court to reduce the conviction for grand theft, a "wobbler" under California law, to a misdemeanor so as to avoid a three strikes sentence. Ewing also asked the trial court to exercise its discretion to dismiss the allegations of some or all of his prior serious or violent felony convictions, again for purposes of avoiding a three strikes sentence. Before sentencing Ewing, the trial court took note of his entire criminal history, including the fact that he was on parole when he committed his latest offense. The court also heard arguments from defense counsel and a plea from Ewing himself.

In the end, the trial judge determined that the grand theft should remain a felony. The court also ruled that the four prior strikes for the three burglaries and the robbery in Long Beach should stand. As a newly convicted felon with two or more "serious" or "violent" felony convictions in his past, Ewing was sentenced under the three strikes law to 25 years to life. . . .

The Eighth Amendment, which forbids cruel and unusual punishments, contains a "narrow proportionality principle" that "applies to non-capital sentences." We have most recently addressed the proportionality principle as applied to terms of years in a series of cases beginning with *Rummel v. Estelle* (1980).

In *Rummel,* we held that it did not violate the Eighth Amendment for a State to sentence a three-time offender to life in prison with the possibility of parole. . . . In *Hutto v. Davis* (1982), the defendant was sentenced to two consecutive terms of 20 years in prison for possession with intent to distribute nine ounces of marijuana and distribution of marijuana. We held that such a sentence was constitutional: . . . In *Solem v. Helm* (1983), we held that the Eighth Amendment prohibited "a life sentence without possibility of parole for a seventh nonviolent felony." The triggering offense in *Solem* was "uttering a 'no account' check for $100." We specifically stated that the Eighth Amendment's ban on cruel and unusual punishments "prohibits . . . sentences that are disproportionate to the crime committed," and that the "constitutional principle of proportionality has been recognized explicitly in this Court for almost a century." . . . [I]n *Solem,* we . . . specifically noted the contrast between that sentence and the sentence in *Rummel,* pursuant to which the defendant was eligible for parole. Indeed, we explicitly declined to overrule *Rummel* . . .

Eight years after *Solem,* we grappled with the proportionality issue again in *Harmelin. Harmelin* . . . involved a first-time offender convicted of possessing 672 grams of cocaine. He was sentenced to life in prison without possibility of parole. A majority of the Court rejected Harmelin's claim that his sentence was so grossly disproportionate that it violated the Eighth Amendment. . . . [In *Harmelin*] Justice Kennedy, joined by two other Members of the Court, concurred in part and concurred in the judgment. Justice Kennedy . . . identified four principles of proportionality review—"the primacy of the legislature, the variety of legitimate penological schemes, the nature of our federal system, and the requirement that proportionality review be guided by objective factors"—that "inform the final one: The Eighth Amendment does not require strict proportionality between crime and sentence. Rather, it forbids only extreme sentences that are 'grossly disproportionate' to the crime."

The proportionality principles in our cases distilled in Justice Kennedy's concurrence guide our application of the Eighth Amendment in the new context that we are called upon to consider. . . .

Throughout the States, legislatures enacting three strikes laws made a deliberate policy choice that individuals who have repeatedly engaged in serious or violent criminal behavior, and whose conduct has not been deterred by more conventional approaches to punishment, must be isolated from society in order to protect the public safety. Though three strikes laws may be relatively new, our tradition of deferring to state legislatures in making and implementing such important policy decisions is longstanding. . . . Our traditional deference to legislative policy choices finds a corollary in the principle that the Constitution "does not mandate adoption of any one penological theory." A sentence can have a variety of justifications, such as incapacitation, deterrence, retribution, or rehabilitation. Some or all of these justifications may play a role in a State's sentencing scheme. Selecting the sentencing rationales is generally a policy choice to be made by state legislatures, not federal courts.

When the California Legislature enacted the three strikes law, it made a judgment that protecting the public safety requires incapacitating criminals who have already been convicted of at least one serious or violent crime. Nothing in the Eighth Amendment prohibits California from making that choice. . . .

California's justification is no pretext. Recidivism is a serious public safety concern in California and throughout the Nation. According to a recent report, approximately 67 percent of former inmates released from state prisons were charged with at least one "serious" new crime within three years of their release. In particular, released property offenders like Ewing had higher recidivism rates than those released after committing violent, drug, or public-order offenses. Approximately 73 percent of the property offenders released in 1994 were arrested again within three years, compared to approximately 61 percent of the violent offenders, 62 percent of the public-order offenders, and 66 percent of the drug offenders.

In 1996, when the *Sacramento Bee* studied 233 three strikes offenders in California, it found that they had an aggregate of 1,165 prior felony convictions, an average of 5 apiece. The prior convictions included 322 robberies and 262 burglaries. About 84 percent of the 233 three strikes offenders had been convicted of at least one violent crime. In all, they were responsible for 17 homicides, 7 attempted slayings, and 91 sexual assaults and child molestations. The *Sacramento Bee* concluded, based on its investigation, that "in the vast majority of the cases, regardless of the third strike, the [three strikes] law is snaring [the] long-term habitual offenders with multiple felony convictions. . . . ."

The State's interest in deterring crime also lends some support to the three strikes law. We have long viewed both incapacitation and deterrence as rationales for recidivism statutes. . . . Four years after the passage of California's three strikes law, the recidivism rate of parolees returned to prison for the commission of a new crime dropped by nearly 25 percent. Even more dramatically: "an unintended but positive consequence of 'Three Strikes' has been the impact on parolees leaving the state. More California parolees are now leaving the state than parolees from other jurisdictions entering California. This striking turnaround started in 1994. It was the first time more parolees left the state than entered since 1976 . . . ."

To be sure, California's three strikes law has sparked controversy. Critics have doubted the law's wisdom, cost-efficiency, and effectiveness in reaching its goals. This criticism is appropriately directed at the legislature, which has primary responsibility for making the difficult policy choices that underlie any criminal sentencing scheme. We do not sit as a "superlegislature" to second-guess these policy choices. It is enough that the State of California has a reasonable basis for believing that dramatically enhanced sentences for habitual felons "advances the goals of [its] criminal justice system in any substantial way."

Against this backdrop, we consider Ewing's claim that his three strikes sentence of 25 years to life is unconstitutionally disproportionate to his offense. . . . In weighing the gravity of Ewing's offense, we must place on the scales not only his current felony, but also his long history of felony recidivism. Any other approach would fail to accord proper deference to the policy judgments that find expression in the legislature's choice of sanctions. In imposing a three strikes sentence, the State's interest is not merely punishing the offense of conviction, or the "triggering" offense: "It is in addition the interest . . . in dealing in a harsher manner with those who by repeated criminal acts have shown that they are simply incapable of con-

forming to the norms of society as established by its criminal law." To give full effect to the State's choice of this legitimate penological goal, our proportionality review of Ewing's sentence must take that goal into account.

Ewing's sentence is justified by the State's public-safety interest in incapacitating and deterring recidivist felons, and amply supported by his own long, serious criminal record. Ewing has been convicted of numerous misdemeanor and felony offenses, served nine separate terms of incarceration, and committed most of his crimes while on probation or parole. His prior "strikes" were serious felonies including robbery and three residential burglaries. To be sure, Ewing's sentence is a long one. But it reflects a rational legislative judgment, entitled to deference, that offenders who have committed serious or violent felonies and who continue to commit felonies must be incapacitated. . . . We hold that Ewing's sentence of 25 years to life in prison, imposed for the offense of felony grand theft under the three strikes law, is not grossly disproportionate and therefore does not violate the Eighth Amendment's prohibition on cruel and unusual punishments. The judgment of the California Court of Appeal is affirmed.

JUSTICE SCALIA, concurring in the judgment.

In my concurring opinion in *Harmelin v. Michigan* (1991), I concluded that the Eighth Amendment's prohibition of "cruel and unusual punishments" was aimed at excluding only certain *modes* of punishment, and was not a "guarantee against disproportionate sentences." Out of respect for the principle of *stare decisis,* I might nonetheless accept the contrary holding of *Solem v. Helm* that the Eighth Amendment contains a narrow proportionality principle—if I felt I could intelligently apply it. This case demonstrates why I cannot.

Proportionality—the notion that the punishment should fit the crime—is inherently a concept tied to the penological goal of retribution. "It becomes difficult even to speak intelligently of 'proportionality,' once deterrence and rehabilitation are given significant weight," not to mention giving weight to the purpose of California's three strikes law: incapacitation. In the present case, the game is up once the plurality has acknowledged that "the Constitution does not mandate adoption of any one penological theory," and that a "sentence can have a variety of justifications, such as incapacitation, deterrence, retribution, or rehabilitation." That acknowledgment having been made, it no longer suffices merely to assess "the gravity of the offense compared to the harshness of the penalty," that classic description of the proportionality principle (alone and in itself quite resistant to policy-free, legal analysis) now becomes merely the "first" step of the inquiry. Having completed that step (by a discussion which, in all fairness, does not convincingly establish that 25-years-to-life is a "proportionate" punishment for stealing three golf clubs), the plurality must then *add* an analysis to show that "Ewing's sentence is justified by the State's public-safety interest in incapacitating and deterring recidivist felons."

Which indeed it is—though why that has anything to do with the principle of proportionality is a mystery. Perhaps the plurality should revise its terminology, so that what it reads into the Eighth Amendment is not the unstated proposition that all punishment should be reasonably proportionate to the gravity of the offense, but rather the unstated proposition that all punishment should reasonably pursue the multiple purposes of the criminal law. That formulation would make it clearer than ever, of course, that the plurality is not applying law but evaluating policy.

Because I agree that petitioner's sentence does not violate the Eighth Amendment's prohibition against cruel and unusual punishments, I concur in the judgment.

JUSTICE THOMAS, concurring in the judgment.

I agree with Justice Scalia's view that the proportionality test announced in *Solem v. Helm* is incapable of judicial application. . . . In my view, the Cruel and Unusual Punishments Clause of the Eighth Amendment contains no proportionality principle. . . . Because the plurality concludes that petitioner's sentence does not violate the Eighth Amendment's prohibition on cruel and unusual punishments, I concur in the judgment.

JUSTICE STEVENS, with whom JUSTICE SOUTER, JUSTICE GINSBURG and JUSTICE BREYER join, dissenting.

. . . I think it clear that the Eighth Amendment's prohibition of "cruel and unusual punishments" expresses a broad and basic proportionality principle that takes into account all of the justifications for penal sanctions. It is this broad proportionality principle that would preclude reliance on any of the justifications for punishment to support, for example, a life sentence for overtime parking.

JUSTICE BREYER, with whom JUSTICE STEVENS, JUSTICE SOUTER, and JUSTICE GINSBURG join, dissenting.

The constitutional question is whether the "three strikes" sentence imposed by California upon repeat-offender Gary Ewing is "grossly disproportionate" to his crime. The sentence amounts to a real prison term of at least 25 years. The sentence-triggering criminal conduct consists of the theft of three golf clubs priced at a total of $1,197. The offender has a criminal history that includes four felony convictions arising out of three separate burglaries (one armed). In *Solem v. Helm,* the Court found grossly disproportionate a somewhat longer sentence imposed on a recidivist offender for triggering criminal conduct that was somewhat less severe. In my view, the differences are not determinative, and the Court should reach the same ultimate conclusion here. . . .

The plurality applies Justice Kennedy's analytical framework in *Harmelin.* And, for present purposes, I will consider Ewing's Eighth Amendment claim on those terms. To implement this approach, courts faced with a "gross disproportionality" claim must first make "a threshold comparison of the crime committed and the sentence imposed." If a claim crosses that threshold—itself a *rare* occurrence—then the court should compare the sentence at issue to other sentences "imposed on other criminals" in the same, or in other, jurisdictions. The comparative analysis will "validate" or invalidate "an initial judgment that a sentence is grossly disproportionate to a crime." . . .

I believe that the case before us is a "rare" case—one in which a court can say with reasonable confidence that the punishment is "grossly disproportionate" to the crime. . . .

Believing Ewing's argument a strong one, sufficient to pass the threshold, I turn to the comparative analysis. A comparison of Ewing's sentence with other sentences requires answers to two questions. First, how would other jurisdictions (or California at other times, *i.e.,* without the three strikes penalty) punish the *same offense conduct*? Second, upon what other conduct would other jurisdictions (or California) impose the *same prison term*? Moreover, since hypothetical punishment is beside the point, the relevant prison time, for comparative purposes, is *real* prison time, *i.e.,* the time that an offender must *actually serve.* . . .

As to California itself, we know the following: First, between the end of World War II and 1994 (when California enacted the three strikes law), *no one* like Ewing could have served more than *10* years in prison. We know that for certain because the maximum sentence for Ewing's crime of conviction, grand theft, was for most of that period 10 years. We also know that the time that any offender actually served was likely far less than 10 years. This is because statistical data shows that the median time actually served for grand theft (other than auto theft) was about two years, and 90 percent of all those convicted of that crime served less than three or four years. Second, statistics suggest that recidivists *of all sorts* convicted during that same time period in California served a small fraction of Ewing's real-time sentence. On average, recidivists served three to four additional (recidivist-related) years in prison, with 90 percent serving less than an additional real seven to eight years. Third, we know that California has reserved, and still reserves, Ewing-type prison time, *i.e.,* at least 25 real years in prison, for criminals convicted of crimes far worse than was Ewing's. Statistics for the years 1945 to 1981, for example, indicate that typical (nonrecidivist) male first-degree murderers served between 10 and 15 real years in prison, with 90 percent of all such murderers serving less than 20 real years. Moreover, California, which has moved toward a real-time sentencing system (where the statutory punishment approximates the time served), still punishes far less harshly those who have engaged in far more serious conduct. It imposes, for example, upon nonrecidivists guilty of arson causing great bodily injury a maximum sentence of nine years in prison, (prison term of 5, 7, or 9 years for arson that causes great bodily injury); it imposes upon those guilty of voluntary manslaughter a maximum sentence of 11 years, (prison term of 3, 6, or 11 years for voluntary manslaughter). It reserves the sentence that it here imposes upon (former-burglar-now-golf-club-thief) Ewing, for non-recidivist, first-degree murderers (sentence of 25 years to life for first-degree murder).

As to other jurisdictions, we know the following: The United States, bound by the federal Sentencing Guidelines, would impose upon a recidivist, such as Ewing, a sentence that, in any ordinary case, would not exceed 18 months in prison. . . .

[W]e do not have before us information about actual time served by Ewing-type offenders in other States. We do know, however, that the law would make it legally impossible for a Ewing-type offender to serve more than 10 years in prison in 33 jurisdictions, as well as the federal courts, more than 15 years in 4 other States, and more than 20 years in 4 additional States. In nine other States, the law *might* make it legally possible to impose a sentence of 25 years or more—though that fact by itself, of course, does not mean that judges have actually done so. . . .

The upshot is that comparison of other sentencing practices, both in other jurisdictions and in California at other times (or in respect to other crimes), validates what an initial threshold examination suggested. Given the information available, given the state and federal parties' ability to provide additional contrary data, and given their failure to do so, we can assume for constitutional purposes that the following statement is true: Outside the California three strikes context, Ewing's recidivist sentence is virtually unique in its harshness for his offense of conviction, and by a considerable degree.

This is not the end of the matter. California sentenced Ewing pursuant to its "three strikes" law. That law represents a deliberate effort to provide stricter punishments for recidivists. And, it is important to consider whether special criminal justice concerns related to California's three strikes policy might justify including Ewing's theft within the class of triggering criminal conduct (thereby imposing a severe punishment), even if Ewing's sentence would otherwise seem disproportionately harsh.

I can find no such special criminal justice concerns that might justify this sentence. . . . Neither do I see any other way in which inclusion of Ewing's conduct (as a "triggering crime") would further a significant criminal justice objective. One might argue that those who commit several *property* crimes should receive long terms of imprisonment in order to "incapacitate" them, *i.e.,* to prevent them from committing further crimes in the future. But that is not the object of this particular three strikes statute. Rather, as the plurality says, California seeks "'to reduce *serious* and *violent* crime.'"

Justice Scalia and Justice Thomas argue that we should not review for gross disproportionality a sentence to a term of years. Otherwise, we make it too difficult for legislators and sentencing judges to determine just when their sentencing laws and practices pass constitutional muster. I concede that a bright-line rule would give legislators and sentencing judges more

guidance. But application of the Eighth Amendment to a sentence of a term of years requires a case-by-case approach. And, in my view, like that of the plurality, meaningful enforcement of the Eighth Amendment demands that application—even if only at sentencing's outer bounds.

A case-by-case approach can nonetheless offer guidance through example. Ewing's sentence is, at a minimum, 2 to 3 times the length of sentences that other jurisdictions would impose in similar circumstances. That sentence itself is sufficiently long to require a typical offender to spend virtually all the remainder of his active life in prison. These and the other factors that I have discussed, along with the questions that I have asked along the way, should help to identify "gross disproportionality" in a fairly objective way—at the outer bounds of sentencing.

In sum, even if I accept for present purposes the plurality's analytical framework, Ewing's sentence (life imprisonment with a minimum term of 25 years) is grossly disproportionate to the triggering offense conduct—stealing three golf clubs—Ewing's recidivism notwithstanding.

For these reasons, I dissent.

8

The Equal Protection Clause and Racial Discrimination

CHAPTER OUTLINE

The Fourteenth Amendment declares that "No state . . . shall deny any person within its jurisdiction the equal protection of the laws." As noted in Chapter 4 of this volume, the meaning of this clause was first explored by the Supreme Court in *The Slaughter-House Cases* (1873), in which case Justice Samuel Miller construed its words narrowly and argued that it prohibited only racial discrimination. At that time, the Court refused to entertain the notion that the Equal Protection Clause could be used to protect the rights of other classes of citizens.

The exact words of the clause, however, guarantee equal protection to all "persons," not simply to ex-slaves or black persons, and, over time, the narrow and spindly equal-protection leg of *Slaughter-House* has grown into a substantial pillar upholding the protection of civil rights. Today, it is viewed as prohibiting all state action that invidiously discriminates against "suspect classifications" or that impinges on "fundamental rights." As a result, the Court is now called on to invoke its protections in cases in which discrimination against African Americans is altogether absent, as in litigation challenging ameliorative racial preference (i.e., affirmative action/reverse discrimination), gender-based classifications, economic inequality, and restrictions on the exercise of the franchise. Chapter 9 takes up these "newer" equal-protection issues and reviews the various analytical frameworks the justices have employed in ruling on these controversial matters. In this chapter, we concentrate exclusively on the race-discrimination issues raised by the Constitution and the Equal Protection Clause.

RACE AND THE FOUNDING

Although the post–Civil War Reconstruction amendments in general, and the Fourteenth Amendment in particular, have figured prominently in most analyses of race and the Constitution, the original Constitution also contains three provisions germane to this issue. The Founders have been heavily criticized because of provisions that set forth the Three-Fifths Compromise, allowed the importation of slaves for twenty years, and mandated the return of fugitive slaves to their masters.

As Herbert Storing put it, the Founders' response to slavery and the problems of race is usually perceived to be "one to be lived down rather than lived up to."[1] This certainly was the view of one element of abolitionist thought, encapsulated in William Lloyd Garrison's pungent observation that "the Constitution is a compact with the Devil." More recently, the eminent black historian John Hope Franklin elaborated this view, charging the Founders with "betraying the ideals to which they gave lip service" by speaking "eloquently at one moment for the brotherhood of man" and denying it "in the next moment . . . to their black brothers." Particularly repugnant was the Framers' apparent willingness to "degrade the human spirit by equating five black men with three white men." Summarizing this moral legacy, Franklin declared: "Having created a tragically flawed revolutionary doctrine and a Constitution that did not bestow the blessings of liberty on its posterity, the Founding Fathers set the stage for every succeeding generation of Americans to apologize, compromise, and temporize on those principles of liberty that were supposed to be the very foundation of our system of government and way of life."[2] Citing as further evidence Chief Justice Roger Taney's pronouncement in *Dred Scott v. Sandford* (1857) that "the right of property in a slave is distinctly and expressly affirmed in the Constitution," advocates of Franklin's viewpoint assert that the Founders first denied blacks the rights of man listed in the Declaration of Independence and then sanctioned slavery and black inferiority in the Constitution.

A strong case can be made, however, for a quite different interpretation. According to this alternative perspective, the Founders clearly understood that all human beings, including blacks, were created equal and endowed with unalienable rights. As Storing points out, "They did not say that all men were actually secured in the exercise of their rights or that they had the power to provide such security; but there was no doubt about the rights."[3] Powerful support for this point of view can be adduced from the final indictment against the British Crown included in Thomas Jefferson's initial draft of the Declaration of Independence:

> He [the King] has waged cruel war against human nature itself, violating its most sacred rights of life and liberty in the persons of a distant people who never offended him, captivating and carrying them into slavery in another hemisphere, or to incure miserable death in their transportation thither. This piratical warfare, the opprobrium of infidel powers, is the warfare of the Christian king of Great Britain. Determined to keep open a market where MEN should be bought and sold, he has prostituted his negative [used his veto power] for suppressing every legislative attempt to prohibit or to restrain this execrable commerce; and that this assemblage of horrors might want no fact of distinguished die, he is now exciting these very people to rise in arms among us, and to purchase that liberty of which he deprived them, by murdering the people upon whom he also obtruded them; thus paying off former crimes committed against the liberties of one people with crimes which he urges them to commit against the lives of another.[4]

This "vehement philippic against negro slavery," as John Adams termed it, eventually was dropped from the Declaration by the Continental Congress, in part because the British Crown was not solely responsible for the evils of slavery: the colonists themselves were willing and active participants in the slave trade. In addition, the Southern states would not have joined in a unanimous Declaration of Independence had it contained language subversive of their "peculiar institution." Opponents of slavery were willing to concede on this point because they recognized that refusal to do so would not free a single slave and would in all likelihood destroy the possibility of political independence and union. Moreover, they comforted themselves with the knowledge that the Declaration's self-evident truth that all men are created equal had in no way been diluted and that the full force of its claims could be asserted and advanced under more propitious circumstances.

Abraham Lincoln expressed this perfectly in a June 26, 1857, speech responding to the *Dred Scott* decision:

> I think the authors of that notable instrument intended to include all men, but they did not intend to declare that all men were equal in all respects. They did not mean to say all were equal in color, size, intellect, moral developments, or social capacity. They defined with tolerable distinctness, in what respects they did consider all men created equal—equal in "certain inalienable rights, among which are life, liberty, and the pursuit of happiness." This they said, and this they meant. They did not mean to assert the obvious untruth, that they were then actually enjoying that equality, nor yet, that they were about to confer it immediately upon them. In fact, they had no power to confer such a boon. They meant simply to declare the *right*, so that the *enforcement* of it might follow as fast as circumstances should permit. They meant to set up a standard maxim for free society, which should be familiar to all, and revered by all; constantly looked to, constantly labored for, and even though never perfectly attained, constantly approximated, and thereby constantly spreading and deepening its influence, and augmenting the happiness and value of life to all people of all colors everywhere.[5]

The Framers of the Constitution conceded no more to slavery than did the signers of the Declaration of Independence. No form of the word *slave* appears in the Constitution, and the text alone gives no clue that it concerns slavery at all. But the Framers did recognize that some concessions to slavery were necessary in order to secure the Union, with its promise of a broad and long-lasting foundation of freedom. Their aim was to make the minimum concessions consistent with that end, to express those concessions in language that would not sanction slavery, and to avoid blotting the Constitution with the stain of slavery. As Frederick Douglass, formerly a slave and then a leading abolitionist, insisted:

> I hold that the Federal Government was never, in its essence, anything but an anti-slavery government. Abolish slavery tomorrow, and not a sentence or syllable of the Constitution need be altered. It was purposely so framed as to give no claim, no sanction to the claim, of property in man. If in its origin slavery had relation to the government, it was only as the scaffolding to the magnificent structure, to be removed as soon as the building was completed.[6]

Douglass's reference to "scaffolding" is illuminating: the Framers' support of slavery was strong enough to allow the structure of the new Union to be built but unobtrusive enough to fade from view when the job was done. A detailed look at the three provisions dealing with slavery demonstrates this.

Article I, Section 2, of the Constitution provides that "Representatives and direct Taxes shall be apportioned among the several States . . . according to their respective Numbers, which shall be determined by adding to the whole Number of free Persons, including those bound to Service for a Term of Years, and excluding Indians not taxed, three fifths of all other Persons." The phrase "three fifths of all other Persons" (referring to slaves) originated in a dispute during the Constitutional Convention over whether legislative representation should be based on population or on wealth. James Madison sought to sidestep that issue by suggesting that population was a good indicator of wealth. The productivity of slave labor, however, was generally understood to be lower than that of free men, and because wealth could claim inclusion in the basis for apportioning representation and was the sole basis for apportioning direct taxes, some reduction for slave labor seemed appropriate. The "three-fifths" figure seemed convenient, having been used under the Articles of Confederation as a guide to apportioning population for purposes of laying requisitions on the states. So the Founders employed the Three-Fifths Clause more as a guideline for measuring wealth than as a method of counting human beings represented in government.

Interestingly, those advocating that slaves be counted as full persons for purposes of representation were the delegates from the slave states, who sought thereby to enhance slave state power in the new national government. To antislavery Founders, the rule was repugnant insofar as it implied that African American slaves lacked full humanity, but they appreciated that the South would not yield to a stronger national government unless its interests were represented at least to the extent of the three-fifths standard. As Martin Diamond noted, "The Convention was faced with the same kind of problem that faced Lincoln later: Not striking the bargain would have freed not a single slave while it would have destroyed the possibility of union. And only a strong union, which would engender a national commercial economy, held out the hope that slavery would gradually be eliminated."[7] To most of the Founders, only the expectation that slavery would become unprofitable in a commercial republic and ultimately wither away rendered the three-fifths compromise palatable as a temporary expedient.

Professor Akhil Amar, however, has pointed out how profoundly and pervasively significant the Three-Fifths Clause was in giving the South extra political clout for every slave it owned or imported. It gave the slaveholding regions an advantage "in every election as far as the eye could see—a political gift that kept giving." It not only caused the House to lean South, but ultimately affected all three branches. The Electoral College of Article II "sat atop the Article I base," as the presidential electors were apportioned according to the number of seats a state had in the House and Senate. Presidents, in turn, nominated Supreme Court justices and other Article III judges. But it does not end there. Georgia, Louisiana, Florida, Maryland, and North Carolina began to use three-fifths as the apportionment ratio in their own state houses, "giving plantation belts extra credit" in the election of their state legislatures, and these "slavery-skewed state legislatures," in turn, elected their US senators. "By the 1840s," Professor Amar reports, "the corrosive effects of the three-fifths Clause had seeped into every branch of the federal government." And, but for the Civil War, these corrosive effects would have long lingered.[8]

The second slavery provision in the Constitution, found in Article I, Section 9, reads: "The Migration or Importation of such Persons as any of the States now existing shall think proper to admit shall not be prohibited by the Congress prior to the year one thousand eight hundred and eight, but a tax or duty may be imposed on such Importation, not exceeding ten dollars for each Person." In *Dred Scott,* Chief Justice Taney relied on this provision to support his claim that the Constitution "distinctly and expressly" affirmed the right of property in a slave. The clause was, in fact, a major concession to slavery: by protecting the importation of new slaves, it guaranteed a substantial increase in the slave population, making the problem of slavery even more intractable. Yet this concession was limited. The provision did not guarantee a right, but merely postponed a power to prohibit. By limiting Congress's power to prohibit only to those states "now existing," the convention indicated that the slave trade was a vested interest to be preserved for a limited time but that Congress did not have to allow it to spread to new states. The second slave provision thus gave only temporary respite to an illicit trade. The presumption was that after twenty years, Congress would forbid this trade—and in fact, it did so.

Article IV, Section 2, contains the third slavery provision in the Constitution, addressing the issue of fugitive slaves: "No person held to Service or Labour in one State, under the Laws thereof, escaping into another, shall, in Consequence of any Law or Regulation thereof, be discharged from such Service or Labour, but shall be delivered up on Claim of the Party to whom such Service or Labour may be due." Another major concession to slavery, this provision amounted to a form of nationalization of slave property, in the sense that residents of free states were obliged to assist in the enforcement of the institution of slavery, at least insofar as fugitive slaves were involved. Like its model in the Northwest Ordinance, which outlawed slavery in the Northwest Territory, the fugitive-slave provision represented the price that had to be paid for a broader freedom: the idea of slaves fleeing to free states made sense only in a system in which states had and exercised the power to outlaw slavery. The Founders were willing to pay this price, although they were intent on defining it narrowly. An early version of this provision, agreed to by the convention, read: "If any person bound to service or labour in any of the U_____ States shall escape into another State, he or she shall not be discharged from such service or labour, in consequence of any regulations subsisting in the State to which they escape, but shall be delivered up to the person justly claiming their service or labour." The Committee on Style subsequently revised it to read: "No person legally held to service or labour in one state, escaping into another, shall in consequence of regulations subsisting therein be discharged from such service or labour, but shall be delivered up on claim of the party to whom such service or labour may be due." The Committee on Style thus withdrew from the master the claim that he "justly claimed" the services of his slave and acknowledged only that the slave's labor "may be due" to the master. This was further revised so that a slave was no longer defined as one "legally held to service or labour," but rather as one "bound to service or labour." The Founders' motivation in these revisions is apparent. Knowing that a provision for the return of fugitive slaves had to be made to win ratification of the Constitution, they carefully chose language that would give as little sanction as possible to the idea that property in slaves had the same moral status as other kinds of property. Overall, the Founders viewed slavery, in the words of Professor Storing, as "an evil to be tolerated, allowed to enter the Constitution only by the back door, grudgingly, unacknowledged, on the presumption that the house would be truly fit to live in only when it was gone, and that it would ultimately be gone."[9]

Ultimately, slavery did disappear. However, it lasted far longer than the Founders anticipated and, contrary to their expectations, was exorcised only by a bloody civil war. In part, the continuation of slavery reflected factors they could not have foreseen, such as the invention of the cotton gin, which made the slavery plantation system economically profitable. In part, too, slavery flourished because the government created by the Constitution, given the political power and single-mindedness of the Southern states, frequently exhibited a proslavery orientation. Constitutional violations that helped sustain slavery, such as the exclusion of antislavery pamphlets from the mail in the South, were ignored. Slavery, initially a matter of state law, increasingly entered into federal law. Thus, Congress adopted a harsh fugitive-slave law in 1793, and it permitted slavery to flourish in Washington, D.C., until 1862. By the time the Supreme Court decided the *Dred Scott* case in 1857, Chief Justice Taney's claim that the Constitution affirmed the right of property in slaves, although inaccurate as to the original understanding, did seem consistent with the living Constitution. Small wonder, then, that some abolitionists, as well as contemporary historians, have viewed the Founders' Constitution as proslavery.

The Civil War and Reconstruction produced fundamental legal changes. The Emancipation Proclamation and the Thirteenth Amendment eventually outlawed slavery. The Fourteenth Amendment expressly overruled *Dred Scott,* affirming that all persons (including African Americans) born in the United States, and subject to the jurisdiction thereof, are citizens of the United States and of the state in which they reside. The Fifteenth Amendment conferred the right to vote to all men, regardless of "race, color, or previous condition of servitude." Finally, the Privileges or Immunities, Due Process, and Equal Protection Clauses of the Fourteenth Amendment protected African Americans—and all others—against discrimination and majority faction at the hands of state governments.

Of the three branches of government, the judiciary has been the most active and influential in interpreting and enforcing the momentous clauses of the Fourteenth Amendment. The Court's emasculation of the Privileges or Immunities Clause was discussed in Chapter 4, and its extensive and varied applications of the Due Process Clause were considered in Chapters 4 through 7 of this volume. Here, we will examine the ways the Equal Protection Clause has been used to protect against racial discrimination.

RACIAL DESEGREGATION

In interpreting the words of the Equal Protection Clause in *The Slaughter-House Cases* (1873), the Court declared that "the existence of laws in the States where the newly emancipated Negroes resided, which discriminated with gross injustice and hardship against them as a class, was the evil to be remedied by this clause, and by it such laws are forbidden." Thus, it argued that the Equal Protection Clause applied only to blacks. But what protection did the clause provide them? As a result of the private and public discriminations perpetrated against the "newly emancipated Negroes," the Court was soon forced to define specifically what it understood the Equal Protection Clause to mean. Its response came in the *Civil Rights Cases* (1883) and in *Plessy v. Ferguson* (1896).

In the landmark *Civil Rights Cases* (see Chapter 7 of Volume I), the Court limited the protection of the Equal Protection Clause to "state action" only. It held that only discrimination by the states was prohibited and that Congress could not penalize private persons for discriminating against blacks. Absent state action (i.e., in the presence of private discrimination alone), the Court held, the Equal Protection Clause could not be invoked for protection. The concept of state action is, in and of itself, a complex issue that is discussed separately below. For the moment, the point to be stressed is that the *Civil Rights Cases* limited the concept of equal protection to a narrow class of cases and left entirely to the states the task of prohibiting private racial discrimination. (Justice Harlan's argument in his dissent in the *Civil Rights Cases*—that Congress has power under Sections 1 and 5 of the Fourteenth Amendment to protect the civil rights of citizens and therefore to prohibit private discrimination—was unavailing.)

At this juncture came the *Plessy* decision, which limited the protections offered by the Equal Protection Clause even in cases in which state action was present. In upholding a Louisiana statute that ordered railroads to provide "equal but separate accommodations for the white and colored races," Justice Henry Brown, speaking for the *Plessy* majority, declared that the clause guaranteed to blacks political and civil equality but that it could not put them "on the same plane" socially with whites. Social equality could not be legislated, Brown argued, for it stemmed from "natural affinities, a mutual appreciation of each other's merits, and a voluntary consent of individuals." What the plaintiff Plessy sought, the Court believed, was social equality. To Plessy's contention that the enforced separation of the races stamped him with the badge of inferiority, the Court responded that nothing in the Louisiana statute pronounced him to be inferior, and if he and others of his race felt inferior, that was because they had chosen to put that construction upon the statute. At play here, the Court suggested, was a psychological problem, not a legal one:

> [Plessy's] argument necessarily assumes that if, as has been more than once the case, and is not unlikely to be so again, the colored race should become the dominant power in the state legislature, and should enact a law in precisely similar terms, it would thereby relegate the white race to an inferior position. We imagine that the white race, at least, would not acquiesce in this assumption.

Part of this psychological understanding of racial discrimination was subsequently "rejected" in *Brown v. Board of Education* (1954) in which the Court held that the "separate but equal" formula is inherently unequal because it generates feelings of inferiority in members of minority groups. It must be emphasized, however, that not all of the psychological understanding of discrimination present in *Plessy* has been repudiated. Justice Brown's belief that whites cannot be discriminated against because they will not feel stigmatized or inferior has never been overruled and, in fact, has been of decisive importance in sustaining the constitutional validity of, among other things, ameliorative racial preference. In *Regents of the University of California v. Bakke* (1978), for instance, Justice William Brennan offered the following observations in seeking to justify the use of racial quotas by the medical school of the University of California at Davis:

> Nor was Bakke in any sense stamped as inferior by the Medical School's rejection of him. . . . [T]here is absolutely no basis for concluding that Bakke's rejection as a result of Davis's use of racial preference will affect him throughout his life in the same way as the segregation of the Negro school children in *Brown I* would have affected them. Unlike discrimination against racial minorities, the use of race preferences for remedial purposes does not inflict a pervasive injury upon individual whites in the sense that wherever they go or whatever they do there is a

significant likelihood that they will be treated as second-class citizens because of their color.

Justice John Marshall Harlan, as the lone dissenter in *Plessy*, rebutted the majority's contention that if blacks felt that Louisiana's "equal but separate" statute branded them as inferior, it was simply because they had put that construction upon it: "Everyone knows that the statute in question had its origin in the purpose, not so much to exclude white persons from railroad cars occupied by blacks, as to exclude colored people from coaches occupied by or assigned to white persons. . . . No one would be so wanting in candor to assert the contrary." More central to his dissent, however, was his eloquent and now-famous declaration that "our Constitution is color-blind, and neither knows nor tolerates classes among citizens." It has become commonplace to assert that these words were finally vindicated by the Court's unanimous decision in *Brown*.[10] But here, too, the Court's post-*Brown* decisions concerning ameliorative racial preference give pause. The principle that the Constitution is color-blind is considered by many to be unduly simplistic and inappropriate for today's complexities; some observers have argued that, although color blindness may be an appropriate long-term goal, "our society cannot be completely color blind in the short term if we are to have a color blind society in the long term."[11]

In sum, *Plessy* limited the protections of the Equal Protection Clause by legitimating the concept of "equal but separate" (or "separate but equal," as it soon came to be known). Once the principle of racial segregation was in place and constitutionally recognized, it proved difficult to remove. Despite decades of noble effort spearheaded in large part by the National Association for the Advancement of Colored People (NAACP),[12] not until the celebrated *Brown* decision, handed down fifty-eight years later, was "separate but equal" finally rooted out. Efforts to overturn *Plessy* largely were confined to, and ultimately prevailed in, the field of education. Although this focus on segregation in education unquestionably was a wise litigation strategy, as the fraudulent character of the protection afforded by "separate but equal" was nowhere more obvious, it did present a certain irony. In *Plessy* Justice Brown relied heavily on the fact there was racial segregation in the schools of Boston and the District of Columbia to sustain racial segregation in railroad coaches in Louisiana: "The establishment of separate schools for white and colored children . . . has been held to be a valid exercise of the legislative power even by courts of States where the political rights of the colored race have been longest and most earnestly enforced."

The initial attempts to overturn *Plessy* and the "separate but equal" doctrine in education were inauspicious. In *Cumming v. Richmond County Board of Education* (1899), in fact, the plaintiffs found that the Court was willing to tolerate even "separate and unequal." This case arose out of a Georgia school board's decision to discontinue the existing black high school in order to use the building and facilities for black elementary education. Whereas no new black high school was established, the white high schools were continued, and black taxpayers and parents brought suit to restrain the school board from using money to support the white high school until equal facilities for black students had been provided. A unanimous Supreme Court sidestepped the question of segregation, denied that the discontinuance of the black school violated the Equal Protection Clause, and stressed that an injunction to close the white schools was not the proper legal remedy, as it would not help the black children.

The problems of reconciling *Cumming* and its progeny with the demands of equal protection finally prompted the Court in the 1930s to emphasize the need for equality in segregation. "Separate but equal" facilities were to be just that; "separate and unequal" treatment, at least in higher education, would no longer be tolerated. *Missouri ex rel Gaines v. Canada* (1938) is significant in this regard. Missouri had refused to admit blacks to the University of Missouri School of Law, providing instead state reimbursement of tuition fees for any of its black citizens who could gain admission to law schools in neighboring states in which segregation was not enforced. Missouri argued that this provision satisfied the "separate but equal" requirement, but the Supreme Court ruled that if facilities within the state were provided for the legal education of white students, equal facilities for black students also had to be made available in the state.

In subsequent cases, the Court continued to insist on equal educational facilities for blacks pursuing post-baccalaureate studies. The most important of these was *Sweatt v. Painter* (1950), which held, in effect, that if educational facilities were segregated, they had to be equal not only quantitatively but also qualitatively. At issue was a law school for blacks that Texas had hastily established as a means of avoiding the desegregation of the University of Texas Law School. In the view of the Court, even if the black school were equal to the all-white law school "in terms of number of the faculty, variety of courses and opportunity for specialization, size of the student body, scope of the library, and availability of law review and other activities"—which it most assuredly was not—it clearly was unequal with respect to those "qualities which are incapable of objective measurement but which make for greatness in a law school. Such qualities, to name but a few, include reputation of the faculty, experience of the administration, position and influence of the alumni, standing in the community, traditions and prestige." The Court's message in *Sweatt* was plain and blunt: segregation per se was not yet unconstitutional, but the requirements of "separate but equal" henceforth would be all but impossible to meet.

The NAACP prudently had begun its assault on segregated education at the postgraduate and professional level, where the inequalities that black students suffered could be documented most easily. Because only a few blacks were seeking admission to these programs, moreover, the public's reaction to the Court's decisions would be uneventful. The *Missouri* and *Sweatt* decisions, however, paved the way for the NAACP's assault on segregation at all levels of public education, which bore fruit in *Brown*. In that landmark decision, handed down on May 17, 1954, by a unanimous Court, Chief Justice Earl Warren held that "in the field of public education the doctrine of 'separate but equal' has no place." Soon after the decision was rendered, the *New York Times* editorialized that "it is fifty-eight years since the Supreme Court, with Justice Harlan dissenting, established the doctrine of 'separate but equal' provision for the white and Negro races on interstate carriers. It is forty-three years since John Marshall Harlan passed from this earth. Now the words he used in his lonely dissent in an 8-to-1 decision in the case of *Plessy v. Ferguson* in 1896 have become a part of the law of the land." Although noting that *Brown* "dealt solely with segregation in the public schools," the *Times* insisted that "there was not one word in Chief Justice Warren's opinion that was inconsistent with the earlier views of Justice Harlan."[13]

The *Times*'s statement expresses the conventional wisdom that *Brown* realized Justice Harlan's famous dissenting dictum. A closer look at the *Brown* opinion, however, belies this claim. Chief Justice Warren did not invalidate "separate but equal" because it departed from the principle that the Constitution is color-blind; he invalidated it because of the psychological damage it caused blacks. "Separate but equal" is inherently unequal, he insisted, because it "generates feelings of inferiority [in blacks] as to their status in the community that may affect their hearts and minds in a way unlikely ever to be undone"—a conclusion he supported by citations to the literature of social psychology. Accordingly, it can be argued that Chief Justice Warren's opinion had more in common with Justice Brown's majority opinion in *Plessy* than with Justice Harlan's dissent.

Central to both Chief Justice Warren and Justice Brown was the question of the psychological damage caused by segregation; they differed only in the answers they gave, not in the questions they asked. Neither understood the Equal Protection Clause in the way that Justice Harlan did—as a flat prohibition against the use of race as the basis for classifying or categorizing individuals. Contrary to commonly held opinion, then, Justice Harlan's dissenting words—that "our Constitution is color-blind"—have never been vindicated. The Supreme Court has continued to regard the Equal Protection Clause as a means for preventing or mitigating the psychological damage caused by racial discrimination, not as a barrier to race-conscious classifications. Grasping this crucial difference will help avoid misunderstanding the bases for future Court decisions.

In *Bolling v. Sharpe* (1954), a companion case to *Brown,* the Court also invalidated racial segregation in the public schools of the District of Columbia. Because the Equal Protection Clause of the Fourteenth Amendment applies only to the states and not to the federal government, the justices based this decision on the Due Process Clause of the Fifth Amendment. In finding it "unthinkable" that the Constitution could impose a lesser duty on the federal government than on the states, they employed a substantive due-process argument to end this practice. Chief Justice Warren reasoned as follows: "Liberty . . . cannot be restricted except for a proper governmental objective. Segregation in public education is not reasonably related to any proper governmental objective, and thus imposes on Negro children of the District of Columbia a burden that constitutes an arbitrary deprivation of their liberty. . . . " The Court has relied on this same line of argument in subsequent cases to impose the standards of the Equal Protection Clause on national legislation—even though, to repeat, the Fourteenth Amendment is not directed toward the national government.

Brown and its companion cases established the fundamental principle that "racial discrimination in public education is unconstitutional"; they did not, however, address the question of how this fundamental principle was to be implemented. Instead, the Court postponed a decision on the application of *Brown,* restored the case to its docket for argument during the next term, and invited all interested parties to present their views on how its decision could be carried out. These hearings were held in April 1955, and on May 31 of that year the Court ruled in what is commonly called *Brown II* that the cases would be remanded to the courts in which they had originated, which were ordered to fashion decrees of enforcement on equitable principles and with regard to "varied local school problems."[14] The Supreme Court directed the lower courts to determine whether the actions or proposals of the various school authorities constituted "good faith implementation of the governing constitutional principles" and charged them with requiring a "prompt and reasonable start toward full compliance" with *Brown I* and with ensuring that the parties to these cases be admitted to public schools "on a racially non-discriminatory basis with all deliberate speed."[15]

Brown I and *Brown II* were met with stiff resistance throughout the South. The resisters redoubled their efforts after the Court, through a series of *per curiam* orders, extended the desegregation requirement, which originally had been confined to public education, to public recreational facilities, golf courses, bus transportation, public parks, athletic contests, airport restaurants, courtroom seating, public auditoriums, and jails.[16] Resistance took a number of forms, including threatened or actual violence. Major incidents involving violence occurred in Clinton, Tennessee, in 1956; in Little Rock, Arkansas, in 1957; in New Orleans in 1960; and at the University of Mississippi in 1962. On these occasions, the Court was quick to act and unequivocal in its condemnation. In the especially significant case of *Cooper v. Aaron* (1958), the Court unanimously held that the violent resistance to the desegregation plan of the schools of Little Rock was "directly traceable" to Arkansas's governor and legislature and warned that the constitutional prohibition of racial discrimination in school admissions "can neither be nullified openly and directly by state legislators or state executive or judicial officers, nor nullified indirectly by them through evasive schemes for segregation." Then, in extraordinary language, the Court explicitly asserted its supreme authority as constitutional expositor. Declaring that *Marbury v. Madison* established "the basic principle that the federal judiciary is supreme in the exposition of the law of the Constitution, and that [this] principle has ever since been respected by this Court and the Country as a permanent and indispensable feature of our Constitutional system," it held that "it follows that the interpretation of the Fourteenth Amendment enunciated by this Court in the *Brown* case is the Supreme Law of the Land, and Art. VI of the Constitution makes it of binding effect on the States."

More often, resistance took the form of delaying tactics by local school boards that, either on their own initiative or under the compulsion of a federal district court order, were charged with preparing desegregation plans. Even those boards willing to act usually preferred to await a court decision requiring that they act—the better to justify their actions to those in the community opposed to *Brown* and to desegregation. When ordered to act, moreover, the boards often instituted measures that stopped short of actual desegregation. "Freedom of choice" plans, under which each pupil supposedly was free to choose the school to be attended but which in fact resulted in very few transfers out of black schools, represented one such measure. For some time, this foot-dragging proved successful—after all, the Supreme Court had seemingly sanctioned these measures in *Brown II,* as it had not required either the school authorities or the lower courts to take immediate steps to "admit pupils to public schools on a racially nondiscriminatory basis" but had only imposed on them the duty to realize this goal "with all deliberate speed." By 1968, however, the Court's patience had run out, and in *Green v. County School Board of New Kent County,* it announced that school boards had a positive duty to eliminate, "root and branch," the historic and pervasive effects of racial discrimination. This required the formulation of plans that promised prompt conversion to a desegregated system. The goal, the Court underlined, was the achievement of a "unitary, nonracial system of public education." The following year, in *Alexander v. Holmes County Board of Education,* the Court more pointedly declared that the "continued operation of segregated schools under a standard of allowing 'all deliberate speed' for desegregation is no longer constitutionally permissible" and demanded that every district immediately end dual school systems and begin to operate unitary schools alone.

The question of exactly what the Court expected when it ordered the operation of unitary school systems has not yet been resolved definitively, but a review of its subsequent decisions yields some indications. In *Swann v. Charlotte-Mecklenburg Board of Education* (1971), it held that where *de jure* segregation existed in the past, school authorities must dismantle the dual school system by taking positive action to create an integrated school system. Among the measures deemed appropriate for eliminating "all vestiges of state-imposed segregation" were remedial altering of attendance zones, clustering, and busing. The Court acknowledged that these measures "may be administratively awkward, inconvenient, and even bizarre in some situations and may impose burdens on some," but it insisted that during this remedial period such inconveniences were necessary evils. In defending this extraordinary use of the judiciary's equity power, the Court emphasized that "absent a constitutional violation there would be no basis for judicially ordering assignment of students on a racial basis. All things being equal, with no history of discrimination, it might well be desirable to assign pupils to schools nearest their homes. But all things are not equal in a system that has been deliberately constructed and maintained to enforce racial segregation."

Soon thereafter, the Court in *Keyes v. School District No. 1, Denver, Colorado* (1973) brought school desegregation and busing to the northern states. Although *de facto* segregation—or, to use Nathan Glazer's phrase, "racial concentration"[17]—undeniably existed in the Denver schools, neither the city nor the state had ever required racial segregation by law. *Keyes* thus provided the Court with the opportunity to rule on whether such *de facto* segregation was unconstitutional, but the justices avoided this question. Noting that the Denver school authorities, in drawing attendance boundaries, assigning teachers, and locating new schools, had acted and were continuing to support *de facto* segregation in a few of the district's schools, the Court argued that the school district had engaged in *de jure* segregation even in the absence of school segregation laws. In separate concurring opinions, however, Justices William Douglas and Lewis Powell argued that the *de jure/de facto* distinction should be abandoned and that segregation, for whatever reason, should be declared unconstitutional.

The Court continued to sidestep the question of whether *de facto* segregation is constitutionally proscribed in *Columbus Board of Education v. Penick* (1979) and *Dayton Board of Education v. Brinkman* (1979). In these companion cases, a badly split Supreme Court affirmed lower federal court rulings ordering wide-scale busing to achieve racial balance in the public school systems of Columbus and Dayton, Ohio. However, the justices did not hold that *de facto* segregation resulting from housing patterns was unconstitutional; they merely accepted lower-court determinations that at the time that *Brown I* was decided, the public school systems of both cities were officially segregated on the basis of race, not by state law but as a consequence of policies pursued by the cities' boards of education.

The breadth of what the Court majority in *Columbus* and *Dayton* was prepared to recognize as *de jure* segregation effectively obviated any need to clarify the constitutional status of *de facto* segregation. It also raised problems, however. As Justice Potter Stewart objected in his dissent, the Court appeared to reason that "if such an officially authorized segregated school system can be found to have existed in 1954, then any current racial separation in the schools will be presumed to have been caused by acts in violation of the Constitution." However, he continued,

> much has changed in 25 years, in the Nation at large and in Dayton and Columbus in particular. Minds have changed with respect to racial relationships. Perhaps more importantly, generations have changed. The prejudices of these School Boards of 1954 (and earlier) cannot realistically be assumed to haunt the school boards of today. Similarly . . . , school systems have changed. Dayton and Columbus are both examples of the dramatic growth and change in urban school districts. It is unrealistic to assume that the hand of 1954 plays any major part in shaping the current school systems in either city.

Continuing on this same theme, Justice William Rehnquist criticized the Court's finding of *de jure* segregation as running counter to the expectations "that the existence of violations of constitutional rights be carefully and clearly defined before a federal court invades the ambit of local control, and that the subsequent displacement of local authority be limited to that necessary to correct the identified violations." Given the majority's encompassing understanding of *de jure* segregation and the sweep of the remedies it was willing to sustain in the *Columbus* and *Dayton* cases, he speculated that "a school system's only hope of avoiding a judicial receivership might be a voluntary dismantling of its neighborhood school program."

In *Milliken v. Bradley* (1974), the Court addressed the question of whether increasingly black city school districts and largely white suburban school districts should be required, in the words of *Green v. New Kent County* (1968), to consolidate into a "single unitary nonracial system of public education." In *Milliken,* however, a five-member majority rejected massive interdistrict busing as a remedy for the *de jure* segregation found in the Detroit school system. Chief Justice Warren Burger, speaking for the majority, ruled that the federal district court's decree bringing fifty-three suburban school districts into Detroit's desegregation plan was unjustified, because the Court had been shown no evidence of significant violations by these outlying school districts or any interdistrict violations: "To approve the remedy ordered by the court would impose on the outlying districts, not shown to have committed any constitutional violation, a wholly impermissible remedy based on a standard not hinted at in *Brown I* and *II* or any holding of this Court." *Milliken v. Bradley* returned to the Supreme Court again in 1977, and at that time the Court upheld a district court order requiring remedial educational programs as part of its desegregation decrees. *Milliken II* marked the Court's first approval of desegregation remedies that not only involved assignment of students to schools on the basis of race but also pierced the core of educational programs; it involved the federal courts more than ever before in educational policy making.

How much more involved the courts were subsequently to become is apparent in *Missouri v. Jenkins* (1990) and *United States v. Fordice* (1992). In *Jenkins* federal district court judge Russell Clark found that the Kansas City school district and the State of Missouri were guilty of operating a segregated school system and issued an order detailing a desegregation remedy and the financing necessary to implement it. His remedy was comprehensive and extraordinarily expensive. Among other things, he mandated that every high school, every middle school, and half of the elementary schools in the school district become magnet schools; costs for implementing his remedial plan were placed between $500 million and $700 million. Justice Kennedy was later to describe Judge Clark's capital improvement plan as follows:

> High schools in which every classroom will have air conditioning, an alarm system, and 15 microcomputers; a 2,000-square-foot planetarium; greenhouses and vivariums; a 25-acre farm with an air-conditioned meeting room for 104 people; a Model United Nations wired for language translation; broadcast-capable radio and television studios with an editing and animation lab; a temperature-controlled art gallery; movie editing and screening rooms; a 3,500-square-foot, dust-free diesel mechanics room; 1,875-square-foot elementary school animal rooms for use in a Zoo Project; swimming pools; and numerous other facilities.

To pay for this remedy, Judge Clark ordered the State of Missouri to cover 75 percent of the costs, with the school district contributing the rest. When it became clear that state tax-limitation laws prohibited the school district from raising property tax rates sufficiently to meet its 25 percent obligation, he enjoined the operation of these state laws and ordered that the district property tax levy be increased from $2.05 to $4.00 per $100 of assessed valuation. When his decree reached the Supreme Court, it unanimously concluded that Judge Clark had abused his discretion; however, a majority held that he abused it only by specifying the tax levy, not by demanding of the school district that it fully fund his remedy.

In *United States v. Fordice*, the Court addressed the efforts of the State of Mississippi to dismantle the dual university system that its laws once mandated. It overturned the conclusion of both the district court and the court of appeals that the adoption and implementation of race-neutral admission policies were sufficient to demonstrate that Mississippi had completely abandoned its prior dual system. In so doing, it placed in potential jeopardy the continued existence of state-supported "historically black institutions." Justice Thomas, in his concurring opinion, attempted to rule out that prospect: "Although I agree that a State is not constitutionally required to maintain its historically black institutions as such, I do not understand our opinion to hold that a State is forbidden from doing so. It would be ironic, to say the least, if the institutions that sustained blacks during segregation were themselves destroyed in an effort to combat its vestiges."

Three additional cases must also be mentioned in this review of the Court's efforts to clarify what *Alexander v. Holmes* requires, for they reveal the Court's ever-increasing commitment to extricate school districts from ongoing judicial supervision and remedial decrees and to restore to state and local authorities control of their systems. The first is *Pasadena City Board of Education v. Spangler* (1976). In it the Court held in a 6–2 decision that, once the affirmative duty to desegregate has been accomplished (i.e., once a unitary school system has been achieved), school authorities are under no compulsion to readjust attendance zones each year to keep up with population shifts. Reaffirming what it had said in *Swann,* the Court declared that once dual school systems have been dismantled, subsequent changes in the racial composition of particular schools within these systems that are caused solely by shifts in population and in no way by segregatory actions by school officials do not justify further district court reassignment and busing orders.

The second case is *Freeman v. Pitts* (1992), in which the Court unanimously concluded that federal district courts have the authority to relinquish supervision and control over school districts in incremental stages before full compliance with its desegregation order has been achieved in every area of school operations. It therefore allowed the US District Court for the Northern District of Georgia to return to the DeKalb County School System (suburban Atlanta) control over student assignment, transportation, physical facilities, and extracurricular activities (areas in which the school system had demonstrated full compliance) but to retain its supervision over the areas of faculty and administrative assignments and the quality of education (where compliance had not been fully achieved).

The third is *Missouri v. Jenkins* (1995), a follow-up case to the 1990 litigation described above. When minority student achievement levels in the Kansas City school district continued to remain below "national norms" despite court-ordered spending of more than $940 million to eliminate the past effects of racial segregation, Judge Clark ordered Missouri to fund salary increases for virtually all instructional and non-instructional staff of the school district and to continue to fund remedial "quality education" programs. He reasoned that these increases would eliminate the vestiges of state-imposed segregation by improving the "desegregative attractiveness" of the city's schools and by reversing "white flight" to the suburbs. The Supreme Court granted certiorari and reversed, holding that Judge Clark's order was "simply too far removed from an acceptable implementation of a permissible means to remedy previous legally mandated segregation." Chief Justice Rehnquist declared, "Just as demographic changes independent of *de jure* segregation will affect the racial composition of student assignments, so too will numerous external factors beyond the control of the . . . school district and the State affect minority student achievement. So long as these external factors are not the result of segregation, they do not figure in the remedial calculus. Insistence upon academic goals unrelated to the effects of legal segregation unwarrantably postpones the day when the . . . school district will be able to operate on its own." In a lengthy and powerful concurring opinion, Justice Thomas harshly criticized Judge Clark for assuming that if "a school district today is black, it must be educationally inferior" and for exercising his "virtually unlimited equitable powers" to "trample upon principles of federalism and separation of powers" as he pursued "other agendas unrelated to the narrow purpose of precisely remedying a constitutional harm."

PRIVATE DISCRIMINATION AND THE CONCEPT OF STATE ACTION

As noted above, the prohibitions of the Equal Protection Clause are limited to "state action" only. Since the *Civil Rights Cases,* the Court has consistently held that private discriminations are not prohibited by the Fourteenth Amendment; only applicable state laws, it has ruled, can address this problem.[18] In hewing to this principle, the justices have had to address the question of what exactly constitutes "state action." The term obviously comprehends statutes enacted by national, state, or local legislative bodies and official actions of all governmental officers, but difficult problems arise when the conduct of private individuals or groups is challenged as racially discriminatory. In such cases the Court has had to determine whether these private actors are performing a government function or are sufficiently involved with or encouraged by the state so that they, too, should be held to the same constitutional obligations as the states themselves.

The "white primary" cases, which involved a series of ploys by the Southern states to bar blacks from participating in primary elections, reflect how the Court has dealt with cases of governmental function. In *Newberry v. United States* (1921), the justices held that primary elections were "in no real sense part of the manner of holding elections" and thus were not subject to constitutional or congressional control. Many states in the "one-party South," aware that winning the Democratic primary was tantamount to winning the general election, thereupon openly set out to discriminate against black voters in primaries. For example, the Texas Legislature in 1923 passed a law flatly prohibiting blacks from voting in that state's Democratic primaries. When the Supreme Court invalidated this statute in *Nixon v. Herndon* (1927) on the grounds that it was "a direct and obvious infringement" of the Equal Protection Clause, segregationist politicians sought to keep blacks from voting in ways that did not involve state action. Again in Texas, the Democratic Party convention, on its own authority and without any state legislation on the subject, adopted a resolution confining party membership to white citizens. The Court unanimously concluded in *Grovey v. Townsend* (1935) that this action did not violate the Fourteenth Amendment because it had been taken by the party and not by the state; the justices thus endorsed the view that political parties were private clubs, uncontrolled by constitutional limitations on official action, and that the primaries they held constitutionally were not part of the election process. This position was abandoned in *United States v. Classic* (1941), a Louisiana ballot-tampering case in which the Court held that the state's election laws made the primary an "integral part" of the process of electing representatives to Congress and that the Democratic primary was actually "the only stage of the election procedure" in which a voter's choice was of any significance. *Classic* did not directly address the issue of the "white primary," but its implications were clear. After acknowledging that primaries performed a governmental function, the Court could no longer persist in the view that the parties conducting them were unaffected with public responsibilities. When the occasion to rule on "white primaries" presented itself in *Smith v. Allwright* (1944), the Court directly reversed the *Grovey* decision, announced that the Democratic Party was "an agency of the State," and declared that the party's use of the "white primary" constituted state action in violation of the Constitution.

State action can also result from state involvement in or encouragement of private discrimination. *Burton v. Wilmington Parking Authority* (1961) concerned a parking facility owned and operated by an agency of the State of Delaware. To help finance the building, the agency leased some of its space to commercial operations, one of which was a segregated restaurant. A majority of the Court held that because of its location in and relationship to the parking facility, the restaurant had lost its "purely private" character. The relationship between the restaurant and parking facility was mutually beneficial—the former provided the latter with revenue, and the latter provided the former with customers. By failing to require the restaurant to serve all customers, the state, in the words of the Court, had "made itself a party to the refusal of service" and had "elected to place its power, property and prestige behind the admitted discrimination."

The sit-in cases present even more dramatic evidence of how state encouragement of private discrimination can become state action. During the 1960s, civil rights advocates frequently staged sit-ins at variety and drug stores that maintained segregated lunch counters. To protest such discrimination, blacks would take seats at lunch counters and, when refused service, continue to sit there until arrested, typically for breach of the peace or trespass. In a series of sit-in cases, the Court consistently reversed the convictions that resulted from these arrests, often on the ground that the policy of segregation that had led to the sit-ins was governmentally inspired and thus amounted to "state action" in violation of the Equal Protection Clause. In *Peterson v. Greenville* (1963), for example, a city ordinance actually required separation of the races in restaurants. *Lombard v. Louisiana* (1963) featured no such ordinance, but the Court ruled that city officials had coerced the restaurant manager to operate a segregated facility. In *Griffin v. Maryland* (1964), the Court held that an amusement park's exclusion of blacks constituted state action because, to enforce this private policy, the park had employed a deputy sheriff who, although off-duty, wore his badge and purported to exercise his official powers.

A more difficult state-action question, which the Court has never answered fully, is whether state action is entirely a negative concept that prohibits states and their agents from practicing racial discrimination, or whether it is also a positive concept that imposes on the states an affirmative obligation to prevent private racial discrimination. Initially, the Court was content to define equal protection negatively and to view the state-action doctrine as simply prohibiting the states from acting in a discriminatory manner against blacks. Since *Shelley v. Kraemer* (1948), however, the Court has increasingly come to hold that the state must take positive steps to prevent racial discrimination by private parties or to overcome the effects of past discrimination.[19]

In *Shelley* the Court held that judicial enforcement of racially restrictive covenants (i.e., agreements entered into by property owners, binding them not to sell or lease their properties to blacks or other minorities) constituted governmental involvement in racial discrimination and thus amounted to state action. The Court reasoned as follows:

> We have no doubt that there has been state action in these cases in the full and complete sense of the phrase. The undisputed facts disclosed that petitioners were willing purchasers of properties upon which they desired to establish homes. The owners of the properties were willing sellers; and contracts of sale were accordingly consummated. It is clear that but for the active intervention of the state courts, supported by the full panoply of state power, petitioners would have been free to occupy the properties in question without restraint.

The Court thus reached the curious conclusion that a contract might be legally valid but unenforceable in court. It appeared to hold that courts would not enforce private property rights, however legal, that had been exercised in a discriminatory manner, on the ground that court enforcement would constitute discriminatory state action.[20] Because private rights count for little unless they can be legally enforced, the Court here came close to destroying the distinction between private action and state action. As a consequence, *Shelley* provoked the following line of inquiry: could a police officer remove a black trespasser from the private residence of a white if the white concedes that the reason he wants the black removed is personal prejudice against blacks?

The Court continued to expand the concept of state action in *Reitman v. Mulkey* (1967). Voting 5–4, the Court concluded in *Reitman* that California was guilty of violating the Equal Protection Clause because its citizens had ratified an amendment to the California state constitution that repealed a law prohibiting racial discrimination in the sale and rental of private dwellings. In his opinion for the Court, Justice Byron White acknowledged that California itself was not guilty of discrimination. He contended, however, that when the voters of California approved the amendment in question, which nullified existing open-housing laws and provided that property owners had "absolute discretion" to sell or rent to persons of their choice, "the right to discriminate, including the right to discriminate on racial grounds, was embodied in the state's basic charter, immune from legislative, executive or judicial regulation at any level of the state government. Those practicing racial discriminations need no longer rely on their personal choice. They could now evoke express constitutional authority."

According to the *Reitman* ruling, discriminatory private action becomes discriminatory state action if the state takes any action allowing such discrimination. Logically, the next step in this chain of reasoning would be the conclusion that discriminatory private action becomes discriminatory state action if the state fails to prohibit such discrimination. As *Moose Lodge No. 107 v. Irvis* (1972) indicated, however, the Court was not willing to take such a step. In this 6–3 decision, the Court held that discrimination by a private club did not constitute state action simply because the club held a state liquor license. In so doing, the Court reaffirmed Justice Arthur Goldberg's statement in *Bell v. Maryland* (1964) that "rights pertaining to privacy and private association are themselves constitutionally protected liberties," and that included among those rights is the right of a person "to close his home or club to any person . . . on the basis of personal prejudices including race."

In *Palmore v. Sidoti* (1984), however, the Court made it clear that this private racial prejudice cannot be invoked by any instrumentality of government to justify racial classifications. In unanimously holding that the reality of private biases and the possible injury they might inflict on children are not permissible considerations for removal of an infant child from the custody of its natural mother in racially mixed household custody cases, the Court offered one of its clearest statements on the constitutional test it employs in racial discrimination cases: racial "classifications are subject to the most exacting scrutiny; to pass constitutional muster, they must be justified by a compelling governmental interest and must be 'necessary to the accomplishment of its legitimate purpose.'"

RACIAL DISCRIMINATION IN JURY TRIALS

Since *Strauder v. West Virginia* (1880), the Supreme Court has held that racial discrimination by the state in jury selection violates the Equal Protection Clause. In *Strauder*, the Court invalidated a state law that allowed only white men to serve as jurors. In *Swain v. Alabama* (1965), it held that black defendants could challenge on equal-protection grounds a state's exercise of peremptory challenges (the rejection of potential jurors without cause, i.e., without providing a reason) to exclude members of their race from their petit juries. To do so, however, they could not rely simply on the pattern of jury strikes in their own particular cases; rather, they would have to introduce evidence of a systematic exclusion of blacks through the use of peremptories over a period of time. In *Batson v. Kentucky* (1986), the Court relaxed the evidentiary requirements of *Swain* and held that a black defendant could establish a *prima facie* case of purposeful discrimination in the selection of jurors based solely on the prosecutor's exercise of peremptory challenges at the defendant's trial. Justice Powell declared for the *Batson* majority, "The harm from discriminatory jury selection extends beyond that inflicted on the defendant and the excluded juror to touch the entire community. Selection procedures that purposefully exclude black persons from juries undermine public confidence in the fairness of our system of justice." In dissent, Justice Rehnquist argued:

> In my view, there is simply nothing "unequal" about the State using its peremptory challenges to strike blacks from the jury in cases involving black defendants, so long as such challenges are also used to exclude whites in cases involving white defendants, Hispanics in cases involving Hispanic defendants, Asians in cases involving Asian defendants, and so on. This case-specific use of peremptory challenges by the State does not single out blacks, or members of any other race for that matter, for discriminatory treatment. Such use of peremptories is at best based upon

seat-of-the-pants instincts, which are undoubtedly crudely stereotypical and may in many cases be hopelessly mistaken. But as long as they are applied across the board to jurors of all races and nationalities, I do not see—and the Court most certainly has not explained—how their use violates the Equal Protection Clause.

In 1991, the Court carried *Batson* to new heights. In *Powers v. Ohio,* it held that a prosecutor in a trial of a white criminal defendant is prohibited from excluding black jurors on the basis of race; in his dissent, Justice Scalia declared himself "unmoved" by "this white defendant's complaint that he sought to be tried by an all-white jury." And in *Edmonson v. Leesville Concrete Company* (1991), the Court held that even private litigants in civil actions cannot exercise their peremptory challenges in a racially discriminatory manner. Justice Kennedy held for a six-member majority that "when private litigants participate in the selection of jurors, they serve an important function within the government and act with its substantial assistance. If peremptory challenges based on race were permitted, persons could be required by summons to be put at risk of open and public discrimination as a condition of their participation in the justice system. The injury to excluded jurors would be the direct result of governmental delegation and participation." Justice O'Connor objected: "Not everything that happens in a courtroom is state action. A trial, particularly a civil trial, is by design largely a stage on which private parties may act; it is a forum through which they can resolve their disputes in a peaceful and ordered manner. The government erects the platform; it does not thereby become responsible for all that occurs upon it. . . . I believe that a peremptory strike by a private litigant is fundamentally a matter of private choice and not state action."

Once *Batson* and *Edmonson* had established that neither prosecutors nor private litigants in civil cases could use their peremptory challenges in a racially discriminatory manner, the next and only remaining question for the Court concerning peremptory strikes came in *Georgia v. McCollum* (1992). In *McCollum,* the Court had to decide whether defendants in criminal cases were likewise prohibited from engaging in racial discrimination in their use of peremptories. Justice Blackmun held for a seven-member majority that they were.[21] In dissent Justice Scalia commented on the "sheer inanity" of the proposition that "a criminal defendant, in the process of defending himself against the state, is held to be acting on behalf of the state."[22]

RACIAL DISCRIMINATION IN PRISONS

In the 1987 case of *Turner v. Safley,* the Supreme Court considered a claim by Missouri prisoners that regulations restricting inmate marriages and inmate-to-inmate correspondence were unconstitutional. The Court rejected the prisoners' arguments that the regulations should be subject to strict scrutiny; the proper question, the Court insisted, was whether the regulations that burdened the prisoners' fundamental rights were "reasonably related" to "legitimate penological interests." In subsequent cases, the Court has relied on *Turner* in dismissing challenges to prison regulations that have restricted such First Amendment rights as freedom of association and receipt of subscription publications, prisoners' access to the courts, and work rules limiting prisoners' attendance at religious services.

In *Johnson v. California* (2005), the Court confronted a prison regulation dealing not with First Amendment or due-process rights but rather with equal protection. To prevent prison violence caused by racial gangs, the California Department of Corrections racially segregated all male prisoners in double cells for up to sixty days each time they entered a correctional facility as a new prisoner or a transferee. Although acknowledging that the

Court had repeatedly insisted that all racial classifications reviewed under the Equal Protection Clause must be strictly scrutinized, the state defended its policy on the ground that the relaxed standard of review the Court had adopted in *Turner* applied to all circumstances in which the needs of prison administration implicated constitutional rights.

Speaking for the majority in a 6–2 decision, Justice O'Connor rejected California's claim, insisting that use of strict scrutiny to enforce "the Fourteenth Amendment's ban on racial discrimination is not only consistent with proper prison administration, but also bolsters the legitimacy of the entire criminal justice system. Race discrimination is 'especially pernicious in the administration of justice.'" Justice Thomas dissented; he found it strange that the Court would defer to the educational judgment of the University of Michigan Law School's faculty and administrators that there was a need for diversity in their student body but not to the judgment of California prison officials that there was a need to classify temporarily prisoners based on their race in a reception center. "Deference would seem all the more warranted in the prison context, for whatever the Court knows of administering educational institutions, it knows much less about administering penal ones. The potential consequences of second-guessing the judgments of prison administrators are also much more severe."

PROOF OF DISCRIMINATION: DISPARATE TREATMENT VERSUS DISPARATE IMPACT

In the celebrated Civil Rights Act of 1964, Congress prohibited, *inter alia,* racial discrimination in the provision of public accommodations (Title II); in programs and activities receiving federal financial assistance, including educational institutions (Title VI); and in employment "affecting commerce" (Title VII). The Civil Rights Act was filled with language addressing "the equal protection of the laws," and Congress clearly understood the act to ban statutorily disparate treatment based on race in the private sector as the Equal Protection Clause banned it constitutionally in the public sector. Nonetheless, in *Griggs v. Duke Power Company* (1971), the Supreme Court unanimously held that an employer violated Title VII, even in the absence of racially disparate treatment of its employees (i.e., in the absence of a racially discriminatory intention), if the facially neutral criteria on which it based its hiring decisions had a racially disparate impact. It held that the Title VII prohibited an employer from requiring a high school education or the passage of a standardized general intelligence test as a condition of employment in or transfer to jobs when these standards had not been shown to be significantly related to successful job performance and when they operated to disqualify black applicants at a substantially higher rate than white applicants.

Nineteen years later, however, in *Wards Cove Packing Co. v. Atonio* (1990), the Court revisited Title VII and implicitly overturned *Griggs.* Justice White held in a 5–4 decision that *Griggs's* "disparate impact theory," in which "a facially neutral employment practice may be deemed violative of Title VII without evidence of the employer's subjective intent to discriminate," was contrary to the language of the statute and its prohibition only of "disparate treatment." Congress, approving of the Court's construction of Title VII in *Griggs,* took exception to White's opinion and one year later passed the Civil Rights Act of 1991, in which it expressly rejected the Court's interpretation in *Wards Cove* and made it clear that the test for the federal judiciary to apply in cases in which the plaintiffs allege discriminatory employment practices is impact, not intent.

But Congress, when it passed the Civil Rights Act of 1991 requiring the Court to use the "disparate impact" test, did not repeal the language in Title VII of the Civil Rights Act of 1964 prohibiting employers from engaging in "disparate treatment." The two can obviously come into conflict, and they did so in *Ricci v. DeStefano* (2009). In this 5–4 decision, the Court held that when the City of New Haven, Connecticut, rejected the results of examinations for firemen seeking promotion to lieutenant and captain because of the fear of disparate-impact litigation brought by lower-scoring black firemen under the Civil Rights Act of 1991, it had actually engaged in disparate-treatment discrimination against higher-scoring white firemen under Title VII.

NOTES

1. Herbert J. Storing, "Slavery and the Moral Foundations of the American Republic," in *The Moral Foundations of the American Republic,* edited by Robert H. Horwitz (Charlottesville: University Press of Virginia, 1977), 214. The discussion that follows relies heavily on this source.

2. John Hope Franklin, "The Moral Legacy of the Founding Fathers," *University of Chicago Magazine* (Summer 1975): 10–13.

3. Storing, "Slavery and the Moral Foundations of the American Republic," 214.

4. See Thomas Jefferson's draft of the Declaration of Independence in *The Founders' Constitution,* edited by Philip B. Kurland and Ralph Lerner, 5 vols. (Chicago: University of Chicago Press, 1987), 1:523–524.

5. Richard N. Current, ed., *The Political Thought of Abraham Lincoln* (New York: Bobbs-Merrill, 1967), 88–89; emphasis in the original.

6. Frederick Douglass, "Address for the Promotion of Colored Enlistments," July 6, 1863, in *The Life and Writings of Frederick Douglass,* edited by Philip S. Foner (New York: International Publishers, 1950), 3:365.

7. Martin Diamond, *The Founding of the Democratic Republic* (Itasca, IL: F. E. Peacock, 1981), 39.

8. Akhil Reed Amar, *America's Constitution: A Biography* (New York: Random House, 2005), 96–98.

9. Storing, "Slavery and the Moral Foundations of the American Republic," 225.

10. See, for example, Alfred H. Kelly and Winfred A. Harbison, *The American Constitution: Its Origins and Development,* 4th ed. (New York: W. W. Norton, 1970), 916.

11. *Associated General Contractors v. Altshuler* (First Cir., 1973).

12. On the critical role played by the NAACP throughout the entire desegregation process, see Daniel M. Berman, *It Is So Ordered: The Supreme Court Rules on School Segregation* (New York: W. W. Norton, 1966); Clement E. Vose, "Litigation as a Form of Pressure Group Activity," *Annals of the American Academy of Political and Social Science* 319 (September 1958); and Richard Kluger, *Simple Justice: The History of* Brown v. Board of Education *and Black America's Struggle for Equality* (New York: Knopf, 1976).

13. *New York Times,* May 23, 1954, E10.

14. The primary responsibility for implementing *Brown* thus fell on the forty-eight federal district court judges serving in the eleven southern states. Nearly all were southern and shared the views of the white southern establishment, and all were subject to the social pressures of their communities. In addition, many were personally unsympathetic to *Brown*. Not surprisingly, in many cases they moved very slowly in implementing school desegregation plans. The ten judges constituting the federal Courts of Appeal for the Fourth and Fifth Circuits, who were responsible for reviewing the district judges' decisions, were somewhat further removed from the pressures of local situations and hence were able to take a more conscientious view of their obligations to enforce the Supreme Court's rulings. As a consequence, they overturned many district court decisions. See Jack W. Peltason, *Fifty-Eight Lonely Men* (New York: Harcourt, Brace & World, 1961).

15. The Court's implementation decision in *Brown II* has been subjected to harsh criticism. See Lino A. Graglia, *Disaster by Decree: The Supreme Court Decisions on Race and the Schools* (Ithaca, NY: Cornell University Press, 1976), 31–45. The Court's use of the phrase *all deliberate speed* has been particularly criticized. See Louis Lusky, "Racial Discrimination and the Federal Law," *Columbia Law Review* 63 (1963): 1172n37: "Conceptually, the 'deliberate speed' formula is impossible to justify. . . . Judicial review has been founded in the judicial duty to give a litigant his rights under the Constitution. But the apparently successful plaintiff in the *Brown* case got no more than a promise that, some time in the indefinite future, other people would be given the rights which the Court said he had." In short, *Brown II* permitted the black plaintiffs in *Brown I* to be denied any relief from the legal wrongs that they were found to have suffered, provided that steps were taken to protect other blacks, at some later date, from similar wrongs.

16. *Mayor of Baltimore v. Dawson* (1955), *Holmes v. City of Atlanta* (1955), *Gayle v. Browder* (1956),

New Orleans City Park Improvement Association v. Detiege (1958), *State Athletic Cmsn. v. Dorsey* (1959), *Turner v. Memphis* (1962), *Johnson v. Virginia* (1963), and *Lee v. Washington* (1968). These cases simply cited *Brown* as the controlling precedent. Because *Brown* addressed only segregation in public education, the Court opened itself up for a barrage of criticism—and not just from those who mourned the passing of segregation—when it failed to spell out constitutional principles and neglected to provide a reasoned argument against segregation in these other areas of public activity. See Herbert Wechsler, "Toward Neutral Principles of Constitutional Law," *Harvard Law Review* 73 (1959): 1, 22.

17. Nathan Glazer, *Affirmative Discrimination* (New York: Basic Books, 1975), 96.

18. However, recall the discussion in Chapter 7 of Volume I concerning *Jones v. Alfred H. Mayer Company* (1968) and *Runyon v. McCrary* (1976) and Congress's enforcement powers under Section 2 of the Thirteenth Amendment.

19. This transformation of the concept of state action is akin to the transformation of the Sixth Amendment's right to counsel, discussed in Chapter 7 of this volume. Originally, the Court had understood the guarantee of right to counsel in a negative sense (i.e., as prohibiting the federal government from denying to a defendant the right to employ counsel); only quite recently has the Court come to understand this right in a more positive or affirmative sense (i.e., as imposing on the government the duty to provide counsel for those who cannot afford private representation).

20. As Professor Lino Graglia has noted, "*Shelley* has been rightly described as constitutional law's *Finnegans Wake*: no one has ever claimed to understand the Court's reasoning or to think that it made sense. The Court purported to find unconstitutional state action in state-court enforcement of a racially restrictive covenant between private parties, even though the Court would not find and has not found state action in state-court enforcement of other private acts of discrimination. A state may, for example, enforce a will making a bequest contingent upon the beneficiary's marrying a person of a particular religious faith." Graglia, "Judicial Review on the Basis of 'Regime Principles': A Prescription for Government by Judiciary," *South Texas Law Journal* 26 (Fall 1985): 450.

21. See *J. E. B. v. Alabama ex rel. T. B.* (1994), in which the Court held that intentional discrimination on the basis of gender by state actors in the use of peremptory strikes violates the Equal Protection Clause.

22. See, however, *Purkett v. Elem* (1995), in which the Court severely limited *Batson* and its progeny by holding, in a *per curiam* opinion, that a challenge to the use of a peremptory strike as racially motivated can be rebutted by an explanation that is neither persuasive nor even plausible, so long as it is race neutral. "What it means to be a 'legitimate reason' is not a reason that makes sense, but a reason that does not deny equal protection."

SELECTED READINGS

The Federalist, Nos. 42, 54.

Amar, Akhil Reed. *America's Constitution: A Biography*. New York: Random House, 2005.

Berger, Raoul. *Government by Judiciary: The Transformation of the Fourteenth Amendment*. Cambridge, MA: Harvard University Press, 1977.

Bickel, Alexander M. "The Original Understanding and the Segregation Decision." *Harvard Law Review* 69 (1955): 1–65.

Cottrol, Robert J., Raymond T. Diamond, and Leland B. Ware, Brown v. Board of Education: *Caste, Culture, and the Constitution*. Lawrence: University Press of Kansas, 2003.

Dunn, Joshua M., *Complex Justice: The Case of* Missouri v. Jenkins. Chapel Hill: University of North Carolina Press, 2008.

———, and Martin R. West (eds.), *From Schoolhouse to Courthouse: The Judiciary's Role in American Education*. Washington, D.C., Brookings Institution Press, 2009.

Freyer, Tony A. *Little Rock on Trial*: Cooper v. Aaron and School Desegregation. Lawrence: University Press of Kansas, 2007.

Graglia, Lino A. *Disaster by Decree: The Supreme Court Decisions on Race and the Schools*. Ithaca, NY: Cornell University Press, 1976.

———. "*Ricci v. DeStefano*: Even Whites Are a Protected Class in the Roberts Court." *Lewis & Clark Law Review* 16 (Summer 2012): 573–603.

Kennedy, Randall. *Race, Crime, and the Law*. New York: Pantheon Books, 1997.

Klarman, Michael J. Brown v. Board of Education *and the Civil Rights Movement*. New York: Oxford University Press, 2007

Kluger, Richard. *Simple Justice*. New York: Knopf, 1976.

Lofgren, Charles A. *The* Plessy *Case: A Legal-Historical Interpretation*. New York: Oxford University Press, 1986.

Maltz, Earl M. *Fugitive Slave at Trial: The Anthony Burns Case and Abolitionist Outrage.* Lawrence: University Press of Kansas, 2010.

McDowell, Gary L. *Equity and the Constitution: The Supreme Court, Equitable Relief, and Public Policy.* Chicago: University of Chicago Press, 1982.

Peltason, Jack. *Fifty-Eight Lonely Men: Southern Federal Judges and School Desegregation.* New York: Harcourt, Brace & World, 1961.

Pizzi, William T. "*Batson v. Kentucky:* Curing the Disease but Killing the Patient." In *1987 Supreme Court Review,* edited by Philip B. Kurland, Gerhard Casper, and Dennis J. Hutchinson. Chicago: University of Chicago Press, 1988.

Rosenberg, Gerald N. *The Hollow Hope: Can Courts Bring About Social Change?* Chicago: University of Chicago Press, 1991.

Rossum, Ralph A. "*Plessy, Brown,* and the Reverse Discrimination Cases: Consistency and Continuity in Judicial Approach." *American Behavioral Scientist 28* (1985): 785–806.

Strauss, David A. "The Myth of Colorblindness." In *1986 Supreme Court Review,* edited by Philip B. Kurland, Gerhard Casper, and Dennis J. Hutchinson. Chicago: University of Chicago Press, 1987.

TenBroek, Jacobus. *Equal Under Law.* Berkeley: University of California Press, 1965.

Thernstrom, Stephan, and Abigail Thernstrom. *America in Black and White: One Nation, Indivisible.* New York: Simon & Schuster, 1997.

Vose, Clement E. *Caucasians Only: The Supreme Court, the NAACP, and the Restrictive Covenant Cases.* Berkeley: University of California Press, 1959.

Walker, Anders. *The Ghost of Jim Crow: How Southern Moderates used* Brown v. Board Education *to Stall Civil Rights.* New York: Oxford University Press, 2009.

Wiecek, William M. "The Witch at the Christening: Slavery and the Constitution's Origins." In *The Framing and Ratification of the Constitution,* edited by Leonard W. Levy and Dennis J. Mahoney. New York: Macmillan, 1987.

Wolf, Eleanor P. *Trial and Error: The Detroit School Segregation Case.* Detroit: Wayne State University Press, 1981.

Wolters, Raymond. *The Burden of* Brown. Knoxville: University of Tennessee Press, 1984.

Woodward, C. Vann. *The Strange Career of Jim Crow.* New York: Oxford University Press, 1966.

Plessy v. Ferguson
163 U.S. 537 (1896)

An 1890 Louisiana statute required railroads to "provide equal but separate accommodations for the white and colored races." The law made it a criminal offense for any passenger to occupy a "coach or compartment to which by race he does not belong." Plessy, who was seven-eighths white and one-eighth black, refused to relinquish a seat assigned to white passengers. He was imprisoned in the parish jail in New Orleans and charged with violating the statute. During the course of his trial, Plessy petitioned the Louisiana Supreme Court to enjoin the trial judge, John Ferguson, from continuing the proceedings against him. After the court rejected his petition, Plessy brought the case to the US Supreme Court on a writ of error. He claimed that Louisiana's statute violated the guarantees of the Thirteenth and Fourteenth Amendments. Opinion of the Court: <u>Brown</u>, Fuller, Field, Gray, Shiras, White, Peckham. Dissenting opinion: <u>Harlan</u>. Not participating: Brewer.

JUSTICE BROWN delivered the opinion of the Court.

The constitutionality of this act is attacked upon the ground that it conflicts both with the Thirteenth Amendment of the Constitution, abolishing slavery, and the Fourteenth Amendment, which prohibits certain restrictive legislation on the part of the States.

1. That it does not conflict with the Thirteenth Amendment, which abolished slavery and involuntary servitude, except as a punishment for crime, is too clear for argument. Slavery implies involuntary servitude—a state of bondage; the ownership of mankind as a chattel, or at least the control of the labor and services of one man for the benefit of another, and the absence of a legal right to the disposal of his own person, property and services. . . .

A statute which implies merely a legal distinction between the white and colored races—a distinction which is founded in the color of the two races, and which must always exist so long as white men are distinguished from the other race by color—has no tendency to destroy the legal equality of the two races, or reestablish a state of involuntary servitude. Indeed, we do not understand that the Thirteenth Amendment is strenuously relied upon by the plaintiff in error in this connection.

2. By the Fourteenth Amendment, all persons born or naturalized in the United States, and subject to the jurisdiction thereof, are made citizens of the United States and of the State wherein they reside; and the States are forbidden from making or enforcing any law which shall abridge the privileges or immunities of citizens of the United States, or shall deprive any person of life, liberty or property without due process of law, or deny to any person within their jurisdiction the equal protection of the laws.

The proper construction of this amendment was first called to the attention of this court in the *Slaughter-House Cases,* . . . which . . . said generally that its main purpose was to establish the citizenship of the negro, to give definitions of citizenship of the United States and of the States, and to protect from the hostile legislation of the States the privileges and immunities of citizens of the United States, as distinguished from those of citizens of the States.

The object of the amendment was undoubtedly to enforce the absolute equality of the two races before the law, but in the nature of things it could not have been intended to abolish distinctions based upon color, or to enforce social, as distinguished from political equality, or a commingling of the two races upon terms unsatisfactory to either. Laws permitting, and even requiring, their separation in places where they are liable to be brought into contact do not necessarily imply the inferiority of either race to the other, and have been generally, if not universally, recognized as within the competency of the state legislatures in the exercise of their police power. The most common instance of this is connected with the establishment of separate schools for white and colored children, which has been held to be a valid exercise of the legislative power even by courts of States where the political rights of the colored race have been longest and most earnestly enforced.

One of the earliest of these cases is that of *Roberts v. City of Boston* (1849), . . . in which the Supreme Judicial Court of Massachusetts held that the general schools committee of Boston had power to make provision for the instruction of colored children in separate schools established exclusively for them, and to prohibit their attendance upon the other schools. . . . Similar laws have been enacted by Congress under its general power of legislation over the District of Columbia, . . . as well as by the legislatures of many of the States, and have been generally, if not uniformly, sustained by the courts. . . .

So far, then, as a conflict with the Fourteenth Amendment is concerned, the case reduces itself to the question whether the statute of Louisiana is a reasonable regulation, and with respect to this there must necessarily be a large discretion on the part of the legislature. In determining the question of reasonableness, it is at liberty to act with reference to the established usages, customs and traditions of the people, and with a view to the promotion of their comfort, and the preservation of the public peace and good order. Gauged by this standard, we cannot say that a law which authorizes or even requires the separation of the two races in public conveyances is unreasonable, or more obnoxious to the Fourteenth Amendment than the acts of Congress requiring separate schools for colored children in the District of Columbia, the constitutionality of which does not seem to have been questioned, or the corresponding acts of state legislatures.

We consider the underlying fallacy of the plaintiff's argument to consist in the assumption that the enforced separation of the two races stamps the colored race with a badge of inferiority. If this be so, it is not by reason of anything found in the act, but solely because the colored race chooses to put that construction upon it. The argument necessarily assumes that if, as has been more than once the case, and is not unlikely to be so again, the colored race should become the dominant power in the state legislature, and should enact a law in precisely similar terms, it would thereby relegate the white race to an inferior position. We imagine that the white race at least would not acquiesce in this assumption. The argument also assumes that social prejudices may be overcome by legislation, and that equal rights cannot be secured to the negro except by an enforced commingling of the two races. We cannot accept this proposition. If the two races are to meet upon terms of social equality, it must be the result of natural affinities, a mutual appreciation of each other's merits and a voluntary consent of individuals. . . . Legislation is powerless to eradicate racial instincts or to abolish distinctions based upon physical differences, and the attempt to do so can only result in accentuating the difficulties of the present situation. If the civil and political rights of both races be equal, one cannot be inferior to the other civilly or politically. If one race be inferior to the other socially, the Constitution of the United States cannot put them upon the same plane. . . .

The judgment of the court below is, therefore,

Affirmed.

JUSTICE HARLAN, dissenting.

The Thirteenth Amendment does not permit the withholding or the deprivation of any right necessarily inhering in freedom. It not only struck down the institution of slavery as previously existing in the United States, but it prevents the imposition of any burdens or disabilities that constitute badges of slavery or servitude. It decreed universal civil freedom in this country. The court has so adjudged. But that amendment having been found inadequate to the protection of the right of those who had been in slavery, it was followed by the Fourteenth Amendment, which added greatly to the dignity and glory of American citizenship and to the security of personal liberty. . . .

It was said in argument that the statute of Louisiana does not discriminate against either race, but prescribes a rule applicable alike to white and colored citizens. But this argument does not meet the difficulty. Every one knows that the statute in question had its origin in the purpose not so much to exclude white persons from railroad cars occupied by blacks, as to exclude colored people from coaches occupied by or assigned to white persons. Railroad corporations of Louisiana did not make discrimination among whites in the matter of accommodation for travellers. The thing to accomplish was, under the guise of giving equal accommodation for whites and blacks, to compel the latter to keep to themselves while travelling in railroad passenger coaches. No one would be so wanting in candor as to assert the contrary. The fundamental objection, therefore, to the statute is that it interferes with the personal freedom of citizens. "Personal liberty," it has been well said, "consists in the power of locomotion, of changing situation, or removing one's person to whatsoever places one's own inclination may direct, without imprisonment or restraint, unless by due course of law." . . . If a white man and a black man choose to occupy the same public conveyance on a public highway, it is their right to do so, and no government, proceeding alone on grounds of race, can prevent it without infringing the personal liberty of each. . . .

The white race deems itself to be the dominant race in this country. And so it is, in prestige, in achievements, in education, in wealth and in power. So, I doubt not, it will continue to be for all time, if it remains true to its great heritage and holds fast to the principles of constitutional liberty. But in view of the Constitution, in the eye of the law, there is in this country no superior dominant ruling class of citizens. There is no caste here. Our Constitution is color-blind, and neither knows nor tolerates classes among citizens. In respect of civil rights, all citizens are equal before the law. The humblest is the peer of the most powerful. The law regards man as man, and

takes no account of his surroundings or of his color when his civil rights as guaranteed by the supreme law of the land are involved. It is, therefore, to be regretted that this high tribunal, the final expositor of the fundamental law of the land, has reached the conclusion that it is competent for a State to regulate the enjoyment by citizens of their civil rights solely upon the basis of race.

In my opinion, the judgment this day rendered will, in time, prove to be quite as pernicious as the decision made by this tribunal in the *Dred Scott* case. . . . The destinies of the two races, in this country, are indissolubly linked together, and the interests of both require that the common government of all shall not permit the seeds of race hate to be planted under the sanction of law. What can more certainly arouse race hate, what more certainly create and perpetuate a feeling of distrust between these races, than state enactments, which, in fact, proceed on the ground that colored citizens are so inferior and degraded that they cannot be allowed to sit in public coaches occupied by white citizens? That, as all will admit, is the real meaning of such legislation as was enacted in Louisiana . . .

The arbitrary separation of citizens, on the basis of race, while they are on a public highway, is a badge of servitude wholly inconsistent with the civil freedom and the equality before the law established by the Constitution. It cannot be justified upon any legal grounds. . . .

Brown v. Board of Education
347 U.S. 483 (1954)

The facts in this landmark case are set out in the opinion. Opinion of the Court: <u>Warren</u>, Black, Reed, Frankfurter, Douglas, Jackson, Burton, Clark, Minton.

THE CHIEF JUSTICE delivered the opinion of the Court.

These cases come to us from the States of Kansas, South Carolina, Virginia, and Delaware. They are premised on different facts and different local conditions, but a common legal question justifies their consideration together in this consolidated opinion.

In each of the cases, minors of the Negro race, through their legal representatives, seek the aid of the courts in obtaining admission to the public schools of their community on a nonsegregated basis. In each instance, they have been denied admission to schools attended by white children under laws requiring or permitting segregation according to race. This segregation was alleged to deprive the plaintiffs of the equal protection of the laws under the Fourteenth Amendment. In each of the cases other than the Delaware case, a three-judge federal district court denied relief to the plaintiffs on the so-called "separate but equal" doctrine announced by this Court in *Plessy v. Ferguson.* . . . Under that doctrine, equality of treatment is accorded when the races are provided substantially equal facilities, even though these facilities be separate. In the Delaware case, the Supreme Court of Delaware adhered to that doctrine, but ordered that the plaintiffs be admitted to the white schools because of their superiority to the Negro schools.

The plaintiffs contend that segregated public schools are not "equal" and cannot be made "equal," and that hence they are deprived of the equal protection of the laws. Because of the obvious importance of the question presented, the Court took jurisdiction. Argument was heard in the 1952 Term, and reargument was heard this Term on certain questions propounded by the Court.

Reargument was largely devoted to the circumstances surrounding the adoption of the Fourteenth Amendment in 1868. It covered exhaustively consideration of the Amendment in Congress, ratification by the states, then existing practices in racial segregation, and the views of proponents and opponents of the Amendment. This discussion and our own investigation convince us that, although these sources cast some light, it is not enough to resolve the problem with which we are faced. At best, they are inconclusive. The most avid proponents of the post-War Amendments undoubtedly intended them to remove all legal distinctions among "all persons born or naturalized in the United States." Their opponents, just as certainly, were antagonistic to both the letter and the spirit of the Amendments and wished them to have the most limited effect. What others in Congress and the state legislatures had in mind cannot be determined with any degree of certainty.

An additional reason for the inconclusive nature of the Amendment's history, with respect to segregated schools, is the status of public education at that time. In the South, the movement toward free common schools, supported by general taxation, had not yet taken hold. Education of white children was largely in the hands of private groups. Education of Negroes was almost nonexistent, and practically all of the race were illiterate. In fact, any education

of Negroes was forbidden by law in some states. Today, in contrast, many Negroes have achieved outstanding success in the arts and sciences as well as in the business and professional world. It is true that public school education at the time of the Amendment had advanced further in the North, but the effect of the Amendment on Northern States was generally ignored in the congressional debates. Even in the North, the conditions of public education did not approximate those existing today. The curriculum was usually rudimentary; ungraded schools were common in rural areas; the school term was but three months a year in many states; and compulsory school attendance was virtually unknown. As a consequence, it is not surprising that there should be so little in the history of the Fourteenth Amendment relating to its intended effect on public education.

In the first cases in this Court construing the Fourteenth Amendment, decided shortly after its adoption, the Court interpreted it as proscribing all state-imposed discriminations against the Negro race.[*] The doctrine of "separate but equal" did not make its appearance in this Court until 1896 in the case of *Plessy v. Ferguson,* . . . involving not education but transportation. American courts have since labored with the doctrine for over half a century. In this Court, there have been six cases involving the "separate but equal" doctrine in the field of public education. In *Cumming v. Board of Education*

---

[*]*Slaughter-House Cases* (1873); *Strauder v. West Virginia* (1880): "It ordains that no State shall deprive any person of life, liberty, or property, without due process of law, or deny to any person within its jurisdiction the equal protection of the laws. What is this but declaring that the law in the States shall be the same for the black as for the white; that all persons, whether colored or white, shall stand equal before the laws of the States, and, in regard to the colored race, for whose protection the amendment was primarily designed, that no discrimination shall be made against them by law because of their color? The words of the amendment, it is true, are prohibitory, but they contain a necessary implication of a positive immunity, or right, most valuable to the colored race, the right to exemption from unfriendly legislation against them distinctively as colored, exemption from legal discriminations, implying inferiority in civil society, lessening the security of their enjoyment of the rights which others enjoy, and discriminations which are steps towards reducing them to the condition of a subject race." See also *Virginia v. Rives* (1880); *Ex parte Virginia* (1880).

of Richmond County (1899) . . . and *Gong Lum v. Rice* (1927) the validity of the doctrine itself was not challenged. In more recent cases, all on the graduate school level, inequality was found in that specific benefits enjoyed by white students were denied to Negro students of the same educational qualifications. . . . In none of these cases was it necessary to re-examine the doctrine to grant relief to the Negro plaintiff. And in *Sweatt v. Painter,* . . . the Court expressly reserved decision on the question whether *Plessy v. Ferguson* should be held inapplicable to public education.

In the instant cases, that question is directly presented. Here, unlike *Sweatt v. Painter,* there are findings below that the Negro and white schools involved have been equalized, or are being equalized, with respect to buildings, curricula, qualifications and salaries of teachers, and other "tangible" factors. Our decision, therefore, cannot turn on merely a comparison of these tangible factors in the Negro and white schools involved in each of the cases. We must look instead to the effect of segregation itself on public education.

In approaching this problem, we cannot turn the clock back to 1868 when the Amendment was adopted, or even to 1896 when *Plessy v. Ferguson* was written. We must consider public education in the light of its full development and its present place in American life throughout the Nation. Only in this way can it be determined if segregation in public schools deprives these plaintiffs of the equal protection of the laws.

Today, education is perhaps the most important function of state and local governments. Compulsory school attendance laws and the great expenditures for education both demonstrate our recognition of the importance of education to our democratic society. It is required in the performance of our most basic public responsibilities, even service in the armed forces. It is the very foundation of good citizenship.

Today it is a principal instrument in awakening the child to cultural values, in preparing him for later professional training, and in helping him to adjust normally to his environment. In these days, it is doubtful that any child may reasonably be expected to succeed in life if he is denied the opportunity of an education. Such an opportunity, where the state has undertaken to provide it, is a right which must be made available to all on equal terms.

We come then to the question presented: Does segregation of children in public schools solely on the basis of race, even though the physical facilities and other "tangible" factors may be equal, deprive the children of the minority group of equal educational opportunities? We believe that it does.

In *Sweatt v. Painter* (1950), . . . , in finding that a segregated law school for Negroes could not provide them equal educational opportunities, this Court relied in large part on "those qualities which are incapable of objective measurement but which make for greatness in a law school." In *McLaurin v. Oklahoma State Regents* (1950), . . . the Court, in requiring that a Negro admitted to a white graduate school be treated like all other students, again resorted to intangible considerations: " . . . his ability to study, to engage in discussions and exchange views with other students, and, in general, to learn his profession." Such considerations apply with added force to children in grade and high schools. To separate them from others of similar age and qualifications solely because of their race generates a feeling of inferiority as to their status in the community that may affect their hearts and minds in a way unlikely ever to be undone. The effect of this separation on their educational opportunities was well stated by a finding in the Kansas case by a court which nevertheless felt compelled to rule against the Negro plaintiffs:

> Segregation of white and colored children in public schools has a detrimental effect upon the colored children. The impact is greater when it has the sanction of the law; for the policy of separating the races is usually interpreted as denoting the inferiority of the negro group. A sense of inferiority affects motivation of a child to learn. Segregation with the sanction of law, therefore, has a tendency to retard the education and mental development of negro children and to deprive them of some of the benefits they would receive in a racially integrated school system.

Whatever may have been the extent of psychological knowledge at the time of *Plessy v. Ferguson*, this finding is amply supported by modern authority.* Any language in *Plessy v. Ferguson* contrary to this finding is rejected.

We conclude that in the field of public education the doctrine of "separate but equal" has no place. Separate educational facilities are inherently unequal. Therefore, we hold that the plaintiffs and others similarly situated for whom the actions have been brought are, by reason of the segregation complained of, deprived of the equal protection of the laws guaranteed by the Fourteenth Amendment. This disposition makes unnecessary any discussion whether such segregation also violates the Due Process Clause of the Fourteenth Amendment.

Because these are class actions, because of the wide applicability of this decision, and because of the great variety of local conditions, the formulation of decrees in these cases presents problems of considerable complexity. On reargument, the consideration of appropriate relief was necessarily subordinated to the primary question—the constitutionality of segregation in public education. We have now announced that such segregation is a denial of the equal protection of the laws. In order that we may have the full assistance of the parties in formulating decrees, the cases will be restored to the docket, and the parties are requested to present further argument on Questions 4 and 5 previously propounded by the Court for the reargument this Term.* The Attorney General of the United States is invited to participate. The Attorneys General of the States requiring or permitting segregation in public education will also be permitted to appear as *amici curiae* upon request to do so by September 15, 1954, and submission of briefs by October 1, 1954. . . .

---

*K. B. Clark, *Effect of Prejudice and Discrimination on Personality Development* (Midcentury White House Conference on Children and Youth, 1950); Witmer and Kotinsky, *Personality in the Making* (1952), c. VI; Deutscher and Chein, The Psychological Effects of Enforced Segregation: A Survey of Social Science Opinion, 26 *J. Psychol.* 259 (1948); Chein, What are the Psychological Effects of Segregation Under Conditions of Equal Facilities?, 3 *Int. J. Opinion and Attitude Res.* 229 (1949); Brameld, Educational Costs, in *Discrimination and National Welfare* (McIver, ed., 1949), 44–48; Frazier, *The Negro in the United States* (1949), 674–81. And see generally Myrdal, *An American Dilemma* (1944).

---

*"4. Assuming it is decided that segregation in public schools violates the Fourteenth Amendment

"(a) would a decree necessarily follow providing that, within the limits set by normal geographic school districting, Negro children should forthwith be admitted to schools of their choice, or

"(b) may this Court, in the exercise of its equity powers, permit an effective gradual adjustment to be brought about from existing segregated systems to a system not based on color distinctions?"

Bolling v. Sharpe
347 U.S. 497 (1954)

In this companion case to Brown v. Board of Education, *the Supreme Court reviewed the validity of segregation in the public schools of the District of Columbia.* Opinion of the Court: <u>Warren</u>, Black, Reed, Frankfurter, Douglas, Jackson, Burton, Clark, Minton.

THE CHIEF JUSTICE delivered the opinion of the Court.

This case challenges the validity of segregation in the public schools of the District of Columbia. The petitioners, minors of the Negro race, allege that such segregation deprives them of due process of law under the Fifth Amendment. They were refused admission to a public school attended by white children solely because of their race. They sought the aid of the District Court for the District of Columbia in obtaining admission. That court dismissed their complaint. We granted a writ of certiorari before judgment in the Court of Appeals because of the importance of the constitutional question presented. . . .

We have this day held that the Equal Protection Clause of the Fourteenth Amendment prohibits the states from maintaining racially segregated public schools. The legal problem in the District of Columbia is somewhat different, however. The Fifth Amendment, which is applicable in the District of Columbia, does not contain an equal protection clause as does the Fourteenth Amendment, which applies only to the states. But the concepts of equal protection and due process, both stemming from our American ideal of fairness, are not mutually exclusive. The "equal protection of the laws" is a more implicit safeguard of prohibited unfairness than "due process of law," and, therefore, we do not imply that the two are always interchangeable phrases. But, as this Court has recognized, discrimination may be so unjustifiable as to be violative of due process.

Classifications based solely upon race must be scrutinized with particular care, since they are contrary to our traditions and hence constitutionally suspect. As long ago as 1896, this Court declared the principle "that the Constitution of the United States, in its present form, forbids, so far as civil and political rights are concerned, discrimination by the General Government, or by the States, against any citizen because of his race." And in *Buchanan v. Warley* (1917), . . . the Court held that a statute which limited the right of a property owner to convey his property to a person of another race was, as an unreasonable discrimination, a denial of due process of law.

Although the Court has not assumed to define "liberty" with any great precision, that term is not confined to mere freedom from bodily restraint. Liberty under law extends to the full range of conduct which the individual is free to pursue, and it cannot be restricted except for a proper governmental objective. Segregation in public education is not reasonably related to any proper governmental objective, and thus it imposes on Negro children of the District of Columbia a burden that constitutes an arbitrary deprivation of their liberty in violation of the Due Process Clause.

In view of our decision that the Constitution prohibits the states from maintaining racially segregated public schools, it would be unthinkable that the same constitution would impose a lesser duty on the Federal Government. We hold that racial segregation in the public schools of the District of Columbia is a denial of the due process of law guaranteed by the Fifth Amendment to the Constitution.

For the reasons set out in *Brown v. Board of Education*, this case will be restored to the docket for reargument on Questions 4 and 5 previously propounded by the Court. . . .

Brown v. Board of Education
349 U.S. 294 (1955)

In this 1955 decision, often referred to as Brown II, *the Supreme Court dealt with the question of how its decision in* Brown I *was to be implemented.* Opinion of the Court: <u>Warren</u>, Black, Reed, Frankfurter, Douglas, Burton, Clark, Minton, Harlan.

THE CHIEF JUSTICE delivered the opinion of the Court.

These cases were decided on May 17, 1954. The opinions of that date, declaring the fundamental principle that racial discrimination in public education is unconstitutional, are incorporated herein by reference. All provisions of federal, state, or local law requiring or permitting such discrimination must yield to this principle. There remains for consideration the manner in which relief is to be accorded. . . .

Full implementation of these constitutional principles may require solution of varied local school problems. School authorities have the primary responsibility for elucidating, assessing, and solving these problems; courts will have to consider whether the action of school authorities constitutes good faith implementation of the governing constitutional principles. Because of their proximity to local conditions and the possible need for further hearing, the courts which originally heard these cases can best perform this judicial appraisal. Accordingly, we believe it appropriate to remand the cases to those courts.

In fashioning and effectuating the decrees, the courts will be guided by equitable principles. Traditionally, equity has been characterized by a practical flexibility in shaping its remedies and by a facility for adjusting and reconciling public and private needs. These cases call for the exercise of these traditional attributes of equity power. At stake is the personal interest of the plaintiffs in admission to public schools as soon as practicable on a nondiscriminatory basis. To effectuate this interest may call for elimination of a variety of obstacles in making the transition to school systems operated in accordance with the constitutional principles set forth in our May 17, 1954, decision. Courts of equity may properly take into account the public interest in the elimination of such obstacles in a systematic and effective manner. But it should go without saying that the vitality of these constitutional principles cannot be allowed to yield simply because of disagreement with them.

While giving weight to these public and private considerations, the courts will require that the defendants make a prompt and reasonable start toward full compliance with our May 17, 1954, ruling. Once such a start has been made, the courts may find that additional time is necessary to carry out the ruling in an effective manner. The burden rests upon the defendants to establish that such time is necessary in the public interest and is consistent with good faith compliance at the earliest practicable date. To that end, the courts may consider problems related to administration, arising from the physical condition of the school plant, the school transportation system, personnel, revision of school districts and attendance areas into compact units to achieve a system of determining admission to the public schools on a nonracial basis, and revision of local laws and regulations which may be necessary in solving the foregoing problems. They will also consider the adequacy of any plans the defendants may propose to meet these problems and to effectuate a transition to a racially nondiscriminatory school system. During this period of transition, the courts will retain jurisdiction of these cases. . . .

. . . The cases . . . are remanded to the district courts to take such proceedings and enter such orders and decrees consistent with this opinion as are necessary and proper to admit to public schools on a racially nondiscriminatory basis with all deliberate speed the parties to these cases.

Swann v. Charlotte-Mecklenburg Board of Education
402 U.S. 1 (1971)

Under a school desegregation plan approved by a federal district court in 1965 for the Charlotte-Mecklenburg County school system (the student population at the time was 71 percent white and 29 percent black), nearly two-thirds of the system's black students attended schools that were at least 99 percent black. Following the Supreme Court's decision in Green v. School District of New Kent County *(1968), which charged school districts with an "affirmative duty" to take whatever steps might be necessary to eliminate all vestiges of a dual school system and establish in its place "a unitary system in which racial discrimination would be eliminated root and branch," John Swann and other petitioners entered federal district court and sought further desegregation of the Charlotte-Mecklenburg system. As a result, the district court ordered the school board in 1969 to provide a plan for faculty and student desegregation. Finding the board's submission unsatisfactory, the court ap-pointed a desegregation expert, Dr. John Finger, to submit a desegregation plan. In 1970, the court adopted a modified version of the board's plan for the faculty and for the junior and senior high schools and the Finger plan for the elementary schools. The school board appealed to the Court of Appeals for the Fourth Circuit, where that part of the district court's orders relating to the faculty and secondary schools was affirmed but that part relating to the elementary schools was vacated. In the estimation of the Fourth Circuit, the Finger plan would have unreasonably burdened elementary school pupils and the board. After further court proceedings and consideration of additional desegregation plans, the district court again ordered that the Finger plan be put into effect. Both parties petitioned the Supreme Court for a writ of certiorari.* Opinion of the Court: <u>Burger</u>, Black, Douglas, Harlan, Brennan, Stewart, White, Marshall, Blackmun.

THE CHIEF JUSTICE delivered the opinion of the Court.

We granted *certiorari* in this case to review important issues as to the duties of school authorities and the scope of powers of federal courts under this Court's mandates to eliminate racially separate public schools established and maintained by state action. . . .

This case and those argued with it arose in states having a long history of maintaining two sets of schools in a single school system deliberately operated to carry out a governmental policy to separate pupils in schools solely on the basis of race. That was what *Brown v. Board of Education* was all about. These cases present us with the problem of defining in more precise terms than heretofore the scope of the duty of school authorities and district courts in implementing *Brown I* and the mandate to eliminate dual systems and establish unitary systems at once. . . .

The problems encountered by the district courts and courts of appeal make plain that we should now try to amplify guidelines, however incomplete and imperfect, for the assistance of school authorities and courts. . . .

The objective today remains to eliminate from the public schools all vestiges of state-imposed segregation. . . . If school authorities fail in their affirmative obligations under [our earlier] holdings, judicial authority may be invoked. Once a right and a violation have been shown, the scope of a district court's equitable powers to remedy past wrongs is broad, for breadth and flexibility are inherent in equitable remedies. . . . In seeking to define even in broad and general terms how far this remedial power extends it is important to remember that judicial powers may be exercised only on the basis of a constitutional violation. . . . Judicial authority enters only when local authority defaults.

The central issue in this case is that of student assignment, and there are essentially four problem areas. . . .

(1) RACIAL BALANCES OR RACIAL QUOTAS

We do not reach in this case the question whether a showing that school segregation is a consequence of other types of state action, without any discriminatory action by the school authorities, is a constitutional violation requiring remedial action by a school desegregation decree.

This case does not present that question and we therefore do not decide it. . . . In this case it is urged that the District Court has imposed a racial balance requirement of 71%–29% on individual schools. The fact that no such objective was actually achieved—and would appear to be impossible—tends to blunt that claim, yet in the opinion and order of the District Court . . . we find that court directing: "that efforts should be made to reach a 71–29 ratio in the various schools so that there will be no basis for contending that one school is racially different from the others. . . . "

The District Judge went on to acknowledge that variation "from that norm may be unavoidable." This contains intimations that the "norm" is a fixed mathematical racial balance reflecting the pupil constituency of the system. If we were to read the holding of the District Court to require, as a matter of substantive constitutional right, any particular degree of racial balance or mixing, that approach would be disapproved and we would be obliged to reverse. The constitutional command to desegregate schools does not mean that every school in every community must always reflect the racial composition of the school system as a whole. . . .

Awareness of the racial composition of the whole school system is likely to be a useful starting point in shaping a remedy to correct past constitutional violations. In sum, the very limited use made of mathematical ratios was within the equitable remedial discretion of the District Court.

(2) ONE-RACE SCHOOLS

The record in this case reveals that familiar phenomenon that in metropolitan areas minority groups are often found concentrated in one part of the city. . . . Schools all or predominately of one race in a district of mixed population will require close scrutiny to determine that school assignments are not part of state-enforced segregation.

In light of the above, it should be clear that the existence of some small number of one-race, or virtually one-race, schools within a district is not in and of itself the mark of a system which still practices segregation by law. . . .

The court should scrutinize such schools, and the burden upon the school authorities will be to satisfy the court that their racial composition is not the result of present or past discriminatory action on their part. . . .

(3) REMEDIAL ALTERING OF ATTENDANCE ZONES

The maps submitted in these cases graphically demonstrate that one of the principal tools employed by school planners and by courts to break up the dual school system has been a frank—and sometimes drastic—gerrymandering of school districts and attendance zones. An additional step was pairing, "clustering," or "grouping" of schools with attendance assignments made deliberately to accomplish the transfer of Negro students out of formerly segregated Negro schools and transfer of white students to formerly all-Negro schools. More often than not, these zones are neither compact nor contiguous; indeed they may be on opposite ends of the city. As an interim corrective measure, this cannot be said to be beyond the broad remedial powers of a court.

Absent a constitutional violation there would be no basis for judicially ordering assignment of students on a racial basis. All things being equal, with no history of discrimination, it might well be desirable to assign pupils to schools nearest their homes. But all things are not equal in a system that has been deliberately constructed and maintained to enforce racial segregation. The remedy for such segregation may be administratively awkward, inconvenient, and even bizarre in some situations and may impose burdens on some; but all awkwardness and inconvenience cannot be avoided in the interim period when remedial adjustments are being made to eliminate the dual school systems.

No fixed or even substantially fixed guidelines can be established as to how far a court can go, but it must be recognized that there are limits. The objective is to dismantle the dual school system. "Racially neutral" assignment plans proposed by school authorities to a district court may be inadequate; such plans may

fail to counteract the continuing effects of past school segregation resulting from discriminatory location of school sites or distortion of school size in order to achieve or maintain an artificial racial separation. When school authorities present a district court with a "loaded game board," affirmative action in the form of remedial altering of attendance zones is proper to achieve truly nondiscriminatory assignments. . . . We hold that the pairing and grouping of noncontiguous school zones is a permissible tool and such action is to be considered in light of the objectives sought. . . .

(4) TRANSPORTATION OF STUDENTS

The scope of permissible transportation of students as an implement of a remedial decree has never been defined by this Court and by the very nature of the problem it cannot be defined with precision. No rigid guidelines as to student transportation can be given for application to the infinite variety of problems presented in thousands of situations. . . . The District Court's conclusion that assignment of children to the school nearest their home serving their grade would not produce an effective dismantling of the dual system is supported by the record.

Thus the remedial techniques used in the District Court's order were within that court's power to provide equitable relief; implementation of the decree is well within the capacity of the school authority.

The decree provided that the buses used to implement the plan would operate on direct routes. . . . The trips for elementary school pupils average about seven miles and the District Court found that they would take "not over 35 minutes at the most." This system compares favorably with the transportation plan previously operated in Charlotte under which each day 23,600 students on all grade levels were transported an average of 15 miles one way for an average trip requiring over an hour. In these circumstances, we find no basis for holding that the local school authorities may not be required to employ bus transportation as one tool of school desegregation. Desegregation plans cannot be limited to the walk-in school.

An objection to transportation of students may have validity when the time or distance of travel is so great as to risk either the health of the children or significantly impinge on the educational process. District courts must weigh the soundness of any transportation plan in light of what is said in subdivisions (1), (2), and (3) above. . . .

On the facts of this case, we are unable to conclude that the order of the District Court is not reasonable, feasible and workable. . . .

It does not follow that the communities served by such systems will remain demographically stable, for in a growing, mobile society, few will do so. Neither school authorities nor district courts are constitutionally required to make year-by-year adjustments of the racial composition of student bodies once the affirmative duty to desegregate has been accomplished and racial discrimination through official action is eliminated from the system. This does not mean that federal courts are without power to deal with future problems, but in the absence of a showing that either the school authorities or some other agency of the State has deliberately attempted to fix or alter demographic patterns to affect the racial composition of the schools, further intervention by a district court should not be necessary.

United States v. Fordice
505 U.S. 717 (1992)

Prior to the Supreme Court's decision in Brown v. Board of Education *(1954), the State of Mississippi operated five universities exclusively for whites (the University of Mississippi, Mississippi State University, Mississippi University for Women, the University of Southern Mississippi, and Delta State University) and three exclusively for blacks (Alcorn State University, Jackson State University, and Mississippi Valley State University). After* Brown, *Mississippi continued its policy of* de jure *segregation in its public university system, maintaining five almost completely white and three almost completely black institutions. Private petitioners initiated litigation in US District Court in 1975, and the US government intervened, charging that state officials had failed to satisfy their obligations under the Equal Protection Clause of the Fourteenth Amendment and Title VI of the Civil Rights Act of 1964 to dismantle the dual system.*

In an attempt to resolve the suit without going to trial through "voluntary dismantlement," the State Board of Trustees in 1981 issued "Mission Statements" for the eight institutions that (1) classified three white institutions (the University of Mississippi, Mississippi State, and Southern Mississippi) as "comprehensive" universities having the most varied degree programs and offering doctoral degrees; (2) redesignated one of the black institutions (Jackson State) as an "urban" university with limited research and degree functions geared toward its urban setting; and (3) characterized the rest as "regional" institutions providing primarily undergraduate education.

Despite these efforts, by the mid-1980s, more than 99 percent of Mississippi's white university students were still enrolled at the state's five historically white institutions. Moreover, the student bodies at these universities also remained predominantly white, averaging between 80 and 91 percent white students. Seventy-one percent of the state's black students continued to attend the three historically black institutions, where the racial composition ranged from 92 to 99 percent black. The suit proceeded to trial, where after voluminous evidence was presented on a full range of educational issues, the district court entered extensive findings of fact on, among other things, admission requirements, institutional classification and mission assignments, duplication of programs, and funding. It concluded, based on its reading of Bazemore v. Friday *(1986), that the affirmative duty of a state to desegregate its institutions of higher education does not include the obligation to restrict student choice or to achieve racial balance. The district court held only that state policies and practices must be racially neutral, be developed and implemented in good faith, and not contribute substantially to the racial identifiability of individual institutions. Employing this test, it concluded that Mississippi had demonstrated conclusively that it was fulfilling its affirmative duty to disestablish its formerly segregated system. The Court of Appeals for the Fifth*

Circuit affirmed, and the Supreme Court granted the writ of certiorari filed by the United States and the private petitioners. Opinion of the Court: White, Rehnquist, Blackmun, Stevens, O'Connor, Kennedy, Thomas, Souter. Concurring opinions: O'Connor; Thomas. Concurring in the judgment and dissenting in part: Scalia.

JUSTICE WHITE delivered the opinion of the Court.

In 1954, this Court held that the concept of "'separate but equal'" has no place in the field of public education. *Brown v. Board of Education (Brown I)* (1954). The following year, the Court ordered an end to segregated public education "with all deliberate speed." *Brown v. Board of Education (Brown II)* (1955). Since these decisions, the Court has had many occasions to evaluate whether a public school district has met its affirmative obligation to dismantle its prior *de jure* segregated system in elementary and secondary schools. In this case we decide what standards to apply in determining whether the State of Mississippi has met this obligation in the university context. . . .

The District Court, the Court of Appeals, and respondents recognize and acknowledge that the State of Mississippi had the constitutional duty to dismantle the dual school system that its laws once mandated. Nor is there any dispute that this obligation applies to its higher education system. If the State has not discharged this duty, it remains in violation of the Fourteenth Amendment. *Brown v. Board of Education* and its progeny clearly mandate this observation. Thus, the primary issue in this case is whether the State has met its affirmative duty to dismantle its prior dual university system.

Our decisions establish that a State does not discharge its constitutional obligations until it eradicates policies and practices traceable to its prior *de jure* dual system that continue to foster segregation.

The Court of Appeals concluded that the State had fulfilled its affirmative obligation to disestablish its prior *de jure* segregated system by adopting and implementing race-neutral policies governing its college and university system. Because students seeking higher education had "real freedom" to choose the institution of their choice, the State need do no more. Even though neutral policies and free choice were not enough to dismantle a dual system of primary or secondary schools, *Green v. New Kent County School Board,* the Court of Appeals thought that universities "differ in character fundamentally" from lower levels of schools sufficiently so that our decision in *Bazemore v. Friday* justified the conclusion that the State had dismantled its former dual system.

Like the United States, we do not disagree with the Court of Appeals' observation that a state university system is quite different in very relevant respects from primary and secondary schools. Unlike attendance at the lower level schools, a student's decision to seek higher education has been a matter of choice. The State historically has not assigned university students to a particular institution. Moreover, like public universities throughout the country, Mississippi's institutions of higher learning are not fungible—they have been designated to perform certain missions. Students who qualify for admission enjoy a range of choices of which institution to attend. Thus, as the Court of Appeals stated, "[i]t hardly needs mention that remedies common to public school desegregation, such as pupil assignments, busing, attendance quotas, and zoning, are unavailable when persons may freely choose whether to pursue an advanced education and, when the choice is made, which of several universities to attend."

We do not agree with the Court of Appeals or the District Court, however, that the adoption and implementation of race-neutral policies alone suffice to demonstrate that the State has completely abandoned its prior dual system. That college attendance is by choice and not by assignment does not mean that a race-neutral admissions policy cures the constitutional violation of a dual system. In a system based on choice, student attendance is determined not simply by admissions policies, but also by many other factors. Although some of these factors clearly cannot be attributed to State policies, many can be. Thus, even after a State dismantles its segregative *admissions* policy, there may still be state action that is traceable to the State's prior *de jure* segregation and that continues to foster segregation. The Equal Protection Clause is offended by "sophisticated as well as simpleminded modes of discrimination." If policies traceable to the *de jure* system are still in force and have discriminatory effects, those policies too must be reformed to the extent practicable and consistent with sound educational practices. We also disagree with respondents that the Court of Appeals and District Court properly relied on our decision in *Bazemore v. Friday* (1986). *Bazemore* neither requires nor justifies the conclusions reached by the two courts below.

Bazemore raised the issue whether the financing and operational assistance provided by a state university's extension service to voluntary 4-H and Homemaker Clubs was inconsistent with the Equal Protection Clause because of the existence of numerous all-white and all-black clubs. Though prior to 1965 the clubs were supported on a segregated basis, the District Court had found that the policy of segregation had been completely abandoned and that no evidence existed of any lingering discrimination in either services or membership; any racial imbalance resulted from the wholly voluntary and unfettered choice of private individuals. In this context, we held inapplicable the *Green* Court's judgment that a voluntary choice program was insufficient to dismantle a *de jure* dual system in public primary and secondary schools, but only after satisfying ourselves that the State had not fostered segregation by playing a part in the decision of which club an individual chose to join.

Bazemore plainly does not excuse inquiry into whether Mississippi has left in place certain aspects of its prior dual system that perpetuate the racially segregated higher education system. If the State perpetuates policies and practices traceable to its prior system that continue to have segregative effects—whether by influencing student enrollment decisions or by fostering segregation in other facets of the university system—and such policies are without sound educational justification and can be practicably eliminated, the State has not satisfied its burden of proving that it has dismantled its prior system. Such policies run afoul of the Equal Protection Clause, even though the State has abolished the legal requirement that

whites and blacks be educated separately and has established racially neutral policies not animated by a discriminatory purpose. Because the standard applied by the District Court did not make these inquiries, we hold that the Court of Appeals erred in affirming the District Court's ruling that the State had brought itself into compliance with the Equal Protection Clause in the operation of its higher education system.

Had the Court of Appeals applied the correct legal standard, it would have been apparent from the undisturbed factual findings of the District Court that there are several surviving aspects of Mississippi's prior dual system which are constitutionally suspect; for even though such policies may be race-neutral on their face, they substantially restrict a person's choice of which institution to enter and they contribute to the racial identifiability of the eight public universities. Mississippi must justify these policies or eliminate them. . . .

We deal first with the current admissions policies of Mississippi's public universities. As the District Court found, the three flagship historically white universities in the system— University of Mississippi, Mississippi State University, and University of Southern Mississippi—enacted policies in 1963 requiring all entrants to achieve a minimum composite score of 15 on the American College Testing Program (ACT). The court described the "discriminatory taint" of this policy, an obvious reference to the fact that, at that time, the average ACT score for white students was 18 and the average score for blacks was 7. The District Court concluded, and the *en banc* Court of Appeals agreed, that present admissions standards derived from policies enacted in the 1970's to redress the problem of student unpreparedness. Obviously, this mid-passage justification for perpetuating a policy enacted originally to discriminate against black students does not make the present admissions standards any less constitutionally suspect.

The present admission standards are not only traceable to the *de jure* system and were originally adopted for a discriminatory purpose, but they also have present discriminatory effects. Every Mississippi resident under 21 seeking admission to the university system must take the ACT. Any applicant who scores at least 15 qualifies for automatic admission to any of the five historically white institutions except Mississippi University for Women, which requires a score of 18 for automatic admission unless the student has a 3.0 high school grade average. Those scoring less than 15 but at least 13 automatically qualify to enter Jackson State University, Alcorn State University, and Mississippi Valley State University. Without doubt, these requirements restrict the range of choices of entering students as to which institution they may attend in a way that perpetuates segregation. Those scoring 13 or 14, with some exceptions, are excluded from the five historically white universities, and if they want a higher education, must go to one of the historically black institutions or attend junior college with the hope of transferring to a historically white institution. Proportionately more blacks than whites face this choice: in 1985, 72 percent of Mississippi's white high school seniors achieved an ACT composite score of 15 or better, while less than 30 percent of black high school seniors earned that score. . . . It is not surprising then that Mississippi's universities remain predominantly identifiable by race. . . .

Another constitutionally problematic aspect of the State's use of the ACT test scores is its policy of denying automatic admission if an applicant fails to earn the minimum ACT score specified for the particular institution, without also resorting to the applicant's high school grades as an additional factor in predicting college performance. The United States produced evidence that the American College Testing Program (ACTP), the administering organization of the ACT, discourages use of ACT scores as the sole admissions criterion on the ground that it gives an incomplete "picture" of the student applicant's ability to perform adequately in college. One ACTP report presented into evidence suggests that "it would be foolish" to substitute a 3- or 4-hour test in place of a student's high school grades as a means of predicting college performance.

The record also indicated that the disparity between black and white students' high school grade averages was much narrower than the gap between their average ACT scores, thereby

suggesting that an admissions formula which included grades would increase the number of black students eligible for automatic admission to all of Mississippi's public universities.

A second aspect of the present system that necessitates further inquiry is the widespread duplication of programs. "Unnecessary" duplication refers, under the District Court's definition, "to those instances where two or more institutions offer the same nonessential or non-core program. Under this definition, all duplication at the bachelor's level of nonbasic liberal arts and sciences course work and all duplication at the master's level and above are considered to be unnecessary." The District Court found that 34.6 percent of the 29 undergraduate programs at historically black institutions are "unnecessarily duplicated" by the historically white universities, and that 90 percent of the graduate programs at the historically black institutions are unnecessarily duplicated at the historically white institutions. In its conclusions of law on this point, the District Court nevertheless determined that "there is no proof" that such duplication "is directly associated with the racial identifiability of institutions," and that "there is no proof that the elimination of unnecessary program duplication would be justifiable from an educational standpoint or that its elimination would have a substantial effect on student choice."

The District Court's treatment of this issue is problematic from several different perspectives. By stating that "there is no proof" that elimination of unnecessary duplication would decrease institutional racial identifiability, affect student choice, and promote educationally sound policies, the court did not make clear whether it had directed the parties to develop evidence on these points, and if so, what that evidence revealed. Finally, by treating this issue in isolation, the court failed to consider the combined effects of unnecessary program duplication with other policies, such as differential admissions standards, in evaluating whether the State had met its duty to dismantle its prior *de jure* segregated system.

We next address Mississippi's scheme of institutional mission classification, and whether it perpetuates the State's formerly *de jure* dual system.

The institutional mission designations adopted in 1981 have as their antecedents the policies enacted to perpetuate racial separation during the *de jure* segregated regime. We do not suggest that absent discriminatory purpose the assignment of different missions to various institutions in a State's higher education system would raise an equal protection issue where one or more of the institutions become or remain predominantly black or white. But here the issue is whether the State has sufficiently dismantled its prior dual system; and when combined with the differential admission practices and unnecessary program duplication, it is likely that the mission designations interfere with student choice and tend to perpetuate the segregated system. On remand, the court should inquire whether it would be practicable and consistent with sound educational practices to eliminate any such discriminatory effects of the State's present policy of mission assignments.

Fourth, the State attempted to bring itself into compliance with the Constitution by continuing to maintain and operate all eight higher educational institutions. The existence of eight instead of some lesser number was undoubtedly occasioned by State laws forbidding the mingling of the races. And as the District Court recognized, continuing to maintain all eight universities in Mississippi is wasteful and irrational. The District Court pointed especially to the facts that Delta State and Mississippi Valley are only 35 miles apart and that only 20 miles separate Mississippi State and Mississippi University for Women. It was evident to the District Court that "the defendants undertake to fund more institutions of higher learning than are justified by the amount of financial resources available to the state," but the court concluded that such fiscal irresponsibility was a policy choice of the legislature rather than a feature of a system subject to constitutional scrutiny.

Unquestionably, a larger rather than a smaller number of institutions from which to choose in itself makes for different choices, particularly when examined in the light of other factors present in the operation of the system, such as admissions, program duplication, and institutional mission designations.

Though certainly closure of one or more institutions would decrease the discriminatory effects of the present system, based on the present record we are unable to say whether such action is constitutionally required. Elimination of program duplication and revision of admissions criteria may make institutional closure unnecessary. However, on remand this issue should be carefully explored by inquiring and determining whether retention of all eight institutions itself affects student choice and perpetuates the segregated higher education system, whether maintenance of each of the universities is educationally justifiable, and whether one or more of them can be practicably closed or merged with other existing institutions.

Because the former *de jure* segregated system of public universities in Mississippi impeded the free choice of prospective students, the State in dismantling that system must take the necessary steps to ensure that this choice now is truly free. The full range of policies and practices must be examined with this duty in mind. That an institution is predominantly white or black does not in itself make out a constitutional violation. But surely the State may not leave in place policies rooted in its prior officially segregated system that serve to maintain the racial identifiability of its universities if those policies can practicably be eliminated without eroding sound educational policies.

If we understand private petitioners to press us to order the upgrading of Jackson State, Alcorn State, and Mississippi Valley *solely* so that they may be publicly financed, exclusively black enclaves by private choice, we reject that request. The State provides these facilities for *all* its citizens and it has not met its burden under *Brown* to take affirmative steps to dismantle its prior *de jure* system when it perpetuates a separate, but "more equal" one. Whether such an increase in funding is necessary to achieve a full dismantlement under the standards we have outlined, however, is a different question, and one that must be addressed on remand.

Because the District Court and the Court of Appeals failed to consider the State's duties in their proper light, the cases must be remanded. To the extent that the State has not met its affirmative obligation to dismantle its prior dual system, it shall be adjudged in violation of the Constitution and Title VI and remedial proceedings shall be conducted. The decision of the Court of Appeals is vacated, and the cases are remanded for further proceedings consistent with this opinion.

JUSTICE THOMAS, concurring.

We must rally to the defense of our schools. We must repudiate this unbearable assumption of the right to kill institutions unless they conform to one narrow standard.
—W. E. B. Du Bois, Schools, 13 *The Crisis* 111, 112 (1917)

I agree with the Court that a State does not satisfy its obligation to dismantle a dual system of higher education merely by adopting race-neutral policies for the future administration of that system. Today, we hold that "[i]f policies traceable to the *de jure* system are still in force and have discriminatory effects, those policies too must be reformed to the extent practicable and consistent with sound educational policies." I agree that this statement defines the appropriate standard to apply in the higher-education context. I write separately to emphasize that this standard is far different from the one adopted to govern the grade-school context in *Green v. New Kent County School Bd.* (1968) and its progeny. In particular, because it does not compel the elimination of all observed racial imbalance, it portends neither the destruction of historically black colleges nor the severing of those institutions from . . . their distinctive histories and traditions.

A challenged policy does not survive under the standard we announce today if it began during the prior *de jure* era, produces adverse impacts, and persists without sound educational justification.

We have no occasion to elaborate upon what constitutes an adequate justification. Nonetheless, I find most encouraging the Court's emphasis on "sound *educational* practices." From the beginning, we have recognized that desegregation remedies cannot be designed to ensure

the elimination of any remnant at any price, but rather must display "a practical flexibility" and "a facility for adjusting and reconciling public and private needs." *Brown v. Board of Education* (1955). Quite obviously, one compelling need to be considered is the *educational* need of the present and future *students* in the Mississippi university system, for whose benefit the remedies will be crafted.

In particular, we do not foreclose the possibility that there exists "sound educational justification" for maintaining historically black colleges *as such*. Despite the shameful history of state-enforced segregation, these institutions have survived and flourished. Indeed, they have expanded as opportunities for blacks to enter historically white institutions have expanded. Between 1954 and 1980, for example, enrollment at historically black colleges increased from 70,000 to 200,000 students, while degrees awarded increased from 13,000 to 32,000. These accomplishments have not gone unnoticed:

The colleges founded for Negroes are both a source of pride to blacks who have attended them and a source of hope to black families who want the benefits of higher learning for their children. They have exercised leadership in developing educational opportunities for young blacks at all levels of instruction, and, especially in the South, they are still regarded as key institutions for enhancing the general quality of the lives of black Americans.
—Carnegie Commission on Higher Education, From Isolation to Mainstream: Problems of the Colleges Founded for Negroes 11 (1971)

I think it undisputable that these institutions have succeeded in part because of their distinctive histories and traditions; for many, historically black colleges have become "a symbol of the highest attainments of black culture." Obviously, a State cannot maintain such traditions by closing particular institutions, historically white or historically black, to particular racial groups. Nonetheless, it hardly follows that a State cannot operate a diverse assortment of institutions—including historically black institutions—open to all on a race-neutral basis, but with established traditions and programs that might disproportionately appeal to one race or another. No one, I imagine, would argue that such institutional *diversity* is without "sound educational justification," or that it is even remotely akin to program *duplication,* which is designed to separate the races for the sake of separating the races. The Court at least hints at the importance of this value when it distinguishes *Green* in part on the ground that colleges and universities "are not fungible." Although I agree that a State is not constitutionally *required* to maintain its historically black institutions as such, I do not understand our opinion to hold that a State is *forbidden* from doing so. It would be ironic, to say the least, if the institutions that sustained blacks during segregation were themselves destroyed in an effort to combat its vestiges.

JUSTICE SCALIA, concurring in the judgment in part and dissenting in part.

With some of what the Court says today, I agree. I agree, of course, that the Constitution compels Mississippi to remove all discriminatory barriers to its state-funded universities. I agree that the Constitution does not compel Mississippi to remedy funding disparities between its historically black institutions (HBIs) and its historically white institutions (HWIs). And I agree that Mississippi's American College Testing Program (ACT) requirements need further review. I reject, however, the effectively unsustainable burden the Court imposes on Mississippi, and all States that formerly operated segregated universities, to demonstrate compliance with *Brown I.* That requirement, which resembles what we prescribed for primary and secondary schools in *Green v. New Kent County School Board* (1968), has no proper application in the context of higher education, provides no genuine guidance to States and lower courts, and is as likely to subvert as to promote the interests of those citizens on whose behalf the present suit was brought. . . .

Whether one consults the Court's description of what it purports to be doing, or what the Court actually does, one must conclude

that the Court is essentially applying to universities the amorphous standard adopted for primary and secondary schools in *Green v. New Kent County School Board* (1968). Like that case, today's decision places upon the State the ordinarily unsustainable burden of proving the negative proposition that *it* is not responsible for extant racial disparity in enrollment. *Green* requires school boards to prove that racially identifiable schools are *not* the consequence of past or present discriminatory state action; today's opinion requires state university administrators to prove that racially identifiable schools are *not* the consequence of any practice or practices (in such impromptu "aggregation" as might strike the fancy of a district judge) held over from the prior *de jure* regime. This will imperil virtually any practice or program plaintiffs decide to challenge—just as *Green* has—so long as racial imbalance remains. And just as under *Green,* so also under today's decision, the only practicable way of disproving that "existing racial identifiability is attributable to the State" *is to eliminate extant segregation, i.e., to assure racial proportionality in the schools.* Failing that, the State's only defense will be to establish an excuse for each challenged practice—either impracticability of elimination or sound educational value.

Application of the standard (or standards) announced today has no justification in precedent, and in fact runs contrary to a case decided six years ago, see *Bazemore v. Friday* (1986). . . . An accurate description of *Bazemore* was set forth in *Richmond v. J. A. Croson Co.* (1989): "mere existence of single-race clubs . . . cannot create a duty to integrate," we said *Bazemore* held, "in absence of *evidence of exclusion* by race"—not "in absence of evidence of state action's playing a part in the decision of which club an individual chose to join." . . .

Bazemore's standard for dismantling a dual system ought to control here: discontinuation of discriminatory practices and adoption of a neutral admissions policy.

It is my view that the requirement of compelled integration (whether by student assignment, as in *Green* itself, or by elimination of nonintegrated options, as the Court today effectively decrees) does not apply to higher education. Only one aspect of an historically segregated university system need be eliminated: discriminatory admissions standards. The burden is upon the formerly *de jure* system to show that that has been achieved. Once that has been done, however, it is not just unprecedented, but illogical as well, to establish that former *de jure* States continue to deny equal protection of the law to students whose choices among public university offerings are unimpeded by discriminatory barriers. Unless one takes the position that *Brown I* required States not only to provide equal access to their universities but also to correct lingering disparities between them, that is, to remedy institutional noncompliance with the "equal" requirement of *Plessy,* a State is in compliance with *Brown I* once it establishes that it has dismantled all discriminatory barriers to its public universities. Having done that, a State is free to govern its public institutions of higher learning as it will, unless it is convicted of discriminating anew— which requires both discriminatory intent and discriminatory causation.

That analysis brings me to agree with the judgment that the Court of Appeals must be reversed in part—for the reason (quite different from the Court's) that Mississippi has not borne the burden of demonstrating that intentionally discriminatory admissions standards have been eliminated. It has been established that Mississippi originally adopted ACT assessments as an admissions criterion because that was an effective means of excluding blacks from the HWIs. Given that finding, the District Court should have required Mississippi to prove that its continued use of ACT requirements does not have a racially exclusionary purpose and effect—a not insubstantial task. What the Court's test is designed to achieve is the elimination of predominantly black institutions. While that may be good social policy, the present petitioners, I suspect, would not agree; and there is much to be said for the Court of Appeals' perception that "if no [state] authority exists to deny [the student] the right to attend the institution of his choice, he is done a severe disservice by remedies which, in seeking to maximize integration, minimize diversity and vitiate his choices." But whether or not the Court's antagonism to

unintegrated schooling is good policy, it is assuredly not good constitutional law. There is nothing unconstitutional about a "black" school in the sense, not of a school that blacks *must* attend and that whites *cannot,* but of a school that, as a consequence of private choice in residence or in school selection, contains, and has long contained, a large black majority. (The Court says this, but does not appear to mean it.) In a perverse way, in fact, the insistence, whether explicit or implicit, that such institutions not be permitted to endure perpetuates the very stigma of black inferiority that *Brown I* sought to destroy. Not only Mississippi but Congress itself seems out of step with the drum that the Court beats today, judging by its passage of an Act entitled "Strengthening Historically Black Colleges and Universities," which authorizes the Education Department to provide money grants to historically black colleges. The implementing regulations designate Alcorn State University, Jackson State University, and Mississippi Valley State University as eligible recipients.

I would not predict, however, that today's opinion will succeed in producing the same result as *Green*—*viz.,* compelling the States to compel racial "balance" in their schools—because of several practical imperfections: because the Court deprives district judges of the most efficient (and perhaps the only effective) *Green* remedy, mandatory student assignment; because some contradictory elements of the opinion (its suggestion, for example, that Mississippi's mission designations foster, rather than deter, segregation) will prevent clarity of application; and because the virtually standardless discretion conferred upon district judges will permit them to do pretty much what they please. What I do predict is a number of years of litigation-driven confusion and destabilization in the university systems of all the formerly *de jure* States, that will benefit neither blacks nor whites, neither predominantly black institutions nor predominantly white ones. Nothing good will come of this judicially ordained turmoil, except the public recognition that any Court that would knowingly impose it must hate segregation. We must find some other way of making that point.

Missouri v. Jenkins
515 U.S. 70 (1995)

*In this eighteen-year-old school desegregation liti-
gation, on the orders of the US District Court for
the Western District of Missouri, the State of Missouri had already spent more than $940 million
to eliminate the past effects of racial segregation in
the Kansas City, Missouri, School District
(KCMSD)—see* Missouri v. Jenkins *(1990). Because of the district court's orders, annual per
pupil costs (excluding capital costs) in the
KCMSD were $9,412—two to three times higher
than for any other school district in the state. In
this particular dispute, the State of Missouri challenged a 1993 order by the district court requiring the state to fund salary increases for virtually
all instructional and noninstructional staff of the
KCMSD and to continue to fund remedial "quality education" programs because student achievement levels were still "at or below national norms
at many grade levels." The Court of Appeals for
the Eighth Circuit rejected the state's challenge,
observing that these increases were designed to
eliminate the vestiges of state-imposed segregation
by improving the "desegregative attractiveness" of
the KCMSD and by reversing "white flight" to
the suburbs. It also rejected the state's request for a
determination of partial unitary status under*
Freeman v. Pitts *(1992). The Supreme Court
granted certiorari. Opinion of the Court:* Rehnquist, *O'Connor, Scalia, Kennedy, Thomas.
Concurring opinions:* O'Connor; Thomas. *
Dissenting opinions:* Souter, *Stevens, Ginsburg, Breyer;* Ginsburg.

THE CHIEF JUSTICE delivered the opinion
of the Court.

As this school desegregation litigation enters
its 18th year, we are called upon again to review the decisions of the lower courts. In this
case, the State of Missouri has challenged the
District Court's order of salary increases for
virtually all instructional and noninstructional
staff within the Kansas City, Missouri, School
District (KCMSD) and the District Court's
order requiring the State to continue to fund
remedial "quality education" programs because
student achievement levels were still "at or
below national norms at many grade levels."
First, the State has challenged the District

Court's requirement that it fund salary increases for KCMSD instructional and noninstructional staff. The State claimed that
funding for salaries was beyond the scope of
the District Court's remedial authority. Second, the State has challenged the District
Court's order requiring it to continue to fund
the remedial quality education programs for
the 1992–1993 school year. The State contended that under *Freeman v. Pitts* (1992), it
had achieved partial unitary status with respect
to the quality education programs already in
place. As a result, the State argued that the District Court should have relieved it of responsibility for funding those programs.

The District Court rejected the State's arguments. It first determined that the salary increases were warranted because "[h]igh quality
personnel are necessary not only to implement
specialized desegregation programs intended to
'improve educational opportunities and reduce
racial isolation' . . . but also to 'ensure that
there is no diminution in the quality of its regular academic program.'" Its "ruling [was]
grounded in remedying the vestiges of segregation by improving the desegregative attractiveness of the KCMSD." The District Court did
not address the State's *Freeman* arguments;
nevertheless, it ordered the State to continue to
fund the quality education programs for the
1992–1993 school year. . . . The Court of Appeals for the Eighth Circuit affirmed. . . .

Because of the importance of the issues, we
granted *certiorari* to consider the following: (1)
whether the District Court exceeded its constitutional authority when it granted salary increases to virtually all instructional and
noninstructional employees of the KCMSD,
and (2) whether the District Court properly
relied upon the fact that student achievement
test scores had failed to rise to some unspecified level when it declined to find that the State
had achieved partial unitary status as to the
quality education programs. . . .

Proper analysis of the District Court's orders
challenged here . . . must rest upon their serving as proper means to the end of restoring the
victims of discriminatory conduct to the

position they would have occupied in the absence of that conduct and their eventual restoration of "state and local authorities to the control of a school system that is operating in compliance with the Constitution." We turn to that analysis.

The State argues that the order approving salary increases is beyond the District Court's authority because it was crafted to serve an "interdistrict goal," in spite of the fact that the constitutional violation in this case is "intradistrict" in nature. . . . The proper response to an intradistrict violation is an intradistrict remedy that serves to eliminate the racial identity of the schools within the effected school district by eliminating, as far as practicable, the vestiges of *de jure* segregation in all facets of their operation.

Here, the District Court has found, and the Court of Appeals has affirmed, that this case involved no interdistrict constitutional violation that would support interdistrict relief. Thus, the proper response by the District Court should have been to eliminate to the extent practicable the vestiges of prior *de jure* segregation within the KCMSD. . . . The District Court and Court of Appeals, however, have felt that because the KCMSD's enrollment remained 68.3% black, a purely *intra*district remedy would be insufficient. But, as noted in *Milliken v. Bradley* (1974), we have rejected the suggestion "that schools which have a majority of Negro students are not 'desegregated' whatever the racial makeup of the school district's population and however neutrally the district lines have been drawn and administered."

Instead of seeking to remove the racial identity of the various schools within the KCMSD, the District Court has set out on a program to create a school district that was equal to or superior to the surrounding [suburban school districts]. Its remedy has focused on "desegregative attractiveness," coupled with "suburban comparability." Examination of the District Court's reliance on "desegregative attractiveness" and "suburban comparability" is instructive for our ultimate resolution of the salary-order issue.

The purpose of desegregative attractiveness has been not only to remedy the system-wide reduction in student achievement, but also to attract nonminority students not presently enrolled in the KCMSD. This remedy has included an elaborate program of capital improvements, course enrichment, and extracurricular enhancement not simply in the formerly identifiable black schools, but in schools throughout the district. The District Court's remedial orders have converted every senior high school, every middle school, and one-half of the elementary schools in the KCMSD into "magnet" schools. The District Court's remedial order has all but made the KCMSD itself into a magnet district.

We previously have approved of intradistrict desegregation remedies involving magnet schools. Magnet schools have the advantage of encouraging voluntary movement of students within a school district in a pattern that aids desegregation on a voluntary basis, without requiring extensive busing and redrawing of district boundary lines. As a component in an intradistrict remedy, magnet schools also are attractive because they promote desegregation while limiting the withdrawal of white student enrollment that may result from mandatory student reassignment.

The District Court's remedial plan in this case, however, is not designed solely to redistribute the students within the KCMSD in order to eliminate racially identifiable schools within the KCMSD. Instead, its purpose is to attract nonminority students from outside the KCMSD schools. But this *inter*district goal is beyond the scope of the *intra*district violation identified by the District Court. In effect, the District Court has devised a remedy to accomplish indirectly what it admittedly lacks the remedial authority to mandate directly: the interdistrict transfer of students. . . .

The District Court's pursuit of the goal of "desegregative attractiveness" results in so many imponderables and is so far removed from the task of eliminating the racial identifiability of the schools within the KCMSD that we believe it is beyond the admittedly broad discretion of the District Court. In this posture, we conclude that the District Court's order of salary increases, which was "grounded in remedying the vestiges of segregation by improving the desegregative attractiveness of the KCMSD," is simply too far removed from an acceptable implementation of a permissible means to remedy previous legally mandated segregation.

Similar considerations lead us to conclude that the District Court's order requiring the State to continue to fund the quality education programs because student achievement levels were still "at or below national norms at many grade levels" cannot be sustained. The State does not seek from this Court a declaration of partial unitary status with respect to the quality education programs. It challenges the requirement of indefinite funding of a quality education program until national norms are met, based on the assumption that while a mandate for significant educational improvement, both in teaching and in facilities, may have been justified originally, its indefinite extension is not.

Our review in this respect is needlessly complicated because the District Court made no findings in its order approving continued funding of the quality education programs. . . . The basic task of the District Court is to decide whether the reduction in achievement by minority students attributable to prior *de jure* segregation has been remedied to the extent practicable. Under our precedents, the State and the KCMSD are "entitled to a rather precise statement of [their] obligations under a desegregation decree. . . . " In reconsidering this order, the District Court should apply our three-part test from *Freeman v. Pitts.* The District Court should consider that the State's role with respect to the quality education programs has been limited to the funding, not the implementation, of those programs. As all the parties agree that improved achievement on test scores is not necessarily required for the State to achieve partial unitary status as to the quality education programs, the District Court should sharply limit, if not dispense with, its reliance on this factor. Just as demographic changes independent of *de jure* segregation will affect the racial composition of student assignments, so too will numerous external factors beyond the control of the KCMSD and the State affect minority student achievement. So long as these external factors are not the result of segregation, they do not figure in the remedial calculus. Insistence upon academic goals unrelated to the effects of legal segregation unwarrantably postpones the

day when the KCMSD will be able to operate on its own. . . .

On remand, the District Court must bear in mind that its end purpose is not only "to remedy the violation" to the extent practicable, but also "to restore state and local authorities to the control of a school system that is operating in compliance with the Constitution." The judgment of the Court of Appeals is reversed.

JUSTICE THOMAS, concurring.

It never ceases to amaze me that the courts are so willing to assume that anything that is predominantly black must be inferior. Instead of focusing on remedying the harm done to those black schoolchildren injured by segregation, the District Court here sought to convert the Kansas City, Missouri, School District (KCMSD) into a "magnet district" that would reverse the "white flight" caused by *de*segregation. In this respect, I join the Court's decision concerning the two remedial issues presented for review. I write separately, however, to add a few thoughts with respect to the overall course of this litigation. In order to evaluate the scope of the remedy, we must understand the scope of the constitutional violation and the nature of the remedial powers of the federal courts.

Two threads in our jurisprudence have produced this unfortunate situation, in which a District Court has taken it upon itself to experiment with the education of the KCMSD's black youth. First, the court has read our cases to support the theory that black students suffer an unspecified psychological harm from segregation that retards their mental and educational development. This approach not only relies upon questionable social science research rather than constitutional principle, but it also rests on an assumption of black inferiority. Second, we have permitted the federal courts to exercise virtually unlimited equitable powers to remedy this alleged constitutional violation. The exercise of this authority has trampled upon principles of federalism and the separation of powers and has freed courts to pursue other agendas unrelated to the narrow purpose of precisely remedying a constitutional harm.

The mere fact that a school is black does not mean that it is the product of a constitutional violation. A "racial imbalance does not itself establish a violation of the Constitution." Instead, in order to find unconstitutional segregation, we require that plaintiffs "prove all of the essential elements of *de jure* segregation—that is, stated simply, a current condition of segregation resulting from *intentional state action directed specifically* to the [allegedly segregated] schools."

In the present case, the District Court inferred a continuing constitutional violation from two primary facts: the existence of *de jure* segregation in the KCMSD prior to 1954, and the existence of *de facto* segregation today. The District Court found that in 1954, the KCMSD operated 16 segregated schools for black students, and that in 1974 39 schools in the district were more than 90% black. Desegregation efforts reduced this figure somewhat, but the District Court stressed that 24 schools remained "racially isolated," that is, more than 90% black, in 1983–1984. For the District Court, it followed that the KCMSD had not dismantled the dual system entirely. The District Court also concluded that because of the KCMSD's failure to "become integrated on a system-wide basis," the dual system still exerted "lingering effects" upon KCMSD black students, whose "general attitude of inferiority" produced "low achievement . . . which ultimately limits employment opportunities and causes poverty."

Without more, the District Court's findings could not have supported a finding of liability against the state. It should by now be clear that the existence of one-race schools is not by itself an indication that the State is practicing segregation. The continuing "racial isolation" of schools after *de jure* segregation has ended may well reflect voluntary housing choices or other private decisions. Here, for instance, the demography of the entire KCMSD has changed considerably since 1954. Though blacks accounted for only 18.9% of KCMSD's enrollment in 1954, by 1983–1984 the school district was 67.7% black. That certain schools are overwhelmingly black in a district that is now more than two-thirds black is hardly a sure sign of intentional state action. . . .

When a district court holds the State liable for discrimination almost 30 years after the last official state action, it must do more than show

that there are schools with high black populations or low test scores. Here, the district judge did not make clear how the high black enrollments in certain schools were fairly traceable to the State of Missouri's actions. I do not doubt that Missouri maintained the despicable system of segregation until 1954. But I question the District Court's conclusion that because the State had enforced segregation until 1954, its actions, or lack thereof, proximately caused the "racial isolation" of the predominantly black schools in 1984. In fact, where, as here, the finding of liability comes so late in the day, I would think it incumbent upon the District Court to explain how more recent social or demographic phenomena did not cause the "vestiges." This the District Court did not do.

Without a basis in any real finding of intentional government action, the District Court's imposition of liability upon the State of Missouri improperly rests upon a theory that racial imbalances are unconstitutional. That is, the court has "indulged the presumption, often irrebuttable in practice, that a presently observed [racial] imbalance has been proximately caused by intentional state action during the prior *de jure* era." In effect, the court found that racial imbalances constituted an ongoing constitutional violation that continued to inflict harm on black students. This position appears to rest upon the idea that any school that is black is inferior, and that blacks cannot succeed without the benefit of the company of whites.

The District Court's willingness to adopt such stereotypes stemmed from a misreading of our earliest desegregation case. In *Brown v. Board of Education* (1954) (*Brown I*), the Court noted several psychological and sociological studies purporting to show that *de jure* segregation harmed black students by generating "a feeling of inferiority" in them. Seizing upon this passage in *Brown I*, the District Court asserted that "forced segregation ruins attitudes and is inherently unequal." The District Court suggested that this inequality continues in full force even after the end of *de jure* segregation. . . . Thus, the District Court seemed to believe that black students in the KCMSD would continue to receive an "inferior education" despite the end of *de jure* segregation, as long as *de facto* segregation persisted. As the

District Court later concluded, compensatory educational programs were necessary "as a means of remedying many of the educational problems which go hand in hand with racially isolated minority student populations." Such assumptions and any social science research upon which they rely certainly cannot form the basis upon which we decide matters of constitutional principle.

It is clear that the District Court misunderstood the meaning of *Brown I*. *Brown I* did not say that "racially isolated" schools were inherently inferior; the harm that it identified was tied purely to *de jure* segregation, not *de facto* segregation. Indeed, *Brown I* itself did not need to rely upon any psychological or social science research in order to announce the simple, yet fundamental truth that the Government cannot discriminate among its citizens on the basis of race. As the Court's unanimous opinion indicated: "[I]n the field of public education the doctrine of 'separate but equal' has no place. Separate educational facilities are inherently unequal." At the heart of this interpretation of the Equal Protection Clause lies the principle that the Government must treat citizens as individuals, and not as members of racial, ethnic or religious groups. It is for this reason that we must subject all racial classifications to the strictest of scrutiny, which (aside from two decisions rendered in the midst of wartime, see *Hirabayashi v. United States* (1943); *Korematsu v. United States* (1944)) has proven automatically fatal.

Segregation was not unconstitutional because it might have caused psychological feelings of inferiority. Public school systems that separated blacks and provided them with superior educational resources—making blacks "feel" superior to whites sent to lesser schools—would violate the Fourteenth Amendment, whether or not the white students felt stigmatized, just as do school systems in which the positions of the races are reversed. Psychological injury or benefit is irrelevant to the question whether state actors have engaged in intentional discrimination—the critical inquiry for ascertaining violations of the Equal Protection Clause. The judiciary is fully competent to make independent determinations concerning the existence of state action without the unnecessary and misleading assistance of the social sciences.

Regardless of the relative quality of the schools, segregation violated the Constitution because the State classified students based on their race. Of course, segregation additionally harmed black students by relegating them to schools with substandard facilities and resources. But neutral policies, such as local school assignments, do not offend the Constitution when individual private choices concerning work or residence produce schools with high black populations. The Constitution does not prevent individuals from choosing to live together, to work together, or to send their children to school together, so long as the State does not interfere with their choices on the basis of race.

Given that desegregation has not produced the predicted leaps forward in black educational achievement, there is no reason to think that black students cannot learn as well when surrounded by members of their own race as when they are in an integrated environment. Indeed, it may very well be that what has been true for historically black colleges is true for black middle and high schools. Despite their origins in "the shameful history of state-enforced segregation," these institutions can be "'both a source of pride to blacks who have attended them and a source of hope to black families who want the benefits of . . . learning for their children.'" Because of their "distinctive histories and traditions," black schools can function as the center and symbol of black communities, and provide examples of independent black leadership, success, and achievement.

Thus, even if the District Court had been on firmer ground in identifying a link between the KCMSD's pre-1954 *de jure* segregation and the present "racial isolation" of some of the district's schools, mere *de facto* segregation (unaccompanied by discriminatory inequalities in educational resources) does not constitute a continuing harm after the end of *de jure* segregation. "Racial isolation" itself is not a harm; only state-enforced segregation is. After all, if separation itself is a harm, and if integration therefore is the only way that blacks can receive a proper education, then there must be something inferior about blacks. Under this theory, segregation injures blacks because blacks, when left on their own, cannot achieve. To my way of thinking, that conclusion is the result of a jurisprudence based upon a theory of black inferiority.

This misconception has drawn the courts away from the important goal in desegregation. The point of the Equal Protection Clause is not to enforce strict race-mixing, but to ensure that blacks and whites are treated equally by the State without regard to their skin color. The lower courts should not be swayed by the easy answers of social science, nor should they accept the findings, and the assumptions, of sociology and psychology at the price of constitutional principle.

We have authorized the district courts to remedy past *de jure* segregation by reassigning students in order to eliminate or decrease observed racial imbalances, even if present methods of pupils assignment are facially neutral. The District Court here merely took this approach to its logical next step. If racial proportions are the goal, then schools must improve their facilities to attract white students until the district's racial balance is restored to the "right" proportions. Thus, fault for the problem we correct today lies not only with a twisted theory of racial injuries, but also with our approach to the remedies necessary to correct racial imbalances.

The District Court's unwarranted focus on the psychological harm to blacks and on racial imbalances has been only half of the tale. Not only did the court subscribe to a theory of injury that was predicted on black inferiority, it also married this concept of liability to our expansive approach to remedial powers. We have given the federal courts the freedom to use any measure necessary to reverse problems—such as racial isolation or low educational achievement—that have proven stubbornly resistant to government policies. We have not permitted constitutional principles such as federalism or the separation of powers to stand in the way of our drive to reform the schools. Thus, the District Court here ordered massive expenditures by local and state authorities, without congressional or executive authorization and without any indication that such measures would attract whites back to KCMSD or raise KCMSD

test scores. The time has come for us to put the genie back in the bottle.

The Constitution extends "[t]he judicial Power of the United States" to "all Cases, in Law and Equity, arising under this Constitution, the Laws of the United States, and Treaties made . . . under their Authority." I assume for purposes of this case that the remedial authority of the federal courts is inherent in the "judicial Power," as there is no general equitable remedial power expressly granted by the Constitution or by statute. As with any inherent judicial power, however, we ought to be reluctant to approve its aggressive or extravagant use, and instead we should exercise it in a manner consistent with our history and traditions. . . .

Motivated by our worthy desire to eradicate segregation, however, we have disregarded this principle and given the courts unprecedented authority to shape a remedy in equity. . . . The judicial overreaching we see before us today perhaps is the price we now pay for our approval of such extraordinary remedies in the past. . . . Such extravagant uses of judicial power are at odds with the history and tradition of the equity power and the Framers' design. . . . Anticipating the growth of our modern doctrine, the Anti-Federalists criticized the Constitution because it might be read to grant broad equitable powers to the federal courts. In response, the defenders of the Constitution "sold" the new framework of government to the public by espousing a narrower interpretation of the equity power. When an attack on the Constitution is followed by an open Federalist effort to narrow the provision, the appropriate conclusion is that the drafters and ratifiers of the Constitution approved the more limited construction offered in response. . . . [G]iven the Federalists' public explanation during the ratification of the federal equity power, we should exercise the power to impose equitable remedies only sparingly, subject to clear rules guiding its use.

Two clear restraints on the use of the equity power—federalism and the separation of powers—derive from the very form of our Government.

Federal courts should pause before using their inherent equitable powers to intrude into the proper sphere of the States. We have long recognized that education is primarily a concern of local authorities. "[L]ocal autonomy of school districts is a vital national tradition. . . . " Federal courts do not possess the capabilities of state and local governments in addressing difficult educational problems. State and local school officials not only bear the responsibility for educational decisions, they also are better equipped than a single federal judge to make the day-to-day policy, curricular, and funding choices necessary to bring a school district into compliance with the Constitution. Federal courts simply cannot gather sufficient information to render an effective decree, have limited resources to induce compliance, and cannot seek political and public support for their remedies. When we presume to have the institutional ability to set effective educational, budgetary, or administrative policy, we transform the least dangerous branch into the most dangerous one.

The separation of powers imposes additional restraints on the judiciary's exercise of its remedial powers. To be sure, this is not a case of one branch of Government encroaching on the prerogatives of another, but rather of the power of the Federal Government over the States. Nonetheless, what the federal courts cannot do at the federal level they cannot do against the States; in either case, Article III courts are constrained by the inherent constitutional limitations on their powers. There simply are certain things that courts, in order to remain courts, cannot and should not do. There is no difference between courts running school systems or prisons and courts running executive branch agencies.

In this case, not only did the District Court exercise the legislative power to tax, it also engaged in budgeting, staffing, and educational decisions, in judgments about the location and aesthetic quality of the schools, and in administrative oversight and monitoring. These functions involve a legislative or executive, rather than a judicial, power. As Alexander Hamilton explained the limited authority of the federal courts: "The courts must declare the sense of the law; and if they should be disposed to exercise WILL instead of JUDGMENT, the consequence would equally be the substitution of their pleasure to that of the legislative body." Federal judges cannot make the fundamentally political decisions as to which priorities are to receive funds and staff, which educational goals are to be sought, and which values are to be taught. When federal judges undertake such local, day-to-day tasks, they detract from the independence and dignity of the federal courts and intrude into areas in which they have little expertise.

It is perhaps not surprising that broad equitable powers have crept into our jurisprudence, for they vest judges with the discretion to escape the constraints and dictates of the law and legal rules. But I believe that we must impose more precise standards and guidelines on the federal equitable power, not only to restore predictability to the law and reduce judicial discretion, but also to ensure that constitutional remedies are actually targeted toward whose who have been injured. . . .

To ensure that district courts do not embark on such broad initiatives in the future, we should demand that remedial decrees be more precisely designed to benefit only those who have been victims of segregation. Race-conscious remedies for discrimination not only must serve a compelling governmental interest (which is met in desegregation cases), but also must be narrowly tailored to further that interest. In the absence of special circumstances, the remedy for *de jure* segregation ordinarily should not include educational programs for students who were not in school (or were even alive) during the period of segregation. Although I do not doubt that all KCMSD students benefit from many of the initiatives ordered by the court below, it is for the democratically accountable state and local officials to decide whether they are to be made available even to those who were never harmed by segregation.

This Court should never approve a State's efforts to deny students, because of their race, an equal opportunity for an education. But the federal courts also should avoid using racial equality as a pretext for solving social problems that do not violate the Constitution. It seems apparent to me that the District Court undertook the worthy task of providing a quality education to the children of KCMSD. As far as I can tell, however, the District Court sought to bring new funds and facilities into the KCMSD by finding a constitutional violation on the part of the State where there was none. Federal courts should not lightly assume that States have caused "racial isolation" in 1984 by maintaining a segregated school system in 1954. We must forever put aside the notion that simply because a school district today is black, it must be educationally inferior. . . .

JUSTICE SOUTER, with whom JUSTICE STEVENS, JUSTICE GINSBURG, and JUSTICE BREYER join, dissenting.

The Court's process of orderly adjudication has broken down in this case. The Court disposes of challenges to only two of the District Court's many discrete remedial orders by declaring that the District Court erroneously provided an interdistrict remedy for an intradistrict violation. In doing so, it resolves a foundational issue going to one element of the District Court's decree that we did not accept for review in this case, that we need not reach in order to answer the questions that we did accept for review, and that we specifically refused to consider when it was presented in a prior petition for *certiorari*. Since, under these circumstances, the respondent school district and pupils naturally came to this Court without expecting that a fundamental premise of a portion of the District Court's remedial order would become the focus of the case, the essence of the Court's misjudgment in reviewing and repudiating that central premise lies in its failure to have warned the respondents of what was really at stake. This failure lulled the respondents into addressing the case without sufficient attention to the foundational issue, and their lack of attention has now infected the Court's decision.

No one on the Court has had the benefit of briefing and argument informed by an appreciation of the potential breadth of the ruling. The deficiencies from which we suffer have led the Court effectively to overrule a unanimous constitutional precedent of 20 years standing, which was not even addressed in argument, was mentioned merely in passing by one of the parties, and discussed by another of them only in a misleading way.

The Court's departures from the practices that produce informed adjudication would call for dissent even in a simple case. But in this one, with a trial history of more than 10 years of litigation, the Court's failure to provide adequate notice of the issue to be decided (or to limit the decision to issues on which *certiorari* was clearly granted) rules out any confidence that today's result is sound, either in fact or in law.

Shelley v. Kraemer
334 U.S. 1 (1948)

J. D. Shelley, an African American, purchased a house from Josephine Fitzgerald in a St. Louis neighborhood in which deeds held by three-fourths of the property owners contained a racially restrictive covenant—that is, an agreement by the property holders not to sell their properties to "people of the Negro or Mongolian Race." The covenant had been in force since 1911, when the holders of the properties in question had entered into a fifty-year contract not to sell to "any person not of the Caucasian race." Neither Shelley nor Fitzgerald was aware of the restrictive covenant at the time of the sale. When Shelley refused to reconsider the purchase after learning of the racial exclusion, Louis Kraemer, a resident of the neighborhood whose deed contained a similar restriction, sued to enjoin Shelley from taking possession of the property. The Missouri Supreme Court ultimately granted Kraemer the relief he sought and directed the trial court to issue the injunction. Shelley appealed to the US Supreme Court, where his case was heard in conjunction with a controversy from Michigan involving a similar restrictive covenant. Opinion of the Court: <u>Vinson</u>, Black, Douglas, Frankfurter, Murphy, Burton. Not participating: Reed, Jackson, Rutledge.

THE CHIEF JUSTICE delivered the opinion of the Court.

These cases present for our consideration questions relating to the validity of court enforcement of private agreements, generally described as restrictive covenants, which have as their purpose the exclusion of persons of designated race or color from the ownership or occupancy of real property. Basic constitutional issues of obvious importance have been raised. . . .

It is well, at the outset, to scrutinize the terms of the restrictive agreements involved in these cases. In the Missouri case, the covenant declares that no part of the affected property shall be "occupied by any person not of the Caucasian race, it being intended hereby to restrict the use of said property . . . against the occupancy as owners or tenants of any portion of said property for resident or other purpose by people of the Negro or Mongolian Race." Not only does the restriction seek to proscribe use and occupancy of the affected properties by members of the excluded class, but as construed by the Missouri courts, the agreement requires that title of any person who uses his property in violation of the restriction shall be divested. The restriction of the covenant in the Michigan case seeks to bar occupancy by persons of the excluded class. It provides that "This property shall not be used or occupied by any person or persons except those of the Caucasian race." . . .

It cannot be doubted that among the civil rights intended to be protected from discriminatory state action by the Fourteenth Amendment are the rights to acquire, enjoy, own and dispose of property. Equality in the enjoyment of property rights was regarded by the framers of that Amendment as an essential precondition to the realization of other basic civil rights and liberties which the Amendment was intended to guarantee. . . .

It is likewise clear that restrictions on the right of occupancy of the sort sought to be created by the private agreements in these cases could not be squared with the requirements of the Fourteenth Amendment if imposed by state statute or local ordinance. We do not understand respondents to urge the contrary. . . .

But the present cases . . . do not involve action by state legislatures or city councils. Here the particular patterns of discrimination and the areas in which the restrictions are to operate, are determined, in the first instance, by the

terms of agreements among private individuals. Participation of the State consists in the enforcement of the restrictions so defined. The crucial issue with which we are here confronted is whether this distinction removes these cases from the operation of the prohibitory provisions of the Fourteenth Amendment.

Since the decision of this Court in the *Civil Rights Cases,* . . . the principle has become firmly embedded in our constitutional law that the action inhibited by the first section of the Fourteenth Amendment is only such action as may fairly be said to be that of the States. That Amendment erects no shield against merely private conduct, however discriminatory or wrongful.

We conclude, therefore, that the restrictive agreements standing alone cannot be regarded as violative of any rights guaranteed to petitioners by the Fourteenth Amendment. So long as the purposes of those agreements are effectuated by voluntary adherence to their terms, it would appear clear that there has been no action by the State and the provisions of the Amendment have not been violated. . . .

But here there was more. These are cases in which the purposes of the agreements were secured only by judicial enforcement by state courts of the restrictive terms of the agreements.

We have no doubt that there has been state action in these cases in the full and complete sense of the phrase. The undisputed facts disclose that petitioners were willing purchasers of properties upon which they desired to establish homes. The owners of the properties were willing sellers; and contracts of sale were accordingly consummated. It is clear that but for the active intervention of the state courts, supported by the full panoply of state power, petitioners would have been free to occupy the properties in question without restraint.

These are not cases, as has been suggested, in which the States have merely abstained from action, leaving private individuals free to impose such discriminations as they see fit. Rather, these are cases in which the States have made available to such individuals the full coercive power of government to deny to petitioners, on the grounds of race or color, the enjoyment of property rights in premises which petitioners are willing and financially able to acquire and which the grantors are willing to sell. The difference between judicial enforcement and nonenforcement of the restrictive covenants is the difference to petitioners between being denied rights of property available to other members of the community and being accorded full enjoyment of those rights on an equal footing. . . .

. . . We have noted that previous decisions of this Court have established the proposition that judicial action is not immunized from the operation of the Fourteenth Amendment simply because it is taken pursuant to the state's common-law policy. Nor is the Amendment ineffective simply because the particular pattern of discrimination, which the State has enforced, was defined initially by the terms of a private agreement. State action, as that phrase is understood for the purposes of the Fourteenth Amendment, refers to exertions of state power in all forms. And when the effect of that action is to deny rights subject to the protection of the Fourteenth Amendment, it is the obligation of this Court to enforce the constitutional commands.

We hold that in granting judicial enforcement of the restrictive agreements in these cases, the States have denied petitioners the equal protection of the laws and that, therefore, the action of the state courts cannot stand. . . .

Respondents urge, however, that since the state courts stand ready to enforce restrictive covenants excluding white persons from the ownership or occupancy of property covered by such agreements, enforcement of covenants excluding colored persons may not be deemed a denial of equal protection of the laws to the colored persons who are thereby affected. This contention does not bear scrutiny. The parties have directed our attention to no case in which a court, state or federal, has been called upon to enforce a covenant excluding members of the white majority from ownership or occupancy of real property on grounds of race or color. But there are more fundamental considerations. The rights created by the first section of the Fourteenth Amendment are, by its terms, guaranteed to the individual. The rights established are personal rights. It is, therefore, no answer to these petitioners to say that the courts may also be induced to deny white persons rights of ownership and occupancy on grounds of race or color. Equal protection of the laws is not achieved through indiscriminate imposition of inequalities. . . .

The historical context in which the Fourteenth Amendment became a part of the Constitution should not be forgotten. Whatever else the framers sought to achieve, it is clear that the matter of primary concern was the establishment of equality in the enjoyment of basic civil and political rights and the preservation of those rights from discriminatory action on the part of the States based on considerations of race or color. Seventy-five years ago this Court announced that the provisions of the Amendment are to be construed with this fundamental purpose in mind. Upon full consideration, we have concluded that in these cases the States have acted to deny petitioners the equal protection of the laws guaranteed by the Fourteenth Amendment. . . .

For the reasons stated, the judgment of the Supreme Court of Missouri and the judgment of the Supreme Court of Michigan must be reversed.

Moose Lodge No. 107 v. Irvis
407 U.S. 163 (1972)

Leroy Irvis, an African American guest at the Moose Lodge in Harrisburg, Pennsylvania, was refused service at its dining room and bar solely because of his race. Irvis sued in federal district court for injunctive relief, charging that the discrimination was state action and thus in violation of the Equal Protection Clause of the Fourteenth Amendment because the Pennsylvania liquor board had issued a liquor license to the Moose Lodge, a private club. The district court agreed with Irvis that state action was present and declared the Moose Lodge's liquor license invalid as long as it continued its discriminatory practices. The Moose Lodge appealed to the Supreme Court. Opinion of the Court: <u>Rehnquist</u>, Burger, Stewart, White, Blackmun,

Powell. Dissenting opinions: <u>Douglas</u>, Marshall; <u>Brennan</u>, Marshall.

JUSTICE REHNQUIST delivered the opinion of the Court.

Moose Lodge is a private club in the ordinary meaning of that term. It is a local chapter of a national fraternal organization having well-defined requirements for membership. It conducts all of its activities in a building that is owned by it. It is not publicly funded. Only members and guests are permitted in any lodge of the order; one may become a guest only by invitation of a member or upon invitation of the house committee.

Appellee, while conceding the right of private clubs to choose members upon a discriminatory basis, asserts that the licensing of Moose Lodge to serve liquor by the Pennsylvania Liquor Control Board amounts to such State involvement with the club's activities as to make its discriminatory practices forbidden by the Equal Protection Clause of the Fourteenth Amendment. The relief sought and obtained by appellee in the District Court was an injunction forbidding the licensing by the liquor authority of Moose Lodge until it ceased its discriminatory practices. We conclude that Moose Lodge's refusal to serve food and beverages to a guest by reason of the fact that he was a Negro does not, under the circumstances here presented, violate the Fourteenth Amendment.

In 1883, this Court in *The Civil Rights Cases* . . . set forth the essential dichotomy between discriminatory action by the State, which is prohibited by the Equal Protection Clause, and private conduct, "however discriminatory or wrongful," against which that clause "erects no shield," *Shelley v. Kraemer* (1948).

While the principle is easily stated, the question of whether particular discriminatory conduct is private, on the one hand, or amounts to "state action," on the other hand, frequently admits of no easy answer. "Only by sifting facts and weighing circumstances can the nonobvious involvement of the State in private conduct be attributed its true significance." . . . Our cases make clear that the impetus for the forbidden discrimination need not originate with the State if it is state action that enforces privately originated discrimination. . . . The

Court held in *Burton v. Wilmington Parking Authority* (1962) that a private restaurant owner who refused service because of a customer's race violated the Fourteenth Amendment, where the restaurant was located in a building owned by a state-created parking authority and leased from the authority.

The Court, after a comprehensive review of the relationship between the lessee and the parking authority concluded that the latter had "so far insinuated itself into a position of interdependence with Eagle [the restaurant owner] that it must be recognized as a joint participant in the challenged activity, which, on that account, cannot be considered to have been so 'purely private' as to fall without the scope of the Fourteenth Amendment." . . . The Court has never held, of course, that discrimination by an otherwise private entity would be violative of the Equal Protection Clause if the private entity receives any sort of benefit or service at all from the State, or if it is subject to state regulation in any degree whatever. Since state-furnished services include such necessities of life as electricity, water, and police and fire protection, such a holding would utterly emasculate the distinction between private as distinguished from State conduct set forth in *The Civil Rights Cases* . . . and adhered to in subsequent decisions. Our holdings indicate that where the impetus for the discrimination is private, the State must have "significantly involved itself with invidious discriminations," . . . in order for the discriminatory action to fall within the ambit of the constitutional prohibition. . . .

Here there is nothing approaching the symbiotic relationship between lessor and lessee that was present in *Burton,* where the private lessee obtained the benefit of locating in a building owned by the state-created parking authority, and the parking authority was enabled to carry out its primary public purpose of furnishing parking space by advantageously leasing portions of the building constructed for that purpose to commercial lessees such as the owner of the Eagle Restaurant. . . .

. . . The Pennsylvania Liquor Control Board plays absolutely no part in establishing or enforcing the membership or guest policies of the club which it licenses to serve liquor. There is no suggestion in this record that the Pennsylvania Act, either as written or as applied, discriminates against minority groups either in their right to apply for club licenses themselves or in their right to purchase and be served liquor in places of public accommodation. The only effect that the state licensing of Moose Lodge to serve liquor can be said to have on the right of any other Pennsylvanian to buy or be served liquor on premises other than those of Moose Lodge is that for some purposes club licenses are counted in the maximum number of licenses which may be issued in a given municipality. Basically each municipality has a quota of one retail license for each 1,500 inhabitants. Licenses issued to hotels, municipal golf courses and airport restaurants are not counted in this quota, nor are club licenses until the maximum number of retail licenses is reached. Beyond that point, neither additional retail licenses nor additional club licenses may be issued so long as the number of issued and outstanding retail licenses remains above the statutory maximum.

The District Court was at pains to point out in its opinion what it considered to be the "pervasive" nature of the regulation of private clubs by the Pennsylvania Liquor Control Board. As that court noted, an applicant for a club license must make such physical alterations in its premises as the board may require, must file a list of the names and addresses of its members and employees, and must keep extensive financial records. The board is granted the right to inspect the licensed premises at any time when patrons, guests or members are present.

However detailed this type of regulation may be in some particulars, it cannot be said to in any way foster or encourage racial discrimination. Nor can it be said to make the State in any realistic sense a partner or even a joint venturer in the club's enterprise. The limited effect of the prohibition against obtaining additional club licenses when the maximum number of retail licenses allotted to a municipality has been issued, when considered together with the availability of liquor from hotel, restaurant, and retail licensees falls far short of conferring upon club licensees a monopoly in the dispensing of liquor in any given municipality or in the State as a whole. We therefore hold that, with the exception hereafter noted, the operation of the regulatory scheme enforced by the Pennsylvania Liquor Control Board does not sufficiently implicate the State in the discriminatory guest policies of Moose Lodge so as to make the latter "state action" within the ambit of the Equal Protection Clause of the Fourteenth Amendment. . . .

JUSTICE DOUGLAS, with whom JUSTICE MARSHALL joins, dissenting. . . .

. . . Liquor licenses in Pennsylvania, unlike driver's licenses, or marriage licenses, are not freely available to those who meet racially neutral qualifications. There is a complex quota system, which the majority accurately describes. . . . What the majority neglects to say is that the Harrisburg quota, where Moose Lodge No. 107 is located, has been full for many years. No more club licenses may be issued in that city.

This state-enforced scarcity of licenses restricts the ability of blacks to obtain liquor, for liquor is commercially available *only* at private clubs for a significant portion of each week. Access by blacks to places that serve liquor is further limited by the fact that the state quota is filled. A group desiring to form a nondiscriminatory club which would serve blacks must purchase a license held by an existing club, which can exact a monopoly price for the transfer. The availability of such a license is speculative at best, however, for, as Moose Lodge itself concedes, without a liquor license a fraternal organization would be hard-pressed to survive.

Thus, the State of Pennsylvania is putting the weight of its liquor license, concededly a valued and important adjunct to a private club, behind racial discrimination.

JUSTICE BRENNAN, with whom JUSTICE MARSHALL joins, dissenting.

When Moose Lodge obtained its liquor license, the State of Pennsylvania became an active participant in the operation of the Lodge bar. Liquor licensing laws are only incidentally revenue measures; they are primarily pervasive regulatory schemes under which the

State dictates and continually supervises virtually every detail of the operation of the licensee's business. Very few, if any, other licensed businesses experience such complete state involvement. . . .

Plainly, the State of Pennsylvania's liquor regulations intertwine the State with the operation of the Lodge bar in a "significant way [and] lend [the State's] authority to the sordid business of racial discrimination." . . .

Georgia v. McCollum
505 U.S. 42 (1992)

Thomas McCollum, William Joseph McCollum, and Ella Hampton McCollum, who were white, were charged with assaulting Jerry and Myra Collins, who were black. Before jury selection began, the trial judge denied the prosecutor's motion to prohibit the defendants from exercising their peremptory challenges to exclude all blacks from participating as jurors in the trial. The Georgia Supreme Court affirmed, distinguishing Edmonson v. Leesville Concrete Co. (1991), in which the US Supreme Court had held that private litigants cannot exercise peremptory challenges in a racially discriminatory manner, on the grounds that Edmonson involved civil litigants rather than criminal defendants. The US Supreme Court granted certiorari. Opinion of the Court: Blackmun, Rehnquist, White, Stevens, Kennedy, Souter. Concurring opinion: Rehnquist. Concurring in the judgment: Thomas. Dissenting opinions: O'Connor; Scalia.

JUSTICE BLACKMUN delivered the opinion of the Court.

For more than a century, this Court consistently and repeatedly has reaffirmed that racial discrimination by the State in jury selection offends the Equal Protection Clause. See, *e.g., Strauder v. West Virginia* (1880). Last Term, this Court held that racial discrimination in a civil litigant's exercise of peremptory challenges also violates the Equal Protection Clause. See *Edmonson v. Leesville Concrete Co.* (1991). Today, we are asked to decide whether the Constitution prohibits a *criminal defendant* from engaging in purposeful racial discrimination in the exercise of peremptory challenges. . . .

Over the last century, in an almost unbroken chain of decisions, this Court gradually has abolished race as a consideration for jury service. In *Strauder v. West Virginia* (1880), the Court invalidated a state statute providing that only white men could serve as jurors. While stating that a defendant has no right to a "petit jury composed in whole or in part of persons of his own race," the Court held that a defendant does have the right to be tried by a jury whose members are selected by nondiscriminatory criteria.

In *Swain v. Alabama* (1965), the Court was confronted with the question whether an African-American defendant was denied equal protection by the State's exercise of peremptory challenges to exclude members of his race from the petit jury. Although the Court rejected the defendant's attempt to establish an equal protection claim premised solely on the pattern of jury strikes in his own case, it acknowledged that proof of systematic exclusion of African Americans through the use of peremptories over a period of time might establish such a violation.

In *Batson v. Kentucky* (1986), the Court discarded *Swain's* evidentiary formulation. The *Batson* Court held that a defendant may establish a *prima facie* case of purposeful discrimination in selection of the petit jury based solely on the prosecutor's exercise of peremptory challenges at the defendant's trial. "Once the defendant makes a *prima facie* showing, the burden shifts to the State to come forward with a neutral explanation for challenging black jurors."

Last Term, this Court applied the *Batson* framework in two other contexts. In *Powers v. Ohio* (1991), it held that in the trial of a white criminal defendant, a prosecutor is prohibited from excluding African-American jurors on the basis of race. In *Edmonson v. Leesville Concrete Co.* (1991), the Court decided that in a civil case, private litigants cannot exercise their peremptory strikes in a racially discriminatory manner.

In deciding whether the Constitution prohibits criminal defendants from exercising racially discriminatory peremptory challenges, we must answer four questions. First, whether a criminal defendant's exercise of peremptory challenges in a racially discriminatory manner inflicts the harms addressed by *Batson*. Second, whether the exercise of peremptory challenges by a criminal defendant constitutes state action. Third, whether prosecutors have standing to raise this constitutional challenge. And fourth, whether the constitutional rights of a criminal defendant nonetheless preclude the extension of our precedents to this case.

The majority in *Powers* recognized that "*Batson* 'was designed to serve multiple ends,'" only one of which was to protect individual defendants from discrimination in the selection of jurors. As in *Powers* and *Edmonson,* the extension of *Batson* in this context is designed to remedy the harm done to the "dignity of persons" and to the "integrity of the courts."

As long ago as *Strauder,* this Court recognized that denying a person participation in jury service on account of his race unconstitutionally discriminates against the excluded juror. While "[a]n individual juror does not have a right to sit on any particular petit jury, . . . he or she does possess the right not to be excluded from one on account of race." Regardless of who invokes the discriminatory challenge, there can be no doubt that the harm is the same—in all cases, the juror is subjected to open and public racial discrimination.

But "the harm from discriminatory jury selection extends beyond that inflicted on the defendant and the excluded juror to touch the entire community." One of the goals of our jury system is "to impress upon the criminal defendant and the community as a whole that a verdict of conviction or acquittal is given in accordance with the law by persons who are fair." Selection procedures that purposefully exclude African Americans from juries undermine that public confidence—as well they should.

The need for public confidence is especially high in cases involving race-related crimes. In such cases, emotions in the affected community will inevitably be heated and volatile. Public confidence in the integrity of the criminal justice system is essential for preserving community peace in trials involving race-related crimes.

Be it at the hands of the State or the defense, if a court allows jurors to be excluded because of group bias, it is a willing participant in a scheme that could only undermine the very foundation of our system of justice—our citizens' confidence in it. Just as public confidence in criminal justice is undermined by a conviction in a trial where racial discrimination has occurred in jury selection, so is public confidence undermined where a defendant, assisted by racially discriminatory peremptory strikes, obtains an acquittal.

The fact that a defendant's use of discriminatory peremptory challenges harms the jurors and the community does not end our equal protection inquiry. Racial discrimination, although repugnant in all contexts, violates the Constitution only when it is attributable to state action. Thus, the second question that must be answered is whether a criminal defendant's exercise of a peremptory challenge constitutes state action for purposes of the Equal Protection Clause.

Until *Edmonson,* the cases decided by this Court that presented the problem of racially discriminatory peremptory challenges involved assertions of discrimination by a prosecutor, a quintessential state actor. In *Edmonson,* by contrast, the contested peremptory challenges were exercised by a private defendant in a civil action. In order to determine whether state action was present in that setting, the Court in *Edmonson* used the analytical framework summarized in *Lugar v. Edmonson Oil Co.* (1982).

The first inquiry is "whether the claimed [constitutional] deprivation has resulted from the exercise of a right or privilege having its source in state authority." "There can be no question" that peremptory challenges satisfy this first requirement, as they "are permitted only when the government, by statute or decisional law, deems it appropriate to allow parties to exclude a given number of persons who otherwise would satisfy the requirements for service on the petit jury."

The second inquiry is whether the private party charged with the deprivation can be described as a state actor. The Court in *Edmonson* found that peremptory challenges perform a traditional function of the government: "Their sole purpose is to permit litigants to assist the government in the selection of an impartial trier of fact." And, as the *Edmonson* Court recognized, the jury system in turn "performs the critical governmental functions of guarding the rights of litigants and 'insur[ing] continued acceptance of the laws by all of the people.'" These same conclusions apply with even greater force in the criminal context because the selection of a jury in a criminal case fulfills a unique and constitutionally compelled governmental function.

Respondents nonetheless contend that the adversarial relationship between the defendant and the prosecution negates the governmental character of the peremptory challenge. In exercising a peremptory challenge, a criminal defendant is wielding the power to choose a quintessential governmental body—indeed, the institution of government on which our judicial system depends. Thus, as we held in *Edmonson*, when "a government confers on a private body the power to choose the government's employees or officials, the private body will be bound by the constitutional mandate of race neutrality."

The fact that a defendant exercises a peremptory challenge to further his interest in acquittal does not conflict with a finding of state action. Whenever a private actor's conduct is deemed "fairly attributable" to the government, it is likely that private motives will have animated the actor's decision. Indeed, in *Edmonson*, the Court recognized that the private party's exercise of peremptory challenges constituted state action, even though the motive underlying the exercise of the peremptory challenge may be to protect a private interest.

Having held that a defendant's discriminatory exercise of a peremptory challenge is a violation of equal protection, we move to the question whether the State has standing to challenge a defendant's discriminatory use of peremptory challenges. In *Powers,* this Court held that a white criminal defendant has standing to raise the equal protection rights of black jurors wrongfully excluded from jury service. While third-party standing is a limited exception, the *Powers* Court recognized that a

litigant may raise a claim on behalf of a third party if the litigant can demonstrate that he has suffered a concrete injury, that he has a close relation to the third party, and that there exists some hindrance to the third party's ability to protect its own interests. In *Edmonson,* the Court applied the same analysis in deciding that civil litigants had standing to raise the equal protection rights of jurors excluded on the basis of their race.

The State's relation to potential jurors in this case is closer than the relationships approved in *Powers* and *Edmonson.* As the representative of all its citizens, the State is the logical and proper party to assert the invasion of the constitutional rights of the excluded jurors in a criminal trial. Indeed, the Fourteenth Amendment forbids the State from denying persons within its jurisdiction the equal protection of the laws. . . . Accordingly, we hold that the State has standing to assert the excluded jurors' rights.

The final question is whether the interests served by *Batson* must give way to the rights of a criminal defendant. As a preliminary matter, it is important to recall that peremptory challenges are not constitutionally protected fundamental rights; rather, they are but one state-created means to the constitutional end of an impartial jury and a fair trial. This Court repeatedly has stated that the right to a peremptory challenge may be withheld altogether without impairing the constitutional guarantee of an impartial jury and a fair trial.

We do not believe that this decision will undermine the contribution of the peremptory challenge to the administration of justice. Nonetheless, "if race stereotypes are the price for acceptance of a jury panel as fair," we reaffirm today that such a "price is too high to meet the standard of the Constitution." It is an affront to justice to argue that a fair trial includes the right to discriminate against a group of citizens based upon their race. . . .

We hold that the Constitution prohibits a criminal defendant from engaging in purposeful discrimination on the ground of race in the exercise of peremptory challenges. Accordingly, if the State demonstrates a *prima facie* case of racial discrimination by the defendants, the defendants must articulate a racially neutral explanation for peremptory challenges. The judgment of the Supreme Court of Georgia is reversed and the case is remanded for further proceedings not inconsistent with this opinion.

THE CHIEF JUSTICE, concurring.

I was in dissent in *Edmonson v. Leesville Concrete Co.* (1991), and continue to believe that case to have been wrongly decided. But so long as it remains the law, I believe that it controls the disposition of this case on the issue of "state action" under the Fourteenth Amendment. I therefore join the opinion of the Court.

JUSTICE THOMAS, concurring in the judgment.

As a matter of first impression, I think that I would have shared the view of the dissenting opinions: A criminal defendant's use of peremptory strikes cannot violate the Fourteenth Amendment because it does not involve state action. Yet, I agree with the Court and the Chief Justice that our decision last term in *Edmonson v. Leesville Concrete Co.* (1991) governs this case and requires the opposite conclusion. Because the respondents do not question *Edmonson,* I believe that we must accept its consequences. I therefore concur in the judgment reversing the Georgia Supreme Court.

I write separately to express my general dissatisfaction with our continuing attempts to use the Constitution to regulate peremptory challenges. In my view, by restricting a criminal defendant's use of such challenges, this case takes us further from the reasoning and the result of *Strauder v. West Virginia* (1880). I doubt that this departure will produce favorable consequences. On the contrary, I am certain that black criminal defendants will rue the day that this court ventured down this road that inexorably will lead to the elimination of peremptory strikes.

In *Strauder,* as the Court notes, we invalidated a state law that prohibited blacks from serving on juries. In the course of the decision, we observed that the racial composition of a jury may affect the outcome of a criminal case. We explained: "It is well known that prejudices often exist against particular classes in the community, which sway the judgment of jurors, and which, therefore, operate in some cases to deny to persons of those classes the full enjoyment of that protection which others enjoy." We thus recognized, over a century ago, the precise point that Justice O'Connor makes today. Simply stated, securing representation of the defendant's race on the jury may help to overcome racial bias and provide the defendant with a better chance of having a fair trial.

I do not think that this basic premise of *Strauder* has become obsolete. The public, in general, continues to believe that the makeup of juries can matter in certain instances. Consider, for example, how the press reports criminal trials. Major newspapers regularly note the number of whites and blacks that sit on juries in important cases. Their editors and readers apparently recognize that conscious and unconscious prejudice persists in our society and that it may influence some juries. Common experience and common sense confirm this understanding.

In *Batson,* however, this Court began to depart from *Strauder* by holding that, without some actual showing, suppositions about the possibility that jurors may harbor prejudice have no legitimacy. We said, in particular, that a prosecutor could not justify peremptory strikes "by stating merely that he challenged jurors of the defendant's race on the assumption—or his intuitive judgment—that they would be partial to the defendant because of their shared race." As noted, however, our decision in *Strauder* rested on precisely such an "assumption" or "intuition." We reasonably surmised, without direct evidence in any particular case, that all-white juries might judge black defendants unfairly.

Our departure from *Strauder* has two negative consequences. First, it produces a serious misordering of our priorities. In *Strauder,* we put the rights of defendants foremost. Today's decision, while protecting jurors, leaves defendants with less means of protecting themselves. Unless jurors actually admit prejudice during *voir dire,* defendants generally must allow them to sit and run the risk that racial animus will affect the verdict. In effect, we have exalted the right of citizens to sit on juries over the rights of the criminal defendant, even though it is the defendant, not the jurors, who faces imprisonment or even death. At a minimum, I think that this inversion of priorities should give us pause.

Second, our departure from *Strauder* has taken us down a slope of inquiry that had no clear stopping point. Today, we decide only that white defendants may not strike black veniremen on the basis of race. Eventually, we will have to decide whether black defendants may strike white veniremen. Next will come the question whether defendants may exercise peremptories on the basis of sex. The consequences for defendants of our decision and of these future cases remain to be seen. But whatever the benefits were that this Court perceived in a criminal defendant's having members of his class on the jury, they have evaporated.

JUSTICE O'CONNOR, dissenting.

The Court reaches the remarkable conclusion that criminal defendants being prosecuted by the State act on behalf of their adversary when they exercise peremptory challenges during jury selection. The Court purports merely to follow precedents, but our cases do not compel this perverse result. To the contrary, our decisions specifically establish that criminal defendants and their lawyers are not government actors when they perform traditional trial functions.

It is well and properly settled that the Constitution's equal protection guarantee forbids prosecutors from exercising peremptory challenges in a racially discriminatory fashion. The Constitution, however, affords no similar protection against private action. "Embedded in our Fourteenth Amendment jurisprudence is a dichotomy between state action, which is subject to scrutiny under the Amendmen[t] . . . , and private conduct, against which the Amendment affords no shield, no matter how unfair that conduct may be." *National Collegiate Athletic Assn. v. Tarkanian* (1988). This distinction appears on the face of the Fourteenth Amendment, which provides that "*No State* shall . . . deny to any person within its jurisdiction the equal protection of the laws." The critical but straightforward question this case presents is whether criminal defendants and their lawyers, when exercising peremptory challenges as part of a defense, are state actors. . . .

From arrest, to trial, to possible sentencing and punishment, the antagonistic relationship between government and the accused is clear for all to see. Rather than squarely facing this fact, the Court, as in *Edmonson*, rests its finding of governmental action on the points that defendants exercise peremptory challenges in a courtroom and judges alter the composition of the jury in response to defendants' choices. I found this approach wanting in the context of civil controversies between private litigants, for reasons that need not be repeated here. But even if I thought *Edmonson* was correctly decided, I could not accept today's simplistic extension of it. The unique relationship between criminal defendants and the State precludes attributing defendants' actions to the State, whatever is the case in civil trials.

That the Constitution does not give federal judges the reach to wipe all marks of racism from every courtroom in the land is frustrating, to be sure. But such limitations are the necessary and intended consequence of the Fourteenth Amendment's state action requirement. Because I cannot accept the Court's conclusion that government is responsible for decisions criminal defendants make while fighting state prosecution, I respectfully dissent.

JUSTICE SCALIA, dissenting.

I agree with the Court that its judgment follows logically from *Edmonson v. Leesville Concrete Co., Inc.* (1991). For the reasons given in the *Edmonson* dissents, however, I think that case was wrongly decided. Barely a year later, we witness its reduction to the terminally absurd: A criminal defendant, in the process of defending himself against the state, is held to be acting on behalf of the state. Justice O'Connor demonstrates the sheer inanity of this proposition (in case the mere statement of it does not suffice), and the contrived nature of the Court's justifications. I see no need to add to her discussion, and differ from her views only in that I do not consider *Edmonson* distinguishable in principle—except in the principle that a bad decision should not be followed logically to its illogical conclusion.

Today's decision gives the lie once again to the belief that an activist, "evolutionary" constitutional jurisprudence always evolves in the direction of greater individual rights. In the interest of promoting the supposedly greater good of race relations in the society as a whole (make no mistake that that is what underlies all of this), we use the Constitution to destroy the ages-old right of criminal defendants to exercise peremptory challenges as they wish, to secure a jury that they consider fair. I dissent.

The Civil Rights Act of 1991
P.L. 102–166

In Wards Cove Packing Co. v. Atonio *(1989), a five-member Court majority implicitly overturned its earlier interpretation of Title VII of the 1964 Civil Rights Act in* Griggs v. Duke Power Co. *(1971) and held that the burden of proving that a defendant company's employment practice discriminates against a protected group always remains with the plaintiff and does not shift to the defendant. In this act, Congress rejects the Court's holding in* Wards Cove *and places the burden of proving that its employment practices do not discriminate squarely on the defendant.*

SECTION 1. SHORT TITLE
This Act may be cited as the "Civil Rights Act of 1991."

SEC. 2. FINDINGS
The Congress finds that—

(1) additional remedies under Federal law are needed to deter unlawful harassment and intentional discrimination in the workplace;

(2) the decision of the Supreme Court in *Wards Cove Packing Co. v. Atonio* (1989) has weakened the scope and effectiveness of Federal civil rights protections; and

(3) legislation is necessary to provide additional protections against unlawful discrimination in employment.

SEC. 3. PURPOSES
The purposes of this Act are—

(1) to provide appropriate remedies for intentional discrimination and unlawful harassment in the workplace;

(2) to codify the concepts of "business necessity" and "job related" enunciated by the Supreme Court in *Griggs v. Duke Power Co.* (1971), and in the other Supreme Court decisions prior to *Wards Cove Packing Co. v. Atonio* (1989);

(3) to confirm statutory authority and provide statutory guidelines for the adjudication of disparate impact suits under Title VII of the Civil Rights Act of 1964 (42 U.S.C. 2000e et seq.); and

(4) to respond to recent decisions of the Supreme Court by expanding the scope of relevant civil rights statutes in order to provide adequate protection to victims of discrimination.

SEC. 104. DEFINITIONS
Section 701 of the Civil Rights Act of 1964 (42 U.S.C. 2000e) is amended by adding at the end the following new subsections:

"(l) The term 'complaining party' means the Commission, the Attorney General, or a person who may bring an action or proceeding under this title.

"(m) The term 'demonstrates' means meets the burdens of production and persuasion.

"(n) The term 'respondent' means an employer, employment agency, labor organization, joint labor-management committee controlling apprenticeship or other training or retraining programs, including an on-the-job training program, or Federal entity subject to section 717."

SEC. 105. BURDEN OF PROOF IN DISPARATE IMPACT CASES
(a) Section 703 of the Civil Rights Act of 1964 (42 U.S.C. 2000e-2) is amended by adding at the end the following new subsection:

"(k)(1)(A) An unlawful employment practice based on disparate impact is established under this title only if—

"(i) a complaining party demonstrates that a respondent uses a particular employment practice that causes a disparate impact on the basis of race, color, religion, sex, or national origin and the respondent fails to demonstrate that the challenged practice is job related for the position in question and consistent with business necessity; or "(ii) the complaining party makes the demonstration described in subparagraph (C) with respect to an alternative employment practice and the respondent refuses to adopt such alternative employment practice.

"(B)(i) With respect to demonstrating that a particular employment practice causes a disparate impact as described in subparagraph (A)(i), the complaining party shall demonstrate that each particular challenged employment practice causes a disparate impact, except that if the complaining party can demonstrate to the court that the elements of a respondent's decision-making process are not capable of separation for analysis, the decisionmaking process may be analyzed as one employment practice.

"(ii) If the respondent demonstrates that a specific employment practice does not cause the disparate impact, the respondent shall not be required to demonstrate that such practice is required by business necessity.

"(C) The demonstration referred to by subparagraph (A)(ii) shall be in accordance with the law as it existed on June 4, 1989 [the date of *Wards Cove*], with respect to the concept of 'alternative employment practice.'"

Ricci v. DeStefano
557 U.S. 557 (2009)

New Haven, Connecticut, uses objective examinations to identify those firefighters best qualified for promotion. The results of such exams administered in 2003 to fill vacant lieutenant and captain positions showed that white candidates had outperformed minority candidates. Seventy-seven candidates completed the lieutenant examination—forty-three whites, nineteen blacks, and fifteen Hispanics. Of those, thirty-four candidates passed—twenty-five whites, six blacks, and three Hispanics. The top ten candidates were eligible for an immediate promotion to lieutenant, and all ten were white. Forty-one candidates completed the captain examination—twenty-five whites, eight blacks, and eight Hispanics. Of those, twenty-two candidates passed—sixteen whites, three blacks, and three Hispanics. The top nine candidates were eligible for an immediate promotion to captain—seven whites and two Hispanics. A rancorous public debate ensued, fed by the demagogic rhetoric of the Reverend Boise Kimber, an influential leader of New Haven's African American community and a close political confidant of New Haven mayor John DeStefano. Confronted with arguments both for and against certifying the test results—and threats of a lawsuit either way—the city threw out the results based on the statistical racial disparity. Petitioners, white and Hispanic firefighters who passed the exams but were denied a chance at promotions by the city's refusal to certify the test results, sued the city, alleging that discarding the test results discriminated against them based on their race in violation of Title VII of the Civil Rights Act of 1964. The defendants responded that had they certified the test results, they could have faced Title VII liability for adopting a practice having a disparate impact on minority firefighters. Without a jury trial, the district court granted summary judgment for the defendants, and the Second Circuit affirmed, in a three-judge panel that included Judge Sonia Sotomayor, in a one-paragraph per curiam opinion: "We affirm, for the reasons stated in the thorough, thoughtful, and well-reasoned opinion of the court below. In this case, the Civil Service Board found itself in the unfortunate position of having no good alternatives. We are not unsympathetic to the plaintiffs' expression of frustration. Mr. Ricci, for example, who is dyslexic, made intensive efforts that appear to have resulted in his scoring highly on one of the exams, only to have it invalidated. But it simply does not follow that he has a viable Title VII claim. To the contrary, because the Board, in refusing to validate the exams, was simply trying to fulfill its obligations under Title VII when confronted with test results that had a disproportionate racial impact, its actions were protected." The Supreme Court granted certiorari. Opinion of the Court: <u>Kennedy</u>, Roberts, Scalia, Thomas, Alito. Concurring opinions: <u>Scalia</u>; <u>Alito</u>, Scalia, Thomas. Dissenting opinion: <u>Ginsburg</u>, Stevens, Souter, Breyer.

JUSTICE KENNEDY delivered the opinion of the Court.

In the fire department of New Haven, Connecticut—as in emergency-service agencies throughout the Nation—firefighters prize their promotion to and within the officer ranks. An agency's officers command respect within the department and in the whole community; and, of course, added responsibilities command increased salary and benefits. Aware of the intense competition for promotions, New Haven, like many cities, relies on objective examinations to identify the best qualified candidates.

In 2003, 118 New Haven firefighters took examinations to qualify for promotion to the rank of lieutenant or captain. Promotion examinations in New Haven (or City) were infrequent, so the stakes were high. The results would determine which firefighters would be considered for promotions during the next two years, and the order in which they would be considered. Many firefighters studied for months, at considerable personal and financial cost.

When the examination results showed that white candidates had outperformed minority candidates, the mayor and other local politicians opened a public debate that turned rancorous. Some firefighters argued the tests should be discarded because the results showed the tests to be discriminatory. They threatened a discrimination lawsuit if the City made promotions based on the tests. Other firefighters said the exams were neutral and fair. And they, in turn, threatened a discrimination lawsuit if the City, relying on the statistical racial disparity, ignored the test results and denied promotions to the candidates who had performed well. In the end the City took the side of those who protested the test results. It threw out the examinations.

Certain white and Hispanic firefighters who likely would have been promoted based on their good test performance sued the City and some of its officials. Theirs is the suit now before us. The suit alleges that, by discarding the test results, the City and the named officials discriminated against the plaintiffs based on their race, in violation of both Title VII of the Civil Rights Act of 1964 and the Equal Protection Clause of the Fourteenth Amendment. The City and the officials defended their actions, arguing that if they had certified the results, they could have faced liability under Title VII for adopting a practice that had a disparate impact on the minority firefighters. The District Court granted summary judgment for the defendants, and the Court of Appeals affirmed.

We conclude that race-based action like the City's in this case is impermissible under Title VII unless the employer can demonstrate a strong basis in evidence that, had it not taken the action, it would have been liable under the disparate-impact statute. The respondents, we further determine, cannot meet that threshold standard. As a result, the City's action in discarding the tests was a violation of Title VII. In light of our ruling under the statutes, we need not reach the question whether respondents' actions may have violated the Equal Protection Clause.

Title VII of the Civil Rights Act of 1964 prohibits employment discrimination on the basis of race, color, religion, sex, or national origin. Title VII prohibits both intentional discrimination (known as "disparate treatment") as well as, in some cases, practices that are not intended to discriminate but in fact have a disproportionately adverse effect on minorities (known as "disparate impact").

As enacted in 1964, Title VII's principal nondiscrimination provision held employers liable only for disparate treatment. That section retains its original wording today. It makes it unlawful for an employer "to fail or refuse to hire or to discharge any individual, or otherwise to discriminate against any individual with respect to his compensation, terms, conditions, or privileges of employment, because of such individual's race, color, religion, sex, or national origin." Disparate-treatment cases . . . occur where an employer has "treated [a] particular person less favorably than others because of" a protected trait. A disparate-treatment plaintiff must establish "that the defendant had a discriminatory intent or motive" for taking a job-related action.

The Civil Rights Act of 1964 did not include an express prohibition on policies or practices that produce a disparate impact. But in *Griggs v. Duke Power Co.* (1971), the Court interpreted the Act to prohibit, in some cases, employers' facially neutral practices that, in fact, are "discriminatory in operation." The *Griggs* Court stated that the "touchstone" for disparate-impact liability is the lack of "business necessity": "If an employment practice which operates to exclude [minorities] cannot be shown to be related to job performance, the practice is prohibited." . . . [I]f an employer met its burden by showing that its practice was job-related, the plaintiff was required to show a legitimate alternative that would have resulted in less discrimination.

Twenty years after *Griggs*, the Civil Rights Act of 1991 was enacted. The Act included a provision codifying the prohibition on disparate-impact discrimination. That provision is now in force along with the disparate-treatment section already noted. Under the disparate-impact statute, a plaintiff establishes a prima facie violation by showing that an employer uses "a particular employment practice that causes a disparate impact on the basis of race, color, religion, sex, or national origin." An employer may defend against liability by demonstrating that the practice is "job related for the position in question and consistent with business necessity." Even if the employer meets that burden, however, a plaintiff may still succeed by showing that the employer refuses to adopt an available alternative employment practice that has less disparate impact and serves the employer's legitimate needs.

Petitioners allege that when the [the City] refused to certify the captain and lieutenant exam results based on the race of the successful candidates, it discriminated against them in violation of Title VII's disparate-treatment provision. The City counters that its decision was permissible because the tests "appear[ed] to violate Title VII's disparate-impact provisions."

Our analysis begins with this premise: The City's actions would violate the disparate-treatment prohibition of Title VII absent some valid defense. All the evidence demonstrates that the City chose not to certify the examination results because of the statistical disparity based on race—*i.e.*, how minority candidates had performed when compared to white candidates. As the District Court put it, the City rejected the test results because "too many whites and not enough minorities would be promoted were the lists to be certified." Without some other justifi-

cation, this express, race-based decision-making violates Title VII's command that employers cannot take adverse employment actions because of an individual's race.

The District Court did not adhere to this principle, however. It held that respondents' "motivation to avoid making promotions based on a test with a racially disparate impact . . . does not, as a matter of law, constitute discriminatory intent." And the Government makes a similar argument in this Court. It contends that the "structure of Title VII belies any claim that an employer's intent to comply with Title VII's disparate-impact provisions constitutes prohibited discrimination on the basis of race." But both of those statements turn upon the City's objective—avoiding disparate-impact liability—while ignoring the City's conduct in the name of reaching that objective. Whatever the City's ultimate aim—however well intentioned or benevolent it might have seemed—the City made its employment decision because of race. The City rejected the test results solely because the higher scoring candidates were white. The question is not whether that conduct was discriminatory but whether the City had a lawful justification for its race-based action.

We consider, therefore, whether the purpose to avoid disparate-impact liability excuses what otherwise would be prohibited disparate-treatment discrimination. Courts often confront cases in which statutes and principles point in different directions. . . . In providing this guidance our decision must be consistent with the important purpose of Title VII—that the workplace be an environment free of discrimination, where race is not a barrier to opportunity.

. . . Petitioners take a strict approach, arguing that under Title VII, it cannot be permissible for an employer to take race-based adverse employment actions in order to avoid disparate-impact liability—even if the employer knows its practice violates the disparate-impact provision. Petitioners would have us hold that, under Title VII, avoiding unintentional discrimination cannot justify intentional discrimination. That assertion, however, ignores the fact that, by codifying the disparate-impact provision in 1991, Congress has expressly prohibited both types of discrimination. We must interpret the statute to give effect to both provisions where possible. We cannot accept petitioners' broad and inflexible formulation.

Petitioners next suggest that an employer in fact must be in violation of the disparate-impact provision before it can use compliance as a defense in a disparate-treatment suit. Again, this is overly simplistic and too restrictive of Title VII's purpose. The rule petitioners offer would run counter to what we have recognized as Congress's intent that "voluntary compliance" be "the preferred means of achieving the objectives of Title VII." Forbidding employers to act unless they know, with certainty, that a practice violates the disparate-impact provision would bring compliance efforts to a near standstill. Even in the limited situations when this restricted standard could be met, employers likely would hesitate before taking voluntary action for fear of later being proven wrong in the course of litigation and then held to account for disparate treatment.

At the opposite end of the spectrum, respondents and the Government assert that an employer's good-faith belief that its actions are necessary to comply with Title VII's disparate-impact provision should be enough to justify race-conscious conduct. But the original, foundational prohibition of Title VII bars employers from taking adverse action "because of . . . race." And when Congress codified the disparate-impact provision in 1991, it made no exception to disparate-treatment liability for actions taken in a good-faith effort to comply with the new, disparate-impact provision in subsection. Allowing employers to violate the disparate-treatment prohibition based on a mere good-faith fear of disparate-impact liability would encourage race-based action at the slightest hint of disparate impact. A minimal standard could cause employers to discard the results of lawful and beneficial promotional examinations even where there is little if any evidence of disparate-impact discrimination. That would amount to a *de facto* quota system, in which a "focus on statistics . . . could put undue pressure on employers to adopt inappropriate prophylactic measures." Even worse, an employer could discard test results (or other employment practices) with the intent of obtaining the employer's preferred racial balance. That operational principle could not be justified, for Title VII is express in disclaiming any interpretation of its requirements as calling for outright racial balancing. The purpose of Title VII "is to promote hiring on the basis of job qualifications, rather than on the basis of race or color."

In searching for a standard that strikes a more appropriate balance, we note that this Court has considered cases similar to this one, albeit in the context of the Equal Protection Clause of the Fourteenth Amendment. The Court has held that certain government actions to remedy past racial discrimination—actions that are themselves based on race—are constitutional only where there is a "'strong basis in evidence'" that the remedial actions were necessary. *Richmond v. J. A. Croson Co.* (1989). . . .

We adopt the strong-basis-in-evidence standard as a matter of statutory construction to resolve any conflict between the disparate-treatment and disparate-impact provisions of Title VII.

Our statutory holding does not address the constitutionality of the measures taken here in purported compliance with Title VII. We also do not hold that meeting the strong-basis-in-evidence standard would satisfy the Equal Protection Clause in a future case. As we explain below, because respondents have not met their burden under Title VII, we need not decide whether a legitimate fear of disparate impact is ever sufficient to justify discriminatory treatment under the Constitution.

Nor do we question an employer's affirmative efforts to ensure that all groups have a fair opportunity to apply for promotions and to participate in the process by which promotions will be made. But once that process has been established and employers have made clear their selection criteria, they may not then invalidate the test results, thus upsetting an employee's legitimate expectation not to be judged on the basis of race. Doing so, absent a strong basis in evidence of an impermissible disparate impact, amounts to the sort of racial preference that Congress has disclaimed and is antithetical to the notion of a workplace where individuals are guaranteed equal opportunity regardless of race.

Title VII does not prohibit an employer from considering, before administering a test or practice, how to design that test or practice in order to provide a fair opportunity for all individuals, regardless of their race. And when, during the test-design stage, an employer invites comments to ensure the test is fair, that process can provide a common ground for open discussions toward that end. We hold only that, under Title VII, before an employer can engage in intentional discrimination for the asserted purpose of avoiding or remedying an unintentional disparate impact, the employer must have a strong basis in evidence to believe it will be subject to disparate-impact liability if it fails to take the race-conscious, discriminatory action. . . .

On this basis, we conclude that petitioners have met their obligation to demonstrate that there is "no genuine issue as to any material fact" and that they are "entitled to judgment as a matter of law." . . . In this Court, the City's only defense is that it acted to comply with Title VII's disparate-impact provision. To succeed on their motion, then, petitioners must demonstrate that there can be no genuine dispute that there was no strong basis in evidence for the City to conclude it would face disparate-impact liability if it certified the examination results.

The racial adverse impact here was significant, and petitioners do not dispute that the City was faced with a prima facie case of disparate-impact liability. . . . Based on the degree of adverse impact reflected in the results, respondents were compelled to take a hard look at the examinations to determine whether certifying the results would have had an impermissible disparate impact. The problem for respondents is that a prima facie case of disparate-impact liability—essentially, a threshold showing of a significant statistical disparity and nothing more—is far from a strong basis in evidence that the City would have been liable under Title VII had it certified the results. That is because the City could be liable for disparate-impact discrimination only if the examinations were not job related and consistent with business necessity, or if there existed an equally valid, less-discriminatory alternative that served the City's needs but that the City refused to

adopt. We conclude there is no strong basis in evidence to establish that the test was deficient in either of these respects. . . .

On the record before us, there is no genuine dispute that the City lacked a strong basis in evidence to believe it would face disparate-impact liability if it certified the examination results. In other words, there is no evidence—let alone the required strong basis in evidence—that the tests were flawed because they were not job-related or because other, equally valid and less discriminatory tests were available to the City. Fear of litigation alone cannot justify an employer's reliance on race to the detriment of individuals who passed the examinations and qualified for promotions. The City's discarding the test results was impermissible under Title VII, and summary judgment is appropriate for petitioners on their disparate-treatment claim.

* * *

The record in this litigation documents a process that, at the outset, had the potential to produce a testing procedure that was true to the promise of Title VII: No individual should face workplace discrimination based on race. Respondents thought about promotion qualifications and relevant experience in neutral ways. They were careful to ensure broad racial participation in the design of the test itself and its administration. As we have discussed at length, the process was open and fair.

The problem, of course, is that after the tests were completed, the raw racial results became the predominant rationale for the City's refusal to certify the results. The injury arises in part from the high, and justified, expectations of the candidates who had participated in the testing process on the terms the City had established for the promotional process. Many of the candidates had studied for months, at considerable personal and financial expense, and thus the injury caused by the City's reliance on raw racial statistics at the end of the process was all the more severe. Confronted with arguments both for and against certifying the test results—and threats of a lawsuit either way—the City was required to make a difficult inquiry. But its hearings produced no strong evidence of a disparate-impact violation, and the City was not entitled to disregard the tests based solely on the racial disparity in the results.

Our holding today clarifies how Title VII applies to resolve competing expectations under the disparate-treatment and disparate-impact provisions. If, after it certifies the test results, the City faces a disparate-impact suit, then in light of our holding today it should be clear that the City would avoid disparate-impact liability based on the strong basis in evidence that, had it not certified the results, it would have been subject to disparate-treatment liability.

Petitioners are entitled to summary judgment on their Title VII claim, and we therefore need not decide the underlying constitutional question. The judgment of the Court of Appeals is reversed, and the cases are remanded for further proceedings consistent with this opinion.

JUSTICE SCALIA, concurring.

I join the Court's opinion in full, but write separately to observe that its resolution of this dispute merely postpones the evil day on which the Court will have to confront the question: Whether, or to what extent, are the disparate-impact provisions of Title VII of the Civil Rights Act of 1964 consistent with the Constitution's guarantee of equal protection? The question is not an easy one.

The difficulty is this: Whether or not Title VII's disparate-treatment provisions forbid "remedial" race-based actions when a disparate-impact violation would *not* otherwise result—the question resolved by the Court today—it is clear that Title VII not only permits but affirmatively *requires* such actions when a disparate-impact violation *would* otherwise result. But if the Federal Government is prohibited from discriminating on the basis of race, *Bolling v. Sharpe*, (1954), then surely it is also prohibited from enacting laws mandating that third parties—*e.g.*, employers, whether private, State, or municipal—discriminate on the basis of race. As the facts of these cases illustrate, Title VII's disparate-impact provisions place a racial thumb on the scales, often requiring employers to evaluate the racial outcomes of their policies, and to make decisions based on (because of) those racial outcomes. That type of

racial decisionmaking is, as the Court explains, discriminatory.

To be sure, the disparate-impact laws do not mandate imposition of quotas, but it is not clear why that should provide a safe harbor. Would a private employer not be guilty of unlawful discrimination if he refrained from establishing a racial hiring quota but intentionally designed his hiring practices to achieve the same end? Surely he would. Intentional discrimination is still occurring, just one step up the chain. Government compulsion of such design would therefore seemingly violate equal protection principles. Nor would it matter that Title VII requires consideration of race on a wholesale, rather than retail, level. "[T]he Government must treat citizens as individuals, not as simply components of a racial, religious, sexual or national class." And of course the purportedly benign motive for the disparate-impact provisions cannot save the statute.

It might be possible to defend the law by framing it as simply an evidentiary tool used to identify genuine, intentional discrimination—to "smoke out," as it were, disparate treatment. But arguably the disparate-impact provisions sweep too broadly to be fairly characterized in such a fashion—since they fail to provide an affirmative defense for good-faith (*i.e.*, nonracially motivated) conduct, or perhaps even for good faith plus hiring standards that are entirely reasonable. This is a question that this Court will have to consider in due course. It is one thing to free plaintiffs from proving an employer's illicit intent, but quite another to preclude the employer from proving that its motives were pure and its actions reasonable.

The Court's resolution of these cases makes it unnecessary to resolve these matters today. But the war between disparate impact and equal protection will be waged sooner or later, and it behooves us to begin thinking about how—and on what terms—to make peace between them.

JUSTICE ALITO, with whom JUSTICE SCALIA and JUSTICE THOMAS join, concurring.

I join the Court's opinion in full. I write separately only because the dissent, while claiming that "[t]he Court's recitation of the facts leaves out important parts of the story," provides an incomplete description of the events that led to New Haven's decision to reject the results of its exam. The dissent's omissions are important because, when all of the evidence in the record is taken into account, it is clear that, even if the legal analysis of the dissent were accepted, affirmance of the decision below is untenable.

As initially described by the dissent, the process by which the City reached the decision not to accept the test results was open, honest, serious, and deliberative. But even the District Court admitted that "a jury could rationally infer that city officials worked behind the scenes to sabotage the promotional examinations because they knew that, were the exams certified, the Mayor would incur the wrath of [Rev. Boise] Kimber and other influential leaders of New Haven's African-American community." This admission finds ample support in the record. Reverend Boise Kimber, to whom the District Court referred, is a politically powerful New Haven pastor and a self-professed "'kingmaker.'" On one occasion, "[i]n front of TV cameras, he threatened a race riot during the murder trial of the black man arrested for killing white Yalie Christian Prince. He continues to call whites racist if they question his actions."

Reverend Kimber's personal ties with seven-term New Haven Mayor John DeStefano (Mayor) stretch back more than a decade. In 1996, for example, Mayor DeStefano testified for Rev. Kimber as a character witness when Rev. Kimber—then the manager of a funeral home—was prosecuted and convicted for stealing prepaid funeral expenses from an elderly woman and then lying about the matter under oath. "Reverend Kimber has played a leadership role in all of Mayor DeStefano's political campaigns, [and] is considered a valuable political supporter and vote-getter." According to the Mayor's former campaign manager (who is currently his executive assistant), Rev. Kimber is an invaluable political asset because "[h]e's very good at organizing people and putting together field operations, as a result of his ties to labor, his prominence in the religious community and his long-standing commitment to roots."

In 2002, the Mayor picked Rev. Kimber to serve as the Chairman of the New Haven Board of Fire Commissioners (BFC), "despite the fact that he had no experience in the profession, fire administration, [or] municipal management." In that capacity, Rev. Kimber told firefighters that certain new recruits would not be hired because "'they just have too many vowels in their name[s].'" After protests about this comment, Rev. Kimber stepped down as chairman of the BFC, but he remained on the BFC and retained "a direct line to the mayor."

Almost immediately after the test results were revealed in "early January" 2004, Rev. Kimber called the City's Chief Administrative Officer, Karen Dubois-Walton, . . . "to express his opinion" about the test results and "to have some influence" over the City's response. As discussed in further detail below, Rev. Kimber adamantly opposed certification of the test results—a fact that he or someone in the Mayor's office eventually conveyed to the Mayor. . . .

On January 22, 2004, the Civil Service Board (CSB) convened its first public meeting. Almost immediately, Rev. Kimber began to exert political pressure on the CSB. He began a loud, minutes-long outburst that required the CSB Chairman to shout him down and hold him out of order three times. Reverend Kimber protested the public meeting, arguing that he and the other fire commissioners should first be allowed to meet with the CSB in private.

Four days after the CSB's first meeting, Mayor DeStefano's executive aide sent an e-mail to Dubois-Walton. . . . The message clearly indicated that the Mayor had made up his mind to oppose certification of the test results (but nevertheless wanted to conceal that fact from the public). . . . On February 5, 2004, the CSB convened its second public meeting. Reverend Kimber again testified and threatened the CSB with political recriminations if they voted to certify the test results: "I look at this [Board] tonight. I look at three whites and one Hispanic and no blacks. . . . I would hope that you would not put yourself in this type of position, *a political ramification that may come back upon you* as you sit on this [Board] and decide the future of a department and the future of those who are being promoted." . . .

One of Rev. Kimber's "friends and allies," Lieutenant Gary Tinney, also exacerbated racial tensions before the CSB. After some firefighters applauded in support of certifying the test results, "Lt. Tinney exclaimed, 'Listen to the Klansmen behind us.'" Tinney also has strong ties to the Mayor's office. After learning that he had not scored well enough on the captain's exam to earn a promotion, Tinney called Dubois-Walton and arranged a meeting in her office. Tinney alleged that the white firefighters had cheated on their exams—an accusation that Dubois-Walton conveyed to the Board without first conducting an investigation into its veracity. The allegation turned out to be baseless.

Dubois-Walton never retracted the cheating allegation, but she and other executive officials testified several times before the CSB. In accordance with directions from the Mayor's office to make the CSB meetings appear deliberative, executive officials remained publicly uncommitted about certification—while simultaneously "work[ing] as a team" behind closed doors with the secretary of the CSB to devise a political message that would convince the CSB to vote against certification. . . .

At some point prior to the CSB's public meeting on March 18, 2004, the Mayor decided to use his executive authority to disregard the test results—*even if* the CSB ultimately voted to certify them. Accordingly, on the evening of March 17th, Dubois-Walton sent an e-mail to the Mayor . . . attaching two alternative press releases. The first would be issued if the CSB voted not to certify the test results; the second would be issued (and would explain the Mayor's invocation of his executive authority) if the CSB voted to certify the test results. Half an hour after Dubois-Walton circulated the alternative drafts, [an aide to the Mayor] replied: "[W]ell, that seems to say it all. Let's hope draft #2 hits the shredder tomorrow nite."

Soon after the CSB voted against certification, Mayor DeStefano appeared at a dinner event and "took credit for the scu[tt]ling of the examination results."

Taking into account all the evidence in the summary judgment record, a reasonable jury could find the following. Almost as soon as the City disclosed the racial makeup of the list of firefighters who scored the highest on the exam, the City administration was lobbied by

an influential community leader to scrap the test results, and the City administration decided on that course of action before making any real assessment of the possibility of a disparate-impact violation. To achieve that end, the City administration concealed its internal decision but worked—as things turned out, successfully—to persuade the CSB that acceptance of the test results would be illegal and would expose the City to disparate-impact liability. But in the event that the CSB was not persuaded, the Mayor, wielding ultimate decision-making authority, was prepared to overrule the CSB immediately. Taking this view of the evidence, a reasonable jury could easily find that the City's real reason for scrapping the test results was not a concern about violating the disparate-impact provision of Title VII but a simple desire to please a politically important racial constituency. It is noteworthy that the Solicitor General—whose position on the principal legal issue in this case is largely aligned with the dissent—concludes that "[n]either the district court nor the court of appeals . . . adequately considered whether, viewing the evidence in the light most favorable to petitioners, a genuine issue of material fact remained whether respondents' claimed purpose to comply with Title VII was a pretext for intentional racial discrimination. . . . "

I will not comment at length on the dissent's criticism of my analysis, but two points require a response.

The first concerns the dissent's statement that I "equat[e] political considerations with unlawful discrimination." The dissent misrepresents my position: I draw no such equation. Of course "there are many ways in which a politician can attempt to win over a constituency—including a racial constituency—without engaging in unlawful discrimination." But—as I assume the dissent would agree—there are some things that a public official cannot do, and one of those is engaging in intentional racial discrimination when making employment decisions.

The second point concerns the dissent's main argument—that efforts by the Mayor and his staff to scuttle the test results are irrelevant because the ultimate decision was made by the CSB. According to the dissent, "[t]he relevant decision was made by the CSB," and there is "scant cause to suspect" that anything done by the opponents of certification, including the Mayor and his staff, "prevented the CSB from evenhandedly assessing the reliability of the exams and rendering an independent, good-faith decision on certification." . . .

Petitioners are firefighters who seek only a fair chance to move up the ranks in their chosen profession. In order to qualify for promotion, they made personal sacrifices. Petitioner Frank Ricci, who is dyslexic, found it necessary to "hir[e] someone, at considerable expense, to read onto audiotape the content of the books and study materials. He "studied an average of eight to thirteen hours a day . . . , even listening to audio tapes while driving his car." Petitioner Benjamin Vargas, who is Hispanic, had to "give up a part-time job," and his wife had to "take leave from her own job in order to take care of their three young children while Vargas studied." "Vargas devoted countless hours to study . . . , missed two of his children's birthdays and over two weeks of vacation time," and "incurred significant financial expense" during the three-month study period. . . .

The dissent grants that petitioners' situation is "unfortunate" and that they "understandably attract this Court's sympathy." But "sympathy" is not what petitioners have a right to demand. What they have a right to demand is even-handed enforcement of the law—of Title VII's prohibition against discrimination based on race. And that is what, until today's decision, has been denied them.

JUSTICE GINSBURG, with whom JUSTICE STEVENS, JUSTICE SOUTER, and JUSTICE BREYER join, dissenting.

In assessing claims of race discrimination, "[c]ontext matters." In 1972, Congress extended Title VII of the Civil Rights Act of 1964 to cover public employment. At that time, municipal fire departments across the country, including New Haven's, pervasively discriminated against minorities. The extension of Title VII to cover jobs in firefighting effected no overnight change. It took decades of persistent effort, advanced by Title VII litigation, to open firefighting posts to members of racial minorities.

The white firefighters who scored high on New Haven's promotional exams understandably attract this Court's sympathy. But they had no vested right to promotion. Nor have other persons received promotions in preference to them. New Haven maintains that it refused to certify the test results because it believed, for good cause, that it would be vulnerable to a Title VII disparate-impact suit if it relied on those results. The Court today holds that New Haven has not demonstrated "a strong basis in evidence" for its plea. In so holding, the Court pretends that "[t]he City rejected the test results solely because the higher scoring candidates were white." That pretension, essential to the Court's disposition, ignores substantial evidence of multiple flaws in the tests New Haven used. The Court similarly fails to acknowledge the better tests used in other cities, which have yielded less racially skewed outcomes.

By order of this Court, New Haven, a city in which African-Americans and Hispanics account for nearly 60 percent of the population, must today be served—as it was in the days of undisguised discrimination—by a fire department in which members of racial and ethnic minorities are rarely seen in command positions. In arriving at its order, the Court barely acknowledges the path-marking decision in *Griggs v. Duke Power Co.* (1971), which explained the centrality of the disparate-impact concept to effective enforcement of Title VII. The Court's order and opinion, I anticipate, will not have staying power. . . .

Moving in a different direction, in *Wards Cove Packing Co. v. Atonio* (1989), a bare majority of this Court significantly modified the *Griggs* . . . delineation of Title VII's disparate-impact proscription. As to business necessity for a practice that disproportionately excludes members of minority groups, *Wards Cove* held, the employer bears only the burden of production, not the burden of persuasion. And in place of the instruction that the challenged practice "must have a manifest relationship to the employment in question," *Wards Cove* said that the practice would be permissible as long as it "serve[d], in a significant way, the legitimate employment goals of the employer."

In response to *Wards Cove* and "a number of [other] recent decisions by the United States Supreme Court that sharply cut back on the scope and effectiveness of [civil rights] laws," Congress enacted the Civil Rights Act of 1991. Among the 1991 alterations, Congress formally codified the disparate-impact component of Title VII. In so amending the statute, Congress made plain its intention to restore "the concepts of 'business necessity' and 'job related' enunciated by the Supreme Court in *Griggs v. Duke Power Co.* . . . and in other Supreme Court decisions prior to *Wards Cove Packing Co. v. Atonio.*" Once a complaining party demonstrates that an employment practice causes a disparate impact, amended Title VII states, the burden is on the employer "to demonstrate that the challenged practice is job related for the position in question and consistent with business necessity." If the employer carries that substantial burden, the complainant may respond by identifying "an alternative employment practice" which the employer "refuses to adopt."

Neither Congress' enactments nor this Court's Title VII precedents (including the now-discredited decision in *Wards Cove*) offer even a hint of "conflict" between an employer's obligations under the statute's disparate-treatment and disparate-impact provisions. Standing on an equal footing, these twin pillars of Title VII advance the same objectives: ending workplace discrimination and promoting genuinely equal opportunity.

Yet the Court today sets at odds the statute's core directives. When an employer changes an employment practice in an effort to comply with Title VII's disparate-impact provision, the Court reasons, it acts "because of race"—something Title VII's disparate-treatment provision generally forbids. This characterization of an employer's compliance-directed action shows little attention to Congress' design or to the *Griggs* line of cases Congress recognized as path-marking.

In codifying the *Griggs* . . . instructions, Congress declared unambiguously that selection criteria operating to the disadvantage of minority group members can be retained only if justified by business necessity.* In keeping with Congress' design, employers who reject

such criteria due to reasonable doubts about their reliability can hardly be held to have engaged in discrimination "because of" race. A reasonable endeavor to comply with the law and to ensure that qualified candidates of all races have a fair opportunity to compete is simply not what Congress meant to interdict. I would therefore hold that an employer who jettisons a selection device when its disproportionate racial impact becomes apparent does not violate Title VII's disparate-treatment bar automatically or at all, subject to this key condition: The employer must have good cause to believe the device would not withstand examination for business necessity. . . .

To "reconcile" the supposed "conflict" between disparate treatment and disparate impact, the Court offers an enigmatic standard. Employers may attempt to comply with Title VII's disparate-impact provision, the Court declares, only where there is a "strong basis in evidence" documenting the necessity of their action. . . .

As a result of today's decision, an employer who discards a dubious selection process can anticipate costly disparate-treatment litigation in which its chances for success—even for surviving a summary-judgment motion—are highly problematic. Concern about exposure to disparate-impact liability, however well grounded, is insufficient to insulate an employer from attack. Instead, the employer must make a "strong" showing that (1) its selection method was "not job related and consistent with business necessity," or (2) that it refused to adopt "an equally valid, less-discriminatory alternative." It is hard to see

---

*"5. On the assumption on which questions 4(a) and (b) are based, and assuming further that this Court will exercise its equity powers to the end described in question 4(b),

"(a) should this Court formulate detailed decrees in these cases;

"(b) if so, what specific issues should decrees reach;

"(c) should this Court appoint a special master to hear evidence with a view to recommending specific terms for such decrees;

"(d) should this Court remand to the courts of first instance with directions to frame decrees in these cases, and if so, what general directions should the decrees of this Court include and what procedures should the courts of first instance follow in arriving at the specific terms of more detailed decrees?"

how these requirements differ from demanding that an employer establish "a provable, actual violation" *against itself*. . . .

The Court's additional justifications for announcing a strong-basis-in-evidence standard are unimpressive. [D]iscarding the results of tests, the Court suggests, calls for a heightened standard because it "upset[s] an employee's legitimate expectation." This rationale puts the cart before the horse. The legitimacy of an employee's expectation depends on the legitimacy of the selection method. If an employer reasonably concludes that an exam fails to identify the most qualified individuals and needlessly shuts out a segment of the applicant pool, Title VII surely does not compel the employer to hire or promote based on the test, however unreliable it may be. Indeed, the statute's prime objective is to prevent exclusionary practices from "operat[ing] to 'freeze' the status quo." . . .

Applying what I view as the proper standard to the record thus far made, I would hold that New Haven had ample cause to believe its selection process was flawed and not justified by business necessity. Judged by that standard, petitioners have not shown that New Haven's failure to certify the exam results violated Title VII's disparate-treatment provision. . . .

Relying heavily on written tests to select fire officers is a questionable practice, to say the least. Successful fire officers, the City's description of the position makes clear, must have the "[a]bility to lead personnel effectively, maintain discipline, promote harmony, exercise sound judgment, and cooperate with other officials." These qualities are not well measured by written tests. . . .

* * *

This case presents an unfortunate situation; one New Haven might well have avoided had it utilized a better selection process in the first place. But what this case does not present is race-based discrimination in violation of Title VII. I dissent from the Court's judgment, which rests on the false premise that respondents showed "a significant statistical disparity," but "nothing more."

9

Substantive Equal Protection

CHAPTER OUTLINE

As Chapter 8 indicated, the Supreme Court initially viewed the Equal Protection Clause simply as a means for prohibiting racial discrimination. In keeping with this understanding, it customarily rejected invitations by counsel to employ the clause to strike down economic and social regulations that introduced distinctions among persons (i.e., that discriminated) on a nonracial basis. Even at the height of the *Lochner* era, when the justices were willing to rely on the Due Process Clause to invalidate what were thought to be unduly restrictive (and hence arbitrary and capricious) regulations, they flatly refused to consider using the Equal Protection Clause for matters unrelated to race. Clearly stating the Court's contempt for such equal protection claims, Justice Oliver Wendell Holmes described them in *Buck v. Bell* (1927) as "the usual last resort of constitutional arguments."

However, the wording of the Equal Protection Clause guarantees equal protection of the laws to *all persons,* not merely to black persons or ex-slaves. In this respect, it advances ends identical to those advanced by the original Constitution: namely, the empowerment and employment of a powerful national government capable of protecting individual rights and liberties from the tyrannical tendencies of the majority while, in the words of *The Federalist,* No. 10, "preserving the spirit and form of popular government." On its face, then, the Equal Protection Clause mandates equality under the law for all persons, regardless of race, gender, socioeconomic condition, nationality, age, place or duration of residence, and so on. Judicial acknowledgment of this fact came under the Warren Court (1953–1969), which for the first time systematically installed the clause as governing in cases involving types of unequal treatment wholly unrelated to traditional forms of racial discrimination. As a result of its seminal decisions, the judiciary has been called on to determine whether the Equal Protection Clause has been violated by state laws and practices that, inter alia, discriminate in favor of (rather than against) members of racial minorities, impose burdens on aliens and illegitimate children, treat the sexes differently, or impinge on the rights to interstate travel, welfare assistance, educational opportunity, and exercise of the franchise.

This increased receptivity to a wide range of equal protection challenges has posed new and difficult questions for the Court. So long as it understood the clause to prohibit only racial classifications, problems of interpretation remained manageable: the justices had only to look at the law or practice in question, determine whether it treated the races differently, and rule accordingly. Once the Court began employing the clause to evaluate other forms of unequal treatment, however, the problems grew in number and difficulty and have become virtually identical to the problems the Court faced in the area of substantive due process. The primary question facing the Court has become, does equal protection of the laws prohibit all legal categories or classifications? In other words, must all people be treated identically with respect to all matters? Because virtually all laws and regulations create legal categories, the Court has understandably refused to respond affirmatively to these questions; to do so would be to render government wholly inoperable. Instead, it has sought to interpret the Equal Protection Clause in such a way as to permit what it considers to be legitimate classifications—which lead inevitably to the question of what constitutes a legitimate classification.

As the justices have grappled with these and other problems, they have found it necessary to develop standards or criteria for interpreting the Equal Protection Clause and for determining whether the laws and practices in question pass constitutional muster. This chapter spells out these standards, examines how and where they have been employed, and identifies the many criticisms that have been leveled against them.

THE TWO-TIER APPROACH

As an aid in determining whether particular classifications are legitimate and hence permissible under the Equal Protection Clause, the Court initially developed what has been commonly called the two-tier approach. The tiers represent the levels of scrutiny that the Court will give to the classification under review. The relatively lenient standard imposed on the lower tier is usually called the rational-basis test. The upper tier imposes a much more stringent standard, referred to as the compelling-state-interest test or the strict-scrutiny standard.

Most statutory categorizations or classifications are reviewed under the rational-basis test, which is governed by the operation of four general principles:

1. The Equal Protection Clause does not prohibit the state from creating legal categories but rather allows a great deal of discretion in this regard; such categories, therefore, should be invalidated only when they lack any reasonable basis and hence are purely arbitrary.
2. A classification having some reasonable basis does not offend against the Equal Protection Clause merely because it is not made with mathematical nicety or because in practice it results in some inequality.
3. When a classification in the law is called into question, it should not be set aside if any state of facts can be conceived to justify it, and the existence of that state of facts at the time the law was enacted must be assumed.
4. The party challenging the classification must carry the burden of showing that it does not rest on any reasonable basis.

Some kinds of classifications, however, have to satisfy much more stringent standards. Under the two-tier system, the Court has subjected to strict scrutiny all laws that create "suspect classifications" or that impinge upon "fundamental rights" and has upheld them only if the state has been able to show that they advanced a compelling governmental interest and are the least restrictive means of achieving that interest.

Whenever suspect classifications or fundamental rights are involved, the Court will reverse the normal presumption of constitutionality and will demand that the state establish a compelling need for these statutory discriminations.[1] And even if such a need is demonstrated, the Court will require the state to show that the classification is narrowly tailored and that no less-restrictive alternatives exist. This is a stringent standard indeed, and it has been applied both to the ends that the state is seeking and to the means it employs to achieve those ends. Initially, this test was appropriately characterized by Professor Gerald Gunther as "'strict' in theory and fatal in practice."[2] As Chief Justice Burger noted in his dissent in *Dunn v. Blumstein* (1972), "To challenge [state policies] by the 'compelling state interest' standard is to condemn them all. So far as I am aware, no state law has ever satisfied this seemingly insurmountable standard and I doubt that one ever will, for it demands nothing less than perfection." Over time, however, certain justices have come to argue that a state has a compelling interest in diversifying the student body of a college or university (initially Justice Powell in *Regents of the University of California v. Bakke* [1978] and more recently Justice O'Connor in *Grutter v. Bolinger* [2003]) or in remedying "unlawful treatment of racial or ethnic groups subject to discrimination" provided the means chosen are "specifically and narrowly framed to accomplish that purpose" (Justices Powell and O'Connor in *Wygant v. Jackson Board of Education* [1986]). This relaxation of what strict scrutiny demands prompted Justice O'Connor in *Adarand Constructors, Inc. v. Peña* (1995) to declare. "We wish to dispel the notion that strict scrutiny is 'strict in theory, but fatal in fact.'

The unhappy persistence of both the practice and the lingering effects of racial discrimination against minority groups in this country is an unfortunate reality, and government is not disqualified from acting in response to it."

THE DEVELOPMENT OF AN INTERMEDIATE LEVEL OF REVIEW

The two-tier approach has caused the Court a number of problems. To begin, under this approach the Court experienced great difficulty in determining which classifications to label suspect. There has been complete agreement that blacks constitute a suspect class; the clear intention of the framers of the Fourteenth Amendment was to have blacks considered as such. Until recently, there also was general agreement that racial classifications of any kind should be considered formally suspect and hence should be subject to scrutiny under the compelling-state-interest test. That agreement, however, has largely broken up on the shoals of the controversy surrounding ameliorative racial preference. Similar controversies have also raged over whether other classifications are suspect, and if so, why. The Court attempted to provide a framework for analyzing these questions when it declared in *Johnson v. Robinson* (1974) that a classification was suspect if based on "an immutable characteristic determined solely by the accident of birth, or a class saddled with such disabilities, or subjected to such a history of purposeful unequal treatment, or relegated to such political powerlessness as to command extraordinary protection from the majoritarian political process." These words, however, failed to bind the Court together, and it has split badly when it has addressed equal protection challenges to classifications based on alienage (the condition of being an alien), illegitimacy, age, gender, and indigency.

A second difficulty with the two-tier approach was its failure to provide the Court with guidance as to the definition of a fundamental right. Over time, the Court has come to recognize as fundamental the right of free speech, the right of freedom of religion, the right of freedom of association, the right of personal privacy, the right to vote, the right to procreate, the right to marry, and the right to travel from state to state. At the same time, it has refused to recognize as fundamental other interests that many people would regard as equally important, including the rights to education, shelter, and food. The Court has defended its position by insisting that only those rights explicitly or implicitly guaranteed in the Constitution are fundamental and that nothing in the Constitution guarantees that the government will provide individuals with an education, a house, or welfare benefits. But as Justice Thurgood Marshall mused in his dissent in *San Antonio v. Rodriguez* (1973), "I would like to know where the Constitution guarantees the right to procreate, or the right to vote in state elections, or the right to appeal a criminal conviction. These are instances in which, due to the importance of the interests at stake, the Court has displayed a strong concern with the existence of discriminatory state treatment. But, the Court has never said or indicated that these are interests which independently enjoy full-blown constitutional protection." Marshall's critique could be underscored with other examples, and his point is well taken. In fact, the Court's method of determining fundamental rights appears to be of greater utility in providing the Court with an explanation for why it has refused to bestow fundamental status on a particular right than in assisting it in ascertaining what rights are indeed fundamental. This approach, in Justice William Rehnquist's words in *Rostker v. Goldberg* (1981), lent itself "all too readily [to] facile abstractions used to justify a result."

Of the several major problems involved in the two-tier approach, perhaps the most serious was its rigid, all-or-nothing character. The lenient rational-basis test almost never results in the invalidation of legislation, whereas the stringent compelling-state-interest standard almost always does. Between these two widely varying levels of scrutiny, there is no room for rights and classes of intermediate importance. As Justice Thurgood Marshall

SUSPECT CLASSIFICATIONS 579

complained in his dissent in *Massachusetts Board of Retirement v. Murgia* (1976), "All interests not fundamental and all classes not suspect are not the same; and it is time for the Court to drop the pretense that, for purposes of the Equal Protection Clause, they are." So long as the Court remained committed to the two-tier approach, however, that pretense could not be dropped, and the only critical decision facing the Court was, as Justice Marshall further remonstrated, "whether strict scrutiny should be invoked at all."

In place of this simplistic and rigid approach, Justice Marshall argued, in both *Murgia* and *San Antonio v. Rodriguez,* for a "more sophisticated" approach in which "concentration is placed upon the character of the classification in question, the relative importance to the individuals in the class discriminated against of the governmental benefits they do not receive, and the asserted state interests in support of the classification." Following Justice Marshall's lead but rejecting his precise formulation, a majority of the Court has, over time, come to acknowledge as legitimate, and to employ, an intermediate level of scrutiny. Under this "middle-tier" approach, the Court will hold that the classification in question must "serve important governmental objectives" and must be "substantially related to the achievement of those objectives." This standard is intermediate with respect both to ends and to means. As Professor Gunther has observed, "Where ends must be 'compelling' to survive strict scrutiny and merely 'legitimate' under the 'old' mode, 'important' objectives are required here, and where means must be 'necessary' under the 'new' equal protection, and merely 'rationally related' under the 'old' equal protection, they must be 'substantially related' to survive the 'intermediate' level of review."[3]

The exact meaning of this new intermediate level of review, however, remains very much in doubt. To begin with, the justices do not agree when the use of this "middle-tier" approach is justified. Some would limit it to classifications based on gender, as in *United States v. Virginia* (1996), or illegitimacy, as in *Clark v. Jeter* (1988); others (Justice Brennan in *Regents of the University of California v. Bakke* [1978], for instance) would extend it as well to cases involving ameliorative racial preference. This has prompted Justice Scalia to quip, "We have no established criterion for 'intermediate scrutiny' . . . , but essentially apply it when it seems like a good idea to load the dice." Additionally, some justices, through imprecision or an intentional desire to hold together fragile Court majorities, have all but obliterated the distinctions between the tiers. Justice Brennan's majority opinion in *Plyler v. Doe* (1982) is a case in point, as it totally blurred the distinctions between the lower and middle tiers. In this 5–4 decision, the Court invalidated on equal-protection grounds a Texas statute that withheld state funds from local school districts for the education of children who were illegal aliens and that further authorized the local school districts to deny enrollment to such children. Mixing language associated with different levels of review, Justice Brennan declared that a state law or practice "can hardly be considered rational unless it furthers some substantial goal of the State." Justice Ginsburg's opinion in *United States v. Virginia* is another. By holding that the "proffered justification" must be "exceedingly persuasive," that it "must be genuine, not hypothesized or invented *post hoc* in response to litigation," and that it "must not rely on overbroad generalizations about the different talents, capacities, or preferences of males and females," Justice Ginsburg so redefined intermediate scrutiny that it became, as Justice Scalia complained in his dissent, "indistinguishable from strict scrutiny."

SUSPECT CLASSIFICATIONS

Ameliorative Racial Preference

Ameliorative racial preference raises two distinct and difficult questions that highlight the difficulties attending the Court's approach to equal-protection analysis: Should racial classifications that burden whites be viewed as suspect? Should classifications employed for the asserted purpose of aiding a minority (typically blacks) be subjected to the strict scrutiny to which invidious classifications have been subjected? The judiciary has split badly on both of these questions.

Some justices reject the contention that discrimination against whites should be subjected to the same stringent review under the Fourteenth Amendment used in cases of discrimination against blacks. They argue that whites as a class have none of the "traditional indicia of suspectness." That is to say, whites as a class have not been subjected to historical and pervasive discriminations and deprivations, have not been stigmatized and set apart, and have not been relegated to a position of political powerlessness. Relying on that portion of *Plessy v. Ferguson* (1896) that *Brown v. Board of Education* (1954) did not repudiate, and on Chief Justice Warren's contention in *Brown* that the Equal Protection Clause merely proscribes classifications that "generate a feeling of inferiority" (i.e., that imply prejudice), advocates of this position have concluded that the clause offers whites no particular protections because discrimination in favor of blacks will not lead whites to assume that they are inferior. The most forceful defenders of this position have been Justice Thurgood Marshall in his dissent in *Richmond v. J. A. Croson Company* (1989) and Justice William Brennan in his opinions in *Bakke* and *Metro Broadcasting v. Federal Communications Commission* (1990).

In *Bakke*, the Court considered a special admission program of the Medical School of the University of California at Davis under which only disadvantaged members of certain minority races were considered for sixteen of the one hundred places in each year's class—it operated quite apart from the school's general admission program under which members of any race could qualify for the other eighty-four places in the class. Allan Bakke, a white plaintiff, argued that he had been denied admission to the school under the general admission program even though applicants with substantially lower entrance examination scores had been admitted under the special admission program. The California Supreme Court found that the special admission program operated as a racial quota because minority applicants in the special program were rated only against one another and sixteen places in the class of one hundred were reserved exclusively for them, and it held, therefore, that the challenged admission program violated the Equal Protection Clause and the Civil Rights Act of 1964. Justice Brennan wrote for a four-member bloc on the Court when he defended this special admission program:

> It is not . . . claimed that Davis' program in any way operates to stigmatize or single out any discrete and insular, or even any identifiable nonminority group. Nor will harm comparable to that imposed upon racial minorities by exclusion or separation on grounds of race be the likely result of the program. It does not, for example, establish an exclusive preserve for minority students apart from and exclusive of whites. Rather, its purpose is to overcome the effects of segregation by bringing the races together. True, whites are excluded from participation in the special admissions program, but this fact only operates to reduce the number of whites to be admitted in the regular admissions program in order to permit admission of a reasonable percentage—less than their proportion of the California population—of otherwise underrepresented qualified minority applicants.
>
> Nor was Bakke in any sense stamped as inferior by the Medical School's rejection of him. . . . Unlike discrimination against racial minorities, the use of racial preferences for remedial purposes does not inflict a pervasive injury upon individual whites in the sense that wherever they go or whatever they do there is a significant likelihood that they will be treated as second-class citizens because of their color. This distinction does not mean that the exclusion of a white resulting from

preferential use of race is not sufficiently serious to require justification; but it does mean that the injury inflicted by such a policy is not distinguishable from disadvantages caused by a wide range of government actions, none of which has ever been thought impermissible for that reason alone.

Four years later in *Metro Broadcasting*, Justice Brennan again argued—this time for a five-member majority—that benign race-conscious measures mandated by Congress, even though not remedial in the sense of being designed to compensate victims of past governmental or societal discrimination, were permissible under the equal-protection component of the Fifth Amendment's Due Process Clause. He concluded that the Federal Communication Commission's policy of giving preference to minority bids in competitive proceedings for new broadcast licenses and permitting limited categories of licenses to be transferred to minority-controlled firms in "distress sales," as mandated by Congress, served an important government interest in promoting broadcasting diversity, was substantially related to the achievement of that objective, and did not violate the Fifth Amendment's equal-protection component.

Other justices insist that discriminations against whites are as suspect as discriminations against blacks. This position is consistent with the first Justice Harlan's famous dictum, in his dissent in *Plessy v. Ferguson*, that "the Constitution is color-blind and neither knows nor tolerates classes among citizens." It was also taken by the California Supreme Court in *Bakke v. Regents of the University of California* (1976) and subsequently by a majority of the US Supreme Court in *Richmond v. J. A. Croson Company* (1989) and *Adarand Constructors, Inc. v. Peña* (1995).

In *Croson*, the Court struck down Richmond's minority set-aside program requiring that 30 percent of the total dollar amount of all city contracts go to minority business enterprises. Justice O'Connor declared that "the standard of review under the Equal Protection Clause is not dependent on the race of those burdened or benefited by a particular classification." For the *Croson* majority, "racial classifications are suspect," regardless of the race of those discriminated against or the reason for the discrimination. In fact, Justice Scalia went so far in his concurrence as to brand all racial classifications impermissible except for those undertaken in response to "a social emergency rising to the level of imminent danger to life or limb—for example, a prison race riot, requiring temporary segregation of inmates." For Scalia, any lesser justification, including the need to ameliorate the effects of past discrimination, is insufficient, for "the difficulty of overcoming the effects of past discrimination is as nothing compared with the difficulty of eradicating from our society the source of those effects, which is the tendency—fatal to a nation such as ours—to classify and judge men and women on the basis of their country of origin or the color of their skin. A solution to the first problem that aggravates the second is no solution at all."

In *Adarand*, the Court applied the same principles announced in *Croson* to the federal government. Justice O'Connor held for the majority that a federal subcontractor compensation clause designed to provide the prime contractor of a federal highway project with a financial incentive to hire disadvantaged business enterprises was suspect and could be sustained only if it passed the strict-scrutiny test. In so doing, she and her fellow colleagues in the majority expressly overturned *Metro Broadcasting* and its use of intermediate scrutiny as the standard of review for congressionally mandated ameliorative racial preference.

Intimately related to the dispute over whether whites are a suspect class has been the question of whether classifications employed for the asserted purpose of aiding minorities should be subjected to the same strict-scrutiny standard as invidious classifications. Justices who have not viewed whites as a suspect class have generally refused to invoke the strict-scrutiny standard in reviewing efforts by the state to remove the lingering effects of past discrimination.[4] Justice Brennan's opinion in *Bakke* reflected this point of view. The use of the compelling-state-interest test, he argued, would result in a denial of the aid that the classification was intended to provide. On the other hand, "because of the significant risk that racial classifications established for ostensibly benign purposes can be misused, causing effects not unlike that created by invidious classifications" (e.g., reinforcement of racial stereotypes), he deemed it inappropriate to inquire only whether there was any conceivable basis on which to sustain such a classification. Instead, he argued that such ameliorative racial preference be upheld if it could be shown that it served "an important and articulated purpose." Such a finding, he concluded, would require the same intermediate level of review appropriate in gender-based classifications—the classification in question "must serve important governmental objectives and be substantially related to the achievement of those objectives." Justice Brennan's opinion in *Metro Broadcasting* employed the same logic and relied on the same intermediate level of review.

By contrast, those justices who have viewed whites as a suspect class have invariably invoked the strict-scrutiny standard, and because classifications intended to aid blacks almost inevitably come at the expense of whites, they have typically invalidated the offending classification as failing to advance a compelling state interest unless its purpose is to remedy the lingering effects of past discrimination for the actual victims of that discrimination.[5]

There has recently arisen, however, one very major exception to this generalization; it was introduced by Justice Powell in his opinion in *Bakke* when he argued that the use of race by a state university in its admission decisions could serve the compelling interest of achieving a diverse student body.

Powell provided an interesting "swing vote" in that case. Four justices in *Bakke* held that both racial quotas and racial preferences in admissions violated the Civil Rights Act of 1964; as a consequence, they never reached the constitutional question of whether they violated the Equal Protection Clause. By contrast, four justices held that both racial quotas and racial preferences in admissions were sustainable under intermediate scrutiny and were permitted under both the Civil Rights Act and the Fourteenth Amendment. Justice Powell rejected the reasoning of both of these camps and stood alone. Using the compelling-state-interest test, he condemned racial quotas for their "disregard of individual rights"; however, he declared that the use by admission programs of racial preferences could pass the strict-scrutiny test if they were like the one at Harvard College, treating race as "a plus"—that is, as "simply one element to be weighed fairly against other elements," because "the attainment of a diverse student body clearly is a constitutionally permissible goal for an institution of higher education."

Although Justice Powell rejected the reasoning of both camps, he agreed with some of each camp's conclusions. He therefore ended up writing the judgment of the Court that found unconstitutional Davis's use of a racial quota in its admission program because it was not the least restrictive means by which to achieve the goal of diversity. For twenty years, his opinion carried great weight and was cited by universities across the country to justify racial preferences in their admission policies—the universities claimed they were free to pursue policies that added to the racial diversity of their student bodies so long as they did not contain explicit racial quotas. However, the significance of Powell's opinion was called into serious question in 1996 by Judge Jerry E. Smith of the Fifth Circuit Court of Appeals in his majority opinion in *Hopwood v. State of Texas* (1996), in which he held unconstitutional the use of racial preferences in admissions at the University of Texas Law School. He declared that those who relied on Justice Powell's opinion in *Bakke* to defend the use of race or ethnicity to achieve a diverse student body had to understand that

"Justice Powell's view is not binding precedent on this issue." As Judge Smith noted, although Justice Powell

> announced the judgment, no other Justice joined in that part of the opinion discussing the diversity rationale. In *Bakke,* the word "diversity" is mentioned nowhere except in Justice Powell's single-Justice opinion. In fact, the four-Justice opinion, which would have upheld the special admissions program under intermediate scrutiny, implicitly rejected Justice Powell's position. ("We also agree with Mr. Justice Powell that a plan like the 'Harvard' plan . . . is constitutional under our approach, at least so long as the use of race to achieve an integrated student body is necessitated by the lingering effects of past discrimination.") Thus, only one Justice concluded that race could be used solely for the reason of obtaining a heterogeneous student body.

The Supreme Court declined to hear the University of Texas's appeal and thereby passed up the opportunity to clarify the significance of Justice Powell's "single-Justice opinion." However, when Judge Boyce F. Martin Jr. of the Sixth Circuit Court of Appeals reached a conclusion in *Grutter v. Bollinger* in 2002 that was diametrically opposed to that of Judge Smith in *Hopwood,* the Court was left with no choice but to resolve the conflict among the federal circuits and address the question of whether Justice Powell's argument that diversity constitutes a compelling interest for a state university to engage in racial preferences in its admission decisions was in fact controlling. Judge Martin gave the Supreme Court no opportunity to skirt the issue, for he expressly asserted that "Justice Powell's opinion is binding on this court" and on that basis upheld as constitutional the University of Michigan Law School's explicit consideration of race and ethnicity in its admissions decisions because it has "a compelling state interest in achieving a diverse student body."

Grutter v. Bollinger was, in fact, one of two cases to come out of the University of Michigan that raised questions concerning the constitutionality of racial preferences; the other was *Gratz v. Bollinger,* which addressed the constitutionality of a far less subtle racial preference program of the university's undergraduate College of Literature, Science, and the Arts. Unlike the law school's use of race, which, Judge Martin insisted, was narrowly tailored because race was merely a "potential 'plus' factor," the undergraduate college's policy challenged in *Gratz* automatically awarded every applicant from an underrepresented racial or ethnic minority group twenty points of the one hundred points needed to guarantee admission. The federal district court that heard *Gratz* found that this policy was the functional equivalent of a racial quota and that it therefore ran afoul of Powell's opinion in *Bakke.* The Supreme Court granted certiorari in both of these cases, even though *Gratz* was still under consideration by the Sixth Circuit, and on June 23, 2003, it handed down decisions in both of these cases.

In *Grutter,* Justice O'Connor held for a five-member majority that Justice Powell's opinion in *Bakke* was indeed "the touchstone for constitutional analysis of race-conscious admissions policies" and that diversity constitutes "a compelling interest that can justify the narrowly tailored use of race in selecting applicants for admission to public universities." Repeatedly invoking Powell's name and his argument in *Bakke,* O'Connor found that the University of Michigan Law School had "a compelling interest in attaining a diverse student body" and that its desire to "enroll a 'critical mass' of minority students" to enhance the educational experience for all of its students survived strict scrutiny. Additionally, she argued that the law school's admission program was "narrowly tailored" in that it used race in a "flexible, nonmechanical way," evaluating each applicant "as an individual and not in a way that makes an applicant's race or ethnicity the defining feature of his or her application."

Until *Grutter* the only governmental use of race that a majority of the Court had held could survive strict scrutiny was remedying past discrimination. This was a very narrow exception to the rule that all race-based classifications are unconstitutional; it was also time bound—once the injury to the actual victims of discrimination was remedied, the justification to classify by race ended. In *Grutter,* however, the Court added a broad and open-ended justification for governmental use of race: diversity. O'Connor praised the benefits of diversity not only in educational settings but also in business ("the skills needed in today's increasingly global marketplace can only be developed through exposure to widely diverse people, cultures, ideas, and viewpoints"), the military ("a highly qualified, racially diverse officer corps is essential to the military's ability to fulfill its principle [*sic*] mission to provide national security"), and politics ("in order to cultivate a set of leaders with legitimacy in the eyes of the citizenry, it is necessary that the path to leadership be visibly open to talented and qualified individuals of every race and ethnicity"). And, further, the benefits of diversity are not time bound (like remedying the effects of past discrimination) but are understood to go on forever. It was clear that O'Connor was troubled by the prospect of the perpetual use of Court-approved racial classifications, and so she introduced her own "sunset" provision. "We expect that 25 years from now, the use of racial preferences will no longer be necessary to further the interest approved today."

O'Connor's majority opinion was met with a series of stinging dissents. Justice Thomas, for example, attacked her sunset provision: although he agreed with "the Court's holding that racial discrimination in higher education admissions will be illegal in 25 years," he insisted that "the Law School's current use of race violates the Equal Protection Clause and that the Constitution means the same thing today as it will in 300 months." He also attacked her conclusion that the law school had a compelling state interest in securing the educational benefits of a diverse student body. He pointed out that the State of Michigan had no compelling interest in having a law school at all—Alaska, Delaware, Massachusetts, New Hampshire, and Rhode Island all get by quite well with no publicly supported law schools; it therefore followed that it had no compelling interest in having an "elite one." The law school, he continued, could have all the diversity it sought by lowering its admission standards for all applicants; that, however, would hurt its "elite status." For Thomas, the Equal Protection Clause requires the law school to choose between diversity and high admission standards—between what he called "its classroom aesthetic [defined by Thomas as "a certain appearance, from the shape of the desks and tables to the color of the students sitting in them"] and its exclusionary admissions system—it cannot have it both ways."

In his dissent, Chief Justice Rehnquist focused primarily on the issue of "critical mass." The law school insisted that it sought to accumulate a "critical mass" of each underrepresented minority group, but, Rehnquist noted, "the record demonstrates that the Law School's admissions practices with respect to these groups differ dramatically and cannot be defended under any consistent use of the term 'critical mass.'" He reviewed the law school's admission data and declared, "If the Law School is admitting between 91 and 108 African Americans in order to achieve 'critical mass,' thereby preventing African-American students from feeling 'isolated or like spokespersons for their race,' one would think that a number of the same order of magnitude would be necessary to accomplish the same purpose for Hispanics and Native Americans." But, in fact, he found that the law school admitted only half that number of Hispanics and only a sixth that number of Native Americans. For Rehnquist, the only explanation for this disparity was that the law school was using "critical mass" as a ruse to cover its real objective: "racial balancing," which O'Connor herself insisted would be "patently unconstitutional."

Although the Court in *Grutter* upheld Michigan's use of race as a "plus" factor to achieve diversity in its law school, in *Gratz* it struck down the state's mechanistic approach for achieving a diverse student body at the undergraduate level. In his majority opinion, Chief Justice Rehnquist was forced to accept the principle announced in *Grutter* that diversity constituted a compelling state interest for employing racial preferences, but he was able to declare for a six-member majority (the four dissenters in *Grutter* plus O'Connor and Breyer) that "the University's policy, which automatically distributes 20 points, or one-fifth of the points needed to guarantee admission, to every single 'underrepresented minority' applicant solely because of race, is not narrowly tailored to achieve the interest in educational diversity that respondents claim justifies their program." In his dissent, Justice Souter took his cues from Justice Powell: "Justice Powell's opinion in *Bakke* rules out a racial quota or set-aside, in which race is the sole fact of eligibility for certain places in a class." Because Michigan's undergraduate admission program did not employ an explicit quota or set-aside, Souter concluded that it was therefore "closer to what *Grutter* approves than to what *Bakke* condemns" and declared that it "should not be held unconstitutional on the current record."

Grutter held that an admission program that uses race to achieve the compelling government interest of diversity can pass the strict scrutiny if it can be shown that it is narrowly tailored. But, as the Court made clear in *Fisher v. University of Texas at Austin* (2013), it will reject lower court judgments that give substantial deference to a university in deciding whether its specific plan was narrowly tailored to achieve its stated goal. After *Hopwood* declared unconstitutional the University of Texas's use of racial preferences, the Texas legislature passed the Top Ten Percent Law that grants automatic admission to the university to all students in the top percent of their class at high schools in Texas. After the passage of this race-neutral law, minority enrollment increased sharply to approximately 20 percent of the student body. But the university was not altogether pleased with the kind of diversity the law produced. The enrolled minority students tended to come from small, rural schools in the poorer parts of the state and were themselves less well-equipped to perform well academically. The university wanted what it called "diversity within the diversity": it wanted the upper-middle-class sons and daughters of successful minority professionals from the state's urban centers who, having attending highly-competitive high schools, were often excellent students even if they were not in the top ten percent of their class. So, the day that *Grutter* was decided, the president of the university announced that it would augment the Top Ten Percent Law and use race as a "plus" factor in admission decisions. When Abigail Fisher, a white student denied admission to the University of Texas, challenged the constitutionality of its policy, the District Court granted summary judgment to the University, and the United States Court of Appeals for the Fifth Circuit affirmed. It held that Fisher could challenge only "whether [the University's] decision to reintroduce race as a factor in admissions was made in good faith." And, it continued, in considering such a challenge, it would "presume the University acted in good faith" and place on Fisher the burden of rebutting that presumption. The Court of Appeals held that to "second-guess the merits" of this aspect of the University's decision was a task it was "ill-equipped to perform" and that it would attempt only to "ensure that [the University's] decision to adopt a race-conscious admissions policy followed from [a process of] good faith consideration." It concluded that "the narrow-tailoring inquiry—like the compelling-interest inquiry—is undertaken with a degree of deference to the Universit[y]." And, because it believed that "the efforts of the University have been studied, serious, and of high purpose," it held that the use of race in the admissions program fell within "a constitutionally protected zone of discretion."

In a 7–1 decision, Justice Kennedy found this deference unacceptable:

These expressions of the controlling standard are at odds with *Grutter*'s command that "all racial classifications imposed by government 'must be analyzed by a reviewing court under strict scrutiny.'" . . . *Grutter* did not hold that good faith would forgive an impermissible consideration of race. It must be remembered that "the mere recitation of a 'benign' or legitimate purpose for a racial classification is entitled to little or no weight." Strict scrutiny does not permit a court to accept a school's assertion that its admissions process uses race in a permissible way without a court giving close analysis to the evidence of how the process works in practice.

Kennedy insisted that, "in order for judicial review to be meaningful, a university must make a showing that its plan is narrowly tailored to achieve the only interest that this Court has approved in this context: the benefits of a student body diversity that "encompasses a . . . broa[d] array of qualifications and characteristics of which racial or ethnic origin is but a single though important element." The Supreme Court vacated the judgment of the Court of Appeals and remanded it for "future proceedings consistent with this opinion."

After the Supreme Court upheld the University of Michigan's law school's use of race-based preferences in *Grutter,* and after the university was compelled to revised its undergraduate admissions process in light of *Gratz,* although doing so in a way that still allowed limited use of race-based preferences, the Michigan voters adopted as an amendment to the state constitution, Proposal 2, which prohibited, among other things, the use of race-based preferences as part of the admissions process for state universities. But, that posed a question: If the use of race serves the compelling government interest of promoting diversity, can the citizens of a state reject that compelling government interest? Can they refuse to implement what the Court said they are permitted to do? The Coalition to Defend Affirmative Action by Any Means Necessary (BAMN) challenged Proposal 2 in federal court, arguing that it violated the Equal Protection Clause. It did so on the basis of what is called the political-process doctrine; by making it unconstitutional for universities to grant preferences in admission decisions based on race but not unconstitutional for universities to grant preferences in admission decisions based on, for example, low-income status or legacy status. Proposal 2 made it more difficult for those seeking racial preferences to achieve their goal (they would first have to gain the political support of the public to repeal Proposal 2) than for those seeking other preferences. The Sixth Circuit Court of Appeal found the political-process argument persuasive and struck down Proposal 2. The Supreme Court, in a 6–2 decision, did not and reversed in *Schuette v. Coalition to Defend Affirmative Action* (2014). Justice Scalia, in his concurrence in the judgment, posed the question before the Court with singular clarity: "Does the Equal Protection Clause forbid a State from banning a practice [i.e., a race-based admission policy] that the Clause barely—and only provisionally—permits? For him, and for a majority of his colleagues, "the question answer[ed] itself."

Bakke, Hopwood, the University of Michigan cases, *Fisher,* and *Schuette* all involved institutions of higher education that attempted to justify the use of race in their admission decisions in order to increase the diversity of their student bodies. In *Parents Involved in Community Schools v. Seattle School District No. 1* (2007), the Court reviewed lower federal court decisions that had employed *Grutter* to affirm voluntary student-assignment plans by school districts that relied on race to determine which schools certain children could attend. These courts held these plans to survive strict scrutiny because they were narrowly tailored to serve the compelling governmental interests of achieving racial diversity and avoiding racial isolation. Five members of the Court found these plans unconstitutional; Chief Justice Roberts held that these school-district plans "are not governed by *Grutter.*" In *Grutter,* he noted, "this Court relied upon considerations unique to institutions of higher education, noting that in light of 'the expansive freedoms of speech and thought associated with the university environment, universities occupy a special niche in our constitutional tradition.' The Court explained that 'context matters' in applying strict scrutiny, and repeatedly noted that it was addressing the use of race 'in the context of higher education.'" (Justice Kennedy supplied the fifth vote to invalidate these plans but found unacceptable Chief Justice Roberts' "all-too-unyielding insistence that race cannot be a factor in instances when, in my view, it may be taken into account.")

Justice Breyer dissented, lamenting that Roberts's opinion broke "the "promise of *Brown,*" which he described as "the promise of true racial equality." Roberts shot back: Quoting *Brown II,* he noted that the promise of *Brown I* was "to achieve a system of determining admission to the public schools on a nonracial basis." And, he continued, that promise was what the Court's decision in *Parents Involved* was keeping. "The way to stop discrimination on the basis of race is to stop discriminating on the basis of race." Justice Thomas agreed in his concurrence and developed at length later in his opinion what he introduced in this sentence: "Disfavoring a color-blind interpretation of the Constitution, the dissent would give school boards a free hand to make decisions on the basis of race—an approach reminiscent of that advocated by the segregationists in *Brown.*"

Alienage

The Court's responses to statutory classifications that deprive aliens of rights enjoyed by citizens have highlighted the problems confronting the justices in consistently applying strict-scrutiny standards to equal-protection challenges. In *Graham v. Richardson* (1971) the Court held that aliens were a suspect class and that restrictions on aliens were to be treated by the Court with "heightened judicial solicitude." With *Graham* as precedent and employing the compelling-state-interest test, the justices subsequently voided a Connecticut law denying aliens the right to practice law (*In re Griffiths* [1973]), a New York statute barring aliens from holding positions in the competitive class of the state civil service (*Sugarman v. Dougall* [1973]), a regulation of the Civil Service Commission limiting employment in the US competitive civil service to citizens of the United States (*Hampton v. Wong* [1976]), and a New York law denying resident aliens financial aid for higher education unless they applied for US citizenship (*Nyquist v. Mauclet* [1977]). In *Foley v. Connelie* (1978), however, the Court sustained a New York law barring aliens from the state police force. And in *Ambach v. Norwick* (1979), it upheld a New York statute forbidding certification as a public school teacher to any person who was not a citizen, unless that person had manifested an intention to apply for citizenship. In both cases, the Court insisted that not all limitations on aliens were suspect and employed the rational-basis test to sustain the challenged classifications.

The Court argued in *Foley* and *Ambach* that some state functions, such as serving as a state trooper and teaching in the public schools, are so bound up with the operation of the state as a governmental entity as to permit the exclusion of all persons who have not become part of the process of self-government. "A discussion of the police function is essentially a description of one of the basic functions of government, especially in a complex modern society where police presence is pervasive," Chief Justice Burger wrote in *Foley.* Justice Powell in *Ambach* saw the teachers as performing an equally important and central function: "Public education, like the police function, 'fulfills a most fundamental obligation of government to its constituency.' The importance of public schools in the preparation of individuals for participation as citizens, and in the preservation of the values on which our society rests, long has been recognized by our decisions."

In recognizing this rule for governmental functions as an exception to the strict-scrutiny standard generally applicable to classifications based on alienage, the Court followed important principles inherent in the Constitution. The distinction between citizens and aliens, though ordinarily irrelevant to private activity, is fundamental to the definition and government of a state, and the constitutional references to such a distinction indicate that the status of citizenship was meant to have significance in the structure of our government. Because of this special significance, the Court ruled in *Foley* and *Ambach,* governmental entities, when exercising the functions of government, must have wide latitude in limiting the participation of aliens. The *Foley* and *Ambach* rulings, however, are difficult to reconcile with the Court's earlier holdings, especially *In re Griffiths.* If a state may bar aliens from law enforcement or teaching because those tasks go to the heart of representative government, it is difficult to understand why a state may not also bar aliens from practicing law. Lawyers, after all, serve as officers of the court and participate directly in the formulation, execution, and review of broad public policy. The Court, however, has never overturned *In re Griffiths* or reconciled its apparently contradictory holdings on the exact status of alienage as a suspect classification.

Illegitimacy

The Court's course in reviewing classifications based on illegitimacy has been even more wavering than its course in reviewing classifications based on alienage. Although it has never labeled illegitimacy a suspect classification, the Court has exercised a degree of heightened scrutiny in most cases involving illegitimacy classifications, which have been struck down with some frequency. Nowhere in its rulings, however, has the Court explained precisely what degree of heightened scrutiny is warranted, and why.

The Court's first encounter with illegitimacy classifications under the two-tier approach came in *Levy v. Louisiana* (1968), in which it held that a law that denied unacknowledged illegitimate children the right to recover damages for the wrongful death of their mothers violated the Equal Protection Clause. The exact reason for the law's unconstitutionality, however, was left in doubt, as Justice Douglas's majority opinion hinted at both the rational-basis test and the compelling-state-interest standard. Three years later, in *Labine v. Vincent* (1971), the Court withdrew from the heightened scrutiny suggested in *Levy* and upheld an intestate succession provision that subordinated the rights of acknowledged illegitimate children to those of the parents' other relatives. Employing the rational-basis test, the *Labine* majority argued that absent an express constitutional guarantee, "it is for the legislature, not this Court, to select from among possible laws." Barely one year later, in *Weber v. Aetna Casualty and Surety Company* (1972), the Court abandoned what it had said in *Labine* and returned to its formulations in *Levy* by holding that the claims of dependent unacknowledged illegitimate children to death benefits under a workmen's compensation law could not be subordinated to the claims of legitimate children.

Such vacillation continued in *Mathews v. Lucas* (1976) and *Trimble v. Gordon* (1977). *Lucas* sustained death-benefits provisions of the Social Security Act that presumed legitimate children to have been dependent on their fathers but required proof of dependency on the part of illegitimate children. In *Trimble,* on the other hand, the Court struck down a provision of the Illinois law governing intestate succession that barred illegitimate children from inheriting from their fathers.

Lucas and *Trimble* illustrate the Court's uneasy search for an articulable and consistently applicable standard of review for illegitimacy classifications. Both cases rejected the strict-scrutiny standard yet indicated that the rational-basis test was only a minimum criterion and that sometimes the Court "requires more." Justice O'Connor's unanimous opinion in *Clark v. Jeter* (1988) identified that something more as the "intermediate" level of review, which the Court then used to conclude that Pennsylvania's six-year statute of limitations for support actions on behalf of illegitimate children "does not withstand heightened scrutiny."

Age

In reviewing classifications based on age, the Court has consistently adopted a deferential posture and employed the rational-basis test. In *Massachusetts Board of Retirement v. Murgia* (1976), the Court upheld a state law mandating that state police officers retire at age fifty. Three years later, in *Vance v. Bradley* (1979), it rejected an equal-protection challenge to a federal law requiring foreign-service personnel to retire at age sixty. The Court has refused to recognize the aged as a suspect class, noting in *Murgia* that old age is a universal condition and that "even if the statute could be said to impose a penalty upon a class defined as the aged, it would not impose a distinction sufficiently akin to those classifications that we have found suspect to call for strict judicial scrutiny." Both *Murgia* and *Vance* elicited strongly worded dissents from Justice Marshall, who urged the adoption of a more flexible approach in which the Court would review the importance of the governmental benefits denied, the character of the class, and the asserted state interests.

Intellectual Disability

In *City of Cleburne, Texas v. Cleburne Living Center* (1985), the Supreme Court in a 6–3 decision refused to apply a "heightened" level of scrutiny to legislation affecting the intellectually disabled. Cleburne Living Center had sought to lease a building for the operation of a group home for the intellectually disabled; when it was denied a special-use permit to do so by the city (which classified the group home under its zoning ordinance as a "hospital for the feebleminded"), it brought suit, alleging that the zoning ordinance in question was unconstitutional, both on its face and as applied. The federal district court rejected its contentions, but the Court of Appeals for the Fifth Circuit reversed, holding that intellectual disability was a "quasi-suspect" classification and that under a "heightened scrutiny equal protection test," the ordinance was unconstitutional, for it did not substantially further an important governmental purpose. Justice White spoke for the Court when he held that where individuals in a group affected by a statute or ordinance have distinguishing characteristics relevant to interests a state has the authority to implement, the Equal Protection Clause requires only that the classification drawn by the statute or ordinance be rationally related to a legitimate government interest. That requirement was met in the case; because intellectually disabled persons have a reduced ability to cope with and function in the everyday world, they are in fact different from other persons, and the state's interest in dealing with and providing for them is legitimate. The Court, nonetheless, struck down Cleburne's zoning ordinance. Justice White found that requiring a permit in this case rested on "an irrational prejudice against the mentally retarded." Justice Marshall concurred in the Court's judgment but objected to its refusal to bring a heightened level of scrutiny to bear on legislation affecting the rights of the intellectually disabled.

Gender-Based Classifications

The problems encountered by the Court in reviewing gender-based classifications clearly exposed the deficiencies of the two-tier approach and were the impetus for the development of the intermediate level of scrutiny.

The Court's traditional stance toward sex-discrimination claims was exhibited in *Goesaert v. Cleary* (1948) when it rejected an attack on a Michigan law that provided that no woman could obtain a bartender's license unless she was "the wife or daughter of the male owner" of a licensed liquor establishment. A radical break with that tradition occurred in 1971, when the Court in *Reed v. Reed* struck down a provision of Idaho's probate code that gave preference to men over women as administrators of estates. Employing the rational-basis test, Chief Justice Burger declared for a unanimous Court in *Reed* that the question before it was "whether a difference in sex of competing applicants for letters of administration bears a rational relationship to a state objective that is sought to be advanced by the operation of [the Idaho law]." Finding no such relationship, he branded the mandatory preference given to men over women as "the very kind of arbitrary legislative choice" forbidden by the Equal Protection Clause.

This apparent consensus that classifications based on sex were to be reviewed under the rational-basis test lasted a scant two years. In *Frontiero v. Richardson* (1973), four members of the Court argued that "classifications based upon sex, like classifications based on race, alienage, and national origin, are inherently suspect." Justices Douglas, White, and Marshall joined Justice Brennan in applying the compelling-state-interest test to find unconstitutional a federal statute under which married servicemen automatically qualified for increased housing allowances and medical and dental benefits for their wives, whereas married servicewomen qualified for those fringe benefits only if their husbands were dependent on them for at least one-half of their support. Four other justices concurred in Brennan's judgment that the statute was unconstitutional but rejected his claim that sex is a suspect classification in favor of *Reed*'s rational-basis test. Justice Powell's concurrence in *Frontiero* was especially interesting in that one of his principal reasons for refusing to view sex as a suspect classification was that the Equal Rights Amendment (ERA) had been approved by Congress and submitted to the states for ratification. If ratified, the amendment would have made sex-based classifications suspect, and Justice Powell saw no reason or need to "preempt by judicial action a major political decision" then in process of resolution.

Had a fifth member joined Justices Brennan, Douglas, White, and Marshall in either *Frontiero* or a subsequent case, a majority of the Court would have been on record as declaring that sex was a suspect classification. Ratification of the ERA would have had the same result. In the absence of either of these developments, sex-based classifications have failed to achieve suspect status, although movement toward what Justice Brennan sought in *Frontiero* has occurred. In *Craig v. Boren* (1976), Brennan was able to prevail on his judicial brethren to heighten somewhat the review given to sex-based classifications. Without formally acknowledging that the Court was about to embrace a new intermediate level of review, he announced that "classifications by gender must serve important governmental objectives and must be substantially related to achievement of those objectives." Using this middle-tier test, he invalidated sections of an Oklahoma statute that allowed females to purchase 3.2 percent beer at age eighteen but prohibited males from doing so until age twenty-one. He found unpersuasive the state's contention that such legislation was the proper way to deal with "the pervasiveness of youthful participation in motor vehicle accidents following the imbibing of alcohol." Then, in *Mississippi University for Women [MUW] v. Hogan* (1982), Justice O'Connor applied an intermediate level of scrutiny to sustain an equal-protection challenge to Mississippi's policy of excluding men from MUW's School of Nursing. Interestingly, O'Connor never mentioned *Craig* and, in fact, offered a different formulation of the middle tier: a governmental classification based on gender will be upheld, she insisted, only if the government meets the burden of showing a "legitimate" and "exceedingly persuasive justification" for the classification and demonstrating "the requisite direct, substantial relationship" between the governmental objective and the means it employs to achieve the objective. This MUW had failed to do, and the result was the perpetuation of "the stereotyped view of nursing as an exclusively woman's job."

In *United States v. Virginia* (1996), the Court employed intermediate review to find unconstitutional Virginia's policy of excluding women from the Virginia Military Institute (VMI), a school whose mission was to produce "citizen-soldiers"—men prepared for leadership in civilian life and in military service. Justice Ginsburg's formulation of the "middle-tier" test was as follows: "The burden of justification is demanding and it rests entirely on the State. The State must show 'at least that the [challenged] classification serves important governmental objectives and that the discriminatory means employed are substantially related to the achievement of those objectives.' The justification must be genuine, not hypothesized or invented *post hoc* in response to litigation. And it must not rely on overbroad generalizations about the different talents, capacities, or preferences of males and females."

Employing this intermediate level of review, the Court has, however, upheld a number of "benevolent" classifications that accord women preferential treatment. In every ruling of this type, the Court has based its decision on the argument that such treatment is a compensation for past economic discrimination. In *Kahn v. Shevin* (1974), for example, the Court sustained a Florida statute granting a $500 property-tax exemption to widows but not to widowers. Justice Douglas wrote for the Court:

> There can be no dispute that the financial difficulties confronting the lone woman . . . exceed those facing the man. Whether from overt discrimination or from the socialization process of a male-dominated culture, the job market is inhospitable to the woman seeking any but the lowest paid jobs. There are, of course, efforts under way to remedy this situation. . . . But firmly entrenched practices are resistant to such pressures. . . . We deal here with a state tax law reasonably designed to further the state policy of cushioning the financial impact of spousal loss upon the sex for whom that loss imposes a disproportionately heavy burden.

Similarly, in *Schlesinger v. Ballard* (1975), the Court sustained a sex classification in a congressional enactment providing for mandatory discharge of naval officers who, after designated periods of service, have failed to gain promotion. The service period was set at nine years for men and thirteen years for women. Ballard, a male officer who failed to receive promotion after nine years, challenged the statute. In sustaining it, the Court pointed out that female officers "because of restriction on their participation in combat . . . do not have equal opportunities for professional service equal to those of male line officers."[6]

Finally, in *Heckler v. Mathews* (1984), the Court upheld a temporary pension-offset provision, applicable to nondependent men but not to similarly situated nondependent women, that required a reduction of spousal benefits by the amount of federal or state government pensions received by Social Security applicants. This provision temporarily revived a gender-based classification that the Court had invalidated earlier in *Califano v. Goldfarb* (1977), but, Justice Brennan insisted, it was "directly and substantially related to the important governmental interest of protecting individuals who planned their retirements in reasonable reliance on the law" invalidated in *Goldfarb*.

The Court has not upheld all "benevolent" classifications, however. Attempts to justify sex-based classifications as compensation for past discrimination against women have been rejected when the classifications involved have penalized women—albeit in unobvious ways. Thus, in *Weinberger v. Wiesenfeld* (1975), the Court held void a provision of the Social Security Act that provided survivor's benefits for the widow of a deceased husband but not for the widower of a deceased wife. And in *Califano v. Goldfarb* (1977), it set aside a gender-based distinction in the Federal Old-Age, Survivors, and Disability Insurance Benefits program, under which a widow automatically received survivors' benefits based on the earnings of a deceased husband but a widower received benefits on the same basis only if he had been receiving at least one-half of his support from his deceased wife. In both cases, the Court rejected the government's claim that the provisions at issue were benevolent because they sought to compensate women beneficiaries as a group for the economic difficulties confronting women who sought to support themselves and their families. Instead, it found that the provisions discriminated against women in that their Social

Security taxes produced less protection for their spouses than was produced by the taxes paid by men. The Court's 1979 decision in *Orr v. Orr* reinforced this approach to gender-based distinctions. Here the Court again employed the intermediate-scrutiny standard, this time to strike down an Alabama law authorizing the payment of alimony to wives but not to husbands. In his opinion for the Court, Justice Brennan stressed that "statutes purportedly designed to compensate for and ameliorate the effects of past discrimination must be carefully tailored," because benevolent gender classifications "carry the inherent risk of reinforcing stereotypes about the 'proper place' of women and their need for special protection." Brennan argued that the state's purposes could as well have been served "by a gender-neutral classification as by one that gender-classifies and therefore carries with it the baggage of sexual stereotypes."

It could be argued that *Wiesenfeld, Goldfarb,* and *Orr* also presented instances of discrimination against men. Although it was not made in those cases, this argument has been employed to challenge the constitutionality of various classifications, and the Court has responded inconsistently. In *Craig,* for example, it held that the Equal Protection Clause can be used to strike down statutory classifications that discriminate against men, at least where no claim of compensation on behalf of women is made to justify them. As Justice Brennan observed in a footnote, "*Kahn v. Shevin* and *Schlesinger v. Ballard,* upholding the use of gender-based classifications, rested upon the Court's perception of the laudatory purposes of those laws as remedying disadvantageous conditions suffered by women in economic and military life. Needless to say, in this case Oklahoma does not suggest that the age-sex differential was enacted to insure the availability of 3.2 percent beer for women as compensation for previous deprivations." In *Michael M. v. Sonoma County Superior Court* (1981), however, the Court upheld a California statutory-rape statute that made it a criminal offense to have sexual intercourse with a female under the age of eighteen. It rejected the petitioner's gender-discrimination challenge that the law was unconstitutional because it did not make it illegal to have sexual intercourse with a male under the age of eighteen. In his opinion announcing the judgment of the Court, Justice Rehnquist declared that the operative standard for reviewing the law in question was "the principle that a legislature may not make overbroad generalizations based on sex which are entirely unrelated to any differences between men and women or which demean the ability or social status of the affected class." Employing this standard, he declared that the statute passed constitutional muster:

> Because virtually all of the significant harmful and inescapably identifiable consequences of teenage pregnancy fall on the young female, a legislature acts well within its authority when it elects to punish only the participant who, by nature, suffers few of the consequences of his conduct. It is hardly unreasonable for a legislature acting to protect minor females to exclude them from punishment. Moreover, risk of pregnancy itself constitutes a substantial deterrence to young females. No similar natural sanctions deter males. A criminal sanction imposed solely on males thus serves to roughly "equalize" the deterrents on the sexes.

Justice Brennan strenuously dissented, insisting that California had not shown that its statutory-rape statute "is any more effective than a gender-neutral law would be in deterring minor females from engaging in sexual intercourse. It has, therefore, not met its burden of proving that the statutory classification is substantially related to the achievement of its asserted goal."

A final case involving gender-based classifications, *Rostker v. Goldberg* (1981), must be dealt with separately because, as the Court majority noted, it arose "in the context of Congress's authority over national defense and military affairs, and perhaps in no other area has the Court accorded Congress greater deference." In this case, the Court concluded that Congress did not violate the equal-protection component of the Fifth Amendment when it authorized the registration of men only under the Military Selective Service Act. In the majority opinion, Justice Rehnquist refused to clarify whether he was employing the rational-relation test or some heightened level of scrutiny: "We do not think that the substantive guarantee of due process or certainty in the law will be advanced by any further 'refinement' in the applicable tests." Such refinement was unnecessary, as "this is not a case of Congress arbitrarily choosing to burden one of two similarly situated groups, such as would be the case with an all-black or all-white, or an all-Catholic or an all-Lutheran, or an all-Republican or an all-Democratic registration. Men and women, because of the combat restrictions on women, are simply not similarly situated for purposes of a draft or a registration for a draft." In his dissent, Justice Marshall accused the Court majority of focusing on the wrong question. What it should have asked, he maintained, was "whether the gender-based classification is itself substantially related to the achievement of the asserted governmental interest. Thus, the Government's task in this case is to demonstrate that excluding women from registration substantially furthers the goal of preparing a draft of combat troops. Or to put it another way, the government must show that drafting women would substantially impede its efforts to prepare for such a draft."

Indigency

In a variety of decisions, primarily in the realm of criminal justice, the Warren Court hinted that classifications based on indigency were suspect. In *Griffin v. Illinois* (1958), for example, it ruled that the state must provide indigent defendants with copies of trial transcripts necessary for filing a criminal appeal, and in *Douglas v. California* (1963), it declared that indigent defendants have a right of court-appointed counsel on appeal. The suspectness of indigency-based classifications seemed all the more clearly established when Justice Douglas declared for the Court in *Harper v. Virginia Board of Elections* (1966) that "lines drawn on the basis of wealth or property, like those of race, are traditionally disfavored," and when the Burger Court invalidated, in *Williams v. Illinois* (1970) and *Tate v. Short* (1971), the imprisonment of indigent defendants who lacked the means to avoid jail by paying fines.

These cases proved to be inconclusive, however. *Griffin* and *Douglas* came in a context involving the fundamental interest of access to the criminal process, *Williams* and *Tate* applied deferential review, and *Harper* involved the fundamental right of exercise of the franchise. In such subsequent decisions as *James v. Valtierra* (1971) and *San Antonio v. Rodriguez* (1973), moreover, the Court indicated that indigency-based classifications were far from being considered suspect. *Valtierra* involved an equal-protection challenge to a California constitutional requirement that prohibited the state from developing low-rent housing projects "without prior approval in a local referendum." In upholding the requirement, Justice Black denied that lawmaking procedures that disadvantage the poor violate equal protection for that reason alone. Justice Powell argued along much the same lines in *Rodriguez,* holding that the Court had never held that "wealth discrimination alone provides an adequate basis for invoking strict scrutiny." Justice Marshall vigorously dissented in both cases. In his *Valtierra* opinion, in which Justices Brennan and Blackmun joined, he insisted that poverty-based classifications were suspect and thus demanded strict scrutiny. For him, "singling out the poor to bear a burden not placed on any other class of citizens tramples the values the Fourteenth Amendment was designed to protect." He resurrected this argument in *Rodriguez,* in which he contended that children living in impoverished school districts "constitute a sufficient class" to justify heightened review.

FUNDAMENTAL RIGHTS

The Court's efforts to identify and defend fundamental rights have sparked controversy but have not been characterized by the vacillation and indecision that have marked its endeavors to define suspect classifications and to determine the level of scrutiny with which those classifications should be reviewed. One of the first rights to be recognized as fundamental under the Warren Court's two-tier approach was the exercise of the franchise. Over time, this right came to embody four distinct principles: (1) each vote must count equally—that is, the one-man, one-vote principle; (2) the franchise must be broadly available; (3) the ballot must reflect a sufficiently representative choice of parties and candidates; and (4) voters must receive equal treatment in recounts. The right to vote is addressed at length in Chapter 10.

Along with the franchise, the Warren Court also recognized as fundamental the right to travel from state to state. In *Shapiro v. Thompson* (1969), it found that this right of a citizen had been burdened for no compelling reason when Connecticut conditioned eligibility to receive public assistance on having satisfied a one-year residency requirement. Justice Harlan, alarmed by this elevation of the right to travel to "fundamental" status, voiced his fear that the Court in *Shapiro* had understood the justification for strict scrutiny to stem entirely from the Equal Protection Clause itself, and not from any independent source elsewhere in the Constitution.[7] The implications of such an understanding disturbed him greatly. Noting that almost all state statutes affect important rights, he charged that if the Court were "to pick out particular human activities, characterize them as 'fundamental,' and give them added protection under an unusually stringent equal protection test," it would soon become a "super-legislature."

Justice Harlan's fears were allayed, however, when the Burger Court refused to build on *Shapiro*. In *Dandridge v. Williams* (1970), it rejected the contention that the right to welfare was fundamental, and in *Lindsey v. Normet* (1972), it rebuffed efforts to establish "decent housing" and "possession of one's home" as fundamental rights. "It is not the province of this Court to create substantive constitutional rights in the name of guaranteeing equal protection of the laws," it declared in *San Antonio Independent School District v. Rodriguez* (1973), a case in which it denied that education is a fundamental right.[8] For a right to be fundamental, the Court insisted, it must be "expressly or implicitly guaranteed by the Constitution."

Nordlinger v. Hahn (1992) was an example of the refusal by the Rehnquist Court as well to build on *Shapiro*. The petitioner claimed that the Supreme Court should strictly scrutinize California's Proposition 13 because it infringed on the constitutional right to travel. Proposition 13 capped real property taxes at 1 percent of the property's full cash value at the time this statewide ballot initiative was passed and thereafter at its appraised value on construction or change of ownership. As housing values in California continued to soar during the late 1970s and 1980s, owners of property purchased before the passage of Proposition 13 ended up paying much lower taxes than owners who built or purchased after its passage. The petitioner claimed that Proposition 13 was unconstitutional, for it impeded her and others from traveling to and settling in California. Justice Blackmun rejected this contention for an eight-member majority, applied the rational-basis test to Proposition 13, and identified "at least two rational or reasonable considerations . . . that justify denying petitioner the benefits of her neighbors' lower assessments." First, "the state has a legitimate interest in local neighborhood preservation, continuity, and stability." And second, "the State legitimately can conclude that a new owner at the time of acquiring his property does not have the same reliance interest warranting protection against higher taxes as does an existing owner." Justice Stevens filed an impassioned dissent, condemning Proposition 13 for irrationally treating "similarly situated persons differently on the basis of the date they joined the class of property owners."

In 2012, in *Armour v. Indianapolis*, the Court cited its decision in *Nordlinger* when it upheld Indianapolis's decision to adopt a new sewer connection policy that forgave previous sewer fees for all home owners who elected to pay in installments for the cost of their upgraded system but provided no reimbursement for those home owners who elected instead (unwisely in retrospect) to pay up front for their entire cost in one lump-sum payment. Justice Breyer for a six-member majority declared, "As long as the City's distinction has a rational basis, that distinction does not violate the Equal Protection Clause. This Court has long held that 'a classification neither involving fundamental rights nor proceeding along suspect lines . . . cannot run afoul of the Equal Protection Clause if there is a rational relationship between the disparity of treatment and some legitimate governmental purpose.' . . . We have repeatedly pointed out that '[l]egislatures have especially broad latitude in creating classifications and distinctions in tax statutes.' *Nordlinger v. Hahn* (1992)." Chief Justice Roberts in dissent also turned to precedent and implicitly denied that what Indianapolis did passed the rational-basis test. "Our precedents do not ask for much from government in this area—only 'rough equality in tax treatment.' . . . Indiana law promised neighboring homeowners that they would be treated equally when it came to paying for sewer hook-ups. The City then ended up charging some homeowners 30 times what it charged their neighbors for the same hook-ups. The equal protection violation is plain."

THE FUTURE OF EQUAL-PROTECTION ANALYSIS

As is apparent, the Court's approach to equal-protection issues is fraught with difficulties that have prompted members of the Court to propose, and on occasion to employ, alternative analytical frameworks for resolving these issues. One such alternative is the "irrebuttable presumptions" doctrine. For a brief time in the mid-1970s, the Court flirted with and even embraced this approach, which asked whether the challenged classification simply presumes something to be the case while preventing an individual so classified from proving otherwise. In *Vlandis v. Kline* (1973), for example, the Court struck down Connecticut's residency requirements for favorable tuition status at state universities on the ground that the requirements did not allow students who had recently arrived in the state a chance to prove that they had in fact become bona fide residents.

The Court's embrace of the irrebuttable-presumptions approach was short-lived, however. In *Weinberger v. Salfi* (1975), it overturned a lower-court decision that had invalidated, on irrebuttable-presumption grounds, a Social Security duration-of-relationship eligibility requirement for surviving wives and stepchildren of deceased wage earners. In like manner, it refused to acknowledge, in *Murgia,* the presence in Massachusetts's mandatory retirement law of an irrebuttable presumption that policemen over the age of fifty are unfit for duty.

Another approach to equal-protection analysis was suggested by Justice Rehnquist in his dissent in *Trimble v. Gordon.* The problems involved in reviewing equal-protection claims, he argued, stemmed "not from the Equal Protection Clause but from the Court's insistence on reading so much into it." To his mind, anything more intensive than the most deferential kind of judicial scrutiny was indefensible, on both theoretical and practical grounds, "except in the area of the law in which the Framers obviously meant it to apply—classifications based on race or on national origin, the first cousin of race." Rehnquist's proposal fell on the deaf ears of those who, with Justice Marshall in *James v. Valtierra* (1971), remained convinced that "it is far too late in the day to contend that the Fourteenth Amendment prohibits only racial discrimination."

In *United States v. Virginia* (1996), Justice Scalia offered still another proposal—not creating a new test, but mooring the present tests in "those constant and unbroken national traditions that embody the people's understanding of ambiguous constitutional texts." He indicated that he had "no problem with a system of abstract tests such as rational-basis, intermediate, and strict scrutiny." He declared that such formulas "are essential to evaluating whether the new restrictions that a changing society constantly imposes upon private conduct comport with that 'equal protection' our society has always accorded in the past." But, he continued, "in my view the function of this Court is to preserve our society's values regarding (among other things) equal protection, not to revise them; to prevent backsliding from the degree of restriction the Constitution imposed upon democratic government, not to prescribe, on our own authority, progressively higher degrees." His deference to tradition, however, is not widely endorsed by his colleagues. And so the Court continues to search for a satisfactory and acceptable approach to the questions posed by substantive equal protection. The need for such an approach is great, for equal protection has gone from the "last resort of constitutional argument" to a prolific source of constitutional litigation. As Archibald Cox noted, "Once loosed, the idea of Equality is not easily cabined."[9]

NOTES

1. The need for strict scrutiny of classifications that are suspect or that burden fundamental rights may be found in Justice Harlan Stone's celebrated *Carolene Products* footnote (1938), which is reprinted in Chapter 4.

2. Gerald Gunther, "The Supreme Court, 1971 Term—Foreword: In Search of Evolving Doctrine on a Changing Court: A Model for a Newer Equal Protection," *Harvard Law Review* 86 (November 1972): 8.

3. Gerald Gunther, *Constitutional Law,* 11th ed. (Mineola, NY: Foundation Press, 1985), 591.

4. *Coalition for Economic Equity v. Wilson* (1997) is an interesting variant on this theme. When the voters of California in November 1996 passed Proposition 209 (barring the state from discriminating against or granting preference to any individual or group on the basis of race, sex, color, ethnicity, or national origin), a federal judge quickly enjoined its implementation on the ground that it prohibited governmental entities at every level from taking voluntary action to remediate past and present discrimination through the use of constitutionally permissible race-and-gender-conscious affirmative action programs. The Ninth Circuit Court of Appeals lifted the injunction and rejected the district court's reasoning. Judge Diarmuid F. O'Scannlain declared, "The Constitution permits the people to grant a narrowly tailored racial preference only if they come forward with a compelling interest to back it up. '[I]n the context of a Fourteenth Amendment challenge, courts must bear in mind the difference between what the law permits, and what it requires.' To hold that a democratically enacted affirmative action program is constitutionally

permissible because the people have demonstrated a compelling state interest is hardly to hold that the program is constitutionally required. The Fourteenth Amendment, lest we lose sight of the forest for the trees, does not require what it barely permits."

5. See also *Martin v. Wilks* (1989), in which the Supreme Court held in a 5–4 decision that white employees who allege that they have been the victims of racial discrimination because of the employment practices their employer has undertaken pursuant to a consent decree cannot be precluded from challenging those practices or the consent decree.

6. Although both *Kahn* and *Ballard* were decided before *Craig v. Boren* and the de facto employment of the middle-tier test, *Califano v. Webster* (1977) left no doubt that the Court considered these earlier cases to be fully consistent with *Craig.*

7. In *Saenz v. Roe* (1999), the Court held that it was a privilege and immunity of national citizenship, as secured by the Privileges and Immunities Clause of Section 1 of the Fourteenth Amendment, for travelers who elect to become permanent residents of a state "to be treated like other citizens of that State." See Chapter 4 for a further discussion of the fundamental right to travel.

8. See, however, *Plyler v. Doe* (1982). Here Justice Brennan, although stating explicitly that education is not a fundamental right and that state denials of educational opportunity are not to be held to the compelling-state-interest test, appeared to argue that the right to education warrants some heightened level of review. The level of review he implicitly employed is the same middle-tier test he used in *Boren* and *Bakke.*

9. Archibald Cox, "The Supreme Court, 1965 Term—Foreword: Constitutional Adjudication and the Promotion of Human Rights," *Harvard Law Review* 82 (November 1966): 91.

SELECTED READINGS

Ackerman, Bruce L. "The Conclusive Presumption Shuffle." *University of Pennsylvania Law Review* 125 (April 1977): 761–810.

Araiza, William D. *Enforcing the Equal Protection Clause: Congressional Power, Judicial Doctrine, and Constitutional Law.* New York: NYU Press, 2016.

Baer, Judith A. *Equality Under the Constitution: Reclaiming the Fourteenth Amendment.* Ithaca, NY: Cornell University Press, 1983.

Ball, Howard. *The* Bakke *Case: Race, Education, and Affirmative Action.* Lawrence: University Press of Kansas 2000.

Belz, Herman. *Equality Transformed: A Quarter-Century of Affirmative Action.* Bowling Green, OH: Transaction Publishers, 1991.

Brown-Nagin, Tomiko. "The Transformative Racial Politics of Justice Thomas: The *Grutter v. Bollinger* Opinion." *University of Pennsylvania Journal of Constitutional Law* 7 (February 2005): 787–807.

Carter, Stephen L. *Reflections of an Affirmative Action Baby.* New York: Basic Books, 1991.

Eastland, Terry, and William J. Bennett. *Counting by Race: Equality from the Founding Fathers to* Bakke *and* Weber. New York: Basic Books, 1979.

Ely, John Hart. *Democracy and Distrust: A Theory of Judicial Review.* Cambridge, MA: Harvard University Press, 1980.

Epstein, Lee, and Jack Knight. "Piercing the Veil: William J. Brennan's Account of *Regents of the University of California v. Bakke.*" *Yale Law & Policy Review* 19 (2001): 341–379.

Eule, Julian N. "Promoting Speaker Diversity: *Austin* and *Metro Broadcasting.*" In *1990 Supreme Court Review,* edited by Gerhard Casper, Dennis J. Hutchinson, and David A. Strauss. Chicago: University of Chicago Press, 1991.

Goldberg, Carole. "American Indians and 'Preferential' Treatment." *UCLA Law Review* 49 (April 2002): 943–989.

Graglia, Lino A. "*Grutter* and *Gratz:* Race Preference to Increase Racial Representation Held 'Patently Unconstitutional' Unless Done Subtly Enough in the Name of Pursuing 'Diversity.'" *Tulane Law Review* 78 (June 2004): 2037–2052.

Grossett, Jeffrey D. "Upholding Racial Diversity in the Classroom as a Compelling Interest." *Case Western Reserve Law Review* 52 (Fall 2001): 339–369.

Jencks, Christopher. "Affirmative Action for Blacks." *American Behavioral Scientist* 28 (July–August 1985): 731–760.

Perry, Barbara. *The Michigan Affirmative Action Cases.* Lawrence: University Press of Kansas, 2007.

Presser, Stephen B. *Recapturing the Constitution: Race, Religion, and Abortion Reconsidered.* Washington, DC: Regnery, 1994.

Rossum, Ralph A. *Reverse Discrimination: The Constitutional Debate.* New York: Marcel Dekker, 1980.

Schuck, Peter H. "Affirmative Action: Past, Present, and Future." *Yale Law & Policy Review* 20 (2002): 1–96.

Sowell, Thomas. *The Economics and Politics of Race: An International Perspective.* New York: Morrow, 1983.

Thernstrom, Abigail, and Stephan Thernstrom. "Secrecy and Dishonesty: The Supreme Court, Racial Preferences, and Higher Education." *Constitutional Commentary* 21 (Spring 2004): 251–274.

West, Thomas G. *Vindicating the Founders: Race, Sex, Class, and Justice in the Origins of America.* Lanham, MD: Rowman & Littlefield, 1997.

Wilkinson, J. Harvie, III. *From* Brown *to* Bakke: *The Supreme Court and School Integration.* New York: Oxford University Press, 1979.

Richmond v. J. A. Croson Company
488 U.S. 469 (1989)

The City of Richmond, Virginia, adopted a Minority Business Utilization Plan requiring prime contractors awarded city construction contracts to subcontract at least 30 percent of the total dollar amount of each contract to one or more Minority Business Enterprises (MBEs), which the city defined to include a business from anywhere in the country, at least 51 percent of which is owned and controlled by black, Spanish-speaking, Oriental, Indian, Eskimo, or Aleut citizens. Although Richmond declared that the plan was "remedial" in nature, the city adopted it after a public hearing at which no direct evidence was presented that the city had discriminated on the basis of race in letting contracts or that its prime contractors had discriminated against minority subcontractors. Material introduced at the hearing consisted of (1) a statistical study indicating that, although the city's population was 50 percent black, only .67 percent of its prime construction contracts had been awarded to minority subcontractors in recent years; (2) figures showing that local contractors' associations had virtually no MBE members; (3) the conclusion of the city's counsel that the plan was constitutional under Fullilove v. Klutznick *(1980); and (4) statements of plan proponents indicating that racial discrimination had been widespread in the local, state, and national construction industries.*

Pursuant to this plan, the city adopted rules requiring individualized consideration of each bid or request for a waiver of the 30 percent set-aside and providing that a waiver could be granted only upon proof that sufficient qualified MBEs were unavailable or unwilling to participate. After J. A. Croson Co., the sole bidder on a city contract, was denied a waiver and lost its contract, it brought suit in US District Court for the Eastern District of Virginia, alleging that the city's plan was unconstitutional under the Fourteenth Amendment's Equal Protection Clause. The district court upheld the plan in all respects, and the Court of Appeals for the Fourth Circuit affirmed, applying a test derived from the Supreme Court's principal opinion in Fullilove, *which accorded great deference to Congress's findings of past societal discrimination in holding that a 10 percent minority set-aside for certain*

federal construction grants did not violate the equal-protection component of the Fifth Amendment. When Croson petitioned the Supreme Court for a writ of certiorari, the Court vacated the judgment from below and remanded the case for further consideration in light of its intervening decision in Wygant v. Jackson Board of Education *(1986), in which a plurality of the Supreme Court applied a strict-scrutiny standard in holding that a race-based layoff program agreed to by a school district and the local teachers union violated the Fourteenth Amendment's Equal Protection Clause. On remand, the court of appeals held that the city's plan violated both prongs of strict scrutiny in that it was not justified by a compelling governmental interest—the record revealed no prior discrimination by the city itself in awarding contracts—and the 30 percent set-aside was not narrowly tailored to accomplish a remedial purpose. The city appealed.* Opinion of the Court: O'Connor, Rehnquist, White, Stevens, Kennedy. Concurring in part and concurring in the judgment: Stevens; Kennedy. Concurring in the judgment: Scalia. Dissenting opinions: Marshall, Brennan, Blackmun; Blackmun, Brennan.

JUSTICE O'CONNOR . . . delivered the opinion of the Court.

In this case, we confront once again the tension between the Fourteenth Amendment's guarantee of equal treatment to all citizens, and the use of racebased measures to ameliorate the effects of past discrimination on the opportunities enjoyed by members of minority groups in our society. In *Fullilove v. Klutznick* . . . (1980), we held that a congressional program requiring that 10% of certain federal construction grants be awarded to minority contractors did not violate the equal protection principles embodied in the Due Process Clause of the Fifth Amendment. Relying largely on our decision in *Fullilove*, some lower federal courts have applied a similar standard of review in assessing the constitutionality of state and local minority set-aside provisions under the Equal Protection Clause of the Fourteenth Amendment. . . . Since our decision two Terms ago in *Wygant v. Jackson*

Board of Education . . . (1986), the lower federal courts have attempted to apply its standards in evaluating the constitutionality of state and local programs which allocate a portion of public contracting opportunities exclusively to minority-owned businesses. . . . We noted probable jurisdiction in this case to consider the applicability of our decision in *Wygant* to a minority set-aside program adopted by the city of Richmond, Virginia. . . .

The parties and their supporting *amici* fight an initial battle over the scope of the city's power to adopt legislation designed to address the effects of past discrimination. Relying on our decision in *Wygant,* appellee argues that the city must limit any race-based remedial efforts to eradicating the effects of its own prior discrimination. This is essentially the position taken by the Court of Appeals below. Appellant argues that our decision in *Fullilove* is controlling, and that as a result the city of Richmond enjoys sweeping legislative power to define and attack the effects of prior discrimination in its local construction industry. We find that neither of these two rather stark alternatives can withstand analysis.

In *Fullilove,* we upheld the minority set-aside contained in §103(f)(2) of the Public Works Employment Act of 1977, . . . against a challenge based on the equal protection component of the Due Process Clause. . . .

The principal opinion in *Fullilove,* written by Chief Justice Burger, did not employ "strict scrutiny" or any other traditional standard of equal protection review. The Chief Justice noted at the outset that although racial classifications call for close examination, the Court was at the same time, "bound to approach [its] task with appropriate deference to the Congress, a co-equal branch charged by the Constitution with the power to 'provide for the . . . general Welfare of the United States' and 'to enforce by appropriate legislation,' the equal protection guarantees of the Fourteenth Amendment." . . . The principal opinion asked two questions: first, were the objectives of the legislation within the power of Congress? Second, was the limited use of racial and ethnic criteria a permissible means for Congress to carry out its objectives within the constraints of the Due Process Clause?

On the issue of congressional power, the Chief Justice found that Congress' commerce power was sufficiently broad to allow it to reach the practices of prime contractors on federally funded local construction projects. . . . Congress could mandate state and local government compliance with the set-aside program under its §5 power to enforce the Fourteenth Amendment. . . .

The Chief Justice next turned to the constraints on Congress' power to employ race-conscious remedial relief. His opinion stressed two factors in upholding the MBE set-aside. First was the unique remedial powers of Congress under §5 of the Fourteenth Amendment:

> Here we deal . . . not with the limited remedial powers of a federal court, for example, but with the broad remedial powers of Congress. It is fundamental that *in no organ of government, state or federal, does there repose a more comprehensive remedial power than in the Congress,* expressly charged by the Constitution with competence and authority to enforce equal protection guarantees. . . .

Because of these unique powers, the Chief Justice concluded that "Congress not only may induce voluntary action to assure compliance with existing federal statutory or constitutional antidiscrimination provisions, but also, where Congress has authority to *declare certain conduct unlawful,* it may, as here, authorize and induce state action to avoid such conduct."

The second factor emphasized by the principal opinion in *Fullilove* was the flexible nature of the 10% set-aside. Two "congressional assumptions" underlay the MBE program: first, that the effects of past discrimination had impaired the competitive position of minority businesses, and second, that "adjustment for the effects of past discrimination" would assure that at least 10% of the funds from the federal grant program would flow to minority businesses. The Chief Justice noted that both of these "assumptions" could be "rebutted" by a grantee seeking a waiver of the 10% requirement. . . . Thus a waiver could be sought where minority businesses were not available to fill the 10% requirement or, more importantly, where an MBE attempted "to exploit the remedial aspects of the program by charging an unreasonable price, *i.e.,* a price not attributable to the present effects of prior discrimination." . . . The Chief Justice indicated that without this fine tuning to remedial purpose, the statute would not have "pass[ed] muster." . . .

Appellant and its supporting *amici* rely heavily on *Fullilove* for the proposition that a city council, like Congress, need not make specific findings of discrimination to engage in race-conscious relief. Thus, appellant argues "[i]t would be a perversion of federalism to hold that the federal government has a compelling interest in remedying the effects of racial discrimination in its own public works program, but a city government does not."

What appellant ignores is that Congress, unlike any State or political subdivision, has a specific constitutional mandate to enforce the dictates of the Fourteenth Amendment. The power to "enforce" may at times also include the power to define situations which *Congress* determines threaten principles of equality and to adopt prophylactic rules to deal with those situations. . . . The Civil War Amendments themselves worked a dramatic change in the balance between congressional and state power over matters of race. Speaking of the Thirteenth and Fourteenth Amendments in *Ex parte Virginia* (1880), the Court stated: "They were intended to be, what they really are, limitations of the powers of the States and enlargements of the power of Congress."

That Congress may identify and redress the effects of society-wide discrimination does not mean that, *a fortiori,* the States and their political subdivisions are free to decide that such remedies are appropriate. Section 1 of the Fourteenth Amendment is an explicit *constraint* on state power, and the States must undertake any remedial efforts in accordance with that provision. To hold otherwise would be to cede control over the content of the Equal Protection Clause to the 50 state legislatures and their myriad political subdivisions. The mere recitation of a benign or compensatory purpose for the use of a racial classification would essentially entitle the States to exercise the full power of Congress under §5 of the Fourteenth Amendment and insulate any racial classification from judicial scrutiny under §1. We believe that such a result would be contrary to the intentions of the Framers of the Fourteenth Amendment, who desired to place clear limits on the States' use of race as a criterion for legislative action, and to have the federal courts enforce those limitations. . . .

It would seem equally clear, however, that a state or local subdivision (if delegated the authority from the State) has the authority to eradicate the effects of private discrimination within its own legislative jurisdiction. This authority must, of course, be exercised within the constraints of §1 of the Fourteenth Amendment. Our decision in *Wygant* is not to the contrary. *Wygant* addressed the constitutionality of the use of racial quotas by local school authorities pursuant to an agreement reached with the local teachers' union. It was in the context of addressing the school board's power to adopt a race-based layoff program affecting its own work force that the *Wygant* plurality indicated that the Equal Protection Clause required "some showing of prior discrimination by the governmental unit involved." . . . As a matter of state law, the city of Richmond has legislative authority over its procurement policies, and can use its spending powers to remedy private discrimination, if it identifies that discrimination with the particularity required by the Fourteenth Amendment. . . .

The Equal Protection Clause of the Fourteenth Amendment provides that "[N]o State shall . . . deny to *any person* within its jurisdiction the equal protection of the laws" (emphasis added). As this Court has noted in the past, the "rights created by the first section of the Fourteenth Amendment are, by its terms, guaranteed to the individual. The rights established are personal rights." *Shelley v. Kraemer,* . . . (1948). The Richmond Plan denies certain citizens the opportunity to compete for a fixed percentage of public contracts based solely upon their race. To whatever racial group these citizens belong, their "personal rights" to be treated with equal dignity and respect are implicated by a rigid rule erecting race as the sole criterion in an aspect of public decision-making.

Absent searching judicial inquiry into the justification for such race-based measures, there is simply no way of determining what classifications are "benign" or "remedial" and what classifications are in fact motivated by illegitimate notions of racial inferiority or simple racial politics. Indeed, the purpose of strict scrutiny is to "smoke out" illegitimate uses of race by assuring that the legislative body is pursuing a goal important enough to warrant use of a highly suspect tool. The test also ensures that the means chosen "fit" this compelling goal so closely that there is little or no possibility that the motive for the classification was illegitimate racial prejudice or stereotype.

Classifications based on race carry a danger of stigmatic harm. Unless they are strictly reserved for remedial settings, they may in fact promote notions of racial inferiority and lead to a politics of racial hostility. . . . We thus reaffirm the view expressed by the plurality in *Wygant* that the standard of review under the Equal Protection Clause is not dependent on the race of those burdened or benefited by a particular classification. . . .

Under the standard proposed by Justice Marshall's dissent, "[r]ace-conscious classifications designed to further remedial goals," . . . are forthwith subject to a relaxed standard of review. How the dissent arrives at the legal conclusion that a racial classification is "designed to further remedial goals," without first engaging in an examination of the factual basis for its enactment and the nexus between its scope and that factual basis we are not told. However, once the "remedial" conclusion is reached, the dissent's standard is singularly deferential, and bears little resemblance to the close examination of legislative purpose we have engaged in when reviewing classifications based either on race or gender. . . . The dissent's watered-down version of equal protection review effectively assures that race will always be relevant in American life, and that the "ultimate goal" of "eliminat[ing] entirely from governmental decision-making such irrelevant factors as a human being's race," . . . will never be achieved.

Even were we to accept a reading of the guarantee of equal protection under which the level of scrutiny varies according to the ability of different groups to defend their interests in the representative process, heightened scrutiny would still be appropriate in the circumstances of this case. One of the central arguments for applying a less exacting standard to "benign" racial classifications is that such measures essentially involve a choice made by dominant racial groups to disadvantage themselves. If one aspect of the judiciary's role under the Equal Protection Clause is to protect "discrete and insular minorities" from majoritarian prejudice or indifference, . . . some maintain that these concerns are not implicated when the "white majority" places burdens upon itself.

In this case, blacks comprise approximately 50% of the population of the city of Richmond. Five of the nine seats on the City Council are held by blacks. The concern that a political majority will more easily act to the disadvantage of a minority based on unwarranted assumptions or incomplete facts would seem to militate for, not against, the application of heightened judicial scrutiny in this case. . . .

Appellant argues that it is attempting to remedy various forms of past discrimination that are alleged to be responsible for the small number of minority businesses in the local contracting industry. Among these the city cites the exclusion of blacks from skilled construction trade unions and training programs. This past discrimination has prevented them "from following the traditional path from laborer to entrepreneur." The city also lists a host of nonracial factors which would seem to face a member of any racial group attempting to establish a new business enterprise, such as deficiencies in working capital, inability to meet bonding requirements, unfamiliarity with bidding procedures, and disability caused by an inadequate track record. . . .

While there is no doubt that the sorry history of both private and public discrimination in this country has contributed to a lack of opportunities for black entrepreneurs, this observation, standing alone, cannot justify a rigid racial quota in the awarding of public contracts in Richmond, Virginia. Like the claim that discrimination in primary and secondary schooling justifies a rigid racial preference in medical school admissions, an amorphous claim that there has been past discrimination in a particular industry cannot justify the use of an unyielding racial quota.

It is sheer speculation how many minority firms there would be in Richmond absent past societal discrimination, just as it was sheer speculation how many minority medical students would have been admitted to the medical school at Davis absent past discrimination in educational opportunities. Defining these sorts of injuries as "identified discrimination" would give local governments license to create a patchwork of racial preferences based on statistical generalizations about any particular field of endeavor.

These defects are readily apparent in this case. The 30% quota cannot in any realistic sense be tied to any injury suffered by anyone. The District Court relied upon five predicate "facts" in reaching its conclusion that there was an adequate basis for the 30% quota: (1) the ordinance declares itself to be remedial; (2) several proponents of the measure stated their views that there had been past discrimination in the construction industry; (3) minority businesses received .67% of prime contracts from the city while minorities constituted 50% of the city's population; (4) there were very few minority contractors in local and state contractors' associations; and (5) in 1977, Congress made a determination that the effects of past discrimination had stifled minority participation in the construction industry nationally. . . .

None of these "findings," singly or together, provide the city of Richmond with a "strong basis in evidence for its conclusion that remedial action was necessary." . . . There is nothing approaching a *prima facie* case of a constitutional or statutory violation by anyone in the Richmond construction industry. . . .

The District Court accorded great weight to the fact that the city council designated the Plan as "remedial." But the mere recitation of a "benign" or legitimate purpose for a racial classification, is entitled to little or no weight. . . . Racial classifications are suspect, and that means that simple legislative assurances of good intention cannot suffice.

The District Court also relied on the highly conclusionary statement of a proponent of the Plan that there was racial discrimination in the construction industry "in this area, and the State, and around the nation." . . . It also noted that the city manager had related his view that

racial discrimination still plagued the construction industry in his home city of Pittsburgh. . . . These statements are of little probative value in establishing identified discrimination in the Richmond construction industry. The factfinding process of legislative bodies is generally entitled to a presumption of regularity and deferential review by the judiciary. . . . But when a legislative body chooses to employ a suspect classification, it cannot rest upon a generalized assertion as to the classification's relevance to its goals. . . . A governmental actor cannot render race a legitimate proxy for a particular condition merely by declaring that the condition exists. . . . The history of racial classifications in this country suggests that blind judicial deference to legislative or executive pronouncements of necessity has no place in equal protection analysis. . . .

Reliance on the disparity between the number of prime contracts awarded to minority firms and the minority population of the city of Richmond is similarly misplaced. There is no doubt that "[w]here gross statistical disparities can be shown, they alone in a proper case may constitute *prima facie* proof of a pattern or practice of discrimination" under Title VII. . . . But it is equally clear that "[w]hen special qualifications are required to fill particular jobs, comparisons to the general population (rather than to the smaller group of individuals who possess the necessary qualifications) may have little probative value." . . .

In the employment context, we have recognized that for certain entry level positions or positions requiring minimal training, statistical comparisons of the racial composition of an employer's work force to the racial composition of the relevant population may be probative of a pattern of discrimination. . . . But where special qualifications are necessary, the relevant statistical pool for purposes of demonstrating discriminatory exclusion must be the number of minorities qualified to undertake the particular task. . . .

In this case, the city does not even know how many MBEs in the relevant market are qualified to undertake prime or subcontracting work in public construction projects. . . . Nor does the city know what percentage of total city construction dollars minority firms now receive as subcontractors on prime contracts let by the city.

To a large extent, the set-aside of subcontracting dollars seems to rest on the unsupported assumption that white prime contractors simply will not hire minority firms. . . . Indeed, there is evidence in this record that overall minority participation in city contracts in Richmond is seven to eight percent, and that minority contractor participation in Community Block Development Grant *construction* projects is 17% to 22%. . . . Without any information on minority participation in subcontracting, it is quite simply impossible to evaluate overall minority representation in the city's construction expenditures.

The city and the District Court also relied on evidence that MBE membership in local contractors' associations was extremely low. Again, standing alone this evidence is not probative of any discrimination in the local construction industry. There are numerous explanations for this dearth of minority participation, including past societal discrimination in education and economic opportunities as well as both black and white career and entrepreneurial choices. Blacks may be disproportionately attracted to industries other than construction. . . . The mere fact that black membership in these trade organizations is low, standing alone, cannot establish a *prima facie* case of discrimination.

In sum, none of the evidence presented by the city points to any identified discrimination in the Richmond construction industry. We, therefore, hold that the city has failed to demonstrate a compelling interest in apportioning public contracting opportunities on the basis of race. To accept Richmond's claim that past societal discrimination alone can serve as the basis for rigid racial preferences would be to open the door to competing claims for "remedial relief" for every disadvantaged group. The dream of a Nation of equal citizens in a society where race is irrelevant to personal opportunity and achievement would be lost in a mosaic of shifting preferences based on inherently unmeasurable claims of past wrongs. . . .

The foregoing analysis applies only to the inclusion of blacks within the Richmond set-aside program. There is *absolutely no evidence* of past discrimination against Spanish-speaking, Oriental, Indian, Eskimo, or Aleut persons in any aspect of the Richmond construction industry. The District Court took judicial notice of the fact that the vast majority of "minority" persons in Richmond were black. . . . It may well be that Richmond has never had an Aleut or Eskimo citizen. The random inclusion of racial groups that, as a practical matter, may never have suffered from discrimination in the construction industry in Richmond, suggests that perhaps the city's purpose was not in fact to remedy past discrimination.

If a 30% set-aside was "narrowly tailored" to compensate black contractors for past discrimination, one may legitimately ask why they are forced to share this "remedial relief" with an Aleut citizen who moves to Richmond tomorrow? The gross overinclusiveness of Richmond's racial preference strongly impugns the city's claim of remedial motivation. . . .

As noted by the court below, it is almost impossible to assess whether the Richmond Plan is narrowly tailored to remedy prior discrimination since it is not linked to identified discrimination in any way. We limit ourselves to two observations in this regard.

First, there does not appear to have been any consideration of the use of race-neutral means to increase minority business participation in city contracting. . . .

Many of the barriers to minority participation in the construction industry relied upon by the city to justify a racial classification appear to be race neutral. If MBEs disproportionately lack capital or cannot meet bonding requirements, a race-neutral program of city financing for small firms would, *a fortiori,* lead to greater minority participation. . . . There is no evidence in this record that the Richmond City Council has considered any alternatives to a race-based quota.

Second, the 30% quota cannot be said to be narrowly tailored to any goal, except perhaps outright racial balancing. It rests upon the "completely unrealistic" assumption that minorities will choose a particular trade in lockstep proportion to their representation in the local population. . . .

Since the city must already consider bids and waivers on a case-by-case basis, it is difficult to see the need for a rigid numerical quota. As noted above, the congressional scheme upheld in *Fullilove* allowed for a waiver of the set-aside provision where an MBE's higher price was not attributable to the effect of past discrimination. Based upon proper findings, such programs are less problematic from an equal protection standpoint because they treat all candidates individually, rather than making the color of an applicant's skin the sole relevant consideration. Unlike the program upheld in *Fullilove,* the Richmond Plan's waiver system focuses solely on the availability of MBEs; there is no inquiry into whether or not the particular MBE seeking a racial preference has suffered from the effects of past discrimination by the city or prime contractors.

Given the existence of an individualized procedure, the city's only interest in maintaining a quota system rather than investigating the need for remedial action in particular cases would seem to be simple administrative convenience. But the interest in avoiding the bureaucratic effort necessary to tailor remedial relief to those who truly have suffered the effects of prior discrimination cannot justify a rigid line drawn on the basis of a suspect classification. . . . Under Richmond's scheme, a successful black, Hispanic, or Oriental entrepreneur from anywhere in the country enjoys an absolute preference over other citizens based solely on their race. We think it obvious that such a program is not narrowly tailored to remedy the effects of prior discrimination. . . .

Because the city of Richmond has failed to identify the need for remedial action in the awarding of its public construction contracts, its treatment of its citizens on a racial basis violates the dictates of the Equal Protection Clause. Accordingly, the judgment of the Court of Appeals for the Fourth Circuit is

Affirmed.

JUSTICE SCALIA, concurring in the judgment.

I agree with much of the Court's opinion, and, in particular, with its conclusion that strict scrutiny must be applied to all governmental classification by race, whether or not its asserted purpose is "remedial" or "benign." . . . I do not agree, however, with the Court's dicta suggesting that, despite the Fourteenth Amendment, state and local governments may in some circumstances discriminate on the basis of race in order (in a broad sense) "to ameliorate the effects of past discrimination." The difficulty of overcoming the effects of past discrimination is as nothing compared with the difficulty of eradicating from our society the source of those effects, which is the tendency—fatal to a nation such as ours—to classify and judge men and women on the basis of their country of origin or the color of their skin. A solution to the first problem that aggravates the second is no solution at all. I share the view expressed by Alexander Bickel that "[t]he lesson of the great decisions of the Supreme Court and the lesson of contemporary history have been the same for at least a generation: discrimination on the basis of race is illegal, immoral, unconstitutional, inherently wrong, and destructive of democratic society." A. Bickel, *The Morality of Consent* 133 (1975). At least where state or local action is at issue, only a social engineering rising to the level of imminent danger to life and limb—for example, a prison race riot, requiring temporary segregation of inmates . . . —can justify an exception to the principle embodied in the Fourteenth Amendment that "[o]ur Constitution is color-blind, and neither knows nor tolerates classes among citizens," . . .

We have in some contexts approved the use of racial classifications by the Federal Government to remedy the effects of past discrimination. I do not believe that we must or should extend these holdings to the States. . . .

A sound distinction between federal and state (or local) action based on race rests not only upon the substance of the Civil War Amendments, but upon social reality and governmental theory. It is a simple fact that what Justice Stewart described in *Fullilove* as "the dispassionate objectivity [and] the flexibility that are needed to mold a race-conscious remedy around the single objective of eliminating the effects of past or present discrimination" . . . are substantially less likely to exist at the state or local level. The struggle for racial justice has historically been a struggle by the national society against oppression in the individual States. . . . What the record shows, in other words, is that racial discrimination against any group finds a more ready expression at the state and local than at the federal level. To the children of the Founding Fathers, this should come as no surprise. An acute awareness of the heightened danger of oppression from political factions in small, rather than large, political units dates to the very beginning of our national history. . . . As James Madison observed in support of the proposed Constitution's enhancement of national powers:

> The smaller the society, the fewer probably will be the distinct parties and interests composing it; the fewer the distinct parties and interests, the more frequently will a majority be found of the same party; and the smaller the number of individuals composing a majority, and the smaller the compass within which they are placed, the more easily will they concert and execute their plan of oppression. Extend the sphere and you take in a greater variety of parties and interests; you make it less probable that a majority of the whole will have a common motive to invade the rights of other citizens; or if such a common motive exists, it will be more difficult for all who feel it to discover their own strength and to act in unison with each other. *The Federalist* No. 10. . . .

The prophesy of these words came to fruition in Richmond in the enactment of a set-aside clearly and directly beneficial to the dominant political group, which happens also to be the dominant racial group. The same thing has no doubt happened before in other cities (though the racial basis of the preference has rarely been made textually explicit)—and blacks have often been on the receiving end of the injustice. Where injustice is the game, however, turn-about is not fair play. . . .

In his final book, Professor Bickel wrote:

> [A] racial quota derogates the human dignity and individuality of all to whom it is applied; it is invidious in principle as well as in practice. Moreover, it can easily be turned against those it purports to help. The history of the racial quota is a history of subjugation, not beneficence. Its evil lies not in its name, but in its effects: a quota is a divider of society, a creator of castes, and it is all the worse for its racial base, especially in a society desperately striving for an equality that will make race irrelevant. Bickel, *The Morality of Consent,* at 133.

Those statements are true and increasingly prophetic. Apart from their societal effects, however, which are "in the aggregate disastrous," . . . it is important not to lose sight of the fact that even "benign" racial quotas have individual victims, whose very real injustice we ignore whenever we deny them enforcement of their right not to be disadvantaged on the basis of race. . . . As Justice Douglas observed: "A DeFunis who is white is entitled to no advantage by virtue of that fact; nor is he subject to any disability, no matter what his race or color. Whatever his race, he had a constitutional right to have his application considered on its individual merits in a racially neutral manner." *DeFunis v. Odegaard* . . . (1974). When we depart from this American principle we play with fire, and much more than an occasional DeFunis . . . or Croson burns.

It is plainly true that in our society blacks have suffered discrimination immeasurably greater than any directed at other racial groups. But those who believe that racial preferences can help to "even the score" display, and reinforce, a manner of thinking by race that was the source of the injustice and that will, if it endures within our society, be the source of more injustice still. The relevant proposition is not that it was blacks, or Jews, or Irish who were discriminated against, but that it was individual men and women, "created equal," who were discriminated against. And the relevant resolve is that that should never happen again. Racial preferences appear to "even the score" (in some small degree) only if one embraces the proposition that our society is appropriately viewed as divided into races, making it right that an injustice rendered in the past to a black man should be compensated for by discriminating against a white. Nothing is worth that embrace. Since blacks have been disproportionately disadvantaged by racial discrimination, any race-neutral remedial program aimed at the disadvantaged *as such* will have a disproportionately beneficial impact on blacks. Only such a program, and not one that operates on the basis of race, is in accord with the letter and the spirit of our Constitution.

Since I believe that the appellee here had a constitutional right to have its bid succeed or fail under a decisionmaking process uninfected with racial bias, I concur in the judgment of the Court.

JUSTICE STEVENS, concurring in part and concurring in the judgment. . . .

The ordinance is . . . vulnerable because of its failure to identify the characteristics of the disadvantaged class of white contractors that justify the disparate treatment. . . . The composition of the disadvantaged class of white contractors presumably includes some who have been guilty of unlawful discrimination, some who practiced discrimination before it was forbidden by law, and some who have never discriminated against anyone on the basis of race. Imposing a common burden on such a disparate class merely because each member of the class is of the same race stems from reliance on a stereotype rather than fact or reason.

There is a special irony in the stereotypical thinking that prompts legislation of this kind. Although it stigmatizes the disadvantaged class with the unproven charge of past racial discrimination, it actually imposes a greater stigma on its supposed beneficiaries. For, as I explained in my *Fullilove* opinion:

> [E]ven though it is not the actual predicate for this legislation, a statute of this kind inevitably is perceived by many as resting on an assumption that those who are granted this special preference are less qualified in some respect that is identified purely by their race. . . .

The risk that habitual attitudes toward classes of persons, rather than analysis of the relevant characteristics of the class, will serve as a basis for a legislative classification is present when benefits are distributed as well as when burdens are imposed. In the past, traditional attitudes too often provided the only explanation for discrimination against women, aliens, illegitimates, and black citizens. Today there is a danger that awareness of past injustice will lead to automatic acceptance of new classifications that are not in fact justified by attributes characteristic of the class as a whole.

When [government] creates a special preference, or a special disability, for a class of persons, it should identify the characteristic that justifies the special treatment. When the classification is defined in racial terms, I believe that such particular identification is imperative.

In this case, only two conceivable bases for differentiating the preferred classes from society as a whole have occurred to me: (1) that they were the victims of unfair treatment in the past and (2) that they are less able to compete in the future. Although the first of these factors would justify an appropriate remedy for past wrongs, for reasons that I have already stated, this statute is not such a remedial measure. The second factor is simply not true. Nothing in the record of this case, the legislative history of the Act, or experience that we may notice judicially provides any support for such a proposition.

JUSTICE MARSHALL, with whom JUSTICE BRENNAN and JUSTICE BLACKMUN join, dissenting.

It is a welcome symbol of racial progress when the former capital of the Confederacy acts forthrightly to confront the effects of racial discrimination in its midst. In my view, nothing in the Constitution can be construed to prevent Richmond, Virginia, from allocating a portion of its contracting dollars for businesses owned or controlled by members of minority groups. Indeed, Richmond's set-aside program is indistinguishable in all meaningful respects from—and in fact was patterned upon—the federal set-aside plan which this Court upheld in *Fullilove v. Klutznick.* . . .

A majority of this Court holds today, however, that the Equal Protection Clause of the Fourteenth Amendment blocks Richmond's initiative. The essence of the majority's position is that Richmond has failed to catalogue adequate findings to prove that past discrimination has impeded minorities from joining or participating fully in Richmond's construction contracting industry. I find deep irony in second-guessing Richmond's judgment on this point. As much as any municipality in the United States, Richmond knows what racial discrimination is; a century of decisions by this and other federal courts has richly documented the city's disgraceful history of public and private racial discrimination. In any event, the Richmond City Council *has* supported its determination that minorities have been wrongly excluded from local construction contracting. Its proof includes statistics showing that minority-owned businesses have received virtually no city contracting dollars and rarely if ever belonged to area trade associations; testimony by municipal officials that discrimination has been widespread in the local construction industry; and the same exhaustive and widely publicized federal studies relied on in *Fullilove,* studies which showed that pervasive discrimination in the Nation's tightknit construction industry had operated to exclude minorities from public contracting. These are precisely the types of statistical and testimonial evidence which, until today, this Court had credited in cases approving of race-conscious measures designed to remedy past discrimination.

More fundamentally, today's decision marks a deliberate and giant step backward in this Court's affirmative action jurisprudence. Cynical of one municipality's attempt to redress the effects of past racial discrimination in a particular industry, the majority launches a grapeshot attack on race-conscious remedies in general. The majority's unnecessary pronouncements will inevitably discourage or prevent governmental entities, particularly States and localities, from acting to rectify the scourge of past discrimination. This is the harsh reality of the majority's decision, but it is not the Constitution's command. . . . My view has long been that race-conscious classifications designed to further remedial goals "must serve important governmental objectives and must be substantially related to achievement of those objectives" in order to withstand constitutional scrutiny. . . . Analyzed in terms of this two-prong standard, Richmond's set-aside, like the federal program on which it was modeled, is "plainly constitutional." . . .

Turning first to the governmental interest inquiry, Richmond has two powerful interests in setting aside a portion of public contracting funds for minority-owned enterprises. The first is the city's interest in eradicating the effects of past racial discrimination. It is far too late in the day to doubt that remedying such discrimination is a compelling, let alone an important, interest. . . .

Richmond has a second compelling interest in setting aside, where possible, a portion of its contracting dollars. That interest is the prospective one of preventing the city's own spending decisions from reinforcing and perpetuating the exclusionary effects of past discrimination.

. . . When government channels all its contracting funds to a white-dominated community of established contractors whose racial homogeneity is the product of private discrimination, it does more than place its imprimatur on the practices which forged and which continue to define that community. It also provides a measurable boost to those economic entities that have thrived within it, while denying important economic benefits to those entities which, but for prior discrimination, might well be better qualified to receive valuable government contracts. In my view, the interest in ensuring that the government does not reflect and reinforce prior private discrimination in dispensing public contracts is every bit as strong as the interest in eliminating private discrimination—an interest which this Court has repeatedly deemed compelling. . . . The more government bestows its rewards on those persons or businesses that were positioned to thrive during a period of private racial discrimination, the tighter the deadhand grip of prior discrimination becomes on the present and future. Cities like Richmond may not be constitutionally required to adopt set-aside plans. . . . But there can be no doubt that when Richmond acted affirmatively to stem the perpetuation of patterns of discrimination through its own decisionmaking, it served an interest of the highest order. . . .

In my judgment, Richmond's set-aside plan also comports with the second prong of the equal protection inquiry, for it is substantially related to the interests it seeks to serve in remedying past discrimination and in ensuring that municipal contract procurement does not perpetuate that discrimination. The most striking aspect of the city's ordinance is the similarity it bears to the "appropriately limited" federal set-aside provision upheld in *Fullilove*. . . .

Today, for the first time, a majority of this Court has adopted strict scrutiny as its standard of Equal Protection Clause review of race-conscious remedial measures. . . . This is an unwelcome development. A profound difference separates governmental actions that themselves are racist, and governmental actions that seek to remedy the effects of prior racism or to prevent neutral governmental activity from perpetuating the effects of such racism. . . .

In concluding that remedial classifications warrant no different standard of review under the Constitution than the most brute and repugnant forms of state-sponsored racism, a majority of this Court signals that it regards racial discrimination as largely a phenomenon of the past, and that government bodies need no longer preoccupy themselves with rectifying racial injustice. . . .

I am also troubled by the majority's assertion that, even if it did not believe generally in strict scrutiny of race-based remedial measures, "the circumstances of this case" require this Court to look upon the Richmond City Council's measure with the strictest scrutiny. . . . The sole such circumstance which the majority cites, however, is the fact that blacks in Richmond are a "dominant racial grou[p]" in the city. . . . In support of this characterization of dominance, the majority observes that "blacks comprise approximately 50% of the population of the city of Richmond" and that "[f]ive of the nine seats on the City Council are held by blacks." . . .

While I agree that the numerical and political supremacy of a given racial group is a factor bearing upon the level of scrutiny to be applied, this Court has never held that numerical inferiority, standing alone, makes a racial group "suspect" and thus entitled to strict scrutiny review. . . .

In my view, the "circumstances of this case" . . . underscore the importance of *not* subjecting to a strict scrutiny straitjacket the increasing number of cities which have recently come under minority leadership and are eager to rectify, or at least prevent the perpetuation of, past racial discrimination. In many cases, these cases will be the ones with the most in the way of prior discrimination to rectify. Richmond's leaders had just witnessed decades of publicly sanctioned racial discrimination in virtually all walks of life—discrimination amply documented in the decisions of the federal judiciary. . . . This history of "purposefully unequal treatment" forced upon minorities, not imposed by them, should raise an inference that minorities in Richmond had much to remedy—and that the 1983 set-aside was undertaken with sincere remedial goals in mind, not "simple racial politics." . . .

The majority today sounds a full-scale retreat from the Court's longstanding solicitude to race-conscious remedial efforts "directed toward deliverance of the century-old promise of equality of economic opportunity." . . . The new and restrictive tests it applies scuttle one city's effort to surmount its discriminatory past, and imperil those of dozens more localities. I, however, profoundly disagree with the cramped vision of the Equal Protection Clause which the majority offers today and with its application of that vision to Richmond, Virginia's, laudable set-aside plan. The battle against pernicious racial discrimination or its effects is nowhere near won. I must dissent.

Adarand Constructors, Inc. v. Peña
515 U.S. 200 (1995)

Adarand Constructors, which submitted the low bid on the guardrail portion of a federal highway project, was not awarded the subcontract because of a federal subcontractor compensation clause designed to provide the prime contractor with a *financial incentive to hire disadvantaged business enterprises. Relying on the reasoning of* Richmond v. J. A. Croson Co. *(1989), Adarand Constructors filed suit against Secretary of Transportation Federico Peña and others, claiming a violation of the equal-protection component of the Fifth Amendment. The US District Court for the District of Colorado granted the respondents' summary judgment, and the Court of Appeals for the Tenth Circuit affirmed, basing its decision on* Fullilove v. Klutznick *(1980) and* Metro Broadcasting, Inc. v. F.C.C. *(1990). The Supreme Court granted certiorari.* Opinion of the Court: <u>O'Connor</u>, Rehnquist, Scalia, Kennedy, Thomas. Concurring in part and concurring in the judgment: <u>Scalia</u>; <u>Thomas</u>. Dissenting opinions: <u>Stevens</u>, Ginsburg; <u>Souter</u>, Ginsburg, Breyer; <u>Ginsburg</u>, Breyer.

JUSTICE O'CONNOR delivered the opinion of the Court.

Petitioner Adarand Constructors, Inc., claims that the Federal Government's practice of giving general contractors on government projects a financial incentive to hire subcontractors controlled by "socially and economically disadvantaged individuals," and in particular, the Government's use of race-based presumptions in identifying such individuals, violates the equal protection component of the Fifth Amendment's Due Process Clause. The Court of Appeals rejected Adarand's claim. We conclude, however, that courts should analyze cases of this kind under a different standard of review than the one the Court of Appeals applied. We therefore vacate the Court of Appeals' judgment and remand the case for further proceedings.

In 1989, the Central Federal Lands Highway Division (CFLHD), which is part of the United States Department of Transportation (DOT), awarded the prime contract for a highway construction project in Colorado to Mountain Gravel & Construction Company. Mountain Gravel then solicited bids from subcontractors for the guardrail portion of the contract. Adarand, a Colorado-based highway construction company specializing in guardrail work, submitted the low bid. Gonzales Construction Company also submitted a bid.

The prime contract's terms provide that Mountain Gravel would receive additional compensation if it hired subcontractors certified as small businesses controlled by "socially and economically disadvantaged individuals." Gonzales is certified as such a business; Adarand is not. Mountain Gravel awarded the subcontract to Gonzales, despite Adarand's low bid, and Mountain Gravel's Chief Estimator has submitted an affidavit stating that Mountain Gravel would have accepted Adarand's bid, had it not been for the additional payment it received by hiring Gonzales instead. Federal law requires that a subcontracting clause similar to the one used here must appear in most federal agency contracts, and it also requires the clause to state that "[t]he contractor shall presume that socially and economically disadvantaged individuals include Black Americans, Hispanic Americans, Native Americans, Asian Pacific Americans, and other minorities, or any other individual found to be disadvantaged by the [Small Business] Administration pursuant to section 8(a) of the Small Business Act." Adarand claims that the presumption set forth in that statute discriminates on the basis of race in violation of the Federal Government's Fifth Amendment obligation not to deny anyone equal protection of the laws. . . .

The Government urges that "[t]he Subcontracting Compensation Clause program is . . . a program based on *disadvantage,* not on race," and thus that it is subject only to "the most relaxed judicial scrutiny." To the extent that the statutes and regulations involved in this case are race neutral, we agree. The Government concedes, however, that "the race-based rebuttable presumption used in some certification determinations under the Subcontracting Compensation Clause" is subject to some heightened level of scrutiny. The parties disagree as to what that level should be.

Adarand's claim arises under the Fifth Amendment to the Constitution, which provides that "No person shall . . . be deprived of life, liberty, or property, without due process of law." Although this Court has always understood that Clause to provide some measure of protection against *arbitrary* treatment by the Federal Government, it is not as explicit a guarantee of *equal* treatment as the Fourteenth Amendment, which provides that "No *State* shall . . . deny to any person within its jurisdiction the equal protection of the laws." Our cases have accorded varying degrees of significance to the difference in the language of those two Clauses. We think it necessary to revisit the issue here. . . .

With *Richmond v. J. A. Croson Co.* (1989), the Court . . . agreed that the Fourteenth Amendment requires strict scrutiny of all race-based action by state and local governments. But *Croson* of course had no occasion to declare what standard of review the Fifth Amendment requires for such action taken by the Federal Government. *Croson* observed simply that the Court's "treatment of an exercise of congressional power in *Fullilove* cannot be dispositive here," because *Croson*'s facts did not implicate Congress' broad power under §5 of the Fourteenth Amendment. . . .

Despite lingering uncertainty in the details, however, the Court's cases through *Croson* had established three general propositions with respect to governmental racial classifications. First, skepticism: "'[A]ny preference based on racial or ethnic criteria must necessarily receive a most searching examination.'" Second, consistency: "The standard of review under the Equal Protection Clause is not dependent on the race of those burdened or benefited by a particular classification." And third, congruence: "[E]qual protection analysis in the Fifth Amendment area is the same as that under the Fourteenth Amendment." Taken together, these three propositions lead to the conclusion that any person, of whatever race, has the right to demand that any governmental actor subject to the Constitution justify any racial classification subjecting that person to unequal treatment under the strictest judicial scrutiny. . . .

A year later, however, the Court took a surprising turn. *Metro Broadcasting, Inc. v. FCC* (1990), involved a Fifth Amendment challenge to two race-based policies of the Federal Communications Commission. In *Metro Broadcasting,* the Court repudiated the long-held notion that "it would be unthinkable that the same Constitution would impose a lesser duty on the Federal Government" than it does on a State to afford equal protection of the laws. It did so by holding that "benign" federal racial classifications need only satisfy intermediate scrutiny, even though *Croson* had recently concluded that such classifications enacted by a State must satisfy strict scrutiny. "[B]enign" federal racial classifications, the Court said, "—even if those measures are not 'remedial' in the sense of being designed to compensate victims of past governmental or societal discrimination—are constitutionally permissible to the extent that they serve *important* governmental objectives within the power of Congress and are *substantially related* to achievement of those objectives." The Court did not explain how to tell whether a racial classification should be deemed "benign," other than to express "confiden[ce] that an 'examination of the legislative scheme and its history' will separate benign measures from other types of racial classifications."

Applying this test, the Court first noted that the FCC policies at issue did not serve as a remedy for past discrimination. Proceeding on the assumption that the policies were nonetheless "benign," it concluded that they served the "important governmental objective" of "enhancing broadcast diversity," and that they were "substantially related" to that objective. It therefore upheld the policies.

By adopting intermediate scrutiny as the standard of review for congressionally mandated "benign" racial classifications, *Metro Broadcasting* departed from prior cases in two significant respects. First, it turned its back on *Croson*'s explanation of why strict scrutiny of all governmental racial classifications is essential:

Absent searching judicial inquiry into the justification for such race-based measures, there is simply no way of determining what classifications are "benign" or "remedial" and what classifications are in fact motivated by illegitimate notions of racial inferiority or simple racial politics. Indeed, the purpose of strict scrutiny is to "smoke out" illegitimate uses of race by assuring that the legislative body is pursuing a goal important enough to warrant use of a highly suspect tool. The test also ensures that the means chosen "fit" this compelling goal so closely that there is little or no possibility that the motive for the classification was illegitimate racial prejudice or stereotype. . . . We adhere to that view today, despite the surface appeal of holding "benign" racial classifications to a lower standard, because "it may not always be clear that a so-called preference is in fact benign."

Second, *Metro Broadcasting* squarely rejected one of the three propositions established by the Court's earlier equal protection cases, namely, congruence between the standards applicable to federal and state racial classifications, and in so doing also undermined the other two—skepticism of all racial classifications, and consistency of treatment irrespective of the race of the burdened or benefited group. Under *Metro Broadcasting,* certain racial classifications ("benign" ones enacted by the Federal Government) should be treated less skeptically than others; and the race of the benefited group is critical to the determination of which standard of review to apply. *Metro Broadcasting* was thus a significant departure from much of what had come before it.

The three propositions undermined by *Metro Broadcasting* all derive from the basic principle that the Fifth and Fourteenth Amendments to the Constitution protect *persons,* not *groups.* It follows from that principle that all governmental action based on race—a *group* classification long recognized as "in most circumstances irrelevant and therefore prohibited,"—should be subjected to detailed judicial inquiry to ensure that the *personal* right to equal protection of the laws has not been infringed. These ideas have long been central to this Court's understanding of equal protection, and holding "benign" state and federal racial classifications to different standards does not square with them. "[A] free people whose institutions are founded upon the doctrine of equality," should tolerate no retreat from the principle that government may treat people differently because of their race only for the most compelling reasons. Accordingly, we hold today that all racial classifications, imposed by whatever federal, state, or local government actor, must be analyzed by a reviewing court under strict scrutiny. In other words, such classifications are constitutional only if they are narrowly tailored measures that further compelling governmental interests. To the extent that *Metro Broadcasting* is inconsistent with that holding, it is overruled.

In dissent, Justice Stevens criticizes us for "deliver[ing] a disconcerting lecture about the evils of governmental racial classifications." With respect, we believe his criticisms reflect a serious misunderstanding of our opinion. . . .

[He] chides us for our "supposed inability to differentiate between 'invidious' and 'benign' discrimination," because it is in his view sufficient that "people understand the difference between good intentions and bad." But, as we have just explained, the point of strict scrutiny is to "differentiate between" permissible and impermissible governmental use of race. And Justice Stevens himself has already explained in his dissent in *Fullilove* why "good intentions" alone are not enough to sustain a supposedly "benign" racial classification: "[E]ven though it is not the actual predicate for this legislation, a statute of this kind inevitably is perceived by many as resting on an assumption that those who are granted this special preference are less qualified in some respect that is identified purely by their race. Because that perception—*especially when fostered by the Congress of the United States*—can only exacerbate rather than reduce racial prejudice, it will delay the time when race will become a truly irrelevant, or at least insignificant, factor. *Unless Congress clearly articulates the need and basis* for a racial classification, *and also tailors the classification to its justification,* the Court should not uphold this kind of statute. . . . These passages make a persuasive case for requiring strict scrutiny of congressional racial classifications.

Perhaps it is not the standard of strict scrutiny itself, but our use of the concepts of "consistency" and "congruence" in conjunction with it, that leads Justice Stevens to dissent. According to Justice Stevens, our view of consistency "equate[s] remedial preferences with invidious discrimination," and ignores the difference between "an engine of oppression" and an effort "to foster equality in society," or, more colorfully, "between a 'No Trespassing' sign and a welcome mat." It does nothing of the kind. The principle of consistency simply means that whenever the government treats any person unequally because of his or her race, that person has suffered an injury that falls squarely within the language and spirit of the Constitution's guarantee of equal protection. It says nothing about the ultimate validity of any particular law; that determination is the job of the court applying strict scrutiny. The principle of consistency explains the circumstances in which the injury requiring strict scrutiny occurs. The application of strict scrutiny, in turn, determines whether a compelling governmental interest justifies the infliction of that injury.

Consistency *does* recognize that any individual suffers an injury when he or she is disadvantaged by the government because of his or her race, whatever that race may be. This Court clearly stated that principle in *Croson*. . . .

Justice Stevens also claims that we have ignored any difference between federal and state legislatures. But requiring that Congress, like the States, enact racial classifications only when doing so is necessary to further a "compelling interest" does not contravene any principle of appropriate respect for a coequal Branch of the Government. . . .

Finally, we wish to dispel the notion that strict scrutiny is "strict in theory, but fatal in fact." The unhappy persistence of both the practice and the lingering effects of racial discrimination against minority groups in this country is an unfortunate reality, and government is not disqualified from acting in response to it. As recently as 1987, for example, every Justice of this Court agreed that the Alabama Department of Public Safety's "pervasive, systematic, and obstinate discriminatory conduct" justified a narrowly tailored race-based remedy. See *United States v. Paradise* (1987). When racebased action is necessary to further a compelling interest, such action is within constitutional constraints if it satisfies the "narrow tailoring" test this Court has set out in previous cases. . . .

The judgment of the Court of Appeals is vacated, and the case is remanded for further proceedings consistent with this opinion.

JUSTICE SCALIA, concurring in part and concurring in the judgment.

I join the opinion of the Court, . . . except insofar as it may be inconsistent with the following: In my view, government can never have a "compelling interest" in discriminating on the basis of race in order to "make up" for past racial discrimination in the opposite direction. Individuals who have been wronged by unlawful racial discrimination should be made whole; but under our Constitution there can be no such thing as either a creditor or a debtor

race. That concept is alien to the Constitution's focus upon the individual, see Amdt. 14, §1 ("[N]or shall any State . . . deny *to any person*" the equal protection of the laws) (emphasis added), and its rejection of dispositions based on race, see Amdt. 15, §1 (prohibiting abridgment of the right to vote "on account of race") or based on blood, see Art. III, §3 ("[N]o Attainder of Treason shall work Corruption of Blood"); Art. I, §9 ("No Title of Nobility shall be granted by the United States"). To pursue the concept of racial entitlement—even for the most admirable and benign of purposes—is to reinforce and preserve for future mischief the way of thinking that produced race slavery, race privilege and race hatred. In the eyes of government, we are just one race here. It is American.

It is unlikely, if not impossible, that the challenged program would survive under this understanding of strict scrutiny, but I am content to leave that to be decided on remand.

JUSTICE THOMAS, concurring in part and concurring in the judgment.

I agree with the majority's conclusion that strict scrutiny applies to *all* government classifications based on race. I write separately, however, to express my disagreement with the premise . . . that there is a racial paternalism exception to the principle of equal protection. I believe that there is a "moral [and] constitutional equivalence" between laws designed to subjugate a race and those that distribute benefits on the basis of race in order to foster some current notion of equality. Government cannot make us equal; it can only recognize, respect, and protect us as equal before the law.

That these programs may have been motivated, in part, by good intentions cannot provide refuge from the principle that under our Constitution, the government may not make distinctions on the basis of race. As far as the Constitution is concerned, it is irrelevant whether a government's racial classifications are drawn by those who wish to oppress a race or by those who have a sincere desire to help those thought to be disadvantaged. There can be no doubt that the paternalism that appears to lie at the heart of this program is at war with the principle of inherent equality that underlies and infuses our Constitution. See Declaration of Independence ("We hold these truths to be self-evident, that all men are created equal, that they are endowed by their Creator with certain unalienable Rights, that among these are Life, Liberty, and the pursuit of Happiness").

These programs not only raise grave constitutional questions, they also undermine the moral basis of the equal protection principle. Purchased at the price of immeasurable human suffering, the equal protection principle reflects our Nation's understanding that such classifications ultimately have a destructive impact on the individual and our society. Unquestionably, "[i]nvidious [racial] discrimination is an engine of oppression." It is also true that "[r]emedial" racial preferences may reflect "a desire to foster equality in society." But there can be no doubt that racial paternalism and its unintended consequences can be as poisonous and pernicious as any other form of discrimination. So-called "benign" discrimination teaches many that because of chronic and apparently immutable handicaps, minorities cannot compete with them without their patronizing indulgence. Inevitably, such programs engender attitudes of superiority or, alternatively, provoke resentment among those who believe that they have been wronged by the government's use of race. These programs stamp minorities with a badge of inferiority and may cause them to develop dependencies or to adopt an attitude that they are "entitled" to preferences. . . .

In my mind, government-sponsored racial discrimination based on benign prejudice is just as noxious as discrimination inspired by malicious prejudice. In each instance, it is racial discrimination, plain and simple.

JUSTICE STEVENS, with whom JUSTICE GINSBURG joins, dissenting.

Instead of deciding this case in accordance with controlling precedent, the Court today delivers a disconcerting lecture about the evils of governmental racial classifications. . . .

The Court's concept of "consistency" assumes that there is no significant difference between a decision by the majority to impose a special burden on the members of a minority race and a decision by the majority to provide a benefit to certain members of that minority notwithstanding its incidental burden on some members of the majority. In my opinion that assumption is untenable. There is no moral or constitutional equivalence between a policy that is designed to perpetuate a caste system and one that seeks to eradicate racial subordination. Invidious discrimination is an engine of oppression, subjugating a disfavored group to enhance or maintain the power of the majority. Remedial race-based preferences reflect the opposite impulse: a desire to foster equality in society. No sensible conception of the Government's constitutional obligation to "govern impartially" should ignore this distinction. . . .

The consistency that the Court espouses would disregard the difference between a "No Trespassing" sign and a welcome mat. It would treat a Dixiecrat Senator's decision to vote against Thurgood Marshall's confirmation in order to keep African Americans off the Supreme Court as on a par with President Johnson's evaluation of his nominee's race as a positive factor. It would equate a law that made black citizens ineligible for military service with a program aimed at recruiting black soldiers. An attempt by the majority to exclude members of a minority race from a regulated market is fundamentally different from a subsidy that enables a relatively small group of newcomers to enter that market. An interest in "consistency" does not justify treating differences as though they were similarities.

The Court's explanation for treating dissimilar race-based decisions as though they were equally objectionable is a supposed inability to differentiate between "invidious" and "benign" discrimination. But the term "affirmative action" is common and well understood. Its presence in everyday parlance shows that people understand the difference between good intentions and bad. As with any legal concept, some cases may be difficult to classify, but our equal protection jurisprudence has identified a critical difference between state action that imposes burdens on a disfavored few and state action that benefits the few "in spite of" its adverse effects on the many. . . .

Moreover, the Court may find that its new "consistency" approach to race-based classifications is difficult to square with its insistence upon rigidly separate categories for discrimination against different classes of individuals. For example, as the law currently stands, the Court will apply "intermediate scrutiny" to cases of invidious gender discrimination and "strict scrutiny" to cases of invidious race discrimination, while applying the same standard for benign classifications as for invidious ones. If this remains the law, then today's lecture about "consistency" will produce the anomalous result that the Government can more easily enact affirmative-action programs to remedy discrimination against women than it can enact affirmative-action programs to remedy discrimination against African Americans—even though the primary purpose of the Equal Protection Clause was to end discrimination against the former slaves. When a court becomes preoccupied with abstract standards, it risks sacrificing common sense at the altar of formal consistency. . . .

The Court's concept of "congruence" assumes that there is no significant difference between a decision by the Congress of the United States to adopt an affirmative-action program and such a decision by a State or a municipality. In my opinion that assumption is untenable. It ignores important practical and legal differences between federal and state or local decisionmakers. . . . [A] reason for giving greater deference to the National Legislature than to a local law-making body is that federal affirmative-action programs represent the will of our entire Nation's elected representatives, whereas a state or local program may have an impact on nonresident entities who played no part in the decision to enact it. Thus, in the state or local context, individuals who were unable to vote for the local representatives who enacted a race-conscious program may nonetheless feel the effects of that program. . . .

Presumably, the majority is now satisfied that its theory of "congruence" between the substantive rights provided by the Fifth and Fourteenth Amendments disposes of the objection based upon divided constitutional powers. But it is one thing to say (as no one seems to dispute) that the Fifth Amendment encompasses a general guarantee of equal protection

as broad as that contained within the Fourteenth Amendment. It is another thing entirely to say that Congress' institutional competence and constitutional authority entitles it to no greater deference when it enacts a program designed to foster equality than the deference due a State legislature. The latter is an extraordinary proposition; and, as the foregoing discussion demonstrates, our precedents have rejected it explicitly and repeatedly. . . .

The Court's holding in *Fullilove* surely governs the result in this case. The Public Works Employment Act of 1977 (1977 Act), which this Court upheld in *Fullilove,* is different in several critical respects from the portions of the Small Business Act and the Surface Transportation and Uniform Relocation Assistance Act of 1987 challenged in this case. Each of those differences makes the current program designed to provide assistance to disadvantaged business enterprises (DBE's) significantly less objectionable than the 1977 categorical grant of $400 million in exchange for a 10% set-aside in public contracts to "a class of investors defined solely by racial characteristics." In no meaningful respect is the current scheme more objectionable than the 1977 Act. Thus, if the 1977 Act was constitutional, then so must be the SBA and STURAA. Indeed, even if my dissenting views in *Fullilove* had prevailed, this program would be valid. . . .

The majority's concept of "consistency" ignores a difference, fundamental to the idea of equal protection, between oppression and assistance. The majority's concept of "congruence" ignores a difference, fundamental to our constitutional system, between the Federal Government and the States. And the majority's concept of *stare decisis* ignores the force of binding precedent. I would affirm the judgment of the Court of Appeals.

JUSTICE SOUTER, with whom JUSTICE GINSBURG and JUSTICE BREYER join, dissenting. . . .

In assessing the degree to which today's holding portends a departure from past practice, it is also worth noting that nothing in today's opinion implies any view of Congress's

§5 power and the deference due its exercise that differs from the views expressed by the *Fullilove* plurality. The Court simply notes the observation in *Croson* "that the Court's 'treatment of an exercise of congressional power in *Fullilove* cannot be dispositive here,' because *Croson*'s facts did not implicate Congress' broad power under §5 of the Fourteenth Amendment," and explains that there is disagreement among today's majority about the extent of the §5 power. . . . Thus, today's decision should leave §5 exactly where it is as the source of an interest of the national government sufficiently important to satisfy the corresponding requirement of the strict scrutiny test. . . .

Grutter v. Bollinger
539 U.S. 306 (2003)

The University of Michigan Law School is one of the nation's top law schools, receiving more than 3,500 applications each year for a class of around 350 students. Through its official admissions policy, it seeks to achieve student-body diversity through compliance with Regents of University of California. v. Bakke *(1978). Focusing on students' academic ability coupled with a flexible assessment of their talents, experiences, and potential, the policy requires admissions officials to evaluate each applicant based on all the information available in the file, including a personal statement, letters of recommendation, an essay describing how the applicant will contribute to law school life and diversity, and the applicant's undergraduate grade point average (GPA) and Law School Admissions Test (LSAT) score. Additionally, it requires officials to look beyond grades and scores to so-called soft variables, such as recommenders' enthusiasm, the quality of the undergraduate institution, the applicant's essay, and the areas and difficulty of undergraduate course selection. Although the policy does not define diversity solely in terms of racial and ethnic status, it does reaffirm the law school's commitment to "one particular type of diversity" with special reference to the inclusion of African American, Hispanic American, and Native American students, who otherwise might not be represented in the student body in meaningful numbers. By enrolling a "critical mass" of underrepresented minority students, the policy seeks to ensure their ability to contribute to the law school's character and to the legal profession.*

When the law school denied admission to Barbara Grutter, a white Michigan resident with a 3.8 GPA and 161 LSAT score, she filed this suit, alleging that the law school had discriminated against her on the basis of race in violation of the Fourteenth Amendment, Title VI of the Civil Rights Act of 1964, and 42 U.S.C. §1981; that she was rejected because the law school uses race as a "predominant" factor, giving applicants belonging to certain minority groups a significantly greater chance of admission than students with similar credentials from disfavored racial groups; and that the law school had no compelling interest to justify that use of race. The US District Court for the Eastern District of Michigan found the law school's use of race as an admissions factor unlawful, but the Sixth Circuit reversed, holding that Justice Powell's opinion in Bakke *was binding precedent, establishing diversity as a compelling state interest, and that the law school's use of race was narrowly tailored because race was merely a "potential 'plus' factor" and because its program was virtually identical to the Harvard admissions program described approvingly by Justice Powell and appended to his* Bakke *opinion. The Supreme Court granted certiorari.* Opinion of the Court: <u>O'Connor</u>, Stevens, Souter, Breyer, Ginsburg. Concurring opinion: <u>Ginsburg</u>, Breyer. Concurring in part and dissenting in part: <u>Scalia</u>, Thomas; <u>Thomas</u>, Scalia. Dissenting opinions: <u>Rehnquist</u>, Scalia, Kennedy, Thomas; <u>Kennedy</u>.

JUSTICE O'CONNOR delivered the opinion of the Court.

. . . We granted certiorari to resolve the disagreement among the Courts of Appeals on a question of national importance: Whether diversity is a compelling interest that can justify the narrowly tailored use of race in selecting applicants for admission to public universities. Compare *Hopwood v. Texas* (CA5 1996) (holding that diversity is not a compelling state interest), with *Smith v. University of Wash. Law School* (CA9 2000) (holding that it is).

We last addressed the use of race in public higher education over 25 years ago. In the landmark *Bakke* case, we reviewed a racial set-aside program that reserved 16 out of 100 seats in a medical school class for members of certain minority groups. The decision produced six separate opinions, none of which commanded a majority of the Court. Four Justices would have upheld the program against all attack on the ground that the government can use race to "remedy disadvantages cast on minorities by past racial prejudice" (joint opinion of Brennan, White, Marshall, and Blackmun, JJ.). Four other Justices avoided the constitutional question altogether and struck down the program on statutory grounds (opinion of Stevens, J., joined by Burger, C. J., and Stewart and Rehnquist, JJ.). Justice Powell provided a fifth vote not only for invalidating the set-aside program, but also for reversing the state court's injunction against any use of race whatsoever. The only holding for the Court in *Bakke* was that a "State has a substantial interest that legitimately may be served by a properly devised admissions program involving the competitive consideration of race and ethnic origin." Thus, we reversed that part of the lower court's judgment that enjoined the university "from any consideration of the race of any applicant."

Since this Court's splintered decision in *Bakke,* Justice Powell's opinion announcing the judgment of the Court has served as the touchstone for constitutional analysis of race-conscious admissions policies. Public and private universities across the Nation have modeled their own admissions programs on Justice Powell's views on permissible race-conscious policies. We therefore discuss Justice Powell's opinion in some detail.

Justice Powell began by stating that "the guarantee of equal protection cannot mean one thing when applied to one individual and something else when applied to a person of another color. If both are not accorded the same protection, then it is not equal." In Justice Powell's view, when governmental decisions "touch upon an individual's race or ethnic background, he is entitled to a judicial determination that the burden he is asked to bear on that basis is precisely tailored to serve a compelling governmental interest." Under this exacting standard, only one of the interests asserted by the university survived Justice Powell's scrutiny. . . . Justice Powell approved the university's use of race to further only one interest: "the attainment of a diverse student body." With the important proviso that "constitutional limitations protecting individual rights may not be disregarded," Justice Powell grounded his analysis in the academic freedom that "long has been viewed as a special concern of the First Amendment." . . . Justice Powell was, however, careful to emphasize that in his view race "is only one element in a range of factors a university properly may consider in attaining the goal of a heterogeneous student body." . . .

. . . [F]or the reasons set out below, today we endorse Justice Powell's view that student body diversity is a compelling state interest that can justify the use of race in university admissions. . . .

We have held that all racial classifications imposed by government "must be analyzed by a reviewing court under strict scrutiny." This means that such classifications are constitutional only if they are narrowly tailored to further compelling governmental interests. "Absent searching judicial inquiry into the justification for such race-based measures," we have no way to determine what "classifications are 'benign' or 'remedial' and what classifications are in fact motivated by illegitimate notions of racial inferiority or simple racial politics."

Strict scrutiny is not "strict in theory, but fatal in fact." Although all governmental uses of race are subject to strict scrutiny, not all are invalidated by it. . . . When race-based action is necessary to further a compelling governmental interest, such action does not violate the constitutional guarantee of equal protection so long as the narrow-tailoring requirement is also satisfied.

Context matters when reviewing race-based governmental action under the Equal Protection Clause. . . . Not every decision influenced by race is equally objectionable and strict scrutiny is designed to provide a framework for carefully examining the importance and the sincerity of the reasons advanced by the governmental decisionmaker for the use of race in that particular context.

With these principles in mind, we turn to the question whether the Law School's use of race is justified by a compelling state interest. Before this Court, as they have throughout this litigation, respondents assert only one justification for their use of race in the admissions process: obtaining "the educational benefits that flow from a diverse student body." In other words, the Law School asks us to recognize, in the context of higher education, a compelling state interest in student body diversity.

We first wish to dispel the notion that the Law School's argument has been foreclosed, either expressly or implicitly, by our affirmative-action cases decided since *Bakke.* It is true that some language in those opinions might be read to suggest that remedying past discrimination is the only permissible justification for race-based governmental action. See, *e.g., Richmond v. J. A. Croson Co.* (1989). But we have never held that the only governmental use of race that can survive strict scrutiny is remedying past discrimination. Nor, since *Bakke,* have we directly addressed the use of race in the context of public higher education. Today, we hold that the Law School has a compelling interest in attaining a diverse student body.

The Law School's educational judgment that such diversity is essential to its educational mission is one to which we defer. The Law School's assessment that diversity will, in fact, yield educational benefits is substantiated by respondents and their *amici.* Our scrutiny of the interest asserted by the Law School is no less strict for taking into account complex educational judgments in an area that lies primarily within the expertise of the university. Our holding today is in keeping with our tradition of giving a degree of deference to a university's academic decisions, within constitutionally prescribed limits.

We have long recognized that, given the important purpose of public education and the expansive freedoms of speech and thought associated with the university environment, universities occupy a special niche in our constitutional tradition. In announcing the principle of student body diversity as a compelling state interest, Justice Powell invoked our cases recognizing a constitutional dimension, grounded in the First Amendment, of educational autonomy: "The freedom of a university to make its own judgments as to education includes the selection of its student body." From this premise, Justice Powell reasoned that by claiming "the right to select those students who will contribute the most to the 'robust exchange of ideas,'" a university "seeks to achieve a goal that is of paramount importance in the fulfillment of its mission." Our conclusion that the Law School has a compelling interest in a diverse student body is informed by our view that attaining a diverse student body is at the heart of the Law School's proper institutional mission, and that "good faith" on the part of a university is "presumed" absent "a showing to the contrary."

As part of its goal of "assembling a class that is both exceptionally academically qualified and broadly diverse," the Law School seeks to "enroll a 'critical mass' of minority students." The Law School's interest is not simply "to assure within its student body some specified percentage of a particular group merely because of its race or ethnic origin." That would amount to outright racial balancing, which is patently unconstitutional. Rather, the Law School's concept of critical mass is defined by reference to the educational benefits that diversity is designed to produce. . . .

The Law School's claim of a compelling interest is further bolstered by its *amici,* who point to the educational benefits that flow from student body diversity. In addition to the expert studies and reports entered into evidence at trial, numerous studies show that student body diversity promotes learning outcomes, and "better prepares students for an increasingly diverse workforce and society, and better prepares them as professionals."

These benefits are not theoretical but real, as major American businesses have made clear that the skills needed in today's increasingly global marketplace can only be developed through exposure to widely diverse people, cultures, ideas, and viewpoints. What is more, high-ranking retired officers and civilian leaders of the United States military assert that, "based on [their] decades of experience," a "highly qualified, racially diverse officer corps . . . is essential to the military's ability to fulfill its principle mission to provide national security." . . .

Moreover, universities, and in particular, law schools, represent the training ground for a large number of our Nation's leaders. Individuals with law degrees occupy roughly half the state governorships, more than half the seats in the United States Senate, and more than a third of the seats in the United States House of Representatives. The pattern is even more striking when it comes to highly selective law schools. A handful of these schools accounts for 25 of the 100 United States Senators, 74 United States Courts of Appeals judges, and nearly 200 of the more than 600 United States District Court judges.

In order to cultivate a set of leaders with legitimacy in the eyes of the citizenry, it is necessary that the path to leadership be visibly open to talented and qualified individuals of every race and ethnicity. All members of our heterogeneous society must have confidence in the openness and integrity of the educational institutions that provide this training. As we have recognized, law schools "cannot be effective in isolation from the individuals and institutions with which the law interacts." Access to legal education (and thus the legal profession) must be inclusive of talented and qualified individuals of every race and ethnicity, so that all members of our heterogeneous society may participate in the educational institutions that provide the training and education necessary to succeed in America.

The Law School does not premise its need for critical mass on "any belief that minority students always (or even consistently) express some characteristic minority viewpoint on any issue." To the contrary, diminishing the force of such stereotypes is both a crucial part of the Law School's mission, and one that it cannot accomplish with only token numbers of minority students. Just as growing up in a particular region or having particular professional experiences is likely to affect an individual's views, so too is one's own, unique experience of being a racial minority in a society, like our

own, in which race unfortunately still matters. The Law School has determined, based on its experience and expertise, that a "critical mass" of underrepresented minorities is necessary to further its compelling interest in securing the educational benefits of a diverse student body.

Even in the limited circumstance when drawing racial distinctions is permissible to further a compelling state interest, government is still "constrained in how it may pursue that end: The means chosen to accomplish the [government's] asserted purpose must be specifically and narrowly framed to accomplish that purpose. The purpose of the narrow tailoring requirement is to ensure that "the means chosen 'fit' . . . the compelling goal so closely that there is little or no possibility that the motive for the classification was illegitimate racial prejudice or stereotype."

Since *Bakke,* we have had no occasion to define the contours of the narrow-tailoring inquiry with respect to race-conscious university admissions programs. That inquiry must be calibrated to fit the distinct issues raised by the use of race to achieve student body diversity in public higher education. . . .

To be narrowly tailored, a race-conscious admissions program cannot use a quota system—it cannot "insulate each category of applicants with certain desired qualifications from competition with all other applicants." Instead, a university may consider race or ethnicity only as a "'plus' in a particular applicant's file," without "insulating the individual from comparison with all other candidates for the available seats." In other words, an admissions program must be "flexible enough to consider all pertinent elements of diversity in light of the particular qualifications of each applicant, and to place them on the same footing for consideration, although not necessarily according them the same weight."

We find that the Law School's admissions program bears the hallmarks of a narrowly tailored plan. As Justice Powell made clear in *Bakke,* truly individualized consideration demands that race be used in a flexible, nonmechanical way. It follows from this mandate that universities cannot establish quotas for members of certain racial groups or put members of those groups on separate admissions tracks. Nor can universities insulate applicants who belong to certain racial or ethnic groups from the competition for admission. Universities can, however, consider race or ethnicity more flexibly as a "plus" factor in the context of individualized consideration of each and every applicant.

We are satisfied that the Law School's admissions program, like the Harvard plan described by Justice Powell, does not operate as a quota. Properly understood, a "quota" is a program in which a certain fixed number or proportion of opportunities are "reserved exclusively for certain minority groups." . . .

Justice Powell's distinction between the medical school's rigid 16-seat quota and Harvard's flexible use of race as a "plus" factor is instructive. Harvard certainly had minimum *goals* for minority enrollment, even if it had no specific number firmly in mind. What is more, Justice Powell flatly rejected the argument that Harvard's program was "the functional equivalent of a quota" merely because it had some "'plus'" for race, or gave greater "weight" to race than to some other factors, in order to achieve student body diversity.

The Law School's goal of attaining a critical mass of underrepresented minority students does not transform its program into a quota. As the Harvard plan described by Justice Powell recognized, there is of course "some relationship between numbers and achieving the benefits to be derived from a diverse student body, and between numbers and providing a reasonable environment for those students admitted." . . .

That a race-conscious admissions program does not operate as a quota does not, by itself, satisfy the requirement of individualized consideration. When using race as a "plus" factor in university admissions, a university's admissions program must remain flexible enough to ensure that each applicant is evaluated as an individual and not in a way that makes an applicant's race or ethnicity the defining feature of his or her application. The importance of this individualized consideration in the context of a race-conscious admissions program is paramount.

Here, the Law School engages in a highly individualized, holistic review of each applicant's file, giving serious consideration to all the ways an applicant might contribute to a diverse educational environment. The Law School affords this individualized consideration to applicants of all races. There is no policy, either *de jure* or *de facto,* of automatic acceptance or rejection based on any single "soft" variable. Unlike the program at issue in *Gratz v. Bollinger,* the Law School awards no mechanical, predetermined diversity "bonuses" based on race or ethnicity. Like the Harvard plan, the Law School's admissions policy "is flexible enough to consider all pertinent elements of diversity in light of the particular qualifications of each applicant, and to place them on the same footing for consideration, although not necessarily according them the same weight."

We also find that, like the Harvard plan Justice Powell referenced in *Bakke,* the Law School's race-conscious admissions program adequately ensures that all factors that may contribute to student body diversity are meaningfully considered alongside race in admissions decisions. With respect to the use of race itself, all underrepresented minority students admitted by the Law School have been deemed qualified. By virtue of our Nation's struggle with racial inequality, such students are both likely to have experiences of particular importance to the Law School's mission, and less likely to be admitted in meaningful numbers on criteria that ignore those experiences. . . .

Petitioner and the United States argue that the Law School's plan is not narrowly tailored because race-neutral means exist to obtain the educational benefits of student body diversity that the Law School seeks. We disagree. Narrow tailoring does not require exhaustion of every conceivable race-neutral alternative. Nor does it require a university to choose between maintaining a reputation for excellence or fulfilling a commitment to provide educational opportunities to members of all racial groups. . . . We agree with the Court of Appeals that the Law School sufficiently considered workable race-neutral alternatives. The District Court took the Law School to task for failing to consider race-neutral alternatives such as "using a lottery system" or "decreasing the emphasis for all applicants on undergraduate GPA and LSAT scores." But these alternatives would require a dramatic sacrifice of diversity, the academic quality of all admitted students, or both. . . .

We acknowledge that "there are serious problems of justice connected with the idea of preference itself." Narrow tailoring, therefore, requires that a race-conscious admissions program not unduly harm members of any racial group. . . . We are satisfied that the Law School's admissions program does not. . . . [I]n the context of its individualized inquiry into the possible diversity contributions of all applicants, the Law School's race-conscious admissions program does not unduly harm nonminority applicants.

We are mindful, however, that "[a] core purpose of the Fourteenth Amendment was to do away with all governmentally imposed discrimination based on race." Accordingly, race-conscious admissions policies must be limited in time. This requirement reflects that racial classifications, however compelling their goals, are potentially so dangerous that they may be employed no more broadly than the interest demands. Enshrining a permanent justification for racial preferences would offend this fundamental equal protection principle. We see no reason to exempt race-conscious admissions programs from the requirement that all governmental use of race must have a logical end point. The Law School, too, concedes that all "race-conscious programs must have reasonable durational limits."

In the context of higher education, the durational requirement can be met by sunset provisions in race-conscious admissions policies and periodic reviews to determine whether racial preferences are still necessary to achieve student body diversity. . . . We take the Law School at its word that it would "like nothing better than to find a race-neutral admissions formula" and will terminate its race-conscious admissions program as soon as practicable. It has been 25 years since Justice Powell first approved the use of race to further an interest in student body diversity in the context of public higher education. Since that time, the number of minority applicants with high grades and test scores has indeed increased. We expect that 25 years from now, the use of racial preferences will no longer be necessary to further the interest approved today.

In summary, the Equal Protection Clause does not prohibit the Law School's narrowly tailored use of race in admissions decisions to further a compelling interest in obtaining the educational benefits that flow from a diverse student body. Consequently, petitioner's statutory claims based on Title VI and 42 U.S.C. §1981 also fail. The judgment of the Court of Appeals for the Sixth Circuit, accordingly, is affirmed.

JUSTICE GINSBURG, with whom JUSTICE BREYER joins, concurring.

The Court's observation that race-conscious programs "must have a logical end point" accords with the international understanding of the office of affirmative action. The International Convention on the Elimination of All Forms of Racial Discrimination, ratified by the United States in 1994 endorses "special and concrete measures to ensure the adequate development and protection of certain racial groups or individuals belonging to them, for the purpose of guaranteeing them the full and equal enjoyment of human rights and fundamental freedoms." But such measures, the Convention instructs, "shall in no case entail as a consequence the maintenance of unequal or separate rights for different racial groups after the objectives for which they were taken have been achieved."

The Court further observes that "it has been 25 years since Justice Powell first approved the use of race to further an interest in student body diversity in the context of public higher education." For at least part of that time, however, the law could not fairly be described as "settled," and in some regions of the Nation, overtly race-conscious admissions policies have been proscribed. See *Hopwood v. Texas* (1996). Moreover, it was only 25 years before *Bakke* that this Court declared public school segregation unconstitutional, a declaration that, after prolonged resistance, yielded an end to a law-enforced racial caste system, itself the legacy of centuries of slavery. See *Brown v. Board of Education* (1954).

It is well documented that conscious and unconscious race bias, even rank discrimination based on race, remain alive in our land, impeding realization of our highest values and ideals.

As to public education, data for the years 2000–2001 show that 71.6% of African-American children and 76.3% of Hispanic children attended a school in which minorities made up a majority of the student body. And schools in predominantly minority communities lag far behind others measured by the educational resources available to them.

However strong the public's desire for improved education systems may be, it remains the current reality that many minority students encounter markedly inadequate and unequal educational opportunities. . . . From today's vantage point, one may hope, but not firmly forecast, that over the next generation's span, progress toward nondiscrimination and genuinely equal opportunity will make it safe to sunset affirmative action.

THE CHIEF JUSTICE, with whom JUSTICE SCALIA, JUSTICE KENNEDY, and JUSTICE THOMAS join, dissenting.

. . . The Law School claims it must take the steps it does to achieve a "'critical mass'" of underrepresented minority students. But its actual program bears no relation to this asserted goal. Stripped of its "critical mass" veil, the Law School's program is revealed as a naked effort to achieve racial balancing. . . .

Before the Court's decision today, we consistently applied the same strict scrutiny analysis regardless of the government's purported reason for using race and regardless of the setting in which race was being used. . . . Although the Court recites the language of our strict scrutiny analysis, its application of that review is unprecedented in its deference.

Respondents' asserted justification for the Law School's use of race in the admissions process is "obtaining 'the educational benefits that flow from a diverse student body.'" They contend that a "critical mass" of underrepresented minorities is necessary to further that interest. Respondents and school administrators explain generally that "critical mass" means a sufficient number of underrepresented minority students to achieve several objectives: To ensure that these minority students do not feel isolated or like spokespersons for their race; to provide adequate opportunities for the type of interaction upon which the educational benefits of diversity depend; and to challenge all students to think critically and reexamine stereotypes. These objectives indicate that "critical mass" relates to the size of the student body. Respondents further claim that the Law School is achieving "critical mass."

In practice, the Law School's program bears little or no relation to its asserted goal of achieving "critical mass." Respondents explain that the Law School seeks to accumulate a "critical mass" of *each* underrepresented minority group. But the record demonstrates that the Law School's admissions practices with respect to these groups differ dramatically and cannot be defended under any consistent use of the term "critical mass."

From 1995 through 2000, the Law School admitted between 1,130 and 1,310 students. Of those, between 13 and 19 were Native American, between 91 and 108 were African Americans, and between 47 and 56 were Hispanic. If the Law School is admitting between 91 and 108 African Americans in order to achieve "critical mass," thereby preventing African-American students from feeling "isolated or like spokespersons for their race," one would think that a number of the same order of magnitude would be necessary to accomplish the same purpose for Hispanics and Native Americans. . . . In order for this pattern of admission to be consistent with the Law School's explanation of "critical mass," one would have to believe that the objectives of "critical mass" offered by respondents are achieved with only half the number of Hispanics and one-sixth the number of Native Americans as compared to African Americans. But respondents offer no race-specific reasons for such disparities. Instead, they simply emphasize the importance of achieving "critical mass," without any explanation of why that concept is applied differently among the three underrepresented minority groups.

These different numbers, moreover, come only as a result of substantially different treatment among the three underrepresented minority groups. . . . [I]n 2000, 12 Hispanics who scored between a 159–160 on the LSAT and earned a GPA of 3.00 or higher applied for admission and only 2 were admitted. Meanwhile, 12 African Americans in the same range of qualifications applied for admission and all 12 were admitted. Likewise, that same year, 16 Hispanics who scored between a 151–153 on the LSAT and earned a 3.00 or higher applied for admission and only 1 of those applicants was admitted. Twenty-three similarly qualified African Americans applied for admission and 14 were admitted.

These statistics have a significant bearing on petitioner's case. Respondents have *never* offered any race-specific arguments explaining why significantly more individuals from one underrepresented minority group are needed in order to achieve "critical mass" or further student body diversity. They certainly have not explained why Hispanics, who they have said are among "the groups most isolated by racial barriers in our country," should have their admission capped out in this manner. . . .

Only when the "critical mass" label is discarded does a likely explanation for these numbers emerge. The Court states that the Law School's goal of attaining a "critical mass" of underrepresented minority students is not an interest in merely "'assuring within its student body some specified percentage of a particular group merely because of its race or ethnic origin.'" The Court recognizes that such an interest "would amount to outright racial balancing, which is patently unconstitutional." The Court concludes, however, that the Law School's use of race in admissions, consistent with Justice Powell's opinion in *Bakke,* only pays "'some attention to numbers.'"

But the correlation between the percentage of the Law School's pool of applicants who are members of the three minority groups and the percentage of the admitted applicants who are members of these same groups is far too precise to be dismissed as merely the result of the school paying "some attention to [the] numbers." . . . [F]rom 1995 through 2000 the percentage of admitted applicants who were members of these minority groups closely tracked the percentage of individuals in the school's applicant pool who were from the same groups. . . . For example, in 1995, when 9.7% of the applicant pool was African American, 9.4% of the admitted class was African American. By 2000, only 7.5% of the applicant pool was African American, and 7.3% of

the admitted class was African American. This correlation is striking. . . . The tight correlation between the percentage of applicants and admittees of a given race, therefore, must result from careful race based planning by the Law School. It suggests a formula for admission based on the aspirational assumption that all applicants are equally qualified academically, and therefore that the proportion of each group admitted should be the same as the proportion of that group in the applicant pool. . . .

I do not believe that the Constitution gives the Law School such free rein in the use of race. The Law School has offered no explanation for its actual admissions practices and, unexplained, we are bound to conclude that the Law School has managed its admissions program, not to achieve a "critical mass," but to extend offers of admission to members of selected minority groups in proportion to their statistical representation in the applicant pool. But this is precisely the type of racial balancing that the Court itself calls "patently unconstitutional."

Finally, I believe that the Law School's program fails strict scrutiny because it is devoid of any reasonably precise time limit on the Law School's use of race in admissions. . . . The Court suggests a possible 25-year limitation on the Law School's current program. Respondents, on the other hand, remain more ambiguous, explaining that "the Law School of course recognizes that race-conscious programs must have reasonable durational limits, and the Sixth Circuit properly found such a limit in the Law School's resolve to cease considering race when genuine race-neutral alternatives become available." These discussions of a time limit are the vaguest of assurances. In truth, they permit the Law School's use of racial preferences on a seemingly permanent basis. Thus, an important component of strict scrutiny— that a program be limited in time—is casually subverted. The Court, in an unprecedented display of deference under our strict scrutiny analysis, upholds the Law School's program despite its obvious flaws. We have said that when it comes to the use of race, the connection between the ends and the means used to attain them must be precise. But here the flaw is deeper than that; it is not merely a question of "fit" between ends and means. Here the means actually used are forbidden by the Equal Protection Clause of the Constitution.

JUSTICE SCALIA, with whom JUSTICE THOMAS joins, concurring in part and dissenting in part.

The "educational benefit" that the University of Michigan seeks to achieve by racial discrimination consists, according to the Court, of "'cross-racial understanding'" and "'better preparation of students for an increasingly diverse workforce and society,'" all of which is necessary not only for work, but also for good "citizenship." This is not, of course, an "educational benefit" on which students will be graded on their Law School transcript (Works and Plays Well with Others: B1) or tested by the bar examiners (Q: Describe in 500 words or less your cross-racial understanding). For it is a lesson of life rather than law—essentially the same lesson taught to (or rather learned by, for it cannot be "taught" in the usual sense) people three feet shorter and twenty years younger than the full-grown adults at the University of Michigan Law School, in institutions ranging from Boy Scout troops to public-school kindergartens. If properly considered an "educational benefit" at all, it is surely not one that is either uniquely relevant to law school or uniquely "teachable" in a formal educational setting. *And therefore:* If it is appropriate for the University of Michigan Law School to use racial discrimination for the purpose of putting together a "critical mass" that will convey generic lessons in socialization and good citizenship, surely it is no less appropriate—indeed, *particularly* appropriate—for the civil service system of the State of Michigan to do so. There, also, those exposed to "critical masses" of certain races will presumably become better Americans, better Michiganders, better civil servants. And surely private employers cannot be criticized—indeed, should be praised—if they also "teach" good citizenship to their adult employees through a patriotic, all-American system of racial discrimination in hiring. The nonminority individuals who are deprived of a legal education, a civil service job, or any job at all by reason of their skin color will surely understand.

Unlike a clear constitutional holding that racial preferences in state educational institutions are impermissible, or even a clear anticonstitutional holding that racial preferences in state educational institutions are OK, today's *Grutter-Gratz* split double header seems perversely designed to prolong the controversy and the litigation. Some future lawsuits will presumably focus on whether the discriminatory scheme in question contains enough evaluation of the applicant "as an individual" and sufficiently avoids "separate admissions tracks" to fall under *Grutter* rather than *Gratz.* Some will focus on whether a university has gone beyond the bounds of a "'good faith effort'" and has so zealously pursued its "critical mass" as to make it an unconstitutional *de facto* quota system, rather than merely "'a permissible goal.'" Other lawsuits may focus on whether, in the particular setting at issue, any educational benefits flow from racial diversity. Still other suits may challenge the bona fides of the institution's expressed commitment to the educational benefits of diversity that immunize the discriminatory scheme in *Grutter.* (Tempting targets, one would suppose, will be those universities that talk the talk of multiculturalism and racial diversity in the courts but walk the walk of tribalism and racial segregation on their campuses—through minority-only student organizations, separate minority housing opportunities, separate minority student centers, even separate minority-only graduation ceremonies.) And still other suits may claim that the institution's racial preferences have gone below or above the mystical *Grutter*-approved "critical mass." Finally, litigation can be expected on behalf of minority groups intentionally short changed in the institution's composition of its generic minority "critical mass." I do not look forward to any of these cases. The Constitution proscribes government discrimination on the basis of race, and state-provided education is no exception.

JUSTICE THOMAS, with whom JUSTICE SCALIA joins, concurring in part and dissenting in part.

Frederick Douglass, speaking to a group of abolitionists almost 140 years ago, delivered a message lost on today's majority:

In regard to the colored people, there is always more that is benevolent, I perceive, than just, manifested towards us. What I ask for the negro is not benevolence, not pity, not sympathy, but simply *justice*. The American people have always been anxious to know what they shall do with us. . . . I have had but one answer from the beginning. Do nothing with us! Your doing with us has already played the mischief with us. Do nothing with us! If the apples will not remain on the tree of their own strength, if they are worm-eaten at the core, if they are early ripe and disposed to fall, let them fall! . . . And if the negro cannot stand on his own legs, let him fall also. All I ask is, give him a chance to stand on his own legs! Let him alone! . . . Your interference is doing him positive injury." What the Black Man Wants: An Address Delivered in Boston, Massachusetts, on 26 January 1865, reprinted in 4 *The Frederick Douglass Papers* 59, 68 (J. Blassingame & J. McKivigan, eds. 1991). (emphasis in original)

Like Douglass, I believe blacks can achieve in every avenue of American life without the meddling of university administrators. Because I wish to see all students succeed whatever their color, I share, in some respect, the sympathies of those who sponsor the type of discrimination advanced by the University of Michigan Law School (Law School). The Constitution does not, however, tolerate institutional devotion to the status quo in admissions policies when such devotion ripens into racial discrimination. Nor does the Constitution countenance the unprecedented deference the Court gives to the Law School, an approach inconsistent with the very concept of "strict scrutiny."

No one would argue that a university could set up a lower general admission standard and then impose heightened requirements only on black applicants. Similarly, a university may not maintain a high admission standard and grant exemptions to favored races. The Law School, of its own choosing, and for its own purposes, maintains an exclusionary admissions system that it knows produces racially disproportionate results. Racial discrimination

is not a permissible solution to the self-inflicted wounds of this elitist admissions policy.

The majority upholds the Law School's racial discrimination not by interpreting the people's Constitution, but by responding to a faddish slogan of the cognoscenti. Nevertheless, I concur in part in the Court's opinion. First, I agree with the Court insofar as its decision, which approves of only one racial classification, confirms that further use of race in admissions remains unlawful. Second, I agree with the Court's holding that racial discrimination in higher education admissions will be illegal in 25 years. I respectfully dissent from the remainder of the Court's opinion and the judgment, however, because I believe that the Law School's current use of race violates the Equal Protection Clause and that the Constitution means the same thing today as it will in 300 months. . . .

Unlike the majority, I seek to define with precision the interest being asserted by the Law School before determining whether that interest is so compelling as to justify racial discrimination. The Law School maintains that it wishes to obtain "educational benefits that flow from student body diversity," . . . One must consider the Law School's refusal to entertain changes to its current admissions system that might produce the same educational benefits. The Law School adamantly disclaims any race-neutral alternative that would reduce "academic selectivity," which would in turn "require the Law School to become a very different institution, and to sacrifice a core part of its educational mission."

In other words, the Law School seeks to improve marginally the education it offers without sacrificing too much of its exclusivity and elite status. The proffered interest that the majority vindicates today, then, is not simply "diversity." Instead the Court upholds the use of racial discrimination as a tool to advance the Law School's interest in offering a marginally superior education while maintaining an elite institution. Unless each constituent part of this state interest is of pressing public necessity, the Law School's use of race is unconstitutional. I find each of them to fall far short of this standard.

A close reading of the Court's opinion reveals that all of its legal work is done through one conclusory statement: The Law School has a "compelling interest in securing the educational benefits of a diverse student body." No serious effort is made to explain how these benefits fit with the state interests the Court has recognized (or rejected) as compelling, or to place any theoretical constraints on an enterprising court's desire to discover still more justifications for racial discrimination. . . .

Justice Powell's opinion in *Bakke* and the Court's decision today rest on the fundamentally flawed proposition that racial discrimination can be contextualized so that a goal, such as classroom aesthetics [defined by Justice Thomas elsewhere in his opinion to mean the Law School's wish "to have a certain appearance, from the shape of the desks and tables in its classrooms to the color of the students sitting at them."], can be compelling in one context but not in another. This "we know it when we see it" approach to evaluating state interests is not capable of judicial application. Today, the Court insists on radically expanding the range of permissible uses of race to something as trivial (by comparison) as the assembling of a law school class. I can only presume that the majority's failure to justify its decision by reference to any principle arises from the absence of any such principle.

Under the proper standard, there is no pressing public necessity in maintaining a public law school at all and, it follows, certainly not an elite law school. Likewise, marginal improvements in legal education do not qualify as a compelling state interest.

While legal education at a public university may be good policy or otherwise laudable, it is obviously not a pressing public necessity when the correct legal standard is applied. Additionally, circumstantial evidence as to whether a state activity is of pressing public necessity can be obtained by asking whether all States feel compelled to engage in that activity. Evidence that States, in general, engage in a certain activity by no means demonstrates that the activity constitutes a pressing public necessity, given the expansive role of government in today's society. The fact that some fraction of the States reject a particular enterprise, however, creates a presumption that the enterprise itself is not a compelling state interest. In this sense,

the absence of a public, American Bar Association (ABA) accredited, law school in Alaska, Delaware, Massachusetts, New Hampshire, and Rhode Island provides further evidence that Michigan's maintenance of the Law School does not constitute a compelling state interest.

As the foregoing makes clear, Michigan has no compelling interest in having a law school at all, much less an *elite* one. Still, even assuming that a State may, under appropriate circumstances, demonstrate a cognizable interest in having an elite law school, Michigan has failed to do so here. . . .

The only cognizable state interests vindicated by operating a public law school are, therefore, the education of that State's citizens and the training of that State's lawyers. . . . The Law School today, however, does precious little training of those attorneys who will serve the citizens of Michigan. In 2002, graduates of the University of Michigan Law School made up less than 6% of applicants to the Michigan bar, even though the Law School's graduates constitute nearly 30% of all law students graduating in Michigan. Less than 16% of the Law School's graduating class elects to stay in Michigan after law school. Thus, while a mere 27% of the Law School's 2002 entering class are from Michigan, only half of these, it appears, will stay in Michigan.

In sum, the Law School trains few Michigan residents and overwhelmingly serves students, who, as lawyers, leave the State of Michigan. . . . The Law School's decision to be an elite institution does little to advance the welfare of the people of Michigan or any cognizable interest of the State of Michigan.

Again, the fact that few States choose to maintain elite law schools raises a strong inference that there is nothing compelling about elite status. . . . The Court never explicitly holds that the Law School's desire to retain the status quo in "academic selectivity" is itself a compelling state interest, and, as I have demonstrated, it is not. Therefore, the Law School should be forced to choose between its classroom aesthetic and its exclusionary admissions system—it cannot have it both ways. . . .

Moreover one would think, in light of the Court's decision in *United States v. Virginia* (1996), that before being given license to use racial discrimination, the Law School would be required to radically reshape its admissions process, even to the point of sacrificing some elements of its character. In *Virginia,* a majority of the Court, without a word about academic freedom, accepted the all-male Virginia Military Institute's (VMI) representation that some changes in its "adversative" method of education would be required with the admission of women, but did not defer to VMI's judgment that these changes would be too great. Instead, the Court concluded that they were "manageable." That case involved sex discrimination, which is subjected to intermediate, not strict, scrutiny. So in *Virginia,* where the standard of review dictated that greater flexibility be granted to VMI's educational policies than the Law School deserves here, this Court gave no deference. Apparently where the status quo being defended is that of the elite establishment—here the Law School—rather than a less fashionable Southern military institution, the Court will defer without serious inquiry and without regard to the applicable legal standard.

Virginia is also notable for the fact that the Court relied on the "experience" of formerly single-sex institutions, such as the service academies, to conclude that admission of women to VMI would be "manageable." Today, however, the majority ignores the "experience" of those institutions that have been forced to abandon explicit racial discrimination in admissions.

The sky has not fallen at Boalt Hall at the University of California, Berkeley, for example. Prior to Proposition 209's adoption which bars the State from "granting preferential treatment . . . on the basis of race . . . in the operation of . . . public education," Boalt Hall enrolled 20 blacks and 28 Hispanics in its first-year class for 1996. In 2002, without deploying express racial discrimination in admissions, Boalt's entering class enrolled 14 blacks and 36 Hispanics. Total underrepresented minority student enrollment at Boalt Hall now exceeds 1996 levels. Apparently the Law School cannot be counted on to be as resourceful. The Court is willfully blind to the very real experience in California and elsewhere, which raises the inference that institutions with "reputations for excellence" rivaling the Law School's have satisfied their sense of mission without resorting to prohibited racial discrimination. . . .

. . . [I]n the national debate on racial discrimination in higher education admissions, much has been made of the fact that elite institutions utilize a so-called "legacy" preference to give the children of alumni an advantage in admissions. This, and other, exceptions to a "true" meritocracy give the lie to protestations that merit admissions are in fact the order of the day at the Nation's universities. The Equal Protection Clause does not, however, prohibit the use of unseemly legacy preferences or many other kinds of arbitrary admissions procedures. What the Equal Protection Clause does prohibit are classifications made on the basis of race. So while legacy preferences can stand under the Constitution, racial discrimination cannot. I will not twist the Constitution to invalidate legacy preferences or otherwise impose my vision of higher education admissions on the Nation. The majority should similarly stay its impulse to validate faddish racial discrimination the Constitution clearly forbids.

Similarly no modern law school can claim ignorance of the poor performance of blacks, relatively speaking, on the Law School Admissions Test (LSAT). Nevertheless, law schools continue to use the test and then attempt to "correct" for black underperformance by using racial discrimination in admissions so as to obtain their aesthetic student body. The Law School's continued adherence to measures it knows produce racially skewed results is not entitled to deference by this Court. The Law School itself admits that the test is imperfect, . . . [a]nd the Law School's *amici* cannot seem to agree on the fundamental question whether the test itself is useful.

Having decided to use the LSAT, the Law School must accept the constitutional burdens that come with this decision. The Law School may freely continue to employ the LSAT and other allegedly merit-based standards in whatever fashion it likes. What the Equal Protection Clause forbids, but the Court today allows, is the use of these standards hand-in-hand with racial discrimination. An infinite variety of admissions methods are available to the Law School. Considering all of the radical thinking that has historically occurred at this country's universities, the Law School's intractable approach toward admissions is striking.

The Court will not even deign to make the Law School try other methods, however, preferring instead to grant a 25-year license to violate the Constitution. And the same Court that had the courage to order the desegregation of all public schools in the South now fears, on the basis of platitudes rather than principle, to force the Law School to abandon a decidedly imperfect admissions regime that provides the basis for racial discrimination.

. . . I must contest the notion that the Law School's discrimination benefits those admitted as a result of it. . . . [N]owhere in any of the filings in this Court is any evidence that the purported "beneficiaries" of this racial discrimination prove themselves by performing at (or even near) the same level as those students who receive no preferences.

The silence in this case is deafening to those of us who view higher education's purpose as imparting knowledge and skills to students, rather than a communal, rubber-stamp, credentialing process. The Law School is not looking for those students who, despite a lower LSAT score or undergraduate grade point average, will succeed in the study of law. The Law School seeks only a facade—it is sufficient that the class looks right, even if it does not perform right. . . .

Beyond the harm the Law School's racial discrimination visits upon its test subjects, no social science has disproved the notion that this discrimination "engenders attitudes of superiority or, alternatively, provokes resentment among those who believe that they have been wronged by the government's use of race." "These programs stamp minorities with a badge of inferiority and may cause them to develop dependencies or to adopt an attitude that they are 'entitled' to preferences."

It is uncontested that each year, the Law School admits a handful of blacks who would be admitted in the absence of racial discrimination. Who can differentiate between those who belong and those who do not? The majority of blacks are admitted to the Law School because of discrimination, and because of this policy all are tarred as undeserving. This problem of stigma does not depend on determinacy as to whether those stigmatized are actually the "beneficiaries" of racial discrimination. When blacks take positions in the highest places of government, industry, or academia, it is an open question today whether their skin color played a part in their advancement. The question itself is the stigma—because either racial discrimination did play a role, in which case the person may be deemed "otherwise unqualified," or it did not, in which case asking the question itself unfairly marks those blacks who would succeed without discrimination. Is this what the Court means by "visibly open"? . . .

The Court also holds that racial discrimination in admissions should be given another 25 years before it is deemed no longer narrowly tailored to the Law School's fabricated compelling state interest. While I agree that in 25 years the practices of the Law School will be illegal, they are, for the reasons I have given, illegal now. The majority does not and cannot rest its time limitation on any evidence that the gap in credentials between black and white students is shrinking or will be gone in that timeframe. In recent years there has been virtually no change, for example, in the proportion of law school applicants with LSAT scores of 165 and higher who are black. In 1993 blacks constituted 1.1% of law school applicants in that score range, though they represented 11.1% of all applicants. In 2000 the comparable numbers were 1.0% and 11.3%. No one can seriously contend, and the Court does not, that the racial gap in academic credentials will disappear in 25 years. Nor is the Court's holding that racial discrimination will be unconstitutional in 25 years made contingent on the gap closing in that time. . . .

For the immediate future, however, the majority has placed its *imprimatur* on a practice that can only weaken the principle of equality embodied in the Declaration of Independence and the Equal Protection Clause. "Our Constitution is color-blind, and neither knows nor tolerates classes among citizens." *Plessy v. Ferguson* (1896) (Harlan, J., dissenting). It has been nearly 140 years since Frederick Douglass asked the intellectual ancestors of the Law School to "do nothing with us!" and the Nation adopted the Fourteenth Amendment.

Now we must wait another 25 years to see this principle of equality vindicated. I therefore respectfully dissent from the remainder of the Court's opinion and the judgment.

Gratz v. Bollinger
539 U.S. 244 (2003)

Jennifer Gratz and Patrick Hamacher, both white residents of Michigan, applied for admission to the University of Michigan's College of Literature, Science, and the Arts (LSA) in 1995 and 1997, respectively. Although the LSA considered Gratz to be well qualified and Hamacher to be within the qualified range, both were denied admission, based on the written guidelines of the university's Office of Undergraduate Admissions (OUA). These guidelines spelled out the weight the OUA would give to a number of factors in making admissions decisions, including high school grades, standardized test scores, high school quality, curriculum strength, geography, alumni relationships, leadership, and race. Although the OUA changed these guidelines a number of times during the period relevant to this litigation, during the entire period the university considered African Americans, Hispanic Americans, and Native Americans to be "underrepresented minorities," and none of the parties disputed that the university admitted virtually every qualified applicant from these groups. The OUA current guidelines when this case went to trial used a selection method under which every applicant from an underrepresented racial or ethnic minority group was automatically awarded twenty points of the one hundred needed to guarantee admission.

Gratz and Hamacher brought a class action in the US District Court for the Eastern District of Michigan on behalf of all individuals who applied for and were denied admission to the LSA for academic year 1995 and forward and who were members of racial or ethnic groups that respondents treated less favorably on the basis of race. Alleging that the university's use of racial preferences in undergraduate admissions violated the Equal Protection Clause of the Fourteenth Amendment, Title VI of the Civil Rights Act of 1964, and 42 U.S.C. §1981, they sought compensatory and punitive damages for past violations, declaratory relief finding that the University of Michigan violated their rights to nondiscrimi-

natory treatment, and an injunction prohibiting it from continuing to discriminate on the basis of race. On cross-motions for summary judgment, the university relied on Justice Powell's principal opinion in Regents of University of California v. Bakke *(1978), which expressed the view that the consideration of race as a factor in admissions might in some cases serve a compelling governmental interest. Respondents contended that the LSA had just such an interest in the educational benefits that result from having a racially and ethnically diverse student body and that its program was narrowly tailored to serve that interest. The district court held that the LSA's current admissions guidelines awarding twenty points for membership in an underrepresented minority group were consistent with Powell's language in* Bakke *and granted the university summary judgment on the constitutionality of its use of the current guidelines. However, concerning the LSA's guidelines for the years 1995 through 1998 that actually "reserved" seats for underrepresented minority applicants, the Court found that they had operated as the functional equivalent of a quota and ran afoul of Powell's* Bakke *opinion; it therefore granted the petitioners summary judgment with respect to the university's admission programs for those years. While appeals were pending in the Sixth Circuit, that court issued an opinion in* Grutter v. Bollinger *(2002), upholding the admissions program used by the university's law school. The Supreme Court granted certiorari in both cases, even though the Sixth Circuit had not yet rendered judgment in this one.* Opinion of the Court: <u>Rehnquist</u>, O'Connor, Scalia, Kennedy, Thomas. Concurring opinions: <u>O'Connor</u>, Breyer (in part); <u>Thomas</u>. Concurring in the judgment: <u>Breyer</u>. Dissenting opinions: <u>Stevens</u>, Souter; <u>Souter</u>, Ginsburg; <u>Ginsburg</u>, Souter, Breyer (in part).

THE CHIEF JUSTICE delivered the opinion of the Court.

We granted certiorari in this case to decide whether "the University of Michigan's use of racial preferences in undergraduate admissions violates the Equal Protection Clause of the Fourteenth Amendment, Title VI of the Civil Rights Act of 1964, or 42 U.S.C. §1981." Because we find that the manner in which the University considers the race of applicants in its undergraduate admissions guidelines violates these constitutional and statutory provisions, we reverse that portion of the District Court's decision upholding the guidelines. . . .

Petitioners argue, first and foremost, that the University's use of race in undergraduate admissions violates the Fourteenth Amendment. Specifically, they contend that this Court has only sanctioned the use of racial classifications to remedy identified discrimination, a justification on which respondents have never relied. Petitioners further argue that "diversity as a basis for employing racial preferences is simply too open-ended, ill-defined, and indefinite to constitute a compelling interest capable of supporting narrowly-tailored means." But for the reasons set forth today in *Grutter v. Bollinger* (2003), the Court has rejected these arguments of petitioners.

Petitioners alternatively argue that even if the University's interest in diversity can constitute a compelling state interest, the District Court erroneously concluded that the University's use of race in its current freshman admissions policy is narrowly tailored to achieve such an interest. Petitioners argue that the guidelines the University began using in 1999 do not "remotely resemble the kind of consideration of race and ethnicity that Justice Powell endorsed in *Bakke*." Respondents reply that the University's current admissions program *is* narrowly tailored and avoids the problems of the Medical School of the University of California at Davis program (U. C. Davis) rejected by Justice Powell. They claim that their program "hews closely" to both the admissions program described by Justice Powell as well as the Harvard College admissions program that he endorsed. Specifically, respondents contend that the LSA's policy provides the individualized consideration that "Justice Powell considered a hallmark of a constitutionally appropriate admissions program." For the reasons set out below, we do not agree.

It is by now well established that "all racial classifications reviewable under the Equal Protection Clause must be strictly scrutinized." *Adarand Constructors, Inc. v. Peña* (1995). This "'standard of review . . . is not dependent on the race of those burdened or benefited by a particular classification.'" Thus, "any person, of whatever race, has the right to demand that any governmental actor subject to the Constitution justify any racial classification subjecting that person to unequal treatment under the strictest of judicial scrutiny."

To withstand our strict scrutiny analysis, respondents must demonstrate that the University's use of race in its current admission program employs "narrowly tailored measures that further compelling governmental interests." Because "racial classifications are simply too pernicious to permit any but the most exact connection between justification and classification," our review of whether such requirements have been met must entail "'a most searching examination.'" We find that the University's policy, which automatically distributes 20 points, or one-fifth of the points needed to guarantee admission, to every single "underrepresented minority" applicant solely because of race, is not narrowly tailored to achieve the interest in educational diversity that respondents claim justifies their program. . . .

Justice Powell's opinion in *Bakke* emphasized the importance of considering each particular applicant as an individual, assessing all of the qualities that individual possesses, and in turn, evaluating that individual's ability to contribute to the unique setting of higher education. The admissions program Justice Powell described, however, did not contemplate that any single characteristic automatically ensured a specific and identifiable contribution to a university's diversity. Instead, under the approach Justice Powell described, each characteristic of a particular applicant was to be considered in assessing the applicant's entire application.

The current LSA policy does not provide such individualized consideration. The LSA's policy automatically distributes 20 points to every single applicant from an "underrepresented minority" group, as defined by the University. The only consideration that accompanies this distribution of points is a factual review of an application to determine whether an individual is a member of one of these minority groups. Moreover, unlike Justice Powell's example, where the race of a "particular black applicant" could be considered without being decisive, the LSA's automatic distribution of 20 points has the effect of making "the factor of race . . . decisive" for virtually every minimally qualified underrepresented minority applicant. . . .

Respondents contend that "the volume of applications and the presentation of applicant information make it impractical for [LSA] to use the . . . admissions system" upheld by the Court today in *Grutter*. But the fact that the implementation of a program capable of providing individualized consideration might present administrative challenges does not render constitutional an otherwise problematic system. Nothing in Justice Powell's opinion in *Bakke* signaled that a university may employ whatever means it desires to achieve the stated goal of diversity without regard to the limits imposed by our strict scrutiny analysis.

We conclude, therefore, that because the University's use of race in its current freshman admissions policy is not narrowly tailored to achieve respondents' asserted compelling interest in diversity, the admissions policy violates the Equal Protection Clause of the Fourteenth Amendment. We further find that the admissions policy also violates Title VI and 42 U.S.C. §1981. Accordingly, we reverse that portion of the District Court's decision granting respondents summary judgment with respect to liability and remand the case for proceedings consistent with this opinion.

JUSTICE SOUTER, with whom JUSTICE GINSBURG joins, dissenting.

. . . The cases now contain two pointers toward the line between the valid and the unconstitutional in race-conscious admissions schemes. *Grutter* reaffirms the permissibility of individualized consideration of race to achieve a diversity of students, at least where race is not assigned a preordained value in all cases. On the other hand, Justice Powell's opinion in *Bakke* rules out a racial quota or set-aside, in which race is the sole fact of eligibility for certain places in a class. Although the freshman admissions system here is subject to argument on the merits, I think it is closer to what *Grutter* approves than to what *Bakke* condemns, and should not be held unconstitutional on the current record.

The record does not describe a system with a quota like the one struck down in *Bakke,* which "insulated" all nonminority candidates from competition from certain seats. The *Bakke* plan "focused *solely* on ethnic diversity" and effectively told nonminority applicants that "no matter how strong their qualifications, quantitative and extracurricular, including their own potential for contribution to educational diversity, they are never afforded the chance to compete with applicants from the preferred groups for the [set-aside] special admissions seats."

The plan here, in contrast, lets all applicants compete for all places and values an applicant's offering for any place not only on grounds of race, but on grades, test scores, strength of high school, quality of course of study, residence, alumni relationships, leadership, personal character, socioeconomic disadvantage, athletic ability, and quality of a personal essay. A nonminority applicant who scores highly in these other categories can readily garner a selection index exceeding that of a minority applicant who gets the 20-point bonus. . . .

The very nature of a college's permissible practice of awarding value to racial diversity means that race must be considered in a way that increases some applicants' chances for admission. Since college admission is not left entirely to inarticulate intuition, it is hard to see what is inappropriate in assigning some stated value to a relevant characteristic, whether it be reasoning ability, writing style, running speed, or minority race. Justice Powell's plus factors necessarily are assigned some values. The college simply does by a numbered scale what the law school accomplishes in its "holistic review"; the distinction does not imply that applicants to the undergraduate college are denied individualized consideration or a fair chance to compete on the basis of all the various merits their applications may disclose.

Nor is it possible to say that the 20 points convert race into a decisive factor comparable to reserving minority places as in *Bakke.* Of course we can conceive of a point system in which the "plus" factor given to minority applicants would be so extreme as to guarantee every minority applicant a higher rank than every nonminority applicant in the university's admissions system. But petitioners do not have a convincing argument that the freshman admissions system operates this way. The present record obviously shows that nonminority applicants may achieve higher selection point totals than minority applicants owing to characteristics other than race, and the fact that the university admits "virtually every qualified under-represented minority applicant" may reflect nothing more than the likelihood that very few qualified minority applicants apply, as well as the possibility that self-selection results in a strong minority applicant pool. It suffices for me, as it did for the District Court, that there are no *Bakke*-like set-asides. . . .

. . . In contrast to the college's forthrightness in saying just what plus factor it gives for membership in an underrepresented minority, it is worth considering the character of one alternative thrown up as preferable, because supposedly not based on race. Drawing on admissions systems used at public universities in California, Florida, and Texas, the United States contends that Michigan could get student diversity in satisfaction of its compelling interest by guaranteeing admission to a fixed percentage of the top students from each high school in Michigan.

While there is nothing unconstitutional about such a practice, it nonetheless suffers from a serious disadvantage. It is the disadvantage of deliberate obfuscation. The "percentage plans" are just as race conscious as the point

scheme (and fairly so), but they get their racially diverse results without saying directly what they are doing or why they are doing it. In contrast, Michigan states its purpose directly and, if this were a doubtful case for me, I would be tempted to give Michigan an extra point of its own for its frankness. Equal protection cannot become an exercise in which the winners are the ones who hide the ball.

JUSTICE GINSBURG, with whom JUSTICE SOUTER joins [and JUSTICE BREYER joins in part], dissenting.

Educational institutions, the Court acknowledges, are not barred from any and all consideration of race when making admissions decisions. But the Court once again maintains that the same standard of review controls judicial inspection of all official race classifications. This insistence on "consistency" would be fitting were our Nation free of the vestiges of rank discrimination long reinforced by law. But we are not far distant from an overtly discriminatory past, and the effects of centuries of law-sanctioned inequality remain painfully evident in our communities and schools.

. . . Actions designed to burden groups long denied full citizenship stature are not sensibly ranked with measures taken to hasten the day when entrenched discrimination and its after effects have been extirpated. . . . [W]here race is considered "for the purpose of achieving equality," no automatic proscription is in order. . . .

Examining in this light the admissions policy employed by the University of Michigan's College of Literature, Science, and the Arts, and for the reasons well stated by Justice Souter, I see no constitutional infirmity.

Parents Involved in Community Schools v. Seattle School District No. 1
551 U.S. 701 (2007)

Seattle School District No. 1 voluntarily adopted a student-assignment plan that relied on race to determine which schools certain children could attend. Although it had never operated legally segregated schools or been subject to court-ordered desegregation, it classified children as white or nonwhite and used the racial classifications as a "tiebreaker" to allocate slots in particular high

schools. In a companion case, the Jefferson County School District (in Louisville, Kentucky), which had been subject to a desegregation decree until 2000 when a federal district court dissolved the decree after finding that the district had achieved unitary status by eliminating the vestiges of prior segregation, adopted a plan in 2001 classifying students as black or "other" in order to make certain elementary school assignments and to rule on transfer requests. The petitioners—Parents Involved, an organization of Seattle parents, and Crystal Meredith, the mother of a Jefferson County student (Joshua)—whose children were denied assignment to particular schools under these plans filed suit, contending that allocating children to different public schools based solely on their race violated the Equal Protection Clause of the Fourteenth Amendment. In the Seattle case, the District Court for the Western District of Washington granted the school district summary judgment, finding that its plan survived strict scrutiny on the federal constitutional claim because it was narrowly tailored to serve the compelling governmental interests of achieving racial diversity and avoiding racial isolation, and the Ninth Circuit affirmed. In the Jefferson County case, the District Court for the Western District of Kentucky found that the school district had asserted a compelling interest in maintaining racially diverse schools and that its plan was narrowly tailored to serve that interest, and the Sixth Circuit affirmed. The Supreme Court granted certiorari. Opinion of the Court: <u>Roberts</u>, Scalia, Kennedy, Thomas, Alito. Concurring opinion: <u>Thomas</u>. Concurring in part and concurring in the judgment: <u>Kennedy</u>. Dissenting opinions: <u>Stevens</u>; <u>Breyer</u>, Stevens, Souter, Ginsburg.

THE CHIEF JUSTICE announced the judgment of the Court, and delivered the opinion of the Court with respect to Parts I, II, III-A, and III-C, and an opinion with respect to Parts III-B and IV, in which JUSTICES SCALIA, THOMAS, and ALITO join.

The school districts in these cases voluntarily adopted student assignment plans that rely upon race to determine which public schools certain children may attend. . . . Parents of students denied assignment to particular schools under these plans solely because of their race brought suit, contending that allocating children to different public schools on the basis of race violated the Fourteenth Amendment guarantee of equal protection. The Courts of Appeals below upheld the plans. We granted certiorari, and now reverse.

I

Both cases present the same underlying legal question—whether a public school that had

not operated legally segregated schools or has been found to be unitary may choose to classify students by race and rely upon that classification in making school assignments. . . .

II

As a threshold matter, we must assure ourselves of our jurisdiction. Seattle argues that Parents Involved lacks standing because none of its current members can claim an imminent injury. . . . This argument is unavailing. . . . [O]ne form of injury under the Equal Protection Clause is being forced to compete in a race-based system that may prejudice the plaintiff, an injury that the members of Parents Involved can validly claim on behalf of their children.

In challenging standing, Seattle also notes that it has ceased using the racial tiebreaker pending the outcome of this litigation. But the district vigorously defends the constitutionality of its race-based program, and nowhere suggests that if this litigation is resolved in its favor it will not resume using race to assign students. Voluntary cessation does not moot a case or controversy. . . .

III
A

It is well established that when the government distributes burdens or benefits on the basis of individual racial classifications, that action is reviewed under strict scrutiny. As the Court recently reaffirmed, "'racial classifications are simply too pernicious to permit any but the most exact connection between justification and classification.'" *Gratz v. Bollinger*, 539 U.S. 244, 270 (2003). In order to satisfy this searching standard of review, the school districts must demonstrate that the use of individual racial classifications in the assignment plans here under review is "narrowly tailored" to achieve a "compelling" government interest.

Without attempting in these cases to set forth all the interests a school district might assert, it suffices to note that our prior cases, in evaluating the use of racial classifications in the school context, have recognized two interests that qualify as compelling. The first is the compelling interest of remedying the effects of past intentional discrimination. Yet the Seattle public schools have not shown that they were ever segregated by law, and were not subject to court-ordered desegregation decrees. The Jefferson County public schools were previously segregated by law and were subject to a desegregation decree entered in 1975. In 2000, the District Court that entered that decree dissolved it, finding that Jefferson County had "eliminated the vestiges associated with the former policy of segregation and its pernicious effects," and thus had achieved "unitary" status. Jefferson County accordingly does not rely upon an interest in remedying the effects of past intentional discrimination in defending its present use of race in assigning students. . . .

The second government interest we have recognized as compelling for purposes of strict scrutiny is the interest in diversity in higher education upheld in *Grutter* [*v. Bollinger*], 539 U.S. 306 at 328 (2003). The specific interest found compelling in *Grutter* was student body diversity "in the context of higher education." The diversity interest was not focused on race alone but encompassed "all factors that may contribute to student body diversity." . . . [*Grutter* noted] . . . that "it is not an interest in simple ethnic diversity, in which a specified percentage of the student body is in effect guaranteed to be members of selected ethnic groups, that can justify the use of race." Instead, what was upheld in *Grutter* was consideration of "a far broader array of qualifications and characteristics of which racial or ethnic origin is but a single though important element."

The entire gist of the analysis in *Grutter* was that the admissions program at issue there focused on each applicant as an individual, and not simply as a member of a particular racial group. The classification of applicants by race upheld in *Grutter* was only as part of a "highly individualized, holistic review." As the Court explained, "the importance of this individualized consideration in the context of a race-conscious admissions program is paramount." The point of the narrow tailoring analysis in which the *Grutter* Court engaged was to ensure that the use of racial classifications was indeed part of a broader assessment of diversity, and not simply an effort to achieve racial balance, which the Court explained would be "patently unconstitutional."

In the present cases, by contrast, race is not considered as part of a broader effort to achieve "exposure to widely diverse people, cultures, ideas, and viewpoints"; race, for some students, is determinative standing alone. The districts argue that other factors, such as student preferences, affect assignment decisions under their plans, but under each plan when race comes into play, it is decisive by itself. It is not simply one factor weighed with others in reaching a decision, as in *Grutter*; it is *the* factor. Like the University of Michigan undergraduate plan struck down in *Gratz*, the plans here "do not provide for a meaningful individualized review of applicants" but instead rely on racial classifications in a "nonindividualized, mechanical" way.

Even when it comes to race, the plans here employ only a limited notion of diversity, viewing race exclusively in white/nonwhite terms in Seattle and black/"other" terms in Jefferson County. The Seattle "Board Statement Reaffirming Diversity Rationale" speaks of the "inherent educational value" in "providing students the opportunity to attend schools with diverse student enrollment." But under the Seattle plan, a school with 50 percent Asian-American students and 50 percent white students but no African-American, Native-American, or Latino students would qualify as balanced, while a school with 30 percent Asian-American, 25 percent African-American, 25 percent Latino, and 20 percent white students would not. It is hard to understand how a plan that could allow these results can be viewed as being concerned with achieving enrollment that is "'broadly diverse.'" . . .

In upholding the admissions plan in *Grutter*, . . . this Court relied upon considerations unique to institutions of higher education, noting that in light of "the expansive freedoms of speech and thought associated with the university environment, universities occupy a special niche in our constitutional tradition." The Court explained that "context matters" in applying strict scrutiny, and repeatedly noted that it was addressing the use of race "in the context of higher education." The Court in *Grutter* expressly articulated key limitations on its holding—defining a specific type of broad-based diversity and noting the unique context of higher education—but these limitations were largely disregarded by the lower courts in extending *Grutter* to uphold race-based assignments in elementary and secondary schools. The present cases are not governed by *Grutter*.

B

Perhaps recognizing that reliance on *Grutter* cannot sustain their plans, both school districts assert additional interests, distinct from the interest upheld in *Grutter*, to justify their race-based assignments. In briefing and argument before this Court, Seattle contends that its use of race helps to reduce racial concentration in schools and to ensure that racially concentrated housing patterns do not prevent nonwhite students from having access to the most desirable schools. Jefferson County has articulated a similar goal, phrasing its interest in terms of educating its students "in a racially integrated environment." Each school district argues that educational and broader socialization benefits flow from a racially diverse learning environment, and each contends that because the diversity they seek is racial diversity—not the broader diversity at issue in *Grutter*—it makes sense to promote that interest directly by relying on race alone.

. . . [I]t is clear that the racial classifications employed by the districts are not narrowly tailored to the goal of achieving the educational and social benefits asserted to flow from racial diversity. In design and operation, the plans are directed only to racial balance, pure and simple, an objective this Court has repeatedly condemned as illegitimate. . . .

Accepting racial balancing as a compelling state interest would justify the imposition of racial proportionality throughout American society, contrary to our repeated recognition that "at the heart of the Constitution's guarantee of equal protection lies the simple command that the Government must treat citizens as individuals, not as simply components of a racial, religious, sexual or national class." Allowing racial balancing as a compelling end in itself would "effectively assure that race will always be relevant in American life, and that the 'ultimate goal' of 'eliminating entirely from governmental decisionmaking such irrelevant factors as a human being's race' will never be achieved."

The validity of our concern that racial balancing has "no logical stopping point" is demonstrated here by the degree to which the districts tie their racial guidelines to their demographics. As the districts' demographics shift, so too will their definition of racial diversity. . . .

The principle that racial balancing is not permitted is one of substance, not semantics. Racial balancing is not transformed from "patently unconstitutional" to a compelling state interest simply by relabeling it "racial diversity." While the school districts use various verbal formulations to describe the interest they seek to promote—racial diversity, avoidance of racial isolation, racial integration—they offer no definition of the interest that suggests it differs from racial balance. . . .

C

The districts assert, as they must, that the way in which they have employed individual racial classifications is necessary to achieve their stated ends. The minimal effect these classifications have on student assignments, however, suggests that other means would be effective. Seattle's racial tiebreaker results, in the end, only in shifting a small number of students between schools. . . . [T]he district could identify only 52 students who were ultimately affected adversely by the racial tiebreaker in that it resulted in assignment to a school they had not listed as a preference and to which they would not otherwise have been assigned. . . .

The districts have also failed to show that they considered methods other than explicit racial classifications to achieve their stated goals. Narrow tailoring requires "serious, good faith consideration of workable race-neutral alternatives," and yet in Seattle several alternative assignment plans—many of which would not have used express racial classifications—were rejected with little or no consideration. Jefferson County has failed to present any evidence that it considered alternatives, even though the district already claims that its goals are achieved primarily through means other than the racial classifications.

IV

Justice Breyer's dissent takes a different approach to these cases, one that fails to ground the result it would reach in law. Instead, it . . . alters and misapplies our well-established legal framework for assessing equal protection challenges to express racial classifications, and greatly exaggerates the consequences of today's decision.

To begin with, Justice Breyer seeks to justify the plans at issue under our precedents recognizing the compelling interest in remedying past intentional discrimination. Not even the school districts go this far, and for good reason. The distinction between segregation by state action and racial imbalance caused by other factors has been central to our jurisprudence in this area for generations. The dissent elides this distinction between *de jure* and *de facto* segregation, casually intimates that Seattle's school attendance patterns reflect illegal segregation, and fails to credit the judicial determination—under the most rigorous standard—that Jefferson County had eliminated the vestiges of prior segregation. The dissent thus alters in fundamental ways not only the facts presented here but the established law. . . .

Justice Breyer's dissent also asserts that these cases are controlled by *Grutter*, claiming that the existence of a compelling interest in these cases "follows *a fortiori*" from *Grutter*, and accusing us of tacitly overruling that case. The dissent overreads *Grutter*, however, in suggesting that it renders pure racial balancing a constitutionally compelling interest; *Grutter* itself recognized that using race simply to achieve racial balance would be "patently unconstitutional." The Court was exceedingly careful in describing the interest furthered in *Grutter* as "not an interest in simple ethnic diversity" but rather a "far broader array of qualifications and characteristics" in which race was but a single element. We take the *Grutter* Court at its word. We simply do not understand how Justice Breyer can maintain that classifying every schoolchild as black or white, and using that classification as a determinative factor in assigning children to achieve pure racial balance, can be regarded as "less burdensome, and hence more narrowly tailored" than the consideration of race in *Grutter* when the Court in *Grutter* stated that "the importance of . . . individualized consideration" in the program was "paramount," and consideration of race was one factor in a "highly individualized, holistic review." Certainly if the constitutionality of the stark use of race in these cases were as established as the dissent would have it, there would have been no need for the extensive analysis undertaken in *Grutter*. In light of the foregoing, Justice Breyer's appeal to *stare decisis* rings particularly hollow.

. . . Justice Breyer's dissent candidly dismisses the significance of this Court's repeated *holdings* that all racial classifications must be reviewed under strict scrutiny, arguing that a different standard of review should be applied because the districts use race for beneficent rather than malicious purposes.

This Court has recently reiterated, however, that "'*all* racial classifications [imposed by government] . . . must be analyzed by a reviewing court under strict scrutiny.'" Justice Breyer nonetheless relies on the good intentions and motives of the school districts, stating that he has found "no case that . . . repudiated this constitutional asymmetry between that which seeks to *exclude* and that which seeks to *include* members of minority races." We have found many. Our cases clearly reject the argument that motives affect the strict scrutiny analysis.

This argument that different rules should govern racial classifications designed to include rather than exclude is not new; it has been repeatedly pressed in the past. The reasons for rejecting a motives test for racial classifications are clear enough. "The Court's emphasis on 'benign racial classifications' suggests confidence in its ability to distinguish good from harmful governmental uses of racial criteria. History should teach greater humility. . . . 'Benign' carries with it no independent meaning, but reflects only acceptance of the current generation's conclusion that a politically acceptable burden, imposed on particular citizens on the basis of race, is reasonable."

Justice Breyer speaks of bringing "the races" together (putting aside the purely black-and-white nature of the plans), as the justification for excluding individuals on the basis of their race. Again, this approach to racial classifications is fundamentally at odds with our precedent, which makes clear that the Equal Protection Clause "protects *persons*, not *groups*."

Justice Breyer's position comes down to a familiar claim: The end justifies the means. He admits that "there is a cost in applying 'a state-mandated racial label,'" but he is confident that the cost is worth paying. Our established strict scrutiny test for racial classifications, however, insists on "detailed examination, both as to ends *and* as to means." Simply because the school districts may seek a worthy goal does not mean they are free to discriminate on the basis of race to achieve it, or that their racial classifications should be subject to less exacting scrutiny.

Despite his argument that these cases should be evaluated under a "standard of review that is not 'strict' in the traditional sense of that word," Justice Breyer still purports to apply strict scrutiny to these cases. It is evident, however, that Justice Breyer's brand of narrow tailoring is quite unlike anything found in our precedents. . . . [T]he dissent suggests that some combination of the development of these plans over time, the difficulty of the endeavor, and the good faith of the districts suffices to demonstrate that these stark and controlling racial classifications are constitutional. The Constitution and our precedents require more.

In keeping with his view that strict scrutiny should not apply, Justice Breyer repeatedly urges deference to local school boards on these issues. Such deference "is fundamentally at odds with our equal protection jurisprudence. We put the burden on state actors to demonstrate that their race-based policies are justified."

Justice Breyer's dissent ends on an unjustified note of alarm. It predicts that today's decision "threatens" the validity of "hundreds of state and federal statutes and regulations." . . . Justice Breyer also suggests that other means for achieving greater racial diversity in schools are necessarily unconstitutional if the racial classifications at issue in these cases cannot survive strict scrutiny. These other means—*e.g.*, where to construct new schools, how to allocate resources among schools, and which academic offerings to provide to attract students to certain schools—implicate different considerations than the explicit racial classifications at issue in these cases, and we express no opinion on their validity—not even in dicta. Rather, we employ the familiar and well-established analytic approach of strict scrutiny to evaluate the plans at issue today, an approach that in no way warrants the dissent's cataclysmic concerns. Under that approach, the school districts have not carried their burden of showing that the ends they seek justify the particular extreme means they have chosen—classifying individual students on the basis of their race and discriminating among them on that basis.

* * *

If the need for the racial classifications embraced by the school districts is unclear, even on the districts' own terms, the costs are undeniable. "Distinctions between citizens solely because of their ancestry are by their very nature odious to a free people whose institutions are founded upon the doctrine of equality." Government action dividing us by race is inherently suspect because such classifications promote "notions of racial inferiority lead to a politics of racial hostility and reinforce the belief held by too many for too much of our history, that individuals should be judged by the color of their skin" and "endorse race-based reasoning and the conception of a Nation divided into racial blocs, thus contributing to an escalation of racial hostility and conflict." As the Court explained in *Rice v. Cayetano*, 528 U.S. 495, 517 (2000), "one of the principal reasons race is treated as a forbidden classification is that it demeans the dignity and worth of a person to be judged by ancestry instead of by his or her own merit and essential qualities."

All this is true enough in the contexts in which these statements were made—government contracting, voting districts, allocation of broadcast licenses, and electing state officers—but when it comes to using race to assign children to schools, history will be heard. In *Brown v. Board of Education*, 347 U.S. 483 (1954) (*Brown I*), we held that segregation deprived black children of equal educational opportunities regardless of whether school facilities and other tangible factors were equal, because government classification and separation on grounds of race themselves denoted inferiority. It was not the inequality of the facilities but the fact of legally separating children on the basis of race on which the Court relied to find a constitutional violation in 1954. The next Term, we accordingly stated that "full compliance" with *Brown I* required school districts "to achieve a system of determining admission to the public schools *on a nonracial basis*." *Brown II* (emphasis added).

The parties and their *amici* debate which side is more faithful to the heritage of *Brown*, but the position of the plaintiffs in *Brown* was spelled out in their brief and could not have been clearer: "The Fourteenth Amendment prevents states from according differential treatment to American children on the basis of their color or race." What do the racial classifications at issue here do, if not accord differential treatment on the basis of race? . . . What do the racial classifications do in these cases, if not determine admission to a public school on a racial basis?

Before *Brown*, schoolchildren were told where they could and could not go to school based on the color of their skin. The school districts in these cases have not carried the heavy burden of demonstrating that we should allow this once again—even for very different reasons. For schools that never segregated on the basis of race, such as Seattle, or that have removed the vestiges of past segregation, such as Jefferson County, the way "to achieve a system of determining admission to the public schools on a nonracial basis" is to stop assigning students on a racial basis. The way to stop discrimination on the basis of race is to stop discriminating on the basis of race.

The judgments of the Courts of Appeals for the Sixth and Ninth Circuits are reversed, and the cases are remanded for further proceedings.

JUSTICE THOMAS, concurring.

Today, the Court holds that state entities may not experiment with race-based means to achieve ends they deem socially desirable. I wholly concur in THE CHIEF JUSTICE's opinion. I write separately to address several of the contentions in JUSTICE BREYER's dissent (hereinafter the dissent). . . . Disfavoring a

color-blind interpretation of the Constitution, the dissent would give school boards a free hand to make decisions on the basis of race— an approach reminiscent of that advocated by the segregationists in *Brown v. Board of Education* (1954). This approach is just as wrong today as it was a half-century ago. The Constitution and our cases require us to be much more demanding before permitting local school boards to make decisions based on race.

I

. . . Because this Court has authorized and required race-based remedial measures to address *de jure* segregation, it is important to define segregation clearly and to distinguish it from racial imbalance. In the context of public schooling, segregation is the deliberate operation of a school system to "carry out a governmental policy to separate pupils in schools solely on the basis of race." In *Brown*, this Court declared that segregation was unconstitutional under the Equal Protection Clause of the Fourteenth Amendment.

Racial imbalance is the failure of a school district's individual schools to match or approximate the demographic makeup of the student population at large. Racial imbalance is not segregation. Although presently observed racial imbalance might result from past *de jure* segregation, racial imbalance can also result from any number of innocent private decisions, including voluntary housing choices. Because racial imbalance is not inevitably linked to unconstitutional segregation, it is not unconstitutional in and of itself.

Although there is arguably a danger of racial imbalance in schools in Seattle and Louisville, there is no danger of resegregation. No one contends that Seattle has established or that Louisville has reestablished a dual school system that separates students on the basis of race. . . .

Despite the dissent's repeated intimation of a remedial purpose, neither of the programs in question qualifies as a permissible race-based remedial measure. Thus, the programs are subject to the general rule that government race-based decisionmaking is unconstitutional.

As the foregoing demonstrates, racial balancing is sometimes a constitutionally permissible remedy for the discrete legal wrong of *de jure* segregation, and when directed to that end, racial balancing is an exception to the general rule that government race-based decisionmaking is unconstitutional. Perhaps for this reason, the dissent conflates the concepts of segregation and racial imbalance: If racial imbalance equates to segregation, then it must also be constitutionally acceptable to use racial balancing to remedy racial imbalance.

For at least two reasons, however, it is wrong to place the remediation of segregation on the same plane as the remediation of racial imbalance. First, as demonstrated above, the two concepts are distinct. Although racial imbalance can result from *de jure* segregation, it does not necessarily, and the further we get from the era of state-sponsored racial separation, the less likely it is that racial imbalance has a traceable connection to any prior segregation.

Second, a school cannot "remedy" racial imbalance in the same way that it can remedy segregation. Remediation of past *de jure* segregation is a one-time process involving the redress of a discrete legal injury inflicted by an identified entity. At some point, the discrete injury will be remedied, and the school district will be declared unitary. Unlike *de jure* segregation, there is no ultimate remedy for racial imbalance. Individual schools will fall in and out of balance in the natural course, and the appropriate balance itself will shift with a school district's changing demographics. Thus, racial balancing will have to take place on an indefinite basis—a continuous process with no identifiable culpable party and no discernable end point. In part for those reasons, the Court has never permitted outright racial balancing solely for the purpose of achieving a particular racial balance.

II

Lacking a cognizable interest in remediation, neither of these plans can survive strict scrutiny because neither plan serves a genuinely compelling state interest. . . . Ultimately, the dissent's entire analysis is corrupted by the considerations that lead it initially to question whether strict scrutiny should apply at all. What emerges is a version of "strict scrutiny" that combines hollow assurances of harmlessness with reflexive acceptance of conventional wisdom. When it comes to government race-based decisionmaking, the Constitution demands more.

The dissent claims that "the law requires application here of a standard of review that is not 'strict' in the traditional sense of that word." . . . These arguments are inimical to the Constitution and to this Court's precedents. We have made it unusually clear that strict scrutiny applies to *every* racial classification. There are good reasons not to apply a lesser standard to these cases. The constitutional problems with government race-based decisionmaking are not diminished in the slightest by the presence or absence of an intent to oppress any race or by the real or asserted well-meaning motives for the race-based decisionmaking. Purportedly benign race-based decisionmaking suffers the same constitutional infirmity as invidious race-based decisionmaking

Even supposing it mattered to the constitutional analysis, the race-based student assignment programs before us are not as benign as the dissent believes. "Racial paternalism and its unintended consequences can be as poisonous and pernicious as any other form of discrimination." As these programs demonstrate, every time the government uses racial criteria to "bring the races together," someone gets excluded, and the person excluded suffers an injury solely because of his or her race. The petitioner in the Louisville case received a letter from the school board informing her that her *kindergartener* would not be allowed to attend the school of petitioner's choosing because of the child's race. . . . This type of exclusion, solely on the basis of race, is precisely the sort of government action that pits the races against one another, exacerbates racial tension, and "provokes resentment among those who believe that they have been wronged by the government's use of race." Accordingly, these plans are simply one more variation on the government race-based decisionmaking we have consistently held must be subjected to strict scrutiny.

Though the dissent admits to discomfort in applying strict scrutiny to these plans, it claims to have nonetheless applied that exacting standard. But in its search for a compelling interest, the dissent casually accepts even the most tenuous interests asserted on behalf of the plans, grouping them all under the term "'integration.'" . . . [T]he dissent argues that the interest in integration has an educational element. The dissent asserts that racially balanced schools improve educational outcomes for black children. . . . In reality, it is far from apparent that coerced racial mixing has any educational benefits, much less that integration is necessary to black achievement.

Scholars have differing opinions as to whether educational benefits arise from racial balancing. Some have concluded that black students receive genuine educational benefits. . . . And some have concluded that there are no demonstrable educational benefits. The *amicus* briefs in the cases before us mirror this divergence of opinion. . . . Given this tenuous relationship between forced racial mixing and improved educational results for black children, the dissent cannot plausibly maintain that an educational element supports the integration interest, let alone makes it compelling.

Perhaps recognizing as much, the dissent argues that the social science evidence is "strong enough to permit a democratically elected school board reasonably to determine that this interest is a compelling one." This assertion is inexplicable. It is not up to the school boards—the very government entities whose race-based practices we must strictly scrutinize—to determine what interests qualify as compelling under the Fourteenth Amendment to the United States Constitution. Rather, this Court must assess independently the nature of the interest asserted and the evidence to support it in order to determine whether it qualifies as compelling under our precedents. . . . The dissent's proposed test—whether sufficient social science evidence supports a government unit's conclusion that the interest it asserts is compelling . . . would leave our equal-protection jurisprudence at the mercy of elected government officials evaluating the evanescent views of a handful of social scientists. To adopt the dissent's deferential approach would be to abdicate our constitutional responsibilities.

III

Most of the dissent's criticisms of today's result can be traced to its rejection of the color-blind Constitution. The dissent attempts to marginalize the notion of a color-blind Constitution by consigning it to me and Members of today's plurality. But I am quite comfortable in the company I keep. My view of the Constitution is Justice Harlan's view in *Plessy:* "Our Constitution is color-blind, and neither knows nor tolerates classes among citizens." And my view was the rallying cry for the lawyers who litigated *Brown.* "The Fourteenth Amendment precludes a state from imposing distinctions or classifications based upon race and color alone."

The dissent appears to pin its interpretation of the Equal Protection Clause to current societal practice and expectations, deference to local officials, likely practical consequences, and reliance on previous statements from this and other courts. Such a view was ascendant in this Court's jurisprudence for several decades. It first appeared in *Plessy,* where the Court asked whether a state law providing for segregated railway cars was "a reasonable regulation." The Court deferred to local authorities in making its determination, noting that in inquiring into reasonableness "there must necessarily be a large discretion on the part of the legislature." The Court likewise paid heed to societal practices, local expectations, and practical consequences by looking to "the established usages, customs and traditions of the people, and with a view to the promotion of their comfort, and the preservation of the public peace and good order." Guided by these principles, the Court concluded: "We cannot say that a law which authorizes or even requires the separation of the two races in public conveyances is unreasonable, or more obnoxious to the Fourteenth Amendment than the acts of Congress requiring separate schools for colored children in the District of Columbia."

The segregationists in *Brown* embraced the arguments the Court endorsed in *Plessy.* Though *Brown* decisively rejected those arguments, today's dissent replicates them to a distressing extent. Thus, the dissent argues that "each plan embodies the results of local experience and community consultation." Similarly, the segregationists made repeated appeals to societal practice and expectation. The dissent argues that today's decision "threatens to substitute for present calm a disruptive round of race-related litigation" and claims that today's decision "risks serious harm to the law and for the Nation." The segregationists also relied upon the likely practical consequences of ending the state-imposed system of racial separation. And foreshadowing today's dissent, the segregationists most heavily relied upon judicial precedent.

The similarities between the dissent's arguments and the segregationists' arguments do not stop there. Like the dissent, the segregationists repeatedly cautioned the Court to consider practicalities and not to embrace too theoretical a view of the Fourteenth Amendment. And just as the dissent argues that the need for these programs will lessen over time, the segregationists claimed that reliance on segregation was lessening and might eventually end.

What was wrong in 1954 cannot be right today. Whatever else the Court's rejection of the segregationists' arguments in *Brown* might have established, it certainly made clear that state and local governments cannot take from the Constitution a right to make decisions on the basis of race by adverse possession. The fact that state and local governments had been discriminating on the basis of race for a long time was irrelevant to the *Brown* Court. The fact that racial discrimination was preferable to the relevant communities was irrelevant to the *Brown* Court. And the fact that the state and local governments had relied on statements in this Court's opinions was irrelevant to the *Brown* Court. The same principles guide today's decision. None of the considerations trumpeted by the dissent is relevant to the constitutionality of the school boards' race-based plans because no contextual detail—or collection of contextual details—can "provide refuge from the principle that under our Constitution, the government may not make distinctions on the basis of race."

In place of the color-blind Constitution, the dissent would permit measures to keep the races together and proscribe measures to keep the races apart. Although no such distinction is apparent in the Fourteenth Amendment, the dissent would constitutionalize today's faddish social theories that embrace that distinction.

The Constitution is not that malleable. Even if current social theories favor classroom racial engineering as necessary to "solve the problems at hand," the Constitution enshrines principles independent of social theories. Indeed, if our history has taught us anything, it has taught us to beware of elites bearing racial theories.

The plans before us base school assignment decisions on students' race. Because "our Constitution is color-blind, and neither knows nor tolerates classes among citizens," such race-based decisionmaking is unconstitutional. I concur in the Chief Justice's opinion so holding.

JUSTICE KENNEDY, concurring in part and concurring in the judgment.

. . . [P]arts of the opinion by THE CHIEF JUSTICE imply an all-too-unyielding insistence that race cannot be a factor in instances when, in my view, it may be taken into account. The plurality opinion is too dismissive of the legitimate interest government has in ensuring all people have equal opportunity regardless of their race. The plurality's postulate that "the way to stop discrimination on the basis of race is to stop discriminating on the basis of race" is not sufficient to decide these cases. Fifty years of experience since *Brown v. Board of Education* should teach us that the problem before us defies so easy a solution. School districts can seek to reach *Brown's* objective of equal educational opportunity. The plurality opinion is at least open to the interpretation that the Constitution requires school districts to ignore the problem of *de facto* resegregation in schooling. I cannot endorse that conclusion. To the extent the plurality opinion suggests the Constitution mandates that state and local school authorities must accept the status quo of racial isolation in schools, it is, in my view, profoundly mistaken.

The statement by Justice Harlan that "our Constitution is color-blind" was most certainly justified in the context of his dissent in *Plessy v. Ferguson* (1896). The Court's decision in that case was a grievous error it took far too long to overrule. *Plessy,* of course, concerned official classification by race applicable to all persons who sought to use railway carriages. And, as an aspiration, Justice Harlan's axiom must command our assent. In the real world, it is regrettable to say, it cannot be a universal constitutional principle.

In the administration of public schools by the state and local authorities it is permissible to consider the racial makeup of schools and to adopt general policies to encourage a diverse student body, one aspect of which is its racial composition. If school authorities are concerned that the student-body compositions of certain schools interfere with the objective of offering an equal educational opportunity to all of their students, they are free to devise race-conscious measures to address the problem in a general way and without treating each student in different fashion solely on the basis of a systematic, individual typing by race.

School boards may pursue the goal of bringing together students of diverse backgrounds and races through other means, including strategic site selection of new schools; drawing attendance zones with general recognition of the demographics of neighborhoods; allocating resources for special programs; recruiting students and faculty in a targeted fashion; and tracking enrollments, performance, and other statistics by race. These mechanisms are race conscious but do not lead to different treatment based on a classification that tells each student he or she is to be defined by race, so it is unlikely any of them would demand strict scrutiny to be found permissible. Executive and legislative branches, which for generations now have considered these types of policies and procedures, should be permitted to employ them with candor and with confidence that a constitutional violation does not occur whenever a decisionmaker considers the impact a given approach might have on students of different races. Assigning to each student a personal designation according to a crude system of individual racial classifications is quite a different matter; and the legal analysis changes accordingly.

Each respondent has asserted that its assignment of individual students by race is permissible because there is no other way to avoid racial isolation in the school districts. Yet, as explained, each has failed to provide the support necessary for that proposition. . . .

The dissent rests on the assumptions that these sweeping race-based classifications of persons are permitted by existing precedents; that its confident endorsement of race categories for each child in a large segment of the community presents no danger to individual freedom in other, prospective realms of governmental regulation; and that the racial classifications used here cause no hurt or anger of the type the Constitution prevents. Each of these premises is, in my respectful view, incorrect. . . .

This Nation has a moral and ethical obligation to fulfill its historic commitment to creating an integrated society that ensures equal opportunity for all of its children. A compelling interest exists in avoiding racial isolation, an interest that a school district, in its discretion and expertise, may choose to pursue. Likewise, a district may consider it a compelling interest to achieve a diverse student population. Race may be one component of that diversity, but other demographic factors, plus special talents and needs, should also be considered. What the government is not permitted to do, absent a showing of necessity not made here, is to classify every student on the basis of race and to assign each of them to schools based on that classification. Crude measures of this sort threaten to reduce children to racial chits valued and traded according to one school's supply and another's demand. . . .

With this explanation I concur in the judgment of the Court.

JUSTICE BREYER, with whom JUSTICE STEVENS, JUSTICE SOUTER, and JUSTICE GINSBURG join, dissenting.

. . . The plurality . . . misapplies the relevant constitutional principles, it announces legal rules that will obstruct efforts by state and local governments to deal effectively with the growing resegregation of public schools, it threatens to substitute for present calm a disruptive round of race-related litigation, and it undermines *Brown*'s promise of integrated primary and secondary education that local communities have sought to make a reality. This cannot be justified in the name of the Equal Protection Clause.

. . . The [Fourteenth] Amendment sought to bring into American society as full members those whom the Nation had previously held in slavery.

There is reason to believe that those who drafted an Amendment with this basic purpose in mind would have understood the legal and practical difference between the use of race-conscious criteria in defiance of that purpose, namely to keep the races apart, and the use of race-conscious criteria to further that purpose, namely to bring the races together. Although the Constitution almost always forbids the former, it is significantly more lenient in respect to the latter.

Sometimes Members of this Court have disagreed about the degree of leniency that the Clause affords to programs designed to include. But I can find no case in which this Court has followed JUSTICE THOMAS' "colorblind" approach. And I have found no case that otherwise repudiated this constitutional asymmetry between that which seeks to *exclude* and that which seeks to *include* members of minority races. . . .

The Court in *Grutter* . . . [held that] "strict scrutiny is not 'strict in theory, but fatal in fact.' Although all governmental uses of race are subject to strict scrutiny, not all are invalidated by it." . . . The upshot [of our past Equal Protection Clause cases] is that . . . though [they] all apply . . . strict scrutiny, [they] do not treat exclusive and inclusive uses the same. Rather, they apply the strict scrutiny test in a manner that is "fatal in fact" only to racial classifications that harmfully *exclude;* they apply the test in a manner that is *not* fatal in fact to racial classifications that seek to *include.*

The plurality cannot avoid this simple fact. Today's opinion reveals that the plurality would rewrite this Court's prior jurisprudence, at least in practical application, transforming the "strict scrutiny" test into a rule that is fatal in fact across the board. In doing so, the plurality parts company from this Court's prior cases, and it takes from local government the longstanding legal right to use race-conscious criteria for inclusive purposes in limited ways.

[A]s *Grutter* specified, "context matters when reviewing race-based governmental action under the Equal Protection Clause." And contexts differ dramatically one from the other. Governmental use of race-based criteria can arise in the context of, for example, census forms, research expenditures for diseases, as-

signments of police officers patrolling predominantly minority-race neighborhoods, efforts to desegregate racially segregated schools, policies that favor minorities when distributing goods or services in short supply, actions that create majority-minority electoral districts, peremptory strikes that remove potential jurors on the basis of race, and others. Given the significant differences among these contexts, it would be surprising if the law required an identically strict legal test for evaluating the constitutionality of race-based criteria as to each of them.

Here, the context is one in which school districts seek to advance or to maintain racial integration in primary and secondary schools. It is a context . . . where history has required special administrative remedies. And it is a context in which the school boards' plans simply set race-conscious limits at the outer boundaries of a broad range.

This context is *not* a context that involves the use of race to decide who will receive goods or services that are normally distributed on the basis of merit and which are in short supply. It is not one in which race-conscious limits stigmatize or exclude; the limits at issue do not pit the races against each other or otherwise significantly exacerbate racial tensions. They do not impose burdens unfairly upon members of one race alone but instead seek benefits for members of all races alike. The context here is one of racial limits that seek, not to keep the races apart, but to bring them together. . . .

The view that a more lenient standard than "strict scrutiny" should apply in the present context would not imply abandonment of judicial efforts carefully to determine the need for race-conscious criteria and the criteria's tailoring in light of the need. And the present context requires a court to examine carefully the race-conscious program at issue. In doing so, a reviewing judge must be fully aware of the potential dangers and pitfalls that Justice Thomas and Justice Kennedy mention. . . .

But unlike the plurality, such a judge would also be aware that a legislature or school administrators, ultimately accountable to the electorate, could *nonetheless* properly conclude that a racial classification sometimes serves a purpose important enough to overcome the risks they mention, for example, helping to end racial isolation or to achieve a diverse student body in public schools. Where that is so, the judge would carefully examine the program's details to determine whether the use of race-conscious criteria is proportionate to the important ends it serves.

In my view, this contextual approach to scrutiny is altogether fitting. I believe that the law requires application here of a standard of review that is not "strict" in the traditional sense of that word, although it does require the careful review I have just described. . . .

Nonetheless, in light of *Grutter* and other precedents, I shall adopt . . . the version of strict scrutiny that those cases embody. I shall consequently ask whether the school boards in Seattle and Louisville adopted these plans to serve a "compelling governmental interest" and, if so, whether the plans are "narrowly tailored" to achieve that interest. If the plans survive this strict review, they would survive less exacting review *a fortiori*. Hence, I conclude that the plans before us pass both parts of the strict scrutiny test. Consequently I must conclude that the plans here are permitted under the Constitution.

The principal interest advanced in these cases to justify the use of race-based criteria goes by various names. Sometimes a court refers to it as an interest in achieving racial "diversity." Other times a court, like the plurality here, refers to it as an interest in racial "balancing." I have used more general terms to signify that interest, describing it, for example, as an interest in promoting or preserving greater racial "integration" of public schools. By this term, I mean the school districts' interest in eliminating school-by-school racial isolation and increasing the degree to which racial mixture characterizes each of the district's schools and each individual student's public school experience.

Regardless of its name, . . . [t]he compelling interest at issue here . . . includes an effort to eradicate the remnants, not of general "societal discrimination" but of primary and secondary school segregation; it includes an effort to create school environments that provide better educational opportunities for all children; it includes an effort to help create citizens better prepared to know, to understand, and to work

with people of all races and backgrounds, thereby furthering the kind of democratic government our Constitution foresees. If an educational interest that combines these three elements is not "compelling," what is?

I next ask whether the plans before us are "narrowly tailored" to achieve these "compelling" objectives. . . . Several factors, taken together, . . . lead me to conclude that the boards' use of race-conscious criteria in these plans passes even the strictest "tailoring" test. . . . [They include] (1) their limited and historically-diminishing use of race, (2) their strong reliance upon other non-race-conscious elements, (3) their history and the manner in which the districts developed and modified their approach, (4) the comparison with prior plans, and (5) the lack of reasonably evident alternatives. [Taken] together [, they] show that the districts' plans are "narrowly tailored" to achieve their "compelling" goals. In sum, the districts' race-conscious plans satisfy "strict scrutiny" and are therefore lawful. . . .

The Founders meant the Constitution as a practical document that would transmit its basic values to future generations through principles that remained workable over time. Hence it is important to consider the potential consequences of the plurality's approach, as measured against the Constitution's objectives. To do so provides further reason to believe that the plurality's approach is legally unsound.

. . . [D]e facto resegregation is on the rise. It is reasonable to conclude that such resegregation can create serious educational, social, and civic problems. Given the conditions in which school boards work to set policy, they may need all of the means presently at their disposal to combat those problems. Yet the plurality would deprive them of at least one tool that some districts now consider vital—the limited use of broad race-conscious student population ranges.

I use the words "may need" here deliberately. The plurality, or at least those who follow JUSTICE THOMAS' "'color-blind'" approach, may feel confident that, to end invidious discrimination, one must end *all* governmental use of race-conscious criteria including those with inclusive objectives. By way of contrast, I do not claim to know how best to stop harmful discrimination; how best to create a society that includes all Americans; how best to overcome our serious problems of increasing *de facto* segregation, troubled inner city schooling, and poverty correlated with race. But, as a judge, I do know that the Constitution does not authorize judges to dictate solutions to these problems. Rather, the Constitution creates a democratic political system through which the people themselves must together find answers. And it is for them to debate how best to educate the Nation's children and how best to administer America's schools to achieve that aim. The Court should leave them to their work. And it is for them to decide, to quote the plurality's slogan, whether the best "way to stop discrimination on the basis of race is to stop discriminating on the basis of race." . . .

Finally, what of the hope and promise of *Brown?* For much of this Nation's history, the races remained divided. It was not long ago that people of different races drank from separate fountains, rode on separate buses, and studied in separate schools. In this Court's finest hour, *Brown v. Board of Education* challenged this history and helped to change it. For *Brown* held out a promise. It was a promise embodied in three Amendments designed to make citizens of slaves. It was the promise of true racial equality—not as a matter of fine words on paper, but as a matter of everyday life in the Nation's cities and schools. It was about the nature of a democracy that must work for all Americans. It sought one law, one Nation, one people, not simply as a matter of legal principle but in terms of how we actually live.

. . . Many parents, white and black alike, want their children to attend schools with children of different races. Indeed, the very school districts that once spurned integration now strive for it. The long history of their efforts reveals the complexities and difficulties they have faced. And in light of those challenges, they have asked us not to take from their hands the instruments they have used to rid their schools of racial segregation, instruments that they believe are needed to overcome the problems of cities divided by race and poverty. The plurality would decline their modest request.

The plurality is wrong to do so. The last half-century has witnessed great strides toward racial equality, but we have not yet realized the promise of *Brown.* To invalidate the plans under review is to threaten the promise of *Brown.* The plurality's position, I fear, would break that promise. This is a decision that the Court and the Nation will come to regret.

I must dissent.

Massachusetts Board of Retirement v. Murgia
427 U.S. 307 (1976)

Robert Murgia, a uniformed officer in the Massachusetts State Police who was in excellent physical and mental health, was forced by state law to retire upon reaching his fiftieth birthday. He challenged the constitutionality of this law, arguing that such compulsory retirement discriminated on the basis of age in violation of the Equal Protection Clause. A three-judge federal district court agreed, holding that the statute lacked "a rational basis in furthering any substantial state interest." The Massachusetts Board of Retirement appealed. Per Curiam: Burger, Brennan, Stewart, White, Blackmun, Powell, Rehnquist. Dissenting opinion: <u>Marshall</u>. Not participating: Stevens.

PER CURIAM. . . .

. . . Uniformed state officers [must] pass a comprehensive physical examination biennially until age 40. After that, until mandatory retirement at age 50, uniformed officers must pass annually a more rigorous examination, including an electrocardiogram and tests for gastrointestinal bleeding. Appellee Murgia had passed such an examination four months before he was retired, and there is no dispute that, when he retired, his excellent physical and mental health still rendered him capable of performing the duties of a uniformed officer.

The record includes the testimony of three physicians . . . that clearly established that the risk of physical failure, particularly in the cardiovascular system, increases with age, and that the number of individuals in a given age group incapable of performing stress functions increases with the age of the group. . . .

In assessing appellee's equal protection claim, the District Court found it unnecessary to apply a strict-scrutiny test, . . . for it determined that the age classification established by the Massachusetts statutory scheme could not in any event withstand a test of rationality. . . . Since there had been no showing that reaching age 50 forecasts even "imminent change" in an officer's physical condition, the District Court held that compulsory retirement at age 50 was irrational under a scheme that assessed the capabilities of officers individually by means of comprehensive annual physical examinations. We agree that rationality is the proper standard by which to test whether compulsory retirement at age 50 violates equal protection. We disagree, however, with the District Court's determination that the age 50 classification is not rationally related to furthering a legitimate state interest.

. . . Equal protection analysis requires strict scrutiny of a legislative classification only when the classification impermissibly interferes with the exercise of a fundamental right or operates to the peculiar disadvantage of a suspect class. Mandatory retirement at age 50 under the Massachusetts statute involves neither situation.

This Court's decisions give no support to the proposition that a right of governmental employment *per se* is fundamental. . . . Accordingly, we have expressly stated that a standard less than strict scrutiny "has consistently been applied to state legislation restricting the availability of employment opportunities."

Nor does the class of uniformed state police officers over 50 constitute a suspect class for purposes of equal protection analysis. . . . A suspect class is one "saddled with such disabilities, or subjected to such a history of purposeful unequal treatment, or relegated to such a position of political powerlessness as to command extraordinary protection from the majoritarian political process." While the treatment of the aged in this Nation has not been wholly free of discrimination, such persons, unlike, say, those who have been discriminated against on the basis of race or national origin, have not experienced a "history of

purposeful unequal treatment" or been subjected to unique disabilities on the basis of stereotyped characteristics not truly indicative of their abilities. The class subject to the compulsory retirement feature of the Massachusetts statute consists of uniformed state police officers over the age of 50. It cannot be said to discriminate only against the elderly. Rather, it draws the line at a certain age in middle life. But even old age does not define a "discrete and insular" group . . . in need of "extraordinary protection from the majoritarian political process." Instead, it marks a stage that each of us will reach if we live out our normal span. Even if the statute could be said to impose a penalty upon a class defined as the aged, it would not impose a distinction sufficiently akin to those classifications that we have found suspect to call for strict judicial scrutiny.

Under the circumstances, it is unnecessary to subject the State's resolution of competing interests in this case to the degree of critical examination that our cases under the Equal Protection Clause recently have characterized as "strict judicial scrutiny." . . .

We turn then to examine this state classification under the rational-basis standard. This inquiry employs a relatively relaxed standard reflecting the Court's awareness that the drawing of lines that create distinctions is peculiarly a legislative task and an unavoidable one. Perfection in making the necessary classifications is neither possible nor necessary. . . . Such action by a legislature is presumed to be valid.

In this case, the Massachusetts statute clearly meets the requirements of the Equal Protection Clause, for the State's classification rationally furthers the purpose identified by the State: Through mandatory retirement at age 50, the legislature seeks to protect the public by assuring physical preparedness of its uniformed police. Since physical ability generally declines with age, mandatory retirement at 50 serves to remove from police service those whose fitness for uniformed work presumptively has diminished with age. This clearly is rationally related to the State's objective. There is no indication that [the statute] has the effect of excluding from service so few officers who are in fact unqualified as to render age 50 a criterion wholly unrelated to the objective of the statute.

That the State chooses not to determine fitness more precisely through individualized testing after age 50 is not to say that the objective of assuring physical fitness is not rationally furthered by a maximum-age limitation. It is only to say that with regard to the interest of all concerned, the State perhaps has not chosen the best means to accomplish this purpose. But where rationality is the test, a State "does not violate the Equal Protection Clause merely because the classifications made by its laws are imperfect." . . .

We do not make light of the substantial economic and psychological effects premature and compulsory retirement can have on an individual; nor do we denigrate the ability of elderly citizens to continue to contribute to society. The problems of retirement have been well documented and are beyond serious dispute. But "[we] do not decide today that the [Massachusetts statute] is wise, that it best fulfills the relevant social and economic objectives that [Massachusetts] might ideally espouse, or that a more just and humane system could not be devised." . . . We decide only that the system enacted by the Massachusetts legislature does not deny appellee equal protection of the laws. . . .

JUSTICE MARSHALL, dissenting. . . .

Although there are signs that its grasp on the law is weakening, the rigid two-tier model still holds sway as the Court's articulated description of the equal protection test. Again, I must object to its perpetuation. The model's two fixed modes of analysis, strict scrutiny and mere rationality, simply do not describe the inquiry the Court has undertaken—or should undertake—in equal protection cases. Rather, the inquiry has been much more sophisticated and the Court should admit as much. It has focused upon the character of the classification in question, the relative importance to individuals in the class discriminated against of the governmental benefits that they do not receive, and the state interests asserted in support of the classification. . . .

Although the Court outwardly adheres to the two-tier model, it has apparently lost interest in recognizing further "fundamental" rights and "suspect" classes. . . . In my view, this result is the natural consequence of the limitations of the Court's traditional equal protection analysis. If a statute invades a "fundamental" right or discriminates against a "suspect" class, it is subject to strict scrutiny. If a statute is subject to strict scrutiny, the statute always, or nearly always, . . . is struck down. Quite obviously, the only critical decision is whether strict scrutiny should be invoked at all. It should be no surprise, then, that the Court is hesitant to expand the number of categories of rights and classes subject to strict scrutiny, when each expansion involves the invalidation of virtually every classification bearing upon a newly covered category.

But however understandable the Court's hesitancy to invoke strict scrutiny, all remaining legislation should not drop into the bottom tier, and be measured by the mere rationality test. For that test, too, when applied as articulated, leaves little doubt about the outcome; the challenged legislation is always upheld. . . . It cannot be gainsaid that there remain rights, not now classified as "fundamental," that remain vital to the flourishing of a free society, and classes, not now classified as "suspect," that are unfairly burdened by invidious discrimination unrelated to the individual worth of their members. Whatever we call these rights and classes, we simply cannot forgo all judicial protection against discriminatory legislation bearing upon them, but for the rare instances when the legislative choice can be termed "wholly irrelevant" to the legislative goal. . . .

While the Court's traditional articulation of the rational-basis test does suggest just such an abdication, happily the Court's deeds have not matched its words. Time and again, met with cases touching upon the prized rights and burdened classes of our society, the Court has acted only after a reasonably probing look at the legislative goals and means, and at the significance of the personal rights and interests invaded. . . .

But there are problems with deciding cases based on factors not encompassed by the applicable standards. First, the approach is rudderless, affording no notice to interested parties of the standards governing particular cases and giving no firm guidance to judges who, as a consequence, must assess the constitutionality of legislation before them on an *ad hoc* basis. Second, and not unrelatedly, the approach is unpredictable and requires holding this Court to standards it has never publicly adopted. Thus, the approach presents the danger that, as I suggest has happened here, relevant factors will be misapplied or ignored. All interests not "fundamental" and all classes not "suspect" are not the same; and it is time for the Court to drop the pretense that, for purposes of the Equal Protection Clause, they are.

The danger of the Court's verbal adherence to the rigid two-tier test, despite its effective repudiation of that test in the cases, is demonstrated by its efforts here. There is simply no reason why a statute that tells able-bodied police officers, ready and willing to work, that they no longer have the right to earn a living in their chosen profession merely because they are 50 years old should be judged by the same minimal standards of rationality that we use to test economic legislation that discriminates against business interests. . . . Yet, the Court today not only invokes the minimal level of scrutiny, it wrongly adheres to it. Analysis of the three factors I have identified above—the importance of the governmental benefits denied, the character of the class, and the asserted state interests—demonstrates the Court's error.

Whether "fundamental" or not, "'the right of the individual . . . to engage in any of the common occupations of life'" has been repeatedly recognized by this Court as falling within the concept of liberty guaranteed by the Fourteenth Amendment. . . .

While depriving any government employee of his job is a significant deprivation, it is particularly burdensome when the person deprived is an older citizen. Once terminated, the elderly cannot readily find alternative employment. The lack of work is not only economically damaging, but emotionally and physically

draining. Deprived of his status in the community and of the opportunity for meaningful activity, fearful of becoming dependent on others for his support, and lonely in his newfound isolation, the involuntarily retired person is susceptible to physical and emotional ailments as a direct consequence of his enforced idleness. . . .

Not only are the elderly denied important benefits when they are terminated on the basis of age, but the classification of older workers is itself one that merits judicial attention. Whether older workers constitute a "suspect" class or not, it cannot be disputed that they constitute a class subject to repeated and arbitrary discrimination in employment. . . .

Of course, the Court is quite right in suggesting that distinctions exist between the elderly and traditional suspect classes such as Negroes, and between the elderly and "quasi-suspect" classes such as women or illegitimates. The elderly are protected not only by certain anti-discrimination legislation, but by legislation that provides them with positive benefits not enjoyed by the public at large. Moreover, the elderly are not isolated in society, and discrimination against them is not pervasive but is centered primarily in employment. The advantage of a flexible equal protection standard, however, is that it can readily accommodate such variables. The elderly are undoubtedly discriminated against, and when legislation denies them an important benefit—employment—I conclude that to sustain the legislation appellants must show a reasonably substantial interest and a scheme reasonably closely tailored to achieving that interest. . . .

. . . The Commonwealth's mandatory retirement law cannot stand when measured against the significant deprivation the Commonwealth's action works upon the terminated employees. I would affirm the judgment of the District Court.

Frontiero v. Richardson
411 U.S. 677 (1973)

Federal statutes provided that married servicemen would automatically qualify to receive increased *quarters allowances and medical and dental benefits for their wives, but that female personnel in the armed services would not receive these fringe benefits unless their husbands were in fact dependent on them for more than 50 percent of their support. Sharron Frontiero, a married US Air Force officer, brought suit in federal district court against Secretary of Defense Elliott Richardson, challenging this sex-based differential treatment. She argued that it violated the equal-protection component of the Due Process Clause of the Fifth Amendment, in that the statutes required a service-woman to prove the actual dependency of her husband. A three-judge court denied relief, and she appealed.* Judgment of the Court: Brennan, Douglas, White, Marshall. Concurring in the judgment: Stewart; Powell, Burger, Blackmun. Dissenting opinion: Rehnquist.

JUSTICE BRENNAN announced the judgment of the Court.

At the outset, appellants contend that classifications based upon sex, like classifications based upon race, alienage, and national origin, are inherently suspect and must therefore be subjected to close judicial scrutiny. We agree and, indeed, find at least implicit support for such an approach in our unanimous decision only last Term in *Reed v. Reed* (1971). . . .

There can be no doubt that our Nation has had a long and unfortunate history of sex discrimination. Traditionally, such discrimination was rationalized by an attitude of "romantic paternalism" which, in practical effect, put women not on a pedestal, but in a cage. . . .

As a result . . . , our statute books gradually became laden with gross, stereotypical distinctions between the sexes and, indeed, throughout much of the 19th century the position of women in our society was, in many respects, comparable to that of blacks under the pre–Civil War slave codes. Neither slaves nor women could hold office, serve on juries, or bring suit in their own names, and married women traditionally were denied the legal capacity to hold or convey property or to serve as legal guardians of their own children. . . . And although blacks were guaranteed the right to vote in 1870, women were denied even that right—which is itself "preservative of other basic civil and political rights"—until adoption of the Nineteenth Amendment half a century

later. It is true, of course, that the position of women in America has improved markedly in recent decades. Nevertheless, it can hardly be doubted that, in part because of the high visibility of the sex characteristic, women still face pervasive, although at times more subtle, discrimination in our educational institutions, on the job market and, perhaps most conspicuously, in the political arena. . . .

Moreover, since sex, like race and national origin, is an immutable characteristic determined solely by the accident of birth, the imposition of special disabilities upon the members of a particular sex because of their sex would seem to violate "the basic concept of our system that legal burdens should bear some relationship to individual responsibility. . . . " And what differentiates sex from such nonsuspect statutes as intelligence or physical disability, and aligns it with the recognized suspect criteria, is that the sex characteristic frequently bears no relation to ability to perform or contribute to society. As a result, statutory distinctions between the sexes often have the effect of invidiously relegating the entire class of females to inferior legal status without regard to the actual capabilities of its individual members. . . .

With these considerations in mind, we can only conclude that classifications based upon sex, like classifications based upon race, alienage, or national origin, are inherently suspect, and must therefore be subjected to strict judicial scrutiny. Applying the analysis mandated by that statutory standard of review, it is clear that the statutory scheme now before us is constitutionally invalid.

The sole basis of the classification established in the challenged statutes is the sex of the individuals involved. . . .

Moreover, the Government concedes that the differential treatment accorded men and women under these statutes serves no purpose other than mere "administrative convenience." In essence, the Government maintains that, as an empirical matter, wives in our society frequently are dependent upon their husbands, while husbands rarely are dependent upon their wives. Thus, the Government argues that Congress might reasonably have concluded that it would be both cheaper and easier simply conclusively to presume that wives of male members are financially dependent upon their husbands, while burdening female members with the task of establishing dependency in fact.

The Government offers no concrete evidence, however, tending to support its views that such differential treatment in fact saves the Government any money. In order to satisfy the demands of strict judicial scrutiny, the Government must demonstrate, for example, that it is actually cheaper to grant increased benefits with respect to *all* male members, than it is to determine which male members are in fact entitled to such benefits and to grant increased benefits only to those members whose wives actually meet the dependency requirement. Here, however, there is substantial evidence that, if put to the test, many of the wives of male members would fail to qualify for benefits. And in light of the fact that the dependency determination with respect to the husbands of female members is presently made solely on the basis of affidavits, rather than through the more costly hearing process, the Government's explanation of the statutory scheme is, to say the least, questionable.

In any case, our prior decisions make clear that, although efficacious administration of governmental programs is not without some importance, "the Constitution recognizes higher values than speed and efficiency." . . . And when we enter the realm of "strict judicial scrutiny," there can be no doubt that "administrative convenience" is not a shibboleth, the mere recitation of which dictates constitutionality. . . . On the contrary, any statutory scheme which draws a sharp line between the sexes, *solely* for the purpose of achieving administrative convenience, necessarily commands "dissimilar treatment for men and women who are . . . similarly situated," and therefore involves the "very kind of arbitrary legislative choice forbidden by the [Constitution]." . . . We therefore conclude that, by according differential treatment to male and female members of the uniformed services for the sole purpose of achieving administrative conve-

nience, the challenged statutes violate the Due Process Clause of the Fifth Amendment insofar as they require a female member to prove the dependency of her husband.

Reversed.

JUSTICE POWELL, with whom THE CHIEF JUSTICE and JUSTICE BLACKMUN join, concurring.

I agree that the challenged statutes constitute an unconstitutional discrimination against service women in violation of the Due Process Clause of the Fifth Amendment, but I cannot join the opinion of Mr. Justice Brennan, which would hold that all classifications based upon sex, "like classifications based upon race, alienage, and national origin," are "inherently suspect and must therefore be subjected to close judicial scrutiny." . . . It is unnecessary for the Court in this case to characterize sex as a suspect classification, with all of the far-reaching implications of such a holding. *Reed v. Reed* (1971), which abundantly supports our decision today, did not add sex to the narrowly limited group of classifications which are inherently suspect. In my view, we can and should decide this case on the authority of *Reed* and reserve for the future any expansion of its rationale.

There is another, and I find compelling, reason for deferring a general categorizing of sex classifications as invoking the strictest test of judicial scrutiny. The Equal Rights Amendment, which if adopted will resolve the substance of this precise question, has been approved by the Congress and submitted for ratification by the States. If this Amendment is duly adopted, it will represent the will of the people accomplished in the manner prescribed by the Constitution. By acting prematurely and unnecessarily, as I view it, the Court has assumed a decisional responsibility at the very time when state legislatures, functioning within the traditional democratic process, are debating the proposed Amendment. It seems to me that this reaching out to pre-empt by judicial action a major political decision which is currently in process of resolution does not reflect appropriate respect for duly prescribed legislature processes.

United States v. Virginia
518 U.S. 515 (1996)

The Virginia Military Institute (VMI) was the sole single-sex school among Virginia's public institutions of higher learning; its mission was to produce "citizen-soldiers," men prepared for leadership in civilian life and in military service. Using an "adversative method" of training not available elsewhere in Virginia, VMI sought to instill physical and mental discipline in its cadets and impart to them a strong moral code. Reflecting the high value alumni placed on their VMI training, VMI had the largest per student endowment of all undergraduate institutions in the nation. The United States sued Virginia and VMI, alleging that VMI's exclusively male admissions policy violated the Fourteenth Amendment's Equal Protection Clause. The district court ruled in VMI's favor. The Court of Appeals for the Fourth Circuit reversed and ordered Virginia to remedy the constitutional violation. In response, Virginia proposed a parallel program for women: Virginia Women's Institute for Leadership (VWIL), located at Mary Baldwin College, a private liberal arts school for women. The district court found that Virginia's proposal satisfied the Constitution's equal-protection requirement, and the Fourth Circuit affirmed. Although the court of appeals acknowledged that the VWIL degree lacked the historical benefit and prestige of a VMI degree, the court nevertheless found the educational opportunities at the two schools sufficiently comparable. The United States petitioned the Supreme Court for a writ of certiorari. Opinion of the Court: Ginsburg, Stevens, O'Connor, Kennedy, Souter, Breyer. Concurring in the judgment: Rehnquist. Dissenting opinion: Scalia. Not participating (because his son was a student at the Citadel, along with VMI, the other public, male-only military academy): Thomas.

JUSTICE GINSBURG delivered the opinion of the Court.

. . . [T]his case present[s] two ultimate issues. First, does Virginia's exclusion of women from the educational opportunities provided by VMI—extraordinary opportunities for military training and civilian leadership development—deny to women "capable of all of the individual activities required of VMI cadets" the equal protection of the laws guaranteed by the Fourteenth Amendment? Second, if VMI's "unique" situation—as Virginia's sole single-sex public institution of higher education—offends the Constitution's equal protection principle, what is the remedial requirement?

We note, once again, the core instruction of this Court's path-marking decisions in *J. E. B. v. Alabama ex rel. T. B.* (1994), and *Mississippi University for Women [v. Hogan]* (1982): Parties who seek to defend gender-based government action must demonstrate an "exceedingly persuasive justification" for that action. . . .

To summarize the Court's current directions for cases of official classification based on gender: Focusing on the differential treatment or denial of opportunity for which relief is sought, the reviewing court must determine whether the proffered justification is "exceedingly persuasive." The burden of justification is demanding and it rests entirely on the State. The State must show "at least that the [challenged] classification serves 'important governmental objectives and that the discriminatory means employed' are 'substantially related to the achievement of those objectives.'" The justification must be genuine, not hypothesized or invented *post hoc* in response to litigation. And it must not rely on overbroad generalizations about the different talents, capacities, or preferences of males and females.

The heightened review standard our precedent establishes does not make sex a proscribed classification. Supposed "inherent differences" are no longer accepted as a ground for race or national origin classifications. Physical differences between men and women, however, are enduring: "[T]he two sexes are not fungible; a community made up exclusively of one [sex] is different from a community composed of both." *Ballard v. United States* (1946).

"Inherent differences" between men and women, we have come to appreciate, remain cause for celebration, but not for denigration of the members of either sex or for artificial constraints on an individual's opportunity. Sex classifications may be used to compensate women "for particular economic disabilities [they have] suffered," *Califano v. Webster* (1977), to "promot[e] equal employment opportunity," see *California Federal Saving & Loan Association v. Guerra* (1987), to advance full development of the talent and capacities of our Nation's people. But such classifications may not be used, as they once were, to create or perpetuate the legal, social, and economic inferiority of women.

Measuring the record in this case against the review standard just described, we conclude that Virginia has shown no "exceedingly persuasive justification" for excluding all women from the citizen-soldier training afforded by VMI. We therefore affirm the Fourth Circuit's initial judgment, which held that Virginia had violated the Fourteenth Amendment's Equal Protection Clause. Because the remedy proffered by Virginia—the Mary Baldwin VWIL program—does not cure the constitutional violation, i.e., it does not provide equal opportunity, we reverse the Fourth Circuit's final judgment in this case.

The Fourth Circuit initially held that Virginia had advanced no state policy by which it could justify, under equal protection principles, its determination "to afford VMI's unique type of program to men and not to women." Virginia challenges that "liability" ruling and asserts two justifications in defense of VMI's exclusion of women. First, the Commonwealth contends, "single-sex education provides important educational benefits," and the option of single-sex education contributes to "diversity in educational approaches." Second, the Commonwealth argues, "the unique VMI method of character development and leadership training," the school's adversative approach, would have to be modified were VMI to admit women. We consider these two justifications in turn.

Single-sex education affords pedagogical benefits to at least some students, Virginia emphasizes, and that reality is uncontested in this litigation. Similarly, it is not disputed that diversity among public educational institutions can serve the public good. But Virginia has not shown that VMI was established, or has been maintained, with a view to diversifying, by its categorical exclusion of women, educational opportunities within the State. . . . A purpose

genuinely to advance an array of educational options, as the Court of Appeals recognized, is not served by VMI's historic and constant plan—a plan to "affor[d] a unique educational benefit only to males." However "liberally" this plan serves the State's sons, it makes no provision whatever for her daughters. That is not equal protection.

Virginia next argues that VMI's adversative method of training provides educational benefits that cannot be made available, unmodified, to women. Alterations to accommodate women would necessarily be "radical," so "drastic," Virginia asserts, as to transform, indeed "destroy" VMI's program. Neither sex would be favored by the transformation, Virginia maintains: Men would be deprived of the unique opportunity currently available to them; women would not gain that opportunity because their participation would "eliminat[e] the very aspects of [the] program that distinguish [VMI] from . . . other institutions of higher education in Virginia." . . .

The United States does not challenge any expert witness estimation on average capacities or preferences of men and women. Instead, the United States emphasizes that time and again since this Court's turning point decision in *Reed v. Reed*, 404 U.S. 71 (1971), we have cautioned reviewing courts to take a "hard look" at generalizations or "tendencies" of the kind pressed by Virginia, and relied upon by the District Court. . . .

The notion that admission of women would downgrade VMI's stature, destroy the adversative system and, with it, even the school, is a judgment hardly proved, a prediction hardly different from other "self-fulfilling prophec[ies]" once routinely used to deny rights or opportunities. . . .

Women's successful entry into the federal military academies, and their participation in the Nation's military forces, indicate that Virginia's fears for the future of VMI may not be solidly grounded. The State's justification for excluding all women from "citizen-soldier" training for which some are qualified, in any event, cannot rank as "exceedingly persuasive," as we have explained and applied that standard. . . .

In the second phase of the litigation, Virginia presented its remedial plan—maintain

VMI as a male-only college and create VWIL as a separate program for women. The plan met District Court approval. The Fourth Circuit, in turn, deferentially . . . concluded that Virginia had arranged for men and women opportunities "sufficiently comparable" to survive equal protection evaluation. The United States challenges this "remedial" ruling as pervasively misguided. . . .

Virginia chose not to eliminate, but to leave untouched, VMI's exclusionary policy. For women only, however, Virginia proposed a separate program, different in kind from VMI and unequal in tangible and intangible facilities. Having violated the Constitution's equal protection requirement, Virginia was obliged to show that its remedial proposal "directly address[ed] and relate[d] to" the violation, the equal protection denied to women ready, willing, and able to benefit from educational opportunities of the kind VMI offers. . . .

VWIL affords women no opportunity to experience the rigorous military training for which VMI is famed. Instead, the VWIL program "deemphasize[s]" military education and uses a "cooperative method" of education "which reinforces self-esteem." VWIL students participate in ROTC and a "largely ceremonial" Virginia Corps of Cadets, but Virginia deliberately did not make VWIL a military institute. The VWIL House is not a military-style residence and VWIL students need not live together throughout the 4-year program, eat meals together, or wear uniforms during the school day. VWIL students thus do not experience the "barracks" life "crucial to the VMI experience," the Spartan living arrangements designed to foster an "egalitarian ethic." "[T]he most important aspects of the VMI educational experience occur in the barracks," the District Court found, yet Virginia deemed that core experience nonessential, indeed inappropriate, for training its female citizen-soldiers.

VWIL students receive their "leadership training" in seminars, externships, and speaker series, episodes and encounters lacking the "[p]hysical rigor, mental stress, . . . minute regulation of behavior, and indoctrination in desirable values" made hallmarks of VMI's citizen-soldier training. Kept away from the pressures, hazards, and psychological bonding characteristic of VMI's adversative training, VWIL students will not know the "feeling of tremendous accomplishment" commonly experienced by VMI's successful cadets.

Virginia maintains that these methodological differences are "justified pedagogically," based on "important differences between men and women in learning and developmental needs," "psychological and sociological differences" Virginia describes as "real" and "not stereotypes." . . . In contrast to the generalizations about women on which Virginia rests, we note again these dispositive realities: VMI's "implementing methodology" is not "inherently unsuitable to women," "some women . . . do well under [the] adversative model," "some women, at least, would want to attend [VMI] if they had the opportunity," "some women are capable of all of the individual activities required of VMI cadets" and "can meet the physical standards [VMI] now impose[s] on men." It is on behalf of these women that the United States has instituted this suit, and it is for them that a remedy must be crafted, a remedy that will end their exclusion from a state-supplied educational opportunity for which they are fit, a decree that will "bar like discrimination in the future."

In myriad respects other than military training, VWIL does not qualify as VMI's equal. VWIL's student body, faculty, course offerings, and facilities hardly match VMI's. Nor can the VWIL graduate anticipate the benefits associated with VMI's 157-year history, the school's prestige, and its influential alumni network. . . .

Virginia's VWIL solution is reminiscent of the remedy Texas proposed 50 years ago, in response to a state trial court's 1946 ruling that, given the equal protection guarantee, African Americans could not be denied a legal education at a state facility. See *Sweatt v. Painter* (1950). Reluctant to admit African Americans to its flagship University of Texas Law School, the State set up a separate school for Herman Sweatt and other black law students. . . . This Court contrasted resources at the new school with those at the school from which Sweatt had been excluded. . . . [But, m]ore important than the tangible features, the Court emphasized, are "those qualities which are incapable of objective measurement but which make for greatness" in a school, including "reputation of the faculty, experience of the administration, position and influence of the alumni, standing in the community, traditions and prestige." Facing the marked differences reported in the *Sweatt* opinion, the Court unanimously ruled that Texas had not shown "substantial equality in the [separate] educational opportunities" the State offered. Accordingly, the Court held, the Equal Protection Clause required Texas to admit African Americans to the University of Texas Law School. In line with *Sweatt,* we rule here that Virginia has not shown substantial equality in the separate educational opportunities the State supports at VWIL and VMI.

When Virginia tendered its VWIL plan, the Fourth Circuit did not inquire whether the proposed remedy, approved by the District Court, placed women denied the VMI advantage in "the position they would have occupied in the absence of [discrimination]." Instead, the Court of Appeals considered whether the State could provide, with fidelity to the equal protection principle, separate and unequal educational programs for men and women. . . .

The Fourth Circuit plainly erred in exposing Virginia's VWIL plan to a deferential analysis, for "all gender-based classifications today" warrant "heightened scrutiny." Valuable as VWIL may prove for students who seek the program offered, Virginia's remedy affords no cure at all for the opportunities and advantages withheld from women who want a VMI education and can make the grade. In sum, Virginia's remedy does not match the constitutional violation; the State has shown no "exceedingly persuasive justification" for withholding from women qualified for the experience premier training of the kind VMI affords. . . .

For the reasons stated, the initial judgment of the Court of Appeals is affirmed, the final judgment of the Court of Appeals is reversed, and the case is remanded for further proceedings consistent with this opinion.

THE CHIEF JUSTICE, concurring in the judgment.

While I agree with [the Court's] conclusions, I disagree with the Court's analysis and so I write separately.

Two decades ago in *Craig v. Boren* (1976), we announced that "[t]o withstand constitutional challenge, . . . classifications by gender must serve important governmental objectives and must be substantially related to achievement of those objectives." We have adhered to that standard of scrutiny ever since. . . .

While terms like "important governmental objective" and "substantially related" are hardly models of precision, they have more content and specificity than does the phrase "exceedingly persuasive justification." That phrase is best confined, as it was first used, as an observation on the difficulty of meeting the applicable test, not as a formulation of the test itself.

Our cases dealing with gender discrimination also require that the proffered purpose for the challenged law be the actual purpose. . . . Before this Court, Virginia has sought to justify VMI's single-sex admissions policy primarily on the basis that diversity in education is desirable, and that while most of the public institutions of higher learning in the State are coeducational, there should also be room for single-sex institutions. I agree with the Court that there is scant evidence in the record that this was the real reason that Virginia decided to maintain VMI as men only. But, unlike the majority, I would consider only evidence that postdates our decision in *Hogan,* and would draw no negative inferences from the State's actions before that time. I think that after *Hogan,* the State was entitled to reconsider its policy with respect to VMI, and to not have earlier justifications, or lack thereof, held against it. . . .

Virginia offers a second justification for the single-sex admissions policy: maintenance of the adversative method. I agree with the Court that this justification does not serve an important governmental objective. A State does not have substantial interest in the adversative methodology unless it is pedagogically beneficial. While considerable evidence shows that a single-sex education is pedagogically beneficial for some students and hence a State may have a valid interest in promoting that methodology, there is no similar evidence in the record that an adversative method is pedagogically beneficial or is any more likely to produce character traits than other methodologies. . . .

[I]t is not the "exclusion of women" that violates the Equal Protection Clause, but the maintenance of an all-men school without providing any—much less a comparable—institution for women. Accordingly, the remedy should not necessarily require either the admission of women to VMI, or the creation of a VMI clone for women. An adequate remedy in my opinion might be a demonstration by Virginia that its interest in educating men in a single-sex environment is matched by its interest in educating women in a single-sex institution. . . . If a state decides to create single-sex programs, the state would, I expect, consider the public's interest and demand in designing curricula. And rightfully so. But the state should avoid assuming demand based on stereotypes; it must not assume *a priori,* without evidence, that there would be no interest in a women's school of civil engineering, or in a men's school of nursing.

In the end, the women's institution Virginia proposes, VWIL, fails as a remedy, because it is distinctly inferior to the existing men's institution and will continue to be for the foreseeable future. VWIL simply is not, in any sense, the institution that VMI is. In particular, VWIL is a program appended to a private college, not a self-standing institution; and VWIL is substantially underfunded as compared to VMI. I therefore ultimately agree with the Court that Virginia has not provided an adequate remedy.

JUSTICE SCALIA, dissenting.

Today the Court shuts down an institution that has served the people of the Commonwealth of Virginia with pride and distinction for over a century and a half. To achieve that desired result, it rejects (contrary to our established practice) the factual findings of two courts below, sweeps aside the precedents of this Court, and ignores the history of our people. As to facts: it explicitly rejects the finding that there exist "gender-based developmental differences" supporting Virginia's restriction of the "adversative" method to only a men's institution, and the finding that the all-male composition of the Virginia Military Institute (VMI) is essential to that institution's character. As to precedent: it drastically revises our established standards for reviewing sex-based classifications. And as to history: it counts for nothing the long tradition, enduring down to the present, of men's military colleges supported by both States and the Federal Government.

Much of the Court's opinion is devoted to deprecating the closed-mindedness of our forebears with regard to women's education, and even with regard to the treatment of women in areas that have nothing to do with education. Closed-minded they were—as every age is, including our own, with regard to matters it cannot guess, because it simply does not consider them debatable. The virtue of a democratic system with a First Amendment is that it readily enables the people, over time, to be persuaded that what they took for granted is not so, and to change their laws accordingly. That system is destroyed if the smug assurances of each age are removed from the democratic process and written into the Constitution. So to counterbalance the Court's criticism of our ancestors, let me say a word in their praise: they left us free to change. The same cannot be said of this most illiberal Court, which has embarked on a course of inscribing one after another of the current preferences of the society (and in some cases only the counter-majoritarian preferences of the society's law-trained elite) into our Basic Law. Today it enshrines the notion that no substantial educational value is to be served by an all-men's military academy—so that the decision by the people of Virginia to maintain such an institution denies equal protection to women who cannot attend that institution but can attend others. Since it is entirely clear that the Constitution of the United States—the old one—takes no sides in this educational debate, I dissent.

[O]ur current equal-protection jurisprudence . . . regards this Court as free to evaluate everything under the sun by applying one of three tests: "rational basis" scrutiny, intermediate scrutiny, or strict scrutiny. These tests are no more scientific than their names suggest, and a further element of randomness is added by the fact that it is largely up to us which test will be applied in each case. Strict scrutiny, we have said, is reserved for state "classifications based on race or national origin and classifications affecting fundamental rights," *Clark v. Jeter,* 486 U.S. 456 (1988). It is my position that the term "fundamental rights" should be limited to "interest[s] traditionally protected by our society." *Michael H. v. Gerald D.* (1989); but the Court has not accepted that view, so that strict scrutiny will be applied to the deprivation of whatever sort of right we consider "fundamental." We have no established criterion for "intermediate scrutiny" either, but essentially apply it when it seems like a good idea to load the dice. So far it has been applied to content-neutral restrictions that place an incidental burden on speech, to disabilities attendant to illegitimacy, and to discrimination on the basis of sex.

I have no problem with a system of abstract tests such as rational-basis, intermediate, and strict scrutiny (though I think we can do better than applying strict scrutiny and intermediate scrutiny whenever we feel like it). Such formulas are essential to evaluating whether the new restrictions that a changing society constantly imposes upon private conduct comport with that "equal protection" our society has always accorded in the past. But in my view the function of this Court is to preserve our society's values regarding (among other things) equal protection, not to revise them; to prevent backsliding from the degree of restriction the Constitution imposed upon democratic government, not to prescribe, on our own authority, progressively higher degrees. For that reason it is my view that, whatever abstract tests we may choose to devise, they cannot supersede—and indeed ought to be crafted so as to reflect—those constant and unbroken national traditions that embody the people's understanding of ambiguous constitutional texts. More specifically, it is my view that "when a practice not expressly prohibited by the text of the Bill of Rights bears the endorsement of a long tradition of open, widespread, and unchallenged use that dates back to the beginning of the Republic, we have no proper basis for striking it down." *Rutan v. Republican Party of Illinois* (1990). The same applies, *mutatis mutandis,* to a practice asserted to be in violation of the post–Civil War Fourteenth Amendment. . . .

Today, . . . change is forced upon Virginia, and reversion to single-sex education is prohibited nationwide, not by democratic processes but by order of this Court. Even while bemoaning the sorry, bygone days of "fixed notions" concerning women's education, the Court favors current notions so fixedly that it is willing to write them into the Constitution of the United States by application of custom-built "tests." This is not the interpretation of a Constitution, but the creation of one.

And the rationale of today's decision is sweeping: for sex-based classifications, a redefinition of intermediate scrutiny that makes it indistinguishable from strict scrutiny. Indeed, the Court indicates that if any program restricted to one sex is "uniqu[e]," it must be opened to members of the opposite sex "who have the will and capacity" to participate in it. I suggest that the single-sex program that will not be capable of being characterized as "unique" is not only unique but nonexistent.

In any event, regardless of whether the Court's rationale leaves some small amount of room for lawyers to argue, it ensures that single-sex public education is functionally dead. The costs of litigating the constitutionality of a single-sex education program, and the risks of ultimately losing that litigation, are simply too high to be embraced by public officials. Any person with standing to challenge any sex-based classification can haul the State into federal court and compel it to establish by evidence (presumably in the form of expert testimony) that there is an "exceedingly persuasive justification" for the classification. Should the courts happen to interpret that vacuous phrase as establishing a standard that is not utterly impossible of achievement, there is considerable risk that whether the standard has been met will not be determined on the basis of the record evidence—indeed, that will necessarily be the approach of any court that seeks to walk the path the Court has trod today. No state official in his right mind will buy such a high-cost, high-risk lawsuit by commencing a single-sex program. The enemies of single-sex education have won; by persuading only seven Justices (five would have been enough) that their view of the world is enshrined in the Constitution, they have effectively imposed that view on all 50 States.

Rostker v. Goldberg
453 U.S. 57 (1981)

The Military Selective Service Act (MSSA) authorizes the president to require the registration for possible military service of males, but not females, the purpose of registration being to facilitate any eventual conscription under the act. Registration for the draft was discontinued by a presidential proclamation in 1975, but President Jimmy Carter decided in 1980 that it was necessary to reactivate the registration process and requested Congress to allocate funds for that purpose. He also recommended that Congress amend the MSSA to permit the registration and conscription of women. Although Congress agreed to reactivate the registration process, it declined to amend the MSSA to permit the registration of women and allocated funds only to register males. Thereafter, the president ordered the registration of specified groups of young men. A lawsuit was brought against Bernard Rostker, director of the Selective Service, by several men, challenging the act's constitutionality. A three-judge district court held that the act's gender-based discrimination violated the Due Process Clause of the Fifth Amendment and enjoined registration under the act, whereupon the US government appealed to the Supreme Court. Opinion of the Court: Rehnquist, Burger, Stewart, Blackmun, Powell, Stevens. Dissenting opinions: White, Brennan; Marshall, Brennan.

JUSTICE REHNQUIST delivered the opinion of the Court.

The question presented is whether the Military Selective Service Act . . . violates the Fifth Amendment to the United States Constitution in authorizing the President to require the registration of males and not females. . . .

Congress is given the power under the Constitution "To raise and support Armies," "To provide and maintain a Navy," and "To make Rules for the Government and Regulation of the land and naval Forces." . . . Pursuant to this grant of authority Congress has enacted the Military Selective Service Act. . . . Section 3 of the Act . . . empowers the President, by proclamation, to require the registration of "every male citizen" and male resident aliens between the ages of 18 and 26. . . . The MSSA registration provision serves no other purpose beyond providing a pool for subsequent induction.

Registration for the draft under §3 was discontinued in 1975. . . . In early 1980, President Carter determined that it was necessary to reactivate the draft registration process. The immediate impetus for this decision was the Soviet armed invasion of Afghanistan. . . . The resulting crisis in Southwestern Asia convinced the President that the "time has come" "to use his present authority to require registration . . . as a necessary step to preserving or enhancing our national security interests." . . . The Selective Service System had been inactive, however, and funds were needed before reactivating registration. The President therefore recommended that funds be transferred from the Department of Defense to the separate Selective Service System. . . . He also recommended that Congress take action to amend the MSSA to permit the registration and conscription of women as well as men. . . .

Congress agreed that it was necessary to reactivate the registration process, and allocated funds for that purpose in a joint resolution which passed the House on April 22 and the Senate on June 12. . . . The resolution did not allocate all the funds originally requested by the President, but only those necessary to register males. . . . Although Congress considered the question at great length, . . . it declined to amend the MSSA to permit the registration of women.

On July 2, 1980, the President, by proclamation, ordered the registration of specified groups of young men pursuant to the authority conferred by §3 of the Act. . . .

Whenever called upon to judge the constitutionality of an Act of Congress—"the gravest and most delicate duty that this Court is called upon to perform" . . . the Court accords "great weight to the decisions of Congress." . . . The Congress is a coequal branch of government whose members take the same oath we do to uphold the Constitution of the United States. . . . The customary deference accorded the judgments of Congress is certainly appropriate when, as here, Congress specifically considered the question of the Act's constitutionality. . . .

This is not, however, merely a case involving the customary deference accorded congressional decisions. The case arises in the context of Congress' authority over national defense and military affairs, and perhaps in no other area has the Court accorded Congress greater deference. In rejecting the registration of women, Congress explicitly relied upon its constitutional powers under Art. I, §8, cls. 12–14. . . . This Court has consistently recognized Congress' "broad constitutional power" to raise and regulate armies and navies, *Schlesinger v. Ballard* (1975).

Not only is the scope of Congress' constitutional power in this area broad, but the lack of competence on the part of the courts is marked. In *Gilligan v. Morgan* . . . (1973), the Court noted: "It is difficult to conceive of an area of governmental activity in which the courts have less competence. The complex, subtle, and professional decisions as to the composition, training, equipping, and control of a military force are essentially professional military judgments, subject always to civilian control of the Legislative and Executive branches." . . .

None of this is to say that Congress is free to disregard the Constitution when it acts in the area of military affairs. In that area, as any other, Congress remains subject to the limitations of the Due Process Clause, . . . but the tests and limitations to be applied may differ because of the military context. We of course do not abdicate our ultimate responsibility to decide the constitutional question, but simply recognize that the Constitution itself requires such deference to congressional choice. . . . In deciding the question before us we must be particularly careful not to substitute our judgment of what is desirable for that of Congress, or our own evaluation of evidence for a reasonable evaluation by the Legislative Branch.

The District Court purported to recognize the appropriateness of deference to Congress when that body was exercising its constitutionally delegated authority over military affairs, . . . but it stressed that "we are not here concerned with military operations or day-to-day conduct of the military into which we have no desire to intrude." . . . Appellees also stress that this case involves civilians, not the military, and that "the impact of registration on the military is only indirect and attenuated." . . . We find these efforts to divorce registration from the military and national defense context, with all the deference called for in that context, singularly unpersuasive. . . . Registration is not an end in itself in the civilian world but rather the first step in the induction process into the military one, and Congress specifically linked its consideration of registration to induction. . . . Congressional judgments concerning registration and the draft are based on judgments concerning military operations and needs . . . and the deference unquestionably due the latter judgments is necessarily required in assessing the former as well.

The Solicitor General argues . . . that this Court should scrutinize the MSSA only to determine if the distinction drawn between men and women bears a rational relation to some legitimate government purpose, . . . and should not examine the Act under the heightened scrutiny with which we have approached gender-based discrimination. . . . We do not think that the substantive guarantee of due process or certainty in the law will be advanced by any further "refinement" in the applicable tests as suggested by the Government. Announced degrees of "deference" to legislative judgments, just as levels of "scrutiny" which this Court announces that it applies to particular classifications made by a legislative body, may all too readily become facile abstractions used to justify a result. In this case the courts are called upon to decide whether Congress, acting under an explicit constitutional grant of authority, has by that action transgressed an explicit guarantee of individual rights which limits the authority so conferred. Simply labelling the legislative decision "military" on the one hand or "gender-based" on the other does not automatically guide a court to the correct constitutional result.

No one could deny that under the test of *Craig v. Boren* [1976] . . . the Government's interest in raising and supporting armies is an "important governmental interest." Congress and its committees carefully considered and debated two alternative means of furthering that interest: the first was to register only males for potential conscription, and the other was to register both sexes. Congress chose the former alternative. When that decision is challenged on equal protection grounds, the question a court must decide is not which alternative it would have chosen, had it been the primary decision-maker, but whether that chosen by Congress denies equal protection of the laws. . . .

This case is quite different from several of the gender-based discrimination cases we have considered in that, despite appellees' assertions, Congress did not act "unthinkingly" or "reflexively and not for any considered reason." . . . The question of registering women for the draft not only received considerable national attention and was the subject of wide-ranging public debate, but also was extensively considered by Congress in hearings, floor debate, and in committee. Hearings held by both Houses of Congress in response to the President's request for authorization to register women adduced extensive testimony and evidence concerning the issue. . . . These hearings built on other hearings held the previous year addressed to the same question.

The House declined to provide for the registration of women when it passed the Joint Resolution allocating funds for the Selective Service System. . . . When the Senate considered the Joint resolution, it defeated, after extensive debate, an amendment which in effect would have authorized the registration of women. . . .

While proposals to register women were being rejected in the course of transferring funds to register males, committees in both Houses which had conducted hearings on the issue were also rejecting the registration of women. The House Subcommittee on Military Personnel of the House Armed Services Committee tabled a bill which would have amended the MSSA to authorize registration of women. . . . The Senate Armed Services Committee rejected a proposal to register women, . . . as it had one year before. . . .

The foregoing clearly establishes that the decision to exempt women from registration was not the "accidental byproduct of a traditional way of thinking about women." . . . The issue

was considered at great length and Congress clearly expressed its purpose and intent. . . .

The MSSA established a plan for maintaining "adequate armed strength . . . to ensure the security of the nation." . . . Registration is the first step "in a united and continuous process designed to raise an army speedily and efficiently," . . . and Congress provided for the reactivation of registration in order to "provide the means for the early delivery of inductees in an emergency." . . . Congress rather clearly linked the need for renewed registration with its views on the character of a subsequent draft. Any assessment of the congressional purpose and its chosen means must therefore consider the registration scheme as a prelude to a draft in a time of national emergency. Any other approach would not be testing the Act in light of the purposes Congress sought to achieve.

Congress determined that any future draft, which would be facilitated by the registration scheme, would be characterized by a need for combat troops. The Senate Report explained, in a specific finding later adopted by both Houses, that "if mobilization were to be ordered in a wartime scenario, the primary manpower need would be for combat replacements." . . .

Women as a group, however, unlike men as a group, are not eligible for combat. The restrictions on the participation of women in combat in the Navy and Air Force are statutory. . . . The Army and Marine Corps preclude the use of women in combat as a matter of established policy. . . . Congress specifically recognized and endorsed the exclusion of women from combat in exempting women from registration. In the words of the Senate Report: "The principle that women should not intentionally and routinely engage in combat is fundamental, and enjoys wide support among our people." . . .

The existence of the combat restrictions clearly indicates the basis for Congress' decision to exempt women from registration. The purpose of registration was to prepare for a draft of combat troops. Since women are excluded from combat, Congress concluded that they would not be needed in the event of a draft, and therefore decided not to register them. . . .

The District Court stressed that the military need for women was irrelevant to the issue of their registration. As that court put it: "Congress could not constitutionally require registration under MSSA of only black citizens or only white citizens, or single out any political or religious group simply because those groups contained sufficient persons to fill the needs of the Selective Service System." . . . This reasoning is beside the point. The reason women are exempt from registration is not because military needs can be met by drafting men. This is not a case of Congress arbitrarily choosing to burden one of two similarly situated groups, such as would be the case with an all-black or all-white, or an all-Catholic or all-Lutheran, or an all-Republican or all-Democratic registration. Men and women, because of the combat restrictions on women, are simply not similarly situated for purposes of a draft or registration for a draft.

Congress' decision to authorize the registration of only men, therefore, does not violate the Due Process Clause. The exemption of women from registration is not only sufficiently but closely related to Congress' purpose in authorizing registration. . . . The fact that Congress and the Executive have decided that women should not serve in combat fully justifies Congress in not authorizing their registration, since the purpose of registration is to develop a pool of potential combat troops. As was the case in *Schlesinger v. Ballard, supra,* "the gender classification is not invidious, but rather realistically reflects the fact that the sexes are not similarly situated" in this case. . . . The Constitution requires that Congress treat similarly situated persons similarly, not that it engage in gestures of superficial equality.

In holding the MSSA constitutionally invalid the District Court relied heavily on the President's decision to seek authority to register women and the testimony of members of the Executive Branch and the military in support of that decision. . . . "As stated by the Administration's witnesses before Congress, however, the President's decision to ask for authority to register women is based on equity." . . . This was also the basis for the testimony by military officials. . . . The Senate Report, evaluating the testimony before the Committee, recognized that "the argument for registration and induction of women . . . is not based on military

necessity, but on considerations of equity." . . . Congress was certainly entitled, in the exercise of its constitutional powers to raise and regulate armies and navies, to focus on the question of military need rather than "equity." . . .

In light of the foregoing, we conclude that Congress acted well within its constitutional authority when it authorized the registration of men, and not women, under the Military Selective Service Act. The decision of the District Court holding otherwise is accordingly

Reversed.

JUSTICE MARSHALL, with whom JUSTICE BRENNAN joins, dissenting.

The Court today places its imprimatur on one of the most potent remaining public expressions of "ancient canards about the proper role of women." . . . It upholds a statute that requires males but not females to register for the draft, and which thereby categorically excludes women from a fundamental civic obligation. Because I believe the Court's decision is inconsistent with the Constitution's guarantee of equal protection of the laws, I dissent.

By now it should be clear that statutes like the MSSA, which discriminate on the basis of gender, must be examined under the "heightened" scrutiny mandated by *Craig v. Boren* (1976). Under this test, a gender-based classification cannot withstand constitutional challenge unless the classification is substantially related to the achievement of an important governmental objective. . . . This test applies whether the classification discriminates against males or females. . . . The party defending the challenged classification carries the burden of demonstrating both the importance of the governmental objective it serves and the substantial relationship between the discriminatory means and the asserted end. . . . Consequently, before we can sustain the MSSA, the Government must demonstrate that the gender-based classification it employs bears "a close and substantial relationship to [the achievement of] important governmental objectives." . . .

. . . I agree with the majority, . . . that "none could deny that . . . the Government's interest in raising and supporting armies is an 'important governmental interest.'" Consequently, the first part of the *Craig v. Boren* test is satisfied.

But the question remains whether the discriminatory means employed itself substantially serves the statutory end. . . . When, as here, a federal law that classifies on the basis of gender is challenged as violating this constitutional guarantee, it is ultimately for this Court, not Congress, to decide whether there exists the constitutionally required "close and substantial relationship" between the discriminatory means employed and the asserted governmental objective. . . . In my judgment, there simply is no basis for concluding in this case that excluding women from registration is substantially related to the achievement of a concededly important governmental interest in maintaining an effective defense. . . .

In the first place, although the Court purports to apply the *Craig v. Boren* test, the "similarly situated" analysis the Court employs is in fact significantly different from the *Craig v. Boren* approach. . . . The Court essentially reasons that the gender classification employed by the MSSA is constitutionally permissible because nondiscrimination is not necessary to achieve the purpose of registration to prepare for a draft of combat troops. In other words, the majority concludes that women may be excluded from registration because they will not be needed in the event of a draft.

This analysis, however, focuses on the wrong question. The relevant inquiry under the *Craig v. Boren* test is not whether a *gender-neutral* classification would substantially advance important governmental interests. Rather, the question is whether the gender-based classification is itself substantially related to the achievement of the asserted governmental interest. Thus, the Government's task in this case is to demonstrate that excluding women from registration substantially furthers the goal of preparing for a draft of combat troops. Or to put it another way, the Government must show that registering women would substantially impede its efforts to prepare for such a draft. Under our precedents, the Government cannot meet this burden without showing that a gender-neutral statute would be a less effective means of attaining this end. . . . In this case, the Government makes no claim that preparing for a draft of combat troops cannot be accomplished just as effectively by *registering* both men and women but *drafting* only men if only men turn out to be needed. Nor can the Government argue that this alternative entails the additional cost and administrative inconvenience of registering women. This Court has repeatedly stated that the administrative convenience of employing a gender classification is not an adequate constitutional justification under the *Craig v. Boren* test. . . .

The fact that registering women in no way obstructs the governmental interest in preparing for a draft of combat troops points up a second flaw in the Court's analysis. The Court essentially reduces the question of the constitutionality of male-only *registration* to the validity of a hypothetical program for *conscripting* only men. The Court posits a draft in which *all* conscripts are either assigned to those specific combat posts presently closed to women or must be available for rotation into such positions. . . . If it could indeed be guaranteed in advance that conscription would be reimposed by Congress only in circumstances where, and in a form under which, all conscripts would have to be trained for and assigned to combat or combat rotation positions from which women are categorically excluded, then it could be argued that registration of women would be pointless.

But of course, no such guarantee is possible. Certainly, nothing about the MSSA limits Congress to reinstituting the draft only in such circumstances. . . .

. . . The discussion and findings in the Senate Report do not enable the Government to carry its burden of demonstrating that *completely* excluding women from the draft by excluding them from registration substantially furthers important governmental objectives. . . . Congressional enactments in the area of military affairs must, like all other laws, be *judged* by the standards of the Constitution. For the Constitution is the supreme law of the land and *all* legislation must conform to the principles it lay down. . . .

Furthermore, "when it appears that an Act of Congress conflicts with [a constitutional] provision, we have no choice but to enforce the paramount commands of the Constitution. We are sworn to do no less. We cannot push back the limits of the Constitution merely to accommodate challenged legislation." . . . In some 106 instances since this court was established it has determined that congressional action exceeded the bounds of the Constitution. I believe the same is true of this statute. In an attempt to avoid its constitutional obligation, the Court today "pushes back the limits of the Constitution" to accommodate an Act of Congress.

I would affirm the judgment of the District Court.

Shapiro v. Thompson
394 U.S. 618 (1969)

Vivian Marie Thompson, a pregnant nineteen-year-old unwed mother who already had one child, moved to Connecticut from Massachusetts in June 1966. Two months later, she applied for public assistance money under the Aid to Families with Dependent Children program. Her application was denied on the sole ground that she had not met the state's one-year residency requirement, which was a prerequisite for eligibility to receive aid. She thereupon brought suit against Bernard Shapiro, the Connecticut welfare commissioner, in federal district court. The three-judge court found the state residency requirement unconstitutional because of its "chilling effect on the right to travel." Shapiro appealed to the Supreme Court. The Court heard this case in conjunction with similar cases from Pennsylvania and the District of Columbia, both of which also involved the validity of one-year residency requirements. Opinion of the Court: Brennan, Douglas, Stewart, White, Fortas, Marshall. Concurring opinion: Stewart. Dissenting opinions: Warren, Black; Harlan.

JUSTICE BRENNAN delivered the opinion of the Court.

There is no dispute that the effect of the waiting-period requirement in each case is to create two classes of needy resident families indistinguishable from each other except that one is composed of residents who have resided a year or more, and the second of residents who have resided less than a year, in the jurisdiction. On the basis of this sole difference the first class is granted and the second class is denied welfare aid upon which may depend the ability of the families to obtain the very means to subsist—food, shelter, and other necessities of life. In each case, the District Court found that appellees met the test for residence in their jurisdictions, as well as all other eligibility requirements except the requirement of residence for a full year prior to their applications. On reargument, appellees' central contention is that the statutory prohibition of benefits to residents of less than a year creates a classification which constitutes an invidious discrimination denying them equal protection of the laws. We agree. The interests which appellants assert are promoted by the classification either may not constitutionally be promoted by government or are not compelling governmental interests.

Primarily, appellants justify the waiting-period requirement as a protective device to preserve the fiscal integrity of state public assistance programs. It is asserted that people who require welfare assistance during their first year of residence in a State are likely to become continuing burdens on state welfare programs. Therefore, the argument runs, if such people can be deterred from entering the jurisdiction by denying them welfare benefits during the first year, state programs to assist long-time residents will not be impaired by a substantial influx of indigent newcomers.

There is weighty evidence that exclusion from the jurisdiction of the poor who need or may need relief was the specific objective of these provisions. In the Congress, sponsors of federal legislation to eliminate all residence requirements have been consistently opposed by representatives of state and local welfare agencies who have stressed the fears of the States that elimination of the requirements would result in a heavy influx of individuals into States providing the most generous benefits. . . .

We do not doubt that the one-year waiting period device is well suited to discourage the influx of poor families in need of assistance. An indigent who desires to migrate, resettle, find a new job, and start a new life will doubtless hesitate if he knows that he must risk making the move without the possibility of falling back on state welfare assistance during his first year of residence when his need may be most acute. But the purpose of inhibiting migration by needy persons into the State is constitutionally impermissible.

This Court long ago recognized that the nature of our Federal Union and our constitutional concepts of personal liberty unite to require that all citizens be free to travel throughout the length and breadth of our land uninhibited by statutes, rules, or regulations which unreasonably burden or restrict this movement. . . .

We have no occasion to ascribe the source of this right to travel interstate to a particular constitutional provision. It suffices that, as Mr. Justice Stewart said for the Court in *United States v. Guest* (1966): "The constitutional right to travel from one State to another . . . occupies a position fundamental to the concept of our Federal Union. It is a right that has been firmly established and repeatedly recognized."

" . . . [The] right finds no explicit mention in the Constitution. The reason, it has been suggested, is that a right so elementary was conceived from the beginning to be a necessary concomitant of the stronger Union the Constitution created. In any event, freedom to travel throughout the United States has long been recognized as a basic right under the Constitution." . . .

Alternatively, appellants argue that even if it is impermissible for a State to attempt to deter the entry of all indigents, the challenged classification may be justified as a permissible state attempt to discourage those indigents who would enter the State solely to obtain larger benefits. We observe first that none of the statutes before us is tailored to serve that objective. Rather, the class of barred newcomers is all-inclusive, lumping the great majority who come to the State for other purposes with those who come for the sole purpose of collecting higher benefits. In actual operation, therefore, the three statutes enact what in effect are nonrebuttable presumptions that every applicant for assistance in his first year of residence came to the jurisdiction solely to obtain higher benefits.

Nothing whatever in any of these records supplies any basis in fact for such a presumption.

More fundamentally, a State may no more try to fence out those indigents who seek higher welfare benefits than it may try to fence out indigents generally. Implicit in any such distinction is the notion that indigents who enter a State with the hope of securing higher welfare benefits are somehow less deserving than indigents who do not take this consideration into account. But we do not perceive why a mother who is seeking to make a new life for herself and her children should be regarded as less deserving because she considers, among other factors, the level of a State's public assistance. Surely such a mother is no less deserving than a mother who moves into a particular State in order to take advantage of its better educational facilities. . . .

We recognize that a State has a valid interest in preserving the fiscal integrity of its programs. It may legitimately attempt to limit its expenditures, whether for public assistance, public education, or any other program. But a State may not accomplish such a purpose by invidious distinctions between classes of its citizens. It could not, for example, reduce expenditures for education by barring indigent children from its schools. Similarly, in the cases before us, appellants must do more than show that denying welfare benefits to new residents saves money. The saving of welfare costs cannot justify an otherwise invidious classification. . . .

Appellants next advance as justification certain administrative and related governmental objectives allegedly served by the waiting-period requirement. They argue that the requirement (1) facilitates the planning of the welfare budget; (2) provides an objective test of residency; (3) minimizes the opportunity for recipients fraudulently to receive payments from more than one jurisdiction; and (4) encourages early entry of new residents into the labor force.

. . . We reject appellants' argument that a mere showing of a rational relationship between the waiting period and these four admittedly permissible state objectives will suffice to justify the classification. . . . Any classification which serves to penalize the exercise of that right, unless shown to be necessary to promote a *compelling* governmental interest, is unconstitutional. . . .

JUSTICE HARLAN, dissenting. . . .

In upholding the equal protection argument, the Court has applied an equal protection doctrine of relatively recent vintage: the rule that statutory classifications which either are based upon certain "suspect" criteria or affect "fundamental rights" will be held to deny equal protection unless justified by a "compelling" governmental interest.

I think that this branch of the "compelling interest" doctrine is sound when applied to racial classifications, for historically the Equal Protection Clause was largely a product of the desire to eradicate legal distinctions founded upon race.

However, I believe that the more recent extensions have been unwise. . . .

The second branch of the "compelling interest" principle is even more troublesome. For it has been held that a statutory classification is subject to the "compelling interest" test if the result of the classification may be to affect a "fundamental right," . . . I think the "compelling interest" doctrine particularly unfortunate and unnecessary. It is unfortunate because it creates an exception which threatens to swallow the standard equal protection rule. Virtually every state statute affects important rights. This Court has repeatedly held, for example, that the traditional equal protection standard is applicable to statutory classifications affecting such fundamental matters as the right to pursue a particular occupation, the right to receive greater or smaller wages or to work more or less hours, and the right to inherit property. Rights such as these are in principle indistinguishable from those involved here, and to extend the "compelling interest" rule to all cases in which such rights are affected would go far toward making this Court a "super-legislature." But when a statute affects only matters not mentioned in the Federal Constitution and is not arbitrary or irrational, I must reiterate that I know of nothing which entitles this Court to pick out particular human activities, characterize them as "fundamental," and give them added protection under an unusually stringent equal protection test. . . .

I do not consider that the factors which have been urged . . . are sufficient to render unconstitutional these state and federal enactments. It is said, first, that this Court . . . has acknowledged that the right to travel interstate is a "fundamental" freedom. Second, it is contended that the governmental objectives mentioned above either are ephemeral or could be accomplished by means which do not impinge as heavily on the right to travel, and hence that the requirements are unconstitutional because they "sweep unnecessarily broadly and thereby invade the area of protected freedoms." . . .

Taking all of these competing considerations into account, I believe that the balance definitely favors constitutionality. In reaching that conclusion, I do not minimize the importance of the right to travel interstate. However, the impact of residence conditions upon that right is indirect and apparently quite insubstantial. On the other hand, the governmental purposes served by the requirements are legitimate and real, and the residence requirements are clearly suited to their accomplishment. To abolish residence requirements might well discourage highly worthwhile experimentation in the welfare field. . . . Moreover, although the appellees assert that the same objectives could have been achieved by less restrictive means, this is an area in which the judiciary should be especially slow to fetter the judgment of Congress and of some 46 state legislatures in the choice of methods. Residence requirements have advantages, such as administrative simplicity and relative certainty, which are not shared by the alternative solutions proposed by the appellees. In these circumstances, I cannot find that the burden imposed by residence requirements upon ability to travel outweighs the governmental interests in their continued employment. Nor do I believe that the period of residence required in these cases— one year—is so excessively long as to justify a finding of unconstitutionality on that score.

I conclude with the following observations. Today's decision, it seems to me, reflects to an unusual degree the current notion that this Court possesses a peculiar wisdom all its own whose capacity to lead this Nation out of its present troubles is contained only by the limits of judicial ingenuity in contriving new constitutional principles to meet each problem as it arises. For anyone who, like myself, believes that it is an essential function of this Court to maintain the constitutional divisions between state and federal authority and among the three branches of the Federal Government, today's decision is a step in the wrong direction. This resurgence of the expansive view of "equal protection" carries the seeds of more judicial interference with the state and federal legislative process, much more indeed than does the judicial application of "due process" according to traditional concepts, . . . about which some members of this Court have expressed fears as to its potentialities for setting us judges "at large." I consider it particularly unfortunate that this judicial roadblock to the powers of Congress in this field should occur at the very threshold of the current discussions regarding the "federalizing" of these aspects of welfare relief.

San Antonio Independent School District v. Rodriguez
411 U.S. 1 (1973)

The financing of public elementary and secondary education in Texas is a product of state and local participation. Almost half of the revenues are derived from a largely state-funded program designed to provide basic minimum education in every school. Each district then supplements this state aid through an ad valorem tax on property within its jurisdiction. Demetrio Rodriguez and others brought a class action on behalf of school-children who were members of poor families that resided in school districts with low property tax bases, claiming that the Texas system's reliance on local property taxation favored the more affluent and that it violated equal-protection requirements because of the substantial interdistrict disparities in per pupil expenditures that resulted primarily from differences in the value of assessable property among the districts. A three-judge federal district court, finding that wealth is a "suspect" classification and that education is a "fundamental right," concluded that the system could be upheld only upon a showing (which appellants failed to make) that there was a compelling state interest for the system. The court further concluded that appellants failed even to demonstrate a rational basis for Texas's system. The state appealed. Opinion of the Court: <u>Powell</u>, Burger, Stewart, Blackmun, Rehnquist. Concurring opinion: <u>Stewart</u>. Dissenting opinions: <u>Brennan</u>; <u>White</u>, Douglas, Brennan; <u>Marshall</u>, Douglas.

JUSTICE POWELL delivered the opinion of the Court.

. . . We must decide, first, whether the Texas system of financing public education operates to the disadvantage of some suspect class or impinges upon a fundamental right explicitly or implicitly protected by the Constitution, thereby requiring strict judicial scrutiny. If so, the judgment of the District Court should be affirmed. If not, the Texas scheme must still be examined to determine whether it rationally furthers some legitimate, articulated state purpose and therefore does not constitute an invidious discrimination in violation of the Equal Protection Clause of the Fourteenth Amendment. . . .

We are unable to agree that this case, which in significant aspects is *sui generis,* may be so neatly fitted into the conventional mosaic of constitutional analysis under the Equal Protection Clause. Indeed, for the several reasons that follow, we find neither the suspect classification nor the fundamental interest analysis persuasive. . . .

The precedents of this Court provide the proper starting point. The individuals or groups of individuals who constituted the class discriminated against in our prior cases shared two distinguishing characteristics: because of their impecunity they were completely unable to pay for some desired benefit, and as a consequence, they sustained an absolute deprivation of a meaningful opportunity to enjoy that benefit. . . .

. . . Even a cursory examination, however, demonstrates that neither of the two distinguishing characteristics of wealth classifications can be found here. First, in support of their charge that the system discriminates against the "poor," appellees have made no effort to demonstrate that it operates to the peculiar disadvantage of any class fairly definable as indigent, or as composed of persons whose incomes are beneath any designated poverty level. Indeed, there is reason to believe that the poorest families are not necessarily clustered in the poorest property districts. A recent and exhaustive study of school districts in Connecticut concluded that "[i]t is clearly incorrect . . . to contend that the 'poor' live in 'poor' districts. . . ." Defining "poor" families as those below the Bureau of the Census "poverty level," the Connecticut study found, not surprisingly, that the poor were clustered around commercial and industrial areas—those same areas that provide the most attractive sources of property tax income for school districts. Whether a similar pattern would be discovered in Texas is not known, but there is no basis on the record in this case for assuming that the poorest people—defined by reference to any level of absolute impecunity—are concentrated in the poorest districts.

Second, neither appellees nor the District Court addressed the fact that, unlike each of the foregoing cases, lack of personal resources has not occasioned an absolute deprivation of the desired benefit. The argument here is not that the children in districts having relatively low assessable property values are receiving no public education; rather, it is that they are receiving a poorer quality education than that available to children in districts having more assessable wealth. Apart from the unsettled and disputed question whether the quality of education may be determined by the amount of money expended for it, a sufficient answer to appellees' argument is that at least where wealth is involved the Equal Protection Clause does not require absolute equality or precisely equal advantages. Nor, indeed, in view of the infinite variables affecting the educational process, can any system assure equal quality of education except in the most relative sense. . . .

For these two reasons—the absence of any evidence that the financing system discriminates against any definable category of "poor" people or that it results in the absolute deprivation of education—the disadvantaged class is not susceptible to identification in traditional terms. . . .

We thus conclude that the Texas system does not operate to the peculiar disadvantage of any

suspect class. But in recognition of the fact that this Court has never heretofore held that wealth discrimination alone provides an adequate basis for invoking strict scrutiny, appellees have not relied solely on this contention. They also assert that the State's system impermissibly interferes with the exercise of a "fundamental" right and that accordingly the prior decisions of this Court require the application of the strict standard of judicial review. . . . It is this question—whether education is a fundamental right, in the sense that it is among the rights and liberties protected by the Constitution—which has so consumed the attention of courts and commentators in recent years.

In *Brown v. Board of Education* (1954), a unanimous Court recognized that "education is perhaps the most important function of state and local governments." . . . What was said there in the context of racial discrimination has lost none of its vitality with the passage of time: "Compulsory school attendance laws and the great expenditures for education both demonstrate our recognition of the importance of education to our democratic society. It is required in the performance of our most basic responsibilities, even service in the armed forces. It is the very foundation of good citizenship. Today it is a principal instrument in awakening the child to cultural values, in preparing him for later professional training, and in helping him to adjust normally to his environment. In these days, it is doubtful that any child may reasonably be expected to succeed in life if he is denied the opportunity of an education. Such an opportunity, where the state has undertaken to provide it, is a right which must be made available to all on equal terms." . . . This theme, expressing an abiding respect for the vital role of education in a free society, may be found in numerous opinions of Justices of this Court writing both before and after *Brown* was decided. . . .

Nothing this court holds today in any way detracts from our historic dedication to public education. We are in complete agreement with the conclusion of the three-judge panel below that "the grave significance of education both to the individual and to our society" cannot be doubted. But the importance of a service performed by the State does not determine whether it must be regarded as fundamental for purposes of examination under the Equal Protection Clause.

. . . It is not the province of this Court to create substantive constitutional rights in the name of guaranteeing equal protection of the laws. Thus the key to discovering whether education is "fundamental" is not to be found in comparisons of the relative societal significance of education as opposed to subsistence or housing. Nor is it to be found by weighing whether education is as important as the right to travel. Rather, the answer lies in assessing whether there is a right to education explicitly or implicitly guaranteed by the Constitution. . . .

Education, of course, is not among the rights afforded explicit protection under our Federal Constitution. Nor do we find any basis for saying it is implicitly so protected. As we have said, the undisputed importance of education will not alone cause this Court to depart from the usual standard for reviewing a State's social and economic legislation. It is appellees' contention, however, that education is distinguishable from other services and benefits provided by the State because it bears a peculiarly close relationship to other rights and liberties accorded protection under the Constitution. Specifically, they insist that education is itself a fundamental personal right because it is essential to the effective exercise of First Amendment freedoms and to intelligent utilization of the right to vote. In asserting a nexus between speech and education, appellees urge that the right to speak is meaningless unless the speaker is capable of articulating his thoughts intelligently and persuasively. The "marketplace of ideas" is an empty forum for those lacking basic communicative tools. Likewise, they argue that the corollary right to receive information becomes little more than a hollow privilege when the recipient has not been taught to read, assimilate, and utilize available knowledge.

A similar line of reasoning is pursued with respect to the right to vote. Exercise of the franchise, it is contended, cannot be divorced from the educational foundation of the voter. The electoral process, if reality is to conform to the democratic ideal, depends on an informed electorate: a voter cannot cast his ballot intelligently unless his reading skills and thought processes have been adequately developed.

We need not dispute any of these propositions. The Court has long afforded zealous protection against unjustifiable governmental interference with the individual's rights to speak and to vote. Yet we have never presumed to possess either the ability or the authority to guarantee to the citizenry the most *effective* speech or the most *informed* electoral choice. That these may be desirable goals of a system of freedom of expression and of a representative form of government is not to be doubted. These are indeed goals to be pursued by a people whose thoughts and beliefs are freed from governmental interference. But they are not values to be implemented by judicial intrusion into otherwise legitimate state activities.

Even if it were conceded that some identifiable quantum of education is a constitutionally protected prerequisite to the meaningful exercise of either right, we have no indication that the present levels of educational expenditure in Texas provide an education that falls short. Whatever merit appellees' argument might have if a State's financing system occasioned an absolute denial of educational opportunities to any of its children, that argument provides no basis for finding an interference with fundamental rights where only relative differences in spending levels are involved and where—as is true in the present case—no charge fairly could be made that the system fails to provide each child with an opportunity to acquire the basic minimal skills necessary for the enjoyment of the rights of speech and of full participation in the political process. . . .

We have carefully considered each of the arguments supportive of the District Court's finding that education is a fundamental right or liberty and have found those arguments unpersuasive. In one further respect we find this a particularly inappropriate case in which to subject state action to strict judicial scrutiny. The present case, . . . involves the most persistent and difficult questions of educational policy, another area in which this Court's lack of specialized knowledge and experience counsels against premature interference with the informed judgments made at the state and local levels. . . . On even the most basic questions in this area the scholars and educational experts are divided. Indeed, one of the hottest sources of controversy concerns the extent to which there is a demonstrable correlation between educational expenditures and the quality of education—an assumed correlation underlying virtually every legal conclusion drawn by the District Court in this case. Related to the questioned relationship between cost and quality is the equally unsettled controversy as to the proper goals of a system of public education. And the question regarding the most effective relationship between state boards of education and local school boards, in terms of their respective responsibilities and degrees of control, is now undergoing searching re-examination. The ultimate wisdom as to these and related problems of education is not likely to be defined for all time even by the scholars who now so earnestly debate the issues. In such circumstances the judiciary is well advised to refrain from interposing on the States inflexible constitutional restraints that could circumscribe or handicap the continued research and experimentation so vital to finding even partial solutions to educational problems and to keeping abreast of ever changing conditions. . . .

The foregoing considerations buttress our conclusion that Texas' system of public school finance is an inappropriate candidate for strict judicial scrutiny. These same considerations are relevant to the determination whether that system, with its conceded imperfections, nevertheless bears some rational relationship to a legitimate state purpose. It is to this question that we next turn our attention. . . .

. . . The Texas plan is not the result of hurried, ill-conceived legislation. It certainly is not the product of purposeful discrimination against any group or class. On the contrary, it is rooted in decades of experience in Texas and elsewhere, and in major part is the product of responsible studies by qualified people. In giving substance to the presumption of validity to which the Texas system is entitled . . . it is important to remember that at every stage of its development it has constituted a "rough accommodation" of interests in an effort to arrive at practical and workable solutions. . . . One

also must remember that the system here challenged is not peculiar to Texas or to any other State. In its essential characteristics the Texas plan for financing public education reflects what many educators for a half century have thought was an enlightened approach to a problem for which there is no perfect solution. We are unwilling to assume for ourselves a level of wisdom superior to that of legislators, scholars, and educational authorities in 49 States, especially where the alternatives proposed are only recently conceived and nowhere yet tested. The constitutional standard under the Equal Protection Clause is whether the challenged state action rationally furthers a legitimate state purpose or interest. . . . We hold that the Texas plan abundantly satisfies this standard.

JUSTICE WHITE, with whom JUSTICE DOUGLAS and JUSTICE BRENNAN join, dissenting. . . .

The Equal Protection Clause permits discriminations between classes but requires that the classification bear some rational relationship to a permissible object sought to be attained by the statute. It is not enough that the Texas system before us seeks to achieve the valid, rational purpose of maximizing local initiative; the means chosen by the State must also be rationally related to the end sought to be achieved. . . .

Neither Texas nor the majority heeds this rule. If the State aims at maximizing local initiative and local choice, by permitting school districts to resort to the real property tax if they choose to do so, it utterly fails in achieving its purpose in districts with property tax bases so low that there is little if any opportunity for interested parents, rich or poor, to augment school district revenues. Requiring the State to establish only that unequal treatment is in furtherance of a permissible goal, without also requiring the State to show that the means chosen to effectuate that goal are rationally related to its achievement, makes equal protection analysis no more than an empty gesture. In my view, the parents and children in Edgewood, and in like districts, suffer from an invidious discrimination violative of the Equal Protection Clause. . . .

JUSTICE MARSHALL, with whom JUSTICE DOUGLAS concurs, dissenting. . . .

This Court has repeatedly held that state discrimination which either adversely affects a "fundamental interest" . . . or is based on a distinction of a suspect character . . . must be carefully scrutinized to ensure that the scheme is necessary to promote a substantial, legitimate state interest. . . . The majority today concludes, however, that the Texas scheme is not subject to such a strict standard of review under the Equal Protection Clause. Instead, in its view, the Texas scheme must be tested by nothing more than that lenient standard of rationality which we have traditionally applied to discriminatory state action in the context of economic and commercial matters. . . . By so doing, the Court avoids the telling task of searching for a substantial state interest which the Texas financing scheme, with its variations in taxable district property wealth, is necessary to further. I cannot accept such an emasculation of the Equal Protection Clause in the context of this case. . . .

To begin, I must once more voice my disagreement with the Court's rigidified approach to equal protection analysis. . . .

I therefore cannot accept the majority's labored efforts to demonstrate that fundamental interests, which call for strict scrutiny of the challenged classification, encompass only established rights which we are somehow bound to recognize from the text of the Constitution itself. To be sure, some interests which the Court has deemed to be fundamental for purposes of equal protection analysis are themselves constitutionally protected rights. . . . But it will not do to suggest that the "answer" to whether an interest is fundamental for purposes of equal protection analysis is *always* determined by whether that interest "is a right . . . explicitly or implicitly guaranteed by the Constitution." . . .

I would like to know where the Constitution guarantees the right to procreate, *Skinner v. Oklahoma ex rel. Williamson* (1942), or the right to vote in state elections, *e.g., Reynolds v. Sims* (1964), or the right to an appeal from a criminal conviction, *e.g., Griffin v. Illinois* (1956). These are instances in which, due to the importance of the interests at stake, the Court has displayed a strong concern with the existence of discriminatory state treatment. But the Court has never said or indicated that these are interests which independently enjoy full-blown constitutional protection.

The majority is, of course, correct when it suggests that the process of determining which interests are fundamental is a difficult one. But I do not think the problem is insurmountable. And I certainly do not accept the view that the process need necessarily degenerate into an unprincipled, subjective "picking-and-choosing" between various interests or that it must involve this Court in creating "substantive constitutional rights in the name of guaranteeing equal protection of the laws." . . . Although not all fundamental interests are constitutionally guaranteed, the determination of which interests are fundamental should be firmly rooted in the text of the Constitution. The task in every case should be to determine the extent to which constitutionally guaranteed rights are dependent on interests not mentioned in the Constitution. As the nexus between the specific constitutional guarantee and the nonconstitutional interest draws closer, the nonconstitutional interest becomes more fundamental and the degree of judicial scrutiny applied when the interest is infringed on a discriminatory basis must be adjusted accordingly. Thus, it cannot be denied that interests such as procreation, the exercise of the state franchise, and access to criminal appellate processes are not fully guaranteed to the citizen by our Constitution. But these interests have nonetheless been afforded special judicial consideration in the face of discrimination because they are, to some extent, interrelated with constitutional guarantees. Procreation is now understood to be important because of its interaction with the established constitutional right of privacy. The exercise of the state franchise is closely tied to basic civil and political rights inherent in the First Amendment. And access to criminal appellate processes enhances the integrity of the range of rights implicit in the Fourteenth Amendment guarantee of due process of law. Only if we closely protect the related interests from state discrimination do we ultimately ensure the integrity of the constitutional guarantee itself. This is the real lesson that must be taken from our previous decisions involving interests deemed to be fundamental. . . .

A similar process of analysis with respect to the invidiousness of the basis on which a particular classification is drawn has also influenced the Court as to the appropriate degree of scrutiny to be accorded any particular case. The highly suspect character of classifications based on race, nationality, or alienage is well established. The reasons why such classifications call for close judicial scrutiny are manifold. Certain racial and ethnic groups have frequently been recognized as "discrete and insular minorities" who are relatively powerless to protect their interests in the political process. . . . Moreover, race, nationality, or alienage is "'in most circumstances irrelevant' to any constitutionally acceptable legislative purpose." . . . Instead, lines drawn on such bases are frequently the reflection of historic prejudices rather than legislative rationality. It may be that all of these considerations, which make for particular judicial solicitude in the face of discrimination on the basis of race, nationality, or alienage, do not coalesce—or at least not to the same degree—in other forms of discrimination. Nevertheless, these considerations have undoubtedly influenced the care with which the Court has scrutinized other forms of discrimination. . . .

In summary, it seems to me inescapably clear that this Court has consistently adjusted the care with which it will review state discrimination in light of the constitutional significance of the interests affected and the invidiousness of the particular classification. In the context of economic interests, we find that discriminatory state action is almost always sustained, for such interests are generally far removed from constitutional guarantees. Moreover, "[t]he extremes to which the Court has gone in dreaming up rational bases for state regulation in that area may in many instances be ascribed to a healthy revulsion from the Court's earlier excesses in using the Constitution to protect interests that

have more than enough power to protect themselves in the legislative halls." . . . But the situation differs markedly when discrimination against important individual interests with constitutional implications and against particularly disadvantaged or powerless classes is involved. The majority suggests, however, that a variable standard of review would give this Court the appearance of a "superlegislature." . . . I cannot agree. Such an approach seems to me a part of the guarantees of our Constitution and of the historic experiences with oppression of and discrimination against discrete, powerless minorities which underlie that Document. In truth, the Court itself will be open to the criticism raised by the majority so long as it continues on its present course of effectively selecting in private which cases will be afforded special consideration without acknowledging the true basis of its action. . . . Such obfuscated action may be appropriate to a political body such as a legislature, but it is not appropriate to this Court. Open debate of the bases for the Court's action is essential to the rationality and consistency of our decision-making process. Only in this way can we avoid the label of legislature and ensure the integrity of the judicial process.

Nevertheless, the majority today attempts to force this case into the same category for purposes of equal protection analysis as decisions involving discrimination affecting commercial interests. By so doing, the majority singles this case out for analytic treatment at odds with what seems to me to be the clear trend of recent decisions in this Court, and thereby ignores the constitutional importance of the interest at stake and the invidiousness of the particular classification, factors that call for far more than the lenient scrutiny of the Texas financing scheme which the majority pursues. Yet if the discrimination inherent in the Texas scheme is scrutinized with the care demanded by the interest and classification present in this case, the unconstitutionality of that scheme is unmistakable.

10

Voting and Representation

CHAPTER OUTLINE

The right to vote is one of the most fundamental rights secured by the Constitution. Article I, Section 2, authorizes any person who is qualified to vote for the lower house of a state's legislature to vote for members of the House of Representatives. The Fourteenth Amendment specifies (in Section 2) that if the right to vote of a citizen is denied or "in any way abridged" by a state, the size of that state's congressional delegation shall be reduced proportionately to the percentage of citizens in that state whose right has been denied or abridged. (Interestingly, the Fourteenth Amendment's Equal Protection Clause was not initially understood as guaranteeing the right to vote; otherwise, Section 2 would have been unnecessary, as would subsequent amendments.) The Constitution also prohibits a state from denying a citizen the right to vote "on account of race, color, or previous condition of servitude" (Fifteenth Amendment); "on account of sex" (Nineteenth Amendment); "by reason of failure to pay any poll tax or other tax" (Twenty-Fourth Amendment); or, for those who are eighteen years of age or older, "on account of age" (Twenty-Sixth Amendment). Each of these amendments gives Congress the "power to enforce," by "appropriate legislation," the right it declares.

Over time, the two constitutional provisions that have figured most prominently in right-to-vote cases have been the Equal Protection Clause of the Fourteenth Amendment and the Fifteenth Amendment. This chapter focuses on how the Court has employed these two provisions not only to guarantee the right to vote but also to establish a right to representation that is as personal as the right to vote itself.

EQUAL PROTECTION AND THE RIGHT TO VOTE

As discussed in Chapter 9, one of the first rights to be recognized as fundamental under the Supreme Court's two-tier approach to equal-protection analysis was the exercise of the franchise. Over time, this right has come to embody four distinct principles: (1) each vote must count equally—that is, the one-person, one-vote principle; (2) the franchise must be broadly available; (3) for the vote to be meaningful, the ballot must reflect a sufficiently representative choice of parties and candidates; and (4) recount procedures, at least with respect to presidential elections, must avoid arbitrary and disparate treatment of voters.

The "One-Person, One-Vote" Decisions

Gray v. Sanders (1963), *Wesberry v. Sanders* (1964), and *Reynolds v. Sims* (1964) collectively introduced the principle of "one man, one vote." *Gray*, decided just one year after the Supreme Court concluded in *Baker v. Carr* that issues of apportionment were justiciable, held that Georgia's county-unit system of primary elections to statewide office violated the Equal Protection Clause. This system was somewhat analogous to the federal Electoral College. Unit votes were allocated among the counties in such a manner that the 8 largest counties had six unit votes each, the next 30 had four unit votes each, and the remaining 121 counties had two unit votes each. The candidate for nomination who received the most popular votes in a primary was awarded the unit votes for that county. The practical consequence of this system was that the vote of citizens counted less and less as the population of their county increased. In fact, a combination of the units from the counties with the smallest populations gave counties having only one-third of the total state population a clear majority of county votes. Justice Douglas wrote the opinion for the eight-member majority; he began by dismissing the analogy of the federal Electoral College as not only inapposite but also unpersuasive. Moreover, he continued, the concept of "we the people" under the Constitution "visualizes no preferred class of voters but equality among those who meet the basic qualifications. . . . Every voter is equal to every other voter in his State." He declared that "the conception of political equality from the Declaration of Independence, to Lincoln's Gettysburg Address, to the Fifteenth, Seventeenth, and Nineteenth Amendments, can mean only one thing—one person, one vote." Applying his conception to the factual setting in *Gray,* he concluded, "Once the geographical unit for which a representative is to be chosen is designated, all who participate in the election are to have an equal vote—whatever their race, whatever their sex, whatever their occupation, whatever their income, and wherever their home may be in that geographical unit. This is required by the Equal Protection Clause of the Fourteenth Amendment."

In *Wesberry v. Sanders,* the Court extended the one-person, one-vote principle to congressional elections. The Georgia district in which the city of Atlanta was located had a 1960 population of 823,680, as compared with the average of 394,312 for all ten Georgia districts. Justice Black held for the Court that such a disparity in the population of congressional districts was contrary to the constitutional requirement of Article I, Section 2, that representatives in Congress be chosen "by the people of the several States," which, Black continued, "means that as nearly as practicable one man's vote in a congressional election is to be worth as much as another's." Black reviewed the history of the adoption and ratification of the Constitution and concluded, among other things, that "it would defeat the principle solemnly embodied in the Great Compromise—equal representation in the House for equal numbers of people—for us to hold that, within the States, legislatures may draw the lines of congressional districts in such a way as to give some voters a greater voice in choosing a Congressman than others. The House of Representatives, the Convention agreed, was to represent the people as individuals, and on the basis of complete equality for each voter." In dissent Justice Harlan accused Black of confusing two issues: "direct election of representatives within the states and the apportionment of representatives among the states." All of Black's historical evidence merely established the latter, which was not the issue, but left altogether unresolved the former, which was the very point of contention. As Harlan complained, "The Great Compromise concerned representation of the States in the Congress. In all the discussion surrounding the basis of representation of the House and all the discussion whether Representatives should be elected by the legislatures or by the people of the states, there is nothing which suggests even remotely that the delegates had in mind the problem of districting within a State."

In *Reynolds v. Sims,* the Court built on *Gray* and *Wesberry* and made "one person, one vote" the constitutional rule for apportioning both houses of a bicameral state legislature. Chief Justice Warren wrote the majority opinion, arguing that in a republican government, "legislators represent people, not trees or acres. Legislators are elected by voters, not farms or cities or economic interests." Representative government is "self-government through the medium of elected representatives." Moreover, "each and every citizen has an inalienable right to full and effective participation in the political processes of his State's legislative bodies." Because most citizens can achieve this participation only as qualified voters through the election of legislators to represent them, Chief Justice Warren went on to declare that "full and effective participation by all citizens in state government requires that each citizen have an equally effective voice in the election of members of his state legislature." Any "infringements" of this right must be "carefully and meticulously scrutinized." Employing the strict-scrutiny standard, the Chief Justice ruled that both houses of a state legislature had to be apportioned strictly according to population.[1]

In his *Reynolds* dissent, Justice Harlan noted that the Court was so busy reading between the lines of the Equal Protection Clause that it failed to read at all the words of Section 2 of the Fourteenth Amendment. "I am unable to understand the Court's utter disregard of the second section which expressly recognizes the States' power to deny 'or in any way' abridge the right of their inhabitants to vote for 'the members of their [State] Legislature,' and its express provision of a remedy for such a denial or abridgement."

What Harlan implied there, he explicitly argued in his dissent in *Wesberry:* namely, that the one-person, one-vote decisions do not involve the right to vote at all, but only the personal right to representation. Justice Frankfurter had made this argument first in his dissent in *Baker:*

> What, then, is this question of legislative apportionment? Appellants invoke the right to vote and to have their votes counted. But they are permitted to vote and their votes are counted. They go to the polls, they cast their ballots, they send their representatives to the state councils. Their complaint is simply that the representatives are not sufficiently numerous or powerful—in short, that Tennessee has adopted a basis of representation with which they are dissatisfied. Talk of "debasement" or "dilution" is circular talk. One cannot speak of "debasement" or "dilution" of the value of a vote until there is first defined a standard or reference as to what a vote should be worth. What is actually asked of the Court in this case is to choose among competing bases of representation—ultimately, really among competing theories of political philosophy—in order to establish an appropriate frame of government for the State of Tennessee and thereby for all the states of the Union.

The Court, in *Gray, Wesberry,* and *Reynolds,* held that citizens have not only the right to vote but also the right to equal representation—a right as personal as the right to vote and that the Court is authorized under the Equal Protection Clause to secure.

The Court acknowledged in *Reynolds* that it would be almost impossible to arrange legislative districts so that each one had an identical number of "residents, or citizens, or voters," and that "mathematical exactness or precision is hardly a workable constitutional requirement." This concession notwithstanding, the Warren Court later struck down a Missouri reapportionment plan that contained no more than a 5.97 percent disparity between the largest and smallest congressional districts.[2] And the Burger Court, in the 1983 case of *Karcher v. Daggett,* invalidated an apportionment plan for congressional districts in New Jersey in which each of the fourteen districts differed from the "ideal" population figure by 0.1384 percent and in which the largest district had a population of 527,472 and the smallest district had a population of 523,798, with the difference between them being only 0.6984 percent of the average district.

Although these decisions were consistent with Chief Justice Warren's argument in *Reynolds* that "population" is not only "the starting point for consideration" but also "the controlling criterion for judgment in legislative apportionment controversies," they conflicted with other statements in *Reynolds.* After all, the Chief Justice declared that "legislators are elected by voters, not farms or cities or economic interests"—or, as he also should have added, by nonvoters, that is, by the entire population. Warren spoke of "residents, or citizens, or voters" interchangeably, as if apportionment on any one of these three bases would result in complete voter equality. However, this blurring of distinct meanings is acceptable only if the ratio of voters to the total population or citizen population or both is constant throughout the state. If no such uniform ratio exists, Warren's language also conflicts with Douglas's pronouncement in *Gray* that "all who participate in the election are to have an equal vote." Ample evidence was available to the Court to establish that widely varying ratios were, in fact, prevalent among the states and that, as a consequence, the use of any population base broader than actual voters would simply magnify the electoral power of the voter who happens to live in a district where relatively large numbers of nonvoters reside. Thus, for example, in the 1962 congressional elections in Missouri, the actual number of voters per 100 adult inhabitants ranged from 7.75 in Pulaski County to 44.41 in Camden County—a ratio of more than 5.7 to 1. Following the Court's directive in *Reynolds* and constructing districts in Missouri that were precisely equal in population, the result would be to give each vote cast in Pulaski County 5.7 times the weight of each vote cast in Camden County. This, of course, raises a serious question: if the Court is willing to allow nonvoters to affect the complete ballot equality of voters, why is it unwilling to allow other factors such as geography and historical subdivisions?

Whereas the Warren Court never explained why it treated "residents, or citizens, or voters" interchangeably, or why it demanded in practice a "mathematical exactness" among congressional districts that it denied in theory, the Burger Court subsequently expanded considerably, at least at the state legislative level, the limits of constitutionally permissible population disparities. In *Mahan v. Howell* (1973), it held a 16.4 percent deviation in the lower house of the Virginia legislature to be justified by "the State's policy of maintaining the integrity of political subdivision lines." And in *Brown v. Thomson* (1983), it upheld an apportionment plan of the Wyoming House of Representatives that allowed an average deviation from population equality of 16 percent and a maximum deviation of 89 percent, noting that "Wyoming's constitutional policy—followed since statehood—of using counties as representative districts and ensuring that each county has one representative is supported by substantial and legitimate state concerns."

One consequence of the Court's one-person, one-vote decisions has been to free those who draw district lines from the need to respect geographical, historical, or political boundaries or to draw districts that are contiguous and compact. This has unleashed a political gerrymandering revolution on the land. In California, for example, congressional district lines were drawn by the Democratic-controlled state legislature after the 1980 census in such a way that, for the next decade, Democratic candidates routinely won two-thirds of the forty-five seats from California in the US House of Representatives, even though they received over that same time period only one-half of the popular vote statewide.

Partisan gerrymandering is, of course, a game that both parties play. In Indiana the Republicans controlled reapportionment and drew lines to benefit themselves. Several Indiana Democrats brought suit in federal court, alleging that the Republicans' partisan gerrymander constituted an equal-protection violation. In *Davis v. Bandemer* (1986), a badly divided Supreme Court rejected their contention. Three justices—Justice O'Connor joined by Chief Justice Burger and Justice Rehnquist—held that claims of partisan gerrymandering raise political questions that have no judicially discernible and manageable standards for resolving; they argued, therefore, that the Democrats' claims should be dismissed as nonjusticiable. Six justices disagreed with that conclusion; however, more important than their disagreement with the other three was their disagreement among themselves, for it deprived the Court of the ability to speak with a majority voice on this issue. Four of them (Justice White, joined by Justices Brennan, Marshall, and Blackmun) found the Democrats' claims justiciable but unavailing, whereas the final two (Justice Powell joined by Justice Stevens) found their claims both justiciable and persuasive. What separated these six was their failure to agree upon what was the proper standard to use when adjudicating claims of political gerrymandering.

In *Bandemer*, six justices were "not persuaded that there are no judicially discernible and manageable standards by which political gerrymandering cases are to be decided." As a group, however, they were unable to persuade themselves as to what these standards were, and the result was that the Supreme Court provided the lower courts with no definitive guidance on how they were to proceed when confronting such cases. Invariably, as cases arose, the lower courts denied relief and relied on the words of Justice White's plurality opinion that "the mere fact that a particular apportionment scheme makes it more difficult for a particular group in a particular district to elect the representatives of its choice does not render that scheme constitutionally infirm." White's plurality opinion noted that "an individual or a group of individuals who votes for a losing candidate is usually deemed to be adequately represented by the winning candidate and to have as much opportunity to influence that candidate as other voters in the district. We cannot presume in such a situation, without actual proof to the contrary, that the candidate elected will entirely ignore the interest of those voters." White's opinion concluded that "a group's electoral power is not unconstitutionally diminished by the simple fact of an apportionment scheme that makes winning elections more difficult." Although White and the plurality agreed that "unconstitutional discrimination" could indeed occur if "the electoral system is arranged in a manner that will consistently degrade a voter's or a group of voters' influence on the political process as a whole," they insisted that such a finding would have to "be supported by evidence of continued frustration of the will of the majority of the voters or effective denial to a minority of voters of a fair chance to influence the political process"—something no lower court has ever found.

When a lower federal court rejected still another political gerrymandering claim, this time arising out of the Republican-controlled Pennsylvania Legislature's adoption of a congressional redistricting plan, the Court was presented in *Vieth v. Jubelirer* (2004) with the opportunity to revisit its decision in *Bandemer* and to address once again whether political gerrymandering claims are justiciable. Once again, however, it found itself badly split. This time four justices—Justice Scalia wrote the plurality opinion and was joined by Chief Justice Rehnquist and Justices O'Connor and Thomas—concluded that "eighteen years of essentially pointless litigation have persuaded us that *Bandemer* is incapable of principled application. We would therefore overrule that case, and decline to adjudicate these political gerrymandering claims." Four other justices—Justice Stevens and Justice Breyer dissented separately, and Justice Ginsburg joined Justice Souter in still a third dissent—insisted that the claim was justiciable; however, they then proceeded to employ three separate standards to establish why the state's redistricting plan was unconstitutional. Justice Kennedy, the ninth justice, was accused by Scalia of playing the role of Hamlet. Although Justice Kennedy conceded that there are "weighty arguments for holding cases like these to be nonjusticiable" and that "those arguments may prevail in the long run"—it was on that basis that he concurred in the judgment—he was unwilling to foreclose all possibility of judicial relief because, over time, "some limited and precise rationale" might be found to "correct an established violation of the Constitution in some redistricting cases."

Invalidating Restrictions on the Franchise

To advance its second principle of the right to vote, that the franchise be broadly available, the Supreme Court has invalidated, on strict-scrutiny grounds, the payment of poll taxes (*Harper v. Virginia Board of Elections* [1966]), military status (*Carrington v. Rush* [1965]), property ownership (*Kramer v. Union Free School District* [1969]), durational residency (*Dunn v. Blumstein* [1972]), and prior party affiliation (*Kusper v. Pontikes* [1973]) as conditions to exercise of the franchise. As Judge J. Harvie Wilkinson III has observed, the Court's decisions involving this principle have implicitly rejected the view that voting is not so much a right as a duty that it is to be engaged in only upon "some demonstration of civic responsibility—whether of interest in public affairs by paying a poll tax, of a stake in political life stemming from ownership of property, or of a familiarity with and commitment to state politics resulting from living within the state's boundaries a respectable period."[3] That view was rejected, Justice Harlan complained in his dissent in *Harper*, because it was "not in accord with current egalitarian notions of how a modern democracy should be organized."

The rejection of this view began with *Harper v. Virginia Board of Elections*. In this case, the Court overruled *Breedlove v. Suttles* (1937) and invalidated Virginia's poll tax. Justice Douglas spoke for a six-member majority when he declared that "voter qualifications have no relation to wealth nor to paying or not paying this or any other tax." He waxed eloquent that "wealth like race, creed, or color, is not germane to one's ability to participate intelligently in the electoral process." Virginia had defended its poll tax on the grounds that it fostered responsible voting. It noted that the convention that had drafted the Virginia Constitution had declared that "the voter has to pay a poll tax, prepare his own application, and cast his own ballot. The plan virtually eliminates the incompetent from politics." Elaborating upon this theme, it stressed in its brief in *Harper* that "the tax . . . only requires an annual payment of $1.50 by December 4 in every year and this serves as a 'simple and objective test of certain minimal capacity for ordering one's own affairs and thus of qualification to participate in the ordering of the affairs of state.'" The Brief for the Appellant complained, however, that "many persons through inadvertence or lack of diligence let the deadline go by without paying their poll taxes, but when the election draws near and candidates and issues are known, find that they cannot vote because they did not pay their poll taxes on time." The *amicus curiae* brief of the United States made much the same argument: the voter must pay the tax well "in advance of the election—at a time, that is, when political activity is relatively quiescent and the actual election campaign has not begun." The Supreme Court held that this means of promoting responsible voting could not withstand strict scrutiny and voided Virginia's poll tax.

The Court's use of the "strict-scrutiny" test to sever the nexus between voting and civic responsibility was also apparent in *Kramer v. Union Free School District* (1969) and *Hill v. Stone* (1975). In these cases, the Supreme Court held that the states of New York and Texas could not deny the franchise to nonproperty owners in municipal elections to approve the issuance of general obligation bonds, even when the general bonded indebtedness of the municipality effectively operated as a lien on all taxable property within its borders. The Union Free School District had defended its property qualification requirement as encouraging more knowledgeable and interested voters. In its brief, it stressed, "It is apodictic that those persons whose properties in the school district are assessed for payment through the local property tax of the cost of rendering services to pupils . . . of the district will have enough of an interest, through the burden on their pocketbooks, to acquire such information as they may need in order to try to evaluate the operation of the public school system and the reasonableness of expenditures." Texas had argued that the qualification protected those who would have a lien placed on their property for the payment of a tax from having that lien placed on them by others who would not. In the words of the Texas Supreme Court, "One who is willing to vote for and impose a tax on the property of another should be willing to assume his distributive share of the burden."[4] The Court rejected these justifications, however, and voided this property qualification, contending that it erected a classification that impermissibly discriminated on the basis of wealth and disenfranchised persons otherwise qualified to vote.

The Court's use of the strict-scrutiny test to free the right to vote from restrictions designed to promote responsible voting is also clear in its consideration of durational residency requirements in *Dunn v. Blumstein*. In a 6–1 decision, it invalidated a Tennessee requirement of residence in the state for one year and in the county for three months as a condition of voting. Tennessee had argued that it had a legitimate interest in securing knowledgeable voters with a genuine interest in the governance of the community and in educating citizens on the importance of casting informed, considered, and responsible votes, and that durational residency requirements contributed to both. Common Cause, in its *amicus curiae* brief for the appellee, disagreed; it insisted that all the knowledge and experience a voter needs to exercise the franchise could be gained in the thirty-day period before an election. "Advertising and news coverage reach and sustain a fever pitch only during the month before an election. Because this is so, a new resident can acquire all the knowledge he wants or needs during that period." Justice Marshall agreed: "Given modern communications, and given the clear indication that campaign spending and voter education occur largely during the month before the election, the state cannot seriously maintain that it is 'necessary' to reside for a year in the state and three months in the county in order to be knowledgeable about congressional, state, or even purely local elections."

Interestingly, however, in *Crawford v. Marion County Election Board* (2008), the Court declined to employ *Harper* and its "strict-scrutiny" standard when it considered the constitutionality of an Indiana election law requiring citizens voting in person to present photo identification issued by the government. The Court divided 6–3 on the issue. Six justices upheld the law, but they split as to the reasons. While Justice Stevens (in an opinion joined by Chief Justice Roberts and Justice Kennedy) applied a balancing test and found Indiana's interests in deterring and detecting voter fraud and in safeguarding voter confidence outweighed the "inconvenience of making a trip to the BMV (Bureau of Motor Vehicles), gathering the required documents, and posing for a [free] photograph," Justice Scalia (in an opinion concurring in the judgment joined by Justices Thomas, and Alito) rejected that "case-by-case" balancing approach because it "naturally encourages constant litigation," arguing instead for the "application of a deferential 'important regulatory interests' standard for non-severe, nondiscriminatory restrictions." Not even the three dissenting justices (Souter, Ginsburg, and Breyer) employed strict scrutiny; they employed the same balancing test as Justice Stevens but reached a different conclusion. In Justice Souter's words, Indiana was imposing "an unreasonable and irrelevant burden on voters who are poor and old" without "a shred of evidence that in-person voter impersonation is a problem in the State."

Guaranteeing Access to the Ballot

The third principle recognized by the Court as implicit in the fundamental right to vote is that the exercise of the franchise must be meaningful as well as available. Among "our most precious freedoms," the Court declared in *Williams v. Rhodes* (1968), is "the right of qualified voters, regardless of their political persuasion, to cast their votes effectively." It therefore invalidated an Ohio election law that allowed the major parties to retain their positions on the ballot simply by obtaining 10 percent of the votes in the last gubernatorial election but required new parties seeking access to the presidential election ballot to file petitions signed by 15 percent of the number of ballots cast in the last gubernatorial election. In addition to greater ballot access for third-party and independent candidates such as George Wallace, John Anderson, and Ross Perot, this principle has required elimination of filing fees for indigent candidates. As the Court held in *Lubin v. Panish* (1974), "it is to be expected that a voter hopes to find on the ballot a candidate who comes near to reflecting his policy preferences on competing issues."[5]

Guaranteeing Fairness in Recounts in Presidential Elections

A fourth and final principle recognized by the Court in *Bush v. Gore* (2000) as implicit in the fundamental right to vote is the right of voters to equal treatment in any recounts of their ballots in presidential elections. When the Florida Elections Canvassing Commission certified the results of the 2000 presidential election for the State of Florida, it found that George W. Bush, governor of Texas and Republican Party candidate for president, had defeated Albert Gore Jr., vice president of the United States and Democratic Party candidate for president by a total of 537 votes (2,912,790 to 2,912,253), and it declared Bush the winner of Florida's 25 electoral votes. Gore contested this certification, arguing, among other things, that Miami–Dade County had failed to tabulate, by manual count, 9,000 ballots on which the counting machines had failed to detect a vote for president—what came to be referred to as "undervotes."

On December 8, the Florida Supreme Court noted the closeness of the election and, after defining a "legal vote" as "one in which there is a 'clear indication of the intent of the voter,'" observed that "on this record, there can be no question that there are legal votes within the 9,000 uncounted votes sufficient to place the results of this election in doubt." It therefore ordered a hand recount of the 9,000 ballots in Miami–Dade County; it further held that relief would require manual recounts in all Florida counties where the so-called undervotes had not been subject to manual tabulation and, with no guidance or instructions on how the intent of the voters was to be ascertained, ordered all manual recounts to begin immediately.

On December 9, the United States Supreme Court granted certiorari and ordered a halt to the recounts until the constitutional issues raised by the case could be resolved. On December 12, a five-member majority (consisting of Chief Justice Rehnquist and Justices Kennedy, O'Connor, Scalia, and Thomas) held that "the use of standardless manual recounts violates the Equal Protection Clause." The *per curiam* opinion noted that the Florida Legislature had expressed its intentions to "participate fully in the federal electoral process" (including the "safe-harbor" provisions, which required that all presidential election contests be completed six days before the meeting of the Electoral College—in the year 2000, by the very day of the Supreme Court's decision, December 12). It therefore held that, even were a recount procedure to be put in place that comported with minimal constitutional standards, there was no time to implement such a recount, and it reversed the judgment of the Florida Supreme Court ordering a recount to proceed.

Two of the dissenting justices (Breyer and Souter) agreed with the majority that there were equal-protection problems with the recount ordered by the Florida Supreme Court. They were obviously troubled by the examples found in the *per curiam* opinion:

> A monitor in Miami–Dade County testified at trial that he observed that three members of the county canvassing board applied different standards in defining a legal vote. And testimony at trial also revealed that at least one county changed its evaluative standards during the counting process. Palm Beach County, for example, began the process with a 1990 guideline which precluded counting completely attached chads, switched to a rule that considered a vote to be legal if any light could be seen through a chad, changed back to the 1990 rule, and then abandoned any pretense of a *per se* rule, only to have a court order that the county consider dimpled chads legal. This is not a process with sufficient guarantees of equal treatment. . . .

Breyer and Souter objected, however, to the majority's decision to end the recount process. As Justice Souter complained, "Unlike the majority, I see no warrant for this Court to assume that Florida could not possibly comply with this requirement before the date set for the meeting of electors, December 18. . . . To recount these manually would be a tall order, but before this Court stayed the effort to do that the courts of Florida were ready to do their best to get that job done. There is no justification for denying the State the opportunity to try to count all disputed ballots now."

The eventual reach of *Bush v. Gore* remains difficult to predict. The equal-protection language of the *per curiam* opinion would seem to cover the fairness of recounts in all state elections, not merely in presidential elections. However, as Chief Justice Rehnquist stressed in his concurring opinion, presidential elections are "exceptional cases." He noted that Article II, Section 1, of the Constitution provides that in presidential elections, the clearly expressed intent of the states' legislatures is to prevail. In this case, however, the Florida Supreme Court had departed from the Florida Legislature's intent concerning the certification of presidential elections and had, therefore, run afoul of the language of Article II.

A total of seven justices seemed to be in agreement that, except for presidential elections, when questions arise concerning the meaning of state election laws, it is, in Justice Stevens's words, the Court's "settled practice to accept the opinions of the highest courts of the States as providing the final answers."

RACE AND REPRESENTATION: THE FIFTEENTH AMENDMENT AND THE VOTING RIGHTS ACT

The Fifteenth Amendment guarantees the right to vote irrespective of "race, color, or previous condition of servitude." Despite this guarantee, prior to 1965, southern states had effectively denied black citizens the franchise through a variety of institutional mechanisms, including white primaries,[6] poll taxes,[7] racial gerrymandering of electoral districts,[8] literacy tests,[9] and grandfather clauses (effectively excepting whites from literacy tests).[10] In some cases, the Supreme Court was able to strike down these barriers; however, neither the Court nor the federal government could keep up with the ingenuity of states intent on keeping African Americans from the polls. Although the Civil Rights Acts of 1957, 1960, and 1964 were, in part, intended to redress voting-rights violations, they did little to achieve this goal. As Chandler Davidson has pointed out, "The burden remained on black voters to seek relief in the courts case by case, a time-consuming and extremely inefficient process," especially given the makeup of the southern district courts.[11] Chief Justice Warren argued similarly in *South Carolina v. Katzenbach* (1966); he declared that these laws

> proved ineffective for a number of reasons. Voting suits are unusually onerous to prepare, sometimes requiring as many as 6,000 man-hours spent combing through registration records in preparation for trial. Litigation has been exceedingly slow, in part because of the ample opportunities for delay afforded by voting officials and others involved in the proceedings. Even when favorable decisions have finally been obtained, some of the States affected have merely switched to discriminatory devices not covered by the federal decrees or have enacted difficult new tests designed to prolong the existing disparity between white and Negro registration. [Alternatively,] certain local officials have defied and evaded court orders or have simply closed their registration offices to freeze the voting rolls.

To overcome these barriers, to fulfill, as Abigail Thernstrom has put it, "the promise of the Fifteenth Amendment ninety-five years late,"[12] Congress passed the Voting Rights Act of 1965 (VRA). The act originally applied to seven southern states (although through the years it has come to have national coverage). In Section 4, it provided a "coverage formula" and defined the "covered jurisdictions" as those States or political subdivisions that maintained tests or devices (such as literacy tests) as prerequisites to voting that had historically been used to deny blacks the franchise and that, as a consequence, had low voter registration or turnout at the time of the Act's initial passage. In Section 5, it prohibited the replacement of old procedures for disenfranchisement with new ones by requiring that new voting procedures in states covered by Section 4 would have to be precleared by the US Department of Justice before they could be implemented.

The Voting Rights Act gave the federal government extraordinary power over the states. The Supreme Court nonetheless affirmed its constitutionality in *South Carolina v. Katzenbach* (1966), holding that the act was a valid exercise of Congress's enforcement power under Section 2 of the Fifteenth Amendment. Chief Justice Warren spoke for the Court: "Congress may use any rational means to effectuate the constitutional prohibition of racial discrimination in voting. The basic test to be applied [with respect to Congress's power under Section 2] is the same as in all cases concerning the express powers of Congress with relation to the reserved powers of the States. *McCulloch v. Maryland.*"

The Voting Rights Act proved to be one of the most successful federal laws ever passed.[13] Reporting in 1975, the US Commission on Civil Rights noted that "minority political participation has increased substantially in the 10 years since the enactment of the Voting Rights Act." It reported that "more than 1 million new black voters were registered in the seven covered Southern states between 1964 and 1972, increasing the percentage of eligible blacks registered from about 29 percent to over 56 percent." In addition, over the same period of time, "the gap between white and black registration rates" was "reduced from 44.1 percentage points to 11.2 percentage points." The number of blacks elected in the seven covered states grew from an estimated "well under 100 black officials" prior to 1965 to 156 by February 1968 and 963 by April 1974.[14]

The very purpose of the Voting Rights Act was fundamentally altered, however, in 1969 when the Supreme Court handed down *Allen v. State Board of Elections.* At issue in *Allen* were proposed changes to state election laws in Mississippi and Virginia. None of the proposed changes related to access to registration or to the counting of ballots; rather, they concerned switching from single-member districts to at-large districts, changing a school superintendent office from being elective to being appointive, and changing the procedures by which independent candidates were to be nominated. Chief Justice Warren, writing for the Court, argued that the remedial powers of the Voting Rights Act were not limited to protecting voter registration and ballot access. The "Act was aimed at the subtle, as well as the obvious, state regulations that had the effect of denying citizens their right to vote because of their race." This meant that electoral practices or procedures that might adversely affect the political effectiveness of black voters were subject to preclearance, not just direct bars to registration and polling booths.

> The right to vote can be affected by a dilution of voting power as well as by an absolute prohibition on casting a ballot. . . . Voters who are members of a racial minority might be in the majority in one district, but in a decided minority in the county as a whole. This type of change could therefore nullify their ability to elect the candidate of their choice just as would prohibiting some of them from voting.

Chief Justice Warren determined that the intent of the Voting Rights Act was "to reach any state enactment which altered the election law of a covered State in even a minor way." It was to ensure that electoral practices neither prevented blacks from voting nor interfered with their ability to elect candidates of their choice. Just as the one-person, one-vote decisions transformed the Constitution's guarantee of the right to vote into the right to representation, so, too, *Allen* transformed the right to vote guaranteed to black citizens by the Voting Rights Act into the right to black representation.

Allen further enlarged the federal power of supervision over state electoral practices. When the Court itself subsequently attempted to curtail somewhat this federal supervisory power in *Mobile v. Bolden* (1980) by holding that the Voting Rights Act applied only to purposeful or intentional discrimination against African Americans' voting rights, Congress responded in 1982 by amending the Voting Rights Act to allow black plaintiffs to show discrimination based solely on the effects of a voting plan. In *Thornburg v. Gingles* (1986), the Court accepted the amended act's "results test" and Congress's decision to invalidate districting plans that have the effect (even if not the intention) of diluting the black vote. Addressing the issue of whether multimember districts are ever permissible or whether they invariably disadvantage minorities, the *Gingles* majority spelled out the circumstances under which it would conclude that multimember districts "operate to impair minority voters' ability to elect representatives of their choice":

These circumstances are necessary preconditions for multimember districts to operate to impair minority voters' ability to elect representatives of their choice for the following reasons. First, the minority group must be able to demonstrate that it is sufficiently large and geographically compact to constitute a majority in a single-member district. If it is not, as would be the case in a substantially integrated district, the *multimember form* of the district cannot be responsible for minority voters' inability to elect its candidates. Second, the minority group must be able to show that it is politically cohesive. If the minority group is not politically cohesive, it cannot be said that the selection of a multimember electoral structure thwarts distinctive minority group interests. Third, the minority must be able to demonstrate that the white majority votes sufficiently as a bloc to enable it—in the absence of special circumstances, such as the minority candidate running unopposed—usually to defeat the minority's preferred candidate. In establishing this last circumstance, the minority group demonstrates that submergence in a white multimember district impedes its ability to elect its chosen representatives.[15]

The 1982 amendments to the Voting Rights Act ban state electoral schemes that have the effect of preventing minority voters from electing "representatives of their choice."[16] How are the courts and the federal government to determine if minority voters have been prevented from electing "representatives of their choice"? The unspoken answer is, if they fail to elect a representative of their own race or ethnicity. Although the 1982 amendments declare that nothing in the Voting Rights Act "establishes a right to have members of a protected class elected in numbers equal to their proportion in the population," any districting scheme that provides for less than proportional representation would seem to fail the "results test."

As the states redrew their congressional and state legislative district lines after the 1990 decennial census, many sought to pass the "results test" by engaging in racial gerrymandering—creating districts that maximized the number of minority candidates who could be elected to office. In *Shaw v. Reno* (1993), however, the Court placed a major roadblock in the path of those who would employ this strategy by declaring that racial gerrymandering would have to survive strict scrutiny. As Justice O'Connor wrote for a five-member majority:

> Racial classifications of any sort pose the risk of lasting harm to our society. They reinforce the belief, held by too many for too much of our history, that individuals should be judged by the color of their skin. Racial classifications with respect to voting carry particular dangers. Racial gerrymandering, even for remedial purposes, may balkanize us into competing racial factions; it threatens to carry us further from the goal of a political system in which race no longer matters—a goal that the Fourteenth and Fifteenth Amendments embody, and to which the Nation continues to aspire. It is for these reasons that race-based districting by our state legislatures demands close judicial scrutiny.

In *Miller v. Johnson* (1995), the prospects that a racial gerrymander could survive strict scrutiny were dealt a serious blow when the Court rejected "the contention that the State has a compelling interest in complying with whatever preclearance mandates the Justice Department issues." Justice Kennedy spoke for the Court when he held:

> When a state governmental entity seeks to justify race-based remedies to cure the effects of past discrimination, we do not accept the government's mere assertion that the remedial action is required. Rather, we insist on a strong basis in evidence

of the harm being remedied. "The history of racial classifications in this country suggests that blind judicial deference to legislative or executive pronouncements of necessity has no place in equal protection analysis." Our presumptive skepticism of all racial classifications prohibits us as well from accepting on its face the Justice Department's conclusion that racial districting is necessary under the Voting Rights Act. Where a State relies on the Department's determination that race-based districting is necessary to comply with the Voting Rights Act, the judiciary retains an independent obligation in adjudicating consequent equal protection challenges to ensure that the State's actions are narrowly tailored to achieve a compelling interest. Were we to accept the Justice Department's objection itself as a compelling interest adequate to insulate racial districting from constitutional review, we would be surrendering to the Executive Branch our role in enforcing the constitutional limits on race-based official action. We may not do so.

What seemed certain in *Shaw v. Reno* and *Miller v. Johnson,* however, began to change with the Court's 1996 decisions in *Shaw v. Hunt* and *Bush v. Vera.* In *Shaw v. Hunt,* Chief Justice Rehnquist accepted "*arguendo,* for the purpose of resolving this case," that compliance with the "results test" mandated by the 1982 amendments to the Voting Rights Act "could be a compelling interest." He continued, however, that even with the benefit of this assumption, North Carolina's racial gerrymander did not survive strict scrutiny because it was not narrowly tailored to that asserted end. Then, in *Bush v. Vera,* Justice O'Connor, the critical fifth vote in *Shaw v. Hunt,* concurred separately to state that "[in] my view, the States have a compelling interest in complying with the results test." Her language seems to contain the very terms of surrender the Court was unwilling to offer up in *Miller.*[17] Whereas the Court in *Miller* refused to surrender "to the Executive Branch our role in enforcing the constitutional limits on race-based official action," O'Connor and the four dissenting justices in *Shaw v. Reno* and the subsequent racial gerrymander cases were apparently willing to surrender that very same role to Congress and its adoption of the "results test." O'Connor insisted, "Although I agree with the dissenters about Section 2's role as part of our national commitment to racial equality, I differ from them in my belief that that commitment can and must be reconciled with the complementary commitment of our Fourteenth Amendment jurisprudence to eliminate the unjustified use of racial stereotypes."

For O'Connor, the "results test" insisted on by Congress had to be squared with the dictates of the Equal Protection Clause banning racial gerrymandering. But how? In *Hunt v. Cromartie* (2001), the Court appeared to answer that question by redefining impermissible racial gerrymanders as permissible political gerrymanders. With Justice O'Connor in complete support, Justice Breyer argued for a five-member majority that because black voters in North Carolina tended to "register and vote Democratic between 95% and 97% of the time," its Democratically controlled state legislature could, in the interests of securing "a safe Democratic seat," draw a majority-black district of highly irregular shape and could do so without offending the Equal Protection Clause because its "reasons would be political rather than racial."

However, the Court's decision in *League of United Latin American Citizens [LULAC] v. Perry* (2006) called the *Cromartie* answer into question. While a majority of the Court rejected LULAC's challenge to Texas's mid-decade political gerrymander, a different majority held that the state must nevertheless guarantee political officeholding to designated racial groups. As Anthony Peacock has observed, *LULAC* held that "the VRA protected not only candidates elected from districts in which minorities were a majority of the voting-age population, but, in certain situations, also those elected from districts where minorities were only a small percentage of the voting-age population."[18]

Much of the Court's attention has focused on Section 2 of the Voting Rights Act and the questions it poses concerning the opportunity for minority voters to elect "representatives of their choice." Section 5 of the Voting Rights Act has also received considerable attention; it requires, for all covered states, that all changes to state election law, however insignificant (for example, going to punch-card ballots from voting machines), be precleared by federal authorities in Washington, D.C.—either the Department of Justice or a three-judge panel of federal district court judges—before they can go into effect. Justice Black found this section unconstitutional in his dissent in *South Carolina v. Katzenbach* (1966): "Section 5, by providing that some of the States cannot pass state laws or adopt state constitutional amendments without first being compelled to beg federal authorities to approve their policies, so distorts our constitutional structure of government as to render any distinction drawn in the Constitution between state and federal power almost meaningless." His objections were unavailing.

A recent and interesting Section 5 case is *Northwest Austin Municipal Utility District Number One* [*Northwest Austin*] *v. Holder* (2009). The appellant in this case was a small utility district with an elected board. Because it is located in Texas, a covered state under Section 4, it was required by Section 5 to seek federal preclearance before it could change anything about its elections, even though there was no evidence it had ever discriminated on the basis of race in those elections. Northwest Austin filed suit in federal district court, seeking relief under the "bailout" provision in Section 4 of the Voting Rights Act, which allows a "political subdivision" to be released from the preclearance requirements if certain conditions are met. It argued in the alternative that if Section 5 were interpreted to render it ineligible for bailout, Section 5 was unconstitutional. The federal court rejected both claims, concluding that bailout under Section 4 is available only to counties, parishes, and subunits that register voters, not to an entity like the district that did not register its own voters. It also concluded that a 2006 congressional amendment extending Section 5 for twenty-five years was constitutional. Chief Justice Roberts for an eight-member majority declined to rule on the constitutionality of that provision, citing the principle of constitutional avoidance; he did conclude, however, that the district was eligible to apply for a bailout from this section because the definition of "political subdivision" included a district of this nature. This decision was consistent with Roberts's embrace of "judicial minimalism," where he attempts to avoid invalidation of federal law or rejection of past judicial precedent unless absolutely necessary. Justice Thomas, however, is no judicial minimalist, and he dissented in part because the Court failed to address the continued constitutionality of Section 5. "For Section 5 to withstand renewed constitutional scrutiny, there must be a demonstrated connection between the 'remedial measures' chosen and the 'evil presented' in the record made by Congress when it renewed the [Voting Rights] Act. 'Strong measures appropriate to address one harm may be an unwarranted response to another, lesser one.'"

Northwest Austin v. Holder paved the way to *Shelby County v. Holder* (2013). The coverage formula of Section 4 and the preclearance requirement of Section 5 of the Voting Right Act of 1965 were initially set to expire after five years, but the Act was reauthorized without change to the coverage formula in 1970, 1975, and 1982. In 2006, the Act was reauthorized for an additional twenty-five years and again without a change to the coverage formula. Coverage still turned on whether a jurisdiction had voting tests at the time of the Act's initial passage that resulted in low minority voter registration or turnout at that time. Shelby County, in the covered jurisdiction of Alabama, sued the Attorney General before a three-judge district court in Washington, D.C., seeking a declaratory judgment that Sections 4 and 5 were facially unconstitutional as well as a permanent injunction against their enforcement. The panel upheld the Act, finding that the evidence before Congress in 2006 was sufficient to justify reauthorizing Section 5 and continuing Section 4's coverage formula. The

D.C. Circuit affirmed; after surveying the evidence in the record, it accepted Congress's conclusion that Section 2 litigation remained inadequate in the covered jurisdictions to protect the rights of minority voters, that Section 5 was therefore still necessary, and that the Section 4's coverage formula continued to pass constitutional muster. In *Shelby County*, Chief Justice Roberts wrote for a five-member majority when he reversed the appellate court decision and declared that what Congress had passed in 2006 was irrational and therefore unconstitutional: "There is no valid reason to insulate the coverage formula from review merely because it was previously enacted 40 years ago. If Congress had started from scratch in 2006, it plainly could not have enacted the present coverage formula. It would have been irrational for Congress to distinguish between States in such a fundamental way based on 40-year-old data, when today's statistics tell an entirely different story. And it would have been irrational to base coverage on the use of voting tests 40 years ago, when such tests have been illegal since that time. But that is exactly what Congress has done." Roberts continued: "We issue no holding on §5 itself [although Justice Thomas in a concurrence would have found it unconstitutional as well], only on the coverage formula. Congress may draft another formula based on current conditions. Such formula is an initial prerequisite to a determination that exceptional conditions still exist justifying such an 'extraordinary departure from the traditional course of relations between the States and the Federal Government.'"

NOTES

1. The Warren Court ultimately came to apply this same one-person, one-vote principle not only to state legislatures but also to local governments (*Avery v. Midland County* [1968]), nominating petitions (*Moore v. Ogilvie* [1969]), and elected junior-college trustees (*Hadley v. Junior College District of Metropolitan Kansas City* [1970]). For a sustained criticism of these decisions, see Ralph A. Rossum, "Representation and Republican Government: Contemporary Court Variations on the Founders' Theme," *American Journal of Jurisprudence* 23 (1978): 88–109.

2. *Kirkpatrick v. Preisler* (1969).

3. J. Harvie Wilkinson III, "The Supreme Court, the Equal Protection Clause, and the Three Faces of Constitutional Equality," *Virginia Law Review* 61 (June 1975): 958.

4. *Montgomery Independent School District v. Martin* (Texas, 1971).

5. However, see *Clements v. Fashing* (1982).

6. See *Nixon v. Herndon* (1927), *Nixon v. Condon* (1932), *Grovey v. Townsend* (1935), *Smith v. Allwright* (1944), and *Terry v. Adams* (1953).

7. See *Breedlove v. Suttles* (1937) and *Harper v. Virginia Board of Elections* (1966).

8. See *Gomillion v. Lightfoot* (1960) and *Wright v. Rockefeller* (1964).

9. See *Schnell v. Davis* (1949), *Alabama v. United States* (1962), and *Louisiana v. United States* (1965).

10. *Guinn v. United States* (1915) and *Myers v. Anderson* (1915).

11. Chandler Davidson, "The Voting Rights Act: A Brief History," in *Controversies in Minority Voting,* edited by Bernard Grofman and Chandler Davidson (Washington, DC: Brookings Institution Press, 1992), 13.

12. Abigail Thernstrom, *Whose Votes Count? Affirmative Action and Minority Voting Rights* (Cambridge, MA: Harvard University Press, 1987), 1.

13. The following discussion relies heavily on Chapter 3 of Anthony A. Peacock, "The Despair of Equality: Voting Rights and the Problem of Representation" (unpublished Ph.D. dissertation, Claremont Graduate School, 1997).

14. U.S. Commission on Civil Rights, *The Voting Rights Act: Ten Years After* (Washington, DC: Government Printing Office, 1975), 39–49.

15. See Justice Thomas's powerful critique of *Gingles* in his concurrence in *Holder v. Hall* (1993).

16. In *Chisom v. Roemer* (1991), the Supreme Court held that the 1982 amendments applied to judicial elections as well, despite the fact that judges are typically not regarded as "representatives" and despite the difficulty of determining whether minorities have had a chance to elect "representatives of their choice" in the absence of judicial districts of equal population. Because the size of judicial districts is determined by the volume and nature of litigation arising in various parts of the state, the Supreme Court has never held that the one-man, one-vote principle must apply to judicial elections. See Ralph A. Rossum, "Applying the Voting Rights Act to Judicial Elections: The Supreme Court's Misconstruction of Section 2 and Misconception of the

Judicial Role," in *Affirmative Action and Representation: Shaw v. Reno and the Future of Voting Rights,* edited by Anthony A. Peacock (Durham, NC: Carolina Academic Press, 1997), 317–341.

17. See Anthony A. Peacock, "The Supreme Court and the Future of Voting Rights," in *Affirmative Action and Representation,* edited by Peacock, 410.

18. Anthony A. Peacock, *Deconstructing the Republic: Voting Rights, the Supreme Court, and the Founders' Republicanism Reconsidered* (Washington, DC: AEI Press, 2008), 136.

SELECTED READINGS

The Federalist, Nos. 52–54, 57.

Ackerman, Bruce A., ed. Bush v. Gore: *A Question of Legitimacy.* New Haven, CT: Yale University Press, 2002.

Adams, Florence. *Latinos and Local Representation: Changing Realities, Emerging Theories.* New York: Garland, 2000.

Aleinikoff, T. Alexander, and Samuel Issacharoff. "Race and Redistricting: Drawing Constitutional Lines after *Shaw v. Reno.*" *Michigan Law Review* 92 (December 1993): 588–651.

Alfange, Dean, Jr. "Gerrymandering and the Constitution: Into the Thorns of the Thicket at Last." In *1986 Supreme Court Review,* edited by Philip B. Kurland, Gerhard Casper, and Dennis J. Hutchinson. Chicago: University of Chicago Press, 1987.

Ceaser, James W., and Andrew E. Busch. *The Perfect Tie.* Lanham, MD: Rowman & Littlefield, 2001.

Clegg, Roger. "Voting Rights and Equal Protection: The Future of the Voting Rights Act after *Bartlett* and *NAMUDNO.*" *Cato Supreme Court Review* (2008–2009): 35–51.

Dionne, E. J., and William Kristol, eds. Bush v. Gore: *The Court Cases and the Commentary.* Washington, DC: Brookings Institution Press, 2001.

Driver, Justin. "Rules, the New Standards: Partisan Gerrymandering and Judicial Manageability." *George Washington Law Review* 73 (August 2005): 1166–1192.

Dworkin, Ronald D., ed. *A Badly Flawed Election: Debating* Bush v. Gore, *the Supreme Court, and American Democracy.* New York: New Press, 2002.

Elliott, Ward E. Y. *The Rise of Guardian Democracy: The Supreme Court's Role in Voting Rights Disputes, 1845–1969.* Cambridge, MA: Harvard University Press, 1974.

Ely, John Hart. "Confounded by *Cromartie:* Are Racial Stereotypes Now Acceptable Across the Board or Only When Used in Support of Partisan Gerrymanders?" *University of Miami Law Review* 56 (April 2002): 489–506.

Galderisi, Peter F., ed. *Redistricting in the New Millennium.* Lanham, MD: Lexington Books, 2005.

Garrow, David J., *Protest at Selma, Martin Luther King, Jr., and the Voting Rights Act of 1965.* New Haven, CT: Yale University Press, 2015.

Grofman, Bernard, ed. *Political Gerrymandering and the Court.* New York: Agathon Press, 1990.

———, and Chandler Davidson, eds. *Controversies in Minority Voting: The Voting Rights Act in Perspective.* Washington, DC: Brookings Institution Press, 1992.

Guinier, Lani. *The Tyranny of the Majority: Fundamental Fairness in Representative Democracy.* New York: Free Press, 1994.

Issacharoff, Samuel. "Judging Politics: The Elusive Quest for Judicial Review of Political Fairness." *Texas Law Review* 71 (June 1993): 1643–1703.

Morgan, Ruth P., *Government by Decree: The Impact of the Voting Rights Act on Dallas.* Lawrence: University Press of Kansas, 2004.

O'Rourke, Timothy G. *The Impact of Reapportionment.* New Brunswick, NJ: Transaction Books, 1980.

Peacock, Anthony A., ed. *Affirmative Action and Representation:* Shaw v. Reno *and the Future of Voting Rights.* Durham, NC: Carolina Academic Press, 1997.

———. *Deconstructing the Republic: Voting Rights, the Supreme Court, and the Founders' Republicanism Reconsidered.* Washington, DC: AEI Press, 2008.

Posner, Richard A. *Breaking the Deadlock: The 2000 Election, the Constitution, and the Courts.* Princeton, NJ: Princeton University Press, 2001.

Rush, Mark E. *Does Redistricting Make a Difference? Partisan Representation and Electoral Behavior.* Baltimore: Johns Hopkins University Press, 1993.

Swain, Carol M. *Black Faces, Black Interests: The Representation of African Americans.* Cambridge, MA: Harvard University Press, 1993.

Thernstrom, Abigail. *Whose Votes Count? Affirmative Action and Minority Voting Rights.* Cambridge, MA: Harvard University Press, 1987.

Withers, Patrick A. "Pouring New Wine into Old Wineskins: The Guaranty Clause and a Federalist Jurisprudence of Voting Rights." *Georgetown Journal of Law and Public Policy* 10 (Winter 2012): 185–213.

Yarbrough, Tinsley E. *Race and Redistricting: The Shaw-Cromartie Cases.* Lawrence: University Press of Kansas, 2002.

Wesberry v. Sanders
376 U.S. 1 (1964)

Georgia had a long-established system of single-member districts for congressional elections, but since 1931 it had failed to realign the state's districts to equalize the population of each district. As a result, the Fifth Congressional District by 1960 had a population of 823,680, more than double the average population of other districts in the state. Several voters in the Fifth District filed a class-action suit in federal court, claiming that the population disparities deprived them and other voters in the district of a right to have their votes for members of Congress given the same weight as the votes of other Georgians. A three-judge district court, though acknowledging that the population of the Fifth District was "grossly out of balance" with those of other districts, dismissed the complaint for "want of equity." The voters then appealed their case to the US Supreme Court. Opinion of the Court: <u>Black</u>, Warren, Douglas, Brennan, White, Goldberg. Concurring opinion: <u>Clark</u>. Dissenting opinion: <u>Harlan</u>, Stewart (in part).

JUSTICE BLACK delivered the opinion of the Court.

Baker v. Carr (1962) considered a challenge to a 1901 Tennessee statute providing for apportionment of State Representatives and Senators under the State's constitution, which called for apportionment among counties or districts "according to the number of qualified voters in each." The complaint there charged that the State's constitutional command to apportion on the basis of the number of qualified voters had not been followed in the 1901 statute and that the districts were so discriminatorily disparate in number of qualified voters that the plaintiffs and persons similarly situated were, "by virtue of the debasement of their votes," denied the equal protection of the laws guaranteed them by the Fourteenth Amendment. The cause there of the alleged "debasement" of votes for state legislators—districts containing widely varying numbers of people—was precisely that which was alleged to debase votes for Congressmen in *Colegrove v. Green* (1946) and in the present case. The Court in *Baker* pointed out that the opinion of

Justice Frankfurter in *Colegrove,* upon the reasoning of which the majority below leaned heavily in dismissing "for want of equity," was approved by only three of the seven Justices sitting. After full consideration of *Colegrove,* the Court in *Baker* held (1) that the District Court had jurisdiction of the subject matter; (2) that the qualified Tennessee voters there had standing to sue; and (3) that the plaintiffs had stated a justiciable cause of action on which relief could be granted.

The reasons which led to these conclusions in *Baker* are equally persuasive here.

This brings us to the merits. We agree with the District Court that the 1931 Georgia apportionment grossly discriminates against voters in the Fifth Congressional District. A single Congressman represents from two to three times as many Fifth District voters as are represented by each of the Congressmen from the other Georgia congressional districts. The apportionment statute thus *contracts* the value of some votes and expands that of others. If the Federal Constitution intends that when qualified voters elect members of Congress each vote be given as much weight as any other vote, then this statute cannot stand.

We hold that, construed in its historical context, the command of Art. I, §2, that Representatives be chosen "by the people of the several States" means that as nearly as is practicable one man's vote in a congressional election is to be worth as much as another's. This rule is followed automatically, of course, when Representatives are chosen as a group on a state-wide basis, as was a widespread *practice* in the first 50 years of our Nation's history. It would be extraordinary to suggest that in such state-wide elections the votes of inhabitants of some parts of a State, for example, Georgia's thinly populated Ninth District, could be weighed at two or three times the value of the votes of people living in more populous parts of the State, for example, the Fifth District around Atlanta. We do not believe that the Framers of the Constitution intended to permit the same vote-diluting discrimination to be accomplished through the device of districts containing widely varied numbers of inhabitants. To say that a vote is worth more in one district than in another would not only run counter to our fundamental ideas of democratic government, it would cast aside the principle of a House of Representatives elected "by the People," a principle tenaciously fought for and established at the Constitutional Convention. The history of the Constitution, particularly that part of it relating to the adoption of Art. I, §2, reveals that those who framed the Constitution meant that, no matter what the mechanics of an election, whether state-wide or by districts, it was population which was to be the basis of the House of Representatives. . . .

No right is more precious in a free country than that of having a voice in the election of those who make the laws under which, as good citizens, we must live. Other rights, even the most basic, are illusory if the right to vote is undermined. Our constitution leaves no room for classification of people in a way that unnecessarily abridges this right. In urging the people to adopt the Constitution, Madison said in No. 57 of *The Federalist*:

Who are to be the electors of the Federal Representatives? Not the rich more than the poor; not the learned more than the ignorant; not the haughty heirs of distinguished names, more than the humble sons of obscure and unpropitious fortune. The electors are to be the great body of the people of the United States. . . .

Readers surely could have fairly taken this to mean "one person, one vote." While it may not be possible to draw congressional districts with mathematical precision, that is no excuse for ignoring our Constitution's plain objective of making equal representation for equal numbers of people the fundamental goal for the House of Representatives. That is the high standard of justice and common sense which the Founders set for us.

JUSTICE HARLAN, dissenting.

I had not expected to witness the day when the Supreme Court of the United States would render a decision which casts grave doubt on the constitutionality of the composition of the House of Representatives. It is not an exaggeration to say that such is the effect of today's decision. The Court's holding that the Constitution requires States to select Representatives either by elections at large or by elections in districts composed "as nearly as is practicable" of equal population places in jeopardy the seats of almost all the members of the present House of Representatives.

In the last congressional election, in 1962, Representatives from 42 States were elected from congressional districts. In all but five of those States, the difference between the populations of the largest and smallest districts exceeded 100,000 persons. A difference of this magnitude in the size of districts the average population of which in each state is less than 500,000 is presumably not equality among districts "as nearly as is practicable," although the Court does not reveal its definition of that phrase. Thus, today's decision impugns the validity of the election of 398 Representatives from 37 States, leaving a "constitutional" House of 37 members now sitting. . . .

The Court holds that the provision in Art. I, §2, for election of Representatives "by the People" *means* that congressional districts are to be "as nearly as is practicable" equal in population. Stripped of rhetoric and a "historical context," which bears little resemblance to the evidence found in the pages of history, the Court's opinion supports its holding only with the bland assertion that "the principle of a House of Representatives elected 'by the People'" would be "cast aside" if "a vote is worth more in one district than in another," if congressional districts within a State, each electing a single Representative, are not equal in population. The fact is, however, that Georgia's 10 Representatives *are* elected "by the People" of Georgia, just as Representatives from other States are elected "by the People of the several States." This is all that the Constitution requires.

Although the Court finds necessity for its artificial construction of Article I in the undoubted importance of the right to vote, that right is not involved in this case. All of the appellants do vote. The Court's talk about "debasement" and "dilution" of the vote is a model of circular reasoning, in which the premises of the argument feed on the conclusion. Moreover, by focusing exclusively on numbers in disregard of the area and shape of a congressional district as well as party affiliations within the district, the Court deals in abstractions which will be recognized even by the politically unsophisticated to have little relevance to the realities of political life.

Far from supporting the Court, the apportionment of Representatives among the States shows how blindly the Court has marched to its decision. Representatives were to be apportioned among the States on the basis of free population plus three-fifths of the slave population. Since no slave voted, the inclusion of three-fifths of their number in the basis of apportionment gave the favored States representation far in excess of their voting population. If, then, slaves were intended to be without representation, Article I did exactly what the Court now says it prohibited: it "weighted" the vote of voters in the slave States. Alternatively, it might have been thought that Representatives elected by free men of a State would speak also for the slaves. But since the slaves added to the representation only of their own State, Representatives from the slave States could have been thought to speak only for the slaves of their own States, indicating both that the Convention believed it possible for a Representative elected by one group to speak for another nonvoting group and that Representatives were in large degree still thought of as speaking for the whole population *of a State.* . . .

Today's decision has portents for our society and the Court itself which should be recognized. This is not a case in which the Court vindicates the kind of individual rights that are assured by the Due Process Clause of the Fourteenth Amendment, whose "vague contours" of course leave much room for constitutional developments necessitated by changing conditions in a dynamic society. Nor is this a case in which an emergent set of facts requires the Court to frame new principles to protect recognized constitutional rights. The claim for judicial relief in this case strikes at one of the fundamental doctrines of our system of government, the separation of powers. In upholding that claim, the Court attempts to effect reforms in a field which the Constitution, as plainly as can be, has committed exclusively to the political process.

This Court, no less than all other branches of the Government, is bound by the Constitution. The Constitution does not confer on the Court blanket authority to step into every situation where the political branch may be thought to have fallen short. The stability of this institution ultimately depends not only upon its being alert to keep the other branches of government within constitutional bounds but equally upon recognition of the limitations on the Court's own functions in the constitutional system.

What is done today saps the political process. The promise of judicial intervention in matters of this sort cannot but encourage popular inertia in efforts for political reform through the political process, with the inevitable result that the process is itself weakened. By yielding to the demand for a judicial remedy in this instance, the Court in my view does a disservice both to itself and to the broader values of our system of government.

Believing that the complaint fails to disclose a constitutional claim, I would affirm the judgment below dismissing the complaint.

Reynolds v. Sims
377 U.S. 533 (1964)

M. O. Sims and other Alabama residents brought suit against B. A. Reynolds and other state election officials, challenging the apportionment of the state legislature. The Alabama Constitution provided that the legislature be reapportioned decennially on the basis of population, but with the qualification that each county be allocated one representative and that no county be apportioned more than one senator. Because no reapportionment had taken place since 1901, however, a substantial degree of malapportionment existed: some highly populous senatorial districts had more than forty-one times as many people as others, and some legislative districts had populations sixteen times larger than others. It was possible, under the existing scheme of apportionment, for 25 percent of the population to elect a majority in the state senate and for approximately the same percentage to elect a majority of the state's representatives. A federal district court held that Alabama's scheme of apportionment violated the Equal Protection Clause of the Fourteenth Amendment. In response to this decision, the Alabama Legislature adopted two alternative reapportionment plans, neither of which apportioned the legislature solely on the basis of population. When the district court also invalidated those plans, the defendants appealed to the Supreme Court. Opinion of the Court: Warren, Black, Douglas, Brennan, White, Goldberg. Concurring in the judgment: Clark; Stewart. Dissenting opinion: Harlan.

THE CHIEF JUSTICE delivered the opinion of the Court.

. . . Our problem is to ascertain . . . whether there are any constitutionally cognizable principles which would justify departures from the basic standard of equality among voters in the apportionment of seats in state legislatures.

A predominant consideration in determining whether a State's legislative apportionment scheme constitutes an invidious discrimination violative of rights asserted under the Equal Protection Clause is that the rights allegedly impaired are individual and personal in nature. . . . While the result of a court decision in a state legislative apportionment controversy may be to require the restructuring of the geographical distribution of seats in a state legislature, the judicial focus must be concentrated upon ascertaining whether there has been any discrimination against certain of the State's citizens which constitutes an impermissible impairment of their constitutionally protected right to vote. . . . Undoubtedly, the right of suffrage is a fundamental matter in a free and democratic society. Especially since the right to exercise the franchise in a free and unimpaired manner is preservative of other basic civil and political rights, any alleged infringement of the right of citizens to vote must be carefully and meticulously scrutinized.

Legislators represent people, not trees or acres. Legislators are elected by voters, not farms or cities or economic interests. As long as ours is a representative form of government, and our legislatures are those instruments of

government elected directly by and directly representative of the people, the right to elect legislators in a free and unimpaired fashion is a bedrock of our political system. It could hardly be gainsaid that a constitutional claim had been asserted by an allegation that certain otherwise qualified voters had been entirely prohibited from voting for members of their state legislature. And, if a State should provide that the votes of citizens in one part of the State should be given two times, or five times, or 10 times the weight of votes of citizens in another part of the State, it could hardly be contended that the right to vote of those residing in the disfavored areas had not been effectively diluted. It would appear extraordinary to suggest that a State could be constitutionally permitted to enact a law providing that certain of the State's voters could vote two, five, or 10 times for their legislative representatives, while voters living elsewhere could vote only once. And it is inconceivable that a state law to the effect that, in counting votes for legislators, the votes of citizens in one part of the State would be multiplied by two, five, or 10, while the votes of persons in another area would be counted only at face value, could be constitutionally sustainable. Of course, the effect of state legislative districting schemes which give the same number of representatives to unequal numbers of constituents is identical. Overweighting and overvaluation of the votes of those living here has the certain effect of dilution and undervaluation of the votes of those living there. The resulting discrimination against those individual voters living in disfavored areas is easily demonstrable mathematically. Their right to vote is simply not the same right to vote as that of those living in a favored part of the State. Two, five, or 10 of them must vote before the effect of their voting is equivalent to that of their favored neighbor. Weighting the votes of citizens differently, by any method or means, merely because of where they happen to reside, hardly seems justifiable. One must be ever aware that the Constitution forbids "sophisticated as well as simple-minded modes of discrimination." . . .

. . . Representative government is in essence self-government through the medium of elected representatives of the people, and each and every citizen has an inalienable right to full and effective participation in the political processes of his State's legislative bodies. Most citizens can achieve this participation only as qualified voters through the election of legislators to represent them. Full and effective participation by all citizens in state government requires, therefore, that each citizen have an equally effective voice in the election of members of his state legislature. Modern and viable state government needs, and the Constitution demands, no less.

Logically, in a society ostensibly grounded on representative government, it would seem reasonable that a majority of the people of a State could elect a majority of that State's legislators. To conclude differently, and to sanction minority control of state legislative bodies, would appear to deny majority rights in a way that far surpasses any possible denial of minority rights that might otherwise be thought to result. Since legislatures are responsible for enacting laws by which all citizens are to be governed, they should be bodies which are collectively responsive to the popular will. And the concept of equal protection has been traditionally viewed as requiring the uniform treatment of persons standing in the same relation to the governmental action questioned or challenged. With respect to the allocation of legislative representation, all voters, as citizens of a State, stand in the same relation regardless of where they live. Any suggested criteria for the differentiation of citizens are insufficient to justify any discrimination, as to the weight of their votes, unless relevant to the permissible purposes of legislative apportionment. Since the achieving of fair and effective representation for all citizens is concededly the basic aim of legislative apportionment, we conclude that the Equal Protection Clause guarantees the opportunity for equal participation by all voters in the election of state legislators. Diluting the weight of votes because of place of residence impairs basic constitutional rights under the Fourteenth Amendment just as much as invidious discriminations based upon factors such as race . . . or economic status. . . . Our constitutional system amply provides for the protection of minorities by means other than giving them majority control of state legislatures. . . .

We are told that the matter of apportioning representation in a state legislature is a complex and many-faceted one. We are advised that States can rationally consider factors other than population in apportioning legislative representation. We are admonished not to restrict the power of the States to impose differing views as to political philosophy on their citizens. We are cautioned about the dangers of entering into political thickets and mathematical quagmires. Our answer is this: a denial of constitutionally protected rights demands judicial protection; our oath and our office require no less of us. . . . To the extent that a citizen's right to vote is debased, he is that much less a citizen. The fact that an individual lives here or there is not a legitimate reason for overweighting or diluting the efficacy of his vote. . . .

. . . Population is, of necessity, the starting point for consideration and the controlling criterion for judgment in legislative apportionment controversies.

We hold that, as a basic constitutional standard, the Equal Protection Clause requires that the seats in both houses of a bicameral state legislature must be apportioned on a population basis. Simply stated, an individual's right to vote for state legislators is unconstitutionally impaired when its weight is in a substantial fashion diluted when compared with votes of citizens living in other parts of the State. . . .

Since neither of the houses of the Alabama Legislature, under any of the three plans considered by the District Court, was apportioned on a population basis, we would be justified in proceeding no further. However, one of the proposed plans . . . at least superficially resembles the scheme of legislative representation followed in the Federal Congress. Under this plan, each of Alabama's 67 counties is allotted one senator, and no counties are given more than one Senate seat. Arguably, this is analogous to the allocation of two Senate seats, in the Federal Congress, to each of the 50 States, regardless of population. . . .

After considering the matter, the court below concluded that no conceivable analogy could be drawn between the federal scheme and the apportionment of seats in the Alabama Legislature under the proposed constitutional amendment. We agree with the District Court, and find the federal analogy inapposite and irrelevant to state legislative districting schemes. Attempted reliance on the federal analogy appears often to be little more than an after-the-fact rationalization offered in defense of maladjusted state apportionment arrangements.

The system of representation in the two Houses of the Federal Congress is one ingrained in our Constitution, as part of the law of the land. It is one conceived out of compromise and concession indispensable to the establishment of our federal republic. Arising from unique historical circumstances, it is based on the consideration that in establishing our type of federalism a group of formerly independent States bound themselves together under one national government. . . .

Political subdivisions of States—counties, cities, or whatever—never were and never have been considered as sovereign entities. Rather, they have been traditionally regarded as subordinate governmental instrumentalities created by the State to assist in the carrying out of state governmental functions. . . .

Since we find the so-called federal analogy inapposite to a consideration of the constitutional validity of state legislative apportionment schemes, we necessarily hold that the Equal Protection Clause requires both houses of a state legislature to be apportioned on a population basis. The right of a citizen to equal representation and to have his vote weighted equally with those of all other citizens in the election of members of one house of a bicameral state legislature would amount to little if States could effectively submerge the equal-population principle in the apportionment of seats in the other house. . . .

JUSTICE HARLAN, dissenting.

The Court's constitutional discussion . . . is remarkable . . . for its failure to address itself at all to the Fourteenth Amendment as a whole. . . .

The Court relies exclusively on that portion of §1 of the Fourteenth Amendment which provides that no State shall "deny to any person within its jurisdiction the equal protection of the laws," and disregards entirely the significance of §2, which reads: "Representatives shall be apportioned among the several States according to their respective numbers, counting the whole number of persons in each State, excluding Indians not taxed. But when the right to vote at any election for the choice of electors for President and Vice President of the United States, Representatives in Congress, the Executive and Judicial officers of a State, or the members of the Legislature thereof, is denied to any of the male inhabitants of such State, being twenty-one years of age, and citizens of the United States, or in any way abridged, except for participation in rebellion, or other crime, the basis of representation therein shall be reduced in the proportion which the number of such male citizens shall bear to the whole number of male citizens twenty-one years of age in such State."

The Amendment is a single text. It was introduced and discussed as such in the Reconstruction Committee, which reported it to the Congress. It was discussed as a unit in Congress and proposed as a unit to the States, which ratified it as a unit. A proposal to split up the Amendment and submit each section to the States as a separate amendment was rejected by the Senate. Whatever one might take to be the application to these cases of the Equal Protection Clause if it stood alone, I am unable to understand the Court's utter disregard of the second section which expressly recognizes the States' power to deny "or in any way" abridge the right of their inhabitants to vote for "the members of the [State] Legislature," and its express provision of a remedy for such denial or abridgment. The comprehensive scope of the second section and its particular reference to the state legislatures preclude the suggestion that the first section was intended to have the result reached by the Court today. If indeed the words of the Fourteenth Amendment speak for themselves, as the majority's disregard of history seems to imply, they speak as clearly as may be against the construction which the majority puts on them. . . .

. . . Note should be taken of the Fifteenth and Nineteenth Amendments. The former prohibited the States from denying or abridging the right to vote "on account of race, color, or previous condition of servitude." The latter, certified as part of the Constitution in 1920, added sex to the prohibited classifications. . . .

. . . Unless one takes the highly implausible view that the Fourteenth Amendment controls methods of apportionment but leaves the right to vote itself unprotected, the conclusion is inescapable that the Court has, for purposes of these cases, relegated the Fifteenth and Nineteenth Amendments to the same limbo of constitutional anachronisms to which the second section of the Fourteenth Amendment has been assigned. . . .

Although the Court—necessarily, as I believe—provides only generalities in elaboration of its main thesis, its opinion nevertheless fully demonstrates how far removed these problems are from fields of judicial competence. Recognizing that "indiscriminate districting" is an invitation to "partisan gerrymandering," . . . the Court nevertheless excludes virtually every basis for the formation of electoral districts other than "indiscriminate districting." . . . So far as presently appears, the *only* factor which a State may consider, apart from numbers, is political subdivisions. But even "a clearly rational state policy" recognizing this factor is unconstitutional if "population is submerged as the controlling consideration." . . .

. . . These decisions give support to a current mistaken view of the Constitution and the constitutional function of this Court. This view, in a nutshell, is that every major social ill in this country can find its cure in some constitutional "principle," and that this Court should "take the lead" in promoting reform when other branches of government fail to act. The Constitution is not a panacea for every blot upon the public welfare, nor should this Court, ordained as a judicial body, be thought of as a general haven for reform movements. The Constitution is an instrument of government, fundamental to which is the premise that in a diffusion of governmental authority lies the greatest promise that this Nation will realize liberty for all its citizens. This Court, limited in function in accordance with that premise, does not serve its high purpose when it exceeds its authority, even to satisfy justified impatience with the slow workings of the political process. For when, in the name of constitutional interpretation, the Court *adds* something to the Constitution that was deliberately excluded from it, the Court in reality substitutes its view of what should be so for the amending process.

Vieth v. Jubelirer
541 U.S. 267 (2004)

After the Republican-controlled Pennsylvania Legislature adopted a congressional redistricting plan, three registered Democrats sued to enjoin the plan's implementation, alleging that it constituted a political gerrymander in violation of Article I of the Constitution and the Fourteenth Amendment's Equal Protection Clause. The three-judge district court dismissed the gerrymandering claim, and the plaintiffs appealed to the Supreme Court. Judgment of the Court: <u>Scalia</u>, Rehnquist, O'Connor, Thomas. Concurring in the judgment: <u>Kennedy</u>. Dissenting opinions: <u>Stevens</u>; <u>Souter</u>, Ginsburg; <u>Breyer</u>.

JUSTICE SCALIA announced the judgment of the Court and delivered an opinion, in which THE CHIEF JUSTICE, JUSTICE O'CONNOR, and JUSTICE THOMAS join.

Plaintiffs-appellants Richard Vieth, Norma Jean Vieth, and Susan Furey challenge a map drawn by the Pennsylvania General Assembly establishing districts for the election of congressional Representatives, on the ground that the districting constitutes an unconstitutional political gerrymander. In *Davis v. Bandemer* (1986), this Court held that political gerrymandering claims are justiciable, but could not agree upon a standard to adjudicate them. The present appeal presents the questions whether our decision in *Bandemer* was in error, and, if not, what the standard should be. . . .

Political gerrymanders are not new to the American scene. One scholar traces them back to the Colony of Pennsylvania at the beginning of the 18th century, where several counties conspired to minimize the political power of the city of Philadelphia by refusing to allow it to merge or expand into surrounding jurisdictions, and denying it additional representatives. The political gerrymander remained alive and well (though not yet known by that name) at the time of the framing. There were allegations that Patrick Henry attempted (unsuccessfully) to gerrymander James Madison out of the First Congress. And in 1812, of course, there occurred the notoriously outrageous political districting in Massachusetts that gave the gerrymander its name—an amalgam of the names of Massachusetts Governor Elbridge Gerry and the creature ("salamander") which the outline of an election district he was credited with forming was thought to resemble. . . .

It is significant that the Framers provided a remedy for such practices in the Constitution. Article 1, §4, while leaving in state legislatures the initial power to draw districts for federal elections, permitted Congress to "make or alter" those districts if it wished. Many objected to the congressional oversight established by this provision. In the course of the debates in the Constitutional Convention, Charles Pinckney and John Rutledge moved to strike the relevant language. James Madison responded in defense of the provision that Congress must be given the power to check partisan manipulation of the election process by the States. . . .

The power bestowed on Congress to regulate elections, and in particular to restrain the practice of political gerrymandering, has not lain dormant. In the Apportionment Act of 1842, Congress provided that Representatives must be elected from single-member districts "composed of contiguous territory." Congress again imposed these requirements in the Apportionment Act of 1862, and in 1872 further required that districts "contain as nearly as practicable an equal number of inhabitants." In the Apportionment Act of 1901, Congress imposed a compactness requirement. The requirements of contiguity, compactness, and equality of population were repeated in the 1911 apportionment legislation, but were not thereafter continued. Today, only the single-member-district-requirement remains. Recent history, however, attests to Congress's awareness of the sort of districting practices appellants protest, and of its power under Article I, §4 to control them. Since 1980, no fewer than five bills have been introduced to regulate gerrymandering in congressional districting.

Eighteen years ago, we held that the Equal Protection Clause grants judges the power—and duty—to control political gerrymandering. It is to consideration of this precedent that we now turn.

As Chief Justice Marshall proclaimed two centuries ago, "it is emphatically the province and duty of the judicial department to say what the law is." *Marbury v. Madison* (1803). Sometimes, however, the law is that the judicial department has no business entertaining the claim of unlawfulness—because the question is entrusted to one of the political branches or involves no judicially enforceable rights. Such questions are said to be "nonjusticiable," or "political questions."

In *Baker v. Carr* (1962), we set forth six independent tests for the existence of a political question. . . . The second [i.e., a lack of judicially discoverable and manageable standards for resolving it] is at issue here, and there is no doubt of its validity. . . . It is the power to act in the manner traditional for English and American courts. One of the most obvious limitations imposed by that requirement is that judicial action must be governed by *standard,* by *rule.* Laws promulgated by the Legislative Branch can be inconsistent, illogical, and ad hoc; law pronounced by the courts must be principled, rational, and based upon reasoned distinctions.

Over the dissent of three Justices, the Court held in *Davis v. Bandemer* that, since it was "not persuaded that there are no judicially discernible and manageable standards by which political gerrymander cases are to be decided," such cases *were* justiciable. The clumsy shifting of the burden of proof for the premise (the Court was "not persuaded" that standards do not exist, rather than "persuaded" that they do) was necessitated by the uncomfortable fact that the six-Justice majority could not discern what the judicially discernible standards might be. There was no majority on that point. Four of the Justices finding justiciability believed that the standard was one thing; two believed it was something else. The lower courts have lived with that assurance of a standard (or more precisely, lack of assurance that there is no standard), coupled with that inability to specify a standard, for the past 18 years. In that time, they have considered numerous political gerrymandering claims; this Court has never revisited the unanswered question of what standard governs.

Nor can it be said that the lower courts have, over 18 years, succeeded in shaping the standard that this Court was initially unable to enunciate. They have simply applied the standard set forth in *Bandemer*'s four-Justice plurality opinion. This might be thought to prove that the four-Justice plurality standard has met the test of time—but for the fact that its application has almost invariably produced the same result (except for the incurring of attorney's fees) as would have obtained if the question were nonjusticiable: judicial intervention has been refused. As one commentary has put it, "throughout its subsequent history, *Bandemer* has served almost exclusively as an invitation to litigation without much prospect of redress."

. . . Eighteen years of judicial effort with virtually nothing to show for it justify us in revisiting the question whether the standard promised by *Bandemer* exists. As the following discussion reveals, no judicially discernible and manageable standards for adjudicating political gerrymandering claims have emerged. Lacking them, we must conclude that political gerrymandering claims are nonjusticiable and that *Bandemer* was wrongly decided.

We begin our review of possible standards with that proposed by Justice White's plurality opinion in *Bandemer* because, as the narrowest ground for our decision in that case, it has been the standard employed by the lower courts. The plurality concluded that a political gerrymandering claim could succeed only where plaintiffs showed "both intentional discrimination against an identifiable political group and an actual discriminatory effect on that group." As to the intent element, the plurality acknowledged that "as long as redistricting is done by a legislature, it should not be very difficult to prove that the likely political consequences of the reapportionment were intended." However, the effects prong was significantly harder to satisfy. Relief could not be based merely upon the fact that a group of persons banded together for political purposes had failed to achieve representation commensurate with its numbers, or that the apportionment scheme made its winning of

elections more difficult. Rather, it would have to be shown that, taking into account a variety of historic factors and projected election results, the group had been "denied its chance to effectively influence the political process" as a whole, which could be achieved even without electing a candidate. . . .

In her *Bandemer* concurrence, Justice O'Connor predicted that the plurality's standard "will over time either prove unmanageable and arbitrary or else evolve towards some loose form of proportionality." That prognostication has been amply fulfilled. Because this standard was misguided when proposed, has not been improved in subsequent application, and is not even defended before us today by the appellants, we decline to affirm it as a constitutional requirement.

Appellants take a run at enunciating their own workable standard based on Article I, §2, and the Equal Protection Clause. We consider it at length not only because it reflects the litigant's view as to the best that can be derived from 18 years of experience, but also because it shares many features with other proposed standards, so that what is said of it may be said of them as well. Appellants' proposed standard retains the two-pronged framework of the *Bandemer* plurality—intent plus effect—but modifies the type of showing sufficient to satisfy each.

To satisfy appellants' intent standard, a plaintiff must "show that the mapmakers acted with a *predominant intent* to achieve partisan advantage," which can be shown "by direct evidence or by circumstantial evidence that other neutral and legitimate redistricting criteria were subordinated to the goal of achieving partisan advantage." As compared with the *Bandemer* plurality's test of mere intent to disadvantage the plaintiff's group, this proposal seemingly makes the standard more difficult to meet—but only at the expense of making the standard more indeterminate.

"Predominant intent" to disadvantage the plaintiff political group refers to the relative importance of that goal as compared with all the other goals that the map seeks to pursue—contiguity of districts, compactness of districts, observance of the lines of political subdivision, protection of incumbents of all parties, cohesion of natural racial and ethnic neighborhoods, compliance with requirements of the Voting Rights Act of 1965 regarding racial distribution, etc. Appellants . . . do not assert that an apportionment fails their intent test if any single district does so. Since "it would be quixotic to attempt to bar state legislatures from considering politics as they redraw district lines," appellants propose a test that is satisfied only when "partisan advantage was the predominant motivation *behind the entire statewide plan.*" Vague as the "predominant motivation" test might be when used to evaluate single districts, it all but evaporates when applied state-wide. Does it mean, for instance, that partisan intent must outweigh all other goals—contiguity, compactness, preservation of neighborhoods, etc.—*state-wide*? And how is the state-wide "outweighing" to be determined? If three-fifths of the map's districts forgo the pursuit of partisan ends in favor of strictly observing political-subdivision lines, and only two-fifths ignore those lines to disadvantage the plaintiffs, is the observance of political subdivisions the "predominant" goal between those two? We are sure appellants do not think so. . . .

The effects prong of appellants' proposal replaces the *Bandemer* plurality's vague test of "denied its chance to effectively influence the political process" with criteria that are seemingly more specific. The requisite effect is established when "(1) the plaintiffs show that the districts systematically 'pack' and 'crack' the rival party's voters *and* (2) the court's examination of the 'totality of circumstances' confirms that the map can thwart the plaintiffs' ability to translate a majority of votes into a majority of seats." This test is loosely based on our cases applying §2 of the Voting Rights Act to discrimination by race. But a person's politics is rarely as readily discernible—and *never* as permanently discernible—as a person's race. Political affiliation is not an immutable characteristic, but may shift from one election to the next; and even within a given election, not all voters follow the party line. We dare say (and hope) that the political party which puts forward an utterly incompetent candidate will lose even in its registration stronghold. These facts make it impossible to

assess the effects of partisan gerrymandering, to fashion a standard for evaluating a violation, and finally to craft a remedy.

Assuming, however, that the effects of partisan gerrymandering can be determined, appellants' test would invalidate the districting only when it prevents a majority of the electorate from electing a majority of representatives. Before considering whether this particular standard is judicially manageable we question whether it is judicially discernible in the sense of being relevant to some constitutional violation. Deny it as appellants may (and do), this standard rests upon the principle that groups (or at least political-action groups) have a right to proportional representation. But the Constitution contains no such principle. It guarantees equal protection of the law to persons, not equal representation in government to equivalently sized groups. It nowhere says that farmers or urban dwellers, Christian fundamentalists or Jews, Republicans or Democrats, must be accorded political strength proportionate to their numbers.

Even if the standard were relevant, however, it is not judicially manageable. To begin with, how is a party's majority status to be established? . . . [I]f we could identify a majority party, we would find it impossible to assure that that party wins a majority of seats—unless we radically revise the States' traditional structure for elections. In any winner-take-all district system, there can be no guarantee, no matter how the district lines are drawn, that a majority of party votes state-wide will produce a majority of seats for that party. The point is proved by the 2000 congressional elections in Pennsylvania, which, according to appellants' own pleadings, were conducted under a judicially drawn district map "free from partisan gerrymandering." On this "neutral playing field," the Democrats' state-wide majority of the major-party vote (50.6%) translated into a minority of seats (10, versus 11 for the Republicans). Whether by reason of partisan districting or not, party constituents may always wind up "packed" in some districts and "cracked" throughout others. Consider, for example, a legislature that draws district lines with no objectives in mind except compactness and respect for the lines of political subdivisions.

Under that system, political groups that tend to cluster (as is the case with Democratic voters in cities) would be systematically affected by what might be called a "natural" packing effect. . . . [R]equiring judges to decide whether a districting system will produce a state-wide majority for a majority party casts them forth upon a sea of imponderables, and asks them to make determinations that not even election experts can agree upon. For these reasons, we find appellants' proposed standards neither discernible nor manageable.

We turn next to consideration of the standards proposed by today's dissenters. We preface it with the observation that the mere fact that these four dissenters come up with three different standards—all of them different from the two proposed in *Bandemer* and the one proposed here by appellants—goes a long way to establishing that there is no constitutionally discernible standard. . . .

Justice Stevens would . . . require courts to consider political gerrymandering challenges at the individual-district level. Much of his dissent is addressed to the incompatibility of severe partisan gerrymanders with democratic principles. We do not disagree with that judgment, any more than we disagree with the judgment that it would be unconstitutional for the Senate to employ, in impeachment proceedings, procedures that are incompatible with its obligation to "try" impeachments. The issue we have discussed is not whether severe partisan gerrymanders violate the Constitution, but whether it is for the courts to say when a violation has occurred, and to design a remedy. On that point, Justice Steven's dissent is less helpful, saying, essentially, that if we can do it in the racial gerrymandering context we can do it here.

. . . Justice Souter recognizes that there is no existing workable standard for adjudicating [these] claims. He proposes a "fresh start": a newly constructed standard loosely based in form on our Title VII cases, see *McDonnell Douglas Corp. v. Green* (1973), and complete with a five-step prima facie test sewn together from parts of, among other things, our Voting Rights Act jurisprudence, law review articles, and apportionment cases. Even if these self-styled "clues" to unconstitutionality could be

manageably applied, which we doubt, there is no reason to think they would detect the constitutional crime which Justice Souter is investigating—an "extremity of unfairness" in partisan competition. . . .

Justice Souter's proposal is doomed to failure for a more basic reason: No test—yea, not even a five-part test—can possibly be successful unless one knows what he is testing *for*. In the present context, the test ought to identify deprivation of that minimal degree of representation or influence to which a political group is constitutionally entitled. As we have seen, the *Bandemer* test sought (unhelpfully, but at least gamely) to specify what that minimal degree was: "[a] chance to effectively influence the political process." So did the appellants' proposed test: "[the] ability to translate a majority of votes into a majority of seats." Justice Souter avoids the difficulties of those formulations by never telling us what his test is looking for, other than the utterly unhelpful "extremity of unfairness." He vaguely describes the harm he is concerned with as vote dilution, a term which usually implies some actual effect on the weight of a vote. But no element of his test looks to the effect of the gerrymander on the electoral success, the electoral opportunity, or even the political influence, of the plaintiff group. We do not know the precise constitutional deprivation his test is designed to identify and prevent. . . .

We agree with much of Justice Breyer's dissenting opinion, which convincingly demonstrates that "political considerations will likely play an important, and proper, role in the drawing of district boundaries." This places Justice Breyer, like the other dissenters, in the difficult position of drawing the line between good politics and bad politics. Unlike them, he would tackle this problem at the state-wide level.

The criterion Justice Breyer proposes is nothing more precise than "the *unjustified* use of political factors to entrench a minority in power." While he invokes in passing the Equal Protection Clause, it should be clear to any reader that what constitutes *unjustified* entrenchment depends on his own theory of effective government. . . .

Justice Kennedy recognizes that we have "demonstrated the shortcomings of the other standards that have been considered to date." He acknowledges, moreover, that we "lack . . . comprehensive and neutral principles for drawing electoral boundaries," and that there is an "absence of rules to limit and confine judicial intervention." From these premises, one might think that Justice Kennedy would reach the conclusion that political gerrymandering claims are nonjusticiable. Instead, however, he concludes that courts should continue to adjudicate such claims because a standard *may* one day be discovered.

The first thing to be said about Justice Kennedy's disposition is that it is not legally available. The District Court in this case considered the plaintiffs' claims *justiciable* but dismissed them because the standard for unconstitutionality had not been met. It is logically impossible to affirm that dismissal without either (1) finding that the unconstitutional-districting standard applied by the District Court, or some other standard that it *should* have applied has not been met, or (2) finding (as we have) that the claim is nonjusticiable. Justice Kennedy seeks to affirm "because, in the case before us, we have no standard." But it is *our* job, not the plaintiffs', to explicate the standard that makes the facts alleged by the plaintiffs adequate or inadequate to state a claim. We cannot nonsuit *them* for our failure to do so.

Justice Kennedy asserts that to declare nonjusticiability would be incautious. Our rush to such a holding after a mere 18 years of fruitless litigation "contrasts starkly" he says, "with the more patient approach" that this Court has taken in the past. We think not. When it has come to determining what areas fall beyond our Article III authority to adjudicate, this Court's practice, from the earliest days of the Republic to the present, has been more reminiscent of Hannibal than of Hamlet.

. . . Reduced to its essence, Justice Kennedy's opinion boils down to this: "As presently advised, I know of no discernible and manageable standard that can render this claim justiciable. I am unhappy about that, and hope that I will be able to change my opinion in the future." What are the lower courts to make of this pronouncement? We suggest that they must treat it as a reluctant fifth vote against justiciability at district and state-wide levels—a

vote that may change in some future case but that holds, for the time being, that this matter is nonjusticiable. . . .

While we do not lightly overturn one of our own holdings, "when governing decisions are unworkable or are badly reasoned, 'this Court has never felt constrained to follow precedent.'" Eighteen years of essentially pointless litigation have persuaded us that *Bandemer* is incapable of principled application. We would therefore overrule that case, and decline to adjudicate these political gerrymandering claims.

The judgment of the District Court is affirmed.

JUSTICE KENNEDY, concurring in the judgment.

. . . While agreeing with the plurality that the complaint the appellants filed in the District Court must be dismissed, and while understanding that great caution is necessary when approaching this subject, I would not foreclose all possibility of judicial relief if some limited and precise rationale were found to correct an established violation of the Constitution in some redistricting cases. . . .

There are . . . weighty arguments [in the plurality opinion] for holding cases like these to be nonjusticiable; and those arguments may prevail in the long run. In my view, however, the arguments are not so compelling that they require us now to bar all future claims of injury from a partisan gerrymander. It is not in our tradition to foreclose the judicial process from the attempt to define standards and remedies where it is alleged that a constitutional right is burdened or denied. Nor is it alien to the Judiciary to draw or approve election district lines. Courts, after all, already do so in many instances. A determination by the Court to deny all hopes of intervention could erode confidence in the courts as much as would a premature decision to intervene. . . .

The plurality says that 18 years, in effect, prove the negative. . . . [B]y the timeline of the law 18 years is rather a short period. In addition, the rapid evolution of technologies in the apportionment field suggests yet unexplored possibilities. Computer assisted districting has become so routine and sophisticated that legislatures, experts, and courts can use databases to map electoral districts in a matter of hours, not months. Technology is both a threat and a promise. On the one hand, if courts refuse to entertain any claims of partisan gerrymandering, the temptation to use partisan favoritism in districting in an unconstitutional manner will grow. On the other hand, these new technologies may produce new methods of analysis that make more evident the precise nature of the burdens gerrymanders impose on the representational rights of voters and parties. That would facilitate court efforts to identify and remedy the burdens, with judicial intervention limited by the derived standards. . . .

JUSTICE STEVENS, dissenting.

The central question presented by this case is whether political gerrymandering claims are justiciable. Although our reasons for coming to this conclusion differ, five Members of the Court are convinced that the plurality's answer to that question is erroneous. Moreover, as is apparent from our separate writings today, we share the view that, even if these appellants are not entitled to prevail, it would be contrary to precedent and profoundly unwise to foreclose all judicial review of similar claims that might be advanced in the future. That we presently have somewhat differing views—concerning both the precedential value of some of our recent cases and the standard that should be applied in future cases—should not obscure the fact that the areas of agreement set forth in the separate opinions are of far greater significance.

Although we reaffirm the central holding of the Court in *Davis v. Bandemer,* we have not reached agreement on the standard that should govern partisan gerrymandering claims. I would decide this case on a narrow ground: . . . Pennsylvania's redistricting plan violates the equal protection principles enunciated in our voting rights cases both before and after *Bandemer.* . . . The plurality's contrary conclusion [concerning justiciability] cannot be squared with our long history of voting rights decisions.

. . . Especially perplexing is the plurality's *ipse dixit* distinction of our racial gerrymandering cases. . . . The critical issue in both racial and political gerrymandering cases is the same: whether a single non-neutral criterion controlled the districting process to such an extent that

the Constitution was offended. . . . [T]oday's plurality has supplied no persuasive reason for distinguishing the justiciability of partisan gerrymanders. Those cases confirm and reinforce the holding that partisan gerrymandering claims are justiciable.

Elected officials in some sense serve two masters: the constituents who elected them and the political sponsors who support them. Their primary obligations are, of course, to the public in general, but it is neither realistic nor fair to expect them wholly to ignore the political consequences of their decisions. "It would be idle . . . to contend that any political consideration taken into account in fashioning a reapportionment plan is sufficient to invalidate it." Political factors are common and permissible elements of the art of governing a democratic society.

But while political considerations may properly influence the decisions of our elected officials, when such decisions disadvantage members of a minority group—whether the minority is defined by its members' race, religion, or political affiliation—they must rest on a neutral predicate. The Constitution enforces "a commitment to the law's neutrality where the rights of persons are at stake." Thus, the Equal Protection Clause implements a duty to govern impartially that requires, at the very least, that every decision by the sovereign serve some nonpartisan public purpose. . . .

In sum, in evaluating a challenge to a specific district, I would . . . ask whether the legislature allowed partisan considerations to dominate and control the lines drawn, forsaking all neutral principles. Under my analysis, if no neutral criterion can be identified to justify the lines drawn, and if the only possible explanation for a district's bizarre shape is a naked desire to increase partisan strength, then no rational basis exists to save the district from an equal protection challenge. Such a narrow test would cover only a few meritorious claims, but it would preclude extreme abuses, and it would perhaps shorten the time period in which the pernicious effects of such a gerrymander are felt. This test would mitigate the current trend under which partisan considerations are becoming the be-all and end-all in apportioning representatives.

... What is clear is that it is not the unavailability of judicially manageable standards that drives today's decision. It is, instead, a failure of judicial will to condemn even the most blatant violations of a state legislature's fundamental duty to govern impartially. Accordingly, I respectfully dissent.

JUSTICE SOUTER, with whom JUSTICE GINSBURG joins, dissenting.

... The plurality says, in effect, that courts have been trying to devise practical criteria for political gerrymandering for nearly 20 years, without being any closer to something workable than we were when *Davis* was decided. While this is true enough, I do not accept it as sound counsel of despair. ...

Since this Court has created the problem no one else has been able to solve, it is up to us to make a fresh start. I would ... preserve *Davis's* holding that political gerrymandering is a justiciable issue, but otherwise start anew. I would adopt a political gerrymandering test analogous to the summary judgment standard crafted in *McDonnell Douglas Corp. v. Green* (1973), calling for a plaintiff to satisfy elements of a prima facie cause of action, at which point the State would have the opportunity not only to rebut the evidence supporting the plaintiff's case, but to offer an affirmative justification for the districting choices, even assuming the proof of the plaintiff's allegations. My own judgment is that we would have better luck at devising a workable *prima facie* case if we concentrated as much as possible on suspect characteristics of individual districts instead of state-wide patterns. It is not that a state-wide view of districting is somehow less important; the usual point of gerrymandering, after all, is to control the greatest number of seats overall. But, as will be seen, we would be able to call more readily on some existing law when we defined what is suspect at the district level, and for now I would conceive of a state-wide challenge as itself a function of claims that individual districts are illegitimately drawn. Finally, in the same interest of threshold simplicity, I would stick to problems of single-member districts; if we could not devise a workable scheme for dealing with claims about these, we would have to forget the complications posed by multimember districts.

For a claim based on a specific single-member district, I would require the plaintiff to make out a *prima facie* case with five elements. First, the resident plaintiff would identify a cohesive political group to which he belonged, which would normally be a major party, as in this case and in *Davis*. There is no reason in principle, however, to rule out a claimant from a minor political party. ... Second, a plaintiff would need to show that the district of his residence paid little or no heed to those traditional districting principles whose disregard can be shown straightforwardly: contiguity, compactness, respect for political subdivisions, and conformity with geographic features like rivers and mountains. ... Third, the plaintiff would need to establish specific correlations between the district's deviations from traditional districting principles and the distribution of the population of his group. ... Fourth, a plaintiff would need to present the court with a hypothetical district including his residence, one in which the proportion of the plaintiff's group was lower (in a packing claim) or higher (in a cracking one) and which at the same time deviated less from traditional districting principles than the actual district. ... Fifth, and finally, the plaintiff would have to show that the defendants acted intentionally to manipulate the shape of the district in order to pack or crack his group. ...

A plaintiff who got this far would have shown that his State intentionally acted to dilute his vote, having ignored reasonable alternatives consistent with traditional districting principles. I would then shift the burden to the defendants to justify their decision by reference to objectives other than naked partisan advantage. They might show by rebuttal evidence that districting objectives could not be served by the plaintiff's hypothetical district better than by the district as drawn, or they might affirmatively establish legitimate objectives better served by the lines drawn than by the plaintiff's hypothetical. ...

The plurality says that my proposed standard would not solve the essential problem of unworkability. It says that "it does not solve the problem [of determining when gerrymandering has gone too far] to break down the original unanswerable question . . . into four more discrete but unanswerable questions." It is common sense, however, to break down a large and intractable issue into discrete fragments as a way to get a handle on the larger one, and the elements I propose are not only tractable in theory, but the very subjects that judges already deal with in practice. . . .

JUSTICE BREYER, dissenting.

. . . By entrenchment I mean a situation in which a party that enjoys only minority support among the populace has nonetheless contrived to take, and hold, legislative power. By *unjustified* entrenchment I mean that the minority's hold on power is purely the result of partisan manipulation and not other factors. These "other" factors that could lead to "justified" (albeit temporary) minority entrenchment include sheer happenstance, the existence of more than two major parties, the unique constitutional requirements of certain representational bodies such as the Senate, or reliance on traditional (geographic, communities of interest, etc.) districting criteria.

The democratic harm of unjustified entrenchment is obvious. . . . Where unjustified entrenchment takes place, voters find it far more difficult to remove those responsible for a government they do not want; and these democratic values are dishonored. . . . Unless some other justification can be found in particular circumstances, political gerrymandering that so entrenches a minority party in power violates basic democratic norms and lacks countervailing justification. For this reason, whether political gerrymandering does, or does not, violate the Constitution in other instances, gerrymandering that leads to entrenchment amounts to an abuse that violates the Constitution's Equal Protection Clause.

Courts need not intervene often to prevent the kind of abuse I have described, because those harmed constitute a political majority, and a majority normally can work its political will. Where a State has improperly gerrymandered legislative or congressional districts to the majority's disadvantage, the majority should be able to elect officials in state-wide races—particularly the Governor—who may help to undo the harm that districting has caused the majority's party, in the next round of districting if not sooner. And where a State has improperly gerrymandered congressional districts, Congress retains the power to revise the State's districting determinations.

Moreover, voters in some States, perhaps tiring of the political boundary-drawing rivalry, have found a procedural solution, confiding the task to a commission that is limited in the extent to which it may base districts on partisan concerns. . . .

But we cannot always count on a severely gerrymandered legislature itself to find and implement a remedy. The party that controls the process has no incentive to change it. And the political advantages of a gerrymander may become ever greater in the future. The availability of enhanced computer technology allows the parties to redraw boundaries in ways that target individual neighborhoods and homes, carving out safe but slim victory margins in the maximum number of districts, with little risk of cutting their margins too thin. . . . When it is necessary, a court should prove capable of finding an appropriate remedy. . . .

The bottom line is that courts should be able to identify the presence of one important gerrymandering evil, the unjustified entrenching in power of a political party that the voters have rejected. They should be able to separate the unjustified abuse of partisan boundary-drawing considerations to achieve that end from their more ordinary and justified use. And they should be able to design a remedy for extreme cases.

Harper v. Virginia State Board of Elections
383 U.S. 663 (1966)

The State of Virginia imposed an annual poll tax of $1.50 on all residents over the age of twenty-one; payment of the tax was a precondition for voting in state elections. Proceeds from *the tax were used to support local government activities, including education. A suit by Harper and others to have the poll tax declared unconstitutional was dismissed by a three-judge* *federal district court on the basis of* Breedlove v. Suttles *(1937), in which the Court had unanimously rejected an equal-protection attack on Georgia's poll tax. Harper appealed to the US Supreme Court.* Opinion of the Court: <u>Douglas</u>, Warren, Clark, Brennan, White, Fortas. Dissenting opinions: <u>Black</u>; <u>Harlan</u>, Stewart.

JUSTICE DOUGLAS delivered the opinion of the Court.

We conclude that a State violates the Equal Protection Clause of the Fourteenth Amendment whenever it makes the affluence of the voter or payment of any fee an electoral standard. Voter qualifications have no relation to wealth nor to paying or not paying this or any other tax. Our cases demonstrate that the Equal Protection Clause of the Fourteenth Amendment restrains the States from fixing voter qualifications which invidiously discriminate. . . .

Long ago in *Yick Wo v. Hopkins* (1886) . . . the Court referred to "the political franchise of voting" as a "fundamental political right, because preservative of all rights." Recently in *Reynolds v. Sims* (1964), . . . we said, "Undoubtedly, the right of suffrage is a fundamental matter in a free and democratic society. Especially since the right to exercise the franchise in a free and unimpaired manner is preservative of other basic civil and political rights, any alleged infringement of the right of citizens to vote must be carefully and meticulously scrutinized." There we were considering charges that voters in one part of the State had greater representation per person in the State Legislature than voters in another part of the State. We concluded: "A citizen, a qualified voter, is no more nor no less so because he lives in the city or on the farm." We say the same whether the citizen, otherwise qualified to vote, has $1.50 in his pocket or nothing at all, pays the fee or fails to pay it. The principle that denies the State the right to dilute a citizen's vote on account of his economic status or other such factors by analogy bars a system which excludes those unable to pay a fee to vote or who fail to pay.

It is argued that a State may exact fees from citizens for many different kind of licenses; that if it can demand from all an equal fee for a driver's license, it can demand from all an equal poll tax for voting. But we must remember that the interest of the State, when it comes to voting, is limited to the power to fix qualifications. Wealth, like race, creed, or color, is not germane to one's ability to participate intelligently in the electoral process. Lines drawn on the basis of wealth or property, like those of race . . . are traditionally disfavored. . . . To introduce wealth or payment of a fee as a measure of a voter's qualifications is to introduce a capricious or irrelevant factor. The degree of the discrimination is irrelevant. In this context—that is, as a condition of obtaining a ballot—the requirement of fee paying causes an "invidious" discrimination . . . that runs afoul of the Equal Protection Clause. Levy "by the poll," as stated in *Breedlove v. Suttles* . . . is an old familiar form of taxation; and we say nothing to impair its validity so long as it is not made a condition to the exercise of the franchise. *Breedlove v. Suttles* sanctioned its use as "a prerequisite of voting." . . . To that extent the *Breedlove* case is overruled. . . .

In a recent searching re-examination of the Equal Protection Clause, we held, as already noted, that "the opportunity for equal participation by all voters in the election of state legislators" is required. . . . We decline to qualify that principle by sustaining this poll tax. Our conclusion, like that in *Reynolds v. Sims,* is founded not on what we think governmental policy should be, but on what the Equal Protection Clause requires.

We have long been mindful that where fundamental rights and liberties are asserted under the Equal Protection Clause, classifications which might invade or restrain them must be closely scrutinized and carefully confined. . . .

Those principles apply here. For to repeat, wealth or fee paying has, in our view, no relation to voting qualifications; the right to vote is too precious, too fundamental to be so burdened or conditioned.

Reversed.

JUSTICE BLACK, dissenting.

In *Breedlove v. Suttles* . . . decided December 6, 1937, a few weeks after I took my seat as a member of this Court, we unanimously upheld the right of the State of Georgia to make payment of its state poll tax a prerequisite to voting in state elections. We rejected at that time contentions that the state law violated the Equal Protection Clause of the Fourteenth Amendment because it put an unequal burden on different groups of people according to their age, sex, and ability to pay. . . . Later, May 28, 1951, I joined the Court's judgment in *Butler v. Thompson* . . . upholding, over the dissent of Mr. Justice Douglas, the Virginia state poll tax law challenged here against the same equal protection challenges. Since the *Breedlove* and *Butler* cases were decided the Federal Constitution has not been amended in the only way it could constitutionally have been, that is, as provided in Article V of the Constitution. I would adhere to the holding of those cases. The Court, however, overrules *Breedlove* in part, but its opinion reveals that it does so not by using its limited power to interpret the original meaning of the Equal Protection Clause, but by giving that clause a new meaning which it believes represents a better governmental policy. From this action I dissent.

It should be pointed out at once that the Court's decision is to no extent based on a finding that the Virginia law as written or as applied is being used as a device or mechanism to deny Negro citizens of Virginia the right to vote on account of their color. . . .

. . . In view of the purpose of the terms to restrain the courts from a wholesale invalidation of state laws under the Equal Protection Clause it would be difficult to say that the poll tax requirement is "irrational" or "arbitrary" or works "invidious discriminations." State poll tax legislation can "reasonably," "rationally" and without an "invidious" or evil purpose to injure anyone be found to rest on a number of state policies including (1) the State's desire to collect its revenue, and (2) its belief that voters who pay a poll tax will be interested in furthering the State's welfare when they vote. . . .

The Court's failure to give any reasons to show that these purposes of the poll tax are "irrational," "unreasonable," "arbitrary," or "invidious" is a pretty clear indication to me that none exist. I can only conclude that the primary, controlling, predominant, if not the exclusive reason for declaring the Virginia law unconstitutional is the Court's deep-seated hostility and antagonism, which I share, to

making payment of a tax a prerequisite to voting. . . .

. . . For us to undertake in the guise of constitutional interpretation to decide the constitutional policy question of this case amounts, in my judgment, to a plain exercise of power which the Constitution has denied us but has specifically granted to Congress. I cannot join in holding that the Virginia state poll tax law violates the Equal Protection Clause.

JUSTICE HARLAN, with whom JUSTICE STEWART joins, dissenting. . . .

. . . Is there a rational basis for Virginia's poll tax as a voting qualification? I think the answer to that question is undoubtedly "yes."

. . . It is certainly a rational argument that payment of some minimal poll tax promotes civic responsibility, weeding out those who do not care enough about public affairs to pay $1.50 or thereabouts a year for the exercise of the franchise. It is also arguable, indeed it was probably accepted as sound political theory by a large percentage of Americans through most of our history, that people with some property have a deeper stake in community affairs, and are consequently more responsible, more educated, more knowledgeable, more worthy of confidence, than those without means, and that the community and Nation would be better managed if the franchise were restricted to such citizens. Nondiscriminatory and fairly applied literacy tests . . . find justification on very similar grounds.

These viewpoints, to be sure, ring hollow on most contemporary ears. Their lack of acceptance today is evidenced by the fact that nearly all of the States, left to their own devices, have eliminated property or poll-tax qualifications; by the cognate fact that Congress and three-quarters of the States quickly ratified the Twenty-Fourth Amendment; and by the fact that rules such as the "pauper exclusion" in Virginia law . . . have never been enforced.

Property and poll-tax qualifications, very simply, are not in accord with current egalitarian notions of how a modern democracy should be organized. It is of course entirely fitting that legislatures should modify the law to reflect such changes in popular attitudes. However, it is all wrong, in my view, for the Court to adopt the political doctrines popularly accepted at a particular moment of our history and to declare all others to be irrational and invidious, barring them from the range of choice by reasonably minded people acting through the political process. It was not too long ago that Mr. Justice Holmes felt impelled to remind the Court that the Due Process Clause of the Fourteenth Amendment does not enact the *laissez-faire* theory of society. . . . The times have changed, and perhaps it is appropriate to observe that neither does the Equal Protection Clause of that Amendment rigidly impose upon America an ideology of unrestrained egalitarianism.

Crawford v. Marion County Election Board
553 U.S. 181 (2008)

After Indiana enacted an election law requiring citizens voting in person to present government-issued photo identification, William Crawford and the Indiana Democratic Party filed suits challenging the law's constitutionality. Following discovery, the US District Court for the Southern District of Indiana granted respondents summary judgment, finding the evidence in the record insufficient to support a facial attack on the statute's validity. In affirming, the Seventh Circuit declined to judge the law by the strict standard set for poll taxes in Harper v. Virginia State Board of Elections *(1966), finding the burden on voters offset by the benefit of reducing the risk of fraud. The Supreme Court granted certiorari.* Judgment of the Court: <u>Stevens</u>, Roberts, Kennedy. Concurring in the judgment: <u>Scalia</u>, Thomas, Alito. Dissenting opinions: <u>Souter</u>, Ginsburg; <u>Breyer</u>.

JUSTICE STEVENS announced the judgment of the Court and delivered an opinion in which THE CHIEF JUSTICE and JUSTICE KENNEDY join.

At issue in these cases is the constitutionality of an Indiana statute requiring citizens voting in person on election day, or casting a ballot in person at the office of the circuit court clerk prior to election day, to present photo identification issued by the government.

Referred to as either the "Voter ID Law" or "SEA 483," the statute applies to in-person voting at both primary and general elections. The requirement does not apply to absentee ballots submitted by mail, and the statute contains an exception for persons living and voting in a state-licensed facility such as a nursing home. A voter who is indigent or has a religious objection to being photographed may cast a provisional ballot that will be counted only if she executes an appropriate affidavit before the circuit court clerk within 10 days following the election. A voter who has photo identification but is unable to present that identification on election day may file a provisional ballot that will be counted if she brings her photo identification to the circuit county clerk's office within 10 days. No photo identification is required in order to register to vote, and the State offers free photo identification to qualified voters able to establish their residence and identity.

Promptly after the enactment of SEA 483 in 2005, the Indiana Democratic Party and the Marion County Democratic Central Committee (Democrats) filed suit in the Federal District Court for the Southern District of Indiana against the state officials responsible for its enforcement, seeking a judgment declaring the Voter ID Law invalid and enjoining its enforcement. A second suit seeking the same relief was brought on behalf of two elected officials and several nonprofit organizations representing groups of elderly, disabled, poor, and minority voters. The cases were consolidated, and the State of Indiana intervened to defend the validity of the statute.

The complaints in the consolidated cases allege that the new law substantially burdens the right to vote in violation of the Fourteenth Amendment; that it is neither a necessary nor appropriate method of avoiding election fraud; and that it will arbitrarily disfranchise qualified voters who do not possess the required identification and will place an unjustified burden on those who cannot readily obtain such identification.

After discovery, District Judge Barker prepared a comprehensive 70-page opinion explaining her decision to grant defendants' motion for summary judgment. She found that petitioners had "not introduced evidence of a single, individual Indiana resident who will be unable to vote as a result of SEA 483 or who will have his or her right to vote unduly burdened by its requirements." She rejected "as utterly incredible and unreliable" an expert's report that up to 989,000 registered voters in Indiana did not possess either a driver's license or other acceptable photo identification. She estimated that as of 2005, when the statute was enacted, around 43,000 Indiana residents lacked a state-issued driver's license or identification card. A divided panel of the Court of Appeals affirmed.

In *Harper v. Virginia Bd. of Elections* (1966), the Court held that Virginia could not condition the right to vote in a state election on the payment of a poll tax of $1.50. We rejected the dissenters' argument that the interest in promoting civic responsibility by weeding out those voters who did not care enough about public affairs to pay a small sum for the privilege of voting provided a rational basis for the tax. Applying a stricter standard, we concluded that a State "violates the Equal Protection Clause of the Fourteenth Amendment whenever it makes the affluence of the voter or payment of any fee an electoral standard." We used the term "invidiously discriminate" to describe conduct prohibited under that standard, noting that we had previously held that while a State may obviously impose "reasonable residence restrictions on the availability of the ballot," it "may not deny the opportunity to vote to a bona fide resident merely because he is a member of the armed services." Although the State's justification for the tax was rational, it was invidious because it was irrelevant to the voter's qualifications.

Thus, under the standard applied in *Harper*, even rational restrictions on the right to vote are invidious if they are unrelated to voter qualifications. In *Anderson v. Celebrezze* (1983), however, we confirmed the general rule that "evenhanded restrictions that protect the integrity and reliability of the electoral process itself" are not invidious and satisfy the standard set forth in *Harper*. Rather than applying any

"litmus test" that would neatly separate valid from invalid restrictions, we concluded that a court must identify and evaluate the interests put forward by the State as justifications for the burden imposed by its rule, and then make the "hard judgment" that our adversary system demands. . . . In later election cases we have followed *Anderson*'s balancing approach.

The State has identified several state interests that arguably justify the burdens that SEA 483 imposes on voters and potential voters. While petitioners argue that the statute was actually motivated by partisan concerns and dispute both the significance of the State's interests and the magnitude of any real threat to those interests, they do not question the legitimacy of the interests the State has identified. Each is unquestionably relevant to the State's interest in protecting the integrity and reliability of the electoral process.

The first is the interest in deterring and detecting voter fraud. The State has a valid interest in participating in a nationwide effort to improve and modernize election procedures that have been criticized as antiquated and inefficient. The State also argues that it has a particular interest in preventing voter fraud in response to a problem that is in part the product of its own maladministration—namely, that Indiana's voter registration rolls include a large number of names of persons who are either deceased or no longer live in Indiana. Finally, the State relies on its interest in safeguarding voter confidence. Each of these interests merits separate comment.

Two recently enacted federal statutes have made it necessary for States to reexamine their election procedures. Both contain provisions consistent with a State's choice to use government-issued photo identification as a relevant source of information concerning a citizen's eligibility to vote.

In the National Voter Registration Act [NVRA] of 1993, Congress established procedures that would both increase the number of registered voters and protect the integrity of the electoral process. The statute requires state motor vehicle driver's license applications to serve as voter registration applications. While that requirement has increased the number of registered voters, the statute also contains a provision restricting States' ability to remove names from the lists of registered voters. These protections have been partly responsible for inflated lists of registered voters. For example, evidence credited by Judge Barker estimated that as of 2004 Indiana's voter rolls were inflated by as much as 41.4%, and data collected by the Election Assistance Committee in 2004 indicated that 19 of 92 Indiana counties had registration totals exceeding 100% of the 2004 voting-age population.

In the Help America Vote Act of 2002 (HAVA), Congress required every State to create and maintain a computerized statewide list of all registered voters. HAVA also requires the States to verify voter information contained in a voter registration application and specifies either an "applicant's driver's license number" or "the last 4 digits of the applicant's social security number" as acceptable verifications. If an individual has neither number, the State is required to assign the applicant a voter identification number.

HAVA also imposes new identification requirements for individuals registering to vote for the first time who submit their applications by mail. If the voter is casting his ballot in person, he must present local election officials with written identification, which may be either "a current and valid photo identification" or another form of documentation such as a bank statement or paycheck. If the voter is voting by mail, he must include a copy of the identification with his ballot. A voter may also include a copy of the documentation with his application or provide his driver's license number or Social Security number for verification. Finally, in a provision entitled "Fail-safe voting," HAVA authorizes the casting of provisional ballots by challenged voters.

Of course, neither HAVA nor NVRA required Indiana to enact SEA 483, but they do indicate that Congress believes that photo identification is one effective method of establishing a voter's qualification to vote and that the integrity of elections is enhanced through improved technology. That conclusion is also supported by a report issued shortly after the enactment of SEA 483 by the Commission on Federal Election Reform chaired by former President Jimmy Carter and former Secretary of State James A. Baker III, which is a part of the record in these cases. . . .

The only kind of voter fraud that SEA 483 addresses is in-person voter impersonation at polling places. The record contains no evidence of any such fraud actually occurring in Indiana at any time in its history. Moreover, petitioners argue that provisions of the Indiana Criminal Code punishing such conduct as a felony provide adequate protection against the risk that such conduct will occur in the future. It remains true, however, that flagrant examples of such fraud in other parts of the country have been documented throughout this Nation's history by respected historians and journalists, that occasional examples have surfaced in recent years, and that Indiana's own experience with fraudulent voting in the 2003 Democratic primary for East Chicago Mayor—though perpetrated using absentee ballots and not in-person fraud—demonstrate that not only is the risk of voter fraud real but that it could affect the outcome of a close election.

There is no question about the legitimacy or importance of the State's interest in counting only the votes of eligible voters. Moreover, the interest in orderly administration and accurate recordkeeping provides a sufficient justification for carefully identifying all voters participating in the election process. While the most effective method of preventing election fraud may well be debatable, the propriety of doing so is perfectly clear. . . .

Finally, the State contends that it has an interest in protecting public confidence "in the integrity and legitimacy of representative government." While that interest is closely related to the State's interest in preventing voter fraud, public confidence in the integrity of the electoral process has independent significance, because it encourages citizen participation in the democratic process. As the Carter-Baker Report observed, the "electoral system cannot inspire public confidence if no safeguards exist to deter or detect fraud or to confirm the identity of voters."

States employ different methods of identifying eligible voters at the polls. Some merely check off the names of registered voters who identify themselves; others require voters to present registration cards or other documentation before they can vote; some require voters to sign their names so their signatures can be compared with those on file; and in recent years an increasing number of States have relied primarily on photo identification. A photo identification requirement imposes some burdens on voters that other methods of identification do not share. For example, a voter may lose his photo identification, may have his wallet stolen on the way to the polls, or may not resemble the photo in the identification because he recently grew a beard. Burdens of that sort arising from life's vagaries, however, are neither so serious nor so frequent as to raise any question about the constitutionality of SEA 483; the availability of the right to cast a provisional ballot provides an adequate remedy for problems of that character.

The burdens that are relevant to the issue before us are those imposed on persons who are eligible to vote but do not possess a current photo identification that complies with the requirements of SEA 483. The fact that most voters already possess a valid driver's license, or some other form of acceptable identification, would not save the statute under our reasoning in *Harper*, if the State required voters to pay a tax or a fee to obtain a new photo identification. But just as other States provide free voter registration cards, the photo identification cards issued by Indiana's BMV are also free. For most voters who need them, the inconvenience of making a trip to the BMV, gathering the required documents, and posing for a photograph surely does not qualify as a substantial burden on the right to vote, or even represent a significant increase over the usual burdens of voting.

Both evidence in the record and facts of which we may take judicial notice, however, indicate that a somewhat heavier burden may be placed on a limited number of persons. They include elderly persons born out-of-state, who may have difficulty obtaining a birth certificate; persons who because of economic or other personal limitations may find it difficult either to secure a copy of their birth certificate or to assemble the other required documentation to obtain a state-issued identification; homeless persons; and persons with a religious objection to being photographed. If we assume, as the evidence suggests, that some members of

these classes were registered voters when SEA 483 was enacted, the new identification requirement may have imposed a special burden on their right to vote.

The severity of that burden is, of course, mitigated by the fact that, if eligible, voters without photo identification may cast provisional ballots that will ultimately be counted. To do so, however, they must travel to the circuit court clerk's office within 10 days to execute the required affidavit. It is unlikely that such a requirement would pose a constitutional problem unless it is wholly unjustified. And even assuming that the burden may not be justified as to a few voters, that conclusion is by no means sufficient to establish petitioners' right to the relief they seek in this litigation.

In sum, on the basis of the record that has been made in this litigation, we cannot conclude that the statute imposes "excessively burdensome requirements" on any class of voters. . . .

The judgment of the Court of Appeals is affirmed.

JUSTICE SCALIA with whom JUSTICE THOMAS and JUSTICE ALITO join, concurring in the judgment.

The lead opinion assumes petitioners' premise that the voter-identification law "may have imposed a special burden on" some voters but holds that petitioners have not assembled evidence to show that the special burden is severe enough to warrant strict scrutiny. That is true enough, but for the sake of clarity and finality (as well as adherence to precedent), I prefer to decide these cases on the grounds that petitioners' premise is irrelevant and that the burden at issue is minimal and justified.

To evaluate a law respecting the right to vote—whether it governs voter qualifications, candidate selection, or the voting process—we use the approach set out in *Burdick v. Takushi* (1992). This calls for application of a deferential "important regulatory interests" standard for non-severe, nondiscriminatory restrictions, reserving strict scrutiny for laws that severely restrict the right to vote. The lead opinion resists the import of *Burdick* by characterizing it as simply adopting "the balancing approach" of *Anderson v. Celebrezze*. Although *Burdick* liberally quoted *Anderson*, *Burdick* forged *Anderson*'s amorphous "flexible standard" into something resembling an administrable rule. Since *Burdick*, we have repeatedly reaffirmed the primacy of its two-track approach. Thus, the first step is to decide whether a challenged law severely burdens the right to vote. Ordinary and widespread burdens, such as those requiring "nominal effort" of everyone, are not severe. Burdens are severe if they go beyond the merely inconvenient.

Of course, we have to identify a burden before we can weigh it. The Indiana law affects different voters differently, but what petitioners view as the law's several light and heavy burdens are no more than the different impacts of the single burden that the law uniformly imposes on all voters. To vote in person in Indiana, everyone must have and present a photo identification that can be obtained for free. The State draws no classifications, let alone discriminatory ones, except to establish optional absentee and provisional balloting for certain poor, elderly, and institutionalized voters and for religious objectors. Nor are voters who already have photo identifications exempted from the burden, since those voters must maintain the accuracy of the information displayed on the identifications, renew them before they expire, and replace them if they are lost.

The Indiana photo-identification law is a generally applicable, nondiscriminatory voting regulation, and our precedents refute the view that individual impacts are relevant to determining the severity of the burden it imposes. . . .

Not all of our decisions predating *Burdick* addressed whether a challenged voting regulation severely burdened the right to vote, but when we began to grapple with the magnitude of burdens, we did so categorically and did not consider the peculiar circumstances of individual voters or candidates. . . .

Insofar as our election-regulation cases rest upon the requirements of the Fourteenth Amendment, weighing the burden of a nondiscriminatory voting law upon each voter and concomitantly requiring exceptions for vulnerable voters would effectively turn back decades of equal-protection jurisprudence. A voter complaining about such a law's effect on him has no valid equal-protection claim because, without proof of discriminatory intent, a generally applicable law with disparate impact is not unconstitutional. The Fourteenth Amendment does not regard neutral laws as invidious ones, even when their burdens purportedly fall disproportionately on a protected class. *A fortiori* it does not do so when, as here, the classes complaining of disparate impact are not even protected.

Even if I thought that *stare decisis* did not foreclose adopting an individual-focused approach, I would reject it as an original matter. This is an area where the dos and don'ts need to be known in advance of the election, and voter-by-voter examination of the burdens of voting regulations would prove especially disruptive. A case-by-case approach naturally encourages constant litigation. . . .

That sort of detailed judicial supervision of the election process would flout the Constitution's express commitment of the task to the States. It is for state legislatures to weigh the costs and benefits of possible changes to their election codes, and their judgment must prevail unless it imposes a severe and unjustified overall burden upon the right to vote, or is intended to disadvantage a particular class. Judicial review of their handiwork must apply an objective, uniform standard that will enable them to determine, ex ante, whether the burden they impose is too severe.

The lead opinion's record-based resolution of these cases, which neither rejects nor embraces the rule of our precedents, provides no certainty, and will embolden litigants who surmise that our precedents have been abandoned. There is no good reason to prefer that course.

* * *

The universally applicable requirements of Indiana's voter-identification law are eminently reasonable. The burden of acquiring, possessing, and showing a free photo identification is simply not severe, because it does not "even represent a significant increase over the usual burdens of voting." And the State's interests are sufficient to sustain that minimal burden. That should end the matter. That the State accommodates some voters by permitting (not requiring) the casting of absentee or provisional ballots, is an indulgence—not a constitutional imperative that falls short of what is required.

JUSTICE SOUTER, with whom JUSTICE GINSBURG joins, dissenting.

. . . Indiana's "Voter ID Law" threatens to impose nontrivial burdens on the voting right of tens of thousands of the State's citizens, and a significant percentage of those individuals are likely to be deterred from voting. The statute is unconstitutional under the balancing standard of *Burdick v. Takushi* (1992): a State may not burden the right to vote merely by invoking abstract interests, be they legitimate, or even compelling, but must make a particular, factual showing that threats to its interests outweigh the particular impediments it has imposed. The State has made no such justification here, and as to some aspects of its law, it has hardly even tried. I therefore respectfully dissent from the Court's judgment sustaining the statute.

Voting-rights cases raise two competing interests, the one side being the fundamental right to vote. . . . As against the unfettered right, however, lies the "[c]ommon sense, as well as constitutional law . . . that government must play an active role in structuring elections; 'as a practical matter, there must be a substantial regulation of elections if they are to be fair and honest and if some sort of order, rather than chaos, is to accompany the democratic processes.'" . . . Given the legitimacy of interests on both sides, we have avoided pre-set levels of scrutiny in favor of a sliding-scale balancing analysis: the scrutiny varies with the effect of the regulation at issue. And whatever the claim, the Court has long made a careful, ground-level appraisal both of the practical burdens on the right to vote and of the State's reasons for imposing those precise burdens. . . . The lead opinion does not disavow these basic principles. But I think it does not insist enough on the hard facts that our standard of review demands. . . .

The first set of burdens shown in these cases is the travel costs and fees necessary to get one of the limited variety of federal or state photo identifications needed to cast a regular ballot under the Voter ID Law. The travel is required for the personal visit to a license branch of the Indiana Bureau of Motor Vehicles (BMV), which is demanded of anyone applying for a driver's license or nondriver photo identification. The need to travel to a BMV branch will affect voters according to their circumstances, with the average person probably viewing it as nothing more than an inconvenience. Poor, old, and disabled voters who do not drive a car, however, may find the trip prohibitive, witness the fact that the BMV has far fewer license branches in each county than there are voting precincts. . . .

The burden of traveling to a more distant BMV office rather than a conveniently located polling place is probably serious for many of the individuals who lack photo identification. They almost certainly will not own cars, and public transportation in Indiana is fairly limited. . . .

For those voters who can afford the roundtrip, a second financial hurdle appears: in order to get photo identification for the first time, they need to present "'a birth certificate, a certificate of naturalization, U. S. veterans photo identification, U. S. military photo identification, or a U. S. passport.'" . . . [M]ost voters must pay at least one fee to get the ID necessary to cast a regular ballot. As with the travel costs, these fees are far from shocking on their face, but . . . it matters that both the travel costs and the fees are disproportionately heavy for, and thus disproportionately likely to deter, the poor, the old, and the immobile. . . .

Indiana's Voter ID Law thus threatens to impose serious burdens on the voting right, even if not "severe" ones, and the next question is whether the number of individuals likely to be affected is significant as well. Record evidence and facts open to judicial notice answer yes. . . . The State shows no discomfort with the District Court's finding that an "estimated 43,000 individuals" (about 1% of the State's voting-age population) lack a qualifying ID. . . . The upshot is this. Tens of thousands of voting-age residents lack the necessary photo identification. A large proportion of them are likely to be in bad shape economically. The Voter ID Law places hurdles in the way of either getting an ID or of voting provisionally, and they translate into nontrivial economic costs. There is accordingly no reason to doubt that a significant number of state residents will be discouraged or disabled from voting. Petitioners, to be sure, failed to nail down precisely how great the cohort of discouraged and totally deterred voters will be, but empirical precision beyond the foregoing numbers has never been demanded for raising a voting-rights claim. While of course it would greatly aid a plaintiff to establish his claims beyond mathematical doubt, he does enough to show that serious burdens are likely. . . .

Without a shred of evidence that in-person voter impersonation is a problem in the State, much less a crisis, Indiana has adopted one of the most restrictive photo identification requirements in the country. The State recognizes that tens of thousands of qualified voters lack the necessary federally issued or state-issued identification, but it insists on implementing the requirement immediately, without allowing a transition period for targeted efforts to distribute the required identification to

individuals who need it. The State hardly even tries to explain its decision to force indigents or religious objectors to travel all the way to their county seats every time they wish to vote, and if there is any waning of confidence in the administration of elections it probably owes more to the State's violation of federal election law than to any imposters at the polling places. It is impossible to say, on this record, that the State's interest in adopting its signally inhibiting photo identification requirement has been shown to outweigh the serious burdens it imposes on the right to vote. . . .

* * *

The Indiana Voter ID Law is thus unconstitutional: the state interests fail to justify the practical limitations placed on the right to vote, and the law imposes an unreasonable and irrelevant burden on voters who are poor and old. I would vacate the judgment of the Seventh Circuit, and remand for further proceedings.

Bush v. Gore
531 U.S. 98 (2000)

By the early hours of November 8, 2000, the day following the presidential election, it had become clear that whoever was declared the winner of the twenty-five electoral votes of the state of Florida would be elected president of the United States. Later that day, the Florida Division of Elections reported that George W. Bush, governor of Texas and Republican candidate for president, had received 2,909,135 votes, and Albert Gore Jr., vice president of the United States and Democratic candidate for president, had received 2,907,351 votes, a margin of 1,784 for Bush. Because Bush's margin of victory was less than "one-half of a percent . . . of the votes cast," an automatic machine recount was conducted under the provisions of the Florida election code; the results showed Bush still winning the race but by a diminished margin. Gore then sought manual recounts in Volusia, Palm Beach, Broward, and Miami–Dade Counties, pursuant to Florida's election-protest provisions. A dispute arose concerning the deadline for local county canvassing boards to submit their returns to the Florida secretary of state. The secretary, Katherine Harris, declined to waive the

November 14 deadline imposed by statute; however, in Palm Beach County Canvassing Board v. Harris, handed down on November 21, the Florida Supreme Court extended the deadline to November 26. The US Supreme Court granted Bush's petition for a writ of certiorari on November 24, and on December 4, in a unanimous per curiam decision in Bush v. Palm Beach County Canvassing Board (2000), it vacated the Florida Supreme Court's decision, finding considerable uncertainty as to the grounds on which it was based.

On November 26, the Florida Elections Canvassing Commission certified the results of the election; it found Bush to have a lead of 537 votes (2,912,790 to 2,912,253) and declared Bush the winner of Florida's twenty-five electoral votes. On November 27, pursuant to the contest provisions of Florida's election code, Gore filed a complaint in Leon County Circuit Court contesting that certification. He sought relief based on Florida statutory language providing that "receipt of a number of illegal votes or rejection of a number of legal votes sufficient to change or place in doubt the result of the election" shall be grounds for a contest. The circuit court denied relief, stating that Gore failed to meet his burden of proof. He appealed to the First District Court of Appeal, which certified the matter to the Florida Supreme Court. The Florida Supreme Court accepted jurisdiction and, on December 8 in Gore v. Harris, *it held that Gore had satisfied his burden of proof with respect to his challenge to Miami–Dade County's failure to tabulate, by manual count, 9,000 ballots on which the machines had failed to detect a vote for president—what came to be referred to as "undervotes." Noting the closeness of the election, the court explained that "on this record, there can be no question that there are legal votes within the 9,000 uncounted votes sufficient to place the results of this election in doubt." A "legal vote," the Florida Supreme Court determined, was "one in which there is a 'clear indication of the intent of the voter.'" The Florida Supreme Court therefore ordered a hand recount of the 9,000 ballots in Miami–Dade County. It also ordered the inclusion in the certified vote totals of 215 votes identified in Palm Beach County and 168 votes identified in Miami–Dade County for Gore. The Florida Supreme Court further held that relief would require manual recounts in all Florida counties where the so-called undervotes had not been subject to manual tabulation, and it ordered all manual recounts to begin at once. Bush filed an emergency application with the US Supreme Court for a stay of this mandate, and on December 9, the Supreme Court granted the application, treated it as a petition for a writ of certiorari, and granted certiorari.* Per Curiam: Rehnquist, O'Connor, Scalia, Kennedy, Thomas. Concurring opinion: <u>Rehnquist</u>, Scalia, Thomas. Dissenting opinions: <u>Stevens</u>, Ginsburg, Breyer; <u>Souter</u>, Stevens (in part), Ginsburg (in part), Breyer; <u>Ginsburg</u>, Stevens, Souter, Breyer (in part); <u>Breyer</u>, Stevens (in part), Souter (in part), Ginsburg (in part).

PER CURIAM.

I

. . . The petition presents the following questions: whether the Florida Supreme Court established new standards for resolving Presidential election contests, thereby violating Art. II, §1, cl. 2, of the United States Constitu-

tion and failing to comply with 3 U.S.C. §5, and whether the use of standardless manual recounts violates the Equal Protection and Due Process Clauses. With respect to the equal protection question, we find a violation of the Equal Protection Clause.

II

The closeness of this election, and the multitude of legal challenges which have followed in its wake, have brought into sharp focus a common, if heretofore unnoticed, phenomenon. Nationwide statistics reveal that an estimated 2% of ballots cast do not register a vote for President for whatever reason, including deliberately choosing no candidate at all or some voter error, such as voting for two candidates or insufficiently marking a ballot. In certifying election results, the votes eligible for inclusion in the certification are the votes meeting the properly established legal requirements.

This case has shown that punch card balloting machines can produce an unfortunate number of ballots which are not punched in a clean, complete way by the voter. After the current counting, it is likely legislative bodies nationwide will examine ways to improve the mechanisms and machinery for voting.

The individual citizen has no federal constitutional right to vote for electors for the President of the United States unless and until the state legislature chooses a state-wide election as the means to implement its power to appoint members of the Electoral College. U.S. Const., Art. II, §1. This is the source for the statement in *McPherson v. Blacker* (1892), that the State legislature's power to select the manner for appointing electors is plenary; it may, if it so chooses, select the electors itself, which indeed was the manner used by State legislatures in several States for many years after the Framing of our Constitution. History has now favored the voter, and in each of the several States the citizens themselves vote for Presidential electors. When the state legislature vests the right to vote for President in its people, the right to vote as the legislature has prescribed is fundamental; and one source of its fundamental nature lies in the equal weight accorded to each vote and the equal dignity owed to each voter. The State, of course, after granting the franchise in the special context of Article II, can take back the power to appoint electors.

The right to vote is protected in more than the initial allocation of the franchise. Equal protection applies as well to the manner of its exercise. Having once granted the right to vote on equal terms, the State may not, by later arbitrary and disparate treatment, value one person's vote over that of another. See, *e.g., Harper v. Virginia Bd. of Elections* (1966) ("Once the franchise is granted to the electorate, lines may not be drawn which are inconsistent with the Equal Protection Clause of the Fourteenth Amendment"). It must be remembered that "the right of suffrage can be denied by a debasement or dilution of the weight of a citizen's vote just as effectively as by wholly prohibiting the free exercise of the franchise." *Reynolds v. Sims,* (1964).

There is no difference between the two sides of the present controversy on these basic propositions. Respondents say that the very purpose of vindicating the right to vote justifies the recount procedures now at issue. The question before us, however, is whether the recount procedures the Florida Supreme Court has adopted are consistent with its obligation to avoid arbitrary and disparate treatment of the members of its electorate.

Much of the controversy seems to revolve around ballot cards designed to be perforated by a stylus but which, either through error or deliberate omission, have not been perforated with sufficient precision for a machine to count them. In some cases a piece of the card—a chad—is hanging, say by two corners. In other cases there is no separation at all, just an indentation.

The Florida Supreme Court has ordered that the intent of the voter be discerned from such ballots. For purposes of resolving the equal protection challenge, it is not necessary to decide whether the Florida Supreme Court had the authority under the legislative scheme for resolving election disputes to define what a legal vote is and to mandate a manual recount implementing that definition. The recount mechanisms implemented in response to the decisions of the Florida Supreme Court do not satisfy the minimum requirement for non-arbitrary treatment of voters necessary to se-cure the fundamental right. Florida's basic command for the count of legally cast votes is to consider the "intent of the voter." This is unobjectionable as an abstract proposition and a starting principle. The problem inheres in the absence of specific standards to ensure its equal application. The formulation of uniform rules to determine intent based on these recurring circumstances is practicable and, we conclude, necessary.

The law does not refrain from searching for the intent of the actor in a multitude of circumstances; and in some cases the general command to ascertain intent is not susceptible to much further refinement. In this instance, however, the question is not whether to believe a witness but how to interpret the marks or holes or scratches on an inanimate object, a piece of cardboard or paper which, it is said, might not have registered as a vote during the machine count. The factfinder confronts a thing, not a person. The search for intent can be confined by specific rules designed to ensure uniform treatment.

The want of those rules here has led to unequal evaluation of ballots in various respects. . . . The record provides some examples. A monitor in Miami–Dade County testified at trial that he observed that three members of the county canvassing board applied different standards in defining a legal vote. And testimony at trial also revealed that at least one county changed its evaluative standards during the counting process. Palm Beach County, for example, began the process with a 1990 guideline which precluded counting completely attached chads, switched to a rule that considered a vote to be legal if any light could be seen through a chad, changed back to the 1990 rule, and then abandoned any pretense of a *per se* rule, only to have a court order that the county consider dimpled chads legal. This is not a process with sufficient guarantees of equal treatment. . . .

The State Supreme Court ratified this uneven treatment. It mandated that the recount totals from two counties, Miami-Dade and Palm Beach, be included in the certified total. The court also appeared to hold *sub silentio* that the recount totals from Broward County, which were not completed until after the original November 14 certification by the Secretary of State, were to be considered part of the new certified vote totals even though the county certification was not contested by Vice President Gore. Yet each of the counties used varying standards to determine what was a legal vote. Broward County used a more forgiving standard than Palm Beach County, and uncovered almost three times as many new votes, a result markedly disproportionate to the difference in population between the counties.

In addition, the recounts in these three counties were not limited to so-called undervotes but extended to all of the ballots. The distinction has real consequences. A manual recount of all ballots identifies not only those ballots which show no vote but also those which contain more than one, the so-called overvotes. Neither category will be counted by the machine. This is not a trivial concern. At oral argument, respondents estimated there are as many as 110,000 overvotes state-wide. As a result, the citizen whose ballot was not read by a machine because he failed to vote for a candidate in a way readable by a machine may still have his vote counted in a manual recount; on the other hand, the citizen who marks two candidates in a way discernible by the machine will not have the same opportunity to have his vote count, even if a manual examination of the ballot would reveal the requisite indicia of intent. Furthermore, the citizen who marks two candidates, only one of which is discernible by the machine, will have his vote counted even though it should have been read as an invalid ballot. The State Supreme Court's inclusion of vote counts based on these variant standards exemplifies concerns with the remedial processes that were under way.

That brings the analysis to yet a further equal protection problem. The votes certified by the court included a partial total from one county, Miami-Dade. The Florida Supreme Court's decision thus gives no assurance that the recounts included in a final certification must be complete. Indeed, it is respondent's submission that it would be consistent with the rules of the recount procedures to include whatever partial counts are done by the time of final certification, and we interpret the Florida Supreme Court's decision to permit this. This accommo-

dation no doubt results from the truncated contest period established by the Florida Supreme Court in *Bush I*, at respondents' own urging. The press of time does not diminish the constitutional concern. A desire for speed is not a general excuse for ignoring equal protection guarantees.

In addition to these difficulties the actual process by which the votes were to be counted under the Florida Supreme Court's decision raises further concerns. That order did not specify who would recount the ballots. . . .

The recount process, in its features here described, is inconsistent with the minimum procedures necessary to protect the fundamental right of each voter in the special instance of a state-wide recount under the authority of a single state judicial officer. Our consideration is limited to the present circumstances, for the problem of equal protection in election processes generally presents many complexities.

The question before the Court is not whether local entities, in the exercise of their expertise, may develop different systems for implementing elections. Instead, we are presented with a situation where a state court with the power to assure uniformity has ordered a state-wide recount with minimal procedural safeguards. When a court orders a state-wide remedy, there must be at least some assurance that the rudimentary requirements of equal treatment and fundamental fairness are satisfied.

Given the Court's assessment that the recount process underway was probably being conducted in an unconstitutional manner, the Court stayed the order directing the recount so it could hear this case and render an expedited decision. The contest provision, as it was mandated by the State Supreme Court, is not well calculated to sustain the confidence that all citizens must have in the outcome of elections. The State has not shown that its procedures include the necessary safeguards. The problem, for instance, of the estimated 110,000 overvotes has not been addressed, although Chief Justice Wells called attention to the concern in his dissenting opinion.

Upon due consideration of the difficulties identified to this point, it is obvious that the recount cannot be conducted in compliance with the requirements of equal protection and due process without substantial additional work. It would require not only the adoption (after opportunity for argument) of adequate state-wide standards for determining what is a legal vote, and practicable procedures to implement them, but also orderly judicial review of any disputed matters that might arise. In addition, the Secretary of State has advised that the recount of only a portion of the ballots requires that the vote tabulation equipment be used to screen out undervotes, a function for which the machines were not designed. If a recount of overvotes were also required, perhaps even a second screening would be necessary. Use of the equipment for this purpose, and any new software developed for it, would have to be evaluated for accuracy by the Secretary of State.

The Supreme Court of Florida has said that the legislature intended the State's electors to "participate fully in the federal electoral process," as provided in 3 U.S.C. §5. *[Note: With respect to the election of the United States president by means of presidential electors, Congress created, in 3 U.S.C. §5, what is called a "safe harbor" by providing that insofar as congressional consideration of a state's electoral votes is concerned, if a state's legislature has provided for final determination of contests or controversies by a law made prior to election day, then that determination shall be conclusive if made at least six days prior to the time of the meeting of the electoral college. For purposes of applying 3 U.S.C. §5 to the presidential election held on November 7, 2000, the "safe-harbor" date, i.e., the date six days prior to the meeting of the electors, was December 12, 2000.]* That statute, in turn, requires that any controversy or contest that is designed to lead to a conclusive selection of electors be completed by December 12. That date is upon us, and there is no recount procedure in place under the State Supreme Court's order that comports with minimal constitutional standards. Because it is evident that any recount seeking to meet the December 12 date will be unconstitutional for the reasons we have discussed, we reverse the judgment of the Supreme Court of Florida ordering a recount to proceed.

Seven Justices of the Court agree that there are constitutional problems with the recount ordered by the Florida Supreme Court that demand a remedy. The only disagreement is as to the remedy. Because the Florida Supreme Court has said that the Florida Legislature intended to obtain the safe-harbor benefits of 3 U.S.C. §5, Justice Breyer's proposed remedy—remanding to the Florida Supreme Court for its ordering of a constitutionally proper contest until December 18—contemplates action in violation of the Florida election code, and hence could not be part of an "appropriate" order. . . .

None are more conscious of the vital limits on judicial authority than are the members of this Court, and none stand more in admiration of the Constitution's design to leave the selection of the President to the people, through their legislatures, and to the political sphere. When contending parties invoke the process of the courts, however, it becomes our unsought responsibility to resolve the federal and constitutional issues the judicial system has been forced to confront.

The judgment of the Supreme Court of Florida is reversed, and the case is remanded for further proceedings not inconsistent with this opinion.

THE CHIEF JUSTICE, with whom JUSTICE SCALIA and JUSTICE THOMAS join, concurring.

We join the *per curiam* opinion. We write separately because we believe there are additional grounds that require us to reverse the Florida Supreme Court's decision. . . .

In most cases, comity and respect for federalism compel us to defer to the decisions of state courts on issues of state law. That practice reflects our understanding that the decisions of state courts are definitive pronouncements of the will of the States as sovereigns. Of course, in ordinary cases, the distribution of powers among the branches of a State's government raises no questions of federal constitutional law, subject to the requirement that the government be republican in character. But there are a few exceptional cases in which the Constitution imposes a duty or confers a power on a particular branch of a State's government. This is one of them. Article II, §1, cl. 2, provides that "each State shall appoint, in such Manner as the *Legislature* thereof may direct," electors for President and Vice President. (Emphasis added.) Thus, the text of the election law itself, and not just its interpretation by the courts of the States, takes on independent significance. . . .

3 U.S.C. §5 informs our application of Art. II, §1, cl. 2, to the Florida statutory scheme, which, as the Florida Supreme Court acknowledged, took that statute into account. Section 5 provides that the State's selection of electors "shall be conclusive, and shall govern in the counting of the electoral votes" if the electors are chosen under laws enacted prior to election day, and if the selection process is completed six days prior to the meeting of the electoral college. As we noted in *Bush v. Palm Beach County Canvassing Bd.,* "Since §5 contains a principle of federal law that would assure finality of the State's determination if made pursuant to a state law in effect before the election, a legislative wish to take advantage of the 'safe harbor' would counsel against any construction of the Election Code that Congress might deem to be a change in the law."

If we are to respect the legislature's Article II powers, therefore, we must ensure that post-election state-court actions do not frustrate the legislative desire to attain the "safe harbor" provided by §5.

In Florida, the legislature has chosen to hold state-wide elections to appoint the State's 25 electors. Importantly, the legislature has delegated the authority to run the elections and to oversee election disputes to the Secretary of State. Isolated sections of the code may well admit of more than one interpretation, but the general coherence of the legislative scheme may not be altered by judicial interpretation so as to wholly change the statutorily provided apportionment of responsibility among these various bodies. In any election but a Presidential election, the Florida Supreme Court can give as little or as much deference to Florida's executives as it chooses, so far as Article II is concerned, and this Court will have no cause to question the court's actions. But, with respect to a Presidential election, the court must be both mindful of the legislature's role under Article II in choosing the manner of appointing electors and deferential to those bodies expressly empowered by the legislature to carry out its constitutional mandate. . . .

Acting pursuant to its constitutional grant of authority, the Florida Legislature has created a detailed, if not perfectly crafted, statutory scheme that provides for appointment of Presidential electors by direct election. Under the statute, "votes cast for the actual candidates for President and Vice President shall be counted as votes cast for the presidential electors supporting such candidates." The legislature has designated the Secretary of State as the "chief election officer," with the responsibility to "obtain and maintain uniformity in the application, operation, and interpretation of the election laws." The state legislature has delegated to county canvassing boards the duties of administering elections. Those boards are responsible for providing results to the state Elections Canvassing Commission, comprising the Governor, the Secretary of State, and the Director of the Division of Elections.

After the election has taken place, the canvassing boards receive returns from precincts, count the votes, and in the event that a candidate was defeated by .5% or less, conduct a mandatory recount. The county canvassing boards must file certified election returns with the Department of State by 5 p.m. on the seventh day following the election. The Elections Canvassing Commission must then certify the results of the election.

The state legislature has also provided mechanisms both for protesting election returns and for contesting certified election results. Section 102.166 governs protests. Any protest must be filed prior to the certification of election results by the county canvassing board. . . .

Contests to the certification of an election, on the other hand, are controlled by §102.168. The grounds for contesting an election include "receipt of a number of illegal votes or rejection of a number of legal votes sufficient to change or place in doubt the result of the election." . . .

In its first decision, *Palm Beach Canvassing Bd. v. Harris (Harris I),* the Florida Supreme Court extended the 7-day statutory certification deadline established by the legislature. . . . The court determined that canvassing boards' decisions regarding whether to recount ballots past the certification deadline (even the certification deadline established by *Harris I*) are to be reviewed *de novo,* although the election code clearly vests discretion whether to recount in the boards, and sets strict deadlines subject to the Secretary's rejection of late tallies and monetary fines for tardiness. . . .

Moreover, the court's interpretation of "legal vote," and hence its decision to order a contest-period recount, plainly departed from the legislative scheme. Florida statutory law cannot reasonably be thought to *require* the counting of improperly marked ballots. Each Florida precinct before election day provides instructions on how properly to cast a vote; each polling place on election day contains a working model of the voting machine it uses; and each voting booth contains a sample ballot. In precincts using punch-card ballots, voters are instructed to punch out the ballot cleanly: "AFTER VOTING, CHECK YOUR BALLOT CARD TO BE SURE YOUR VOTING SELECTIONS ARE CLEARLY AND CLEANLY PUNCHED AND THERE ARE NO CHIPS LEFT HANGING ON THE BACK OF THE CARD." No reasonable person would call it "an error in the vote tabulation" or a "rejection of legal votes" when electronic or electromechanical equipment performs precisely in the manner designed, and fails to count those ballots that are not marked in the manner that these voting instructions explicitly and prominently specify. . . .

But as we indicated in our remand of the earlier case, in a Presidential election the clearly expressed intent of the legislature must prevail. . . .

The scope and nature of the remedy ordered by the Florida Supreme Court jeopardizes the "legislative wish" to take advantage of the safe harbor provided by 3 U.S.C. §5. December 12, 2000, is the last date for a final determination of the Florida electors that will satisfy §5. Yet in the late afternoon of December 8th—four days before this deadline—the Supreme Court of Florida ordered recounts of tens of thousands of so-called "undervotes" spread through 64 of the State's 67 counties. This was done in a search for elusive—perhaps delusive—certainty as to the exact count of 6 million votes. But no one claims that these ballots had not previously been tabulated; they were initially read by voting machines at the time of the election, and thereafter reread by virtue of Florida's automatic recount provision. No one claims there was any fraud in the election. The Supreme Court of Florida ordered this additional recount under the provision of the election code giving the circuit judge the authority to provide relief that is "appropriate under such circumstances."

Surely when the Florida Legislature empowered the courts of the State to grant "appropriate" relief, it must have meant relief that would have become final by the cutoff date of 3 U.S.C. §5. In light of the inevitable legal challenges and ensuing appeals to the Supreme Court of Florida and petitions for certiorari to this Court, the entire recounting process could not possibly be completed by that date. . . .

Given all these factors, and in light of the legislative intent identified by the Florida Supreme Court to bring Florida within the "safe harbor" provision of 3 U.S.C. §5, the remedy prescribed by the Supreme Court of Florida cannot be deemed an "appropriate" one as of December 8. It significantly departed from the statutory framework in place on November 7, and authorized open-ended further proceedings which could not be completed by December 12, thereby preventing a final determination by that date.

For these reasons, in addition to those given in the *per curiam,* we would reverse.

JUSTICE STEVENS, with whom JUSTICE GINSBURG and JUSTICE BREYER join, dissenting.

The Constitution assigns to the States the primary responsibility for determining the manner of selecting the Presidential electors. When questions arise about the meaning of state laws, including election laws, it is our settled practice to accept the opinions of the highest courts of the States as providing the final answers. On rare occasions, however, either federal statutes or the Federal Constitution may require federal judicial intervention in state elections. This is not such an occasion.

The federal questions that ultimately emerged in this case are not substantial. Article

II provides that "each *State* shall appoint, in such Manner as the Legislature *thereof* may direct, a Number of Electors." (emphasis added). It does not create state legislatures out of whole cloth, but rather takes them as they come—as creatures born of, and constrained by, their state constitutions. Lest there be any doubt, we stated over 100 years ago in *McPherson v. Blacker,* (1892), that "what is forbidden or required to be done by a State" in the Article II context "is forbidden or required of the legislative power under state constitutions as they exist." In the same vein, we also observed that "the [State's] legislative power is the supreme authority except as limited by the constitution of the State." The legislative power in Florida is subject to judicial review pursuant to Article V of the Florida Constitution, and nothing in Article II of the Federal Constitution frees the state legislature from the constraints in the state constitution that created it. Moreover, the Florida Legislature's own decision to employ a unitary code for all elections indicates that it intended the Florida Supreme Court to play the same role in Presidential elections that it has historically played in resolving electoral disputes. The Florida Supreme Court's exercise of appellate jurisdiction therefore was wholly consistent with, and indeed contemplated by, the grant of authority in Article II.

. . . §5 provides a safe harbor for States to select electors in contested elections "by judicial or other methods" established by laws prior to the election day. Section 5, like Article II, assumes the involvement of the state judiciary in interpreting state election laws and resolving election disputes under those laws. Neither §5 nor Article II grants federal judges any special authority to substitute their views for those of the state judiciary on matters of state law. . . .

Even assuming that aspects of the remedial scheme might ultimately be found to violate the Equal Protection Clause, I could not subscribe to the majority's disposition of the case. As the majority explicitly holds, once a state legislature determines to select electors through a popular vote, the right to have one's vote counted is of constitutional stature. As the majority further acknowledges, Florida law holds that all ballots that reveal the intent of the voter constitute valid votes. Recognizing these principles, the majority nonetheless orders the termination of the contest proceeding before all such votes have been tabulated. Under their own reasoning, the appropriate course of action would be to remand to allow more specific procedures for implementing the legislature's uniform general standard to be established. . . .

Finally, neither in this case, nor in its earlier opinion in *Palm Beach County Canvassing Bd. v. Harris* did the Florida Supreme Court make any substantive change in Florida electoral law. Its decisions were rooted in long-established precedent and were consistent with the relevant statutory provisions, taken as a whole. It did what courts do—it decided the case before it in light of the legislature's intent to leave no legally cast vote uncounted. In so doing, it relied on the sufficiency of the general "intent of the voter" standard articulated by the state legislature, coupled with a procedure for ultimate review by an impartial judge, to resolve the concern about disparate evaluations of contested ballots. If we assume—as I do—that the members of that court and the judges who would have carried out its mandate are impartial, its decision does not even raise a colorable federal question.

What must underlie petitioners' entire federal assault on the Florida election procedures is an unstated lack of confidence in the impartiality and capacity of the state judges who would make the critical decisions if the vote count were to proceed. Otherwise, their position is wholly without merit. The endorsement of that position by the majority of this Court can only lend credence to the most cynical appraisal of the work of judges throughout the land. It is confidence in the men and women who administer the judicial system that is the true backbone of the rule of law. Time will one day heal the wound to that confidence that will be inflicted by today's decision. One thing, however, is certain. Although we may never know with complete certainty the identity of the winner of this year's Presidential election, the identity of the loser is perfectly clear. It is the Nation's confidence in the judge as an impartial guardian of the rule of law.

I respectfully dissent.

JUSTICE SOUTER, with whom JUSTICE BREYER joins and with whom JUSTICE STEVENS and JUSTICE GINSBURG join with regard to all but Part C, dissenting.

. . . Petitioners have raised an equal protection claim (or, alternatively, a due process claim), in the charge that unjustifiably disparate standards are applied in different electoral jurisdictions to otherwise identical facts. It is true that the Equal Protection Clause does not forbid the use of a variety of voting mechanisms within a jurisdiction, even though different mechanisms will have different levels of effectiveness in recording voters' intentions; local variety can be justified by concerns about cost, the potential value of innovation, and so on. But evidence in the record here suggests that a different order of disparity obtains under rules for determining a voter's intent that have been applied (and could continue to be applied) to identical types of ballots used in identical brands of machines and exhibiting identical physical characteristics (such as "hanging" or "dimpled" chads). I can conceive of no legitimate state interest served by these differing treatments of the expressions of voters' fundamental rights. The differences appear wholly arbitrary.

In deciding what to do about this, we should take account of the fact that electoral votes are due to be cast in six days. I would therefore remand the case to the courts of Florida with instructions to establish uniform standards for evaluating the several types of ballots that have prompted differing treatments, to be applied within and among counties when passing on such identical ballots in any further recounting (or successive recounting) that the courts might order.

Unlike the majority, I see no warrant for this Court to assume that Florida could not possibly comply with this requirement before the date set for the meeting of electors, December 18. . . . To recount these manually would be a tall order, but before this Court stayed the effort to do that the courts of Florida were ready to do their best to get that job done. There is no justification for denying the State the opportunity to try to count all disputed ballots now.

I respectfully dissent.

JUSTICE GINSBURG, with whom JUSTICE STEVENS joins, and with whom JUSTICE SOUTER and JUSTICE BREYER join as to Part I, dissenting.

I

The Chief Justice acknowledges that provisions of Florida's Election Code "may well admit of more than one interpretation." *Ante*, at 3. But instead of respecting the state high court's province to say what the State's Election Code means, The Chief Justice maintains that Florida's Supreme Court has veered so far from the ordinary practice of judicial review that what it did cannot properly be called judging. My colleagues have offered a reasonable construction of Florida's law. Their construction coincides with the view of one of Florida's seven Supreme Court justices. I might join The Chief Justice were it my commission to interpret Florida law. But disagreement with the Florida court's interpretation of its own State's law does not warrant the conclusion that the justices of that court have legislated. There is no cause here to believe that the members of Florida's high court have done less than "their mortal best to discharge their oath of office" and no cause to upset their reasoned interpretation of Florida law. . . .

The Chief Justice says that Article II, by providing that state legislatures shall direct the manner of appointing electors, authorizes federal superintendence over the relationship between state courts and state legislatures, and licenses a departure from the usual deference we give to state court interpretations of state law. The Framers of our Constitution, however, understood that in a republican government, the judiciary would construe the legislature's enactments. See U.S. Const., Art. III; *The Federalist* No. 78 (A. Hamilton). In light of the constitutional guarantee to States of a "Republican Form of Government," U.S. Const., Art. IV, §4, Article II can hardly be read to invite this Court to disrupt a State's republican regime. Yet The Chief Justice today would reach out to do just that. By holding that Article II requires our revision of a state court's construction of state laws in order to protect one organ of the State from another, The Chief Justice contradicts the basic principle that a State may organize itself as it sees fit. Article II does not call for the scrutiny undertaken by this Court.

The extraordinary setting of this case has obscured the ordinary principle that dictates its proper resolution: Federal courts defer to state high courts' interpretations of their state's own law. This principle reflects the core of federalism, on which all agree. . . . The Chief Justice's solicitude for the Florida Legislature comes at the expense of the more fundamental solicitude we owe to the legislature's sovereign. Were the other members of this Court as mindful as they generally are of our system of dual sovereignty, they would affirm the judgment of the Florida Supreme Court.

II

I agree with Justice Stevens that petitioners have not presented a substantial equal protection claim. Ideally, perfection would be the appropriate standard for judging the recount. But we live in an imperfect world, one in which thousands of votes have not been counted. I cannot agree that the recount adopted by the Florida court, flawed as it may be, would yield a result any less fair or precise than the certification that preceded that recount. . . .

Even if there were an equal protection violation, I would agree with Justice Stevens, Justice Souter, and Justice Breyer that the Court's concern about "the December 12 deadline" is misplaced. Time is short in part because of the Court's entry of a stay on December 9, several hours after an able circuit judge in Leon County had begun to superintend the recount process. More fundamentally, the Court's reluctance to let the recount go forward—despite its suggestion that "the search for intent can be confined by specific rules designed to ensure uniform treatment"—ultimately turns on its own judgment about the practical realities of implementing a recount, not the judgment of those much closer to the process.

Equally important, as Justice Breyer explains, the December 12 "deadline" for bringing Florida's electoral votes into 3 U.S.C. §5's safe harbor lacks the significance the Court assigns it. Were that date to pass, Florida would still be entitled to deliver electoral votes Congress *must* count unless both Houses find that the

votes "had not been . . . regularly given." The statute identifies other significant dates. See, *e.g.,* §7 (specifying December 18 as the date electors "shall meet and give their votes"); §12 (specifying "the fourth Wednesday in December"—this year, December 27—as the date on which Congress, if it has not received a State's electoral votes, shall request the state secretary of state to send a certified return immediately). But none of these dates has ultimate significance in light of Congress' detailed provisions for determining, on "the sixth day of January," the validity of electoral votes. §15.

The Court assumes that time will not permit "orderly judicial review of any disputed matters that might arise" . . . [T]he Court's conclusion that a constitutionally adequate recount is impractical is a prophecy the Court's own judgment will not allow to be tested. Such an untested prophecy should not decide the Presidency of the United States.

I dissent.

JUSTICE BREYER, with whom JUSTICE STEVENS and JUSTICE GINSBURG join except as to Part I-A-1, and with whom JUSTICE SOUTER joins as to Part I, dissenting.

The Court was wrong to take this case. It was wrong to grant a stay. It should now vacate that stay and permit the Florida Supreme Court to decide whether the recount should resume.

I

The political implications of this case for the country are momentous. But the federal legal questions presented, with one exception, are insubstantial.

The majority raises three Equal Protection problems with the Florida Supreme Court's recount order: first, the failure to include overvotes in the manual recount; second, the fact that *all* ballots, rather than simply the undervotes, were recounted in some, but not all, counties; and third, the absence of a uniform, specific standard to guide the recounts. As far as the first issue is concerned, petitioners presented no evidence, to this Court or to any Florida court, that a manual recount of overvotes would identify additional legal votes. The same is true of the second, and, in addition, the majority's reasoning would seem to invalidate any state provision for a manual recount of individual counties in a state-wide election.

The majority's third concern does implicate principles of fundamental fairness. The majority concludes that the Equal Protection Clause requires that a manual recount be governed not only by the uniform general standard of the "clear intent of the voter," but also by uniform subsidiary standards (for example, a uniform determination whether indented, but not per-forated, "undervotes" should count). The opin-ion points out that the Florida Supreme Court ordered the inclusion of Broward County's un-dercounted "legal votes" even though those votes included ballots that were not perforated but simply "dimpled," while newly recounted ballots from other counties will likely include only votes determined to be "legal" on the basis of a stricter standard. In light of our pre-vious remand, the Florida Supreme Court may have been reluctant to adopt a more specific standard than that provided for by the legisla-ture for fear of exceeding its authority under Article II. However, since the use of different standards could favor one or the other of the candidates, since time was, and is, too short to permit the lower courts to iron out significant differences through ordinary judicial review, and since the relevant distinction was embod-ied in the order of the State's highest court, I agree that, in these very special circumstances, basic principles of fairness may well have coun-seled the adoption of a uniform standard to address the problem. In light of the majority's disposition, I need not decide whether, or the extent to which, as a remedial matter, the Con-stitution would place limits upon the content of the uniform standard.

Nonetheless, there is no justification for the majority's remedy, which is simply to reverse the lower court and halt the recount entirely. An appropriate remedy would be, instead, to remand this case with instructions that, even at this late date, would permit the Florida Su-preme Court to require recounting *all* under-counted votes in Florida, including those from Broward, Volusia, Palm Beach, and Miami-Dade Counties, whether or not previously re-counted prior to the end of the protest period, and to do so in accordance with a single-uniform substandard.

The majority justifies stopping the recount entirely on the ground that there is no more time. In particular, the majority relies on the lack of time for the Secretary to review and ap-prove equipment needed to separate under-votes. But the majority reaches this conclusion in the absence of *any* record evidence that the recount could not have been completed in the time allowed by the Florida Supreme Court. The majority finds facts outside of the record on matters that state courts are in a far better position to address. Of course, it is too late for any such recount to take place by December 12, the date by which election disputes must be decided if a State is to take advantage of the safe harbor provisions of 3 U.S.C. §5. Whether there is time to conduct a recount prior to De-cember 18, when the electors are scheduled to meet, is a matter for the state courts to deter-mine. And whether, under Florida law, Florida could or could not take further action is obvi-ously a matter for Florida courts, not this Court, to decide.

By halting the manual recount, and thus en-suring that the uncounted legal votes will not be counted under any standard, this Court crafts a remedy out of proportion to the as-serted harm. . . .

II

. . . [T]he selection of the President is of fun-damental national importance. But that im-portance is political, not legal. And this Court should resist the temptation unnecessarily to resolve tangential legal disputes, where doing so threatens to determine the outcome of the election.

The Constitution and federal statutes them-selves make clear that restraint is appropriate. They set forth a road map of how to resolve disputes about electors, even after an election as close as this one. That road map foresees res-olution of electoral disputes by *state* courts. See 3 U.S.C. §5 (providing that, where a "State shall have provided, by laws enacted prior to [election day], for its final determination of any controversy or contest concerning the ap-pointment of . . . electors . . . by *judicial* or other methods," the subsequently chosen electors enter a safe harbor free from congres-sional challenge). But it nowhere provides for involvement by the United States Supreme Court.

To the contrary, the Twelfth Amendment commits to Congress the authority and responsibility to count electoral votes. A federal statute, the Electoral Count Act, enacted after the close 1876 Hayes-Tilden Presidential election, specifies that, after States have tried to resolve disputes (through "judicial" or other means), Congress is the body primarily authorized to resolve remaining disputes. See Electoral Count Act of 1887, 24 Stat. 373, 3 U.S.C. §§5, 6, and 15.

The legislative history of the Act makes clear its intent to commit the power to resolve such disputes to Congress, rather than the courts: "The two Houses are, by the Constitution, authorized to make the count of electoral votes. They can only count legal votes, and in doing so must determine, from the best evidence to be had, what are legal votes. . . . The power to determine rests with the two Houses, and there is no other constitutional tribunal." H. Rep. No. 1638, 49th Cong., 1st Sess., 2 (1886) (report submitted by Rep. Caldwell, Select Committee on the Election of President and Vice-President). . . .

The Act goes on to set out rules for the congressional determination of disputes about those votes. If, for example, a state submits a single slate of electors, Congress must count those votes unless both Houses agree that the votes "have not been . . . regularly given." If, as occurred in 1876, one or more states submits two sets of electors, then Congress must determine whether a state has entered the safe harbor of §5, in which case its votes will have "conclusive" effect. If, as also occurred in 1876, there is controversy about "which of two or more of such State authorities . . . is the lawful tribunal" authorized to appoint electors, then each House shall determine separately which votes are "supported by the decision of such State so authorized by its law." If the two Houses of Congress agree, the votes they have approved will be counted. If they disagree, then "the votes of the electors whose appointment shall have been certified by the executive of the State, under the seal thereof, shall be counted."

Given this detailed, comprehensive scheme for counting electoral votes, there is no reason to believe that federal law either foresees or requires resolution of such a political issue by this Court. Nor, for that matter, is there any reason to think that the Constitution's Framers would have reached a different conclusion. Madison, at least, believed that allowing the judiciary to choose the presidential electors "was out of the question."

The decision by both the Constitution's Framers and the 1886 Congress to minimize this Court's role in resolving close federal presidential elections is as wise as it is clear. However awkward or difficult it may be for Congress to resolve difficult electoral disputes, Congress, being a political body, expresses the people's will far more accurately than does an unelected Court. And the people's will is what elections are about. . . .

I fear that in order to bring this agonizingly long election process to a definitive conclusion, we have not adequately attended to that necessary "check upon our own exercise of power," "our own sense of self-restraint." Justice Brandeis once said of the Court, "The most important thing we do is not doing." What it does today, the Court should have left undone. I would repair the damage done as best we now can, by permitting the Florida recount to continue under uniform standards.

I respectfully dissent.

The United States Supreme Court handed down its decision just before 10:00 p.m. on December 12. On December 13, Gore ended his campaign and conceded the election. On December 18, the Electoral College voted and cast 271 votes for Bush and 266 for Gore.

Katzenbach v. Morgan
384 U.S. 641 (1966)

Voters of New York City entered US District Court for the District of Columbia, seeking *declaratory and injunctive relief restraining enforcement of §4(e) of the Voting Rights Act of*

1965. That section provided that no person who had successfully completed the sixth grade in an American-flag school in which the predominant language of instruction was other than English could be disqualified from voting under any literacy test. It was being applied to prohibit enforcement against Puerto Ricans living in New York City of a New York election law requiring the ability to read and write English as a condition of voting. The three-judge district court granted relief, and an appeal was taken directly to the United States Supreme Court. Opinion of the Court: <u>Brennan</u>, Warren, Black, Douglas, Clark, White, Fortas. Dissenting opinion: <u>Harlan</u>, Stewart.

JUSTICE BRENNAN delivered the opinion of the Court.

We hold that, in the application challenged in these cases, §4(e) is a proper exercise of the powers granted to Congress by §5 of the Fourteenth Amendment and that by force of the Supremacy Clause, Article VI, the New York English literacy requirement cannot be enforced to the extent that it is inconsistent with §4(e). . . .

The Attorney General of the State of New York argues that an exercise of congressional power under §5 of the Fourteenth Amendment that prohibits the enforcement of a state law can only be sustained if the judicial branch determines that the state law is prohibited by the provisions of the Amendment that Congress sought to enforce. More specifically, he urges that §4(e) cannot be sustained as appropriate legislation to enforce the Equal Protection Clause unless the judiciary decides—even with the guidance of a congressional judgment—that the application of the English literacy requirement prohibited by §4(e) is forbidden by the Equal Protection Clause itself. We disagree. Neither the language nor history of §5 supports such a construction. As was said with regard to §5 in *Ex parte Com. of Virginia* (1880): "It is the power of Congress which has been enlarged. Congress is authorized to *enforce* the prohibitions by appropriate legislation. Some legislation is contemplated to make the amendments fully effective." A construction of §5 that would require a judicial determination that the en-

forcement of the state law precluded by Congress violated the Amendment, as a condition of sustaining the congressional enactment, would depreciate both congressional resourcefulness and congressional responsibility for implementing the Amendment. It would confine the legislative power in this context to the insignificant role of abrogating only those state laws that the judicial branch was prepared to adjudge unconstitutional, or of merely informing the judgment of the judiciary by particularizing the "majestic generalities" of §1 of the Amendment.

Thus our task in this case is not to determine whether the New York English literacy requirement as applied to deny the right to vote to a person who successfully completed the sixth grade in a Puerto Rican school violates the Equal Protection Clause. Accordingly, our decision in *Lassiter v. Northampton County Bd. of Election* (1959), sustaining the North Carolina English literacy requirement as not in all circumstances prohibited by the first sections of the Fourteenth and Fifteenth Amendments, is inapposite. *Lassiter* did not present the question before us here: Without regard to whether the judiciary would find that the Equal Protection Clause itself nullifies New York's English literacy requirement as so applied, could Congress prohibit the enforcement of the state law by legislating under §5 of the Fourteenth Amendment? In answering this question, our task is limited to determining whether such legislation is, as required by §5, appropriate legislation to enforce the Equal Protection Clause.

By including §5 the draftsmen sought to grant to Congress, by a specific provision applicable to the Fourteenth Amendment, the same broad powers expressed in the Necessary and Proper Clause, Art. I, §8, cl. 18.

Correctly viewed, §5 is a positive grant of legislative power authorizing Congress to exercise its discretion in determining whether and what legislation is needed to secure the guarantees of the Fourteenth Amendment.

We therefore proceed to the consideration whether §4(e) is "appropriate legislation" to enforce the Equal Protection Clause, that is, under the *McCulloch v. Maryland* standard, whether §4(e) may be regarded as an enactment to enforce the Equal Protection Clause, whether it is "plainly adapted to that end" and whether it is not prohibited by but is consistent with "the letter and spirit of the constitution."*

There can be no doubt that §4(e) may be regarded as an enactment to enforce the Equal Protection Clause. Congress explicitly declared that it enacted §4(e) "to secure the rights under the fourteenth amendment of persons educated in American-flag schools in which the predominant classroom language was other than English." More specifically, §4(e) may be viewed as a measure to secure for the Puerto Rican community residing in New York nondiscriminatory treatment by government—both in the imposition of voting qualifications and the provision or administration of governmental services, such as public schools, public housing, and law enforcement.

It was for Congress, as the branch that made this judgment, to assess and weigh the various conflicting considerations—the risk or pervasiveness of the discrimination in governmental services, the effectiveness of eliminating the state restriction on the right to vote as a means of dealing with the evil, the adequacy or availability of alternative remedies, and the nature and significance of the state interests that would be affected by the nullification of the English literacy requirement as applied to residents who have successfully completed the sixth grade in a Puerto Rican school. It is not for us to review the congressional resolution of these factors. It is enough that we be able to perceive a basis upon which the Congress might resolve the conflict as it did. There plainly was such a basis to support §4(e) in the application in question in this case. Any contrary conclusion would require us to be blind to the realities familiar to the legislators.

---

*Contrary to the suggestion of the dissent, §5 does not grant Congress power to exercise discretion in the other direction and to enact "statutes so as in effect to dilute equal protection and due process decisions of this Court." We emphasize that Congress' power under §5 is limited to adopting measures to enforce the guarantees of the Amendment; §5 grants Congress no power to restrict, abrogate, or dilute these guarantees. Thus, for example, an enactment authorizing the States to establish racially segregated systems of education would not be—as required by §5—a measure to "enforce" the Equal Protection Clause, since that clause, of its own force, prohibits such state laws.

Section 4(e) does not restrict or deny the franchise but in effect extends the franchise to persons who otherwise would be denied it by state law. Thus we need not decide whether a state literacy law conditioning the right to vote on achieving a certain level of education in an American-flag school (regardless of the language of instruction) discriminates invidiously against those educated in non-American-flag schools. We need only decide whether the challenged limitation on the relief effected in §4(e) was permissible. In deciding that question, the principle that calls for the closest scrutiny of distinctions in laws *denying* fundamental rights is inapplicable; for the distinction challenged by appellees is presented only as a limitation on a reform measure aimed at eliminating an existing barrier to the exercise of the franchise. Rather, in deciding the constitutional propriety of the limitations in such a reform measure we are guided by the familiar principles that a "statute is not invalid under the Constitution because it might have gone farther than it did," that a legislature need not "strike at all evils at the same time," and that "reform may take one step at a time, addressing itself to the phase of the problem which seems most acute to the legislative mind."

Guided by these principles, we are satisfied that appellees' challenge to this limitation in §4(e) is without merit.

We therefore conclude that §4(e), in the application challenged in this case, is appropriate legislation to enforce the Equal Protection Clause and that the judgment of the District Court must be and hereby is reversed.

JUSTICE HARLAN, with whom JUSTICE STEWART joins, dissenting.

Worthy as its purposes may be thought by many, I do not see how §4(e) of the Voting Rights Act of 1965 can be sustained except at the sacrifice of fundamentals in the American constitutional system—the separation between the legislative and judicial function and the boundaries between federal and state political authority.

I believe the Court has confused the issue of how much enforcement power Congress possesses under §5 with the distinct issue of what questions are appropriate for congressional determination and what questions are essentially judicial in nature.

When recognized state violations of federal constitutional standards have occurred, Congress is of course empowered by §5 to take appropriate remedial measures to redress and prevent the wrongs. But it is a judicial question whether the condition with which Congress has thus sought to deal is in truth an infringement of the Constitution, something that is the necessary prerequisite to bringing the §5 power into play at all.

The question here is not whether the statute is appropriate remedial legislation to cure an established violation of a constitutional command, but whether there has in fact been an infringement of that constitutional command, that is, whether a particular state practice or, as here, a statute is so arbitrary or irrational as to offend the command of the Equal Protection Clause of the Fourteenth Amendment. That question is one for the judicial branch ultimately to determine. Were the rule otherwise, Congress would be able to qualify this Court's constitutional decisions under the Fourteenth and Fifteenth Amendments, let alone those under other provisions of the Constitution, by resorting to congressional power under the Necessary and Proper Clause. In view of this Court's holding in *Lassiter* that an English literacy test is a permissible exercise of state supervision over its franchise, I do not think it is open to Congress to limit the effect of that decision as it has undertaken to do by §4(e). In effect the Court reads §5 of the Fourteenth Amendment as giving Congress the power to define the *substantive* scope of the Amendment. If that indeed be the true reach of §5, then I do not see why Congress should not be able as well to exercise its §5 "discretion" by enacting statutes so as in effect to dilute equal protection and due process decisions of this Court. In all such cases there is room for reasonable men to differ as to whether or not a denial of equal protection or due process has occurred, and the final decision is one of judgment. Until today this judgment has always been one for the judiciary to resolve.

Shaw v. Reno
509 U.S. 630 (1993)

As a result of population growth during the 1980s, North Carolina's congressional delegation was increased from eleven to twelve after the 1990 census. The North Carolina Legislature redrew the state's congressional district lines in such a way that it protected the state's eleven incumbent congressmen and simultaneously carved out a new majority-black district, thereby ensuring the election of the state's first African American member of Congress since Reconstruction. The attorney general of the United States, enforcing the Voting Rights Act of 1965 as amended in 1982, rejected the state's plan, however, on the grounds that a second majority-black congressional district could also be created. The state revised its plan and created a second majority-black district. It came to be known as the Interstate 85 District—a district that stretched more than 160 miles along I-85 and that for much of its length was no wider than the I-85 corridor. Five state residents filed suit against this plan, alleging that the state had created a racial gerrymander in violation of the Fourteenth Amendment. A three-judge district court for the Eastern District of North Carolina dismissed the appellants' complaint, and an appeal was taken to the US Supreme Court. *Opinion of the Court:* O'Connor, *Rehnquist, Scalia, Kennedy, Thomas. Dissenting opinions:* White, *Blackmun, Stevens;* Blackmun; Stevens; Souter.

JUSTICE O'CONNOR delivered the opinion of the Court.

This case involves two of the most complex and sensitive issues this Court has faced in recent years: the meaning of the constitutional "right" to vote, and the propriety of race-based state legislation designed to benefit members of historically disadvantaged racial minority groups. As a result of the 1990 census, North Carolina became entitled to a twelfth seat in the United States House of Representatives. The General Assembly enacted a reapportionment plan that included one majority-black congressional district. After the Attorney

General of the United States objected to the plan pursuant to §5 of the Voting Rights Act of 1965, the General Assembly passed new legislation creating a second majority-black district. Appellants allege that the revised plan, which contains district boundary lines of dramatically irregular shape, constitutes an unconstitutional racial gerrymander. The question before us is whether appellants have stated a cognizable claim.

The voting age population of North Carolina is approximately 78% white, 20% black, and 1% Native American; the remaining 1% is predominantly Asian. The black population is relatively dispersed; blacks constitute a majority of the general population in only 5 of the State's 100 counties. Geographically, the State divides into three regions: the eastern Coastal Plain, the central Piedmont Plateau, and the western mountains. The largest concentrations of black citizens live in the Coastal Plain, primarily in the northern part. The General Assembly's first redistricting plan contained one majority-black district centered in that area of the State.

Forty of North Carolina's one hundred counties are covered by §5 of the Voting Rights Act of 1965, which prohibits a jurisdiction subject to its provisions from implementing changes in a "standard, practice, or procedure with respect to voting" without federal authorization. The jurisdiction must obtain either a judgment from the United States District Court for the District of Columbia declaring that the proposed change "does not have the purpose and will not have the effect of denying or abridging the right to vote on account of race or color" or administrative preclearance from the Attorney General. Because the General Assembly's reapportionment plan affected the covered counties, the parties agree that §5 applied. The State chose to submit its plan to the Attorney General for preclearance.

The Attorney General, acting through the Assistant Attorney General for the Civil Rights Division, interposed a formal objection to the General Assembly's plan. The Attorney General specifically objected to the configuration of boundary lines drawn in the south-central to southeastern region of the State. In the Attorney General's view, the General Assembly could have created a second majority-minority district "to give effect to black and Native American voting strength in this area" by using boundary lines "no more irregular than [those] found elsewhere in the proposed plan" but failed to do so for "pretextual reasons."

Under §5, the State remained free to seek a declaratory judgment from the District Court for the District of Columbia notwithstanding the Attorney General's objection. It did not do so. Instead, the General Assembly enacted a revised redistricting plan that included a second majority-black district. The General Assembly located the second district not in the south-central to southeastern part of the State, but in the north-central region along Interstate 85.

The first of the two majority-black districts contained in the revised plan, District 1, is somewhat hook shaped. Centered in the northeast portion of the State, it moves southward until it tapers to a narrow band; then, with finger-like extensions, it reaches far into the southernmost part of the State near the South Carolina border. District 1 has been compared to a "Rorschach inkblot test," and a "bug splattered on a windshield."

The second majority-black district, District 12, is even more unusually shaped. It is approximately 160 miles long and, for much of its length, no wider than the I-85 corridor. It winds in snakelike fashion through tobacco country, financial centers, and manufacturing areas "until it gobbles in enough enclaves of black neighborhoods." Northbound and southbound drivers on I-85 sometimes find themselves in separate districts in one county, only to "trade" districts when they enter the next county. Of the 10 counties through which District 12 passes, five are cut into three different districts; even towns are divided. At one point the district remains contiguous only because it intersects at a single point with two other districts before crossing over them. One state legislator has remarked that "[i]f you drove down the interstate with both car doors open, you'd kill most of the people in the district." The district even has inspired poetry: "Ask not for whom the line is drawn; it is drawn to avoid thee."

The Attorney General did not object to the General Assembly's revised plan. But numerous North Carolinians did. Appellants instituted the present action in the United States District Court for the Eastern District of North Carolina. Appellants alleged not that the revised plan constituted a political gerrymander, nor that it violated the "one-person, one-vote" principle, but that the State had created an unconstitutional *racial* gerrymander. Appellants are five residents of Durham County, North Carolina, all registered to vote in that county. Under the General Assembly's plan, two will vote for congressional representatives in District 12 and three will vote in neighboring District 2.

Appellants contended that the General Assembly's revised reapportionment plan violated several provisions of the United States Constitution, including the Fourteenth Amendment. They alleged that the General Assembly deliberately "create[d] two Congressional Districts in which a majority of black voters was concentrated arbitrarily—without regard to any other considerations, such as compactness, contiguousness, geographical boundaries, or political subdivisions" with the purpose "to create Congressional Districts along racial lines" and to assure the election of two black representatives to Congress.

By a 2-to-1 vote, the District Court . . . dismissed the complaint against the state appellees. . . . An understanding of the nature of appellants' claim is critical to our resolution of this case. In their complaint, appellants did not claim that the General Assembly's reapportionment plan unconstitutionally "diluted" white voting strength. They did not even claim to be white. Rather, appellants' complaint alleged that the deliberate segregation of voters into separate districts on the basis of race violated their constitutional right to participate in a "color-blind" electoral process.

Despite their invocation of the ideal of a "color-blind" Constitution, see *Plessy v. Ferguson* (1896) (Justice Harlan, dissenting), appellants appear to concede that race-conscious redistricting is not always unconstitutional. That concession is wise: This Court never has held that race-conscious state decisionmaking is impermissible in *all* circumstances. What appellants object to is redistricting legislation that is so extremely irregular on its face that it

rationally can be viewed only as an effort to segregate the races for purposes of voting, without regard for traditional districting principles and without sufficiently compelling justification. For the reasons that follow, we conclude that appellants have stated a claim upon which relief can be granted under the Equal Protection Clause.

The Equal Protection Clause provides that "[n]o State shall . . . deny to any person within its jurisdiction the equal protection of the laws." Its central purpose is to prevent the States from purposefully discriminating between individuals on the basis of race. Laws that explicitly distinguish between individuals on racial grounds fall within the core of that prohibition.

Classifications of citizens solely on the basis of race "are by their very nature odious to a free people whose institutions are founded upon the doctrine of equality." They threaten to stigmatize individuals by reason of their membership in a racial group and to incite racial hostility. Accordingly, we have held that the Fourteenth Amendment requires state legislation that expressly distinguishes among citizens because of their race to be narrowly tailored to further a compelling governmental interest.

These principles apply not only to legislation that contains explicit racial distinctions, but also to those "rare" statutes that, although race-neutral, are, on their face, "unexplainable on grounds other than race." Appellants contend that redistricting legislation that is so bizarre on its face that it is "unexplainable on grounds other than race," demands the same close scrutiny that we give other state laws that classify citizens by race. Our voting rights precedents support that conclusion. . . .

We believe that reapportionment is one area in which appearances do matter. A reapportionment plan that includes in one district individuals who belong to the same race, but who are otherwise widely separated by geographical and political boundaries, and who may have little in common with one another but the color of their skin, bears an uncomfortable resemblance to political apartheid. It reinforces the perception that members of the same racial group—regardless of their age, education, economic status, or the community in which they live—think alike, share the same political interests, and will prefer the same candidates at the polls. We have rejected such perceptions elsewhere as impermissible racial stereotypes. By perpetuating such notions, a racial gerrymander may exacerbate the very patterns of racial block voting that majority-minority districting is sometimes said to counteract.

The message that such districting sends to elected representatives is equally pernicious. When a district obviously is created solely to effectuate the perceived common interests of one racial group, elected officials are more likely to believe that their primary obligation is to represent only the members of that group, rather than their constituency as a whole. This is altogether antithetical to our system of representative democracy.

For these reasons, we conclude that a plaintiff challenging a reapportionment statute under the Equal Protection Clause may state a claim by alleging that the legislation, though race-neutral on its face, rationally cannot be understood as anything other than an effort to separate voters into different districts on the basis of race, and that the separation lacks sufficient justification. We hold only that, on the facts of this case, plaintiffs have stated a claim sufficient to defeat the state appellees' motion to dismiss. . . .

Justice Souter apparently believes that racial gerrymandering is harmless unless it dilutes a racial group's voting strength. As we have explained, however, reapportionment legislation that cannot be understood as anything other than an effort to classify and separate voters by race injures voters in other ways. It reinforces racial stereotypes and threatens to undermine our system of representative democracy by signaling to elected officials that they represent a particular racial group rather than their constituency as a whole. Justice Souter does not adequately explain why these harms are not cognizable under the Fourteenth Amendment. . . .

The dissenters make two other arguments that cannot be reconciled with our precedents. First, they suggest that a racial gerrymander of the sort alleged here is functionally equivalent to gerrymanders for nonracial purposes, such as political gerrymanders. This Court has held

political gerrymanders to be justiciable under the Equal Protection Clause. But nothing in our case law compels the conclusion that racial and political gerrymanders are subject to precisely the same constitutional scrutiny. In fact, our country's long and persistent history of racial discrimination in voting—as well as our Fourteenth Amendment jurisprudence, which always has reserved the strictest scrutiny for discrimination on the basis of race, would seem to compel opposite conclusions.

Second, Justice Stevens argues that racial gerrymandering poses no constitutional difficulties when district lines are drawn to favor the minority, rather than the majority. We have made clear, however, that equal protection analysis "is not dependent on the race of those burdened or benefitted by a particular classification." Indeed, racial classifications receive close scrutiny even when they may be said to burden or benefit the races equally.

Racial classifications of any sort pose the risk of lasting harm to our society. They reinforce the belief, held by too many for too much of our history, that individuals should be judged by the color of their skin. Racial classifications with respect to voting carry particular dangers. Racial gerrymandering, even for remedial purposes, may balkanize us into competing racial factions; it threatens to carry us further from the goal of a political system in which race no longer matters—a goal that the Fourteenth and Fifteenth Amendments embody, and to which the Nation continues to aspire. It is for these reasons that race-based districting by our state legislatures demands close judicial scrutiny.

In this case, the Attorney General suggested that North Carolina could have created a reasonably compact second majority-minority district in the south-central to southeastern part of the State. We express no view as to whether appellants successfully could have challenged such a district under the Fourteenth Amendment. We also do not decide whether appellants' complaint stated a claim under constitutional provisions other than the Fourteenth Amendment. Today we hold only that appellants have stated a claim under the Equal Protection Clause by alleging that the North Carolina General Assembly adopted a reapportionment scheme so irrational on its face that it can be understood only as an effort to segregate voters into separate voting districts because of their race, and that the separation lacks sufficient justification. If the allegation of racial gerrymandering remains uncontradicted, the District Court further must determine whether the North Carolina plan is narrowly tailored to further a compelling governmental interest. Accordingly, we reverse the judgment of the District Court and remand the case for further proceedings consistent with this opinion.

JUSTICE WHITE, with whom JUSTICE BLACKMUN and JUSTICE STEVENS join, dissenting.

The grounds for my disagreement with the majority are simply stated: Appellants have not presented a cognizable claim, because they have not alleged a cognizable injury. To date, we have held that only two types of state voting practices could give rise to a constitutional claim. The first involves direct and outright deprivation of the right to vote, for example by means of a poll tax or literacy test. Plainly, this variety is not implicated by appellants' allegations and need not detain us further. The second type of unconstitutional practice is that which "affects the political strength of various groups," *Mobile v. Bolden* (1980), in violation of the Equal Protection Clause. As for this latter category, we have insisted that members of the political or racial group demonstrate that the challenged action have the intent and effect of unduly diminishing their influence on the political process.

It strains credulity to suggest that North Carolina's purpose in creating a second majority-minority district was to discriminate against members of the majority group by "impair[ing] or burden[ing their] opportunity . . . to participate in the political process." The State has made no mystery of its intent, which was to respond to the Attorney General's objections by improving the minority group's prospects of electing a candidate of its choice. I doubt that this constitutes a discriminatory purpose as defined in the Court's equal protection case—*i.e.,* an intent to aggravate "the unequal distribution of electoral power." But even assuming that it does, there is no question that appellants

have not alleged the requisite discriminatory effects. Whites constitute roughly 76 percent of the total population and 79 percent of the voting age population in North Carolina. Yet, under the State's plan, they still constitute a voting majority in 10 (or 83 percent) of the 12 congressional districts. Though they might be dissatisfied at the prospect of casting a vote for a losing candidate—a lot shared by many, including a disproportionate number of minority voters—surely they cannot complain of discriminatory treatment.

Part of the majority's explanation of its holding is related to its simultaneous discomfort and fascination with irregularly shaped districts. Lack of compactness or contiguity, like uncouth district lines, certainly is a helpful indicator that some form of gerrymandering (racial or other) might have taken place and that "something may be amiss." Disregard for geographic divisions and compactness often goes hand in hand with partisan gerrymandering.

But while district irregularities may provide strong indicia of a potential gerrymander, they do no more than that. In particular, they have no bearing on whether the plan ultimately is found to violate the Constitution. Given two districts drawn on similar, race-based grounds, the one does not become more injurious than the other simply by virtue of being snakelike, at least so far as the Constitution is concerned and absent any evidence of differential racial impact. The majority's contrary view is perplexing in light of its concession that "compactness or attractiveness has never been held to constitute an independent federal constitutional requirement for state legislative districts." It is shortsighted as well, for a regularly shaped district can just as effectively effectuate racially discriminatory gerrymandering as an odd-shaped one. By focusing on looks rather than impact, the majority "immediately casts attention in the wrong direction—toward superficialities of shape and size, rather than toward the political realities of district composition."

Limited by its own terms to cases involving unusually shaped districts, the Court's approach nonetheless will unnecessarily hinder to some extent a State's voluntary effort to ensure a modicum of minority representation. This will be true in areas where the minority population is geographically dispersed. It also will be true where the minority population is not scattered but, for reasons unrelated to race—for example incumbency protection—the State would rather not create the majority-minority district in its most "obvious" location. When, as is the case here, the creation of a majority-minority district does not unfairly minimize the voting power of any other group, the Constitution does not justify, much less mandate, such obstruction.

Although I disagree with the holding that appellants' claim is cognizable, the Court's discussion of the level of scrutiny it requires warrants a few comments. I have no doubt that a State's compliance with the Voting Rights Act clearly constitutes a compelling interest.

JUSTICE STEVENS, dissenting.

The duty to govern impartially is abused when a group with power over the electoral process defines electoral boundaries solely to enhance its own political strength at the expense of any weaker group. That duty, however, is not violated when the majority acts to facilitate the election of a member of a group that lacks such power because it remains underrepresented in the state legislature—whether that group is defined by political affiliation, by common economic interests, or by religious, ethnic, or racial characteristics. The difference between constitutional and unconstitutional gerrymanders has nothing to do with whether they are based on assumptions about the groups they affect, but whether their purpose is to enhance the power of the group in control of the districting process at the expense of any minority group, and thereby to strengthen the unequal distribution of electoral power. When an assumption that people in particular a minority group (whether they are defined by the political party, religion, ethnic group, or race to which they belong) will vote in a particular way is used to *benefit* that group, no constitutional violation occurs. Politicians have always relied on assumptions that people in particular groups are likely to vote in a particular way when they draw new district lines, and I cannot believe that anything in today's opinion will stop them from doing so in the future.

JUSTICE SOUTER, dissenting.

In districting, the mere placement of an individual in one district instead of another denies no one a right or benefit provided to others. All citizens may register, vote, and be represented. In whatever district, the individual voter has a right to vote in each election, and the election will result in the voter's representation. As we have held, one's constitutional rights are not violated merely because the candidate one supports loses the election or because a group (including a racial group) to which one belongs winds up with a representative from outside that group.

It may be that the terms for pleading this cause of action will be met so rarely that this case will wind up an aberration. The shape of the district at issue in this case is indeed so bizarre that few other examples are ever likely to carry the unequivocal implication of impermissible use of race that the Court finds here. It may therefore be that few electoral districting cases are ever likely to employ the strict scrutiny the Court holds to be applicable on remand if appellants' allegations are "not contradicted." I would not respond to the seeming egregiousness of the redistricting now before us by untethering the concept of racial gerrymander in such a case from the concept of harm exemplified by dilution. In the absence of an allegation of such harm, I would affirm the judgment of the District Court. I respectfully dissent.

Shelby County v. Holder
570 U.S. ___ (2013)

Congress enacted the Voting Rights Act of 1965 to address entrenched racial discrimination in voting—what the Supreme Court in South Carolina v. Katzenbach *(1966) described as "an insidious and pervasive evil which had been perpetuated in certain parts of our country through unremitting and ingenious defiance of the Constitution." Section 2 of the Act bans any "standard, practice, or procedure" that "results in a denial or abridgement of the right of any citizen . . . to vote on account of race or color," applies nationwide, is permanent, and is not at issue in this case. Other sections apply only to some parts of the country. Section 4 of the Act provides a "coverage formula," defining the "covered jurisdictions" as States or political subdivisions that maintained tests or devices as prerequisites to voting, and had low voter registration or turnout at the time of the Act's initial passage. In those covered jurisdictions, Section 5 of the Act provides that no change in voting procedures can take effect until precleared by the United States Department of Justice, through an administrative procedure, or a three-judge panel of the United States District Court for the District of Columbia, through a declaratory judgment action. The coverage formula and preclearance requirement were initially set to expire after five years, but the Act was reauthorized without change to the coverage formula in 1970, 1975, and 1982. In 2006, the Act was reauthorized for an additional twenty-five years and again without change to the coverage formula. Coverage still turned on whether a jurisdiction had a voting test at the time of the Act's initial passage and had low voter registration or turnout at that time. Shortly after the 2006 reauthorization, a Texas utility district sought to bail out from the Act's coverage and, in the alternative, challenged the Act's constitutionality. In* Northwest Austin Municipal Utility District Number One v. Holder *(2009), Chief Justice John Roberts wrote for an eight-member majority of the Supreme Court resolving the challenge on statutory grounds but expressing serious doubts about the Act's continued constitutionality. Justice Thomas concurred in part and dissented in part; in a lengthy opinion, he argued that Section 5 of the Act should be declared unconstitutional.*

Petitioner Shelby County, in the covered jurisdiction of Alabama, sued the Attorney General in Federal District Court in Washington, D.C., seeking a declaratory judgment that Sections 4 and 5 are facially unconstitutional as well as a permanent injunction against their enforcement. The District Court upheld the Act, finding that the evidence before Congress in 2006 was sufficient to justify reauthorizing Section 5 and

continuing Section 4's coverage formula. The D.C. Circuit affirmed. After surveying the evidence in the record, that court accepted Congress's conclusion that Section 2 litigation remained inadequate in the covered jurisdictions to protect the rights of minority voters, that Section 5 was therefore still necessary, and that the coverage formula of Section 4 continued to pass constitutional muster. The Supreme Court granted certiorari. Opinion of the Court: <u>Roberts</u>, Scalia, Kennedy, Thomas, Alito. Concurring opinion: <u>Thomas</u>. Dissenting opinion: <u>Ginsburg</u>, Breyer, Sotomayor, Kagan.

CHIEF JUSTICE ROBERTS delivered the opinion of the Court.

The Voting Rights Act of 1965 employed extraordinary measures to address an extraordinary problem. Section 5 of the Act required States to obtain federal permission before enacting any law related to voting—a drastic departure from basic principles of federalism. And Section 4 of the Act applied that requirement only to some States—an equally dramatic departure from the principle that all States enjoy equal sovereignty. This was strong medicine, but Congress determined it was needed to address entrenched racial discrimination in voting, "an insidious and pervasive evil which had been perpetuated in certain parts of our country through unremitting and ingenious defiance of the Constitution." *South Carolina v. Katzenbach* (1966). As we explained in upholding the law, "exceptional conditions can justify legislative measures not otherwise appropriate." Reflecting the unprecedented nature of these measures, they were scheduled to expire after five years.

Nearly 50 years later, they are still in effect; indeed, they have been made more stringent, and are now scheduled to last until 2031. There is no denying, however, that the conditions that originally justified these measures no longer characterize voting in the covered jurisdictions. By 2009, "the racial gap in voter registration and turnout [was] lower in the States originally covered by §5 than it [was] nationwide." Since that time, Census Bureau data indicate that African-American voter turnout has come to exceed white voter turnout in five of the six States originally covered by §5, with a gap in the sixth State of less than one half of one percent.

At the same time, voting discrimination still exists; no one doubts that. The question is whether the Act's extraordinary measures, including its disparate treatment of the States, continue to satisfy constitutional requirements. As we put it a short time ago, "the Act imposes current burdens and must be justified by current needs."

II

In *Northwest Austin*, we stated that "the Act imposes current burdens and must be justified by current needs." And we concluded that "a departure from the fundamental principle of equal sovereignty requires a showing that a statute's disparate geographic coverage is sufficiently related to the problem that it targets." These basic principles guide our review of the question before us.

A

. . . Outside the strictures of the Supremacy Clause, States retain broad autonomy in structuring their governments and pursuing legislative objectives. Indeed, the Constitution provides that all powers not specifically granted to the Federal Government are reserved to the States or citizens. This "allocation of powers in our federal system preserves the integrity, dignity, and residual sovereignty of the States." But the federal balance "is not just an end in itself: Rather, federalism secures to citizens the liberties that derive from the diffusion of sovereign power."

More specifically, "the Framers of the Constitution intended the States to keep for themselves, as provided in the Tenth Amendment, the power to regulate elections." Of course, the Federal Government retains significant control over federal elections. For instance, the Constitution authorizes Congress to establish the time and manner for electing Senators and Representatives. But States have "broad powers to determine the conditions under which the right of suffrage may be exercised." *Carrington v. Rash* (1965). And "[e]ach State has the power to prescribe the qualifications of its officers and the manner in which they shall be chosen."

Not only do States retain sovereignty under the Constitution, there is also a "fundamental principle of equal sovereignty" among the States. Over a hundred years ago, this Court explained that our Nation "was and is a union of States, equal in power, dignity and authority." *Coyle v. Smith* (1911). Indeed, "the constitutional equality of the States is essential to the harmonious operation of the scheme upon which the Republic was organized." . . . [A]s we made clear in *Northwest Austin*, the fundamental principle of equal sovereignty remains highly pertinent in assessing subsequent disparate treatment of States.

The Voting Rights Act sharply departs from these basic principles. It suspends "all changes to state election law—however innocuous—until they have been precleared by federal authorities in Washington, D.C." States must beseech the Federal Government for permission to implement laws that they would otherwise have the right to enact and execute on their own, subject of course to any injunction in a §2 action. The Attorney General has 60 days to object to a preclearance request, longer if he requests more information. If a State seeks preclearance from a three-judge court, the process can take years.

And despite the tradition of equal sovereignty, the Act applies to only nine States (and several additional counties). While one State waits months or years and expends funds to implement a validly enacted law, its neighbor can typically put the same law into effect immediately, through the normal legislative process. Even if a noncovered jurisdiction is sued, there are important differences between those proceedings and preclearance proceedings; the preclearance proceeding "not only switches the burden of proof to the supplicant jurisdiction, but also applies substantive standards quite different from those governing the rest of the nation."

All this explains why, when we first upheld the Act in 1966, we described it as "stringent" and "potent." We recognized that it "may have been an uncommon exercise of congressional power," but concluded that "legislative measures not otherwise appropriate" could be justified by "exceptional conditions." We have since noted that the Act "authorizes federal intrusion into sensitive areas of state and local policy-making" and represents an "extraordinary departure from the traditional course of relations between the States and the Federal Government." As we reiterated in *Northwest Austin*, the Act constitutes "extraordinary legislation otherwise unfamiliar to our federal system.

B

In 1966, we found these departures from the basic features of our system of government justified. The "blight of racial discrimination in voting" had "infected the electoral process in parts of our country for nearly a century." Several States had enacted a variety of requirements and tests "specifically designed to prevent" African-Americans from voting. Case-by-case litigation had proved inadequate to prevent such racial discrimination in voting, in part because States "merely switched to discriminatory devices not covered by the federal decrees," "enacted difficult new tests," or simply "defied and evaded court orders." Shortly before enactment of the Voting Rights Act, only 19.4 percent of African-Americans of voting age were registered to vote in Alabama, only 31.8 percent in Louisiana, and only 6.4 percent in Mississippi. Those figures were roughly 50 percentage points or more below the figures for whites.

In short, we concluded that "[u]nder the compulsion of these unique circumstances, Congress responded in a permissibly decisive manner." We also noted then and have emphasized since that this extraordinary legislation was intended to be temporary, set to expire after five years.

At the time, the coverage formula—the means of linking the exercise of the unprecedented authority with the problem that warranted it—made sense. We found that "Congress chose to limit its attention to the geographic areas where immediate action seemed necessary." The areas where Congress found "evidence of actual voting discrimination" shared two characteristics: "the use of tests and devices for voter registration, and a voting rate in the 1964 presidential election at least 12 points below the national average." We explained that "[t]ests and devices are relevant to voting discrimination because of their long history as a tool for

perpetrating the evil; a low voting rate is pertinent for the obvious reason that widespread disenfranchisement must inevitably affect the number of actual voters." We therefore concluded that "the coverage formula [was] rational in both practice and theory." It accurately reflected those jurisdictions uniquely characterized by voting discrimination "on a pervasive scale," linking coverage to the devices used to effectuate discrimination and to the resulting disenfranchisement. The formula ensured that the "stringent remedies [were] aimed at areas where voting discrimination ha[d] been most flagrant."

C

Nearly 50 years later, things have changed dramatically. Shelby County contends that the preclearance requirement, even without regard to its disparate coverage, is now unconstitutional. Its arguments have a good deal of force. In the covered jurisdictions, "[v]oter turnout and registration rates now approach parity. Blatantly discriminatory evasions of federal decrees are rare. And minority candidates hold office at unprecedented levels." The tests and devices that blocked access to the ballot have been forbidden nationwide for over 40 years.

Those conclusions are not ours alone. Congress said the same when it reauthorized the Act in 2006, writing that "[s]ignificant progress has been made in eliminating first generation barriers experienced by minority voters, including increased numbers of registered minority voters, minority voter turnout, and minority representation in Congress, State legislatures, and local elected offices." . . .

There is no doubt that these improvements are in large part because of the Voting Rights Act. The Act has proved immensely successful at redressing racial discrimination and integrating the voting process. . . . Yet the Act has not eased the restrictions in Section 5 or narrowed the scope of the coverage formula in Section 4 along the way. Those extraordinary and unprecedented features were reauthorized—as if nothing had changed. In fact, the Act's unusual remedies have grown even stronger. When Congress reauthorized the Act in 2006, it did so for another 25 years on top of the previous

40—a far cry from the initial five-year period. Congress also expanded the prohibitions in Section 5. We had previously interpreted Section 5 to prohibit only those redistricting plans that would have the purpose or effect of worsening the position of minority groups. In 2006, Congress amended Section 5 to prohibit laws that could have favored such groups but did not do so because of a discriminatory purpose, even though we had stated that such broadening of Section 5 coverage would "exacerbate the substantial federalism costs that the preclearance procedure already exacts, perhaps to the extent of raising concerns about Section 5's constitutionality." In addition, Congress expanded Section 5 to prohibit any voting law "that has the purpose of or will have the effect of diminishing the ability of any citizens of the United States," on account of race, color, or language minority status, "to elect their preferred candidates of choice." In light of those two amendments, the bar that covered jurisdictions must clear has been raised even as the conditions justifying that requirement have dramatically improved. . . .

Respondents do not deny that there have been improvements on the ground, but argue that much of this can be attributed to the deterrent effect of Section 5, which dissuades covered jurisdictions from engaging in discrimination that they would resume should Section 5 be struck down. Under this theory, however, Section 5 would be effectively immune from scrutiny; no matter how "clean" the record of covered jurisdictions, the argument could always be made that it was deterrence that accounted for the good behavior.

The provisions of Section 5 apply only to those jurisdictions singled out by Section 4. We now consider whether that coverage formula is constitutional in light of current conditions.

III
A

When upholding the constitutionality of the coverage formula in 1966, we concluded that it was "rational in both practice and theory." The formula looked to cause (discriminatory tests) and effect (low voter registration and turnout), and tailored the remedy (preclearance) to those jurisdictions exhibiting both.

By 2009, however, we concluded that the "coverage formula raise[d] serious constitutional questions." As we explained, a statute's "current burdens" must be justified by "current needs," and any "disparate geographic coverage" must be "sufficiently related to the problem that it targets." The coverage formula met that test in 1965, but no longer does so.

Coverage today is based on decades-old data and eradicated practices. The formula captures States by reference to literacy tests and low voter registration and turnout in the 1960s and early 1970s. But such tests have been banned nationwide for over 40 years. And voter registration and turnout numbers in the covered States have risen dramatically in the years since. Racial disparity in those numbers was compelling evidence justifying the preclearance remedy and the coverage formula. There is no longer such a disparity.

In 1965, the States could be divided into two groups: those with a recent history of voting tests and low voter registration and turnout, and those without those characteristics. Congress based its coverage formula on that distinction. Today the Nation is no longer divided along those lines, yet the Voting Rights Act continues to treat it as if it were. . . .

B

. . . The Fifteenth Amendment commands that the right to vote shall not be denied or abridged on account of race or color, and it gives Congress the power to enforce that command. The Amendment is not designed to punish for the past; its purpose is to ensure a better future. To serve that purpose, Congress—if it is to divide the States—must identify those jurisdictions to be singled out on a basis that makes sense in light of current conditions. It cannot rely simply on the past. We made that clear in *Northwest Austin*, and we make it clear again today. . . .

D

The dissent proceeds from a flawed premise. It quotes the famous sentence from *McCulloch v. Maryland* (1819), with the following emphasis: "Let the end be legitimate, let it be within the scope of the constitution, and all means which are appropriate, which are plainly adapted to that end, which are not prohibited, but consist with the letter and spirit of the constitution, are constitutional." But this case is about a part of the sentence that the dissent does not emphasize—the part that asks whether a legislative means is "consist[ent] with the letter and spirit of the constitution." The dissent states that "[i]t cannot tenably be maintained" that this is an issue with regard to the Voting Rights Act, but four years ago, in an opinion joined by two of today's dissenters, the Court expressly stated that "[t]he Act's preclearance requirement and its coverage formula raise serious constitutional questions." *Northwest Austin*. The dissent does not explain how those "serious constitutional questions" became untenable in four short years.

The dissent treats the Act as if it were just like any other piece of legislation, but this Court has made clear from the beginning that the Voting Rights Act is far from ordinary. At the risk of repetition, *Katzenbach* indicated that the Act was "uncommon" and "not otherwise appropriate," but was justified by "exceptional" and "unique" conditions. Multiple decisions since have reaffirmed the Act's "extraordinary" nature. Yet the dissent goes so far as to suggest instead that the preclearance requirement and disparate treatment of the States should be upheld into the future "unless there [is] no or almost no evidence of unconstitutional action by States." . . .

There is no valid reason to insulate the coverage formula from review merely because it was previously enacted 40 years ago. If Congress had started from scratch in 2006, it plainly could not have enacted the present coverage formula. It would have been irrational for Congress to distinguish between States in such a fundamental way based on 40-year-old data, when today's statistics tell an entirely different story. And it would have been irrational to base coverage on the use of voting tests 40 years ago, when such tests have been illegal since that time. But that is exactly what Congress has done.

* * *

Striking down an Act of Congress "is the gravest and most delicate duty that this Court is called on to perform." We do not do so lightly.

That is why, in 2009, we took care to avoid ruling on the constitutionality of the Voting Rights Act when asked to do so, and instead resolved the case then before us on statutory grounds. But in issuing that decision, we expressed our broader concerns about the constitutionality of the Act. Congress could have updated the coverage formula at that time, but did not do so. Its failure to act leaves us today with no choice but to declare Section 4 unconstitutional. The formula in that section can no longer be used as a basis for subjecting jurisdictions to preclearance.

Our decision in no way affects the permanent, nationwide ban on racial discrimination in voting found in Section 2. We issue no holding on Section 5 itself, only on the coverage formula. Congress may draft another formula based on current conditions. Such a formula is an initial prerequisite to a determination that exceptional conditions still exist justifying such an "extraordinary departure from the traditional course of relations between the States and the Federal Government." Our country has changed, and while any racial discrimination in voting is too much, Congress must ensure that the legislation it passes to remedy that problem speaks to current conditions.

The judgment of the Court of Appeals is reversed.

JUSTICE THOMAS, concurring.

I join the Court's opinion in full but write separately to explain that I would find Section 5 of the Voting Rights Act unconstitutional as well. The Court's opinion sets forth the reasons. . . . While the Court claims to "issue no holding on Section 5 itself," its own opinion compellingly demonstrates that Congress has failed to justify "'current burdens'" with a record demonstrating "'current needs.'" By leaving the inevitable conclusion unstated, the Court needlessly prolongs the demise of that provision. For the reasons stated in the Court's opinion, I would find Section 5 unconstitutional.

JUSTICE GINSBURG, with whom JUSTICE BREYER, JUSTICE SOTOMAYOR, and JUSTICE KAGAN join, dissenting.

In the Court's view, the very success of Section 5 of the Voting Rights Act demands its dormancy. Congress was of another mind. Recognizing that large progress has been made, Congress determined, based on a voluminous record, that the scourge of discrimination was not yet extirpated. The question this case presents is who decides whether, as currently operative, Section 5 remains justifiable, this Court, or a Congress charged with the obligation to enforce the post–Civil War Amendments "by appropriate legislation." With overwhelming support in both Houses, Congress concluded that, for two prime reasons, Section 5 should continue in force, unabated. First, continuance would facilitate completion of the impressive gains thus far made; and second, continuance would guard against backsliding. Those assessments were well within Congress' province to make and should elicit this Court's unstinting approbation.

II

. . . It is well established that Congress' judgment regarding exercise of its power to enforce the Fourteenth and Fifteenth Amendments warrants substantial deference. The VRA addresses the combination of race discrimination and the right to vote, which is "preservative of all rights." When confronting the most constitutionally invidious form of discrimination, and the most fundamental right in our democratic system, Congress' power to act is at its height.

The basis for this deference is firmly rooted in both constitutional text and precedent. The Fifteenth Amendment, which targets precisely and only racial discrimination in voting rights, states that, in this domain, "Congress shall have power to enforce this article by appropriate legislation." In choosing this language, the Amendment's framers invoked Chief Justice Marshall's formulation of the scope of Congress' powers under the Necessary and Proper Clause: "Let the end be legitimate, let it be within the scope of the constitution, and all means which are appropriate, which are plainly adapted to that end, which are not prohibited, but consist with the letter and spirit of the constitution, are constitutional." *McCulloch v. Maryland* (1819).

It cannot tenably be maintained that the VRA, an Act of Congress adopted to shield the right to vote from racial discrimination, is inconsistent with the letter or spirit of the Fifteenth Amendment, or any provision of the Constitution read in light of the Civil War Amendments. Nowhere in today's opinion, or in *Northwest Austin*, is there clear recognition of the transformative effect the Fifteenth Amendment aimed to achieve. Notably, "the Founders' first successful amendment told Congress that it could 'make no law' over a certain domain"; in contrast, the Civil War Amendments used "language [that] authorized transformative new federal statutes to uproot all vestiges of unfreedom and inequality" and provided "sweeping enforcement powers . . . to enact 'appropriate' legislation targeting state abuses."

The stated purpose of the Civil War Amendments was to arm Congress with the power and authority to protect all persons within the Nation from violations of their rights by the States. In exercising that power, then, Congress may use "all means which are appropriate, which are plainly adapted" to the constitutional ends declared by these Amendments. So when Congress acts to enforce the right to vote free from racial discrimination, we ask not whether Congress has chosen the means most wise, but whether Congress has rationally selected means appropriate to a legitimate end. "It is not for us to review the congressional resolution of [the need for its chosen remedy]. It is enough that we be able to perceive a basis upon which the Congress might resolve the conflict as it did."

Until today, in considering the constitutionality of the VRA, the Court has accorded Congress the full measure of respect its judgments in this domain should garner. *South Carolina v. Katzenbach* supplies the standard of review: "As against the reserved powers of the States, Congress may use any rational means to effectuate the constitutional prohibition of racial discrimination in voting." Faced with subsequent reauthorizations of the VRA, the Court has reaffirmed this standard. Today's Court does not purport to alter settled precedent establishing that the dispositive question is whether Congress has employed "rational means."

For three reasons, legislation reauthorizing an existing statute is especially likely to satisfy the minimal requirements of the rational-basis test. First, when reauthorization is at issue, Congress has already assembled a legislative record justifying the initial legislation. Congress is entitled to consider that preexisting record as well as the record before it at the time of the vote on reauthorization. This is especially true where, as here, the Court has repeatedly affirmed the statute's constitutionality and Congress has adhered to the very model the Court has upheld.

Second, the very fact that reauthorization is necessary arises because Congress has built a temporal limitation into the Act. It has pledged to review, after a span of years (first 15, then 25) and in light of contemporary evidence, the continued need for the VRA. Cf. *Grutter v. Bollinger* (2003) anticipating, but not guaranteeing, that, in 25 years, "the use of racial preferences [in higher education] will no longer be necessary."

Third, a reviewing court should expect the record supporting reauthorization to be less stark than the record originally made. Demand for a record of violations equivalent to the one earlier made would expose Congress to a catch-22. If the statute was working, there would be less evidence of discrimination, so opponents might argue that Congress should not be allowed to renew the statute. In contrast, if the statute was not working, there would be plenty of evidence of discrimination, but scant reason to renew a failed regulatory regime.

This is not to suggest that congressional power in this area is limitless. It is this Court's responsibility to ensure that Congress has used appropriate means. The question meet for judicial review is whether the chosen means are "adapted to carry out the objects the amendments have in view." *Ex parte Virginia* (1880). The Court's role, then, is not to substitute its judgment for that of Congress, but to determine whether the legislative record sufficed to show that "Congress could rationally have determined that [its chosen] provisions were appropriate methods."

In summary, the Constitution vests broad power in Congress to protect the right to vote, and in particular to combat racial discrimina- tion in voting. This Court has repeatedly reaffirmed Congress' prerogative to use any rational means in exercise of its power in this area. And both precedent and logic dictate that the rational-means test should be easier to satisfy, and the burden on the statute's challenger should be higher, when what is at issue is the reauthorization of a remedy that the Court has previously affirmed, and that Congress found, from contemporary evidence, to be working to advance the legislature's legitimate objective.

IV

Congress approached the 2006 reauthorization of the VRA with great care and seriousness. The same cannot be said of the Court's opinion today. The Court makes no genuine attempt to engage with the massive legislative record that Congress assembled. Instead, it relies on increases in voter registration and turnout as if that were the whole story. Without even identifying a standard of review, the Court dismissively brushes off arguments based on "data from the record," and declines to enter the "debat[e about] what [the] record shows." One would expect more from an opinion striking at the heart of the Nation's signal piece of civil-rights legislation.

I note the most disturbing lapses. First, by what right, given its usual restraint, does the Court even address Shelby County's facial challenge to the VRA? Second, the Court veers away from controlling precedent regarding the "equal sovereignty" doctrine without even acknowledging that it is doing so. Third, hardly showing the respect ordinarily paid when Congress acts to implement the Civil War Amendments, and as just stressed, the Court does not even deign to grapple with the legislative record.

C

. . . The sad irony of today's decision lies in its utter failure to grasp why the VRA has proven effective. The Court appears to believe that the VRA's success in eliminating the specific devices extant in 1965 means that preclearance is no longer needed. With that belief, and the argument derived from it, history repeats itself. The same assumption—that the problem could be solved when particular methods of voting discrimination are identified and eliminated—was indulged and proved wrong repeatedly prior to the VRA's enactment. Unlike prior statutes, which singled out particular tests or devices, the VRA is grounded in Congress' recognition of the "variety and persistence" of measures designed to impair minority voting rights. In truth, the evolution of voting discrimination into more subtle second-generation barriers is powerful evidence that a remedy as effective as preclearance remains vital to protect minority voting rights and prevent backsliding.

Beyond question, the VRA is no ordinary legislation. It is extraordinary because Congress embarked on a mission long delayed and of extraordinary importance: to realize the purpose and promise of the Fifteenth Amendment. For a half century, a concerted effort has been made to end racial discrimination in voting. Thanks to the Voting Rights Act, progress once the subject of a dream has been achieved and continues to be made.

The record supporting the 2006 reauthorization of the VRA is also extraordinary. It was described by the Chairman of the House Judi-ciary Committee as "one of the most extensive considerations of any piece of legislation that the United States Congress has dealt with in the 27½ years" he had served in the House. (statement of Rep. Sensenbrenner). After exhaustive evidence-gathering and deliberative process, Congress reauthorized the VRA, including the coverage provision, with overwhelming bipartisan support. It was the judgment of Congress that "40 years has not been a sufficient amount of time to eliminate the vestiges of discrimination following nearly 100 years of disregard for the dictates of the 15th amendment and to ensure that the right of all citizens to vote is protected as guaranteed by the Constitution." That determination of the body empowered to enforce the Civil War Amendments "by appropriate legislation" merits this Court's utmost respect. In my judgment, the Court errs egregiously by overriding Congress' decision.

* * *

For the reasons stated, I would affirm the judgment of the Court of Appeals.

11

The Right to Privacy, Personal Autonomy, and Dignity

CHAPTER OUTLINE

Any consideration of the right to privacy must begin with Louis D. Brandeis. In a pioneering exposition, Brandeis, then a young legal scholar, asserted in the 1890 *Harvard Law Review* that the right to privacy means fundamentally "the right to be let alone."[1] The significance of this article, which he wrote with Samuel Warren, cannot be overstated; it is generally regarded as the most influential law-review article ever published. Thirty-eight years later, as a justice of the Supreme Court, Brandeis expanded on the theme of the article in his dissent in *Olmstead v. United States* (1928): "The right to be let alone . . . is the most comprehensive of rights and the right most valued by civilized men. To protect that right, every unjustified intrusion of the government upon the privacy of the individual, whatever the means employed, must be deemed a constitutional violation." Another thirty-seven years would pass before Justice Brandeis's words were vindicated in *Griswold v. Connecticut* (1965), a landmark case in which the Court for the first time acknowledged the individual's constitutional right to privacy. Once vindicated, however, Brandeis's words, along with the right they declare, came to have a profound and troubling impact, for the right to privacy has figured prominently in some of the most controversial and divisive decisions the Court has ever rendered—those on abortion, homosexual rights, and the right to die. This chapter explores three principal issues arising out of this right to privacy:

1. Is there a constitutional right to privacy, and, if so, what is its constitutional basis?
2. What exactly does this right protect? Does the privacy to be protected inhere in places, relationships, or people?
3. What qualifications, if any, limit this right?

THE CONSTITUTIONAL BASIS

In his *Olmstead* dissent, Justice Brandeis considered the right to privacy to be "the most comprehensive of rights," and so it may well be. That same comprehensive nature, however, has made it exceedingly difficult for the Court to ascertain precisely what provision (or provisions) of the Constitution protects this right. Various justices have identified and relied on different constitutional bases. Justice Brandeis, in his dissent in *Olmstead* (discussed in Chapter 7 of this volume), based the right to privacy on the Fourth Amendment's protections against unreasonable searches and seizures and on the Fifth Amendment's guarantee against self-incrimination. But Justice John Marshall Harlan, in his concurrence in *Griswold,* and Justice Harry Blackmun, in his opinion for the Court in *Roe v. Wade* (1973), declared that privacy claims were protected by the Due Process Clause of the Fourteenth Amendment; Justice William Brennan, in both his opinion for the Court in *Eisenstadt v. Baird* (1972) and his dissent in *Harris v. McRae* (1980), and Justice Sandra Day O'Connor, in her concurrence in *Lawrence v. Texas* (2003), based the right to privacy on the Equal Protection Clause of the Fourteenth Amendment; Justice Arthur Goldberg, in his *Griswold* concurrence, relied on the Ninth Amendment; and Justice William Douglas, in his majority opinion in *Griswold,* unable to identify any single constitutional provision but taking comfort in the fact that "specific guarantees in the Bill of Rights have penumbras, formed by emanations from those guarantees that help give them life and substance," argued that a penumbral right of privacy emanates from particular guarantees found in the First, Third, Fourth, Fifth, and Ninth Amendments.

These initial differences of opinion over the constitutional basis of the right to privacy reflected a clear reluctance on the part of the Court to rely on the Due Process Clause. To many of these justices, grounding the right to privacy on the Due Process Clause and then employing that provision to bar legislative regulation of an entire area of conduct—as exemplified in *Griswold*—raised the specter of substantive due process and provided too many parallels to the Court's pre-1937 espousal of "liberty of contract" as a defense against business regulation (see *Lochner v. New York* [1905] in Chapter 4 of this volume). Therefore, they pressed into service other constitutional provisions, including the Equal Protection Clause, the Ninth Amendment, and Justice Douglas's "penumbras." Reliance on these provisions enabled the justices to provide the same level of protection for the right to privacy as would have been provided by substantive due process. As Justice William Rehnquist noted in the wake of *Roe v. Wade*, these provisions—at least insofar as they have been employed by the Court in privacy cases—are "sisters under the skin" to substantive due process.[2] By invoking them, the justices apparently believed they would escape the onus so often attached to substantive due process. Consider, for example, the following statement by Justice Douglas in *Griswold*, in which he publicly repudiated substantive due process yet embraced it *sub silentio*.

> We are met with a wide range of questions that implicate the Due Process Clause of the Fourteenth Amendment. Overtones of some arguments suggest that *Lochner v. State of New York* . . . should be our guide. But we decline that invitation. . . . We do not sit as a super-legislature to determine the wisdom, need, and propriety of laws that touch economic problems, business affairs, or social conditions.

As *Troxel v. Granville* (2000) so well demonstrates, however, the recent Court has lost all fear of being accused of practicing substantive due process. When a judge pursuant to a State of Washington statute granted visitation rights to the grandparents of her two daughters, Tommie Granville claimed the provision infringed on the fundamental right of parents to rear their children. A *Griswold*-era Court would doubtless have found the law unconstitutional based on the "right to privacy" that inheres in a protected family relationship, but the Court in the year 2000 matter-of-factly relied on the Due Process Clause. That clause, the Court announced, "includes a substantive component that 'provides heightened protection against governmental interference with certain fundamental rights and liberty interests,'" and it employed it to find the offending statute unconstitutional.

WHAT THE RIGHT TO PRIVACY PROTECTS

A second major issue arising out of the right to privacy centers on the question of what exactly this right protects. In its initial decisions regarding privacy, the Court tended to view the right to privacy as place oriented and property based, and hence as narrow in the range of its protections. This tendency was understandable in view of the fact that these decisions invariably concerned questions of criminal procedure and the meaning and reach of the Fourth Amendment's protections against unreasonable searches and seizures. In the landmark *Olmstead* decision, for example, the Court majority upheld the courtroom use of wiretap evidence that had been obtained without a search warrant, arguing that because there had been no "actual physical invasion" or trespass of the defendants' homes or offices, there had been no search involved, and hence no violation of the Fourth Amendment and the privacy it guarantees. Justice Brandeis, in dissent, argued that privacy inheres in the individual (i.e., the person) and involves nothing less than the "right to be let alone." Despite this eloquent plea, the majority opinion in *Olmstead* remained in force well into the 1960s. A long line of cases, stretching from *Olmstead* through *Goldman v. United States* (1942) to *Silverman v. United States* (1961), consistently presented privacy as place oriented and property based. (The frequent repetition by the courts of the aphorism "A man's home is his castle" underscored the judiciary's identification of privacy with property rights.) Anything less than physical trespass onto private premises, these cases held, fell outside the ambit of Fourth Amendment protection.

In the mid-1960s, however, this long-standing approach to privacy questions underwent drastic changes. In *Griswold*, the Court declared that privacy inheres in legally protected relationships (in this case, marriage). It went further in *Katz v. United States* (1967), declaring that the privacy component of the "Fourth Amendment protects people, not places,"[3] thus broadening considerably the scope of coverage of the right to privacy.

Griswold struck down a Connecticut statute that had made it a criminal offense either to use birth control devices or to give information or instruction on their use. In defending this decision, Justice Douglas observed that to enforce the law, the police would have to search the bedrooms of married couples for evidence of contraceptive use—an idea that struck him as "repulsive to the notions of privacy surrounding the marriage relationship." Justice Douglas placed heavy emphasis on the "intimate relation of husband and wife": the privacy he sought to protect inhered in neither places nor persons, but in a relationship. He waxed poetic concerning this relationship: "Marriage is a coming together for better or for worse, hopefully enduring [Douglas remained hopeful even after three divorces], and intimate to the degree of being sacred." Ironically, his efforts to protect the privacy of the conjugal bed by stressing the sacred intimacy of marriage were soon rendered superfluous by *Eisenstadt v. Baird* (1972), in which the Court invalidated a Massachusetts law that had made it a felony to give anyone other than a married person contraceptive medicines or devices. Justice Brennan, speaking for the Court, argued that the right to privacy inheres in the person and is not limited to certain relationships:

> If under *Griswold* the distribution of contraceptives to married persons cannot be prohibited, a ban on distribution to unmarried persons would be equally impermissible. It is true that in *Griswold* the right of privacy in question inhered in the marital relationship. Yet the marital couple is not an independent entity with a mind and heart of its own, but an association of two individuals each with a separate intellectual and emotional make-up. If the right of privacy means anything, it is the right of the individual, married or single, to be free from unwarranted governmental intrusion into matters so fundamentally affecting a person as the decision whether to bear or beget a child.

The ground for the Court's claim in *Eisenstadt* that the right to privacy inheres in the person and not necessarily in the relationship had been prepared in the *Katz* ruling that the privacy component of the Fourth Amendment "protects people, not places." Writing for the *Katz* majority, Justice Stewart had abandoned the line of cases from *Olmstead* through *Silverman* that had limited the reach of the Fourth Amendment to "constitutionally protected areas" and declared that "what a person knowingly exposes to the public, even in his own home or office, is not a subject of Fourth Amendment protection. . . . But what he seeks to preserve as private, even in an area accessible to the public, may be constitutionally protected."

Abortion Rights

Because it emerged in a Fourth Amendment case, this new person-oriented right to privacy was initially limited to cases involving unreasonable searches and seizures. In subsequent cases, however, the Court used this expanded conception of privacy not only to regulate particular practices in law enforcement and criminal procedure but also (and more important) to invalidate substantive governmental regulation of entire areas of conduct. Thus, it employed a broad conception of the right to privacy in banning legislative restrictions of birth control in *Eisenstadt* and in invalidating antiabortion statutes in the highly controversial case of *Roe v. Wade* (1973).

By declaring that "the personal right of privacy includes the abortion decision," *Roe,* together with the companion case of *Doe v. Bolton* (1973), generated a firestorm of controversy that has enveloped the Court ever since. To begin with, critics have charged that *Roe* and *Doe* gave an entirely new meaning to the term *privacy*. As Justice Rehnquist noted in his dissent, "A transaction resulting in an operation such as this is not 'private' in the ordinary usage of the word." Professor Louis Henkin elaborated:

> What the Court has been talking about is not at all what most people mean by privacy. . . . Ms. Roe sought her abortion openly, "publicly." In a word, the Court has been vindicating not a right to freedom from official intrusion, but to freedom from official regulation. . . . [T]hey are, I think, different notions conceptually, with different philosophical, political and social (and, one might have thought, legal) assumptions and consequences; they may look different also if viewed as aspects of the confrontation of private right with public good.[4]

This point leads to a second criticism. If what was at stake in *Roe v. Wade* was "freedom from official regulation," the Court was guilty of "*Lochnering,*" that is, of superimposing its own views of wise social policy on those of the legislature. The remarkable similarities between *Roe* and *Lochner v. New York* (1905) have led critics to ask why the right to be let alone should give a woman control over her body with regard to an abortion but not, since the Court's repudiation of *Lochner,* control over her body concerning the sale of her labor (i.e., the wages she shall receive and the hours she shall work).

Roe and *Doe* also have been attacked on the grounds that in them, the Court paid insufficient attention to protecting the interests of the fetus—that in protecting the woman's right to be let alone, it unnecessarily jeopardized the fetus's "right to be." Justice Harry Blackmun's majority opinion attempted with little success to parry this criticism. Blackmun admitted that if a fetus is a person, its right to life is guaranteed by the Fourteenth Amendment.[5] But he then skirted the question of whether a fetus is a person (i.e., the question of when the life of a person begins): "We need not resolve the difficult question of when life begins. When those trained in the respective disciplines of medicine, philosophy, and theology are unable to arrive at any consensus, the judiciary, at this point in the development of man's knowledge, is not in a position to speculate as to the answer."[6]

Despite these criticisms, the Court has consistently supported *Roe* in subsequent decisions. *Planned Parenthood of Central Missouri v. Danforth* (1976), an especially important case in this respect, involved a Missouri abortion statute passed in response to *Roe*. Although the Court upheld the statute's flexible definition of viability; affirmed the state's right to require the informed, voluntary, and written consent of the woman; and sustained the reporting and record-keeping provisions of the law, it emasculated the statute by declaring unconstitutional the following crucial elements:

1. the requirement that written consent must also be obtained from the spouse in nontherapeutic abortions
2. the requirement that written consent must be obtained from the woman's parents if she is under eighteen and unmarried, except in a lifesaving situation
3. the blanket prohibition on the use of saline amniocentesis as a technique for inducing abortion
4. the imposition of a criminal penalty on the attending physicians for any failure on their part to exercise due care and skill to preserve the life and health of the fetus, insofar as that is possible

Here, as in *Roe v. Wade,* the Court's decision hinged on the priority it placed on guaranteeing to the pregnant woman the right to be let alone. As for spousal consent, Justice Blackmun noted that the majority could not hold that the state "has the constitutional authority to give the spouse unilaterally the ability to prohibit the wife from terminating her pregnancy, when the State itself lacks that right." The spouse, then, was viewed as having no more of an interest in the abortion decision than the state had. And as to the parental consent requirement, Blackmun observed that "any independent interest the parent may have in the termination of the minor daughter's pregnancy is no more weighty than the right of privacy of the competent minor mature enough to have become pregnant." The Court thereby held, for the first time, that minors have constitutional rights as against their parents.

In *Akron v. Akron Center for Reproductive Health* (1983), the Court dramatically reaffirmed *Roe v. Wade,* going so far as to announce that a woman has a "fundamental right" to have an abortion. The City of Akron had passed an ordinance that imposed a number of restrictions on the abortion process. Perhaps the most important was a requirement that any abortion performed after the first trimester of pregnancy had to be performed in a hospital. A six-member majority invalidated this requirement because it placed "a significant obstacle in the path of women seeking an abortion," a burden not justifiable as a reasonable health regulation. Although hospitalization for abortions performed after the first trimester was recommended at the time of *Roe,* the safety of such abortions had "increased dramatically" since then because of improved technology and procedures, and there was no compelling reason these abortions could not be performed on an outpatient basis in appropriate nonhospital settings. As Justice Powell declared for the majority, "Present medical knowledge convincingly undercuts *Akron's* justification for requiring that all second-trimester abortions be performed in a hospital." Justice O'Connor dissented, observing that it was not until 1982, four years after *Akron* had passed its ordinance, that even the American College of Obstetricians and Gynecologists revised its standards and no longer recommended that all midtrimester abortions be performed in a hospital. Her real objection, however, was with *Roe* itself. As she noted:

> The *Roe* framework . . . is clearly on a collision course with itself. As the medical risks of various abortion procedures decrease, the point at which the State may regulate for reasons of maternal health is moved further forward to actual childbirth. As medical science becomes better able to provide for the separate existence of the fetus, the point of viability is moved further back toward conception. Moreover, it is clear that the trimester approach violates the fundamental aspiration of judicial decision making through the application of neutral principles "sufficiently absolute to give them roots throughout the community and continuity over significant periods of time. . . ." The *Roe* framework is inherently tied to the state of medical technology that exists whenever particular litigation ensues. Although legislatures are better suited to make the necessary factual judgments in this area, the Court's framework forces legislatures, as a matter of constitutional law, to speculate about what constitutes "acceptable medical practice" at any given time. Without the necessary expertise or ability, courts must then pretend to act as science review boards and examine those legislative judgments.

Interestingly, when the opportunity for Justice O'Connor to help overturn *Roe* presented itself in *Webster v. Reproductive Health Services* (1989), she declined to do so on grounds of judicial self-restraint. The Missouri Legislature had passed an abortion statute that, among other things, declared in its preamble that human life begins at conception and that "unborn children have protectable interests in life, health, and well-being." The law required medical tests to ascertain whether any fetus over twenty weeks old was viable and prohibited the use of public employees and facilities to perform abortions not necessary to save the life of the mother. Chief Justice Rehnquist wrote the judgment of the Court upholding all sections of the law. He favored overturning *Roe* but lacked the necessary fifth vote that Justice O'Connor could have supplied to do so. O'Connor concurred in the judgment but did so because Missouri's statute did not, in her estimation, "conflict with any of the Court's past decisions concerning state regulation of abortion." Her actions left Justice Scalia furious; wishing the Court to overturn *Roe* completely and explicitly, he lamented that "the mansion of constitutionalized abortion law, constructed overnight in *Roe v. Wade,* must be disassembled doorjamb by doorjamb, and never entirely brought down, no matter how wrong it may be."

By the time the next major abortion case, *Planned Parenthood of Southern Pennsylvania v. Casey* (1992), was heard by the Court, the conventional wisdom was that Chief Justice Rehnquist and Justice Scalia would finally have their way and that *Roe* would be overturned. Two new justices had been added to the Court since *Webster*—David Souter and Clarence Thomas, both appointed by President George H. W. Bush, who had made no secret of his opposition to *Roe* and abortion. For Rehnquist and Scalia, however, *Casey* proved to be a major disappointment. In *Casey* the Court considered the five key provisions of the Pennsylvania Abortion Control Act of 1982 which together required informed consent of, and imposed a twenty-four-hour waiting period on, all women seeking an abortion; required the informed consent of one parent for a minor to obtain an abortion (but also provided for a judicial bypass procedure); required that wives seeking abortions notify their husbands; provided that the previous requirements could be waived in a "medical emergency"; and imposed certain reporting requirements on facilities providing abortions. The Court ended up sustaining the constitutionality of all the act's provisions except for the one requiring spousal notification. Although it shifted the jurisprudential grounds for the right of a woman to obtain an abortion from it being part of the "right to privacy" articulated in *Griswold* to it being at "the heart of the liberty protected by the Due Process Clause," abandoned *Roe*'s "rigid trimester framework," emphasized the "state's profound interest in potential life," and adopted a new "undue burden" test to evaluate restrictions on abortion, it nevertheless insisted that it was affirming the "central holding of *Roe v. Wade*" and remaining faithful to precedent.

Justice O'Connor, who refused to depart from precedent in *Webster,* refused to do so once again in *Casey.* She joined with Justices Kennedy and Souter in an unusual, jointly signed plurality opinion that concluded that even though *Roe* was probably wrongly decided, it should not be overturned. They argued that if the Court were to overturn *Roe* merely because newly appointed justices regarded it as a bad decision, it would create the impression that the justices yielded to political pressure and more generally that constitutional decisions are determined by politics.[7] That, they insisted, would result in "both profound and unnecessary damage to the Court's legitimacy, and to the Nation's commitment to the rule of law. It is therefore imperative to adhere to the essence of *Roe*'s original decision, and we do so today." Chief Justice Rehnquist objected: "Our constitutional watch does not cease merely because we have spoken before on an issue; when it becomes clear that a prior constitutional interpretation is unsound we are obliged to reexamine the question." Rehnquist's objection, however, was unavailing. To overturn the precedent that *Roe* had set would, the plurality insisted, jeopardize the very "character of a Nation of people who aspire to live according to the rule of law. Their belief in themselves as such a people is not readily separable from their understanding of the Court invested with the authority to decide their constitutional cases and speak before all others for their constitutional ideals. The Court's concern with legitimacy is not for the sake of the Court but for the sake of the Nation to which it is responsible."

In the name of precedent, therefore, Justices O'Connor, Kennedy, and Souter upheld *Roe,* even as they discarded the trimester framework that *Roe* had created and sustained a variety of restrictions on abortion contrary to the Court's original holding in *Roe.* Chief Justice Rehnquist complained in his dissent that, instead of adhering to precedent, the three justices' joint opinion revised it. "*Roe* continues to exist, but only in the way a store-front on a western movie set exists: a mere facade to give the illusion of reality." He also objected to the plurality's "undue burden" test, labeling it "a standard that is not built to last." Justice Scalia likewise filed an especially vigorous dissent. He responded to the joint opinion's argument that "to overrule under fire would subvert the Court's legitimacy" by thundering: "The Imperial Judiciary lives. It is instructive to compare this Nietzschean vision of us unelected, life-tenured judges—leading a Volk who will be 'tested by following,' and whose very 'belief in themselves' is mystically bound up in their 'understanding' of a Court that 'speak[s] before all others for their constitutional ideals'—with the somewhat more modest role envisioned for these lawyers by the Founders: 'The judiciary . . . has neither FORCE nor WILL but merely judgment.' *The Federalist,* No. 78."

Justice Blackmun objected in *Casey* to the plurality's substitution of the "undue burden" test for the "strict scrutiny" test and to its abandonment of *Roe*'s trimester framework, fearing that the Court's commitment to guaranteeing a woman's right to an abortion was faltering. As events unfolded, however, Blackmun had little reason to worry. Until 2007 in *Gonzales v. Carhart,* not even laws prohibiting "partial birth abortion" were held by the Supreme Court to pass the "undue burden" test. In this case, Justice Kennedy wrote for a five-member majority, "Where it has a rational basis to act, and it does not impose an undue burden, the State may use its regulatory power to bar certain procedures and substitute others, all in furtherance of its legitimate interests in regulating the medical profession in order to promote respect for life, including life of the unborn." It therefore upheld Congress's enactment of the Partial-Birth Abortion Ban Act of 2003, proscribing a particular method of ending the life of the unborn in the late stages of pregnancy.

The Court's commitment to guaranteeing a woman's constitutional right to an abortion has been as unwavering as its refusal to hold that the government is compelled to fund abortions for women in financial need. In *Maher v. Roe* (1977), the Court held that Connecticut's decision not to pay for nontherapeutic abortions for indigent women, despite the fact that it did pay for childbirth, did not violate the Constitution. Justice Powell held for a six-member majority that the state's policy did not impinge on *Roe*'s recognition of a woman's fundamental right to protection "from unduly burdensome interference with her freedom to decide whether to terminate her pregnancy." That right, he declared, "implies no limitation on the authority of a State to make a value judgment favoring childbirth over abortion, and to implement that judgment by the allocation of public funds." He continued:

> The Connecticut regulation places no obstacles—absolute or otherwise—in the pregnant woman's path to an abortion. An indigent woman who desires an abortion suffers no disadvantage as a consequence of Connecticut's decision to fund childbirth; she continues as before to be dependent on private sources for the services she desires. The State may have made childbirth a more attractive alternative, thereby influencing the woman's decision, but it has imposed no restriction on access to abortions that was not already there. The indigency that may make it difficult—and in some cases, perhaps, impossible—for some women to have abortions is neither created nor in any way affected by the Connecticut regulation.

Justice Brennan, in dissent, accused the majority of a "distressing insensitivity to the plight of impoverished pregnant women."

In its 5–4 decision in *Harris v. McRae* (1980), the Court not only reaffirmed *Maher,* but also carried Justice Powell's argument one step further. Whereas *Maher* dealt only with nontherapeutic abortions, *Harris* sustained the constitutionality of the Hyde Amendment, which drastically limited federal funding for most medically necessary abortions as well. Justice Stewart's majority opinion relied heavily on the analysis in *Maher:*

> Although the liberty protected by the Due Process Clause affords protection against unwarranted governmental interference with freedom of choice in the context of certain personal decisions, it does not confer an entitlement to such funds as may be necessary to realize all the advantages of that freedom. To hold otherwise would make a drastic change in our understanding of the Constitution.

Justice Brennan again dissented:

> Abortion and childbirth, when stripped of the sensitive moral arguments surrounding the abortion controversy, are simply two alternative medical methods of dealing with pregnancy. In every pregnancy, one of these two courses of treatment is medically necessary and the poverty-stricken woman depends on the Medicaid Act to pay for the expenses associated with that procedure. But under the Hyde Amendment, the Government will fund only those procedures incidental to childbirth. By thus injecting coercive financial incentives favoring childbirth into a decision that is constitutionally guaranteed to be free from governmental intrusion, the Hyde Amendment deprives the indigent woman of her freedom to choose abortion over maternity, thereby impinging on the due process liberty right recognized in *Roe v. Wade.*

Same-Sex Marriage

Professor Paul Freund once observed that privacy is a "greedy legal concept."[8] In light of *Roe* and its progeny, his observation seems apt. And in light of the Court's 1996 decision in *Romer v. Evans* and its 2003 decision in *Lawrence v. Texas,* his observation seems understated. Both cases dealt with homosexual rights and were decided against the backdrop of the Court's 1986 decision in *Bowers v. Hardwick.*

In *Bowers,* the Supreme Court overturned a decision of the Eleventh Circuit Court of Appeals that had invalidated a Georgia statute that made consensual homosexual sodomy a criminal offense. Justice White spoke for a five-member majority when he rejected the claim that the federal Constitution confers a "fundamental right upon homosexuals to engage in sodomy." He insisted that there should be "great resistance to expand the substantive reach" of the Due Process Clause, "particularly if it requires redefining the category of rights deemed to be fundamental. Otherwise, the Judiciary necessarily takes to itself further authority to govern the country without express constitutional authority. The claimed right pressed on us today falls far short of overcoming this resistance."

In his dissent, Justice Blackmun charged that although the Court "claims that its decision today merely refuses to recognize a fundamental right to engage in homosexual sodomy, what the Court really has refused to recognize is the fundamental interest all individuals have in controlling the nature of their intimate associations with others." Justice Stevens also dissented, holding that Georgia's statute failed not only the compelling-state-interest test but the rational-basis test as well: "The fact that the governing majority in a State has traditionally viewed a particular practice as immoral is not a sufficient reason for upholding a law prohibiting the practice."

The status of *Bowers* was subsequently called into serious question in *Romer v. Evans* when the Court held, 6–3, that the Equal Protection Clause of the Fourteenth

Amendment was violated by Colorado's Amendment 2. After various Colorado municipalities including Aspen, Boulder, and the City and County of Denver passed ordinances banning discrimination based on sexual orientation in housing, employment, education, public accommodations, health and welfare services, and other transactions and activities, Colorado voters in 1992 adopted by statewide referendum Amendment 2 to the Colorado Constitution, which precluded all legislative, executive, or judicial action at any level of state or local government designed to protect the status of persons based on their "homosexual, lesbian or bisexual orientation, conduct, practices or relationships." Justice Kennedy spoke for the Court when he declared: "Amendment 2 classifies homosexuals not to further a proper legislative end but to make them unequal to everyone else. This Colorado cannot do. A State cannot so deem a class of persons a stranger to its laws." Justice Kennedy refused to hold that Amendment 2 burdened a fundamental right or targeted a suspect class; in his mind, there was no need to go that far, as there was no rational relationship between the ballot measure and a legitimate governmental purpose. Amendment 2, he continued, inflicted on gays and lesbians "immediate, continuing, and real injuries that outrun and belie any legitimate justifications that may be claimed for it."

Interestingly, in Justice Kennedy's majority opinion in *Romer, Bowers* was the dog that did not bark. As Justice Scalia pointed out in his dissent: "The case most relevant to the issue before us today is not even mentioned in the Court's opinion: In *Bowers v. Hardwick,* we held that the Constitution does not prohibit what virtually all States had done from the founding of the Republic until very recent years—making homosexual conduct a crime." *Bowers,* he continued, "is a given in the present case: Respondents' briefs did not urge overruling *Bowers,* and at oral argument respondents' counsel expressly disavowed any intent to seek such overruling. If it is constitutionally permissible for a State to make homosexual conduct criminal, surely it is constitutionally permissible for a State to enact other laws merely disfavoring homosexual conduct."

Scalia also defended Amendment 2 as "an entirely reasonable provision." As he pointed out in a dissent joined by Chief Justice Rehnquist and Justice Thomas, "The amendment prohibits special treatment of homosexuals, and nothing more. It would not affect, for example, a requirement of state law that pensions be paid to all retiring state employees with a certain length of service; homosexual employees, as well as others, would be entitled to that benefit. But it would prevent the State or any municipality from making death-benefit payments to the 'life partner' of a homosexual when it does not make such payments to the long-time roommate of a nonhomosexual employee." The amendment was, he insisted, "a modest attempt by seemingly tolerant Coloradans to preserve traditional sexual mores against the efforts of a politically powerful minority to revise those mores through use of the laws. That objective, and the means chosen to achieve it, are not only unimpeachable under any constitutional doctrine hitherto pronounced; they have been specifically approved by the Congress of the United States and by this Court."

In *Lawrence v. Texas,* Justice Kennedy wrote for the same six-member majority present in *Romer* and held unconstitutional a Texas statute forbidding anal sex with a member of the same sex. *Bowers* barked furiously in the case, and Justice Kennedy, no longer able to overlook it, overruled it. Quoting from the three-member plurality opinion in *Casey,* Kennedy declared that the Georgia statute in *Bowers* and the Texas statute in *Lawrence* interfered with "personal dignity and autonomy" and with "the right to define one's own concept of existence, of meaning, of the universe, and of the mystery of human life." He then turned to international sources and cited as "authoritative" and therefore persuasive a decision of the European Court of Human Rights that held that laws prohibiting consensual homosexual conduct were invalid under the European Convention on Human Rights. Finally, he referenced approvingly Justice Stevens's analysis in his *Bowers* dissent that the promotion of majoritarian sexual morality is not a legitimate state interest that can justify its intrusion into the personal and private life of the individual. Stevens's analysis, he insisted, "should have been controlling" there and was "control[ling] here." "The petitioners are entitled to respect for their private lives. The State cannot demean their existence or control their destiny by making their private sexual conduct a crime. Their right to liberty under the Due Process Clause gives them the full right to engage in their conduct without intervention of the government."

Justice Scalia filed the lead dissent. He vigorously attacked the Court for undermining all morals legislation. The Texas statute "undoubtedly imposes constraints on liberty. So do laws prohibiting prostitution, recreational use of heroin, and, for that matter, working more than 60 hours per week in a bakery. But there is no right to 'liberty' under the Due Process Clause, though today's opinion repeatedly makes that claim. The Fourteenth Amendment *expressly allows* States to deprive their citizens of 'liberty,' *so long as 'due process of law' is provided.'*" He continued:

> The Texas statute undeniably seeks to further the belief of its citizens that certain forms of sexual behavior are "immoral and unacceptable"—the same interest furthered by criminal laws against fornication, bigamy, adultery, adult incest, bestiality, and obscenity. *Bowers* held that this *was* a legitimate state interest. The Court today reaches the opposite conclusion. The Texas statute, it says, "furthers *no legitimate state interest* which can justify its intrusion into the personal and private life of the individual."

For Scalia, "this effectively decrees the end of all morals legislation. If, as the Court asserts, "the promotion of majoritarian sexual morality is not even a *legitimate* state interest, none of the above-mentioned laws can survive rational-basis review."

Justice Kennedy was eager to point out that *Lawrence* did not "involve whether the government must give formal recognition to any relationship that homosexual persons seek to enter," but Scalia was not buying his argument: "Do not believe it." Scalia confidently predicted that *Lawrence* would pave the way for judicial recognition of same-sex marriage. "More illuminating than this bald, unreasoned disclaimer is the progression of thought displayed by an earlier passage in the Court's opinion, which notes the constitutional protections afforded to 'personal decisions relating to *marriage,* procreation, contraception, family relationships, child rearing, and education,' and then declares that 'persons in a homosexual relationship may seek autonomy for these purposes, just as heterosexual persons do.'"

Scalia insisted that *Lawrence* effectively dismantled "the structure of constitutional law that has permitted a distinction to be made between heterosexual and homosexual unions, insofar as formal recognition in marriage is concerned. If moral disapprobation of homosexual conduct is 'no legitimate state interest' for purposes of proscribing that conduct, and if, as the Court coos (casting aside all pretense of neutrality), 'when sexuality finds overt expression in intimate conduct with another person, the conduct can be but one element in a personal bond that is more enduring'; what justification could there possibly be for denying the benefits of marriage to homosexual couples exercising 'the liberty protected by the Constitution'?" Scalia concluded by observing, "This case 'does not involve' the issue of homosexual marriage only if one entertains the belief that principle and logic have nothing to do with the decisions of this Court. Many will hope that, as the Court comfortingly assures us, this is so."

As *Goodridge v. Department of Public Health* (2003) would soon show, however, the Massachusetts Supreme Court was eager to follow the "principle and logic" of *Lawrence,* even if Justice Kennedy and his colleagues in the majority were not. In *Goodridge,* handed down less than five months later, Chief Justice Margaret H. Marshall immediately cited

Lawrence and its affirmation that "the core concept of common human dignity protected by the Fourteenth Amendment to the United States Constitution precludes government intrusion into the deeply personal realms of consensual adult expressions of intimacy and one's choice of an intimate partner." *Lawrence,* she continued, "also reaffirmed the central role that decisions whether to marry or have children bear in shaping one's identity." Then, noting that "the Massachusetts Constitution is, if anything, more protective of individual liberty and equality," demands "broader protection for fundamental rights," and "is less tolerant of government intrusion into the protected spheres of private life" than the federal Constitution, she concluded for the majority in a 4–3 decision that Massachusetts's law barring same-sex marriage violated the Massachusetts Constitution. "Barred access to the protections, benefits, and obligations of civil marriage, a person who enters into an intimate, exclusive union with another of the same sex is arbitrarily deprived of membership in one of our community's most rewarding and cherished institutions. That exclusion is incompatible with the constitutional principles of respect for individual autonomy and equality under law."

Goodridge was followed by the California Supreme Court's 2008 decision in *In re Marriage Cases.* In another 4–3 decision, Chief Justice Ronald George held an initiative statute, Proposition 22, which was adopted in 2000 by a 61.4 percent popular vote and read, "Only marriage between a man and a woman is valid or recognized in California," was unconstitutional because, even though the California Legislature had passed laws that granted same-sex couples the right to enter into an officially recognized family relationship that afforded all of the significant legal rights and obligations traditionally associated under state law with the institution of marriage, the union of a same-sex couple was officially designated a "domestic partnership," whereas the union of an opposite-sex couple was officially designated a "marriage." George argued, "One of the core elements of the right to establish an officially recognized family that is embodied in the California constitutional right to marry is a couple's right to have their family relationship accorded dignity and respect equal to that accorded other officially recognized families, and assigning a different designation for the family relationship of same-sex couples while reserving the historic designation of 'marriage' exclusively for opposite-sex couples poses at least a serious risk of denying the family relationship of same-sex couples such equal dignity and respect." The opinion was especially far-reaching in that it declared sexual orientation to be a suspect classification and held that laws that classify on that basis must be subjected to strict scrutiny.[9]

Prior to the May 2008 California Supreme Court decision, opponents of same-sex marriage had already begun their efforts to qualify an initiative constitutional amendment, Proposition 8, for the ballot. The text of Proposition 8 was identical to Proposition 22: "Only marriage between a man and a woman is valid or recognized in California." Their reasoning at the time was that since Proposition 22 was only a statute, it was subject to judicial review in a way that an amendment to the constitution would not be. *In re Marriage Cases* validated their worries and assisted them in gathering 1,120,801 petition signatures (they needed only 694,354), thereby qualifying Proposition 8 for the November 4, 2008, election ballot. The campaign was highly contentious and expensive. The campaigns for and against Proposition 8 raised $35.8 million and $37.6 million, respectively. Even though the ballot title of Proposition 8, as prepared by the California secretary of state, was "Eliminates Right of Same-Sex Couples to Marry," it passed with 52.3 percent of the vote.

After the California Supreme Court in *Strauss v. Horton* (2009) upheld the constitutionality of Proposition 8 under the provisions of the California Constitution, a variety of plaintiffs brought suit in federal district court and successfully challenged its constitutionality under the Due Process and Equal Protection Clauses of the Fourteenth Amendment. And when California's governor and attorney general refused to defend the constitutional provision on appeal, the proponents of Proposition 8 took over the appeal before both the Ninth Circuit Court of Appeals and the US Supreme Court, only to be told in *Hollingsworth v. Perry* (2013) that they lacked standing to challenge the district court's decision.

Goodridge and *Perry v. Brown* raised the question of whether other states that did not permit same-sex marriage must give binding legal effect to these unions under Article IV, Section 1, of the US Constitution, which declares that "Full Faith and Credit shall be given in each State to the public Acts, Records, and judicial Proceedings of every other State." Those words would suggest that same-sex marriages performed in Massachusetts must be recognized as legally binding in all the other states. But Article IV, Section 1, also states: "And the Congress may by general Laws prescribe the Manner in which such Acts, Records, and Proceedings shall be proved, and the Effect thereof." Those words would suggest that Congress could relieve other states of the obligation to recognize these marriages.

Congress, in fact, had so acted. When, as a result of its decision in *Baehr v. Lewin* (1993), it appeared (incorrectly as it turned out) that the Hawaii Supreme Court was on the verge of requiring that state to issue marriage licenses to same-sex couples, Congress responded with the Defense of Marriage Act (DOMA) of 1996. Approved in the House of Representatives by a vote of 342 to 67 and in the Senate by a vote of 85 to 14, and signed into law by President Clinton, the act provided that no state is required to accord full faith and credit to a marriage license issued by another state if it pertains to a relationship between persons of the same sex, and it defined the terms *marriage* and *spouse,* for purposes of federal law only, to apply exclusively to relationships between persons of the opposite sex.

In two recent decisions, however, the Supreme Court has invalidated both provisions of DOMA and has declared that, under the Due Process and Equal Protection Clauses of the Fourteenth Amendment, couples of the same sex have a fundamental right to marry. In *United States v. Windsor* (2013), in an opinion for a five-member majority, Justice Kennedy struck down that provision of DOMA that limited marriage to a "legal union between one man and one woman." He found that Congress was "motivated by an improper animus" when it passed this provision, and he held that the states and not the federal government have the power to define marriage. This led him to the following conclusion:

> The class to which DOMA directs its restrictions and restraints are those persons who are joined in same-sex marriages made lawful by the State. DOMA singles out a class of persons deemed by a State entitled to recognition and protection to enhance their own liberty. It imposes a disability on the class by refusing to acknowledge a status the State finds to be dignified and proper. DOMA instructs all federal officials, and indeed all persons with whom same-sex couples interact, including their own children, that their marriage is less worthy than the marriages of others. The federal statute is invalid, for no legitimate purpose overcomes the purpose and effect to disparage and to injure those whom the State, by its marriage laws, sought to protect in personhood and dignity. By seeking to displace this protection and treating those persons as living in marriages less respected than others, the federal statute is in violation of the [Due Process Clause of the] Fifth Amendment.

And, then in *Obergefell v. Hodges* (2015), Justice Kennedy, writing for the same five-member majority, found unconstitutional all state laws that prohibited same-sex marriage. He wrote: "The right to marry is a fundamental right inherent in the liberty of the person, and under the Due Process and Equal Protection Clauses of the Fourteenth Amendment couples of the same-sex may not be deprived of that right and that liberty. The Court now holds that same-sex couples may exercise the fundamental right to marry.

No longer may this liberty be denied to them. . . . The State laws challenged by Petitioners in these cases are now held invalid to the extent they exclude same-sex couples from civil marriage on the same terms and conditions as opposite-sex couples." This conclusion left the constitutionality of the other provision of DOMA open to question, to which Kennedy provided the answer: "These cases also present the question whether the Constitution requires States to recognize same-sex marriages validly performed out of State. . . . As counsel for the respondents acknowledged at argument, if States are required by the Constitution to issue marriage licenses to same-sex couples, the justifications for refusing to recognize those marriages performed elsewhere are undermined. The Court, in this decision, holds same-sex couples may exercise the fundamental right to marry in all States. It follows that the Court also must hold—and it now does hold—that there is no lawful basis for a State to refuse to recognize a lawful same-sex marriage performed in another State on the ground of its same-sex character."

QUALIFICATIONS ON THE RIGHT TO PRIVACY

To date, the Court's most expansive interpretations of the right to personal autonomy have come in the areas of sexual behavior and same-sex marriage. Claims in other areas of life have met with a less favorable reception. *Kelley v. Johnson* and *Paul v. Davis,* both decided in 1976, are cases in point. In *Kelley,* decided 6–2, Justice Rehnquist held for the Court that a county regulation limiting the length of county policemen's hair did not violate any right guaranteed by the Fourteenth Amendment. In particular, he denied that the regulation impermissibly limited the right of privacy or the personal autonomy of the policemen, maintaining that the protections of this right were limited to "infringements on the individual's freedom of choice with respect to certain basic matters of procreation, marriage, and family life." Justice Marshall strenuously dissented: "To say that the liberty guarantee of the Fourteenth Amendment does not encompass matters of personal appearance would be fundamentally inconsistent with the values of privacy, self-identity, autonomy, and personal integrity that I have always assumed the Constitution was designed to protect." In *Paul,* Justice Rehnquist again spoke for the Court, this time to reject, among other things, a privacy claim made by a person who had been listed as an "active shoplifter" in a flyer made up by the Louisville police and distributed to city merchants. He had been arrested for shoplifting but never tried, and the charges against him had ultimately been dropped. Rehnquist held that because the police had not invaded any area traditionally regarded as private, such as "matters related to marriage, procreation, contraception, family relationships, and child rearing and education," there had been no constitutional violation of the right to privacy.

In *Whalen v. Roe* (1977), a related case, the Court unanimously sustained a New York statute requiring that the names of persons receiving dangerous prescription drugs be kept in a computer file. The statute had been challenged by an individual who claimed that such lists violated his right to privacy because of the risk that the information might become public. Justice Stevens noted for the Court that privacy cases involve, at minimum, two different types of interests: the individual interest in avoiding disclosure of a personal matter, of which the *Griswold* decision was representative, and the interest in securing independence in making certain kinds of important decisions, of which *Roe v. Wade* was illustrative. He concluded that "the New York program does not, on its face, pose a sufficiently grievous threat to either interest to establish a constitutional violation." With respect to a disclosure of personal matters, he emphasized the careful security provisions in the law and insisted that there was no justification for assuming that those provisions would be administered improperly. And with respect to an infringement of the interest in making important decisions independently, he dismissed the claim that patients would decline needed medication in order to keep their names out of the computerized file, insisting that the law did not significantly inhibit the patient-physician decision regarding needed medication.

PERSONAL AUTONOMY AND THE RIGHT TO DIE

In his classic work *The Nature of the Judicial Process,* Benjamin Cardozo observed that there is a tendency for a legal principle "to expand to the limits of its logic." That this tendency is especially true of a "greedy concept" such as the "right to be let alone" is apparent in what have come to be called the "right to die" cases.[10]

In *In re Karen Ann Quinlan* (1976), the New Jersey Supreme Court held that the "right to be let alone" extended to the right to die with dignity and that the State of New Jersey could not prevent Karen Ann Quinlan, existing in a "persistent vegetative state," on the request of her legal guardian, from being disconnected from her respirator. To date, the United States Supreme Court has taken a less expansive view. In *Cruzan v. Director, Missouri Department of Health* (1990), it held, in a 5–4 decision, that the State of Missouri could involve itself in the decision of whether to terminate the artificial nutrition and hydration procedures keeping incompetent patients alive by demanding the production of clear and convincing evidence of the incompetent's wishes as to the withdrawal of treatment. And in *Washington v. Glucksberg* (1997) and *Vacco v. Quill* (1997), it overturned court of appeals decisions from the Ninth and Second Circuits that had declared unconstitutional laws banning physician-assisted suicide.[11] In *Glucksberg*, it rejected the Ninth Circuit's reliance on *Planned Parenthood of Southeastern Pennsylvania v. Casey* and its contention that, "like the decision of whether or not to have an abortion, the decision how and when to die is one of 'the most intimate and personal choices a person may make in a lifetime,' a choice 'central to personal dignity and autonomy.'" In *Vacco*, it rejected the Second Circuit's insistence that the Equal Protection Clause is violated when "some terminally ill people—those who are on life-support systems—are treated differently than those who are not, in that the former may 'hasten death' by ending treatment, but the latter may not 'hasten death' through physician-assisted suicide." As Justice Souter's concurring opinions in *Glucksberg* and *Vacco* make clear, however, he and several of his colleagues were unwilling to deny categorically the existence of a right to die with dignity or to concede anything more than that this is a question best left for now in the hands of state legislators rather than judges. As he wrote in *Glucksberg*, "While I do not decide for all time that respondents' claim should not be recognized, I acknowledge the legislative institutional competence as the better one to deal with that claim at this time."

NOTES

1. Samuel D. Warren and Louis D. Brandeis, "The Right to Privacy," *Harvard Law Review* 4, no. 5 (1890): 193.

2. William H. Rehnquist, "Is an Expanded Right to Privacy Consistent with Fair and Effective Law Enforcement? or, Privacy, You've Come a Long Way, Baby," *Kansas Law Review* 23 (1974): 6.

3. It should be noted that these decisions, which conceptualized privacy as inhering in the relationship or in the person, supplemented but did not supplant the earlier view that privacy inheres in the place. In *Stanley v. Georgia* (1969), for example, the Court operated from the assumption that privacy inheres in the place when it declared that "whereas the States retain broad power to regulate obscenity, that power simply does not extend to mere possession by the individual in the privacy of his own home."

4. Louis Henkin, "Privacy and Autonomy," *Columbia Law Review* 74 (1974): 1410, 1424–1427.

5. Consider, however, Professor John Hart Ely's observations that a determination of whether a fetus is a "Fourteenth Amendment person" is irrelevant to the question of whether a fetus can be protected: "It has never been held or even asserted that the state interest needed to justify forcing a person to refrain from an activity, whether or not that activity is constitutionally protected, must implicate either the life or the constitutional rights of another person. Dogs are not 'persons in the whole sense' nor have they constitutional rights, but that does not mean the state cannot prohibit killing them. It does not even mean the state cannot prohibit killing them in the exercise of the First Amendment right of political protest. Come to think of it, draft cards aren't persons either." Ely, "The Wages of Crying Wolf: A Comment on *Roe v. Wade*," *Yale Law Journal* 82 (1973): 929.

6. The Court's language here was of critical importance to the proponents of the Human Life Statute, which would have declared that "the life of each human being begins at conception." They claimed that the Court's refusal in *Roe* to treat the fetus as a person merely represented an admission that the judiciary was incapable of deciding the question of when human life begins. Further, they argued, under Section 5 of the Fourteenth Amendment, which empowers Congress to enforce by appropriate legislation the provisions of the amendment, that Congress is the appropriate body to resolve that question and, if it were to find life to begin at conception, to enforce the obligation of the states under the Fourteenth Amendment not to deprive persons (including unborn children) of life without due process of law. See Stephen H. Galebach, "A Human Life Statute," *Human Life Review* 5 (1981): 3.

7. As Justices O'Connor, Kennedy, and Souter readily acknowledged in their joint opinion, abortion has proved to be an especially "divisive" issue. Organizations opposed to the morality of abortion, such as Operation Rescue, have adopted the tactic of protesting in front of abortion clinics and illegally obstructing access to them in the hopes of thereby dissuading pregnant women seeking abortions from entering. This tactic was challenged by abortion clinics and supporting organizations in *Bray v. Alexandria Women's Health Clinic* (1993). They sought a permanent injunction against Operation Rescue, enjoining them from trespassing on, impeding, or obstructing ingress to or egress from Washington, D.C.–area abortion clinics. They claimed that Operation Rescue was conspiring to deprive women seeking abortions of their right to interstate travel and was therefore in violation of the

first clause of 42 U.S.C. §1985—the surviving version of §2 of the Civil Rights Act of 1871 (otherwise known as the Ku Klux Klan Act of 1871)—which prohibited private conspiracies to deprive "any person or class of persons of the equal protection of the laws, or of equal privileges and immunities under the law." In a 5–4 decision, the Supreme Court rejected this challenge. As Justice Scalia noted for the majority in *Bray*, Operation Rescue's demonstrations were not directed toward any "class of persons." "Whatever one thinks of abortion, it cannot be denied that there are common and respectable reasons for opposing it, other than hatred of or condescension toward (or indeed any view at all concerning) women as a class—as is evident from the fact that men and women are on both sides of the issues, just as men and women are on both sides of petitioners' unlawful demonstrations." *Bray*, however, was followed by *National Organization of Women v. Scheidler* (1994), in which the Court unanimously allowed a different kind of challenge to the obstructionist tactics of antiabortion groups; it held that abortion clinics had standing to bring an action against the Pro-Life Action Network and other antiabortion groups for allegedly conspiring to use force to dissuade pregnant women from receiving the clinics' abortion services and therefore to injure the clinics' business and property interests in violation of the Racketeer Influenced and Corrupt Organizations Act (RICO). The antiabortion groups argued that RICO did not apply to them because they were engaged in "non-economic crimes committed in furtherance of non-economic motives." In *Scheidler v. National Organization of Women* (2006), a unanimous Court agreed with them, holding that Congress did not intend to create a freestanding physical-violence offense or to forbid acts or threats of physical violence unrelated to robbery or extortion.

8. Paul Freund, "Privacy: One Concept or Many," in *Privacy*, edited by J. Roland Pennock and John W. Chapman (New York: Atherton Press, 1971), 192.

9. See also the Connecticut Supreme Court decision in *Kerrigan v. Commissioner of Public Health*, 957 A.2d 407 (2008). In still another 4–3 decision, Justice Richard N. Palmer declared that "because the institution of marriage carries with it a status and significance that the [State of Connecticut's] newly created classification of civil unions does not embody, the segregation of heterosexual and homosexual couples into separate institutions constitutes a cognizable harm." He found that sexual orientation constitutes a "quasi-suspect classifica-

tion," that Connecticut's "statutes discriminating against gay persons are subject to heightened or intermediate judicial scrutiny," and that "the state's disparate treatment of same sex couples is constitutionally deficient under an intermediate level of scrutiny."

10. See also *American Motorcycle Association v. Davids* (1968), in which the Michigan Court of Appeals invalidated a state law requiring motorcyclists and riders to wear crash helmets by citing Brandeis in *Olmstead* and quoting his language: "The makers of our Constitution . . . conferred, as against the government, the right to be let alone—the most comprehensive of rights and the right most valued by civilized men."

11. An issue opposite to physician-assisted suicide was raised in the case of Theresa Marie Schiavo. Concerned that the Florida state courts were insufficiently attentive to protecting the life of Schiavo, a severely brain-damaged woman, by allowing her husband to withdraw food and fluids necessary to sustain her life, Congress passed P.L. 109–3 (2005), granting the United States District Court for the Middle District of Florida the "jurisdiction to hear, determine, and render judgment on a suit or claim by or on behalf of Theresa Marie Schiavo for the alleged violation of any right of Theresa Marie Schiavo under the Constitution or laws of the United States relating to the withholding or withdrawal of food, fluids, or medical treatment necessary to sustain her life," and conferring standing on "any parent of Theresa Marie Schiavo . . . to bring a suit under this Act." A possible constitutional challenge to the act was avoided when neither the US District Court nor the Court of Appeals for the Eleventh Circuit found any violations of Schiavo's rights, the US Supreme Court refused to hear her parents' appeal, and Schiavo died of dehydration and starvation soon thereafter.

SELECTED READINGS

Ball, Howard, *The Supreme Court in the Intimate Lives of Americans: Birth, Sex, Marriage, and Death.* New York: NYU Press, 2004.

Barnett, Randy, ed. *The Rights Retained by the People: The History and Meaning of the Ninth Amendment.* Fairfax, VA: George Mason University Press, 1989.

Berger, Raoul. "The Ninth Amendment." *Cornell Law Review* 66 (1980): 1–26.

Bork, Robert H. *The Tempting of America: The Political Seduction of Law.* New York: Free Press, 1990.

Burgess, Susan R. *Contest for Constitutional Authority: The Abortion and War Powers Debates.* Lawrence: University Press of Kansas, 1992.

Colloquium: "The Boundaries of Liberty after *Lawrence v. Texas.*" *Michigan Law Review* 102 (June 2004): 1447–1666.

DeRosa, Marshall L. *The Ninth Amendment and the Politics of Creative Jurisprudence.* New Brunswick, NJ: Transaction Publishers, 1996.

Ely, John Hart. "The Wages of Crying Wolf: A Comment on *Roe v. Wade.*" *Yale Law Journal* 82 (1973): 920–949.

Epstein, Lee. *The Supreme Court and Legal Change: Abortion and the Death Penalty.* Chapel Hill: University of North Carolina Press, 1992.

Galebach, Stephan H. "A Human Life Statute." *Human Life Review* 5 (1981): 3–31.

Gardner, Martin R. "Adoption by Homosexuals in the Wake of *Lawrence v. Texas.*" *Journal of Law & Family Studies* 6 (2004): 19–58.

Garrow, David J. "Significant Risks: *Gonzales v. Carhart* and the Future of Abortion Law." In *2007 Supreme Court Review,* edited by Dennis J. Hutchinson, David A. Strauss, and Geoffrey R. Stone. Chicago: University of Chicago Press, 2008.

Glendon, Mary Ann. *Abortion and Divorce in Western Law.* Cambridge, MA: Harvard University Press, 1987.

Hixson, Richard F. *Privacy in a Public Society: Human Rights in Conflict.* New York: Oxford University Press, 1987.

Hull, N. E. H., and Peter Charles Hoffer, Roe v. Wade: *The Abortion Rights Controversy in American History.* Lawrence: University Press of Kansas, 2010.

Judges, Donald P. *Hard Choices, Lost Voices: How the Abortion Conflict Has Divided America, Distorted Constitutional Law, and Damaged the Courts.* Chicago: Ivan R. Dee, 1993.

McConnell, Michael W. "The Selective Funding Problem: Abortions and Religious Schools." *Harvard Law Review* 104 (1991): 989–1050.

McWhirter, Darien A. *Privacy as a Constitutional Right: Sex, Drugs, and the Right to Life.* New York: Quorum Books, 1992.

Posner, Richard A. *Sex and Reason.* Cambridge, MA: Harvard University Press, 1992.

Presser, Stephen B. *Recapturing the Constitution: Race, Religion, and Abortion Reconsidered.* Washington, DC: Regnery, 1994.

Rubin, Eva R. *Abortion, Politics, and the Courts:* Roe v. Wade *and Its Aftermath.* New York: Greenwood, 1987.

Seidman, Louis Michael. "Confusion at the Border: *Cruzan,* 'the Right to Die,' and the Public/Private Distinction." In *1991 Supreme Court Review,* edited by Dennis J. Hutchinson, David A. Strauss, and Geoffrey R. Stone. Chicago: University of Chicago Press, 1992.

Uhlmann, Michael M. *Last Rights? Assisted Suicide and Euthanasia Debated.* Grand Rapids, MI: Eerdmans, 1998.

Warren, Samuel D., and Louis D. Brandeis. "The Right to Privacy." *Harvard Law Review* 4 (1890): 193.

Westin, Alan F. *Privacy and Freedom.* New York: Atheneum, 1967.

Troxel v. Granville
530 U.S. 57 (2000)

Section 26.10.160(3) of the Revised Code of Washington permits "[a]ny person" to petition for visitation rights "at any time" and authorizes state superior courts to grant such rights whenever visitation may serve a child's best interest. Jennifer and Gary Troxel petitioned for the right to visit their deceased son's daughters, Isabelle and Natalie Troxel. Tommie Granville, the girls' mother, did not oppose all visitation but objected to the amount sought by the Troxels. The superior court ordered more visitation than Granville desired, and she appealed. The state court of appeals reversed and dismissed the Troxels' petition, and the state supreme court affirmed, holding that §26.10.160(3) unconstitutionally infringed on the fundamental right of parents to rear their children. Reasoning that the federal Constitution permits a state to interfere with this right only to prevent harm or potential harm to the child, it found that §26.10.160(3) did not require a threshold showing of harm and therefore swept too broadly by permitting any person to petition at any time with the only requirement being that the visitation serve the best interest of the child. The US Supreme Court granted certiorari. Judgment of the Court: <u>O'Connor</u>, Rehnquist, Ginsburg, Breyer. Concurring in the judgment: <u>Souter</u>; <u>Thomas</u>. Dissenting opinions: <u>Stevens</u>; <u>Scalia</u>; <u>Kennedy</u>.

JUSTICE O'CONNOR announced the judgment of the Court and delivered an opinion, in which THE CHIEF JUSTICE, JUSTICE GINSBURG, and JUSTICE BREYER join.

The Fourteenth Amendment provides that no State shall "deprive any person of life, liberty, or property, without due process of law." We have long recognized that the Amendment's Due Process Clause, like its Fifth Amendment counterpart, "guarantees more than fair process." *Washington v. Glucksberg* (1997). The Clause also includes a substantive component that "provides heightened protection against government interference with certain fundamental rights and liberty interests."

The liberty interest at issue in this case—the interest of parents in the care, custody, and control of their children—is perhaps the oldest of the fundamental liberty interests recognized by this Court. More than 75 years ago, in *Meyer v. Nebraska* (1923), we held that the "liberty" protected by the Due Process Clause includes the right of parents to "establish a home and bring up children" and "to control the education of their own." Two years later, in *Pierce v. Society of Sisters* (1925), we again held that the "liberty of parents and guardians" includes the right "to direct the upbringing and education of children under their control." We explained in *Pierce* that "[t]he child is not the mere creature of the State; those who nurture him and direct his destiny have the right, coupled with the high duty, to recognize and prepare him for additional obligations." We returned to the subject in *Prince v. Massachusetts* (1944), and again confirmed that there is a constitutional dimension to the right of parents to direct the upbringing of their children. "It is cardinal with us that the custody, care and nurture of the child reside first in the parents, whose primary function and freedom include preparation for obligations the state can neither supply nor hinder." Section 26.10.160(3), as applied to Granville and her family in this case, unconstitutionally infringes on that fundamental parental right. The Washington nonparental visitation statute is breathtakingly broad. According to the statute's text, "[a]ny person may petition the court for visitation rights *at any time*," and the court may grant such visitation rights whenever "visitation may serve *the best interest of the child*" (emphasis added). That language effectively permits any third party seeking visitation to subject any decision by a parent concerning visitation of the parent's children to state-court review. Once the visitation petition has been filed in court and the matter is placed before a judge, a parent's decision that visitation would not be in the child's best interest is accorded no deference.

Section 26.10.160(3) contains no requirement that a court accord the parent's decision any presumption of validity or any weight whatsoever. Instead, the Washington statute places the best-interest determination solely in the hands of the judge. Should the judge disagree with the parent's estimation of the child's best interests, the judge's view necessarily prevails. Thus, in practical effect, in the State of Washington a court can disregard and overturn any decision by a fit custodial parent concerning visitation whenever a third party affected by the decision files a visitation petition, based solely on the judge's determination of the child's best interests. . . .

Turning to the facts of this case, . . . the combination of several factors here compels our conclusion that §26.10.160(3), as applied, exceeded the bounds of the Due Process Clause. . . .

First, the Troxels did not allege, and no court has found, that Granville was an unfit parent. That aspect of the case is important, for there is a presumption that fit parents act in the best interests of their children. . . . So long as a parent adequately cares for his or her children (i.e., is fit), there will normally be no reason for the State to inject itself into the private realm of the family to further question the ability of that parent to make the best decisions concerning the rearing of that parent's children. . . .

The problem here is not that the Washington Superior Court intervened, but that when it did so, it gave no special weight at all to Granville's determination of her daughters' best interests. More importantly, it appears that the Superior Court applied exactly the opposite presumption. . . .

The decisional framework employed by the Superior Court directly contravened the traditional presumption that a fit parent will act in the best interest of his or her child. In that respect, the court's presumption failed to provide any protection for Granville's fundamental constitutional right to make decisions concerning the rearing of her own daughters. . . .

Finally, we note that there is no allegation that Granville ever sought to cut off visitation entirely. Rather, the present dispute originated when Granville informed the Troxels that she would prefer to restrict their visitation with Isabelle and Natalie to one short visit per month and special holidays. In the Superior Court proceedings Granville did not oppose visitation but instead asked that the duration of any visitation order be shorter than that requested by the Troxels. While the Troxels requested two weekends per month and two full weeks in the summer, Granville asked the Superior Court to order only one day of visitation per month (with no overnight stay) and participation in the Granville family's holiday celebrations. . . .

Considered together with the Superior Court's reasons for awarding visitation to the Troxels, the combination of these factors demonstrates that the visitation order in this case was an unconstitutional infringement on Granville's fundamental right to make decisions concerning the care, custody, and control of her two daughters. . . . [T]he Due Process Clause does not permit a State to infringe on the fundamental right of parents to make child-rearing decisions simply because a state judge believes a "better" decision could be made. Neither the Washington nonparental visitation statute generally—which places no limits on either the persons who may petition for visitation or the circumstances in which such a petition may be granted—nor the Superior Court in this specific case required anything more. Accordingly, we hold that §26.10.160(3), as applied in this case, is unconstitutional.

JUSTICE SOUTER, concurring in the judgment.

. . . I concur in the judgment affirming the decision of the Supreme Court of Washington, whose facial invalidation of its own state statute is consistent with this Court's prior cases addressing the substantive interests at stake. I would say no more. The issues that might well be presented by reviewing a decision addressing the specific application of the state statute by the trial court are not before us and do not call for turning any fresh furrows in the "treacherous field" of substantive due process.

JUSTICE THOMAS, concurring in the judgment.

I write separately to note that neither party has argued that our substantive due process cases were wrongly decided and that the original understanding of the Due Process Clause precludes judicial enforcement of unenumerated rights under that constitutional provision. As a result, I express no view on the merits of this matter, and I understand the plurality as well to leave the resolution of that issue for another day.

Consequently, I agree with the plurality that this Court's recognition of a fundamental right of parents to direct the upbringing of their children resolves this case. Our decision in *Pierce v. Society of Sisters,* (1925), holds that parents have a fundamental constitutional right to rear their children, including the right to determine who shall educate and socialize them. The opinions of the plurality, Justice Kennedy, and Justice Souter recognize such a right, but curiously none of them articulates the appropriate standard of review. I would apply strict scrutiny to infringements of fundamental rights. Here, the State of Washington lacks even a legitimate governmental interest—to say nothing of a compelling one—in second-guessing a fit parent's decision regarding visitation with third parties. On this basis, I would affirm the judgment below.

JUSTICE STEVENS, dissenting.

The Court today wisely declines to endorse either the holding or the reasoning of the Supreme Court of Washington. In my opinion, the Court would have been even wiser to deny *certiorari.* Given the problematic character of the trial court's decision and the uniqueness of the Washington statute, there was no pressing need to review a State Supreme Court decision that merely requires the state legislature to draft a better statute.

Having decided to address the merits, however, the Court should begin by recognizing that the State Supreme Court rendered a federal constitutional judgment holding a state law invalid on its face. In light of that judgment, I believe that we should confront the federal questions presented directly.

In response to Tommie Granville's federal constitutional challenge, the State Supreme Court broadly held that Wash. Rev. Code §26.10.160(3) (Supp. 1996) was invalid on its face under the Federal Constitution. Despite the nature of this judgment, Justice O'Connor would hold that the Washington visitation statute violated the Due Process Clause of the Fourteenth Amendment only as applied. I agree with Justice Souter that this approach is untenable. . . .

While I thus agree with Justice Souter in this respect, I do not agree with his conclusion that the State Supreme Court made a definitive construction of the visitation statute that necessitates the constitutional conclusion he would draw.

We are thus presented with the unconstrued terms of a state statute and a State Supreme Court opinion that, in my view, significantly misstates the effect of the Federal Constitution upon any construction of that statute. Given that posture, I believe the Court should identify and correct the two flaws in the reasoning of the state court's majority opinion, and remand for further review of the trial court's disposition of this specific case.

In my view, the State Supreme Court erred in its federal constitutional analysis because neither the provision granting "any person" the right to petition the court for visitation nor the absence of a provision requiring a "threshold . . . finding of harm to the child" provides a sufficient basis for holding that the statute is invalid in all its applications. I believe that a facial challenge should fail whenever a statute has "a 'plainly legitimate sweep.'"

The second key aspect of the Washington Supreme Court's holding—that the Federal Constitution requires a showing of actual or potential "harm" to the child before a court may order visitation continued over a parent's objections—finds no support in this Court's case law. While, as the Court recognizes, the Federal Constitution certainly protects the parent-child relationship from arbitrary impairment by the State . . .

. . . Far from guaranteeing that parents' interests will be trammeled in the sweep of cases arising under the statute, the Washington law merely gives an individual—with whom a child may have an established relationship—the procedural right to ask the State to act as arbiter, through the entirely well-known best-interests standard, between the parent's protected interests and the child's. It seems clear to me that the Due Process Clause of the Fourteenth Amendment leaves room for States to consider the impact on a child of possibly arbitrary parental decisions that neither serve nor are motivated by the best interests of the child.

Accordingly, I respectfully dissent.

JUSTICE SCALIA, dissenting.

In my view, a right of parents to direct the upbringing of their children is among the "unalienable Rights" with which the Declaration of Independence proclaims "all Men . . . are endowed by their Creator." And in my view that right is also among the "othe[r] [rights] retained by the people" which the Ninth Amendment says the Constitution's enumeration of rights "shall not be construed to deny or disparage." The Declaration of Independence, however, is not a legal prescription conferring powers upon the courts; and the Constitution's refusal to "deny or disparage" other rights is far removed from affirming any one of them, and even farther removed from authorizing judges to identify what they might be, and to enforce the judges' list against laws duly enacted by the people. Consequently, while I would think it entirely compatible with the commitment to representative democracy set forth in the founding documents to argue, in legislative chambers or in electoral campaigns, that the state has no power to interfere with parents' authority over the rearing of their children, I do not believe that the power which the Constitution confers upon me as a judge entitles me to deny legal effect to laws that (in my view) infringe upon what is (in my view) that unenumerated right. . . .

Judicial vindication of "parental rights" under a Constitution that does not even mention them requires (as Justice Kennedy's opinion rightly points out) not only a judicially crafted definition of parents, but also—unless, as no one believes, the parental rights are to be absolute—judicially approved assessments of "harm to the child" and judicially defined gradations of other persons (grandparents, extended family, adoptive family in an adoption later found to be invalid, long-term guardians, etc.) who may have some claim against the wishes of the parents. If we embrace this unenumerated right, I think it obvious—whether we affirm or reverse the judgment here, or remand as Justice Stevens or Justice Kennedy would do—that we will be ushering in a new regime of judicially prescribed, and federally prescribed, family law. I have no reason to believe that federal judges will be better at this than state legislatures; and state legislatures have the great advantages of doing harm in a more circumscribed area, of being able to correct their mistakes in a flash, and of being removable by the people.

For these reasons, I would reverse the judgment below.

JUSTICE KENNEDY, dissenting.

Given the error I see in the State Supreme Court's central conclusion that the best interests of the child standard is never appropriate in third-party visitation cases, that court should have the first opportunity to reconsider this case. I would remand the case to the state court for further proceedings. If it then found the statute has been applied in an unconstitutional manner because the best interests of the child standard gives insufficient protection to a parent under the circumstances of this case, or if it again declared the statute a nullity because the statute seems to allow any person at all to seek visitation at any time, the decision would present other issues which may or may not warrant further review in this Court. These include not only the protection the Constitution gives parents against state-ordered visitation but also the extent to which federal rules for facial challenges to statutes control in state courts. These matters, however, should await some further case. The judgment now under review should be vacated and remanded on the sole ground that the harm ruling that was so central to the Supreme Court of Washington's decision was in error, given its broad formulation.

Griswold v. Connecticut
381 U.S. 479 (1965)

A Connecticut statute proscribed the use of birth control devices and made it a criminal offense for anyone to give information or instruction on their use. *Estelle Griswold, executive director of the Planned Parenthood League of Connecticut, and Dr. Buxton, its medical director and a professor* *at the Yale Medical School, were convicted of dispensing such information to married persons in violation of the law and were fined $100. After a state appellate court and the Connecticut Supreme Court of Errors affirmed the convictions, the defendants appealed to the United States Supreme Court. It should be noted that the same statute had previously been unsuccessfully challenged in* Tileston v. Ullman *(1943), and* Poe v. Ullman *(1961).* Opinion of the Court: Douglas, Warren, Clark, Brennan, Goldberg. Concurring opinion: Goldberg, Warren, Brennan. Concurring in the judgment: Harlan; White. Dissenting opinions: Black, Stewart; Stewart, Black.

JUSTICE DOUGLAS delivered the opinion of the Court.

. . . We are met with a wide range of questions that implicate the Due Process Clause of the Fourteenth Amendment. Overtones of some arguments suggest that *Lochner v. State of New York* (1905) . . . should be our guide. But we decline that invitation as we did in *West Coast Hotel Co. v. Parrish* (1937). . . . We do not sit as a superlegislature to determine the wisdom, need, and propriety of laws that touch economic problems, business affairs, or social conditions. This law, however, operates directly on an intimate relation of husband and wife and their physician's role in one aspect of that relation.

The association of people is not mentioned in the Constitution nor in the Bill of Rights. The right to educate a child in a school of the parents' choice—whether public or private or parochial—is also not mentioned. Nor is the right to study any particular subject or any foreign language. Yet the First Amendment has been construed to include certain of those rights. . . .

[Previous] cases suggest that specific guarantees in the Bill of Rights have penumbras, formed by emanations from those guarantees that help give them life and substance. . . . Various guarantees create zones of privacy. The right of association contained in the penumbra of the First Amendment is one. . . . The Third Amendment in its prohibition against the quartering of soldiers "in any house" in time of peace without the consent of the owner is another facet of that privacy. The Fourth Amend-

ment explicitly affirms the "right of the people to be secure in their persons, houses, papers, and effects, against unreasonable searches and seizures." The Fifth Amendment in its Self-Incrimination Clause enables the citizen to create a zone of privacy which government may not force him to surrender to his detriment. The Ninth Amendment provides: "The enumeration in the Constitution, of certain rights, shall not be construed to deny or disparage others retained by the people."

The Fourth and Fifth Amendments were described in *Boyd v. United States* (1886) . . . as protection against all governmental invasions "of the sanctity of a man's home and the privacies of life." We recently referred in *Mapp v. Ohio* (1961) . . . to the Fourth Amendment as creating a "right to privacy, no less important than any other right carefully and particularly reserved to the people." . . .

We have had many controversies over these penumbral rights of "privacy and repose." . . . These cases bear witness that the right of privacy which presses for recognition here is a legitimate one.

The present case, then, concerns a relationship lying within the zone of privacy created by several fundamental constitutional guarantees. And it concerns a law which, in forbidding the *use* of contraceptives rather than regulating their manufacture or sale, seeks to achieve its goals by means having a maximum destructive impact upon that relationship. Such a law cannot stand in light of the familiar principle, so often applied by this Court, that a "governmental purpose to control or prevent activities constitutionally subject to state regulation may not be achieved by means which sweep unnecessarily broadly and thereby invade the area of protected freedoms." . . . Would we allow the police to search the sacred precincts of marital bedrooms for telltale signs of the use of contraceptives? The very idea is repulsive to the notions of privacy surrounding the marriage relationship.

We deal with a right of privacy older than the Bill of Rights—older than our political parties, older than our school system. Marriage is a coming together for better or worse, hopefully enduring, and intimate to the degree of being sacred. It is an association that promotes a way of life, not causes; a harmony in living, not political faiths; a bilateral loyalty, not commercial or social projects. Yet it is an association for as noble a purpose as any involved in our prior decisions.

Reversed.

JUSTICE GOLDBERG, with whom THE CHIEF JUSTICE and JUSTICE BRENNAN join, concurring.

I agree with the Court that Connecticut's birth-control law unconstitutionally intrudes upon the right of marital privacy, and I join in its opinion and judgment. Although I have not accepted the view that "due process" as used in the Fourteenth Amendment includes all of the first eight Amendments, . . . I do agree that the concept of liberty protects those personal rights that are fundamental, and is not confined to the specific terms of the Bill of Rights. My conclusion that the concept of liberty is not so restricted and that it embraces the right of marital privacy though that right is not mentioned explicitly in the Constitution is supported both by numerous decisions of this Court, referred to in the Court's opinion, and by the language and history of the Ninth Amendment. In reaching the conclusion that the right of marital privacy is protected, as being within the protected penumbra of specific guarantees of the Bill of Rights, the Court refers to the Ninth Amendment. . . . I add these words to emphasize the relevance of that Amendment to the Court's holding.

The Court stated many years ago that the Due Process Clause protects those liberties that are "so rooted in the traditions and conscience of our people as to be ranked as fundamental." . . . This Court, in a series of decisions, has held that the Fourteenth Amendment absorbs and applies to the States those specifics of the first eight amendments which express fundamental personal rights. The language and history of the Ninth Amendment reveal that the Framers of the Constitution believed that there are additional fundamental rights, protected from governmental infringement, which exist alongside those fundamental rights specifically mentioned in the first eight constitutional amendments.

. . . It was proffered to quiet expressed fears that a bill of specifically enumerated rights could not be sufficiently broad to cover all essential rights and that the specific mention of certain rights would be interpreted as a denial that others were protected. . . .

A dissenting opinion suggests that my interpretation of the Ninth Amendment somehow "broaden[s] the powers of this Court." . . . I do not mean to imply that the Ninth Amendment is applied against the States by the Fourteenth. Nor do I mean to state that the Ninth Amendment constitutes an independent source of rights protected from infringement by either the States or the Federal Government. Rather, the Ninth Amendment shows a belief of the Constitution's authors that fundamental rights exist that are not expressly enumerated in the first eight amendments and an intent that the list of rights included there not be deemed exhaustive. As any student of this Court's opinions knows, this Court has held, often unanimously, that the Fifth and Fourteenth Amendments protect certain fundamental personal liberties from abridgment by the Federal Government or the States. . . . The Ninth Amendment simply shows the intent of the Constitution's authors that other fundamental personal rights should not be denied such protection or disparaged in any other way simply because they are not specifically listed in the first eight constitutional amendments. I do not see how this broadens the authority of the Court; rather it serves to support what this Court has been doing in protecting fundamental rights.

Nor am I turning somersaults with history in arguing that the Ninth Amendment is relevant in a case dealing with a *State's* infringement of a fundamental right. While the Ninth Amendment—and indeed the entire Bill of Rights—originally concerned restrictions upon *federal* power, the subsequently enacted Fourteenth Amendment prohibits the States as well from abridging fundamental personal liberties. And, the Ninth Amendment, in indicating that not all such liberties are specifically mentioned in the first eight amendments, is surely relevant in showing the existence of other fundamental personal rights, now protected from state, as well as federal, infringement. In sum, the

Ninth Amendment simply lends strong support to the view that the "liberty" protected by the Fifth and Fourteenth Amendments from infringement by the Federal Government or the States is not restricted to rights specifically mentioned in the first eight amendments. . . .

The entire fabric of the Constitution and the purposes that clearly underlie its specific guarantees demonstrate that the rights to marital privacy and to marry and raise a family are of similar order and magnitude as the fundamental rights specifically protected.

Although the Constitution does not speak in so many words of the right of privacy in marriage, I cannot believe that it offers these fundamental rights no protection. The fact that no particular provision of the Constitution explicitly forbids the State from disrupting the traditional relation of the family—a relation as old and as fundamental as our entire civilization—surely does not show that the Government was meant to have the power to do so. Rather, as the Ninth Amendment expressly recognizes, there are fundamental personal rights such as this one, which are protected from abridgment by the Government though not specifically mentioned in the Constitution. . . .

The logic of the dissents would sanction federal or state legislation that seems to me even more plainly unconstitutional than the statute before us. Surely the Government, absent a showing of a compelling subordinating state interest, could not decree that all husbands and wives must be sterilized after two children have been born to them. Yet by their reasoning such an invasion of marital privacy would not be subject to constitutional challenge because, while it might be "silly," no provision of the Constitution specifically prevents the Government from curtailing the marital right to bear children and raise a family. While it may shock some of my Brethren that the Court today holds that the Constitution protects the right of marital privacy, in my view it is far more shocking to believe that the personal liberty guaranteed by the Constitution does not include protection against such totalitarian limitation of family size, which is at complete variance with our constitutional concepts. Yet, if upon a showing of a slender basis of rationality, a law outlawing voluntary birth control by married persons is valid, then, by the same reasoning, a law requiring compulsory birth control also would seem to be valid. In my view, however, both types of law would unjustifiably intrude upon rights of marital privacy which are constitutionally protected.

In sum, I believe that the right of privacy in the marital relation is fundamental and basic—a personal right "retained by the people" within the meaning of the Ninth Amendment. Connecticut cannot constitutionally abridge this fundamental right, which is protected by the Fourteenth Amendment from infringement by the States. I agree with the Court that petitioners' convictions must therefore be reversed.

JUSTICE HARLAN, concurring.

I fully agree with the judgment of reversal, but find myself unable to join the Court's opinion. . . .

In my view, the proper constitutional inquiry in this case is whether this Connecticut statute infringes the Due Process Clause of the Fourteenth Amendment because the enactment violates basic values "implicit in the concept of ordered liberty," *Palko v. State of Connecticut* (1937). . . . I believe that it does. While the relevant inquiry may be aided by resort to one or more of the provisions of the Bill of Rights, it is not dependent on them or any of their radiations. The Due Process Clause of the Fourteenth Amendment stands, in my opinion, on its own bottom. . . .

While I could not more heartily agree that judicial "self restraint" is an indispensable ingredient of sound constitutional adjudication, I do submit that the formula suggested for achieving it is more hollow than real. "Specific" provisions of the Constitution, no less than "due process," lend themselves as readily to "personal" interpretations by judges whose constitutional outlook is simply to keep the Constitution in supposed "tune with the times." . . .

Judicial self-restraint will not, I suggest, be brought about in the "due process" area by the historically unfounded incorporation formula long advanced by my Brother Black, and now in part espoused by my Brother Stewart. It will be achieved in this area, as in other constitutional areas, only by continual insistence upon respect for the teachings of history, solid recognition of the basic values that underlie our society, and wise appreciation of the great roles that the doctrines of federalism and separation of powers have played in establishing and preserving American freedoms. . . . Adherence to these principles will not, of course, obviate all constitutional differences of opinion among judges, nor should it. Their continued recognition will, however, go farther toward keeping most judges from roaming at large in the constitutional field than will the interpolation into the Constitution of an artificial and largely illusory restriction on the content of the Due Process Clause.

JUSTICE BLACK, with whom JUSTICE STEWART joins, dissenting.

I agree with my Brother Stewart's dissenting opinion. And like him I do not to any extent whatever base my view that this Connecticut law is constitutional on a belief that the law is wise or that its policy is a good one. In order that there may be no room at all to doubt why I vote as I do, I feel constrained to add that the law is every bit as [personally] offensive to me as it is my Brethren. . . .

. . . I get nowhere in this case by talk about a constitutional "right of privacy" as an emanation from one or more constitutional provisions. I like my privacy as well as the next one, but I am nevertheless compelled to admit that government has a right to invade it unless prohibited by some specific constitutional provision. For these reasons I cannot agree with the Court's judgment and the reasons it gives for holding this Connecticut law unconstitutional. . . .

I realize that many good and able men have eloquently spoken and written, sometimes in rhapsodical strains, about the duty of this Court to keep the Constitution in tune with the times. The idea is that the Constitution must be changed from time to time and that this Court is charged with a duty to make those changes. For myself, I must with all deference reject that philosophy. The Constitution makers knew the need for change and provided for it. Amendments suggested by the people's elected representatives can be submitted to the people or their selected agents for ratification. That method of change was good for our

Fathers, and being somewhat old-fashioned I must add it is good enough for me. And so, I cannot rely on the Due Process Clause or the Ninth Amendment or any mysterious and uncertain natural law concept as a reason for striking down this state law. The Due Process Clause with an "arbitrary and capricious" or "shocking to the conscience" formula was liberally used by this Court to strike down economic legislation in the early decades of this century, threatening, many people thought, the tranquility and stability of the Nation. . . . That formula, based on subjective considerations of "natural justice," is no less dangerous when used to enforce this Court's views about personal rights than those about economic rights. I had thought that we had laid that formula, as a means for striking down state legislation to rest once and for all in cases like *West Coast Hotel Co. v. Parrish.*

JUSTICE STEWART, with whom JUSTICE BLACK joins, dissenting.

Since 1879 Connecticut has had on its books a law which forbids the use of contraceptives by anyone. I think this is an uncommonly silly law. As a practical matter, the law is obviously unenforceable, except in the oblique context of the present case. . . . But we are not asked in this case to say whether we think this law is unwise, or even asinine. We are asked to hold that it violates the United States Constitution. And that I cannot do.

In the course of its opinion the Court refers to no less than six Amendments to the Constitution: the First, the Third, the Fourth, the Fifth, the Ninth, and the Fourteenth. But the Court does not say which of these Amendments, if any, it thinks is infringed by this Connecticut law. . . .

The Court also quotes the Ninth Amendment, and my Brother Goldberg's concurring opinion relies heavily upon it. But to say that the Ninth Amendment has anything to do with this case is to turn somersaults with history. The Ninth Amendment, like its companion the Tenth, which this Court held "states but a truism that all is retained which has not been surrendered," *United States v. Darby* (1941), was framed by James Madison and adopted by the States simply to make clear that the adoption of the Bill of Rights did not alter the plan that the Federal Government was to be a government of express and limited powers, and that all rights and powers not delegated to it were retained by the people and the individual States. Until today no member of this Court has ever suggested that the Ninth Amendment meant anything else, and the idea that a federal court could ever use the Ninth Amendment to annul a law passed by the elected representatives of the people of the State of Connecticut would have caused James Madison no little wonder.

What provision of the Constitution, then, does make this state law invalid? The Court says it is the right of privacy "created by several fundamental constitutional guarantees." With all deference, I can find no such general right of privacy in the Bill of Rights, in any other part of the Constitution, or in any case ever before decided by this Court. . . .

Roe v. Wade
410 U.S. 113 (1973)

A Texas abortion statute made it a felony for anyone to destroy a fetus except on "medical advice for the purpose of saving the life of the mother." This law was typical of abortion statutes in effect in most states for approximately a century. Jane Roe (the pseudonym for an unmarried pregnant woman) brought suit against District Attorney Wade of Dallas County for declaratory and injunctive relief. She challenged the statute on grounds that it denied equal protection (in that it forced women who did not have the money to have a baby when those who had money could go elsewhere and procure a safe, legal abortion), due process (because the statute was vague as to what "saving the life of the mother" actually meant), and the mother's right of privacy guaranteed under the First, Fourth, Fifth, Ninth, and Fourteenth Amendments. A three-judge federal district court found the statute unconstitutional, and Texas appealed to the Supreme Court. The Court heard Roe *in conjunction with* Doe v. Bolton *(1973), in which a modern "reform" abortion statute from Georgia was also challenged. Opinion of the Court:* Blackmun, *Burger, Douglas, Brennan, Stewart, Marshall, Powell. Concurring opinions:* Burger, *Douglas;* Stewart. *Dissenting opinions:* White, *Rehnquist;* Rehnquist.

JUSTICE BLACKMUN delivered the opinion of the Court.

We forthwith acknowledge our awareness of the sensitive and emotional nature of the abortion controversy, of the vigorous opposing views, even among physicians, and of the deep and seemingly absolute convictions that the subject inspires. One's philosophy, one's experiences, one's exposure to the raw edges of human existence, one's religious training, one's attitudes toward life and family and their values, and the moral standards one establishes and seeks to observe, are all likely to influence and to color one's thinking and conclusions about abortion.

In addition, population growth, pollution, poverty, and racial overtones tend to complicate and not to simplify the problem.

Our task, of course, is to resolve the issue by constitutional measurement, free of emotion and of predilection. We seek earnestly to do this, and, because we do, we have inquired into, and in this opinion place some emphasis upon, medical and medical-legal history and what that history reveals about man's attitudes toward the abortion procedure over the centuries. We bear in mind, too, Mr. Justice Holmes' admonition in his now-vindicated dissent in *Lochner v. New York* (1905): "[The Constitution] is made for people of fundamentally differing views, and the accident of our finding certain opinions natural and familiar or novel and even shocking ought not to conclude our judgment upon the question whether statutes embodying them conflict with the Constitution of the United States." . . .

The principal thrust of appellant's attack on the Texas statutes is that they improperly invade a right, said to be possessed by the pregnant woman, to choose to terminate her pregnancy. Appellant would discover this right in the concept of personal "liberty" embodied in the Fourteenth Amendment's Due Process Clause; or in personal, marital, familial, and sexual privacy said to be protected by the Bill of Rights or its penumbras, . . . or among those rights reserved to the people by the Ninth Amendment. . . . Before addressing this claim, we feel it desirable briefly to survey, in several aspects, the history of abortion, for such insight as that history may afford us, and then to examine the state purposes and interests behind the criminal abortion laws. . . .

It perhaps is not generally appreciated that the restrictive criminal abortion laws in effect in a majority of States today are of relatively recent vintage. Those laws, generally proscribing abortion or its attempt at any time during pregnancy except when necessary to preserve the pregnant woman's life, are not of ancient or even of common-law origin. Instead, they derive from statutory changes effected, for the most part, in the latter half of the 19th century. . . .

Three reasons have been advanced to explain historically the enactment of criminal abortion laws in the 19th century and to justify their continued existence.

It has been argued occasionally that these laws were the product of a Victorian social concern to discourage illicit sexual conduct. Texas, however, does not advance this justification in the present case, and it appears that no court or commentator has taken the argument seriously. . . .

A second reason is concerned with abortion as a medical procedure. When most criminal abortion laws were first enacted, the procedure was a hazardous one for the woman. . . . Thus, it has been argued that a State's real concern in enacting a criminal abortion law was to protect the pregnant woman, that is, to restrain her from submitting to a procedure that placed her life in serious jeopardy.

Modern medical techniques have altered this situation. . . .

The third reason is the State's interest—some phrase it in terms of duty—in protecting prenatal life. Some of the argument for this justification rests on the theory that a new human life is present from the moment of conception. The State's interest and general obligation to protect life then extends, it is argued, to prenatal life. Only when the life of the pregnant mother herself is at stake, balanced against the life she carries within her, should the interest of the embryo or fetus not prevail. Logically, of course, a legitimate state interest in this area need not stand or fall on acceptance of the belief that life begins at conception or at some other point prior to live birth. In assessing the State's interest, recognition may be given to the less rigid claim that as long as at least *potential* life is involved, the State may assert interests beyond the protection of the pregnant woman alone. . . .

It is with these interests, and the weight to be attached to them, that this case is concerned. . . .

The Constitution does not explicitly mention any right of privacy. In a line of decisions, however, going back perhaps as far as . . . 1891, the Court has recognized that a right of personal privacy, or a guarantee of certain areas or zones of privacy, does exist under the Constitution. In varying contexts, the Court or individual Justices have, indeed, found at least the roots of that right in the First Amendment, . . . in the Fourth and Fifth Amendments, . . . in the penumbras of the Bill of Rights, . . . in the Ninth Amendment, . . . or in the concept of liberty guaranteed by the first section of the Fourteenth Amendment. . . . These decisions make it clear that only personal rights that can be deemed "fundamental" or "implicit in the concept of ordered liberty" . . . are included in this guarantee of personal privacy. They also make it clear that the right has some extension to activities relating to marriage, . . . procreation, . . . contraception, . . . family relationships, . . . and child rearing and education. . . .

This right of privacy, whether it be founded in the Fourteenth Amendment's concept of personal liberty and restrictions upon state action, as we feel it is, or, as the District Court determined, in the Ninth Amendment's reservation of rights to the people, is broad enough to encompass a woman's decision whether or not to terminate her pregnancy. The detriment that the State would impose upon the pregnant woman by denying this choice altogether is apparent. Specific and direct harm medically diagnosable even in early pregnancy may be involved. Maternity, or additional offspring, may force upon the woman a distressful life and future. Psychological harm may be imminent. Mental and physical health may be taxed by child care. There is also the distress, for all concerned, associated with the unwanted child, and there is the problem of bringing a child into a family already unable, psychologically and otherwise, to care for it. In other cases, as in this one, the additional difficulties and continuing stigma of unwed motherhood may be involved. All these are factors the woman and her responsible physician necessarily will consider in consultation.

On the basis of elements such as these, appellant and some *amici* argue that the woman's right is absolute and that she is entitled to terminate her pregnancy at whatever time, in whatever way, and for whatever reason she alone chooses. With this we do not agree. Appellant's arguments that Texas either has no valid interest at all in regulating the abortion decision, or no interest strong enough to support any limitation upon the woman's sole determination, is unpersuasive. The Court's decisions recognizing a right of privacy also acknowledge that some state regulation in areas protected by that right is appropriate. As noted above, a State may properly assert important interests in safeguarding health, in maintaining medical standards, and in protecting potential life. At some point in pregnancy, these respective interests become sufficiently compelling to sustain regulation of the factors that govern the abortion decision. The privacy right involved, therefore, cannot be said to be absolute. In fact, it is not clear to us that the claim asserted by some *amici* that one has an unlimited right to do with one's body as one pleases bears a close relationship to the right of privacy previously articulated in the Court's decisions. The Court has refused to recognize an unlimited right of this kind in the past. . . .

We, therefore, conclude that the right of personal privacy includes the abortion decision, but that this right is not unqualified and must be considered against important state interests in regulation. . . .

Where certain "fundamental rights" are involved, the Court has held that a regulation limiting these rights may be justified only by a "compelling state interest" . . . and that legislative enactments must be narrowly drawn to express only the legitimate state interests at stake. . . .

The District Court held that the appellee failed to meet his burden of demonstrating that the Texas statute's infringement upon Roe's rights was necessary to support a compelling state interest, and that, although the appellee presented "several compelling justifications for state presence in the area of abortions," the statutes outstripped these justifications and swept "far beyond any areas of compelling state interest." . . . Appellant and appellee both contest that holding. Appellant, as has been indicated, claims an absolute right that bars any state imposition of criminal penalties in the area. Appellee argues that the State's determination to recognize and protect prenatal life from and after conception constitutes a compelling state interest. . . . We do not agree fully with either formulation.

A. The appellee and certain *amici* argue that the fetus is a "person" within the language and meaning of the Fourteenth Amendment. In support of this, they outline at length and in detail the well-known facts of fetal development. If this suggestion of personhood is established, the appellant's case, of course, collapses, for the fetus' right to life is then guaranteed specifically by the Amendment. The appellant conceded as much on reargument. On the other hand, the appellee conceded on reargument that no case could be cited that holds that a fetus is a person within the meaning of the Fourteenth Amendment.

The Constitution does not define "persons" in so many words. . . . [I]n nearly all . . . instances [in which the word *person* is used], the use of the word is such that it has application only postnatally. None indicates, with any assurance, that it has any possible pre-natal application.

All this, together with our observation . . . that throughout the major portion of the 19th century prevailing legal abortion practices were far freer than they are today, persuades us that the word "person," as used in the Fourteenth Amendment, does not include the unborn. . . .

This conclusion, however, does not of itself fully answer the contentions raised by Texas, and we pass on to other considerations.

B. The pregnant woman cannot be isolated in her privacy. She carries an embryo and, later, a fetus, if one accepts the medical definitions of the developing young in the human uterus. . . . The situation therefore is inherently different from marital intimacy, or bedroom possession of obscene material, or marriage, or procreation, or education. . . . As we have intimated above, it is reasonable and appropriate for a State to decide that at some point in time another interest, that of health of the mother or that of potential human life, becomes significantly involved. The woman's privacy is no longer sole and any right of privacy she possesses must be measured accordingly.

Texas urges that, apart from the Fourteenth Amendment, life begins at conception and is present throughout pregnancy, and that, therefore, the State has a compelling interest in protecting that life from and after conception. We need not resolve the difficult question of when life begins. When those trained in the respective disciplines of medicine, philosophy, and theology are unable to arrive at any consensus, the judiciary, at this point in the development of man's knowledge, is not in a position to speculate as to the answer. . . .

In view of . . . this, we do not agree that, by adopting one theory of life, Texas may override the rights of the pregnant woman that are at stake. We repeat, however, that the State does have an important and legitimate interest in preserving and protecting the health of the pregnant woman, whether she be a resident of the State or a nonresident who seeks medical consultation and treatment there, and that it has still *another* important and legitimate interest in protecting the potentiality of human life. These interests are separate and distinct. Each grows in substantiality as the woman approaches term and, at a point during pregnancy, each becomes "compelling."

With respect to the State's important and legitimate interest in the health of the mother, the "compelling" point, in the light of present medical knowledge, is at approximately the end of the first trimester. This is so because of the now-established medical fact . . . that until the end of the first trimester mortality in abortion may be less than mortality in normal childbirth. It follows that, from and after this point, a State may regulate the abortion procedure to the extent that the regulation reasonably relates to the preservation and protection of maternal health. Examples of permissible state regulation in this area are requirements as to the qualifications of the person who is to perform the abortion; as to the licensure of that person; as to the facility in which the procedure is to be performed, that is, whether it must be a hospital or may be a clinic or some other place of less-than-hospital status; as to the licensing of the facility; and the like.

This means, on the other hand, that, for the period of pregnancy prior to this "compelling" point, the attending physician, in consultation with his patient, is free to determine, without regulation by the State, that, in his medical judgment, the patient's pregnancy should be terminated. If that decision is reached, the judgment may be effectuated by an abortion free of interference by the State. With respect to the State's important and legitimate interest in potential life, the "compelling" point is at viability. This is so because the fetus then presumably has the capability of meaningful life outside the mother's womb. State regulation protective of fetal life after viability thus has both logical and biological justifications. If the State is interested in protecting fetal life after viability, it may go so far as to proscribe abortion during that period, except when it is necessary to preserve the life or health of the mother.

Measured against these standards, Art. 1196 of the Texas Penal Code, in restricting legal abortions to those "procured or attempted by medical advice for the purpose of saving the life of the mother," sweeps too broadly. The statute makes no distinction between abortions performed early in pregnancy and those performed later, and it limits to a single reason, "saving" the mother's life, the legal justification for the procedure. The statute, therefore, cannot survive the constitutional attack made upon it here. . . .

To summarize and to repeat: 1. A state criminal abortion statute of the current Texas type, that excepts from criminality only a *lifesaving* procedure on behalf of the mother, without regard to pregnancy stage and without recognition of the other interests involved, is violative of the Due Process Clause of the Fourteenth Amendment. (*a*) For the stage prior to approximately the end of the first trimester, the abortion decision and its effectuation must be left to the medical judgment of the pregnant woman's attending physician. (*b*) For the stage subsequent to approximately the end of the first trimester, the State, in promoting its interest in the health of the mother, may, if it chooses, regulate the abortion procedure in ways that are reasonably related to maternal health. (*c*) For the stage subsequent to viability, the State in promoting its interest in the potentiality of human life may, if it chooses, regulate, and even proscribe, abortion except where it is necessary, in appropriate medical judgment, for the preservation of the life or health of the mother. . . .

This holding, we feel, is consistent with the relative weights of the respective interests involved, with the lessons and examples of medical and legal history, with the lenity of the common law, and with the demands of the profound problems of the present day. . . .

JUSTICE REHNQUIST, dissenting.

. . . I have difficulty in concluding, as the Court does, that the right of "privacy" is involved in this case. Texas, by the statute here challenged, bars the performance of a medical abortion by a licensed physician on a plaintiff such as Roe. A transaction resulting in an operation such as this is not "private" in the ordinary usage of that word. Nor is the "privacy" that the Court finds here even a distant relative of the freedom from searches and seizures protected by the Fourth Amendment to the Constitution, which the Court has referred to as embodying a right to privacy. . . .

If the Court means by the term "privacy" no more than that the claim of a person to be free from unwanted state regulation of consensual transactions may be a form of "liberty" protected by the Fourteenth Amendment, there is no doubt that similar claims have been upheld in our earlier decisions on the basis of that liberty. I agree with the statement of Mr. Justice Stewart in his concurring opinion that the "liberty," against deprivation of which without due process the Fourteenth Amendment protects, embraces more than the rights found in the Bill of Rights. But that liberty is not guaranteed absolutely against deprivation, only against deprivation without due process of law. The test traditionally applied in the area of social and economic legislation is whether or not a law such as that challenged has a rational relation to a valid state objective. . . . The Due Process Clause of the Fourteenth Amendment undoubtedly does place a limit, albeit a broad one, on legislative power to enact laws such as this. If the Texas statute were to prohibit an abortion even where the mother's life is in jeopardy, I have little doubt that such a statute would lack a rational relation to a valid state objective. . . . But the Court's sweeping invalidation of any restrictions on abortion during the first trimester is impossible to justify under that standard, and the conscious weighing of competing factors that the Court's opinion apparently substitutes for the established test is far more appropriate to a legislative judgment than to a judicial one.

The Court eschews the history of the Fourteenth Amendment in its reliance on the "compelling state interest" test. . . . But the Court adds a new wrinkle to this test by transposing it from the legal considerations associated with the Equal Protection Clause of the Fourteenth Amendment to this case arising under the Due Process Clause of the Fourteenth Amendment. Unless I misapprehend the consequences of this transplanting of the "compelling state interest test," the Court's opinion will accomplish the seemingly impossible feat of leaving this area of the law more confused than it found it.

While the Court's opinion quotes from the dissent of Mr. Justice Holmes in *Lochner v. New York,* . . . the result it reaches is more closely attuned to the majority opinion of Mr. Justice Peckham in that case. As in *Lochner* and similar cases applying substantive due process standards to economic and social welfare legislation, the adoption of the compelling state interest standard will inevitably require this Court to examine the legislative policies and pass on the wisdom of these policies in the very process of deciding whether a particular state interest put forward may or may not be "compelling." The decision here to break pregnancy into three distinct terms and to outline the permissible restrictions the State may impose in each one, for example, partakes more of judicial legislation than it does of a determination of the intent of the drafters of the Fourteenth Amendment.

Planned Parenthood of Southeastern Pennsylvania v. Casey
505 U.S. 833 (1992)

Central to this case were five provisions of the Pennsylvania Abortion Control Act of 1982. One required that a woman seeking an abortion give her informed consent prior to the procedure and specified that she be provided with certain information at least twenty-four hours before the abortion was performed; the second mandated the informed consent of one parent for a minor to obtain an abortion, but provided for a judicial bypass procedure; the third required, subject to certain exceptions, that a married woman seeking an abortion must sign a statement indicating that she had notified her husband; the fourth defined a "medical emergency" that would excuse compliance with the foregoing requirements; and the fifth imposed certain reporting requirements on facilities providing abortion services.

Before any of these provisions took effect, five abortion clinics and a physician, representing himself and a class of doctors who provided abortion services, brought suit in US District Court for the Eastern District of Pennsylvania, seeking a declaratory judgment that each of these provisions was unconstitutional, as well as injunctive relief. On the basis of Roe v. Wade *(1973),* Akron v. Akron Center for Reproductive Health *(1983), and* Thornburgh v. American College of Obstetricians and Gynecologists *(1986), the district court held all of the provisions unconstitutional and permanently enjoined their enforcement. The Court of Appeals for the Third Circuit reversed in part and affirmed in part, upholding all of the act's provisions with the exception of spousal notification. The Supreme Court granted certiorari. Judgment of the Court and opinion of the Court in part:* O'Connor, Kennedy, Souter. *Concurring in the opinion in part and the judgment in part and dissenting in part:* Blackmun; Stevens. *Concurring in the judgment in part and dissenting in part:* Rehnquist, *White, Scalia, Thomas;* Scalia, *Rehnquist, White, Thomas.*

JUSTICE O'CONNOR, JUSTICE KENNEDY, and JUSTICE SOUTER announced the judgment of the Court and delivered the opinion of the Court [in part].

After considering the fundamental constitutional questions resolved by *Roe,* principles of institutional integrity, and the rule of *stare decisis,* we are led to conclude this: the essential holding of *Roe v. Wade* should be retained and once again reaffirmed.

It must be stated at the outset and with clarity that *Roe's* essential holding, the holding we reaffirm, has three parts. First is a recognition of the right of the woman to choose to have an abortion before viability and to obtain it without undue interference from the State. Before viability, the State's interests are not strong enough to support a prohibition of abortion or the imposition of a substantial obstacle to the woman's effective right to elect the procedure. Second is a confirmation of the State's power to restrict abortions after fetal viability, if the law contains exceptions for pregnancies which endanger a woman's life or health. And third is the principle that the State has legitimate interests from the outset of the pregnancy in protecting the health of the woman and the life of the fetus that may become a child. These principles do not contradict one another; and we adhere to each.

Constitutional protection of the woman's decision to terminate her pregnancy derives from the Due Process Clause of the Fourteenth Amendment. It declares that no State shall "deprive any person of life, liberty, or property, without due process of law." The controlling word in the cases before us is "liberty." Although a literal reading of the Clause might suggest that it governs only the procedures by which a State may deprive persons of liberty, for at least 105 years, since *Mugler v. Kansas* (1887), the Clause has been understood to contain a substantive component as well, one barring certain government actions regardless of the fairness of the procedures used to implement them. . . .

The most familiar of the substantive liberties protected by the Fourteenth Amendment are those recognized by the Bill of Rights. We have held that the Due Process Clause of the Fourteenth Amendment incorporates most of the Bill of Rights against the States. It is tempting, as a means of curbing the discretion of federal judges, to suppose that liberty encompasses no more than those rights already guaranteed to the individual against federal interference by the express provisions of the first eight Amendments to the Constitution. But of course this Court has never accepted that view.

It is also tempting, for the same reason, to suppose that the Due Process Clause protects only those practices, defined at the most specific level, that were protected against government interference by other rules of law when the Fourteenth Amendment was ratified. But such a view would be inconsistent with our law. It is a promise of the Constitution that there is a realm of personal liberty which the government may not enter. We have vindicated this principle before. Marriage is mentioned nowhere in the Bill of Rights and interracial marriage was illegal in most States in the 19th century, but the Court was no doubt correct in finding it to be an aspect of liberty protected against state interference by the substantive component of the Due Process Clause in *Loving v. Virginia* (1967). . . .

Neither the Bill of Rights nor the specific practices of States at the time of the adoption of the Fourteenth Amendment marks the outer limits of the substantive sphere of liberty which the Fourteenth Amendment protects. See U.S. Const., Amdt. 9. . . .

The inescapable fact is that adjudication of substantive due process claims may call upon the Court in interpreting the Constitution to exercise that same capacity which by tradition courts always have exercised: reasoned judgment. Its boundaries are not susceptible of expression as a simple rule. That does not mean we are free to invalidate state policy choices with which we disagree; yet neither does it permit us to shrink from the duties of our office. . . .

Our law affords constitutional protection to personal decisions relating to marriage, procreation, contraception, family relationships, child rearing, and education. *Carey v. Population Services International.* Our cases recognize the right of the *individual,* married or single, to be free from unwarranted governmental intrusion into matters so fundamentally affecting a person as the decision whether to bear or beget a child. *Eisenstadt v. Baird,* (emphasis in original). Our precedents "have respected the private realm of family life which the state cannot enter." These matters, involving the most intimate and personal choices a person may make in a lifetime, choices central to personal dignity and autonomy, are central to the liberty protected by the Fourteenth Amendment. At the heart of liberty is the right to define one's own concept of existence, of meaning, of the universe, and of the mystery of human life. Beliefs about these matters could not define the attributes of personhood were they formed under compulsion of the State. . . .

It should be recognized, moreover, that in some critical respects the abortion decision is of the same character as the decision to use contraception, to which *Griswold v. Connecticut, Eisenstadt v. Baird,* and *Carey v. Population Services International* afford constitutional protection. We have no doubt as to the correctness of those decisions. They support the reasoning in *Roe* relating to the woman's liberty because they involve personal decisions concerning not only the meaning of procreation but also human responsibility and respect for it. As with abortion, reasonable people will have differences of opinion about these matters. One view is based on such reverence for the wonder of creation that any pregnancy ought to be welcomed and carried to full term no matter how difficult it will be to provide for the child and ensure its well-being. Another is that the inability to provide for the nurture and care of the infant is a cruelty to the child and an anguish to the parent. These are intimate views with infinite variations, and their deep, personal character underlay our decisions in *Griswold, Eisenstadt,* and *Carey.* The same concerns are present when the woman confronts the reality that, perhaps despite her attempts to avoid it, she has become pregnant. . . .

While we appreciate the weight of the arguments made on behalf of the State in the cases before us, arguments which in their ultimate formulation conclude that *Roe* should be over-ruled, the reservations any of us may have in reaffirming the central holding of *Roe* are outweighed by the explication of individual liberty we have given combined with the force of *stare decisis.* We turn now to that doctrine.

The obligation to follow precedent begins with necessity, and a contrary necessity marks its outer limit. With Cardozo, we recognize that no judicial system could do society's work if it eyed each issue afresh in every case that raised it. Indeed, the very concept of the rule of law underlying our own Constitution requires such continuity over time that a respect for precedent is, by definition, indispensable. At the other extreme, a different necessity would make itself felt if a prior judicial ruling should come to be seen so clearly as error that its enforcement was for that very reason doomed. . . .

So in this case we may inquire whether *Roe's* central rule has been found unworkable; whether the rule's limitation on state power could be removed without serious inequity to those who have relied upon it or significant damage to the stability of the society governed by the rule in question; whether the law's growth in the intervening years has left *Roe's* central rule a doctrinal anachronism discounted by society; and whether *Roe's* premises of fact have so far changed in the ensuing two decades as to render its central holding somehow irrelevant or unjustifiable in dealing with the issue it addressed.

Although *Roe* has engendered opposition, it has in no sense proven "unworkable," representing as it does a simple limitation beyond which a state law is unenforceable. While *Roe* has, of course, required judicial assessment of state laws affecting the exercise of the choice guaranteed against government infringement, and although the need for such review will remain as a consequence of today's decision, the required determinations fall within judicial competence.

The inquiry into reliance counts the cost of a rule's repudiation as it would fall on those who have relied reasonably on the rule's continued application. . . . [F]or two decades of economic and social developments, people have organized intimate relationships and made choices that define their views of themselves and their

places in society, in reliance on the availability of abortion in the event that contraception should fail. The ability of women to participate equally in the economic and social life of the Nation has been facilitated by their ability to control their reproductive lives. The Constitution serves human values, and while the effect of reliance on *Roe* cannot be exactly measured, neither can the certain cost of overruling *Roe* for people who have ordered their thinking and living around that case be dismissed.

No evolution of legal principle has left *Roe's* doctrinal footings weaker than they were in 1973. No development of constitutional law since the case was decided has implicitly or explicitly left *Roe* behind as a mere survivor of obsolete constitutional thinking. . . .

We have seen how time has overtaken some of *Roe's* factual assumptions: advances in maternal health care allow for abortions safe to the mother later in pregnancy than was true in 1973, and advances in neonatal care have advanced viability to a point somewhat earlier. But these facts go only to the scheme of time limits on the realization of competing interests, and the divergences from the factual premises of 1973 have no bearing on the validity of *Roe's* central holding, that viability marks the earliest point at which the State's interest in fetal life is constitutionally adequate to justify a legislative ban on nontherapeutic abortions. The soundness or unsoundness of that constitutional judgment in no sense turns on whether viability occurs at approximately 28 weeks, as was usual at the time of *Roe,* at 23 to 24 weeks, as it sometimes does today. . . .

The sum of the precedential inquiry to this point shows *Roe's* underpinnings unweakened in any way affecting its central holding. While it has engendered disapproval, it has not been unworkable. An entire generation has come of age free to assume *Roe's* concept of liberty in defining the capacity of women to act in society, and to make reproductive decisions; no erosion of principle going to liberty or personal autonomy has left *Roe's* central holding a doctrinal remnant; *Roe* portends no developments at odds with other precedent for the analysis of personal liberty; and no changes of fact have rendered viability more or less appropriate as the point at which the balance of interests tips.

Within the bounds of normal *stare decisis* analysis, then, and subject to the considerations on which it customarily turns, the stronger argument is for affirming *Roe*'s central holding, with whatever degree of personal reluctance any of us may have, not for overruling it. . . .

. . . Our analysis would not be complete, however, without explaining why overruling *Roe*'s central holding would not only reach an unjustifiable result under principles of *stare decisis,* but would seriously weaken the Court's capacity to exercise the judicial power and to function as the Supreme Court of a Nation dedicated to the rule of law. To understand why this would be so it is necessary to understand the source of this Court's authority, the conditions necessary for its preservation, and its relationship to the country's understanding of itself as a constitutional Republic.

The root of American governmental power is revealed most clearly in the instance of the power conferred by the Constitution upon the Judiciary of the United States and specifically upon this Court. As Americans of each succeeding generation are rightly told, the Court cannot buy support for its decisions by spending money and, except to a minor degree, it cannot independently coerce obedience to its decrees. The Court's power lies, rather, in its legitimacy, a product of substance and perception that shows itself in the people's acceptance of the Judiciary as fit to determine what the Nation's law means and to declare what it demands. . . .

The Court must take care to speak and act in ways that allow people to accept its decisions on the terms the Court claims for them, as grounded truly in principle, not as compromises with social and political pressures having, as such, no bearing on the principled choices that the Court is obliged to make. Thus, the Court's legitimacy depends on making legally principled decisions under circumstances in which their principled character is sufficiently plausible to be accepted by the Nation.

The need for principled action to be perceived as such is implicated to some degree whenever this, or any other appellate court, overrules a prior case. This is not to say, of course, that this Court cannot give a perfectly satisfactory explanation in most cases. People understand that some of the Constitution's language is hard to fathom and that the Court's Justices are sometimes able to perceive significant facts or to understand principles of law that eluded their predecessors and that justify departures from existing decisions. However upsetting it may be to those most directly affected when one judicially derived rule replaces another, the country can accept some correction of error without necessarily questioning the legitimacy of the Court.

In two circumstances, however, the Court would almost certainly fail to receive the benefit of the doubt in overruling prior cases. There is, first, a point beyond which frequent overruling would overtax the country's belief in the Court's good faith. Despite the variety of reasons that may inform and justify a decision to overrule, we cannot forget that such a decision is usually perceived (and perceived correctly) as, at the least, a statement that a prior decision was wrong. There is a limit to the amount of error that can plausibly be imputed to prior courts. If that limit should be exceeded, disturbance of prior rulings would be taken as evidence that justifiable reexamination of principle had given way to drives for particular results in the short term. The legitimacy of the Court would fade with the frequency of its vacillation.

That first circumstance can be described as hypothetical; the second is to the point here and now. Where, in the performance of its judicial duties, the Court decides a case in such a way as to resolve the sort of intensely divisive controversy reflected in *Roe* and those rare, comparable cases, its decision has a dimension that the resolution of the normal case does not carry. It is the dimension present whenever the Court's interpretation of the Constitution calls the contending sides of a national controversy to end their national division by accepting a common mandate rooted in the Constitution.

The Court is not asked to do this very often, having thus addressed the Nation only twice in our lifetime, in the decisions of *Brown* and *Roe*. But when the Court does act in this way, its decision requires an equally rare precedential force to counter the inevitable efforts to overturn it and to thwart its implementation. Some of those efforts may be mere unprincipled emotional reactions; others may proceed from principles worthy of profound respect. But whatever the premises of opposition may be, only the most convincing justification under accepted standards of precedent could suffice to demonstrate that a later decision overruling the first was anything but a surrender to political pressure, and an unjustified repudiation of the principle on which the Court staked its authority in the first instance. So to overrule under fire in the absence of the most compelling reason to reexamine a watershed decision would subvert the Court's legitimacy beyond any serious question. . . .

It is true that diminished legitimacy may be restored, but only slowly. Unlike the political branches, a Court thus weakened could not seek to regain its position with a new mandate from the voters, and even if the Court could somehow go to the polls, the loss of its principled character could not be retrieved by the casting of so many votes. Like the character of an individual, the legitimacy of the Court must be earned over time. So, indeed, must be the character of a Nation of people who aspire to live according to the rule of law. Their belief in themselves as such a people is not readily separable from their understanding of the Court invested with the authority to decide their constitutional cases and speak before all others for their constitutional ideals. If the Court's legitimacy should be undermined, then, so would the country be in its very ability to see itself through its constitutional ideals. The Court's concern with legitimacy is not for the sake of the Court but for the sake of the Nation to which it is responsible.

The Court's duty in the present case is clear. In 1973, it confronted the already-divisive issue of governmental power to limit personal choice to undergo abortion, for which it provided a new resolution based on the due process guaranteed by the Fourteenth Amendment. Whether or not a new social consensus is developing on that issue, its divisiveness is no less today than in 1973, and pressure to overrule the decision, like pressure to retain it, has grown only more intense. A decision to overrule Roe's essential holding under the existing circumstances would address error, if error

there was, at the cost of both profound and unnecessary damage to the Court's legitimacy, and to the Nation's commitment to the rule of law. It is therefore imperative to adhere to the essence of Roe's original decision, and we do so today.

From what we have said so far it follows that it is a constitutional liberty of the woman to have some freedom to terminate her pregnancy. We conclude that the basic decision in Roe was based on a constitutional analysis which we cannot now repudiate. The woman's liberty is not so unlimited, however, that from the outset the State cannot show its concern for the life of the unborn, and at a later point in fetal development the State's interest in life has sufficient force so that the right of the woman to terminate the pregnancy can be restricted.

That brings us, of course, to the point where much criticism has been directed at Roe, a criticism that always inheres when the Court draws a specific rule from what in the Constitution is but a general standard. We conclude, however, that the urgent claims of the woman to retain the ultimate control over her destiny and her body, claims implicit in the meaning of liberty, require us to perform that function. Liberty must not be extinguished for want of a line that is clear. And it falls to us to give some real substance to the woman's liberty to determine whether to carry her pregnancy to full term.

We conclude the line should be drawn at viability, so that before that time the woman has a right to choose to terminate her pregnancy. We adhere to this principle for two reasons. First, as we have said, is the doctrine of *stare decisis*. Any judicial act of line-drawing may seem somewhat arbitrary, but Roe was a reasoned statement, elaborated with great care. We have twice reaffirmed it in the face of great opposition. . . .

The second reason is that the concept of viability, as we noted in Roe, is the time at which there is a realistic possibility of maintaining and nourishing a life outside the womb, so that the independent existence of the second life can in reason and all fairness be the object of state protection that now overrides the rights of the woman. Consistent with other constitutional norms, legislatures may draw lines which appear arbitrary without the necessity of offering a justification. But courts may not. We must justify the lines we draw. And there is no line other than viability which is more workable. To be sure, as we have said, there may be some medical developments that affect the precise point of viability, but this is an imprecision within tolerable limits given that the medical community and all those who must apply its discoveries will continue to explore the matter. The viability line also has, as a practical matter, an element of fairness. In some broad sense, it might be said that a woman who fails to act before viability has consented to the State's intervention on behalf of the developing child.

The woman's right to terminate her pregnancy before viability is the most central principle of *Roe v. Wade.* It is a rule of law and a component of liberty we cannot renounce. . . .

Yet it must be remembered that *Roe v. Wade* speaks with clarity in establishing not only the woman's liberty but also the State's "important and legitimate interest in potential life." That portion of the decision in *Roe* has been given too little acknowledgment and implementation by the Court in its subsequent cases. Those cases decided that any regulation touching upon the abortion decision must survive strict scrutiny, to be sustained only if drawn in narrow terms to further a compelling state interest. Not all of the cases decided under that formulation can be reconciled with the holding in *Roe* itself that the State has legitimate interests in the health of the woman and in protecting the potential life within her. In resolving this tension, we choose to rely upon *Roe,* as against the later cases.

Roe established a trimester framework to govern abortion regulations. Under this elaborate but rigid construct, almost no regulation at all is permitted during the first trimester of pregnancy; regulations designed to protect the woman's health, but not to further the State's interest in potential life, are permitted during the second trimester; and during the third trimester, when the fetus is viable, prohibitions are permitted provided the life or health of the mother is not at stake. Most of our cases since *Roe* have involved the application of rules derived from the trimester framework.

The trimester framework no doubt was erected to ensure that the woman's right to choose not become so subordinate to the State's interest in promoting fetal life that her choice exists in theory but not in fact. We do not agree, however, that the trimester approach is necessary to accomplish this objective. A framework of this rigidity was unnecessary and in its later interpretation sometimes contradicted the State's permissible exercise of its powers.

Though the woman has a right to choose to terminate or continue her pregnancy before viability, it does not at all follow that the State is prohibited from taking steps to ensure that this choice is thoughtful and informed. Even in the earliest stages of pregnancy, the State may enact rules and regulations designed to encourage her to know that there are philosophic and social arguments of great weight that can be brought to bear in favor of continuing the pregnancy to full term and that there are procedures and institutions to allow adoption of unwanted children as well as a certain degree of state assistance if the mother chooses to raise the child herself. "[T]he Constitution does not forbid a State or city, pursuant to democratic processes, from expressing a preference for normal childbirth." . . .

It follows that States are free to enact laws to provide a reasonable framework for a woman to make a decision that has such profound and lasting meaning. This, too, we find consistent with *Roe*'s central premises, and indeed the inevitable consequence of our holding that the State has an interest in protecting the life of the unborn.

We reject the trimester framework, which we do not consider to be part of the essential holding of *Roe.* . . . Measures aimed at ensuring that a woman's choice contemplates the consequences for the fetus do not necessarily interfere with the right recognized in *Roe,* although those measures have been found to be inconsistent with the rigid trimester framework announced in that case. A logical reading of the central holding in *Roe* itself, and a necessary reconciliation of the liberty of the woman and the interest of the State in promoting prenatal life, require, in our view, that we abandon the trimester framework as a rigid prohibition on all pre-viability regulation aimed at the protection of fetal life. The trimester framework suffers from these basic flaws: in its formulation it misconceives the nature of the pregnant woman's interest; and in practice it undervalues the State's interest in potential life, as recognized in *Roe.*

As our jurisprudence relating to all liberties save perhaps abortion has recognized, not every law which makes a right more difficult to exercise is, *ipso facto,* an infringement of that right. An example clarifies the point. We have held that not every ballot access limitation amounts to an infringement of the right to vote. Rather, the States are granted substantial flexibility in establishing the framework within which voters choose the candidates for whom they wish to vote.

The abortion right is similar. Numerous forms of state regulation might have the incidental effect of increasing the cost or decreasing the availability of medical care, whether for abortion or any other medical procedure. The fact that a law which serves a valid purpose, one not designed to strike at the right itself, has the incidental effect of making it more difficult or more expensive to procure an abortion cannot be enough to invalidate it. Only where state regulation imposes an undue burden on a woman's ability to make this decision does the power of the State reach into the heart of the liberty protected by the Due Process Clause. . . .

The very notion that the State has a substantial interest in potential life leads to the conclusion that not all regulations must be deemed unwarranted. Not all burdens on the right to decide whether to terminate a pregnancy will be undue. In our view, the undue burden standard is the appropriate means of reconciling the State's interest with the woman's constitutionally protected liberty.

The concept of an undue burden has been utilized by the Court as well as individual members of the Court, including two of us, in ways that could be considered inconsistent. Because we set forth a standard of general application to which we intend to adhere, it is important to clarify what is meant by an undue burden.

A finding of an undue burden is a shorthand for the conclusion that a state regulation has the purpose or effect of placing a substantial obstacle in the path of a woman seeking an abortion of a nonviable fetus. A statute with this purpose is invalid because the means chosen by the State to further the interest in potential life must be calculated to inform the woman's free choice, not hinder it. And a statute which, while furthering the interest in potential life or some other valid state interest, has the effect of placing a substantial obstacle in the path of a woman's choice cannot be considered a permissible means of serving its legitimate ends. . . . In our considered judgment, an undue burden is an unconstitutional burden. Understood another way, we answer the question, left open in previous opinions discussing the undue burden formulation, whether a law designed to further the State's interest in fetal life which imposes an undue burden on the woman's decision before fetal viability could be constitutional. The answer is no.

Some guiding principles should emerge. What is at stake is the woman's right to make the ultimate decision, not a right to be insulated from all others in doing so. Regulations which do no more than create a structural mechanism by which the State, or the parent or guardian of a minor, may express profound respect for the life of the unborn are permitted, if they are not a substantial obstacle to the woman's exercise of the right to choose. Unless it has that effect on her right of choice, a state measure designed to persuade her to choose childbirth over abortion will be upheld if reasonably related to that goal. Regulations designed to foster the health of a woman seeking an abortion are valid if they do not constitute an undue burden.

Even when jurists reason from shared premises, some disagreement is inevitable. That is to be expected in the application of any legal standard which must accommodate life's complexity. We do not expect it to be otherwise with respect to the undue burden standard. We give this summary:

(a) To protect the central right recognized by *Roe v. Wade* while at the same time accommodating the State's profound interest in potential life, we will employ the undue burden analysis as explained in this opinion. An undue burden exists, and therefore a provision of law is invalid, if its purpose or effect is to place a substantial obstacle in the path of a woman seeking an abortion before the fetus attains viability.

(b) We reject the rigid trimester framework of *Roe v. Wade.* To promote the State's profound interest in potential life, throughout pregnancy, the State may take measures to ensure that the woman's choice is informed, and measures designed to advance this interest will not be invalidated as long as their purpose is to persuade the woman to choose childbirth over abortion. These measures must not be an undue burden on the right.

(c) As with any medical procedure, the State may enact regulations to further the health or safety of a woman seeking an abortion. Unnecessary health regulations that have the purpose or effect of presenting a substantial obstacle to a woman seeking an abortion impose an undue burden on the right.

(d) Our adoption of the undue burden analysis does not disturb the central holding of *Roe v. Wade,* and we reaffirm that holding. Regardless of whether exceptions are made for particular circumstances, a State may not prohibit any woman from making the ultimate decision to terminate her pregnancy before viability.

(e) We also reaffirm *Roe's* holding that "subsequent to viability, the State in promoting its interest in the potentiality of human life may, if it chooses, regulate, and even proscribe, abortion except where it is necessary, in appropriate medical judgment, for the preservation of the life or health of the mother."

These principles control our assessment of the Pennsylvania statute, and we now turn to the issue of the validity of its challenged provisions.

The Court of Appeals applied what it believed to be the undue burden standard and upheld each of the provisions except for the husband notification requirement. We agree generally with this conclusion, but refine the undue burden analysis in accordance with the principles articulated above. We now consider the separate statutory sections at issue.

Because it is central to the operation of various other requirements, we begin with the statute's definition of medical emergency. Under the statute, a medical emergency is

[t]hat condition which, on the basis of the physician's good faith clinical

judgment, so complicates the medical condition of a pregnant woman as to necessitate the immediate abortion of her pregnancy to avert her death or for which a delay will create serious risk of substantial and irreversible impairment of a major bodily function.

. . . We adhere to that course today, and conclude that, as construed by the Court of Appeals, the medical emergency definition imposes no undue burden on a woman's abortion right.

We next consider the informed consent requirement. Except in a medical emergency, the statute requires that at least 24 hours before performing an abortion a physician inform the woman of the nature of the procedure, the health risks of the abortion and of childbirth, and the "probable gestational age of the unborn child." The physician or a qualified non-physician must inform the woman of the availability of printed materials published by the State describing the fetus and providing information about medical assistance for childbirth, information about child support from the father, and a list of agencies which provide adoption and other services as alternatives to abortion. An abortion may not be performed unless the woman certifies in writing that she has been informed of the availability of these printed materials and has been provided them if she chooses to view them. . . .

We also see no reason why the State may not require doctors to inform a woman seeking an abortion of the availability of materials relating to the consequences to the fetus, even when those consequences have no direct relation to her health. . . . [R]equiring that the woman be informed of the availability of information relating to fetal development and the assistance available should she decide to carry the pregnancy to full term is a reasonable measure to insure an informed choice, one which might cause the woman to choose childbirth over abortion. This requirement cannot be considered a substantial obstacle to obtaining an abortion, and, it follows, there is no undue burden. . . .

All that is left of petitioners' argument is an asserted First Amendment right of a physician not to provide information about the risks of abortion, and childbirth, in a manner mandated by the State. To be sure, the physician's First Amendment rights not to speak are implicated, but only as part of the practice of medicine, subject to reasonable licensing and regulation by the State. We see no constitutional infirmity in the requirement that the physician provide the information mandated by the State here.

. . . Our analysis of Pennsylvania's 24-hour waiting period between the provision of the information deemed necessary to informed consent and the performance of an abortion under the undue burden standard requires us to reconsider the premise behind the decision in *Akron I* invalidating a parallel requirement. In *Akron I* we said: "Nor are we convinced that the State's legitimate concern that the woman's decision be informed is reasonably served by requiring a 24-hour delay as a matter of course." We consider that conclusion to be wrong. The idea that important decisions will be more informed and deliberate if they follow some period of reflection does not strike us as unreasonable, particularly where the statute directs that important information become part of the background of the decision. The statute, as construed by the Court of Appeals, permits avoidance of the waiting period in the event of a medical emergency and the record evidence shows that in the vast majority of cases, a 24-hour delay does not create any appreciable health risk. In theory, at least, the waiting period is a reasonable measure to implement the State's interest in protecting the life of the unborn, a measure that does not amount to an undue burden. . . .

. . . Pennsylvania's abortion law provides, except in cases of medical emergency, that no physician shall perform an abortion on a married woman without receiving a signed statement from the woman that she has notified her spouse that she is about to undergo an abortion. The woman has the option of providing an alternative signed statement certifying that her husband is not the man who impregnated her; that her husband could not be located; that the pregnancy is the result of spousal sexual assault which she has reported; or that the woman believes that notifying her husband will cause

him or someone else to inflict bodily injury upon her. A physician who performs an abortion on a married woman without receiving the appropriate signed statement will have his or her license revoked, and is liable to the husband for damages. . . . [T]here are millions of women in this country who are the victims of regular physical and psychological abuse at the hands of their husbands. Should these women become pregnant, they may have very good reasons for not wishing to inform their husbands of their decision to obtain an abortion. . . .

The spousal notification requirement is thus likely to prevent a significant number of women from obtaining an abortion. It does not merely make abortions a little more difficult or expensive to obtain; for many women, it will impose a substantial obstacle. We must not blind ourselves to the fact that the significant number of women who fear for their safety and the safety of their children are likely to be deterred from procuring an abortion as surely as if the Commonwealth had outlawed abortion in all cases. . . .

The husband's interest in the life of the child his wife is carrying does not permit the State to empower him with . . . authority over his wife. The contrary view leads to consequences reminiscent of the common law. A husband has no enforceable right to require a wife to advise him before she exercises her personal choices. If a husband's interest in the potential life of the child outweighs a wife's liberty, the State could require a married woman to notify her husband before she uses a postfertilization contraceptive. Perhaps next in line would be a statute requiring pregnant married women to notify their husbands before engaging in conduct causing risk to the fetus. After all, if the husband's interest in the fetus's safety is a sufficient predicate for state regulation, the State could reasonably conclude that pregnant wives should notify their husbands before drinking alcohol or smoking. Perhaps married women should notify their husbands before using contraceptives or before undergoing any type of surgery that may have complications affecting the husband's interest in his wife's reproductive organs. . . . A State may not give to a man the kind of dominion over his wife that parents exercise over their children.

[The act] embodies a view of marriage consonant with the common law status of married women but repugnant to our present understanding of marriage and of the nature of the rights secured by the Constitution. Women do not lose their constitutionally protected liberty when they marry. The Constitution protects all individuals, male or female, married or unmarried, from the abuse of governmental power, even where that power is employed for the supposed benefit of a member of the individual's family. These considerations confirm our conclusion that the spousal notification provision is invalid.

We next consider the parental consent provision. Except in a medical emergency, an unemancipated young woman under 18 may not obtain an abortion unless she and one of her parents (or guardian) provides informed consent as defined above. If neither a parent nor a guardian provides consent, a court may authorize the performance of an abortion upon a determination that the young woman is mature and capable of giving informed consent and has in fact given her informed consent, or that an abortion would be in her best interests.

We have been over most of this ground before. Our cases establish, and we reaffirm today, that a State may require a minor seeking an abortion to obtain the consent of a parent or guardian, provided that there is an adequate judicial bypass procedure. Under these precedents, in our view, the one-parent consent requirement and judicial bypass procedure are constitutional. . . .

Under the recordkeeping and reporting requirements of the statute, every facility which performs abortions is required to file a report stating its name and address as well as the name and address of any related entity, such as a controlling or subsidiary organization. In the case of state-funded institutions, the information becomes public.

For each abortion performed, a report must be filed identifying: the physician (and the second physician where required); the facility; the referring physician or agency; the woman's age; the number of prior pregnancies and prior abortions she has had; gestational age; the type of abortion procedure; the date of the abortion; whether there were any pre-existing medical conditions which would complicate pregnancy; medical complications with the abortion; where applicable, the basis for the determination that the abortion was medically necessary; the weight of the aborted fetus; and whether the woman was married, and if so, whether notice was provided or the basis for the failure to give notice. Every abortion facility must also file quarterly reports showing the number of abortions performed broken down by trimester. In all events, the identity of each woman who has had an abortion remains confidential. . . .

We think that all the provisions at issue here except that relating to spousal notice are constitutional. Although they do not relate to the State's interest in informing the woman's choice, they do relate to health. The collection of information with respect to actual patients is a vital element of medical research, and so it cannot be said that the requirements serve no purpose other than to make abortions more difficult. Nor do we find that the requirements impose a substantial obstacle to a woman's choice. At most they might increase the cost of some abortions by a slight amount. While at some point increased cost could become a substantial obstacle, there is no such showing on the record before us. . . .

Our Constitution is a covenant running from the first generation of Americans to us and then to future generations. It is a coherent succession. Each generation must learn anew that the Constitution's written terms embody ideas and aspirations that must survive more ages than one. We accept our responsibility not to retreat from interpreting the full meaning of the covenant in light of all of our precedents. We invoke it once again to define the freedom guaranteed by the Constitution's own promise of liberty.

The judgment . . . is affirmed in part and reversed in part, and the case is remanded for proceedings consistent with this opinion, including consideration of the question of severability.

JUSTICE STEVENS, concurring in part and dissenting in part.

Serious questions arise when a State attempts to "persuade the woman to choose childbirth over abortion." Decisional autonomy must limit the State's power to inject into a woman's most personal deliberations its own views of what is best. The State may promote its preferences by funding childbirth, by creating and maintaining alternatives to abortion, and by espousing the virtues of family; but it must respect the individual's freedom to make such judgments.

The 24-hour waiting period required by . . . the Pennsylvania statute raises even more serious concerns. [E]ven in those cases in which the delay is not especially onerous, it is, in my opinion, "undue" because there is no evidence that such a delay serves a useful and legitimate purpose. [T]here is no legitimate reason to require a woman who has agonized over her decision to leave the clinic or hospital and return again another day. While a general requirement that a physician notify her patients about the risks of a proposed medical procedure is appropriate, a rigid requirement that all patients wait 24 hours or (what is true in practice) much longer to evaluate the significance of information that is either common knowledge or irrelevant is an irrational and, therefore, "undue" burden.

JUSTICE BLACKMUN, concurring in part, concurring in the judgment in part, and dissenting in part.

. . . Today, no less than yesterday, the Constitution and decisions of this Court require that a State's abortion restrictions be subjected to the strictest of judicial scrutiny. Our precedents and the joint opinion's principles require us to subject all non–*de minimis* abortion regulations to strict scrutiny. Under this standard, the Pennsylvania statute's provisions requiring content-based counseling, a 24-hour delay, informed parental consent, and reporting of abortion-related information must be invalidated.

. . . Strict scrutiny of state limitations on reproductive choice still offers the most secure protection of the woman's right to make her own reproductive decisions, free from state coercion. No majority of this Court has ever agreed upon an alternative approach. The factual premises of the trimester framework have not been undermined, and the *Roe* framework is far more administrable, and far less manipu-

lable, than the "undue burden" standard adopted by the joint opinion. . . . *Roe*'s requirement of strict scrutiny as implemented through a trimester framework should not be disturbed. No other approach has gained a majority, and no other is more protective of the woman's fundamental right. Lastly, no other approach properly accommodates the woman's constitutional right with the State's legitimate interests. . . .

If there is much reason to applaud the advances made by the joint opinion today, there is far more to fear from the Chief Justice's opinion. The Chief Justice's criticism of *Roe* follows from his stunted conception of individual liberty. While recognizing that the Due Process Clause protects more than simple physical liberty, he then goes on to construe this Court's personal-liberty cases as establishing only a laundry list of particular rights, rather than a principled account of how these particular rights are grounded in a more general right of privacy. This constricted view is reinforced by the Chief Justice's exclusive reliance on tradition as a source of fundamental rights. . . .

In one sense, the Court's approach is worlds apart from that of the Chief Justice and Justice Scalia. And yet, in another sense, the distance between the two approaches is short—the distance is but a single vote.

I am 83 years old. I cannot remain on this Court forever, and when I do step down, the confirmation process for my successor well may focus on the issue before us today. That, I regret, may be exactly where the choice between the two worlds will be made.

THE CHIEF JUSTICE, with whom JUSTICE WHITE, JUSTICE SCALIA, and JUSTICE THOMAS join, concurring in the judgment in part and dissenting in part.

The joint opinion, following its newly minted variation on *stare decisis,* retains the outer shell of *Roe v. Wade* (1973), but beats a wholesale retreat from the substance of that case. We believe that *Roe* was wrongly decided, and that it can and should be overruled consistently with our traditional approach to *stare decisis* in constitutional cases. We would adopt the approach of the plurality in *Webster v.*

Reproductive Health Services (1989), and uphold the challenged provisions of the Pennsylvania statute in their entirety. . . .

The joint opinion of Justices O'Connor, Kennedy, and Souter cannot bring itself to say that *Roe* was correct as an original matter, but the authors are of the view that the immediate question is not the soundness of *Roe*'s resolution of the issue, but the precedential force that must be accorded to its holding. Instead of claiming that *Roe* was correct as a matter of original constitutional interpretation, the opinion therefore contains an elaborate discussion of *stare decisis.* This discussion of the principle of *stare decisis* appears to be almost entirely *dicta,* because the joint opinion does not apply that principle in dealing with *Roe. Roe* decided that a woman had a fundamental right to an abortion. The joint opinion rejects that view. *Roe* decided that abortion regulations were to be subjected to "strict scrutiny" and could be justified only in the light of "compelling state interests." The joint opinion rejects that view. *Roe* analyzed abortion regulation under a rigid trimester framework, a framework which has guided this Court's decisionmaking for 19 years. The joint opinion rejects that framework. . . . While purporting to adhere to precedent, the joint opinion instead revises it. *Roe* continues to exist, but only in the way a storefront on a western movie set exists: a mere facade to give the illusion of reality.

The joint opinion discusses several *stare decisis* factors which, it asserts, point toward retaining a portion of *Roe.* Two of these factors are that the main "factual underpinning" of *Roe* has remained the same, and that its doctrinal foundation is no weaker now than it was in 1973. Of course, what might be called the basic facts which give rise to *Roe* have remained the same—women become pregnant, there is a point somewhere, depending on medical technology, where a fetus becomes viable, and women give birth to children. But this is only to say that the same facts which gave rise to *Roe* will continue to give rise to similar cases. It is not a reason, in and of itself, why those cases must be decided in the same incorrect manner as was the first case to deal with the question. And surely there is no requirement, in considering whether to depart from *stare decisis* in a constitutional case, that a decision be more wrong now than it was at the time it was rendered. If that were true, the most outlandish constitutional decision could survive forever, based simply on the fact that it was no more outlandish later than it was when originally rendered.

Nor does the joint opinion faithfully follow this alleged requirement. The opinion frankly concludes that *Roe* and its progeny were wrong in failing to recognize that the State's interests in maternal health and in the protection of unborn human life exist throughout pregnancy. But there is no indication that these components of *Roe* are any more incorrect at this juncture than they were at its inception. . . .

In the end, having failed to put forth any evidence to prove any true reliance, the joint opinion's argument is based solely on generalized assertions about the national psyche, on a belief that the people of this country have grown accustomed to the *Roe* decision over the last 19 years and have "ordered their thinking and living around" it. As an initial matter, one might inquire how the joint opinion can view the "central holding" of *Roe* as so deeply rooted in our constitutional culture, when it so casually uproots and disposes of that same decision's trimester framework. Furthermore, at various points in the past, the same could have been said about this Court's erroneous decisions that the Constitution allowed "separate but equal" treatment of minorities, see *Plessy v. Ferguson* (1896), or that "liberty" under the Due Process Clause protected "freedom of contract." See *Adkins v. Children's Hospital* (1923). . . .

Apparently realizing that conventional *stare decisis* principles do not support its position, the joint opinion advances a belief that retaining a portion of *Roe* is necessary to protect the "legitimacy" of this Court. Because the Court must take care to render decisions "grounded truly in principle," and not simply as political and social compromises, the joint opinion properly declares it to be this Court's duty to ignore the public criticism and protest that may arise as a result of a decision. Few would quarrel with this statement, although it may be doubted that Members of this Court, holding their tenure as they do during constitutional "good behavior," are at all likely to be intimidated by such public protests.

But the joint opinion goes on to state that when the Court "resolve[s] the sort of intensely divisive controversy reflected in *Roe* and those rare, comparable cases," its decision is exempt from reconsideration under established principles of *stare decisis* in constitutional cases. This is so, the joint opinion contends, because in those "intensely divisive" cases, the Court has "call[ed] the contending sides of a national controversy to end their national division by accepting a common mandate rooted in the Constitution," and must therefore take special care not to be perceived as "surrender[ing] to political pressure" and continued opposition. This is a truly novel principle, one which is contrary to both the Court's historical practice and to the Court's traditional willingness to tolerate criticism of its opinions. Under this principle, when the Court has ruled on a divisive issue, it is apparently prevented from overruling that decision for the sole reason that it was incorrect, unless opposition to the original decision has died away. . . .

There are other reasons why the joint opinion's discussion of legitimacy is unconvincing as well. In assuming that the Court is perceived as "surrender[ing] to political pressure" when it overrules a controversial decision, the joint opinion forgets that there are two sides to any controversy. The joint opinion asserts that, in order to protect its legitimacy, the Court must refrain from overruling a controversial decision lest it be viewed as favoring those who oppose the decision. But a decision to adhere to prior precedent is subject to the same criticism, for in such a case one can easily argue that the Court is responding to those who have demonstrated in favor of the original decision. The decision in *Roe* has engendered large demonstrations, including repeated marches on this Court and on Congress, both in opposition to and in support of that opinion. A decision either way on *Roe* can therefore be perceived as favoring one group or the other. But this perceived dilemma arises only if one assumes, as the joint opinion does, that the Court should make its decisions with a view toward speculative public perceptions.

If one assumes instead, that the Court's legitimacy is enhanced by faithful interpretation of the Constitution irrespective of public opposition, such self-engendered difficulties may be put to one side.

Roe is not this Court's only decision to generate conflict. Our decisions in some recent capital cases, and in *Bowers v. Hardwick* (1986), have also engendered demonstrations in opposition. The joint opinion's message to such protesters appears to be that they must cease their activities in order to serve their cause, because their protests will only cement in place a decision which by normal standards of *stare decisis* should be reconsidered. . . . Strong and often misguided criticism of a decision should not render the decision immune from reconsideration, lest a fetish for legitimacy penalize freedom of expression.

The end result of the joint opinion's paeans of praise for legitimacy is the enunciation of a brand new standard for evaluating state regulation of a woman's right to abortion—the "undue burden" standard. As indicated above, *Roe v. Wade* adopted a "fundamental right" standard under which state regulations could survive only if they met the requirement of "strict scrutiny." While we disagree with that standard, it at least had a recognized basis in constitutional law at the time *Roe* was decided. The same cannot be said for the "undue burden" standard, which is created largely out of whole cloth by the authors of the joint opinion. It is a standard which even today does not command the support of a majority of this Court. And it will not, we believe, result in the sort of "simple limitation," easily applied, which the joint opinion anticipates. In sum, it is a standard which is not built to last.

In evaluating abortion regulations under that standard, judges will have to decide whether they place a "substantial obstacle" in the path of a woman seeking an abortion. In that this standard is based even more on a judge's subjective determinations than was the trimester framework, the standard will do nothing to prevent "judges from roaming at large in the constitutional field" guided only by their personal views. Because the undue burden standard is plucked from nowhere, the question of what is a "substantial obstacle" to abortion will undoubtedly engender a variety of conflicting views. For example, in the very matter before us now, the authors of the joint opinion would uphold Pennsylvania's 24-hour waiting period, concluding that a "particular burden" on some women is not a substantial obstacle. But the authors would at the same time strike down Pennsylvania's spousal notice provision, after finding that in a "large fraction" of cases the provision will be a substantial obstacle. And, while the authors conclude that the informed consent provisions do not constitute an "undue burden," Justice Stevens would hold that they do.

Furthermore, while striking down the spousal notice regulation, the joint opinion would uphold a parental consent restriction that certainly places very substantial obstacles in the path of a minor's abortion choice. The joint opinion is forthright in admitting that it draws this distinction based on a policy judgment that parents will have the best interests of their children at heart, while the same is not necessarily true of husbands as to their wives. This may or may not be a correct judgment, but it is quintessentially a legislative one. The "undue burden" inquiry does not in any way supply the distinction between parental consent and spousal consent which the joint opinion adopts. . . .

The sum of the joint opinion's labors in the name of *stare decisis* and "legitimacy" is this: *Roe v. Wade* stands as a sort of judicial Potemkin Village, which may be pointed out to passersby as a monument to the importance of adhering to precedent. But behind the facade, an entirely new method of analysis, without any roots in constitutional law, is imported to decide the constitutionality of state laws regulating abortion. Neither *stare decisis* nor "legitimacy" are truly served by such an effort.

We have stated above our belief that the Constitution does not subject state abortion regulations to heightened scrutiny. Accordingly, we think that the correct analysis is that . . . [a] woman's interest in having an abortion is a form of liberty protected by the Due Process Clause, but States may regulate abortion procedures in ways rationally related to a legitimate state interest. . . .

[With this rule in mind] . . . we therefore would hold that each of the challenged provisions of the Pennsylvania statute is consistent with the Constitution. It bears emphasis that our conclusion in this regard does not carry with it any necessary approval of these regulations. Our task is, as always, to decide only whether the challenged provisions of a law comport with the United States Constitution. If, as we believe, these do, their wisdom as a matter of public policy is for the people of Pennsylvania to decide.

JUSTICE SCALIA, with whom THE CHIEF JUSTICE, JUSTICE WHITE, and JUSTICE THOMAS join, concurring in the judgment in part and dissenting in part.

The States may, if they wish, permit abortion-on-demand, but the Constitution does not require them to do so. The permissibility of abortion, and the limitations upon it, are to be resolved like most important questions in our democracy: by citizens trying to persuade one another and then voting. As the Court acknowledges, "where reasonable people disagree the government can adopt one position or the other." The Court is correct in adding the qualification that this "assumes a state of affairs in which the choice does not intrude upon a protected liberty"—but the crucial part of that qualification is the penultimate word. A State's choice between two positions on which reasonable people can disagree is constitutional even when (as is often the case) it intrudes upon a "liberty" in the absolute sense. Laws against bigamy, for example— which entire societies of reasonable people disagree with—intrude upon men and women's liberty to marry and live with one another. But bigamy happens not to be a liberty specially "protected" by the Constitution.

That is, quite simply, the issue in this case: not whether the power of a woman to abort her unborn child is a "liberty" in the absolute sense; or even whether it is a liberty of great importance to many women. Of course it is both. The issue is whether it is a liberty protected by the Constitution of the United States. I am sure it is not. I reach that conclusion not because of anything so exalted as my views concerning the "concept of existence, of meaning, of the universe, and of the mystery of human life." Rather, I reach it for the same reason I reach the conclusion that bigamy is not constitutionally protected—because of two simple facts: (1) the Constitution says absolutely nothing about it, and (2) the long-standing traditions of American society have permitted it to be legally proscribed. . . .

I cannot agree with, indeed I am appalled by, the Court's suggestion that the decision whether to stand by an erroneous constitutional decision must be strongly influenced—against overruling, no less—by the substantial and continuing public opposition the decision has generated. The Court's judgment that any other course would "subvert the Court's legitimacy" must be another consequence of reading the error-filled history book that described the deeply divided country brought together by *Roe.* In my history book, the Court was covered with dishonor and deprived of legitimacy by *Dred Scott v. Sandford* (1857), an erroneous (and widely opposed) opinion that it did not abandon, rather than by *West Coast Hotel Co. v. Parrish* (1937), which produced the famous "switch in time" from the Court's erroneous (and widely opposed) constitutional opposition to the social measures of the New Deal. (Both *Dred Scott* and one line of the cases resisting the New Deal rested upon the concept of "substantive due process" that the Court praises and employs today.)

In truth, I am as distressed as the Court is about the "political pressure" directed to the Court: the marches, the mail, the protests aimed at inducing us to change our opinions. How upsetting it is, that so many of our citizens (good people, not lawless ones, on both sides of this abortion issue, and on various sides of other issues as well) think that we Justices should properly take into account their views, as though we were engaged not in ascertaining an objective law but in determining some kind of social consensus. The Court would profit, I think, from giving less attention to the fact of this distressing phenomenon, and more attention to the cause of it. That cause permeates today's opinion: a new mode of constitutional adjudication that relies not upon text and traditional practice to

determine the law, but upon what the Court calls "reasoned judgment," which turns out to be nothing but philosophical predilection and moral intuition. All manner of "liberties," the Court tells us, inhere in the Constitution and are enforceable by this Court—not just those mentioned in the text or established in the traditions of our society.

What makes all this relevant to the bothersome application of "political pressure" against the Court are the twin facts that the American people love democracy and the American people are not fools. As long as this Court thought (and the people thought) that we Justices were doing essentially lawyers' work up here—reading text and discerning our society's traditional understanding of that text—the public pretty much left us alone. Texts and traditions are facts to study, not convictions to demonstrate about. But if in reality our process of constitutional adjudication consists primarily of making value judgments; if we can ignore a long and clear tradition clarifying an ambiguous text; . . . if, as I say, our pronouncement of constitutional law rests primarily on value judgments, then a free and intelligent people's attitude towards us can be expected to be (ought to be) quite different. The people know that their value judgments are quite as good as those taught in any law school—maybe better. If, indeed, the "liberties" protected by the Constitution are, as the Court says, undefined and unbounded, then the people should demonstrate, to protest that we do not implement their values instead of ours. Not only that, but confirmation hearings for new Justices should deteriorate into question-and-answer sessions in which Senators go through a list of their constituents' most favored and most disfavored alleged constitutional rights, and seek the nominee's commitment to support or oppose them. Value judgments, after all, should be voted on, not dictated; and if our Constitution has somehow accidentally committed them to the Supreme Court, at least we can have a sort of plebiscite each time a new nominee to that body is put forward. Justice Blackmun not only regards this prospect with equanimity, he solicits it.

Gonzales v. Carhart
550 U.S. 124 (2007)

Following the Supreme Court's decision in Stenberg v. Carhart *(2000) that Nebraska's "partial birth abortion" statute violated the federal Constitution, as interpreted in* Planned Parenthood of Southeastern Pennsylvania v. Casey *(1992), and* Roe v. Wade *(1973), Congress passed the Partial-Birth Abortion Ban Act of 2003 to proscribe a particular method of ending fetal life in the later stages of pregnancy. The specific provisions of the act are spelled out in the majority opinion below. In* Gonzales v. Carhart, *the US District Court for the District of Nebraska found the act unconstitutional because, inter alia, it lacked an exception allowing the prohibited procedure where necessary for the mother's health. The Eighth Circuit affirmed, finding that a lack of consensus existed in the medical community as to the banned procedure's necessity, and thus Stenberg required legislatures to err on the side of protecting women's health by including a health exception. In the companion case of* Gonzales v. Planned Parenthood Federation of America, *the District Court for the Northern District of California likewise concluded that the act was unconstitutional on its face because it unduly burdened a woman's ability to choose a second-trimester abortion, was too vague, and lacked a health exception as required by Stenberg. The Ninth Circuit also agreed and affirmed. The Supreme Court granted certiorari.* Opinion of the Court: <u>Kennedy,</u> Roberts, Scalia, Thomas, Alito. Concurring opinion: <u>Thomas,</u> Scalia. Dissenting opinion: <u>Ginsburg,</u> Stevens, Souter, Breyer.

JUSTICE KENNEDY delivered the opinion of the Court.

These cases require us to consider the validity of the Partial-Birth Abortion Ban Act of 2003, a federal statute regulating abortion procedures. In recitations preceding its operative provisions the Act refers to the Court's opinion in *Stenberg v. Carhart* (2000), which also addressed the subject of abortion procedures used in the later stages of pregnancy. Compared to the state statute at issue in *Stenberg*, the Act is more specific concerning the instances to which it applies and in this respect more

precise in its coverage. We conclude the Act should be sustained against the objections lodged by the broad, facial attack brought against it. . . .

I

The Act proscribes a particular manner of ending fetal life, so it is necessary here, as it was in *Stenberg*, to discuss abortion procedures in some detail. Three United States District Courts heard extensive evidence describing the procedures. In addition to the two courts involved in the instant cases the District Court for the Southern District of New York also considered the constitutionality of the Act. *National Abortion Federation v. Ashcroft* (2004). It found the Act unconstitutional and the Court of Appeals for the Second Circuit affirmed, *National Abortion Federation v. Gonzales* (2006). The three District Courts relied on similar medical evidence; indeed, much of the evidence submitted to the *Carhart* court previously had been submitted to the other two courts. We refer to the District Courts' exhaustive opinions in our own discussion of abortion procedures.

Abortion methods vary depending to some extent on the preferences of the physician and, of course, on the term of the pregnancy and the resulting stage of the unborn child's development. Between 85 and 90 percent of the approximately 1.3 million abortions performed each year in the United States take place in the first three months of pregnancy, which is to say in the first trimester. The most common first-trimester abortion method is vacuum aspiration (otherwise known as suction curettage) in which the physician vacuums out the embryonic tissue. Early in this trimester an alternative is to use medication, such as mifepristone (commonly known as RU-486), to terminate the pregnancy. The Act does not regulate these procedures.

Of the remaining abortions that take place each year, most occur in the second trimester. The surgical procedure referred to as "dilation and evacuation" or "D&E" is the usual abortion method in this trimester. Although individual techniques for performing D&E differ, the general steps are the same.

A doctor must first dilate the cervix at least to the extent needed to insert surgical instruments into the uterus and to maneuver them to evacuate the fetus. The steps taken to cause dilation differ by physician and gestational age of the fetus. A doctor often begins the dilation process by inserting osmotic dilators, such as laminaria (sticks of seaweed), into the cervix. The dilators can be used in combination with drugs, such as misoprostol, that increase dilation. The resulting amount of dilation is not uniform, and a doctor does not know in advance how an individual patient will respond. In general the longer dilators remain in the cervix, the more it will dilate. Yet the length of time doctors employ osmotic dilators varies. Some may keep dilators in the cervix for two days, while others use dilators for a day or less.

After sufficient dilation the surgical operation can commence. The woman is placed under general anesthesia or conscious sedation. The doctor, often guided by ultrasound, inserts grasping forceps through the woman's cervix and into the uterus to grab the fetus. The doctor grips a fetal part with the forceps and pulls it back through the cervix and vagina, continuing to pull even after meeting resistance from the cervix. The friction causes the fetus to tear apart. For example, a leg might be ripped off the fetus as it is pulled through the cervix and out of the woman. The process of evacuating the fetus piece by piece continues until it has been completely removed. A doctor may make 10 to 15 passes with the forceps to evacuate the fetus in its entirety, though sometimes removal is completed with fewer passes. Once the fetus has been evacuated, the placenta and any remaining fetal material are suctioned or scraped out of the uterus. The doctor examines the different parts to ensure the entire fetal body has been removed.

Some doctors, especially later in the second trimester, may kill the fetus a day or two before performing the surgical evacuation. They inject digoxin or potassium chloride into the fetus, the umbilical cord, or the amniotic fluid. Fetal demise may cause contractions and make

greater dilation possible. Once dead, moreover, the fetus' body will soften, and its removal will be easier. Other doctors refrain from injecting chemical agents, believing it adds risk with little or no medical benefit.

The abortion procedure that was the impetus for the numerous bans on "partial-birth abortion," including the Act, is a variation of this standard D&E. The medical community has not reached unanimity on the appropriate name for this D&E variation. It has been referred to as "intact D&E," "dilation and extraction" (D&X), and "intact D&X." For discussion purposes this D&E variation will be referred to as intact D&E. The main difference between the two procedures is that in intact D&E a doctor extracts the fetus intact or largely intact with only a few passes. There are no comprehensive statistics indicating what percentage of all D&Es are performed in this manner.

Intact D&E, like regular D&E, begins with dilation of the cervix. Sufficient dilation is essential for the procedure. To achieve intact extraction some doctors thus may attempt to dilate the cervix to a greater degree. This approach has been called "serial" dilation. Doctors who attempt at the outset to perform intact D&E may dilate for two full days or use up to 25 osmotic dilators.

In an intact D&E procedure the doctor extracts the fetus in a way conducive to pulling out its entire body, instead of ripping it apart. One doctor, for example, testified: "If I know I have good dilation and I reach in and the fetus starts to come out and I think I can accomplish it, the abortion with an intact delivery, then I use my forceps a little bit differently. I don't close them quite so much, and I just gently draw the tissue out attempting to have an intact delivery, if possible."

Rotating the fetus as it is being pulled decreases the odds of dismemberment. A doctor also "may use forceps to grasp a fetal part, pull it down, and re-grasp the fetus at a higher level—sometimes using both his hand and a forceps—to exert traction to retrieve the fetus intact until the head is lodged in the [cervix]."

Intact D&E gained public notoriety when, in 1992, Dr. Martin Haskell gave a presentation describing his method of performing the operation. In the usual intact D&E the fetus' head lodges in the cervix, and dilation is insufficient to allow it to pass. Haskell explained the next step as follows:

At this point, the right-handed surgeon slides the fingers of the left [hand] along the back of the fetus and "hooks" the shoulders of the fetus with the index and ring fingers (palm down).

While maintaining this tension, lifting the cervix and applying traction to the shoulders with the fingers of the left hand, the surgeon takes a pair of blunt curved Metzenbaum scissors in the right hand. He carefully advances the tip, curved down, along the spine and under his middle finger until he feels it contact the base of the skull under the tip of his middle finger.

The surgeon then forces the scissors into the base of the skull or into the foramen magnum. Having safely entered the skull, he spreads the scissors to enlarge the opening.

The surgeon removes the scissors and introduces a suction catheter into this hole and evacuates the skull contents. With the catheter still in place, he applies traction to the fetus, removing it completely from the patient.

This is an abortion doctor's clinical description. Here is another description from a nurse who witnessed the same method performed on a 26-week fetus and who testified before the Senate Judiciary Committee:

Dr. Haskell went in with forceps and grabbed the baby's legs and pulled them down into the birth canal. Then he delivered the baby's body and the arms—everything but the head. The doctor kept the head right inside the uterus. . . .

The baby's little fingers were clasping and unclasping, and his little feet were kicking. Then the doctor stuck the scissors in the back of his head, and the baby's arms jerked out, like a startle reaction, like a flinch, like a baby does when he thinks he is going to fall.

The doctor opened up the scissors, stuck a high-powered suction tube into the opening, and sucked the baby's brains out. Now the baby went completely limp. . . .

He cut the umbilical cord and delivered the placenta. He threw the baby in a pan, along with the placenta and the instruments he had just used.

Dr. Haskell's approach is not the only method of killing the fetus once its head lodges in the cervix, and "the process has evolved" since his presentation. Another doctor, for example, squeezes the skull after it has been pierced "so that enough brain tissue exudes to allow the head to pass through." Still other physicians reach into the cervix with their forceps and crush the fetus' skull. Others continue to pull the fetus out of the woman until it disarticulates at the neck, in effect decapitating it. These doctors then grasp the head with forceps, crush it, and remove it.

Some doctors performing an intact D&E attempt to remove the fetus without collapsing the skull. Yet one doctor would not allow delivery of a live fetus younger than 24 weeks because "the objective of [his] procedure is to perform an abortion," not a birth. The doctor thus answered in the affirmative when asked whether he would "hold the fetus' head on the internal side of the [cervix] in order to collapse the skull" and kill the fetus before it is born. Another doctor testified he crushes a fetus' skull not only to reduce its size but also to ensure the fetus is dead before it is removed. For the staff to have to deal with a fetus that has "some viability to it, some movement of limbs," according to this doctor, "[is] always a difficult situation."

D&E and intact D&E are not the only second-trimester abortion methods. Doctors also may abort a fetus through medical induction. The doctor medicates the woman to induce labor, and contractions occur to deliver the fetus. Induction, which unlike D&E should occur in a hospital, can last as little as 6 hours but can take longer than 48. It accounts for about five percent of second-trimester abortions before 20 weeks of gestation and 15 percent of those after 20 weeks. Doctors turn to two other methods of second-trimester abortion, hysterotomy and hysterectomy, only in emergency situations because they carry increased risk of complications. In a hysterotomy, as in a cesarean section, the doctor removes the fetus by making an incision through the abdomen and uterine wall to gain access to the uterine cavity. A hysterectomy requires the removal of the entire uterus. These two procedures represent about .07% of second-trimester abortions.

After Dr. Haskell's procedure received public attention, with ensuing and increasing public concern, bans on "'partial birth abortion'" proliferated. By the time of the *Stenberg* decision, about 30 States had enacted bans designed to prohibit the procedure. In 1996, Congress also acted to ban partial-birth abortion. President Clinton vetoed the congressional legislation, and the Senate failed to override the veto. Congress approved another bill banning the procedure in 1997, but President Clinton again vetoed it. In 2003, after this Court's decision in *Stenberg*, Congress passed the Act at issue here. On November 5, 2003, President Bush signed the Act into law. It was to take effect the following day.

The Act responded to *Stenberg* in two ways. First, Congress made factual findings. Congress determined that this Court in *Stenberg* "was required to accept the very questionable findings issued by the district court judge" but that Congress was "not bound to accept the same factual findings." Congress found, among other things, that "[a] moral, medical, and ethical consensus exists that the practice of performing a partial-birth abortion . . . is a gruesome and inhumane procedure that is never medically necessary and should be prohibited."

Second, and more relevant here, the Act's language differs from that of the Nebraska statute struck down in *Stenberg*. The operative provisions of the Act provide in relevant part:

(a) Any physician who, in or affecting interstate or foreign commerce, knowingly performs a partial-birth abortion and thereby kills a human fetus shall be fined under this title or imprisoned not more than 2 years, or both. This subsection does not apply to a partial-birth abortion that is necessary to save the life of a mother whose life is endangered by a physical disorder, physical illness, or physical injury, including a life-endangering physical condition caused by or arising from the pregnancy itself. This subsection takes effect 1 day after the enactment.

(b) As used in this section—

(1) the term 'partial-birth abortion' means an abortion in which the person performing the abortion—

(A) deliberately and intentionally vaginally delivers a living fetus until, in the case of a head-first presentation, the entire fetal head is outside the body of the mother, or, in the case of breech presentation, any part of the fetal trunk past the navel is outside the body of the mother, for the purpose of performing an overt act that the person knows will kill the partially delivered living fetus; and

(B) performs the overt act, other than completion of delivery, that kills the partially delivered living fetus; and

(2) the term 'physician' means a doctor of medicine or osteopathy legally authorized to practice medicine and surgery by the State in which the doctor performs such activity, or any other individual legally authorized by the State to perform abortions: *Provided, however,* that any individual who is not a physician or not otherwise legally authorized by the State to perform abortions, but who nevertheless directly performs a partial-birth abortion, shall be subject to the provisions of this section.

    . . . .

(d) (1) A defendant accused of an offense under this section may seek a hearing before the State Medical Board on whether the physician's conduct was necessary to save the life of the mother whose life was endangered by a physical disorder, physical illness, or physical injury, including a life-endangering physical condition caused by or arising from the pregnancy itself.

(2) The findings on that issue are admissible on that issue at the trial of the defendant. Upon a motion of the defendant, the court shall delay the beginning of the trial for not more than 30 days to permit such a hearing to take place.

(e) A woman upon whom a partial-birth abortion is performed may not be prosecuted under this section, for a conspiracy to violate this section, or for an offense under section 2, 3, or 4 of this title based on a violation of this section.

The District Court in *Carhart* concluded the Act was unconstitutional for two reasons. First, it determined the Act was unconstitutional because it lacked an exception allowing the procedure where necessary for the health of the mother. Second, the District Court found the Act deficient because it covered not merely intact D&E but also certain other D&Es.

The Court of Appeals for the Eighth Circuit addressed only the lack of a health exception. The court began its analysis with what it saw as the appropriate question—"whether 'substantial medical authority' supports the medical necessity of the banned procedure." This was the proper framework, according to the Court of Appeals, because "when a lack of consensus exists in the medical community, the Constitution requires legislatures to err on the side of protecting women's health by including a health exception." The court rejected the Attorney General's attempt to demonstrate changed evidentiary circumstances since *Stenberg* and considered itself bound by *Stenberg*'s conclusion that a health exception was required. It invalidated the Act.

The District Court in *Planned Parenthood* concluded the Act was unconstitutional "because it (1) posed an undue burden on a woman's ability to choose a second trimester abortion; (2) [was] unconstitutionally vague; and (3) required a health exception as set forth by . . . *Stenberg*.

The Court of Appeals for the Ninth Circuit agreed. Like the Court of Appeals for the Eighth Circuit, it concluded the absence of a health exception rendered the Act unconstitutional. The court interpreted *Stenberg* to require a health exception unless "there is *consensus in the medical community* that the banned procedure is never medically necessary to preserve the health of women." Even after applying a deferential standard of review to Congress' factual findings, the Court of Appeals determined "substantial disagreement exists in the medical community regarding whether" the procedures prohibited by the Act are ever necessary to preserve a woman's health.

The Court of Appeals concluded further that the Act placed an undue burden on a woman's ability to obtain a second-trimester abortion. The court found the textual differences between the Act and the Nebraska statute struck down in *Stenberg* insufficient to distinguish D&E and intact D&E. As a result, according to the Court of Appeals, the Act imposed an undue burden because it prohibited D&E.

Finally, the Court of Appeals found the Act void for vagueness. Abortion doctors testified they were uncertain which procedures the Act made criminal. The court thus concluded the Act did not offer physicians clear warning of its regulatory reach . . . and held the Act was unconstitutional on its face and should be permanently enjoined.

II

The principles set forth in the joint opinion in *Planned Parenthood of Southeastern Pennsylvania v. Casey* (1992), did not find support from all those who join the instant opinion. (See [Justice Scalia's opinion, joined by Justice Thomas], concurring in judgment in part and dissenting in part). Whatever one's views concerning the *Casey* joint opinion, it is evident a premise central to its conclusion—that the government has a legitimate and substantial interest in preserving and promoting fetal life—would be repudiated were the Court now to affirm the judgments of the Courts of Appeals.

Casey involved a challenge to *Roe v. Wade* (1973). The opinion contains this summary:

It must be stated at the outset and with clarity that *Roe*'s essential holding, the holding we reaffirm, has three parts. First is a recognition of the right of the woman to choose to have an abortion before viability and to obtain it without undue interference from the State. Before viability, the State's interests are not strong enough to support a prohibition of abortion or the imposition of a substantial obstacle to the woman's effective right to elect the procedure. Second is a confirmation of the State's power to restrict abortions after fetal viability, if the law contains exceptions for pregnancies which endanger the woman's life or health. And third is the principle that the State has legitimate interests from the outset of the pregnancy in protecting the health of the woman and the life of the fetus that may become a child. These principles do not contradict one another; and we adhere to each.

Though all three holdings are implicated in the instant cases, it is the third that requires the most extended discussion; for we must determine whether the Act furthers the legitimate interest of the Government in protecting the life of the fetus that may become a child. To implement its holding, *Casey* rejected both *Roe*'s rigid trimester framework and the interpretation of *Roe* that considered all previability regulations of abortion unwarranted. On this point *Casey* overruled the holdings in two cases because they undervalued the State's interest in potential life.

We assume the following principles for the purposes of this opinion. Before viability, a State "may not prohibit any woman from making the ultimate decision to terminate her pregnancy." It also may not impose upon this right an undue burden, which exists if a regulation's "purpose or effect is to place a substantial obstacle in the path of a woman seeking an abortion before the fetus attains viability." On the other hand, "regulations which do no more than create a structural mechanism by which the State, or the parent or guardian of a minor, may express profound respect for the life of the unborn are permitted, if they are not a substantial obstacle to the woman's exercise of the right to choose." *Casey*, in short, struck a balance. The balance was central to its holding. We now apply its standard to the cases at bar.

III

We begin with a determination of the Act's operation and effect. A straightforward reading of the Act's text demonstrates its purpose and the scope of its provisions: It regulates and proscribes, with exceptions or qualifications to be discussed, performing the intact D&E procedure.

Respondents agree the Act encompasses intact D&E, but they contend its additional reach is both unclear and excessive. Respondents assert that, at the least, the Act is void for vagueness because its scope is indefinite. In the alternative, respondents argue the Act's text proscribes all D&Es. Because D&E is the most common second-trimester abortion method, respondents suggest the Act imposes an undue burden. In this litigation the Attorney General does not dispute that the Act would impose an undue burden if it covered standard D&E.

We conclude that the Act is not void for vagueness, does not impose an undue burden from any overbreadth, and is not invalid on its face.

The Act punishes "knowingly performing" a "partial-birth abortion." It defines the unlawful abortion in explicit terms.

First, the person performing the abortion must "vaginally deliver a living fetus." The Act does not restrict an abortion procedure involving the delivery of an expired fetus. The Act, furthermore, is inapplicable to abortions that do not involve vaginal delivery (for instance, hysterotomy or hysterectomy). The Act does apply both previability and postviability because, by common understanding and scientific terminology, a fetus is a living organism while within the womb, whether or not it is viable outside the womb. We do not understand this point to be contested by the parties.

Second, the Act's definition of partial-birth abortion requires the fetus to be delivered "until, in the case of a head-first presentation, the entire fetal head is outside the body of the mother, or, in the case of breech presentation, any part of the fetal trunk past the navel is outside the body of the mother." The Attorney General concedes, and we agree, that if an abortion procedure does not involve the delivery of a living fetus to one of these "anatomical 'landmarks'"—where, depending on the presentation, either the fetal head or the fetal trunk past the navel is outside the body of the mother—the prohibitions of the Act do not apply.

Third, to fall within the Act, a doctor must perform an "overt act, other than completion of delivery, that kills the partially delivered living fetus." For purposes of criminal liability, the overt act causing the fetus' death must be separate from delivery. And the overt act must occur after the delivery to an anatomical landmark. This is because the Act proscribes killing "the partially delivered" fetus, which, when read in context, refers to a fetus that has been delivered to an anatomical landmark.

Fourth, the Act contains scienter requirements concerning all the actions involved in the prohibited abortion. To begin with, the physician must have "deliberately and intentionally" delivered the fetus to one of the Act's anatomical landmarks. If a living fetus is delivered past the critical point by accident or inadvertence, the Act is inapplicable. In addition, the fetus must have been delivered "for the purpose of performing an overt act that the [doctor] knows will kill [it]." If either intent is absent, no crime has occurred. This follows from the general principle that where scienter is required no crime is committed.

Respondents contend the language described above is indeterminate, and they thus argue the Act is unconstitutionally vague on its face. "As generally stated, the void-for-vagueness doctrine requires that a penal statute define the criminal offense with sufficient definiteness that ordinary people can understand what conduct is prohibited and in a manner that does not encourage arbitrary and discriminatory enforcement." The Act satisfies both requirements.

The Act provides doctors "of ordinary intelligence a reasonable opportunity to know what is prohibited." Indeed, it sets forth "relatively clear guidelines as to prohibited conduct" and provides "objective criteria" to evaluate whether a doctor has performed a prohibited procedure. Unlike the statutory language in *Stenberg* that prohibited the delivery of a "'substantial portion'" of the fetus—where a doctor might question how much of the fetus is a substantial portion—the Act defines the line between potentially criminal conduct on the one hand and lawful abortion on the other. Doctors performing D&E will know that if they do not deliver a living fetus to an anatomical landmark they will not face criminal liability.

This conclusion is buttressed by the intent that must be proved to impose liability. The Court has made clear that scienter requirements alleviate vagueness concerns. The Act requires the doctor deliberately to have delivered the fetus to an anatomical landmark. Because a doctor performing a D&E will not face criminal liability if he or she delivers a fetus beyond the prohibited point by mistake, the Act cannot be described as "a trap for those who act in good faith." . . .

We next determine whether the Act imposes an undue burden, as a facial matter, because its restrictions on second-trimester abortions are too broad. A review of the statutory text discloses the limits of its reach. The Act prohibits intact D&E; and, notwithstanding respondents' arguments, it does not prohibit the D&E procedure in which the fetus is removed in parts. . . .

The Act excludes most D&Es in which the fetus is removed in pieces, not intact. If the doctor intends to remove the fetus in parts from the outset, the doctor will not have the requisite intent to incur criminal liability. A doctor performing a standard D&E procedure can often "take about 10–15 'passes' through the uterus to remove the entire fetus." Removing the fetus in this manner does not violate the Act because the doctor will not have delivered the living fetus to one of the anatomical landmarks or committed an additional overt act that kills the fetus after partial delivery.

A comparison of the Act with the Nebraska statute struck down in *Stenberg* confirms this point. The statute in *Stenberg* prohibited "'deliberately and intentionally delivering into the vagina a living unborn child, or a substantial portion thereof, for the purpose of performing a procedure that the person performing such procedure knows will kill the unborn child and does kill the unborn child.'" The Court concluded that this statute encompassed D&E because "D&E will often involve a physician pulling a 'substantial portion' of a still living fetus, say, an arm or leg, into the vagina prior to the death of the fetus." The Court also rejected the limiting interpretation urged by Nebraska's Attorney General that the statute's reference to a "procedure" that "'kills the unborn child'" was to a distinct procedure, not to the abortion procedure as a whole.

Congress, it is apparent, responded to these concerns because the Act departs in material ways from the statute in *Stenberg*. It adopts the phrase "delivers a living fetus" instead of "'delivering . . . a living unborn child, or a substantial portion thereof.'" The Act's language, unlike the statute in *Stenberg*, expresses the usual meaning of "deliver" when used in connection with "fetus," namely, extraction of an entire fetus rather than removal of fetal pieces. The Act thus displaces the interpretation of "delivering" dictated by the Nebraska statute's reference to a "substantial portion" of the fetus. In interpreting statutory texts courts use the ordinary meaning of terms unless context requires a different result. Here, unlike in *Stenberg*, the language does not require a departure from the ordinary meaning. D&E does not involve the delivery of a fetus because it requires the removal of fetal parts that are ripped from the fetus as they are pulled through the cervix.

The identification of specific anatomical landmarks to which the fetus must be partially delivered also differentiates the Act from the statute at issue in *Stenberg*. . . .

Under the [*Casey*] principles accepted as controlling here, the Act, as we have interpreted it, would be unconstitutional "if its purpose or effect is to place a substantial obstacle in the path of a woman seeking an abortion before the fetus attains viability." The abortions affected by the Act's regulations take place both previability and postviability; so the quoted language and the undue burden analysis it relies upon are applicable. The question is whether the Act, measured by its text in this facial attack imposes a substantial obstacle to late-term, but previability, abortions. The Act does not on its face impose a substantial obstacle, and we reject this further facial challenge to its validity.

The Act's purposes are set forth in recitals preceding its operative provisions. A description of the prohibited abortion procedure demonstrates the rationale for the congressional enactment. The Act proscribes a method of abortion in which a fetus is killed just inches before completion of the birth process. Congress stated as follows: "Implicitly approving such a brutal and inhumane procedure by choosing not to prohibit it will further coarsen society to the humanity of not only newborns, but all vulnerable and innocent human life, making it increasingly difficult to protect such life." The Act expresses respect for the dignity of human life.

Congress was concerned, furthermore, with the effects on the medical community and on its reputation caused by the practice of partial-birth abortion. The findings in the Act explain: "Partial-birth abortion . . . confuses the medical, legal, and ethical duties of physicians to preserve and promote life, as the physician acts directly against the physical life of a child, whom he or she had just delivered, all but the head, out of the womb, in order to end that life."

There can be no doubt the government "has an interest in protecting the integrity and ethics of the medical profession." Under our precedents it is clear the State has a significant role to play in regulating the medical profession.

Casey reaffirmed these governmental objectives. The government may use its voice and its regulatory authority to show its profound respect for the life within the woman. A central premise of the opinion was that the Court's precedents after *Roe* had "undervalued the State's interest in potential life." The plurality opinion indicated "the fact that a law which serves a valid purpose, one not designed to strike at the right itself, has the incidental effect of making it more difficult or more expensive to procure an abortion cannot be enough to invalidate it." This was not an idle assertion. The three premises of *Casey* must coexist. The third premise, that the State, from the inception of the pregnancy, maintains its own regulatory interest in protecting the life of the fetus that may become a child, cannot be set at naught by interpreting *Casey*'s requirement of a health exception so it becomes tantamount to allowing a doctor to choose the abortion method he or she might prefer. Where it has a rational basis to act, and it does not impose an undue burden, the State may use its regulatory power to bar certain procedures and substitute others, all in furtherance of its legitimate interests in regulating the medical profession in order to promote respect for life, including life of the unborn.

The Act's ban on abortions that involve partial delivery of a living fetus furthers the Government's objectives. No one would dispute that, for many, D&E is a procedure itself laden with the power to devalue human life. Congress could nonetheless conclude that the type of abortion proscribed by the Act requires specific regulation because it implicates additional ethical and moral concerns that justify a special prohibition. Congress determined that the abortion methods it proscribed had a "disturbing similarity to the killing of a newborn infant," and thus it was concerned with "drawing a bright line that clearly distinguishes abortion and infanticide." The Court has in the past confirmed the validity of drawing boundaries to prevent certain practices that extinguish life and are close to actions that are condemned.

Respect for human life finds an ultimate expression in the bond of love the mother has for her child. The Act recognizes this reality as well. Whether to have an abortion requires a difficult and painful moral decision. While we find no reliable data to measure the phenomenon, it seems unexceptionable to conclude some women come to regret their choice to abort the infant life they once created and sustained. Severe depression and loss of esteem can follow. In a decision so fraught with emotional consequence some doctors may prefer not to disclose precise details of the means that will be used, confining themselves to the required statement of risks the procedure entails. From one standpoint this ought not to be surprising. Any number of patients facing imminent surgical procedures would prefer not to hear all details, lest the usual anxiety preceding invasive medical procedures become the more intense. This is likely the case with the abortion procedures here in issue.

It is, however, precisely this lack of information concerning the way in which the fetus will be killed that is of legitimate concern to the State. The State has an interest in ensuring so grave a choice is well informed. It is self-evident that a mother who comes to regret her choice to abort must struggle with grief more anguished and sorrow more profound when she learns, only after the event, what she once did not know: that she allowed a doctor to pierce the skull and vacuum the fast-developing brain of her unborn child, a child assuming the human form. . . .

It is objected that the standard D&E is in some respects as brutal, if not more, than the intact D&E, so that the legislation accomplishes little. What we have already said,

however, shows ample justification for the regulation. Partial-birth abortion, as defined by the Act, differs from a standard D&E because the former occurs when the fetus is partially outside the mother to the point of one of the Act's anatomical landmarks. It was reasonable for Congress to think that partial-birth abortion, more than standard D&E, "undermines the public's perception of the appropriate role of a physician during the delivery process, and perverts a process during which life is brought into the world." . . . In sum, we reject the contention that the congressional purpose of the Act was "to place a substantial obstacle in the path of a woman seeking an abortion."

The Act's furtherance of legitimate government interests bears upon, but does not resolve, the next question: whether the Act has the effect of imposing an unconstitutional burden on the abortion right because it does not allow use of the barred procedure where "'necessary, in appropriate medical judgment, for [the] preservation of the . . . health of the mother.'" . . . [W]hether the Act creates significant health risks for women has been a contested factual question. The evidence presented in the trial courts and before Congress demonstrates both sides have medical support for their position. . . .

The question becomes whether the Act can stand when this medical uncertainty persists. The Court's precedents instruct that the Act can survive this facial attack. The Court has given state and federal legislatures wide discretion to pass legislation in areas where there is medical and scientific uncertainty.

This traditional rule is consistent with *Casey*, which confirms the State's interest in promoting respect for human life at all stages in the pregnancy. Physicians are not entitled to ignore regulations that direct them to use reasonable alternative procedures. The law need not give abortion doctors unfettered choice in the course of their medical practice, nor should it elevate their status above other physicians in the medical community. . . .

Medical uncertainty does not foreclose the exercise of legislative power in the abortion context any more than it does in other contexts. The medical uncertainty over whether the Act's prohibition creates significant health risks provides a sufficient basis to conclude in this facial attack that the Act does not impose an undue burden.

. . . [While] *Stenberg* has been interpreted to leave no margin of error for legislatures to act in the face of medical uncertainty [, such a] zero tolerance policy would strike down legitimate abortion regulations, like the present one, if some part of the medical community were disinclined to follow the proscription. This is too exacting a standard to impose on the legislative power, exercised in this instance under the Commerce Clause, to regulate the medical profession. Considerations of marginal safety, including the balance of risks, are within the legislative competence when the regulation is rational and in pursuit of legitimate ends. When standard medical options are available, mere convenience does not suffice to displace them; and if some procedures have different risks than others, it does not follow that the State is altogether barred from imposing reasonable regulations. The Act is not invalid on its face where there is uncertainty over whether the barred procedure is ever necessary to preserve a woman's health, given the availability of other abortion procedures that are considered to be safe alternatives.

V

. . . As the previous sections of this opinion explain, respondents have not demonstrated that the Act would be unconstitutional in a large fraction of relevant cases. . . . The Act is open to a proper as-applied challenge in a discrete case. No as-applied challenge need be brought if the prohibition in the Act threatens a woman's life because the Act already contains a life exception.

Respondents have not demonstrated that the Act, as a facial matter, is void for vagueness, or that it imposes an undue burden on a woman's right to abortion based on its overbreadth or lack of a health exception. For these reasons the judgments of the Courts of Appeals for the Eighth and Ninth Circuits are reversed.

JUSTICE THOMAS, with whom JUSTICE SCALIA joins, concurring.

I join the Court's opinion because it accurately applies current jurisprudence, including

Planned Parenthood of Southeastern Pennsylvania v. Casey. I write separately to reiterate my view that the Court's abortion jurisprudence, including *Casey* and *Roe v. Wade*, has no basis in the Constitution. I also note that whether the Act constitutes a permissible exercise of Congress' power under the Commerce Clause is not before the Court. The parties did not raise or brief that issue; it is outside the question presented; and the lower courts did not address it.

JUSTICE GINSBURG, with whom JUSTICE STEVENS, JUSTICE SOUTER, and JUSTICE BREYER join, dissenting.

In *Planned Parenthood of Southeastern Pennsylvania v. Casey*, the Court declared that "liberty finds no refuge in a jurisprudence of doubt." There was, the Court said, an "imperative" need to dispel doubt as to "the meaning and reach" of the Court's 7-to-2 judgment, rendered nearly two decades earlier in *Roe v. Wade*. . . . Seven years ago, in *Stenberg v. Carhart*, the Court invalidated a Nebraska statute criminalizing the performance of a medical procedure that, in the political arena, has been dubbed "partial-birth abortion." With fidelity to the *Roe-Casey* line of precedent, the Court held the Nebraska statute unconstitutional in part because it lacked the requisite protection for the preservation of a woman's health.

Today's decision is alarming. It refuses to take *Casey* and *Stenberg* seriously. It tolerates, indeed applauds, federal intervention to ban nationwide a procedure found necessary and proper in certain cases by the American College of Obstetricians and Gynecologists (ACOG). It blurs the line, firmly drawn in *Casey*, between previability and postviability abortions. And, for the first time since *Roe*, the Court blesses a prohibition with no exception safeguarding a woman's health.

I dissent from the Court's disposition. Retreating from prior rulings that abortion restrictions cannot be imposed absent an exception safeguarding a woman's health, the Court upholds an Act that surely would not survive under the close scrutiny that previously attended state-decreed limitations on a woman's reproductive choices.

I

As *Casey* comprehended, at stake in cases challenging abortion restrictions is a woman's "control over her [own] destiny." . . . Thus, legal challenges to undue restrictions on abortion procedures . . . center on a woman's autonomy to determine her life's course, and thus to enjoy equal citizenship stature.

In keeping with this comprehension of the right to reproductive choice, the Court has consistently required that laws regulating abortion, at any stage of pregnancy and in all cases, safeguard a woman's health. We have thus ruled that a State must avoid subjecting women to health risks not only where the pregnancy itself creates danger, but also where state regulation forces women to resort to less safe methods of abortion. In *Stenberg*, we expressly held that a statute banning intact D&E was unconstitutional in part because it lacked a health exception. . . . [W]e reasoned, division in medical opinion "at most means uncertainty, a factor that signals the presence of risk, not its absence." "[A] statute that altogether forbids [intact D&E]. . . . consequently must contain a health exception."

In 2003, a few years after our ruling in *Stenberg*, Congress passed the Partial-Birth Abortion Ban Act—without an exception for women's health. The congressional findings on which the Partial-Birth Abortion Ban Act rests do not withstand inspection, as the lower courts have determined and this Court is obliged to concede. ([As the District Court in *Carhart v. Ashcroft* noted:] "None of the six physicians who testified before Congress had ever performed an intact D&E. Several did not provide abortion services at all; and one was not even an obgyn. . . . The oral testimony before Congress was not only unbalanced, but intentionally polemic.")

Many of the Act's recitations are incorrect. For example, Congress determined that no medical schools provide instruction on intact D&E. But in fact, numerous leading medical schools teach the procedure. More important, Congress claimed there was a medical consensus that the banned procedure is never necessary. There was, however, a substantial body of medical opinion presented to Congress in opposition. If anything . . . the congressional record establishes that there was a 'consensus' in favor of the banned procedure.

Similarly, Congress found that "there is no credible medical evidence that partial-birth abortions are safe or are safer than other abortion procedures." But the congressional record includes letters from numerous individual physicians stating that pregnant women's health would be jeopardized under the Act, as well as statements from nine professional associations, including ACOG, the American Public Health Association, and the California Medical Association, attesting that intact D&E carries meaningful safety advantages over other methods. . . .

The Court acknowledges some of this evidence but insists that, because some witnesses disagreed with the . . . other experts' assessment of risk, the Act can stand. . . . Even indulging the assumption that the Government witnesses were equally qualified to evaluate the relative risks of abortion procedures, their testimony could not erase the "significant medical authority supporting the proposition that in some circumstances, [intact D&E] would be the safest procedure."

II

The Court offers flimsy and transparent justifications for upholding a nationwide ban on intact D&E *sans* any exception to safeguard a women's health. Today's ruling, the Court declares, advances "a premise central to [*Casey's*] conclusion"—*i.e.*, the Government's "legitimate and substantial interest in preserving and promoting fetal life." But the Act scarcely furthers that interest: The law saves not a single fetus from destruction, for it targets only a *method* of performing abortion. . . .

As another reason for upholding the ban, the Court emphasizes that the Act does not proscribe the nonintact D&E procedure. But why not, one might ask. Nonintact D&E could equally be characterized as "brutal," involving as it does "tearing [a fetus] apart" and "ripping off" its limbs. "The notion that either of these two equally gruesome procedures . . . is more akin to infanticide than the other, or that the State furthers any legitimate interest by banning one but not the other, is simply irrational."

Delivery of an intact, albeit nonviable, fetus warrants special condemnation, the Court maintains, because a fetus that is not dismembered resembles an infant. But so, too, does a fetus delivered intact after it is terminated by injection a day or two before the surgical evacuation, or a fetus delivered through medical induction or cesarean. Yet, the availability of those procedures—along with D&E by dismemberment—the Court says, saves the ban on intact D&E from a declaration of unconstitutionality. Never mind that the procedures deemed acceptable might put a woman's health at greater risk.

Ultimately, the Court admits that "moral concerns" are at work, concerns that could yield prohibitions on any abortion. Notably, the concerns expressed are untethered to any ground genuinely serving the Government's interest in preserving life. By allowing such concerns to carry the day and case, overriding fundamental rights, the Court dishonors our precedent. See, *e.g.*, . . . *Lawrence v. Texas* (2003). (Though "for many persons [objections to homosexual conduct] are not trivial concerns but profound and deep convictions accepted as ethical and moral principles," the power of the State may not be used "to enforce these views on the whole society through operation of the criminal law.")

Revealing in this regard, the Court invokes an antiabortion shibboleth for which it concededly has no reliable evidence: Women who have abortions come to regret their choices, and consequently suffer from "severe depression and loss of esteem." Because of women's fragile emotional state and because of the "bond of love the mother has for her child," the Court worries, doctors may withhold information about the nature of the intact D&E procedure. The solution the Court approves, then, is *not* to require doctors to inform women, accurately and adequately, of the different procedures and their attendant risks. Instead, the Court deprives women of the right to make an autonomous choice, even at the expense of their safety.

This way of thinking reflects ancient notions about women's place in the family and under the Constitution—ideas that have long since been discredited. Though today's majority may

regard women's feelings on the matter as "self-evident," this Court has repeatedly confirmed that "the destiny of the woman must be shaped . . . on her own conception of her spiritual imperatives and her place in society."

In cases on a "woman's liberty to determine whether to [continue] her pregnancy," this Court has identified viability as a critical consideration. "There is no line [more workable] than viability," the Court explained in *Casey*, for viability is "the time at which there is a realistic possibility of maintaining and nourishing a life outside the womb, so that the independent existence of the second life can in reason and all fairness be the object of state protection that now overrides the rights of the woman. . . . In some broad sense it might be said that a woman who fails to act before viability has consented to the State's intervention on behalf of the developing child."

Today, the Court blurs that line, maintaining that "the Act [legitimately] applies both previability and postviability because . . . a fetus is a living organism while within the womb, whether or not it is viable outside the womb." Instead of drawing the line at viability, the Court refers to Congress' purpose to differentiate "abortion and infanticide" based not on whether a fetus can survive outside the womb, but on where a fetus is anatomically located when a particular medical procedure is performed.

One wonders how long a line that saves no fetus from destruction will hold in face of the Court's "moral concerns." The Court's hostility to the right *Roe* and *Casey* secured is not concealed. Throughout, the opinion refers to obstetrician-gynecologists and surgeons who perform abortions not by the titles of their medical specialties, but by the pejorative label "abortion doctor." A fetus is described as an "unborn child," and as a "baby"; second-trimester, previability abortions are referred to as "late-term"; and the reasoned medical judgments of highly trained doctors are dismissed as "preferences" motivated by "mere convenience." Instead of the heightened scrutiny we have previously applied, the Court determines that a "rational" ground is enough to uphold the Act. And, most troubling, *Casey*'s principles, confirming the continuing vitality of "the essential holding of *Roe,*" are merely "assumed" for the moment rather than "retained" or "reaffirmed."

III

. . . If there is anything at all redemptive to be said of today's opinion, it is that the Court is not willing to foreclose entirely a constitutional challenge to the Act. "The Act is open," the Court states, "to a proper as-applied challenge in a discrete case." But the Court offers no clue on what a "proper" lawsuit might look like. . . . The Court's allowance only of an "as-applied challenge in a discrete case"—jeopardizes women's health and places doctors in an untenable position. Even if courts were able to carve-out exceptions through piecemeal litigation for "discrete and well-defined instances," women whose circumstances have not been anticipated by prior litigation could well be left unprotected. In treating those women, physicians would risk criminal prosecution, conviction, and imprisonment if they exercise their best judgment as to the safest medical procedure for their patients. The Court is thus gravely mistaken to conclude that narrow as-applied challenges are "the proper manner to protect the health of the woman.

IV

As the Court wrote in *Casey,* "overruling *Roe's* central holding would not only reach an unjustifiable result under principles of *stare decisis,*

but would seriously weaken the Court's capacity to exercise the judicial power and to function as the Supreme Court of a Nation dedicated to the rule of law."

Though today's opinion does not go so far as to discard *Roe* or *Casey,* the Court, differently composed than it was when we last considered a restrictive abortion regulation, is hardly faithful to our earlier invocations of "the rule of law" and the "principles of *stare decisis.*" Congress imposed a ban despite our clear prior holdings that the State cannot proscribe an abortion procedure when its use is necessary to protect a woman's health. Although Congress' findings could not withstand the crucible of trial, the Court defers to the legislative override of our Constitution-based rulings. A decision so at odds with our jurisprudence should not have staying power.

In sum, the notion that the Partial-Birth Abortion Ban Act furthers any legitimate governmental interest is, quite simply, irrational. The Court's defense of the statute provides no saving explanation. In candor, the Act, and the Court's defense of it, cannot be understood as anything other than an effort to chip away at a right declared again and again by this Court—and with increasing comprehension of its centrality to women's lives. When "a statute burdens constitutional rights and all that can be said on its behalf is that it is the vehicle that legislators have chosen for expressing their hostility to those rights, the burden is undue."

Lawrence v. Texas
539 U.S. 558 (2003)

In response to a reported weapons disturbance in a private residence, Houston police entered John Geddes Lawrence's apartment and saw him and another adult man engaging in a private, consensual sexual act. They were arrested and charged with deviate sexual intercourse in violation of a Texas statute forbidding anal sex with a member of the same sex. They entered a plea of nolo contendere and were each fined $200 and assessed court costs. They appealed to the state court of appeals, which relied on Bowers v. Hardwick *(1986) as controlling and held that the statute was not unconstitutional under the Due Process*

Clause of the Fourteenth Amendment. The Supreme Court granted certiorari. Opinion of the Court: <u>Kennedy</u>, Stevens, Souter, Ginsburg, Breyer. Concurring in the judgment: <u>O'Connor</u>. Dissenting opinions: <u>Scalia</u>, Rehnquist, Thomas; <u>Thomas</u>.

JUSTICE KENNEDY delivered the opinion of the Court.

Liberty protects the person from unwarranted government intrusions into a dwelling or other private places. In our tradition the State is not omnipresent in the home. And there are other spheres of our lives and existence, outside the home, where the State should not be a dominant presence. Freedom extends beyond spatial bounds. Liberty presumes an autonomy of self that includes freedom of thought, belief, expression, and certain intimate conduct. The instant case involves liberty of the person both in its spatial and more transcendent dimensions.

The question before the Court is the validity of a Texas statute making it a crime for two persons of the same sex to engage in certain intimate sexual conduct. . . .

We conclude the case should be resolved by determining whether the petitioners were free as adults to engage in the private conduct in the exercise of their liberty under the Due Process Clause of the Fourteenth Amendment to the Constitution. For this inquiry we deem it necessary to reconsider the Court's holding in *Bowers*.

There are broad statements of the substantive reach of liberty under the Due Process Clause in earlier cases, including *Pierce v. Society of Sisters* (1925), and *Meyer v. Nebraska* (1923); but the most pertinent beginning point is our decision in *Griswold v. Connecticut* (1965).

In *Griswold* the Court invalidated a state law prohibiting the use of drugs or devices of contraception and counseling or aiding and abetting the use of contraceptives. The Court described the protected interest as a right to privacy and placed emphasis on the marriage relation and the protected space of the marital bedroom.

After *Griswold* it was established that the right to make certain decisions regarding sexual conduct extends beyond the marital relationship. In *Eisenstadt v. Baird*, (1972), the Court invalidated a law prohibiting the distribution of contraceptives to unmarried persons. . . . The opinions in *Griswold* and *Eisenstadt* were part of the background for the decision in *Roe v. Wade* (1973). As is well known, the case involved a challenge to the Texas law prohibiting abortions, but the laws of other States were affected as well. . . . In *Carey v. Population Services Int'l.* (1977), the Court confronted a New York law forbidding sale or distribution of contraceptive devices to persons under 16 years of age. Although there was no single opinion for the

Court, the law was invalidated. Both *Eisenstadt* and *Carey*, as well as the holding and rationale in *Roe*, confirmed that the reasoning of *Griswold* could not be confined to the protection of rights of married adults. This was the state of the law with respect to some of the most relevant cases when the Court considered *Bowers v. Hardwick*.

The facts in *Bowers* had some similarities to the instant case. A police officer, whose right to enter seems not to have been in question, observed Hardwick, in his own bedroom, engaging in intimate sexual conduct with another adult male. The conduct was in violation of a Georgia statute making it a criminal offense to engage in sodomy. One difference between the two cases is that the Georgia statute prohibited the conduct whether or not the participants were of the same sex, while the Texas statute, as we have seen, applies only to participants of the same sex. Hardwick was not prosecuted, but he brought an action in federal court to declare the state statute invalid. He alleged he was a practicing homosexual and that the criminal prohibition violated rights guaranteed to him by the Constitution. The Court . . . sustained the Georgia law. . . .

The Court began its substantive discussion in *Bowers* as follows: "The issue presented is whether the Federal Constitution confers a fundamental right upon homosexuals to engage in sodomy and hence invalidates the laws of the many States that still make such conduct illegal and have done so for a very long time." That statement, we now conclude, discloses the Court's own failure to appreciate the extent of the liberty at stake. To say that the issue in *Bowers* was simply the right to engage in certain sexual conduct demeans the claim the individual put forward, just as it would demean a married couple were it to be said marriage is simply about the right to have sexual intercourse. The laws involved in *Bowers* and here are, to be sure, statutes that purport to do no more than prohibit a particular sexual act. Their penalties and purposes, though, have more far-reaching consequences, touching upon the most private human conduct, sexual behavior, and in the most private of places, the home. The statutes do seek to control a personal relationship that, whether or not entitled to formal recognition in the law, is within the liberty of persons to choose without being punished as criminals.

This, as a general rule, should counsel against attempts by the State, or a court, to define the meaning of the relationship or to set its boundaries absent injury to a person or abuse of an institution the law protects. It suffices for us to acknowledge that adults may choose to enter upon this relationship in the confines of their homes and their own private lives and still retain their dignity as free persons. When sexuality finds overt expression in intimate conduct with another person, the conduct can be but one element in a personal bond that is more enduring. The liberty protected by the Constitution allows homosexual persons the right to make this choice. . . .

. . . Almost five years before *Bowers* was decided the European Court of Human Rights considered a case with parallels to *Bowers* and to today's case. An adult male resident in Northern Ireland alleged he was a practicing homosexual who desired to engage in consensual homosexual conduct. The laws of Northern Ireland forbade him that right. He alleged that he had been questioned, his home had been searched, and he feared criminal prosecution. The court held that the laws proscribing the conduct were invalid under the European Convention on Human Rights. *Dudgeon v. United Kingdom,* 45 Eur. Ct. H. R. (1981) P52. Authoritative in all countries that are members of the Council of Europe (21 nations then, 45 nations now), the decision is at odds with the premise in *Bowers* that the claim put forward was insubstantial in our Western civilization.

In our own constitutional system the deficiencies in *Bowers* became even more apparent in the years following its announcement. The 25 States with laws prohibiting the relevant conduct referenced in the *Bowers* decision are reduced now to 13, of which 4 enforce their laws only against homosexual conduct. In those States where sodomy is still proscribed, whether for same-sex or heterosexual conduct, there is a pattern of nonenforcement with respect to consenting adults acting in private. The State of Texas admitted in 1994 that as of

that date it had not prosecuted anyone under those circumstances.

Two principal cases decided after *Bowers* cast its holding into even more doubt. In *Planned Parenthood of Southeastern Pa. v. Casey* (1992), the Court reaffirmed the substantive force of the liberty protected by the Due Process Clause. The *Casey* decision again confirmed that our laws and tradition afford constitutional protection to personal decisions relating to marriage, procreation, contraception, family relationships, child rearing, and education. In explaining the respect the Constitution demands for the autonomy of the person in making these choices, we stated as follows:

These matters, involving the most intimate and personal choices a person may make in a lifetime, choices central to personal dignity and autonomy, are central to the liberty protected by the Fourteenth Amendment. At the heart of liberty is the right to define one's own concept of existence, of meaning, of the universe, and of the mystery of human life. Beliefs about these matters could not define the attributes of personhood were they formed under compulsion of the State.

Persons in a homosexual relationship may seek autonomy for these purposes, just as heterosexual persons do. The decision in *Bowers* would deny them this right.

The second post-*Bowers* case of principal relevance is *Romer v. Evans,* (1996). There the Court struck down class-based legislation directed at homosexuals as a violation of the Equal Protection Clause. . . . We concluded that the provision was "born of animosity toward the class of persons affected" and further that it had no rational relation to a legitimate governmental purpose.

As an alternative argument in this case, counsel for the petitioners and some *amici* contend that *Romer* provides the basis for declaring the Texas statute invalid under the Equal Protection Clause. That is a tenable argument, but we conclude the instant case requires us to address whether *Bowers* itself has continuing validity. Were we to hold the statute invalid under the Equal Protection Clause some might question whether a prohibition would be valid if drawn differently, say, to prohibit the conduct both between same-sex and different-sex participants.

Equality of treatment and the due process right to demand respect for conduct protected by the substantive guarantee of liberty are linked in important respects, and a decision on the latter point advances both interests. If protected conduct is made criminal and the law which does so remains unexamined for its substantive validity, its stigma might remain even if it were not enforceable as drawn for equal protection reasons. When homosexual conduct is made criminal by the law of the State, that declaration in and of itself is an invitation to subject homosexual persons to discrimination both in the public and in the private spheres. The central holding of *Bowers* has been brought in question by this case, and it should be addressed. Its continuance as precedent demeans the lives of homosexual persons. . . .

To the extent *Bowers* relied on values we share with a wider civilization, it should be noted that the reasoning and holding in *Bowers* have been rejected elsewhere. The European Court of Human Rights has followed not *Bowers* but its own decision in *Dudgeon v. United Kingdom*. Other nations, too, have taken action consistent with an affirmation of the protected right of homosexual adults to engage in intimate, consensual conduct. The right the petitioners seek in this case has been accepted as an integral part of human freedom in many other countries. There has been no showing that in this country the governmental interest in circumscribing personal choice is somehow more legitimate or urgent.

The doctrine of *stare decisis* is essential to the respect accorded to the judgments of the Court and to the stability of the law. It is not, however, an inexorable command. *Payne v. Tennessee* (1991) . . . The rationale of *Bowers* does not withstand careful analysis. In his dissenting opinion in *Bowers* Justice Stevens came to these conclusions: "[T]he fact that the governing majority in a State has traditionally viewed a particular practice as immoral is not a sufficient reason for upholding a law prohibiting the practice; . . . individual decisions by married persons, concerning the intimacies of their physical relationship, even when not intended to produce offspring, are a form of 'liberty' protected by the Due Process Clause of the Fourteenth Amendment. Moreover, this protection extends to intimate choices by unmarried as well as married persons." Justice Stevens' analysis, in our view, should have been controlling in *Bowers* and should control here. *Bowers* was not correct when it was decided, and it is not correct today. It ought not to remain binding precedent. *Bowers v. Hardwick* should be and now is overruled.

The present case does not involve minors. It does not involve persons who might be injured or coerced or who are situated in relationships where consent might not easily be refused. It does not involve public conduct or prostitution. It does not involve whether the government must give formal recognition to any relationship that homosexual persons seek to enter. The case does involve two adults who, with full and mutual consent from each other, engaged in sexual practices common to a homosexual lifestyle. The petitioners are entitled to respect for their private lives. The State cannot demean their existence or control their destiny by making their private sexual conduct a crime. Their right to liberty under the Due Process Clause gives them the full right to engage in their conduct without intervention of the government. "It is a promise of the Constitution that there is a realm of personal liberty which the government may not enter." The Texas statute furthers no legitimate state interest which can justify its intrusion into the personal and private life of the individual.

Had those who drew and ratified the Due Process Clauses of the Fifth Amendment or the Fourteenth Amendment known the components of liberty in its manifold possibilities, they might have been more specific. They did not presume to have this insight. They knew times can blind us to certain truths and later generations can see that laws once thought necessary and proper in fact serve only to oppress. As the Constitution endures, persons in every generation can invoke its principles in their own search for greater freedom.

The judgment of the Court of Appeals for the Texas Fourteenth District is reversed, and the case is remanded for further proceedings not inconsistent with this opinion.

JUSTICE O'CONNOR, concurring in the judgment.

The Court today overrules *Bowers v. Hardwick* (1986). I joined *Bowers,* and do not join the Court in overruling it. Nevertheless, I agree with the Court that Texas' statute banning same-sex sodomy is unconstitutional. Rather than relying on the substantive component of the Fourteenth Amendment's Due Process Clause, as the Court does, I base my conclusion on the Fourteenth Amendment's Equal Protection Clause. . . .

The statute at issue here makes sodomy a crime only if a person "engages in deviate sexual intercourse with another individual of the same sex." Sodomy between opposite-sex partners, however, is not a crime in Texas. That is, Texas treats the same conduct differently based solely on the participants. Those harmed by this law are people who have a same-sex sexual orientation and thus are more likely to engage in behavior prohibited by [the statute].

A law branding one class of persons as criminal solely based on the State's moral disapproval of that class and the conduct associated with that class runs contrary to the values of the Constitution and the Equal Protection Clause, under any standard of review. I therefore concur in the Court's judgment that Texas' sodomy law banning "deviate sexual intercourse" between consenting adults of the same sex, but not between consenting adults of different sexes, is unconstitutional.

JUSTICE SCALIA, with whom THE CHIEF JUSTICE and JUSTICE THOMAS join, dissenting.

. . . Most of the rest of today's opinion has no relevance to its actual holding—that the Texas statute "furthers no legitimate state interest which can justify" its application to petitioners under rational-basis review. Though there is discussion of "fundamental propositions" and "fundamental decisions," nowhere does the Court's opinion declare that homosexual sodomy is a "fundamental right" under the Due Process Clause; nor does it subject the

Texas law to the standard of review that would be appropriate (strict scrutiny) if homosexual sodomy *were* a "fundamental right." Thus, while overruling the *outcome* of *Bowers,* the Court leaves strangely untouched its central legal conclusion: "Respondent would have us announce . . . a fundamental right to engage in homosexual sodomy. This we are quite unwilling to do." Instead the Court simply describes petitioners' conduct as "an exercise of their liberty"—which it undoubtedly is—and proceeds to apply an unheard-of form of rational-basis review that will have far-reaching implications beyond this case. . . .

Texas['s statute] undoubtedly imposes constraints on liberty. So do laws prohibiting prostitution, recreational use of heroin, and, for that matter, working more than 60 hours per week in a bakery. But there is no right to "liberty" under the Due Process Clause, though today's opinion repeatedly makes that claim. The Fourteenth Amendment *expressly allows* States to deprive their citizens of "liberty," *so long as "due process of law" is provided.* . . . Our opinions applying the doctrine known as "substantive due process" hold that the Due Process Clause prohibits States from infringing *fundamental* liberty interests, unless the infringement is narrowly tailored to serve a compelling state interest. We have held repeatedly, in cases the Court today does not overrule, that *only* fundamental rights qualify for this so-called "heightened scrutiny" protection—that is, rights which are "'deeply rooted in this Nation's history and tradition.'" All other liberty interests may be abridged or abrogated pursuant to a validly enacted state law if that law is rationally related to a legitimate state interest.

Bowers held, first, that criminal prohibitions of homosexual sodomy are not subject to heightened scrutiny because they do not implicate a "fundamental right" under the Due Process Clause. Noting that "proscriptions against that conduct have ancient roots," that "sodomy was a criminal offense at common law and was forbidden by the laws of the original 13 States when they ratified the Bill of Rights," and that many States had retained their bans on sodomy, *Bowers* concluded that a right to engage in homosexual sodomy was not "'deeply rooted in this Nation's history and tradition.'"

The Court today does not overrule this holding. Not once does it describe homosexual sodomy as a "fundamental right" or a "fundamental liberty interest," nor does it subject the Texas statute to strict scrutiny. Instead, having failed to establish that the right to homosexual sodomy is "'deeply rooted in this Nation's history and tradition,'" the Court concludes that the application of Texas's statute to petitioners' conduct fails the rational-basis test, and overrules *Bowers*' holding to the contrary. . . . This proposition is so out of accord with our jurisprudence—indeed, with the jurisprudence of *any* society we know—that it requires little discussion.

The Texas statute undeniably seeks to further the belief of its citizens that certain forms of sexual behavior are "immoral and unacceptable"—the same interest furthered by criminal laws against fornication, bigamy, adultery, adult incest, bestiality, and obscenity. *Bowers* held that this *was* a legitimate state interest. The Court today reaches the opposite conclusion. The Texas statute, it says, "furthers *no legitimate state interest* which can justify its intrusion into the personal and private life of the individual" (emphasis added). The Court embraces instead Justice Stevens' declaration in his *Bowers* dissent, that "the fact that the governing majority in a State has traditionally viewed a particular practice as immoral is not a sufficient reason for upholding a law prohibiting the practice." This effectively decrees the end of all morals legislation. If, as the Court asserts, the promotion of majoritarian sexual morality is not even a *legitimate* state interest, none of the above-mentioned laws can survive rational-basis review.

Finally, I turn to petitioners' equal-protection challenge, which no Member of the Court save Justice O'Connor embraces: On its face [the Texas statute] applies equally to all persons. Men and women, heterosexuals and homosexuals, are all subject to its prohibition of deviate sexual intercourse with someone of the same sex. To be sure, [it] does distinguish between the sexes insofar as concerns the partner with whom the sexual acts are performed: men can violate the law only with other men, and

women only with other women. But this cannot itself be a denial of equal protection, since it is precisely the same distinction regarding partner that is drawn in state laws prohibiting marriage with someone of the same sex while permitting marriage with someone of the opposite sex. . . .

Today's opinion is the product of a Court, which is the product of a law-profession culture, that has largely signed on to the so-called homosexual agenda, by which I mean the agenda promoted by some homosexual activists directed at eliminating the moral opprobrium that has traditionally attached to homosexual conduct. . . . One of the most revealing statements in today's opinion is the Court's grim warning that the criminalization of homosexual conduct is "an invitation to subject homosexual persons to discrimination both in the public and in the private spheres." It is clear from this that the Court has taken sides in the culture war, departing from its role of assuring, as neutral observer, that the democratic rules of engagement are observed. Many Americans do not want persons who openly engage in homosexual conduct as partners in their business, as scoutmasters for their children, as teachers in their children's schools, or as boarders in their home. They view this as protecting themselves and their families from a lifestyle that they believe to be immoral and destructive. The Court views it as "discrimination" which it is the function of our judgments to deter. So imbued is the Court with the law profession's anti-anti-homosexual culture, that it is seemingly unaware that the attitudes of that culture are not obviously "mainstream"; that in most States what the Court calls "discrimination" against those who engage in homosexual acts is perfectly legal; that proposals to ban such "discrimination" under Title VII have repeatedly been rejected by Congress; that in some cases such "discrimination" is *mandated* by federal statute (mandating discharge from the armed forces of any service member who engages in or intends to engage in homosexual acts); and that in some cases such "discrimination" is a constitutional right, see *Boy Scouts of America v. Dale* (2000).

Let me be clear that I have nothing against homosexuals, or any other group, promoting their agenda through normal democratic means. Social perceptions of sexual and other morality change over time, and every group has the right to persuade its fellow citizens that its view of such matters is the best. That homosexuals have achieved some success in that enterprise is attested to by the fact that Texas is one of the few remaining States that criminalize private, consensual homosexual acts. But persuading one's fellow citizens is one thing, and imposing one's views in absence of democratic majority will is something else. I would no more *require* a State to criminalize homosexual acts—or, for that matter, display *any* moral disapprobation of them—than I would *forbid* it to do so. What Texas has chosen to do is well within the range of traditional democratic action, and its hand should not be stayed through the invention of a brand-new "constitutional right" by a Court that is impatient of democratic change. It is indeed true that "later generations can see that laws once thought necessary and proper in fact serve only to oppress"; and when that happens, later generations can repeal those laws. But it is the premise of our system that those judgments are to be made by the people, and not imposed by a governing caste that knows best.

. . . At the end of its opinion—after having laid waste the foundations of our rational-basis jurisprudence—the Court says that the present case "does not involve whether the government must give formal recognition to any relationship that homosexual persons seek to enter." Do not believe it. More illuminating than this bald, unreasoned disclaimer is the progression of thought displayed by an earlier passage in the Court's opinion, which notes the constitutional protections afforded to "personal decisions relating to *marriage,* procreation, contraception, family relationships, child rearing, and education," and then declares that "persons in a homosexual relationship may seek autonomy for these purposes, just as heterosexual persons do." Today's opinion dismantles the structure of constitutional law that has permitted a distinction to be made between heterosexual and homosexual unions, insofar as formal recognition

in marriage is concerned. If moral disapprobation of homosexual conduct is "no legitimate state interest" for purposes of proscribing that conduct, and if, as the Court coos (casting aside all pretense of neutrality), "when sexuality finds overt expression in intimate conduct with another person, the conduct can be but one element in a personal bond that is more enduring"; what justification could there possibly be for denying the benefits of marriage to homosexual couples exercising "the liberty protected by the Constitution"? Surely not the encouragement of procreation, since the sterile and the elderly are allowed to marry. This case "does not involve" the issue of homosexual marriage only if one entertains the belief that principle and logic have nothing to do with the decisions of this Court. Many will hope that, as the Court comfortingly assures us, this is so.

The matters appropriate for this Court's resolution are only three: Texas's prohibition of sodomy neither infringes a "fundamental right" (which the Court does not dispute), nor is unsupported by a rational relation to what the Constitution considers a legitimate state interest, nor denies the equal protection of the laws. I dissent.

JUSTICE THOMAS, dissenting.

I join Justice Scalia's dissenting opinion. I write separately to note that the law before the Court today "is . . . uncommonly silly." *Griswold v. Connecticut* (1965) (Stewart, J., dissenting). If I were a member of the Texas Legislature, I would vote to repeal it. Punishing someone for expressing his sexual preference through noncommercial consensual conduct with another adult does not appear to be a worthy way to expend valuable law enforcement resources.

Notwithstanding this, I recognize that as a member of this Court I am not empowered to help petitioners and others similarly situated. My duty, rather, is to "decide cases 'agreeably to the Constitution and laws of the United States.'" And, just like Justice Stewart, I "can find [neither in the Bill of Rights nor any other part of the Constitution a] general right of privacy," or as the Court terms it today, the "liberty of the person both in its spatial and more transcendent dimensions."

Defense of Marriage Act of 1996
P.L. 104–199

As a result of its decision to hear Baehr v. Lewin *(1993), the Hawaii Supreme Court appeared to be on the verge of requiring that state to issue marriage licenses to same-sex couples. Although the court ultimately rejected the plaintiffs' claims, the case prompted other states that do not permit homosexuals to marry to consider the issue of whether they would nonetheless be obligated under the Full Faith and Credit Clause of Article IV, Section 1, of the United States Constitution to give binding legal effect to such unions. Likewise, with regard to federal law, the case raised the question of whether a decision by one state to authorize same-sex marriage would entitle such couples to federal benefits that depend on marital status. In the Defense of Marriage Act of 1996, Congress answered these questions by providing that no state shall be required to accord full faith and credit to a marriage license issued by another state if it relates to a relationship between persons of the same sex and by defining the terms marriage and spouse, for purposes of federal law only, to reaffirm that they refer exclusively to relationships between persons of the opposite sex.*

An Act to define and protect the institution of marriage.

SECTION 1. SHORT TITLE.

This Act may be cited as the "Defense of Marriage Act."

SEC. 2. POWERS RESERVED TO THE STATES.

(a) . . . No State, territory, or possession of the United States, or Indian tribe, shall be required to give effect to any public act, record, or judicial proceeding of any other State, territory, possession, or tribe respecting a relationship between persons of the same sex that is treated as a marriage under the laws of such other State, territory, possession, or tribe, or a right or claim arising from such relationship.

SEC. 3. DEFINITION OF MARRIAGE.

(a) . . . In determining the meaning of any Act of Congress, or of any ruling, regulation, or interpretation of the various administrative bureaus and agencies of the United States, the word "marriage" means only a legal union between one man and one woman as husband and wife, and the word "spouse" refers only to a person of the opposite sex who is a husband or a wife.

Obergefell v. Hodges
576 U.S. ___ (2015)

Michigan, Kentucky, Ohio, and Tennessee defined marriage as a union between one man and one woman. The petitioners, fourteen same-sex couples and two men whose same-sex partners are deceased, filed suits in Federal District Courts in their home States, claiming that respondent state officials violated the Fourteenth Amendment by denying them the right to marry or to have marriages lawfully performed in another State given full recognition. Each District Court ruled in petitioners' favor, but the Sixth Circuit consolidated the cases and reversed. The Supreme Court granted certiorari. Opinion of the Court: Kennedy, *Breyer, Sotomayor, Kagan. Dissenting opinions:* Roberts, *Scalia, Thomas;* Scalia, *Thomas;* Thomas, *Scalia;* Alito, *Scalia, Thomas.*

JUSTICE KENNEDY delivered the opinion of the Court.

The Constitution promises liberty to all within its reach, a liberty that includes certain specific rights that allow persons, within a lawful realm, to define and express their identity. The petitioners in these cases seek to find that liberty by marrying someone of the same sex and having their marriages deemed lawful on the same terms and conditions as marriages between persons of the opposite sex. . . .

II

Before addressing the principles and precedents that govern these cases, it is appropriate to note the history of the subject now before the Court.

A

From their beginning to their most recent page, the annals of human history reveal the transcendent importance of marriage. The life-long union of a man and a woman always has promised nobility and dignity to all persons, without regard to their station in life. Marriage is sacred to those who live by their religions and offers unique fulfillment to those who find meaning in the secular realm. Its dynamic allows two people to find a life that could not be found alone, for a marriage becomes greater than just the two persons. Rising from the most basic human needs, marriage is essential to our most profound hopes and aspirations.

The centrality of marriage to the human condition makes it unsurprising that the institution has existed for millennia and across civilizations. Since the dawn of history, marriage has transformed strangers into relatives, binding families and societies together. Confucius taught that marriage lies at the foundation of government. This wisdom was echoed centuries later and half a world away by Cicero, who wrote, "The first bond of society is marriage; next, children; and then the family." There are untold references to the beauty of marriage in religious and philosophical texts spanning time, cultures, and faiths, as well as in art and literature in all their forms. It is fair and necessary to say these references were based on the understanding that marriage is a union between two persons of the opposite sex.

That history is the beginning of these cases. The respondents say it should be the end as well. To them, it would demean a timeless institution if the concept and lawful status of marriage were extended to two persons of the same sex. Marriage, in their view, is by its nature a gender-differentiated union of man and woman. This view long has been held—and continues to be held—in good faith by reasonable and sincere people here and throughout the world.

The petitioners acknowledge this history but contend that these cases cannot end there. Were their intent to demean the revered idea and reality of marriage, the petitioners' claims would be of a different order. But that is neither their purpose nor their submission. To the contrary, it is the enduring importance of marriage that underlies the petitioners' contentions. This, they say, is their whole point. Far from seeking to devalue marriage, the petitioners seek it for themselves because of their respect—and need—for its privileges and responsibilities. And their immutable nature dictates that same-sex marriage is their only real path to this profound commitment. . . .

B

The ancient origins of marriage confirm its centrality, but it has not stood in isolation from developments in law and society. The history of marriage is one of both continuity and change. That institution—even as confined to opposite-sex relations—has evolved over time.

For example, marriage was once viewed as an arrangement by the couple's parents based on political, religious, and financial concerns; but by the time of the Nation's founding it was understood to be a voluntary contract between a man and a woman. As the role and status of women changed, the institution further evolved. Under the centuries-old doctrine of coverture, a married man and woman were treated by the State as a single, male-dominated legal entity. As women gained legal, political, and property rights, and as society began to understand that women have their own equal dignity, the law of coverture was abandoned. These and other developments in the institution of marriage over the past centuries were not mere superficial changes. Rather, they worked deep transformations in its structure, affecting aspects of marriage long viewed by many as essential.

These new insights have strengthened, not weakened, the institution of marriage. Indeed, changed understandings of marriage are characteristic of a Nation where new dimensions of freedom become apparent to new generations, often through perspectives that begin in pleas or protests and then are considered in the political sphere and the judicial process.

This dynamic can be seen in the Nation's experiences with the rights of gays and lesbians. Until the mid-20th century, same-sex intimacy long had been condemned as immoral by the state itself in most Western nations, a belief often embodied in the criminal law. For this reason, among others, many persons did not deem homosexuals to have dignity in their own distinct identity. A truthful declaration by same-sex couples of what was in their hearts had to remain unspoken. Even when a greater awareness of the humanity and integrity of homosexual persons came in the period after World War II, the argument that gays and lesbians had a just claim to dignity was in conflict with both law and widespread social conventions. Same-sex intimacy remained a crime in many States. Gays and lesbians were prohibited from most government employment, barred from military service, excluded under immigration laws, targeted by police, and burdened in their rights to associate.

For much of the 20th century, moreover, homosexuality was treated as an illness. When the American Psychiatric Association published the first Diagnostic and Statistical Manual of Mental Disorders in 1952, homosexuality was classified as a mental disorder, a position adhered to until 1973. Only in more recent years have psychiatrists and others recognized that sexual orientation is both a normal expression of human sexuality and immutable.

In the late 20th century, following substantial cultural and political developments, same-sex couples began to lead more open and public lives and to establish families. This development was followed by a quite extensive discussion of the issue in both governmental and private sectors and by a shift in public attitudes toward greater tolerance. As a result, questions about the rights of gays and lesbians soon reached the courts, where the issue could be discussed in the formal discourse of the law.

This Court first gave detailed consideration to the legal status of homosexuals in *Bowers v. Hardwick* (1986). There it upheld the constitutionality of a Georgia law deemed to criminalize certain homosexual acts. Ten years later, in *Romer v. Evans* (1996), the Court invalidated an amendment to Colorado's Constitution that sought to foreclose any branch or political subdivision of the State from protecting persons against discrimination based on sexual orientation. Then, in 2003, the Court overruled *Bowers*, holding that laws making same-sex intimacy a crime "demea[n] the lives of homosexual persons." *Lawrence v. Texas.*

Against this background, the legal question of same-sex marriage arose. In 1993, the Hawaii Supreme Court held Hawaii's law restricting marriage to opposite-sex couples constituted a classification on the basis of sex and was therefore subject to strict scrutiny under the Hawaii Constitution. Although this decision did not mandate that same-sex marriage be allowed, some States were concerned by its implications and reaffirmed in their laws that marriage is defined as a union between opposite-sex partners. So too in 1996, Congress passed the Defense of Marriage Act (DOMA) defining marriage for all federal-law purposes as "only a legal union between one man and one woman as husband and wife."

The new and widespread discussion of the subject led other States to a different conclusion. In 2003, the Supreme Judicial Court of Massachusetts held the State's Constitution guaranteed same-sex couples the right to marry. See *Goodridge v. Department of Public Health* (2003). After that ruling, some additional States granted marriage rights to same-sex couples, either through judicial or legislative processes. . . . Two Terms ago, in *United States v. Windsor* (2013), this Court invalidated DOMA to the extent it barred the Federal Government from treating same-sex marriages as valid even when they were lawful in the State where they were licensed. DOMA, the Court held, impermissibly disparaged those same-sex couples "who wanted to affirm their commitment to one another before their children, their family, their friends, and their community."

Numerous cases about same-sex marriage have reached the United States Courts of Appeals in recent years. In accordance with the judicial duty to base their decisions on principled reasons and neutral discussions, without scornful or disparaging commentary, courts have written a substantial body of law considering all sides of these issues. That case law helps to explain and formulate the underlying principles this Court now must consider. With the exception of the opinion here under review . . . , the Courts of Appeals have held that excluding same-sex couples from marriage violates the Constitution. There also have been many thoughtful District Court decisions addressing same-sex marriage—and most of them, too, have concluded same-sex couples must be allowed to marry. In addition the highest courts of many States have contributed to this ongoing dialogue in decisions interpreting their own State Constitutions. . . .

III

Under the Due Process Clause of the Fourteenth Amendment, no State shall "deprive any person of life, liberty, or property, without due process of law." The fundamental liberties protected by this Clause include most of the rights enumerated in the Bill of Rights. In addition these liberties extend to certain personal choices central to individual dignity and autonomy, including intimate choices that define personal identity and beliefs.

The identification and protection of fundamental rights is an enduring part of the judicial duty to interpret the Constitution. That responsibility, however, "has not been reduced to any formula." Rather, it requires courts to exercise reasoned judgment in identifying interests of the person so fundamental that the State must accord them its respect. That process is guided by many of the same considerations relevant to analysis of other constitutional provisions that set forth broad principles rather than specific requirements. History and tradition guide and discipline this inquiry but do not set its outer boundaries. That method respects our history and learns from it without allowing the past alone to rule the present.

The nature of injustice is that we may not always see it in our own times. The generations that wrote and ratified the Bill of Rights and the Fourteenth Amendment did not presume to know the extent of freedom in all of its dimensions, and so they entrusted to future generations a charter protecting the right of all persons to enjoy liberty as we learn its meaning. When new insight reveals discord between the Constitution's central protections and a received legal stricture, a claim to liberty must be addressed.

Applying these established tenets, the Court has long held the right to marry is protected by the Constitution. In *Loving v. Virginia* (1967), which invalidated bans on interracial unions, a unanimous Court held marriage is "one of the vital personal rights essential to the orderly pursuit of happiness by free men." . . . Over time and in other contexts, the Court has reiterated that the right to marry is fundamental under the Due Process Clause.

It cannot be denied that this Court's cases describing the right to marry presumed a relationship involving opposite-sex partners. The Court, like many institutions, has made assumptions defined by the world and time of which it is a part. This was evident in *Baker v. Nelson*, a one-line summary decision issued in 1972, holding the exclusion of same-sex couples from marriage did not present a substantial federal question.

Still, there are other, more instructive precedents. This Court's cases have expressed constitutional principles of broader reach. In defining the right to marry these cases have identified essential attributes of that right based in history, tradition, and other constitutional liberties inherent in this intimate bond. And in assessing whether the force and rationale of its cases apply to same-sex couples, the Court must respect the basic reasons why the right to marry has been long protected.

This analysis compels the conclusion that same-sex couples may exercise the right to marry. The four principles and traditions to be discussed demonstrate that the reasons marriage is fundamental under the Constitution apply with equal force to same-sex couples.

A first premise of the Court's relevant precedents is that the right to personal choice regarding marriage is inherent in the concept of individual autonomy. This abiding connection between marriage and liberty is why *Loving* invalidated interracial marriage bans under the Due Process Clause. . . . Choices about marriage shape an individual's destiny. . . . The nature of marriage is that, through its enduring bond, two persons together can find other freedoms, such as expression, intimacy, and spirituality. This is true for all persons, whatever their sexual orientation. There is dignity in the bond between two men or two women who seek to marry and in their autonomy to make such profound choices.

A second principle in this Court's jurisprudence is that the right to marry is fundamental because it supports a two-person union unlike any other in its importance to the committed individuals. . . . Marriage responds to the universal fear that a lonely person might call out only to find no one there. It offers the hope of companionship and understanding and assurance that while both still live there will be someone to care for the other.

As this Court held in *Lawrence*, . . . "[w]hen sexuality finds overt expression in intimate conduct with another person, the conduct can be but one element in a personal bond that is more enduring." But while *Lawrence* confirmed a dimension of freedom that allows individuals to engage in intimate association without criminal liability, it does not follow that freedom stops there. Outlaw to outcast may be a step forward, but it does not achieve the full promise of liberty.

A third basis for protecting the right to marry is that it safeguards children and families and thus draws meaning from related rights of childrearing, procreation, and education. . . . By giving recognition and legal structure to their parents' relationship, marriage allows children "to understand the integrity and closeness of their own family and its concord with other families in their community and in their daily lives." *Windsor*. Marriage also affords the permanency and stability important to children's best interests.

As all parties agree, many same-sex couples provide loving and nurturing homes to their children, whether biological or adopted. And hundreds of thousands of children are presently being raised by such couples. Most States have allowed gays and lesbians to adopt, either as individuals or as couples, and many adopted and foster children have same-sex parents. This provides powerful confirmation from the law itself that gays and lesbians can create loving, supportive families.

Excluding same-sex couples from marriage thus conflicts with a central premise of the right to marry. Without the recognition, stability, and predictability marriage offers, their children suffer the stigma of knowing their families are somehow lesser. They also suffer the significant material costs of being raised by unmarried parents, relegated through no fault of their own to a more difficult and uncertain family life. The marriage laws at issue here

thus harm and humiliate the children of same-sex couples.

That is not to say the right to marry is less meaningful for those who do not or cannot have children. An ability, desire, or promise to procreate is not and has not been a prerequisite for a valid marriage in any State. In light of precedent protecting the right of a married couple not to procreate, it cannot be said the Court or the States have conditioned the right to marry on the capacity or commitment to procreate. The constitutional marriage right has many aspects, of which childbearing is only one.

Fourth and finally, this Court's cases and the Nation's traditions make clear that marriage is a keystone of our social order. . . . For that reason, just as a couple vows to support each other, so does society pledge to support the couple, offering symbolic recognition and material benefits to protect and nourish the union. Indeed, while the States are in general free to vary the benefits they confer on all married couples, they have throughout our history made marriage the basis for an expanding list of governmental rights, benefits, and responsibilities. These aspects of marital status include: taxation; inheritance and property rights; rules of intestate succession; spousal privilege in the law of evidence; hospital access; medical decision-making authority; adoption rights; the rights and benefits of survivors; birth and death certificates; professional ethics rules; campaign finance restrictions; workers' compensation benefits; health insurance; and child custody, support, and visitation rules. Valid marriage under state law is also a significant status for over a thousand provisions of federal law. The States have contributed to the fundamental character of the marriage right by placing that institution at the center of so many facets of the legal and social order.

There is no difference between same- and opposite-sex couples with respect to this principle. Yet by virtue of their exclusion from that institution, same-sex couples are denied the constellation of benefits that the States have linked to marriage. This harm results in more than just material burdens. Same-sex couples are consigned to an instability many opposite-sex couples would deem intolerable in their own lives. As the State itself makes marriage all the more precious by the significance it attaches to it, exclusion from that status has the effect of teaching that gays and lesbians are unequal in important respects. It demeans gays and lesbians for the State to lock them out of a central institution of the Nation's society. Same-sex couples, too, may aspire to the transcendent purposes of marriage and seek fulfillment in its highest meaning.

The limitation of marriage to opposite-sex couples may long have seemed natural and just, but its inconsistency with the central meaning of the fundamental right to marry is now manifest. With that knowledge must come the recognition that laws excluding same-sex couples from the marriage right impose stigma and injury of the kind prohibited by our basic charter. . . .

The right to marry is fundamental as a matter of history and tradition, but rights come not from ancient sources alone. They rise, too, from a better informed understanding of how constitutional imperatives define a liberty that remains urgent in our own era. Many who deem same-sex marriage to be wrong reach that conclusion based on decent and honorable religious or philosophical premises, and neither they nor their beliefs are disparaged here. But when that sincere, personal opposition becomes enacted law and public policy, the necessary consequence is to put the imprimatur of the State itself on an exclusion that soon demeans or stigmatizes those whose own liberty is then denied. Under the Constitution, same-sex couples seek in marriage the same legal treatment as opposite-sex couples, and it would disparage their choices and diminish their personhood to deny them this right.

The right of same-sex couples to marry that is part of the liberty promised by the Fourteenth Amendment is derived, too, from that Amendment's guarantee of the equal protection of the laws. The Due Process Clause and the Equal Protection Clause are connected in a profound way, though they set forth independent principles. Rights implicit in liberty and rights secured by equal protection may rest on different precepts and are not always co-extensive, yet in some instances each may be instructive as to the meaning and reach of the other. In any

particular case one Clause may be thought to capture the essence of the right in a more accurate and comprehensive way, even as the two Clauses may converge in the identification and definition of the right. This interrelation of the two principles furthers our understanding of what freedom is and must become. . . .

Indeed, in interpreting the Equal Protection Clause, the Court has recognized that new insights and societal understandings can reveal unjustified inequality within our most fundamental institutions that once passed unnoticed and unchallenged.. . . . It is now clear that the challenged laws burden the liberty of same-sex couples, and it must be further acknowledged that they abridge central precepts of equality. Here the marriage laws enforced by the respondents are in essence unequal: same-sex couples are denied all the benefits afforded to opposite-sex couples and are barred from exercising a fundamental right. Especially against a long history of disapproval of their relationships, this denial to same-sex couples of the right to marry works a grave and continuing harm. The imposition of this disability on gays and lesbians serves to disrespect and subordinate them. And the Equal Protection Clause, like the Due Process Clause, prohibits this unjustified infringement of the fundamental right to marry.

These considerations lead to the conclusion that the right to marry is a fundamental right inherent in the liberty of the person, and under the Due Process and Equal Protection Clauses of the Fourteenth Amendment couples of the same-sex may not be deprived of that right and that liberty. The Court now holds that same-sex couples may exercise the fundamental right to marry. No longer may this liberty be denied to them. *Baker v. Nelson* must be and now is overruled, and the State laws challenged by Petitioners in these cases are now held invalid to the extent they exclude same-sex couples from civil marriage on the same terms and conditions as opposite-sex couples.

IV

There may be an initial inclination in these cases to proceed with caution—to await further legislation, litigation, and debate. The respondents warn there has been insufficient democratic discourse before deciding an issue so basic as the definition of marriage. . . . Yet there has been far more deliberation than this argument acknowledges. There have been referenda, legislative debates, and grassroots campaigns, as well as countless studies, papers, books, and other popular and scholarly writings. There has been extensive litigation in state and federal courts. Judicial opinions addressing the issue have been informed by the contentions of parties and counsel, which, in turn, reflect the more general, societal discussion of same-sex marriage and its meaning that has occurred over the past decades. . . .

Of course, the Constitution contemplates that democracy is the appropriate process for change, so long as that process does not abridge fundamental rights. . . . The dynamic of our constitutional system is that individuals need not await legislative action before asserting a fundamental right. The Nation's courts are open to injured individuals who come to them to vindicate their own direct, personal stake in our basic charter. An individual can invoke a right to constitutional protection when he or she is harmed, even if the broader public disagrees and even if the legislature refuses to act. The idea of the Constitution "was to withdraw certain subjects from the vicissitudes of political controversy, to place them beyond the reach of majorities and officials and to establish them as legal principles to be applied by the courts." This is why "fundamental rights may not be submitted to a vote; they depend on the outcome of no elections." Ibid. It is of no moment whether advocates of same-sex marriage now enjoy or lack momentum in the democratic process. The issue before the Court here is the legal question whether the Constitution protects the right of same-sex couples to marry. . . .

Finally, it must be emphasized that religions, and those who adhere to religious doctrines, may continue to advocate with utmost, sincere conviction that, by divine precepts, same-sex marriage should not be condoned. The First Amendment ensures that religious organizations and persons are given proper protection as they seek to teach the principles that are so fulfilling and so central to their lives and faiths, and to their own deep aspirations to continue the family structure they have long revered. The same is true of those who oppose same-sex marriage for other reasons. In turn, those who believe allowing same-sex marriage is proper or indeed essential, whether as a matter of religious conviction or secular belief, may engage those who disagree with their view in an open and searching debate. The Constitution, however, does not permit the State to bar same-sex couples from marriage on the same terms as accorded to couples of the opposite sex.

V

These cases also present the question whether the Constitution requires States to recognize same-sex marriages validly performed out of State. . . . As counsel for the respondents acknowledged at argument, if States are required by the Constitution to issue marriage licenses to same-sex couples, the justifications for refusing to recognize those marriages performed elsewhere are undermined. The Court, in this decision, holds same-sex couples may exercise the fundamental right to marry in all States. It follows that the Court also must hold—and it now does hold—that there is no lawful basis for a State to refuse to recognize a lawful same-sex marriage performed in another State on the ground of its same-sex character.

* * *

No union is more profound than marriage, for it embodies the highest ideals of love, fidelity, devotion, sacrifice, and family. In forming a marital union, two people become something greater than once they were. As some of the petitioners in these cases demonstrate, marriage embodies a love that may endure even past death. It would misunderstand these men and women to say they disrespect the idea of marriage. Their plea is that they do respect it, respect it so deeply that they seek to find its fulfillment for themselves. Their hope is not to be condemned to live in loneliness, excluded from one of civilization's oldest institutions. They ask for equal dignity in the eyes of the law. The Constitution grants them that right.

The judgment of the Court of Appeals for the Sixth Circuit is reversed.

It is so ordered.

CHIEF JUSTICE ROBERTS, with whom JUSTICE SCALIA and JUSTICE THOMAS join, dissenting.

Petitioners make strong arguments rooted in social policy and considerations of fairness. They contend that same-sex couples should be allowed to affirm their love and commitment through marriage, just like opposite-sex couples. That position has undeniable appeal; over the past six years, voters and legislators in eleven States and the District of Columbia have revised their laws to allow marriage between two people of the same sex.

But this Court is not a legislature. Whether same-sex marriage is a good idea should be of no concern to us. Under the Constitution, judges have power to say what the law is, not what it should be. The people who ratified the Constitution authorized courts to exercise "neither force nor will but merely judgment." *The Federalist* No. 78.

Although the policy arguments for extending marriage to same-sex couples may be compelling, the legal arguments for requiring such an extension are not. The fundamental right to marry does not include a right to make a State change its definition of marriage. And a State's decision to maintain the meaning of marriage that has persisted in every culture throughout human history can hardly be called irrational. In short, our Constitution does not enact any one theory of marriage. The people of a State are free to expand marriage to include same-sex couples, or to retain the historic definition.

Today, however, the Court takes the extraordinary step of ordering every State to license and recognize same-sex marriage. Many people will rejoice at this decision, and I begrudge none their celebration. But for those who believe in a government of laws, not of men, the majority's approach is deeply disheartening. Supporters of same-sex marriage have achieved considerable success persuading their fellow citizens—through the democratic process—to adopt their view. That ends today. Five lawyers have closed the debate and enacted their own vision of marriage as a matter of constitutional law. Stealing this issue from the people will for many cast a cloud over same-sex marriage, making a dramatic social change that much more difficult to accept.

The majority's decision is an act of will, not legal judgment. The right it announces has no basis in the Constitution or this Court's precedent. The majority expressly disclaims judicial "caution" and omits even a pretense of humility, openly relying on its desire to remake society according to its own "new insight" into the "nature of injustice." As a result, the Court invalidates the marriage laws of more than half the States and orders the transformation of a social institution that has formed the basis of human society for millennia, for the Kalahari Bushmen and the Han Chinese, the Carthaginians and the Aztecs. Just who do we think we are?

It can be tempting for judges to confuse our own preferences with the requirements of the law. But as this Court has been reminded throughout our history, the Constitution "is made for people of fundamentally differing views." *Lochner v. New York* (Holmes, J., dissenting). Accordingly, "courts are not concerned with the wisdom or policy of legislation." The majority today neglects that restrained conception of the judicial role. It seizes for itself a question the Constitution leaves to the people, at a time when the people are engaged in a vibrant debate on that question. And it answers that question based not on neutral principles of constitutional law, but on its own "understanding of what freedom is and must become." I have no choice but to dissent.

Understand well what this dissent is about: It is not about whether, in my judgment, the institution of marriage should be changed to include same-sex couples. It is instead about whether, in our democratic republic, that decision should rest with the people acting through their elected representatives, or with five lawyers who happen to hold commissions authorizing them to resolve legal disputes according to law. The Constitution leaves no doubt about the answer. . . .

II

Petitioners first contend that the marriage laws of their States violate the Due Process Clause. . . . The Solicitor General of the United States, appearing in support of petitioners, expressly disowned that position before this Court. The majority nevertheless resolves these cases for petitioners based almost entirely on the Due Process Clause.

The majority purports to identify four "principles and traditions" in this Court's due process precedents that support a fundamental right for same-sex couples to marry. In reality, however, the majority's approach has no basis in principle or tradition, except for the unprincipled tradition of judicial policymaking that characterized discredited decisions such as *Lochner v. New York*. Stripped of its shiny rhetorical gloss, the majority's argument is that the Due Process Clause gives same-sex couples a fundamental right to marry because it will be good for them and for society. If I were a legislator, I would certainly consider that view as a matter of social policy. But as a judge, I find the majority's position indefensible as a matter of constitutional law.

A

Petitioners' "fundamental right" claim falls into the most sensitive category of constitutional adjudication. Petitioners do not contend that their States' marriage laws violate an enumerated constitutional right, such as the freedom of speech protected by the First Amendment. There is, after all, no "Companionship and Understanding" or "Nobility and Dignity" Clause in the Constitution. They argue instead that the laws violate a right implied by the Fourteenth Amendment's requirement that "liberty" may not be deprived without "due process of law."

This Court has interpreted the Due Process Clause to include a "substantive" component that protects certain liberty interests against state deprivation "no matter what process is provided." The theory is that some liberties are "so rooted in the traditions and conscience of our people as to be ranked as fundamental," and therefore cannot be deprived without compelling justification.

Allowing unelected federal judges to select which unenumerated rights rank as "fundamental"—and to strike down state laws on the basis of that determination—raises obvious concerns about the judicial role. Our precedents have accordingly insisted that judges "exercise the utmost care" in identifying implied fundamental rights, "lest the liberty protected by the Due Process Clause be subtly transformed into the policy preferences of the Members of this Court."

The need for restraint in administering the strong medicine of substantive due process is a lesson this Court has learned the hard way. The Court first applied substantive due process to strike down a statute in *Dred Scott v. Sandford* (1857). There the Court invalidated the Missouri Compromise on the ground that legislation restricting the institution of slavery violated the implied rights of slaveholders. The Court relied on its own conception of liberty and property in doing so. It asserted that "an act of Congress which deprives a citizen of the United States of his liberty or property, merely because he came himself or brought his property into a particular Territory of the United States . . . could hardly be dignified with the name of due process of law." In a dissent that has outlasted the majority opinion, Justice Curtis explained that when the "fixed rules which govern the interpretation of laws [are] abandoned, and the theoretical opinions of individuals are allowed to control" the Constitution's meaning, "we have no longer a Constitution; we are under the government of individual men, who for the time being have power to declare what the Constitution is, according to their own views of what it ought to mean."

Dred Scott's holding was overruled on the battlefields of the Civil War and by constitutional amendment after Appomattox, but its approach to the Due Process Clause reappeared. In a series of early 20th-century cases, most prominently *Lochner v. New York*, this Court invalidated state statutes that presented "meddlesome interferences with the rights of the individual," and "undue interference with liberty of person and freedom of contract." . . . The majority's contrary conclusion required adopting as constitutional law "an economic theory which a large part of the country does not entertain." As Justice Holmes memorably put it, "The Fourteenth Amendment does not enact Mr. Herbert Spencer's Social Statics," a leading work on the philosophy of Social Darwinism. The Constitution "is not intended to embody a particular economic theory. . . . It is made for people of fundamentally differing views, and the accident of our finding certain opinions natural and familiar or novel and even shocking ought not to conclude our judgment upon the question whether statutes embodying them conflict with the Constitution."

In the decades after *Lochner*, the Court struck down nearly 200 laws as violations of individual liberty, often over strong dissents contending that "[t]he criterion of constitutionality is not whether we believe the law to be for the public good." By empowering judges to elevate their own policy judgments to the status of constitutionally protected "liberty," the *Lochner* line of cases left "no alternative to regarding the court as a . . . legislative chamber."

Eventually, the Court recognized its error and vowed not to repeat it. "The doctrine that . . . due process authorizes courts to hold laws unconstitutional when they believe the legislature has acted unwisely," we later explained, "has long since been discarded. We have returned to the original constitutional proposition that courts do not substitute their social and economic beliefs for the judgment of legislative bodies, who are elected to pass laws." Thus, it has become an accepted rule that the Court will not hold laws unconstitutional simply because we find them "unwise, improvident, or out of harmony with a particular school of thought."

Rejecting *Lochner* does not require disavowing a doctrine of implied fundamental rights, and this Court has not done so. But to avoid repeating *Lochner*'s error of converting personal preferences into constitutional mandates, our modern substantive due process cases have stressed the need for "judicial self-restraint." Our precedents have required that implied fundamental rights be "objectively, deeply rooted in this Nation's history and tradition," and "implicit in the concept of ordered liberty, such that neither liberty nor justice would exist if they were sacrificed." . . .

B

The majority acknowledges none of this doctrinal background, and it is easy to see why: Its aggressive application of substantive due process breaks sharply with decades of precedent and returns the Court to the unprincipled approach of *Lochner*.

1

The majority's driving themes are that marriage is desirable and petitioners desire it. The opinion describes the "transcendent importance" of marriage and repeatedly insists that petitioners do not seek to "demean," "devalue," "denigrate," or "disrespect" the institution. Nobody disputes those points. Indeed, the compelling personal accounts of petitioners and others like them are likely a primary reason why many Americans have changed their minds about whether same-sex couples should be allowed to marry. As a matter of constitutional law, however, the sincerity of petitioners' wishes is not relevant.

When the majority turns to the law, it relies primarily on precedents discussing the fundamental "right to marry." These cases do not hold, of course, that anyone who wants to get married has a constitutional right to do so. They instead require a State to justify barriers to marriage as that institution has always been understood. In *Loving*, the Court held that racial restrictions on the right to marry lacked a compelling justification. . . .

None of the laws at issue in those cases purported to change the core definition of marriage as the union of a man and a woman. The . . . interracial marriage ban at issue in *Loving* define marriage as "the union of a man and a woman of the same race." Removing racial barriers to marriage therefore did not change what a marriage was any more than integrating schools changed what a school was. As the majority admits, the institution of "marriage" discussed in every one of these cases "presumed a relationship involving opposite-sex partners."

In short, the "right to marry" cases stand for the important but limited proposition that particular restrictions on access to marriage as traditionally defined violate due process. These precedents say nothing at all about a right to make a State change its definition of marriage, which is the right petitioners actually seek here. Neither petitioners nor the majority cites a single case or other legal source providing any basis for such a constitutional right. None exists, and that is enough to foreclose their claim.

2

The majority suggests that "there are other, more instructive precedents" informing the right to marry. Although not entirely clear, this reference seems to correspond to a line of cases discussing an implied fundamental "right of privacy." . . . The Court invoked the right to privacy in *Lawrence v. Texas* (2003), which struck down a Texas statute criminalizing homosexual sodomy. *Lawrence* relied on the position that criminal sodomy laws, like bans on contraceptives, invaded privacy by inviting "unwarranted government intrusions" that "touc[h] upon the most private human conduct, sexual behavior . . . in the most private of places, the home."

Neither *Lawrence* nor any other precedent in the privacy line of cases supports the right that petitioners assert here. Unlike criminal laws banning . . . sodomy, the marriage laws at issue here involve no government intrusion. They create no crime and impose no punishment. Same-sex couples remain free to live together, to engage in intimate conduct, and to raise their families as they see fit. No one is "condemned to live in loneliness" by the laws challenged in these cases—no one. At the same time, the laws in no way interfere with the "right to be let alone." . . .

In sum, the privacy cases provide no support for the majority's position, because petitioners do not seek privacy. Quite the opposite, they seek public recognition of their relationships, along with corresponding government benefits. Our cases have consistently refused to allow litigants to convert the shield provided by constitutional liberties into a sword to demand positive entitlements from the State. Thus, although the right to privacy recognized by our precedents certainly plays a role in protecting the intimate conduct of same-sex couples, it provides no affirmative right to redefine marriage and no basis for striking down the laws at issue here. . . .

Ultimately, only one precedent offers any support for the majority's methodology: *Lochner v. New York*. The majority opens its opinion by announcing petitioners' right to "define and express their identity." The majority later explains that "the right to personal choice regarding marriage is inherent in the concept of individual autonomy." This freewheeling notion of individual autonomy echoes nothing so much as "the general right of an individual to be free in his person and in his power to contract in relation to his own labor." *Lochner*.

. . . One immediate question invited by the majority's position is whether States may retain the definition of marriage as a union of two people. Although the majority randomly inserts the adjective "two" in various places, it offers no reason at all why the two-person element of the core definition of marriage may be preserved while the man-woman element may not. Indeed, from the standpoint of history and tradition, a leap from opposite-sex marriage to same-sex marriage is much greater than one from a two-person union to plural unions, which have deep roots in some cultures around the world. If the majority is willing to take the big leap, it is hard to see how it can say no to the shorter one.

It is striking how much of the majority's reasoning would apply with equal force to the claim of a fundamental right to plural marriage. If "[t]here is dignity in the bond between two men or two women who seek to marry and in their autonomy to make such profound choices," why would there be any less dignity in the bond between three people who, in exercising their autonomy, seek to make the profound choice to marry? If a same-sex couple has the constitutional right to marry because their children would otherwise "suffer the stigma of knowing their families are somehow lesser," why wouldn't the same reasoning apply to a family of three or more persons raising children? If not having the opportunity to marry "serves to disrespect and subordinate" gay and lesbian couples, why wouldn't the same "imposition of this disability" serve to disrespect and subordinate people who find fulfillment in polyamorous relationships?

I do not mean to equate marriage between same-sex couples with plural marriages in all respects. There may well be relevant differences that compel different legal analysis. But if there are, petitioners have not pointed to any. When asked about a plural marital union at oral argument, petitioners asserted that a State "doesn't have such an institution." But that is exactly the point: the States at issue here do not have an institution of same-sex marriage, either. . . .

III

In addition to their due process argument, petitioners contend that the Equal Protection

Clause requires their States to license and recognize same-sex marriages. The majority does not seriously engage with this claim. . . . [T]he majority fails to provide even a single sentence explaining how the Equal Protection Clause supplies independent weight for its position, nor does it attempt to justify its gratuitous violation of the canon against unnecessarily resolving constitutional questions. In any event, the marriage laws at issue here do not violate the Equal Protection Clause, because distinguishing between opposite-sex and same-sex couples is rationally related to the States' "legitimate state interest" in "preserving the traditional institution of marriage." *Lawrence* (O'Connor, J., concurring in judgment).

I V

Those who founded our country would not recognize the majority's conception of the judicial role. They after all risked their lives and fortunes for the precious right to govern themselves. They would never have imagined yielding that right on a question of social policy to unaccountable and unelected judges. . . . The Court's accumulation of power does not occur in a vacuum. It comes at the expense of the people. And they know it. Here and abroad, people are in the midst of a serious and thoughtful public debate on the issue of same-sex marriage. They see voters carefully considering same-sex marriage, casting ballots in favor or opposed, and sometimes changing their minds. They see political leaders similarly reexamining their positions, and either reversing course or explaining adherence to old convictions confirmed anew. They see governments and businesses modifying policies and practices with respect to same-sex couples, and participating actively in the civic discourse. They see countries overseas democratically accepting profound social change, or declining to do so. This deliberative process is making people take seriously questions that they may not have even regarded as questions before.

When decisions are reached through democratic means, some people will inevitably be disappointed with the results. But those whose views do not prevail at least know that they have had their say, and accordingly are—in the tradition of our political culture—reconciled to the result of a fair and honest debate. In addition, they can gear up to raise the issue later, hoping to persuade enough on the winning side to think again. "That is exactly how our system of government is supposed to work."

But today the Court puts a stop to all that. By deciding this question under the Constitution, the Court removes it from the realm of democratic decision. There will be consequences to shutting down the political process on an issue of such profound public significance. Closing debate tends to close minds. People denied a voice are less likely to accept the ruling of a court on an issue that does not seem to be the sort of thing courts usually decide. As a thoughtful commentator observed about another issue, "The political process was moving . . . , not swiftly enough for advocates of quick, complete change, but majoritarian institutions were listening and acting. Heavy-handed judicial intervention was difficult to justify and appears to have provoked, not resolved, conflict." Indeed, however heartened the proponents of same-sex marriage might be on this day, it is worth acknowledging what they have lost, and lost forever: the opportunity to win the true acceptance that comes from persuading their fellow citizens of the justice of their cause. And they lose this just when the winds of change were freshening at their backs.

Federal courts are blunt instruments when it comes to creating rights. They have constitutional power only to resolve concrete cases or controversies; they do not have the flexibility of legislatures to address concerns of parties not before the court or to anticipate problems that may arise from the exercise of a new right. Today's decision, for example, creates serious questions about religious liberty. Many good and decent people oppose same-sex marriage as a tenet of faith, and their freedom to exercise religion is—unlike the right imagined by the majority—actually spelled out in the Constitution.

Respect for sincere religious conviction has led voters and legislators in every State that has adopted same-sex marriage democratically to include accommodations for religious practice. The majority's decision imposing same-sex marriage cannot, of course, create any such accommodations. The majority graciously suggests that religious believers may continue to "advocate" and "teach" their views of marriage. The First Amendment guarantees, however, the freedom to "exercise" religion. Ominously, that is not a word the majority uses.

Hard questions arise when people of faith exercise religion in ways that may be seen to conflict with the new right to same-sex marriage—when, for example, a religious college provides married student housing only to opposite-sex married couples, or a religious adoption agency declines to place children with same-sex married couples. Indeed, the Solicitor General candidly acknowledged that the tax exemptions of some religious institutions would be in question if they opposed same-sex marriage. There is little doubt that these and similar questions will soon be before this Court. Unfortunately, people of faith can take no comfort in the treatment they receive from the majority today.

Perhaps the most discouraging aspect of today's decision is the extent to which the majority feels compelled to sully those on the other side of the debate. The majority offers a cursory assurance that it does not intend to disparage people who, as a matter of conscience, cannot accept same-sex marriage. That disclaimer is hard to square with the very next sentence, in which the majority explains that "the necessary consequence" of laws codifying the traditional definition of marriage is to "demea[n] or stigmatiz[e]" same-sex couples. The majority reiterates such characterizations over and over. By the majority's account, Americans who did nothing more than follow the understanding of marriage that has existed for our entire history—in particular, the tens of millions of people who voted to reaffirm their States' enduring definition of marriage—have acted to "lock . . . out," "disparage," "disrespect and subordinate," and inflict "[d]ignitary wounds" upon their gay and lesbian neighbors.

* * *

If you are among the many Americans—of whatever sexual orientation—who favor expanding same-sex marriage, by all means celebrate today's decision. Celebrate the achievement of a desired goal. Celebrate the opportunity for a new expression of commitment to a partner. Celebrate the availability of new benefits. But do not celebrate the Constitution. It had nothing to do with it.

I respectfully dissent.

JUSTICE SCALIA, with whom JUSTICE THOMAS joins, dissenting.

I join The Chief Justice's opinion in full. I write separately to call attention to this Court's threat to American democracy.

The substance of today's decree is not of immense personal importance to me. The law can recognize as marriage whatever sexual attachments and living arrangements it wishes, and can accord them favorable civil consequences, from tax treatment to rights of inheritance. Those civil consequences—and the public approval that conferring the name of marriage evidences—can perhaps have adverse social effects, but no more adverse than the effects of many other controversial laws. So it is not of special importance to me what the law says about marriage. It is of overwhelming importance, however, who it is that rules me. Today's decree says that my Ruler, and the Ruler of 320 million Americans coast-to-coast, is a majority of the nine lawyers on the Supreme Court. The opinion in these cases is the furthest extension in fact—and the furthest extension one can even imagine—of the Court's claimed power to create "liberties" that the Constitution and its Amendments neglect to mention. This practice of constitutional revision by an unelected committee of nine, always accompanied (as it is today) by extravagant praise of liberty, robs the People of the most important liberty they asserted in the Declaration of Independence and won in the Revolution of 1776: the freedom to govern themselves.

I

. . . The Constitution places some constraints on self-rule—constraints adopted by the People themselves when they ratified the Constitution and its Amendments. Forbidden are laws "impairing the Obligation of Contracts," denying "Full Faith and Credit" to the "public Acts" of other States, prohibiting the free exercise of religion, abridging the freedom of speech, infringing the right to keep and bear arms, authorizing unreasonable searches and seizures, and so forth. Aside from these limitations, those powers "reserved to the States respectively, or to the people" can be exercised as the States or the People desire. These cases ask us to decide whether the Fourteenth Amendment contains a limitation that requires the States to license and recognize marriages between two people of the same sex. Does it remove that issue from the political process?

Of course not. It would be surprising to find a prescription regarding marriage in the Federal Constitution since, as the author of today's opinion reminded us only two years ago (in an opinion joined by the same Justices who join him today): "[R]egulation of domestic relations is an area that has long been regarded as a virtually exclusive province of the States." "[T]he Federal Government, through our history, has deferred to state-law policy decisions with respect to domestic relations."

But we need not speculate. When the Fourteenth Amendment was ratified in 1868, every State limited marriage to one man and one woman, and no one doubted the constitutionality of doing so. That resolves these cases. When it comes to determining the meaning of a vague constitutional provision—such as "due process of law" or "equal protection of the laws"—it is unquestionable that the People who ratified that provision did not understand it to prohibit a practice that remained both universal and uncontroversial in the years after ratification. We have no basis for striking down a practice that is not expressly prohibited by the Fourteenth Amendment's text, and that bears the endorsement of a long tradition of open, widespread, and unchallenged use dating back to the Amendment's ratification. Since there is no doubt whatever that the People never decided to prohibit the limitation of marriage to opposite-sex couples, the public debate over same-sex marriage must be allowed to continue. . . .

II

But what really astounds is the hubris reflected in today's judicial Putsch. The five Justices who compose today's majority are entirely comfortable concluding that every State violated the Constitution for all of the 135 years between the Fourteenth Amendment's ratification and Massachusetts' permitting of same-sex marriages in 2003. They have discovered in the Fourteenth Amendment a "fundamental right" overlooked by every person alive at the time of ratification, and almost everyone else in the time since. They see what lesser legal minds—minds like Thomas Cooley, John Marshall Harlan, Oliver Wendell Holmes, Jr., Learned Hand, Louis Brandeis, William Howard Taft, Benjamin Cardozo, Hugo Black, Felix Frankfurter, Robert Jackson, and Henry Friendly—could not. They are certain that the People ratified the Fourteenth Amendment to bestow on them the power to remove questions from the democratic process when that is called for by their "reasoned judgment." These Justices know that limiting marriage to one man and one woman is contrary to reason; they know that an institution as old as government itself, and accepted by every nation in history until 15 years ago, cannot possibly be supported by anything other than ignorance or bigotry. And they are willing to say that any citizen who does not agree with that, who adheres to what was, until 15 years ago, the unanimous judgment of all generations and all societies, stands against the Constitution.

JUSTICE THOMAS, with whom JUSTICE SCALIA joins, dissenting.

The Court's decision today is at odds not only with the Constitution, but with the principles upon which our Nation was built. Since well before 1787, liberty has been understood as freedom from government action, not entitlement to government benefits. The Framers created our Constitution to preserve that understanding of liberty. Yet the majority invokes our Constitution in the name of a "liberty" that the Framers would not have recognized, to the detriment of the liberty they sought to protect. Along the way, it rejects the idea—captured in our Declaration of Independence—that human dignity is innate and suggests instead that it comes from the Government. This distortion of our Constitution not only ignores the text, it inverts the relationship between the individual and the state in our Republic. I cannot agree with it. . . .

II

. . . The majority claims these state laws deprive petitioners of "liberty," but the concept of "liberty" it conjures up bears no resemblance to any plausible meaning of that word as it is used in the Due Process Clauses. . . . As used in the Due Process Clauses, "liberty" most likely refers to "the power of locomotion, of changing situation, or removing one's person to whatsoever place one's own inclination may direct; without imprisonment or restraint, unless by due course of law." 1 W. Blackstone, *Commentaries on the Laws of England* 130 (1769) That definition is drawn from the historical roots of the Clauses and is consistent with our Constitution's text and structure. . . . Even assuming that the "liberty" in those Clauses encompasses something more than freedom from physical restraint, it would not include the types of rights claimed by the majority. In the American legal tradition, liberty has long been understood as individual freedom from governmental action, not as a right to a particular governmental entitlement. . . .

Whether we define "liberty" as locomotion or freedom from governmental action more broadly, petitioners have in no way been deprived of it.

Petitioners cannot claim, under the most plausible definition of "liberty," that they have been imprisoned or physically restrained by the States for participating in same-sex relationships. To the contrary, they have been able to cohabitate and raise their children in peace. They have been able to hold civil marriage ceremonies in States that recognize same-sex marriages and private religious ceremonies in all States. They have been able to travel freely around the country, making their homes where they please. Far from being incarcerated or physically restrained, petitioners have been left alone to order their lives as they see fit.

Nor, under the broader definition, can they claim that the States have restricted their ability to go about their daily lives as they would be able to absent governmental restrictions. Petitioners do not ask this Court to order the States to stop restricting their ability to enter same-sex relationships, to engage in intimate behavior, to make vows to their partners in public ceremonies, to engage in religious wedding ceremonies, to hold themselves out as married, or to raise children. The States have imposed no such restrictions. Nor have the States prevented petitioners from approximating a number of incidents of marriage through private legal means, such as wills, trusts, and powers of attorney.

Instead, the States have refused to grant them governmental entitlements. Petitioners claim that as a matter of "liberty," they are entitled to access privileges and benefits that exist solely because of the government. They want, for example, to receive the State's imprimatur on their marriages—on state issued marriage licenses, death certificates, or other official forms. And they want to receive various monetary benefits, including reduced inheritance taxes upon the death of a spouse, compensation if a spouse dies as a result of a work-related injury, or loss of consortium damages in tort suits. But receiving governmental recognition and benefits has nothing to do with any understanding of "liberty" that the Framers would have recognized.

To the extent that the Framers would have recognized a natural right to marriage that fell within the broader definition of liberty, it would not have included a right to governmental recognition and benefits. Instead, it would have included a right to engage in the very same activities that petitioners have been left free to engage in—making vows, holding religious ceremonies celebrating those vows, raising children, and otherwise enjoying the society of one's spouse—without governmental interference. At the founding, such conduct was understood to predate government, not to flow from it. . . .

In a concession to petitioners' misconception of liberty, the majority characterizes petitioners' suit as a quest to "find . . . liberty by marrying someone of the same sex and having their marriages deemed lawful on the same terms and conditions as marriages between persons of the opposite sex." But "liberty" is not lost, nor can it be found in the way petitioners seek. As a philosophical matter, liberty is only freedom from governmental action, not an entitlement to governmental benefits. And as a constitutional matter, it is likely even narrower than that, encompassing only free-dom from physical restraint and imprison-ment. The majority's "better informed understanding of how constitutional impera-tives define . . . liberty"—better informed, we must assume, than that of the people who rati-fied the Fourteenth Amendment—runs head-long into the reality that our Constitution is a "collection of 'Thou shalt nots,'" not "Thou shalt provides."

III

B

. . . Numerous amici—even some not sup-porting the States—have cautioned the Court that its decision here will "have unavoidable and wide-ranging implications for religious lib-erty." In our society, marriage is not simply a governmental institution; it is a religious insti-tution as well. Today's decision might change the former, but it cannot change the latter. It appears all but inevitable that the two will come into conflict, particularly as individuals and churches are confronted with demands to participate in and endorse civil marriages be-tween same-sex couples.

The majority appears unmoved by that inev-itability. It makes only a weak gesture toward religious liberty in a single paragraph. And even that gesture indicates a misunderstand-ing of religious liberty in our Nation's tradition. Religious liberty is about more than just the protection for "religious organizations and persons . . . as they seek to teach the principles that are so fulfilling and so central to their lives and faiths." Religious liberty is about freedom of action in matters of religion gener-ally, and the scope of that liberty is directly correlated to the civil restraints placed upon religious practice.

IV

. . . [T]he majority goes to great lengths to as-sert that its decision will advance the "dignity" of same-sex couples. The flaw in that reasoning, of course, is that the Constitution contains no "dignity" Clause, and even if it did, the govern-ment would be incapable of bestowing dignity.

Human dignity has long been understood in this country to be innate. When the Framers proclaimed in the Declaration of Indepen-dence that "all men are created equal" and "en-dowed by their Creator with certain unalienable Rights," they referred to a vision of mankind in which all humans are created in the image of God and therefore of inherent worth. That vi-sion is the foundation upon which this Nation was built.

The corollary of that principle is that human dignity cannot be taken away by the govern-ment. Slaves did not lose their dignity (any more than they lost their humanity) because the government allowed them to be enslaved. Those held in internment camps did not lose their dignity because the government confined them. And those denied governmental benefits certainly do not lose their dignity because the government denies them those benefits. The government cannot bestow dignity, and it can-not take it away. . . .

JUSTICE ALITO, with whom JUSTICE SCA-LIA and JUSTICE THOMAS join, dissenting.

The Constitution says nothing about a right to same-sex marriage. . . . Attempting to cir-cumvent the problem presented by the new-ness of the right found in these cases, the majority claims that the issue is the right to equal treatment. Noting that marriage is a fun-damental right, the majority argues that a State has no valid reason for denying that right to same-sex couples. . . . This understanding of marriage, which focuses almost entirely on the happiness of persons who choose to marry, is shared by many people today, but it is not the traditional one. For millennia, marriage was inextricably linked to the one thing that only an opposite-sex couple can do: procreate.

. . . [T]he States defending their adherence to the traditional understanding of marriage have explained their position using the prag-matic vocabulary that characterizes most American political discourse. Their basic argu-ment is that States formalize and promote marriage, unlike other fulfilling human rela-tionships, in order to encourage potentially procreative conduct to take place within a last-ing unit that has long been thought to provide the best atmosphere for raising children. They thus argue that there are reasonable secular grounds for restricting marriage to opposite-sex couples.

If this traditional understanding of the purpose of marriage does not ring true to all ears today, that is probably because the tie between marriage and procreation has frayed. Today, for instance, more than 40% of all children in this country are born to unmarried women. This development undoubtedly is both a cause and a result of changes in our society's understanding of marriage.

While, for many, the attributes of marriage in 21st-century America have changed, those States that do not want to recognize same-sex marriage have not yet given up on the traditional understanding. They worry that by officially abandoning the older understanding, they may contribute to marriage's further decay. It is far beyond the outer reaches of this Court's authority to say that a State may not adhere to the understanding of marriage that has long prevailed, not just in this country and others with similar cultural roots, but also in a great variety of countries and cultures all around the globe. . . .

Cruzan v. Director, Missouri Department of Health
497 U.S. 261 (1990)

Nancy Cruzan was thrown from her car and sustained severe injuries in an automobile accident in 1983. Before paramedics arrived on the scene and restored her heartbeat and breathing, her brain had been deprived of oxygen for twelve to fourteen minutes. She remained in a coma for about three weeks and then fell into a persistent vegetative state, exhibiting motor reflexes but evincing no indications of significant cognitive function. When subsequent rehabilitative efforts proved unsuccessful, she was moved to a Missouri state hospital and cared for at state expense. As it became increasingly apparent that she had virtually no chance of regaining her mental faculties, her parents asked the state hospital employees to terminate the artificial nutrition and hydration procedures keeping her alive. They refused, without a court order, to honor the parents' request, since that would result in her death. A state court judge authorized the termination, finding that Cruzan had a fundamental right under the Fourteenth Amendment to direct or refuse the withdrawal of life-prolonging procedures and that Cruzan's expression to a former housemate that she would not wish to continue her life if sick or injured unless she could live "at least halfway normally" suggested that she would not wish to continue on with artificial nutrition and hydration. The Missouri Supreme Court reversed; it declined to read into either the Missouri Constitution or the US Constitution a broad right to privacy that would support an unrestricted right to refuse treatment, and it rejected the argument that her parents were entitled to order the termination of her medical treatment, concluding that no person can assume that choice for an incompetent in the absence of a living will or clear and convincing evidence of the patient's wishes. The Supreme Court granted certiorari. Opinion of the Court: <u>Rehnquist</u>, White, O'Connor, Scalia, Kennedy. Concurring opinions: <u>O'Connor</u>; <u>Scalia</u>. Dissenting opinions: <u>Brennan</u>, Marshall, Blackmun; <u>Stevens</u>.

THE CHIEF JUSTICE delivered the opinion of the Court.

. . . This is the first case in which we have been squarely presented with the issue of whether the United States Constitution grants what is in common parlance referred to as a "right to die." We follow the judicious counsel of our decision in *Twin City Bank v. Nebeker* (1897), where we said that in deciding "a question of such magnitude and importance . . . it is the [better] part of wisdom not to attempt, by any general statement, to cover every possible phase of the subject."

The Fourteenth Amendment provides that no State shall "deprive any person of life, liberty, or property, without due process of law." The principle that a competent person has a constitutionally protected liberty interest in refusing unwanted medical treatment may be inferred from our prior decisions. In *Jacobson v. Massachusetts* (1905), for instance, the Court balanced an individual's liberty interest in declining an unwanted smallpox vaccine against the State's interest in preventing disease. . . .

But determining that a person has a "liberty interest" under the Due Process Clause does not end the inquiry; "whether respondent's constitutional rights have been violated must be determined by balancing his liberty interests against the relevant state interests."

[F]or purposes of this case, we assume that the United States Constitution would grant a competent person a constitutionally protected right to refuse lifesaving hydration and nutrition.

Petitioners go on to assert that an incompetent person should possess the same right in this respect as is possessed by a competent person. . . .

The difficulty with petitioners' claim is that in a sense it begs the question: an incompetent person is not able to make an informed and voluntary choice to exercise a hypothetical right to refuse treatment or any other right. Such a "right" must be exercised for her, if at all, by some sort of surrogate. Here, Missouri has in effect recognized that under certain circumstances a surrogate may act for the patient in electing to have hydration and nutrition withdrawn in such a way as to cause death, but it has established a procedural safeguard to assure that the action of the surrogate conforms as best it may to the wishes expressed by the patient while competent. Missouri requires that evidence of the incompetent's wishes as to the withdrawal of treatment be proved by clear and convincing evidence. The question, then, is whether the United States Constitution forbids the establishment of this procedural requirement by the State. We hold that it does not.

Whether or not Missouri's clear and convincing evidence requirement comports with the United States Constitution depends in part on what interests the State may properly seek to protect in this situation. Missouri relies on its interest in the protection and preservation of human life, and there can be no gainsaying this interest. As a general matter, the States—indeed, all civilized nations—demonstrate their commitment to life by treating homicide as serious crime. Moreover, the majority of States in this country have laws imposing criminal penalties on one who assists another to commit suicide. We do not think a State is required to remain neutral in the face of an informed and voluntary decision by a physically able adult to starve to death.

But in the context presented here, a State has more particular interests at stake. The choice between life and death is a deeply personal decision of obvious and overwhelming finality. We believe Missouri may legitimately seek to safeguard the personal element of this choice through the imposition of heightened evidentiary requirements. It cannot be disputed that the Due Process Clause protects an interest in life as well as an interest in refusing life-sustaining medical treatment. Not all incompetent patients will have loved ones available to serve as surrogate decisionmakers.

In our view, Missouri has permissibly sought to advance these interests through the adoption of a "clear and convincing" standard of proof to govern such proceedings. "The function of a standard of proof, as that concept is embodied in the Due Process Clause and in the realm of factfinding, is to 'instruct the factfinder concerning the degree of confidence our society thinks he should have in the correctness of factual conclusions for a particular type of adjudication.'"

We think it self-evident that the interests at stake in the instant proceedings are more substantial, both on an individual and societal level, than those involved in a run-of-the-mill civil dispute. But not only does the standard of proof reflect the importance of a particular adjudication, it also serves as "a societal judgment about how the risk of error should be distributed between the litigants." The more stringent the burden of proof a party must bear, the more that party bears the risk of an erroneous decision. We believe that Missouri may permissibly place an increased risk of an erroneous decision on those seeking to terminate an incompetent individual's life-sustaining treatment. An erroneous decision not to terminate results in a maintenance of the status quo; the possibility of subsequent developments such as advancements in medical science, the discovery of new evidence regarding the patient's intent, changes in the law, or simply the unexpected death of the patient despite the administration of life-sustaining treatment, at least create the potential that a wrong decision will eventually be corrected or its impact mitigated. An erroneous decision to withdraw life-sustaining treatment, however, is not susceptible of correction. . . .

In sum, we conclude that a State may apply a clear and convincing evidence standard in proceedings where a guardian seeks to discontinue nutrition and hydration of a person diagnosed to be in a persistent vegetative state. We note that many courts which have adopted some sort of substituted judgment procedure in situations like this, whether they limit consideration of evidence to the prior expressed wishes of the incompetent individual, or whether they allow more general proof of what the individual's decision would have been, require a clear and convincing standard of proof for such evidence. . . .

No doubt is engendered by anything in this record but that Nancy Cruzan's mother and father are loving and caring parents. If the State were required by the United States Constitution to repose a right of "substituted judgment" with anyone, the Cruzans would surely qualify. But we do not think the Due Process Clause requires the State to repose judgment on these matters with anyone but the patient herself. Close family members may have a strong feeling—a feeling not at all ignoble or unworthy, but not entirely disinterested, either—that they do not wish to witness the continuation of the life of a loved one which they regard as hopeless, meaningless, and even degrading. But there is no automatic assurance that the view of close family members will necessarily be the same as the patient's would have been had she been confronted with the prospect of her situation while competent. All of the reasons previously discussed for allowing Missouri to require clear and convincing evidence of the patient's wishes lead us to conclude that the State may choose to defer only to those wishes, rather than confide the decision to close family members.

The judgment of the Supreme Court of Missouri is

Affirmed.

JUSTICE O'CONNOR concurring.

I agree that a protected liberty interest in refusing unwanted medical treatment may be inferred from our prior decisions, and that the refusal of artificially delivered food and water is encompassed within that liberty interest. I write separately to clarify why I believe this to be so.

As the Court notes, the liberty interest in refusing medical treatment flows from decisions involving the State's invasions into the body. Because our notions of liberty are inextricably entwined with our idea of physical freedom and self-determination, the Court has often deemed state incursions into the body repugnant to the interests protected by the Due Process Clause. . . .

Accordingly, the liberty guaranteed by the Due Process Clause must protect, if it protects anything, an individual's deeply personal decision to reject medical treatment, including the artificial delivery of food and water.

I also write separately to emphasize that the Court does not today decide the issue whether a State must also give effect to the decisions of a surrogate decisionmaker. In my view, such a duty may well be constitutionally required to protect the patient's liberty interest in refusing medical treatment. Few individuals provide explicit oral or written instructions regarding their intent to refuse medical treatment should they become incompetent. States which decline to consider any evidence other than such instructions may frequently fail to honor a patient's intent. Such failures might be avoided if the State considered an equally probative source of evidence: the patient's appointment of a proxy to make health care decisions on her behalf. Delegating the authority to make medical decisions to a family member or friend is becoming a common method of planning for the future. . . .

Today's decision, holding only that the Constitution permits a State to require clear and convincing evidence of Nancy Cruzan's desire to have artificial hydration and nutrition withdrawn, does not preclude a future determination that the Constitution requires the States to implement the decisions of a patient's duly appointed surrogate. Nor does it prevent States from developing other approaches for protecting an incompetent individual's liberty interest in refusing medical treatment. As is evident from the Court's survey of state court decisions, no national consensus has yet emerged on the best solution for this difficult and sensitive problem. Today we decide only that one State's practice does not violate the Constitution; the more challenging task of crafting appropriate procedures for safeguarding incompetents' liberty interests is entrusted to the "laboratory" of the States in the first instance.

JUSTICE SCALIA, concurring.

The various opinions in this case portray quite clearly the difficult, indeed agonizing, questions that are presented by the constantly increasing power of science to keep the human body alive for longer than any reasonable person would want to inhabit it. The States have begun to grapple with these problems through legislation. I am concerned, from the tenor of today's opinions, that we are poised to confuse that enterprise as successfully as we have confused the enterprise of legislating concerning abortion—requiring it to be conducted against a background of federal constitutional imperatives that are unknown because they are being newly crafted from Term to Term. That would be a great misfortune.

While I agree with the Court's analysis today, and therefore join in its opinion, I would have preferred that we announce, clearly and promptly, that the federal courts have no business in this field; that American law has always accorded the State the power to prevent, by force if necessary, suicide—including suicide by refusing to take appropriate measures necessary to preserve one's life; that the point at which life becomes "worthless," and the point at which the means necessary to preserve it become "extraordinary" or "inappropriate," are neither set forth in the Constitution nor known to the nine Justices of this Court any better than they are known to nine people picked at random from the Kansas City telephone directory; and hence, that even when it *is* demonstrated by clear and convincing evidence that a patient no longer wishes certain measures to be taken to preserve her life, it is up to the citizens of Missouri to decide, through their elected representatives, whether that wish will be honored. It is quite impossible (because the Constitution says nothing about the matter) that those citizens will decide upon a line less lawful than the one we

would choose; and it is unlikely (because we know no more about "life-and-death" than they do) that they will decide upon a line less reasonable.

The text of the Due Process Clause does not protect individuals against deprivations of liberty *simpliciter*. It protects them against deprivations of liberty "without due process of law." To determine that such a deprivation would not occur if Nancy Cruzan were forced to take nourishment against her will, it is unnecessary to reopen the historically recurrent debate over whether "due process" includes substantive restrictions. . . . It is at least true that no "substantive due process" claim can be maintained unless the claimant demonstrates that the State has deprived him of a right historically and traditionally protected against State interference. *Bowers v. Hardwick* (1986). . . . That cannot possibly be established here. . . .

I assert only that the Constitution has nothing to say about [a "right to die"]. To raise up a constitutional right here we would have to create out of nothing (for it exists neither in text nor tradition) some constitutional principle whereby, although the State may insist that an individual come in out of the cold and eat food, it may not insist that he take medicine; and although it may pump his stomach empty of poison he has ingested, it may not fill his stomach with food he has failed to ingest. Are there, then, no reasonable and humane limits that ought not to be exceeded in requiring an individual to preserve his own life? There obviously are, but they are not set forth in the Due Process Clause. What assures us that those limits will not be exceeded is the same constitutional guarantee that is the source of most of our protection—what protects us, for example, from being assessed a tax of 100% of our income above the subsistence level, from being forbidden to drive cars, or from being required to send our children to school for 10 hours a day, none of which horribles is categorically prohibited by the Constitution. Our salvation is the Equal Protection Clause, which requires the democratic majority to accept for themselves and their loved ones what they impose on you and me. This Court need not, and has no authority to, inject itself into every field of human activity where irrationality and oppression may theoretically occur, and if it tries to do so it will destroy itself.

JUSTICE BRENNAN, with whom JUSTICE MARSHALL and JUSTICE BLACKMUN join, dissenting.

Because I believe that Nancy Cruzan has a fundamental right to be free of unwanted artificial nutrition and hydration, which right is not outweighed by any interests of the State, and because I find that the improperly biased procedural obstacles imposed by the Missouri Supreme Court impermissibly burden that right, I respectfully dissent. Nancy Cruzan is entitled to choose to die with dignity. . . .

The question before this Court is a relatively narrow one: whether the Due Process Clause allows Missouri to require a now-incompetent patient in an irreversible persistent vegetative state to remain on life-support absent rigorously clear and convincing evidence that avoiding the treatment represents the patient's prior, express choice. . . .

The starting point for our legal analysis must be whether a competent person has a constitutional right to avoid unwanted medical care. Earlier this Term, this Court held that the Due Process Clause of the Fourteenth Amendment confers a significant liberty interest in avoiding unwanted medical treatment. Today, the Court concedes that our prior decisions "support the recognition of a general liberty interest in refusing medical treatment." . . .

But if a competent person has a liberty interest to be free of unwanted medical treatment, as both the majority and Justice O'Connor concede, it must be fundamental. "We are dealing here with [a decision] which involves one of the basic civil rights of man." The right to be free from medical attention without consent, to determine what shall be done with one's own body, *is* deeply rooted in this Nation's traditions, as the majority acknowledges.

This right has long been "firmly entrenched in American tort law" and is securely grounded in the earliest common law. That there may be serious consequences involved in refusal of the medical treatment at issue here does not vitiate the right under our common law tradition of medical self-determination. . . .

The right to be free from unwanted medical attention is a right to evaluate the potential benefit of treatment and its possible consequences according to one's own values and to make a personal decision whether to subject oneself to the intrusion. For a patient like Nancy Cruzan, the sole benefit of medical treatment is being kept metabolically alive. Neither artificial nutrition nor any other form of medical treatment available today can cure or in any way ameliorate her condition. Irreversibly vegetative patients are devoid of thought, emotion and sensation; they are permanently and completely unconscious. . . .

There are also affirmative reasons why someone like Nancy might choose to forgo artificial nutrition and hydration under these circumstances. Dying is personal. And it is profound. For many, the thought of an ignoble end, steeped in decay, is abhorrent. A quiet, proud death, bodily integrity intact, is a matter of extreme consequence. . . .

Although the right to be free of unwanted medical intervention, like other constitutionally protected interests, may not be absolute, no State interest could outweigh the rights of an individual in Nancy Cruzan's position. Whatever a State's possible interests in mandating life-support treatment under other circumstances, there is no good to be obtained here by Missouri's insistence that Nancy Cruzan remain on life-support systems if it is indeed her wish not to do so. Missouri does not claim, nor could it, that society as a whole will be benefited by Nancy's receiving medical treatment. No third party's situation will be improved and no harm to others will be averted.

The only state interest asserted here is a general interest in the preservation of life. But the State has no legitimate general interest in someone's life, completely abstracted from the interest of the person living that life, that could outweigh the person's choice to avoid medical treatment. . . . Thus, the State's general interest in life must accede to Nancy Cruzan's particularized and intense interest in self-determination in her choice of medical treatment. There is simply nothing legitimately within the State's purview to be gained by superseding her decision. . . .

This is not to say that the State has no legitimate interests to assert here. As the majority recognizes, Missouri has a *parens patriae* interest in providing Nancy Cruzan, now incompetent, with as accurate as possible a determination of how she would exercise her rights under these circumstances. Second, if and when it is determined that Nancy Cruzan would want to continue treatment, the State may legitimately assert an interest in providing that treatment. But *until* Nancy's wishes have been determined, the only state interest that may be asserted is an interest in safeguarding the accuracy of that determination.

Accuracy, therefore, must be our touchstone. Missouri may constitutionally impose only those procedural requirements that serve to enhance the accuracy of a determination of Nancy Cruzan's wishes or are at least consistent with an accurate determination. The Missouri "safeguard" that the Court upholds today does not meet that standard. The determination needed in this context is whether the incompetent person would choose to live in a persistent vegetative state on life-support or to avoid this medical treatment. Missouri's rule of decision imposes a markedly asymmetrical evidentiary burden. Only evidence of specific statements of treatment choice made by the patient when competent is admissible to support a finding that the patient, now in a persistent vegetative state, would wish to avoid further medical treatment. Moreover, this evidence must be clear and convincing. No proof is required to support a finding that the incompetent person would wish to continue treatment.

The majority offers several justifications for Missouri's heightened evidentiary standard. First, the majority explains that the State may constitutionally adopt this rule to govern determinations of an incompetent's wishes in order to advance the State's substantive interests, including its unqualified interest in the preservation of human life. Missouri's evidentiary standard, however, cannot rest on the State's own interest in a particular substantive result. To be sure, courts have long erected clear and convincing evidence standards to place the greater risk of erroneous decisions on those bringing disfavored claims. In such cases, however, the choice to discourage certain claims was a legitimate, constitutional policy choice. In contrast, Missouri has no such power to disfavor a choice by Nancy Cruzan to avoid medical treatment, because Missouri has no legitimate interest in providing Nancy with treatment until it is established that this represents her choice. Just as a State may not override Nancy's choice directly, it may not do so indirectly through the imposition of a procedural rule.

The majority claims that the allocation of the risk of error is justified because it is more important not to terminate life-support for someone who would wish it continued than to honor the wishes of someone who would not. An erroneous decision to terminate life-support is irrevocable, says the majority, while an erroneous decision not to terminate "results in a maintenance of the status quo." But, from the point of view of the patient, an erroneous decision in either direction is irrevocable. An erroneous decision to terminate artificial nutrition and hydration, to be sure, will lead to failure of that last remnant of physiological life, the brain stem, and result in complete brain death. An erroneous decision not to terminate life-support, however, robs a patient of the very qualities protected by the right to avoid unwanted medical treatment. His own degraded existence is perpetuated; his family's suffering is protracted; the memory he leaves behind becomes more and more distorted. . . .

Even more than its heightened evidentiary standard, the Missouri court's categorical exclusion of relevant evidence dispenses with any semblance of accurate factfinding. The court adverted to no evidence supporting its decision, but held that no clear and convincing, inherently reliable evidence had been presented to show that Nancy would want to avoid further treatment. In doing so, the court failed to consider statements Nancy had made to family members and a close friend. The court also failed to consider testimony from Nancy's mother and sister that they were certain that Nancy would want to discontinue artificial nutrition and hydration, even after the court found that Nancy's family was loving and without malignant motive. The court also failed to consider the conclusions of the guardian *ad litem,* appointed by the trial court, that there was clear and convincing evidence that Nancy would want to discontinue medical treatment and that this was in her best interests. The court did not specifically define what kind of evidence it would consider clear and convincing, but its general discussion suggests that only a living will or equivalently formal directive from the patient when competent would meet this standard. . . .

Too few people execute living wills or equivalently formal directives for such an evidentiary rule to ensure adequately that the wishes of incompetent persons will be honored. While it might be a wise social policy to encourage people to furnish such instructions, no general conclusion about a patient's choice can be drawn from the absence of formalities. The probability of becoming irreversibly vegetative is so low that many people may not feel an urgency to marshal formal evidence of their preferences. Some may not wish to dwell on their own physical deterioration and mortality. Even someone with a resolute determination to avoid life-support under circumstances such as Nancy's would still need to know that such things as living wills exist and how to execute one. Often legal help would be necessary, especially given the majority's apparent willingness to permit States to insist that a person's wishes are not truly known unless the particular medical treatment is specified. . . .

I do not suggest that States must sit by helplessly if the choices of incompetent patients are in danger of being ignored. Even if the Court had ruled that Missouri's rule of decision is unconstitutional, as I believe it should have, States would nevertheless remain free to fashion procedural protections to safeguard the interests of incompetents under these circumstances. The Constitution provides merely a framework here: protections must be genuinely aimed at ensuring decisions commensurate with the will of the patient, and must be reliable as instruments to that end. Of the many States which have instituted such protections, Missouri is virtually the only one to have fashioned a rule that lessens the likelihood of accurate determinations. In contrast, nothing in the Constitution prevents States from reviewing the advisability of a family decision, by requiring a court proceeding or by appointing an impartial guardian *ad litem*. . . .

Finally, I cannot agree with the majority that where it is not possible to determine what choice an incompetent patient would make, a State's role as *parens patriae* permits the State automatically to make that choice itself. . . .

The majority justifies its position by arguing that, while close family members may have a strong feeling about the question, "there is no automatic assurance that the view of close family members will necessarily be the same as the patient's would have been had she been confronted with the prospect of her situation while competent." I cannot quarrel with this observation. But it leads only to another question: Is there any reason to suppose that a State is *more* likely to make the choice that the patient would have made than someone who knew the patient intimately? To ask this is to answer it. As the New Jersey Supreme Court observed: "Family members are best qualified to make substituted judgments for incompetent patients not only because of their peculiar grasp of the patient's approach to life, but also because of their special bonds with him or her. . . . It is . . . they who treat the patient as a person, rather than a symbol of a cause." The State, in contrast, is a stranger to the patient.

I respectfully dissent.

JUSTICE STEVENS, dissenting.

Nancy Cruzan's interest in life, no less than that of any other person, includes an interest in how she will be thought of after her death by those whose opinions mattered to her. There can be no doubt that her life made her dear to her family, and to others. How she dies will affect how that life is remembered. The trial court's order authorizing Nancy's parents to cease their daughter's treatment would have permitted the family that cares for Nancy to bring to a close her tragedy and her death. Missouri's objection to that order subordinates Nancy's body, her family, and the lasting significance of her life to the State's own interests. The decision we review thereby interferes with constitutional interests of the highest order.

To be constitutionally permissible, Missouri's intrusion upon these fundamental liberties must, at a minimum, bear a reasonable relationship to a legitimate state end. Missouri asserts that its policy is related to a state interest in the protection of life. In my view, however, it is an effort to define life, rather than to protect it, that is the heart of Missouri's policy. Missouri insists, without regard to Nancy Cruzan's own interests, upon equating her life with the biological persistence of her bodily functions. Nancy Cruzan, it must be remembered, is not now simply incompetent. She is in a persistent vegetative state, and has been so for seven years. The trial court found, and no party contested, that Nancy has no possibility of recovery and no consciousness.

It seems to me that the Court errs insofar as it characterizes this case as involving "judgments about the 'quality' of life that a particular individual may enjoy." Nancy Cruzan is obviously "*alive*" in a physiological sense. But for patients like Nancy Cruzan, who have no consciousness and no chance of recovery, there is a serious question as to whether the mere persistence of their bodies is "*life*" as that word is commonly understood, or as it is used in both the Constitution and the Declaration of Independence. The State's unflagging determination to perpetuate Nancy Cruzan's physical existence is comprehensible only as an effort to define life's meaning, not as an attempt to preserve its sanctity.

This much should be clear from the oddity of Missouri's definition alone. Life, particularly human life, is not commonly thought of as a merely physiological condition or function. Its sanctity is often thought to derive from the impossibility of any such reduction. When people speak of life, they often mean to describe the experiences that comprise a person's history, as when it is said that somebody "led a good life." They may also mean to refer to the practical manifestation of the human spirit, a meaning captured by the familiar observation that somebody "added life" to an assembly. If there is a shared thread among the various opinions on this subject, it may be that life is an activity which is at once the matrix for and an integration of a person's interests. In any event, absent some theological abstraction, the idea of life is not conceived separately from the idea of a living person. Yet, it is by precisely such a separation that Missouri asserts an interest in Nancy Cruzan's life in opposition to Nancy Cruzan's own interests. The resulting definition is uncommon indeed.

Washington v. Glucksberg
521 U.S. 702 (1997)

Since its first territorial legislature outlawed "assisting another in the commission of self-murder" in 1854, it has always been a crime to assist a suicide in the state of Washington. The state's present law makes "[p]romoting a suicide attempt" a felony, and provides: "A person is guilty of [that crime] when he knowingly causes or aids another person to attempt suicide." Dr. Harold Glucksberg and three other Washington physicians who occasionally treated terminally ill, suffering patients declared that they would assist these patients in ending their lives were it not for the state's assisted-suicide ban. They, along with three gravely ill plaintiffs who subsequently died and a nonprofit organization that counsels people considering physician-assisted suicide, filed suit in US District Court against the petitioners, the state, and its attorney general, seeking a declaration that the ban is, on its face, unconstitutional.

They asserted a liberty interest protected by the Fourteenth Amendment's Due Process Clause, which extends to a mentally competent, terminally ill adult the personal choice to commit physician-assisted suicide. Relying primarily on Planned Parenthood of Southeastern Pennsylvania v. Casey (1992) and Cruzan v. Director, Missouri Department of Health (1990), the federal district court agreed, concluding that Washington's assisted-suicide ban was unconstitutional because it places an undue burden on the exercise of that constitutionally protected liberty interest. A panel of the Court of Appeals for the Ninth Circuit reversed, emphasizing, "In the two hundred and five years of our existence no constitutional right to aid in killing oneself has ever been asserted and upheld by a court of final jurisdiction." The Ninth Circuit reheard the case en banc, reversed the panel's decision, and affirmed the district court. Like the district court, the en banc court of appeals emphasized the Casey and Cruzan decisions. The Supreme Court granted certiorari and heard it in conjunction with Vacco v. Quill *(which follows next), a case in which the Second Circuit invalidated New York's ban on assisted suicide on equal-protection grounds. Except for Chief Justice Rehnquist's separate majority opinions in the two cases, and Justice Souter's separate concurrences, all of the other justices who wrote opinions in these cases wrote combined concurrences, which are found here.* Opinion of the Court: <u>Rehnquist</u>, O'Connor, Scalia, Kennedy, Thomas. Concurring opinion: <u>O'Connor</u>, Ginsburg, Breyer. Concurring in the judgment: <u>Stevens</u>; <u>Souter</u>; <u>Ginsburg</u>; <u>Breyer</u>.

THE CHIEF JUSTICE delivered the opinion of the Court.

The question presented in this case is whether Washington's prohibition against "caus[ing]" or "aid[ing]" a suicide offends the Fourteenth Amendment to the United States Constitution. We hold that it does not. . . .

We begin, as we do in all due process cases, by examining our Nation's history, legal traditions, and practices. In almost every State—indeed, in almost every western democracy—it is a crime to assist a suicide. The States' assisted-suicide bans are not innovations. Rather, they are longstanding expressions of the States' commitment to the protection and preservation of all human life. Indeed, opposition to and condemnation of suicide—and, therefore, of assisting suicide—are consistent and enduring themes of our philosophical, legal, and cultural heritages.

More specifically, for over 700 years, the Anglo-American common-law tradition has punished or otherwise disapproved of both suicide and assisting suicide. . . . Though deeply rooted, the States' assisted-suicide bans have in recent years been reexamined and, generally, reaffirmed. Because of advances in medicine and technology, Americans today are increasingly likely to die in institutions, from chronic illnesses. Public concern and democratic action are therefore sharply focused on how best to protect dignity and independence at the end of life, with the result that there have been many significant changes in state

laws and in the attitudes these reflect. Many States, for example, now permit "living wills," surrogate health care decisionmaking, and the withdrawal or refusal of life-sustaining medical treatment. At the same time, however, voters and legislators continue for the most part to reaffirm their States' prohibitions on assisting suicide.

The Washington statute at issue in this case was enacted in 1975 as part of a revision of that State's criminal code. Four years later, Washington passed its Natural Death Act, which specifically stated that the "withholding or withdrawal of life-sustaining treatment . . . shall not, for any purpose, constitute a suicide" and that "[N]othing in this chapter shall be construed to condone, authorize, or approve every mercy killing. . . ." In 1991, Washington voters rejected a ballot initiative which, had it passed, would have permitted a form of physician-assisted suicide. Washington then added a provision to the Natural Death Act expressly excluding physician-assisted suicide.

California voters rejected an assisted-suicide initiative similar to Washington's in 1993. On the other hand, in 1994, voters in Oregon enacted, also through ballot initiative, that State's "Death With Dignity Act," which legalized physician-assisted suicide for competent, terminally ill adults. Since the Oregon vote, many proposals to legalize assisted suicide have been and continue to be introduced in the States' legislatures, but none has been enacted. And just last year, Iowa and Rhode Island joined the overwhelming majority of States explicitly prohibiting assisted suicide. Also, on April 30, 1997, President Clinton signed the Federal Assisted Suicide Funding Restriction Act of 1997, which prohibits the use of federal funds in support of physician-assisted suicide.

Thus, the States are currently engaged in serious, thoughtful examinations of physician-assisted suicide and other similar issues. . . .

Attitudes toward suicide itself have changed [over the centuries], but our laws have consistently condemned, and continue to prohibit, assisting suicide. Despite changes in medical technology and notwithstanding an increased emphasis on the importance of end-of-life decisionmaking, we have not retreated from this prohibition. Against this backdrop of history, tradition, and practice, we now turn to respondents' constitutional claim.

The Due Process Clause guarantees more than fair process, and the "liberty" it protects includes more than the absence of physical restraint. The Clause also provides heightened protection against government interference with certain fundamental rights and liberty interests. In a long line of cases, we have held that, in addition to the specific freedoms protected by the Bill of Rights, the "liberty" specially protected by the Due Process Clause includes the rights to marry, *Loving v. Virginia* (1967); to have children, *Skinner v. Oklahoma ex rel. Williamson* (1942); to direct the education and upbringing of one's children, *Meyer v. Nebraska* (1923); *Pierce v. Society of Sisters* (1925); to marital privacy, *Griswold v. Connecticut* (1965); to use contraception, *ibid; Eisenstadt v. Baird* (1972); to bodily integrity, *Rochin v. California* (1952); and to abortion, *Casey.* We have also assumed, and strongly suggested, that the Due Process Clause protects the traditional right to refuse unwanted lifesaving medical treatment.

But we "ha[ve] always been reluctant to expand the concept of substantive due process because guideposts for responsible decision-making in this unchartered area are scarce and open-ended." By extending constitutional protection to an asserted right or liberty interest, we, to a great extent, place the matter outside the arena of public debate and legislative action. We must therefore "exercise the utmost care whenever we are asked to break new ground in this field," lest the liberty protected by the Due Process Clause be subtly transformed into the policy preferences of the members of this Court.

Our established method of substantive-due-process analysis has two primary features: First, we have regularly observed that the Due Process Clause specially protects those fundamental rights and liberties which are, objectively, "deeply rooted in this Nation's history and tradition." Second, we have required in substantive-due-process cases a "careful description" of the asserted fundamental liberty interest. . . . This approach tends to rein in the subjective elements that are necessarily present in due process judicial review. In addition, by

establishing a threshold requirement—that a challenged state action implicate a fundamental right—before requiring more than a reasonable relation to a legitimate state interest to justify the action, it avoids the need for complex balancing of competing interests in every case.

Turning to the claim at issue here, the Court of Appeals stated that "[p]roperly analyzed, the first issue to be resolved is whether there is a liberty interest in determining the time and manner of one's death," or, in other words, "[i]s there a right to die?" Similarly, respondents assert a "liberty to choose how to die" and a right to "control of one's final days" and describe the asserted liberty as "the right to choose a humane, dignified death" and "the liberty to shape death." . . .

We now inquire whether this asserted right has any place in our Nation's traditions. Here, as discussed above, we are confronted with a consistent and almost universal tradition that has long rejected the asserted right, and continues explicitly to reject it today, even for terminally ill, mentally competent adults. To hold for respondents, we would have to reverse centuries of legal doctrine and practice, and strike down the considered policy choice of almost every State.

Respondents contend, however, that the liberty interest they assert *is* consistent with this Court's substantive-due-process line of cases, if not with this Nation's history and practice. Pointing to *Casey* and *Cruzan,* respondents read our jurisprudence in this area as reflecting a general tradition of "self-sovereignty" and as teaching that the "liberty" protected by the Due Process Clause includes "basic and intimate exercises of personal autonomy." . . . The question presented in this case, however, is whether the protections of the Due Process Clause include a right to commit suicide with another's assistance. With this "careful description" of respondents' claim in mind, we turn to *Casey* and *Cruzan.*

In *Cruzan,* we considered whether Nancy Beth Cruzan, who had been severely injured in an automobile accident and was in a persistive vegetative state, "ha[d] a right under the United States Constitution which would require the hospital to withdraw life-sustaining treatment" at her parents' request. . . . "[F]or purposes of [that] case, we assume[d] that the United States Constitution would grant a competent person a constitutionally protected right to refuse lifesaving hydration and nutrition." We concluded that, notwithstanding this right, the Constitution permitted Missouri to require clear and convincing evidence of an incompetent patient's wishes concerning the withdrawal of life-sustaining treatment. . . . In *Cruzan* itself, we recognized that most States outlawed assisted suicide—and even more do today—and we certainly gave no intimation that the right to refuse unwanted medical treatment could be somehow transmuted into a right to assistance in committing suicide.

Respondents also rely on *Casey*. There, the Court's opinion . . . discussed in some detail this Court's substantive-due-process tradition of interpreting the Due Process Clause to protect certain fundamental rights and "personal decisions relating to marriage, procreation, contraception, family relationships, child rearing, and education," and noted that many of those rights and liberties "involv[e] the most intimate and personal choices a person may make in a lifetime."

The Court of Appeals, like the District Court, found *Casey* "'highly instructive'" and "'almost prescriptive'" for determining "'what liberty interest may inhere in a terminally ill person's choice to commit suicide'":

Like the decision of whether or not to have an abortion, the decision how and when to die is one of "the most intimate and personal choices a person may make in a lifetime," a choice "central to personal dignity and autonomy"

Similarly, respondents emphasize the statement in *Casey* that:

At the heart of liberty is the right to define one's own concept of existence, of meaning, of the universe, and of the mystery of human life. Beliefs about these matters could not define the attributes of personhood were they formed under compulsion of the State.

. . . That many of the rights and liberties protected by the Due Process Clause [are grounded] in personal autonomy does not warrant the sweeping conclusion that any and all important, intimate, and personal decisions are so protected, and *Casey* did not suggest otherwise.

The history of the law's treatment of assisted suicide in this country has been and continues to be one of the rejection of nearly all efforts to permit it. That being the case, our decisions lead us to conclude that the asserted "right" to assistance in committing suicide is not a fundamental liberty interest protected by the Due Process Clause. The Constitution also requires, however, that Washington's assisted-suicide ban be rationally related to legitimate government interests. This requirement is unquestionably met here. . . .

First, Washington has an "unqualified interest in the preservation of human life." The State's prohibition on assisted suicide, like all homicide laws, both reflects and advances its commitment to this interest. . . .

The State also has an interest in protecting the integrity and ethics of the medical profession. In contrast to the Court of Appeals' conclusion that "the integrity of the medical profession would [not] be threatened in any way by [physician-assisted suicide]," the American Medical Association, like many other medical and physicians' groups, has concluded that "[p]hysician-assisted suicide is fundamentally incompatible with the physician's role as healer." . . .

Next, the State has an interest in protecting vulnerable groups—including the poor, the elderly, and disabled persons—from abuse, neglect, and mistakes. The Court of Appeals dismissed the State's concern that disadvantaged persons might be pressured into physician-assisted suicide as "ludicrous on its face." We have recognized, however, the real risk of subtle coercion and undue influence in end-of-life situations. . . .

The State's interest here goes beyond protecting the vulnerable from coercion; it extends to protecting disabled and terminally ill people from prejudice, negative and inaccurate stereotypes, and "societal indifference." The State's assisted-suicide ban reflects and reinforces its policy that the lives of terminally ill, disabled, and elderly people must be no less valued than the lives of the young and healthy, and that a seriously disabled person's suicidal impulses should be interpreted and treated the same way as anyone else's. . . .

Finally, the State may fear that permitting assisted suicide will start it down the path to voluntary and perhaps even involuntary euthanasia. The Court of Appeals struck down Washington's assisted-suicide ban only "as applied to competent, terminally ill adults who wish to hasten their deaths by obtaining medication prescribed by their doctors." Washington insists, however, that the impact of the court's decision will not and cannot be so limited. If suicide is protected as a matter of constitutional right, it is argued, "every man and woman in the United States must enjoy it." The Court of Appeals' decision, and its expansive reasoning, provide ample support for the State's concerns. . . .

This concern is further supported by evidence about the practice of euthanasia in the Netherlands. The Dutch government's own study revealed that in 1990, there were 2,300 cases of voluntary euthanasia (defined as "the deliberate termination of another's life at his request"), 400 cases of assisted suicide, and more than 1,000 cases of euthanasia without an explicit request. In addition to these latter 1,000 cases, the study found an additional 4,941 cases where physicians administered lethal morphine overdoses without the patients' explicit consent. This study suggests that, despite the existence of various reporting procedures, euthanasia in the Netherlands has not been limited to competent, terminally ill adults who are enduring physical suffering, and that regulation of the practice may not have prevented abuses in cases involving vulnerable persons, including severely disabled neonates and elderly persons suffering from dementia. . . .

Throughout the Nation, Americans are engaged in an earnest and profound debate about the morality, legality, and practicality of physician-assisted suicide. Our holding permits this debate to continue, as it should in a democratic society. The decision of the *en banc* Court of Appeals is reversed, and the case is remanded for further proceedings consistent with this opinion.

JUSTICE O'CONNOR, with whom JUSTICE GINSBURG and JUSTICE BREYER join, concurring.

. . . Every one of us at some point may be affected by our own or a family member's terminal illness. There is no reason to think the democratic process will not strike the proper balance between the interests of terminally ill, mentally competent individuals who would seek to end their suffering and the State's interests in protecting those who might seek to end life mistakenly or under pressure. As the Court recognizes, States are presently undertaking extensive and serious evaluation of physician-assisted suicide and other related issues. In such circumstances, "the . . . challenging task of crafting appropriate procedures for safeguarding . . . liberty interests is entrusted to the 'laboratory' of the States . . . in the first instance."

JUSTICE BREYER, concurring in the judgments.

. . . I do not agree . . . with the Court's formulation of that claimed "liberty" interest. The Court describes it as a "right to commit suicide with another's assistance." But I would not reject the respondents' claim without considering a different formulation, for which our legal tradition may provide greater support. That formulation would use words roughly like a "right to die with dignity." But irrespective of the exact words used, at its core would lie personal control over the manner of death, professional medical assistance, and the avoidance of unnecessary and severe physical suffering—combined. . . .

I do not believe, however, that this Court need or now should decide whether or not such a right is "fundamental." That is because, in my view, the avoidance of severe physical pain (connected with death) would have to comprise an essential part of any successful claim and because the laws before us do not *force* a dying person to undergo that kind of pain. Rather, the laws of New York and of Washington do not prohibit doctors from providing patients with drugs sufficient to control pain despite the risk that those drugs themselves will kill. And under these circumstances the laws of New York and Washington would overcome any remaining significant interests and would be justified, regardless.

JUSTICE STEVENS, concurring in the judgments.

The Court ends its opinion with the important observation that our holding today is fully consistent with a continuation of the vigorous debate about the "morality, legality, and practicality of physician-assisted suicide" in a democratic society. I write separately to make it clear that there is also room for further debate about the limits that the Constitution places on the power of the States to punish the practice. . . .

[J]ust as our conclusion that capital punishment is not always unconstitutional did not preclude later decisions holding that it is sometimes impermissibly cruel, so is it equally clear that a decision upholding a general statutory prohibition of assisted suicide does not mean that every possible application of the statute would be valid. A State, like Washington, that has authorized the death penalty and thereby has concluded that the sanctity of human life does not require that it always be preserved, must acknowledge that there are situations in which an interest in hastening death is legitimate. Indeed, not only is that interest sometimes legitimate, I am also convinced that there are times when it is entitled to constitutional protection. . . .

In New York, a doctor must respect a competent person's decision to refuse or to discontinue medical treatment even though death will thereby ensue, but the same doctor would be guilty of a felony if she provided her patient assistance in committing suicide. Today we hold that the Equal Protection Clause is not violated by the resulting disparate treatment of two classes of terminally ill people who may have the same interest in hastening death. I agree that the distinction between permitting death to ensue from an underlying fatal disease and causing it to occur by the administration of medication or other means provides a constitutionally sufficient basis for the State's classification. Unlike the Court, however, see *Vacco,* I am not persuaded that in all cases there will in fact be a significant difference between the intent of the physicians, the patients or the families in the two situations.

There may be little distinction between the intent of a terminally-ill patient who decides to remove her life support and one who seeks the assistance of a doctor in ending her life; in both situations, the patient is seeking to hasten a certain, impending death. The doctor's intent might also be the same in prescribing lethal medication as it is in terminating life support. . . .

There remains room for vigorous debate about the outcome of particular cases that are not necessarily resolved by the opinions announced today. How such cases may be decided will depend on their specific facts. In my judgment, however, it is clear that the so-called "unqualified interest in the preservation of human life" is not itself sufficient to outweigh the interest in liberty that may justify the only possible means of preserving a dying patient's dignity and alleviating her intolerable suffering.

JUSTICE SOUTER, concurring in the judgment.

. . . The argument supporting respondents' position . . . progresses through three steps of increasing forcefulness. First, it emphasizes the decriminalization of suicide. Reliance on this fact is sanctioned under the standard that looks not only to the tradition retained, but to society's occasional choices to reject traditions of the legal past. . . . The second step in the argument is to emphasize that the State's own act of decriminalization gives a freedom of choice much like the individual's option in recognized instances of bodily autonomy. One of these, abortion, is a legal right to choose in spite of the interest a State may legitimately invoke in discouraging the practice, just as suicide is now subject to choice, despite a state interest in discouraging it. The third step is to emphasize that respondents claim a right to assistance not on the basis of some broad principle that would be subject to exceptions if that continuing interest of the State's in discouraging suicide were to be recognized at all. Respondents base their claim on the traditional right to medical care and counsel, subject to the limiting conditions of informed, responsible choice when death is imminent, conditions that support a strong analogy to rights of care in other situations in which medical counsel and assistance have been available as a matter of course. There can be no stronger claim to a physician's assistance than at the time when death is imminent, a moral judgment implied by the State's own recognition of the legitimacy of medical procedures necessarily hastening the moment of impending death.

In my judgment, the importance of the individual interest here, as within that class of "certain interests" demanding careful scrutiny of the State's contrary claim, cannot be gainsaid. Whether that interest might in some circumstances, or at some time, be seen as "fundamental" to the degree entitled to prevail is not, however, a conclusion that I need draw here, for I am satisfied that the State's interests described in the following section are sufficiently serious to defeat the present claim that its law is arbitrary or purposeless. . . .

I take it that the basic concept of judicial review with its possible displacement of legislative judgment bars any finding that a legislature has acted arbitrarily when the following conditions are met: there is a serious factual controversy over the feasibility of recognizing the claimed right without at the same time making it impossible for the State to engage in an undoubtedly legitimate exercise of power; facts necessary to resolve the controversy are not readily ascertainable through the judicial process; but they are more readily subject to discovery through legislative fact-finding and experimentation. It is assumed in

this case, and must be, that a State's interest in protecting those unable to make responsible decisions and those who make no decisions at all entitles the State to bar aid to any but a knowing and responsible person intending suicide, and to prohibit euthanasia. How, and how far, a State should act in that interest are judgments for the State, but the legitimacy of its action to deny a physician the option to aid any but the knowing and responsible is beyond question. . . .

Now it is enough to say that our examination of legislative reasonableness should consider the fact that the Legislature of the State of Washington is no more obviously at fault than this Court is in being uncertain about what would happen if respondents prevailed today. We therefore have a clear question about which institution, a legislature or a court, is relatively more competent to deal with an emerging issue as to which facts currently unknown could be dispositive. The answer has to be, for the reasons already stated, that the legislative process is to be preferred. There is a closely related further reason as well. . . . The experimentation that should be out of the question in constitutional adjudication displacing legislative judgments is entirely proper, as well as highly desirable, when the legislative power addresses an emerging issue like assisted suicide. The Court should accordingly stay its hand to allow reasonable legislative consideration. While I do not decide for all time that respondents' claim should not be recognized, I acknowledge the legislative institutional competence as the better one to deal with that claim at this time.

Vacco v. Quill
521 U.S. 793 (1997)

New York State made it a crime to aid another to commit or attempt suicide; however, it allowed competent patients to refuse "medical treatment, even if the withdrawal of such treatment will result in death." Dr. Timothy Quill and two other New York physicians asserted that although it would be consistent with the standards of their medical practices to prescribe lethal medication for mentally competent, terminally ill patients who are suffering great pain and desire a doctor's

help in taking their own lives, they were deterred from doing so by New York's assisted-suicide ban. They and three gravely ill patients who subsequently died entered New York District Court for the Southern District of New York and sued Dennis C. Vacco, the state's attorney general, claiming that the ban violated the Fourteenth Amendment's Equal Protection Clause. The federal district court disagreed, but the Second Circuit reversed. It held that New York accorded different treatment to those competent, terminally ill persons who wished to hasten their deaths by self-administering prescribed drugs than it did to those who wished to do so by directing the removal of life-support systems. This unequal treatment, it held, was not rationally related to any legitimate state interests. The Supreme Court granted certiorari and heard it in conjunction with Washington v. Glucksberg *(which precedes this case), a case in which the Ninth Circuit invalidated Washington State's ban on assisted suicide on due-process grounds. Except for Chief Justice Rehnquist's majority opinions in the two cases, and Justice Souter's separate concurrences, all of the other justices who wrote opinions in these cases wrote combined concurrences, which can be found with the* Glucksberg *decision.* Opinion of the Court: Rehnquist, O'Connor, Scalia, Kennedy, Thomas. Concurring opinion: O'Connor, Ginsburg, Breyer. Concurring in the judgment: Stevens; Souter; Ginsburg; Breyer.

THE CHIEF JUSTICE delivered the opinion of the Court.

In New York, as in most States, it is a crime to aid another to commit or attempt suicide, but patients may refuse even lifesaving medical treatment. The question presented by this case is whether New York's prohibition on assisting suicide therefore violates the Equal Protection Clause. . . .

The Equal Protection Clause commands that no State shall "deny to any person within its jurisdiction the equal protection of the laws." This provision creates no substantive rights. Instead, it embodies a general rule that States must treat like cases alike but may treat unlike cases accordingly. If a legislative classification or distinction "neither burdens a fundamental right nor targets a suspect class, we will uphold [it] so long as it bears a rational relation to some legitimate end."

New York's statutes outlawing assisting suicide affect and address matters of profound significance to all New Yorkers alike. They neither infringe fundamental rights nor involve suspect classifications. . . . On their faces, neither New York's ban on assisting suicide nor its statutes permitting patients to refuse medical treatment treat anyone differently than anyone else or draw any distinctions between persons.

Everyone, regardless of physical condition, is entitled, if competent, to refuse unwanted lifesaving medical treatment; *no one* is permitted to assist a suicide. Generally speaking, laws that apply evenhandedly to all "unquestionably comply" with the Equal Protection Clause.

The Court of Appeals, however, concluded that some terminally ill people—those who are on life-support systems—are treated differently than those who are not, in that the former may "hasten death" by ending treatment, but the latter may not "hasten death" through physician-assisted suicide. This conclusion depends on the submission that ending or refusing lifesaving medical treatment "is nothing more nor less than assisted suicide." Unlike the Court of Appeals, we think the distinction between assisting suicide and withdrawing life-sustaining treatment, a distinction widely recognized and endorsed in the medical profession and in our legal traditions, is both important and logical; it is certainly rational.

The distinction comports with fundamental legal principles of causation and intent. First, when a patient refuses life-sustaining medical treatment, he dies from an underlying fatal disease or pathology; but if a patient ingests lethal medication prescribed by a physician, he is killed by that medication. . . . Furthermore, a physician who withdraws, or honors a patient's refusal to begin, life-sustaining medical treatment purposefully intends, or may so intend, only to respect his patient's wishes and "to cease doing useless and futile or degrading things to the patient when [the patient] no longer stands to benefit from them." The same is true when a doctor provides aggressive palliative care; in some cases, painkilling drugs may hasten a patient's death, but the physician's purpose and intent is, or may be, only to ease his patient's pain. A doctor who assists a suicide, however, "must, necessarily and indubitably, intend primarily that the patient be made dead." . . .

Given these general principles, it is not surprising that many courts, including New York courts, have carefully distinguished refusing life-sustaining treatment from suicide. . . . Similarly, the overwhelming majority of state legislatures have drawn a clear line between assisting suicide and withdrawing or permitting the refusal of unwanted lifesaving medical treatment by prohibiting the former and permitting the latter. . . .

This Court has also recognized, at least implicitly, the distinction between letting a patient die and making that patient die. . . . For all these reasons, we disagree with respondents' claim that the distinction between refusing lifesaving medical treatment and assisted suicide is "arbitrary" and "irrational." . . . By permitting everyone to refuse unwanted medical treatment while prohibiting anyone from assisting a suicide, New York law follows a longstanding and rational distinction.

New York's reasons for recognizing and acting on this distinction—including prohibiting intentional killing and preserving life; preventing suicide; maintaining physicians' role as their patients' healers; protecting vulnerable people from indifference, prejudice, and psychological and financial pressure to end their lives; and avoiding a possible slide towards euthanasia— are discussed in greater detail in our opinion in *Glucksberg*. These valid and important public interests easily satisfy the constitutional requirement that a legislative classification bear a rational relation to some legitimate end.

The judgment of the Court of Appeals is reversed.

JUSTICE SOUTER, concurring in the judgment.

Even though I do not conclude that assisted suicide is a fundamental right entitled to recognition at this time, I accord the claims raised by the patients and physicians in this case and *Washington v. Glucksberg* a high degree of importance, requiring a commensurate justification. The reasons that lead me to conclude in *Glucksberg* that the prohibition on assisted suicide is not arbitrary under the due process standard also support the distinction between assistance to suicide, which is banned, and practices such as termination of artificial life support and death-hastening pain medication, which are permitted. I accordingly concur in the judgment of the Court.

⚜

The Constitution of the United States of America

We the People of the United States, in Order to form a more perfect Union, establish Justice, insure domestic Tranquility, provide for the common defence, promote the general Welfare, and secure the Blessings of Liberty to ourselves and our Posterity, do ordain and establish this CONSTITUTION for the United States of America.

ARTICLE I

SECTION 1. All legislative Powers herein granted shall be vested in a Congress of the United States, which shall consist of a Senate and House of Representatives.

SECTION 2. [1] The House of Representatives shall be composed of Members chosen every second Year by the People of the several States, and the Electors in each State shall have the Qualifications requisite for Electors of the most numerous Branch of the State Legislature.

[2] No person shall be a Representative who shall not have attained to the Age of twenty five Years, and been seven Years a Citizen of the United States, and who shall not, when elected, be an Inhabitant of that State in which he shall be chosen.

[3] Representatives and direct Taxes shall be apportioned among the several States which may be included within this Union, according to their respective Numbers, which shall be determined by adding to the whole Number of free Persons, including those bound to Service for a Term of Years, and excluding Indians not taxed, three fifths of all other Persons. The actual Enumeration shall be made within three Years after the first Meeting of the Congress of the United States, and within every subsequent Term of ten Years, in such Manner as they shall by Law direct. The Number of Representatives shall not exceed one for every thirty Thousand, but each State shall have at Least one Representative; and until such enumeration shall be made, the State of New Hampshire shall be entitled to chuse three, Massachusetts eight, Rhode-Island and Providence Plantations one, Connecticut five, New-York six, New Jersey four, Pennsylvania eight, Delaware one, Maryland six, Virginia ten, North Carolina five, South Carolina five, and Georgia three.

[4] When vacancies happen in the Representation from any State, the Executive

Authority thereof shall issue Writs of Election to fill such Vacancies.

[5] The House of Representatives shall chuse their Speaker and other Officers; and shall have the sole Power of Impeachment.

SECTION 3. [1] The Senate of the United States shall be composed of two Senators from each State, chosen by the Legislature thereof, for six Years; and each Senator shall have one Vote.

[2] Immediately after they shall be assembled in Consequence of the first Election, they shall be divided as equally as may be into three Classes. The Seats of the Senators of the first Class shall be vacated at the Expiration of the Second Year, of the second Class at the Expiration of the fourth Year, and of the third Class at the Expiration of the sixth Year, so that one third may be chosen every second Year; and if Vacancies happen by Resignation, or otherwise, during the Recess of the Legislature of any State, the Executive thereof may make temporary Appointments until the next Meeting of the Legislature, which shall then fill such Vacancies.

[3] No person shall be a Senator who shall not have attained to the Age of thirty Years, and been nine Years a Citizen of the United States, and who shall not, when elected, be an Inhabitant of that State for which he shall be chosen.

[4] The Vice President of the United States shall be President of the Senate, but shall have no Vote, unless they be equally divided.

[5] The Senate shall chuse their other Officers, and also a President pro tempore, in the absence of the Vice President, or when he shall exercise the Office of the President of the United States.

[6] The Senate shall have the sole Power to try all Impeachments. When sitting for that Purpose, they shall be on Oath or Affirmation. When the President of the United States is tried, the Chief Justice shall preside: And no Person shall be convicted without the Concurrence of two thirds of the Members present.

[7] Judgment in Cases of Impeachment shall not extend further than to removal from Office, and disqualification to hold and enjoy any Office of honor, Trust or Profit under the United States: but the Party convicted shall nevertheless be liable and subject to Indictment, Trial, Judgment and Punishment, according to Law.

SECTION 4. [1] The Times, Places and Manner of holding Elections for Senators and Representatives, shall be prescribed in each State by the Legislature thereof; but the Congress may at any time by Law make or alter such Regulations, except as to the Places of chusing Senators.

[2] The Congress shall assemble at least once in every Year, and such Meeting shall be on the first Monday in December, unless they shall by Law appoint a different Day.

SECTION 5. [1] Each House shall be the Judge of the Elections, Returns and Qualifications of its own Members, and a Majority of each shall constitute a Quorum to do Business, but a smaller Number may adjourn from day to day, and may be authorized to compel the Attendance of absent Members, in such Manner, and under such Penalties as each House may provide.

[2] Each House may determine the Rules of its Proceedings, punish its Members for disorderly Behavior, and, with the Concurrence of two thirds, expel a Member.

[3] Each House shall keep a Journal of its Proceedings, and from time to time publish the same, excepting such Parts as may in their Judgment require Secrecy; and the Yeas and Nays of the Members of either House on any question shall, at the Desire of one fifth of those Present, be entered on the Journal.

[4] Neither House, during the Session of Congress, shall, without the Consent of the other, adjourn for more than three days, nor to any other Place than that in which the two Houses shall be sitting.

SECTION 6. [1] The Senators and Representatives shall receive a Compensation for their Services, to be ascertained by Law, and paid out of the Treasury of the United States. They shall in all Cases, except Treason, Felony and Breach of the Peace, be privileged from Arrest during their Attendance at the Session of their respective Houses, and in going to and returning from the same; and for any Speech or Debate in either House, they shall not be questioned in any other Place.

[2] No Senator or Representative shall, during the Time for which he was elected, be appointed to any civil Office under the Authority of the United States, which shall have been created, or the Emoluments whereof shall have been encreased during such time; and no Person holding any Office under the United States, shall be a Member of either House during his Continuance in Office.

SECTION 7. [1] All Bills for raising Revenue shall originate in the House of Representatives; but the Senate may propose or concur with Amendments as on other Bills.

[2] Every Bill which shall have passed the House of Representatives and the Senate, shall, before it become a Law, be presented to the President of the United States: If he approve he shall sign it, but if not he shall return it, with his Objections to that House in which it shall have originated, who shall enter the Objections at large on their Journal, and proceed to reconsider it. If after such Reconsideration two thirds of that House shall agree to pass the Bill, it shall be sent, together with the Objections, to the other House, by which it shall likewise be reconsidered, and if approved by two thirds of that House, it shall become a Law. But in all such Cases the Votes of both Houses shall be determined by Yeas and Nays, and the Names of the Persons voting for and against the Bill shall be entered on the Journal of each House respectively. If any Bill shall not be returned by the President within ten Days (Sundays excepted) after it shall have been presented to him, the Same shall be a Law, in like Manner as if he had signed it, unless the Congress by their Adjournment prevent its Return, in which Case it shall not be a Law.

[3] Every Order, Resolution, or Vote to which the Concurrence of the Senate and House of Representatives may be necessary (except on a question of Adjournment) shall be presented to the President of the United States;

and before the Same shall take Effect, shall be approved by him, or being disapproved by him, shall be repassed by two thirds of the Senate and House of Representatives, according to the Rules and Limitations prescribed in the Case of a Bill.

SECTION 8. The Congress shall have Power

[1] To lay and collect Taxes, Duties, Imposts and Excises, to pay the Debts and provide for the common Defence and general Welfare of the United States, but all Duties, Imposts and Excises shall be uniform throughout the United States;

[2] To borrow Money on the credit of the United States;

[3] To regulate Commerce with foreign Nations, and among the several States, and with the Indian Tribes;

[4] To establish an uniform Rule of Naturalization, and uniform Laws on the subject of Bankruptcies throughout the United States;

[5] To coin Money, regulate the Value thereof, and of foreign Coin, and fix the Standard of Weights and Measures;

[6] To provide for the Punishment of counterfeiting the Securities and current Coin of the United States;

[7] To Establish Post Offices and post Roads;

[8] To promote the Progress of Science and useful Arts, by securing for limited Times to Authors and Inventors the exclusive Right to their respective Writings and Discoveries;

[9] To constitute Tribunals inferior to the supreme Court;

[10] To define and punish Piracies and Felonies committed on the high Seas, and Offenses against the Law of Nations;

[11] To declare War, grant Letters of Marque and Reprisal, and make Rules concerning Captures on Land and Water;

[12] To raise and support Armies, but no Appropriation of Money to that Use shall be for a longer Term than two Years;

[13] To provide and maintain a Navy;

[14] To make Rules for the Government and Regulation of the land and naval Forces;

[15] To provide for calling forth the Militia to execute the Laws of the Union, suppress Insurrections and repel Invasions;

[16] To provide for organizing, arming, and disciplining, the Militia, and for Governing such Part of them as may be employed in the Service of the United States, reserving to the States respectively, the Appointment of the Officers, and the Authority of training the Militia according to the discipline prescribed by Congress;

[17] To exercise exclusive Legislation in all Cases whatsoever, over such District (not exceeding ten Miles square) as may, by Cession of particular States, and the Acceptance of Congress, become the Seat of the Government of the United States, and to exercise like Authority over all Places purchased by the Consent of the Legislature of the State in which the Same shall be, for the Erection of Forts, Magazines, Arsenals, dock-Yards, and other needful Buildings;—And

[18] To make all Laws which shall be necessary and proper for carrying into Execution the foregoing Powers, and all other Powers vested by this Constitution in the Government of the United States, or in any Department or Officer thereof.

SECTION 9. [1] The Migration or Importation of Such Persons as any of the States now existing shall think proper to admit, shall not be prohibited by the Congress prior to the Year one thousand eight hundred and eight, but a Tax or duty may be imposed on such Importation, not exceeding ten dollars for each Person.

[2] The Privilege of the Writ of *Habeas Corpus* shall not be suspended, unless when in Cases of Rebellion or Invasion the public Safety may require it.

[3] No Bill of Attainder or *ex post facto* Law shall be passed.

[4] No Capitation, or other direct, Tax shall be laid, unless in Proportion to the Census or enumeration herein before directed to be taken.

[5] No Tax or Duty shall be laid on Articles exported from any State.

[6] No preference shall be given by any Regulation of Commerce or Revenue to the Ports of one State over those of another; nor shall Vessels bound to, or from, one State be obliged to enter, clear, or pay Duties in another.

[7] No money shall be drawn from the Treasury, but in Consequence of Appropriations made by Law; and a regular Statement and Account of the Receipts and Expenditures of all public Money shall be published from time to time.

[8] No Title of Nobility shall be granted by the United States: And no Person holding any Office of Profit or Trust under them, shall, without the Consent of the Congress, accept of any present, Emolument, Office, or Title, of any kind whatever, from any King, Prince, or foreign State.

SECTION 10. [1] No State shall enter into any Treaty, Alliance, or Confederation; grant Letters of Marque and Reprisal; coin Money; emit Bills of Credit; make any Thing but gold and silver Coin a Tender in Payment of Debts; pass any Bill of Attainder, *ex post facto* Law, or Law impairing the Obligation of Contracts, or grant any Title of Nobility.

[2] No State shall, without the Consent of the Congress, lay any Imposts or Duties on Imports or Exports, except what may be absolutely necessary for executing its inspection Laws: and the net Produce of all Duties and Imposts, laid by any State on Imports or Exports, shall be for the Use of the Treasury of the United States; and all such Laws shall be subject to the Revision and Control of the Congress.

[3] No State shall, without the Consent of Congress, lay any Duty of Tonnage, keep Troops, or Ships of War in time of Peace, enter into any Agreement or Compact with another State, or with a foreign Power, or engage in War, unless actually invaded, or in such imminent Danger as will not admit of delay.

ARTICLE II

SECTION 1. [1] The executive Power shall be vested in a President of the United States of America. He shall hold his Office during the Term of four Years, and together with the Vice President, chosen for the same Term, be elected, as follows:

[2] Each State shall appoint, in such Manner as the Legislature thereof may direct, a Number of Electors, equal to the whole Number of Senators and Representatives to which the

State may be entitled in the Congress: but no Senator or Representative, or Person holding an Office of Trust or Profit under the United States, shall be appointed an Elector.

[3] The Electors shall meet in their respective States, and vote by Ballot for two Persons, of whom one at least shall not be an Inhabitant of the same State with themselves. And they shall make a List of all the Persons voted for, and of the Number of Votes for each; which List they shall sign and certify, and transmit sealed to the Seat of the Government of the United States, directed to the President of the Senate. The President of the Senate shall, in the Presence of the Senate and House of Representatives, open all the Certificates, and the Votes shall then be counted. The Person having the greatest Number of Votes shall be the President, if such Number be a Majority of the whole Number of Electors appointed; and if there be more than one who have such Majority, and have an equal Number of Votes, then the House of Representatives shall immediately chuse by Ballot one of them for President; and if no Person have a Majority, then from the five highest on the List the said House shall in like Manner chuse the President. But in chusing the President, the Votes shall be taken by States, the Representation from each State having one Vote; A quorum for this purpose shall consist of a Member or Members from two thirds of the States, and a Majority of all the States shall be necessary to a Choice. In every Case, after the Choice of the President, the Person having the greatest Number of Votes of the Electors shall be the Vice President. But if there should remain two or more who have equal Votes, the Senate shall chuse from them by Ballot the Vice President.

[4] The Congress may determine the Time of chusing the Electors, and the Day on which they shall give their Votes; which Day shall be the same throughout the United States.

[5] No person except a natural born Citizen, or a Citizen of the United States, at the time of the Adoption of this Constitution, shall be eligible to the Office of President; neither shall any Person be eligible to that Office who shall

not have attained to the Age of thirty five Years, and been fourteen Years a Resident within the United States.

[6] In Case of the Removal of the President from Office, or of his Death, Resignation, or Inability to discharge the Powers and Duties of the said Office, the Same shall devolve on the Vice President, and the Congress may by Law provide for the Case of Removal, Death, Resignation or Inability, both of the President and Vice President, declaring what Officer shall then act as President, and such Officer shall act accordingly, until the Disability be removed, or a President shall be elected.

[7] The President shall, at stated Times, receive for his Services, a Compensation, which shall neither be increased nor diminished during the Period for which he shall have been elected, and he shall not receive within that Period any other Emolument from the United States, or any of them.

[8] Before he enter on the Execution of his Office, he shall take the following Oath or Affirmation:—"I do solemnly swear (or affirm) that I will faithfully execute the Office of President of the United States, and will to the best of my Ability, preserve, protect and defend the Constitution of the United States."

SECTION 2. [1] The President shall be Commander in Chief of the Army and Navy of the United States, and of the Militia of the several States, when called into the actual Service of the United States; he may require the Opinion, in writing, of the Principal Officer in each of the executive Departments, upon any Subject relating to the Duties of their respective Offices, and he shall have Power to grant Reprieves and Pardons for Offenses against the United States, except in Cases of Impeachment.

[2] He shall have Power, by and with the Advice and Consent of the Senate, to make Treaties, provided two thirds of the Senators present concur; and he shall nominate, and by and with the Advice and Consent of the Senate, shall appoint Ambassadors, other public Ministers and Consuls, Judges of the supreme Court, and all other Officers of the United States, whose Appointments are not herein

otherwise provided for, and which shall be established by Law, but the Congress may by Law vest the Appointment of such inferior Officers, as they think proper, in the President alone, in the Courts of Law, or in the Heads of Departments.

[3] The President shall have Power to fill up all Vacancies that may happen during the Recess of the Senate, by granting Commissions which shall expire at the End of their next Session.

SECTION 3. He shall from time to time give to the Congress Information of the State of the Union, and recommend to their Consideration such Measures as he shall judge necessary and expedient; he may, on extraordinary Occasions, convene both Houses, or either of them, and in Case of Disagreement between them, with Respect to the Time of Adjournment, he may adjourn them to such Time as he shall think proper; he shall receive Ambassadors and other public Ministers; he shall take Care that the Laws be faithfully executed, and shall Commission all the Officers of the United States.

SECTION 4. The President, Vice President and all civil Officers of the United States, shall be removed from Office on Impeachment for, and Conviction of, Treason, Bribery, or other high Crimes and Misdemeanors.

ARTICLE III

SECTION 1. The judicial Power of the United States, shall be vested in one supreme Court, and in such inferior Courts as the Congress may from time to time ordain and establish. The Judges, both of the supreme and inferior Courts, shall hold their Offices during good Behaviour, and shall, at stated Times, receive for their Services a Compensation which shall not be diminished during their Continuance in Office.

SECTION 2. [1] The judicial Power shall extend to all Cases, in Law and Equity, arising under this Constitution, the Laws of the United States, and Treaties made, or which shall be made, under their Authority;—to all Cases affecting Ambassadors, other public Ministers and Consuls;—to all Cases of admiralty and maritime Jurisdiction;—to Controversies to which the United States shall be a Party;—to Controversies between two or more States;—between a State and Citizens of another State;—between Citizens of different States;—between Citizens of the same State claiming Lands under Grants of different States, and between a State, or the Citizens thereof, and foreign States, Citizens or Subjects.

[2] In all Cases affecting Ambassadors, other public Ministers and Consuls, and those in which a State shall be Party, the supreme Court shall have original Jurisdiction. In all the other Cases before mentioned, the supreme Court shall have appellate Jurisdiction, both as to Law and Fact, with such Exceptions, and under such Regulations as the Congress shall make.

[3] The Trial of all Crimes, except in Cases of Impeachment, shall be by Jury; and such Trial shall be held in the State where the said Crimes shall have been committed, but when not committed within any State, the Trial shall be at such Place or Places as the Congress may by Law have directed.

SECTION 3. [1] Treason against the United States, shall consist only in levying War against them, or in adhering to their Enemies, giving them Aid and Comfort. No Person shall be convicted of Treason unless on the Testimony of two Witnesses to the same overt Act, or on Confession in open Court.

[2] The Congress shall have power to declare the Punishment of Treason, but no Attainder of Treason shall work Corruption of Blood, or Forfeiture except during the Life of the Person attained.

ARTICLE IV

SECTION 1. Full Faith and Credit shall be given in each State to the public Acts, Records, and judicial Proceedings of every other State. And the Congress may by general Laws prescribe the Manner in which such Acts, Records and Proceedings shall be proved, and the Effect thereof.

SECTION 2. [1] The Citizens of each State shall be entitled to all Privileges and Immunities of Citizens in the several States.

[2] A Person charged in any State with Treason, Felony, or other Crime, who shall flee from Justice, and be found in another State, shall on Demand of the executive Authority of the State from which he fled, be delivered up, to be removed to the State having Jurisdiction of the Crime.

[3] No Person held to Service or Labour in one State, under the Laws thereof, escaping into another, shall, in Consequence of any Law or Regulation therein, be discharged from such Service or Labour, but shall be delivered up on Claim of the Party to whom such Service or Labour may be due.

SECTION 3. [1] New States may be admitted by the Congress into this Union; but no new State shall be formed or erected within the Jurisdiction of any other State; nor any State be formed by the Junction of two or more States, or parts of States, without the Consent of the Legislature of the States concerned as well as of the Congress.

[2] The Congress shall have Power to dispose of and make all needful Rules and Regulations respecting the Territory or other Property belonging to the United States; and nothing in this Constitution shall be so construed as to Prejudice any Claims of the United States, or of any particular State.

SECTION 4. The United States shall guarantee to every State in this Union a Republican Form of Government, and shall protect each of them against Invasion; and on Application of the Legislature, or of the Executive (when the Legislature cannot be convened), against domestic Violence.

ARTICLE V

The Congress, whenever two thirds of both Houses shall deem it necessary, shall propose Amendments to this Constitution, or, on the Application of the Legislatures of two thirds of the several States, shall call a Convention for proposing Amendments, which, in either Case, shall be valid to all Intents and Purposes, as part of this Constitution, when ratified by the Legislatures of three fourths of the several States, or by Conventions in three fourths thereof, as the one or the other Mode of Ratification may be proposed by the Congress; Provided that no Amendment which may be made prior to the Year One thousand eight hundred and eight shall in any Manner affect the first and fourth Clauses in the Ninth Section of the first Article; and that no State, without its Consent, shall be deprived of its equal Suffrage in the Senate.

ARTICLE VI

[1] All Debts contracted and Engagements entered into, before the Adoption of this Constitution, shall be as valid against the United States under this Constitution, as under the Confederation.

[2] This Constitution, and the Laws of the United States which shall be made in Pursuance thereof; and all Treaties made, or which shall be made, under the Authority of the United States, shall be the supreme Law of the Land; and the Judges in every State shall be bound thereby, any Thing in the Constitution or Laws of any State to the Contrary notwithstanding.

[3] The Senators and Representatives before mentioned, and the Members of the several State Legislatures, and all executive and judicial Officers, both of the United States and of the several States, shall be bound by Oath or Affirmation, to support this Constitution; but no religious Test shall ever be required as a Qualification to any Office or public Trust under the United States.

ARTICLE VII

The Ratification of the Conventions of nine States shall be sufficient for the Establishment of this Constitution between the States so ratifying the Same.

Done in Convention by the Unanimous Consent of the States present the Seventeenth Day of September in the Year of our Lord one thousand seven hundred and Eighty seven and of the Independence of the United States of America the Twelfth In witness whereof We have hereunto subscribed our Names,

G° WASHINGTON—
Presdt and deputy from
Virginia

Delaware	Geo: Reed
	Gunning Bedford jun
	John Dickson
	Jaco: Broom
	James McHenry
Maryland	Dan of St Thos. Jenifer
	Danl. Carroll
Virginia	John Blair
	James Madison Jr.
	Wm. Blount
North Carolina	Richd. Dobbs Spaight
	Hu Williamson
	J. Rutledge
South Carolina	Charles Cotesworth
	Pinckney
	Charles Pinckney
	Pierce Butler
Georgia	Willian Few
	Abr Baldwin
New Hampshire	John Langdon
	Nicholas Gilman
Massachusetts	Nathaniel Gorham
	Rufus King
Connecticut	Wm. Saml. Johnson
	Roger Sherman
New York	Alexander Hamilton
	Wil: Livingston
New Jersey	David Brearley
	Wm. Paterson
	Jona: Dayton
Pennsylvania	B Franklin
	Thomas Mifflin
	Robt. Morris
	Geo. Clymer
	Thos. FitzSimons
	Jared Ingersoll
	James Wilson
	Gouv Morris

ARTICLES IN ADDITION TO, AND AMENDMENT OF, THE CONSTITUTION OF THE UNITED STATES OF AMERICA, PROPOSED BY CONGRESS, AND RATIFIED BY THE LEGISLATURES OF THE SEVERAL STATES, PURSUANT TO THE FIFTH ARTICLE OF THE ORIGINAL CONSTITUTION

AMENDMENT I [1791]

Congress shall make no law respecting an establishment of religion, or prohibiting the free exercise thereof; or abridging the freedom of speech, or of the press; or the right of the people peaceably to assemble, and to petition the Government for a redress of grievances.

AMENDMENT II [1791]

A well regulated Militia, being necessary to the security of a free State, the right of the people to keep and bear Arms, shall not be infringed.

AMENDMENT III [1791]

No Soldier shall, in time of peace be quartered in any house, without the consent of the Owner, nor in time of war, but in a manner to be prescribed by Law.

AMENDMENT IV [1791]

The right of the people to be secure in their persons, houses, papers, and effects, against unreasonable searches and seizures, shall not be violated, and no Warrants shall issue, but upon probable cause, supported by Oath or affirmation, and particularly describing the place to be searched, and the persons or things to be seized.

AMENDMENT V [1791]

No person shall be held to answer for a capital, or otherwise infamous crime, unless on a presentment or indictment of a Grand Jury, except in cases arising in the land or naval forces, or in the Militia, when in actual service in time of War or public danger; nor shall any person be subject for the same offence to be twice put in jeopardy of life or limb; nor shall be compelled in any criminal case to be a witness against himself, nor be deprived of life, liberty, or property, without due process of law; nor shall private property be taken for public use, without just compensation.

AMENDMENT VI [1791]

In all criminal prosecutions, the accused shall enjoy the right to a speedy and public trial, by an impartial jury of the State and district wherein the crime shall have been committed, which district shall have been previously ascertained by law, and to be informed of the nature and cause of the accusation; to be confronted with the witnesses against him; to have compulsory process for obtaining witnesses in his favor, and to have the Assistance of Counsel for his defense.

AMENDMENT VII [1791]

In suits at common law, where the value in controversy shall exceed twenty dollars, the right of trial by jury shall be preserved, and no fact tried by jury, shall be otherwise reexamined in any Court of the United States, than according to the rules of the common law.

AMENDMENT VIII [1791]

Excessive bail shall not be required, nor excessive fines imposed, nor cruel and unusual punishments inflicted.

AMENDMENT IX [1791]

The enumeration in the Constitution, of certain rights, shall not be construed to deny or disparage others retained by the people.

AMENDMENT X [1791]

The powers not delegated to the United States by the Constitution, nor prohibited by it to the States, are reserved to the States respectively, or to the people.

AMENDMENT XI [1798]

The Judicial power of the United States shall not be construed to extend to any suit in law or equity, commenced or prosecuted against one of the United States by Citizens of another State, or by Citizens or Subjects of any Foreign State.

AMENDMENT XII [1804]

The electors shall meet in their respective states and vote by ballot for President and Vice-President, one of whom, at least, shall not be an inhabitant of the same state with themselves; they shall name in their ballots the person voted for as President, and in distinct ballots the person voted for as Vice-President, and they shall make distinct lists of all persons voted for as President, and of all persons voted for as Vice-President, and of the number of votes for each, which lists they shall sign and certify, and transmit sealed to the seat of the government of the United States, directed to the President of the Senate;—The President of the Senate shall, in presence of the Senate and House of Representatives, open all the certificates and the votes shall then be counted;—The person having the greatest number of votes for President, shall be the President, if such number be a majority of the whole number of Electors appointed; and if no person have such majority, then from the persons having the highest numbers not exceeding three on the list of those voted for as President, the House of Representatives shall choose immediately, by ballot, the President. But in choosing the President, the votes shall be taken by states, the representation from each state having one vote; a quorum for this purpose shall consist of a member or members from two-thirds of the states, and a majority of all the states shall be necessary to a choice. And if the House of Representatives shall not choose a President whenever the right of choice shall devolve upon them, before the fourth day of March next following, then the Vice-President shall act as President, as in case of the death or other constitutional disability of the President.—The person having the greatest number of votes as Vice-President, shall be the Vice-President, if such number be a majority of the whole number of Electors appointed, and if no person have a majority, then from the two highest numbers on the list, the Senate shall choose the Vice-President; a quorum for the purpose shall consist of two-thirds of the whole number of Senators, and a majority of the whole number shall be necessary to a choice. But no person constitutionally ineligible to the office of President shall be eligible to that of Vice-President of the United States.

AMENDMENT XIII [1865]

SECTION 1. Neither slavery nor involuntary servitude, except as a punishment for crime whereof the party shall have been duly convicted, shall exist within the United States, or any place subject to their jurisdiction.

SECTION 2. Congress shall have power to enforce this article by appropriate legislation.

AMENDMENT XIV [1868]

SECTION 1. All persons born or naturalized in the United States, and subject to the jurisdiction thereof, are citizens of the United States and of the State wherein they reside. No State shall make or enforce any law which shall abridge the privileges or immunities of citizens of the United States; nor shall any State deprive any person of life, liberty, or property, without due process of law; nor deny to any person within its jurisdiction the equal protection of the laws.

SECTION 2. Representatives shall be apportioned among the several States according to their respective numbers, counting the whole number of persons in each State, excluding Indians not taxed. But when the right to vote at any election for the choice of electors for President and Vice-President of the United States, Representatives in Congress, the Executive and Judicial officers of a State, or the members of the Legislature thereof, is denied to any of the male inhabitants of such State, being twenty-one years of age, and citizens of the United States, or in any way abridged, except for participation in rebellion, or other crime, the basis of representation therein shall be reduced in the proportion which the number of such male citizens shall bear to the whole number of male citizens twenty-one years of age in such State.

SECTION 3. No person shall be a Senator or Representative in Congress, or elector of President and Vice-President, or hold any office, civil or military, under the United States, or under any State, who, having previously taken an oath, as a member of Congress, or as an officer of the United States, or as a member of any State legislature, or as an executive or judicial officer of any State, to support the Constitution of the United States, shall have engaged in insurrection or rebellion against the same, or given aid or comfort to the enemies thereof.

But Congress may by a vote of two-thirds of each House, remove such disability.

SECTION 4. The validity of the public debt of the United States, authorized by law, including debts incurred for payment of pensions and bounties for services in suppressing insurrection or rebellion, shall not be questioned. But neither the United States nor any State shall assume or pay any debt or obligation incurred in aid of insurrection or rebellion against the United States, or any claim for the loss or emancipation of any slave; but all such debts, obligations and claims shall be held illegal and void.

SECTION 5. The Congress shall have power to enforce, by appropriate legislation, the provisions of this article.

AMENDMENT XV [1870]

SECTION 1. The right of citizens of the United States to vote shall not be denied or abridged by the United States or by any State on account of race, color, or previous condition of servitude.

SECTION 2. The Congress shall have power to enforce this article by appropriate legislation.

AMENDMENT XVI [1913]

The Congress shall have power to lay and collect taxes on incomes, from whatever source derived, without apportionment among the several States, and without regard to any census or enumeration.

AMENDMENT XVII [1913]

The Senate of the United States shall be composed of two Senators from each State, elected by the people thereof, for six years, and each Senator shall have one vote. The electors in each State shall have the qualifications requisite for electors of the most numerous branch of the State legislatures.

When vacancies happen in the representation of any State in the Senate, the executive authority of such State shall issue writs of election to fill such vacancies: *Provided,* That the legislature of any State may empower the executive thereof to make temporary appointments until the people fill the vacancies by election as the legislature may direct.

This amendment shall not be so construed as to affect the election or term of any Senator chosen before it becomes valid as part of the Constitution.

AMENDMENT XVIII [1919]

SECTION 1. After one year from the ratification of this article the manufacture, sale, or transportation of intoxicating liquors within, the importation thereof into, or the exportation thereof from the United States and all territory subject to the jurisdiction thereof for beverage purposes is hereby prohibited.

SECTION 2. The Congress and the several States shall have concurrent power to enforce this article by appropriate legislation.

SECTION 3. This article shall be inoperative unless it shall have been ratified as an amendment to the Constitution by the legislatures of the several States, as provided in the Constitution, within seven years from the date of the submission hereof to the States by the Congress.

AMENDMENT XIX [1920]

The right of citizens of the United States to vote shall not be denied or abridged by the United States or by any State on account of sex.

Congress shall have the power to enforce this article by appropriate legislation.

AMENDMENT XX [1933]

SECTION 1. The terms of the President and Vice President shall end at noon on the 20th day of January, and the terms of Senators and Representatives at noon on the 3rd day of January, of the years in which such terms would have ended if this article had not been ratified; and the terms of their successors shall then begin.

SECTION 2. The Congress shall assemble at least once in every year, and such meeting shall begin at noon on the 3d day of January, unless they shall by law appoint a different day.

SECTION 3. If, at the time fixed for the beginning of the term of the President, the President elect shall have died, the Vice President elect shall become President. If a President shall not have been chosen before the time fixed for the beginning of his term, or if the President elect shall have failed to qualify, then the Vice President elect shall act as President until a President shall have qualified; and the Congress may by law provide for the case wherein neither a President elect nor a Vice President elect shall have qualified, declaring who shall then act as President, or the manner in which one who is to act shall be selected, and such person shall act accordingly until a President or Vice President shall have qualified.

SECTION 4. The Congress may by law provide for the case of the death of any of the persons from whom the House of Representatives may choose a President whenever the right of choice shall have devolved upon them, and for the case of the death of any of the persons from whom the Senate may choose a Vice President whenever the right of choice shall have devolved upon them.

SECTION 5. Sections 1 and 2 shall take effect on the 15th day of October following the ratification of this article.

SECTION 6. This article shall be inoperative unless it shall have been ratified as an amendment to the Constitution by the legislatures of three-fourths of the several States within seven years from the date of its submission.

AMENDMENT XXI [1933]

SECTION 1. The eighteenth article of amendment to the Constitution of the United States is hereby repealed.

SECTION 2. The transportation or importation into any State, Territory, or possession of the United States for delivery of use therein of intoxicating liquors, in violation of the laws thereof, is hereby prohibited.

SECTION 3. This article shall be inoperative unless it shall have been ratified as an amendment to the Constitution by conventions in the several States, as provided in the Constitution, within seven years from the date of the submission hereof to the States by the Congress.

AMENDMENT XXII [1951]

SECTION 1. No person shall be elected to the office of the President more than twice, and no person who has held the office of President, or acted as President, for more than two years of a term to which some other person was elected President shall be elected to the office of President more than once. But this Article shall not apply to any person holding the office of President when this Article was proposed by the Congress, and shall not prevent any person who may be holding the office of President, or acting as President, during the term within which this Article becomes operative from holding the office of President or acting as President during the remainder of such term.

SECTION 2. This article shall be inoperative unless it shall have been ratified as an amendment to the Constitution by the legislatures of three-fourths of the several States within seven years from the date of its submission to the States by the Congress.

AMENDMENT XXIII [1961]

SECTION 1. The District constituting the seat of Government of the United States shall appoint in such manner as Congress may direct: A number of electors of President and Vice President equal to the whole number of Senators and Representatives in Congress to which the District would be entitled if it were a State, but in no event more than the least populous State; they shall be in addition to those appointed by the States, but they shall be considered, for the purposes of the election of President and Vice President, to be electors appointed by a State; and they shall meet in the District and perform such duties as provided by the twelfth article of amendment.

SECTION 2. The Congress shall have power to enforce this article by appropriate legislation.

AMENDMENT XXIV [1964]

SECTION 1. The right of citizens of the United States to vote in any primary or other election for President or Vice President, for electors for President or Vice President, or for Senator or Representative in Congress, shall not be denied or abridged by the United States or any State by reason of failure to pay any poll tax or other tax.

SECTION 2. The Congress shall have power to enforce this article by appropriate legislation.

AMENDMENT XXV [1967]

SECTION 1. In case of the removal of the President from office or his death or resignation, the Vice President shall become President.

SECTION 2. Whenever there is a vacancy in the office of the Vice President, the President shall nominate a Vice President who shall take office upon confirmation by a majority vote of both Houses of Congress.

SECTION 3. Whenever the President transmits to the President pro tempore of the Senate and the Speaker of the House of Representatives his written declaration that he is unable to discharge the powers and duties of his office, and until he transmits to them a written declaration to the contrary, such powers and duties shall be discharged by the Vice President as Acting President.

SECTION 4. Whenever the Vice President and a majority of either the principal officers of the executive departments or of such other body as Congress may by law provide, transmit to the President pro tempore of the Senate and the Speaker of the House of Representatives their written declaration that the President is unable to discharge the powers and duties of his office, the Vice President shall immediately assume the powers and duties of the office as Acting President.

Thereafter, when the President transmits to the President pro tempore of the Senate and the Speaker of the House of Representatives his written declaration that no inability exists, he shall resume the powers and the duties of his office unless the Vice President and a majority of either the principal officers of the executive department or of such other body as Congress may by law provide, transmit within four days to the President pro tempore of the Senate and the Speaker of the House of Representatives their written declaration that the President is unable to discharge the powers and duties of his office. Thereupon Congress shall decide the issue, assembling within forty-eight hours for that purpose if not in session. If the Congress, within twenty-one days after receipt of the latter written declaration, or, if Congress is not in session, within twenty-one days after Congress is required to assemble, determines by two-thirds vote of both Houses that the President is unable to discharge the powers and duties of his office, the Vice President shall continue to discharge the same as Acting President; otherwise, the President shall resume the powers and duties of his office.

AMENDMENT XXVI [1971]

SECTION 1. The right of citizens of the United States, who are eighteen years of age or older, to vote shall not be denied or abridged by the United States or by any State on account of age.

SECTION 2. The Congress shall have power to enforce this article by appropriate legislation.

AMENDMENT XXVII [1992]

No law, varying the compensation for the services of the Senators and Representatives, shall take effect, until an election of representatives shall have intervened.*

---

*Adopted in 1992, 203 years after it was first proposed by James Madison and approved by the First Congress. Six states ratified the amendment in 1792, a seventh in 1873, an eighth in 1978, and thirty-two more recently, with Illinois becoming the thirty-eighth state to ratify it on May 12, 1992.

Justices of the Supreme Court

	Term	Appointed by	Replaced
*John Jay**	1789–1795	Washington	
John Rutledge	1789–1791	Washington	
William Cushing	1789–1810	Washington	
James Wilson	1789–1798	Washington	
John Blair	1789–1796	Washington	
James Iredell	1790–1799	Washington	
Thomas Johnson	1791–1793	Washington	Rutledge
William Paterson	1793–1806	Washington	Johnson
John Rutledge	1795	Washington	Jay
Samuel Chase	1796–1811	Washington	Blair
Oliver Ellsworth	1796–1800	Washington	Rutledge
Bushrod Washington	1798–1829	J. Adams	Wilson
Alfred Moore	1799–1804	J. Adams	Iredell
John Marshall	1801–1835	J. Adams	Ellsworth
William Johnson	1804–1834	Jefferson	Moore

*The names of the chief justices are italicized.

	Term	Appointed by	Replaced
Brockholst Livingston	1806–1823	Jefferson	Paterson
Thomas Todd	1807–1826	Jefferson	(new seat)
Gabriel Duval	1811–1835	Madison	Chase
Joseph Story	1811–1845	Madison	Cushing
Smith Thompson	1823–1843	Monroe	Livingston
Robert Trimble	1826–1828	J. Q. Adams	Todd
John McLean	1829–1861	Jackson	Trimble
Henry Baldwin	1830–1844	Jackson	Washington
James Wayne	1835–1867	Jackson	Johnson
Roger Taney	1836–1864	Jackson	Marshall
Philip Barbour	1836–1841	Jackson	Duval
John Catron	1837–1865	Van Buren	(new seat)
John McKinley	1837–1852	Van Buren	(new seat)
Peter Daniel	1841–1860	Van Buren	Barbour
Samuel Nelson	1845–1872	Tyler	Thompson
Levi Woodbury	1845–1851	Polk	Story
Robert Grier	1846–1870	Polk	Baldwin
Benjamin Curtis	1851–1857	Fillmore	Woodbury
John Campbell	1853–1861	Pierce	McKinley
Nathan Clifford	1858–1881	Buchanan	Curtis
Noah Swayne	1862–1881	Lincoln	McLean
Samuel Miller	1862–1890	Lincoln	Daniel
David Davis	1862–1877	Lincoln	Campbell
Stephen Field	1863–1897	Lincoln	(new seat)

	Term	Appointed by	Replaced
Salmon Chase	1864–1873	Lincoln	Taney
William Strong	1870–1880	Grant	Grier
Joseph Bradley	1870–1892	Grant	Wayne
Ward Hunt	1872–1882	Grant	Nelson
Morrison Waite	1874–1888	Grant	Chase
John Marshall Harlan	1877–1911	Hayes	Davis
William Woods	1880–1887	Hayes	Strong
Stanley Matthews	1881–1889	Garfield	Swayne
Horace Gray	1881–1902	Arthur	Clifford
Samuel Blatchford	1882–1893	Arthur	Hunt
Lucius Lamar	1888–1893	Cleveland	Woods
Melville Fuller	1888–1910	Cleveland	Waite
David Brewer	1889–1910	Harrison	Matthews
Henry Brown	1890–1906	Harrison	Miller
George Shiras	1892–1903	Harrison	Bradley
Howell Jackson	1893–1895	Harrison	Lamar
Edward White	1894–1910	Cleveland	Blatchford
Rufus Peckham	1895–1909	Cleveland	Jackson
Joseph McKenna	1898–1925	McKinley	Field
Oliver Wendell Holmes	1902–1932	T. Roosevelt	Gray
William Day	1903–1922	T. Roosevelt	Shiras
William Moody	1906–1910	T. Roosevelt	Brown
Horace Lurton	1909–1914	Taft	Peckham
Charles Evans Hughes	1910–1916	Taft	Brewer

	Term	Appointed by	Replaced
Edward White	1910–1921	Taft	Fuller
Willis Van Devanter	1910–1937	Taft	White
Joseph Lamar	1910–1916	Taft	Moody
Mahlon Pitney	1912–1922	Taft	Harlan
James McReynolds	1914–1941	Wilson	Lurton
Louis Brandeis	1916–1939	Wilson	Lamar
John Clarke	1916–1922	Wilson	Hughes
William Howard Taft	1921–1930	Harding	White
George Sutherland	1922–1938	Harding	Clarke
Pierce Butler	1922–1939	Harding	Day
Edward Sanford	1923–1930	Harding	Pitney
Harlan Stone	1925–1941	Coolidge	McKenna
Charles Evans Hughes	1930–1941	Hoover	Taft
Owen Roberts	1932–1945	Hoover	Sanford
Benjamin Cardozo	1932–1938	Hoover	Holmes
Hugo Black	1937–1971	F. Roosevelt	Van Devanter
Stanley Reed	1938–1957	F. Roosevelt	Sutherland
Felix Frankfurter	1939–1962	F. Roosevelt	Cardozo
William Douglas	1939–1975	F. Roosevelt	Brandeis
Frank Murphy	1940–1949	F. Roosevelt	Butler
James Byrnes	1941–1942	F. Roosevelt	McReynolds
Harlan Stone	1941–1946	F. Roosevelt	Hughes
Robert Jackson	1941–1954	F. Roosevelt	Stone
Wiley Rutledge	1943–1949	F. Roosevelt	Byrnes

	Term	Appointed by	Replaced
Harold Burton	1945–1958	Truman	Roberts
Fred Vinson	1946–1953	Truman	Stone
Tom Clark	1949–1967	Truman	Murphy
Sherman Minton	1949–1956	Truman	Rutledge
Earl Warren	1953–1969	Eisenhower	Vinson
John Harlan	1955–1971	Eisenhower	Jackson
William Brennan	1956–1990	Eisenhower	Minton
Charles Whittaker	1957–1962	Eisenhower	Reed
Potter Stewart	1958–1981	Eisenhower	Burton
Arthur Goldberg	1962–1965	Kennedy	Frankfurter
Byron White	1962–1993	Kennedy	Whittaker
Abe Fortas	1965–1969	Johnson	Goldberg
Thurgood Marshall	1967–1991	Johnson	Clark
Warren Burger	1969–1986	Nixon	Warren
Harry Blackmun	1970–1994	Nixon	Fortas
Lewis Powell	1972–1987	Nixon	Black
William Rehnquist	1972–1986	Nixon	Harlan
John Paul Stevens	1975–2010	Ford	Douglas
Sandra Day O'Connor	1981–2005	Reagan	Stewart
William Rehnquist	1986–2005	Reagan	Burger
Antonin Scalia	1986–2016	Reagan	Rehnquist
Anthony Kennedy	1988–	Reagan	Powell
David Souter	1990–2009	G. H. W. Bush	Brennan
Clarence Thomas	1991–	G. H. W. Bush	Marshall

	Term	Appointed by	Replaced
Ruth Bader Ginsburg	1993–	Clinton	White
Stephen Breyer	1994–	Clinton	Blackmun
John Roberts	2005–	G. W. Bush	Rehnquist
Samuel Alito	2006–	G. W. Bush	O'Connor
Sonia Sotomayor	2009–	Obama	Souter
Elena Kagan	2010–	Obama	Stevens

Glossary of Common
Legal Terms

Abstention The doctrine under which the US Supreme Court and other federal courts choose not to rule on state cases, even when empowered to do so, so as to allow the issue to be decided on the basis of state law.

Advisory Opinion A legal opinion rendered at the request of the government or another party indicating how the court would rule if the issue arose in an adversary context.

Amicus Curiae "Friend of the court." A person or group not directly involved in a particular case that volunteers or is requested by the court to supply its views on the case (usually through the submission of a brief).

Appeal The procedure whereby a case is brought from an inferior to a superior court. In the Supreme Court, certain cases are designated as appeals under federal law and must be heard formally by the Court.

Appellant The party who appeals a decision from a lower to a higher court.

Appellate Jurisdiction The authority of a court to hear, determine, and render judg-

ment in an action on appeal from an inferior court.

Appellee The party against whom an appeal to a superior court is taken and who has an interest in upholding the lower court's decision.

Arraignment The formal process of charging a person with a crime, reading the charge, and asking for and entering the plea.

Bail The security (cash or a bail bond) given as a guarantee that a released prisoner will appear at trial.

Bill of Attainder A legislative act declaring a person guilty of a crime and passing sentence without benefit of trial.

Brief A document prepared by counsel as the basis for an argument in court. It sets forth the facts of the case and the legal arguments in support of the party's position.

Case Law The law as defined by previously decided cases.

Certification A method of appeal whereby a lower court requests a higher court to rule on certain legal questions so that the lower court can make the correct decision in light of the answer given.

Certiorari, Writ of An order from a superior court to an inferior court to forward the entire record of a case to the superior court for review. The US Supreme Court can issue such writs at its discretion.

Civil Action A lawsuit, usually brought by a private party, seeking redress for a noncriminal act (e.g., a suit in negligence, contract, or defamation).

Class Action A lawsuit brought by one person or by a group on behalf of all persons similarly situated.

Comity Courtesy and respect. In the legal sense, the respect federal courts give to the decisions of state courts.

Common Law Principles and rules of action, particularly from unwritten English law, whose authority stems from long-standing usage and custom or from judicial recognition and enforcement of those customs.

Concurrent Powers Powers that can be exercised by both the national government and state governments.

Concurring Opinion An opinion submitted by a member of a court who agrees with the result by the court in a case but either disagrees with the court's reasons for the decision or wishes to address matters not touched on in the opinion of the court.

Declaratory Judgment A judicial pronouncement declaring the legal rights of the parties involved in an actual case or controversy but not ordering a specific action.

De Facto "In fact." The existence of something in fact or reality, as opposed to de jure (by right).

Defendant The person against whom a civil or criminal charge is brought.

De Jure "By right." Lawful, rightful, legitimate; as a result of official action, as opposed to de facto (in fact).

Dissenting Opinion An opinion submitted by a member of a court who disagrees with the result reached by the court.

Distinguish To point out why a previous decision is not applicable.

Diversity Jurisdiction The authority of federal courts to hear cases involving citizens of different states.

Dual Federalism The view that national powers should be interpreted so as not to invade traditional spheres of state activity.

Equity The administration of justice based upon principles of fairness rather than upon strictly applied rules found in the law.

Error, Writ of A writ issued by a superior court directing a lower court to send to the superior court the record of a case in which the lower court has entered a final judgment, for the purpose of reviewing alleged errors made by the lower court.

Exclusionary Rule The rule that evidence obtained by illegal means, such as unreasonable searches and seizures, cannot be introduced by the prosecution in a criminal trial.

Ex parte "From (or on) one side." A hearing in the presence of only one of the parties to a case, such as a hearing to review a petition for a writ of habeas corpus.

Ex Post Facto "After the fact." A law that makes an action a crime after it has already been committed.

Ex Rel. "By (or on) the information of." The designation of suit instituted by a state but at the instigation of a private individual interested in the matter.

Federal Question A case that contains a major issue involving the US Constitution, or US laws or treaties. (The jurisdiction of the federal courts is limited to federal questions and diversity suits.)

Habeas Corpus "You have the body." A writ inquiring of an official who has custody of a person whether that person is imprisoned or detained lawfully.

In Camera "In chambers." The hearing of a case or part of a case in private (without spectators).

Incorporation The process by which provisions of the Bill of Rights were applied as limitations on state governments through the Due Process Clause of the Fourteenth Amendment.

In Forma Pauperis "In the manner of a pauper." Permission for indigents to bring legal action without payment of the required fees.

Injunction A writ prohibiting the person to whom it is directed from performing some specified act.

In re "In the matter of; concerning." The designation of judicial proceedings in which there are no adversaries.

Judgment of the Court The ruling of the court (independent of the reasons for the court's ruling).

Judicial Review The power of a court to review legislation or other governmental action in order to determine its validity with respect to the US Constitution or state constitutions.

Juris Belli "Under the law of war." That part of the law of nations that defines the rights of belligerent and neutral nations during wartime.

Jurisdiction The authority of a court to hear, determine, and render final judgment in an action, and to enforce its judgments by legal process.

Justiciability The question of whether a matter is appropriate for judicial decision. A justiciable issue is one that appropriately can be decided by a court.

Litigant An active participant in a lawsuit.

Mandamus, Writ of "We command." A court order directing an individual or organization to perform a particular act.

Moot Unsettled, undecided. A moot question is one in which either the result sought by the lawsuit has occurred or the conditions have so changed as to render it impossible for the court to grant the relief sought.

Obiter Dicta (also called dictum or dicta) That part of the reasoning in a judicial opinion that is not necessary to resolve the case. Dicta are not necessarily binding in future cases.

Opinion of the Court The opinion that announces the court's decision and is adhered to by a majority of the participating judges.

Original Jurisdiction The authority of a court to hear, determine, and render judgment in an action as a trial court.

Per Curiam "By the court." An unsigned opinion by the court, or a collectively authored opinion.

Petitioner The party who files a petition with a court seeking action.

Plaintiff The party who brings a civil action or sues to obtain a remedy for an injury to his or her rights.

Plea Bargain Negotiations between the prosecution and defense aimed at exchanging a plea of guilty for concessions by the prosecution.

Police Power The power of the states to protect the health, safety, welfare, and morals of their citizens.

Political Question An issue that the court believes should be decided by a nonjudicial unit of government.

Precedent A prior case relied upon in deciding a present dispute.

Preemption The doctrine under which issues previously subject to state control are brought, through congressional action, within the primary or exclusive jurisdiction of the national government.

Prima Facie "At first sight." Evidence that, unless contradicted, is sufficient to establish a claim without investigation or evaluation.

Pro Bono "For the good." Legal services rendered without charge.

Ratio Decidendi "Reason for the decision." The principle of the case.

Remand To send back. In remanding a decision, a higher court sends it, for further action, back to the court from which it came.

Respondent The party against whom a legal action is taken.

Special Master A person designated by a court to hear evidence and submit findings and recommendations based on that evidence. The Supreme Court typically uses special masters in original jurisdiction cases.

Standing The qualifications needed to bring or participate in a case. To have standing to sue, plaintiffs must demonstrate the existence of a controversy in which they personally have suffered or are about to suffer an injury or infringement of a legally protected right.

Stare Decisis "Let the decision stand." The doctrine that a point settled in a previous case is a precedent that should be followed in subsequent cases with similar facts.

State Action Action by the state or by a private entity closely associated with it ("under color of state law"). The basis for redress under the Due Process and Equal Protection Clauses of the Fourteenth Amendments.

Stay To halt or suspend further judicial proceedings.

Subpoena An order to present oneself and to testify before a court, grand jury, or legislative hearing.

Subpoena *Duces Tecum* An order by a court or other authorized body that specified documents or papers be produced.

Tort Willful or negligent injury to the person, property, or reputation of another.

Ultra Vires "Beyond power." An action beyond the legal authority of the person or body performing it.

Vacate To make void, annul, or rescind.

Venue The jurisdiction in which a case is to be heard.

Vested Rights Long-established rights that government should recognize and protect and that a person cannot be deprived of without injustice.

Writ A written court order commanding the recipient to perform or refrain from performing acts specified in the order.

Table of Cases

Case titles in capital letters indicate cases that are reprinted in this volume. ***Bold italic*** page numbers indicate where the case is reprinted in this volume.